# Instructor's Edition
# Findings
## *Readings for Critical Writing*

*Lewis Meyers*
Hunter College

D. C. Heath and Company
Lexington, Massachusetts    Toronto

Address editorial correspondence to:

D.C. Heath and Company
125 Spring Street
Lexington, MA 02173

| | |
|---|---|
| Acquisitions Editor: | Paul A. Smith |
| Development Editor: | Linda M. Bieze |
| Production Editor: | Rosemary R. Jaffe |
| Designer: | Kenneth Hollman |
| Production Coordinator: | Richard Tonachel |
| Permissions Editor: | Margaret Roll |
| Cover photo researcher: | Ann Barnard |

To
*Diana Tietjens Meyers*

# TO THE INSTRUCTOR

*F*indings: *Readings for Critical Writing* is an anthology of essays, short stories, and poems designed for college composition students whose instructors share the belief that reading, writing, and thinking are inextricably linked functions of the inquiring mind. The thematic divisions of the book as well as the specific contents reflect this view.

Following a general introduction, the book is divided into six parts: Myths of Existence, Personal Identity, The Natural World, Social Reality, Moral Action and Spiritual Life, and—a mixed thematic section—Further Writing Assignments. The reading selections in Parts I through V incorporate these themes variously. They do so most often directly, sometimes subtly, but always, I hope, in a revelatory manner that expressly serves students' literate interests.

The themes that shape the book reflect enduring cultural concerns, are emblematic of humane letters generally, and meet the legitimate if sometimes neglected interests of students in investigating matters that give them a full sense of being in the world.

The reading selections represent an outpouring of literary art and intellectual and practical ideas from various nations of the world as well as from diverse cultures within the United States. The readings therefore represent a wide band of views and perspectives on themes and topics to which we universally address ourselves. And yet, although such a multicultural distribution naturally speaks to the idea of separate identity, it also embodies the commonality of issues that produces a sense of unity for writers despite their making different approaches to these issues.

I have tried to include in *Findings* texts that are accessible yet sustain such a consistently high level of language and thought that students will recognize their authenticity. Moreover, these texts were selected on the basis of their intrinsic ability to promote critical thinking, instill practical knowledge, serve argument, and otherwise aid students in developing reading and writing skills essential to academic success. Finally, the texts, I believe, are a pleasure to read.

Each division of the book begins with an introduction whose aim is to orient students to the readings. The introduction concludes with three suggested approaches to the theme at hand. Next, three brief primary texts sample different perspectives on the theme. The readings proper are for the most part independent selections, but some are "linked" readings. These texts by different hands are combined either because they reflect on the same general concern (rape and the issue of its attendent publicity, found in Part IV, for instance) or because they address the identical topic (such as the story of Prometheus in Part I). Although many of the texts and writing assignments in *Findings* serve the purpose of critical thinking, the linked readings do so most forcefully by providing larger contexts for questioning and viewing particular issues.

Whether linked or independent, each reading selection is preceded by a biographical sketch of the author and by three preview suggestions for reading (Looking Ahead). Following each reading are ten study questions (Looking Back) and three detailed writing assignments based on the text.

Each thematic part of the book also presents a follow-up student essay based on one of the readings. The student essay is a preliminary, unedited draft that responds to one of the writing assignments for the reading it follows (for instance, Gwen Caras' "Dirty Boulevard," written in response to James Baldwin's "The Discovery of What It Means to Be an American," in Part II). Along with the student essay is a list of analytical questions on revision possibilities so students can both see the need to revise and practice that skill on work similar to what they themselves might initially produce.

Part VI, Further Writing Assignments, offers for each previous part of the book and its overarching theme five challenging writing projects intended to result in somewhat longer student papers. The first three of each set direct students to read specific texts from different parts of the book and to write an essay based on a common topic. The remaining two assignments ask students to expand on topics introduced in the book by doing library research.

In the *Instructor's Guide for Findings,* I take up the above features in considerably more detail and make suggestions for their classroom use. I also address the practical value of the book in enabling critical thinking, in helping students form arguments, and in pursuing writing as process.

I am very grateful for the many helpful suggestions and comments I have received from readers of this book in its developing stages. I would particularly like to thank Stephen Behrendt, University of Nebraska; Stanley J. H. Crowe, Furman University; Robert W. Funk, Eastern Illinois University; Paula Gillespie, Marquette University; Dona J. Hickey, University of Richmond; Francis A. Hubbard, Marquette University; George Kennedy, Washington State University; Douglas Krienke, Sam Houston State University; Bob Land, University of California—Irvine; Diane LeBow, Cañada College; Harvey Lillywhite, Towson State University; Keith Lloyd, University of Louisville; Joseph Lostracco, Austin Community College; Michael G. Moran, University of Georgia; Terry R. Otten, Wittenberg University; Thomas Recchio, University of Connecticut; Barbara Traister, Lehigh University; and Richard J. Zbaracki, Iowa State University.

Lewis Meyers

# CONTENTS

**TO THE STUDENT**   1

**INTRODUCTION**   7

*The Essay*   7

*From (Their) Text to (Your) Text*   10

   FRED NEUROHR, *Now and Zen*   17

*Critical Thinking*   22

*Prewriting*   25

*The Audience for Writing*   29

*Drafting and Revising*   30

   SARAH AVERILL, *On Moving On*   32

**I  MYTHS OF EXISTENCE**   43

*Primary Texts*   44

MIRCEA ELIADE, from *Myth and Reality*   44
EDITH HAMILTON, from *Mythology*   45
PAUL RADIN, from *African Folktales*   46

   KEVIN CROSSLEY-HOLLAND, *The Creation*   47
   "So the earth was fashioned and filled with men and giants and dwarfs, surrounded by the sea and covered by the sky."

   PÄR LAGERKVIST, *Paradise*   52
   " 'You have no idea what it's like down in paradise,' he said."

   **Follow-Up: An Essay for Analysis**   56
   SHERYL MUIRHEAD, *Intelligence Does Not Equal Wisdom*   56

   J. ALDEN MASON, *The Legendary Empire*   58
   "The Spanish chroniclers recount several different and mutually contradictory legends of Manco Capac and of the origins of the Inca dynasty and empire, all of them containing supernatural elements."

**Linked Readings**   66

THOMAS BULFINCH, *Prometheus and Pandora*   67

"Prometheus was one of the Titans, a gigantic race who inhabited the earth before the creation of man."

H. A. GUERBER, *The Story of Prometheus* and *Deucalion and Pyrrha*   72

"In a world of wicked mortals these two had lived righteously; and when Zeus saw them there alone, and remembered their goodness, he decided not to include them in the general destruction, but to save their lives."

AL ROSS, *To the Woman Who Discovered Fire*   77

A toast.

KAREL CAPEK, *The Punishment of Prometheus*   78

" 'You have heard a number of witnesses who have deposed that in trying Prometheus's boyish invention they have suffered serious burns and in some cases even damage to property.' "

FRANZ KAFKA, *Prometheus*   81

"The legend tried to explain the inexplicable."

❊

DINO BUZZATI, *The Bewitched Jacket*   85

"The more one gets, the more one wants."

J. IDRIES SHAH, *The Fisherman and the Genie*   91

"The bottle was not very large. On the top was inscribed a strange symbol, the Seal of Solomon, King and Master."

ROMAN CZERWCZAK, *A Summer*   95

"There was a feeling of desperation in this whole derelict neighborhood and even the lively *Salsa* coming from empty barber shops and bars could not change it."

**Linked Readings**   100

PAUL RADIN (ed.), *The Origin of Death: Krachi, Akamba, Hottentot*   101

"And so men become old and die; they do not rise again."

MARGOT ASTROV (ed.), *The Origin of Death: Coeur D'Alène; Coyote and the Origin of Death: Caddo*   104

"In the beginning of the world there was no such thing as death."

C. G. JUNG, *On Life After Death*   106

"A man should be able to say he has done his best to form a conception of life after death, or to create some image of it—even if he must confess his failure."

MARGOT ASTROV (ed.), *A Speech to the Dead: Fox*     125
"Think only of what is good."


## II PERSONAL IDENTITY     131

*Primary Texts*     132

GLORIA STEINEM, from *Revolution from Within: A Book of Self-Esteem*     132
ROBERT W. WHITE, from *The Abnormal Personality*     134
HERBERT READ, from *Icon and Idea*     136

**Linked Readings**     137

ANONYMOUS, *The Baby Boomer*     137
"You should decide against getting that tattoo on your ankle . . ."

SAINT AUGUSTINE OF HIPPO, *As a Baby*     139
"Who can recall to me the sins I committed as a baby?"

CAMARA LAYE, *I Was Very Young*     142
"The blackboard's blank surface was an exact replica of our minds."

CATHERINE S. MANEGOLD, *Crystal*     152
" 'Kids who study are all nerds,' she said dismissively."

LEO TOLSTOY, *Boyhood*     159
"My mind went round in circles. . . ."

ROGELIO R. GOMEZ, *Foul Shots*     163
"Now and then I can still see their faces, snickering and laughing, their eyes mocking me."

ONDINE GALSWORTH, *Air Raid*     167
"For one, my mother was beautiful, gorgeous, a sexbomb, a real looker."

FRANÇOIS, DUC DE LA ROCHEFOUCAULD, *Self-Portrait*     173
"I am intelligent, and I make no bones about saying so, for what is the good of being coy about it?"

JAMES BALDWIN, *The Discovery of What It Means to Be An American*     177
"The fact that I am the son of a slave and they were the sons of free men meant less, by the time we confronted each other on European soil, then the fact that we were both searching for our separate identities."

**Follow-Up: An Essay for Analysis**    **183**
GWEN CARAS, *Dirty Boulevard*    183

BHARATI MUKHERJEE, *The World According to Hsü*    186
"He had paid five thousand dollars in airfare so they could hold hands on a beach under the Southern Cross, but already she was accusing him of selfishness and bigotry."

F. SCOTT FITZGERALD, *Early Success*    199
"Rage and bliss alternated hour by hour."

IDA FINK, *Night of Surrender*    205
" 'But listen, the war is over. You have to learn to believe in people, in happiness and goodness.' "

TIM O'BRIEN, *On the Rainy River*    212
"In June of 1968, a month after graduating from Macalester College, I was drafted to fight a war I hated."

DIANE ARBUS, *My Favorite Thing Is to Go Where I've Never Been*    227
*A Family One Evening in a Nudist Camp, Pa., 1965*
". . . I really believe there are things which nobody would see unless I photographed them."

**III  THE NATURAL WORLD**    **241**

*Primary Texts*    *243*
OVID, from *Metamorphoses*    243
ARISTOTLE, from *De Partibus Animalium*    244
RALPH WALDO EMERSON, from "Nature"    245

LEWIS THOMAS, *The Music of This Sphere*    247
"We are only saved by music from being overwhelmed by nonsense."

**Follow-Up: An Essay for Analysis**    **252**
PAMELA COREY, *A Debt to Animals*    252

CARL SAGAN, *Can We Know the Universe? Reflections on a Grain of Salt*    254
"If the universe had natural laws that governed its behavior to the same degree of regularity that determines a crystal of salt, then, of course, the universe would be knowable."

**Linked Readings**     260

HERMAN HESSE, *Trees*     261

"Trees are sanctuaries."

CLAUDE LÉVI-STRAUSS, *In the Forest*     262

"What attracts me now is the forest."

THE AUDUBON SOCIETY, *An Aerial View*     270

". . . why the heck do they keep cutting them down?"

LAUREN STRUTZEL, *The Evolution of Allegiance to the Green Concern*     274

"Recently our company received a letter written on the back of an envelope, from a doctor who very clearly stated that he would not do business with a company that did not use recycled paper."

BERYL MARKHAM, *Royal Exile*     283

"He was a Thoroughbred stallion and he knew nothing of remorse."

ANNIE DILLARD, *Living Like Weasels*     290

"I would like to learn, or remember, how to live."

NATALIE ANGIER, *The Cockroach*     295

" 'I love cockroaches, and I don't know where I'd be without them,' said Dr. Schal. 'But unfortunately I'm starting to get slightly allergic to them.' "

THE NEW YORK TIMES, *Animal Rights Raiders Destroy Years of Work*     303

"The slogans were signed 'A.L.F.,' for Animal Liberation Front."

WALLACE STEGNER, *Thoughts in a Dry Land*     307

"You have to get over the color green; you have to quit associating beauty with gardens and lawns; you have to get used to an inhuman scale; you have to understand geological time."

**Linked Readings**     316

LEONARDO DA VINCI, *The Nature of Water*     317

"But in what tongue or with what words am I to express or describe the awful ruin, the inconceivable and pitiless havoc wrought by the deluges of ravening rivers, against which no human resource can avail?"

FERNAND BRAUDEL, *Something to Drink*     320

"Many fountains were built in Istanbul as a result of the religious requirement to wash frequently every day under running water."

JOAN DIDION, *Holy Water*   324

"A pool is water, made available and useful, and is, as such, infinitely soothing to the western eye."

ALAIN ROBBE-GRILLET, *Reflected Vision: The Wrong Direction*   328

"Someone, walking noiselessly on the mulchy carpet of the woods, has appeared on the right, moving toward the water."

❊

LOREN EISELEY, *The Brown Wasps*   333

"Prematurely I am one of the brown wasps and I often sit with them in the great droning hive of the station . . ."

D. H. LAWRENCE, *Reflections on the Death of a Porcupine*   340

"As far as existence goes, that life-species is the highest which can devour, or destroy, or subjugate every other life-species against which it is pitted in contest."

## IV  SOCIAL REALITY   355

*Primary Texts*   *356*

RAYMOND WILLIAMS, from *Keywords*   356
CICERO, from *On Government*   359
LESZEK KOLAKOWSKI, from *Toward a Marxist Humanism*   362

LAURIE ANDERSON, *Politics & Music*   362

"I mean, just how do people convince each other of things that are basically quite preposterous?"

**Linked Readings**   **366**

PAULINE KAEL, ROBERT GARD, CHANCE STONER, *Campus Life*   367

"I was a troublemaker then. (Laughs.) I wish I still were."

STUDENTS FOR A DEMOCRATIC SOCIETY, *The Port Huron Statement*   370

"We are people of this generation, bred in at least modest comfort, housed now in universities, looking uncomfortably to the world we inherit."

NICOLA CHIAROMONTE, *The Student Revolt*   382

"You can talk about right only when you talk reasonably, person to person. A rioting crowd never reasons, nor can it ever be right . . ."

❊

ANDREW L. SHAPIRO, *Reading, Writing, and Ignorance: Education and Achievement*    390

"The effects of a deteriorating educational system are already apparent."

VERA BRITTAIN, *Woman Workers, Today and Tomorrow*    405

"Women will find themselves part of a far greater revolution which will involve society as a whole in its results."

RONALD TAKAKI, *Different Shores*    411

"To use the term *reverse discrimination* to describe affirmative action is both confusing and incorrect."

MARY MAN-KONG, *Memories of My Mother*    420

"In addition, all the things I had ever learned and believed from school differed from what she said and thought."

STANLEY CROUCH, *Nationalism of Fools*    426

"The appearance of Louis Farrakhan at this time seems a comment on the failure of black, liberal, and conservative politics since the Nixon era."

PATRICIA WILLIAMS, *The Death of the Profane*    438

"I pressed my round brown face to the window and my finger to the buzzer."

**Follow-Up: An Essay for Analysis**    445
ROSEMARY WAIKUNY, *Weight*    445

**Linked Readings**    447
ALDOUS HUXLEY, *British Honduras*    448

"In practice we are able to do things with a light heart, because we never know very clearly what we are doing, and are happily incapable of imagining how our deeds will affect other people or our future selves."

KATHA POLLITT, *Media Goes Wilding in Palm Beach*    450

"But even if I'm unduly cynical and the media sincerely wish to conduct a teach-in on rape, the interests of the public can be served without humiliating the complainant."

ANNA QUINDLEN, *Making a Case*    459

" 'The way to fight back is to show our faces,' she says."

BELL HOOKS, *Feminist Movement to End Violence*    463

"It is essential for continued feminist struggle to end violence against women that this struggle be viewed as a component of an overall movement to end violence."

RANDY SHILTS, *Heterosexuals and AIDS*   475

" 'How did you end up like this?' the reporter asked, as he drove Silvana back
to her Jones Street hotel room."

**Linked Readings**   487

GEORGE ORWELL, *A Hanging*   487

"We all had a drink together, native and European alike, quite amicably. The
dead man was a hundred yards away."

WILLIAM BRADFORD, *Anno Dom: 1638* [*Englishmen Executed
for Murdering an Indian*]   491

"And some of the Narragansett Indians and of the party's friends were present
when it was done, which gave them and all the county a good satisfaction."

**Linked Readings**   495

VACLAV HAVEL, *The End of the Modern Era*   495

"We must try harder to understand than to explain."

ROBERT L. MELTZER, STUART A. NEWMAN, FELIPE C.
CABELLO, GREGORY HEDBURG, *With Apologies to Havel,
Let Reason Rule*   498

"His call to irrationalism will be of little help. . . ."


**V  MORAL ACTION AND SPIRITUAL LIFE**   503

*Primary Texts*   504

RAYMOND M. SMULLYAN, from "Why Do You Help Your Fellow Man?"   504
PLUTARCH, from "On Being Aware of Moral Progress"   506
STEPHEN MITCHELL, from *The Gospel According to Jesus*   507

**Linked Readings**   508

SAINT MATTHEW, *The Sermon on the Mount*   508

"Blessed are the pure in heart, because they shall see God."

MARTIN BUBER (ed.), *Walking the Tight Rope*   512

"Tell us, dear rabbi, how should we serve God?"

AGNES MARTIN, *What We Do Not See If We Do Not See*   515

"In this life we are struggling from death into life."

HELMUTH JAMES VON MOLTKE, *Letters to Freya*   524

"Dear heart, my life is finished and I can say of myself: He died in the fullness
of years and of life's experiences."

BERTOLT BRECHT, *Two Sons* 536

"In January 1945, as Hitler's war was drawing to a close, a farmer's wife in Thuringia dreamt that her son at the front was calling her . . ."

JULIAN BARNES, *The Visitors* 540

"Ten minutes later there came the noise of shooting."

N. SCOTT MOMADAY, *The Priest of the Sun* 559

" 'May the Great Spirit—can we knock off that talking in back there?—be with you always.' "

HEINRICH BÖLL, *Like a Bad Dream* 565

"But I never did understand. It is beyond understanding."

ERIC ROHMER, *The Baker's Girl* 571

"I moved over to her and with one finger touched her bare back."

ALBERT CAMUS, *The Growing Stone* 582

" 'And you, have you never called out, made a promise?' "

ANONYMOUS, *Is That So?* 604

"She told her parents the truth—that the real father of the child was a young man who worked in the fishmarket."

MARGOT OLAVARRIA, *Remembering John* 606

"John worked very hard to finish the play he was working on before his eyes couldn't handle the word processor screen."

JOAN DIDION, *On Morality* 612

"You see I want to be quite obstinate about insisting that we have no way of knowing—beyond that fundamental loyalty to the social code—what is 'right' and what is 'wrong,' what is 'good' and what is 'evil.' "

**Follow-Up: An Essay for Analysis** 617

EILEEN WHITEHEAD, *Words in the English Language* 617

DIANA TIETJENS MEYERS, *Work and Self-Respect* 620

"In recognizing the autonomy of employees, these rights make work a source of self-respect and, as such, a site of personal meaning."

GARY SNYDER, *Buddhism and the Coming Revolution* 630

"There is nothing in human nature or the requirements of human social organization which intrinsically requires that a culture be contradictory, repressive and productive of violent and frustrated personalities."

**Linked Readings**    634

THE BROTHERS GRIMM, *The Water of Life*    634

"Then she further told him where the spring with the Water of Life was, but he'd have to hurry and draw the water before it struck twelve."

CHUANG TZU, *Supreme Happiness*    638

"I look at what ordinary people find happiness in, what they all make a mad dash for, racing around as though they couldn't stop—they all say they're happy with it."


**VI  FURTHER WRITING ASSIGNMENTS    645**

*Myths of Existence*    645

*Personal Identity*    647

*The Natural World*    649

*Social Reality*    651

*Moral Action and Spiritual Life*    652


**ACKNOWLEDGMENTS    655**

**INDEX    661**

# RHETORICAL AND TYPOLOGICAL
## TABLE OF CONTENTS

The reason for the word *typological,* which is unusual in this context, is that besides the accustomed rhetorical means of development, three types of written discourse—that which emphasizes critical thinking, the personal essay, and the critical essay—are included here for the convenience of teachers and students. You will notice that some listings are much fuller than others. Because critical thinking assumes such importance in this book, the list of works in which it is present naturally is larger. Also, focus or emphasis decides what is included where, not the superficial presence of a particular element. In addition, three literary genres—myth/folk tale, fiction, and personal reflection (a less structured form than the typological *personal essay*)—are listed here.

## CRITICAL THINKING

J. IDRIES SHAH, *The Fisherman and the Genie*  91

C. G. JUNG, *On Life After Death*  106

CAMARA LAYE, *I Was Very Young*  142

LEO TOLSTOY, *Boyhood*  159

JAMES BALDWIN, *The Discovery of What It Means to Be An American*  177

CARL SAGAN, *Can We Know the Universe? Reflections on a Grain of Salt*  254

WALLACE STEGNER, *Thoughts in a Dry Land*  307

LOREN EISELEY, *The Brown Wasps*  333

STUDENTS FOR A DEMOCRATIC SOCIETY, *The Port Huron Statement*  370

NICOLA CHIAROMONTE, *The Student Revolt*  382

VERA BRITTAIN, *Woman Workers, Today and Tomorrow*  405

RONALD TAKAKI, *Different Shores*      411

STANLEY CROUCH, *Nationalism of Fools*      426

PATRICIA WILLIAMS, *The Death of the Profane*      438

KATHA POLLITT, *Media Goes Wilding in Palm Beach*      450

VACLAV HAVEL, *The End of the Modern Era*      495

JOAN DIDION, *On Morality*      612

DIANA TIETJENS MEYERS, *Work and Self-Respect*      620

## THE PERSONAL ESSAY

ROMAN CZERWCZAK, *A Summer*      95

C. G. JUNG, *On Life After Death*      106

ROGELIO R. GOMEZ, *Foul Shots*      163

FRANÇOIS, DUC DE LA ROCHEFOUCAULD, *Self-Portrait*      173

JAMES BALDWIN, *The Discovery of What It Means to Be An American*      177

F. SCOTT FITZGERALD, *Early Success*      199

LAUREN STRUTZEL, *The Evolution of Allegiance to the Green Concern*      274

JOAN DIDION, *Holy Water*      324

LOREN EISELEY, *The Brown Wasps*      333

RONALD TAKAKI, *Different Shores*      411

GEORGE ORWELL, *A Hanging*      487

JOAN DIDION, *On Morality*      612

## THE CRITICAL ESSAY

RONALD TAKAKI, *Different Shores*      411

BELL HOOKS, *Feminist Movement to End Violence*      463

ROBERT L. MELTZER, STUART A. NEWMAN, FELIPE C. CABELLO, GREGORY HEDBURG, *With Apologies to Havel, Let Reason Rule*   498


## ARGUMENTATION

JAMES BALDWIN, *The Discovery of What It Means to Be An American*   177

LEWIS THOMAS, *The Music of This Sphere*   247

LAUREN STRUTZEL, *The Evolution of Allegiance to the Green Concern*   274

ANNIE DILLARD, *Living Like Weasels*   290

D. H. LAWRENCE, *Reflections on the Death of a Porcupine*   340

STUDENTS FOR A DEMOCRATIC SOCIETY, *The Port Huron Statement*   370

NICOLA CHIAROMONTE, *The Student Revolt*   382

ANDREW L. SHAPIRO, *Reading, Writing, and Ignorance: Education and Achievement*   390

RONALD TAKAKI, *Different Shores*   411

STANLEY CROUCH, *Nationalism of Fools*   426

KATHA POLLITT, *Media Goes Wilding in Palm Beach*   450

BELL HOOKS, *Feminist Movement to End Violence*   463

VACLAV HAVEL, *The End of the Modern Era*   495

ROBERT L. MELTZER, STUART A. NEWMAN, FELIPE C. CABELLO, GREGORY HEDBURG, *With Apologies to Havel, Let Reason Rule*   498

AGNES MARTIN, *What We Do Not See If We Do Not See*   515

JOAN DIDION, *On Morality*   612

DIANA TIETJENS MEYERS, *Work and Self-Respect*   620

GARY SNYDER, *Buddhism and the Coming Revolution*    630

## ANALYSIS

J. ALDEN MASON, *The Legendary Empire*    58

CATHERINE S. MANEGOLD, *Crystal*    152

ROGELIO R. GOMEZ, *Foul Shots*    163

JAMES BALDWIN, *The Discovery of What It Means to Be An American*    177

CARL SAGAN, *Can We Know the Universe? Reflections on a Grain of Salt*    254

CLAUDE LÉVI-STRAUSS, *In the Forest*    262

NATALIE ANGIER, *The Cockroach*    295

WALLACE STEGNER, *Thoughts in a Dry Land*    307

LEONARDO DA VINCI, *The Nature of Water*    317

FERNAND BRAUDEL, *Something to Drink*    320

STUDENTS FOR A DEMOCRATIC SOCIETY, *The Port Huron Statement*    370

ANDREW L. SHAPIRO, *Reading, Writing, and Ignorance: Education and Achievement*    390

VERA BRITTAIN, *Woman Workers, Today and Tomorrow*    405

PATRICIA WILLIAMS, *The Death of the Profane*    438

ALDOUS HUXLEY, *British Honduras*    448

KATHA POLLITT, *Media Goes Wilding in Palm Beach*    450

DIANA TIETJENS MEYERS, *Work and Self-Respect*    620

## ILLUSTRATION BY EXAMPLE

ONDINE GALSWORTH, *Air Raid*    167

CARL SAGAN, *Can We Know the Universe? Reflections on a Grain of Salt*    254

NATALIE ANGIER, *The Cockroach*   295

WALLACE STEGNER, *Thoughts in a Dry Land*   307

FERNAND BRAUDEL, *Something to Drink*   320

LOREN EISELEY, *The Brown Wasps*   333

MARY MAN-KONG, *Memories of My Mother*   420

RANDY SHILTS, *Heterosexuals and AIDS*   475

JOAN DIDION, *On Morality*   612

## COMPARISON AND CONTRAST

CLAUDE LÉVI-STRAUSS, *In the Forest*   262

NATALIE ANGIER, *The Cockroach*   295

LOREN EISELEY, *The Brown Wasps*   333

## DEFINITION

FRANÇOIS DUC DE LA ROCHEFOUCAULD,
*Self-Portrait*   173

CARL SAGAN, *Can We Know the Universe? Reflections on a
Grain of Salt*   254

D. H. LAWRENCE, *Reflections on the Death of a
Porcupine*   340

JOAN DIDION, *On Morality*   612

DIANA TIETJENS MEYERS, *Work and
Self-Respect*   620

## NARRATION

J. ALDEN MASON, *The Legendary Empire*   58

CAMARA LAYE, *I Was Very Young*   142

ROGELIO R. GOMEZ, *Foul Shots*   163

ONDINE GALSWORTH, *Air Raid*   167

CLAUDE LÉVI-STRAUSS, *In the Forest*   262

ANNIE DILLARD, *Living Like Weasels*   290

THE NEW YORK TIMES, *Animal Rights Raiders Destroy Years of Work*    303

D. H. LAWRENCE, *Reflections on the Death of a Porcupine*    340

PATRICIA WILLIAMS, *The Death of the Profane*    438

GEORGE ORWELL, *A Hanging*    487

WILLIAM BRADFORD, *Anno Dom: 1638 [Englishmen Executed for Murdering an Indian]*    491

MARGOT OLAVARRIA, *Remembering John*    606

## DESCRIPTION

ROMAN CZERWCZAK, *A Summer*    95

CLAUDE LÉVI-STRAUSS, *In the Forest*    262

ANNIE DILLARD, *Living Like Weasels*    290

NATALIE ANGIER, *The Cockroach*    295

LOREN EISELEY, *The Brown Wasps*    333

ALAIN ROBBE-GRILLET, *Reflected Vision: The Wrong Direction*    328

D. H. LAWRENCE, *Reflections on the Death of a Porcupine*    340

## MYTH/FOLK TALE

KEVIN CROSSLEY-HOLLAND, *The Creation*    47

PÄR LAGERKVIST, *Paradise*    52

THOMAS BULFINCH, *Prometheus and Pandora*    67

H. A. GUERBER, *The Story of Prometheus* and *Deucalion and Pyrrha*    72

PAUL RADIN (ed.), *The Origin of Death*    101

MARGOT ASTROV (ed.), *The Origin of Death*    104

ANONYMOUS, *Is That So?*    604

THE BROTHERS GRIMM, *The Water of Life*    634

CHUANG TZU, *Supreme Happiness*    638

## FICTION

AL ROSS, *To the Woman Who Discovered Fire* (drawing)    77

KAREL CAPEK, *The Punishment of Prometheus*    78

FRANZ KAFKA, *Prometheus*    81

DINO BUZZATI, *The Bewitched Jacket*    85

BHARATI MUKHERJEE, *The World According to Hsü*    186

IDA FINK, *Night of Surrender*    205

TIM O'BRIEN, *On the Rainy River*    212

BERTOLT BRECHT, *Two Sons*    536

JULIAN BARNES, *The Visitors*    540

N. SCOTT MOMADAY, *The Priest of the Sun*    559

HEINRICH BÖLL, *Like a Bad Dream*    565

ERIC ROHMER, *The Baker's Girl*    571

ALBERT CAMUS, *The Growing Stone*    582

## PERSONAL REFLECTION

SAINT AUGUSTINE OF HIPPO, *As a Baby*    139

DIANE ARBUS, *My Favorite Thing Is to Go Where I've Never Been*    227

HERMAN HESSE, *Trees*    261

THE AUDUBON SOCIETY, *An Aerial View* (drawing)    270

BERYL MARKHAM, *Royal Exile*    283

LAURIE ANDERSON, *Politics & Music*    362

PAULINE KAEL, ROBERT GARD, and CHANCE STONER, *Campus Life*    367

ANNA QUINDLEN, *Making a Case*    459

SAINT MATTHEW, *The Sermon on the Mount*    508

HELMUTH JAMES VON MOLTKE, *Letters to Freya*    524

# To the Student

When readers look back on the books in their lives, those that seem most precious are often the ones that were so good they called for an articulate response, whether in speech or in writing. It seemed necessary to these readers to tell *somebody* about what they had read, and sometimes to tell many people, to spread the word. Doing so is to act on the conviction—which many have held—that literature can transform the world. First it is the reader's personal world that grows larger, fuller, and richer. But later, if that world is not to shrink back to its original, prereading dimensions, other people must be receptive to the reader's enthusiasms and make room for them. So, as readers, we speak to people, write for them, and if we convince them, their worlds also expand and deepen. There's room for everybody.

*Findings* is a collection of essays, short fiction, and poems that will increase your intellectual space and populate it with new, animated presences. The book's title has a double meaning. It points to the literary works themselves, each representing an author's discovering and understanding of some part of life; and it points to your own activity as a reader: the investigations you make and the results you come up with.

The book is divided into six parts: Myths of Existence, Personal Identity, The Natural World, Social Reality, Moral Action and Spiritual Life, and—a nonthematic part—Further Writing Assignments, which are based on readings in the previous parts of the book.

## PART I: MYTHS OF EXISTENCE

Myth, with which the thematic contents start, displays the original and still extraordinarily powerful method human beings have used to structure their understanding of their lives. To be aware of myth, of the forms it takes and the functions it serves, is to perceive how certain realities, such as the mystery of human origins and the inescapability of physical death, continue both to haunt and to unify consciousness. To be thus aware is also to realize that all our concerns, pursuits, and studies exist in the light of these realities. Such a realization humbles and exalts at once: we see that we're just the latest actors on an old stage, but we see as well that the stage, though ancient, is a grand one, and human destiny has its magnificence.

# PART II: PERSONAL IDENTITY

Out of this background, the human being emerges as more than a biological type, but rather as a creature capable of personhood, of having a personal identity. No doubt, the possibility of having a self developed slowly, throughout eons of human existence. By now, however, it seems to have triumphed. Individualism is a social and political value many people share. But individualism does not guarantee individuality. The first, as a doctrine, protects against the loss of rights and the decay of justice. The second, the distinction between one person and another, results from the way each of us independently shapes our own life. Without individuality, individualism is not a secure holding (although too much individuality, perhaps, gives individualism a bad name). Are we and the people we know "individuals"? Those who think they should persist in asking this question need to have before them cases, records, discussions, and narratives of the assertive, reflective self. Part II of *Findings* presents these.

# PART III: THE NATURAL WORLD

Throughout history, in the attempt to be themselves, people have found it necessary to break free from the constraints of nature because nature insists that human beings are a biological species only, not a collection of unique selves. That dispute we can safely leave aside here. However, what we can and do consider is that the heroic attempt to be individuals has frequently been at the expense of the natural world. We have set out to "conquer" nature, and to the extent we have succeeded, we have buried even its memory. Yet, natural disasters like earthquakes and ecological threats like the hole in the ozone layer remind us of how limited our control actually is. We would do well, no doubt, to be reminded in less drastic ways of what comprises our true world. For, as paradoxical as it may sound, we human beings do not discover our selves by denying the reality of what we need to distinguish ourselves from, nor by negating it through destruction, but rather by seeing it as the very ground of our existence.

# PART IV: SOCIAL REALITY

If Part III presents evidence of what we have dubbed the "*true* world," Part IV does the same for what many people, particularly college students, call the "*real* world," the social one. Human society—as much as nature—is our environment. It is hard to escape the conclusion that it is also the more intricate and complicated environment of the two. In society, we constantly interact with others and become for them what they are for us. The social world is not inert, static, and unchanging; it is not simply acted on; it does not obey a number of observable laws that hold true at all times and in all places. Although in different countries, certain kinds of institutions and certain patterns of social relations may appear so similar that we are half-convinced there is one social foundation for the world, closer study reveals the existence of enormously varied forms of association and administration. These often take cultural forms—distinct networks of behaviors, attitudes, and values—that further the sense of multiplicity. It would be foolish to think such a huge collection could be adequately represented in one part of one book, but it can be sampled, as it is here, and can thus lead to continued investigation on your part.

# PART V: MORAL ACTION AND SPIRITUAL LIFE

In the midst of society, dreaming mythically, in uneasy alliance with nature, and busy creating a self, the individual discovers still more to cope with: the spiritual life as a dimension of existence and moral action as a theater of operations. Along with artistic endeavors, and not definitively separated from them, spirituality and morality represent refinements of human capacity. They are not refinements in the sense of the luxurious and the inessential. Instead we refer to refinements as the priority humans put on basic affinities and blessed states like lovingkindness, mutual aid, innocence, and goodness, and on conduct that preserves and continues these. It is appropriate, therefore, that this highly developed quality bind together the readings in the last thematic part of the book.

In this part, as in the previous ones, the reading selections have been chosen for their individual merit as well as for their clear reflection of a common theme. These criteria result in a table of contents that, except for the Linked Readings, does not present texts grouped around a few particular subjects, such as the abortion controversy or ways to define the good person. Rather, each text exists in its own right, as individuals do in a family. Thus, the collection in *Findings* presents a range of viewpoints on a variety of topics, leaving you free to discover what interests you now and, possibly, what will continue to do so.

# SUGGESTIONS FOR USING THIS BOOK

Approaching the book for the first time in a college course, you should preview the table of contents in order to get an idea of the offerings. Read the general introduction, then turn to a particular part of the book and read its introduction. Look for particular works that have caught your eye. Go to different sections of the book to sample the varied thematic organization. Read one or two pieces, perhaps even one of the groups called Linked Readings, and take note of the instructional aids and the writing assignments that come before and after each text.

At this point, let's look in a more detailed way at these standard features of the book.

*Introduction.*   Each part of the book begins with introductory remarks. These will orient you to the particular subject matter by establishing the terms, issues, and concerns that typically are present within it. Each introduction concludes with a list of three general suggestions for reading the material that lies ahead.

*Primary Texts.*   A group of brief Primary Texts represents different perspectives on the theme that organizes the subsequent reading selections. These texts will alert you to the complex nature of the subject.

*Biographical Sketch.*   Heading each reading selection is a brief note about the author, often identifying his or her chief works, including the one from which the present text is taken.

*Looking Ahead.*   Preceding each reading selection are three suggestions for finding your way through the work. Often, these will hint at what to look for as you read; sometimes they identify concerns that the writing assignments will take up. You will read more effectively if you keep these guides in mind.

*Looking Back.*   Ten study questions are appended to each reading selection. These sometimes require only a literal comprehension of parts of the text. More often they ask you to make inferences and interpret meaning. Typically, questions take up concerns in the order of their appearance in the text. Thus, this section can help you monitor your reading *as* you proceed, so that you can focus on matters of most importance (though you should feel free to attend to what interests and intrigues you whether or not a question touches on it). Very often, questions tie in with writing assignments, and so writing out your answers at some length will directly contribute to the essay you produce.

*Writing Assignments.*   Three proposals for writing follow each reading selection. For each assignment, the phrase "write an essay" is accompanied by directions for a specific writing task. You can discover on your own (or as a result of joint preparation in the classroom) the particular approach you think best in terms of essay organization, methods of development, the extent of your treatment of the subject, and how you will refer to and build on the original reading. You should make sure you fully understand an assignment before undertaking it. It will prove useful—if you know the assignment beforehand—to keep it in mind while you read the text on which it is based.

As mentioned above, in each part of the book a group of the readings will have a specific topic in common; such groups are called Linked Readings. Frequently, you will be asked to read such a unit in its entirety. When you do so, notice that although a separate Looking Ahead section precedes each text, one biographical sketch includes information on all the authors. Likewise, a single Looking Back section follows the group of readings. The three Writing Assignments are broad enough to cover all the Linked Readings, but there are also individual assignments, one based on each reading selection in case you are assigned just one of the linked texts.

However you use *Findings* in your composition course, it is to be hoped that you will find your reading both instructive and entertaining—to employ the familiar but nonetheless precise terms that describe our expectations of literature. In the Introduction that follows, we will look more specifically at certain strategies for reading and writing and, in particular, at the ways in which writing emerges from reading.

# *Introduction*

What value do our formal uses of language—writing and reading—have? Practical value, certainly. Some of the earliest writing has been discovered on bills of lading, or cargo lists. But cultural value, also: the planting in the rich soil of our social groupings of a permanent human speech. Greek civilization, it has been claimed, arose with the invention of the subordinate clause. And because it is hard to imagine a complex syntax (exemplified by the subordinate clause) having much of a life outside of written language, it looks as if writing itself is essential to civilization. All modern, civilized societies produce books. Thus, reading and writing about what is read are hallmarks of the civilized—that is, educated—person, and thus writing and reading together not only help us live but direct the manner in which we do so.

Starting from such assumptions about language's value and use, and as a student of these high literate arts, you face the problem everyone does when confronting a text: "What do I make of this?" It's the word *make* in this question that is significant. It points simultaneously to reading and writing: to understanding what you read and to doing something with it. But this wording is deceptively simple. To understand what you read is to recognize its meaning, but meaning occurs in various ways, on various levels, and with different purposes in mind. To do something with your understanding—to write—establishes certain links with your sense of a text, takes place in gradual stages, and turns back to the original text or—on the strength of it—away from it, in diverse ways.

This introduction to *Findings* is devoted to answering the question posed above by describing ways you can approach it. It is good, however, to start with a description of the essay as a form, since it is the kind of writing you will be doing in this course.

## THE ESSAY

An **essay** is a relatively brief, nonfiction, written discourse, usually prose, devoted to a particular subject about which, usually, the author presents definite ideas in a new fashion.

Saying this, we define a **form**. As with all definitions, we limit our conception in ways that may become too confining when we wish to use the form in inventive and original ways. Description comes to the rescue. Expanding on the terms in the definition can increase the essay writer's scope without violating the proper limits of the art.

Let us, then, take up and examine the most important terms in our definition of the essay.

**Brief.**   *Relatively* is the important word here. Although it is generally understood that essays are shorter than most books, book-length essays are not unheard of. Remember this when you want to extend your treatment of a particular subject to a length you have not previously attempted and that is, therefore, a trifle daunting. Although editors and teachers often set limits on the length of a piece, at times you are free to set them yourself. The rule of thumb is to write as much as you think the subject demands. Knowing how much is enough comes with the kind of experience you will be acquiring in this course.

**Nonfiction.**   Although the American novelist and essayist Gore Vidal has quipped that nonfiction is merely "fiction about actual people," it is possible to draw a more distinct line. In short stories, novels, and plays, the characters, events, speech, and action are imagined; they do not correspond precisely to actuality. The reverse is true for nonfiction. This fact, however, does not rule out the use of the imagination. Besides employing such stylistic devices as metaphor and visual imagery, and such rhetorical techniques as the inclusion of dialogue and quotation, the essayist is free to use hypothesis, conjecture, speculation, imaginative sympathy, and even prediction—all of which move the writer past observed fact into the realm of the possible, not into imaginative literature but into the literary imagination.

**Written.**   Gilbert Ryle, a British philosopher, comments in his *The Concept of Mind,* "Much of our ordinary thinking is conducted in internal monologues or silent soliloquy, usually accompanied by an internal cinematograph-show of visual imagery." Speech and pictures. The one is characterized by informality and presence, and the other by the mere appearance of things. Both must yield in writing to the formal organization of language, to the interpretation of meaning, and to the separation of performer and audience. The key to this development is calculation. The writer carefully plans and places material, divides and balances sections of a composition, decides on the amount and degree of emphasis, and does all this not just beforehand but in the middle of things and after the fact as well (see the sections below on Prewriting, Drafting, and Revising essays).

**Prose.**   Although you are hardly likely to attempt an essay in verse, still it is useful to focus on the prose medium as the one that lends itself most readily to explaining, arguing, and analyzing. These are prime functions of the essayist engaged by ideas. The prose writer is greatly concerned to achieve clear syntax and effective diction on the level of precision, concision, and aptness. Sentence variety, parallel structure, necessary subordination of points, idiomatic expression, and other virtues of good prose become language targets for the essayist who wishes to *create* the best sense of a subject as well as to *communicate* that sense to others.

**Particular.**  This term and the noun it modifies, *subject,* should probably be mentioned together. Used as an adjective, *particular* corrects a tendency many writers have to let a subject overflow the essay's relatively narrow bounds and lose all definition. But *particular* used as a noun, especially when it is made plural—as in, "Would you please state all the particulars of the case?"—points also to a world of separate facts, objects, names, shapes, sensations—in short, to the enormously variegated and concrete actuality of existence that forms the basis for ideas and reminds us that we live in a real world.

**Subject.**  Two problems face the essayist here. One is the problem of wandering off the subject. The other is failing to allow matters that may seem unrelated, but are not, to enter. Often, you will find that these problems are solvable at once if an identical principle links them together: issues, ideas, events, and so on that you feel the urge to introduce in your essay are trustworthy inclusions if they have **thematic unity** and untrustworthy if they lack it. For instance, your subject might be state-imposed conditions on abortions. The theme is reproductive freedom. Whatever pursues this theme is a candidate for inclusion in your essay, though you must show its specific connection to your subject. The French abortifacient RU-486 might well be a matter for discussion in such an essay, since its adoption in the United States could greatly decrease the demand for clinical abortions and thus render moot the issue of conditions. But a discussion of single parenting and the difficulties a friend has had in this regard would violate thematic unity *unless* you can show that abortion and single parenting were related and that the two came together on the issue of conditions in the friend's life. All this could be the case, but it might not be, and merely to bring her up in the essay as a person who needs help would be to wander off theme.

**Definite.**  Again, this adjective and the *ideas* it describes cannot easily be separated in this discussion. Yet we should consider *definiteness* in isolation, especially because it is both a highly desirable quality in writing *and* a possible source of trouble. To be definite means to state your meaning precisely, without ambiguity and with conviction. There's a definite (not vaguely possible) chance of rain, according to meteorological observation. The national debt in 1995 was definitely still on the rise, not showing signs of decline. But to say the national debt will never go down, or to say it will never stop raining, is to be too definite. You would properly *qualify* such statements by adding the clause "unless spending is cut and taxes go up" to the first and "it seems as if" to the second. The flexible writer, the one who can modulate expression, is the one who nicely balances definiteness and qualification.

*Ideas.*   Because the essay is rather gemlike (compared to the great rock formation of a book), it is perfectly suited to examine a very few linked ideas at one time, without having to integrate the discussion with numerous other, complex matters. In fact, because of this very serviceability, essays exist for the sake of ideas. It is easy to lose sight of this fact when writing an essay. Telling a story or describing a place, we may become so involved with plot or concrete detail that we forget that they should yield ideas, illustrate ideas, demonstrate how ideas work out in the world, or otherwise firmly establish the importance of ideas. An idea results from the thoughts that we collect from disparate sources and relate to each other. It is not rare to have an idea, but the question is, How do we know that the idea is our own, that it is therefore . . .

*New.*   Generally in life, there seems little reason merely to repeat what others have said. We want to be ourselves, and therefore we want to say something new. Inexperience of various kinds may discourage this desire, though no one is ever possessed of enough experience to count on it alone for ideas. Furthermore, particularly in an academic setting where teaching (rather than learning) and collaborative learning (rather than teaching) both seem endlessly to *supply* ideas, you may feel that everything you think reflects the thoughts of others. But, in fact, it is the particular glory of the essay form to give us a chance to try out a personal voice, to make our own stylistic decisions, to reach our own insights. These are sources of value, and these, you will discover, provide new dimensions of meaning and distinguish your presentation from anyone else's. As a result, if you do take advantage of the opportunities afforded you—if the sources of value in writing become your *resources*—you will make what you do new. The experience essential to generating new ideas is the experience of investigating whatever subject matter is at issue and coming up with findings that lead to definite conclusions on your part. If it is your investigation, the idea will be yours too.

How to make the investigation your own and arrive at new ideas is the specific focus of the next section of this introduction.

# FROM (THEIR) TEXT TO (YOUR) TEXT

When a film is broken down into its separate frames, we can follow and understand action as one gesture leading to the next; we cannot do this very easily if the film remains a continuous flow. In the latter case, *what* happens, not *how* it happens, impresses itself upon us. The same applies to moving from reading to writing, from someone else's sentences to your own, from another's meaning to your own. Learning how best to move in this way requires an analysis of the process in which we see the actual stages of progress from text to text.

Here is a brief story that composition student Fred Neurohr read, responded to, and reflected on to create his own meaning.

## A Parable

Buddha told a parable in a sutra:

A man traveling across a field encountered a tiger. He fled, the tiger after him. Coming to a precipice, he caught hold of the root of a wild vine and swung himself down over the edge. The tiger sniffed at him from above. Trembling, the man looked down to where, far below, another tiger was waiting to eat him. Only the vine sustained him.                                                                          5

Two mice, one white and one black, little by little started to gnaw away at the vine. The man saw a lucious strawberry near him. Grasping the vine with one hand, he plucked the strawberry with the other. How sweet it tasted!

Neurohr's essay based on this text began like this:

```
"A Parable" is a story that we as westerners stand to
learn a lot from.  Once it is unpacked, "A Parable"
contains many interesting points that can help raise
the spiritual quality of life.  In the story we read
about a man crossing a field.  He spots a tiger and     5
flees.  He jumps over a precipice and catches the
root of a tree.  He dangles there.  The man soon
finds himself with a tiger above him, a tiger below
him and two mice chewing away at the very root from
which he hangs.  With his death close at hand, rather   10
than scream, pray or panic, he picks a nearby straw-
berry and eats it.  This is a type of story that is
supposed to illustrate a moral attitude or a reli-
gious principle.  The one resounding principle that
comes across is that we should do what the man in the   15
story did and partake of life's offerings.  Another
not so obvious idea is that of living in the present.
It is exactly this Zen idea that allowed that man to
partake and, in many ways, allows us to partake as
well.                                                   20
```

It is very typical of westerners to struggle to live according to a future event or fret about something in the past. In eastern culture there is an antecedent spiritual attitude that pervades all ac-
25 tions and in which all experiences take on special significance. We do not find in "A Parable" any sense of regret that the man didn't take another route rather than the field he chose. He is also not anticipating his certain and very painful and violent
30 demise. The important feature of this story is that he is living in the present. This is exactly why he can partake in the sweetness of the strawberry. The present moment is the only moment. In reading the story, we see that there is no reference to anything
35 outside the story. No past tenses are used that refer to an occurence happening at a time prior to the time of the tale; nothing in the future is referred to.

It is easy to see how many of the modern-day prob-
40 lems of westerners are a result of either worrying about the future or brooding over things that happened in the past. Emotional states such as adolescence and mid-life crises are western phenomena that attest to this. The former is the result of pressure
45 put on children to concern themselves with a time in their lives that has not arrived while the latter comes from a lingering insecurity in past actions. Worry, regret, avarice, and grudges are all everyday sentiments and common conditions that focus on a time
50 other than the one we happen to be in. All detract from the present and, consequently, the quality of life in one way or another.

In these three paragraphs alone, Neurohr moves through these five stages of reading and writing:

1. Particular recognitions
2. Literal comprehension
3. Interpretative understanding
4. Stating the meaning and significance of the text
5. Extrapolating and/or interpolating meaning

Now let us follow him through this process, explaining the above terms as we go along.

*Particular Recognitions.*    When reading, you can't go very far or fast unless the language and its presentation are, or become, clear and familiar to you. "A Parable" is translated from Japanese into English. In translation, the language presents no problem, nor does the typical use of full sentences and paragraphing. If some foreign words had remained, however, or if the text displayed an uncommon typography, you would be facing language on the elementary level of appearance that would require some adjustments on your part. On this level, you always need to recognize cultural references and allusions and all vocabulary words. In "A Parable," the term *parable* itself, *sutra,* and the attribution of the story to Buddha might all be obstacles to immediate recognition and thus to literal comprehension.

*Literal Comprehension.*    Neurohr does not find it necessary (though you might) to define *sutra* as a religious speech or to identify the Buddha as Siddhartha Gautama, the fifth century B.C.E. founder of one of the world's great religions. Apparently, he doesn't feel the reader needs this information. But he might well have originally consulted his dictionary for his own benefit. In his notes for this essay, he does define *parable* as "a short fictitious story that illustrates a moral attitude or a religious principle," and he goes so far as to define *precipice* as "a very steep or overhanging place or a hazardous situation; brink." As a reader, you need to understand the meaning of these terms and references.

Also as a reader, you must understand all syntactical constructions and logical connections. Because "A Parable" employs relatively short sentences, the **syntax**—the orderly and meaningful association of words within sentence units—is not complicated. But for such a brief story, a large number of participles appear (*traveling, Coming, Trembling,* and *Grasping*), and it might be useful to consider how these adjectival constructions establish the idea of action.

The logic of the text is that of time: chronology. **Narratives,** which recount an event or series of related events, are perhaps the simplest logical structures to follow. The sequential logic of analytic reasoning and the associative logic of literary art present greater challenges. But you should notice in "A Parable" the symmetry of the situation at the heart of the action: the tiger behind matched by the tiger ahead, and the vine as a line connecting them, flanked by mice whose colors cancel each other out. The asymmetry of the strawberry, however, produces the action that is the key to an interpretative understanding.

*Interpretative Understanding.*    Everyone needs to know what particular words mean. But we also need to know what *combinations* of words mean— not just the identity of the Buddha or the dictionary meaning of *sutra* but, on the basis of the text, what the Buddha communicates and what the sutra explains. Neurohr does not feel compelled to explain to the reader that the twin tigers symbolize birth and death and the mice night and day, but in the notes he made for himself he writes:

"A Parable" . . . makes a statement about what the
whole of life really is.

It is the idea of the cynic that each moment in life
is one closer to death.  That each sensation, each
experience, good or bad, only takes our life breath
away.

"A Parable" represents the end of a conflict, a surrender.

The ancient idea of time is circular, while ours
is linear.  Birth is a death and death is a birth.
If we reverse the ideas in the story this becomes
clear.  The vine is an umbilical cord.  Once the umbilical cord is cut, life begins, but once this vine
is cut, life ends.  Since time is cyclical, birth and
death are not considered as conflicting ideas, but
are very closely related.  Just as night and day are
not contraries, but complements.  This synthesis
carries over to the man's not struggling, because
facing death is not something to fight; it is something expected and not to be feared.

In his essay proper, mentions of time—of the past and the future—and of
death suffice for him. But notice the emphasis he places on the man's central
position, which is central to his interpretation and thus to the essay he will
write.

"A Parable" requires the reader to move from concrete symbols (like the
strawberry) to abstract concepts (like "partake of life's offerings"). In other texts,
you will need to put together separate points an author makes, points you have
literally comprehended, to form a general idea of the intended meaning. For instance, an author citing high unemployment figures, negative job growth, loss
of consumer confidence, and decaying infrastructure obviously believes that the
economic situation is a dire one. If the author has shown causal connections between these factors, we are probably meant to understand that a solution must
reflect these links. The author may state such conclusions outright, in which
case our task is the relatively simple one of digesting someone else's interpretation. But if these conclusions are unstated, or if we realize that explicit statements are mere preliminaries to further thinking on our part, then we must
make **inferences**—detect what is suggested but not actually expressed—or otherwise expand on meaning through our own analytic reasoning.

Neurohr performs the second of these two interpretative functions. He perceives the tigers in the story to symbolize birth and death. Death is not a difficult interpretation to make, but why birth? Neurohr's reasoning can be found in
his notes quoted above. We might reach a similar conclusion by making the fol-

lowing connections: the threats to the man's life are opposite each other spatially, but they are both tigers and therefore what they represent could also be identical. If each means his death, the death represented by the one chasing the man across the meadow could be seen as the death he has left (as opposed to the death he is approaching). But what death do we leave behind? Before birth is nonexistence; after death is extinction. Each is a form of death. Roughly speaking, therefore, the tiger at the man's back is his own birth.

### *Stating the Meaning and Significance of the Text.*   To inform the reader of meaning and significance is a chief task of writers who work from texts, sometimes *the* chief task. We might be tempted to say that this stage of producing your own writing consists only of shaping in sentences that are meant for public consumption what you have already thought or noted down in more fragmentary form. But, as we see if we compare Neurohr's notes with the portion of his essay quoted above, this stage calls for more than that.

For one thing, you cannot convey your ideas about the contents of a work until you have described its form—what happens, who is present, how events unfold, and so on. Otherwise, the reader will be able neither to judge the accuracy and value of your interpretation nor to understand later references to the original text. Neurohr **paraphrases** "A Parable." He puts the story in his own words. He doesn't feel it necessary to quote directly, evidently because he considers none of the original prose so irreplaceable that he must reproduce it; nor does he summarize the story, which he might have done if it were longer, by identifying the *kinds* of events that occur and saying what their interrelationship amounts to. Both quotation and summary are generally valuable, however, and you should certainly use them when they seem appropriate.

What we do find is that Neurohr's report of the original story reduces it to a very few words. His so doing reflects the writer's principle of **selectivity**: he chooses to report only what is essential to the meaning of "A Parable."

From paraphrase, Neurohr springs directly into the following statement of meaning.

```
The one resounding principle that comes across is
that we should do what the man in the story did and
partake of life's offerings. Another not so obvious
idea is of living in the present.
```

Here we see Neurohr *making connections between points* (partaking and living in the present), which is another useful principle of stating meaning.

In some instances, facing some writing tasks, you may feel the need to go to greater lengths in connecting the author's points. Equally, you will sometimes see the benefit of reporting an author's general attitudes and approaches to producing his or her meaning, as Neurohr does when he comments on "eastern culture." And sometimes it is graceful as well as useful to state a critical appreciation of the author's thinking and of its expression.

The meaning of a text takes a step up, toward becoming significant, when you show how major ideas have an important relation to other ideas, events, situations, or persons, especially your readers. In Neurohr's reaction to the two sentences quoted on the previous page,

```
It is exactly this Zen idea that allowed that man to
partake and, in many ways, allows us to partake as
well.
```

he points to the important relation between "partaking" and "us," giving the original meaning its true significance. This statement takes Neurohr to extrapolating and interpolating meaning. We define these terms and explain these functions of writing next.

### *Extrapolating and/or Interpolating Meaning.*   To **extrapolate** is to take what you have learned in one place and apply it in another place, one that at first seemed unrelated but that you now recognize as connected after all. In her book *Empty Places,* pop singer Laurie Anderson comments as follows:

> Even though the backstage door scene is sort of corny, signing autographs on someone's arm, etc., I'm very grateful to people who take the time to talk to me after a performance. Sometimes they tell me, "Oh, I got so many ideas from your work!" Then they tell me what the ideas were and they have nothing whatever to do with what I said or did. This tells me that the work was really a success—when other people take it and use it in a way I'd never dreamed of.

Anderson's fans, in a no doubt informal way, are extrapolating.

Neurohr also uses his knowledge in a new way when he applies his interpretation of "A Parable" to western society. No mention of western society exists in the original text. Nonetheless, it seems obvious to Neurohr to contrast western ways with the eastern culture from which the text emerges. The point of contrast is the idea of living in the present. Not only do westerners typically not do this, according to Neurohr, but their failure to do so is the source of many of their troubles. "Worry, regret, avarice, and grudges," he points out, "are all everyday sentiments and common conditions that focus on a time other than the one we happen to be in."

By this time, we are pretty far from the original text, but because Neurohr has established a new line of communication between it and his later concerns (western culture), we never balk at the application he makes of his ideas. Although parables, moral tales, allegories, and the like are expressly intended to produce such applications, making them is still a matter of independent thinking. It is also a matter of being responsible to the original text, of making sure a logical connection exists between where you get to and where you started from.

In the rest of his essay (see below), Neurohr examines case studies of people he believes are wasting the present time. Doing so extends his extrapolation, but here, as well as in his introductory paragraphs, he also interpolates meaning. To **interpolate** is to bring external ideas, issues, concerns, and so on *into* the text so that they can illuminate it and, in effect, provide a commentary on its subject matter. Neurohr, having established that western and eastern cultures are starkly different, goes back to "A Parable" and refers to the character's lack of regret for the past or apprehension of the future, and notes the absence of tense other than present.

In the final sentences of the essay, Neurohr mixes interpolation and extrapolation so skillfully that we are hard put to distinguish them.

```
At every single moment we find ourselves on a cliff
edge of experience.  It's just like the man in the
story who suddenly found himself on a precipice.  We
too have a choice.  Do we look back?  Do we look
ahead?  Or do we just look?
```

Perhaps now we can say that the original text of "A Parable" and the next text, "Now and Zen," combine to produce a fresh understanding and, possibly, a third text—the one you might write in response to the two.

Here is the whole of Fred Neurohr's essay:

NOW AND ZEN

Fred Neurohr

Zen

```
"A Parable" is a story that we as westerners stand to
learn a lot from.  Once it is unpacked, "A Parable"
contains many interesting points that can help raise
the spiritual quality of life.  In the story we read
about a man crossing a field.  He spots a tiger and       5
flees.  He jumps over a precipice and catches the
root of a tree.  He dangles there.  The man soon
finds himself with a tiger above him, a tiger below
him and two mice chewing away at the very root from
which he hangs.  With his death close at hand, rather     10
than scream, pray or panic, he picks a nearby straw-
berry and eats it.  This is a type of story that is
supposed to illustrate a moral attitude or a reli-
gious principle.  The one resounding principle that
comes across is that we should do what the man in the     15
story did and partake of life's offerings.  Another
```

not so obvious idea is that of living in the present.
It is exactly this Zen idea that allowed that man to
partake and, in many ways, allows us to partake as
20  well.

It is very typical of westerners to struggle to
live according to a future event or fret about something in the past.  In eastern culture there is an
antecedent spiritual attitude that pervades all ac-
25  tions and in which all experiences take on special
significance.  We do not find in "A Parable" any
sense of regret that the man didn't take another
route rather than the field he chose.  He is also not
anticipating his certain and very painful and violent
30  demise.  The important feature of this story is that
he is living in the present.  This is exactly why he
can partake in the sweetness of the strawberry.  The
present moment is the only moment.  In reading the
story, we see that there is no reference to anything
35  outside the story.  No past tenses are used that refer to an occurrence happening at a time prior to
the time of the tale; nothing in the future is
referred to.

It is easy to see how many of the modern-day prob-
40  lems of westerners are a result of either worrying
about the future or brooding over things that happened in the past.  Emotional states such as adolescence and mid-life crises are western phenomena that
attest to this.  The former is the result of pressure
45  put on children to concern themselves with a time in
their lives that has not arrived while the latter
comes from a lingering insecurity in past actions.
Worry, regret, avarice, and grudges are all everyday
sentiments and common conditions that focus on a time
50  other than the one we happen to be in.  All detract
from the present and, consequently, the quality of
life in one way or another.

## Then

Last year my uncle Terry, my mother's only brother,
made a rare trip to New York City from his home in
55  rural New Hampshire.  It had been years since he and
my mom had gotten together.  The last time was the
spring of 1978 when Terry, also my Godfather, stood
beside me as my sponsor during the sacrament of Con-

firmation at Our Lady of Perpetual Help in Brooklyn.
Uncle Terry had undergone several eye operations at
Massachusetts General Hospital. He had lost most of
his vision due to his diabetes. His daughter Kelly
told me he wanted to visit me and my mom while he
could still see.

He looked good, fit. My mother seemed happy to
see him. It was a warm fall day, so my mother and I,
having picked him up from his friend's house in
Brooklyn, went to the South Street Seaport for lunch.
He and my mom talked about how New York had changed
so much and about all the people in our family who
had died, some I'd never even heard of. Then there
was the big debate about New York sports teams and
Boston sports teams. I was lying in a lounge chair
next to them, listening, looking across the East
River at the Brooklyn Bridge and the Watchtower
Building. I noticed that there was all this conversation between a brother and sister, who see each
other about once every ten or twelve years, that
never ran deeper than discussing Patrick Ewing and
Larry Bird, Don Mattingly and Wade Boggs. I found
that strange.

I went to Brooklyn alone the following evening to
see Terry again. I was to stay over and take him to
Port Authority the next morning. We ate in a diner
that evening. I insisted on taking him to Peter
Luger's or somewhere special, but he said that he
couldn't go home without eating at a classic New York
"greasy spoon." Later, he and I shared a bed together at his friend Eddie Wade's house and he told
me how he wished my mom would call, she almost never
did, and how he wanted her to see Erin, his first
grandchild. His wishes soon turned to snores and the
next thing I knew his bus was backing out of the
gate, bound for Boston.

Back at home, I chatted with my mother about Terry
and told her all the stuff we talked about. "How
come you don't call him?" I asked.

"Because I can't forgive him for what he did."
She said that when my maternal grandmother died in
1971, Terry never showed up at the funeral. He did
come down to visit everyone while the funeral was going on, but word was that he couldn't bear the pain

of seeing his mother dead. That's why he never
showed up at the actual service. I tried to explain
105   that to my mom to no avail. "All I know," she said,
"is I had to go through all that shit on my own.
Your **God**father was having a ball at your aunt
Loretta's house!" "I don't see how he could have
been having a good time mom, Grandma did die you
110   know!" "You didn't even know your grandmother. You
didn't know all that she did for Terry, so what do
you care." Well my hopes of an intelligent conversation were gone at that point. It was the last time
we spoke about uncle Terry.
115       I still call him about once a month. I may go
fishing with him this year at Lake Winnipesaukee,
N. H., just a short drive from where his daughter and
granddaughter live, near Goose Rocks Beach, Maine,
just north of Kennebunkport. I don't know if I'll
120   tell him what my mom said. Why bring up the past
when we're so far away? Just fishing.
My mother is unable to move out of the past to
truly partake in the here and now with her brother.
The grudge she holds is a prohibitive element rooted
125   in the past that she continues to let detract from
the present. She is dwelling on the past, a time
that only has the reality and all the importance that
my mother assigns to it. Talking things out with my
uncle would be the equivalent of tasting the sweet-
130   ness of the strawberry like the man in the story. As
long as she concentrates on things in the past, they
will eat away at her like the mice on the vine.

### Yet to Come

Steve Drucker and I worked together at a storage
warehouse when I was a freshman in college. He and I
135   used to run the warehouse alone on Saturdays and Sun-
days. There wasn't much to do, so we played a lot of
football in the parking lot. He was nice enough, but
I always wondered about him. He was a good looking
fellow with an outstanding physique, carrot-red hair
140   and freckles. What puzzled me was how he kept to
himself in so many ways. I hardly knew anything
about him. I mean I knew where he lived and how many
brothers and sisters he had and all that, but I never
knew about him. The only things were the obvious.

He worked out, you could tell by his build, he was            145
computer literate, you could tell by the way he
messed with the PC in the office.  But there was
something else.  He was afraid of opening up at all,
even a little bit.
      He avoided anything that could turn into a male       150
bonding session.  He would always decline invitations
to go out to a bar or club, for example, or to watch
a football game on television with a bunch of guys.
He was also notoriously cheap.  I always kidded him,
telling him he had "short arms and deep pockets."           155
Never spent cash.  If he didn't bring lunch from
home, he starved.  It's not that he didn't have
money.  He worked lots of overtime, made good money
and lived at home.  Sometimes I'd buy him lunch just
as a nice gesture, yet he never returned any of the         160
gestures I offered.
      There was a certain defensiveness about the way he
operated, everything was a shortcut, a scam.  He had
little maneuvers around given systems or sets of
rules that he would defend and make work until he           165
saved a few dollars on something.  As an example,
he bought a used car.  It was an expensive high performance sports car.  In order to get by paying the
sales tax that we are all required to pay, he claimed
he bought the car for $50.00.  He told the Department       170
of Motor Vehicles that the car was a wreck, useless.
He had to dig it out of six inches of mud and tow it
on a flatbed to his garage.  It had no engine, no
suspension, no wheels and no axles.  The story went
on and on.  The D.M.V. looked into it, and I guess          175
his plot to save a few dollars backfired because I
didn't see him drive that car for the rest of our acquaintance.  He never told me what happened.
      When Steve and I left the warehouse, he got a job
as a systems analyst at Citibank, I went to work as a       180
market analyst for a publishing company.  We never
really spoke again after that, but I do keep in touch
with our old boss; she and I have cocktails together
now and then.  She said that Steve "worked like a
dog" and he finally bought his house.  "His house?"         185
I said, "Steve bought a house?"  "That guy?  That's
all he lived for."  She asked, "How could you not
know?  You never saw him spend money. . . ."  All I

190 could think was what a waste.  The guy hadn't made a
friend as long as I knew him and the ones he had
stopped calling after getting the brush off so many
times.  The funny part is, now that he has his house,
he still doesn't call.

195 I don't think it's wrong, as Jesse Jackson says,
to "keep your eyes on the prize."  Planning is an integral part of success and there's no getting around
it.  It's when it becomes an obsession, that the
problems start.  You can wind up paying far more for
a house than the asking price.

### Zen and Now

200 The future is such a ruling force in Steve's life
that it clouds his present.  If he were the man dangling from the root, he would be so wrapped up in en-
visioning his fate, I'm sure he would not even realize that the strawberry was near him to begin with.

205 My mother and Steve Drucker, by concentrating on a
time other than the one in which they live, are unable to truly partake in life.  The past and future
are only as real as we imagine them to be.  The only
things we can really savor are in the present.  At

210 every single moment we find ourselves on a cliff edge
of experience.  It's just like the man in the story
who suddenly found himself on a precipice.  We too
have a choice.  Do we look back?  Do we look ahead?
Or do we just look?

The process described above and illustrated by Fred Neurohr's essay outlines the development on a practical level of what may be designated **critical
thinking**: the conscious movement by the writer from true understanding to
original statement. Because the ability to think critically is such an important intellectual achievement, crowning the writer's efforts with creative freedom, let
us now focus more specifically on this concept.

# CRITICAL THINKING

The word *critical* can be misleading if we think of it exclusively as a negative
term. It is partially that, to be sure. We adversely criticize something when we
expose its faults or shortcomings. But we also can reach a critical understanding
of the same thing when, rather than simply rejecting it out of hand, we discover

its positive characteristics as well or, if it lacks these, we frame it in a context that more fully explains its nature.

For example, it would be extremely difficult for most people to find anything good to say about Adolf Hitler. Yet we don't get very far if all we say is that he was evil. In fact, reducing comment to that obvious level probably weakens our condemnation of him, since our audience's eyes glaze when they encounter truisms (statements that hardly need to be made). We more strongly accuse him, we do not excuse him, when we see him as a radical purveyor of racism, nationalism, and militarism, traditions that had a long history in Germany and a ready reception among many people. And we go even further in this direction when we add knowledge of post–World War I Germany and begin to explain how Hitler and his gang[1] exploited this situation.

We can say at this point, then, that critical thinkers try to view a person, text, theory, event, or anything else they focus on, with as wide a lens as possible to capture a sense of its entirety. The desired view is a balanced one. It is fair to every aspect of the situation, never allowing personal or other bias to magnify one detail at the expense of another. (Of course, an unbiased and objective view might well find such a difference in importance.) This approach is basic, but it is also preliminary. The aim of critical thinkers is to reexamine and revalue the subject of their inquiry. In the end, they may reaffirm *or* deny what others have thought. But the result will be *their* new configuration of the subject—*their* thoughts taking shape in writing. This originality gives them their status as critical thinkers.

Like everyone else, the critical thinker begins at the beginning. As Albert Camus, one of the authors represented in this book, has observed, "Thinking is learning all over again how to see, directing one's consciousness . . ." (*The Myth of Sisyphus,* p. 43). To start with, we will discuss seeing in terms of *reading* critically, an activity that corresponds to the kind of interpretative understanding discussed earlier (pp. 13–15).

**Reading Critically.**    When reading, we often find it pleasurable to let ourselves be swept away by the subject matter, never questioning the direction it takes. This is especially so when reading fiction. Plot, character, dialogue, situation become visible and moving, and if we want to maintain the pace the author has set, we rarely pause to consider matters of sense and sensibility. But it is always possible, even here, to do so, to stop and question, to ask what background views the author holds, what the characters' behavior and language reveals, what ideology or general worldview the work may be attempting to validate. Understanding these matters can only enrich the act of reading. We experience the text more completely in itself, and we also may now compare it more tellingly with other texts.

---

1. If you balked even slightly at the use of the word *gang* here instead of, say, colleagues or fellow Nazis, you are thinking critically. This was a test. *Gang* has negative connotations and decides the issue before it is joined.

What is possible with fiction is doubly so with nonfiction. The statements of nonfiction authors are frequently more direct, their reasoning is (or should be) clearly on display, and the sources of their ideas are safely attributed. It is easier for readers, therefore, to isolate these in the text and evaluate them. Here are some criteria to use:

- Test statements of meaning for their logical consistency (whether they contradict themselves or otherwise interrupt a normal sequence), their germaneness (whether they really apply to the topic), and their effectiveness (whether they are clearly put in appropriate and precise language so as to further the author's point of view).

- Test reasoning for its basic assumptions (either fair or unwarranted, the latter possibly in the mistaken belief that everyone shares a particular view), the use of evidence (the relevance and sufficiency of the support), and the ideas formed by the reasoning process (their power to combine logic free from fallacies and to mount evidence toward confirmation of the writer's points).

- Test sources of ideas for their examined quality (have they been opened up for discussion and, if necessary, corrected by objective commentators?), their authoritativeness (do they reflect careful weighing of evidence and balanced judgment?), and their reliability (have they stood the test of time as indicators of value and meaning, or have they merely survived because they satisfied an emotional need?).

Once readers increase their understanding of texts in these ways (and understanding that their own written work will be similarly judged), they can move on to writing *from* their reading. Doing so corresponds to the stages described above in the sections on Stating the Meaning and Significance of the Text and Extrapolating and/or Interpolating Meaning (pp. 15–17).

**Writing Critically.**   The greater the number of angles writers approach a subject from, the more comprehensive a view they can offer of it. If developed in sufficient detail, each of these approaches can create a new context for the subject. In each, the subject takes on a new coloring, giving us a new way to see it, as if it were a person moving through a series of rooms and reacting differently to each. However, these contexts do not simply multiply; they add up. Enough of the right ones, meaningfully connected, produce a new way of thinking about the subject. To return to our previous example, a writer can say something original to explain Hitler's rise to power if the German dictator's experience in World War I and his postwar failure to earn a living—two different contexts for study—are on the one hand connected and, on the other, presented as corresponding to the same experiences on a much larger, national scale involving hundreds of thousands of people.

More factors than these are essential to a full explanation, but even at this point, it is possible to emerge with a new idea. It is that Hitler owed his early success in part to the way his own life mirrored general social and economic conditions, and to his subsequent ability to claim to be the soul of Germany, to understand its needs implicitly.

The critical reading a writer would no doubt have applied to this subject would have supplied most of the material for writing. We can imagine a writer making such a historical investigation, finding in one text a balanced view of one aspect of the matter and, in another text, a biased view. The first could go some way toward correcting the second, but the second might nonetheless provide valuable additional facts and information. With other, less distant subjects than our Hitler example, the writer can add to the mix personal experience or that of someone he or she knows or interviews. Experience forms another context. It cannot usually supplant those that reading creates, but it can temper them—be a moderating influence—just as texts can exert this pressure on experience. Collecting facts from authoritative sources (such as a single text you focus on or multiple texts you research), opinions from interested parties (such as fellow students with whom you confer in classroom group work), and answers to questions that probe the issue at hand (such as those appended to the present readings, but also those you yourself may generate)—all these also can open up a subject to your having varying perspectives on it and producing a number of contexts in which to place it. In this book, all these possibilities are present.

When writers have enough to go on, they can go beyond reportage and even beyond interpretation of another's works. As we have seen, now they can break into new intellectual territory, in which they have fresh ideas on their subject. Although they have found part of their ideas in one place and part in another, discovering the interactions between these ideas, which excites new thinking on the subject, is precisely the way all thinking advances on what has preceded it. Interpolation to illuminate an existing body of knowledge and extrapolation to produce a new one are key methods of making such an advance (see pp. 16–17).

Writing and reading critically are the material steps taken by the writer whose mental operations involve critical thinking. Such combined abilities are quite evident in Fred Neurohr's essay, as is his clear movement from another's text to his own. However, Neurohr's essay, as we might guess, did not spring to life in the finished form reprinted here. Neurohr made earlier, prewriting approaches to his essay and later returned to his work to make certain improvements. These matters are what we turn to now.

# PREWRITING

Few writers start adding sentence to sentence and paragraph to paragraph without some preliminary groundwork. Although writers use different means to prepare, three major techniques are most popular: note taking, free writing, and conferring with others. These strategies are popular because they answer the greatest needs writers have, needs that you will soon discover for yourself. These are (1) having key ideas, notable quotations, and important facts at your fingertips; (2) having the freedom to experiment with your own thoughts before committing yourself to their more formal expression; and, (3) having an early audience for untested ideas and a later one for your way of putting these ideas in writing. Let us examine these techniques.

***Note Taking.*** On page 14, we see examples of Fred Neurohr's notes on his reading of "A Parable." His notes are chiefly interpretative. Also, they are written on separate pages and in full sentences. Evidently he felt these approaches best served his interests in moving from what he read to what he made of it in writing. Other purposes and other practical uses are possible, however, and we should look at them as well.

Commenting on your reading in the text margins is one useful method of note taking. The meaning of a statement you read may suddenly occur to you. If you delay in jotting it down, you may lose it. The same applies to connections you may perceive between your reading and the writing you plan to base on it. You may have entirely new ideas that you want to stand in their fragmentary form next to a textual passage. Sometimes, posing a question or merely placing a question mark in the margin will alert you to reexamine a particular passage later. Other times, the important points a writer makes begin to emerge in a text along with paragraphs explaining each such point. To keep track of these points, you may want to number the points in the margin. Significant terms, names, dates, and places may also call for marginal notes or text highlighting.

Such notes as these are usually fragmentary, often limited to a kind of shorthand that suits the narrow space of a margin. Notes on cards or separate pieces of paper, however, can be fuller, and often you will want to transfer marginal notes to cards just to have room to expand an idea, interpret an author's meaning in more detail, define a term, and so on. At times, inspired by your reading, you may find yourself going directly to another piece of paper and beginning to write original thoughts on it. This may become a form of free writing, but you should probably still regard it as a collection of notes to make use of later.

Note taking while you read—and afterward as well—can help you clarify your thinking about the text at hand. The key is putting into your own words what someone else's words say and mean and lead to. That is, this practice aids in reading itself, which is a much more effective activity when you make the text as much your own as possible through sheer absorption of its contents. It is then that you can legitimately claim the title of spokesperson for the text.

But it is the use you *finally* put your notes to that gives them most value. They should contribute both to your reporting what a text says and to your producing ideas of your own. If some notes make no such contribution, it may be that your purpose in writing has changed to some extent from what it originally was. Such an outcome is actually a good sign. It means that your note taking in the first place was *directed*. You knew what you were aiming at (writing an essay according to the directions in a particular assignment), and the energy you put into your reading and thinking was focused on your goal.

Sometimes you may find your notes inadequate to either your original or current purpose in writing. When this happens, return to the text to fill in the gaps and refresh your approach. Once you are satisfied that your note taking measures a complete and directed reading, you still may discard some notes that are repetitive or that become less useful in later drafts and revisions. Put the notes you retain into an order that roughly follows the plan of your essay. With marginal notes, this may mean copying them over. Ordering your notes will make writing more convenient and efficient. It will also help ensure that you don't overlook anything in your notes when you use them.

*Free Writing.*   Moving directly into the first draft of an essay is seldom the best course. A valuable activity is first to try out some of your ideas in writing. Or you may want to sketch a report of what a text you have read says, in part or altogether. Or you may simply decide to practice writing, either on your subject or on anything that comes to mind. In any of these cases, free writing is a handy instrument.

The term means what it says: to write freely, without feeling pressured to organize your thoughts, state your meaning absolutely clearly, produce grammatical sentences, spell correctly, or otherwise impose foresight, oversight, and hindsight. Obviously, this freedom does not mean that order, clarity, correctness, and accuracy are any less important in writing. Far from it. But each of these qualities is a virtue, and virtues take time to develop—here, the duration of writing through various drafts of an essay (see below for a discussion of drafting). Before you begin this process, you may want to stake your claim to writing as a concrete presence on the page, a physical reality, language that no one will judge but that you eventually may be able to make something out of. Write for a while on any subject and you can say, sitting back from your desk, "Look, there it is, a stream of words, a flow of ink, images and ideas, sense and nonsense, my own intellectual energy lighting up the page!"

As implied above, you can go in either of two important directions in free writing: you can put down whatever you think of as it comes, hardly knowing what will happen on the page before it does; or you can express yourself freely on some aspect of your projected essay. You may sometimes be asked to free write at the beginning of a writing class. Other times, you can free write at home to loosen up before attempting a first draft. You can free write in a journal you may be keeping or in a notebook expressly intended for free writing. Later, you can return to these efforts and exploit them for whatever value they may have as ideas and language.

If your free writing is to have value, though, you should let yourself go while doing it. Try out new images and figures of speech. Think of crazy reasons for your arguments (on later inspection, more effective reasons will stand out in contrast). Try endlessly long sentences and extremely brief ones. Invent. Stay loose.

It is best to set a time limit for your free writing—five or ten minutes but probably not more than that; the strain might prove too great. Fix your eyes on your paper and let your pen hover above it. Decide whether you want to embark on a set course (say, one connected to your essay) or plunge into the deep grass (where anything goes). Touch pen to paper and keep writing for the time allotted without stopping.

Soon after you have finished (or later, depending on your needs), look at your free writing to see what, if you have addressed your essay subject, may be usable. One way to discover this is by reading your writing aloud to other people. Of course, your listeners must agree that what you read doesn't have to pass any test for accomplished prose. But writers naturally form subjective judgments about their own work, so other people's views might even here be valuable because they can be more objective.

Turning to others for advice is generally a sound idea, saying which leads naturally to the third important prewriting activity we will discuss: conferring with other people.

***Conferring with Others.***    Although conferring appears here as a prewriting activity, it can help at any stage of the writing process, from your original interpretation of a text to your polished revisions of an essay based on it. We know that talking things over with someone else is generally a good idea. Isolation is not a happy state. Alone and under pressure by the immediate circumstances of our lives, we often are unable to imagine different perspectives to adopt or alternate courses of action to take. These same difficulties also occur in reading and writing. And here, we can examine the places where conferring helps most.

1. *Talking about reading.*    Two or more people reading the same story or essay can easily conceive of it differently. Perhaps the main reasons for this difference are the range of meaning and the number of connections that readers may perceive within a text. Not everyone can see everything. Separate investigations, therefore, produce partial findings that, joined together, can make a wholly sufficient reading. You and your friends don't have to end up agreeing on every particular of such a reading. But once the joint reading exists, you will have before you—especially if you have taken notes on the discussion—choices and possibilities that you might previously have been unaware of.

2. *Generating ideas.*    Ideas don't come out of the blue. They have various sources, usually other people. Each of us gets a little here, a little there, from the thinking of others. We pick up cues from their suggestions and finish thoughts that they begin. We form ideas that in part represent the contributions of our sympathizers. The end result demonstrates an old truth: writing, though each of us does it alone, is inherently social. However, do not fear that the part others play in shaping your ideas will tarnish your own creativity and originality. Ultimately, your own insights, perceived connections, and ways of expressing things will combine to produce work that does not closely resemble anyone else's, just as theirs will not look like yours.

3. *Reading and discussing drafts.* How do we learn most quickly that a version of an essay is not final but still on the way—still a draft? It's when we present it to someone else to read or hear and that person sees problems that we had overlooked. This revelation is not always welcome, but it is always useful. It reminds us that authors naturally love their own creations and can be blind to their faults. This blindness can deflect the original purpose in writing and seriously impair the hoped-for result. Professional writers are well aware of this fact and thus most often submit their work to others' inspection. These writers, and you, are free to accept or reject recommendations as they see fit, but they try to avoid being defensive in order to profit from the advice they get.

The best advice, of course, comes from people who are in the same field and know what the writer is trying to accomplish. In the classroom, this is not a problem since all are aware of the assignment and the generally preferred means of fulfilling it. However, because you will be making one specific approach and someone else another, every commentator has to be sensitive to the individuality of the author, a trait that gives thinking and writing its great value. It is also necessary to know what to look for in another's work that pertains to the universal craft of writing, matters such as clear expression, coherent organization, pointed ideas and supporting evidence, sufficient development in terms of explanation and descriptive detail, and standard English grammar. Let us mention also that, often enough, you will read your paper aloud to a group who may have before them a photocopy of it. Seeing is somewhat useful at this stage, and eventually we rely on it entirely. But with early versions, hearing is indispensable in that it produces more of an actual presence than seeing. If we listen to ourselves as well as to others, we can often catch by ear where we went wrong and where we did right.

Conferring on drafts manufactures an audience for your writing: the people facing you in the classroom. But another audience exists at that point and even earlier in the process of writing. This audience is more general; it is composed of people you may never meet but whom you want to know your view on things and to understand your reasoning, people who are "out there." But just who are these people, and how do we get in touch with them? To answer these questions, let us now focus on the topic of audience.

# THE AUDIENCE FOR WRITING

Everyone wants to know who's on the other end of the telephone he or she picks up. After all, who would say much of what we do on the phone to an anonymous as well as invisible person? Rather, we shape our speeches to our knowledge of the recipient. The writer's position is not identical to the speaker's in this respect, but it is very similar. Writers cannot control the membership of their audience—anyone may choose to read their work—but writers do work with a strong sense of the readers they *hope* to reach, and this sense is responsible for much of the form and content of what they produce.

Personal letters, for instance, are aimed at someone known to the letter writer. The knowledge each has of the other means that to explain some matters a word or two suffice. But even such letters point to the other's absence and distance. The letter writer has had experiences the recipient cannot be expected to have shared, and these need describing; they cannot simply be referred to in the way other common matters may be. And if personal correspondents must take special pains to communicate, think of how much more is required of other kinds of writers. The distance between these writers and their readers—the absence and silence of the latter—creates problems from the very beginning that the writer must solve.

For instance, if you are arguing a position on capital punishment, you probably envision an audience that does not necessarily agree with you but whose views you would like to influence. Otherwise why write such a paper? Some of your classmates are probably on the other side from you. Thus, you find yourself needing not only to persuade them but, in order to do so, to remind them of certain positions taken in a reading you have all done. Perhaps you realize also, however, that the accommodations you make for them can serve to greatly increase your potential audience—expanding beyond the classroom—if you are even more careful to fill in this newly imagined audience about what your class has mutually experienced. At this point, you are writing for the larger audience, the one most writers address.

As you progress as a writer, you will cultivate more refinements in imagining an audience. At times, you will want to write for people interested in a specific activity or topic, and then you will have to decide on what level you want to meet them. Do you assume their general ignorance of the subject, or are you writing to a sophisticated audience eager for the latest and most advanced views? Other ways to define and limit an audience will also present themselves—some, for practice, in this book—but at this point you will probably do best to think of your readers as people who are patient and curious, who want to know what you think but won't have much of a chance unless you carefully report where you have started from, fully state your ideas on the subject, and gently explain their meaning and significance.

Doing these things, you produce a draft of your essay. Since few of us achieve perfection the first time around, you should consider this writing a preliminary version in probable need of revision. Drafting and revision are topics we turn to now.

# DRAFTING AND REVISING

Here are three different comments on the need to redo what is not yet quite right:

Motivated entirely by greed I stay in the hotel room all day writing a 1000-word piece about [Stephen] Frears for an American film magazine. They promise me $1000. On finishing it, sending it round and listening to their reservations, I realize how rarely any kind of writing is simple and how few easy bucks there are to be made. Whenever you write you always have to go back and rethink and rewrite. And you have to be prepared to do that. You never get away with anything.

—Harif Kureishi, from "Some Time with Stephen"

*"This is definitely the last time for Chapter Seventeen!"*

—Drawing by Booth; ©1992 The New Yorker Magazine, Inc.

It seems useless, but
Don't throw it away;
Sour young grapes
Finally grow into
Sweet raisins.

—Anonymous Zen poet

Kureishi counsels us not to harbor false hopes about writing to a *T* the first time around. Booth portrays the natural frustration writers feel in going around again, and sometimes yet again. And Anonymous says we don't go around for nothing. Taken together, these are the psychological stages of revision. The corresponding practical stages are these: realistically appraising what you've written and seeing room for improvement, battling—sometimes against yourself— to get it right, and at last triumphantly bringing something valuable to light.

Let us see how this is done by examining a student essay. Here is the final draft:

## ON MOVING ON

### Sarah Averill

```
    I come from a family of nomads, people cut off from
    their own history, half lost and half found.  As
    such, I am addicted to change, to moving on.  My pri-
    mary instinct is to run; it has been bred into my
 5  genes for generations.
    As a child--by definition a person humiliated with
    lack of choice--I learned to love these nomadic ways,
    as had those that came before me.  Great-grandma Van
    Azletine came from Holland, great-grandpa Lawrence
10  came from Ireland and in search of what--a new hope,
    a new place, a dream of betterment.  They and their
    children and grandchildren left a trail of watermelon
    seeds, arsoned homes, ruined dairy farms, and gold
    cows down blue highways of New York State.  Sometimes
15  they even left their children with other relatives
    momentarily caught like flies in a web of stability.
    They believed still that they were moving up.  My
    mother, with us in the back seat of her most recent
    junker, searched the Americas under the influence of
20  the same dream--a drug, a hope of progress, that elu-
    sive American collective delusion.
    Leaving was a ritual for us, midnight the pre-
    ferred time of departure.  Like bandits, we needed
    the cover of night to hide our shame for merely ex-
25  isting.  We were not good enough for the light of
    day.  Not yet.  We had not yet arrived.  We hoped
    still that progress was not a bankrupt idea, like
    those people today that cling stubbornly to the no-
    tion that bootstraps are something you are born with.
30  Through deserted city streets that were barely damp
```

with evening dew and smelled slightly of tar, we
slipped and snuck on to the great American highway
system, designed to accommodate a constantly migrat-
ing population, forever in search of the golden
arches of opportunity.

The first big trip I remember started just before
my fifth birthday. We drove non-stop from Syracuse,
New York, to Saltillo, Nuevo Leon. Along the way,
we lost a couple of suitcases off the roof of our
Oldsmobile 88. They landed in a field of black-eyed
Susans. I remember looking back. We all saw them
go, but we never stopped.

That trip we started late at night like so many
that were to follow. We left when the air was light
and fresh and the roads were deserted. My mother
wanted to go to medical school and figured that in
Mexico it would be affordable. The dream of advancing herself, of becoming a professional, was what motivated her. On that day as on many after she was
reaching for those famous bootstraps.

During the middle of the third day, somewhere in
the desert, the car overheated again under that big
Texas sky with its blistering sun. In front of a
tumbledown shack with a rain barrel, Hank, my
mother's second husband, asked for some water to re-
fill the radiator. There was nothing else in sight,
just fields of cactus to infinity. A large man in
overalls gave us a jug of water and we drove on,
never turning the motor off. In fact, fearing it
might not start again, Mom refused to turn it off
until we arrived in Saltillo.

She was and still is that way, afraid that if she
isn't moving she is rusting in a junk yard.

That journey traversing the United States from
north to south is too clear in my mind: sitting in
the back seat with my brother Patrick while Mom and
Hank took turns driving, listening to Jim Croce and
Janis Joplin blaring from 8-track tapes, the night
air blowing in the back, the bounce of the car and
the whir of the engine rocking and singing us to
sleep. It was too exciting.

That is when I started developing my taste for the
move. I wasn't even big enough to see out the window
to watch the tail lights of the cars ahead or the
headlights on the cars behind.

35

40

45

50

55

60

65

70

75

Always quietly discontented at the roots, not satisfied with her relationship to others, with her educational status, her pay, her job, or herself, mom was
often gripped by fits, to go someplace new.  She
80   wanted a change of scene, change of weather, a geographical fix.  When she got that way there was no
way of knowing if we were going to stay or leave with
the next nightfall.  All through my childhood, I
stayed up and listened to her talk herself into a de-
85   cision one way or the other.  I felt the dreams that
she spun through wisps of smoke; I inhaled them and
·       they seeped into my bloodstream.  When it all comes
back--the adrenaline, the excitement, the idea that
it will be better if we/I just find the right place
90   to start over--part of me wants to believe in it, the
way we all want to believe in Santa Claus.  But it
has become harder and harder to believe that as we
move forward life gets better.
       My mother, now in her late forties, has arrived in
95   a small town in New Mexico.  She is a medical doctor
with a large house, a swimming pool, a new car, and
thirteen cats.  When I talk to her on the phone she
says she is happy.  She's been there over a year now.
But I can hear the tightness in her voice, a tight-
100  ness I can recognize.  She visits her sisters in California and me in New York, and dreams of moving
again.  She sounds on the verge of tears.

When I started high school, my mother used to ask
me to sit on her bed before I went to sleep.  She
105  propped herself up on three down pillows and talked
to me, asking me what I thought of her latest scheme.
I used to stare into the rows of half-empty coffee
cups on her night stand and the saucers filled with
grey ash, and envision the life she dreamed of: the
110  peace, the calm of that perfect place we were going
to find, that Camelot that my mother could see three
inches in front of her nose.
       "Alaska sounds like such a nice place, doesn't it,
Sarah?  So wild.  We could live in Anchorage and you
115  could take classes at the university while you finish
high school.  We'll get sealskin coats for the winter.  I hear it is very cold there.  We'll load up
the new Saab with tons of canned food and drive all
the way.  We've been in Buffalo for almost five years

now--five times longer than we've been in any other      120
town or city.  We've done the stability thing.  I
could use a change of scene.  So restless these
days."

     It was like watching someone suffering from DT's.
She desperately needed a drink.  The fits came on        125
sometimes unexpectedly driving home at night from the
movies.  If the air was cool and it was late we would
all feel it--we would remember the excitement of having a packed car and a long road trip ahead.  My
brother Patrick navigated, riding shotgun to my Gypsy    130
mother.  Sometimes it passed in a few days and we
stayed wherever we happened to be at the time: Houston, Auburn, Monterrey, Syracuse, Buffalo, Saltillo.

And sometimes it didn't.

The last major move that I made with my mother,          135
brother and sister (my basic unit of mobility) was
just after my twelfth birthday.  At twelve, I was old
enough to want girl friends to talk to about all the
things you can't talk to your mother or brother or
little sister about--not yet anyway.  I was at that      140
age when young girls put on their first bras and
start wondering about shaving their legs.  I needed
friends and I had made them when, suddenly, we moved
again.  I was angry for a year.  Mom did not hear the
words "I love you" from my mouth for the next twelve     145
months.  I found refuge in books, and my gray-spotted
cat became my only confidant.  The next couple of
years were difficult; they were years of conscious
suffering.  I knew that I had outgrown my family's
way of life.                                             150

Yet it still runs in my veins.  At twenty-two, I get
the same fits that my mother did, the ones that kept
her up late into the night chain-smoking and swallow-
ing pots of dark coffee at the kitchen table.
     I am filled with her voice sometimes and imagine    155
that in America many are filled with such voices going back generations.  I imagine my great-grandfather
Lawrence listened to his parents and was filled with
their voice before he came to America.  I envision
him sitting at a crooked kitchen table and listening    160
to voices.  My grandfather, I know, is filled with

the stories of his father Lawrence and my mother of her father's stories and a brand of his peculiar rambling ways.

165     I listened to other voices, too, the voices in the wind, the howls in the night, the beckoning American dream that politicians would have us believe in. And now I wonder how many have listened and heeded and how many have chosen not to listen. How many chil-
170 dren of Irish carpenters, Welsh coal miners, Italian bricklayers, Cuban cigar makers, watched their parents over cups of steaming liquids discuss their dreams of finding a better life, of progress, of motion, of revolution late into the night and listened
175 with their bones so hard that they shook as if a train were about to pass them by? Once moved, transported, indentured, and filled with loneliness, how many repented, regretted, wished that as children they had been deaf to their parents' enlightened
180 ideas? I for one.

    In my darker moments, I picture myself as a helium balloon on a child's wrist slipping free and floating up into the stratosphere. I drift and wander across the sky, too free, almost out of sight and then I
185 burst. I fall back to earth a withered bit of plastic. People find me on the beach and in the street. They smile faintly, remembering the helium balloons that they have lost, not realizing that the little shriveled-up piece of rubber is me--used up, lost,
190 exploded from the inside out.

    I dream now that my mother tries to burn my house down, a house that she and I both live in, though it has been five years now since I left home. This house, which is riddled with little fires under the
195 floor boards and between the walls, is filled with friends and family. This repeated dream is a projection onto the past; it tells me how destructive it was to keep moving--that really a move is like setting fire to friendships, to the fabric of our human
200 relations, to the stuff that life is made of. These dreams speak to me, they warn me that I too have access to that fire, and I too can be an arsonist.

    I fight the fits that grip me with such violence and demand my obedience. I run in circles to beat
205 them back, I take long walks until I sweat and am too tired to think, to move, I sleep. I fight them the

way I fight the notion that you can pull yourself up
by your bootstraps. I've found too often that even
when the bootstraps are in sight, my arms have been
tied behind my back.

I've gotten tired, worn down, by running, and                              210
now, I find I'm holding on, even as I'm running, to
threads of my past, to my friends, memories, places.
Even as I run, I carry on my back a dozen houses,
half a dozen apartments, and a few abandoned shacks,        215
secret hideouts in the backwoods where fields of
black-eyed Susans desperately try to put down roots.

I never perfected the fine art of leaving a place
behind, of not looking back. I can no longer let go,
forget, leave things behind. It is too painful, so I        220
hold on to each place, to each friendship and love
affair.

Tenaciously, I hold onto the houses, apartments,
states and climates that I have lived in, hoping that
somehow, if I carry those places around in my head          225
and heart I will know who I am, be complete, whole,
sane.

To get a glimpse into the way this essay came about, we can look at a paragraph from a preliminary draft and compare that sample to the way it appears in
the final draft. We can then listen to Averill herself on the process of writing.

## Preliminary Draft

Alaska sounds like such a nice place doesn't it
Sarah? we could live in Anchorage and you could take
classes at the university while you finish your last
year of highschool. we'll get seal skin coats for
the winter. i hear it is very cold there. we've
been in Buffalo for almost five years now--five
times longer that we've been in any other town or
city. We've done the stability thing. I could use
a change of scene. I've got ants in my pants--so
wrestless these days.

## Final Draft

"Alaska sounds like such a nice place, doesn't it
Sarah? So wild. We could live in Anchorage and you
could take classes at the university while you finish high school. We'll get sealskin coats for the
winter. I hear it is very cold there. We'll load up
the new Saab with tons of canned food and drive all

the way. We've been in Buffalo for almost five years
now--five times longer than we've been in any other
town or city. We've done the stability thing. I
could use a change of scene. So restless these
days."

Here is a list of the types of revisions Averill made between these two versions, with a commentary on them.

1. *Editing.*   Correcting spelling, typographical errors, punctuation, and word form should come last. We'll look at them first here, though, because they stick out most. These are mechanical problems, and although they are important to fix so that they do not impair communication, they ought not to take precedence over more serious concerns. Notice, however, that by her final draft Averill has enclosed this whole speech in quotation marks, added commas, capitalized the beginnings of sentences and the first-person pronoun, separated *highschool* into two words and made *seal skin* one, and spelled *restless* correctly.

2. *Cutting.*   An early draft may contain more material than you need for your specific purpose. Sometimes the excess is the result of **redundancy,** covering the same ground twice; sometimes, it is caused by wandering off the subject, sometimes by putting in material that actually works better elsewhere in the essay (in which case, to cut is really to transfer). When you or your critics perceive a problem in one of these areas, you ought to cut the offending material, even if it is dear to your heart. It has to work in the context of that part of the essay where it appears and in the context of the essay as a whole. Between Averill's two drafts, she cuts "I've got ants in my pants." Probably she considered it a vulgar statement—a different reason from those cited above—and felt it could safely be cut as not absolutely necessary to the point her mother was making—which *is* one of the reasons given.

3. *Adding.*   One of the chief motives for revision is to develop points at greater length in order to bring out their meaning and clarify their connection to your subject. Writers add more details to description, remember more events, fill in the gaps in a logical sequence, explain a comparison more fully, and so on. Averill adds to her final draft a sentence not in the preliminary one: "We'll load up the new Saab with tons of canned food and drive all the way." The new car is mentioned two paragraphs earlier as one element of the mother's supposed contented state. Here, it appears as a way out of actual discontent. Thus Averill reemphasizes her mother's restlessness. The same purpose no doubt applies to the addition of "So wild" near the paragraph opening.

4. *Changing language and meaning.*   Averill's Alaska paragraph contains no example of this kind of revision, but look ahead to the samples she gives us in her own remarks on revision (pp. 39–42) and to her reasons for making changes. Very often, you will realize later that you haven't used the most precise

language possible to make your point, or that your syntax could be better arranged. Sometimes you will perceive a problem in logic and want to correct it, and sometimes you will even change your mind entirely about a point you made earlier. Remember, however, that revising for meaning may involve not just the immediate context of an improvement but may affect the whole essay. That is, you will have to be sure that what you've said beforehand allows this change, and that what comes afterward reflects it. If it does not, you will need to revise further, both backward and forward from the change. The whole essay is what matters, not just a part of it, and when you revise, this sense of what is needed often surfaces only after one or more preliminary drafts.

Frequently, you will find that the prewriting you have done—the free writing, note taking, brainstorming, and the like—has helped you accumulate many ideas, images, quotations, observations, and insights about your subject. Next, you need to order these materials according to how you think they should appear in your essay: you need to lay out a plan of action. But once you begin writing, you will find that some of your original material no longer fits, or that you require new material, or—as you really get into your essay—that you need to develop your ideas more effectively, by adding or by cutting or by restating.

As you move from one draft to the next, often in response to your readers' comments, sometimes changing small matters and sometimes rewriting whole sections, you may doubt whether you are making progress. In fact, sometimes writers do revise too much and, on reflection, return to an earlier version of a sentence or a paragraph. On the whole, however, if you give thought to the changes you make, if you don't simply cut wholesale what may not seem good enough, if you rather work confidently to make it better, your essay will develop in a positive direction.

Like everyone engaged in any art, you may never be quite satisfied with your final product. Nevertheless, your readers will be surprisingly generous, chiefly because they can tell when a written work has been brought to a high pitch of perfection, when the writer has flattered their legitimate desire for logic, coherence, and clarity, when meaning shines through with the power of intellect.

But why don't we let Sarah Averill speak for herself and all of us at this point? We'll end with the comments that she prepared for an oral presentation about the experience of writing "On Moving On."

My original intent in writing this essay was to explore the effect that frequent moving during my childhood has had on me. I tried to capture the essence of the way of thinking that dominated my immediate family, which consisted solely of my mother. 5
This led me to look at her family more closely than

I had in the past.  I also tried to link my family's behavior to predominant ideals in this society in order to capture the more universal aspects of my experi-
10  ence.  I started the essay looking at moving from the perspective of a social disease which can be transmitted.

When I started, I didn't have a plan.  I just started writing down all of my thoughts on the matter.  I
15  carried a notebook and a pen everywhere so that when something occurred to me I would be able to write it down.  I ended up with twenty pages of handwritten notes.  This is when I started to plan because I knew that I was going to have to cut a lot of the
20  material out.
     I sorted through the material, choosing for the essay the most vivid images and those that were truest to my life experience.  I looked for themes in my notes that I could follow.
25     A large part of the organization of the essay came late in the writing process.  I had to put my drafts aside for several days in order to get a fresh look at them and in the end it became obvious which parts went together.  I could see where I was repeating my-
30  self and where I was jumping around too much.
     The workshops in class gave me a couple of ideas on how to organize the essay.  One of my classmates suggested that I try to follow a strict chronological order.  I tried that and didn't like the result, but
35  it gave me a fresh perspective and I ended up putting a large part of the essay in chronological order.
     I think that had more of my classmates showed up for the workshops, I would have gotten more out of them.  Only two people commented on my essay and
40  then, only briefly.  Their comments were not specific enough to be helpful in most cases.  I had one friend outside of class read it and he made a few useful suggestions on how to streamline some of my convoluted sentences and to condense some of the para-
45  graphs that were too wordy.

I have copies of all my drafts, which allows me to closely examine some of the changes I have made.  One of my greatest successes in revising is on page eight of the final version.  It originally read:

I envision a helium balloon on a child's wrist slip-        50
ping free and floating up into the stratosphere.  It
drifts and wanders across the sky, almost out of
sight and then it bursts--it was too free and could
not withstand the freedom.  It falls back to earth a
withered bit of plastic and we find them on the         55
beach, in the street.  They evoke a faint smile.
We've all lost such balloons.  When I see those little bits I shudder; I could be that little shriveled
up piece of rubber--used up lost, exploded from the
inside out.                                                        60

The final version of this paragraph reads:

In my darker moments, I picture myself as a helium
balloon on a child's wrist, slipping free and floating up into the stratosphere.  I drift and wander
across the sky, too free, almost out of sight and         65
then I burst.  I fall back to earth a withered bit
of plastic.  People find me on the beach and in the
street.  They smile faintly, remembering the helium
balloons that they have lost, not realizing that the
little shriveled up piece of plastic is me--used up,      70
lost, exploded from the inside out.

By making the connection between the exploded helium balloon and myself more personal, the image became powerful and more clearly represents what I feel
about having no roots, no home.                                    75
There are revisions elsewhere in the essay which
served to strengthen it.  For example, on page [36],
in the last paragraph, the sentence that begins "How
many children . . ." originally ended with "shook as
if a train were within three inches of their precious      80
faces."  I changed the sentence to end "shook as if a
train were about to pass them by."  The latter image
ties in with the idea of progress.  The "I have a
train to catch" mentality.  It says, "I want to go
somewhere and I'm afraid if I don't keep moving I'll       85
get left behind," and ties into the earlier observation about my mother being afraid to turn the car off
because she would end up stuck in the mud with her
tires spinning.

On the whole, I am pleased with the way that I depict      90
events in the essay.  I have captured successfully
the scenes I remember from my childhood.  I think
that I have also captured some of my feelings as a

95  child, such as the excitement I felt and learned to
    like.

    The more universal theme was difficult to weave into
    the essay.  I had a difficult time choosing a tack
    that would parallel the idea of moving as a disease.
    I saw elements within our society that were equally
100 disturbing.  Twelve years listening to Reagan and
    Bush spout the virtues of supply-side economics and
    the evils of people collecting unemployment made
    clear to me that the idea that if you try hard you
    can be always advancing was alive and well.  I tried
105 to take this idea down a notch in the parts where I
    talked about immigrants.

    I am not so sure, however, that I have accurately
    captured what motivated my mother, and the way that
    she thinks about those years that we shared together.
110 Much of my family history remains unknown to me.  I
    tried to capture that by remaining vague about my
    knowledge, using such words as "imagine" and "envi-
    sion."  The essay might have been strengthened had I
    spent some time talking to my relatives about general
115 family history and to my mother about how she regards
    her life in connection to her family.

    During one of the workshops one of my group members
    asked me about the main metaphor I chose for the es-
    say: progress.  He questioned whether the immigrants'
120 moving was comparable to my family's moving.  I have
    thought about it and I am still unsure.  There is a
    basis for comparison, but I think that he was right
    to question how closely they are related.  It would
    have been better had I made the distinction clearer.
125 I tried to make clear that my family has taken the
    dream of progress beyond any reasonable limit.  Some
    of that reflected back on the way I write about immi-
    gration.  I don't think that that is entirely inaccu-
    rate.  Many immigrants were deceived into thinking
130 that in the U.S. they would find much more than they
    did and were gravely disappointed.  I could improve
    those sections of the essay related to immigration by
    choosing my words more carefully and more fully ex-
    plicating the differences I see between the immi-
135 grants' dreams of progress and my family's.

# I

# *Myths of Existence*

M yths are stories. But they are also more than that. Their characters, events, and situations transcend common experience. They trace the origin and explain the nature of the major aspects—and many of the minor elements—of human existence. The world hustles into being, fire is expropriated, death makes an appearance one fine day. But also, the white narcissus flower sighs upward from the earth, the laurel blooms, the hunter finds his place as a star in the sky. Although these stories are magical, they are not unreal, because reality is the outcome of our most permanent tendencies, and these are just what myths describe. Similarly, though they are fictional, myths are not lies. Rather, they say what is the case about human beings throughout time in all places. They embody *essential* truths, symbolic of the human condition.

However, just as truths go in and out of fashion, or are revealed as only culturally bound, so some myths lose their force over time while others gain in power. For many people, Eve springing from Adam's rib into subordination no longer captures the imagination. The myth is not dead but dark. Its reality and truth have retreated, departed, perhaps into an indefinite cold storage; we no longer automatically appeal to the myth to justify behavior or to frame our understanding of relations between male and female.

On the other hand, Orpheus descending into the underworld to regain his lost love, Eurydice, continues to engage us. Who among us has not seen, or will not see, love slip from his or her grasp? Who doesn't look for love everywhere, even in the unconscious, where the sweetest music of human reason, like Orpheus's singing, must placate the monsters, must dispel the passionate misunderstanding that lies at the heart of our pain? Who is not Orpheus?

Whether they fall behind us forever or for a while, cling to us in the present, or lie in wait for us to reach them, myths track our movements. They emerge at all times, from all cultures and from all countries. And although the stories they tell involve people with particular names who take specific actions, their character and plot are universal: we can dissolve our own names and the plot of our own lives, or even what it means to be human at a certain time, into a given myth. As a result, our own existence is exalted; we break out of our fragmented lives into the general greatness of existence.

**Mythologizing**—transfiguring the human condition by making it bigger than life—is a powerful impulse and, like all such urges, has its dangers. We may be tempted to exaggerate our own importance by identifying too strongly with a mythic character. We may begin to undervalue the ordinariness of our daily life. We may tend to freeze our ideas of human action into certain formal and traditional patterns not open to intelligent scrutiny and end up with only half a brain. Yet, particularly in this day and age, none of these possibilities seems too menacing. It is rare indeed that individuals or cultures are able to transcend themselves for long. Therefore, when those moments do come in which a myth seems to be just our size, there seems to be no harm in trying it on and becoming a new creation.

Whether you find yourself close to or distant from the myths you are about to read, keep in mind the following considerations:

1. Myths are not intended to compete with science for verifiability, or with history for factuality. Read them purely for their power to create an emotional and psychological sense of human existence.

2. Like most narratives, myths include dramatic action, meaningful relationships, and strict consequences. The better you understand these elements, the more you will grasp the symbolic import of the myth.

3. Finding a parallel between at least some parts of a myth and your own history is often possible and always fascinating. You might try to see what applies to your life.

## PRIMARY TEXTS

It would be hard to find a definition of myth that would be acceptable to all scholars and at the same time intelligible to nonspecialists. Then, too, is it even possible to find *one* definition that will cover all the types and functions of myths in all traditional and archaic societies? Myth is an extremely complex cultural reality, which can be approached and interpreted from various and complementary viewpoints.

5

Speaking for myself, the definition that seems least inadequate because most embracing is this: Myth narrates a sacred history; it relates an event that took place in primordial Time, the fabled time of the "beginnings." In other words, myth tells how, through the deeds of Supernatural Beings, a reality came into existence, be it the whole of reality, the Cosmos, or only a fragment of reality—an island, a species of plant, a particular kind of human behavior, an insti-

10

tution. Myth, then, is always an account of a "creation"; it relates how something was produced, began to *be*. Myth tells only of that which *really* happened, which manifested itself completely. The actors in myths are Supernatural Beings. They are known primarily by what they did in the transcendent times of the "beginnings." Hence myths disclose their creative activity and reveal the sacredness (or simply the "supernaturalness") of their works. In short, myths describe the various and sometimes dramatic breakthroughs of the sacred (or the "supernatural") into the World. It is this sudden breakthrough of the sacred that really *establishes* the World and makes it what it is today. Furthermore, it is as a result of the intervention of Supernatural Beings that man himself is what he is today, a mortal, sexed, and cultural being.

We shall later have occasion to enlarge upon and refine these few preliminary indications, but at this point it is necessary to emphasize a fact that we consider essential: the myth is regarded as a sacred story, and hence a "true history," because it always deals with *realities*. The cosmogonic myth is "true" because the existence of the World is there to prove it; the myth of the origin of death is equally true because man's mortality proves it, and so on. . . .

—Mircea Eliade, from *Myth and Reality*

*Of old the Hellenic race was marked off from the barbarian as more keen-witted and more free from nonsense.*

—Herodotus I: 60.

Greek and Roman mythology is quite generally supposed to show us the way the human race thought and felt untold ages ago. Through it, according to this view, we can retrace the path from civilized man who lives so far from nature, to man who lived in close companionship with nature; and the real interest of the myths is that they lead us back to a time when the world was young and people had a connection with the earth, with trees and seas and flowers and hills, unlike anything we ourselves can feel. When the stories were being shaped, we are given to understand, little distinction had as yet been made between the real and the unreal. The imagination was vividly alive and not checked by the reason, so that anyone in the woods might see through the trees a fleeing nymph, or bending over a clear pool to drink behold in the depths a naiad's face.

The prospect of traveling back to this delightful state of things is held out by nearly every writer who touches upon classical mythology, above all by the poets. In that infinitely remote time primitive man could

Have sight of Proteus rising from the sea;
Or hear old Triton blow his wreathèd horn.

And we for a moment can catch, through the myths he made, a glimpse of that strangely and beautifully animated world.

20    But a very brief consideration of the ways of uncivilized peoples everywhere and in all ages is enough to prick that romantic bubble. Nothing is
clearer than the fact that primitive man, whether in New Guinea today or eons
ago in the prehistoric wilderness, is not and never has been a creature who peoples his world with bright fancies and lovely visions. Horrors lurked in the
primeval forest, not nymphs and naiads. Terror lived there, with its close atten-
25    dant, Magic, and its most common defense, Human Sacrifice. Mankind's chief
hope of escaping the wrath of whatever divinities were then abroad lay in some
magical rite, senseless but powerful, or in some offering made at the cost of pain
and grief.

—Edith Hamilton, from *Mythology*


Briefly stated, these assumptions are the following: All peoples are endowed
in equal degree with the mythopoeic imagination. The type of mythology
found today is not necessarily, nor even probably, the only type a given people
ever possessed. Myths and *Märchen* have changed as the social-economic struc-
5    ture of a civilization and the ideas developed in connection with it have
changed. The change in their content and style may be ascribed primarily to
two factors: the extent to which transformations in the social-economic structure have enabled the specific ideologies flowing from and accompanying such
structures to become dominant, and the extent to which the old cultural tradi-
10    tions and background have been reorganized, reinterpreted, and given new
forms, particularly by artistically gifted individuals. All the evidence at our disposal today—and it is not inconsiderable—justifies our assuming that, from
the very beginning of man's history, artistically gifted individuals have existed
among all peoples.
15    Now for the great historic civilizations of Asia and Europe, it has been contended by some theorists[1] that the mythopoeic imagination has been most profoundly stirred and has found its richest expression at three historic periods and
in three specific areas, India, Greece, and Christian Europe of the Middle Ages.
It is always dangerous to hazard precise dates, but I do not think it would be far
20    from wrong to assign the Indian period to somewhere in the early part of the
second millennium B.C., the Greek to the early part of the first millennium B.C.
Moreover, according to the same theorists, it is not really of much importance
whether or not the plots, themes, and motifs found among the Greeks and in
the Christian Middle Ages did or did not come ultimately from India, as the
25    great scholar Benfey[2] once contended. What is important is the nature and the
intensity of a people's preoccupation with them.
That reputable folklorists and culture-historians should have taken it upon
themselves thus to limit and restrict this stirring of the so-called mythopoeic

---

1. Especially by the members of the Finnish school of folklore.

2. Theodor Benfey, introduction to his translation: *Pantschatantra* (Leipzig, 1859).

imagination to just a few periods in the history of specific peoples is almost incomprehensible. Possibly it can be explained by the well known limitations of     30
the academic mind and the narrowness of its vision. Needless to say, nothing is
actually further from the truth.

On the basis of data obtained in the nineteenth and twentieth centuries
concerning the unwritten literatures of aboriginal peoples, it is now quite clear
that at certain periods in their history, the mythopoeic imagination had been as     35
vitally stirred and had expressed itself among them as richly and voluminously
as was ever the case in Greece, India, and Christian medieval Europe. It would
be erroneous, however, to suppose that the mythopoeic imagination has been at
work among aboriginal peoples from the beginning of their history and that it
was still in evidence when they were discovered by the Europeans. This would     40
be a dangerous illusion. No aboriginal tribe exists that does not assign its myth-
making to an earlier and very distant epoch in its history. . . .

—Paul Radin, from *African Folktales*

# Kevin Crossley-Holland

# The Creation

Kevin Crossley-Holland, a British poet, has numerous books to his credit dealing with
northern European myths, sagas, and heroic poems. Also a writer of children's
books, in 1985 he was awarded the Carnegie Medal for outstanding work in this
field. In his introduction to *The Norse Myths,* from which "The Creation" is taken, he
remarks that most of these myths, though they took shape at least a thousand years
before the birth of Christ, were not written down until much later in time by "poets
and antiquarians 'out on the end of an event, waving goodbye'" to the original
tellers.

## Looking Ahead

1. Although not as well known as Greek mythology, Norse mythology comprises one
   of the most important bodies of myths in the world. This fact is useful to recall as
   you seek to discover the particular grandeur of this creation myth and its general
   similarity to others you know.

2. Many of the names in "The Creation" will sound foreign to your ears; try pronounc-
   ing them aloud to gain familiarity with them.

3. If you can, think of the original teller as reaching into every pocket of imagination
   and observation of nature to construct a narrative that combines poetry with systematic explanation.

Burning ice, biting flame; that is how life began.

In the south is a realm called Muspell. That region flickers with dancing flames. It seethes and it shines. No one can endure it except those born into it. Black Surt is there; he sits on the furthest reach of that land, brandishing a flaming sword; he is already waiting for the end when he will rise and savage the gods and whelm the whole world with fire.

In the north is a realm called Niflheim. It is packed with ice and covered with vast sweeps of snow. In the heart of that region lies the spring Hvergelmir and that is the source of eleven rivers named the Elivagar: they are cool Svol and Gunnthra the defiant, Fjorm and bubbling Fimbulthul, fearsome Slid and storming Hrid, Sylg, Ylg, broad Vid and Leipt which streaks like lightning, and freezing Gjoll.

Between these realms there once stretched a huge and seeming emptiness; this was Ginnungagap. The rivers that sprang from Hvergelmir streamed into the void. The yeasty venom in them thickened and congealed like slag, and the rivers turned into ice. That venom also spat out drizzle—an unending dismal hagger that, as soon as it settled, turned into rime. So it went on until all the northern part of Ginnungagap was heavy with layers of ice and hoar frost, a desolate place haunted by gusts and skuthers of wind.

Just as the northern part was frozen, the southern was molten and glowing, but the middle of Ginnungagap was as mild as hanging air on a summer evening. There, the warm breath drifting north from Muspell met the rime from Niflheim; it touched it and played over it, and the ice began to thaw and drip. Life quickened in those drops, and they took the form of a giant. He was called Ymir.

Ymir was a frost giant; he was evil from the first. While he slept, he began to sweat. A man and woman grew out of the ooze under his left armpit, and one of his legs fathered a son on the other leg. Ymir was the forefather of all the frost giants, and they called him Aurgelmir.

As more of the ice in Ginnungagap melted, the fluid took the form of a cow. She was called Audumla. Ymir fed off the four rivers of milk that coursed from her teats, and Audumla fed off the ice itself. She licked the salty blocks and by the evening of the first day a man's hair had come out of the ice. Audumla licked more and by the evening of the second day a man's head had come. Audumla licked again and by the evening of the third day the whole man had come. His name was Buri.

Buri was tall and strong and good-looking. In time he had a son called Bor and Bor married a daughter of Bolthor, one of the frost giants. Her name was Bestla and she mothered three children, all of them sons. The first was Odin, the second was Vili, and the third was Ve.

All this was in the beginning, before there were waves of sand, the sea's cool waves, waving grass. There was no earth and no heaven above; only Muspell and Niflheim and, between them, Ginnungagap.

The three sons of Bor had no liking for Ymir and the growing gang of unruly, brutal frost giants; as time went on, they grew to hate them. At last they at-

tacked Ymir and killed him. His wounds were like springs; so much blood      45
streamed from them, and so fast, that the flood drowned all the frost giants except Bergelmir and his wife. They embarked in their boat—it was made out of a
hollowed tree trunk—and rode on a tide of gore.

   Odin and Vili and Ve hoisted the body of the dead frost giant on to their
shoulders and carted it to the middle of Ginnungagap. That is where they made      50
the world from his body. They shaped the earth from Ymir's flesh and the
mountains from his unbroken bones; from his teeth and jaws and the fragments
of his shattered bones they made rocks and boulders and stones.

   Odin and Vili and Ve used the welter of blood to make landlocked lakes
and to make the sea. After they had formed the earth, they laid the rocking      55
ocean in a ring right round it. And it is so wide that most men would dismiss
the very idea of crossing it.

   Then the three brothers raised Ymir's skull and made the sky from it and
placed it so that its four corners reached to the ends of the earth. They set a
dwarf under each corner, and their names are East and West and North and      60
South. Then Odin and Vili and Ve seized on the sparks and glowing embers
from Muspell and called them sun and moon and stars; they put them high in
Ginnungagap to light heaven above and earth below. In this way the brothers
gave each star its proper place; some were fixed in the sky, others were free to
follow the paths appointed for them.      65

   The earth was round and lay within the ring of the deep sea. Along the
strand the sons of Bor marked out tracts of land and gave them to the frost giants and the rock giants; and there, in Jotunheim, the giants settled and remained. They were so hostile that the three brothers built an enclosure further
inland around a vast area of the earth. They shaped it out of Ymir's eyebrows,      70
and called it Midgard. The sun warmed the stones in the earth there, and the
ground was green with sprouting leeks. The sons of Bor used Ymir's brains as
well; they flung them up into the air and turned them into every kind of cloud.

   One day, Odin and Vili and Ve were striding along the frayed edge of the
land, where the earth meets the sea. They came across two fallen trees with their      75
roots ripped out of the ground; one was an ash, the other an elm. Then the sons
of Bor raised them and made from them the first man and woman. Odin
breathed into them the spirit of life; Vili offered them sharp wits and feeling
hearts; and Ve gave them the gifts of hearing and sight. The man was called Ask
and the woman Embla and they were given Midgard to live in. All the families      80
and nations and races of men are descended from them.

   One of the giants living in Jotunheim, Narvi, had a daughter called Night
who was as dark eyed, dark haired and swarthy as the rest of her family. She
married three times. Her first husband was a man called Naglfari and their son
was Aud; her second husband was Annar and their daughter was Earth; and her      85
third husband was shining Delling who was related to the sons of Bor. Their son
was Day and, like all his father's side of the family, Day was radiant and fair of
face.

Then Odin took Night and her son Day, sat them in horse-drawn chariots,
90   and set them in the sky to ride round the world every two half-days. Night leads
the way and her horse is frosty-maned Hrimfaxi. Day's horse is Skinfaxi; he has
a gleaming mane that lights up sky and earth alike.

A man called Mundilfari living in Midgard had two children and they were
so beautiful that he called his son Moon and his daughter Sun; Sun married a
95   man called Glen. Odin and his brothers and their offspring, the Aesir, were angered at such daring. They snatched away both children and placed them in the
sky to guide the chariots of the sun and moon—the constellations made by the
sons of Bor to light the world out of the sparks from Muspell.

Moon leads the way. He guides the moon on its path and decides when he
100   will wax and wane. He does not travel alone, as you can see if you look into the
sky; for Moon in turn plucked two children from Midgard, Bil and Hjuki,
whose father is Vidfinn. They were just walking away from the well Byrgir, carrying between them the water cask Soeg on the pole Simul, when Moon
swooped down and carried them off.

105   Sun follows behind. One of her horses is called Arvak because he rises so
early, and the other Alsvid because he is immensely strong. The Aesir inserted
iron-cold bellows under their shoulder-blades to keep them cool. Sun always
seems to be in a great hurry, and that is because she is chased by Skoll, the wolf
who is always snapping and growling close behind her. In the end he will catch
110   her. And the wolf that races in front of Sun is called Hati; he is after Moon and
will run him down in the end. Both wolves are the sons of an aged giantess who
lived in Iron Wood, east of Midgard.

After the sons of Bor had made the first man and woman, and set Night and
Day, Moon and Sun in the sky, they remembered the maggots that had
115   squirmed and swarmed in Ymir's flesh and crawled out over the earth. Then
they gave them wits and the shape of men, but they live under the hills and
mountains in rocky chambers and grottoes and caverns. These man-like maggots are called dwarfs. Modsognir is their leader and his deputy is Durin.

So the earth was fashioned and filled with men and giants and dwarfs, sur-
120   rounded by the sea and covered by the sky. Then the sons of Bor built their own
realm of Asgard—a mighty stronghold, a place of green plains and shining
palaces high over Midgard. The two regions were linked by Bifrost, a flaming
rainbow bridge; it was made of three colours with magic and great skill, and it is
wonderfully strong. All the Aesir, the guardians of men, crossed over and set-
125   tled in Asgard. Odin, Allfather, is the oldest and greatest of them all; there are
twelve divine gods and twelve divine goddesses, and a great assembly of other
Aesir. And this was the beginning of all that has happened, remembered or forgotten, in the regions of the world.

And all that has happened, and all the regions of the world, lie under the
130   branches of the ash Yggdrasill, greatest and best of trees. It soars over all that is;
its three roots delve into Asgard and Jotunheim and Niflheim, and there is a
spring under each. A hawk and eagle sit in it, a squirrel scurries up and down it,
deer leap within it and nibble at it, a dragon devours it, and it is sprinkled with

dew. It gives life to itself, it gives life to the unborn. The winds whirl round it
and Yggdrasill croons or groans. Yggdrasill always was and is and will be.      135

## Looking Back

1. Why do you think the teller gave some of the first rivers human characteristics (lines 9–12)?
2. How was Ymir, the frost giant, created?
3. Does it seem that Ymir and Buri were created by accident or design? What evidence can you find in the text for your answer?
4. In lines 76–77, we read that the first man and woman were created, but a human couple came into being earlier (see line 26). What does this seeming contradiction imply about the construction of this narrative?
5. What do various details reveal about the conditions of human life at the time this myth was made?
6. How, according to this myth, was the world created?
7. Is there an important difference between a story in which one god creates both the world and human beings, and a myth in which several godlike beings (Odin and his brothers) do the creating? How can you explain the difference?
8. What do the frost giants seem to represent that causes Odin and his brothers to despise them?
9. How do you interpret the great ash tree Yggdrasill of the final paragraph?
10. Does having a complete account of existence serve a human need? What need? How does the myth satisfy the need?

## Writing Assignments

1. Creation myths often trace the origin of human life to a single couple. Adam and Eve come immediately to mind. The Norse, as we see, produce Ask and Embla (note the first initials, coincidentally the same). No doubt, one reason for this practice is the available model of parents, grandparents, or other known ancestors. Also, stories are easier to tell when the characters are limited in number and have names. Finally, perhaps we can better understand what it is to be a human being when we can identify original character traits. Ask and Embla, for instance, have "sharp wits and feeling hearts" (lines 78–79). This last reason, the desire to learn about ourselves, is compelling and can guide your own investigation. Write an essay in which you imagine a first couple. Give them names and supply any other facts of their existence you wish. Your main task, however, is to describe their character traits and to explain how these define the human species.

2. In the first book of the Old Testament, Genesis, "God" creates the world. In "The Creation," a number of "gods" do the same. Odin, Vili, and Ve, however, unlike the Old Testament God, are humanly recognizable. They are the sons of a mother, they have human anatomies (line 50), and they make accidental discoveries, just as humans do (lines 75–76). In a sense, they are men who *become* gods. This distinction

raises anew this old question about how best to exist in the world: Should we live in fear and humility before the great creator God, interfering as little as possible with the world as it is given to us, or dare we assume godlike powers of creation (think of genetic engineering) and destruction (think of nuclear weaponry) to remake the world in our image? The answer is probably not an either/or one, but we may certainly lean one way or the other. Write an essay explaining the problems arising from either choice.

3. We read in "The Creation" that all human beings—"All the families and nations"—are descended from the first man, Ask, and the first woman, Embla. Although most of us can climb part of the way down our family tree to find our ancestry, obviously none of us can plunge this far back into the mists of time. At a certain point we draw a blank. This fact, however, does not deter many people from searching for their roots—the beginnings and continuation of their bloodline up to the present day. Why do people conduct such a search? What do they hope to find besides the actual names of their forebears? How can the knowledge of their past relatives help them to live in the present? Is it mere vanity that motivates people, or can they take a justifiable pride in discovering their origins? Write an essay that explores whether there is true value in tracing your family tree and that addresses the other questions listed above.

# Pär Lagerkvist

## Paradise

The Swedish writer Pär Lagerkvist (1891–1974) won the Nobel Prize in literature in 1951. Most famous for his novels, particularly *The Dwarf* and *Barabbas*, he is also the author of plays, essays, and short stories. In his work, Lagerkvist is concerned chiefly with eternal themes of existence, such as love, war, evil, death, ignorance, and self-sacrifice. Frequently, as in this story, first published in 1935, he narrates the lives of mythical figures. In so doing, he produces a kind of grid that we can place over contemporary events to plot their meaning more accurately.

### Looking Ahead

1. Unlike the more abstract version in Genesis, this story portrays "the Lord" as a definite character with a clear personality.
2. The characters' speech is hardly biblical in tone. Read critically to discover how this fact affects your reading of a story with biblical roots.
3. The author introduces various philosophical points that are useful to grasp.

And the Lord said: "Now I have arranged things for you here as best I can; planted rice, peas and potatoes, many edible plants which you will find useful, various kinds of grain for baking bread, cocoanut palms, sugar cane and turnips; marked out ground suitable for pasture land and gardening; provided

animals that are easy to tame and wild animals for hunting; laid out plains, val-  5
leys and mountainous regions, terraces that can well be used for growing grapes
and olives; set out pines, eucalyptus trees and fair acacia groves; devised birch
woods, lotus flowers and breadfruit trees, violet slopes and wild strawberry
patches; invented the sunshine—which you'll find will please you; put the
moon in the heavens so that you'll have something to go by till you're big  10
enough to get a clock; hung up the stars to guide you on the sea and lead your
thoughts—those that are not of the earth; seen that there are clouds to give rain
and shade, thought out the seasons and determined their pleasant changing,
and one thing and another. I hope you will like it.

"But remember to eat of the tree of knowledge, so that you will be really  15
sensible and wise."

And the first human beings bowed deeply and humbled themselves before
their Lord. "Thank you very much," they said.

They began to dig and cultivate the soil, to reap, multiply themselves and
fill the whole of paradise, and they liked it very much. They ate freely of the tree  20
of knowledge, as the Lord had told them, but did not grow noticeably sensible.
They became very sly and artful and intelligent, and well-informed and excellent in many ways, but they did not become sensible. And this made their existence increasingly complicated and troublesome, and they got into more and
more of a muddle.  25

At last a resolute man appeared who was grieved by the way things were
going, and he stepped forward before the Lord and said: "The people are behaving so strangely down there, it seems to me; it's true they grow more intelligent
and shrewd every day, but they prefer to turn their cunning and great learning
to evil and senseless uses; I don't know, but there must be something wrong  30
with the tree of knowledge."

"What," said the Lord, "something wrong with the tree of knowledge, did
you say? Certainly not. It must be like that, don't you see? It's the best I could
do. If you think you know what it ought to be like, then please say."

No, he didn't know. But all was not as it should be down there, and how-  35
ever well-thought-out the tree of knowledge might be, it did seem as though
eating from it made them a little foolish.

"But the tree cannot be otherwise," the Lord said. "Admittedly, it's rather
complicated learning how to eat of it, but it must be complicated; it can't be
helped. Some things you must find out for yourselves, or what's the point of  40
your existence? You can't be spoon-fed the whole time. Personally, I think the
tree is the finest thing I've created, and if you don't show yourselves worthy of
it, human life won't be much to speak of. Tell them that."

And with that answer the man had to be content.

But when he had gone the Lord sat there quite distressed. If they had found  45
fault with anything else he had made, it wouldn't have mattered so much, but
the tree of knowledge was especially dear to his heart, perhaps because it had
been so much more difficult to make than the other trees and everything else on
the earth. Like the great artist he was, he was thinking at this moment not of his

50   generally recognized achievements but only of this misunderstood work into
which he thought he had secretly put his whole soul, without having any joy of
it. And just because this very work of his seemed to him so extremely important, he couldn't imagine that humanity could do without it—its real, deep
significance.

55      And perhaps he was right. He was, after all, a great creative spirit and ought
to know best himself. He ought to know what he had put his soul into.

He sat thinking that people were ungrateful to him and his most outstanding work.

It is not easy to know how long he sat thus. Perhaps time passes quickly in
60   eternity and the wingbeats of the Lord's thought are perhaps as thousands of
years for us. Then a man came again before him, but this time it was the
archangel Gabriel himself who came.

"You have no idea what it's like down in paradise," he said. "It is quite incredible. They are trying to destroy everything for you and they think of the
65   worst imaginable deeds of villainy to bring it about. There is a deafening noise
and they hurl the hideous fruits of the tree of knowledge at each other so that
they burst with a horrible roar, and, worst of all, uproot all the vegetation. They
bluster and brag so that it's shameful to hear them and they say they're much
cleverer than God himself, for they invent much greater things than you, and
70   they have frightful monsters that shatter everything in their path, everything
that you have created, and in the air they have huge imitation birds that vomit
fire and devastation. I have never been in hell—I'm glad to say—but that's what
it must look like. It is an abomination. And it's all the fault of that tree of knowledge. You should never have given it to them—and come to that, I said so from
75   the outset. Think what you like, but have a look at how things are there!"

And the Lord looked down onto the earth and saw that it was true. Then
wrath was kindled in his mighty, pained creator's soul and lightning flashed
from his eyes and he sent out his hosts and they drove the people out, together
with all their evil and devilish works, into the great desert of Savi, where noth-
80   ing grows. And he set a fence around paradise, and two angels at its gate, each
with his machine gun and flaming sword. And the desert lay right next to paradise and the fence round about.

Inside, life was delightful with its sun and verdure, fresh and springlike
now that the people had been driven out; the meadows smelled sweet and the
85   air was full of bird song. And the banished stood looking in between the bars
and saw it, but they could not get in.

And the angels—those who were not on guard—retired to rest after the battle and fell asleep, exhausted. But under the best-loved tree in paradise the Lord
sat in deep contemplation, and its branches shaded him with their great peace.

## Looking Back

1. What is the effect of introducing clocks (line 11) and machine guns (line 81) in the
narrative?

2. Who does "the Lord" sound like when, in line 14, he says about paradise to the first humans, "I hope you like it"?

3. How does being "sensible and wise" (line 16) differ from being "sly and artful and intelligent, and well-informed and excellent in many ways" (lines 22–23)?

4. What exactly goes wrong in paradise?

5. Why does the Lord place so much importance on the tree of knowledge?

6. What does he mean when he says, about human beings, "You can't be spoon-fed the whole time" (line 41)?

7. This story assumes that God makes mistakes. If this were true, what must we conclude about such a God?

8. How do you interpret Gabriel's report to God about human behavior?

9. How may the deity be compared to an artist (see lines 49–58)?

10. What do you think the Lord is contemplating at the end of the story?

## Writing Assignments

1. Dictionary definitions of even the most common abstract words take us only so far and no further in our attempts to understand a particular use these words are put to. *Intelligence* is one such word. Previously we may have been content with a written definition, but when the word suddenly appears in an unaccustomed context, its meaning there may puzzle us. In "Paradise," the positive qualities we usually attribute to intelligence lessen when the word is tied to the terms *sly* and *artful* (line 22). We begin to realize that intelligence is not as high a mental achievement as wisdom and, in fact, may detract from it. But how, we might ask, can this be? Can intelligence actually be harmful? Sometimes or always? When and how? Should we try not to be *too* intelligent? If intelligence differs from wisdom, what does it mean to be wise? Write an essay in which you distinguish intelligence from wisdom in order to define each term separately and to show any connection between them. Conceive of your audience as one that may not normally make distinctions such as these and that therefore needs to be shown the usefulness of doing so.

2. At the end of "Paradise," after the first inhabitants of the world have been driven into the desert for their sins, the Lord sinks into deep thought about what has happened to his creation. We are not told what passes through his mind, but we can imagine his disappointment and chagrin. He may even have second thoughts about having created people in the first place. After all, they seem to have proved unequal to the tasks set before them and to have spoiled what they were given so generously—in fact, to have made a hell of heaven on earth. We see this most clearly in the powerful speech Gabriel delivers late in the story (lines 63–75). Particularly in light of the angel's indictment, the question arises whether it would have been better for the planet generally if our species had never evolved. Interpolating your view into the events of the story, write an essay addressing this question: Would things be better without us? Remember, of course, that as a human being you are an interested party, so try to weigh the evidence as objectively as you can.

3. Defending his creation of the tree of knowledge, the Lord answers his critic by saying, "Some things you must find out for yourselves, or what's the point of your existence? You can't be spoon-fed the whole time" (lines 40–41). In effect, he is defend-

ing his gift to humans of free will. The theory of free will states that the lives of human beings are not absolutely determined by the control of the deity, by biology, or by the psyche. Rather, people can make moral choices, they have a decision-making capacity, and they can change not only their behavior but the shape of their personal selves. Accepting this definition of human existence, write a persuasive essay in which you explain as concretely as possible the importance to human beings of having free will.

# Follow-Up: An Essay for Analysis

## INTELLIGENCE DOES NOT EQUAL WISDOM

A person may be quite intelligent; however, intelligence does not necessarily infer wisdom. Contrastly, a wise person is not simply intelligent, but prudent in having the intelligence to use his or her knowl-
5    edge and experience sensibly, with discretion and foresight. In other words, wisdom is the path or choice a person takes in using intelligence. Intelligence is therefore the lesser mental achievement.

For example, to distinguish between an intelligent
10  person and a wise person, a story of two men will be helpful to clarify the concepts. Two men receive the same training and education in chemical engineering at a local university. Both men graduate the same year. One ventures off in a field using the knowledge
15  and understanding to do work benefiting  himself and the community at large. The other fellow takes the knowledge and understanding acquired and uses it in a destructive manner; he turns to illegal drug manufacturing or bomb making for drug dealers and terrorists
20  respectfully. Both men are intelligent enough to have the capacity to learn and understand the mechanics of chemical engineering, and both know the destruction that can result if the knowledge is misrepresented or used for illegal activities. However, one man chooses
25  to warp his knowledge and use it in a way not intended for its official use. The wise man uses his knowledge sensibly. The intelligent fool manipulates and contorts the knowledge acquired.

One does not necessarily have to be educated to be
30  intelligent or even wise for that matter. There are none as wise as our elders, who have acquired their

knowledge and wisdom from lifes' experiences. Better yet, wise is the person who learns from the experiences of others. Therefore, one would be wise in observing the mistakes of others, learning from them too, so as not to make the same mistakes. Those with wisdom use their learning and understanding in a constructive fashion. 35

But to get back to intelligence, intelligence is not harmful. It is the person, who uses his intelligence for harmful things, that is harmful. Not the intelligence. The harmful include devious, sly and artful persons. These are the persons with intelligence that make foolish choices that create unnecessary hardships for themselves and their fellow human beings. 40 45

As Walt Whitman once wrote, "Wisdom is not finally tested by the schools . . . nor can it be passed from one having it to another not having it. Wisdom is of the soul, is not susceptible of proof, is its own proof." In closing, intelligence is evident in the articulation and application of knowledge. To be wise is to use knowledge prudently, not carelessly or viciously. 50

--Sheryl Muirhead, composition student

## Critical Inquiry

Sheryl Muirhead wrote this essay in response to Pär Lagerkvist's "Paradise," Writing Assignment 1 (p. 55). Muirhead's essay is a preliminary draft. That is, it needs revision on a number of levels before it can be judged acceptable. To help you become more aware of your own writing needs as well as those of this student writer, analyze this essay using the following questions. But first, go back and reread Lagerkvist's text and the writing assignment Muirhead responded to.

## Questions for Analysis

1. In your judgment, has Muirhead done what the writing assignment asked? If so, what supports your view? If not, what has the writer failed to address?

2. Has Muirhead referred to Lagerkvist's text sufficiently for someone who has *not* read "Paradise" to understand its intent and chief ideas? Why do you think this?

3. Are any paragraphs underdeveloped, overloaded, or disunified? Should the sentences in any of the paragraphs be reordered? Is the point of each paragraph clear?

4. Do the paragraphs connect with one another, or are more explicit transitions between them needed?

5. Does Muirhead's logic hold up throughout, or are there places where it falls down? Be specific.

6. Is Muirhead's argument generally convincing, or should she work to make it more so? Would you suggest that, in later drafts, Muirhead develop some parts of her essay in greater detail? Which parts?

7. How would you evaluate Muirhead's word choices? Does any language need elucidation or replacement in the next draft? Are there any redundancies? Identify them.

8. Generally, do you believe a little or a lot of work remains to be done on this draft? Explain your answer.

# J. Alden Mason

# The Legendary Empire

John Alden Mason (1885–1967) was an archaeologist, museum curator, and chronicler of native American folklore. He made a number of research expeditions to Latin America and in 1957 published the first of several editions of his *The Ancient Civilizations of Peru*, from which this piece is taken. The book describes political, social, and economic structures before the time of Columbus. It also relates the historical development of Inca civilization as the record was transcribed from oral accounts by the Spanish conquerors.

## Looking Ahead

1. To gain familiarity with the names of people and places that are especially foreign, keep a running list for future reference and use in writing.

2. Notice in this piece how myth melts into history and how, to ennoble itself, history preserves elements of myth.

3. As you read, identify and test political insights to discover to what degree they are as applicable to present-day as to past societies.

Manco Capac was a demigod who was considered the founder of the Inca dynasty. He was turned to stone, but the dried bodies or mummies of the next ten emperors—or at least bodies that were claimed and believed to be theirs—were preserved in Cuzco until the time of Pizarro.

5       The Spanish chroniclers recount several different and mutually contradictory legends of Manco Capac and of the origins of the Inca dynasty and empire, all of them containing supernatural elements. The best known of these is somewhat as follows:

About 18 miles south-east of Cuzco, at a place called Paccari Tampu ("Dawn Tavern"), is a hill known as Tampu-Tocco ("Tavern Hole"), in which there were three openings.[1] From these openings emerged the founders of the empire, the ancestors of some of the Inca *ayllus* ("clans") from the side holes, Manco Capac and his brothers and sisters from the central or "Splendid Opening." His three brothers were named Ayar Auca, Ayar Cachi, and Ayar Uchu; the four sisters Mama Ocllo, Mama Huaco, Mama Cora, and Mama Raua; Manco Capac himself was then known as Ayar Manco.

The eight assumed leadership of the ten ayllus that had come out of the side holes, and led them towards the valley of Cuzco. The exodus occupied a number of years, for the migrants paused for a year or two in several villages on the way, in one of which Sinchi Roca, the second emperor, was born to Manco Capac and his eldest sister, Mama Ocllo. Also *en route* Manco succeeded in getting rid of his three brothers. Cachi was a husky fellow and the others feared him. He climbed to the top of the hill of Huanacauri (which Inca boys also had to climb in their puberty tests), and from there threw sling-stones with such force that he created new ravines. So they sent him back to the origin hole to fetch the sacred llama, and another man went back to help him and to wall him up in the hole—where he is yet. Uchu remained at Huanacauri where he turned to stone, the *huaca*[2] of the shrine there. Auca went on to Cuzco where he became the stone field-guardian huaca of the city. That left only Manco.

Manco and his sisters continued on to the valley of Cuzco where they tested the ground with a golden staff. Finding the soil a little to the east of modern Cuzco to be fertile, they decided to settle there. The valley, of course, was inhabited, but the Inca were the chosen people of the Sun, and wanted their land of corn and llamas. The several small tribes or ayllus in the region were attacked and driven out. The amazonian Mama Huaco killed one man with a bola stone, cut out his lungs and inflated them, which horrid sight frightened the rest away. Then Manco and his four sisters built their first houses on the site of the later Coricancha, and Temple of the Sun.

Naturally several versions of the origin myth, differing considerably in details, were recorded by the Spanish. Garcilaso gives a rather different story in which Manco Capac and his sister were created by the Sun on an island in Lake Titicaca. Manco was a culture hero rather than a conqueror, and he and Mama Ocllo taught the people industries and arts and gathered them together to found Cuzco.

Manco Capac may have been a purely mythological character, invented in later years to give paternity and supernatural origin to the real quasi-historical founder of the Inca empire, Sinchi Roca.

---

1. The word *tocco* is translated "window" by some, "cave mouth" by others. Three "windows" in a wall at Machu Picchu are identified by Bingham as the traditional site; others consider the reference to be to natural small caves in a hill.

2. *Huaca*: sacred object or place. Pronounced "waca," which phonetic but non-standard form will be used herein.

Garcilaso de la Vega is one of the most famous of the many Spanish chroniclers who wrote down the Inca legends, and his version was followed by many
50    of his successors and accepted by many modern writers. Thus Means[3] adopts
the Garcilassan accounts. According to this, the Emperor Sinchi Roca began the
expansion of the Inca empire, Lloque Yupanqui extended it to Lake Titicaca,
Mayta Capac reached Tiahuanaco and the headwaters of the coastal rivers, and
Capac Yupanqui conquered some of the coastal peoples.

55    Garcilaso's account is not supported by most of the earlier chroniclers, and
the modern opinion is against its acceptance and inclined to believe that it was
not until the reign of Yahuar Huacac that the expansion of the empire began.
Even regarding this time the various accounts are rather contradictory.

If the account of Garcilaso is to be credited, the predecessors of Pachacuti[4]
60    had already conquered and incorporated in the Inca empire a large part of Peru
and Bolivia, and yet we find, in the time of Viracocha Inca,[5] the Inca waging a
life-and-death struggle with their rivals for ascendancy, the Chanca, Lupaca,
and Colla, Cuzco besieged, and Emperor Pachacuti beginning his great conquests in the close vicinity of Cuzco. Garcilaso's accounts seem to be hardly
65    compatible with these facts, and it appears more likely that the pre-Pachacuti
wars were local ones, without permanent subjugation by the Inca of any enemy
people.

The historical accounts of Pedro Sarmiento de Gamboa and of the Jesuit Father Bernabé Cobo seem to be more logical and reliable, and are supported by a
70    number of the other chroniclers. They are accepted in general by the modern
authority Rowe[6] instead of the Garcilaso-Means version, and are here adopted,
with the understanding that they are not presented with any claim to exactitude
or finality.

According to the versions here accepted, during the reigns of the first eight
75    Inca emperors, Manco Capac to Viracocha Inca, the Inca did not extend their
sway or political influence beyond the immediate region of Cuzco. There were
many independent small groups in this area, probably physically identical with
the Inca, speaking slightly variant dialects or varieties of the same language, and
enjoying very much the same culture, economic and non-material. That is to
80    say, at this time the Inca were but one of a number of equally unimportant
groups in their habitat. They were constantly in competition and often at war
with their neighbours, but no group had any thought of establishing permanent
hegemony over the others; the imperial concept had not yet developed. The vic-
tor in inter-tribal or inter-city wars looted the vanquished and possibly imposed

---

3. Philip Means, *Ancient Civilizations of the Andes* (1931).

4. *Pachacuti*: the ninth Inca emperor in 1438, who began an expansion of the empire; see lines
183–184. (*ed.*)

5. *Viracocha Inca*: was the eighth emperor; see lines 169–170. (*ed.*)

6. John H. Rowe, et al., "Reconnaissance Notes on the Site of Huari, Near Ayacucho, Peru"
(1946).

a tribute on them, and then let them alone until, possibly, they again acquired    85
enough power to become a menace. The traditions of the Inca record no defeats
suffered, but such set-backs are readily forgotten; only victories are remembered. All of the great empires of antiquity had a similar rise from unimportance
among the obscure. Possibly the Inca custom of hereditary succession for their
leaders had something to do with their later rise; it is not known whether the    90
neighbouring groups followed a similar pattern or not.

Sinchi Roca, second emperor and son of Manco Capac and his sister Mama
Ocllo, was probably an historical character, but the legends say little about him.
He was not warlike and made no military campaigns, adding nothing to the
Inca dominions. He succeeded Manco Capac by his father's nomination. There    95
is disagreement among the chroniclers as to whether or not he followed his father's example of marrying his sister. His son, Lloque Yupanqui, succeeded
him; Lloque is said to mean "left-handed." Lloque Yupanqui had an elder
brother; why in this case Manco Capac's rule of primogeniture was not followed
is a question. Like his father he did nothing of historical importance and per-    100
formed no military exploits. According to the legend, he had no children in
spite of his advanced age. Like the early biblical patriarchs, they lived to a really
ripe old age in that period; Sarmiento has all the early emperors living to an age
of over one hundred! So they got old Lloque Yupanqui another wife—not his
sister, it seems—and by her he had a son, Mayta Capac.    105

Mayta Capac was a strong character like his great-grandfather, Manco Capac, and so fabulous myths grew up about him, as in the case of Manco Capac.
A vigorous three-month baby, he was born with a full set of teeth. At the age of
one year he was as big as an average eight-year-old, and at two years he was
fighting with big lads. When only a few years older he got into a quarrel with    110
some boys of the Alcahuiza group, the nearest neighbours of the Inca, which
developed into a full-scale battle and finally into a war in which, of course, the
Inca were victorious. Still in early childhood, Mayta Capac gave a good account
of himself in these battles, and so went through the maturity rites at that tender
age. Like most kindly fathers, Lloque Yupanqui could not understand his bel-    115
ligerent brat and chided him, fearing that he would involve his family and people in disaster. However, the Inca were quite ready for a fight at any time and
gave Mayta Capac enthusiastic support, especially after Lloque Yupanqui died
and Mayta became emperor. Garcilaso makes him the first great conqueror,
who subdued the country from Lake Titicaca to the headwaters of the coastal    120
rivers, but later historical events, as well as the testimony of earlier and more reliable chroniclers, do not support this claim, and it is more probable that the
wars under Mayta Capac did not extend more than a few miles beyond Cuzco
and had few results beyond the taking of booty, the imposition of tribute, and
the cultivation of hostility.    125

The chroniclers are in even greater disagreement than usual regarding the
identity of Mayta Capac's *coya* or principal wife, no less than five different
women being named; only one writer states that he married his sister. He followed the precedent of his father in making an inspection tour of his entire

130     realm immediately after his inauguration, which custom was followed by all his successors. He also, according to one of the chroniclers, legitimized the great body of soothsayers, medicine men, and the like who had hitherto been accustomed to practise clandestinely their age-old professions.

The fifth emperor, Capac Yupanqui, was appointed by his father Mayta Ca-
135     pac just before his death. He also, apparently, was not the eldest son, but was selected because his older brother was ugly. Though his annals are short and simple, he is reported to have been the first emperor who made conquests beyond the valley of Cuzco, though these were only a dozen miles away.

Inca Roca, his son, also waged war with neighbouring peoples and subju-
140     gated some groups within twenty miles south of Cuzco. For the greater part, however, he preferred the flesh-pots of Cuzco and idleness therein.

Inca Roca begat a number of legitimate—or, let us say, royal—sons, among whom Titu Cusi Hualpa and Vicaquirao left their marks on Peruvian history. The former succeeded to the throne under a new name, Yahuar Huacac, "He
145     Who Weeps Blood," for the origin of which name a legend—doubtless apocryphal except, possibly, in skeleton—was told.

Titu Cusi Hualpa's mother, Mama Micay, was a beautiful Huayllaca woman who, it was said, had first been promised to the chief of a neighbouring group, the Ayamarca. As this promise was broken, the Ayamarca went to war with the
150     Huayllaca and were besting them. As the price of peace the Huayllaca agreed to deliver Mama Micay's child to the Ayamarca. Inducing Inca Roca to send the boy, then about eight years old, to a neighbouring town, he was seized and taken to the chief of the Ayamarca, the rejected suitor of his mother. With indignation beyond his years Titu Cusi Hualpa wept tears of blood and threatened
155     a curse upon his captors if he were injured. It was several years before he was returned to his father, Inca Roca, the Inca "emperor," which illustrates the slight power of the Inca in those days.

That Yahuar Huacac was chosen emperor is strange, for he seems to have been quite unsuited for the post, unenterprising and even cowardly. His
160     brother (cousin, according to some accounts) Vicaquirao apparently was much more capable, as well as likeable. He led some campaigns against the groups south and east of Cuzco, and probably for the first time consolidated and organized these near-by regions as integral parts of the Inca empire. Another brother or cousin, Apo Mayta, is mentioned as a successful general; according to other
165     accounts, Apu Mayta was merely another name for Vicaquirao.

Most of the chroniclers agree—for the first time—regarding the name and identity of the coya or queen of Yahuar Huacac; she was not his sister, indicating that at that time sister marriage was at least not a rule.

Hatun Tupac Inca, the eighth emperor, more commonly known by his later
170     name of Viracocha Inca, was the most famous of the sons of Yahuar Huacac; on accession to the throne he assumed his new name in honour of Viracocha, the Creator, his reputed divine ancestor, who had appeared to him in a vision in his youth.

Viracocha was apparently the first true imperialist, the first emperor who planned permanent rule over foreign non-Inca peoples. Up until his time neighbouring groups had been conquered, but no garrisons had been placed among them, no Inca officials put over them; they were left alone, and eventually were again attacked and defeated. Viracocha began making them integral parts of his realm. With his experienced and efficient generals Vicaquirao and Apo Mayta he began a series of systematic conquests. He had passed his prime, however, before he had extended the empire more than some twenty-five miles around Cuzco. The larger expansion, more aptly compared with an explosion, began toward the end of his reign, and was animated by his even more capable and imperialistically minded son, Pachacuti.

Peru had by this time reached the economic and cultural stage when it was ripe for imperialism; it was in the air and in the cards. The Inca were but one of three or four rival strong groups in the Andean region, each about equally ready to progress towards imperialism and to gain ascendancy over the others. It was one of those times when the course of history depended on the outcome of a battle or two, and the latter largely upon the quality of leadership. The Inca under Pachacuti and Viracocha's generals had the experience and were the victors.

First it might be well to introduce some of the *dramatis personae*. Aged Emperor Viracocha's favourite child was the natural son Urco, or Urcon, whom he nominated as his successor, much to the disgust of the eldest royal son Inca Roca and the generals. The latter preferred the virile third royal son Cusi Inca Yupanqui, later known to Peruvian history as the great conqueror emperor Pachacuti.

Two Aymara-speaking groups of the Lake Titicaca region far to the southeast of Cuzco were then, with the Inca, the strong nations of the area. These were the Lupaca and the Colla. With that fatuous short-sightedness that has ever induced a people to solicit the aid of a more foreign and potentially more dangerous group in order to overcome a more closely related rival, each hoped for Inca aid to subdue the other. So did the Tlaxcaltec join with Cortés to crush the Aztec; so do today (1966) Chinese Nationalists seek Western aid to overcome the Communists; so would almost any nation today ally with beings from Mars to defeat its pet terrestrial enemy. Anyway, Emperor Viracocha formed an alliance with the Lupaca. The Colla, however, learning of this, attacked the Lupaca before Viracocha could send aid, but were defeated in a great battle at Paucarcolla; that eliminated them from the race for hegemony.

Immediately to the west of Cuzco were the Quechua, and to the west of the latter the Chanca, in the province of Andahuaylas. The Quechua, as the name suggests, were of the same blood, language, and culture as the Inca, and enjoyed friendly relations with the latter; the Chanca were a rather different people, and old enemies of the Quechua-Inca. In the early part of Viracocha's reign the Chanca had overcome the Quechua and established suzerainty over them, so that the Inca and Chanca territories were contiguous; they could not long remain so without conflict. Emperor Viracocha had strengthened his position by cultivating friendship with the Quechua and by taking his queen from that region.

220  Finally, towards the end of Viracocha's reign, the Chanca felt strong enough to attack, hoping that Inca leadership would be weak. They advanced on Cuzco with such a large army that many of the leaders, including Viracocha himself and his son and heir-apparent Urcon, believed the cause to be lost, and barricaded themselves in a fortress in Caquia-Xaquixahuana, which they be-
225  lieved could be defended better than the city. However, the two royal sons, Roca and Cusi Yupanqui, refused to yield and, together with the old generals Vicaquirao and Apo Mayta and a band of other last-ditchers, planned a desperate defence of Cuzco; Cusi Yupanqui was the leader. The Chanca attack was finally repulsed by resistance so heroic that the defenders believed that the stones
230  of the battlefield must have turned into men to aid them; Cusi Inca Yupanqui had some of them taken and placed in the city's shrines as sacred *wacas*. After their repulse from the city, the Chanca were defeated in several other battles and disappeared as rivals to Inca power.

About this time, apparently, Viracocha died and was succeeded by his son,
235  Inca Urcon, half-brother of Cusi Inca Yupanqui. His reign was short, however, for Cusi Yupanqui refused to recognize him, had himself enthroned in his place and ordered Urcon's name removed from the official list of emperors. Cusi Yupanqui took the new name of Pachacuti, by which he is known to history, the first of the really great Inca emperors.

240  There are, of course, several different versions of the story of the accession of Pachacuti. According to Sarmiento he twice journeyed to Xaquixahuana to offer the spoils of the Chanca war to Emperor Viracocha, but his father kept insisting that his favourite son and nominee Urcon should receive them. Pachacuti finally, on the generals' urging, took the throne, without his father's con-
245  sent or approval. The latter never again resided in Cuzco, which he had deserted.

The death of Viracocha Inca marks the close of the Middle period and of the legendary era of Inca history. Up until this time the many chroniclers have been in great disagreement, few details can be given as incontrovertible, and in
250  most cases the truth is beyond assurance. With the advent of the next emperor, Pachacuti, all the major and more reliable authorities are in virtual agreement.

## Looking Back

1. Why is it significant that the founding dynasty of the Incas emerges from the earth?

2. Does it surprise you that the founders' incestuous and murderous activities are recounted as if they were normal? Why or why not?

3. What distinguishes a culture hero from a conqueror (see line 42)?

4. What political ends might be served by giving a nation a mythological origin (see lines 45–47)?

5. Can you summarize what we learn in lines 74–91 about the rise of nations?

6. What political lesson does Mason teach in lines 200–206? Give another example of this principle in operation.
7. How is Sincha Roca related to Manco Capac?
8. How do the Incan myths seem to influence accounts of people who actually lived?
9. Starting from the beginning, trace the stages of development of the Inca empire.
10. Overall, what is your evaluation of the Incas?

## Writing Assignments

1. We learn from their mythology that the Incas considered themselves the "chosen people of the sun" (line 33), chosen to dominate other peoples, who are not similarly the darlings of fortune or destined to rule. The basis for this dominance is the preferred group's common bloodline; the consequence is the subjugation, oppression, and sometimes annihilation of other groups. The Incas were neither the first nor the last people to claim racial or national superiority over others. Throughout history and into contemporary life other examples of this phenomenon abound. Yet, although most of us are critical of it, we do not always articulate its evils as clearly as we might. Do this now. Extrapolating from the views and practices of the Incas, write an essay that attempts to explain how ethnocentrism and ultranationalism work. Conceive of your audience as one that has not been victimized; convince them that even they may not always be safe.

2. Behind the foundation of nation states, and behind the founders themselves, often lies a body of myth. We see this in the story of the original Incas emerging from the earth. We remember Romulus and Remus, the founders of Rome, being suckled by the she-wolf. We even recall, less sensationally, George Washington's virtue in confessing to chopping down the cherry tree. These myths confer on persons and states a kind of legitimacy, a notion that the nation is blessed and its founders righteous. But how do myths accomplish this? One way to answer this question is by contrasting mythical and historical accounts and asking, What beliefs does one account supply that the other does not? For instance, we could contrast the mythical origins of the Incas as told here with their actual origins, part of which Mason provides and the rest of which we can research or make educated guesses about. Write an essay, referring to "The Legendary Empire," that sets up this contrast. Tell what different ideas of themselves derived from myth and history worked to convince the Incas of their legitimacy as that term is defined above.

3. Referring to both myth and history, we discover that the Incas' rise to power involved incest, murder, warfare, invasion, and conquest. These actions make one wonder. They are hardly admirable, at least by today's standards. Yet—with the exception of incest, perhaps—these tactics seem always to have prepared the way for the emergence of powerful nations and great civilizations. We believe that power is useful and that science, industry, and art—the products of civilization—are essential. But does their value outweigh the means necessary to gain them? Or does another alternative exist in which greatness and peace may coexist? Is it better to be less great but more virtuous? Or does a country that does not try to outstrip others risk defeat at their hands? Referring first to the Inca empire and later to the United States, write an essay addressing these questions.

# Linked Readings

Thomas Bulfinch
PROMETHEUS AND PANDORA

H. A. Guerber
THE STORY OF PROMETHEUS

DEUCALION AND PYRRHA

Al Ross
TO THE WOMAN WHO DISCOVERED FIRE!

Karel Capek
THE PUNISHMENT OF PROMETHEUS

Franz Kafka
PROMETHEUS

When the same story is told more than once, it inevitably changes in the telling. Some events, descriptive passages, and even characters drop out; others appear. More significantly, the **emphasis** the author places on one or more of these matters shifts to become more or less. This fact of reading is an instructive one for writers. Not only does it show how subjective individual authors may be, but it demonstrates, through contrast, the importance to writing of point of view, language choices, cultural attitudes, and stylistic purpose. These elements undergo a number of changes in the four narratives and the cartoon caption that follow.

Each of these texts focuses on Prometheus, the giant in the earth and fire-bringer who, in the original myth, first created human beings and then replenished their life with the gift of fire. Zeus (in the Greek, Jupiter in Latin) thought the fire gift went too far, and Prometheus was harshly punished for his deed. Besides Prometheus, other characters who figure in the myth are Pandora, the first woman, and Deucalion and Pyrrha, descendants of Prometheus.

Thomas Bulfinch (1796–1867), a Harvard professor, became and continues to be a household name for having popularized the Greek myths, the legends of King Arthur, and the tales of Charlemagne. H. A. Guerber's *The Myths of Greece and Rome* was first published in 1907. Extensively revised thirty years later, its many reprints attest to its great popularity. Al Ross is a cartoonist whose work frequently appears in the *New Yorker*, the source of this drawing. Czech playwright and novelist Karel Capek (1890–1938) introduced the word *robot* (from the play *R.U.R.*) into the language. His modern version of Prometheus is from his *Apocryphal Stories*. Franz Kafka (1883–1924), author of *The Trial* and *The Castle,* also wrote numerous short pieces like the one included here. The mythological imagination is characteristic of all Kafka's works.

# PROMETHEUS AND PANDORA

## *Looking Ahead*

1. Bulfinch's language is built on a relatively simple vocabulary but a fairly elaborate way of putting words together in sentences. His **syntax** is more characteristic of the nineteenth century than ours and may require your careful attention.

2. Notice that Bulfinch, like many mythographers, includes different versions of some details of his story. Here, the variations have to do with Pandora. This flexibility should alert you to the fact that different cultures interpret myths differently, often to suit the ideas of the time.

3. Read critically to test the reliability of Bulfinch's point of view on the Bible, on women, on the nature of Jupiter (that is, on supreme authority), and on rebellion.

The creation of the world is a problem naturally fitted to excite the liveliest interest of man, its inhabitant. The ancient pagans, not having the information on the subject which we derive from the pages of Scripture, had their own way of telling the story, which is as follows:

Before earth, and sea, and heaven were created, all things wore one aspect,    5
to which we give the name of Chaos—a confused and shapeless mass, nothing but dead weight, in which, however, slumbered the seeds of things. Earth, sea, and air were all mixed up together; so the earth was not solid, the sea was not fluid, and the air was not transparent. God and Nature at last interposed and put an end to this discord, separating earth from sea, and heaven from both.    10
The fiery part, being the lightest, sprang up and formed the skies; the air was next in weight and place. The earth, being heavier, sank below, and the water took the lowest place, and buoyed up the earth.

Here, some god—it is not known which—gave his good offices in arranging and disposing the earth. He appointed rivers and bays their places, raised    15
mountains, scooped out valleys, distributed woods, fountains, fertile fields, and stony plains. The air being cleared, the stars began to appear, fishes took possession of the sea, birds of the air, and four-footed beasts of the land.

But a nobler animal was wanted, and Man was made. It is not known whether the Creator made him of divine materials, or whether in the earth, so    20
lately separated from heaven, there lurked still some heavenly seeds. Prometheus took some of this earth, and kneading it up with water, made man in the image of the gods. He gave him an upright stature, so that while all other animals turn their faces downward and look to the earth, he raises his to heaven and gazes on the stars.
                                                                                                            25
Prometheus was one of the Titans, a gigantic race who inhabited the earth before the creation of man. To him and his brother Epimetheus was committed the office of making man, and providing him and all other animals with the faculties necessary for their preservation. Epimetheus undertook to do this, and

30 Prometheus was to overlook his work, when it was done. Epimetheus accordingly proceeded to bestow upon the different animals the various gifts of courage, strength, swiftness, sagacity; wings to one, claws to another, a shelly[1] covering to a third, etc. But when man came to be provided for, who was to be superior to all other animals, Epimetheus had been so prodigal of his resources

35 that he had nothing left to bestow upon him. In his perplexity he resorted to his brother Prometheus, who, with the aid of Minerva,[2] went up to heaven, and lighted his torch at the chariot of the sun, and brought down fire to man. With this gift man was more than a match for all other animals. It enabled him to make weapons wherewith to subdue them; tools with which to cultivate the

40 earth; to warm his dwelling, so as to be comparatively independent of climate; and finally to introduce the arts and to coin money, the means of trade and commerce.

Woman was not yet made. The story (absurd enough!) is that Jupiter made her and sent her to Prometheus and his brother, to punish them for their pre-

45 sumption in stealing fire from heaven; and man, for accepting the gift. The first woman was named Pandora. She was made in heaven, every god contributing something to perfect her. Venus gave her beauty, Mercury persuasion, Apollo[3] music, etc. Thus equipped, she was conveyed to earth and presented to Epimetheus, who gladly accepted her, though cautioned by his brother to be-

50 ware of Jupiter and his gifts. Epimetheus had in his house a jar, in which were kept certain noxious articles, for which, in fitting man for his new abode, he had had no occasion. Pandora was seized with an eager curiosity to know what this jar contained; and one day she slipped off the cover and looked in. Forthwith there escaped a multitude of plagues for hapless man—such as gout,

55 rheumatism, and colic for his body, and envy, spite, and revenge for his mind— and scattered themselves far and wide. Pandora hastened to replace the lid; but alas! the whole contents of the jar had escaped, one thing only excepted, which lay at the bottom, and that was *hope*. So we see at this day, whatever evils are abroad, hope never entirely leaves us; and while we have *that,* no amount of

60 other ills can make us completely wretched.

Another story is that Pandora was sent in good faith, by Jupiter, to bless man; that she was furnished with a box, containing her marriage presents, into which every god had put some blessing. She opened the box incautiously, and the blessings all escaped, *hope* only excepted. This story seems more probable

65 than the former; for how could *hope*, so precious a jewel as it is, have been kept in a jar full of all manner of evils, as in the former statement?

---

1. *shelly:* the adjectival form of *shell. (ed.)*

2. *Minerva:* the Roman goddess of wisdom. *(ed.)*

3. *Venus:* the goddess of love; *Mercury:* the messenger of the gods, among whose talents was the art of rhetoric (persuasion); *Apollo:* the sun god, who exercised the power of music. *(ed.)*

The world being thus furnished with inhabitants, the first age was an age of innocence and happiness, called the *Golden Age.* Truth and right prevailed, though not enforced by law, nor was there any magistrate to threaten or punish. The forest had not yet been robbed of its trees to furnish timbers for vessels, nor had men built fortifications round their towns. There were no such things as swords, spears, or helmets. The earth brought forth all things necessary for man, without his labor in ploughing or sowing. Perpetual spring reigned, flowers sprang up without seed, the rivers flowed with milk and wine, and yellow honey distilled from the oaks. 70

Then succeeded the *Silver Age,* inferior to the golden, but better than that of brass. Jupiter shortened the spring and divided the year into seasons. Then, first, men had to endure the extremes of hot and cold, and houses became necessary. Caves were the first dwellings, and leafy coverts of the woods, and huts woven of twigs. Crops would no longer grow without planting. The farmer was obliged to sow the seed, and the toiling ox to draw the plough. 75

Next came the *Brazen Age,* more savage of temper and readier to the strife of arms yet not altogether wicked. The hardest and worst was the *Iron Age.* Crime burst in like a flood; modesty, truth, and honor fled. In their places came fraud and cunning, violence, and the wicked love of gain. Then seamen spread sails to the wind, and the trees were torn from the mountains to serve for keels to ships, and vex the face of ocean. The earth, which till now had been cultivated in common, began to be divided off into possessions. Men were not satisfied with what the surface produced, but must dig into its bowels, and draw forth from thence the ores of metals. Mischievous *iron,* and more mischievous *gold,* were produced. War sprang up, using both as weapons; the guest was not safe in his friend's house; and sons-in-law and fathers-in-law, brothers and sisters, husbands and wives, could not trust one another. Sons wished their fathers dead, that they might come to the inheritance; family love lay prostrate. The earth was wet with slaughter, and the gods abandoned it, one by one, till Astræa[4] alone was left, and finally she also took her departure. 80 85 90 95

Jupiter, seeing this state of things, burned with anger. He summoned the gods to council. They obeyed the call and took the road to the palace of heaven.

---

4. *Astræa:* The goddess of innocence and purity. After leaving earth, she was placed among the stars, where she became the constellation Virgo—the Virgin. Themis (Justice) was the mother of Astræa. She is represented as holding aloft a pair of scales, in which she weighs the claims of opposing parties.

It was a favorite idea of the old poets that these goddesses would one day return and bring back the Golden Age. Even in a Christian hymn, the Messiah of Pope, this idea occurs.

> All crimes shall cease, and ancient fraud shall fail,
> Returning Justice lift aloft her scale,
> Peace o'er the world her olive wand extend,
> And white-robed Innocence from heaven descend.

See also Milton's Hymn to the Nativity, stanzas xiv and xv.

The road, which any one may see in a clear night, stretches across the face of the sky and is called the Milky Way. Along the road stand the palaces of the illustri-
100    ous gods; the common people of the skies live apart, on either side. Jupiter addressed the assembly. He set forth the frightful condition of things on the earth and closed by announcing his intention to destroy the whole of its inhabitants, and provide a new race, unlike the first, who would be more worthy of life and much better worshippers of the gods. So saying he took a thunderbolt, and was
105    about to launch it at the world, and destroy it by burning; but recollecting the danger that such a conflagration might set heaven itself on fire, he changed his plan and resolved to drown it. The north wind, which scatters the clouds, was chained up; the south was sent out, and soon covered all the face of heaven with a cloak of pitchy darkness. The clouds, driven together, resound with a crash;
110    torrents of rain fall; the crops are laid low; the year's labor of the husbandman perishes in an hour. Jupiter, not satisfied with his own waters, calls on his brother Neptune[5] to aid him with his. He lets loose the rivers and pours them over the land. At the same time, he heaves the land with an earthquake and brings in the reflux of the ocean over the shores. Flocks, herds, men, and
115    houses are swept away, and temples, with their sacred enclosures, profaned. If any edifice remained standing, it was overwhelmed, and its turrets lay hid beneath the waves. Now all was sea, sea without shore. Here and there an individual remained on a projecting hill-top, and a few, in boats, pulled the oar where they had lately driven the plough. The fishes swim among the tree-tops; the an-
120    chor is let down into a garden. Where the graceful lambs played but now unwieldy sea calves gambol. The wolf swims among the sheep, the yellow lions and tigers struggle in the water. The strength of the wild boar serves him not, nor his swiftness the stag. The birds fall with weary wing into the water, having found no land for a resting-place. These living beings whom the water spared
125    fell a prey to hunger.

Parnassus alone, of all the mountains, overtopped the waves; and there Deucalion, and his wife Pyrrha, of the race of Prometheus, found refuge—he a just man, and she a faithful worshipper of the gods. Jupiter, when he saw none left alive but this pair, and remembered their harmless lives and pious de-
130    meanor, ordered the north winds to drive away the clouds, and disclose the skies to earth, and earth to the skies. Neptune also directed Triton[6] to blow on his shell and sound a retreat to the waters. The waters obeyed, and the sea returned to its shores, and the rivers to their channels. Then Deucalion thus addressed Pyrrha: "Oh, wife, only surviving woman, joined to me first by the ties
135    of kindred and marriage, and now by a common danger, would that we possessed the power of our ancestor Prometheus, and could renew the race as he at first made it! But as we cannot, let us seek yonder temple, and inquire of the

---

5. *Neptune:* the god of the oceans. (*ed.*)

6. *Triton:* Neptune's fish-tailed offspring. (*ed.*)

gods what remains for us to do." They entered the temple, deformed as it was with slime, and approached the altar, where no fire burned. There they fell prostrate on the earth and prayed the goddess to inform them how they might   140
retrieve their miserable affairs. The oracle answered, "Depart from the temple with head veiled and garments unbound, and cast behind you the bones of your mother." They heard the words with astonishment. Pyrrha first broke silence: "We cannot obey; we dare not profane the remains of our parents." They sought the thickest shades of the wood, and revolved the oracle in their minds. At   145
length Deucalion spoke: "Either my sagacity deceives me, or the command is one we may obey without impiety. The earth is the great parent of all; the stones are her bones; these we may cast behind us; and I think this is what the oracle means. At least, it will do no harm to try." They veiled their faces, unbound their garments, and picked up stones, and cast them behind them. The stones   150
(wonderful to relate) began to grow soft, and assume shape. By degrees, they put on a rude resemblance to the human form, like a block half finished in the hands of the sculptor. The moisture and slime that were about them became flesh; the stony part became bones; the veins remained veins, retaining their name, only changing their use. Those thrown by the hand of the man became   155
men, and those by the woman became women. It was a hard race, and well adapted to labor, as we find ourselves to be at this day, giving plain indications of our origin.

The comparison of Eve to Pandora is too obvious to have escaped Milton, who introduces it in Book IV of *Paradise Lost:*[7]   160

> More lovely than Pandora, whom the gods
> Endowed with all their gifts; and O, too like
> . In sad event, when to the unwiser son
> Of Japhet brought by Hermes, she insnared
> Mankind with her fair looks, to be avenged   165
> On him who had stole Jove's authentic fire.

Prometheus and Epimetheus were sons of Iapetus, which Milton changes to Japhet.
Prometheus has been a favorite subject with the poets. He is represented as the friend of mankind, who interposed in their behalf when Jove[8] was incensed   170
against them and who taught them civilization and the arts. But as, in so doing, he transgressed the will of Jupiter, he drew down on himself the anger of the ruler of gods and men. Jupiter had him chained to a rock on Mount Caucasus, where a vulture preyed on his liver, which was renewed as fast as devoured. This state of torment might have been brought to an end at any time by   175

---

7. *John Milton* (1608–1674): one of the greatest English poets, whose masterpiece, *Paradise Lost,* describes the expulsion of Adam and Eve from Eden. (*ed.*)

8. *Jove:* a name for Jupiter in his juvenile aspect. (*ed.*)

Prometheus, if he had been willing to submit to his oppressor; for he possessed a secret which involved the stability of Jove's throne, and if he would have revealed it, he might have been at once taken into favor. But that he disdained to do. He has therefore become the symbol of magnanimous endurance of unmer-
180    ited suffering, and strength of will resisting oppression.

Byron and Shelley[9] have both treated this theme. The following are Byron's lines:

> Titan! to whose immortal eyes
>     The sufferings of mortality,
185 >         Seen in their sad reality,
> Were not as things that gods despise,
> What was thy pity's recompense?
> A silent suffering, and intense;
> The rock, the vulture, and the chain;
190 > All that the proud can feel of pain;
> The agony they do not show,
> The suffocating sense of woe.
>
> Thy godlike crime was to be kind;
>     To render why thy precepts less
195 >         The sum of human wretchedness,
> And strengthen man with his own mind
>     And, baffled as thou wert from high.
>     Still, in thy patient energy
> In the endurance and repulse
200 >         Of thine impenetrable spirit,
> Which earth and heaven could not convulse,
>     A mighty lesson we inherit.

Byron also employs the same allusion, in his ode to Napoleon Bonaparte:

> Or, like the thief of fire from heaven,
205 >         Wilt thou withstand the shock?
> And share with him—the unforgiven—
>     His vulture and his rock?

## THE STORY OF PROMETHEUS
## DEUCALION AND PYRRHA

### Looking Ahead

1. It is instructive to test a writer's basic assumptions. Note that Guerber *chooses* to accept the negative view of womankind presented in this version of the myth.

---

9. *George Gordon Lord Byron* (1788–1824) and *Percy Bysshe Shelley* (1792–1822): English poets of the romantic era. (*ed.*)

2. Observing the parallel between the Noah story and the story of Deucalion and Pyrrha will give you a sense of the origin, at different times and in different places, of the same myths.

3. Guerber's inclusion of illustrative quotations from poems, a common practice of earlier writers, indicates the impressive level of cultural knowledge and appreciation readers at this time were assumed to have.

## The Story of Prometheus

In the great conflict between Cronus and Zeus Prometheus, unlike his father Iapetus, had ranged himself with the Olympian gods. He was now chosen by Zeus to direct the important task of creating living beings to inhabit the empty though beautiful world. In this undertaking he was aided by his brother Epimetheus. Together they made birds, beasts, and fishes, giving to each gifts    5 of strength, swiftness, beauty, or intelligence according to their different needs, but it was Prometheus who last of all brought into existence the most intelligent though not the strongest, or the swiftest, or the most beautiful of creatures—Man.

From a lump of clay kneaded with water Prometheus wrought an image re-    10 sembling the high gods themselves, an image standing upright, with its head lifted to gaze upon the stars. But Epimetheus had been so lavish with his gifts to the other new beings that his elder brother decided to endow Man with a gift which should surpass all the rest—the gift of fire. Prometheus soared heaven-ward and lit his torch at the eternal lamp of the sun. Then he descended to earth    15 and bestowed upon humanity the divine spark which, in the fullness of time, was to flame up into knowledge, art, commerce, and civilization. Hence the metaphor, so dear to poets, of "Promethean fire."

Then, according to the ancient poets, came the true Age of Gold, when men were, as they have never been since, happy, sinless, and peaceful. This was the    20 legend in Milton's mind when, speaking of the angels' song "On the Morning of Christ's Nativity," he wrote:

> For, if such holy song
> Enwrap our fancy long,
>    Time will run back, and fetch the Age of Gold;    25
> And speckled Vanity
> Will sicken soon and die,
>    And leprous Sin will melt from earthly mould;
> And Hell itself will pass away,
> And leave her dol'rous mansions to the peering Day.    30
>
> Yea, Truth and Justice then
> Will down return to Men,
>    Orbed in a rainbow; and, like glories wearing,
> Mercy will sit between,
> Throned in celestial sheen,    35
>    With radiant feet the tissued clouds down-steering;

And Heav'n, as at some festival,
Will open wide the gates of her high palace hall.

This Age of Gold was in some ways a rather monotonous time. The year
40    was not divided into seasons, and perpetual spring reigned. The men who dwelt
in this paradise had neither wives nor daughters—they were like Adam before
the creation of Eve. They did not work—why should they, when the earth
brought forth everything that they needed? They had no arts or crafts. The
plough, the loom, the potter's wheel, were as yet unknown.
45    Then came the Age of Silver, when Zeus divided the year into seasons, and
for the first time mankind suffered the hardships of wind and weather. They
took refuge in caves, instead of dwelling happily in the open air. They had to
plough and sow instead of harvesting rich crops which had sprung up of their
own accord. The discipline of rough weather and hard work seems to have had
50    anything but a good effect upon men. Soon they began to neglect the altars of the
Olympian gods, and presently they had the audacity to dispute with Zeus himself, and to claim greater privileges than the All-Highest was disposed to grant.
Prometheus sided with the presumptuous creatures he had made, and, en-
deavouring to settle one disagreement in their favour, he played upon Zeus a
55    trick which the god never forgot or forgave. The question at issue was what portions of an animal sacrifice should be dedicated to the gods, and what should
belong to man. Prometheus divided a sacrificial ox into two, and having stuffed
the eatable parts into the skin he slyly put a heap of ugly odd bits on the top;
then he covered the bones with what looked like fat, and invited Zeus to choose
60    between the two.
According to one version of the story, the god chose the more attractive alternative, and was very wroth when he found nothing but bones inside; according to another version, he saw through the trick, but pretended to be deceived,
in order to have an excuse for punishing the now detested human race. This
65    punishment was to deprive them of fire, but once more Prometheus came to
their rescue, and brought the precious flame down from the sky in a hollow
fennel-stalk. Such a hollow stalk is still used as a primitive means of carrying a
light in some of the isles of Greece.
Zeus inflicted upon the Titan a terrible penalty. Chained to a craggy peak of
70    Mount Caucasus, Prometheus was doomed to have his liver gnawed all day by a
vulture. By night what had been devoured grew again, so that the ghastly
process should be renewed the next morning. This agony continued for many
centuries, until at least Herakles (Hercules) slew the vulture and set its victim
free. According to Æschylus the Titan suffered for thirty thousand years.

75                    Titan! to whose immortal eyes
                        The sufferings of mortality,
                        Seen in their sad reality,
                    Were not as things that gods despise;

What was thy pity's recompense?
A silent suffering and intense;                                                  80
The rock, the vulture, and the chain,
All that the proud can feel of pain.

—Byron, *Prometheus*

Meanwhile the vindictive Zeus had resolved, with the aid and approval of
his fellow-gods, to mete out an overwhelming punishment to man. This was the    85
creation of woman!

Having endowed her with beauty, charm, a sweet voice, a graceful walk, an
appealing manner, they called her Pandora, the gift of *all* the gods, and Hermes
(Mercury), the messenger of the immortals, escorted her down to earth and presented her to Prometheus, who was not then fettered to his Caucasian crag. Dis-  90
trustful of Zeus and all his works, Prometheus turned his back resolutely on the
lovely newcomer; but his more confiding young brother Epimetheus received
her with joy.

By way of a dowry Pandora had brought with her, as a gift from Zeus himself, a sealed casket, which she had been solemnly warned not to open. The All-   95
Highest had apparently realized that curiosity would be one of the characteristics
of the new creature which he had invented to be the curse of man, for it was his
intention that she *should* open the mysterious casket, and before very long she
*did*. And then, alack! out flew a swarm of evil sprites, all the bodily and mental
ills that ever since have tormented the human race: out flew rheumatism, gout,   100
blindness, and deafness; out flew malice, pride, cruelty, and covetousness, each
uglier and more malignant than the last. They darkened the air with their dusky
wings, and Pandora recoiled in terror from what she had done. But in the very
bottom of the casket there remained one sprite whose wings were not dusky—a
little golden being whose name was Hope. Thus did the gods, with a torch of di-   105
vine pity, light up the shadow which then descended upon man.

After the Age of Silver came the Age of Brass, or Bronze, wilder than the earlier ages, yet not wholly evil. And then came the graceless and sinister Age of
Iron, when men's ways were so wicked that one by one the good divinities deserted them, the last to depart being Astræa, the goddess of innocence, daughter  110
of Themis, the goddess of justice. Ancient poets used to prophesy that these goddesses would return to earth when another Golden Age should dawn. This is the
idea behind the title of John Dryden's poem on the Restoration, *Astræa Redux*.

Zeus had kept a close watch over men's actions during all these years; and
their evil conduct aroused his wrath to such a point that he vowed he would       115
blot out the human race. But as he could not decide which would be the best
way to do this, he summoned the gods to aid him by their counsels. The first
suggestion offered was to destroy the world by fire, kindled by Zeus's much-
dreaded thunderbolts; and the king of gods was about to put it into instant execution, when his arm was stayed by the reminder that the rising flames might     120

set fire to his own dwelling-place, and reduce its magnificence to ashes. He therefore rejected the plan as impracticable, and bade the gods devise other means of destruction.

125     After much delay and discussion the immortals agreed to wash mankind off the face of the earth by a mighty flood. The winds were instructed to gather the rain-clouds over the earth. Poseidon let loose the waves of the sea, bidding them rise, overflow, and deluge the land. No sooner had the gods spoken than the elements obeyed: the winds blew; the rain fell in torrents; lakes, seas, rivers, and oceans broke their bonds; and terrified mortals, forgetting their petty quar-
130 rels in a common impulse to flee from the death which threatened them, climbed the highest mountains, clung to uprooted trees, and even took refuge in the light skiffs they had constructed in happier days. Their efforts were all in vain, however, for the waters rose higher and higher, overtook them one after another in their ineffectual efforts to escape, closed over the homes where they
135 might have been so happy, and drowned their last despairing cries in their seething depths.

## Deucalion and Pyrrha

The rain continued to fall, until, after many days, the waves covered all the surface of the earth except the summit of Mount Parnassus, the highest peak in Greece. On this mountain, surrounded by the ever-rising flood, stood the son of
140 Prometheus, Deucalion, with his faithful wife Pyrrha, a daughter of Epimetheus and Pandora. From thence they, the sole survivors, viewed the universal desolation with tear-dimmed eyes.

    In a world of wicked mortals these two had lived righteously; and when Zeus saw them there alone, and remembered their goodness, he decided not to
145 include them in the general destruction, but to save their lives. He therefore bade the winds return to their cave and the rain to cease. Poseidon blew a re-sounding blast upon his conch-shell to recall the wandering waves, which im-mediately returned within their usual bounds.

    Deucalion and Pyrrha followed the receding waves step by step down the
150 steep mountain-side.

> At length the world was all restor'd to view,
> But desolate, and of a sickly hue;
> Nature beheld herself, and stood aghast,
> A dismal desert and a silent waste.

155                                 —Ovid (*Dryden's translation*)

    As they talked upon how they should repeople the desolate earth they came to the shrine of Delphi, the dwelling of a famous oracle, which alone had been able to resist the force of the waves. There they entered to consult the wishes of the gods. Their surprise and horror were unbounded, however, when a voice

exclaimed, "Depart from hence with veiled heads, and cast your mothers' bones 160
behind you!" To obey such a command seemed nothing less than sacrilege; for
the dead had always been held in deep veneration by the Greeks, and the dese-
cration of a grave was considered a heinous crime, and punished accordingly.
But, they reasoned, the god's oracles can seldom be accepted in a literal sense;
and Deucalion, after due thought, explained to Pyrrha what he conceived to be 165
the meaning of this mysterious command.

"The Earth," said he, "is the mother of all, and the stones may be considered
her bones." Husband and wife speedily decided to act upon this theory, and
continued their descent, casting stones behind them. All those thrown by Deucalion were immediately changed into men, while those cast by Pyrrha became 170
women.

Thus the earth was peopled for the second time with a race of good men,
sent to replace the wicked beings slain by Zeus. Deucalion and Pyrrha shortly
after became the happy parents of a son named Hellen, who gave his name to all
the Hellenic or Greek race; while his sons, Æolus and Dorus, and grandsons, 175
Ion and Achæus, became the ancestors of the Æolian, Dorian, Ionian, and Acha-
ian nations.

Other mythologists, in treating of the flood myths, state that Deucalion and
Pyrrha took refuge in an ark, which, after sailing about for many days, was
stranded on the top of Mount Parnassus. This version was far less popular with 180
the Greeks, although it betrays still more plainly the common source whence all
these myths are derived.

## TO THE WOMAN WHO DISCOVERED FIRE!

### Looking Ahead

1. Context is always an important consideration in understanding speech or writing.
   Here, *where* the speaker gives her toast is significant.

2. Read the expression on the listeners' faces to see how their dismay adds meaning to
   the speaker's words.

3. An enlightening aspect of this drawing is its informal demonstration that, even in
   casual settings, myths form the background of our common culture.

*"To the woman who discovered fire!"*

—Drawing by Ross; ©1992 The New Yorker Magazine, Inc.

## THE PUNISHMENT OF PROMETHEUS

### Looking Ahead

1. As you read, test a principle of language use—that words must be appropriate to the situation—by observing how the modernization of the Prometheus myth is managed entirely by the speaker's **diction** (choice of words).

2. Read critically to perceive, first, how the nature of the speakers' accusations reveals their character and, second, how the positions they defend reveal their politics.

3. This story contains a denouement, starting with line 108. Look up *denouement* in the dictionary so you will understand and appreciate the structural function of this part of the narrative.

With much coughing and clearing of throats and after prolonged proceedings for the collection of evidence, the extraordinary Senate betook itself to the meeting, which was held in the shade of the sacred olive grove.

"Well, gentlemen," yawned Hypometheus, the president of the Senate, "what a confoundedly long time all this has taken! I think I hardly need to sum up; however, to obviate any formal objections—The accused, Prometheus, a citizen of this place, being summoned before the court on a charge of inventing fire and thereby—hm, hm—upsetting the existing order of things, confessed, firstly, that he actually invented fire; further, that he is able to produce the same

at any time by the action called kindling; thirdly, that he did not keep this mys-   10
tery—this shocking phenomenon—secret or report it to the appropriate authority but deliberately revealed it, in fact handed it over to the use of unauthorized persons, as is proved by the evidence of the persons concerned, whom we
have just interrogated. I think that is all and that we can proceed at once to declare him guilty and to pronounce the sentence."                                  15

"Excuse me, Mr. President," objected the lay magistrate Apometheus, "but I
consider that in view of the importance of this extraordinary tribunal it would
have been more suitable if we proceeded to pronounce judgement after deliber-
ation and, so to speak, general discussion."

"As you please, gentlemen," assented the conciliatory Hypometheus. "The   20
case is perfectly clear, but if any of you wish to make a remark, please do so."

"I would venture to point out," said Ametheus, a member of the tribunal,
coughing primly, "that in my opinion one aspect of the whole matter should be
specially emphasized. Gentlemen, I am thinking of the religious aspect. I ask
you, what is this fire? What is this kindled spark? As Prometheus himself ad-   25
mits, it is nothing other than lightning, and lightning, as we all know, is the expression of the extraordinary power of Zeus the Thunderer. Will you explain to
me, gentlemen, how an ordinary fellow like Prometheus had access to this divine fire? By what right did he seize it? Where did he get it from? Prometheus
has tried to persuade us that he simply invented it; but that is a silly excuse—if   30
it were as simple and innocent as all that, why should not one of us have invented fire? I am convinced, gentlemen, that Prometheus simply stole this fire
from our gods. His denial and prevarication do not mislead us. I would describe
his crime as common theft on the one hand, and as the crime of blasphemy and
sacrilege on the other. We are here to punish with the utmost severity this impi-   35
ous presumptuousness and to protect the sacred property of our national gods.
That is all I wished to say," concluded Ametheus, and blew his nose energetically on the corner of his chlamys.[1]

"Well said," agreed Hypometheus. "Does anyone else wish to make a remark?"

"I ask your indulgence," said Apometheus, "but I cannot agree with the ar-   40
gument of my esteemed colleague. I watched how the said Prometheus kindled
this fire; and I tell you frankly, gentlemen, that—between ourselves—there's
absolutely nothing in it. The discovery of fire could have been made by any
idler, loafer or goatherd; we ourselves did not happen upon it simply because a
serious man hasn't the time and doesn't dream of playing about with stones to   45
make fire. I assure my colleague Ametheus that these are quite ordinary natural
forces which it is beneath the dignity of a thinking man, much less a god, to occupy himself with. In my opinion fire is too insignificant to affect in any way
matters which are sacred to us all. But the case has another aspect, to which I
must call the attention of my distinguished colleagues. It appears that fire is a   50

---

1. *chlamys:* a kind of vest worn by men in ancient Greece. (*ed.*)

very dangerous element, in fact even harmful. You have heard a number of witnesses who have deposed that in trying Prometheus's boyish invention they have suffered serious burns and in some cases even damage to property. Gentlemen, if through the fault of Prometheus the use of fire becomes general, which
55  now, unfortunately, seems impossible to prevent, neither the property nor even the lives of any of us will be safe; and that, gentlemen, may mean the end of all civilization. It needs only the least carelessness—and at what will this mischief-working element stop? Prometheus, gentlemen, has committed an act of criminal irresponsibility in bringing into the world so harmful a thing. I should de-
60  scribe his crime as the causing of grievous bodily harm and endangering the public safety. In view of this I am in favour of a life sentence of imprisonment with a hard pallet and manacles. I have finished, Mr. President."

"You are perfectly right, sir," granted Hypometheus. "And I would just like to say, gentlemen, what did we need this fire for, anyway? Did our forefathers
65  use fire? To invent such a thing is simply disrespect to the inherited order, it is—hm, merely revolutionary activity. Playing about with fire, who ever heard of such a thing? And consider, gentlemen, what it leads to: people will relax by the fire, they will wallow in warmth and comfort instead of—well, instead of fighting and things like that. It can only lead to effeminacy, the degeneration of
70  morals and—hm, general disorder and so on. In a word, something must be done against such unhealthy signs. The times are grave, very grave. That is all I wished to point out."

"Most rightly said," declared Antimetheus. "We all certainly agree with our President that Prometheus's fire may have unforeseeable consequences. Gentle-
75  men, do not let us conceal the fact from ourselves, it is a tremendous thing. To have fire in one's power—what new possibilities open out before one! I will only mention a few of them haphazard: to burn the enemy's crop, set fire to his olive groves and so on. In fire, gentlemen, our people have been given a new force and a new weapon; through fire we shall become almost equal to the
80  gods," whispered Antimetheus, and suddenly exploded fiercely. "I accuse Prometheus of having entrusted this divine and irresistible element of fire to shepherds and slaves, to the first comer; I accuse him of not giving it up into authorized hands which would have guarded it as a treasure of the state and governed by its means. I accuse Prometheus of thus being a dishonest trustee of
85  the discovery of fire, which should be a secret of the priesthood. I accuse Prometheus," shouted Antimetheus, carried away by emotion, "of teaching even foreigners how to kindle fire! of not concealing it even from our enemies! Prometheus stole fire from us by giving it to everyone! I accuse Prometheus of high treason! I accuse him of conspiracy against the community!" His voice rose
90  to a scream and he broke off, coughing. "I propose the death sentence," he managed to get out.

"Well, gentlemen," said Hypometheus, "does anyone else wish to speak? Then in the opinion of the court the accused Prometheus is found guilty firstly of the crime of blasphemy and sacrilege, secondly of the crime of inflicting
95  grievous bodily harm, causing damage to the property of others and endanger-

ing the public safety, and thirdly of the crime of high treason. Gentlemen, I propose to pass sentence upon him either of life imprisonment, rendered more rigorous by hard pallet and manacles, or sentence of death. Ahem."

"Or both," said Ametheus thoughtfully, "so as to comply with both proposals."

"How do you mean, both sentences?" asked the president.                                    100

"I've just been thinking it over," grunted Ametheus. "Perhaps we could manage it like this . . . condemn Prometheus to be chained to a rock for the rest of his life . . . perhaps let vultures peck out his godless liver, does Your Excellency understand?"

"That would do," said Hypometheus placidly. "Gentlemen, that would be     105
an exemplary punishment for such a—ahem—criminal eccentricity, wouldn't it? Has anyone any objection? Then the session is closed."

"And why did you condemn Prometheus to death, Daddy?" Hypometheus's son, Epimetheus, asked him at supper.

"You wouldn't understand," grunted Hypometheus, gnawing a leg of mut-    110
ton as he spoke. "Upon my word, this mutton tastes better roasted than raw; so you see, this fire is some use after all. It was for reasons of public interest, do you see? Where should we be if anyone who liked was allowed to come along with great, new inventions unpunished? See what I mean? But there's something this meat still needs—ah, I've got it!" he exclaimed delightedly. "Roast    115
mutton ought to be salted and rubbed with garlic! That's the right way to do it! Now that is a real discovery! You know, a fellow like Prometheus would never have thought of that!"

## PROMETHEUS

### *Looking Ahead*

1. Look up the word *legend,* which Kafka uses. Note its different connotation from the word *myth.*

2. *Entropy* is a term that might describe both the content and the form of Kafka's reading of the myth. Find the word in your dictionary and consider how it applies here.

3. Kafka's final sentence establishes a strange but convincing relationship between truth and mystery, or the inexplicable. Think about other examples from life of this relationship.

There are four legends concerning Prometheus:

According to the first he was clamped to a rock in the Caucasus for betraying the secrets of the gods to men, and the gods sent eagles to feed on his liver, which was perpetually renewed.

According to the second Prometheus, goaded by the pain of the tearing     5
beaks, pressed himself deeper and deeper into the rock until he became one with it.

According to the third his treachery was forgotten in the course of thousands of years, the gods forgotten, the eagles, he himself forgotten.

10      According to the fourth every one grew weary of the meaningless affair. The gods grew weary, the eagles grew weary, the wound closed wearily.

There remained the inexplicable mass of rock.—The legend tried to explain the inexplicable. As it came out of a substratum of truth it had in turn to end in the inexplicable.

## Looking Back

1. Which of these treatments of the Prometheus myth do you prefer? Why?
2. How does the tone of voice differ from one author to another?
3. Do you find it helpful or distracting when authors interpolate other texts into their own, as Bulfinch and Guerber do? Explain.
4. What do Capek's and Ross's modernization of the Prometheus myth tell you about the lasting power of myths generally? How does Kafka's retelling modify this sense?
5. What do you make of the distinction Bulfinch draws in his first paragraph between myth and Scripture (the Bible)?
6. Why do you think human beings imagine that their original condition was a paradise, a Golden Age (see Bulfinch, lines 67–74, and Guerber, lines 39–44)?
7. How do these authors differ in their attitudes toward Pandora and, perhaps, toward women in general (remembering that conscious omission may well indicate an attitude)?
8. The destruction of the created world figures in Bulfinch's and Guerber's narratives (see lines 96–126 and lines 114–136, respectively). How do you account for this human impulse to imagine an earlier, worldwide catastrophe?
9. In your estimation, is Prometheus as the inventor of technology—the thief of fire— a positive or a negative figure?
10. Does Prometheus deserve the punishment Zeus metes out to him? Why or why not?

## Writing Assignments (Linked Readings)

1. "Promethean man" (never, it turns out, Promethean woman) is a term often used to characterize the historical human tendency to make technological advances. From the shaping of the wheel to the slicking down of the space shuttle, from the discovery of fire to the harnessing of the atom, the human species has sought easier, more powerful, more efficient ways of satisfying its needs and desires. This is hardly news, of course. We see the results all around us, every day, of the extension of our basic abilities to speak, move, and make things happen. Many delight in this technology. Others doubt the essential value, if not the practical utility, of inventions ranging from the ballpoint pen to the fax machine. We blame or praise Prometheus. The question continues to arise: Have we gone too far in technological development and what has it cost us? Write an essay giving your answer to this question. Illustrate your points by referring exclusively to common machines and implements, such as the personal computer or the VCR.

2. Bulfinch, Guerber, and Ross all comment on Woman (with a capital W) as she relates to Prometheus. According to the first two authors, she is Pandora, meaning

trouble; to the third, she is the rightful Prometheus, meaning justice. Capek and Kafka hold their tongue about Woman; their silence itself may be a kind of comment. Write an essay that compares the different ways these authors treat women and that finds in the Prometheus myth some of the basic attitudes our society has held toward the female sex. Imagine an audience that has little or no cultural knowledge of American society. Include any pertinent personal experiences and refer if you wish to other mythical and actual female figures.

3. In addition to being the father of invention, Prometheus is the brother of men and women. His chief aim is to help the highly vulnerable race of humans. To be of use, however, Prometheus, like so many since, has to rebel against authority. He found it necessary to steal the fire of heaven; more recent rebels have found it necessary to question received (automatically accepted) values, to disobey commands, to disrupt social order, to commit crimes to finance opposition parties, to wage guerilla warfare. Whether mild or wild, such rebellion operates on the two related principles named above: helping human beings and opposing authority. It can be argued, however, that some of the activities listed above are self-defeating. Write an essay that, starting from the case of Prometheus, discusses when and under what conditions these activities are justifiable. You may want to refer to related texts in this book, like "Campus Life" (page 367), "The Port Huron Statement" (page 370), and "The Student Revolt" (page 382).

## *Writing Assignments (Individual Readings)*
### PROMETHEUS AND PANDORA

Bulfinch gives us two different accounts of Pandora's box (lines 43–67). The second version of the story—in which the contents of the box are blessings, not curses—is intended to make the presence of hope in the box more acceptable. "This story seems more probable than the former," Bulfinch assures us, "for how could *hope,* so precious a jewel as it is, have been kept in a jar full of all manner of evils, as in the former statement?" A very different view of hope emerges in this passage from "Summer in Algiers," an essay by French novelist Albert Camus:

> From Pandora's box, where all the ills of humanity swarmed, the Greeks drew out hope after all the others, as the most dreadful of all. I know no more stirring symbol; for, contrary to the general belief, hope equals resignation. And to live is not to resign oneself.

Write an essay discussing your own preference for Bulfinch's or Camus's view of hope, expressing your own view.

## THE STORY OF PROMETHEUS
## DEUCALION AND PYRRHA

Deucalion and Pyrrha, we read, were spared the destruction visited on the rest of the human race because they alone "had lived righteously" (line 143). A similar situation occurs in other world literatures where, although the details may change, the basic theme is the same. A sinning humanity so incenses the deity that He or She engulfs them in flood or fire, sparing only those few people who have remembered the Law and continued to be virtuous. Today, numbers of religious fundamentalists hold the same belief in themselves as the sole candidates for salvation. Religious thinking of this sort results in a startlingly new view of the world and of human society, a view that we may consider, on one hand, accurate and even necessary, or, on the other, wholly negative, intolerant, and divisive. Write an essay discussing your opinion. Conceive of your audience as one that has largely been exposed to different views from your own but that, in the interests of education, wants to experience a new perspective on the matter.

## TO THE WOMAN WHO DISCOVERED FIRE!

Native Americans, African Americans, Asian Americans, and numerous other minorities have had the experience of being oppressed or ignored solely because of who they are. So have women, though by no means a minority of the population. As Al Ross's drawing strongly implies, a historical view of women has been that their particular gender characteristics are less important and useful than men's and that therefore women cannot achieve as much as men. Questions that arise from these assumptions have to do with men's and women's innate differences, comparative abilities, and final value. What accounts for the view American and other societies have held that women are inferior to men? What do you think of this view? Write an essay that examines the issue of equality between men and women. Imagine your audience as one consisting of the opposite gender from you.

## THE PUNISHMENT OF PROMETHEUS

The term *prometheus* means "forethought." In Capek's story, Antimetheus (antithought) accuses Prometheus, in effect, of taking too much thought for the future of humanity by sharing the secret of fire (lines 80–91). Prometheus is a "traitor to the community" for not having seen that his primary duty is to the state and to his own class; he should have preferred their interests above all others. The underlying issue here is the nature of the individual's moral responsibility. We can see this more clearly if we think of the stolen fire as corresponding not to atomic secrets leaked by a spy but to a truth about life whose disclosure might enlighten people generally and free them from the autocratic control their ignorance made possible. In this sense, Prometheus indeed can be seen as a deliverer. As Ralph Waldo Emerson puts it in his essay "History," Prometheus is "the Jesus of the old mythology . . . the friend of man." Accepting this view, write an interpolative essay that defends Prometheus (who in Capek's story has no opportunity to defend himself) against the accusations leveled at him by Antimetheus.

## PROMETHEUS

Kafka takes us through various stages of the drama of Prometheus's punishment to show us that gradually everyone loses interest in the case. The truth of Prometheus's original situation remains in all its complexity (like the rock to which he was chained), but the crime is forgotten as time goes by, and all the hullaballoo that once surrounded it now seems meaningless. This outcome brings up an interesting problem regarding the crimes for which mandatory sentences are imposed, such as life without possibility of parole for drug dealing. The problem is this: At an earlier time in a person's life, when she first was sentenced, her character might well have been a criminal one. But now, years later, she may no longer be the same self who committed that crime. Yet her later self is still imprisoned for what her earlier self did. Can this be fair? Can it be argued that mandatory sentences are themselves unfair? On the other hand, even accepting the possibility that people may change for the better, mandatory sentences can be defended on the grounds that only drastic and unrelenting penalties can deter certain kinds of crimes. Write an essay arguing a position on the use of mandatory sentences.

# Dino Buzzati

# The Bewitched Jacket

Dino Buzzati (1906–1972), Italian novelist, short story writer, and journalist, was particularly interested in fantasy, which allows the literary imagination to extend human action past the limits of logical expectation and in this way to examine humankind's potential for good and evil. In 1958, he won the prestigious Premio Strega literary prize. One of his most important novels is *The Tartar Steppes*.

## Looking Ahead

1. As you read, be aware of the fact that the narrator is not Buzzati himself but, rather, his main character. The narrator's **point of view**—which we depend on for understanding—is of course influenced by his own nature, by his part in the plot, and by his own understanding, which is necessarily more limited than the author's.

2. Readers of fiction are called on to suspend disbelief, that is, to accept the author's inventions as real. Doing this is particularly useful when reading a fantasy like this one.

3. A good deal of the story's interest lies in its combination of genres: the folktale of the inexhaustible purse is linked to the myth of selling one's soul to the devil.

Although I appreciate elegant dress, I don't usually pay attention to the perfection (or imperfection) with which my companions' clothing is cut.

Nonetheless, one night during a reception at a house in Milan, I met a man about forty years old who literally shone because of the simple and decisive beauty of his clothes.

5

I don't know who he was, I was meeting him for the first time, and at the introduction, as always happens, it was impossible to get his name. But at a certain point during the evening, I found myself near him, and we began to talk. He seemed a civil, well-bred man, but with an air of sadness. Perhaps with exaggerated familiarity—God should have stopped me—I complimented him on his elegance; and I even dared to ask him who his tailor might be.

He smiled curiously, as if he had expected my question. "Nearly no one knows him," he said. "Still, he's a great master. And he works only when it comes to him. For a few initiates."

"So that I couldn't . . . ?"

"Oh, try, try. His name is Corticella, Alfonso Corticella, via Ferrara 17."

"He will be expensive, I imagine."

"I believe so, but I swear I don't know. He made me this suit three years ago, and he still hasn't sent me the bill."

"Corticella? Via Ferrara 17, did you say?"

"Exactly," the stranger answered. And he left me to join another group of people.

At via Ferrara 17, I found a house like so many others and like those of so many other tailors; it was the residence of Alfonso Corticella. It was he who came to let me in. He was a little old man with black hair, which was, however, obviously dyed.

To my surprise, he was not hard to deal with. In fact, he seemed eager for me to be his customer. I explained to him how I had gotten his address, praised his cutting, and asked him to make me a suit. We selected a gray wool, then he took my measurements, and offered to come to my apartment for the fitting. I asked him the price. There was no hurry, he answered, we could always come to an agreement. What a congenial man, I thought at first. Nevertheless, later, while I was returning home, I realized that the little old man had left me feeling uneasy (perhaps because of his much too warm and persistent smiles). In short, I had no desire at all to see him again. But now the suit had been ordered. And after about three weeks it was ready.

When they brought it to me, I tried it on in front of a mirror for a little while. It was a masterpiece. Yet, I don't know why, perhaps because of my memory of the unpleasant old man, I didn't have any desire to wear it. And weeks passed before I decided to do so.

That day I shall remember forever. It was a Tuesday in April and it was raining. When I had slipped into the clothes—jacket, trousers, and vest—I was pleased to observe that they didn't pull and weren't tight anywhere, as almost always happens with new suits. And yet they wrapped me perfectly.

As a rule I put nothing in the right jacket pocket; in the left one, I keep my cards. This explains why, only after a couple of hours at the office, casually slipping my hand into the right pocket, I noticed that there was a piece of paper inside. Was it maybe the tailor's bill?

No. It was a ten thousand lire note.

I was astounded. I certainly had not put it there. On the other hand, it was   50
absurd to think it a joke of the tailor Corticella. Much less did it seem a gift from
my maid, the only person, other than the tailor, who had occasion to go near
my suit. Or was it a counterfeit note? I looked at it in the light, I compared it to
other ones. It couldn't be any better than these.

There was a single possible explanation: Corticella's absent-mindedness.   55
Perhaps a customer had come to make a payment. The tailor didn't have his
wallet with him just then, and so to avoid leaving the money around, he
slipped it into my jacket, which was hanging on a mannequin. These things can
happen.

I rang for my secretary. I wanted to write a letter to Corticella, returning the   60
money that was not mine. Yet (and I can't say why I did it) I slipped my hand
into the pocket again.

"Is anything wrong, sir? Do you feel ill?" asked my secretary, who entered
at that moment. I must have turned pale as death. In my pocket my fingers
touched the edge of another strip of paper—which had not been there a few   65
minutes before.

"No, no, it's nothing," I said. "A slight dizziness. It happens to me sometimes. Maybe I'm a little tired. You can go now, dear, I wanted to dictate a letter,
but we'll do it later."

Only after my secretary had gone did I dare remove the piece of paper from   70
my pocket. It was another ten thousand lire note. Then I tried a third time. And
a third banknote came out.

My heart began to race. I had the feeling that for some mysterious reason I
was involved in the plot of a fairy tale, like those that are told to children and
that no one believes are true.   75

On the pretext that I was not feeling well, I left the office and went home. I
needed to be alone. Luckily, my maid had already gone. I shut the doors, lowered the blinds. I began to take out the notes one after another, very quickly. My
pocket seemed inexhaustible.

I worked in a spasmodic nervous tension, with the fear that the miracle   80
might stop at any moment. I wanted it to continue all day and night, until I had
accumulated billions. But at a certain point the flow diminished.

Before me stood an impressive heap of banknotes. The important thing
now was to hide them, so no one might get wind of the affair. I emptied an old
trunk full of rugs and put the money, arranged in many little piles, at the bot-   85
tom. Then I slowly began counting. There were 58 million lire.

I awoke the next morning after the maid arrived. She was amazed to find
me in bed still completely dressed. I tried to laugh, explaining that I had drunk
a little too much the night before and sleep had suddenly seized me.

A new anxiety arose: she asked me to take off the suit, so she could at least   90
give it a brushing.

I answered that I had to go out immediately and didn't have time to change. Then I hurried to a store selling ready-to-wear clothes to buy another suit made of a similar material; I would leave this one in the maid's care; "mine," the suit
95    that in the course of a few days would make me one of the most powerful men in the world, I would hide in a safe place.

I didn't know whether I was living in a dream, whether I was happy or rather suffocating under the burden of too hard a fate. On the street, I was continually feeling the magic pocket through my raincoat. Each time I breathed a
100   sigh of relief. Beneath the cloth answered the comforting crackle of paper money.

But a singular coincidence cooled my joyous delirium. News of a robbery that occurred the day before headlined the morning papers. A bank's armored car, after making the rounds of the branches, was carrying the day's deposits to the main office when it was seized and cleaned out in viale Palmanova by four crim-
105   inals. As people swarmed around the scene, one of the gangsters began to shoot to keep them away. A passerby was killed. But, above all, the amount of the loot struck me: it was exactly 58 million—like the money I had put in the trunk.

Could there be a connection between my sudden wealth and the criminal raid that happened almost simultaneously? It seemed foolish to think so. What's
110   more, I am not superstitious. All the same, the incident left me very confused.

The more one gets, the more one wants. I was already rich, considering my modest habits. But the illusion of a life of unlimited luxury was compelling. And that same evening I set to work again. Now I proceeded more slowly, with less torture to my nerves. Another 135 million was added to my previous treasure.
115   That night I couldn't close my eyes. Was it the presentiment of danger? Or the tormented conscience of one who undeservedly wins a fabulous fortune? Or was it a kind of confused remorse? At dawn I leaped from the bed, dressed, and ran outside to get a newspaper.

As I read, I lost my breath. A terrible fire, which had begun in a naphtha
120   warehouse, had half-destroyed a building on the main street, via San Cloro. The flames had consumed, among other things, the safes of a large real estate company which contained more than 130 million in cash. Two firemen met their deaths in the blaze.

Should I now, perhaps, list my crimes one by one? Yes, because now I knew
125   that the money the jacket gave me came from those crimes, from blood, from desperation and death, from hell. But I was still within the snare of reason, which scornfully refused to admit that I was in any way responsible. And then the temptation resumed, then the hand—it was so easy!—slipped into the pocket, and the fingers, with the quickest delight, grasped the edges of always
130   another banknote. The money, the divine money!

Without moving out of my old apartment (so as not to attract attention), I soon bought a huge villa, owned a precious collection of paintings, drove around in luxurious automobiles, and having left my firm for "reasons of health," traveled back and forth throughout the world in the company of marvelous women.

I knew that whenever I drew money from the jacket, something base and painful happened in the world. But it was still always a vague awareness, not supported by logical proofs. Meanwhile, at each new collection, my conscience was degraded, becoming more and more vile. And the tailor? I telephoned him to ask for the bill, but no one answered. In via Ferrara, where I went to search for him, they told me that he had emigrated abroad, they didn't know where. Everything then conspired to show me that without knowing it, I was bound in a pact with the Devil.

Until one morning, in the building where I lived for many years, they found a sixty-year-old retired woman asphyxiated by gas; she had killed herself for having mislaid her monthly pension of 30 thousand lire, which she had collected the day before (and which had ended up in my hands).

Enough, enough! In order not to sink to the depths of the abyss, I had to rid myself of the jacket. And not by surrendering it to someone else, because the horror would continue (who would ever be able to resist such enticement?). Its destruction was absolutely necessary.

By car I arrived at a secluded valley in the Alps. I left the car in a grassy clearing and set out in the direction of the forest. There wasn't a living soul in sight. Having gone beyond the forest, I reached the rocky ground of the moraine. Here, between two gigantic boulders, I pulled the wicked jacket from the knapsack, sprinkled it with kerosene, and lit it. In a few minutes only ashes were left.

But at the last flicker of the flames, behind me—it seemed about two or three meters away—a human voice resounded: "Too late, too late!" Terrified, I turned around with a serpent's snap. But I saw no one. I explored the area, jumping from one huge rock to another, to hunt out the damned person. Nothing. There were only rocks.

Notwithstanding the fright I experienced, I went back down to the base of the valley with a feeling of relief. I was free at last. And rich, luckily.

But my car was no longer in the grassy clearing. And after I returned to the city, my sumptuous villa had disappeared; in its place was an uncultivated field with some poles that bore the notice "Municipal Land For Sale." My savings accounts were also completely drained, but I couldn't explain how. The big packets of deeds in my numerous safe-deposit boxes had vanished too. And there was dust, nothing but dust, in the old trunk.

I now resumed working with difficulty, I hardly get through a day, and what is stranger, no one seems to be amazed by my sudden ruin.

And I know that it's still not over, I know that one day my doorbell will ring, I'll answer it and find that cursed tailor before me, with his contemptible smile, asking for the final settling of my account.

## Looking Back

1. How are we alerted by the adverb *literally* (line 4) to events that are out of the ordinary?

2. Given the context of the meeting between the narrator and the stranger, what is disturbing about the latter's "air of sadness" (line 9) and his description of his tailor (lines 12–14)?

3. Returning from the last lines of the story to the stranger's speech in lines 18–19, what do you surmise about the stranger's probable fate?

4. Why does Buzzati have the narrator draw money from his pocket instead of, say, magical formulas or state secrets, either of which might also make him "one of the most powerful men in the world" (lines 95–96)?

5. What *moral* connection does the narrator perceive between particular losses of money by other people and his own sudden riches?

6. How do you understand the narrator's words, "Meanwhile, at each new collection, my conscience was degraded, becoming more and more vile" (lines 138–139)?

7. If it is true that "[t]he more one gets, the more one wants" (line 111), what comment does this make on human beings generally?

8. How does the narrator use his wealth? How might he have used it differently?

9. If the narrator had used his wealth more selflessly, say by giving huge sums to charity, would the devil have had any less a claim on him? Why or why not?

10. Considering the final events, what moral can we draw from this story?

## Writing Assignments

1. The old adage seems to hold universally true: One person's gain is another person's loss. This certainly is the case in "The Bewitched Jacket," in which the issue is the profit motive. Should people be able to profit at the expense of others? Is the condemnation of profiting we might read into the story convincing, or is it unreal and impractical to expect that people will ever forgo profits? Is it reasonable to place a limit on profitability, or should people be able to take what they can get? Are certain forms of profiting legitimate and others not? Is an economic life possible that does not include the profit motive? Write an essay examining the profit motive in terms of these questions. Your audience consists of citizens of a country attempting to institute a market economy and therefore eager to hear the opinions of someone already familiar with such a system.

2. Buzzati's narrator confesses that he spent his money on luxury housing, on traveling the world, on acquiring beautiful and expensive objects, and on using his wealth to attractive "marvelous" women. If we are honest with ourselves, we probably will admit that, within limits, we too would like to be able to do what he does. "Within limits," we say, because we have more modest expectations and because we recognize the moral defects of ostentation, materialism, and exploitation. Or do we? Perhaps we would also go whole hog. Or perhaps, again to be honest with our better selves, we would reject these conceited uses of money and instead practice philanthropy. What would you do if you suddenly inherited a fortune? Beginning by refer-

ring to the story, write an essay describing your probable course of action and explaining your reasons for pursuing it.

3. One character in "The Bewitched Jacket" is the Devil, who impersonates a tailor. Whether we suspend disbelief when meeting him in the story (see number 2 in Looking Ahead, above) or believe implicitly in his existence, one thing is certain: If the Devil (or what he stands for) exists, then so does God (or what He or She stands for). And if we live in a world in which both God and the Devil exist (and perhaps even if we don't), then each of us has a soul, which we are always putting on the line. We may define the soul as the imperishable part of ourselves, the most precious part, where the truth of our being lies. The danger of losing one's soul and the need to preserve it intact thus set the scene for high spiritual drama. Having such a soul makes the world and our place in it very different from what they might be if there were nothing to lose. To understand what this sense and this place might be, write an essay describing the narrator's view of the soul and how it compares to your own view.

# J. Idries Shah

# The Fisherman and the Genie

J. Idries Shah (b. 1924) is a respected Sufi scholar and anthropologist, the author of *The Dermis Probe, The Magic Monastery, The Sufis,* and *Tales of the Dervishes,* from which this story is taken. Shah's interests range widely over religious beliefs in the Orient and the ancient Near East. He has collected "teaching stories" such as "The Fisherman and the Genie" to demonstrate their use by religious masters to give neophytes insight into the hidden recesses of life and the sources of wisdom. Quoting one master in his introduction to *Tales of the Dervishes,* Shah tells us, "To be a Sufi is to detach from fixed ideas and from preconceptions, and not to try to avoid what is your lot." We find these precepts acted on in this mythic tale, in which proverbs are considered dynamic, not static, ideas and in which the fisherman recognizes his human limitations.

## Looking Ahead

1. "The Fisherman and the Genie," as noted above, is primarily a teaching story; you certainly want to discover its lesson.

2. The story goes beyond the life of the main character but builds on it. Therefore, read critically to grasp the import of the fisherman's actions in order to understand the logical extension of the narrative.

3. You may recall that, in the *Arabian Nights* version of this story, the genie during his first thousand years of imprisonment intends to reward his liberator; only as he fails to be freed does he determine to kill that person instead. Also, as Shahrazad tells it, the fisherman profits from his association with the genie.

A lone fisherman one day brought up a brass bottle, stoppered with lead, in his net. Though the appearance of the bottle was quite different from what he was used to finding in the sea, he thought it might contain something of value. Besides, he had not had a good catch, and at the worst he could sell the bottle to a
5   brass-merchant.

The bottle was not very large. On the top was inscribed a strange symbol, the Seal of Solomon, King and Master. Inside had been imprisoned a fearsome genie; and the bottle had been cast into the sea by Solomon himself so that men should be protected from the spirit until such time as there came one who could
10   control it, assigning it to its proper role of service of mankind.

But the fisherman knew nothing of this. All he knew was that here was something which he could investigate, which might be of profit to him. Its outside shone and it was a work of art. "Inside," he thought, "there may be diamonds."

15   Forgetting the adage, "Man can use only what he has learned to use," the fisherman pulled out the leaden stopper.

He inverted the bottle, but there seemed to be nothing in it, so he set it down and looked at it. Then he noticed a faint wisp as of smoke, slowly becoming denser, which swirled and formed itself into the appearance of a huge and
20   threatening being, which addressed him in a booming voice:

"I am the Chief of the Jinns who know the secrets of miraculous happenings, imprisoned by order of Solomon against whom I rebelled, and I shall destroy you!"

The fisherman was terrified, and, casting himself upon the sand, cried out: "Will you destroy him who gave you your freedom?"

25   "Indeed I shall," said the genie, "for rebellion is my nature, and destruction is my capacity, although I may have been rendered immobile for several thousand years."

The fisherman now saw that, far from profit from this unwelcome catch, he was likely to be annihilated for no good reason that he could fathom.

30   He looked at the seal upon the stopper, and suddenly an idea occurred to him. "You could never have come out of that bottle," he said. "It is too small."

"What! Do you doubt the word of the Master of the Jinns?" roared the apparition. And he dissolved himself again into wispy smoke and went back into the bottle. The fisherman took up the stopper and plugged the bottle with it.

35   Then he threw it back, as far as he could, into the depths of the sea.

Many years passed, until one day another fisherman, grandson of the first, cast his net in the same place, and brought up the self-same bottle.

He placed the bottle upon the sand and was about to open it when a thought struck him. It was the piece of advice which had been passed down to
40   him by his father, from *his* father.

It was: "Man can use only what he has learned to use."

And so it was that when the genie, aroused from his slumbers by the movement of his metal prison, called through the brass: "Son of Adam, whoever you may be, open the stopper of this bottle and release me: for I am the Chief of the
45   Jinns who know the secrets of miraculous happenings," the young fisherman,

remembering his ancestral adage, placed the bottle carefully in a cave and scaled the heights of a near-by cliff, seeking the cell of a wise man who lived there.

He told the story to the wise man, who said: "Your adage is perfectly true: and you have to do this thing yourself, though you must know how to do it."

"But what do I have to do?" asked the youth.

"There is something, surely, that you feel you want to do?" said the other.

"What I want to do is to release the jinn, so that he can give me miraculous knowledge: or perhaps mountains of gold, and seas made from emeralds, and all the other things which jinns can bestow."

"It has not, of course, occurred to you," said the sage, "that the jinn might not give you these things when released; or that he may give them to you and then take them away because you have no means to guard them; quite apart from what might befall you if and when you did have such things, since 'Man can use only what he has learned to use.'"

"Then what should I do?"

"Seek from the jinn a sample of what he can offer. Seek a means of safe-guarding that sample and testing it. Seek knowledge, not possessions, for possessions without knowledge are useless, and that is the cause of all our distractions."

Now, because he was alert and reflective, the young man worked out his plan on the way back to the cave where he had left the jinn.

He tapped on the bottle, and the jinn's voice answered, tinny through the metal, but still terrible: "In the name of Solomon the Mighty, upon whom be peace, release me, son of Adam!"

"I don't believe that you are who you say and that you have the powers which you claim," answered the youth.

"Don't believe me! Do you not know that I am incapable of telling a lie?" the jinn roared back.

"No, I do not," said the fisherman.

"Then how can I convince you?"

"By giving me a demonstration. Can you exercise any powers through the wall of the bottle?"

"Yes," admitted the jinn, "but I cannot release myself through these powers."

"Very well, then: give me the ability to know the truth of the problem which is on my mind."

Instantly, as the jinn exercised his strange craft, the fisherman became aware of the source of the adage handed down by his grandfather. He saw, too, the whole scene of the release of the jinn from the bottle; and he also saw how he could convey to others how to gain such capacities from the jinns. But he also realized that there was no more that he could do. And so the fisherman picked up the bottle and, like his grandfather, cast it into the ocean.

And he spent the rest of his life not as a fisherman but as a man who tried to explain to others the perils of "Man trying to use what he has not learned to use."

But, since few people ever came across jinns in bottles, and there was no wise man to prompt them in any case, the successors of the fisherman garbled

what they called his "teachings," and mimed his descriptions. In due course
they became a religion, with brazen bottles from which they sometimes drank
housed in costly and well-adorned temples. And, because they respected the
behaviour of this fisherman, they strove to emulate his actions and his deport-
95  ment in every way.

The bottle, now many centuries later, remains the holy symbol and mystery
for these people. They try to love each other only because they love this fisherman; and in the place where he settled and built a humble shack they deck
themselves with finery and move in elaborate rituals.

100  Unknown to them the disciples of the wise man still live, the descendants
of the fisherman are unknown. The brass bottle lies at the bottom of the sea
with the genie slumbering within.

## Looking Back

1. How do you interpret the adage that the fisherman has forgotten (lines 15–16)?
2. What distinction does the genie draw between nature and capacity (lines 25–26)?
3. The original fisherman's grandson recalls the adage his grandfather forgot; what does this tell us about the power of proverbial wisdom in Near Eastern culture?
4. What does the existence in this culture of wise men reveal about it?
5. Can you use the text to support the notion that the wise man is an analytic thinker—that is, someone who attempts to understand the component parts and function of what he studies?
6. Do you agree or disagree with the moral lesson the wise man teaches in lines 62–64? Explain your answer.
7. How does the sage's statement combine with the earlier adage to form a larger, more complex admonition?
8. Why does the young fisherman return the bottle, with the genie still inside, to the ocean?
9. In what way do the fisherman's experiences form the basis for the development of a full-blown religion?
10. What comment do the last three paragraphs make on established religion generally?

## Writing Assignments

1. Between the two of them, the fisherman and the sage come up with a fairly powerful formula for avoiding pitfalls and continuing on a solid path through life. The fisherman contributes the insight of the adage, "Man can use only what he has learned to use." And the wise man adds this advice: "Seek knowledge, not possessions, for possessions without knowledge are useless, and that is the cause of all our distractions" (lines 58–64). Using their remarks as a text, write an essay that performs two major functions: one is to interpret the two men's commentary; the other is to apply your interpretation, by way of a critical appraisal, to the emphasis in American life on consumer goods. Be sure to

define such terms as *knowledge* and *distraction* (knowledge of what? distraction from what?), and to describe how one can gain knowledge and suffer by being distracted.

2. It is a long-accepted truism that established religions frequently distort the teachings of their founders. The mere passage of time, the institutionalization of what were basic practices, the entrance into complex relations with other social institutions—all are responsible for the kind of "garbling" and "miming" of the original message (lines 89–91). In the last three paragraphs of "The Fisherman and the Genie," this process is given concrete form that has universal application. That is, the fisherman's disciples act in ways that all do who have lost sight of where they started from. Beginning with these followers specifically and defining their situation, write an essay that explains how a religion or any other social institution, though it fans the old fire, often loses the true flame.

3. Cultural values greatly influence our thinking and guide our actions, often without our being quite aware of the fact. (An example would be the value that our culture places on the idea of individualism.) But it would be far from accurate to say that we always exist within a culture as if it were our element, unconsciously, like fish in water. We frequently have cause to examine particular values and end up redefining their current status or reassessing their viability. Sometimes we criticize one value by contrasting it with another. Sometimes we argue that a new value should be more widely accepted. That is, we become conscious of cultural values and seek, by one means or another, to change the way people think about them and are influenced by them. This can be your project. Write an essay in which you imagine cultural value placed on the sage (as in "The Fisherman and the Genie") and describe the likely effect of such a value on society at large.

❋

# Roman Czerwczak

## A Summer

Born in Poland in 1959, Roman Czerwczak emigrated to the United States in 1982. Previously, he worked as an actor and director in France, where he lived for some years after training at the Film School in Lodz, Poland. He is currently studying theater in New York and is planning to be a teacher. Czerwczak has written plays and movie scripts that he hopes someday to see produced.

### Looking Ahead

1. Czerwczak mythologizes himself (see the Introduction to Part I, page 43, and writing assignment 3 below). This fact helps explain how he can find himself at the heart of matters that we normally examine from a distance.

2. It is interesting to note the *dignity* of Czerwczak's prose, a formality he himself attributes to the fact that he writes English as a second language and is not yet quite attuned to the idiom.

3. At the real, though not necessarily actual, center of this essay is a parable written by Franz Kafka, which Czerwczak quotes in full. Images and narrative portions of the essay are linked to the parable in ways you should read critically to discover.

Six years ago, I got a job in a poor Hispanic neighborhood on Amsterdam Avenue between 109th and 110th Streets. At that time, it was a desolate area filled with half-burned buildings, ruined coffee-shops, and dirty delis. English was hardly spoken there and the whole district, stretching from the rear of Colum-
5  bia University farther north, seemed a country within a city. In the mornings, in this part of the zone where I worked, deli owners would lay out, in torn brown cartons, strange gourds and roots on dirty pavement in front of their stores. Old people would come out of the buildings and sit on the stairs without a word and look at piled-up black garbage bags and various debris. Here and there, at the
10  horizon of the street, a drunken man or woman would navigate the way home trying to end the night which was long and desperate, or full of unexpected joys. A bum, dressed in the heat of the summer as though it was a cold winter, would search for remnants of pizza or half empty beer-cans. And a passer-by would whisper in your ear: "Coke, man? Grass?" There was a feeling of despera-
15  tion in this whole derelict neighborhood and even the lively *Salsa* coming from empty barber shops and bars could not change it. Even the three neighborhood funeral parlors, which were the most sharp-looking establishments there, seemed dirty and abandoned. Summer was sending days like bright angels to glare at decay, death, and ruin.
20      There was one more thing in that area which especially attracted my atten-tion: an inhabited building of unknown purpose made out of plates of grey marble standing on the east side of Amsterdam Avenue between 109th and 110th Streets: THE BUILDING.
        Most people hate summers in New York but to be forced, out of need of
25  money, to work for $5.50 an hour, as I was that summer six years ago, carrying old furniture and garbage out of vacant apartments in over 90-degree heat, that was something else. Besides my poverty and my job, a book which I just had read contributed to my feeling of global depression. A book about cryonics.[1] Death in different forms seemed to haunt me that summer.
30      I quickly discovered that the company I worked for abounded in men-on-the-verge-of-nervous-break-downs of my kind. We formed a brigade and, whenever possible, went on beer trips. There were plenty of delis around that were open during work-time, and after work as well. Some of them even all night. The cold beer seemed to quench my thirst and some of the mental an-
35  guish of that summer.
        In the blazing heat, and in a hallucinogenic state of mind produced by a hangover which had already lasted for a few weeks, my attention was rarely

---

1. *cryonics:* the science of freezing dead bodies with the hope of bringing them back to life at a time when the diseases that killed them have been conquered (*ed.*)

drawn to the things that were carried out of the empty apartments. And, after all, it was somebody's life: the ghosts of wardrobes, tables, chairs, sometimes a paper reproduction of Van Gogh's *Flowers*. Occasionally, a bag would break 40 open and I would get a closer look at this "life," as remnants of personal things would scatter on the floor or on the staircase: an old lipstick, a hazy mirror, a worn toothbrush, or a faded purse. But one day the things which fell out of a torn suitcase weren't just mere trash but family photos collected with care by someone over the years. Looking at these pictures scattered on the floor I could 45 see, unfolding in front of my eyes, a history of a family. That is when the words of Franz Kafka's parable, "The Next Village," came clearly to my mind:

> My grandfather used to say: "Life is astoundingly short. To me, looking back over it, life seems so foreshortened that I scarcely understand, for instance, how a young man can decide to ride over to the next village without being 50 afraid that—not to mention accidents—even the span of a normal happy life may fall far short of the time needed for such a journey."

Nothing will alter the current of time which carries you to your end. And time is so precious that it might be better to focus on "pure" existence, unobstructed by any "actions," to "reflect" rather than "live." The lesson is vague because it 55 doesn't stop there. The parable acknowledges the attractions of life: there *are* other villages, towns, hopes, and immediate pleasures that youth *will* seek. But none of this will bring anybody closer to the mystery of life. It will be all in vain. As in vain were the lives that I saw in these pictures scattered on the floor in the now empty apartment. 60

First there were photographs from the homeland—Europe, as far as I could make out, Austria or Germany. These pictures had the unique, brownish hue characteristic of photographs from the beginning of the century. The most interesting was a picture of the whole family, children and adults, lined up in two rows. The event of the picture-taking, which attempted to perpetuate this fam- 65 ily into eternity, must have been a very important one, as the dead ancestors were present as well. There was an easel portrait of a man, who was apparently the grandfather, standing high among the family. I also liked a photo of a man in a military uniform in front of a huge cannon with enormous wooden wheels. He was looking somewhere up into the distance, his right hand proudly grip- 70 ping a pair of field glasses that hung from his neck.

Viewed in these images, the history of this family followed to America, to New York in the 1930s. I found a picture of two young women whom I recognized from the family photo from Europe. They were standing on a street in New York posing in obviously new outfits, maybe the first ones they bought 75 here. Then I witnessed and sensed the whole vitality of these women's lives. In the pictures, as in a phantasmagoric dream, appeared new people, new friendships. Then came husbands, cars, children, a vacation at sea side, a family reunion for a birthday.

80   It seemed that both women lived near each other, maybe even next door. Their families led a very similar life. With the progression of time, however, which I could clearly see on the aging faces of the two women, the pictures become less interesting. Domestic animals replaced friends and loved ones. The two of them—I guess they were sisters—became fattish and old. Suddenly the
85   men disappeared from the pictures and the eyes of the two women became tiny drops of tragedy. The two women were left alone. And one day my boss, I imagine, knocked on the door and proposed a sale so that the old ladies could live alone in a nursing home. Or maybe my boss bought the vacant apartment from a son or a daughter who did not care for the family albums.

90   It was around this time that I started to notice the specifics of the neighborhood. Between 106th and 110th Streets on Amsterdam Avenue there are three funeral homes. Passing by them on my way to work, I could not help thinking that the lives of these people, some of which just had passed in front of my eyes faster than any movie, ended up in one of these establishments. There is noth-
95   ing wrong with that. However unnatural death may seem, it *is* natural and I, passing in front of a funeral parlor with a beer firmly connected to my hand, could even imagine that, as Freud maintained, the instincts of sex and death lie close to each other in the brain, which explains the sexual urge in the proximity of a corpse. But suddenly I was stricken by the realization that funeral homes
100  are always built in poor neighborhoods. As if the misery of life is not enough for lower class people, they are also persecuted by *memento mori* each time they go to a grocery store. It seemed to me that summer that only the poor people were dying. There might be one or two funeral parlors in the whole of mid-Manhattan but there one cannot cross three intersections on Lexington or Madi-
105  son Avenue and encounter three families dressed in black, not because it is an elegant and always fashionable (some people say sexy) color, but because they are in mourning. This does not happen in central Manhattan. There, the illusion of life has to be perfect. Besides, the ground is too expensive, the rent too high.

     My constant hangover and the feeling that I was trapped in some impossible sit-
110  uation without a way out tormented me. I could not get out of my head the simple possibility that my life could actually have—if not exactly the same—to some degree at least a similar fate as that of these two women and their husbands. I am certain that I was growing slightly insane that summer. My fears, the neighborhood, the futility of a quite normal life that I had witnessed in such
115  a strange way, and my general depression found in the end a visible symbol. It was THE BUILDING.
        It wasn't any of the funeral homes that I passed each morning with a shiver. It wasn't the building in which the two women had lived either. THE BUILDING is not an average building. It is a freestanding structure built out of blocks
120  of marble put together as if by some giant hand. There are no windows in the whole edifice—only some sinister, silver circles assembled within huge rectangular forms placed on the walls of grey marble imitation windows. The whole

structure resembles an enormous mausoleum built in the center of a neighborhood afflicted by death. And I could not believe that a book about cryonics could be a solution to any of it.

I became afraid of this building and I still am. It is still there, on the east side of Amsterdam Avenue between 109th and 110th Streets, mysterious and horrifying. I am afraid to ask what is in there, for someone might enlighten me and say that this is one of the cryonics centers and then the ghosts dead and half-dead could break out again and mix with those alive or half-alive. I live in this neighborhood now and I'm afraid I am being subjected to the same pattern of life as the two women. Kafka's parable continues to haunt me.

125

130

## Looking Back

1. How does the opening picture of the neighborhood set the scene for what follows?
2. Why the choice of *glare* in line 19?
3. In what way do the family photographs relate to the Kafka parable?
4. Does the author appropriately extend his interpretation of "The Next Village," as found in lines 56–60? Explain your answer.
5. What is the effect on the reader of Czerwczak's observations of the family photographs and his speculations about them?
6. Can you accept the author's linkage between sex and death (lines 95–99)? Why or why not?
7. What importance does THE BUILDING assume?
8. Does his failure to further investigate THE BUILDING further produce an unnecessary mystery, or is this refusal a requirement of the imagination and thus a good idea? Explain your answer.
9. Who or what are the ghosts "alive or half-alive" mentioned in line 130?
10. How does the final mention of Kafka's parable (line 132) crystallize the author's summer for him and tie together the themes of the essay?

## Writing Assignments

1. Mythologizing yourself is like switching on a table lamp: your ordinary experience, like a dull lampshade, suddenly is lit up from inside; it glows with new, symbolic meaning, able to illuminate other existences besides your own. Like Czerwczak, you find yourself at the center of life, not at the edge. You are suddenly conscious that great forces like death, time, and fear have a bearing on your life; these magnify the intensity of your experience and make it significant for others. To mythologize yourself, you do not have to exaggerate the nature of your experience, nor to overdramatize it. Rather, it is enough to discover its connections to some of the major themes of human life that now you seem to exemplify, themes to which your experience gives new importance and urgency. To do this, write an essay about a personal experience that you feel could resonate in this way. Describe the experience in sufficient detail so that your audience can confirm its authenticity, and explain how the experience gathers to it a greater significance.

2. After a long and sometimes harrowing description of a New York neighborhood he once worked in, Czerwczak slips in at the end of his essay the surprising but unexplained detail that he has since moved there. This fact is important because it allows us to evaluate his view of the neighborhood in a different way. He now seems not simply a critical, appalled outsider but, rather, an inhabitant, someone whose life is bound up with the place and whose version of it, although it may not be shared by all his neighbors, is reliable. We trust his report and find in it the *thereness*, the "local habitation and a name" (to use Shakespeare's phrase), that can only be created by someone who not only talks the talk, but walks the walk. Write an essay about the neighborhood you live in, disclosing the findings of your own lengthy investigation of the place. You may not have realized till now that you *were* making such an investigation, but, like Czerwczak, you can discover in retrospect that day by day you gathered facts and impressions, images and thoughts, which you can now put to good use.

3. Death is a resounding theme in "A Summer." Although some might accuse Czerwczak of morbidity, we can defend his obsession by pointing out that his preoccupation effectively counters the all-too-human tendency to reduce death to a mere fact, forgetting that it is rich in associations, in emotion, in explanations and promises, in mysteries, in symbols and images, in rituals and rites. Never is it *merely* itself. By rescuing the power of the phenomenon of death, Czerwczak faces its terrors. And though he may not overcome them in his own life, he restores to death its dramatic meaning and its almost mythical status. But making death a significant event requires work, not primarily the work of tomb-builders but of writers and other artists, work for which new hands constantly are needed. Like yours. Write an essay that first attempts to define death and that then extends this necessarily limited definition to explore your sense of death's fullest meaning. Refer to your own experience if that proves useful, and think in terms of ceremonies, survivors, religion, nature, the deceased's past life, and whatever else makes us want to write the word Death with a capital D.

# Linked Readings

Paul Radin (editor)
THE ORIGIN OF DEATH:
KRACHI, AKAMBA, HOTTENTOT

Margot Astrov (editor)
THE ORIGIN OF DEATH: COEUR D'ALÊNE

COYOTE AND THE ORIGIN OF DEATH: CADDO

C. G. Jung
ON LIFE AFTER DEATH

Margot Astrov (editor)
A SPEECH TO THE DEAD: FOX

Krachi, Akamba, and Hottentot are names of African tribes, and Coeur d'Alêne, Caddo, and Fox are names of Native American tribes. Paul Radin (1883–1954) was an American anthropologist whose books include *The Trickster: A Study of American Indian Mythology* and several collections of sub-Saharan African stories. In his introduction to *African Tales,* Radin points out that "all people are endowed in equal degree with the mythopoeic imagination." He finds typical of African myths a demanding realism in which, when the gods appear, they descend to earth rather than waiting in heaven for humans to ascend to them. Margot Astrov (b. 1908) published her edited collection, *American Indian Prose and Poetry,* in 1946. Although she is quick to inform us that "the idea of the Indian is an abstraction"—meaning that throughout early American history particular tribal identities predominated—she nonetheless observes that generally Native Americans believed that the word, language itself, was sacred, a fact that elevates the cultural importance of stories like those printed here. "On Life After Death" is a chapter from C. G. Jung's autobiography. Jung (1875–1961) was a Swiss psychiatrist and one-time disciple of Sigmund Freud. He is most famous for developing the concepts of the collective unconscious, as opposed to a purely personal one, and mythic archetypes, figures who symbolize original states of being (e.g., a mother figure).

## THE ORIGIN OF DEATH: KRACHI, AKAMBA, HOTTENTOT

*Looking Ahead*

1. Read critically to gauge the effect in these stories of **personification**—bestowing human habits and traits on animals, inanimate objects, and abstract concepts.
2. Attitudes toward death vary greatly; therefore, the consistency of the attitudes toward death in these stories holds cultural interest.
3. Notice that these stories end with what purport to be statements of universal truths, an important characteristic of myths generally.

Long, long ago there was a great famine in the world, and a certain young man, while wandering in search of food, strayed into a part of the bush where he had never been before. Presently he perceived a strange mass lying on the ground. He approached and saw that it was the body of a giant whose hair resembled that of white men in that it was silky rather than woolly. It was of an incredible length and stretched as far as from Krachi to Salaga. The young man was properly awed at the spectacle, and wished to withdraw, but the giant, noticing him, asked what he wanted. 5

The young man told about the famine and begged the giant to give him some food. The latter agreed on condition that the youth would serve him for a while. This matter having been arranged, the giant said that his name was Owuo, or Death, and he then gave the boy some meat. 10

Never before had the latter tasted such fine food, and he was well pleased with his bargain. He served his master for a long time and received plenty of meat, but one day he grew homesick, and he begged his master to give him a short holiday. The latter agreed, if the youth would promise to bring another boy in his place. So the youth returned to his village and there persuaded his brother to go with him into the bush, and he gave him to Owuo.

In course of time the youth became hungry again and longed for the meat which Owuo had taught him to like so much. So one day he made up his mind to return to his master, and, leaving the village, he made his way back to the giant's abode. The latter asked him what he wanted, and when the youth told him that he wanted to taste once more of the good meat, the giant bade him enter the hut and take as much as he liked, but added that he would have to work for him again.

The youth agreed and entered the hut. He ate as much as he could and went to work at the task which his master set him. The work continued for a long time and the boy ate his fill every day. But, to his surprise, he never saw anything of his brother, and, whenever he asked about him, the giant told him that the lad was away on business.

Once more the youth grew homesick and asked for leave to return to his village. The giant agreed on condition that he would bring a girl for him, Owuo, to wed. So the youth went home and there persuaded his sister to go into the bush and marry the giant. The girl agreed, and took with her a slave companion, and they all repaired to the giant's abode. There the youth left the two girls and went back to the village.

It was not very long after that he again grew hungry and longed for a taste of the meat. So he made his way once more into the bush and found the giant. The latter did not seem overpleased to see the boy and grumbled at being bothered a third time. However, he told the boy to go into the inner chamber of his hut and take what he wanted. The youth did so and took up a bone which he began to devour. To his horror he recognized it at once as being the bone of his sister. He looked around at all the rest of the meat and saw that it was that of his sister and her slave girl.

Thoroughly frightened, he escaped from the house and ran back to the village. There he told the elders what he had done and the awful thing he had seen. At once the alarm was sounded and all the people went out into the bush to see for themselves the dreadful thing they had heard about. When they drew near to the giant they grew afraid at the sight of so evil a monster. They went back to the village and consulted among themselves what they had best do. At last it was agreed to go to Salaga, where the end of the giant's hair was, and set a light to it. This was done, and when the hair was burning well they returned to the bush and watched the giant.

Presently the latter began to toss about and to sweat. It was quite evident that he was beginning to feel the heat. The nearer the flames advanced, the more he tossed and grumbled. At last the fire reached his head and for the moment the giant was dead.

The villagers approached him cautiously, and the young man noticed magic powder which had been concealed in the roots of the giant's hair. He took it and called the others to come and see what he had found. No one could say what power this medicine might have, but an old man suggested that no harm would be done if they sprinkled some of it on the bones and meat in the hut. This idea was carried out, and to the surprise of everyone, the girls and the boy at once returned to life.

The youth, who had still some of the powder left, proposed to put it on the giant. But at this there was a great uproar as the people feared Owuo might come to life again. The boy, therefore, by way of compromise, sprinkled it into the eye of the dead giant. At once the eye opened and the people fled in terror. But alas, it is from that eye that death comes, for every time that Owuo shuts that eye a man dies, and, unfortunately for us, he is forever blinking and winking.

[Krachi]

And how did it happen?

It is God who created men. And since God had pity, He said, "I do not wish men to die altogether. I wish that men, having died, should rise again." And so He created men and placed them in another region. But He stayed at home.

And then God saw the chameleon and the weaver-bird. After He had spent three days with the chameleon and the weaver-bird, He recognized that the weaver-bird was a great maker of words compounded of lies and truth. Now of lies there were many, but of the words of truth there were few.

Then He watched the chameleon and recognized that he had great intelligence. He did not lie. His words were true. So he spoke to the chameleon, "Chameleon, go into that region where I have placed the men I created, and tell them that when they have died, even if they are altogether dead, still they shall rise again—that each man shall rise after he dies."

The chameleon said, "Yes, I will go there." But he went slowly, for it is his fashion to go slowly. The weaver-bird had stayed behind with God.

The chameleon travelled on, and when he had arrived at his destination, he said, "I was told, I was told, I was told. . . ." But he did not say what he had been told.

The weaver-bird said to God, "I wish to step out for a moment."

And God said to him, "Go!"

But the weaver-bird, since he is a bird, flew swiftly, and arrived at the place where the chameleon was speaking to the people and saying, "I was told. . . ." Everyone was gathered there to listen. When the weaver-bird arrived, he said, "What was told to us? Truly, we were told that men, when they are dead, shall perish like the roots of the aloe."

Then the chameleon exclaimed, "But we were told, we were told, we were told, that when men are dead, they shall rise again."

Then the magpie interposed and said, "The first speech is the wise one."

And now all the people left and returned to their homes. This was the way
30   it happened.

And so men become old and die; they do not rise again.

[Akamba]

The moon, it is said, once sent an insect to men, saying, "Go to men and tell
them, 'As I die, and dying live; so you shall also die, and dying live.'"

The insect started with the message, but, while on his way, was overtaken
by the hare, who asked, "On what errand are you bound?"
5   The insect answered, "I am sent by the Moon to men, to tell them that as
she dies and dying lives, so shall they also die and dying live."

The hare said, "As you are an awkward runner, let me go." With these
words he ran off, and when he reached men, he said, "I am sent by the Moon to
tell you, 'As I die and dying perish, in the same manner you also shall die and
10   come wholly to an end.'"

The hare then returned to the Moon and told her what he had said to men.
The Moon reproached him angrily, saying, "Do you dare tell the people a thing
which I have not said?"

With these words the moon took up a piece of wood and struck the hare on
15   the nose. Since that day the hare's nose has been slit, but men believe what Hare
had told them.

[Hottentot]

## THE ORIGIN OF DEATH: COEUR D'ALÊNE COYOTE AND THE ORIGIN OF DEATH: CADDO

### Looking Ahead

1. Margot Astrov's comment on the topic of these readings (from her introduction to
   *American Indian Prose and Poetry*) is noteworthy: "All over the world we meet with
   the belief that whatever is valued most highly among a people is connected in some
   way or other with the dead."
2. Notice how the Coeur d'Alêne tale traces the origin of death to a specific event, a
   form of explanation generally pleasing to human beings.
3. The *necessity* of death is an edifying theme introduced in the Caddo story.

Once a woman had twin children who fainted away. Possibly they only slept.
Their mother left them in the morning; and when she returned in the evening,
they were still lying there. She noticed their tracks around the house: therefore
she thought they must come to life and play during her absence. One day she

stole on them unseen and found them arguing with each other inside the lodge. 5
One said, "It is much better to be dead." And the other said, "It is better to be
alive." When they saw her, they stopped talking, and since then people die from
time to time. There are always some being born and some dying at the same
time, always some living ones and some dead ones. Had she remained hidden
and allowed them to finish their argument, one would have prevailed over the 10
other, and there would have been either no life or no death.

[Coeur d'Alêne]

In the beginning of this world there was no such thing as death. Everyone continued to live until there were so many people that there was no room for any
more on the earth. The chiefs held a council to determine what to do. One man
arose and said that he thought it would be a good plan to have the people die
and be gone for a little while, and then to return. As soon as he sat down Coyote 5
jumped up and said that he thought that people ought to die forever, for this little world was not large enough to hold all of the people, and if the people who
died came back to life, there would not be food enough for all. All of the other
men objected, saying that they did not want their friends and relatives to die
and be gone forever, for then people would grieve and worry and there would 10
not be any happiness in the world. All except Coyote decided to have the people die and be gone for a little while, and then to come back to life again.

The medicine men built a large grass house facing the east, and when they
had completed it they called the men of the tribe together and told them that
they had decided to have the people who died come to the medicine house and 15
there be restored to life. The chief medicine man said they would sing a song that
would call the spirit of the dead to the grass house, and when the spirit came
they would . . . restore it to life again. All of the people were glad, for they were
anxious for the dead to be restored to life and come again and live with them.

After a time—when the first man had died—the medicine men assembled 20
in the grass house and sang. In about ten days a whirlwind blew from the west
and circled about the grass house. Coyote saw it. And as the whirlwind was
about to enter the house, he closed the door. The spirit in the whirlwind, finding the door closed, whirled on by. Death forever was then introduced, and
people from that time on grieved about the dead and were unhappy. 25

Now whenever anyone meets a whirlwind or hears the wind whistle he
says: "There is someone wandering about." Ever since Coyote closed the door,
the spirits of the dead have wandered over the earth, trying to find some place
to go, until at last they find the road to Spirit Land.

Coyote jumped up and ran away and never came back, for when he saw 30
what he had done he was afraid. Ever after that he ran from one place to another, always looking back first over one shoulder and then over the other, to
see if anyone was pursuing him, and ever since then he has been starving, for no
one will give him anything to eat.

[Caddo]

# ON LIFE AFTER DEATH

*Looking Ahead*

1. To follow Jung more effectively, look up in your dictionary these terms that he uses: *rationalism, unconscious* (noun), *ego, psyche, anima, monad,* and *karma.*

2. Although use of the first person singular is hardly surprising in an autobiographical essay, note the unusual effect of subjectivity implied by use of that voice on such a significant topic as life after death.

3. Along with his personal testimony, Jung conducts an argument for believing in an afterlife. Read critically to discover the logic of his argument and to test its soundness.

What I have to tell about the hereafter, and about life after death, consists entirely of memories, of images in which I have lived and of thoughts which have buffeted me. These memories in a way also underlie my works; for the latter are fundamentally nothing but attempts, ever renewed, to give an answer to the
5   question of the interplay between the "here" and the "hereafter." Yet I have never written expressly about a life after death; for then I would have had to document my ideas, and I have no way of doing that. Be that as it may, I would like to state my ideas now.

Even now I can do no more than tell stories—"mythologize." Perhaps one
10   has to be close to death to acquire the necessary freedom to talk about it. It is not that I wish we had a life after death. In fact, I would prefer not to foster such ideas. Still, I must state, to give reality its due, that, without my wishing and without my doing anything about it, thoughts of this nature move about within me. I can't say whether these thoughts are true or false, but I do know they are
15   there, and can be given utterance, if I do not repress them out of some prejudice. Prejudice cripples and injures the full phenomenon of psychic life. And I know too little about psychic life to feel that I can set it right out of superior knowledge. Critical rationalism has apparently eliminated, along with so many other mythic conceptions, the idea of life after death. This could only have hap-
20   pened because nowadays most people identify themselves almost exclusively with their consciousness, and imagine that they are only what they know about themselves. Yet anyone with even a smattering of psychology can see how limited this knowledge is. Rationalism and doctrinairism are the disease of our time; they pretend to have all the answers. But a great deal will yet be discov-
25   ered which our present limited view would have ruled out as impossible. Our concepts of space and time have only approximate validity, and there is therefore a wide field for minor and major deviations. In view of all this, I lend an attentive ear to the strange myths of the psyche, and take a careful look at the varied events that come my way, regardless of whether or not they fit in with my
30   theoretical postulates.

Unfortunately, the mythic side of man is given short shrift nowadays. He can no longer create fables. As a result, a great deal escapes him; for it is important and salutary to speak also of incomprehensible things. Such talk is like the telling of a good ghost story, as we sit by the fireside and smoke a pipe.

What the myths or stories about a life after death really mean, or what kind of reality lies behind them, we certainly do not know. We cannot tell whether they possess any validity beyond their indubitable value as anthropomorphic projections. Rather, we must hold clearly in mind that there is no possible way for us to attain certainty concerning things which pass our understanding.

We cannot visualize another world ruled by quite other laws, the reason being that we live in a specific world which has helped to shape our minds and establish our basic psychic conditions. We are strictly limited by our innate structure and therefore bound by our whole being and thinking to this world of ours. Mythic man, to be sure, demands a "going beyond all that," but scientific man cannot permit this. To the intellect, all my mythologizing is futile speculation. To the emotions, however, it is a healing and valid activity; it gives existence a glamour which we would not like to do without. Nor is there any good reason why we should.

Parapsychology holds it to be a scientifically valid proof of an afterlife that the dead manifest themselves—either as ghosts, or through a medium—and communicate things which they alone could possibly know. But even though there do exist such well-documented cases, the question remains whether the ghost or the voice is identical with the dead person or is a psychic projection, and whether the things said really derive from the deceased or from knowledge which may be present in the unconscious.

Leaving aside the rational arguments against any certainty in these matters, we must not forget that for most people it means a great deal to assume that their lives will have an indefinite continuity beyond their present existence. They live more sensibly, feel better, and are more at peace. One has centuries, one has an inconceivable period of time at one's disposal. What then is the point of this senseless mad rush?

Naturally, such reasoning does not apply to everyone. There are people who feel no craving for immortality, and who shudder at the thought of sitting on a cloud and playing the harp for ten thousand years! There are also quite a few who have been so buffeted by life, or who feel such disgust for their own existence, that they far prefer absolute cessation to continuance. But in the majority of cases the question of immortality is so urgent, so immediate, and also so ineradicable that we must make an effort to form some sort of view about it. But how?

My hypothesis is that we can do so with the aid of hints sent to us from the unconscious—in dreams, for example. Usually we dismiss these hints because we are convinced that the question is not susceptible to answer. In response to this understandable skepticism, I suggest the following considerations. If there is something we cannot know, we must necessarily abandon it as an intellectual problem. For example, I do not know for what reason the universe has come into being, and shall never know. Therefore I must drop this question as a

scientific or intellectual problem. But if an idea about it is offered to me—in dreams or in mythic traditions—I ought to take note of it. I even ought to build up a conception on the basis of such hints, even though it will forever remain a
80  hypothesis which I know cannot be proved.

A man should be able to say he has done his best to form a conception of life after death, or to create some image of it—even if he must confess his failure. Not to have done so is a vital loss. For the question that is posed to him is the age-old heritage of humanity: an archetype, rich in secret life, which seeks
85  to add itself to our own individual life in order to make it whole. Reason sets the boundaries far too narrowly for us, and would have us accept only the known—and that too with limitations—and live in a known framework, just as if we were sure how far life actually extends. As a matter of fact, day after day we live far beyond the bounds of our consciousness; without our knowledge, the life of
90  the unconscious is also going on within us. The more the critical reason dominates, the more impoverished life becomes; but the more of the unconscious, and the more of myth we are capable of making conscious, the more of life we integrate. Overvalued reason has this in common with political absolutism: under its dominion the individual is pauperized.
95  The unconscious helps by communicating things to us, or making figurative allusions. It has other ways, too, of informing us of things which by all logic we could not possibly know. Consider synchronistic phenomena, premonitions, and dreams that come true. I recall one time during the Second World War when I was returning home from Bollingen. I had a book with me, but
100  could not read, for the moment the train started to move I was overpowered by the image of someone drowning. This was a memory of an accident that had happened while I was on military service. During the entire journey I could not rid myself of it. It struck me as uncanny, and I thought, "What has happened? Can there have been an accident?"
105  I got out at Erlenbach and walked home, still troubled by this memory. My second daughter's children were in the garden. The family was living with us, having returned to Switzerland from Paris because of the war. The children stood looking rather upset, and when I asked, "Why, what is the matter?" they told me that Adrian, then the youngest of the boys, had fallen into the water in
110  the boathouse. It is quite deep there, and since he could not really swim he had almost drowned. His older brother had fished him out. This had taken place at exactly the time I had been assailed by that memory in the train. The unconscious had given me a hint. Why should it not be able to inform me of other things also?
115  I had a somewhat similar experience before a death in my wife's family. I dreamed that my wife's bed was a deep pit with stone walls. It was a grave, and somehow had a suggestion of classical antiquity about it. Then I heard a deep sigh, as if someone were giving up the ghost. A figure that resembled my wife sat up in the pit and floated upward. It wore a white gown into which curious
120  black symbols were woven. I awoke, roused my wife, and checked the time. It was three o'clock in the morning. The dream was so curious that I thought at

once that it might signify a death. At seven o'clock came the news that a cousin of my wife had died at three o'clock in the morning.

Frequently foreknowledge is there, but not recognition. Thus I once had a dream in which I was attending a garden party. I saw my sister there, and that greatly surprised me, for she had died some years before. A deceased friend of mine was also present. The rest were people who were still alive. Presently I saw that my sister was accompanied by a lady I knew well. Even in the dream I had drawn the conclusion that the lady was going to die. "She is already marked," I thought. In the dream I knew exactly who she was. I knew also that she lived in Basel. But as soon as I woke up I could no longer, with the best will in the world, recall who she was, although the whole dream was still vivid in my mind. I pictured all my acquaintances in Basel to see whether the memory images would ring a bell. Nothing!

A few weeks later I received news that a friend of mine had had a fatal accident. I knew at once that she was the person I had seen in the dream but had been unable to identify. My recollection of her was perfectly clear and richly detailed, since she had been my patient for a considerable time up to a year before her death. In my attempt to recall the person in my dream, however, hers was the one picture which did not appear in my portrait gallery of Basel acquaintances, although by rights it should have been one of the first.

When one has such experiences—and I will tell of others like them—one acquires a certain respect for the potentialities and arts of the unconscious. Only, one must remain critical and be aware that such communications may have a subjective meaning as well. They may be in accord with reality, and then again they may not. I have, however, learned that the views I have been able to form on the basis of such hints from the unconscious have been most rewarding. Naturally, I am not going to write a book of revelations about them, but I will acknowledge that I have a "myth" which encourages me to look deeper into this whole realm. Myths are the earliest form of science. When I speak of things after death, I am speaking out of inner prompting, and can go no farther than to tell you dreams and myths that relate to this subject.

Naturally, one can contend from the start that myths and dreams concerning continuity of life after death are merely compensating fantasies which are inherent in our natures—all life desires eternity. The only argument I can adduce in answer to this is the myth itself.

However, there are indications that at least a part of the psyche is not subject to the laws of space and time. Scientific proof of that has been provided by the well-known J. B. Rhine experiments.[1] Along with numerous cases of spontaneous foreknowledge, non-spatial perceptions, and so on—of which I have given a number of examples from my own life—these experiments prove that the psyche at times functions outside of the spatio-temporal law of causality. This indicates that our conceptions of space and time, and therefore of causality

1. *Extra-sensory Perception* (Boston, 1934); *The Reach of the Mind* (New York, 1947).

also, are incomplete. A complete picture of the world would require the addition of still another dimension; only then could the totality of phenomena be
given a unified explanation. Hence it is that the rationalists insist to this day that
parapsychological experiences do not really exist; for their world-view stands or
falls by this question. If such phenomena occur at all, the rationalistic picture of
the universe is invalid, because incomplete. Then the possibility of an other-
valued reality behind the phenomenal world becomes an inescapable problem,
and we must face the fact that our world, with its time, space, and causality, relates to another order of things lying behind or beneath it, in which neither
"here and there" nor "earlier and later" are of importance. I have been convinced
that at least a part of our psychic existence is characterized by a relativity of
space and time. This relativity seems to increase, in proportion to the distance
from consciousness, to an absolute condition of timelessness and spacelessness.

Not only my own dreams, but also occasionally the dreams of others,
helped to shape, revise, or confirm my views on a life after death. I attach particular importance to a dream which a pupil of mine, a woman of sixty,
dreamed about two months before her death. She had entered the hereafter.
There was a class going on, and various deceased women friends of hers sat on
the front bench. An atmosphere of general expectation prevailed. She looked
around for a teacher or lecturer, but could find none. Then it became plain that
she herself was the lecturer, for immediately after death people had to give accounts of the total experience of their lives. The dead were extremely interested
in the life experiences that the newly deceased brought with them, just as if the
acts and experiences taking place in earthly life, in space and time, were the decisive ones.

In any case, the dream describes a most unusual audience whose like could
scarcely be found on earth: people burningly interested in the final psychological results of a human life that was in no way remarkable, any more than were
the conclusions that could be drawn from it—to our way of thinking. If, however, the "audience" existed in a state of relative non-time, where "termination,"
"event," and "development" had become questionable concepts, they might very
well be most interested precisely in what was lacking in their own condition.

At the time of this dream the lady was afraid of death and did her best to
fend off any thoughts about it. Yet death is an important interest, especially to
an aging person. A categorical question is being put to him, and he is under an
obligation to answer it. To this end he ought to have a myth about death, for
reason shows him nothing but the dark pit into which he is descending. Myth,
however, can conjure up other images for him, helpful and enriching pictures
of life in the land of the dead. If he believes in them, or greets them with some
measure of credence, he is being just as right or just as wrong as someone who
does not believe in them. But while the man who despairs marches toward
nothingness, the one who has placed his faith in the archetype follows the
tracks of life and lives right into his death. Both, to be sure, remain in uncertainty, but the one lives against his instincts, the other with them.

The figures from the unconscious are uninformed too, and need man, or contact with consciousness, in order to attain to knowledge. When I began working with the unconscious, I found myself much involved with the figures of Salome and Elijah.[2] Then they receded, but after about two years they reappeared. To my enormous astonishment, they were completely unchanged; they spoke and acted as if nothing had happened in the meanwhile. In actuality the most incredible things had taken place in my life. I had, as it were, to begin from the beginning again, to tell them all about what had been going on, and explain things to them. At the time I had been greatly surprised by this situation. Only later did I understand what had happened: in the interval the two had sunk back into the unconscious and into themselves—I might equally well put it, into timelessness. They remained out of contact with the ego and the ego's changing circumstances, and therefore were ignorant of what had happened in the world of consciousness.

Quite early I had learned that it was necessary for me to instruct the figures of the unconscious, or that other group which is often indistinguishable from them, the "spirits of the departed." The first time I experienced this was on a bicycle trip through upper Italy which I took with a friend in 1911. On the way home we cycled from Pavia to Arona, on the lower part of Lake Maggiore, and spent the night there. We had intended to pedal on along the lake and then through the Tessin as far as Faido, where we were going to take the train to Zürich. But in Arona I had a dream which upset our plans.

In the dream I was in an assemblage of distinguished spirits of earlier centuries; the feeling was similar to the one I had later toward the "illustrious ancestors" in the black rock temple of my 1944 vision. The conversation was conducted in Latin. A gentleman with a long, curly wig addressed me and asked a difficult question, the gist of which I could no longer recall after I woke up. I understood him, but did not have a sufficient command of the language to answer him in Latin. I felt so profoundly humiliated by this that the emotion awakened me.

At the very moment of awakening I thought of the book I was then working on, *The Psychology of the Unconscious,* and had such intense inferiority feelings about the unanswered question that I immediately took the train home in order to get back to work. It would have been impossible for me to continue the bicycle trip and lose another three days. I had to work, to find the answer.

Not until years later did I understand the dream and my reaction. The bewigged gentleman was a kind of ancestral spirit, or spirit of the dead, who had addressed questions to me—in vain! It was still too soon, I had not yet come so far, but I had an obscure feeling that by working on my book I would be answering the question that had been asked. It had been asked by, as it were, my

210

215

220

225

230

235

240

245

---

2. *Salome and Elijah:* Salome was the biblical princess who demanded and got the head of Saint John the Baptist. Elijah was a Hebrew prophet. (*ed.*)

spiritual forefathers, in the hope and expectation that they would learn what
they had not been able to find out during their time on earth, since the answer
250   had first to be created in the centuries that followed. If question and answer had
already been in existence in eternity, had always been there, no effort on my
part would have been necessary, and it could all have been discovered in any
other century. There does seem to be unlimited knowledge present in nature, it
is true, but it can be comprehended by consciousness only when the time is ripe
255   for it. The process, presumably, is like what happens in the individual psyche: a
man may go about for many years with an inkling of something, but grasps it
clearly only at a particular moment.

Later, when I wrote the *Septem Sermones ad Mortuos*,[3] once again it was the
dead who addressed crucial questions to me. They came—so they said—"back
260   from Jerusalem, where they found not what they sought." This had surprised
me greatly at the time, for according to the traditional views the dead are the
possessors of great knowledge. People have the idea that the dead know far
more than we, for Christian doctrine teaches that in the hereafter we shall "see
face to face." Apparently, however, the souls of the dead "know" only what they
265   knew at the moment of death, and nothing beyond that. Hence their endeavor
to penetrate into life in order to share in the knowledge of men. I frequently
have a feeling that they are standing directly behind us, waiting to hear what answer we will give to them, and what answer to destiny. It seems to me as if they
were dependent on the living for receiving answers to their questions, that is,
270   on those who have survived them and exist in a world of change: as if omniscience or, as I might put it, omniconsciousness, were not at their disposal, but
could flow only into the psyche of the living, into a soul bound to a body. The
mind of the living appears, therefore, to hold an advantage over that of the dead
in at least one point: in the capacity for attaining clear and decisive cognitions.
275   As I see it, the three-dimensional world in time and space is like a system of co-
ordinates; what is here separated into ordinates and abscissae[4] may appear
"there," in space-timelessness, as a primordial image with many aspects, perhaps as a diffuse cloud of cognition surrounding an archetype. Yet a system of
co-ordinates is necessary if any distinction of discrete contents is to be possible.
280   Any such operation seems to us unthinkable in a state of diffuse omniscience,
or, as the case may be, of subjectless consciousness, with no spatio-temporal
demarcations. Cognition, like generation, presupposes an opposition, a here
and there, an above and below, a before and after.

If there were to be a conscious existence after death, it would, so it seems to
285   me, have to continue on the level of consciousness attained by humanity, which
in any age has an upper though variable limit. There are many human beings
who throughout their lives and at the moment of death lag behind their own

---

3. *Septem Semones ad Mortuos:* seven sermons to the dead. (*ed.*)

4. *ordinates and abscissae:* mathematical measurements used to plot the distance of points on a
horizontal line from points on a vertical line that crosses it. (*ed.*)

potentialities and—even more important—behind the knowledge which has been brought to consciousness by other human beings during their own lifetimes. Hence their demand to attain in death that share of awareness which they failed to win in life.    290

I have come to this conclusion through observation of dreams about the dead. I dreamed once that I was paying a visit to a friend who had died about two weeks before. In life, this friend had never espoused anything but a conventional view of the world, and had remained stuck in this unreflecting attitude.    295
In the dream his home was on a hill similar to the Tüllinger hill near Basel. The walls of an old castle surrounded a square consisting of a small church and a few smaller buildings. It reminded me of the square in front of the castle of Rapperswil. It was autumn. The leaves of the ancient trees had turned gold, and the whole scene was transfigured by gentle sunlight. My friend sat at a table    300
with his daughter, who had studied psychology in Zürich. I knew that she was telling him about psychology. He was so fascinated by what she was saying that he greeted me only with a casual wave of the hand, as though to intimate: "Don't disturb me." The greeting was at the same time a dismissal. The dream told me that now, in a manner which of course remains incomprehensible to    305
me, he was required to grasp the reality of his psychic existence, which he had never been capable of doing during his life.

I had another experience of the evolution of the soul after death when—about a year after my wife's death—I suddenly awoke one night and knew that I had been with her in the south of France, in Provence, and had spent an entire    310
day with her. She was engaged on studies of the Grail there. That seemed significant to me, for she had died before completing her work on this subject. Interpretation on the subjective level—that my anima had not yet finished with the work she had to do—yielded nothing of interest; I know quite well that I am not yet finished with that. But the thought that my wife was continuing after    315
death to work on her further spiritual development—however that may be conceived—struck me as meaningful and held a measure of reassurance for me.

Ideas of this sort are, of course, inaccurate, and give a wrong picture, like a body projected on a plane or, conversely, like the construction of a four-dimensional model out of a three-dimensional body. They use the terms of a    320
three-dimensional world in order to represent themselves to us. Mathematics goes to great pains to create expressions for relationships which pass empirical comprehension. In much the same way, it is all-important for a disciplined imagination to build up images of intangibles by logical principles and on the basis of empirical data, that is, on the evidence of dreams. The method    325
employed is what I have called "the method of the necessary statement." It represents the principle of *amplification* in the interpretation of dreams, but can most easily be demonstrated by the statements implicit in simple whole numbers.

One, as the first numeral, is unity. But it is also "*the* unity," the One, All-Oneness, individuality and non-duality—not a numeral but a philosophical    330
concept, an archetype and attribute of God, the monad. It is quite proper that

335 the human intellect should make these statements; but at the same time the intellect is determined and limited by its conception of oneness and its implications. In other words, these statements are not arbitrary. They are governed by the nature of oneness and therefore are necessary statements. Theoretically, the same logical operation could be performed for each of the following conceptions of number, but in practice the process soon comes to an end because of the rapid increase in complications, which become too numerous to handle.

340 Every further unit introduces new properties and new modifications. Thus, it is a property of the number four that equations of the fourth degree can be solved, whereas equations of the fifth degree cannot. The necessary statement of the number four, therefore, is that, among other things, it is an apex and simultaneously the end of a preceding ascent. Since with each additional unit one or

345 more new mathematical properties appear, the statements attain such a complexity that they can no longer be formulated.

The infinite series of natural numbers corresponds to the infinite number of individual creatures. That series likewise consists of individuals, and the properties even of its first ten members represent—if they represent anything at

350 all—an abstract cosmogony derived from the monad. The properties of numbers are, however, simultaneously properties of matter, for which reason certain equations can anticipate its behavior.

Therefore I submit that other than mathematical statements (i.e., statements implicit in nature) are likewise capable of pointing to irrepresentable re-

355 alities beyond themselves—such, for example, as those products of the imagination which enjoy universal acceptance or are distinguished by the frequency of their occurrence, like the whole class of archetypal motifs. Just as in the case of some factors in mathematical equations we cannot say to what physical realities they correspond, so in the case of some mythological products we do not

360 know at first to what psychic realities they refer. Equations governing the turbulence of heated gases existed long before the problems of such gases had been precisely investigated. Similarly, we have long been in possession of mythologems which express the dynamics of certain subliminal processes, though these processes were only given names in very recent times.

365 The maximum awareness which has been attained anywhere forms, so it seems to me, the upper limit of knowledge to which the dead can attain. That is probably why earthly life is of such great significance, and why it is that what a human being "brings over" at the time of his death is so important. Only here, in life on earth, where the opposites clash together, can the general level of con-

370 sciousness be raised. That seems to be man's metaphysical task—which he cannot accomplish without "mythologizing." Myth is the natural and indispensable intermediate stage between unconscious and conscious cognition. True, the unconscious knows more than consciousness does; but it is knowledge of a special sort, knowledge in eternity, usually without reference to the here and now, not

375 couched in language of the intellect. Only when we let its statements amplify

themselves, as has been shown above by the example of numerals, does it come within the range of our understanding; only then does a new aspect become perceptible to us. This process is convincingly repeated in every successful dream analysis. That is why it is so important not to have any preconceived, doctrinaire opinions about the statements made by dreams. As soon as a certain "monotony of interpretation" strikes us, we know that our approach has become doctrinaire and hence sterile.

380

Although there is no way to marshal valid proof of continuance of the soul after death, there are nevertheless experiences which make us thoughtful. I take them as hints, and do not presume to ascribe to them the significance of insights.

385

One night I lay awake thinking of the sudden death of a friend whose funeral had taken place the day before. I was deeply concerned. Suddenly I felt that he was in the room. It seemed to me that he stood at the foot of my bed and was asking me to go with him. I did not have the feeling of an apparition; rather, it was an inner visual image of him, which I explained to myself as a fantasy. But in all honesty, I had to ask myself, "Do I have any proof that this is a fantasy? Suppose it is not a fantasy, suppose my friend is really here and I decided he was only a fantasy—would that not be abominable of me?" Yet I had equally little proof that he stood before me as an apparition. Then I said to myself, "Proof is neither here nor there! Instead of explaining him away as a fantasy, I might just as well give him the benefit of the doubt and for experiment's sake credit him with reality." The moment I had that thought, he went to the door and beckoned me to follow him. So I was going to have to play along with him! That was something I hadn't bargained for. I had to repeat my argument to myself once more. Only then did I follow him in my imagination.

390

395

400

He led me out of the house, into the garden, out to the road, and finally to his house. (In reality it was several hundred yards away from mine.) I went in, and he conducted me into his study. He climbed on a stool and showed me the second of five books with red bindings which stood on the second shelf from the top. Then the vision broke off. I was not acquainted with his library and did not know what books he owned. Certainly I could never have made out from below the titles of the books he had pointed out to me on the second shelf from the top.

405

This experience seemed to me so curious that next morning I went to his widow and asked whether I could look up something in my friend's library. Sure enough, there was a stool standing under the bookcase I had seen in my vision, and even before I came closer I could see the five books with red bindings. I stepped up on the stool so as to be able to read the titles. They were translations of the novels of Emile Zola. The title of the second volume read: "The Legacy of the Dead." The contents seemed to me of no interest. Only the title was extremely significant in connection with this experience.

410

415

Equally important to me were the dream-experiences I had before my mother's death. News of her death came to me while I was staying in the Tessin.

420   I was deeply shaken, for it had come with unexpected suddenness. The night before her death I had a frightening dream. I was in a dense, gloomy forest; fantastic, gigantic boulders lay about among huge jungle-like trees. It was a heroic, primeval landscape. Suddenly I heard a piercing whistle that seemed to resound through the whole universe. My knees shook. Then there were crashings in the
425   underbrush, and a gigantic wolfhound with a fearful, gaping maw burst forth. At the sight of it, the blood froze in my veins. It tore past me, and I suddenly knew: the Wild Huntsman had commanded it to carry away a human soul. I awoke in deadly terror, and the next morning I received the news of my mother's passing.

430   Seldom has a dream so shaken me, for upon superficial consideration it seemed to say that the devil had fetched her. But to be accurate the dream said that it was the Wild Huntsman, the *"Grünhütl,"* or Wearer of the Green Hat, who hunted with his wolves that night—it was the season of Föhn storms in January. It was Wotan, the god of my Alemannic forefathers, who had gathered my
435   mother to her ancestors—negatively to the "wild horde," but positively to the *"sälig lüt,"* the blessed folk. It was the Christian missionaries who made Wotan into a devil. In himself he is an important god—a Mercury or Hermes, as the Romans correctly realized, a nature spirit who returned to life again in the Merlin of the Grail legend and became, as the *spiritus Mercurialis,* the sought-after
440   arcanum of the alchemists. Thus the dream says that the soul of my mother was taken into that greater territory of the self which lies beyond the segment of Christian morality, taken into that wholeness of nature and spirit in which conflicts and contradictions are resolved.

I went home immediately, and while I rode in the night train I had a feeling
445   of great grief, but in my heart of hearts I could not be mournful, and this for a strange reason: during the entire journey I continually heard dance music, laughter, and jollity, as though a wedding were being celebrated. This contrasted violently with the devastating impression the dream had made on me. Here was gay dance music, cheerful laughter, and it was impossible to yield en-
450   tirely to my sorrow. Again and again it was on the point of overwhelming me, but the next moment I would find myself once more engulfed by the merry melodies. One side of me had a feeling of warmth and joy, and the other of terror and grief; I was thrown back and forth between these contrasting emotions.

This paradox can be explained if we suppose that at one moment death was
455   being represented from the point of view of the ego, and at the next from that of the psyche. In the first case it appeared as a catastrophe; that is how it so often strikes us, as if wicked and pitiless powers had put an end to a human life.

And so it is—death is indeed a fearful piece of brutality; there is no sense pretending otherwise. It is brutal not only as a physical event, but far more so
460   psychically: a human being is torn away from us, and what remains is the icy stillness of death. There no longer exists any hope of a relationship, for all the bridges have been smashed at one blow. Those who deserve a long life are cut off in the prime of their years, and good-for-nothings live to a ripe old age. This

is a cruel reality which we have no right to sidestep. The actual experience of the cruelty and wantonness of death can so embitter us that we conclude there is no merciful God, no justice, and no kindness.    465

From another point of view, however, death appears as a joyful event. In the light of eternity, it is a wedding, a *mysterium coniunctionis.* The soul attains, as it were, its missing half, it achieves wholeness. On Greek sarcophagi the joyous element was represented by dancing girls, on Etruscan tombs by banquets.    470
When the pious Cabbalist[5] Rabbi Simon ben Jochai came to die, his friends said that he was celebrating his wedding. To this day it is the custom in many regions to hold a picnic on the graves on All Souls' Day. Such customs express the feeling that death is really a festive occasion.

Several months before my mother's death, in September 1922, I had a    475
dream which presaged it. It concerned my father, and made a deep impression upon me. I had not dreamed of my father since his death in 1896. Now he once more appeared in a dream, as if he had returned from a distant journey. He looked rejuvenated, and had shed his appearance of paternal authoritarianism. I went into my library with him, and was greatly pleased at the prospect of finding out what he had been up to. I was also looking forward with particular joy    480
to introducing my wife and children to him, to showing him my house, and to telling him all that had happened to me and what I had become in the meanwhile. I wanted also to tell him about my book on psychological types, which had recently been published. But I quickly saw that all this would be inopportune, for my father looked preoccupied. Apparently he wanted something from    485
me. I felt that plainly, and so I refrained from talking about my own concerns.

He then said to me that since I was after all a psychologist, he would like to consult me about marital psychology. I made ready to give him a lengthy lecture on the complexities of marriage, but at this point I awoke. I could not properly    490
understand the dream, for it never occurred to me that it might refer to my mother's death. I realized that only when she died suddenly in January 1923.

My parents' marriage was not a happy one, but full of trials and difficulties and tests of patience. Both made the mistakes typical of many couples. My dream was a forecast of my mother's death, for here was my father who, after an    495
absence of twenty-six years, wished to ask a psychologist about the newest insights and information on marital problems, since he would soon have to resume this relationship again. Evidently he had acquired no better understanding in his timeless state and therefore had to appeal to someone among the living who, enjoying the benefits of changed times, might have a fresh approach    500
to the whole thing.

Such was the dream's message. Undoubtedly, I could have found out a good deal more by looking into its subjective meaning—but why did I dream it

---

5. *Cabbalist:* (usually spelled Kabbalist) a believer and participant in a mystical Jewish sect. (*ed.*)

just before the death of my mother, which I did not foresee? It plainly referred
to my father, with whom I felt a sympathy that deepened as I grew older.

Since the unconscious, as the result of its spatio-temporal relativity, possesses better sources of information than the conscious mind—which has only sense perceptions available to it—we are dependent for our myth of life after death upon the meager hints of dreams and similar spontaneous revelations from the unconscious. As I have already said, we cannot attribute to these allusions the value of knowledge, let alone proof. They can, however, serve as suitable bases for mythic amplifications; they give the probing intellect the raw material which is indispensable for its vitality. Cut off the intermediary world of mythic imagination, and the mind falls prey to doctrinaire rigidities. On the other hand, too much traffic with these germs of myth is dangerous for weak and suggestible minds, for they are led to mistake vague intimations for substantial knowledge, and to hypostatize mere phantasms.

One widespread myth of the hereafter is formed by the ideas and images centering on reincarnation. In one country whose intellectual culture is highly complex and much older than ours—I am, of course, referring to India—the idea of reincarnation is as much taken for granted as, among us, the idea that God created the world, or that there is a *spiritus rector*.[6] Cultivated Hindus know that we do not share their ideas about this, but that does not trouble them. In keeping with the spirit of the East, the succession of birth and death is viewed as an endless continuity, as an eternal wheel rolling on forever without a goal. Man lives and attains knowledge and dies and begins again from the beginning. Only with the Buddha does the idea of a goal emerge, namely, the overcoming of earthly existence.

The mythic needs of the Occidental call for an evolutionary cosmogony with a *beginning* and a *goal*. The Occidental rebels against a cosmogony with a beginning and mere *end*, just as he cannot accept the idea of a static, self-contained, eternal cycle of events. The Oriental, on the other hand, seems able to come to terms with this idea. Apparently there is no unanimous feeling about the nature of the world, any more than there is general agreement among contemporary astronomers on this question. To Western man, the meaninglessness of a merely static universe is unbearable. He must assume that it has meaning. The Oriental does not need to make this assumption; rather, he himself embodies it. Whereas the Occidental feels the need to complete the meaning of the world, the Oriental strives for the fulfillment of meaning in man, stripping the world and existence from himself (Buddha).

I would say that both are right. Western man seems predominantly extraverted, Eastern man predominantly introverted. The former projects the meaning and considers that it exists in objects; the latter feels the meaning in himself. But the meaning is both without and within.

---

6. *spiritus rector:* ruling spirit. (*ed.*)

The idea of rebirth is inseparable from that of karma. The crucial question   545
is whether a man's karma is personal or not. If it is, then the preordained destiny with which a man enters life represents an achievement of previous lives,
and a personal continuity therefore exists. If, however, this is not so, and an impersonal karma is seized upon in the act of birth, then that karma is incarnated
again without there being any personal continuity.   550

Buddha was twice asked by his disciples whether man's karma is personal
or not. Each time he fended off the question, and did not go into the matter; to
know this, he said, would not contribute to liberating oneself from the illusion
of existence. Buddha considered it far more useful for his disciples to meditate
upon the Nidâna chain, that is, upon birth, life, old age, and death, and upon   555
the cause and effect of suffering.

I know no answer to the question of whether the karma which I live is the
outcome of my past lives, or whether it is not rather the achievement of my ancestors, whose heritage comes together in me. Am I a combination of the lives of
these ancestors and do I embody these lives again? Have I lived before in the   560
past as a specific personality, and did I progress so far in that life that I am now
able to seek a solution? I do not know. Buddha left the question open, and I like
to assume that he himself did not know with certainty.

I could well imagine that I might have lived in former centuries and there
encountered questions I was not yet able to answer; that I had to be born again   565
because I had not fulfilled the task that was given to me. When I die, my deeds
will follow along with me—that is how I imagine it. I will bring with me what I
have done. In the meantime it is important to insure that I do not stand at the
end with empty hands. Buddha, too, seems to have had this thought when he
tried to keep his disciples from wasting time on useless speculation.   570

The meaning of my existence is that life has addressed a question to me.
Or, conversely, I myself am a question which is addressed to the world, and I
must communicate my answer, for otherwise I am dependent upon the world's
answer. That is a suprapersonal life task, which I accomplish only by effort and
with difficulty. Perhaps it is a question which preoccupied my ancestors, and   575
which they could not answer. Could that be why I am so impressed by the fact
that the conclusion of *Faust* contains no solution? Or by the problem on which
Nietzsche foundered: the Dionysian side of life, to which the Christian seems to
have lost the way?[7] Or is it the restless Wotan-Hermes of my Alemannic and
Frankish ancestors who poses challenging riddles?   580

---

7. *Faust:* a play by Johann Wolfgang Von Goethe (1749–1832) in which Faust, a medieval
philosopher, sells his soul to the devil in exchange for knowledge and power on earth; *Friedrich
Nietzsche* (1844–1900): German philosopher who conceived of the "superman" and who wrote *Thus
Spake Zarathustra, Beyond Good and Evil,* and *Ecce Homo,* among other books. He was also a composer, and recently his music has been issued on CD in the United States; *Dionysius:* in Greek
mythology, the god of wine and fertility. (*ed.*)

What I feel to be the resultant of my ancestors' lives, or a karma acquired in a previous personal life, might perhaps equally well be an impersonal archetype which today presses hard on everyone and has taken a particular hold upon me—an archetype such as, for example, the development over the centuries of the divine triad and its confrontation with the feminine principle; or the still pending answer to the Gnostic[8] question as to the origin of evil, or, to put it another way, the incompleteness of the Christian God-image.

I also think of the possibility that through the achievement of an individual a question enters the world, to which he must provide some kind of answer. For example, my way of posing the question as well as my answer may be unsatisfactory. That being so, someone who has my karma—or I myself—would have to be reborn in order to give a more complete answer. It might happen that I would not be reborn again so long as the world needed no such answer, and that I would be entitled to several hundred years of peace until someone was once more needed who took an interest in these matters and could profitably tackle the task anew. I imagine that for a while a period of rest could ensue, until the stint I had done in my lifetime needed to be taken up again.

The question of karma is obscure to me, as is also the problem of personal rebirth or of the transmigration of souls. "With a free and open mind" I listen attentively to the Indian doctrine of rebirth, and look around in the world of my own experience to see whether somewhere and somehow there is some authentic sign pointing toward reincarnation. Naturally, I do not count the relatively numerous testimonies, here in the West, to the belief in reincarnation. A belief proves to me only the phenomenon of belief, not the content of the belief. This I must see revealed empirically in order to accept it. Until a few years ago I could not discover anything convincing in this respect, although I kept a sharp lookout for any such signs. Recently, however, I observed in myself a series of dreams which would seem to describe the process of reincarnation in a deceased person of my acquaintance. But I have never come across any such dreams in other persons, and therefore have no basis for comparison. Since this observation is subjective and unique, I prefer only to mention its existence and not to go into it any further. I must confess, however, that after this experience I view the problem of reincarnation with somewhat different eyes, though without being in a position to assert a definite opinion.

If we assume that life continues "there," we cannot conceive of any other form of existence except a psychic one; for the life of the psyche requires no space and no time. Psychic existence, and above all the inner images with which we are here concerned, supply the material for all mythic speculations about a life in the hereafter, and I imagine that life as a continuance in the world of im-

---

8. *Gnostic:* refers to religious teaching in the first century after the death of Christ that promulgated truths that supposedly revealed the hidden reality of the world. (*ed.*)

ages. Thus the psyche might be that existence in which the hereafter or the land of the dead is located.

From the psychological point of view, life in the hereafter would seem to be a logical continuation of the psychic life of old age. With increasing age, contemplation, and reflection, the inner images naturally play an ever greater part in man's life. "Your old men shall dream dreams."[9] That, to be sure, presupposes that the psyches of the old men have not become wooden, or entirely petrified—*sero medicina paratur cum mala per longas convaluere moras.*[10] In old age one begins to let memories unroll before the mind's eye and, musing, to recognize oneself in the inner and outer images of the past. This is like a preparation for an existence in the hereafter, just as, in Plato's view, philosophy is a preparation for death.

The inner images keep me from getting lost in personal retrospection. Many old people become too involved in their reconstruction of past events. They remain imprisoned in these memories. But if it is reflective and is translated into images, retrospection can be a *reculer pour mieux sauter.*[11] I try to see the line which leads through my life into the world, and out of the world again.

In general, the conception people form of the hereafter is largely made up of wishful thinking and prejudices. Thus in most conceptions the hereafter is pictured as a pleasant place. That does not seem so obvious to me. I hardly think that after death we shall be spirited to some lovely flowering meadow. If everything were pleasant and good in the hereafter, surely there would be some friendly communication between us and the blessed spirits, and an outpouring upon us of goodness and beauty from the prenatal state. But there is nothing of the sort. Why is there this insurmountable barrier between the departed and the living? At least half the reports of encounters with the dead tell of terrifying experiences with dark spirits; and it is the rule that the land of the dead observes icy silence, unperturbed by the grief of the bereaved.

To follow out the thought that involuntarily comes to me: the world, I feel, is far too unitary for there to be a hereafter in which the rule of opposites is completely absent. There, too, is nature, which after its fashion is also God's. The world into which we enter after death will be grand and terrible, like God and like all of nature that we know. Nor can I conceive that suffering should entirely cease. Granted that what I experienced in my 1944 visions—liberation from the burden of the body, and perception of meaning—gave me the deepest bliss. Nevertheless, there was darkness too, and a strange cessation of human warmth. Remember the black rock to which I came! It was dark and of the

620

625

630

635

640

645

650

655

---

9. Acts 2:17; Joel 2:28.

10. *sero . . . moras:* The medicine is prepared too late, when the illness has grown strong by long delay.

11. *reculer . . . sauter:* drawing back so as to leap (to see imaginatively) farther. (*ed.*)

hardest granite. What does that mean? If there were no imperfections, no primordial defect in the ground of creation, why should there be any urge to create, any longing for what must yet be fulfilled? Why should the gods be the least
660   bit concerned about man and creation? About the continuation of the Nidâna
chain to infinity? After all, the Buddha opposes to the painful illusion of existence his *quod non,*[12] and the Christian hopes for the swift coming of this
world's end.

It seems probable to me that in the hereafter, too, there exist certain limita-
665   tions, but that the souls of the dead only gradually find out where the limits of
the liberated state lie. Somewhere "out there" there must be a determinant, a necessity conditioning the world, which seeks to put an end to the after-death
state. This creative determinant—so I imagine it—must decide what souls
will plunge again into birth. Certain souls, I imagine, feel the state of three-
670   dimensional existence to be more blissful than that of Eternity. But perhaps that
depends upon how much of completeness or incompleteness they have taken
across with them from their human existence.

It is possible that any further spell of three-dimensional life would have no
more meaning once the soul had reached a certain stage of understanding; it
675   would then no longer have to return, fuller understanding having put to rout
the desire for re-embodiment. Then the soul would vanish from the three-
dimensional world and attain what the Buddhists call nirvana. But if a karma
still remains to be disposed of, then the soul relapses again into desires and returns to life once more, perhaps even doing so out of the realization that some-
680   thing remains to be completed.

In my case it must have been primarily a passionate urge to reward understanding which brought about my birth. For that is the strongest element in my
nature. This insatiable drive toward understanding has, as it were, created a
consciousness in order to know what is and what happens, and in order to
685   piece together mythic conceptions from the slender hints of the unknowable.

We lack concrete proof that anything of us is preserved for eternity. At
most we can say that there is some probability that something of our psyche
continues beyond physical death. Whether what continues to exist is conscious
of itself, we do not know either. If we feel the need to form some opinion on this
690   question, we might possibly consider what has been learned from the phenomena of psychic dissociation. In most cases where a split-off complex manifests
itself it does so in the form of a personality, as if the complex had a consciousness of itself. Thus the voices heard by the insane are personified. I dealt long
ago with this phenomenon of personified complexes in my doctoral disserta-
695   tion. We might, if we wish, adduce these complexes as evidence for a continuity
of consciousness. Likewise in favor of such an assumption are certain astonishing observations in cases of profound syncope after acute injuries to the brain

---

12. *quod non:* which is nothing. (*ed.*)

and in severe states of collapse. In both situations, total loss of consciousness can be accompanied by perceptions of the outside world and vivid dream experiences. Since the cerebral cortex, the seat of consciousness, is not functioning 700 at these times, there is as yet no explanation for such phenomena. They may be evidence for at least a subjective persistence of the capacity for consciousness—even in a state of apparent unconsciousness.

The thorny problem of the relationship between eternal man, the self and earthly man in time and space was illuminated by two dreams of mine. 705

In one dream, which I had in October 1958, I caught sight from my house of two lens-shaped metallically gleaming disks, which hurtled in a narrow arc over the house and down to the lake. They were two UFOs (Unidentified Flying Objects). Then another body came flying directly toward me. It was a perfectly circular lens, like the objective of a telescope. At a distance of four or five hun- 710 dred yards it stood still for a moment, and then flew off. Immediately afterward, another came speeding through the air: a lens with a metallic extension which led to a box—a magic lantern. At a distance of sixty or seventy yards it stood still in the air, pointing straight at me. I awoke with a feeling of astonishment. Still half in the dream, the thought passed through my head: "We always think 715 that the UFOs are projections of ours. Now it turns out that we are their projections. I am projected by the magic lantern as C. G. Jung. But who manipulates the apparatus?"

I had dreamed once before of the problem of the self and the ego. In that earlier dream I was on a hiking trip. I was walking along a little road through a 720 hilly landscape; the sun was shining and I had a wide view in all directions. Then I came to a small wayside chapel. The door was ajar, and I went in. To my surprise there was no image of the Virgin on the altar, and no crucifix either, but only a wonderful flower arrangement. But then I saw that on the floor in front of the altar, facing me, sat a yogi—in lotus posture, in deep meditation. 725 When I looked at him more closely, I realized that he had my face. I started in profound fright, and awoke with the thought: "Aha, so he is the one who is meditating me. He has a dream, and I am it." I knew that when he awakened, I would no longer be.

I had this dream after my illness in 1944. It is a parable: My self retires into 730 meditation and meditates my earthly form. To put it another way: it assumes human shape in order to enter three-dimensional existence, as if someone were putting on a diver's suit in order to dive into the sea. When it renounces existence in the hereafter, the self assumes a religious posture, as the chapel in the dream shows. In earthly form it can pass through the experiences of the 735 three-dimensional world, and by greater awareness take a further step toward realization.

The figure of the yogi, then, would more or less represent my unconscious prenatal wholeness, and the Far East, as is often the case in dreams, a psychic state alien and opposed to our own. Like the magic lantern, the yogi's medita- 740 tion "projects" my empirical reality. As a rule, we see this causal relationship in reverse: in the products of the unconscious we discover mandala symbols, that is, circular and quaternary figures which express wholeness, and whenever we wish to express wholeness, we employ just such figures. Our basis is ego-consciousness, our world the field of light centered upon the focal point of the ego. From that point we look out upon an enigmatic world of obscurity, never knowing to what extent the shadowy forms we see are caused by our consciousness, or possess a reality of their own. The superficial observer is content with the first assumption. But closer study shows that as a rule the images of the unconscious are not produced by consciousness, but have a reality and spontaneity of their own. Nevertheless, we regard them as mere marginal phenomena.

The aim of both these dreams is to effect a reversal of the relationship between ego-consciousness and the unconscious, and to represent the unconscious as the generator of the empirical personality. This reversal suggests that in the opinion of the "other side," our unconscious existence is the real one and our conscious world a kind of illusion, an apparent reality constructed for a specific purpose, like a dream which seems a reality as long as we are in it. It is clear that this state of affairs resembles very closely the Oriental conception of Maya.[13]

Unconscious wholeness therefore seems to me the true *spiritus rector* of all biological and psychic events. Here is a principle which strives for total realization—which in man's case signifies the attainment of total consciousness. Attainment of consciousness is culture in the broadest sense, and self-knowledge is therefore the heart and essence of this process. The Oriental attributes unquestionably divine significance to the self, and according to the ancient Christian view self-knowledge is the road to knowledge of God.

The decisive question for man is: Is he related to something infinite or not? That is the telling question of his life. Only if we know that the thing which truly matters is the infinite can we avoid fixing our interest upon futilities, and upon all kinds of goals which are not of real importance. Thus we demand that the world grant us recognition for qualities which we regard as personal possessions: our talent or our beauty. The more a man lays stress on false possessions, and the less sensitivity he has for what is essential, the less satisfying is his life. He feels limited because he has limited aims, and the result is envy and jealousy. If we understand and feel that here in this life we already have a link with the infinite, desires and attitudes change. In the final analysis, we count for something only because of the essential we embody, and if we do not embody that, life is wasted. In our relationships to other men, too, the crucial question is whether an element of boundlessness is expressed in the relationship.

The feeling for the infinite, however, can be attained only if we are bounded to the utmost. The greatest limitation for man is the "self"; it is manifested in the experience: "I am *only* that!" Only consciousness of our narrow confinement in the self forms the link to the limitlessness of the unconscious. In

_____

13. *Maya:* the illusory nature of what most people take for reality. (*ed.*)

such awareness we experience ourselves concurrently as limited and eternal, as both the one and the other. In knowing ourselves to be unique in our personal combination—that is, ultimately limited—we possess also the capacity for becoming conscious of the infinite. But only then! 785

In an era which has concentrated exclusively upon extension of living space and increase of rational knowledge at all costs, it is a supreme challenge to ask man to become conscious of his uniqueness and his limitation. Uniqueness and limitation are synonymous. Without them, no perception of the unlimited is possible—and, consequently, no coming to consciousness either—merely a delusory identity with it which takes the form of intoxication with large numbers and an avidity for political power. 790

Our age has shifted all emphasis to the here and now, and thus brought about a daemonization of man and his world. The phenomenon of dictators and all the misery they have wrought springs from the fact that man has been robbed of transcendence by the shortsightedness of the super-intellectuals. Like them, he has fallen a victim to unconsciousness. But man's task is the exact opposite: to become conscious of the contents that press upward from the unconscious. Neither should he persist in his unconsciousness, nor remain identical with the unconscious elements of his being, thus evading his destiny, which is to create more and more consciousness. As far as we can discern, the sole purpose of human existence is to kindle a light in the darkness of mere being. It may even be assumed that just as the unconscious affects us, so the increase in our consciousness affects the unconscious. 795 800 805

## A SPEECH TO THE DEAD: FOX

### Looking Ahead

1. If you glance at the In Memoriam tributes found on most newspaper obituary pages, you will see how common it is for the living to address the dead directly, as happens here.

2. According to the speaker, the dead have a particular power, which you should pause to contemplate.

3. As you read this short piece—and as you reread it, aloud, to experience its incantatory effect—try to recognize the general attitude toward the dead that it expresses.

> Now this day you have ceased to see daylight.
> Think only of what is good.
> Do not think of anything uselessly.
> You must think all the time of what is good.
> You will go and live with our nephew.
> And do not think evil towards these your relatives. 5
> When you start to leave them this day you must not
> think backwards of them with regret.

And do not think of looking back at them.
10   And do not feel badly because you have lost sight of
      this daylight.
      This does not happen today to you alone, so that you
      thus be alone when you die.
15   Bless the people so that they may not be sick.
      This is what you will do.
      You must merely bless them so that they may live as
      mortals here.
      You must always think kindly.
20   Today is the last time I shall speak to you.
      Now I shall cease speaking to you, my relative.

                                                    [Fox]


## Looking Back

1. What do we learn about human psychology from the fact that, in the African and Native American tales (except for the Fox speech), error or maliciousness, not nature itself, is responsible for death's entering the world?

2. How is the idea of the resurrection of the dead represented differently in these stories?

3. In what way do Jung's sympathy for myth, distrust of pure rationality, and belief in the power of the unconscious combine to produce in him an inquiring mind?

4. Why, according to Jung, do some people desire a life after death whereas others find the idea repugnant?

5. What is your opinion of Jung's position on reason and rationality, particularly as he outlines it in lines 85–91, 157–176, and 197–207?

6. As found in lines 365–372, what important functions does Jung ascribe to myth?

7. What sense is Jung making in lines 514–517?

8. How does Jung's vision of the hereafter differ from popular versions?

9. In Jung's view (see lines 767–806), what positive moral and political consequences derive from a belief in the infinite?

10. What attitude toward the dead does the Fox speech reveal?


## Writing Assignments (Linked Readings)

1. Often, when we remember our dreams, we discover that the movie theater in our heads has given us—for no admission fee except our life experiences—such a show that we are touched, bored, made thoughtful, alarmed, awed by the vivid images we recall, haunted long afterward, and more. Yet we all dream differently. How do you dream? What notable dreams do you recall? Further, what is your personal view of dreaming? What does it mean to dream? Do dreams have meaning? Write an essay generally structured along the lines of these questions. If by chance you can't re-

member any of your dreams, you can refer to one or more dreams Jung reports, and you can regard the African and Native American myths as if they were dreams.

2. "Reason sets the boundaries far too narrowly for us, and would have us accept only the known—and that too with limitations—and live in a known framework, just as if we were sure how far life extends." Although Jung is the author of these words (see lines 85–88), the thought could equally have come from any one of the anonymous storytellers whose myths of the origin of death we read here. Their dreamlike accounts certainly go beyond the boundaries of the known, and one could imagine these authors, like Jung, criticizing the faculty of reason for overly restricting imagination, belief, and the capacity of human beings to transcend their physical lives. On the other hand, it might be argued, reason enables us to make accurate appraisals of our true condition as living creatures, to plan our lives, to act rationally, and to predict probable outcomes. Without it, we are lost. Although most of us combine some elements both of reason and a belief in the unknown to get through our days, the two can conflict, as Jung points out, and then we must gravitate to one or the other. Write an essay that takes off from such a dilemma. Argue that reason or a belief in the unknown or some combination you define is the best policy to adopt toward one of the following concepts: death, love, God, children (the future), the national interest as appealed to by a political leader, voting for a political candidate.

3. Throughout the history of human cultures, the idea of life after death has been remarkably attractive. Why do you think this is so? Jung answers this question fairly explicitly. Other answers come from the *ways* in which some of the African and Native American myths presented here imagine death. These answers involve the emotions of fear and hope, but fear of what, hope for what? What is it about the idea of life ending with physical death that has proved so unacceptable to so many generations of people? Is it that life is too short for what we want out of it? Is our general quality of life inadequate, compared to what it might be in a different form? Are we dismayed by the apparent final loss of people we love? Write an essay that, referring to Jung and to the myths read here, examines the notion of an afterlife by addressing the above questions and others that may occur to you.

## *Writing Assignments (Individual Readings)*
### THE ORIGIN OF DEATH: KRACHI, AKAMBA, HOTTENTOT

Although true myths are anonymous, known authors have tried their hand at telling them. Sometimes these mythmakers keep the original plot intact, and sometimes they make subtle changes in it. Sometimes they modernize the narrative by making contemporary references or by introducing a psychology unknown at the time of the myth itself. Sometimes—Jorge Luis Borges and Franz Kafka come to mind—they write entirely new narratives to present ancient mythic ideas. The origin of death is one such subject that could use a new treatment, perhaps utilizing one of the methods just described. Write a relatively brief mythic narrative to account for the origin of death (you may want to use the African tales as a model), and then—to make this a veritable essay—comment on the *idea* about death that your myth illustrates. To do this successfully, you probably need to have your idea in mind before you write your story.

## THE ORIGIN OF DEATH: COEUR D'ALÊNE; COYOTE AND THE ORIGIN OF DEATH: CADDO

These Native American myths convey the idea that death is an evil. Write an essay with this format: in the introduction, state how this idea emerges differently in each myth; in the body of your paper, go on to examine both the merits and defects of looking at death that way. Keep in mind that the attitude expressed in these texts is a *cultural* one. It does not result from ignorance of nature or willful denial of the facts, but from a generally shared view—translated into the concrete terms found here—that death is repugnant and unwelcome, the enemy of humankind. Your argument, therefore, cannot simply dismiss this view; it must contend with it as representing a given worldview. The society that holds this view is "theirs," but you may also find it is "ours"; that is, not all ideas change over time. Nonetheless, people can stand outside cultures, their own and others, and criticize them. So you are perfectly at liberty to accept or reject this idea of death as long as you can defend your opinion.

## ON LIFE AFTER DEATH

Near the end of his discourse, Jung writes that the destiny—that is, the natural aim—of human beings is "to create more and more consciousness." In fact, according to Jung, "As far as we can discern, the sole purpose of human existence is to kindle a light in the darkness of mere being" (lines 803–804). This is the language of an essentially independent thinker, one who refuses to accept conventional ideas merely because many people hold them and who rebels against political or other authority that attempts to smother thought and its free expression. It is *not* the language of one who believes in received values—those that are handed to one by parents, teachers, or others, unexamined for their truthfulness because they have a long history or powerful backing. And it is *not* the language of one who takes the easy path of letting other people tell him or her what to think or do. All of us, at one time or another, and in one way or another, have kindled Jung's light by thinking on our own and acting according to our own reasoning. How have you done this? Write an essay describing a personal experience in which you asserted independence of mind and spirit. Explain the exact circumstances, and say why your action was necessary and good.

## A SPEECH TO THE DEAD: FOX

In this speech, the dead person, who is about to embark on the journey that all dead people take, is admonished, "Think only of what is good" (line 2). In a prefatory note to *The Tibetan Book of the Dead*, editor W. Y. Evans-Wentz remarks that "Buddhists and Hindus alike believe that the last thought at the moment of death determines the character of the next incarnation." In his poem "The Dry Salvages" from *Four Quartets*, T. S. Eliot similarly alludes to Indian mythology, telling us that a person's dying thought will strongly influence the lives of other people and that "the time of death is every moment." By now in the above movement of ideas, we have reached this point: Death can be viewed as a metaphor for time passing in a human life, and for the inheritance of our thoughts—which reflect our actions—by those who know us or know of us. We have thus returned to life and to the ethical duty to live an exemplary life, one that others may look to for positive guidance. Thus the question arises, How do I shape my life so that it can help others? Write an essay answering this question. Try to focus on concrete situations in which right and wrong actions are at issue so that your discussion does not become abstract and general.

# II

# *Personal Identity*

Gradually, as the years pass, we become who we are. It sometimes seems as if we put on different articles of clothing, one by one, until we were finally dressed to kill. Unfortunately for this theory of acquiring personal identity, if not for the analogy itself, there is always more apparel to put on or take off, not to mention the possibility of changing to an entirely new outfit.

We can change. But how much can we change? Isn't there some basic type of clothing, common to everyone despite differences in style, that we will never escape wearing? And even if we go naked, won't our upbringing, our social conditioning, our general predispositions, and learned responses survive? Won't we end up pretty much as we were before, when we thought we knew ourselves?

Without expecting a definite answer to these questions, we may nonetheless be mindful of them as we consider the problem of personhood. Clearly, to be human means to be biologically assimilable to a type. Yet, as the Austrian novelist Thomas Bernhard says about that type, "Every person is a unique and autonomous person and actually, considered independently, the greatest artwork of all time." These words may encourage us as, balancing nature and culture, we go forward in life to become a self.

The self is a locus of sensations, desires, memories, beliefs, and more. The self plans and acts. It wakes up in the morning and slowly distinguishes itself from its surroundings. It is a consciousness and therefore subjective. It knows it is just a term in relations involving other terms, yet it cannot escape the feeling that, as in a heliocentric universe, everything else revolves around it. It tries to correct this error and illusion by occupying a position, even if only for moments at a time, from which it can look at itself objectively, as if it were not itself but one of the others. All too soon it is only itself again, but at least for the space of a ten-second thought or of a ten-page memoir, it got outside and saw itself as others see it. It had a vision of itself.

That vision may be encouraging or distressing, but those who look hard enough will discover their personal identity. Their findings are the stuff of much of the literature that we read. Whether a fictional character or an actual personage, the hero or heroine of experience and investigation is an individual who, as existentialist philosopher Jean-Paul Sartre says, "is faced in his own lifetime with the task of wresting his life from the various forms of night." Each self, Sartre implies, is beleaguered by the external world, a world that assumes many guises, including finally death, to dissolve the self into its indistinguishable mass. Defending its borders against these intrusions, the self cherishes its inner life and asserts its own identity in social relations.

With such an idea of the individual self in mind, it is hardly surprising that no one can answer the question "Who are you?" merely by pulling a laminated photo ID from a wallet. Personal identity is a far more complex matter. It involves names, continuity in time, stability of image, memory and anticipation, irreducible qualities and fluid adaptability, and so much more, all the crystallized product of experience, of having lived long enough to be someone.

The pieces that follow in this section all say "I" in one way or another, each different. Your reading will prosper if you keep in mind the following general guidelines:

1. The self is a network of connections, but these are formed by subtle processes and by indirect routes. Thus, not all writers addressing the subject of the self and personal identity are explicit. You must be prepared in some cases to make the connections yourself.

2. Social context is an important factor to keep in mind as you read. Individuals define themselves by discovering the boundaries between themselves and others.

3. It is natural, as you read about others' experience of personhood, to ponder your own. Doing so increases your empathy with others and provides material for your writing.

# PRIMARY TEXTS

Everyone has a word for it. Indeed, there has always been a way of saying it.

In France and French-speaking parts of the world, self-esteem is *amour-propre,* "love of self," in Italian it's *autostima,* in Danish *selvvaerd,* and Spanish speakers everywhere call it *autoestima.* To the Germans it's *selbstachtung,* to the Dutch, *zelfwaardering.* Arabic speakers say *al-jtibar al-dhati.* In Hebrew it's *haaracha atzmit;* and in Yiddish, *zelbst gloibn.*

*Samouvazhenie* is the single word in Russian; *kujistahi* in Swahili; and *swavhimani* in Hindi. The Chinese combine the pictogram for self (pronounced *zi*) with the one for esteem or respect (pronounced *zun*) and say *zizun.* The Japanese say *ji son shin.*

But however different the words, their meaning is the same. *The Oxford English Dictionary* gives the primary definition as a "favourable appreciation or opinion of oneself," and cites uses of "selfe-esteem" from the 1600s. North American dictionaries shorten its meaning to "belief in oneself," or "self-respect." Thesaurus synonyms are "self-reliance," "self-consequence," "poise," "confidence," "assurance," "pride," or "self-sufficiency." Antonyms run the negative gamut from "self-doubt" and "self-effacement" to "self-hatred" and "shame."

Tracing the English word even further back, we find unfamiliar spellings: *silfe, soelf, suelf;* and *extyme, aesteam, extseme.* By 1657, when Augustine Baker, a mystical theologian and Benedictine monk, declared "Selfe-esteem, Selfe-judgment, & selfe-will" to be the three requisites of independence, the term had been used by scholars in Latin and by common people in English for centuries, with origins in the Western world dating back at least to the ancient Greeks. *Allotriosis,* "self-alienation," for instance, was the greatest evil in Greek philosophy, and *oikeiosis* ("self-love," "self-acceptance," or "self-contentedness") was the greatest goal. Plato called "rational self-love" crucial to progress because it alone "requires a man [sic] to be concerned for his own future condition." Aristotle equated self-contentedness with happiness. For him, the full realization of one's own specific nature was the ultimate good. Indeed, in that Golden Age of Greece more than three centuries before the birth of Christ, *oikeiosis* was seen as the root of almost everything positive. From this center radiated successive circles of love: first for oneself, then for one's children, then for one's family, and finally for the whole human species.

The Stoics added another circle to this progression: love of nature. Thus, self-love became the keystone of their belief that unity with nature was a greater good than obedience to social convention. Self-alienation was seen as destructive far beyond the boundaries of the individual self: it prevented one from honoring the natural world.

But even this thinking came relatively late in written history. Some 2,500 years before the birth of Christ in what is believed to be the first formal book, a priest named Ptahhotep, a sage and prime minister of Egypt, recorded wisdom gathered during his 110 years of life, and its core was: "Follow your heart."

In the same era, Asian religions were exploring an outer circle that extended even beyond nature in radiating out from the self: the universe, the cosmos, the mind of God. The idea that self-knowledge was God-knowledge—that the self was a microcosm of the universe, and that knowing the self was our individual way of knowing the mind of God—was central to the origins of Hinduism, and thus to Buddhism, Sufism, and the many other religions that sprang from it. Self-realization became a goal placed over caste duties, external rules, obedience—everything.

In the Upanishads, dialogues that codified the wisdom of the Vedic period in India from 2500 to 600 B.C., there is one central text from which all else derives: *Tat tvam asi,* "That art Thou," a circular statement that is often translated,

55   "Truth is within us." Instead of creating a hierarchy in which humans were
     placed above nature, and kinds of knowledge were ranked, Vedic teaching de-
     scribed a circle: starting at any point could complete the whole. Thus, *Brahman*
     (the truth discovered objectively through observation) and *Atman* (the truth
     discovered subjectively through introspection) could become one and the same.
60   As scholar Sarvepalli Radhakrishnan summed up the belief at the core of these
     ancient commentaries: "The real which is at the heart of the universe is reflected
     in the infinite depths of the self."
         This quest for universal understanding through self-understanding has
     been misused to create the uncaring, navel-contemplating stereotype of Eastern
65   philosophies. In fact, their turn toward passivity had more to do with the poli-
     tics of poverty and despair superimposed upon them. Even in rich countries, re-
     ligion, psychoanalysis, and self-help theories have been used to justify passivity
     and enshrine external injustices. In many ways, Freud's biological determinism
     is a simpler and more passivity-producing theory than Eastern ideas of a present
70   life set in the context of past lives and the forces of the universe.
         It seems that the older the teaching, the more it presents self-wisdom and
     self-honor as a source of strength, rebellion, and a kind of meta-democracy—a
     oneness with all living things and with the universe itself. Returning to this con-
     cept of circularity and oneness that preceded patriarchy, racism, class systems,
75   and other hierarchies that ration self-esteem—and that create obedience to ex-
     ternal authority by weakening belief in our natural and internal wisdom—is
     truly a revolution from within.
         "When we realize the universal Self in us," ask the Upanishads defiantly,
     "when and what may anybody fear or worship?"

     —Gloria Steinem, from *Revolution from Within: A Book of Self-Esteem*

## Formation of the Self

There can be no doubt that the self, like everything else in an organism, develops and changes a great deal in the course of life. Its nucleus appears to be what
is experienced as "I" and "me," as distinguished from everything else that is "not
me." This distinction, whatever its primitive basis, is amplified and strength-
5   ened by learning: children find out by investigation that the foot is part of "me"
and the favorite toy is not. As time goes on, "myself" assumes a fuller and richer
meaning. It is compounded of bodily sensations, feelings, the image of one's
body, the sound of one's name, the continuity of one's memories, all leading to
the experience of oneself as a unique and separate person having a continuous
10   existence. Particularly important is the feeling of activity and initiative. One's
self is experienced not only as an object but as an agent. This feeling of activity,
whatever its nature, is a highly characteristic feature of the ego system. In experiments using hypnotism it is possible to divest behavior temporarily of the feeling of active participation. It is then experienced as occurring of its own accord,
15   and the experience is indeed a curious one.

Around this enduring nucleus are presently gathered many accretions. Awareness of oneself and knowledge about oneself are heavily influenced by social interaction. A child builds up his sense of self out of the responses made to him by other people; through their acts and attitudes he learns how they perceive him and is influenced to perceive himself in the same way. This process can be observed in bald form when parents apply adjectives to children and children begin to apply them to each other. The child's knowledge that he is strong, naughty, smart, or silly becomes formulated to a considerable extent through the labels applied by others. Gardner Murphy describes the situation as follows:

> Children are forever classifying one another by the use of good and bad names, applying to one another the nouns and adjectives which they have heard used in such a tone as to make them appropriate for praising or damning. . . . Most of the trait names that are used represent general action tendencies; and as soon as they are applied to oneself, or as soon as one finds himself applying them to others, they stimulate a trait psychology in their user. . . . Generalities are evoked by means of labels; the child lives up to the terms employed. . . . The child forms general ideas about himself. *In short, the self becomes less and less a pure perceptual object, and more and more a conceptual trait system.*[1]

These accretions to the enduring nucleus of the self are subject to continuous change. The pattern is formed and reformed many times in the course of life. You may remember but little of what you were like as a child, though you do remember it as *your* childhood continuous with your life today. You may remember more clearly yourself as a high-school sophomore, though only with a pleasant sense that you are not like that any more. A less sympathetic observer might point out more continuities than you would care to admit, but certainly you are not just the same from year to year. A particularly large reworking occurs at adolescence, when family membership weakens and social acceptability becomes a more vital attribute of self. In the course of time the pattern of selfhood becomes more stable. In this it is assisted by social pressure. "With age and greater responsibility, the individual organism is persuaded more and more to act like a unit, to phrase the multiplicity and incongruity of its wants in terms of the multiple expressions of a fixed self."[2] It is easier to live with others when they function as unified selves, and we encourage them to do so. The self is thus shaped into a unity from both directions at once. On the one hand it is attached to the enduring nucleus represented by one's sense of personal identity. On the other hand its various accretions are pressed toward unity by the requirements of social living.

—Robert W. White, from *The Abnormal Personality*

---

1. G. Murphy, *Personality: A Biosocial Approach to Origins and Structure* (New York: Harper & Row, 1947), pp. 505–6.

2. *Ibid.*, p. 489.

*And is it not true that even the small step of a glimpse through the micro-
scope reveals to us images which we should deem fantastic and overimagina-
tive if we were to see them somewhere accidentally, and lacked the sense to
understand them?*

—Paul Klee

The self has been defined as "simply that which knows and wills and feels." As
such it is not a thing of which we can be aware, even by introspection. "I am
quite unable to convince myself," writes Professor Paton, the author of the definition I have just quoted,

5      that introspection ever takes place at all. I can observe a color, I can even
       perhaps observe a table, but what I cannot observe is my act of seeing or
       observing. I can remember, but I cannot observe remembering; I can think,
       but I cannot observe thinking. I can also will, and I can distinguish between
       voluntary and involuntary movement of my body but, curiously enough, in
10     spite of the utmost efforts to do so, I have never been able to observe will-
       ing. In all cases of attempted introspection I seem to find myself observing
       not a mental activity but the object to which it is directed or by which it is
       accompanied.

And Professor Paton concludes that

15     we have no direct or relatively immediate acquaintance with a special object or
       fact called the self which is capable of being observed in isolation from other
       objects as sound or color can be said to be observed in isolation from other
       objects.

And yet, at some stage in human development, man conceived the idea of a
20   self, of a distinct personal identity, and made this self an object of pride, an object to be exhibited as separate, and valued for its separateness, its distinctive-
ness, its eccentricity. How did this awareness of a self come about; how was it
isolated from the continuity and wholeness of experience which is characteristic
of man as an animal and as a member of a social group?

25     The philosopher's answer to this question is somewhat tautological. Professor Paton, for example, who will not admit (rightly, in my opinion) that we can
have any knowledge of the self by immediate observation, or introspection,
substitutes words like "reflection" or "inference" which are logically, or philo-
sophically, more exact, but which do not give us much idea of the genetic
30   process involved. "The distinction between self and objects or the consciousness of objects as objects arises . . . only from a self which has reflected. It is by
reflection that the self makes itself a self and makes its objects objects." But
there is no clear definition of this key word, "reflection"—it is just the activity
by means of which we become aware of the distinctions between subject and

object, the knowing and the known, and in spite of his protest to the contrary, it   35
seems to me that Professor Paton is merely introducing the idea of introspection
under another name.

The distinction he tries to make between these two terms is based on the
definitions of another British philosopher, Samuel Alexander, who held that
the *awareness* involved in the relation between subject and object, between the   40
knowing and the known, was one of enjoyment. Self-knowledge is, according
to Professor Paton, this kind of awareness—it is a primitive feeling of enjoyment
of which we become conscious by dwelling on it:

> To say that a mind enjoys itself and contemplates its objects is to describe not a
> primitive unreflective experience but a highly developed and reflective experi-   45
> ence. The distinction between self and objects or the consciousness of objects
> as objects arises . . . only from a self that has reflected. . . . The self is not a self
> till it is self-conscious. And there are no objects until they are distinguished
> from the self.

I will leave aside for the moment the problem of what is happening   50
in the mind in the intermediate or transitive stages between one reflective
experience and another—there is, for example, an anticipatory state of consciousness which is the intention-to-reflect. We speak of "absence of mind,"
of gaps in consciousness. As William James observed, "there are innumerable
consciousnesses of emptiness no one of which taken in itself has a name,   55
but all different from each other. The ordinary way is to assume that they
are emptiness of consciousness, and so the same state. But the feeling of
an absence is *toto coelo* other than the absence of a feeling." In other words,
there are perceptions which never become articulate to the conscious mind,
and these too, we must assume, are an essential part of the self. Is it possible   60
that one of the functions of art is to bring these inarticulate perceptions into
consciousness?

—Herbert Read, from *Icon and Idea*

# *Linked Readings*

### Anonymous
### THE BABY BOOMER

### Saint Augustine of Hippo
### AS A BABY

The Baby Boomer pictured here is anonymous, as is the author of her horoscope. The
most famous books by Saint Augustine (A.D. 354–430) are *Confessions* and *City of God*.
Baptized at age thirty-three, he gave up his old life as a professor of rhetoric and

returned to his native Africa, where he became a leading bishop and spent the rest of his life. Together, these two pieces provide opportunities for critical thinking by producing a new context in which to view the major themes of freedom and determinism addressed by the authors.

# THE BABY BOOMER

## *Looking Ahead*

1. Whenever photographs accompany texts, it is necessary to perceive the relationship between them, which is not always mere illustration or explanation. Here, a critical view will uncover a logical relationship more complex than these.
2. Even if you have never read a horoscope before, you will notice in this one details that seem a little too particular and, for that reason, are unsettling.
3. Notice the difference between this use of horoscopes to cover birthdays and the use meant to guide the reader on a daily basis.

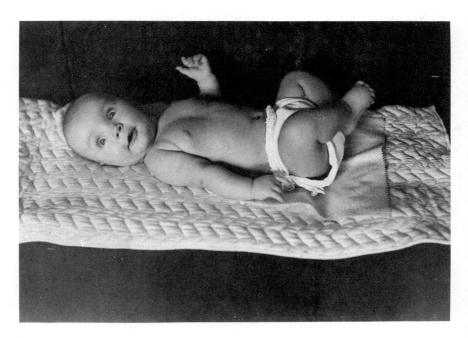

Welcome to the world! You've come a long way and arrived at just the right moment. The stars foretell that, as an adult, your life will be a busy one, full of domestic joys and high achievement in a professional career of your choosing. You may not reap the greatest financial rewards, but others in your field will recognize your indisputable merit and respect you for it (though you should decide against getting that tattoo on your ankle and not wear more than one earring in each ear). Before you enter a demanding career, however, you will have to guard against certain tendencies that often surface in babies born on this day. These are skipping breakfast, making trains with no time to spare, and reading too many books at once. If you can break these habits, your life will be orderly    10 and satisfying.

## AS A BABY

### *Looking Ahead*

1. Because the so-called sinfulness of babies is an unusual concept to many people, you should search carefully to discover Saint Augustine's views on this matter.
2. Try to find the connection between the author's critical approach to babies and his praise of God, testing his reasoning for its basic assumptions.
3. As you read, notice Saint Augustine's effective use of **rhetorical questions**—questions not intended to produce a reply but, rather, to impress the reader with their importance.

Hear me, O God! How wicked are the sins of men! Men say this and you pity them, because you made man, but you did not make sin in him.

Who can recall to me the sins I committed as a baby? For in your sight no man is free from sin, not even a child who has lived only one day on earth. Who can show me what my sins were? Some small baby in whom I can see all that I    5 do not remember about myself? What sins, then, did I commit when I was a baby myself? Was it a sin to cry when I wanted to feed at the breast? I am too old now to feed on mother's milk, but if I were to cry for the kind of food suited to my age, others would rightly laugh me to scorn and remonstrate with me. So then too I deserved a scolding for what I did; but since I could not have under-    10 stood the scolding, it would have been unreasonable, and most unusual, to rebuke me. We root out these faults and discard them as we grow up, and this is proof enough that they are faults, because I have never seen a man purposely throw out the good when he clears away the bad. It can hardly be right for a child, even at that age, to cry for everything, including things which would    15 harm him; to work himself into a tantrum against people older than himself and not required to obey him; and to try his best to strike and hurt others who know better than he does, including his own parents, when they do not give in to him and refuse to pander to whims which would only do him harm. This shows that, if babies are innocent, it is not for lack of will to do harm, but for lack of    20 strength.

I have myself seen jealousy in a baby and know what it means. He was not old enough to talk, but whenever he saw his foster-brother at the breast, he would grow pale with envy. This much is common knowledge. Mothers and

25  nurses say that they can work such things out of the system by one means or another, but surely it cannot be called innocence, when the milk flows in such abundance from its source, to object to a rival desperately in need and depending for his life on this one form of nourishment? Such faults are not small or unimportant, but we are tender-hearted and bear with them because we know

30  that the child will grow out of them. It is clear that they are not mere peccadilloes, because the same faults are intolerable in older persons.

You, O Lord my God, gave me my life and my body when I was born. You gave my body its five senses; you furnished it with limbs and gave it its proper proportions; and you implanted in it all the instincts necessary for the welfare

35  and safety of a living creature. For these gifts you command me to acknowledge you and *praise you and sing in honour of your name,* because you are Almighty God, because you are good, and because I owe you praise for these things, even if you had done nothing else. No one but you can do these things, because you are the one and only mould in which all things are cast and the perfect form which shapes all things, and everything takes its place according to your law.

40  

I do not remember that early part of my life, O Lord, but I believe what other people have told me about it and from watching other babies I can conclude that I also lived as they do. But, true though my conclusions may be, I do not like to think of that period as part of the same life I now lead, because it is

45  dim and forgotten and, in this sense, it is no different from the time I spent in my mother's womb. But if *I was born in sin and guilt was with me already when my mother conceived me,* where, I ask you, Lord, where or when was I, your servant, ever innocent? But I will say no more about that time, for since no trace of it remains in my memory, it need no longer concern me.

## *Looking Back*

1. What immediate, general impression of babies do you get from the photograph accompanying the Baby Boomer horoscope?

2. When you look back at your baby pictures in the family album, how (other than in a physical sense) do they contrast with your present sense of yourself?

3. Do you think it would be helpful to be given at birth a set of warnings like those expressed in the horoscope? Why or why not?

4. How do the various elements of the Baby Boomer's horoscope cohere in a unified prediction, or if they fail to, how do they fall apart?

5. Can you gauge the effect of Saint Augustine's peppering God with questions (lines 3–7)?

6. Do you agree with Saint Augustine that "We root out these faults and discard them as we grow up" (line 12), or do you think we do not essentially change as we grow up? Explain your answer.

7. What is his view of a baby's innocence?

8. Does his claim that babies can be jealous ring true to you? Explain your answer.

9. How does his praise of God bear on his ideas about babyhood (lines 32–40)?

10. Do you think he is right to dismiss a past time (here his babyhood) because he can barely remember it? Explain your answer.

## Writing Assignments (Linked Readings)

1. Who we are in actuality is often more clearly disclosed to us when we consider other possibilities—identities we might have had but do not, directions we might have gone in but did not, roles we might have played in life but will not. Imagining these unrealized versions of our lives, we can isolate our real self for examination. We can conceive of it the way it is and become newly conscious of its value to us. Referring when it is useful to do so to the Baby Boomer and Saint Augustine, write an essay in which you try to say who you are and how you like being yourself. Do so, as suggested above, by presenting other possible versions of your self, contrasting your situation with them, and weighing the merits and defects of the self—your own—that emerges. Regard your audience as one that has never met you before and that therefore needs a full explanation.

2. The Baby Boomer's horoscope and Saint Augustine's views on babyhood make us think about the freedom to choose and change and about the claim that we are born innocent and will remain so until proven guilty by the acts of our life. How do these conceptions relate to these authors to give us a sense of how the self is formed? Based on your own experience, write an essay interpolating your views of how the self is formed in order to comment at length on both the Baby Boomer and Saint Augustine.

3. The Baby Boomer's horoscope and Saint Augustine's meditation address, in different ways, the moral capacity of children. If we agree that children have a moral sense, the question arises for adults of justifying "orders and prohibitions" that they give to children. Should adults make a practice of explaining their directions? Address this issue by writing an essay in which you attempt to say how much moral judgment children probably have, and therefore how much explanation adults owe them, as well as what, if anything, they should explain. Refer in your essay to the readings and to your own memories of childhood.

## Writing Assignments (Individual Readings)
### THE BABY BOOMER

Horoscopes appearing in newspapers and magazines are widely consulted by the general public. Many people believe implicitly that their predictions are accurate and useful. Even people who do not think so can hardly stop themselves from sneaking a look at theirs when they happen on it. Yet, despite its popularity, critics shake their heads over astrology, claiming it is superstitious to believe in it. What is your view of astrology and the practical use of horoscopes? Write an essay expressing your general opinion on the subject. Refer to the Baby Boomer's photograph and text, and find another example of a horoscope—perhaps one specifying astrological data—for examination and comparison.

## AS A BABY

Saint Augustine's ideas about natal innocence, or the lack thereof, remind us that childhood may be regarded as at least as serious and responsible a time of life as adulthood. The sins of newborns may be nonexistent, but it *is* possible to interpret certain tendencies in children as early signs of character faults. If these are not corrected, the theory runs, they will follow into adult life and complicate it unnecessarily for the person and for others. Accepting this view—that early behavior problems are not necessarily innocent but may be the precursors of adult trouble—we may try to raise children in a totally disciplined manner. But some argue that full-scale discipline destroys a child's developing imagination, initiative, and freedom. The child will not be able to form his or her own identity but will be forced to adopt someone else's idea of a proper self. No doubt, given the bad practical consequences of going to either extreme, it is possible to strike a balance between severity and permissiveness. Referring to Saint Augustine's views, write an essay in which you strike such a balance, saying how much freedom and discipline a child needs, in what areas of life these should exist, and how early in life such training should start.

# Camara Laye

# I Was Very Young

Born in French Guinea in 1928, Camara Laye was sent to France by his tribe, while in his mid-twenties, to study engineering. There, in 1954, he published *The Dark Child,* an autobiographical memoir in which "I Was Very Young" is one chapter. Several of Laye's memories reveal the biased points of view of the characters, including Laye himself. Although he stops short of expressing judgments on these biases, the fact that he presents them at all shows an underlying critical aim to reexamine the situation from which they arose. His nonfiction work *A Dream of Africa* appeared in 1971.

## Looking Ahead

1. As you read, compare your own elementary school education with Laye's in order to appreciate the distinct character of his.

2. In a number of ways, a child's experience, however limited, reflects the development of human societies and cultures. A critical reading will reveal signs of that universality here.

3. You may find it useful to form your own critical ideas of the proper social environment for early school life.

I was very young when I began school, first attending the Koran school,[1] and, shortly afterwards, transferring to the French. Neither my mother nor I had the slightest suspicion how long I would be a student in the latter. Had she known, I am sure she would have kept me at home. Perhaps my father knew already.

Immediately after breakfast my sister and I would start out, carrying our books and notebooks in a raffia satchel. On the way we would be joined by our friends, and the closer we got to school the more of us there would be. My sister walked with the girls, I stayed with the boys. Like all young boys we loved to tease the girls, but they gave as good as they got, and when we pulled their hair they fought back, scratching and biting us, although this did not dampen our enthusiasm noticeably. There was, however, a truce between my sister and myself; her friend, Fanta, also let me alone, but I did not return the compliment.

One day when we were alone in the school yard, she asked me, "Why do you pull my hair?"

"Because you're a girl."

"I don't pull yours."

I stopped to think for a moment. Only then did I realize that she was the only one, with the exception of my sister, who didn't.

"Well, why don't you?" I asked.

"Because!"

"Because! What kind of an answer's that?"

"I wouldn't hurt you, no matter what."

"Well, I'm going to pull *your* hair."

But then it seemed foolish to do it when none of my classmates was around. She burst into laughter when I did not carry out my threat.

"You just wait until school's out," I threatened.

But again I did not make good my threat. Something restrained me, and from then on I rarely bothered her. My sister was not long in noticing this.

"I don't see you pulling Fanta's hair," she said.

"Why should I? She leaves me alone."

"Yes, I've noticed."

"Then, why should I?"

"Oh, I don't know. I thought there might be some other reason."

What was she getting at? I shrugged my shoulders. Girls were crazy; all girls were.

"Oh, Fanta makes me sick," I said. "And you make me sick too."

She only laughed at me.

"Now, you watch out," I said. "If you don't stop laughing—"

She avoided my grasp and shouted from a distance: "Fanta! Fanta!"

"Oh, shut up."

She paid no attention to me, and I rushed at her.

"Fanta! Fanta!"

---

1. *Koran school:* Islamic parochial school. (*ed.*)

Unfortunately I couldn't find a stone to throw at her, but I made a resolution to take care of that matter later.

Once at school, we went straight to our seats, boys and girls side by side, their quarrels over. So motionless and attentive did we sit, that it would have been wonderful to see what would have happened had we stirred. Our teacher moved like quicksilver, here, there, everywhere. His flow of talk would have bewildered less attentive pupils; but we were extraordinarily attentive. Young though we were, we regarded our school work as a deadly serious matter. Nothing that we learned was old or expected; all came as though from another planet, and we never tired of listening. But even if we had wearied, this omnipresent teacher would never have given us an opportunity to interrupt. Interruption was out of the question; the idea did not even occur to us. We wanted to be noticed as little as possible, for we lived in continual dread of being sent to the blackboard.

This was our nightmare. The blackboard's blank surface was an exact replica of our minds. We knew little, and the little that we knew came out haltingly. The slightest thing could inhibit us. When we were called to the blackboard we had to take the chalk and really work, if we were to avoid a beating. The smallest detail was of the utmost importance, and the blackboard magnified everything. If we made one downward stroke not precisely of the same height as the others, we were required to do extra lessons on Sunday, or were sent during recess to the first grade for a caning—a caning, I should add, one did not easily forget. Irregular downward strokes made our teacher furious. He examined our exercises under a magnifying glass, and dealt out his blows accordingly. He was indeed quicksilver, and he wielded his rod with joyous *élan*.

This was how things were in the primary grades. There were fewer beatings in the upper classes; other kinds of punishment, no more pleasant, took their place. I underwent a vast variety of punishments in that school, and only one thing did not vary—my anguish. One's love of knowledge had to be very strong to survive these ordeals.

For second-year students, the customary punishment was sweeping the school yard. It was then that we comprehended how truly spacious that yard was, what an enormous number of guava trees it possessed. It seemed to us certain that the trees had been planted there for the specific purpose of littering the ground, for certainly we never received any of the fruit. In the third and fourth years our punishment was to work in the kitchen garden; and it would have been difficult to find cheaper labor. During our last two years, the school authorities had such confidence in us—a confidence, I might add, we would have gladly forgone—that we were entrusted with the herd of cattle which belonged to the school.

This last task was no sinecure.[2] The herd we tended was famous for miles around. Did a farmer have a vicious cow, it inevitably ended up in our herd.

---

2. *sinecure:* paid position that requires no work. (*ed.*)

There was a good reason for this; the farmer, desperate to be rid of the beast,    85
would accept almost any price, and the school authorities were only too anxious to take advantage of such a windfall. So the real reason was stinginess, and
the result was that our school owned the most complete collection of sly, ornery
creatures in existence. When we cried out, "Right!" it was just natural for them
to veer left.
                                                                                   90
   The way they galloped about in the bush, it seemed as if a swarm of flies
were constantly irritating them. We galloped after them, incredible distances.
They were always much more intent on wandering off, or battling among themselves, than foraging for food. However, their picturesque behavior was no pleasure to us. We knew that, on our return, the school authorities would carefully    95
survey their bellies to see how well they had eaten. And woe to us should the
stomachs of those raw-boned creatures not be full.
   But heaven help us indeed, should a single head be missing from this, the
devil's own herd. We would return home at nightfall, exhausted, since we had
to whip them into a lather in order to get them to move at all in the right direc-  100
tion. This, of course, did not improve the dispositions of these fantastic animals.
To make up for their not having eaten very much, we would gorge them with
water. Footsore, we would appear with the entire herd. We would not have
dared come back without every one of them. The consequences would have
been too dreadful.
                                                                                   105
   That's how it was with our teachers—at any rate, when things were at their
worst—and it is understandable enough that we could scarcely wait to finish
school and receive that famous certificate of studies which proclaimed us
"learned." And yet it seems that as yet I have scarcely said anything about the
dark side of our school life, since the worst was what the older pupils made us    110
younger ones suffer. These older students—I can not call them "comrades"
since they were older and stronger than we, and less strictly supervised—persecuted us in every conceivable way. They were a haughty lot, and with reason,
since no doubt they were repaying the treatment they had themselves received:
Excessively harsh treatment is not precisely the best method of inculcating        115
kindness.
   I remember—my hands and fingertips can not forget—what lay in store for
us when we returned to school after vacation. The guava trees in the yard would
be in leaf again and last year's leaves would be strewn about the ground in scattered heaps. In places there would be great piles of them.
                                                                                   120
   "Sweep these up," the director would say. "This yard must be cleaned
immediately."
   Immediately! And there was enough work there, damnable work, for more
than a week. There was more work than there should have been, since the only
tools we had were our hands—our hands, and our fingers, and our fingernails.      125
   "Now, be quick about it," the director would say to the older students, "or
you'll be hearing from me."
   At an order from the older boys, we would line up like peasants about to
reap a field, but we did not work like peasants; we worked like galley slaves.

130   This in a school yard! There were open spaces between the guava trees, but
      there was also a place where the guava trees grew so close together that their
      branches intertwined. Here the sun did not penetrate, and the acrid odor of de-
      cay lingered when the weather was fine.
          Even when the work was not proceeding as quickly as the director had or-
135   dered, the older boys refused to help. They considered it easier to pull branches
      from the trees with which to beat us. Guava wood is extremely flexible, and
      when skillfully handled the whips whistled as they moved through the air;
      our backs felt as though they were on fire. Our flesh smarted, and tears fell from
      our eyes.
140       There was only one way to avoid these blows, and that was to bribe our
      tyrants with the lunches we had brought from home; the savory cakes of Indian
      corn, the wheat, the *couscous* made of meat or fish. If we had any money, that
      also changed hands. Anyone who refused to give up his lunch, mindful of his
      empty stomach, found himself the recipient of a dreadful beating. It was admin-
145   istered so violently, in such a diabolical rhythm, that even a deaf man would
      have understood that these blows were given not to speed up the work but to
      extort food and money.
          Occasionally one of us, worn out by the deliberate cruelty, would dare to
      complain to the director. The director would become very angry, but the pun-
150   ishment he inflicted on the culprits was nothing compared to what they had ad-
      ministered. At any rate, our complaints did nothing to remedy the situation.
      Possibly it would have been wiser to have informed our parents of what we
      were undergoing, but somehow or other this never occurred to us. Perhaps we
      remained silent because of pride, or because of loyalty to the school. I know
155   now that whatever the reason, it was stupid of us to keep silent. Such beatings
      were utterly alien to my people's passion for independence and equality.
          One day, one of my playmates, Kouyaté Karmoko, having been the recipi-
      ent of a particularly brutal beating, declared that he had had enough of this sort
      of thing. Kouyaté was extremely small and thin—so small that we joked that he
160   must have the stomach of a bird, that is, a gizzard. One thing is certain, whether
      Kouyaté was the owner of a gizzard or some other form of stomach, he put very
      little into it. He cared only for fruit, and at lunch was satisfied if he were able to
      trade his *couscous* for guavas and oranges. This minimum even he required, and
      it was obvious that, if he were forced to give up his fruit, he would inevitably
165   have to turn in his gizzard for something smaller, perhaps the stomach of an in-
      sect. This did not bother the older boys; their insistent demands forced Kouyaté
      into a rigorous period of fasting. That day, hunger, in combination with the
      welts on his buttocks, made him rebel.
          "I've taken all I intend to," he sniffled through his tears. "I'm going to tell
170   my father."
          "It won't do you any good to make a fuss," I said.
          "You really don't think it will?"
          "Don't forget that the older boys—"
          But he would not let me finish.

"I don't care—I'm going to tell him," he shouted at the top of his voice.    175
"For heaven's sake, keep your voice down."

He was my best friend, and I was afraid that this outburst would only earn
him another beating.

"You know my father—you know he'll do something."

I knew Kouyaté's father well; he was one of the most respected praise-    180
singers in the district. Although he no longer practiced his profession, he had a
special standing in the community—a sort of scholar and praise-singer emeritus. There was no house that was not open to him.

"Kouyaté, your father's an old man."

"A very strong man," he replied proudly, drawing his thin little body up to    185
its full height.

"You're being stupid," I warned him.

He left off whining, and I finished the conversation by telling him to do as
he pleased.

The next day, no sooner had Kouyaté arrived at the school yard than he    190
went over to Himourana, the boy who had thrashed him so brutally the day
before.

"My father is most anxious to meet the upper form boy who has been kindest to me. I thought of you at once. Can you come to dinner this evening?"

"I'll be happy to," Himourana said.    195

Himourana's brutality was only matched by his stupidity. He was probably
a glutton as well.

And that evening, sure enough, the dunce showed up at Kouyaté's concession. One of the most sturdily built in Kouroussa, it had only one gate, and the
wall around it, instead of being made of reeds, was constructed of masonry with    200
pieces of broken glass strewn along the top. One entered or left it only by permission of the master of the house. That evening Kouyaté's father came to open
the gate in person, and, when Himourana had entered it, it was carefully bolted
behind him.

"Do sit down," said Kouyaté's father. "Our whole family is expecting you."    205

Himourana glanced quickly at the cooking utensils, which seemed to
promise a most satisfactory meal, and sat down in the yard. He prepared himself for the compliments that were about to be addressed to him. And then
Kouyaté arose.

"Father," he said, pointing at the guest. "That's the one who always takes    210
my food and money."

"Now, now, Kouyaté, that's not a nice thing to say," his father replied. "Are
you sure you're telling the truth?" And he turned to Himourana. "Young man,
you hear what my son has said? What do you have to say in your defense? Do
speak quickly. I don't have too much time to give you, but I don't want to be    215
ungenerous."

It was as if a thunderbolt had dropped at Himourana's feet. He couldn't understand a word of what was being said. He thought only of fleeing, which
would have been a reasonable enough idea if there had not been that wall. One

220    had to be as big a boob as Himourana to attempt to put the idea into execution. He was caught before he had taken ten steps.

    "Now, get this into your head," Kouyaté's father said. "I am not sending my son to school for you to make a slave out of him."

225    And then Himourana found himself raised aloft by his arms and legs and held extended, while Kouyaté's father gave him a sound thrashing. Shamefaced, his rear end aflame, he was then permitted to go.

    The next day at school the story of Himourana's punishment spread like wildfire. It created a scandal. Never before had such a thing happened, and we could scarcely believe that it had happened. All of us younger boys felt that

230    Kouyaté's father had avenged us. The upshot was that the older boys held a meeting and decided that Kouyaté and his sister, Mariama, were to be ostracized. The edict was extended to us younger students—we also were not to talk to our playmate. However, we noted that they were very careful not to touch either Kouyaté or his sister, and even the stupidest of us was aware that they were afraid. An era

235    had ended, we sensed, and we prepared to breathe the air of liberty.

    At noon I went up to Kouyaté, having decided to defy our oppressors.

    "Be careful," he said. "You know what's likely to happen."

    "Oh, to hell with them."

    I gave him the oranges I had brought for lunch.

240    "Do go away. I'm afraid they'll beat you."

    I had no time to answer. Several of them were coming toward us, and I hesitated, unable to decide whether to run or not. I made my decision, and suddenly I felt their blows upon me. Then I ran, and didn't stop until I had come to the other end of the school yard. I cried as much from anger as from pain.

245    When I had left off crying, I found Fanta sitting next to me.

    "What are you doing here?"

    "I've brought you a wheat-cake."

    I took it and ate it almost without noticing what I was eating, although Fanta's mother was famous for making the best wheat-cakes in the district.

250    When I had finished I went and drank some water and washed my face. Then I returned and sat down again.

    "I don't like you to sit beside me when I'm crying," I said.

    "Were you crying? I didn't notice."

    I looked at her. She was lying. Obviously to spare my pride. I smiled at her.

255    "Do you want another wheat-cake?" she asked.

    "No, I'm too angry. Doesn't it make you angry, too?"

    "Yes," and her eyes filled with tears.

    "I hate them!" I cried. "You can't imagine how I hate them. Do you know what I'm going to do? I'm going to quit school. I'm going to grow up fast, and

260    then I'm going to come back. And for every beating I've received, I'm going to pay them back with a thousand."

    She stopped crying and looked at me admiringly.

    That evening I sought out my father under the veranda.

"Father, I don't want to go to school any more."

"What?"

"No," I said.

But by this time the scandal had gone the rounds of the concessions in Kouroussa.

"What's going on in that school?" my father asked.

"I'm afraid of the older boys."

"I thought you weren't afraid of anyone."

"I'm afraid of them."

"What do they do to you?"

"They take away our money and eat our lunches."

"Do they? And they whip you?"

"Yes."

"Yes, I'll have a word with those bullies tomorrow. So that's what's up?"

The next day my father and his apprentices accompanied me to school, and they stood with me at the school door. Each time one of the older boys passed, my father asked, "Is that one of them?"

"No," I answered, although there were many among them who had beaten and robbed me. But I was waiting for one boy in particular, the one who had treated me most savagely. When I saw him I cried out, "There's the worst of all."

Without further ado, the apprentices threw themselves on him and stripped him bare. They handled him so roughly that my father had to come to his rescue.

"The director and I are going to have a chat about you," he said. "What I want to find out is whether you bigger fellows are here for any other reason than to beat up the smaller boys and steal their money."

That day the business of not speaking to Kouyaté or his sister ended. They played with us, and none of the older boys attempted to interfere. They did not even seem to notice us. Was a new era beginning? It seemed so. The older boys kept to themselves; it seemed almost, since we were the more numerous, that they were the ones who were being ostracized. That they were none too pleased with the way things were going was evident. And certainly they were in none too happy a situation. Up to now their parents had been unaware of their nasty practices. If the parents were informed—and there was a very good chance that everything would become public—the culprits could expect only scoldings and punishments.

When school was recessed that afternoon, my father arrived. As he had said he would, he went immediately to the director who was in the yard with the other teachers. Without bothering to say: "Good-day," my father asked, "do you have any idea what's going on in this school?"

"Why, of course I do," the director answered. "Everything's proceeding as it should."

"Then the older boys are supposed to whip the younger ones and steal their money? Are you blind, or is that really your intention?"

"Why don't you stay out of what doesn't concern you?"

"Doesn't concern me? Is it no concern of mine that my son is treated like a
310  slave?"

"It most certainly is not."

"That you shouldn't have said!"

And my father marched closer to the director.

"Now I suppose I'm to be beaten the way your apprentices beat one of my
315  students this morning," said the director.

He put up his fists. He was a strong man but quite fat, and my father, who
was slender and quick, would have had no trouble with him at all. In fact, he
did knock him down, but the assistants pulled them apart before the thing
really got under way.

320  The director stood feeling his jaw and saying nothing; and my father, having dusted himself off, took me by the hand and led me from the yard. I walked
proudly beside him to our concession. But later I felt much less proud, when,
walking by myself in the city, I heard people say as I passed, "Look! There's the
boy whose father beat up the director in the school yard."

325  This was not at all comparable to the incident in which Kouyaté's father
had been involved. This was a scandal, occurring as it had in the presence of the
teachers and students, and with the director as the principal victim. No, it was
not at all like the other, and it seemed to me lucky if it should end with no more
than my being expelled from school. I hurried back to my father.

330  "Why did you have to fight with him? I'll never be able to go back again!"

"But that's what you want! Didn't you say so yourself?" And my father
laughed loudly.

"I don't see anything to laugh about."

"Sleep well, little dunce. If we don't hear the put-put of a certain motor-
335  cycle at our gates by tomorrow, I shall complain to the district administration."

There was no need to make this complaint. The next day, sure enough, the
director's motorcycle drove up to our gate. He came in, and my father, as well as
the rest, greeted him amiably: "Good evening, sir."

A chair was offered the guest, and he and my father sat down. At a motion
340  from the latter we withdrew and watched from a distance. Their conversation
appeared to be friendly, and evidently it was, for from that time on, my sister
and I experienced no further horrors at school.

Yet, for all that, the scandal was not hushed up. A few months later the director was forced to resign because of a petition signed by all of the parents. The
345  rumor had gotten about that he was using some of the students as houseboys
for the convenience of his wives. These students had been boarded with him by
their parents so that they might receive special attention, and their board had
been paid for with cattle. I don't know if anything further came of it. All I know
is that it was the straw that broke the camel's back, and that we were never
350  again bullied by the older boys.

## Looking Back

1. From Laye's day to our own, what has changed regarding school discipline?
2. What does Laye mean by referring to his teacher as "quicksilver" (lines 48 and 68)?
3. Would you say the school exploited the students' labor, or were students being given an opportunity to take responsibility for their own environment? Explain your answer.
4. Is it a good idea for agricultural duties to be part of the curriculum, as they were of Laye's? Why or why not?
5. The "tribute" Laye and his young schoolmates pay to placate the older boys also figures, on a grander scale, in the history of nations. What does this practice say about history?
6. How do you understand Laye's statement, in lines 155–156, that "Such beatings were utterly alien to my people's passion for independence and equality"?
7. How does Fanta's obvious affection for young Camara reflect a maturity beyond her years?
8. Do you think a father's intervening to settle his child's disputes helps the child in the long run? Explain your answer.
9. Does Laye's style of writing, plain and unembellished, contribute to or detract from this piece? Refer to the text to support your answer.
10. What terms would you use to judge the overall quality of life for students at Laye's school?

## Writing Assignments

1. Their early schooling is a topic many autobiographical writers dwell on at some length in their works. They feel that the formative experience of the primary years is crucial to understanding the people they have become. They see that a discernible line can be drawn between what Laye speaks of as "the blank surface" of their minds then and the much-written-on surface of their minds now. Looking back to this time for this purpose makes good sense when we consider what elementary school typically exposes children to and involves them in. Such experiences help form the child's developing self; they helped form Laye's and no doubt they contributed to your own. Extrapolating from Laye, write an essay telling how your early school experiences influenced you. If you can, select a single major trait of your character, and describe the early school experience that you think helped shape it.

2. In the early 1990s, it became more clear than ever to educators that American public schools were not, on the whole, serving their students' needs. Students were not learning and they were not being properly socialized. At the same time, the rising costs of education made the miseducation of students even less tolerable. In response to these conditions, a number of plans for model schools were devised, plans that call for reforms ranging from sharply limiting class size to providing students with telephones and VCRs. These model schools would attempt to be cost-efficient

in such ways as having students help clean the restrooms, classrooms, and corridors to reduce the need for janitorial services. This particular proposal has a precedent in the French school Laye attended. There, however, cleaning was a punishment inflicted on certain students. To make it instead a common duty, especially in hard times, is altogether different. It also may raise the following questions: Even if donated labor of this sort would benefit society, isn't it an unfair imposition on students? Can it contribute to the development of students' character? How would it do so? If it would not, what alternative nonacademic activities can you suggest for students that would serve the same end? Referring to Laye's experience, write an essay answering these questions.

3. In this chapter from *The Dark Child,* Laye tells us, "Nothing that we learned was old or expected" (lines 50–51). Although he never tells us how *well* he and his fellow students learned, we begin to wonder if the kind of school environment he describes might possibly have eased their task. The question of proper environment is a crucial one for education. The challenges that real learning poses for students can hardly be met, their need to enter new intellectual territory can barely be satisfied, if the setting is wrong. Write an essay explaining what a proper learning environment would look like. You might take up such general concerns as the physical plant, the decor and architecture of classrooms, class size, teacher-student ratio, and whatever other factors you consider important.

# Catherine S. Manegold

# Crystal

Catherine S. Manegold is a reporter for *The New York Times.* She wrote this piece, which appeared in the *Times,* on April 8, 1993, as one article in a ten-part series entitled "Children of the Shadows." Each article focused on a different young person and attempted to find in the life of its subject a reflection of social conditions as they affect an entire generation. Manegold's detailed investigation of her subject demonstrates the extent to which journalism may go in preparing the ground for further critical thinking. From this article, we can derive a new contextual understanding, putting together a person with different aspects of her environment to enable us to reevaluate both.

## Looking Ahead

1. Although Cavallaro Junior High School, where Crystal is a student, may or may not resemble the school you attended, you should be able to recognize problems that are generally shared.

2. As you read, analyze Crystal's home environment and try to judge its probable effect on her school life.

3. One topic to think about is the threat posed by life on the streets and its impact on teenagers' education.

Crystal Rossi wears two streaks of bright magenta in her hair. They hang, stains of Kool-Aid, down her loose, long strands of blond like a seventh grader's twist of punk: Don't come too close. Don't mess with me. Don't tell me what to do. I'm not like you.

At her Brooklyn public school, a kaleidoscope of teen-age rage, Crystal's   5 teachers see a young girl with an attitude.[1] They focus on her slouch, her Kool-Aid streaks, her grunge clothes and sullen anger and see all the signs of trouble. But those vivid slashes say the most, communicating a basic paradox of adolescence, the double-edged message: "bug off" and "LOOK AT ME."

This is the time, this tender age of 12, when every major decision on the   10 treacherous road to adulthood looms. It is also the time, in the sixth and seventh grades, when some students start a long, slow fall away from school.

On the surface, Crystal hardly seems the sort of child who would stumble.

Her family is stable. Her stepfather works. Her mother takes care of the home. Her father lives just blocks away. Her school is typical, chaotic, under-   15 financed and overcrowded, but it is clean and relatively safe.

But in a competition between the street and her Bensonhurst[2] school, the street seems to be winning.

"The classes are boring!" Crystal exploded one afternoon. "And the teachers are mean!" Her eyes downcast, she complained that too much class time was   20 spent on discipline. "They are always yelling," she said. "I wish they would all just shut up."

Her face to the world is one of toughness. But in fact she is a child trying to navigate a difficult and often lonely road. In a whisper one day, her head cast down and fingers playing across a desk top, she admitted that she was often   25 nervous.

"Sometimes I can't even sleep," she said. "I stay up all night, and then I'm too tired to get up in the morning."

She rarely allows herself to express such vulnerability. Instead, she tends toward bravado; in a rare moment of exuberance she tells her mother that she is   30 a "leader" who sets the pace in school. Her mother does not buy it. "No," her mother says as she shakes her head. "You are a follower."

Such deflations are consistent. What is absent is a quiet, steady voice of encouragement, a single figure to lead Crystal through the minefields of a childhood in Bensonhurst. Pressures abound, applied by teachers, parents and even   35 friends, but Crystal seems without a touchstone to guide her and give her a sense of her potential.

---

1. *attitude:* an "attitude," at least in the New York area, does not require the adjective *bad* to convey the sense of hostility, anger, and irritability. (*ed.*)

2. *Bensonhurst:* a neighborhood in Brooklyn, New York. (*ed.*)

At home, three other daughters occupy her mother's time and worry. Crystal's sister, Colette, 15, is failing the ninth grade. Her halfsisters, Candice, 5, and Jovan, 2, demand attention and dominate family life, especially when their dad comes home and lifts them in a warm embrace. Crystal, lonely and lackluster, hides in plain sight.

Crystal says she wants to be a lawyer. But she has never actually met a lawyer and is now flunking most of her classes. That career appeals because, she says, "you get to talk back to people" and "you make a lot of money."

Her teachers worry that she might not even make it to her high school graduation. They already see the signs. In class she ducks competition and is losing focus. Outside of school hers is a childhood of temptations and dangers: drugs, alcohol, gangs and older kids who linger on street corners wanting everything from sex to the coat off a 12-year-old's back.

There was a fleeting moment when Crystal's academic future seemed full of promise. Her 34-year-old mother, Colleen Ficalora, said Crystal was once slated for a kindergarten for gifted students, "but she would have had to take a bus." Now, in the seventh grade at the Joseph B. Cavallaro Junior High School in Bensonhurst, Crystal is often restless, angry and tuned out.

Mrs. Ficalora wants Crystal to break a family pattern. Not one of her own 14 brothers and sisters graduated from high school. Neither did she. Nor did Crystal's father or stepfather. If Crystal gets her diploma she will stand apart.

At school, some teachers are trying to help. But sitting in one class, a "resource room" tailored to give troubled students individual attention, Crystal slumped on her desk. "We just sit there," she said later. "They are supposed to help you with stuff you don't understand. But I understand everything so I just sit there."

"Kids who study are all nerds," she said dismissively. "Who'd want to be like that? Everybody makes fun of them."

But the kids make fun of one another for failing, too.

"Stoooopid," Crystal taunted a friend in the resource room one morning.

"No, you're stupid, stupid," the girl retorted.

"No. You. You're stupid," Crystal shot back, her head resting on her desk top.

Most days, Crystal says, she is usually happy only at lunch, when she and her friends bend over pizza and sandwiches "just talking." The time brings them together, jostling and punching and trading stories of their day. Sometimes they vanish into a bathroom and plant thick lipstick kisses—perfect O's—on one another's foreheads. Their mark of solidarity against a world too often hostile.

Of the 950 or so students at Cavallaro Junior High School on any given day, says Rose P. Molinelli, the principal, 300 or more are at risk of everything from dropping out to doping up to slashing their wrists and watching their lives literally drain right out of them. One of the school's seventh-grade classes last year had five suicide attempts. This year has been quieter, but the threats remain. 80

"You can walk out this door any afternoon and get hurt," Mrs. Molinelli said as she stooped on a busy stairwell to scoop up a bit of litter. Other pressures are subtler.

"The kids all know who is abused and who is having trouble at home and who is in a gang," Mrs. Molinelli said. "They know who gets high. They know who gets killed. It gets to them. I think all kids today are at risk. And parents are overwhelmed. A lot of kids get lost." 85

Three years ago Cavallaro, on 24th Avenue and Cropsey Avenue, was a place where gangs lurked in hallways and teachers lived in fear. Then Mrs. Molinelli came, the gangs were banished and a new sense of order was imposed. Today the halls are clean and orderly and, unlike the local high school where a metal detector was recently installed to screen out guns and knives, students can move about with a sense of ease and safety. A guard monitors everyone entering and leaving the building, and Mrs. Molinelli herself quizzes every child she finds wandering the hallways during class time. 90 95

Crystal glides through the environment as though untouched. When a fight breaks out in the hall, she slips around the corner. But privately, she whispers about the gangs, the kids who have been robbed or hurt or are threatened by bullies, and of friends with "troubles" at home. 100

"I know a kid who just got shot," she said starkly. "He got shot and he is dead."

Mrs. Molinelli changed the school hours—ending the day a half-hour earlier—to let her students out before the local high school students have a chance to victimize the younger children. Other problems are more intractable. 105

Classes run at or near their maximum of 30 children each, and teachers have to struggle just to keep order, much less provide individual attention. Budget cuts have whittled resources, and although Mrs. Molinelli says her teachers have come up with creative ways to compensate for the shortages, she knows the children could use more. 110

"We're on the edge," she said. "We're already on the edge and now they are talking about more funding cuts. Right now, we've only got one guidance counselor for 700 students. That's not enough."

Crystal's schedule includes one-on-one tutoring in a "rap class" where Cathy Searao, a school drug counselor, spends time talking with troubled students partly as a mentor and partly as a friend. Shrugging, embarrassed and monosyllabic, Crystal says she likes the program because there "the teacher really talks to you." One afternoon Ms. Searao taught Crystal and a friend how to develop film. It was the one moment in her school day when Crystal smiled. She shyly admits that she also enjoys science and a dance program she goes to after school. 115 120

Mrs. Molinelli would like to see more individualized programs in the school. But in the meantime, she fights cutbacks.

125 Crystal's mother wants more from the public school as well. "I feel like I try my hardest," she said, "but I still need someone there education-wise who can back me up."

130 Early on a wintry afternoon, teachers chatted about the bitter cold and a new problem it had spawned. Some students arrived in class wearing ski masks and it was scaring the staff stiff. A warning went out over the public-address system: Henceforth, ski masks were forbidden. It was too unnerving for the teachers not to be able to identify potential assailants.

In science, as a substitute teacher tried to teach the difference between fact and opinion, Crystal spent her time, lipstick in one hand, a mirror in the other, tracing streaks of red along her lips.

135 The toll of her inattention is already becoming all too clear. In the first semester, Crystal passed every major class but science. But as the school year progressed, she started drifting. In September Crystal made her way to class on time on every day but one. In January she was late 12 days out of 20.

140 Her mother says it is a constant battle just to get Crystal up and out. As she and her husband begin the day, the tone is set.

"I start trying to wake her up at 7 A.M.," Mrs. Ficalora said. "By 7:30, I am really screaming."

145 Crystal's February report card included a 65 in social studies. She failed English, math, science, foreign language and physical education. "We have already sent the family an 'at risk' letter," said Diane Costaglioli, the assistant principal in charge of the seventh grade. "She's on a decline."

At home, her mother tells her to do her homework but rarely checks, and her stepfather, Louie Ficolara, an electrician at ABC, rarely asks about it. But together they provide a raft of high-tech toys that keep Crystal occupied but

150 unmotivated.

The basement room she shares with Colette has all the comforts—and distractions—of a fully equipped apartment. "Sometimes my mom punishes me by making me go to my room," Crystal said. "But that's O.K. We've got a television, a VCR, Nintendo, a radio, books, magazines, our own phone line and a bunch

155 of other stuff down there."

Upstairs, there are distractions, too. The television comes on just after Crystal gets home at 3. It stays on well into the night.

Mrs. Ficalora complains that the family is not brought in to the school's daily rhythms. "We don't even have to see the homework," she said. "So we

160 don't know what they're dealing with."

Somehow, though, there has been a breakdown in communication. Last fall, Crystal's school gave each student a homework planner that encouraged parents to be involved in each day's assignment. Crystal says she lost hers and her mother concedes that although she at times helps with homework, she usu-

165 ally is involved only at report-card time.

For Crystal, though, homework can seem almost quaint in a life that whirls through a landscape full of real and perceived dangers. Outside school, her world stretches from glass-strewn lots where friends drink and smash bottles against brick walls to street corners where gang members pick fights. Her friends are an ethnic stew of Italian-Americans, Puerto Ricans, blacks and immigrants—a multiracial bond that in coming years may well be tested.    170

So far, though, they face their fears together. Temptations and highs lurk everywhere. Though Crystal says she has not yet tried marijuana, LSD or crack, she talks about such drugs the way children used to talk of trolls and ice cream cones. Like most of her friends, she has already sampled alcohol and cigarettes.    175 Other temptations await. "Everybody drinks," she said with a knowing shrug. "They drink and do acid in the park."

Crystal knows the varied routes to dropping out. But they do not scare her. "They hang out," she said of the students who leave school. "They do weed. They drink. They do acid. Everybody knows what they are doing."    180

Sex looms, too. So far, boys don't seem to be her problem. Her mother prohibits her from dating. But Crystal points out coolly, "When I'm out there you don't know where I am." Crystal's mother assumes that her 12-year-old can take care of herself. "I let her know that she has an independence," she said.

Yet just surviving is a constant struggle. Teachers, the police and parents    185 say they are often stunned by the casualness of the violence both inside and outside school. Hallways are full of a steady stream of students who sniffle that a friend has hit or kicked them. Students are called from class for fighting. Friends poke, trip and slap.

On the streets, fights start over nothing. Many boys link up with gangs.    190 Crystal lists their names, neighborhood by neighborhood, including two for girls, Bitches on a Mission, and the Five Million Hoodlums, to which some of her friends belong. "They can protect you," Crystal said somewhat admiringly. "They can keep you safe."

But it is toward her sister Colette that Crystal most often turns for protec-    195 tion. "She watches out for me," she said. "If somebody bothers me, she sends people after them."

Colette may be failing, but she has another quality that Crystal values far more than grades. She is the one older person who always listens—and never punishes.    200

Still, anxiety pervades. "I'm always nervous," she said quietly one day at school, her head cast down, her hands clasped tightly between her legs. "I get nervous over nothing. And then I'll get a really big headache."

One moment of ease comes in the minutes between school and life after school. When the last bell rings, Crystal and her friends linger outside the    205 building to remind one another that they care. Linking arms and passing gum and cigarettes around, they laugh and poke and share their secrets, their fears, their triumphs. Then they reach forward, one to the next, to kiss, almost somberly, and wish one another well.

## Looking Back

1. From the first three paragraphs, what sense do you get of Crystal as a person?

2. Based on your experience, are Crystal's complaints about school (see lines 19–22) justified? Explain your answer.

3. How might having at least one high school graduate in her family affect a person like Crystal?

4. Does Crystal appear to you too intelligent or not intelligent enough to do well in her school? Explain your answer.

5. What does the number of "at risk" students tell you about Cavallaro Junior High School?

6. Although we aren't told why the students who attempted suicide did so, what educated guesses can you make about their reasons? How do your answers contribute to a general sense of the teenage life Crystal shares?

7. How do you reconcile the claim that the school halls are "clean and orderly" (line 92) and the report of violence in the school (see lines 185–189)?

8. In addition to smaller classes and more counselors, which Manegold mentions as desirable changes, what other improvements in school conditions might make a difference in the educational lives of students?

9. In your view, is Crystal's home life conducive to a successful education? Why or why not?

10. Do you think anyone who starts out with school problems like Crystal's can solve them while living in a neighborhood like hers? Explain your answer.

## Writing Assignments

1. Seen through the eyes of a junior high or high school student, education no doubt seems quite different from the way it appears to even the most sympathetic teachers and parents. Crystal has specific complaints on this score, and as a probably recent high school graduate, you yourself are in a good position to suggest curriculum and support service changes that could make school a better experience for students (see number 8 in Looking Back). Referring to Crystal's problems and the situation at her school, write an essay that attempts to persuade school authorities to make the changes you would recommend.

2. In a couple of places in this article (lines 70–75 and 204–209), we see Crystal bonding with her friends against "a world too often hostile." Write an essay describing the particular sources of this hostility in Crystal's life—in school, at home, and on the street. Extrapolate from these sources to explain why teenagers seek solidarity with certain of their peers. What forms does this solidarity take? Is it effective or futile? Can it make the situation worse, or only better? Refer to your own past or present experience, as well as to Crystal's, if it is helpful to do so.

3. Manegold invites us into Crystal's home environment but only rarely employs terms that characterize its quality. How do you judge the life that Crystal faces at home? In your estimation, what would constitute a good home environment for the social and educational purposes of a young person who, like Crystal, is "at risk" (see number 9 in Looking Back)? Write an essay that addresses the relationship between home and school in the lives of teenagers. You might begin by describing Crystal's specific situation in your own words, and you shouldn't hesitate to cite your own experience, but try also to think in terms of junior high and high school students generally.

# Leo Tolstoy

# Boyhood

Leo Tolstoy (1828–1910) is considered one of Russia's finest authors, and indeed one of the great writers of all time. In addition to the well-known novels *Anna Karenina* and *War and Peace*, he also published numerous short works, including "The Death of Ivan Ilyich," whose spiritual message relates to the meditations in this excerpt from *Childhood, Boyhood, and Youth*. Although in later life Tolstoy became a Christian pacifist and moralist, his thought settling into a fairly dogmatic mold, in his best work he convincingly portrays a constant anguished search by his characters for identity and meaning. "Boyhood" is a case study of critical thinking on Tolstoy's part, in which the author questions basic assumptions in order to free himself of those that do not stand the test of reason.

## Looking Ahead

1. Tolstoy stops us at points with statements that push out from the text and seem to stand alone. To grasp the import of these thoughts is to comprehend his mature ideas.

2. Similarly, you will become more receptive to his boyhood meditations as you recognize how precocious they are.

3. One purpose of Tolstoy's writing that you should be aware of here is self-criticism, subtly presented but perceptible. Take the opportunity to examine along with the author the kind of reasoning he employs.

People will scarcely believe what were the favorite and most constant subjects of my meditations during boyhood—so incongruous were they with my age and situation. But, in my opinion, incongruity between a man's situation and his moral activity is the surest sign of truth.

In the course of the year during which I led a solitary moral life, turned in upon myself, I was already confronted by all the abstract questions concerning man's destiny, the future life, and the immortality of the soul; and my feeble    5 childish mind endeavored with all the ardor of inexperience to comprehend those questions whose formulation constitutes the highest degree that man's mind can attain, but whose resolution is not granted to him.

It seems to me that the human mind in each individual follows the same path in its development as that of whole generations, that the ideas which serve as the basis of various philosophical theories constitute inalienable attributes of that mind, and that each man is more or less aware of them before he even knows of the existence of philosophical theories.

These thoughts occurred to my mind with such clarity and vividness that I even attempted to apply them in life, imagining that I was the *first* to discover such great and useful truths.

Once I had the idea that happiness does not depend on external causes but on our attitude to them, that a man accustomed to enduring suffering cannot be unhappy, and so, in order to accustom myself to hardship, I held, despite the terrible pain, Tatishchev's dictionaries outstretched at arm's length for five minutes at a time, or else went off to the box room and lashed my bare back with a rope so painfully that my eyes involuntarily filled with tears.

Another time, recollecting suddenly that death awaited me at any hour, at any minute, I decided, unable to understand how people had not realized it before, that man could not otherwise be happy than by taking full advantage of the present and not thinking of the past—and for three days, under the influence of this idea, I abandoned my lessons and occupied myself solely with lying on the bed, enjoying myself reading some novel or other, and eating gingerbread and honey, which I had bought with my last pocket money.

On one occasion I was standing before the blackboard and chalking various figures on it when I was suddenly struck by the thought: Why is symmetry pleasant to the eye? What is symmetry? It is an inborn feeling, I answered myself. But what is it based on? Not everything in life is symmetrical, is it? On the contrary, here is life—and I drew an oval figure on the board. After life the soul passes into infinity; here is infinity—and from one side of the oval I drew a line to the very edge of the board. Why is there no such line on the other side? And indeed, how can there be infinity on one side only? We must have existed before this life, although we've lost all recollection of it.

This argument—which seemed extraordinarily new and clear to me and whose thread I can only just manage to capture now—pleased me extraordinarily, and taking up a sheet of paper I thought to expound it in writing, but at this point such a welter of thoughts surged into my head that I was obliged to stand up and walk about the room. When I came to the window my attention was attracted by the water horse, which the coachman was harnessing at this moment, and all my thoughts concentrated on resolving the question: Into what animal or person will the soul of this water horse go when it expires? At that moment Volodya passed through the room and smiled when he noticed that I was meditating about something, and this smile was enough for me to realize that everything I was thinking was the most awful rubbish.

I have related this incident, which for some reason I find memorable, merely in order to give the reader an idea of the nature of my philosophizing.

But not one of the philosophical trends carried me away so completely as did skepticism, which at one time brought me to a condition bordering on madness. I imagined that, besides myself, nothing and no one existed in the whole world, that objects were not objects but images, which appeared only when I turned my attention to them, and that as soon as I ceased thinking of them these images disappeared. In short, I agreed with Schelling[1] in the conviction that it was not objects that existed but only my attitude to them. There were moments when, under the influence of this *idée fixe,*[2] I reached such a stage of lunacy that sometimes I would look quickly in the opposite direction, hoping to catch nothingness (*néant*) unawares while I was not there.

What a pitiful worthless spring of moral action is the mind of man!

My feeble mind was unable to penetrate the impenetrable and in this impossible labor it lost, one after the other, beliefs that, for my happiness in life, I ought never to have dared to touch.

From all this heavy moral labor I derived nothing except an agility of mind that diminished my will power and a habit of perpetual moral analysis that destroyed freshness of feeling and clearness of judgment.

Abstract ideas are formed as a result of man's ability to apprehend with his consciousness at any given moment the state of his mind and to transfer it to his memory. My fondness for abstract reasoning developed my consciousness to such an unnatural degree that frequently, when starting to think of the simplest thing, I entered a vicious circle of mental self-analysis, so that I no longer thought of the original question, but thought only of what I was thinking about. Asking myself: What am I thinking of? I would reply: I am thinking of what I am thinking. And what am I thinking of now? I am thinking that I am thinking of what I am thinking, and so on. My mind went round in circles. . . .

Nevertheless, the philosophical discoveries I made were extraordinarily flattering to my self-esteem: I frequently imagined myself to be a great man, discovering new truths for the good of all mankind, and I gazed at other mortals with proud consciousness of my merit; but, strange to say, when coming into contact with these mortals, I was shy in the presence of all of them and the higher I rated myself in my own opinion, not only was I the less capable with others of displaying my consciousness of this merit, but I could not even accustom myself to not feeling ashamed of every little word and gesture.

---

1. *Friedrich Wilhelm Joseph Schelling* (1774–1854): German philosopher who propounded theories of the self. (*ed.*)

2. *idée fixe:* fixed idea. (*ed.*)

## Looking Back

1. How would you explain the reasoning behind the opinion Tolstoy states in lines 3–4?
2. Do you agree with Tolstoy that raising questions about destiny, the future, and immortality is a great mental achievement, even though these questions cannot be answered? Why or why not?
3. What do you think of the author's claim that happiness is a state of mind (lines 19–24)?
4. Tolstoy's decision to plunge into hedonism (lines 25–31) reveals what developing character trait in him?
5. Can you mount a critique of his "proof" of what in effect is reincarnation (lines 32–40)?
6. Why did Volodya's smile (lines 48–51) so humble Tolstoy?
7. Why does Tolstoy offer such an unsparing judgment of humanity in line 65?
8. What were the effects of Tolstoy's philosophizing on the formation of his self?
9. If the author was so proud of his mental acuity, why did he feel so inadequate in the company of others?
10. Can you think of any mental experiences in your own childhood that, within limits, resembled Tolstoy's? Describe them.

## Writing Assignments

1. We might say that intellectually Tolstoy went off the deep end a number of times in his youth, sliding into beliefs in reincarnation, in hedonism, in skepticism, among others. He defines the generally negative effects of this habit on his character, but we can imagine that there was a positive side as well. That is, his early studies prepared him for his extraordinary accomplishments later in life. Write an essay that argues in favor of giving everybody who shows signs of mental acuity in youth the opportunity at that point to develop his or her intellect as rapidly as possible. Extrapolating from Tolstoy in this way, state as concretely as possible the probable long-term effects of such early intellectual adventures. What would open up to the inquiring mind that might have remained closed to it under normal schooling conditions? What slow, dull, repetitive labors would give way to what new mental challenges? How might the life of the mind shoot forward? In personal terms, what particular studies would you like to have pursued during your childhood?

2. To use the contemporary idiom, happiness is a state of mind; so also Tolstoy says he once thought (see number 3 in Looking Back). Many people accept this definition, while many others reject it out of hand. What seems certain is that everybody wants to be happy, and therefore everybody wants to know what will guarantee happiness. However, because we face so many obstacles to happiness, we also face this problem: Is happiness a state of mind, a positive way of looking at life no matter what it tosses our way, or is happiness the product of fortunate circumstances and of them alone? If the first, we surely must cultivate this way of looking; we must develop the proper attitude and philosophic approach. But if happiness is circumstantial, we

must take certain measures; we must act to ensure those circumstances and guard against unhappiness by avoiding experiences that are likely to produce it. How do you approach the problem? Referring to Tolstoy, write an essay saying what you think produces happiness: the right attitudes or the right experiences.

3. *Hedonism,* derived from the Greek word for pleasure, is the belief that enjoyment is the most desirable good in life and should be the goal that guides action. In an informal manner, Tolstoy, precociously confronting the inevitability of death, converts—for three days!—to this philosophical view. He ceases intellectual labor, lazes in bed, and stuffs his face with luxury food he has spent his last dime to purchase (lines 25–31). He enjoys himself, he tells us, but we can imagine that if he had continued this regimen for very long, he would have failed his courses, developed bed sores, and suffered a terrific stomachache. That is, his pleasure would have become its opposite, pain. Hedonism, therefore, may not be the answer, at least if indulged too long or too consistently. But the question remains: How should we live? Write an essay discussing how we should live, given that one day we will die and *given that we want to be one kind of person rather than another.*

☙

# Rogelio R. Gomez
# Foul Shots

Rogelio Gomez is a fiction writer living in San Antonio. In this piece, which appeared in *The New York Times,* Gomez realizes the aim of the critical thinker to reevaluate ideas or events and the aim of the writer of memoirs to see himself or herself anew.

## Looking Ahead

1. Although this piece is almost entirely a narrative, notice that it fulfills its critical function as an essay by producing a commentary on events.
2. Try to see the connection between the central event of the narrative and the conditions of Gomez's life that surrounded it.
3. As you read, ask yourself whether your own experience confirms the author's in any way.

Now and then I can still see their faces, snickering and laughing, their eyes mocking me. And it bothers me that I should remember. Time and maturity should have diminished the pain, because the incident happened more than 20 years ago. Occasionally, however, a smug smile triggers the memory, and I think, "I should have done something." Some act of defiance could have killed and buried the memory of the incident. Now it's too late.    5

In 1969, I was a senior on the Luther Burbank High School basketball team. The school is on the south side of San Antonio, in one of the city's many barrios. After practice one day our coach announced that we were going to spend the following Saturday scrimmaging with the ball club from Winston Churchill High, located in the city's rich, white north side. After the basketball game, we were to select someone from the opposing team and "buddy up"— talk with him, have lunch with him and generally spend the day attempting friendship. By telling us that this experience would do both teams some good, I suspect our well-intentioned coach was thinking about the possible benefits of integration and of learning to appreciate the differences of other people. By integrating us with this more prosperous group, I think he was also trying to inspire us.

But my teammates and I smiled sardonically at one another, and our sneakers squeaked as we nervously rubbed them against the waxed hardwood floor of our gym. The prospect of a full day of unfavorable comparisons drew from us a collective groan. As "barrio boys," we were already acutely aware of the differences between us and them. Churchill meant "white" to us: It meant shiny new cars, two-story homes with fireplaces, pedigreed dogs and manicured hedges. In other words, everything that we did not have. Worse, traveling north meant putting up a front, to ourselves as well as to the Churchill team. We felt we had to pretend that we were cavalier about it all, tough guys who didn't care about "nothin.'"

It's clear now that we entered the contest with negative images of ourselves. From childhood, we must have suspected something was inherently wrong with us. The evidence wrapped itself around our collective psyche like a noose. In elementary school, we were not allowed to speak Spanish. The bladed edge of a wooden ruler once came crashing down on my knuckles for violating this dictum. By high school, however, policies had changed, and we could speak Spanish without fear of physical reprisal. Still, speaking our language before whites brought on spasms of shame—for the supposed inferiority of our language and culture—and guilt at feeling shame. That mixture of emotions fueled our burning sense of inferiority.

After all, our mothers in no way resembled the glamorized models of American TV mothers—Donna Reed baking cookies in high heels. My mother's hands were rough and chafed, her wardrobe drab and worn. And my father was preoccupied with making ends meet. His silence starkly contrasted with the glib counsel Jim Anderson offered in "Father Knows Best." And where the Beaver worried about trying to understand some difficult homework assignment, for me it was an altogether different horror, when I was told by my elementary school principal that I did not have the ability to learn.

After I failed to pass the first grade, my report card read that I had a "learning disability." What shame and disillusion it brought my parents! To have carried their dream of a better life from Mexico to America, only to have their hopes quashed by having their only son branded inadequate. And so somewhere during my schooling I assumed that saying I had a "learning disability" was just another way of saying that I was "retarded." School administrators didn't care that I could not speak English.

As teen-agers, of course, my Mexican-American friends and I did not consciously understand why we felt inferior. But we might have understood if we had fathomed our desperate need to trounce Churchill. We viewed the prospect of beating a white, north-side squad as a particularly fine coup. The match was clearly racial, our need to succeed born of a defiance against prejudice. I see now that we used the basketball court to prove our "blood." And who better to confirm us, if not those whom we considered better? In retrospect, I realize the only thing confirmed that day was that we saw ourselves as negatively as they did.

After we won the morning scrimmage, both teams were led from the gym into an empty room where everyone sat on a shiny linoleum floor. We were supposed to mingle—rub the colors together. But the teams sat separately, our backs against concrete walls. We faced one another like enemies, the empty floor between us a no man's land. As the coaches walked away, one reminded us to share lunch. God! The mere thought of offering them a taco from our brown bags when they had refrigerated deli lunches horrified us.

Then one of their players tossed a bag of Fritos at us. It slid across the slippery floor and stopped in the center of the room. With hearts beating anxiously, we Chicanos stared at the bag as the boy said with a sneer, "Y'all probably like 'em"—the "Frito Bandito" commercial being popular then. And we could see them, smiling at each other, giggling, jabbing their elbows into one another's ribs at the joke. The bag seemed to grow before our eyes like a monstrous symbol of inferiority.

We won the afternoon basketball game as well. But winning had accomplished nothing. Though we had wanted to, we couldn't change their perception of us. It seems, in fact, that defeating them made them meaner. Looking back, I feel these young men needed to put us "in our place," to reaffirm the power they felt we had threatened. I think, moreover, that they felt justified, not only because of their inherent sense of superiority, but because our failure to respond to their insult underscored our worthlessness in their eyes.

Two decades later, the memory of their gloating lives on in me. When a white person is discourteous, I find myself wondering what I should do, and afterward, if I've done the right thing. Sometimes I argue when a deft comment would suffice. Then I reprimand myself, for I am no longer a boy. But my impulse to argue bears witness to my ghosts. For, invariably, whenever I feel insulted I'm reminded of that day at Churchill High. And whenever the past encroaches upon the present, I see myself rising boldly, stepping proudly across the years and crushing, underfoot, a silly bag of Fritos.

## Looking Back

1. How do you explain Gomez's structural decision to begin and end his essay about a long-past event in the present tense?

2. Under what conditions might the coach's "integrationist" strategy have worked?

3. What do you think was the reason for forbidding children to speak Spanish in elementary school, then allowing them to do so in high school?

4. In what way might a "collective psyche" (line 31) determine an individual's sense of self?

5. Can you explain the emotional line Gomez traces, in lines 35–38, from inferiority to shame to guilt and back to inferiority? At what point, and in what way, could this damaging cycle have been halted?

6. What problem of personal identity does the author introduce in his comments on television programming (lines 39–46)?

7. Why did Gomez fail the first grade?

8. If winning the basketball games against Churchill was so important to Gomez and his teammates, why does he mention their victories almost in passing, as if they hardly matter?

9. How does the bag of Fritos function in the narrative? What lesson about using concrete details in writing does its use disclose?

10. At the conclusion, what is the power of the past that Gomez reveals?

## Writing Assignments

1. Gomez measures his own family against the American family encountered in TV sitcoms (see number 6 in Looking Back). The resulting contrast is a stark one. As the author points out, the images on the home screen are "glamorized models." They are idealized representations meant to persuade the viewer that they constitute the norm and should therefore be accepted as the reality. But it is not the reality, many people would argue. In fact, far from being the rule, the televised version of the family is the exception, if it exists at all. Even so, the medium somehow retains its powerful sway over people's idea of themselves and of who they should be. Inevitably a number of serious problems emerge. Referring to Gomez's discussion, write an essay examining the negative or positive influence that television's images can exert on the formation of the self.

2. There is little doubt that "the supposed inferiority of our language and culture" that Gomez speaks of (lines 36–37) is a harmful burden to bear, and an unjust one. It stigmatizes an entire group of people and, through membership in that group, individuals who internalize a belief in their own inferiority may be blocked from realizing their true potential. Believing that one is racially or ethnically inferior may further encourage oppression by others at the same time that it disarms oneself. Because prejudice of this sort begins early in life, perhaps the first line of resistance should be established before children have adapted to it. But how? One traditional answer is to stress, in schools and at home, the universal values of equality, democracy, and freedom, with the hope that this will influence children from all backgrounds to grow into adults who respect one another's rights. Another currently popular answer is to impress on children the value of their group membership. Knowing their roots and the history of their people, the argument runs, will empower individuals by giving them pride in their origins and their racial, ethnic, or

gender identity. Thus, they will be able to withstand stereotyping and bias, which at the same time will diminish as the identities in question achieve social legitimacy. Write an essay discussing these two programmatic approaches to ending prejudice and discrimination and saying whether, in your view, one or the other or a combination is best. Refer to Gomez's situation and, if you can, illustrate your points with personal examples.

3. Those who are insulted and injured by others often cannot return the favor. Sometimes they are cowed by those who humiliate them, afraid of those people's apparent power to do harm. At other times, their own sensitivity—evidenced by their ability to register these sorts of injuries in the first place—prevents them from responding in kind. But at times they see the need to protect themselves somehow. Gomez does, as we learn in the last paragraph of his essay. We see that unless the injured party manages to take some action, the memory of not having done so will haunt that person, weakening him or her even more. For instance, Gomez did *not* trample the bag of Fritos when he was a boy; he has to step "across the years," that is, fantasize a past action, to rewrite history. Write an essay explaining how past hurt can continue to do harm in the present. Discuss how taking action at the time, when it counts, may save the person from remorse in the future. Conceive of your audience as people who will gain in some way by heightening their consciousness of the situation described above.

# Ondine Galsworth

# Air Raid

Ondine Galsworth (b. 1963) entered college at the age of twenty-five and at last sighting was majoring in English and dance at the University of California, Irvine. Although she has "bought into the California lifestyle with an embarrassing amount of willingness" (her words), Galsworth grew up in Chicago and New York. Galsworth plans to be a writer.

## Looking Ahead

1. The fact that a very troubled person can still be admired and loved may not be too surprising, but it is always good to get fresh evidence of it, as we do here.
2. As you read this essay, watch for the author's structural shift between past and present and analyze her reason for it.
3. Notice the connection between Galsworth's language and her approach to her subject, and try to judge the appropriateness of her language.

The doorbell rings—we hit the deck. On my belly I expertly crawl across the carpet towards the TV to lower the volume. My mother is kneeling, wide-eyed, with her ear against the door. "I wonder who the hell it is," she whispers.

"Shhh!" I say. "What if they hear?" She puts her fingertips to her mouth and
slithers away from the door. The bell again. This time two long deliberate rings.
We are paralyzed in mid-crawl. "Don't move!" I gasp. "It's probably those fuck-
ing Jehovah Witnesses or something," she says. Staring at the door we lie there
in silence until five minutes pass. Then we cautiously peer out the edge of the
window. The coast is clear. The air raid is over. We speak freely now about who
it might have been and about how we should probably keep the shades down
from now on. It never occurs to us that we might have answered the door. Of
course not. Only when we know someone is coming and have time to prepare
for their visit do we ever answer the door. We need time to fix up the house,
which is always in a state of chaos, and also to make ourselves presentable for
the public. Our dress code at home is not something to be witnessed by an innocent outsider. Our severe attachment to threadbare rummage sale garb is as
private as the rest of our relationship. My mother and I have our own little
world. A secret magical little place that is impenetrable and does not welcome
intruders. Intruders are anybody else.

My mother was sick, that I knew. We called it the illness. I also knew what the
illness was. I knew she was a diagnosed paranoid schizophrenic. I knew she was
a manic-depressive. I knew she had been an abused child. I knew about the sexual abuse, the emotional abuse, the physical abuse. I knew she was addicted to
prescription drugs. I knew she had problems with men. I knew she didn't like
to be touched. I knew she cried every day. I knew that she hated her mother
and that she had never felt love until she had me. I knew that I had a big responsibility. I knew all this and I knew it all by the time I was eight.

My relationship with my mother was like a love affair. It was passionate and
full of drama. We cherished it like a rare jewel. As a child I never thought of our
behavior or life-style as unhealthy in any way; I just knew it was different. It was
special. It needed to be protected. I adored my mother; she was my heart as I
was hers.

The severity of my mother's condition was never out of my awareness. This
was part of my daily life and in a sense I was used to it. The fact that my mother
was always suffering was very clear to me. It blended in with the rest of my daily
existence, making my moment-to-moment childhood reality a blur of joy and
pain. Being a child, I possessed that wonderful childlike ability to lose myself in
my imagination despite the harsh realities of life. My fantasy life was active and
powerful. My imagination brought me to many places that were warm and safe,
and helped me to create a gauze to cover my raw emotions. When people ask
me how I could have managed under such harsh circumstances, I always answer, "What choice did I have?" The survival instinct in children is infinite.

Through all the smoke and mirrors of my childhood experiences, I still have
crystal clear memories of many a fun and loving time with my eccentric mother.
My tiny mom and my tiny self plowing through the snow with our enormous

eighteen-dollar Christmas tree. It always had a side with a few branches missing that we would face toward the wall. Decorating it was a slow and careful project—standing back with a squinted eye until finally hanging the shiny ball on the appropriate branch. There was also staying up every Saturday night, huddling on the couch watching rock concerts till two. Then there was our famed     50
excursion to see Alice Cooper (the man of my dreams at the time) when I was ten. We swooned over Tom Jones (the man of my mother's dreams), we struck dramatic poses to Ravel's *Bolero,* we baked apple turnovers every Friday (the frozen kind). I never once wished that I had a different mother when I was a child.     55

Aside from the fact that she was a schizophrenic, I must mention two things about my mother that influenced my impression of her greatly. For one, my mother was beautiful, gorgeous, a sexbomb, a real looker. She came from Colombia; she had dark skin but very classical European features. She looked like a dark-eyed, dark-haired version of Catherine Deneuve with a dash of Cher     60
thrown in. She didn't need any make-up. She had thick long lashes surrounding her bedroom eyes, and wonderfully arched eyebrows that tapered out into a pencil-thin line over her perfectly protruding browbone. Her cheekbones were high and round as plums, her nose was straight and long enough to look refined and not cute. Her mouth always seemed carved out of stone—still and even.     65
Then there was her hair—a full black mass that never tangled. She had intense movie star looks, either that or of an Egyptian princess, I always thought. What she didn't possess was elegance or grace. Not a drop. Her fancy equipment was glazed with a comical layer of goofiness. She showed off her fine lines about as gracefully as a penguin. This eased any threat of intimidation or envy. Still it     70
was great having a mother who, even though she couldn't bake or sew like other housewives, could kick butt in the looks department. Definitely. I, on the other hand, was not a lovely child. I did have my moments of adorableness but then came those five or six years when my features sat quite uncomfortably on my face. It was during this awkward period that I found beautiful people mysteri-     75
ous and fascinating. I was thrilled by my mother's beauty and even more thrilled when in my teens I began to resemble her slightly.

My mother was also an artist, a painter. She was a star pupil in art school, winning awards and respect from her peers. After I was born she continued to paint sporadically for about ten years. There was always a room filled with     80
paints, easels, canvases, and the smell of turpentine. There were art books scattered around the house along with charcoal sketches of crazed women. She raved over all my drawings of butterflies, comparing me to Picasso. I always wondered if Picasso drew butterflies wearing boots and hair ribbons. I was exposed to the rich culture of the art world and the fact that my mother was very     85
talented. She was good at something. She eventually gave it up with the same indifference she had toward her beauty. It did not bring her happiness.

I can remember feeling a tightness in my jaw while contemplating my mother's tragic side. For a little girl I had a very serious side, very grown up. I

90  started to identify strongly with the notion that I was the only one with real strength in my family, and that I could handle anything. I was the one in control.

During my early twenties is when I first learned that my "I can handle it" self-image was typical of a child from a dysfunctional family, *dysfunctional* being a general term used to describe families plagued by alcoholism, mental illness, drug abuse, and other unhealthy behavior. Through books, insightful friends, 95  and self-help groups like Al-Anon, I became aware of how my relationship with my mother had affected my perception of myself and my ability to function.

Lying around in bed for a few days on end had a lot to do with why my productivity level hovered around zero. Of course there were the occasional bursts 100  of enthusiasm, backed up by fresh resolutions and intricate schedules. These would carry me through a couple of gratifying days, but eventually some fear or resentment would swallow up the whole batch of optimism and it would be back to bed. My mother always went to bed when she couldn't deal with life and I learned to deal with anxiety the same way. I often still feel that my pillows 105  and blankets are trying to lure me back to the comforts of hiding, but it has gotten much easier to reject such invitations. To let myself be seduced by my bed is to enter a world of self-loathing and hopelessness.

Facing the reality of how my mother's illness has affected me has been a grueling task. It has also been a rewarding one beyond belief, and continues to be.

110  It is amazing how much progress one can make and at the same time have habits that go virtually unchanged, like a crocodile's evolution since the days of the dinosaur. A couple of weeks ago I was hanging around the apartment in an old housecoat with a paisley print that my mother found in a bag in church. This has been my favorite thing to wear at home lately, along with a pair of two-115  dollar terrycloth slippers that are frayed and stained with tomato sauce. I chose this outfit over the four beautiful robes given to me by various family members (excluding my mother). There's the luxurious flowing velvet one; very Garbo, it forces me to glide around and light up cigarettes. Then there's the amazing hand-embroidered robe from India, and the big, pink, fluffy terrycloth bathrobe 120  that is way too clean for my bathroom. And, of course, there's my perky little turquoise robe that hangs officially on a hook by the sink. This one is for drying my hands with when reading in the tub. Basically I use these robes for sleepovers and unexpected visits with a ten-minute warning. It was in my beloved, old-lady house coat, though, that a few weeks ago I was challenged by an unex-125  pected doorbell ring around nine o'clock. Anyone who knows me knows that this is too early. I stopped dead in my tracks. The fact that I'm four flights up did not stop me from keeping perfectly still and silent. It rang again. I glared at the intercom, this time spewing profanity. About thirty minutes later it rang again. My mind raced. My mother? She wouldn't dare, not without calling first. 130  A burglar trying to see if I'm home? What if he tries to rob the place and I'll be found murdered in this outfit? Another hour passed and the barbaric bell buzzed again. By this time I was so full of contempt for this creature that had vi-

olated me from four flights down that I made indecent gestures towards the intercom and stormed around with my slippers flapping behind me. When I finally left the apartment I found a little note from UPS stating that they had tried   135
three times to deliver a package and that they would try again at ten-thirty the
following morning. "Wow, a package," I mumbled foolishly. I carefully noted
down ten-thirty in my day-book.

The next day I was ready and waiting. I was dressed and had aired out the
apartment all night. My mother was over for a morning visit when the doorbell   140
rang. "Who's that?" she asked suspiciously. "Oh, I'm expecting a package," I said,
playing it cool. I signed for it and then brought in this weightless box. My
mother and I stared at it as if we were waiting for it to speak. It did not occur to
me that it might be a birthday present even though it was the day before my
birthday. It was from my friend Barbara from California. I tore it open and there   145
it was. A birthday present! As it turned out, the only one I got this year. It was a
beautiful red hat with a black ribbon around it, and a silk skirt stuffed inside it.
Underneath there was a card. It read, "Happy Birthday—hope this gets there on
time." I was flabbergasted. I had almost blown this effort to get this present to me
on time because of my absurd allergic reaction to doorbells. I might as well still   150
be crawling around on the rug like a soldier! Time to change my programming.

I haven't worn my housecoat since the birthday present incident, but I
haven't thrown it out. It's rolled up in a ball under the television. I am now giving my robe from India a trial period and have been wearing a pair of twelve-
dollar booties that I stole from my in-laws' country house. I've tried to stop   155
screening my calls with my phone machine and occasionally take the risk of just
answering the phone. Things are coming along slowly. Perhaps there will even
be a time without air raids.

## Looking Back

1. How is the importance of titles pointed up by this one, "Air Raid"?
2. Do you think the author's plunging into a dramatic scene to begin her essay works well? Why or why not?
3. What rhetorical effect does the repetition of "I knew" in the second paragraph have? (**Rhetorical** refers to the way language directly influences the reader's response.)
4. How does Galsworth account for her ability as a child to bear her mother's difficulties?
5. In what way do the images Galsworth conjures up in lines 43–55 contribute to our sense of her family life?
6. What do you think of Galsworth's choice of words like "sexbomb" (line 58), "bed-room eyes" (line 62), and "kick butt in the looks department" (line 72)?
7. Besides her mental illness, what strikes you as particularly tragic about the author's mother?
8. Since Galsworth, by her own admission, was adversely affected by living with her mother, should she have been allowed to do so?

9. How does the humorous self-deprecation of the last section of the essay (starting with line 110) mask a serious concern of the author?

10. Although Galsworth's mother obviously is an extreme case (which does not necessarily mean atypical), do you think that a parent's strongly marked personality complicates life for a child? Explain your answer.

## Writing Assignments

1. In a poem about witnessing, as a child, his uncle dying of Hodgkin's disease, Robert Lowell writes, "I cowered in terror. I wasn't a child at all—" Lowell lived at a time when children generally didn't speak unless they were spoken to, as the saying goes, and so—unlike Ondine Galsworth, who was her mother's active companion—he was a witness only, not a participant in the drama. Yet both Lowell and Galsworth are alike in that, despite being children, they knew the score and bore the burden of that knowledge. From these examples—a convincing case always requires more than one—we can assume that children's ability to register facts, gain psychological knowledge, and have a surprisingly sophisticated awareness of adult lives is much greater than popularly supposed. Write an essay confirming this assumption with examples from your own childhood and referring to Galsworth's as well. Then go on to explain the implications of your findings for the way we should view this time of life.

2. Children carry into their adult lives the manifold influences of their childhood. We find Galsworth as a young woman just as afraid of answering the unexpected ring of a doorbell as her mother was years earlier. Revealing this seemingly paranoid fear, which has survived the progress she has otherwise made so far, is part of Galsworth's project of "facing the reality of how my mother's illness has affected me" (line 108). Like the author, we all must confront the fact that who we *are* is partially who we *were,* and that to know fully who we are we must find the link between our childhood and adult life. Consult your own memory and write an autobiographical essay that uncovers—in as much concrete detail as possible—an important connection between past and present in your life, and explain the effect of this connection on you.

3. Often, people distinguish a father's love from a mother's love on the basis of the conditions the father places on that love. The father, according to this view, grants his love depending on the child's meeting certain standards of behavior and performance that he has set. The mother's love, on the other hand, is unconditional, meaning that her emotions flow toward her child irrespective of the child's coming up to the mark, a mark she would never dream of setting in the first place. Undoubtedly, no parents or anyone else perfectly fits this gendered description; yet the two types of love seem to exist in the world, and we often prefer to give one or the other. Galsworth, setting no conditions on her love for her mother, nonetheless knew what conditions she could have set. Building on a description of Galsworth's love for her mother, write an essay examining the merits of conditional love—with its self-defensiveness and demands for responsibility—and unconditional love—with its all-embracing acceptance.

◈

# François, duc de La Rochefoucauld
## Self-Portrait

La Rochefoucauld (1613–1680) is most famous for his **aphorisms,** brief sentences that sting with their insights and truth, yet, despite their brevity, derive from thoughtful consideration of experience. In the introduction to a collection of these, Leonard Tancock writes, "At heart an observer, a speculator about human nature, [La Rochefoucauld was] a quiet witness of the human comedy and tragedy." La Rochefoucauld published his *Memoirs* in 1662 and *Maxims* in 1665.

## Looking Ahead

1. As you read, keep in mind the age-old desire for self-knowledge, a yearning that distinguishes this self-portrait.

2. Note that the author avoids mere self-regard—that is, taking undue satisfaction from looking at himself—yet read critically to decide whether his assertions about himself are sufficient or whether more evidence supporting them is needed.

3. Because his writing is sometimes incisive to the point of shorthand, be prepared to meet the author halfway in order to fully understand his self-disclosures.

I am of medium height, well set-up and proportioned, my complexion dark but fairly uniform; my forehead is lofty and reasonably broad, eyes black, small and deep-set with thick, black but well-shaped brows. I should be hard put to it to say what sort of a nose I have, for it is neither flat nor aquiline, fleshy nor pointed—at least I do not think so—all I know is that it is big rather than small    5
and comes down a little too low. I have a wide mouth with lips usually rather red and neither good nor bad in shape; my teeth are white and tolerably regular. I have been told that my chin is somewhat too prominent, and having just felt myself and looked in the glass to find out, I do not quite know what to make of it. As for shape of face, mine is either square or oval, but which of the two it    10
would be very hard to say. My hair is dark and naturally wavy, thick and long enough for me to claim to have a fine crop. My expression has something melancholy and aloof about it which makes most people think I am supercilious, although I am nothing of the kind. I am very much given to movement, perhaps a bit too much, to the point of gesticulating a good deal when talking.    15
That, in plain terms, is what I believe I am like from the outside, and I think it will be found that my own opinion of myself in this respect is not far from the truth. I will deal equally faithfully with the rest of my portrait, for I have studied myself as much as is needful for self-knowledge and am not wanting in either

20   confidence to state freely such good qualities as I may have or candour to own
up to such defects as I certainly possess. To speak first about my temperament,
I am melancholic, and to such a degree that I have scarcely been seen to laugh
more than three or four times in the past three or four years. Yet, I think, my
melancholy would be pretty mild and easy to put up with if its only source were
25   in my temperament, but so much depression comes from other sources and fills
my imagination and dominates my mind to such an extent that most of the time
I am either dreaming without uttering a word or have scarcely any conscious
knowledge of what I am saying. I am very reserved with strangers and not remarkably forthcoming even with the majority of the people I know. It is a fail-
30   ing, I realize that, and I will leave nothing untried to cure myself, but as a certain sullen expression on my face helps to make me look even more reserved
than I am, and as it is not in our power to rid ourselves of a forbidding expression due to the natural arrangement for our features, I think that when I have
corrected myself within I shall still keep unfortunate signs without. I am intelli-
35   gent, and I make no bones about saying so, for what is the good of being coy
about it? So much beating about the bush and toning down when it is a question of stating the advantages we possess looks to me like concealing a bit of
vanity behind externals of modesty, and resorting to artful wiles to make others
think much better of us than we actually claim. For my part, I am content not to
40   be thought handsomer than I make myself out to be, better humoured than I
portray myself, or wittier and more sensible than I say I am. Very well then, I
am intelligent, but my intelligence is spoilt by melancholy, for although I have
quite a fluent tongue, a retentive memory, and am not given to muddled thinking, yet I am so preoccupied with my gloomy thoughts that I often express my
45   ideas very badly. The conversation of well-bred people is one of the pleasures I
enjoy most keenly. I like talk to be serious and mainly concerned with moral
questions, but I can enjoy it when it is amusing, and if I do not throw in many
little jokes myself it is at any rate not for want of appreciating the value of nicely
turned frivolities or of getting much amusement out of this kind of light banter
50   that some nimble minds can succeed in so well. If I were interested in literary
glory I think that with a little trouble I could make quite a name, for I can write
good prose and make up decent verse.

I am fond of all kinds of reading, but especially that in which there is something to train the mind and toughen the soul; and above all I find very great en-
55   joyment in sharing my reading with an intelligent person, for in so doing one
can continually reflect upon what is being read, and such reflections form the
basis of the most delightful and profitable conversation. I can criticize quite
justly works in prose or verse submitted to me, although perhaps I express my
opinion a trifle too freely. Another weak point of mine is that I sometimes go in
60   for excessively fine distinctions and over-severe criticism. I am not averse from
listening to arguments, indeed I often enter into them myself, but as a rule I defend my own opinion too heatedly, and when somebody is upholding an unjust
cause against me I sometimes stand up so passionately for the cause of reason
that I become most unreasonable myself.

Right-thinking and naturally inclined towards good, I am so anxious to be     65
socially acceptable that my friends could give me no greater pleasure than to
point out my shortcomings in all sincerity. Those who know me at all intimately
and have been kind enough to express opinions on this matter are aware that I
have always welcomed such opinions with all the joy imaginable and as submis-
sively as could be desired. My passions are all moderate and sufficiently under     70
control: hardly ever have I been seen in a temper and I have never entertained
feelings of hatred for anybody. Yet I am not incapable of taking revenge if I am
wronged and it is a matter of honour not to let an insult pass unnoticed. On the
contrary, I am told that my sense of duty would so effectively take over the
function of hatred that I would pursue my revenge more vigorously than many     75
another. Ambition does not worry me in the least. There are few things I fear,
and death is not one of them. I am not easily touched by pity, and wish I were
not at all, although there is nothing I would not do to comfort people in affliction, and indeed I believe that one should do everything, even to the point of
showing great compassion for their sufferings, for misery makes people so stu-     80
pid that such pity does them all the good in the world. But I also hold that one
should not go beyond showing pity, and take the greatest care not to feel it
oneself. This passion should have no place in a noble soul, for it only makes one
soft-hearted, and it should be left to the common people, for they never do anything because of reason and have to be moved to action by their emotions.     85

I am fond of my friends, so fond that I would not hesitate a moment to
put their interests before my own. I fit in with their wishes, patiently put up
with their less agreeable moods, hasten to excuse their every act, but I do not
make much show of affection, neither am I very much upset by their absence.
By nature I have very little curiosity for most of the things that inspire curios-     90
ity in others. I am very secretive, and nobody could find it easier to keep to
himself anything told him in confidence. Most punctilious about keeping my
word, I never break it however important the matter may be, and I have made
this an inviolable rule all through my life. I am scrupulously polite with
women, and I do not think I have ever said a word in their presence that could     95
have caused them embarrassment. When they are intelligent I prefer their
conversation to men's, for there is a kind of smooth ease about it that is not
found in us men, and moreover it seems to me that they express themselves
more clearly and give a more graceful turn to what they say. I was formerly
something of a ladies' man, but although I am still young that is no longer the     100
case. I have given up making pretty compliments and am only amazed that
there are so many serious-minded men who still do. I have the greatest admiration for noble passions, for they denote greatness of soul, and although the
emotional stress they involve us in is hardly compatible with wise moderation,
yet they are so conducive to austere virtue that they cannot rightly be     105
condemned. Being well versed in all the delicacy and strength of deep feelings
of love, I feel that if ever I fall in love it will be in this way, but knowing how I
am made, I do not think this knowledge of mine will ever pass from my head
to my heart.

## Looking Back

1. How does La Rochefoucauld's sudden presence in lines 8–10 affect your reading?
2. What do you think of his seeming inability at times to say just what he looks like, as in lines 10–11?
3. Is it probable that most people, at some time in their lives, examine themselves "as much as is needful for self-knowledge" (lines 18–19)? What might be the consequence of failing to do so?
4. What do we mean by saying that melancholy, as described in lines 21–45, is a *humor*?
5. Do the frequent distinctions the author makes between inner feelings and their outward expression ring true to you? Why or why not?
6. Can you summarize La Rochefoucauld's general evaluation of his own intelligence?
7. In what way do his points about his critical faculties and his debating skills (lines 57–64) apply to your own essay writing?
8. How do you understand his discussion of pity (lines 77–85)?
9. In what way do the last lines of this piece echo a theme introduced earlier?
10. What personal qualities that the author does *not* claim nonetheless come into view as a result of what he *does* disclose?

## Writing Assignments

1. It is untrue that "nobody knows us as we know ourselves." It would be better said that nobody knows us as we *can* know ourselves and, perhaps, as we should. All too rarely do we put ourselves in the harsh light of self-examination, much less publish the results, as La Rochefoucauld did. After all, picking ourself apart is often uncomfortable, sometimes even painful, and we may feel there is no compelling reason to do so. Yet, consider that few of us would carry a backpack or suitcase everywhere we go without knowing its contents. How much more pressing it is to know our own contents, from which we can never be separated. With this encouragement, write an essay attempting a self-portrait on the model of La Rochefoucauld's. Take up his topics: physical appearance, temperament, degree and uses of intelligence, passions, vices and virtues. Notice, before you begin, that he is personal, not private; you, too, should not reveal what you think others have no call to hear. There is a difference between disclosing the self and exposing it.

2. "Moderation cures all the vices," wrote Leonardo da Vinci. "My passions are all moderate," La Rochefoucauld tells us, "and sufficiently under control: hardly ever have I been seen in a temper and I have never entertained feelings of hatred for anybody" (lines 70–72). The golden mean and the middle way are other terms, derived from other cultures, that also praise moderation, as earlier in this century a group of American literary theorists known as humanists also did. Yet, responding to them, Ernest Hemingway asked rhetorically who could possibly make love moderately. And although "moderation in all things" seems to be regaining popularity in our age of excess, still impulsiveness, spontaneity, passion retain their appeal. As best you can say at this point, which do you favor, moderation or immoderation or some combination? Write an essay addressing this question.

3. The uses to which people put their intelligence are legion, and we hardly have to cast our eyes in any direction before we notice these uses in such diverse areas as architecture, college curricula, political leadership, and so on. Let us here consider not the *uses*—with that word's connotations of practicality, duty, and manipulation—but the *entitlements* of our intelligence—those almost magical abilities that the intelligence gives us to enrich our lives and, in turn, those of others. La Rochefoucauld discusses four major entitlements of his own intelligence: good conversation, reading, criticism, and debate of issues (see lines 41–64). Extrapolating from his discussion of these, write an essay that analyzes objectively these entitlements of intelligence and points out their value to the development of the self.

## James Baldwin

# The Discovery of What It Means to Be an American

James Baldwin (1924–1987) was a leading American essayist and novelist. His best-known collections of essays are. *Notes of a Native Son, The Fire Next Time,* and *Nobody Knows My Name,* from which this piece is taken. In these essays, as well as in novels like *Another Country,* Baldwin is deeply concerned with the social condition and personal identity of the African American. Baldwin won Guggenheim and Ford Foundation awards, among others, and was made a commander of the Legion of Honor in France, where he lived and wrote for many years. In this piece, Baldwin questions basic assumptions about his identity by providing a new context (Europe) within which to test them.

## *Looking Ahead*

1. Baldwin considers issues of personal identity in terms of race and profession, not simply nationality, as the title implies.

2. Though focusing on his own experience, Baldwin also reveals much of what it means for anyone to be an American. Read critically to test his reasoning in this respect.

3. The idea of expatriation—of voluntarily removing oneself from one's native land— is a subject Baldwin reflects on here and one that has concerned many another writer, indicating its universal significance.

"It is a complex fate to be an American," Henry James[1] observed, and the principal discovery an American writer makes in Europe is just how complex this fate is. America's history, her aspirations, her peculiar triumphs, her even more peculiar defeats, and her position in the world—yesterday and today—are all so

---

1. *Henry James* (1811–1882): American novelist. (*ed.*)

5   profoundly and stubbornly unique that the very word "America" remains a new,
almost completely undefined and extremely controversial proper noun. No one
in the world seems to know exactly what it describes, not even we motley millions who call ourselves Americans.

I left America because I doubted my ability to survive the fury of the color
10  problem here. (Sometimes I still do.) I wanted to prevent myself from becoming
*merely* a Negro; or, even, merely a Negro writer. I wanted to find out in what
way the *specialness* of my experience could be made to connect me with other
people instead of dividing me from them. (I was as isolated from Negroes as I
was from whites, which is what happens when a Negro begins, at bottom, to be-
15  lieve what white people say about him.)

In my necessity to find the terms on which my experience could be related
to that of others, Negroes and whites, writers and nonwriters, I proved, to my
astonishment, to be as American as any Texas G.I. And I found my experience
was shared by every American writer I knew in Paris. Like me, they have been
20  divorced from their origins, and it turned out to make very little difference that
the origins of white Americans were European and mine were African—they
were no more at home in Europe than I was.

The fact that I was the son of a slave and they were the sons of free men meant
less, by the time we confronted each other on European soil, than the fact that
25  we were both searching for our separate identities. When we had found these,
we seemed to be saying, why, then, we would no longer need to cling to the
shame and bitterness which had divided us so long.

It became terribly clear in Europe, as it never had been here, that we knew
more about each other than any European ever could. And it also became clear
30  that, no matter where our fathers had been born, or what they had endured, the
fact of Europe had formed us both was part of our identity and part of our
inheritance.

I had been in Paris a couple of years before any of this became clear to me.
When it did, I, like many a writer before me upon the discovery that his props
35  have all been knocked out from under him, suffered a species of breakdown
and was carried off to the mountains of Switzerland. There, in that absolutely
alabaster landscape, armed with two Bessie Smith[2] records and a typewriter, I
began to try to re-create the life that I had first known as a child and from which
I had spent so many years in flight.

40  It was Bessie Smith, through her tone and her cadence, who helped me to
dig back to the way I myself must have spoken when I was a pickaninny, and to
remember the things I had heard and seen and felt. I had buried them very
deep. I had never listened to Bessie Smith in America (in the same way that, for
years, I would not touch watermelon), but in Europe she helped to reconcile me
45  to being a "nigger."

---

2. *Bessie Smith* (1894–1937): American blues singer. (*ed.*)

I do not think that I could have made this reconciliation here. Once I was able to accept my role—as distinguished, I must say, from my "place"—in the extraordinary drama which is America, I was released from the illusion that I hated America.

The story of what can happen to an American Negro writer in Europe simply illustrates, in some relief, what can happen to any American writer there. It is not meant, of course, to imply that it happens to them all, for Europe can be very crippling, too; and, anyway, a writer, when he has made his first breakthrough, has simply won a crucial skirmish in a dangerous, unending and unpredictable battle. Still, the breakthrough is important, and the point is that an American writer, in order to achieve it, very often has to leave this country. 55

The American writer, in Europe is released, first of all, from the necessity of apologizing for himself. It is not until he *is* released from the habit of flexing his muscles and proving that he is just a "regular guy" that he realizes how crippling this habit has been. It is not necessary for him, there, to pretend to be something he is not, for the artist does not encounter in Europe the same suspicion he encounters here. Whatever the Europeans may actually think of artists, they have killed enough of them off by now to know that they are as real—and as persistent—as rain, snow, taxes or businessmen. 60

Of course, the reason for Europe's comparative clarity concerning the different functions of men in society is that European society has always been divided into classes in a way that American society never has been. A European writer considers himself to be part of an old and honorable tradition—of intellectual activity, of letters—and his choice of a vocation does not cause him any uneasy wonder as to whether or not it will cost him all his friends. But this tradition does not exist in America. 65

On the contrary, we have a very deep-seated distrust of real intellectual effort (probably because we suspect that it will destroy, as I hope it does, that myth of America to which we cling so desperately). An American writer fights his way to one of the lowest rungs on the American social ladder by means of pure bull-headedness and an indescribable series of odd jobs. He probably *has* been a "regular fellow" for much of his adult life, and it is not easy for him to step out of that lukewarm bath. 70

We must, however, consider a rather serious paradox: though American society is more mobile than Europe's, it is easier to cut across social and occupational lines there than it is here. This has something to do, I think, with the problem of status in American life. Where everyone has status, it is also perfectly possible, after all, that no one has. It seems inevitable, in any case, that a man may become uneasy as to just what his status is. 80

But Europeans have lived with the idea of status for a long time. A man can be as proud of being a good waiter as of being a good actor, and, in neither case, feel threatened. And this means that the actor and the waiter can have a freer and more genuinely friendly relationship in Europe than they are likely to have here. The waiter does not feel, with obscure resentment, that the actor has "made it," and the actor is not tormented by the fear that he may find himself, tomorrow, once again a waiter. 85

90

This lack of what may roughly be called social paranoia causes the American writer in Europe to feel—almost certainly for the first time in his life—that he can reach out to everyone, that he is accessible to everyone and open to everything. This is an extraordinary feeling. He feels, so to speak, his own
95   weight, his own value.

It is as though he suddenly came out of a dark tunnel and found himself beneath the open sky. And, in fact, in Paris, I began to see the sky for what seemed to be the first time. It was borne in on me—and it did not make me feel melancholy—that this sky had been there before I was born and would be there when
100   I was dead. And it was up to me, therefore, to make of my brief opportunity the most that could be made.

I was born in New York, but have lived only in pockets of it. In Paris, I lived in all parts of the city—on the Right Bank and the Left, among the bourgeoisie and among *les misérables,* and knew all kinds of people, from pimps and prosti-
105   tutes in Pigalle to Egyptian bankers in Neuilly.[3] This may sound extremely unprincipled or even obscurely immoral: I found it healthy. I love to talk to people, all kinds of people, and almost everyone, as I hope we still know, loves a man who loves to listen.

This perpetual dealing with people very different from myself caused a
110   shattering in me of preconceptions I scarcely knew I held. The writer is meeting in Europe people who are not American, whose sense of reality is entirely different from his own. They may love or hate or admire or fear or envy this country—they see it, in any case, from another point of view, and this forces the writer to reconsider many things he had always taken for granted. This reassess-
115   ment, which can be very painful, is also very valuable.

This freedom, like all freedom, has its dangers and its responsibilities. One day it begins to be borne in on the writer, and with great force, that he is living in Europe as an American. If he were living there as a European, he would be living on a different and far less attractive continent.

120   This crucial day may be the day on which an Algerian taxi-driver tells him how it feels to be an Algerian in Paris. It may be the day on which he passes a café terrace and catches a glimpse of the tense, intelligent and troubled face of Albert Camus.[4] Or it may be the day on which someone asks him to explain Little Rock[5] and he begins to feel that it would be simpler—and, corny as the words
125   may sound, more honorable—to *go* to Little Rock than sit in Europe, on an American passport, trying to explain it.

---

3. *Pigalle:* a somewhat seedy section of Paris where prostitution is common; *Neuilly:* an affluent suburb of Paris. (*ed.*)

4. *Albert Camus* (1913–1960): French novelist, essayist, and dramatist. (*ed.*)

5. *Little Rock:* refers to conflict over the desegregation of Little Rock, Arkansas, high school in the 1950s. (*ed.*)

This is a personal day, a terrible day, the day to which his entire sojourn has been tending. It is the day he realizes that there are no untroubled countries in this fearfully troubled world; that if he has been preparing himself for anything in Europe, he has been preparing himself—for America. In short, the freedom that the American writer finds in Europe brings him, full circle, back to himself, with the responsibility for his development where it always was: in his own hands.

Even the most incorrigible maverick has to be born somewhere. He may leave the group that produced him—he may be forced to—but nothing will efface his origins, the marks of which he carries with him everywhere. I think it is important to know this and even find it a matter for rejoicing, as the strongest people do, regardless of their station. On this acceptance, literally, the life of a writer depends.

The charge has often been made against American writers that they do not describe society, and have no interest in it. They only describe individuals in opposition to it, or isolated from it. Of course, what the American writer is describing is his own situation. But what is *Anna Karenina*[6] describing if not the tragic fate of the isolated individual, at odds with her time and place?

The real difference is that Tolstoy was describing an old and dense society in which everything seemed—to the people in it, though not to Tolstoy—to be fixed forever. And the book is a masterpiece because Tolstoy was able to fathom, and make us see, the hidden laws which really governed this society and made Anna's doom inevitable.

American writers do not have a fixed society to describe. The only society they know is one in which nothing is fixed and in which the individual must fight for his identity. This is a rich confusion, indeed, and it creates for the American writer unprecedented opportunities.

That the tensions of American life, as well as the possibilities, are tremendous is certainly not even a question. But these are dealt with in contemporary literature mainly compulsively; that is, the book is more likely to be a symptom of our tension than an examination of it. The time has come, God knows, for us to examine ourselves, but we can only do this if we are willing to free ourselves of the myth of America and try to find out what is really happening here.

Every society is really governed by hidden laws, by unspoken but profound assumptions on the part of the people, and ours is no exception. It is up to the American writer to find out what these laws and assumptions are. In a society much given to smashing taboos without thereby managing to be liberated from them, it will be no easy matter.

It is no wonder, in the meantime, that the American writer keeps running off to Europe. He needs sustenance for his journey and the best models he can

---

6. *Anna Karenina:* a novel published in 1876 by Russian writer Leo Tolstoy (1828–1910). (*ed.*)

find. Europe has what we do not have yet, a sense of the mysterious and inexorable limits of life, a sense, in a word, of tragedy. And we have what they sorely need: a new sense of life's possibilities.

170    In this endeavor to wed the vision of the Old World with that of the New, it is the writer, not the statesman, who is our strongest arm. Though we do not wholly believe it yet, the interior life is a real life, and the intangible dreams of people have a tangible effect on the world.

## Looking Back

1. How does the "fate" of being an American (line 1) connect to the *destiny* Americans may share (lines 168–169)? What do you make of the fact that Baldwin begins with the one and ends with the other?

2. What does Baldwin mean by his remark that in the United States his *"specialness"* separated him from other people instead of joining him to them (lines 12–15)?

3. Why does Baldwin need to "reconcile" himself to his racial identity if, as he says, Europe not Africa had formed him (see lines 28–45)?

4. What "suspicion" of writers is characteristic of Americans (see lines 56–70)? Why does it not exist in Europe?

5. What are some advantages of the "odd jobs" Baldwin says American writers take to survive?

6. Why does he consider class lines easier to cross in Europe than in the United States?

7. Does Baldwin convince you that expatriation is a wise course of action for a writer? Could his advice extend to nonwriters as well? Explain your answer.

8. How, according to Baldwin, does expatriation bring someone "back to himself" (lines 131–132)?

9. Are you encouraged or distressed by Baldwin's contention that American society "is one in which nothing is fixed and in which the individual must fight for his identity" (lines 151–152)? Explain your answer.

10. Can you describe in your own words the approach Baldwin says the American writer—and, we might say, any thinking individual—must take toward his or her society (see lines 157–164)?

## Writing Assignments

1. James Baldwin opens by quoting Henry James on what it is to be an American and closes by suggesting that "a new sense of life's possibilities" is an enduring characteristic of American identity (see lines 1 and 168–169, respectively, and question 1 in Looking Back). Extrapolating from these two comments, write an essay that explains—in concrete as well as abstract terms—what you believe it means to be an American. Just as Baldwin does, take into consideration not only racial and ethnic origins but also roles such as worker or student. See if your essay can earn the title Baldwin gives his.

2. Leaving home is an ancient theme in literature and, historically, a common impulse among young people who feel suffocated by their environment. Such people, propelled by motives more or less complicated than Baldwin's, are like him trying to

find themselves. But what does it mean to find yourself? And how does leaving familiar surroundings serve this purpose? What may a new place possibly offer that the old one failed to? Are there problems in the search for self to which leaving home offers no solution, or only a partial one? Write an essay that attempts to answer these questions. Review Baldwin's experience, and use your own if appropriate, but also take an analytic approach to the issues suggested by these questions.

3. According to Baldwin, writers and intellectuals have a significant place in European society, but quite the reverse in the United States. Abroad, they may not be liked, but they are at least taken seriously. Here, the writer "fights his way to one of the lowest rungs on the American social ladder" (lines 73–74, and see question 4 in Looking Back). Although this neglect is often painful to American writers, we can also imagine that they can benefit from the lack of official recognition and from the need to struggle on their own for the acclaim of their readers (see question 5 in Looking Back). Which on balance, do you think is the better situation for writers, the European or the American one? Write an essay that reports Baldwin's negative findings, discusses the positive slant suggested above, and decides which is more convincing and why.

# *Follow-Up: An Essay for Analysis*

### DIRTY BOULEVARD

At times I have felt like a novelty, since I moved to
New York that is.  Some people have found quite interesting the girl off the turnip truck from Utah,
the Mormon.  I was insistent on being a maverick, on
making something of myself.  So I took the leap out          5
of the stifling ennui of farm country and flew over
the protecting shield of Rocky Mountains.  Through
whatever pains or troubles I would huddle with the
masses; I would help the poor; I would make a new
life with the open minded, the liberated.  Instead, I          10
was forced to swallow my effervescent Laguardia landing when I realized the indigestible glint from a
dirty boulevard.
      I was in New York a while before I really realized
what I was missing and why I didn't understand what          15
was going on.  I had never known anyone who was
African-American, Jewish, Italian or Catholic and I
never thought it important.  I hadn't participated
much in the world, but where I was from there was no
one different from me to fear enough to hate.  My only          20
concern was getting far enough away from the boredom,
sexism and religion that I might feel free to be anything I want to be.  But, "Do Mormons still practice

polygamy?" my fellow New Yorkers would ask. They knew
25 as much about me as I knew about them. Those spacious
skies began to storm over me as I realized the open
minded, the liberated, whom I expected to huddle with,
were in self-imposed, sequestered segments giving us
a bunch of cleaves, colonies, satellites whom abhor
30 each other. Most recently, I was disappointed to find
my fiancé Mark's family to be such a tight community
of a people, so different from me that my difference
is seen as a threat to them. "Can't you see she is
trying to break up the family," Gerildine, his sister,
35 asked. Yes, too me, it was a dirty boulevard.

Everyone has a comfort zone: the place inside
themselves inscribed with the personal regulations of
what in life they can deal with and what they cannot.
I've got mine, you've got yours and James Baldwin had
40 his. However vast and complex the subject of Mr.
Baldwin's essay "The discovery of What It Means to Be
an American," it broaches his finding himself through
his becoming an expatriate. It was dealing with people different than himself that helped him reexamine
45 what being an American meant to him and thereby
helped him widen the margins of his own comfort zone.
As a writer in Europe he witnessed a freedom and
openness among the people which he compared with what
he saw as "social paranoia," the pity and pomp be-
50 tween power brokers and "regular guys" in America.
His observations  helped him come to terms with the
racism he was subject to in America. He discovered
that finding oneself is realizing that the only one
who can hold you back is yourself.
55 I kept running, from boulevard to boulevard, Manhattan to Flushing to Bensonhurst to my latest stop
Staten Island looking for a place I would fit in, but
failing to realize the importance of my origin, how it
shaped me, how it helped me understand you. Baldwin
60 denied himself his Bessie Smith and watermelon and
trained himself not to fit in with anybody until he
got to Europe; He resented his own origins. But he
realized you can only blame others until you have the
social consciousness to empower yourself. My recog-
65 nizing that Baldwin's troubles were different from
mine helps me to understand that they were also different, or the same, as yours. By doing this I have a
better understanding of my, and your, origins, and,

moreover, why we are such a threat to each other. We are all our own troubled countries "in this fearfully troubled world," and as long as we realize this we can try to understand our own pain and that of others. Some people, I believe, can understand this without leaving their own surroundings, but for me New York, like Europe for Baldwin, no matter how painful a real- ization was not only healthy but the only way. Going to the dirty boulevard is the first step, but when you get there learning to understand and accept the fears and pain of those who walk on it is the first step in finding yourself. It is how you react and by your own example that those who do not know you can learn to accept you. Leaving our own familiar communities will not teach us everything we need to know in his life, it will never guarantee that others will accept you for who you are, but if you can accept this fact, and yourself, then you have found yourself. Your life is how you react to your surroundings, and Baldwin would say that is in your own hands.

70
75
80
85

--Gwen Caras, composition student

## Critical Inquiry

Gwen Caras wrote the essay "Dirty Boulevard" in response to James Baldwin's "The Dis-covery of What It Means to Be an American," Writing Assignment 2 (p. 182). Caras's es-say is a preliminary draft. That is, it needs revision on a number of levels before it can be judged acceptable. To help you become more aware of your own writing needs as well as those of this student writer, use this list of questions to analyze her essay. Before answer-ing them, you should reread the text and writing assignment Caras responded to.

## Questions for Analysis

1. To what degree do you think Caras has fully absorbed and understood Baldwin's text? Why do you think so?

2. In your judgment, has Caras done what the writing assignment called for? If so, what supports your view? If not, what matters has she left unaddressed?

3. Has Caras referred to Baldwin's text sufficiently for someone who has *not* read his essay to understand his intent and chief idea? Why do you think this?

4. How would you evaluate the overall structure of this draft? Is there a clear begin-ning, middle, and end? Does Caras need to position some materials differently?

5. Does Caras's logic hold up throughout, or are there places where it falls down? Be specific.

6. Is any part of the discussion irrelevant to Caras's purpose? If so, which part, and how is it irrelevant?

7. Have you detected surface errors—grammar, sentence structure, punctuation, spelling, and capitalization—that need to be edited? If so, correct them by rewriting the sentences in which they occur.

8. Do you think Caras has come close, in this draft, to discussing the topic of finding oneself in a creative and original way? Would you have thought things out differently than she did? Support your view.

# Bharati Mukherjee

# The World According to Hsü

Born in Calcutta in 1940, Bharati Mukherjee is a short story writer and novelist. Her novels include *Jasmine* and *The Tiger's Daughter*. "The World According to Hsü," from her first collection *Darkness* (1985), won a Canadian journalism award. In the introduction to this volume, Mukherjee's comments on her immigrant status cast light on the story printed here.

> In the years that I spent in Canada—1966 to 1980—I discovered that the country is hostile to its citizens who had been born in hot, moist continents like Asia; that the country proudly boasts of its opposition to the whole concept of cultural assimilation. . . .

> I was frequently taken for a prostitute or shoplifter, frequently assumed to be a domestic, praised by astonished auditors that I didn't have a "sing-song" accent. . . . In the United States, however, I see *myself* in these same outcasts. . . .

> I see myself as an American writer in the tradition of other American writers whose parents or grandparents had passed through Ellis Island. . . .

Mukherjee has taught at Columbia University and Queens College. Currently she is a Distinguished Professor on the English department faculty of the University of California, Berkeley.

## Looking Ahead

1. Although references likely to be unfamiliar are explained in footnotes, observe the sense of internationalism that remains as a key element in the story.

2. As in much fiction, the characters' past history is mixed with the chronology of the present narrative to help us read critically to understand who these people are.

3. The title of the story comments on the emotional crisis at the heart of the story, a fact to keep in mind since the title emerges in the text.

They had come to this island off the coast of Africa for simple reasons: he to see the Southern Cross[1] and she to take stock of a life that had until recently seemed to her manageably capricious. Their travel agent, a refugee from Beirut, morbidly sensitive to political and epidemical tremors, had not warned them of the latest crisis in the capital. Coups and curfews visited with seasonal regularity, but like nearly everything else about the island, went unreported in the press. The most recent, involving melancholy students and ungenerous bureaucrats, had been especially ferocious; people had died and shops had been sacked but nothing had stained the island's reputation for languor and spices.

The Claytons did not blame Camille Lioon, the travel agent. No one could have told them about the revolution, this thing called, alternatively (in the island's morning daily), *les événements de soixante-dix-huit,* and *l'aventure des forces contre-revolutionnaires, impérialistes, et capitalistes.*[2] Continents slide, no surface is permanent. Today's ballooning teenager is tomorrow's anorexic. The island should have been a paradise.

They had wanted an old-fashioned vacation on the shores of a vast new ocean. They had planned to pick shells, feed lemurs on the balcony of a hotel managed by a paunchy Indian, visit a colonial museum or two, where, under glass, the new guardians of the nation enshrined the whips and chains of their unnatural past. They had readied themselves for small misadventures—lost bags, cancelled hotel reservations—the kind that Graeme Clayton could tell with some charm on their return to Canada.

But Ratna Clayton, groping for the wisdom that should have descended on her in her thirty-third year, hoped for something more from this journey to the island below the equator. Surely simple tourist pleasures, for instance, watching the big pink sun fall nightly into calm pink waters, would lighten the shadows of the past six months? She imagined herself in her daring new bikini on a shoreline tangled with branches and cattle skulls. The landscape was always narcotically beautiful. But always, Graeme was just behind her, training his Nikon on that chaotic greenery to extract from it some definitive order.

In Montreal, each Ektachrome transparency of the island, she knew, would command a commentary, every slide a mini-lecture. Lecturing was Graeme's business. For his friends he would shape and reshape the tropical confusion. Ratna would serve her cashew-lamb pilaf and begin hesitant anecdotes about pickpockets and beggars. The friends would listen with civil, industrious faces until Graeme, having set up the projector, was free to entertain and instruct. The burned-out buses, they would learn, were Hungarian; the plump young paratroopers with flat African faces were coastal people, a reminder of the island's proximity to the Dark Continent. The ducks in the rice paddies did not

1. *Southern Cross:* a four-star constellation that is visible only over the southern hemisphere. (*ed.*)

2. *les événements . . . capitalistes:* the events of '78; the adventure of imperialist and capitalist counterrevolutionary forces. (*ed.*)

40 yet answer to genus and species; Graeme would have to look it up. And bitter,
terrified, politicized Freddie McLaren, Graeme's colleague at McGill,[3] would
find an opportune moment to pipe up, "I don't know why you two went to
Africa. If you wanted trouble you could've found it right here in Canada." Freddie
with his talk of Belfast and Beirut, and what the future held for Montreal. "It's
45 not going to matter one damn bit to them that you speak French and hate Ontario as much as they do," he'd say, and Graeme would answer, "But Freddie—I
don't hate Ontario." Ratna Clayton would add, quietly, "And I don't hate Quebec." And soon the McLarens would lead the Claytons back from Africa and its
riots to the safe disasters of letter-bombs and budget cuts.
50 Camille Lioon had prepared them for lesser dangers. "No, m'sieur, you
should not make the *escale*[4] in Zanzibar, where I have heard there is much
cholera." Camille had contacts in World Health, in banks, in subministries
around the world. Ratna pictured a small army of sallow Lioons frenziedly
sending telegrams to all parts of the French-speaking world: *disaster imminent.*
55 *Don't come. Hide.* And to Ratna he'd whispered, "No, madame, if I were Hindu I
would cancel the *escale* in Jiddah. Those Saudis, they're so insensible." Ratna
smiled, suspecting that Camille had slipped on a tangled cognate.
"Insensitive?" she'd asked.
"Yes, yes, insensitive."
60 "Unfeeling?" Ratna pursued.
"That's it! *Un peu brutale.*"[5]
In Riyadh,[6] chopped-off hands were lying on the street. The street was
black with flies, feasting on hands, according to Camille. "I am no less an Arab
than they, but if I land in Mecca—phfft—they slit my throat, no questions
65 asked. Not even in anger. No, I would definitely not stop in Jiddah." The trouble with the Saudis, Graeme had thought, was not with their quaint notions of
punishment. It was that they had lost some of their wayward mystery. In spite
of their genial floggings and stoical dismemberments, petro-dollars had opened
them up, made them accessible to Rotarians and the covers of *Time*. And so the
70 Claytons had given up their earlier itinerary, not because Camille's caution was
infectious, but because they yearned for once to be simple-minded travellers
yielding to every expensive and off-beat prompting. This island of spices, this
misplaced Tahiti, this gorgeous anachronism, would serve them beautifully,
they'd thought.
75 Graeme had reserved his strength, which came to him in paroxysms much
like panic, for this voyage of a lifetime to what everyone called *la grande île au
bout du monde.*[7] Islands and endings were Graeme's business too, and he de-

3. McGill: a Canadian university located in Montreal. (*ed.*)

4. *escale:* port of call. (*ed.*)

5. *un peu brutale:* slightly brutal. (*ed.*)

6. *Riyadh:* city in Saudi Arabia. (*ed.*)

7. *la grande . . . monde:* the great island at the bottom of the world. (*ed.*)

manded, in his leisure, a certain consonance with his discipline. He was thirty-
five, the youngest full professor of psychology at McGill, an authority on a
whole rainbow of dysfunctions, and he had a need for something which he in
his old-fashioned way called romance. It was not the opposite of reality; it was
more a sharpening of line and color, possible only in the labs or on a carefully
researched, fully cooperative, tropical island. In the place of a heart he should
have had a Nikon.

Besides, he hoped the vacation would be the right setting for persuading
Ratna to move to Toronto, where he'd been offered—quite surprisingly in a year
when English Montrealers would leap at just about anything—the chair in Personality Development. So far, she'd been obdurate. She claimed to be happy
enough in Montreal, less perturbed by the impersonal revenges of Quebec
politicians than personal attacks by Toronto racists. In Montreal she was merely
"English," a grim joke on generations of British segregationists. It was thought
charming that her French was just slightly short of fluent. In Toronto, she was
not Canadian, not even Indian. She was something called, after the imported idiom of London, a Paki. And for Pakis, Toronto was hell.

She had only a secondhand interest in the English language and a decided
aversion to British institutions; English had been a mutually agreed upon second language in her home, in her first city, in her first country, in her career and
it had remained so, even in her marriage. Frenchification was quaint, not threatening. She'd even voted for the separatists. She had claimed reluctance to chop
off what tentative roots she had in Montreal. *La grande île* was to be a refuge
from just such fruitless debates.

So, having picked their archipelago to get away to, the Claytons had flown
in on schedule one wintry June morning (it was cool; sweater weather, though
many of the islanders at the airport had been wearing overcoats, gloves and caps
with tied-down earflaps) and immediately found themselves prisoners of an unreported revolution.

Their prison, a twenty-five-dollar a day double room with a bath and bidet
at the Hotel Papillon,[8] was not uncomfortable. In a time of lesser crisis they
might have complained, among themselves, of the lumps in the mattress or the
pale stains on the towel. They might have wondered at the new gray wall-to-
wall carpeting, the Simenon novels on the window ledge, the Cinzano ashtrays
("This is Africa? This is a People's Republic?"). But now, on their first day in the
capital, still convalescing from thirty hours' flying and the teetering ride in the
airport taxi, the Papillon appeared a triumph of French obstinacy in the face of
antipodean distraction.

The entrance to the hotel, whose walls were ochre deepening to brown
where the water pipes had rusted, was off a sidewalk choked with stalls. Around
the entrance were pyramids of tomatoes, green peppers, dried fish, fried
grasshoppers, safety pins and chipped buttons. The sidewalk directly in front of

---

8. *Papillon:* French for "butterfly"; perhaps a symbolic name for the proprietor. (*ed.*)

120   it was gouged and fissured, as though islanders walking by had wrenched up
the paving stones and put them to more urgent, if unrecorded, use. The gouges
were coated with the pulp of chewed rotting food spat out by the stallkeepers.
An opaque glass door behind a sidewalk tangle of metal tables and chairs had
announced in neat black lettering:

125                                     HOTEL PAPILLON                            ·
                                    Prop: M J-P Papillon

       Monsieur Jean-Paul Papillon, the Claytons learned from Justin, the taxi-
driver, had died thirteen years before. The hotel had been declining with his
health. Why hadn't they chosen the new Hilton? The Hilton was a touch of
130   Paris.
       "In the old days," Justin said, "this place was better than anything in Mar-
seilles. The French called it the pearl of the Indian Ocean. The restaurant of the
Papillon had two stars from Michelin." Then, turning to Ratna Clayton, he'd
asked, "Do you want me to drive you to the Hilton?"
135          They had gotten off at the Papillon to spite the driver. To Justin, the Claytons had seemed American or German, part of the natural Hilton crowd. The
Hilton had four dining rooms and a rooftop casino. From late October through
to the beginning of autumn, in April, it maintained an outdoor pool. Graeme
understood the type-casting and decided not to forgive him.
140          "Papillon," Graeme had ordered, having studied all the guide books on the
flight from Paris. "L'avenue d'Albert Camus."
       "M'sieur-dame, you don't understand," Justin had pleaded, placing a pink re-
straining palm on their luggage. "The Papillon is in the center of the marketplace."
       "*Tant mieux*,"9 Ratna had said, nudging a suitcase out of his grip.
145          "But madame, *les manifesteurs*10 . . . there might be trouble again tonight."
       "We'll manage," Graeme had said. Other people's revolutions could not
shock or dismay. He wondered if tourists in Montreal, those few who still came,
counted themselves equally bold.
       "But m'sieur," Justin begged, now flushed from his coyness, "all the Indi-
150   ans, they stay at the Hilton. In times like these, it's the safest place."
       "I am a Canadian," Ratna said arrogantly. "I'm a Canadian tourist and I
want to stay at the Papillon in the marketplace, okay?"
       The truth was, she knew, that even on this island she could not escape the
consequences of being half—the dominant half—Indian. Her mother, a Czech
155   nurse, had found love or perhaps only escape in a young Indian medical student on holiday in Europe in 1936, and she had sailed with him to Calcutta.
She'd died there last year, a shrunken widow in a white sari, allegedly a happy
woman. The European strain had appeared and disappeared, leaving no genetic

---

     9.  *Tant mieux:* so much the better. (*ed.*)

     10.  *les manifesteurs:* the demonstrators. (*ed.*)

souvenir (for her first two years, family legend had it, Ratna had been a pale, scrawny blonde, shunned by her father's family as a "white rat"). Ratna's Euro-     160
peanness lay submerged like an ancient city waiting to be revealed by shallow-water archeology. Her show of unaccustomed fervor apparently satisfied Justin.

*"Alors, madame, vous n'êtes pas indienne?"*[11] He had then swung the bag out of her hand and carried it to the hotel entrance.

"Are the nights cloudy in June?" Graeme had asked, paying him off. "I've     165
come a long way to see the Southern Cross."

That's when they'd learned the cruncher. Justin pointed to a hastily scrawled sign, pasted to the door. COUVRE-FEU 17h.

"All-night curfew, m'sieur. *Tout est fermé*[12] . . . No stars, no nothing."

"God!" muttered Graeme Clayton.     170

"That explains those paratroopers tramping around the paddy-fields," Ratna remarked. She was a freelance journalist grateful for good copy. There had been paratroopers everywhere, black faces from the coast, ubiquitous sentinels among the copper-skinned, straw-hatted natives of the capital. Descending on the adobe villages like Van Gogh's crows, they had squatted in the clean greenness of ba-     175
nana groves, kicked the muddy flanks of water buffalo and sped down the air-port road in their frail Renaults. They had even stopped Justin's taxi a few miles outside the city and ordered a half-hearted search of the Claytons' baggage. She'd not realized, until seeing the curfew sign, that she and Graeme might have been in danger, that the soldiers' comments in a different language, obviously directed     180
to Justin about her, could have led to untraceable tragedy in a paddy-field.

Justin seemed reluctant to leave them. "You want me to come back for you this afternoon? I'll make you a cheap excursion?"

"How much?"

"Ten thousand francs. I'll give you the two-hour tour, bring you back be-     185
fore the curfew."

Ratna had not yet calibrated the local currency. Ten thousand was, roughly, thirty dollars. At the sound of ten thousand she had snapped instinctively, "Too much."

"Eight thousand."

"Come for us at three."     190

Still Justin hung around. He had become transformed from taxi-driver to gracious host. She wondered if they owed him their lives; that if they'd not been cheerful and approving and engaging in that brief ride from the airport to the informal roadblock, and if he had not said something preventive to the troops,     195
she and Graeme would have been slaughtered, their travellers' checks and local currency and Canadian dollars and gold chains and Nikon apportioned as the usual supplemental wages.

---

11. *"Alors . . . indienne?"*: "So, madam, you aren't Indian?" (*ed.*)

12. *Toute est fermé*: Everything is closed. (*ed.*)

The lobby was narrow, dark, no more than a corridor partitioned off the
200   hotel's former dining room. Three islanders were still breakfasting on *café au
lait,* croissants and a Gauloise: each at his table replicating France. Compared to
them, Ratna thought, the Montrealers they had left behind at Charles de Gaulle
Airport—those for whom Paris and not the end of the world had been the
destination—were nothing but wonderstruck Americans, accidental French-
205   speakers with Quebec fleurs-de-lis sewn on their bulging hip pockets. Far less
Gallic than these Peruvian-looking Africans waiting out another bizarre crisis at
the Papillon.
       The proprietress sat at the end of the dark corridor, behind an uneven
counter and under a cardboard arrow that said: Caisse.[13] She was obese, with
210   densely powdered, flour-white skin.
       Justin preceded the Canadians. He asked first after Madame Papillon's
daughter, who had apparently been sent back to France for *traitements.* Treatments for what? Graeme was about to ask, then suppressed it. Madame Papillon
asked Justin about *les événements:* had there been much looting? He reassured
215   her. Nothing new. Only two blocks burned. The epicenter of the looting was
only a block away; Madame Papillon was evidently reclusive. The shops of the
Indians in la Place del l'Indépendance and along the Faubourg. *Les indiens,* they
had fled as usual to the Hilton, to lock up their gold and money in the hotel's
safe. "Ah, toujours les indiens," wheezed Madame, "les juifs de l'Afrique."[14] Stu-
220   dents were gathering again in front of the Secretariat building. Possibly, another
outbreak might occur that night. (Later, during the sightseeing trip, Justin explained that Madame Papillon, a model of Vichy rectitude, had not stepped
from the hotel since her husband's death thirteen years before. "I bring her
news like infusions," he said.)
225   After the bellboy had left, cautioning them that the tap water was not
potable and that mineral water could be secured through him more cheaply
than through room service, they forced open the window shutters for their first
private view of the city.
       "Don't worry about the smoke," Graeme said. "The fires are out."
230   "I'm not worrying about this island," Ratna said from the closet where she
was checking the wallpaper seams for roaches. "I'm worrying about Toronto." A
week before their flight, a Bengali woman was beaten and nearly blinded on the
street. And the week before that an eight-year-old Punjabi boy was struck by a
car announcing on its bumper: KEEP CANADA GREEN. PAINT A PAKI.
235   He knew from the deadness of her voice what was to come. "It won't happen to you," he said quickly. He resented this habit she had of injecting bitterness into every new scene. He had paid five thousand dollars in airfare so they
could hold hands on a beach under the Southern Cross, but already she was accusing him of selfishness and bigotry.

---

13. *Caisse:* cashier. (*ed.*)

14. *"Ah . . . de l'Afrique":* "Ah, always Indians, the Jews of Africa." (*ed.*)

"That's not the point." 240

"Look—violence is everywhere. Toronto's the safest city on the continent."

"Sure," she said, "for you." She hung a cotton dress in the closet. She had married him for a trivial reason—his blue eyes—then discovered in him tenderness, affection, decency. Once not long ago she had believed in the capacity of these virtues to restore symmetry to lives mangled by larger, blunter an- 245 tipathies. "An Indian professor's wife was jumped at a red light, right in her car. They threw her groceries on the street. They said Pakis shouldn't drive big cars."

"If you don't want to go to Toronto, we won't go."

"But you want to go. It's the best place for you. You said Montreal's finished."

"Can we just relax and enjoy the vacation?" 250

Ratna nodded. He deserved a truce.

Justin returned for them at 3:05. He had borrowed his brother's Peugeot. His brother sold polished stones; he could give them a good price. He drove them to a lookout point near an old French fort. The city lay spilled over the greenish-red hills like bushels of stone eggs, clinging to ledges and piling up in color- 255 ful heaps in the valleys. In the afternoon light, the oranges and yellows of the buildings were brilliant. They counted thirty-seven churches, Lutheran predominating. "Swedish missionaries in the 19th century," Justin explained. "Very successful, before the massacre." Graeme asked if all the islanders were Christian, and Justin said they were; religion was called *la troisième force*.[15] They were 260 reluctant to inquire about the first two. *"Mais les peuples de côte nord, ils sont un peu musulman au même temps."*[16]

The heat of the June sun was gentle. The people wore their winter clothes capriciously, as though experimenting with other nations' castoffs. It was hard to think of them as revolutionaries, but in that morning's paper, the riots of the 265 night before had been termed counterrevolutionary, the work of enemies of the revolution, fueled by agents of international capitalism. The only foreign country with influence besides France, according to Justin, was North Korea.

He showed them the legitimate sights: the President's house, the squares where various presidents had been assassinated or executed, a housing project, 270 an artificial lake and the Hilton Hotel which was the tallest building in the city.

The zoo was closed to the public because of the disturbances. The museum too was closed indefinitely. The mission school, run by Quebec fathers, was closed. At the Monday market they walked around two burned trucks and bought mangoes. 275

Finally, Justin said, "If you like, we can drive past the Indian shops."

They drove behind a truckload of jeering paratroopers who pointed their rifles and fired mock salvos into their taxi. Justin appeared worried and Graeme

---

15. *la troisième force:* the third force (between capitalism and communism). (*ed.*)

16. *"Mais . . . temps":* "But the people living on the northern coast are slightly Muslim at the same time." (*ed.*)

cringed, but Ratna felt safer than she had in the subway stations of Toronto.
280 They swung onto a wide boulevard, la Place de l'Indépendance, lined with gutted shops. In one ruined shop, a mannequin in lavender silk stuck an intact head out of a jagged hole in the display case. The signboard was splashed with tomatoes:

LUI ET ELLE
285 Importeurs
Props. K. Mourardji Desai et Fils

A paratrooper, daubed in garish greens and browns, waved them on.

"Drive slowly," Graeme whispered. He hid his Nikon half in his shirt and snapped the paratrooper beside the mannequin.

290 Justin had promised them a two-hour trip but he had shown them the city in forty-five minutes. Too many things were closed, too many sections of town under guard. So they asked him to drive out into the country.

For miles the road was nothing more than an untidy gash, an aid-project miscalculation, on the side of an endless red hill. They feared the road might
295 strand them among wet rice fields and blood-red adobes. Then, without warning, the flaccid gash acquired a scab of gray; it became an oddly formal *grande allée* wider than a runway, lined with jacaranda and light standards. The boulevard terminated at the iron gate of a wooden house with painted columns.

"*Et voilà*," Justin announced. "*Le palais de roi.*"
300 "Where's the King?" Ratna asked.

"The French threw him out in 1767. He was seven feet tall and used to kill missionaries by biting their heads off—phfft."

"Where's that music coming from?" Graeme asked. Faint, almost familiar, it seemed to be coming from the royal grounds.
305 "Oh, that? It is a recital by the King's band."

"But you have no king."

"We still have his band. Only the best musicians are allowed to play."

"It is open to the public?"

"No, no," said Justin, throwing up his hands. "The public is not allowed.
310 No photography is allowed."

"Then who the hell are they playing for? Are they practicing for a special occasion?"

"Yes, they are rehearsing," said Justin.

"For a holiday?"
315 "No, no, the revolution outlawed all the old holidays. Now they give recitals here everyday."

"For themselves?" asked Ratna.

"Yes, yes, only for themselves. They rehearse for when the holidays come back and they give recitals everyday for themselves."
320 The Claytons walked up the shallow steps that led to the iron gate. Heavy chains and an ornamental lock were looped around its rusty trelliswork. It was hard to think of that entrance or of that wooden house as royal. There were no

guards, not even the gaudy paratroopers in open-topped boots. The Claytons searched the wooden structure—the wood turned out to be just a facade for another large adobe box—for clues to its forgotten history, but all the plaques had been taken down. The walls showed no flags, no heraldic signs, not even the mysterious wounds of battle. Over to one side, under the shade of jacaranda trees, sat the King's band. Their uniforms were splendidly gallant, red satin with gold braid. It was a brass band; the bandmaster wore a yachting cap and a bright red tunic. His white beard was neatly trimmed. The band knew the piece well, whatever it was; this was a recital, not a practice. The notes meandered in the wintry twilight, refusing to coalesce into anything familiar. The music revealed no hurt, no quiet suffering—it was intended for pomp and public celebration, it was music of the plazas and reviewing stands. The moment held no pathos, only dust and gallantry. When the visitors had to leave because it was too perilously close to the curfew deadline, the man playing the tuba tipped his instrument in Ratna's direction. 325

330

335

At 5:30, Madame Papillon taped down the windows of the dining hall so that even if stones were thrown later that night, the glass would not shatter. At 6:30, she locked the glass-fronted entrance to the hotel. At seven, the Claytons came down for dinner. 340

Graeme brought his copy of *Scientific American* that he had begun to read on the plane. This was his light reading; he had brought no psych or medical journals with him.

"Did you know that it's always irritated me, I mean your reading at the table?" 345

"I'm not reading," he said, meaning *you're free to interrupt me, I'm not advancing my career; I'm being open and conversational, this is just the sports page to me.* "Did you know, according to . . ."

She couldn't catch the name, but it sounded like a dry sneeze. Hsü? Could it be Hsü? 350

". . . that six million years ago the Mediterranean basin was a desert? And it took the Atlantic a million years to break through and fill it again? Gibraltar for a million years was the most spectacular waterfall the world will ever see. The old sea was called Tethys and it connected the Atlantic with the Indian Ocean." 355

At the table to her right a German communications expert was teaching an English folksong to three Ismaili-Indian children.

"Row, row, row your boat," the children shouted, before collapsing in giggles.

"In the last Ice Age the Black Sea was a freshwater lake. They have fossil crustaceans to prove it." 360

The children's father, a small handsome man, scraped his chair back and said, "Watch me. Here is Bob Hope playing golf." The children giggled again. How, Ratna wondered, how in the world had they seen or heard of Bob Hope? Or golf? Or had they, or did it matter? It struck her as unspeakably heroic, gallant. 365

Graeme asked her if she was crying.

An American at the next table looked up at her from the paperback he was pretending to read and winked at her. He was tanned like a marine biologist.

Graeme slid the magazine across to her. She read the title: "When the Black Sea Was Drained," by Kenneth J. Hsü.

"He writes very well," said Graeme. This, she realized, was a concession to her; he was appreciating something remotely journalistic, though still respectably scientific.

An African chef, in a flowered shirt, carried a casserole to their table. Ratna had ordered "the National Dish." She found it a concoction of astonishing crudity.

A waiter turned on the television set for the World Cup scores, relayed from Dar es Salaam,[17] *en provenance de*[18] Buenos Aires, on another cold night under the Southern Cross. The Claytons had not expected color television on such an island. The German (East or West, Ratna wondered), overhearing the Canadians, informed them that it was cheaper to install the latest color system than an obsolete black-and-white one. It had to do with the island's profound underdevelopment. They could not even manufacture their own spare parts, and the industrialized countries no longer turned out components for black-and-white. That's why he was on the island, he said; to install a complete microwave transmitting system. Given her mood, it struck Ratna as one of the most brutal stories she had ever heard.

"What about India?" she asked.

"Oh, India is technologically sophisticated," he said. And she was faintly, absurdly, assured. India would keep its sophisticated black-and-white system for the foreseeable future and leave color to the basket-cases.

A woman news announcer said in carefully articulated French that there had been a coup on a nearby archipelago. Counterrevolutionary forces led by neocolonialist intriguers had killed the popular, progressive prime minister and placed the islands under martial law. Progressive people everywhere expressed their concern, and from Pyongyang, Kim Il Sung[19] spoke for the whole world in denouncing this act of capitalist desperation. Demonstrations in support of the true revolutionaries would be held tomorrow in the capital, at the municipal football stadium. No mention was made of the riots on the island, which led Graeme to speculate that things were getting worse.

"According to Hsü," he said, "the last time the world was one must have been about six million years ago. Now Africa and Asia are colliding. India got smashed into Asia—that's why the Himalayas got wrinkled up. This island is just part of the debris."

---

17. *Dar es Salaam:* a coastal city in Tanzania. (*ed.*)

18. *en provenance de:* by way of. (*ed.*)

19. *Pyongyang; Kim Il Sung:* capital of North Korea; North Korean communist head of state until 1994. (*ed.*)

Ratna played with forkfuls of the national dish. Why did the Black Sea have to  405
drain? Why did continents have to collide? Why did they have to move to Toronto?

On that small island, in that besieged dining hall, she felt that with effort
she might become an expert on the plate tectonics of emotion. As long as she
could sit and listen to the other guests converse in a mutually agreed-upon
second language, she would be all right. Like her, they were nonislanders,  410
refugees.

She heard Graeme ask Madame Papillon, "Is it safe to go outside for a moment? I've spent a fortune to see the Southern Cross."

At nine, while they were lingering over a local red wine, a waiter burst in
with news. Snipers had shot the Bulgarian ambassador's wife. She had been  415
watching the riot from her balcony and phfft—a sniper had got her in the chest.
Now the paratroopers would probably go on a rampage.

"It's always the same thing," Madame Papillon sighed. "The students want
to overthrow the government. You can't carry on an honest business on this island." She left, to sit again at her desk.  420

Graeme poured more wine, draining the bottle. "An acceptable red wine—
surprising, eh, from such a place?"

"It used to be French," Ratna said. At least the French left palpable legacies,
despite the profound underdevelopment.

"By the way," Graeme said, "I wrote to Toronto before we left. I've accepted  425
the Chair. And don't worry, if anything happens to you there I promise we'll
leave. Immediately, okay?"

"What can I say?"

"Will you come see the stars with me?"

"Not tonight."  430

He signaled for the waiter and ordered another half-bottle of red wine. He
poured her a glass, then called the waiter back. She heard the waiter mention *La
Voie lactée* and *les sacs de charbon,* and Graeme's eyes lit up. "The Coal sack! I
didn't think I'd ever see it." And just below the coal sacks in that luminous tropical Milky Way, low on the horizon, the waiter told him he'd see the Southern  435
Cross.

They went out, through the kitchen and the service entrance.

He'd be all right, she thought. Wherever he went.

The American leaned toward her from his table. "What's this," he asked,
"this *champignons farcis?*" He looked drunk, but courteous. She had to look  440
where he was pointing.

"Mushrooms," she said, smiling. From that odd opening on that odd island
a conversation could go anywhere. Not all North Americans were forced to fear
the passionate consequences of their unilingualism.

For the first time she saw that the label on the bottle read: Côte de Cassan-  445
dre. A superior red table wine that no one had ever heard of; perhaps the lone
competent industry on the island. Better, she thought, than the Quebec cider
she and Graeme made such a patriotic point of always serving.

450 She poured herself another glass, feeling for the moment at home in that collection of Indians and Europeans babbling in English and remembered dialects. No matter where she lived, she would never feel so at home again.

## Looking Back

1. When do the events reported here occur?
2. What early picture do we get of Graeme and Ratna Clayton?
3. How is our view of Graeme affected by his belief that "other people's revolutions could not shock or dismay" (lines 146–147)? How does this attitude compare with Ratna's as hers becomes clear in the story?
4. Does Ratna's ostracism because of her childhood blondness (see lines 159–160) have parallels with problems of racial identity that you know of? What are they?
5. What do we gather from Mme. Papillon's remarks about the relative positions in society of whites, Indians, and blacks (see lines 211–224)?
6. What is the difference between the "truce" Ratna concedes to Graeme (line 251) and peace?
7. How does Ratna's emotional crisis (over the racism she expects in Toronto) account for the way she observes the other diners at the Papillon (see lines 338–392)?
8. What do the questions Ratna asks in lines 405–406 have in common?
9. How does Graeme's sudden announcement that he's accepted the job in Toronto strike you?
10. Can you explain why Ratna feels that "No matter where she lived, she would never feel so at home again" (line 451)?

## Writing Assignments

1. Cultural diversity is seen by many people as positive—good for society at large, good for the historical development of a nation, and good for the individual who brings to a new place elements of an original culture. Many other people, however—and Mme. Papillon and Graeme himself may number among them—are indifferent and sometimes even hostile to the idea of varied nationalities coming together to produce a new mix. Because of such opposition, the need remains to define, illustrate, and justify the idea and practices of cultural diversity. Referring to the story when useful, write an essay discussing cultural diversity as a good. One question you might consider is just how much of one's ethnic inheritance ought to be preserved and how much given up.

2. Marriage between two individuals from different cultures can become a problem when one partner, like Graeme in the story, does not consider the history and heritage of the other partner. Some people object to intermarriage on this very ground, arguing that it further complicates the basic relationship, which is never trouble-free anyhow. Other people have other objections to intermarriage, such as the need for particular groups to maintain their purity. Still others say that love does not recognize such

boundaries and such abstract requirements. What do you say? Write an essay interpolating your response to these views as a means of discussing Graeme and Ratna's marriage and extrapolating from that discussion to comment on intermarriage generally.

3. Ratna, we discover, was scorned as a child by members of her family because her physical appearance varied from the racial norm. This phenomenon seems not to be limited to Indians. In the United States today, some African Americans make distinctions between individuals based on how dark or light they are. At one moment, lightness is preferred for its closeness to Caucasian color; at another moment, darkness is valued as a testimony to the pure blood of the individual. That is, there seem to be cultural and political reasons for this valuation. Should there be, or should individuals be accepted or rejected on other grounds, like personal character, no matter what their hue? Write an essay addressing this question.

# F. Scott Fitzgerald
# Early Success

Although he felt that he had wasted his early promise as a writer, F(rancis) Scott Fitzgerald (1896–1940) produced in his short lifetime a novel that has become an American classic, *The Great Gatsby*, the relatively underestimated but fine *Tender Is the Night*, and the posthumously published and unfinished work, *The Last Tycoon*. His second novel, *The Beautiful and the Damned*, is less important. *This Side of Paradise* is the book whose publication "Early Success" chronicles. At the time Fitzgerald wrote this essay, he had just arrived in Hollywood to begin a screenwriting career as a last attempt to recoup his failing fortunes. His wife had gone insane, he was a recovering alcoholic, his books had already been largely forgotten, and so this nostalgic gaze back at the romantic dreams of his youth is hardly surprising. "Early Success" goes beyond nostalgia to exhibit Fitzgerald's critical thinking on a number of scores. For example, he questions the commonly shared veneration of the Jazz Age of the 1920s, the era most associated with his name. And he reevaluates his overnight popularity as an author, finding in that popularity losses as well as gains. The connection he makes between the social scene and his personal career produces a new perspective of the kind that marks a writer for originality.

## Looking Ahead

1. In this piece, Fitzgerald compresses the events he covers into a very few sentences, so it is necessary to let each sentence resonate in your mind for full effect.
2. Ernest Hemingway criticized Fitzgerald as self-pitying for writing confessions like this one. Read to test Hemingway's reasoning. See whether you agree with him or, instead, find redeeming value in the insights in Fitzgerald's essay.

3. The tragic sense of loss permeating this essay may seem slightly mysterious unless you perceive Fitzgerald's underlying conviction that, in life, whatever we gain we lose.

*October, 1937*

Seventeen years ago this month I quit work or, if you prefer, I retired from business. I was through—let the Street Railway Advertising Company carry along under its own power. I retired, not on my profits, but on my liabilities, which included debts, despair, and a broken engagement and crept home to St. Paul to
5 "finish a novel."
 That novel, begun in a training camp late in the war, was my ace in the hole. I had put it aside when I got a job in New York, but I was as constantly aware of it as of the shoe with cardboard in the sole, during all one desolate spring. It was like the fox and goose and the bag of beans. If I stopped working
10 to finish the novel, I lost the girl.
 So I struggled on in a business I detested and all the confidence I had garnered at Princeton and in a haughty career as the army's worst aide-de-camp melted gradually away. Lost and forgotten, I walked quickly from certain places—from the pawn shop where one left the field glasses, from prosperous
15 friends whom one met when wearing the suit from before the war—from restaurants after tipping with the last nickel, from busy cheerful offices that were saving the jobs for their own boys from the war.
 Even having a first story accepted had not proved very exciting. Dutch Mount and I sat across from each other in a car-card slogan advertising office,
20 and the same mail brought each of us an acceptance from the same magazine— the old *Smart Set*.[1]
 "My check was thirty—how much was yours?"
 "Thirty-five."
 The real blight, however, was that my story had been written in college two
25 years before, and a dozen new ones hadn't even drawn a personal letter. The implication was that I was on the down-grade at twenty-two. I spent the thirty dollars on a magenta feather fan for a girl in Alabama.
 My friends who were not in love or who had waiting arrangements with "sensible" girls, braced themselves patiently for a long pull. Not I—I was in love
30 with a whirlwind and I must spin a net big enough to catch it out of my head, a head full of trickling nickels and sliding dimes, the incessant music box of the poor. It couldn't be done like that, so when the girl threw me over I went home and finished my novel. And then, suddenly, everything changed, and this article is about that first wild wind of success and the delicious mist it brings with
35 it. It is a short and precious time—for when the mist rises in a few weeks, or a few months, one finds that the very best is over.

---

1. *Smart Set*: a magazine edited by American writer H. L. Mencken. (*ed.*)

It began to happen in the autumn of 1919 when I was an empty bucket, so mentally blunted with the summer's writing that I'd taken a job repairing car roofs at the Northern Pacific shops. Then the postman rang, and that day I quit work and ran along the streets, stopping automobiles to tell friends and acquaintances about it—my novel *This Side of Paradise* was accepted for publication. That week the postman rang and rang, and I paid off my terrible small debts, bought a suit, and woke up every morning with a world of ineffable toploftiness and promise.                40

While I waited for the novel to appear, the metamorphosis of amateur into professional began to take place—a sort of stitching together of your whole life into a pattern of work, so that the end of one job is automatically the beginning of another. I had been an amateur before; in October, when I strolled with a girl among the stones of a southern graveyard, I was a professional and my enchantment with certain things that she felt and said was already paced by an anxiety to set them down in a story—it was called *The Ice Palace* and it was published later. Similarly, during Christmas week in St. Paul, there was a night when I had stayed home from two dances to work on a story. Three friends called up during the evening to tell me I had missed some rare doings: a well-known man-about-town had disguised himself as a camel and, with a taxi-driver as the rear half, managed to attend the wrong party. Aghast with myself for not being there, I spent the next day trying to collect the fragments of the story.                45    50    55

"Well, all I can say is it was funny when it happened." "No, I don't know where he got the taxi-man." "You'd have to know him well to understand how funny it was."                60

In despair, I said:

"Well, I can't seem to find out exactly what happened but I'm going to write about it as if it was ten times funnier than anything you've said." So I wrote it, in twenty-two consecutive hours, and wrote it "funny," simply because I was so emphatically told it was funny. *The Camel's Back* was published and still crops up in the humorous anthologies.                65

With the end of the winter set in another pleasant pumped-dry period, and, while I took a little time off, a fresh picture of life in America began to form before my eyes. The uncertainties of 1919 were over—there seemed little doubt about what was going to happen—America was going on the greatest, gaudiest spree in history and there was going to be plenty to tell about it. The whole golden boom was in the air—its splendid generosities, its outrageous corruptions and the tortuous death struggle of the old America in prohibition.[2] All the stories that came into my head had a touch of disaster in them—the lovely young creatures in my novels went to ruin, the diamond mountains of my short                70    75

---

2. *prohibition:* a reference to the laws forbidding the manufacture and sale of liquor, in effect from 1920–1933. (*ed.*)

stories blew up, my millionaires were as beautiful and damned as Thomas Hardy's[3] peasants. In life these things hadn't happened yet, but I was pretty sure living wasn't the reckless, careless business these people thought—this generation just younger than me.

80      For my point of vantage was the dividing line between the two generations, and there I sat—somewhat self-consciously. When my first big mail came in—hundreds and hundreds of letters on a story about a girl who bobbed her hair—it seemed rather absurd that they should come to me about it. On the other hand, for a shy man it was nice to be somebody except oneself again: to be "the

85  Author" as one had been "the Lieutenant." Of course one wasn't really an author any more than one had been an army officer, but nobody seemed to guess behind the false face.

All in three days I got married and the presses were pounding out *This Side of Paradise* like they pound out extras in the movies.

90      With its publication I had reached a stage of manic depressive insanity. Rage and bliss alternated hour by hour. A lot of people thought it was a fake, and perhaps it was, and a lot of others thought it was a lie, which it was not. In a daze I gave out an interview—I told what a great writer I was and how I'd achieved the heights. Heywood Broun,[4] who was on my trail, simply quoted it

95  with the comment that I seemed to be a very self-satisfied young man, and for some days I was notably poor company. I invited him to lunch and in a kindly way told him that it was too bad he had let his life slide away without accomplishing anything. He had just turned thirty and it was about then that I wrote a line which certain people will not let me forget: "She was a faded but still lovely

100  woman of twenty-seven."

In a daze I told the Scribner Company that I didn't expect my novel to sell more than twenty thousand copies and when the laughter died away I was told that a sale of five thousand was excellent for a first novel. I think it was a week after publication that it passed the twenty thousand mark, but I took myself so

105  seriously that I didn't even think it was funny.

These weeks in the clouds ended abruptly a week later when Princeton turned on the book—not undergraduate Princeton but the black mass of faculty and alumni. There was a kind but reproachful letter from President Hibben, and a room full of classmates who suddenly turned on me with condemnation.

110  We had been part of a rather gay party staged conspicuously in Harvey Firestone's car of robin's-egg blue, and in the course of it I got an accidental black eye trying to stop a fight. This was magnified into an orgy and in spite of a delegation of undergraduates who went to the board of Governors, I was suspended from my club for a couple of months. The *Alumni Weekly* got after my book and

---

3. *Thomas Hardy* (1840–1928): English novelist and poet who chronicled country life in his work. (*ed.*)

4. *Heywood Broun* (1888–1939): American journalist. (*ed.*)

only Dean Gauss had a good word to say for me. The unctuousness and hypocrisy of the proceedings was exasperating and for seven years I didn't go to Princeton. Then a magazine asked me for an article about it and when I started to write it, I found I really loved the place and that the experience of one week was a small item in the total budget. But on that day in 1920 most of the joy went out of my success.

But one was now a professional—and the new world couldn't possibly be presented without bumping the old out of the way. One gradually developed a protective hardness against both praise and blame. Too often people liked your things for the wrong reasons or people liked them whose dislike would be a compliment. No decent career was ever founded on a public and one learned to go ahead without precedents and without fear. Counting the bag, I found that in 1919 I had made $800 by writing, that in 1920 I had made $18,000, stories, picture rights and book. My story price had gone from $30 to $1,000. That's a small price to what was paid later in the Boom, but what it sounded like to me couldn't be exaggerated.

The dream had been early realized and the realization carried with it a certain bonus and a certain burden. Premature success gives one an almost mystical conception of destiny as opposed to will power—at its worst the Napoleonic delusion. The man who arrives young believes that he exercises his will because his star is shining. The man who only asserts himself at thirty has a balanced idea of what will power and fate have each contributed, the one who gets there at forty is liable to put the emphasis on will alone. This comes out when the storms strike your craft.

The compensation of a very early success is a conviction that life is a romantic matter. In the best sense one stays young. When the primary objects of love and money could be taken for granted and a shaky eminence had lost its fascination, I had fair years to waste, years that I can't honestly regret, in seeking the eternal Carnival by the Sea. Once in the middle twenties I was driving along the High Corniche Road through the twilight with the whole French Riviera twinkling on the sea below. As far ahead as I could see was Monte Carlo, and though it was out of season and there were no Grand Dukes left to gamble and E. Phillips Oppenheim was a fat industrious man in my hotel, who lived in a bathrobe—the very name was so incorrigibly enchanting that I could only stop the car and like the Chinese whisper: "Ah me! Ah me!" It was not Monte Carlo I was looking at. It was back into the mind of the young man with cardboard soles who had walked the streets of New York. I was him again—for an instant I had the good fortune to share his dreams, I who had no more dreams of my own. And there are still times when I creep up on him, surprise him on an autumn morning in New York or a spring night in Carolina when it is so quiet that you can hear a dog barking in the next county. But never again as during that all too short period when he and I were one person, when the fulfilled future and the wistful past were mingled in a single gorgeous moment—when life was literally a dream.

## Looking Back

1. What dilemma does Fitzgerald recall in lines 9–10?

2. In your estimation, is his description of himself as "Lost and forgotten" (line 13) frank or self-pitying? Explain your answer.

3. Can you explain how the metaphor in lines 33–36 works?

4. What implicit advice to writers does Fitzgerald give in lines 45–48?

5. Why does he include anecdotes about writing two short stories (lines 45–66)?

6. In the face of society's postwar turn toward pleasure-seeking, how did Fitzgerald retain the perspective of the writer (lines 67–79)? What is this perspective?

7. Given his publications, how can he say "one wasn't really an author" (line 85)?

8. Does it seem reasonable that, as a result of his alma mater's adverse reaction to his novel, "most of the joy went out" of his success (lines 119–120)? Why?

9. What distinctions does Fitzgerald draw between achieving success at one age in life or another (lines 131–138)?

10. At the end of the essay, why does he picture himself again in New York, young, poor, and struggling?

## Writing Assignments

1. In more than one place in "Early Success," Fitzgerald proclaims the virtues of youth, implying its superiority over any other period in life. But is it superior? Or is this a view that only people who are no longer young can have about their past? Is it best, as Fitzgerald thought, to be always on the brink of fulfillment? Or is that notion a self-deception, a false belief stemming from a preference for a half-formed identity over the one you are now pretty much stuck with? Is it fun to be young, or do people in time forget its pains? Referring to Fitzgerald's ideas and experiences, write an essay answering these questions in order to examine the contention that youth is the best time of one's life. Your audience consists of people your own age.

2. Fitzgerald brings up a certain problem of personal identity when he remarks, recalling the fan mail he got in response to a short story, that "it seemed rather absurd that they should come to me about it."

   > On the other hand, for a shy man it was nice to be somebody except myself again: to be "the Author" as one had been "the Lieutenant." Of course one wasn't really an author any more than one had been an army officer, but nobody seemed to guess behind the false face. (lines 83–87)

   That is, although public recognition pleases him, he knows it greets what he appears to be rather than what he is. To his readers, he exists within a category—"Author"—that smooths out all individual differences; to himself, he is an individual who keeps his rough edges—his uniqueness as a person—despite the way others see him. Somehow he must solve the problem: he must be himself without ceasing to do what gives a false impression of his self, writing. And in some way, we all face this problem. Whether in the classroom or the workplace, at home or in the street, we know we do not look at ourselves the way others look at us. How do you experience this division? Write an essay describing an encounter or situation that demonstrates the split between how we see ourselves and how others see us. Use your own experience, but broaden your essay to portray the situation as an objective problem of personal identity.

3. Remarking on the Jazz Age, a term he coined for America's devotion to intense relaxation (insofar as the term was accurate) in the decade following the unprecedented shocks of World War I, Fitzgerald tells us that the stories he wrote at the time reflected his critical stance on the search for pleasure: "I was pretty sure living wasn't the reckless, careless business these people thought" (lines 77–78). Like many intellectuals and artists, he was able to situate himself consciously outside the age to get a better view of it. Because it is difficult to see out and around from the middle of things, detaching or distancing oneself is the only way to see accurately. Yet, like keeping a diary your friends know they figure in, this detachment can alienate other people and divorce you from the human community. You can end up, in the words of poet-critic Randall Jarrell, "seeing through everything except seeing through everything." Thus arises the problem of *how* to be in the world and which vantage point to choose, the inside or the outside. Assuming that you must be mainly in one place or the other, write an essay explaining the strengths and weaknesses of both wholehearted participation and objective detachment. Extrapolate from Fitzgerald's essay and Jarrell's quoted remark, and use examples from your own experience as focal points for your discussion.

# Ida Fink

# Night of Surrender

Ida Fink (b. 1921) is a Polish Jew who survived the Nazi occupation and since 1957 has lived in Israel. A writer of short stories and radio plays, she won the Anne Frank Prize for Literature in 1985 for her collection of stories *A Scrap of Time,* from which "Night of Surrender" is taken. In 1992, her novel *The Journey* was published. One function of critical thinking is to reappraise past actions in order to better understand them. This kind of thinking achieves particular importance in Fink's story by opening up a new way of thinking about personal identity, one of her central concerns.

## Looking Ahead

1. The title of this story applies to two related realms, the public and the personal, a conjunction often found in dramas of the self. Read critically to understand the logic binding these two areas of experience.

2. Although the action is transparent, particularly toward the close of the story, imagining the mentality of survivors of the Nazi extermination policy might help you grasp the narrator's situation.

3. The psychological distance between the two main characters is a key element to notice in this story.

I met Mike in a park, in a pretty little town on the Alsatian[1] border. I had been imprisoned there briefly in 1943, which was complicated, considering that I was a Jew using Aryan papers. Now the war was ending, the front was falling apart around Stuttgart,[2] and the surrender was expected any day.

5     Mike was a very nice fellow, and in those first days of freedom I was feeling very lonely and sad. I used to go to the park every day. It was immaculately kept and the rhododendrons were in full bloom, covered with pale violet flowers. I would walk to the park, sit on a bench, and tell myself that I should be happy to have survived, but I wasn't happy, and I was upset to be so sad. I went there

10    every day and the girls from the camp figured that I had met a boy; they were envious and curious. Their suspicions were confirmed on the day Mike walked me back to the camp; and from then on he would come to get me every day at four and we would go for a stroll.

      Michael was very tall, he had funny long legs, his uniform trousers fit

15    tightly, his waist was as slender as a girl's. He wore large eyeglasses with rectanglar frames. He smiled like a child, and if he wasn't so big, you could have mistaken him for a teenager; but he was a serious grown man, a professor of mathematics, already twenty-seven, ten years older than I.

      He would take my hand—my head came up to his elbow—and we would

20    go strolling in the park or along the Rhine, and he would always whistle the same tune. Much later, I found out that it was Smetana's *Moldau*,[3] but at that time I didn't know its name or who had composed it. My knowledge of the world and of life was one-sided: I knew death, terror, cunning, how to lie and trick, but nothing about music or poetry or love.

25    This is how I met him: One day I was sitting on the bench beside the pale violet rhododendrons. It was evening and I should have gotten up and returned to the camp for supper, but I kept on sitting there, I didn't feel like getting up even though I was hungry, and I didn't notice the lanky boy with the glasses and the American uniform who had sat down on the edge of the bench. When

30    he asked, "What are you thinking about?" I was terrified, and he burst out laughing.

      I answered in my broken English, "I was in a German prison here,"—though I hadn't been thinking of that at all, only about supper, because I was hungry.

      "Did they beat you?"

---

1. *Alsatian:* refers to Alsace, a border region between France and Germany. (*ed.*)

2. *Stuttgart:* a provincial capital and major city in southwestern Germany. (*ed.*)

3. *Bedřich Smetana* (1824–1884): a Czech composer; *Moldau:* Smetana's symphonic masterpiece. (*ed.*)

"No."

He looked closely at me, then said, "That's funny." 35

I didn't know what was funny—the fact that I had been in prison or that they hadn't beaten me. Some kind of moron, I thought, but he kept on asking me questions.

"And why did the Germans lock you up in prison?" 40

I looked at him as if he were a creature from another world.

"Don't worry. I just wanted to know what it was like for you."

He looked at me seriously, and his eyes shone with a warm, golden light. Maybe he's not such a fool, I thought. But watch out, I told myself, wait a bit. You held out for so many years, you can hold out for another week or two. The 45 war is still going on.

But already I anticipated the enormous relief it would be to say those three words—their weight was growing more unbearable each day. I smiled faintly, and in that teary voice befitting the revelation of one's life story, said: "Ah, my history is very sad, why return to those matters? I don't want to." 50

"Poor child!" He stroked my hair and took some chocolate out of his pocket. "But you will tell me some day, won't you?"

It was milk chocolate. I love milk chocolate; it's light and melts in your mouth. The last time I ate chocolate was before the war, but I didn't say anything, I just got up to go to supper—the potatoes and canned meat in gravy we 55 got every day.

The next afternoon Mike brought me some enormous, dark violets, and I rewarded him with the life story I had patched together over the last three years; it moved him as it was meant to. I was sorry that I was still lying, but consoled myself with the fact that the true story would have been a hundred times more 60 horrifying.

The girls from the camp were jealous, and in the evening they would ask in detail about everything. After a week, they asked, "Has he kissed you?" and when I answered, "No," they were very disappointed. And that was the truth. Mike brought me more chocolate (because I had told him, after all, that not 65 since before the war . . .). He bought me ice cream, he held my hand, and sometimes, when we lay near the Rhine, he stroked my hair and said it was silken and shiny. He also told me about his home and the school where he taught, and about the garden he worked himself. It all sounded like a fairy tale from a storybook for well-brought-up children, and sometimes I smiled to myself, espe- 70 cially when he talked about flowers and mowed grass. I never asked him if he had a girlfriend in America. It was obvious that he did, but he never mentioned her.

Sometimes we didn't say anything. The water in the Rhine glittered like fish scales, the weeds flowered in the ruins, airplanes circled overhead and they too 75 were silvery and long, like fish. But there was no reason to fear them, and now, without getting that tightness in your throat, you could watch them dive, grow huge, and mark the earth with the shadow of a cold black cross.

"Ann," Mike would say, giving my name, Anna, its English form, "isn't this
80   nice?"

"Very nice," I would answer, and he would say, "Very, very nice, my dear,"
but it wasn't very nice at all and it couldn't be very nice as long as I was lying
to him.

That day, when we were returned from the park, the rhododendrons were
85   already yellow and withered. Mike asked, "Why won't you tell me everything
about yourself? It would make you feel better."

I was well trained. I replied instantly, "But I told you."

"Not everything, Ann. I'm sure that was only a part, maybe not even the
most important part. Why don't you trust me?"

90   Again he had that warm, golden glow in his eyes, and I thought: I am mean
and nasty.

"The war taught all of you not to trust anyone. I'm not surprised. But listen, the war is over. You have to learn to believe in people, in happiness and
goodness."

95   "You're talking like a professor, and a stupid one. You think everything can
change just like that? Believe in people? It makes me laugh"—I wanted to say
throw up—"when I hear such idiotic stuff."

"Ann, I want to ask you something."

My heart began to pound, because that was what every one said before they
100   asked, "Are you a Jew?"

"Well, ask," I said, but he didn't say anything; he just looked at me and I
couldn't help seeing the tenderness and concern in his glance. I felt like touching his face, pressing close to him, asking him not to go away, telling him that I
didn't want to be alone anymore, that I was tired of standing outside myself and
105   watching every move.

"Well, ask. I'm waiting," I said.

We were standing at the gate to the camp. It was suppertime. A crowd of
DPs[4] with aluminum mess kits for their potatoes and canned meat with gravy
were crossing the large square where, every morning, roll call and edifying
110   prayers were held.

I looked at Mike and noticed that a muscle in his right cheek was quivering.

"Would you go away with me?"

"With you? Well . . . where?" I asked only to gain time and calm down. I
knew very well what he meant.

115   "Where? Where? To the moon!" All at once, he grew serious. "You know
what I'm asking and you know that I mean it. I've thought about it for a long
time and I've come to the conclusion that it's very nice for us both when we're
together. Right?"

"You're saying this out of pity, aren't you?" I laughed. "A poor victim of the
120   war, she lost her parents in the uprising, she's all alone in the world."

---

4. *DPs*: displaced persons, or refugees. (*ed.*)

"Stop it, that's horrible. You know that isn't true. It's not pity, I just want things to be nice for us. I know that together . . . Don't answer now. Think about it. I'll come tomorrow. You can tell me then. We've known each other for almost a month, and I want you to stay with me. But Ann," he didn't let go of my hand, "get rid of all those defenses. Trust me. I want to bring you up all over again, teach you to live again." 125

For the first time he looked like a serious, grown-up man.

"All right, Professor," I said, and then ran away. The next day the surrender came and everyone was going wild. I waited for Mike for a whole hour on the low wall in front of the camp. By the time he arrived that evening, I had lost 130 hope. Lying on my bunk in the empty room—all the girls had gone to a party— I thought, with the army you never can tell, they might have transferred him suddenly, and goodbye! I lay there dazed, trying to recall the melody he always whistled, and which I still didn't know the name of. But I couldn't, so I tried to summon up his smile and his long funny legs. When he walked into the room, I 135 was very happy—but only for the second it took me to remember that today I had to tell him everything. Though I very much wanted to be rid of the burden of those three words, I was frightened. Mike seemed like a total stranger. But that feeling, too, lasted only a moment, because he said, "My God, you look like a schoolgirl, like a child, and I'm an old man." He began singing to that *Moldau* 140 melody, "Such an old man, but so very much in love," and we laughed till tears came to our eyes. Only on the way to the Rhine did I remember the gnawing fear inside me and though the night was quite warm, I felt cold.

The river no longer looked like a silver scale; it was dark and the water babbled against the shore. From the direction of town came songs, shouts, the 145 noise of fireworks.

I thought, what a shame to ruin this night. We should be drinking and celebrating like normal people.

"Ann," Mike said softly, "today is doubly important. Right? The war has ended and we are beginning a new life. The two of us. I know your answer; I 150 can read it in your eyes. I know—you'll stay with me."

He kissed me tenderly on the mouth; his lips were soft and gentle.

"Michael," I said, "before I tell you I'll stay with you, you have to know the truth about me. You have to know who I am."

"Do you think I don't know? You're a small, lost child of the war. You're sev- 155 enteen years old, but you're just a little girl who needs protection and tenderness."

I looked at the sky. A rain of man-made stars showered down, falling like fiery fountains. The water in the river was sparkling with color, the ruins of the town were colored, the whole night was colored.

"Michael." I looked into his eyes. Now I couldn't afford to miss even the 160 tremor of an eyelid. "I am Jewish."

Perhaps it was because I was hearing those words for the first time in three years, those words I had carried inside myself constantly, or because none of the things I had feared registered on Mike's face, but I felt tears well up, and I opened my eyes wide so as not to burst out crying. 165

"And that's what you were hiding from me so carefully? Whatever for?"

I spoke quickly, feeling lighter with every word.

"You don't know, and you can't know. You don't know what it means to say, 'I am Jewish.' For three years I heard those words day and night but never, not even when I was alone, did I dare to say them aloud. Three years ago I swore that until the war ended no one would hear them from me. Do you know what it means to live in fear, lying, never speaking your own language, or thinking with your own brain, or looking with your own eyes? Michael, it's not true that my parents died in the uprising. They were killed right in front of me. I was hiding in the wardrobe that the Germans forgot—just think, they forgot!—to open. You don't know what an action means. You don't know anything, and I won't tell you. When I came out of the wardrobe, I found my parents' bodies on the floor. I ran out of the house. I left them there just as they were, it was night, deathly still. I ran to the village where friends of my father lived and they gave me their daughter Anna's birth certificate. I got on the train and got off in a big city, but there was a round-up in the station—you don't even know what a round-up is!—and they shipped me directly to Germany to do forced labor. I was lucky, very few people had such good luck, because others saw their parents' bodies and then were tortured and killed. But I milked cows, mowed grass, knew how to lie, to invent stories at the drop of a hat. I was lucky, no one found me out, and except for the few days spent in prison, I lived in peace until the end of the war. But at night I dreamed all the time that I was hiding in a wardrobe and was afraid to come out. But I don't want to tell you about it, why did I tell you? Tonight is such a joyous night, and I've ruined it completely."

His kind eyes were so sad. He didn't stop stroking my hand and I didn't want him to stop. I longed to go to sleep, I felt as if I had been in labor, with its healthy pain and healthy exhaustion.

"What's your real name?" he asked.

"Klara."

"Klara," he repeated. "Clear one . . . but you'll always be Ann to me."

The sky above us was golden and red. We could hear the noise of the rockets, and red stars were falling into the river. I bowed my head and heard that wondrous music: the beating of a human heart.

"I will do everything to make you forget that nightmare. And you will forget," Mike said after a moment. "You're very young. You'll see, time will cover over all this the way grass grows over the earth. But promise me one thing: that you will remain Ann—and not just in name. It will be better that way, believe me."

I felt a chill down to my fingertips.

"For whom?" I asked clearly, because suddenly it seemed to me that the river was making a lot of noise and that my words were drowning in that noise.

"For you, for us. The world is so strange, Ann, it will be better if no one other than me knows about Klara."

"Michael, *you too?*"

"Oh, you child, it's not a question of anti-Semitism. I have no prejudices, 210
it'll simply be easier that way. You'll avoid a lot of problems, it'll be simpler for
you to cast off the burden of your experiences. You've suffered so much already!
I'm not saying this out of prejudice, but for your own good. And since you've already left it behind . . ."

The river was still roaring, the river that was flowing inside me. 215

"If you don't want to I won't insist. You can decide for yourself, but believe
me, I have experience, it'll be easier for you this way."

He touched his lips to my hair; in the glare of the rocket exploding into
light above us I saw the anxiety in his eyes. I felt cold and once again I didn't
know how to cry. 220

"Let's not talk about this now, it's not important," he pleaded. "Not tonight,
the night of the surrender . . ."

He didn't finish. He wasn't stupid.

I silently shook my head. Maybe he didn't notice, maybe he didn't
understand. 225

The water in the river was burning with the fire of victory and in the pure
air of the May night we could clearly hear the singing that welcomed the end of
the war.

## Looking Back

1. Why does Ann say that being a Jew with Aryan papers was complicated (lines 2–3)?
2. How would you characterize someone who describes herself as knowing "death, terror, cunning, how to lie and trick, but nothing about music or poetry or love" (lines
   23–24)?
3. We learn that the "three words" she will not pronounce for Mike are "I am Jewish."
   How can they be likened, in other circumstances, to the words "I love you"?
4. In what essential way do Mike and Ann/Klara differ?
5. Is Mike's insistence that she trust him a reasonable request? Why or why not?
6. Why does Mike urge Ann to keep her pseudonym and her false identity?
7. Do you think that Mike, despite his denials, is anti-Semitic? Explain your answer.
8. What are the psychological effects on Ann/Klara of Mike's attempt to persuade her
   to hide the truth?
9. How does the image of the river that is both outside and inside Ann (line 215) relate
   to the theme of the story?
10. Does Ann/Klara go along with Mike? Is her choice the right one? Why or why not?

## Writing Assignments

1. The particular circumstances of our lives help shape our identities. As these circumstances change, so do we. Sometimes, just becoming more aware of them can affect

our sense of who we are. The greatest pressure brought to bear on personal identity seems to come from catastrophe. It may be the Nazi plague, or it may be impoverishment and confinement to an urban slum; it may be suffering rape, or it may be getting laid off in mid-career. People who undergo disastrous experiences are altered by them. But how are they altered? Write an essay answering this question by interpolating your explanation into Ann/Klara's case and by extrapolating from it to tragedies of everyday life such as those mentioned above.

2. Although Jewish identity and not gender identity is the focal point of the story, the latter becomes an issue, or should, when Mike refers to Ann/Klara as a "small lost child" and a "little girl" (lines 155–156). These are the obvious signs of his attitude toward her as a female and, perhaps, of his general approach to women. Most women and more and more men would recognize a problem here, but just what is it? Write an essay that tries to state what general attitude, viewpoint, or philosophy lies behind his words. Describe the probable effects on women, and say what sense of themselves women must have who accept this kind of depiction and treatment by men. Say how you think women should see themselves, and what men can do to accommodate them. Explain as best you can how a failure to do so affects women's place in society.

3. Most of us are familiar, at least from newspaper stories, with the worst aspects of racial and ethnic disharmony. The vocabulary of its causes and effects is equally familiar: *stereotyping, bias, bigotry, prejudice, discrimination, racism, inequality, oppression, persecution.* The list grows worse as it grows longer, as dislike and fear and ignorance become hatred. But the list (which is not necessarily exhaustive) is valuable because it offers people of good will specific concepts to examine, to comprehend, and to try to render obsolete as descriptions of reality. At the root of the evil lies a blindness to individual identities, an insistence that within a certain group each member wears the same face. This is stereotyping. Starting with a description of how this works in respect to members of a specific group—one you choose to discuss—write an essay that analyzes the causes of racial or ethnic hatred and attempts to say what people can do to end it. Conceive of your audience as consisting primarily of people outside the group you focus on as stereotyped.

# Tim O'Brien

# On the Rainy River

Tim O'Brien (b. 1947) is a combat veteran of the Vietnam War, a war that caused a major rupture in American as well as Asian life, and to which O'Brien has devoted a number of works, including the personal memoir *If I Die in a Combat Zone* and *The Things They Carried,* the source of "On the Rainy River." His novel *Going After Cacciato* won the National Book Award; his other novels are *Northern Lights, The Nuclear Age,* and, published in 1994, *In the Lake of the Woods,* a novel that won immediate critical acclaim. O'Brien was born in Minnesota and educated at Harvard University. He has worked as a national affairs reporter for the *Washington Post*. "On the Rainy River" is a story in which critical thinking is as much the subject as are the events of the plot. O'Brien must question his townfolks' assumptions about patriotism and courage and must balance his own views against theirs in order to find an acceptable way to conceive of his life and the action he contemplates.

## Looking Ahead

1. O'Brien uses his own name and follows the contours of his own experience, but still this is fiction: he changes enough details to make it a work of the imagination (a different version of these events appears in *If I Die in a Combat Zone*). Read critically to try to conclude whether this story, though not factual, is nevertheless truthful.

2. An important theme to follow here is that of moral crisis.

3. Since to a large extent we are what we do in life, you can trace the development of the main character of the story to understand his true identity.

This is one story I've never told before. Not to anyone. Not to my parents, not to my brother or sister, not even to my wife. To go into it, I've always thought, would only cause embarrassment for all of us, a sudden need to be elsewhere, which is the natural response to a confession. Even now, I'll admit, the story makes me squirm. For more than twenty years I've had to live with it, feeling    5
the shame, trying to push it away, and so by this act of remembrance, by putting the facts down on paper, I'm hoping to relieve at least some of the pressure on my dreams. Still, it's a hard story to tell. All of us, I suppose, like to believe that in a moral emergency we will behave like the heroes of our youth, bravely and forthrightly, without thought of personal loss or discredit. Cer-    10
tainly that was my conviction back in the summer of 1968. Tim O'Brien: a secret hero. The Lone Ranger. If the stakes ever became high enough—if the evil were evil enough, if the good were good enough—I would simply tap a secret reservoir of courage that had been accumulating inside me over the years. Courage, I seemed to think, comes to us in finite quantities, like an inheritance,    15
and by being frugal and stashing it away and letting it earn interest, we steadily increase our moral capital in preparation for that day when the account must be drawn down. It was a comforting theory. It dispensed with all those bothersome little acts of daily courage; it offered hope and grace to the repetitive coward; it justified the past while amortizing the future.    20
    In June of 1968, a month after graduating from Macalester College,[1] I was drafted to fight a war I hated. I was twenty-one years old. Young, yes, and politically naive, but even so the American war in Vietnam seemed to me wrong.

---

1. *Macalester College:* located in St. Paul, Minnesota. (*ed.*)

Certain blood was being shed for uncertain reasons. I saw no unity of purpose,
25  no consensus on matters of philosophy or history or law. The very facts were
shrouded in uncertainty: Was it a civil war? A war of national liberation or simple aggression? Who started it, and when, and why? What really happened to
the USS *Maddox* on that dark night in the Gulf of Tonkin? Was Ho Chi Minh a
Communist stooge, or a nationalist savior, or both, or neither? What about the
30  Geneva Accords? What about SEATO and the Cold War? What about dominoes?[2] America was divided on these and a thousand other issues, and the debate had spilled out across the floor of the United States Senate and into the
streets, and smart men in pinstripes could not agree on even the most fundamental matters of public policy. The only certainty that summer was moral con-
35  fusion. It was my view then, and still is, that you don't make war without knowing why. Knowledge, of course, is always imperfect, but it seemed to me that
when a nation goes to war it must have reasonable confidence in the justice and
imperative of its cause. You can't fix your mistakes. Once people are dead, you
can't make them undead.

40  In any case those were my convictions, and back in college I had taken a
modest stand against the war. Nothing radical, no hothead stuff, just ringing a
few doorbells for Gene McCarthy,[3] composing a few tedious, uninspired editorials for the campus newspaper. Oddly, though, it was almost entirely an intellectual activity. I brought some energy to it, of course, but it was the energy that
45  accompanies almost any abstract endeavor; I felt no personal danger; I felt no
sense of an impending crisis in my life. Stupidly, with a kind of smug removal
that I can't begin to fathom, I assumed that the problems of killing and dying
did not fall within my special province.

The draft notice arrived on June 17, 1968. It was a humid afternoon, I re-
50  member, cloudy and very quiet, and I'd just come in from a round of golf. My
mother and father were having lunch out in the kitchen. I remember opening
up the letter, scanning the first few lines, feeling the blood go thick behind my
eyes. I remember a sound in my head. It wasn't thinking, just a silent howl. A
million things all at once—I was too *good* for this war. Too smart, too compas-
55  sionate, too everything. It couldn't happen. I was above it. I had the world
dicked—Phi Beta Kappa and summa cum laude and president of the student
body and a full-ride scholarship for grad studies at Harvard. A mistake,
maybe—a foul-up in the paperwork. I was no soldier. I hated Boy Scouts. I

---

2. *USS Maddox:* American warship purportedly attacked by North Vietnamese torpedo boats
in August 1964, leading to retaliatory U.S. strikes and the Tonkin Bay Resolution, passed by both
houses of Congress and giving the president broad executive powers to aid South Vietnam; *Ho Chi
Minh* (1890–1969): the president of North Vietnam; *Geneva Accords:* refers to the settlement in
1954 of the war between France and Vietnam after the French defeat; *SEATO:* acronym for the
Southeast Asia Treaty Organization; *dominoes:* refers to the "domino theory," which held that if one
country fell to communism, so would the next, and the next, and so forth, falling like dominoes.
(ed.)

3. *Eugene McCarthy* (b. 1916): U.S. Senator and antiwar presidential candidate in 1968. (ed.)

hated camping out. I hated dirt and tents and mosquitoes. The sight of blood made me queasy, and I couldn't tolerate authority, and I didn't know a rifle   60
from a slingshot. I was a *liberal,* for Christ sake: If they needed fresh bodies, why not draft some back-to-the-stone-age hawk? Or some dumb jingo in his hard hat and Bomb Hanoi button, or one of LBJ's pretty daughters, or West-moreland's[4] whole handsome family—nephews and nieces and baby grandson. There should be a law, I thought. If you support a war, if you think it's worth   65
the price, that's fine, but you have to put your own precious fluids on the line. You have to head for the front and hook up with an infantry unit and help spill the blood. And you have to bring along your wife, or your kids, or your lover. A *law,* I thought.

I remember the rage in my stomach. Later it burned down to a smoldering   70
self-pity, then to numbness. At dinner that night my father asked what my plans were.

"Nothing," I said. "Wait."

I spent the summer of 1968 working in an Armour meatpacking plant in my hometown of Worthington, Minnesota. The plant specialized in pork products,   75
and for eight hours a day I stood on a quarter-mile assembly line—more prop-erly, a disassembly line—removing blood clots from the necks of dead pigs. My job title, I believe, was Declotter. After slaughter, the hogs were decapitated, split down the length of the belly, pried open, eviscerated, and strung up by the hind hocks on a high conveyer belt. Then gravity took over. By the time a car-   80
cass reached my spot on the line, the fluids had mostly drained out, everything except for thick clots of blood in the neck and upper chest cavity. To remove the stuff, I used a kind of water gun. The machine was heavy, maybe eighty pounds, and was suspended from the ceiling by a heavy rubber cord. There was some bounce to it, an elastic up-and-down give, and the trick was to maneuver   85
the gun with your whole body, not lifting with the arms, just letting the rubber cord do the work for you. At one end was a trigger; at the muzzle end was a small nozzle and a steel roller brush. As a carcass passed by, you'd lean forward and swing the gun up against the clots and squeeze the trigger, all in one mo-tion, and the brush would whirl and water would come shooting out and you'd   90
hear a quick splattering sound as the clots dissolved into a fine red mist. It was not pleasant work. Goggles were a necessity, and a rubber apron, but even so it was like standing for eight hours a day under a lukewarm blood-shower. At night I'd go home smelling of pig. It wouldn't go away. Even after a hot bath, scrubbing hard, the stink was always there—like old bacon, or sausage, a dense   95
greasy pig-stink that soaked deep into my skin and hair. Among other things, I remember, it was tough getting dates that summer. I felt isolated; I spent a lot of time alone. And there was also that draft notice tucked away in my wallet.

---

4. *LBJ*: President Lyndon Baines Johnson; *William C. Westmoreland* (b. 1914): U.S. general who commanded American forces in Vietnam. (*ed.*)

In the evenings I'd sometimes borrow my father's car and drive aimlessly
100    around town, feeling sorry for myself, thinking about the war and the pig factory and how my life seemed to be collapsing toward slaughter. I felt paralyzed.
All around me the options seemed to be narrowing, as if I were hurtling down a
huge black funnel, the whole world squeezing in tight. There was no happy way
out. The government had ended most graduate school deferments; the waiting
105    lists for the National Guard and Reserves were impossibly long; my health was
solid; I didn't qualify for CO status—no religious grounds, no history as a pacifist. Moreover, I could not claim to be opposed to war as a matter of general
principle. There were occasions, I believed, when a nation was justified in using
military force to achieve its ends, to stop a Hitler or some comparable evil, and I
110    told myself that in such circumstances I would've willingly marched off to the
battle. The problem, though, was that a draft board did not let you choose
your war.
         Beyond all this, or at the very center, was the raw fact of terror. I did not
want to die. Not ever. But certainly not then, not there, not in a wrong war.
115    Driving up Main Street, past the courthouse and the Ben Franklin store, I sometimes felt the fear spreading inside me like weeds. I imagined myself dead. I
imagined myself doing things I could not do—charging an enemy position, taking aim at another human being.
         At some point in mid-July I began thinking seriously about Canada. The
120    border lay a few hundred miles north, an eight-hour drive. Both my conscience
and my instincts were telling me to make a break for it, just take off and run like
hell and never stop. In the beginning the idea seemed purely abstract, the word
Canada printing itself out in my head; but after a time I could see particular
shapes and images, the sorry details of my own future—a hotel room in Win-
125    nipeg, a battered old suitcase, my father's eyes as I tried to explain myself over
the telephone. I could almost hear his voice, and my mother's. Run, I'd think.
Then I'd think, Impossible. Then a second later I'd think, *Run.*
         It was a kind of schizophrenia. A moral split. I couldn't make up my mind.
I feared the war, yes, but I also feared exile. I was afraid of walking away from
130    my own life, my friends and my family, my whole history, everything that mattered to me. I feared losing the respect of my parents. I feared the law. I feared
ridicule and censure. My hometown was a conservative little spot on the prairie,
a place where tradition counted, and it was easy to imagine people sitting
around a table down at the old Gobbler Café on Main Street, coffee cups poised,
135    the conversation slowly zeroing in on the young O'Brien kid, how the damned
sissy had taken off for Canada. At night, when I couldn't sleep, I'd sometimes
carry on fierce arguments with those people. I'd be screaming at them, telling
them how much I detested their blind, thoughtless, automatic acquiescence to
it all, their simple-minded patriotism, their prideful ignorance, their love-it-or-
140    leave-it platitudes, how they were sending me off to fight a war they didn't understand and didn't want to understand. I held them responsible. By God, yes, I
*did.* All of them—I held them personally and individually responsible—the

polyestered Kiwanis boys, the merchants and farmers, the pious churchgoers, the chatty housewives, the PTA and the Lions club and the Veterans of Foreign Wars and the fine upstanding gentry out at the country club. They didn't know Bao Dai[5] from the man in the moon. They didn't know history. They didn't know the first thing about Diem's[6] tyranny, or the nature of Vietnamese nationalism, or the long colonialism of the French—this was all too damned complicated, it required some reading—but no matter, it was a war to stop the Communists, plain and simple, which was how they liked things, and you were a treasonous pussy if you had second thoughts about killing or dying for plain and simple reasons.

I was bitter, sure. But it was so much more than that. The emotions went from outrage to terror to bewilderment to guilt to sorrow and then back again to outrage. I felt a sickness inside me. Real disease.

Most of this I've told before, or at least hinted at, but what I have never told is the full truth. How I cracked. How at work one morning, standing on the pig line, I felt something break open in my chest. I don't know what it was. I'll never know. But it was real, I know that much, it was a physical rupture—a cracking-leaking-popping feeling. I remember dropping my water gun. Quickly, almost without thought, I took off my apron and walked out of the plant and drove home. It was midmorning, I remember, and the house was empty. Down in my chest there was still that leaking sensation, something very warm and precious spilling out, and I was covered with blood and hog-stink, and for a long while I just concentrated on holding myself together. I remember taking a hot shower. I remember packing a suitcase and carrying it out to the kitchen, standing very still for a few minutes, looking carefully at the familiar objects all around me. The old chrome toaster, the telephone, the pink and white Formica on the kitchen counters. The room was full of bright sunshine. Everything sparkled. My house, I thought. My life. I'm not sure how long I stood there, but later I scribbled out a short note to my parents.

What it said, exactly, I don't recall now. Something vague. Taking off, will call, love Tim.

I drove north.

It's a blur now, as it was then, and all I remember is a sense of high velocity and the feel of the steering wheel in my hands. I was riding on adrenaline. A giddy feeling, in a way, except there was the dreamy edge of impossibility to it—like running a dead-end maze—no way out—it couldn't come to a happy conclusion and yet I was doing it anyway because it was all I could think of to do. It was pure flight, fast and mindless. I had no plan. Just hit the border at

---

5. *Bao Dai:* the emperor of Indochina during France's colonial rule. (*ed.*)

6. *Ngo Dinh Diem:* South Vietnam's chief of state; he was assassinated in 1963. (*ed.*)

high speed and crash through and keep on running. Near dusk I passed through Bemidji, then turned northeast toward International Falls. I spent the night in the car behind a closed-down gas station a half mile from the border. In the morning, after gassing up, I headed straight west along the Rainy River, which separates Minnesota from Canada, and which for me separated one life from another. The land was mostly wilderness. Here and there I passed a motel or bait shop, but otherwise the country unfolded in great sweeps of pine and birch and sumac. Though it was still August, the air already had the smell of October, football season, piles of yellow-red leaves, everything crisp and clean. I remember a huge blue sky. Off to my right was the Rainy River, wide as a lake in places, and beyond the Rainy River was Canada.

For a while I just drove, not aiming at anything, then in the late morning I began looking for a place to lie low for a day or two. I was exhausted, and scared sick, and around noon I pulled into an old fishing resort called the Tip Top Lodge. Actually it was not a lodge at all, just eight or nine tiny yellow cabins clustered on a peninsula that jutted northward into the Rainy River. The place was in sorry shape. There was a dangerous wooden dock, an old minnow tank, a flimsy tar paper boathouse along the shore. The main building, which stood in a cluster of pines on high ground, seemed to lean heavily to one side, like a cripple, the roof sagging toward Canada. Briefly, I thought about turning around, just giving up, but then I got out of the car and walked up to the front porch.

The man who opened the door that day is the hero of my life. How do I say this without sounding sappy? Blurt it out—the man saved me. He offered exactly what I needed, without questions, without any words at all. He took me in. He was there at the critical time—a silent, watchful presence. Six days later, when it ended, I was unable to find a proper way to thank him, and I never have, and so, if nothing else, this story represents a small gesture of gratitude twenty years overdue.

Even after two decades I can close my eyes and return to that porch at the Tip Top Lodge. I can see the old guy staring at me. Elroy Berdahl: eighty-one years old, skinny and shrunken and mostly bald. He wore a flannel shirt and brown work pants. In one hand, I remember, he carried a green apple, a small paring knife in the other. His eyes had the bluish gray color of a razor blade, the same polished shine, and as he peered up at me I felt a strange sharpness, almost painful, a cutting sensation, as if his gaze were somehow slicing me open. In part, no doubt, it was my own sense of guilt, but even so I'm absolutely certain that the old man took one look and went right to the heart of things—a kid in trouble. When I asked for a room, Elroy made a little clicking sound with his tongue. He nodded, led me out to one of the cabins, and dropped a key in my hand. I remember smiling at him. I also remember wishing I hadn't. The old man shook his head as if to tell me it wasn't worth the bother.

"Dinner at five-thirty," he said. "You eat fish?"

"Anything," I said.

Elroy grunted and said, "I'll bet."

We spent six days together at the Tip Top Lodge. Just the two of us. Tourist season was over and there were no boats on the river, and the wilderness seemed to withdraw into a great permanent stillness. Over those six days Elroy Berdahl and I took most of our meals together. In the mornings we sometimes went out on long hikes into the woods, and at night we played Scrabble or listened to  230
records or sat reading in front of his big stone fireplace. At times I felt the awkwardness of an intruder, but Elroy accepted me into his quiet routine without fuss or ceremony. He took my presence for granted, the same way he might've sheltered a stray cat—no wasted sighs or pity—and there was never any talk about it. Just the opposite. What I remember more than anything is the man's  235
willful, almost ferocious silence. In all that time together, all those hours, he never asked the obvious questions: Why was I there? Why alone? Why so preoccupied? If Elroy was curious about any of this, he was careful never to put it into words.

My hunch, though, is that he already knew. At least the basics. After all, it  240
was 1968, and guys were burning draft cards, and Canada was just a boat ride away. Elroy Berdahl was no hick. His bedroom, I remember, was cluttered with books and newspapers. He killed me at the Scrabble board, barely concentrating, and on those occasions when speech was necessary he had a way of compressing large thoughts into small, cryptic packets of language. One evening,  245
just at sunset, he pointed up at an owl circling over the violet-lighted forest to the west.

"Hey, O'Brien," he said. "There's Jesus."

The man was sharp—he didn't miss much. Those razor eyes. Now and then he'd catch me staring out at the river, at the far shore, and I could almost hear  250
the tumblers clicking in his head. Maybe I'm wrong, but I doubt it.

One thing for certain, he knew I was in desperate trouble. And he knew I couldn't talk about it. The wrong word—or even the right word—and I would've disappeared. I was wired and jittery. My skin felt too tight. After supper one evening I vomited and went back to my cabin and lay down for a few  255
moments and then vomited again; another time, in the middle of the afternoon, I began sweating and couldn't shut it off. I went through whole days feeling dizzy with sorrow. I couldn't sleep; I couldn't lie still. At night I'd toss around in bed, half awake, half dreaming, imagining how I'd sneak down to the beach and quietly push one of the old man's boats out into the river and start paddling my  260
way toward Canada. There were times when I thought I'd gone off the psychic edge. I couldn't tell up from down, I was just falling, and late in the night I'd lie there watching weird pictures spin through my head. Getting chased by the Border Patrol—helicopters and searchlights and barking dogs—I'd be crashing through the woods, I'd be down on my hands and knees—people shouting out  265
my name—the law closing in on all sides—my hometown draft board and the FBI and the Royal Canadian Mounted Police. It all seemed crazy and impossible. Twenty-one years old, an ordinary kid with all the ordinary dreams and ambitions, and all I wanted was to live the life I was born to—a mainstream

270 life—I loved baseball and hamburgers and cherry Cokes—and now I was off on the margins of exile, leaving my country forever, and it seemed so impossible and terrible and sad.

I'm not sure how I made it through those six days. Most of it I can't remember. On two or three afternoons, to pass some time, I helped Elroy get the place
275 ready for winter, sweeping down the cabins and hauling in the boats, little
chores that kept my body moving. The days were cool and bright. The nights
were very dark. One morning the old man showed me how to split and stack
firewood, and for several hours we just worked in silence out behind his house.
At one point, I remember, Elroy put down his maul and looked at me for a long
280 time, his lips drawn as if framing a difficult question, but then he shook his
head and went back to work. The man's self-control was amazing. He never
pried. He never put me in a position that required lies or denials. To an extent, I
suppose, his reticence was typical of that part of Minnesota, where privacy still
held value, and even if I'd been walking around with some horrible deformity—
285 four arms and three heads—I'm sure the old man would've talked about everything except those extra arms and heads. Simple politeness was part of it. But
even more than that, I think, the man understood that words were insufficient.
The problem had gone beyond discussion. During that long summer I'd been
over and over the various arguments, all the pros and cons, and it was no longer
290 a question that could be decided by an act of pure reason. Intellect had come up
against emotion. My conscience told me to run, but some irrational and powerful force was resisting, like a weight pushing me toward the war. What it came
down to, stupidly, was a sense of shame. Hot, stupid shame. I did not want people to think badly of me. Not my parents, not my brother and sister, not even
295 the folks down at the Gobbler Café. I was ashamed to be there at the Tip Top
Lodge. I was ashamed of my conscience, ashamed to be doing the right thing.

Some of this Elroy must've understood. Not the details, of course, but the
plain fact of crisis.

Although the old man never confronted me about it, there was one occa-
300 sion when he came close to forcing the whole thing out into the open. It was
early evening, and we'd just finished supper, and over coffee and dessert I asked
him about my bill, how much I owed so far. For a long while the old man
squinted down at the tablecloth.

"Well, the basic rate," he said, "is fifty bucks a night. Not counting meals.
305 This makes four nights, right?"

I nodded. I had three hundred and twelve dollars in my wallet.

Elroy kept his eyes on the tablecloth. "Now that's an on-season price. To be
fair, I suppose we should knock it down a peg or two." He leaned back in his
chair. "What's a reasonable number, you figure?"

310 "I don't know," I said. "Forty?"

"Forty's good. Forty a night. Then we tack on food—say another hundred?
Two hundred sixty total?"

"I guess."

He raised his eyebrows. "Too much?"

"No, that's fair. It's fine. Tomorrow, though . . . I think I'd better take off    315
tomorrow."

Elroy shrugged and began clearing the table. For a time he fussed with the
dishes, whistling to himself as if the subject had been settled. After a second he
slapped his hands together.

"You know what we forgot?" he said. "We forgot wages. Those odd jobs you    320
done. What we have to do, we have to figure out what your time's worth. Your
last job—how much did you pull in an hour?"

"Not enough," I said.

"A bad one?"

"Yes. Pretty bad."    325

Slowly then, without intending any long sermon, I told him about my days
at the pig plant. It began as a straight recitation of the facts, but before I could
stop myself I was talking about the blood clots and the water gun and how the
smell had soaked into my skin and how I couldn't wash it away. I went on for a
long time. I told him about wild hogs squealing in my dreams, the sounds of    330
butchery, slaughterhouse sounds, and how I'd sometimes wake up with that
greasy pig-stink in my throat.

When I was finished, Elroy nodded at me.

"Well, to be honest," he said, "when you first showed up here, I wondered
about all that. The aroma, I mean. Smelled like you was awful damned fond of    335
pork chops." The old man almost smiled. He made a snuffling sound, then sat
down with a pencil and a piece of paper. "So what'd this crud job pay? Ten
bucks an hour? Fifteen?"

"Less."

Elroy shook his head. "Let's make it fifteen. You put in twenty-five hours    340
here, easy. That's three hundred seventy-five bucks total wages. We subtract the
two hundred sixty for food and lodging, I still owe you a hundred and fifteen."

He took four fifties out of his shirt pocket and laid them on the table.

"Call it even," he said.

"No."    345

"Pick it up. Get yourself a haircut."

The money lay on the table for the rest of the evening. It was still there when
I went back to my cabin. In the morning, though, I found an envelope tacked to
my door. Inside were the four fifties and a two-word note that said EMERGENCY
FUND.    350

The man knew.

Looking back after twenty years, I sometimes wonder if the events of that summer didn't happen in some other dimension, a place where your life exists before you've lived it, and where it goes afterward. None of it ever seemed real.
During my time at the Tip Top Lodge I had the feeling that I'd slipped out of my    355
own skin, hovering a few feet away while some poor yo-yo with my name and
face tried to make his way toward a future he didn't understand and didn't
want. Even now I can see myself as I was then. It's like watching an old home

360 movie: I'm young and tan and fit. I've got hair—lots of it. I don't smoke or drink. I'm wearing faded blue jeans and a white polo shirt. I can see myself sitting on Elroy Berdahl's dock near dusk one evening, the sky a bright shimmering pink, and I'm finishing up a letter to my parents that tells what I'm about to do and why I'm doing it and how sorry I am that I'd never found the courage to talk to them about it. I ask them not to be angry. I try to explain some of my

365 feelings, but there aren't enough words, and so I just say that it's a thing that has to be done. At the end of the letter I talk about the vacations we used to take up in this north country, at a place called Whitefish Lake, and how the scenery here reminds me of those good times. I tell them I'm fine. I tell them I'll write again from Winnipeg or Montreal or wherever I end up.

370 On my last full day, the sixth day, the old man took me out fishing on the Rainy River. The afternoon was sunny and cold. A stiff breeze came in from the north, and I remember how the little fourteen-foot boat made sharp rocking motions as we pushed off from the dock. The current was fast. All around us, I remember, there was a vastness to the world, an unpeopled rawness, just the trees and

375 the sky and the water reaching out toward nowhere. The air had the brittle scent of October.

For ten or fifteen minutes Elroy held a course upstream, the river choppy and silver-gray, then he turned straight north and put the engine on full throttle. I felt the bow lift beneath me. I remember the wind in my ears, the sound of

380 the old outboard Evinrude. For a time I didn't pay attention to anything, just feeling the cold spray against my face, but then it occurred to me that at some point we must've passed into Canadian waters, across that dotted line between two different worlds, and I remember a sudden tightness in my chest as I looked up and watched the far shore come at me. This wasn't a daydream. It

385 was tangible and real. As we came in toward land, Elroy cut the engine, letting the boat fishtail lightly about twenty yards off shore. The old man didn't look at me or speak. Bending down, he opened up his tackle box and busied himself with a bobber and a piece of wire leader, humming to himself, his eyes down.

It struck me then that he must've planned it. I'll never be certain, of course,

390 but I think he meant to bring me up against the realities, to guide me across the river and to take me to the edge and to stand a kind of vigil as I chose a life for myself.

I remember staring at the old man, then at my hands, then at Canada. The shoreline was dense with brush and timber. I could see tiny red berries on the

395 bushes. I could see a squirrel up in one of the birch trees, a big crow looking at me from a boulder along the river. That close—twenty yards—and I could see the delicate latticework of the leaves, the texture of the soil, the browned needles beneath the pines, the configurations of geology and human history. Twenty yards. I could've done it. I could've jumped and started swimming for

400 my life. Inside me, in my chest, I felt a terrible squeezing pressure. Even now, as I write this, I can still feel that tightness. And I want you to feel it—the wind

coming off the river, the waves, the silence, the wooded frontier. You're at the bow of a boat on the Rainy River. You're twenty-one years old, you're scared, and there's a hard squeezing pressure in your chest.

What would you do?

Would you jump? Would you feel pity for yourself? Would you think about your family and your childhood and your dreams and all you're leaving behind? Would it hurt? Would it feel like dying? Would you cry, as I did?

I tried to swallow it back. I tried to smile, except I was crying.

Now, perhaps, you can understand why I've never told this story before. It's not just the embarrassment of tears. That's part of it, no doubt, but what embarrasses me much more, and always will, is the paralysis that took my heart. A moral freeze: I couldn't decide, I couldn't act, I couldn't comport myself with even a pretense of modest human dignity.

All I could do was cry. Quietly, not bawling, just the chest-chokes.

At the rear of the boat Elroy Berdahl pretended not to notice. He held a fishing rod in his hands, his head bowed to hide his eyes. He kept humming a soft, monotonous little tune. Everywhere, it seemed, in the trees and water and sky, a great worldwide sadness came pressing down on me, a crushing sorrow, sorrow like I had never known it before. And what was so sad, I realized, was that Canada had become a pitiful fantasy. Silly and hopeless. It was no longer a possibility. Right then, with the shore so close, I understood that I would not do what I should do. I would not swim away from my hometown and my country and my life. I would not be brave. That old image of myself as a hero, as a man of conscience and courage, all that was just a threadbare pipe dream. Bobbing there on the Rainy River, looking back at the Minnesota shore, I felt a sudden swell of helplessness come over me, a drowning sensation, as if I had toppled overboard and was being swept away by the silver waves. Chunks of my own history slashed by. I saw a seven-year-old boy in a white cowboy hat and a Long Ranger mask and a pair of holstered six-shooters; I saw a twelve-year-old Little League shortstop pivoting to turn a double play; I saw a sixteen-year-old kid decked out for his first prom, looking spiffy in a white tux and a black bow tie, his hair cut short and flat, his shoes freshly polished. My whole life seemed to spill out into the river, swirling away from me, everything I had ever been or ever wanted to be. I couldn't get my breath; I couldn't stay afloat; I couldn't tell which way to swim. A hallucination, I suppose, but it was as real as anything I would ever feel. I saw my parents calling to me from the far shoreline. I saw my brother and sister, all the townsfolk, the mayor and the entire Chamber of Commerce and all my old teachers and girlfriends and high school buddies. Like some weird sporting event: everybody screaming from the sidelines, rooting me on—a loud stadium roar. Hotdogs and popcorn—stadium smells, stadium heat. A squad of cheerleaders did cartwheels along the banks of the Rainy River; they had megaphones and pompoms and smooth brown thighs. The crowd swayed left and right. A marching band played fight songs. All my aunts and uncles were there, and Abraham Lincoln, and Saint George, and a nine-year-old

girl named Linda who had died of a brain tumor back in fifth grade, and several members of the United States Senate, and a blind poet scribbling notes, and LBJ, and Huck Finn, and Abbie Hoffman, and all the dead soldiers back from the grave, and the many thousands who were later to die—villagers with terri-
450  ble burns, little kids without arms or legs—yes, and the Joint Chiefs of Staff were there, and a couple of popes, and a first lieutenant named Jimmy Cross, and the last surviving veteran of the American Civil War, and Jane Fonda dressed up as Barbarella, and an old man sprawled beside a pigpen, and my grandfather, and Gary Cooper, and a kind-faced woman carrying an umbrella
455  and a copy of Plato's *Republic,* and a million ferocious citizens waving flags of all shapes and colors—people in hard hats, people in headbands—they were all whooping and chanting and urging me toward one shore or the other. I saw faces from my distant past and distant future. My wife was there. My unborn daughter waved at me, and my two sons hopped up and down, and a drill
460  sergeant named Blyton sneered and shot up a finger and shook his head. There was a choir in bright purple robes. There was a cabbie from the Bronx. There was a slim young man I would one day kill with a hand grenade along a red clay trail outside the village of My Khe.[7]

The little aluminum boat rocked softly beneath me. There was the wind
465  and the sky.

I tried to will myself overboard.

I gripped the edge of the boat and leaned forward and thought, *Now.*

I did try. It just wasn't possible.

All those eyes on me—the town, the whole universe—and I couldn't risk
470  the embarrassment. It was as if there were an audience to my life, that swirl of faces along the river, and in my head I could hear people screaming at me. Trai-tor! they yelled. Turncoat! Pussy! I felt myself blush. I couldn't tolerate it. I couldn't endure the mockery, or the disgrace, or the patriotic ridicule. Even in my imagination, the shore just twenty yards away, I couldn't make myself be
475  brave. It had nothing to do with morality. Embarrassment, that's all it was.

And right then I submitted.

I would go to the war—I would kill and maybe die—because I was embar-rassed not to.

That was the sad thing. And so I sat in the bow of the boat and cried.
480  It was loud now. Loud, hard crying.

Elroy Berdahl remained quiet. He kept fishing. He worked his line with the tips of his fingers, patiently, squinting out at his red and white bobber on the Rainy River. His eyes were flat and impassive. He didn't speak. He was simply there, like the river and the late-summer sun. And yet by his presence, his mute
485  watchfulness, he made it real. He was the true audience. He was a witness, like

---

7. *My Khe:* a settlement within Son My village, close to My Lai, where in 1968 U.S. troops un-der Lt. William Calley massacred some 400 Vietnamese civilians. (*ed.*)

God, or like the gods, who look on in absolute silence as we live our lives, as we make our choices or fail to make them.

"Ain't biting," he said.

Then after a time the old man pulled in his line and turned the boat back toward Minnesota.

490

I don't remember saying goodbye. That last night we had dinner together, and I went to bed early, and in the morning Elroy fixed breakfast for me. When I told him I'd be leaving, the old man nodded as if he already knew. He looked down at the table and smiled.

At some point later in the morning it's possible that we shook hands—I just don't remember—but I do know that by the time I'd finished packing the old man had disappeared. Around noon, when I took my suitcase out to the car, I noticed that his old black pickup truck was no longer parked in front of the house. I went inside and waited for a while, but I felt a bone certainty that he wouldn't be back. In a way, I thought, it was appropriate. I washed up the breakfast dishes, left his two hundred dollars on the kitchen counter, got into the car, and drove south toward home.

495

500

The day was cloudy. I passed through towns with familiar names, through the pine forests and down to the prairie, and then to Vietnam, where I was a soldier, and then home again. I survived, but it's not a happy ending. I was a coward. I went to the war.

505

## Looking Back

1. According to O'Brien, how can we hope to display courage on that future day when it will be needed (see lines 8–20)?

2. What picture does he draw of his own view, and undoubtedly that of many other Americans, of the Vietnam War in 1968 (see lines 21–39)?

3. O'Brien's immediate reaction to his draft notice was that people like him—with intelligence, sensitivity, and firm beliefs—should not be forced to serve in the military. Is he right? Explain your answer.

4. How does his work in the meatpacking plant affect his state of mind?

5. What are the horns of O'Brien's moral dilemma?

6. In what way is his crisis one of personal identity as well as of moral action?

7. Can you say what he means by the townspeople's "simple-minded patriotism, their prideful ignorance, their love-it-or-leave-it platitudes" (lines 139–140)?

8. The old man at Tip Top Lodge never gives O'Brien a word of advice about what to do. Why then does O'Brien say that Elroy Berdahl is "the hero of my life" (line 203)? What does he do for O'Brien?

9. How do you account for O'Brien's decision not to flee to Canada?

10. In your estimation, did O'Brien make the right or the wrong decision? Explain your answer.

## Writing Assignments

1. The character named O'Brien in this story roundly condemns himself as a coward for allowing himself to be drafted. However, given the extreme pressures he was under, we may be somewhat less ready to blame him, at least not before examining how we would act in the same situation. Write an essay speculating on what you would do, and *why,* by answering these questions he puts to the reader in lines 405–408:

   What would you do?
   Would you jump? Would you feel pity for yourself? Would you think about your family and your childhood and your dreams and all you're leaving behind? Would it hurt? Would it feel like dying?
   Would you cry, as I did?

   On the basis of your answers, say how you now feel about his action (see number 10 in Looking Back).

2. Moral courage is the great virtue O'Brien seeks and, by his own admission, fails to realize. Otherwise, he would have fled to Canada. More than that, however, at least in terms of definition, we don't know. And just what *does* it mean—for anybody—to have moral courage? Write an essay mapping out a definition of the term. You might take into consideration factors present in the story, namely, social pressure, individual conscience, personal emotions, and the need to decide between right and wrong action; you may also want to use examples from outside the story. But your main job is to show how these factors come together to produce something called moral courage. Conceive of an audience who, without your essay, would draw a blank at mention of the term.

3. Although each of us desires strongly to form a definite self, a self all our own, it seems that we inevitably need other people to help us do so. Specifically, quite often we need one other person. Why? Why can't we rely wholly on ourselves, our own judgment, our own resources? Is the single self always inadequate to this task? Write an essay that interpolates your own views into a reading of "On the Rainy River" by analyzing O'Brien's need for Elroy Berdahl and explaining Berdahl's contribution to O'Brien. Attempt to answer the above questions, to explain why personal identity is always formed in the framework of relationships, not only in O'Brien's case but—extrapolating from it—in anybody's.

# Diane Arbus

# My Favorite Thing Is to Go Where I've Never Been

# A Family One Evening in a Nudist Camp, Pa., 1965

Born and raised in New York City, Diane Arbus (1923–1971) began her career as a fashion photographer. However, her fame rests on the portraits she shot of people we rarely see— or saw, prior to her work—in serious photography. In her pictures of "freaks," we begin to see the ordinary, and in her pictures of ordinary people, we begin to see the freakish. In all of her work, the individual emerges from the type. Arbus won Guggenheim Fellowships in 1963 and 1966. A year after her death by suicide, a retrospective show at the Museum of Modern Art in New York established her reputation as a major American photographer. The text presented here was compiled from tape recordings of classes she taught, interviews she gave, and written materials. Together, these present a critical thinking project of the highest kind. The mind that considers what the eye looks at and the camera records is transformed by challenging habitual ways of *not* seeing and by approaching subjects from a fresh perspective.

## Looking Ahead

1. As you read, you may discover that the text is fragmented and apparently discontinuous, but this is on the surface only: there is an underlying unity deriving from Arbus's sensibility and her art itself.

2. Grappling with the intricacies of one's self is difficult; presenting these to others is more so. Therefore, read this piece both critically and deliberately, pausing when necessary to find in the more private views Arbus expresses meaningful statements that apply generally.

3. Note the way the opening sentence and the photograph on page 230 not only frame her remarks generally but also reflect on each other and comment on much of what she says about herself and others.

My favorite thing is to go where I've never been. For me there's something about just going into somebody else's house. When it comes time to go, if I have to take a bus to somewhere or if I have to take a cab uptown, it's like I've got a blind date. It's always seemed something like that to me. And sometimes I have a sinking feeling of, Oh God it's time and I really don't want to go. And then, once I'm on my way, something terrific takes over      5 about the sort of queasiness of it and how there's absolutely no method for control.

If I were just curious, it would be very hard to say to someone, "I want to
10 come to your house and have you talk to me and tell me the story of your life." I mean people are going to say, "You're crazy." Plus they're going to keep mighty guarded. But the camera is a kind of license. A lot of people, they want to be paid that much attention and that's a reasonable kind of attention to be paid.

15 Actually, they tend to like me. I'm extremely likeable with them. I think I'm kind of two-faced. I'm very ingratiating. It really kind of annoys me. I'm just sort of a little too nice. Everything is Oooo. I hear myself saying, "How terrific," and there's this woman making a face. I really *mean* it's terrific. I don't mean I wish I looked like that. I don't mean I wish my children looked like that. I don't
20 mean in my private life I want to kiss you. But I mean that's amazingly, undeniably something.

There are always two things that happen. One is recognition and the other is that it's totally peculiar. But there's some sense in which I always identify with them.

Everybody has that thing where they need to look one way but they come out
25 looking another way and that's what people observe. You see someone on the street and essentially what you notice about them is the flaw. It's just extraordinary that we should have been given these peculiarities. And, not content with what we were given, we create a whole other set. Our whole guise is like giving a sign to the world to think of us in a certain way but there's a point between
30 what you want people to know about you and what you can't help people knowing about you. And that has to do with what I've always called the gap between intention and effect. I mean if you scrutinize reality closely enough, if in some way you really, really get to it, it becomes fantastic. You know it really is totally fantastic that we look like this and you sometimes see that very clearly in
35 a photograph. Something is ironic in the world and it has to do with the fact that what you intend never comes out like you intend it.

What I'm trying to describe is that it's impossible to get out of your skin into somebody else's. And that's what all this is a little bit about. That somebody else's tragedy is not the same as your own.

40 Another thing is a photograph has to be specific. I remember a long time ago when I first began to photograph I thought, There are an awful lot of people in the world and it's going to be terribly hard to photograph all of them, so if I photograph some kind of generalized human being, everybody'll recog-

nize it. It'll be like what they used to call the common man or something. It was my teacher, Lisette Model, who finally made it clear to me that the more 45 specific you are, the more general it'll be. You really have to face that thing. And there are certain evasions, certain nicenesses that I think you have to get out of.

The process itself has a kind of exactitude, a kind of scrutiny that we're not normally subject to. I mean that we don't subject each other to. We're nicer to each 50 other than the intervention of the camera is going to make us. It's a little bit cold, a little bit harsh.

Now, I don't mean to say that all photographs have to be mean. Sometimes they show something really nicer in fact than what you felt, or oddly different. But in a way this scrutiny has to do with not evading facts, not evading what it really 55 looks like.

Freaks was a thing I photographed a lot. It was one of the first things I photographed and it had a terrific kind of excitement for me. I just used to adore them. I still do adore some of them. I don't quite mean they're my best friends but they made me feel a mixture of shame and awe. There's a quality of legend 60 about freaks. Like a person in a fairy tale who stops you and demands that you answer a riddle. Most people go through life dreading they'll have a traumatic experience. Freaks were born with their trauma. They've already passed their test in life. They're aristocrats.

I'm very little drawn to photographing people that are known or even subjects 65 that are known. They fascinate me when I've barely heard of them and the minute they get public, I become terribly blank about them.

Sometimes I can see a photograph or a painting, I see it and I think, That's not the way it is. I don't mean a feeling of, I don't like it. I mean the feeling that this is fantastic, but there's something wrong. I guess it's my own sense of what a 70 fact is. Something will come up in me very strongly of No, a terrific No. It's a totally private feeling I get of how different it really is.

I'm not saying I get it only from pictures I don't like. I also get it from pictures I like a lot. You come outdoors and all you've got is you and all photographs begin to fall away and you think, My God, it's really totally differ- 75 ent. I don't mean you can do it precisely like it is, but you can do it more like it is.

I used to have this notion when I was a kid that the minute you said anything, it was no longer true. Of course it would have driven me crazy very rapidly if I

80  hadn't dropped it, but there's something similar in what I'm trying to say. That once it's been done, you want to go someplace else. There's just some sense of straining.

Nudist camps was a terrific subject for me. I've been to three of them over a period of years. The first time I went was in 1963 when I stayed a whole week and
85  that was really thrilling. It was the seediest camp and for that reason, for some reason, it was also the most terrific. It was really falling apart. The place was mouldy and the grass wasn't growing.

I had always wanted to go but I sort of didn't dare tell anybody. The director met me at the bus station because I didn't have a car so I got in his car and I was
90  very nervous. He said, "I hope you realize you've come to a nudist camp." Well, I hope I realized I had. So we were in total agreement there. And then he gave me this speech saying, "You'll find the moral tone here is higher than that of the outside world." His rationale for this had to do with the fact that the human body is really not as beautiful as it's cracked up to be and when you look at it,
95  the mystery is taken away.

They have these rules. I remember at one place there were two grounds for expulsion. A man could get expelled if he got an erection or either sex could get expelled for something like staring. They had a phrase for it. I mean you were

A Family One Evening in a Nudist Camp, Pa., 1965

allowed to look at people but you weren't allowed to somehow make a big deal of it.                                                                                                        100

It's a little bit like walking into an hallucination without being quite sure whose it is. I was really flabbergasted the first time. I had never seen that many men naked, I had never seen that many people naked all at once. The first man I saw was mowing his lawn.

You think you're going to feel a little silly walking around with nothing on but     105
your camera. But that part is really sort of fun. It just takes a minute, you learn how to do it, and then you're a nudist. You may think you're not but you are.

They seem to wear more clothes than other people. I mean the men wear shoes and socks when they go down to the lake and they have their cigarettes tucked into their socks. And the women wear earrings, hats, bracelets, watches, high     110
heels. Sometimes you'll see someone with nothing on but a bandaid.

After a while you begin to wonder. I mean there'll be an empty pop bottle or a rusty bobby pin underfoot, the lake bottom oozes mud in a particularly nasty way, the outhouse smells, the woods look mangy. It gets to seem as if way back in the Garden of Eden after the Fall, Adam and Eve had begged the Lord to for-     115
give them and He, in his boundless exasperation had said, "All right, then. Stay. Stay in the Garden. Get civilized. Procreate. Muck it up." And they did.

One of the things I felt I suffered from as a kid was I never felt adversity. I was confirmed in a sense of unreality which I could only feel as unreality. And the sense of being immune was, ludicrous as it seems, a painful one. It was as if I     120
didn't inherit my own kingdom for a long time. The world seemed to me to be-long to the world. I could learn things but they never seemed to be my own experience.

I wasn't a child with tremendous yearnings. I didn't worship heroes. I didn't long to play the piano or anything. I did paint but I hated painting and I quit     125
right after high school because I was continually told how terrific I was. It was like self-expression time and I was in a private school and their tendency was to say, "What would you like to do?" And then you did something and they said, "How terrific." It made me feel shaky. I remember I hated the smell of the paint and the noise it would make when I put my brush to the paper. Sometimes I     130
wouldn't really look but just listen to this horrible sort of squish squish squish. I didn't want to be told I was terrific. I had the sense that if I was so terrific at it, it wasn't worth doing.

135   It's always seemed to me that photography tends to deal with facts whereas film tends to deal with fiction. The best example I know is when you go to the movies and you see two people in bed, you're willing to put aside the fact that you perfectly well know that there was a director and a cameraman and assorted lighting people all in that same room and the two people in bed weren't really alone. But when you look at a photograph, you can never put that aside.

140   A whore I once knew showed me a photo album of Instamatic color pictures she'd taken of guys she'd picked up. I don't mean kissing ones. Just guys sitting on beds in motel rooms. I remember one of a man in a bra. He was just a man, the most ordinary, milktoast sort of man, and he had just tried on a bra. Like anybody would try on a bra, like anybody would try on what the other

145   person had that he didn't have. It was heartbreaking. It was really a beautiful photograph.

There've been a couple of times that I've had an experience that's absolutely like a photograph to me even though it's totally non-visual. I don't know if I can describe it. There was one that was sensational. I had gone to a dance for handi-

150   capped people. I didn't have my camera. At first I'd come in and I was incredibly bored. I was sort of holding myself very in and really dreading the whole evening. I couldn't photograph and there wasn't even much I wanted to photograph. There were all different kinds of handicapped people. In fact, one woman told me this terrific thing which was that the cerebral palsies don't like

155   the polios and they both dislike the retardeds. Anyway, after a while somebody asked me to dance and then I danced with a number of people. I began to have an absolutely sensational time. I can't really explain it. One sort of unpleasant aspect of it was that it was a little bit like being Jean Shrimpton[1] all of a sudden. I mean you had this feeling that you were totally sensational suddenly because

160   of the circumstances. Something had shifted and suddenly you were a remarkable creature. But the other thing was that my whole relation to people changed and I really had the most marvelous time.

Then the woman who had brought me pointed out this man. She said, "Look at that man. He's dying to dance with somebody but he's afraid." He was a sixty

165   year old man and he was retarded and visually he was not interesting to me at all because there was nothing about him that looked strange. He just looked like any sixty year old man. He just looked sort of ordinary. We started to dance and he was very shy. In fact there was something about him that was left over from being eleven. I asked him where he lived and he told me he lived in Coney Is-

170   land with his father who was eighty and I asked him if he worked and he said in

---

1. *Jean Shrimpton:* a glamorous, high-fashion model of the 1960s. (*ed.*)

the summer he sold Good Humors. And then he said this incredible sentence. It was something like, "I used to worry about"—it was very slow—"I used to worry about being like this. Not knowing more. But now"—and his eyes sort of lit up—"now I don't worry anymore." Well, it was just totally knockout for me.

I like to put things up around my bed all the time, pictures of mine that I like   175
and other things and I change it every month or so. There's some funny sublim- inal thing that happens. It isn't just looking at it. It's looking at it when you're not looking at it. It really begins to act on you in a funny way.

I suppose a lot of these observations are bound to be after the fact. I mean they're nothing you can do to yourself to get yourself to work. You can't make   180
yourself work by putting up something beautiful on the wall or by knowing yourself. Very often knowing yourself isn't really going to lead you anywhere. Sometimes it's going to leave you kind of blank. Like, here I am, there is a me, I've got a history, I've got things that are mysterious to me in the world, I've got things that bug me in the world. But there are moments when all that doesn't   185
seem to avail.

Another thing I've worked from is reading. It happens very obliquely. I don't mean I read something and rush out and make a picture of it. And I hate that business of illustrating poems. But here's an example of something I've never photographed that's like a photograph to me. There's a Kafka story called "In-   190
vestigations of a Dog" which I read a long, long time ago and I've read it since a number of times. It's a terrific story written by the dog and it's the real dog life of a dog.

Actually, one of the first pictures I ever took must have been related to that story because it was of a dog. This was about twenty years ago and I was living   195
in the summer on Martha's Vineyard. There was a dog that came at twilight every day. A big dog. Kind of a mutt. He had sort of Weimaraner eyes, grey eyes. I just remember it was very haunting. He would come and just stare at me in what seemed a very mythic way. I mean a dog, not barking, not licking, just looking right through you. I don't think he liked me. I did take a picture of him   200
but it wasn't very good.

I don't particularly like dogs. Well, I love stray dogs, dogs who don't like peo- ple. And that's the kind of dog picture I would take if I ever took a dog picture.

One thing I would never photograph is dogs lying in the mud.

In the beginning of photographing I used to make very grainy things. I'd be fas-   205
cinated by what the grain did because it would make a kind of tapestry of all these little dots and everything would be translated into this medium of dots.

Skin would be the same as water would be the same as sky and you were dealing mostly in dark and light, not so much in flesh and blood.

210   But when I'd been working for a while with all these dots, I suddenly wanted terribly to get through there. I wanted to see the real differences between things. I'm not talking about textures. I really hate that, the idea that a picture can be interesting simply because it shows texture. I mean that just kills me. I don't see what's interesting about texture. It really bores the hell out of me. But I wanted
215   to see the difference between flesh and material, the densities of different kinds of things: air and water and shiny. So I gradually had to learn different techniques to make it come clear. I began to get terribly hyped on clarity.

I used to have a theory about photographing. It was a sense of getting in between two actions, or in between action and repose. I don't mean to make a big
220   deal of it. It was just like an expression I didn't see or wouldn't have seen. One of the excitements of strobe at one time was that you were essentially blind at the moment you took the picture. I mean it alters the light enormously and reveals things you don't see. In fact that's what made me really sick of it. I began to miss light like it really is and now I'm trying to get back to some kind of ob-
225   scurity where at least there's normal obscurity.

Lately I've been struck with how I really love what you can't see in a photograph. An actual physical darkness. And it's very thrilling for me to see darkness again.

What's thrilling to me about what's called technique—I hate to call it that be-
230   cause it sounds like something up your sleeve—but what moves me about it is that it comes from some mysterious deep place. I mean it can have something to do with the paper and the developer and all that stuff, but it comes mostly from some very deep choices somebody has made that take a long time and keep haunting them.

235   Invention is mostly this kind of subtle, inevitable thing. People get closer to the beauty of their invention. They get narrower and more particular in it. Invention has a lot to do with a certain kind of light some people have and with the print quality and the choice of subject. It's a million choices you make. It's luck in a sense, or even ill luck. Some people hate a certain kind of complexity. Oth-
240   ers only want that complexity. But none of that is really intentional. I mean it comes from your nature, your identity. We've all got an identity. You can't avoid it. It's what's left when you take everything else away. I think the most beautiful inventions are the ones you don't think of.

Some pictures are tentative forays without your even knowing it. They become
245   methods. It's important to take bad pictures. It's the bad ones that have to do

with what you've never done before. They can make you recognize something you hadn't seen in a way that will make you recognize it when you see it again.

I hate the idea of composition. I don't know what good composition is. I mean I guess I must know something about it from doing it a lot and feeling my way into it and into what I like. Sometimes for me composition has to do with a cer- 250 tain brightness or a certain coming to restness and other times it has to do with funny mistakes. There's a kind of rightness and wrongness and sometimes I like rightness and sometimes I like wrongness. Composition is like that.

Recently I did a picture—I've had this experience before—and I made rough prints of a number of them. There was something wrong in all of them. I felt I'd 255 sort of missed it and I figured I'd go back. But there was one that was just totally peculiar. It was a terrible dodo of a picture. It looks to me a little as if the lady's husband took it. It's terribly head-on and sort of ugly and there's something ter-rific about it. I've gotten to like it better and better and now I'm secretly sort of nutty about it. 260

I think the camera is something of a nuisance in a way. It's recalcitrant. It's de-termined to do one thing and you may want to do something else. You have to fuse what you want and what the camera wants. It's like a horse. Well, that's a bad comparison because I'm not much of a horseback rider, but I mean you get to learn what it will do. I've worked with a couple of them. One will be terrific 265 in certain situations, or I can make it be terrific. Another will be very dumb but sometimes I kind of like that dumbness. It'll do, you know. I get a great sense that they're different from me. I don't feel that total identity with the machine. I mean I can work it fine, although I'm not so great actually. Sometimes when I'm winding it, it'll get stuck or something will go wrong and I just start click- 270 ing everything and suddenly very often it's all right again. That's my feeling about machines. If you sort of look the other way, they'll get fixed. Except for certain ones.

There used to be this moment of panic which I still can get where I'd look in the ground glass and it would all look ugly to me and I wouldn't know what was 275 wrong. Sometimes it's like looking in a kaleidoscope. You shake it around and it just won't shake out right. I used to think if I could jumble it up, it would all go away. But short of that, since I couldn't do that, I'd just back up or start to talk or, I don't know, go someplace else. But I don't think that's the sort of thing you can calculate on because there's always this mysterious thing in the process. 280

Very often when you go to photograph it's like you're going for an event. Say it's a beauty contest. You picture it in your mind a little bit, that there'll be these people who'll be the judges and they'll be choosing the winner from all these contestants and then you go there and it's not like that at all.

285   Very often an event happens scattered and the account of it will look to you in your mind like it's going to be very straight and photographable. But actually one person is over there and another person is over here and they don't get together. Even when you go to do a family, you want to show the whole family, but how often are the mother and father and the two kids all on the same side of
290   the room? Unless you tell them to go there.

I work from awkwardness. By that I mean I don't like to arrange things. If I stand in front of something, instead of arranging it, I arrange myself.

I remember one summer I worked a lot in Washington Square Park. It must have been about 1966. The park was divided. It has these walks, sort of like a
295   sunburst, and there were these territories staked out. There were young hippie junkies down one row. There were lesbians down another, really tough amazingly hard-core lesbians. And in the middle were winos. They were like the first echelon and the girls who came from the Bronx to become hippies would have to sleep with the winos to get to sit on the other part with the junkie hippies. It
300   was really remarkable. And I found it very scary. I mean I could become a nudist, I could become a million things. But I could never become that, whatever all those people were. There were days I just couldn't work there and then there were days I could. And then, having done it a little, I could do it more. I got to know a few of them. I hung around a lot. They were a lot like sculptures in a
305   funny way. I was very keen to get close to them, so I had to ask to photograph them. You can't get that close to somebody and not say a word, although I have done that.

I have this funny thing which is that I'm never afraid when I'm looking in the ground glass. This person could be approaching with a gun or something like
310   that and I'd have my eyes glued to the finder and it wasn't like I was really vulnerable. It just seemed terrific what was happening. I mean I'm sure there are limits. God knows, when the troops start advancing on me, you do approach that stricken feeling where you perfectly well can get killed.

But there's a kind of power thing about the camera. I mean everyone knows
315   you've got some edge. You're carrying some slight magic which does something to them. It fixes them in a way.

I used to think I was shy and I got incredibly persistent in the shyness. I remember enjoying enormously the situation of being put off and having to wait. I still do. I suppose I use that waiting time for a kind of nervousness, for getting
320   calm or, I don't know, just waiting. It isn't such a productive time. It's a really boring time. I remember once I went to this female impersonator show and I waited about four hours backstage and then I couldn't photograph and they

told me to come back another night. But somehow I learned to like that experience because, while being bored I was also entranced. I mean it *was* boring, but it was also mysterious, people would pass. And also I had a sense of what there was to photograph that I couldn't actually photograph which I think is quite enjoyable sometimes. 325

The Chinese have a theory that you pass through boredom into fascination and I think it's true. I would never choose a subject for what it means to me or what I think about it. You've just got to choose a subject, and what you feel about it, what it means, begins to unfold if you just plain choose a subject and do it enough. 330

There's this person I've photographed a lot. I just saw her on the street one day. I was riding my bicycle on Third Avenue and she was with a friend of hers. They were enormous, both of them, almost six feet tall, and fat. I thought they were big lesbians. They went into a diner and I followed them and asked if I could photograph them. They said, "Yes, tomorrow morning." Subsequently they were apparently arrested and they spent the night in jail being booked. So the next morning I got to their house around eleven and they were just coming up the stairs after me. The first thing they said was, "I think we should tell you"—I don't know why they felt so obligated—"we're men." I was very calm but I was really sort of pleased. 335 340

I got to know one of them pretty well. She lives always dressed as a woman and she whores as a woman. I would never think she was a man. I can't really see the man in her. Most of the time I absolutely know but she has none of the qualities of female impersonators that I can recognize. I have gone into restaurants with her and every man in the place has turned around to look at her and made all kinds of hoots and whistles. And it was her, it wasn't me. 345

The last time I saw her I went to her birthday party. She called me up and said it was her birthday party and would I come and I said, "How terrific." It was a hotel on Broadway and 100th Street. I've never been in a place like that in my life. I've been in some pretty awful places but the lobby was really like Hades. There were people lounging around with the whites of their eyes sort of purple and their faces all somehow violety black and it was scary. The elevator was broken and so finally I decided to walk. It was the fourth floor and there were these people dead on their feet on the stairs. You had to step over about three or four people every flight. And then I came into her room. The birthday party was me and her, a whore friend of hers and her pimp, and the cake. 350 355

The thing that's important to know is that you never know. You're always sort of feeling your way. 360

One thing that struck me very early is that you don't put into a photograph what's going to come out. Or, vice versa, what comes out is not what you put in.

I never have taken a picture I've intended. They're always better or worse.

365  For me the subject of the picture is always more important than the picture. And more complicated. I do have a feeling for the print but I don't have a holy feeling for it. I really think what it is, is what it's about. I mean it has to be *of* something. And what it's of is always more remarkable than what it is.

370  I do feel I have some slight corner on something about the quality of things. I mean it's very subtle and a little embarrassing to me, but I really believe there are things which nobody would see unless I photographed them.

## Looking Back

1. As she describes it from the beginning to line 23, how would you paraphrase Arbus's complex relation to her photographic subjects?

2. What is the "gap between intention and effect" (lines 31–32) that Arbus refers to?

3. In what way might her comment that "the more specific you are, the more general it'll [the subject] be" apply to writing as well as to photography?

4. Why are "freaks" aristocratic, according to Arbus (line 64)?

5. Can you explain the problematic tie between reality and depictions of it—particularly by means of photography—that Arbus describes in lines 68–82?

6. Why do you think the handicapped man's speech reported in lines 172–174 represents for Arbus the truest approach to understanding one's own personal identity?

7. What does she mean by the statement, "We've all got an identity. . . . It's what's left when you take everything else away" (lines 241–243)? What is this "everything else"?

8. What do you discover in the text about the importance of subjectivity and the uniqueness of experience?

9. How do you interpret her comment, "The thing that's important to know is that you never know. You're always sort of feeling your way" (lines 359–360)?

10. In what way does Arbus's photograph of a nudist family support her criticism of the search nudists conduct for a pure, unadulterated existence? Do you think she would apply this criticism to everyone?

## Writing Assignments

1. Diane Arbus strongly implies that people we traditionally see as occupying the margins of life have more to teach about human existence, about personal identity and social reality, than people we normally place in the mainstream. She is never patronizing to "freaks" and others; she doesn't "adopt" them as a group or as individuals.

In fact, she clearly rejects the idea that some marginal types, like nudists and "junkie hippies," have any value at all. Yet, as a result of her investigations, we come to understand that it is these people's very identity deriving from their membership in a particular group that enables them to illuminate aspects of life that "ordinary" people cannot reveal. Why this is so? What gives them this special faculty? Referring to Arbus, write an essay that analyzes the particular nature of such marginalized people, shows their relation to the mainstream, and finds in both their nature and these relationships an answer to our questions.

2. Nudists pursue an existence uncorrupted by the wearing of clothes. In this way, they are similar to other groups, such as vegetarians and celibate religionists, who reject certain parts of life and seek to purify themselves. Some of these groups base their practices on reason, some on faith, some on intuition. All, though each in a different way, seem to believe that they have hit on the right path to salvation. This path, as it turns out, necessarily leads away from the ordinary lives of most people. It is this conscious aim to be apart (which is not the same as having been shoved aside) and to be pure whose wisdom Arbus seems to doubt. Do you share her doubts? Write an essay arguing that the "purified" life is or is not worthwhile if it means being separated from most people and no longer experiencing what they do.

3. "The thing that's important to know is that you never know. You're always sort of feeling your way," writes Diane Arbus (lines 259–260). Extrapolating from the interpretation you made in answering number 9 in Looking Back, write an essay that analyzes her comment as a piece of wisdom. *Why* is it important? *How* are we always feeling our way? Point out, with as many concrete details, illustrative examples, and revealing comparisons as you feel are useful, whether acting on such wisdom—the wisdom of Socrates and of the Zen Buddhist masters alike—can be enlightening for the individual and steer him or her in the right direction. Conceive of an audience of people younger than you, people who might make good use of the advice you can give them.

# III

## *The Natural World*

In the final words of Mary McCarthy's novel *Birds of America,* one of the characters states, "Nature is dead, *mein kind*" (my child). As a factual report, this is probably not altogether accurate. Still, things certainly could be better, and as a vision of the future, these words are not to be taken lightly. In fact, the sentiment is not so taken anymore. From protecting species in Kenya to saving rain forests in Brazil to recycling trash in Fort Worth, more and more people are acting to preserve the environment. They have realized how irreplaceable are the mysteries and beauties of the natural world, not to mention that we can't soldier on in this world without oxygen and a dependably temperate climate.

This concern does not mean that there cannot be valid differences about what and how much should be done. It *does* mean that for fewer of us than ever is nature beneath our notice. Nor is nature over our heads, as it would be if we accepted the claim of one sociologist that "Nature is an idea," a phenomenon we think up. Ideas are intellectual constructions placed on things, persons, and happenings to abstract them and make them significant. We can have ideas about nature, but the physical world itself is a given reality of our lives, in the way a person we love might be. We may well have an idea of that love, but the person and the emotional charge are actual.

The actuality of nature is its force, its palpability, its odors, its sounds, and its colors. Historically, we have thrashed the brushwood and slain rattlesnakes, raised windbreaks and trampled daisies, all to carve out our own space and walk in it without impediment or peril. Yet, as George Orwell puts it, we keep the aspidistra flying. The potted plants and windowboxes in our city apartments testify that we must stay in contact with the nature we have subdued, with vegetation, with streams and meadows, and also with animals (pets are tokens, yes, but isn't that a rooster crowing next door?). We bring nature back to ourselves, and we go out to meet it, even if our farthest excursion is only to the zoo. But why do we do this? What is the attraction? Isn't it, perhaps, that we recognize that the natural world is irrefutable? It is never wrong, nor mistaken; it is never of two minds, nor is it logical, nor does it ever present a contradiction in terms. It simply is. And when we take it for what it is, we may, for moments that we all want to prolong, find the source of our deepest being.

This understanding of nature is not always consoling. Although nature sometimes appears to us as a home, with its shade trees and its unmade beaches, other times it is far from that. Glaciers grind their teeth across a valley from ponds of gentians; winds descend to tear off the roof; the supple doe, even, carries nasty ticks. Nature is red in tooth and claw, and we feel betrayed by that. We retreat from sentimentalizing it to find it is indifferent to our longings, heedless of our desires to be at one with the universe. We're on our own again.

But as the letters from home drop off, we realize that the individual freedom we prize so much stems from our very separation from nature. We need it, we go back to it, it flows within us, and yet the distinction we draw, for example, between ourselves and the "lower" animals shows who we think we are—human beings who can think that they think and who know they will die. This detachment allows us to *conceive* of nature—not to mistake it for an idea, but to enclose it in one. We are prevented thus from losing ourselves in nature, while we are led constantly to renegotiate our ties to it. We lend it some of our subjectivity and, at times, we become a willing object of its scrutiny; it seems, perhaps at our most precious moments, that we are watched—not watched over—by tigers and lilies.

As you read the selections in this part of the book, it will be useful to consider the following:

1. Environmental concerns and objections to animal testing continue to make headlines. Reading such articles when they appear can help you put in the proper context all of these readings, not just those dealing with this specific issue.

2. Some of the authors represented here are more subjective than others in their approaches to nature. Their differences indicate two common human tendencies: to draw closer to nature, and to withdraw further from it.

3. Since each of us is implicated in the natural world, you may want to accompany your reading with a constant self-reminder of your own proximity or involvement and of how that contributes to your life.

# PRIMARY TEXTS

## *The Creation*

Before the ocean was, or earth, or heaven
Nature was all alike, a shapelessness,
Chaos, so-called, all rude and lumpy matter,
Nothing but bulk, inert, in whose confusion
Discordant atoms warred: there was no sun                    5
To light the universe; there was no moon
With slender silver crescents filling slowly;
No earth hung balanced in surrounding air;
No sea reached far along the fringe of shore.
Land, to be sure, there was, and air, and ocean,            10
But land on which no man could stand, and water
No man could swim in, air no man could breathe,
Air without light, substance forever changing,
Forever at war: within a single body
Heat fought with cold, wet fought with dry, the hard        15
Fought with the soft, things having weight contended
With weightless things.
                        Till God, or kindlier Nature,
Settled all argument, and separated
Heaven from earth, water from land, our air                 20
From the high stratosphere, a liberation
So things evolved, and out of blind confusion
Found each its place, bound in eternal order.
The force of fire, that weightless element,
Leaped up and claimed the highest place in heaven;          25
Below it, air; and under them the earth
Sank with its grosser portions; and the water,
Lowest of all, held up, held in, the land.

Whatever god it was, who out of chaos
Brought order to the universe, and gave it                  30
Division, subdivision, he molded earth,
In the beginning, into a great globe,
Even on every side, and bade the waters
To spread and rise, under the rushing winds,
Surrounding earth; he added ponds and marshes,             35
He banked the river-channels, and the waters
Feed earth or run to sea, and that great flood
Washes on shores, not banks. He made the plains
Spread wide, the valleys settle, and the forest
Be dressed in leaves; he made the rocky mountains          40
Rise to full height, and as the vault of Heaven
Has two zones, left and right, and one between them
Hotter than these, the Lord of all Creation

45

Marked on the earth the same design and pattern.
The torrid zone too hot for men to live in,
The north and south too cold, but in the middle
Varying climate, temperature and season.
Above all things the air, lighter than earth,

50

Lighter than water, heavier than fire,
Towers and spreads; there mist and cloud assemble,
And fearful thunder and lightning and cold winds,
But these, by the Creator's order, held
No general dominion; even as it is,

55

These brothers brawl and quarrel; though each one
Has his own quarter, still, they come near tearing
The universe apart. Eurus is monarch
Of the lands of dawn, the realms of Araby,
The Persian ridges under the rays of morning.

60

Zephyrus holds the west that glows at sunset,
Boreus, who makes men shiver, holds the north,
Warm Auster governs in the misty southland,
And over them all presides the weightless ether,
Pure without taint of earth.
                                        These boundaries given,

65

Behold, the stars, long hidden under darkness,
Broke through and shone, all over the spangled heaven,
Their home forever, and the gods lived there,
And shining fish were given the waves for dwelling
And beasts the earth, and birds the moving air.

70

But something else was needed, a finer being,
More capable of mind, a sage, a ruler,
So Man was born, it may be, in God's image,
Or Earth, perhaps, so newly separated
From the old fire of Heaven, still retained

75

Some seed of the celestial force which fashioned
Gods out of living clay and running water.
All other animals look downward; Man,
Alone, erect, can raise his face toward Heaven.

—Ovid, from *Metamorphoses*

Of all beings naturally composed, some are ungenerated and imperishable for the whole of eternity, but others are subject to coming-to-be and perishing. It has come about that in relation to the former, which possess value—indeed divinity—the studies we can make are less, because both the starting-points of the
5   inquiry and the things we long to know about present extremely few appearances to observation. We are better equipped to acquire knowledge about the perishable plants and animals because they grow beside us: much can be

learned about each existing kind if one is willing to take sufficient pains. Both studies have their attractions. Though we grasp only a little of the former, yet because the information is valuable we gain more pleasure than from everything around us, just as a small and random glimpse of those we love pleases us more than seeing many other things large and in detail. But the latter, because the information about them is better and more plentiful, take the advantage in knowledge. Also, because they are closer to us and belong more to our nature, they have their own compensations in comparison with the philosophy concerned with the divine things. And since we have completed the account of our views concerning these, it remains to speak about animal nature, omitting nothing if possible whether of lesser or greater value. For even in the study of animals unattractive to the senses, the nature that fashioned them offers immeasurable pleasures in the same way to those who can learn the causes and are naturally lovers of wisdom. It would be unreasonable, indeed absurd, to enjoy studying their representations on the grounds that we thereby study the art that fashioned them (painting or sculpture), but not to welcome still more the study of the actual things composed by nature, at least when we can survey their causes. Therefore we must avoid a childish distaste for examining the less valued animals. For in all natural things there is something wonderful. And just as Heraclitus is said to have spoken to the visitors, who were wanting to meet him but stopped as they were approaching when they saw him warming himself at the oven—he kept telling them to come in and not worry, "for there are gods here too"—so we should approach the inquiry about each animal without aversion, knowing that in all of them there is something natural and beautiful. For the non-random, the *for-something's-sake,* is present in the works of nature most of all, and the end for which they have been composed or have come to be occupies the place of the beautiful. If anyone has thought the study of the other animals valueless, he should think the same about himself; for one cannot without considerable distaste view the parts that compose the human kind, such as blood, flesh, bones, veins, and the like. Just as in any discussion of parts or equipment we must not think that it is the matter to which attention is being directed or which is the object of the discussion, but rather the conformation as a whole (a house, for example, rather than bricks, mortar, and timber), in the same way we must think that a discussion of nature is about the composition and the being as a whole, not about parts that can never occur in separation from the being they belong to.

—Aristotle, from *De Partibus Animalium*

Nature is always consistent, though she feigns to contravene her own laws. She keeps her laws, and seems to transcend them. She arms and equips an animal to find its place and living in the earth, and, at the same time, she arms and equips another animal to destroy it. Space exists to divide creatures; but by clothing the

5    sides of a bird with a few feathers, she gives him a petty omnipresence. The direction is forever onward, but the artist still goes back for materials, and begins
again with the first elements on the most advanced stage: otherwise, all goes to
ruin. If we look at her work, we seem to catch a glance of a system in transition.
Plants are the young of the world, vessels of health and vigor; but they grope
10   ever upward towards consciousness; the trees are imperfect men, and seem to
bemoan their imprisonment, rooted in the ground. The animal is the novice and
probationer of a more advanced order. The men, though young, having tasted
the first drop from the cup of thought, are already dissipated: the maples and
ferns are still uncorrupt; yet no doubt, when they come to consciousness, they
15   too will curse and swear. Flowers so strictly belong to youth, that we adult men
soon come to feel, that their beautiful generations concern not us: we have had
our day; now let the children have theirs. The flowers jilt us, and we are old
bachelors with our ridiculous tenderness.

    Things are so strictly related, that according to the skill of the eye, from any
20   one object the parts and properties of any other may be predicted. If we had
eyes to see it, a bit of stone from the city wall would certify us of the necessity
that man must exist, as readily as the city. That identity makes us all one, and
reduces to nothing great intervals on our customary scale. We talk of deviations
from natural life, as if artificial life were not also natural. The smoothest curled
25   courtier in the boudoirs of a palace has an animal nature, rude and aboriginal as
a white bear, omnipotent to its own ends, and is directly related, there amid
essences and billetsdoux, to Himmaleh mountain-chains, and the axis of the
globe. If we consider how much we are nature's, we need not be superstitious
about towns, as if that terrific or benefic force did not find us there also, and
30   fashion cities. Nature who made the mason, made the house. We may easily
hear too much of rural influences. The cool disengaged air of natural objects,
makes them enviable to us, chafed and irritable creatures with red faces, and we
think we shall be as grand as they, if we camp out and eat roots; but let us be
men instead of woodchucks, and the oak and the elm shall gladly serve us,
35   though we sit in chairs of ivory on carpets of silk.

    This guiding identity runs through all the surprises and contrasts of the
piece, and characterizes every law. Man carries the world in his head, the whole
astronomy and chemistry suspended in a thought. Because the history of nature
is charactered in his brain, therefore is he the prophet and discoverer of her se-
40   crets. Every known fact in natural science was divined by the presentiment of
somebody, before it was actually verified. A man does not tie his shoe without
recognising laws which bind the farthest regions of nature: moon, plant, gas,
crystal, are concrete geometry and numbers. Common sense knows its own,
and recognises the fact at first sight in chemical experiment. The common sense
45   of Franklin, Dalton, Davy, and Black, is the same common sense which made
the arrangements which now it discovers.

—Ralph Waldo Emerson, from "Nature"

# Lewis Thomas

## The Music of *This* Sphere[1]

Lewis Thomas (1913–1993), essayist and physician, wrote *Et Cetera Et Cetera, The Fragile Species, Late Night Thoughts on Listening to Mahler's Ninth Symphony, The Medusa and the Snail,* and *The Lives of a Cell,* from which this essay is taken. He was president of Memorial Sloan-Kettering Cancer Center and past professor of pediatrics, medicine, pathology, and biology. He also served as dean of the New York University and Yale medical schools. In "The Music of *This* Sphere," Thomas affirms the universal presence of music; the importance he places on the transmutation of sound into music brings to his essay a critical awareness of the world that leads him, and us, to a new sense of physical existence.

## Looking Ahead

1. The term *music,* you will notice, has a special sense and meaning to Thomas. Read critically to determine what that is and to test the validity of this finding on his part.

2. Try to identify Thomas's attitude toward the sounds animals make. It is this general approach that enables him to intrigue us.

3. Thomas's view of nature, gained through the investigation of animal sounds, is an optimistic one that you might attempt to put in your own words as you read.

It is one of our problems that as we become crowded together, the sounds we make to each other, in our increasingly complex communication systems, become more random-sounding, accidental or incidental, and we have trouble selecting meaningful signals out of the noise. One reason is, of course, that we do not seem able to restrict our communication to information-bearing, relevant signals. Given any new technology for transmitting information, we seem bound to use it for great quantities of small talk. We are only saved by music from being overwhelmed by nonsense.                                                                                   5

It is a marginal comfort to know that the relatively new science of bioacoustics must deal with similar problems in the sounds made by other animals to each other. No matter what sound-making device is placed at their disposal, creatures in general do a great deal of gabbling, and it requires long patience and observation to edit out the parts lacking syntax and sense. Light social conversation, designed to keep the party going, prevails. Nature abhors a long silence.                                               10

---

1. *The Music of* This *Sphere:* The title refers to the harmonies purportedly heard at high altitudes and coming from other worlds. (*ed.*)

15      Somewhere, underlying all the other signals, is a continual music. Termites make percussive sounds to each other by beating their heads against the floor in the dark, resonating corridors of their nests. The sound has been described as resembling, to the human ear, sand falling on paper, but spectrographic analysis of sound records has recently revealed a high degree of organization in the

20      drumming; the beats occur in regular, rhythmic phrases, differing in duration, like notes for a tympani section.

From time to time, certain termites make a convulsive movement of their mandibles to produce a loud, high-pitched clicking sound, audible ten meters off. So much effort goes into this one note that it must have urgent meaning, at

25      least to the sender. He cannot make it without such a wrench that he is flung one or two centimeters into the air by the recoil.

There is obvious hazard in trying to assign a particular meaning to this special kind of sound, and problems like this exist throughout the field of bioacoustics. One can imagine a woolly-minded Visitor from Outer Space, inter-

30      ested in human beings, discerning on his spectrograph the click of that golf ball on the surface of the moon, and trying to account for it as a call of warning (unlikely), a signal of mating (out of the question), or an announcement of territory (could be).

Bats are obliged to make sounds almost ceaselessly, to sense, by sonar, all

35      the objects in their surroundings. They can spot with accuracy, on the wing, small insects, and they will home onto things they like with infallibility and speed. With such a system for the equivalent of glancing around, they must live in a world of ultrasonic bat-sound, most of it with an industrial, machinery sound. Still, they communicate with each other as well, by clicks and high-

40      pitched greetings. Moreover, they have been heard to produce, while hanging at rest upside down in the depths of woods, strange, solitary, and lovely bell-like notes.

Almost anything that an animal can employ to make a sound is put to use. Drumming, created by beating the feet, is used by prairie hens, rabbits, and

45      mice; the head is banged by woodpeckers and certain other birds; the males of deathwatch beetles make a rapid ticking sound by percussion of a protuberance on the abdomen against the ground; a faint but audible ticking is made by the tiny beetle *Lepinotus inquilinus,* which is less than two millimeters in length. Fish make sounds by clicking their teeth, blowing air, and drumming with special

50      muscles against tuned inflated air bladders. Solid structures are set to vibrating by toothed bows in crustaceans and insects. The proboscis of the death's-head hawk moth is used as a kind of reed instrument, blown through to make high-pitched, reedy notes.

Gorillas beat their chests for certain kinds of discourse. Animals with loose

55      skeletons rattle them, or, like rattlesnakes, get sounds from externally placed structures. Turtles, alligators, crocodiles, and even snakes make various more or less vocal sounds. Leeches have been heard to tap rhythmically on leaves, en-

gaging the attention of other leeches, which tap back, in synchrony. Even earthworms make sounds, faint staccato notes in regular clusters. Toads sing to each
other, and their friends sing back in antiphony.

Birdsong has been so much analyzed for its content of business communication that there seems little time left for music, but it is there. Behind the glos-
saries of warning calls, alarms, mating messages, pronouncements of territory,
calls for recruitment, and demands for dispersal, there is redundant, elegant
sound that is unaccountable as part of the working day. The thrush in my backyard sings down his nose in meditative, liquid runs of melody, over and over
again, and I have the strongest impression that he does this for his own pleasure. Some of the time he seems to be practicing, like a virtuoso in his apartment. He starts a run, reaches a midpoint in the second bar where there should
be a set of complex harmonics, stops, and goes back to begin over, dissatisfied.
Sometimes he changes his notation so conspicuously that he seems to be im-
provising sets of variations. It is a meditative, questioning kind of music, and I
cannot believe that he is simply saying, "thrush here."

The robin sings flexible songs, containing a variety of motifs that he rearranges to his liking; the notes in each motif constitute the syntax, and the possibilities of variation produce a considerable repertoire. The meadow lark, with
three hundred notes to work with, arranges these in phrases of three to six notes
and elaborates fifty types of song. The nightingale has twenty-four basic songs,
but gains wild variety by varying the internal arrangement of phrases and the
length of pauses. The chaffinch listens to other chaffinches, and incorporates
into his memory snatches of their songs.

The need to make music, and to listen to it, is universally expressed by human beings. I cannot imagine, even in our most primitive times, the emergence
of talented painters to make cave paintings without there having been, near at
hand, equally creative people making song. It is, like speech, a dominant aspect
of human biology.

The individual parts played by other instrumentalists—crickets or earthworms, for instance—may not have the sound of music by themselves, but we
hear them out of context. If we could listen to them all at once, fully orches-
trated, in their immense ensemble, we might become aware of the counterpoint,
the balance of tones and timbres and harmonics, the sonorities. The recorded
songs of the humpback whale, filled with tensions and resolutions, ambiguities
and allusions, incomplete, can be listened to as a *part* of music, like an isolated
section of an orchestra. If we had better hearing, and could discern the descants
of sea birds, the rhythmic tympani of schools of mollusks, or even the distant
harmonics of midges hanging over meadows in the sun, the combined sound
might lift us off our feet.

There are, of course, other ways to account for the songs of whales. They
might be simple, down-to-earth statements about navigation, or sources
of krill, or limits of territory. But the proof is not in, and until it is shown

that these long, convoluted, insistent melodies, repeated by different singers with ornamentations of their own, are the means of sending through several hundred miles of undersea such ordinary information as "whale here," I shall believe otherwise. Now and again, in the intervals between songs, the whales
105 have been seen to breach, leaping clear out of the sea and landing on their backs, awash in the turbulence of their beating flippers. Perhaps they are pleased by the way the piece went, or perhaps it is celebration at hearing one's own song returning after circumnavigation; whatever, it has the look of jubilation.
110    I suppose that my extraterrestrial Visitor might puzzle over my records in much the same way, on first listening. The 14th Quartet might, for him, be a communication announcing, "Beethoven here," answered, after passage through an undersea of time and submerged currents of human thought, by another long signal a century later, "Bartok here."
115    If, as I believe, the urge to make a kind of music is as much a characteristic of biology as our other fundamental functions, there ought to be an explanation for it. Having none at hand, I am free to make one up. The rhythmic sounds might be the recapitulation of something else—an earliest memory, a score for the transformation of inanimate, random matter in chaos into the
120 improbable, ordered dance of living forms. Morowitz has presented the case, in thermodynamic terms, for the hypothesis that a steady flow of energy from the inexhaustible source of the sun to the unfillable sink of outer space, by way of the earth, is mathematically destined to cause the organization of matter into an increasingly ordered state. The resulting balancing act involves a
125 ceaseless clustering of bonded atoms into molecules of higher and higher complexity, and the emergence of cycles for the storage and release of energy. In a nonequilibrium steady state, which is postulated, the solar energy would not just flow to the earth and radiate away; it is thermodynamically inevitable that it must rearrange matter into symmetry, away from probabil-
130 ity, against entropy, lifting it, so to speak, into a constantly changing condition of rearrangement and molecular ornamentation. In such a system, the outcome is a chancy kind of order, always on the verge of descending into chaos, held taut against probability by the unremitting, constant surge of energy from the sun.
135    If there were to be sounds to represent this process, they would have the arrangement of the Brandenburg Concertos for my ear, but I am open to wonder whether the same events are recalled by the rhythms of insects, the long, pulsing runs of birdsong, the descants of whales, the modulated vibrations of a million locusts in migration, the tympani of gorilla breasts, termite heads,
140 drumfish bladders. A "grand canonical ensemble" is, oddly enough, the proper term for a quantitative model system in thermodynamics, borrowed from music by way of mathematics. Borrowed back again, provided with notation, it would do for what I have in mind.

## Looking Back

1. Why does Thomas emphasize the word *This* in his title?
2. What criticism does Thomas make in the first paragraph of the uses of human speech?
3. If the so-called Visitor from Outer Space would be baffled by the sound of a bouncing golf ball (lines 27–33), what problem lies in assigning meaning to sound?
4. What do you infer about Thomas's attitude toward animal sounds from his attribution to bats of "lovely bell-like notes" (lines 41–42)?
5. What place in his essay does his inventory of animal sounds have (lines 43–60)?
6. Why is his claim that "Even earthworms make sounds" (lines 58–59) particularly effective?
7. Can you explain what Thomas means by the "redundant, elegant sound" of birdsong (lines 64–65)? How does he elaborate on this claim?
8. Why does he find it necessary to imagine the "immense ensemble" of musical animals (line 90)?
9. Thomas contends that since no explanation exists for the music of animals, he is "free to make one up" (line 117)? Do you agree? Explain your answer.
10. What *is* Thomas's explanation for nature's urge to make music? How does it help him argue for the contribution of animal sounds to a bearable existence?

## Writing Assignments

1. The world is a sounding board, according to Lewis Thomas, and anyone willing to lend an ear would hardly argue with him on this score. Thomas mostly describes the sounds animals make and the music he hears in them, but he refers as well to human sounds. You can make a similar investigation of animal or human sounds, or both, depending on where you live and what is available to you. Extrapolating from Thomas's theory of music, write an essay in which you take note of the sounds around you, give your specific and general impressions of them, and comment on how much or how little music you find they make together.

2. Thomas's idea of the "contribution of animal sounds to a bearable existence" (number 10 in Looking Back) alerts us to the indispensable position in the world of so-called lower animals. It is possible to imagine ways other than the music animals make in which continued animal life is essential to the planet in general and to human beings in particular. Write an essay that does imagine (and describes) how it is essential. Either start with or incorporate a discussion of Thomas's theory of animal sounds. Try to be as concrete in looking at animals as he is in listening to them, but also try to convey a more abstract sense of what their appearance and behavior mean to us.

3. Although Thomas's subject is animal sounds, at the beginning of his essay he makes a few choice remarks on human speech. He is critical of the ways in which we misuse and waste our ability to communicate through language. But because our chatter is not his main focus, he does not detail his findings on the topic; he

merely suggests that our speech is "random-sounding, accidental, or incidental" (line 3). Adopting his critical perspective, write an essay in which you *do* go into detail to describe and comment on the wasteful and inconsequential uses we put speech to. (Small talk is one example he gives; just turn on your television set or listen to your radio for more.)

## *Follow-Up: An Essay for Analysis*

### A DEBT TO ANIMALS

Manhattan's Central Park is a necessary oasis in the middle of the crowded, ugly city. I am rejuvenated, relieved of stress, by a simple walk in the park, where I can encounter nature in the form of an ani-
5   mal. I walk past the zoo to see the sea lions swim and dive, and I've discovered that besides the ducks, pigeons and seagulls, a majestic heron occasionally visits one of the man-made ponds. In a city of mil-lions of people, I need these examples of nonhuman
10   animals to remind me of the diversity of life.

Lewis Thomas presents us, in his essay, a theory of animal sounds that equates them with a biological urge to make music. He tells us that all animals make sounds; together these noises can be seen as the
15   remnants of a huge ensemble that played music to ac-company the creation of life on this planet. An overture of evolution. And just as the individual members of an orchestra are integral to the whole, each animal and its particular sound contributes to
20   this symphony of nature.

When we look at the earth and its huge population of life forms, its easy to see why some of the so-called "lower" animals are disappearing. It might seem hard to make a case for every member of the or-
25   chestra. I don't agree with the idea that animals should be viewed in terms of their functions, but hu-man beings still depend on many animals for food, clothing and manual labor. Whether we benefit di-rectly or not, there is an important role in nature
30   for all creatures, even those that seem most insignif-icant. As Thomas points out, even the earthworm con-tributes a sound to the "grand canonical ensemble." In fact, earthworms are especially important to human

beings because of their activity in the soil. Worms, spiders and other "creepy-crawly" animals contribute to the balance of nature in ways most of us ignore. The backyard garden, or park, is a small ecosystem with a food chain of insects, birds and small mammals. Plants are pollinated, the earth is aerated and nature grows and flourishes.

Despite our hindering presence, nature and its animal life proceeds in its age-old cycle. Just as Thomas takes note, with appreciation, of the varied sounds of the animal world, I look for animals to relieve the stress of the urban environment. Even in the city, I notice that the activity levels of birds and squirrels can herald the changing seasons. Interaction with the park inhabitants can be a relaxing diversion; there are always people throwing breadcrumbs to the ducks and pigeons.

I always wonder why so many city people own dogs, considering that their living spaces are so small. But I think, when I see the romping canines on Central Park's "dog hill," that is the answer: the dogs get them outside. The dogs are happy playing with each other while their human companions relax in the fresh air, surrounded by trees, birds, and squirrels instead of concrete and taxicabs. It is here, in the park with the animals, that one can appreciate and feel included in, the diversity of nature.

--Pamela Corey, composition student

## Critical Inquiry

Pamela Corey wrote the above essay in response to Lewis Thomas's "The Music of *This Sphere*," Writing Assignment number 2 (p. 251). Corey's essay is an early draft. That is, it needs revision on a number of levels before it can be judged acceptable. To help you become more aware of your own writing needs as well as those of this student writer, use the following list of questions to analyze this essay. Before answering them, you should go back and reread Thomas's text and the writing assignment Corey responded to.

## Questions for Analysis

1. In your judgment, has Corey done what the writing assignment called for? If so, what supports your view? If not, what matters has she not addressed?
2. Has Corey referred to Thomas's text sufficiently for someone who has *not* read it to understand Thomas's intent and chief ideas? Why do you think this?

3. Are any of the paragraphs in Corey's essay overloaded or disunified? Do the sentences in any of the paragraphs need reordering? Is the point of each paragraph clear?

4. Do the paragraphs connect smoothly with one another, or does she need to add more explicit transitions between them?

5. Does Corey's logic hold up throughout, or are there places where it falls down? Be specific.

6. Would you suggest that, in later drafts, Corey develop some parts of the essay in greater detail? If so, which parts?

7. Is Corey's point of view generally convincing? What might she do to make it more so? Be specific.

8. Are there any particular achievements in language, organizational structure, or thought on which you would commend this composition student?

## Carl Sagan

# Can We Know the Universe?
# Reflections on a Grain of Salt

David Duncan Professor of Astronomy and Space Science, Carl Sagan (b. 1934) has taught at Cornell University for many years. He is the author of *Cosmos, The Dragon of Eden,* and *Broca's Brain,* from which this essay was taken. Its title is a variant on Walt Whitman's "universe in a grain of sand" and is, with some obvious differences, reminiscent of this poem by Alfred, Lord Tennyson:

> Flower in the crannied wall,
> I pluck you out of the crannies:—
> Hold you here, root and all, in my hand,
> Little flower—but if I could understand
> What you are, root and all, and all in all,
> I should know what God and man is.

Sagan defines scientific method as a species of critical thinking, in that it seeks "to question the conventional wisdom" and to discover a new and more probing way to regard its objects of inquiry.

### Looking Ahead

1. Science and superstition (the latter notion discussed by Sagan in another chapter of *Broca's Brain*) are opposed concepts. Keeping this opposition in mind will bring you closer to Sagan's definition of *science* and enable you to test the reliability of that definition.

2. As you read, consider how Sagan's answer to his title question reflects on cultural values and social relations as well as on the natural world.

3. Note the structural framework of this essay: a question posed at the beginning (here in the title) and an answer reached near the end. This is a classical approach in writing to elucidate a difficult point or to suggest the solution to a problem.

*Nothing is rich but the inexhaustible wealth of nature. She shows us only surfaces, but she is a million fathoms deep.*

—Ralph Waldo Emerson

Science is a way of thinking much more than it is a body of knowledge. Its goal is to find out how the world works, to seek what regularities there may be, to penetrate to the connections of things—from subnuclear particles, which may be the constituents of all matter, to living organisms, the human social community, and thence to the cosmos as a whole. Our intuition is by no means an infallible guide. Our perceptions may be distorted by training and prejudice or merely because of the limitations of our sense organs, which, of course, perceive directly but a small fraction of the phenomena of the world. Even so straightforward a question as whether in the absence of friction a pound of lead falls faster than a gram of fluff was answered incorrectly by Aristotle and almost everyone else before the time of Galileo. Science is based on experiment, on a willingness to challenge old dogma, on an openness to see the universe as it really is. Accordingly, science sometimes requires courage—at the very least the courage to question the conventional wisdom.

Beyond this the main trick of science is to *really* think of something: the shape of clouds and their occasional sharp bottom edges at the same altitude everywhere in the sky; the formation of a dewdrop on a leaf; the origin of a name or a word—Shakespeare, say, or "philanthropic"; the reason for human social customs—the incest taboo, for example; how it is that a lens in sunlight can make paper burn; how a "walking stick" got to look so much like a twig; why the Moon seems to follow us as we walk; what prevents us from digging a hole down to the center of the Earth; what the definition is of "down" on a spherical Earth; how it is possible for the body to convert yesterday's lunch into today's muscle and sinew; or how far is up—does the universe go on forever, or if it does not, is there any meaning to the question of what lies on the other side? Some of these questions are pretty easy. Others, especially the last, are mysteries to which no one even today knows the answer. They are natural questions to ask. Every culture has posed such questions in one way or another. Almost always the proposed answers are in the nature of "Just So Stories,"[1]

---

1. *"Just So Stories"*: tales by English author Rudyard Kipling (1865–1936) that gave fanciful explanations of basic animal characteristics. (*ed.*)

30   attempted explanations divorced from experiment, or even from careful comparative observations.

But the scientific cast of mind examines the world critically as if many alternative worlds might exist, as if other things might be here which are not. Then
we are forced to ask why what we see is present and not something else. Why
35   are the Sun and the Moon and the planets spheres? Why not pyramids, or
cubes, or dodecahedra? Why not irregular, jumbly shapes? Why so symmetrical, worlds? If you spend any time spinning hypotheses, checking to see
whether they make sense, whether they conform to what else we know, thinking of tests you can pose to substantiate or deflate your hypotheses, you will
40   find yourself doing science. And as you come to practice this habit of thought
more and more you will get better and better at it. To penetrate into the heart of
the thing—even a little thing, a blade of grass, as Walt Whitman said—is to experience a kind of exhilaration that, it may be, only human beings of all the beings on this planet can feel. We are an intelligent species and the use of our in-
45   telligence quite properly gives us pleasure. In this respect the brain is like a
muscle. When we think well, we feel good. Understanding is a kind of ecstasy.

But to what extent can we *really* know the universe around us? Sometimes
this question is posed by people who hope the answer will be in the negative,
who are fearful of a universe in which everything might one day be known. And
50   sometimes we hear pronouncements from scientists who confidently state that
everything worth knowing will soon be known—or even is already known—
and who paint pictures of a Dionysian or Polynesian age in which the zest for
intellectual discovery has withered, to be replaced by a kind of subdued languor, the lotus eaters drinking fermented coconut milk or some other mild hal-
55   lucinogen. In addition to maligning both the Polynesians, who were intrepid
explorers (and whose brief respite in paradise is now sadly ending), as well as
the inducements to intellectual discovery provided by some hallucinogens, this
contention turns out to be trivially mistaken.

Let us approach a much more modest question: not whether we can know
60   the universe or the Milky Way Galaxy or a star or a world. Can we know, ultimately and in detail, a grain of salt? Consider one microgram of table salt, a
speck just barely large enough for someone with keen eyesight to make out
without a microscope. In that grain of salt there are about $10^{16}$ sodium and
chlorine atoms. This is a 1 followed by 16 zeros, 10 million billion atoms. If we
65   wish to know a grain of salt, we must know at least the three-dimensional positions of each of these atoms. (In fact, there is much more to be known—for example, the nature of the forces between the atoms—but we are making only a
modest calculation.) Now, is this number more or less than the number of
things which the brain can know?

70   How much *can* the brain know? There are perhaps $10^{11}$ neurons in the
brain, the circuit elements and switches that are responsible in their electrical
and chemical activity for the functioning of our minds. A typical brain neuron
has perhaps a thousand little wires, called dendrites, which connect it with its

fellows. If, as seems likely, every bit of information in the brain corresponds to one of these connections, the total number of things knowable by the brain is no more than $10^{14}$, one hundred trillion. But this number is only one percent of the number of atoms in our speck of salt.

So in this sense the universe is intractable, astonishingly immune to any human attempt at full knowledge. We cannot on this level understand a grain of salt, much less the universe.

But let us look a little more deeply at our microgram of salt. Salt happens to be a crystal in which, except for defects in the structure of the crystal lattice, the position of every sodium and chlorine atom is predetermined. If we could shrink ourselves into this crystalline world, we would see rank upon rank of atoms in an ordered array, a regularly alternating structure—sodium, chlorine, sodium, chlorine, specifying the sheet of atoms we are standing on and all the sheets above us and below us. An absolutely pure crystal of salt could have the position of every atom specified by something like 10 bits of information.[2] This would not strain the information-carrying capacity of the brain.

If the universe had natural laws that governed its behavior to the same degree of regularity that determines a crystal of salt, then, of course, the universe would be knowable. Even if there were many such laws, each of considerable complexity, human beings might have the capability to understand them all. Even if such knowledge exceeded the information-carrying capacity of the brain, we might store the additional information outside our bodies—in books, for example, or in computer memories—and still, in some sense, know the universe.

Human beings are, understandably, highly motivated to find regularities, natural laws. The search for rules, the only possible way to understand such a vast and complex universe, is called science. The universe forces those who live in it to understand it. Those creatures who find everyday experience a muddled jumble of events with no predictability, no regularity, are in grave peril. The universe belongs to those who, at least to some degree, have figured it out.

It is an astonishing fact that there *are* laws of nature, rules that summarize conveniently—not just qualitatively but quantitatively—how the world works. We might imagine a universe in which there are no such laws, in which the $10^{80}$ elementary particles that make up a universe like our own behave with utter and uncompromising abandon. To understand such a universe we would need a brain at least as massive as the universe. It seems unlikely that such a universe could have life and intelligence, because beings and brains require some degree of internal stability and order. But even if in a much more random universe there were such beings with an intelligence much greater than our own, there could not be much knowledge, passion or joy.

2. Chlorine is a deadly poison gas employed on European battlefields in World War I. Sodium is a corrosive metal which burns upon contact with water. Together they make a placid and unpoisonous material, table salt. Why each of these substances has the properties it does is a subject called chemistry, which requires more than 10 bits of information to understand.

Fortunately for us, we live in a universe that has at least important parts
115    that are knowable. Our common-sense experience and our evolutionary history
have prepared us to understand something of the workaday world. When we go
into other realms, however, common sense and ordinary intuition turn out to
be highly unreliable guides. It is stunning that as we go close to the speed of
light our mass increases indefinitely, we shrink toward zero thickness in the di-
120    rection of motion, and time for us comes as near to stopping as we would like.
Many people think that this is silly, and every week or two I get a letter from
someone who complains to me about it. But it is a virtually certain consequence
not just of experiment but also of Albert Einstein's brilliant analysis of space and
time called the Special Theory of Relativity. It does not matter that these effects
125    seem unreasonable to us. We are not in the habit of traveling close to the speed
of light. The testimony of our common sense is suspect at high velocities.

Or consider an isolated molecule composed of two atoms shaped something like a dumbbell—a molecule of salt, it might be. Such a molecule rotates
about an axis through the line connecting the two atoms. But in the world of
130    quantum mechanics, the realm of the very small, not all orientations of our
dumbbell molecule are possible. It might be that the molecule could be oriented
in a horizontal position, say, or in a vertical position, but not at many angles in
between. Some rotational positions are forbidden. Forbidden by what? By the
laws of nature. The universe is built in such a way as to limit, or quantize, rota-
135    tion. We do not experience this directly in everyday life; we would find it startling as well as awkward in sitting-up exercises, to find arms outstretched from
the sides or pointed up to the skies permitted but many intermediate positions
forbidden. We do not live in the world of the small, on the scale of $10^{-13}$ centimeters, in the realm where there are twelve zeros between the decimal place
140    and the one. Our common-sense intuitions do not count. What does count is
experiment—in this case observations from the far infrared spectra of molecules. They show molecular rotation to be quantized.

The idea that the world places restrictions on what humans might do is
frustrating. Why *shouldn't* we be able to have intermediate rotational positions?
145    Why *can't* we travel faster than the speed of light? But so far as we can tell, this
is the way the universe is constructed. Such prohibitions not only press us toward a little humility; they also make the world more knowable. Every restric-
tion corresponds to a law of nature, a regularization of the universe. The more
restrictions there are on what matter and energy can do, the more knowledge
150    human beings can attain. Whether in some sense the universe is ultimately
knowable depends not only on how many natural laws there are that encom-
pass widely divergent phenomena, but also on whether we have the openness
and the intellectual capacity to understand such laws. Our formulations of the
regularities of nature are surely dependent on how the brain is built, but also,
155    and to a significant degree, on how the universe is built.

For myself, I like a universe that includes much that is unknown and, at the
same time, much that is knowable. A universe in which everything is known
would be static and dull, as boring as the heaven of some weak-minded theolo-

gians. A universe that is unknowable is no fit place for a thinking being. The ideal universe for us is one very much like the universe we inhabit. And I would guess that this is not really much of a coincidence.   160

## Looking Back

1. When you add to the first two sentences of this essay other descriptive statements Sagan makes about science, what is the resulting definition of *science?*
2. How may "experiment," "challenge," and "openness," three qualities Sagan says are basic to scientific method, be thought of as useful approaches to life generally?
3. Is it surprising to you that "human social customs—the incest taboo, for example" (lines 18–19) are proper subjects for scientific investigation? Why or why not?
4. In what way does the writer who makes language choices resemble the scientist who "examines the world critically, as if many alternative worlds might exist" (lines 32–33)?
5. What does Sagan's repetition of the title question in line 47 reveal about the function of the essay up to that point?
6. Why, according to the author, do some people (including himself) hope that the universe will never wholly be known?
7. How does he use the example of a grain of salt to demonstrate that gaining scientific knowledge of the natural world, which seems a daunting task, is actually comparatively simple? Does he answer the title question?
8. Does his claim that "The universe belongs to those who, at least to some degree, have figured it out" (lines 102–103) ring true? Explain your answer.
9. What criticism does Sagan level at common sense and intuition as guides to knowledge (see lines 114–142)?
10. How do you interpret the last sentence of the essay?

## Writing Assignments

1. To paraphrase Sagan, knowledge is power (see number 8 in Looking Back). The obverse of this statement is that ignorance is impotence. Sagan is hardly the first person to say this, and no doubt will not be the last, probably because ignorance can be so comfortable that people have to be reminded constantly of how debilitating it is. One way to remind ourselves, as well as others, is to analyze the ways in which knowledge empowers and ignorance enfeebles. Referring to Sagan, write an essay conducting such an analysis. Choose as the main focus for your essay any area of life you wish: it may be some aspect of nature, but it may be as various as knowing the history and social reality of your own ethnic or racial group, knowing a particular academic subject, or knowing yourself.

2. Common sense and intuition, Sagan points out, are serviceable tools for the "workaday world," the world of ordinary experience and practical tasks, but they blunder somewhat in "other realms," for example, the physical universe (see number 9 in Looking Back). And when it comes to social relations, sole reliance on common sense and intuition as paths to knowledge may be not at all useful. This is particularly so when,

accepting dominant cultural values and social practices, we mistake what is customary for what is natural. One example is the belief that a woman's place is in the home, cooking, cleaning, and raising children. Although this conviction has lost much ground in recent years, it still is popular, and many people who hold it are known to say things like, "It's just common sense that children need a mother," meaning by this that only women are able to perform the mother's traditional services. Using this example or any others, and extrapolating from Sagan's ideas, write an essay that explains how common sense and intuition may cause us to mistake what is normal for what is natural.

3. Science questions the "givens" in the world, like nature itself, and tries to discover if there is more to the story than what appears on the surface (see the epigraph from Emerson heading Sagan's essay). Origins, true functions, interconnections—these, as well as the proven or theoretically convincing inevitability of a specific phenomenon, are what science is seeking, according to Sagan. However, opposed to the scientific method (see lines 37–40), and to science itself, are such beliefs as creationism (the anti-evolutionary account of human development), astrology, fortune telling, and a host of superstitions, such as the belief that breaking a mirror brings seven years of bad luck unless you quickly throw salt over your left shoulder. How would the ideas of experiment, challenge, and openness, which characterize the scientific spirit (see number 2 in Looking Back), confront these unscientific beliefs? How would the scientific method itself do so? Choose one or more "unscientific" beliefs (those named above or others) and write an essay answering these questions.

# Linked Readings

### Hermann Hesse
### TREES

### Claude Lévi-Strauss
### IN THE FOREST

### The Audubon Society
### AN AERIAL VIEW

Most famous for his novels *Steppenwolf, Magister Ludi,* and *Siddhartha,* Hermann Hesse (1877–1962) won the Nobel Prize for literature in 1946. Throughout his life, Hesse, a German expatriate to Switzerland, was interested in eastern mysticism and in the division in human beings between emotion and intellect. However, as Eric Peters points out in the introduction to *Magister Ludi,* Hesse also had a "remarkable capacity to pull back into the world of light and air, of lakes, mountains and streams." Claude Lévi-Strauss (b. 1908) is the founder of structural anthropology (which makes a study of like elements in different cultures). He is the author of *Tristes Tropiques,* from which "In the Forest" is taken, *The Raw and the Cooked,* and numerous other books and articles. He taught at the New School for Social Research in New York and at the University of São Paulo in Brazil, and served as cultural attaché to the French embassy in Washington, D.C. The Audubon Society, an organization concerned to preserve nature, was named after John James Audubon (1785–1851), an American naturalist who observed and drew the birds of North America. Together, these pieces produce a new context in which we can view trees and, therefore, introduce the possibility of thinking differently about them.

# TREES

## *Looking Ahead*

1. See what you think of Hesse's projecting human characteristics onto nature—in this case, onto trees.

2. Hesse reflects a strand of traditional German culture in which nature is viewed from an almost religious standpoint. Read to test this basic assumption as one that does or does not lead to conclusions that have value.

3. It is interesting to find a connection between Hesse's exalted tone of voice–a kind of "Ah!" continuously sighed—and the noble claim he makes for nature.

For me, trees have always been the most penetrating preachers. I revere them when they live in tribes and families, in forests and groves. And even more I revere them when they stand alone. They are like lonely persons. Not like hermits who have stolen away out of some weakness, but like great, solitary men, like Beethoven and Nietzsche.[1] In their highest boughs the world rustles, their roots 5 rest in infinity; but they do not lose themselves there, they struggle with all the force of their lives for one thing only: to fulfill themselves according to their own laws, to build up their own form, to represent themselves. Nothing is holier, nothing is more exemplary than a beautiful, strong tree. When a tree is cut down and reveals its naked death-wound to the sun, one can read its whole 10 history in the luminous, inscribed disk of its trunk: in the rings of its years, its scars, all the struggle, all the suffering, all the sickness, all the happiness and prosperity stand truly written, the narrow years and the luxurious years, the attacks withstood, the storms endured. And every young farmboy knows that the hardest and noblest wood has the narrowest rings, that high on the mountains 15 and in continuing danger the most indestructible, the strongest, the ideal trees grow.

Trees are sanctuaries. Whoever knows how to speak to them, whoever knows how to listen to them, can learn the truth. They do not preach learning and precepts, they preach, undeterred by particulars, the ancient law of life. 20

A tree says: A kernel is hidden in me, a spark, a thought, I am life from eternal life. The attempt and the risk that the eternal mother took with me is unique, unique the form and veins of my skin, unique the smallest play of

---

1. *Ludwig van Beethoven* (1770–1827): one of the foremost German composers, whose greatest works are probably his ninth symphony, his later piano sonatas, and his last string quartets; *Friedrich Nietzsche* (1844–1900): German philosopher and author of such works as *Thus Spake Zarathustra, Beyond Good and Evil,* and *The Genealogy of Morals. (ed.)*

leaves in my branches and the smallest scar on my bark. I was made to form and
25   reveal the eternal in my smallest special detail.

A tree says: My strength is trust. I know nothing about my fathers, I know
nothing about the thousand children that every year spring out of me. I live out
the secret of my seed to the very end, and I care for nothing else. I trust that
God is in me. I trust that my labor is holy. Out of this trust I live.

30   When we are stricken and cannot bear our lives any longer, then a tree has
something to say to us: Be still! Be still! Look at me! Life is not easy, life is not
difficult. Those are childish thoughts. Let God speak within you, and your
thoughts will grow silent. You are anxious because your path leads away from
mother and home. But every step and every day lead you back again to the
35   mother. Home is neither here nor there. Home is within you, or home is
nowhere at all.

A longing to wander tears my heart when I hear trees rustling in the wind at
evening. If one listens to them silently for a long time, this longing reveals its
kernel, its meaning. It is not so much a matter of escaping from one's suffering,
40   though it may seem to be so. It is a longing for home, for a memory of the
mother, for new metaphors for life. It leads home. Every path leads homeward,
every step is birth, every step is death, every grave is mother.

So the tree rustles in the evening, when we stand uneasy before our own
childish thoughts. Trees have long thoughts, long-breathing and restful, just as
45   they have longer lives than ours. They are wiser than we are, as long as we do
not listen to them. But when we have learned how to listen to trees, then the
brevity and the quickness and the childlike hastiness of our thoughts achieve an
incomparable joy. Whoever has learned how to listen to trees no longer wants
to be a tree. He wants to be nothing except what he is. That is home. That is
50   happiness.

## IN THE FOREST

### Looking Ahead

1. Criticizing the fruits of civilization without seeming heavy-handed is a delicate task;
using narrative is a comparatively subtle way to do so, as we see here.

2. Lévi-Strauss's view, you should note, is that of a cultivated, complex individual, a
fact that marks the character of his writing.

3. The author's sense of wonder is apparent but restrained: he holds back somewhat.
Read critically to perceive how this restraint accounts for the precision of his language and how this precision reinforces this restraint.

Ever since my childhood, the sea has aroused mixed feelings in me. The shore
itself, and that marginal area ceded from time to time by the reflux which pro-
longs it—these I find attractive by reason of the challenge which they offer to

our undertakings, the unexpected universe which lies hidden within them, and
the possibilities which they offer of observations and discoveries most flattering          5
to the imagination. Like Benvenuto Cellini, whom I find more sympathetic than
the masters of the Quattrocento,[1] I enjoy walking on shores left bare by the re-
ceding tide, following, round some steep slope, the itinerary which that tide has
imposed upon me; picking up stones with holes through the middle of them,
shells whose geometry has been reshaped by the motion of the waves, or spec-          10
tral fragments of sea-wrack, and making a private museum of these things: a
museum which, for a moment, seems quite the equal of those other museums to
which only masterpieces are admitted. Perhaps, after all, those masterpieces derive from methods of work which, though rooted in the mind rather than in the
palpable world, may not be fundamentally different from those with which Na-          15
ture amuses herself.

But as I am neither sailor nor fisherman, I feel myself diminished by this
mass of water which robs me of half my universe—more than half, indeed,
since it makes its presence known some way inland, giving the landscape, as often as not, a touch of austerity. It seems to me that the sea destroys the normal          20
variety of the earth. Enormous spaces and supplementary colours it may offer
to the eye—but at the price of a deadening monotony, a flat sameness, where
never a hidden valley keeps in reserve the surprises on which my imagination
feeds.

And, what is more, the pleasures which the sea has to offer are now no          25
longer available to us. Like an animal whose carapace thickens with age, forming an impenetrable crust through which the epidermis can no longer breathe,
thus hastening the onset of old age, most European countries have allowed their
coasts to become cluttered with villas, hotels, and casinos. Whereas the littoral
once gave a foretaste of the ocean's great solitudes, it has become a kind of front          30
line, where mankind from time to time mobilizes all its forces for a full-scale attack on liberty: but the value of that liberty is marked down by the very conditions in which we allow ourselves to grasp hold of it. A beach was once a place
where the sea yielded up the results of commotions many thousands of years in
the making, admitting us, in this way, to an astonishing museum in which Na-          35
ture always ranked herself with the avant-garde; today that same beach is trod-
den by great crowds and serves merely as a depository for their rubbish.

So I prefer the mountains to the sea; and for some years past this preference
has taken the form of a jealous passion. I hated all those who shared my
predilection, for they were a menace to the solitude I value so highly; and I de-          40
spised those others for whom mountains meant merely physical exhaustion and
a constricted horizon and who were, for that reason, unable to share in my emotions. The only thing that would have satisfied me would have been for the entire world to admit to the superiority of mountains and grant me the monopoly

---

1. *Benvenuto Cellini* (1500–1571): Italian sculptor and goldsmith; *Quattrocento:* the fifteenth
century; especially refers to the art and literature produced during that period. (*ed.*)

45  of their enjoyment. I must add that my feelings did not extend to *high* mountains: these had already disappointed me, because of the ambiguous character
of the delights—and I do not deny them—that they have to offer; these delights
are physical in the extreme—organic, one might say, in view of the efforts involved. But they have a formal, almost an abstract quality in so much as one's
50  attention, absorbed by problems of a technical character, is often drawn away
from the splendours of Nature and entirely engrossed by preoccupations relating rather to mechanics or geometry. What I liked best were pasture-mountains
and, above all, the zone between four thousand five hundred and six thousand
seven hundred and fifty feet: the heights are not great enough, as yet, to impov-
55  erish the landscape, as is the case higher up, and while they make it difficult to
cultivate the land they seem, in other respects, to urge Nature on to an activity
more vivid, more sharply contrasted than that found in the valley below. On
these lofty balconies, and with that undomesticated landscape before one, it is
easy, though doubtless erroneous, to imagine that Man in his beginnings was
60  confronted with just such a sight as meets one's eyes.

 If the sea presents, in my opinion, a landscape many degrees below proof,
mountains offer, by contrast, a world in a state of intense concentration. Concentrated it is, in fact, in the strict sense of the word, in that the earth is pleated
and folded in such a way as to offer the maximum amount of surface for a given
65  area. A denser universe, it keeps its promises longer: the instability of the climate and the differences due to the height, the nature of the soil, and the fact of
its exposure to the air—all favour a sharp and direct contrast between one season and another, and likewise between level ground and steep slopes. Unlike so
many people, I was not at all depressed by a sojourn in a narrow valley where
70  the slopes, so close to one another as to take on the look of high walls, allowed
one to glimpse only a small section of the sky and to enjoy at most a few hours
of sunlight. On the contrary, I found an immense vitality in the upended landscape. Instead of submitting passively to my gaze, like a picture that can be
studied without one's giving anything of oneself, the mountain scene invited me
75  to a conversation, as it were, in which we both had to give of our best. I made
over to the mountains the physical effort that it cost me to explore them, and in
return their true nature was revealed to me. At once rebellious and provocative,
never revealing more than half of itself at any one time, keeping the other half
fresh and intact for those complementary perspectives which would open up as
80  I clambered up or down its slopes, the mountain scene joined with me in a kind
of dance—and a dance in which, I felt, I could move the more freely for having
so firm a grasp of the great truths which had inspired it.

 And yet I have to admit that, although I do not feel that I myself have
changed, my love for the mountains is draining away from me like a wave run-
85  ning backwards down the sand. My thoughts are unchanged, but the mountains
have taken leave of me. Their unchanging joys mean less and less to me, so long
and so intently have I sought them out. Surprise itself has become familiar to
me as I follow my oft-trodden routes. When I climb, it is not among bracken

and rock-face, but among the phantoms of my memories. Those memories have
lost their charm for me, on two separate counts: first, because long usage has   90
robbed them of all novelty; and second, because a pleasure which grows a little
less vivid with each repetition can only be had at the price of an effort which
grows greater and greater with the years. I am getting older, but the only evidence of it is that the cutting edge of my projects is growing steadily blunter. I
can still carry them through, but their fulfilment no longer brings me the satis-   95
faction on which I could so often and so undisappointedly count.

What attracts me now is the forest. It has the same magic as the mountains,
but in a more peaceable, more welcoming form. Having to cross and recross the
desert-like savannahs of central Brazil has taught me to appreciate anew the luxuriant Nature beloved of the ancients: young grass, flowers, and the dewy fresh-   100
ness of brakes. No longer could I look to the stony Cevennes[2] with the intransi-
gent passion of old; and I realized that my generation's enthusiasm for
Provence[3] was a ruse of which we were first the authors and later the victims. In
the interests of discovery—that greatest of joys, and one of which civilization
was soon to deprive us—we sacrificed to novelty the objective which should   105
justify it. We had neglected that department of Nature, while there were others
for us to batten on. Now that the finest was no longer available to us, we had to
scale down our ambitions to those which were still within our reach, and set
ourselves to glorify what was dry and hard, since nothing else remained to us.

But in that forced march we had forgotten the forest. As dense as our cities,   110
it was inhabited by other beings—beings organized in a society which, better
than either the high peaks or the sun-baked flatlands, had known how to keep
us at a distance: a collectivity of trees and plants that covered our tracks as soon
as we had passed. Often difficult to penetrate, the forest demands of those who
enter it concessions every bit as weighty, if less spectacular, than those exacted   115
by the mountains from the walker. Its horizon, less extensive than that of the
great mountain ranges, closes in on the traveller, isolating him as completely as
any of the desert's empty perspectives. A world of grasses, flowers, mushrooms,
and insects leads there an independent life of its own, to which patience and
humility are our only passports. A hundred yards from the edge of the forest,   120
and the world outside is abolished. One universe gives place to another—less
agreeable to look at, but rich in rewards for senses nearer to the spirit: hearing, I
mean, and smell. Good things one had thought never to experience again are
restored to one: silence, coolness, peace. In our intimacy with the vegetable
world, we enjoy those things which the sea can no longer give us and for which   125
the mountains exact too high a price.

For me to have been convinced of this, it may well have been indispensable
that the forest should first appear to me in its most virulent form, so that its universal traits were immediately evident. For between the forest as we know it in

---

2. *Cevennes:* mountain range in France. (*ed.*)

3. *Provence:* region in southwestern France noted for its desert-like climate. (*ed.*)

130   Europe, and the forest into which I plunged en route to the Tupi-Kawahibs,[4]
the distance is so great that I do not know how best to express it.

Seen from outside, the Amazonian forest looks like a great heap of station-
ary bubbles, a vertical accumulation of green blisters. It is as if the river-marge
had been visited, everywhere and at the same time, by some pathological afflic-
135   tion. But once the film is broken, and the traveller penetrates into the interior,
all is changed: seen from within, the confused mass becomes a monumental
universe. The forest is no longer a scene of terrestrial disorder and could rather
be taken for a new planetary world, which is as rich as our own and has taken
its place.

140   Once the eye has adjusted itself to the nearness of one plane to another, and
the mind has overcome its first sensation of being overwhelmed, a complicated
system presents itself. Storeys superimposed one on the other may be discerned, and for all the abrupt changes of level and intermittent mulching which
interfere with their alignment, these are all constructed in the same way. First
145   comes the head-high crest of plants and grasses. Next, the pale trunks of trees
and liana, free for a brief space to grow untrammelled by vegetation. Shortly,
however, these trunks vanish, masked by the foliage of bushes or the scarlet
flowers of the wild banana or *pacova.* The trunks re-emerge fleetingly, only to
disappear again among the palm-leaves, and make a third appearance at the
150   point where their first branches stand out horizontally. They are leafless; but,
just as a ship has its rigging, so have these branches an outcrop of epiphytal
plants—orchids or bromeliaceae. And finally, almost out of sight, the forest-
universe ends in huge cupolas, some green, some shorn of their leaves; these
latter are covered with flowers—white, yellow, orange, purple, or mauve—in
155   which a European spectator is amazed to recognize the freshness of the European spring, but on a scale so disproportionate that he can only compare it
with, if anything, the majestic and luxurious blaze of colour which we associate
with autumn.

To these aerial storeys others closely corresponding may be found beneath
160   the traveller's feet. For it would be an illusion to suppose that he is walking "on
the ground." That ground is buried deep beneath tangle upon tangle of roots,
suckers, mosses, and tufts of grass. Let him tread too heavily on unsteady
ground, and he may find himself falling—disconcertingly far, at times. In my
case, Lucinda's presence added a further complication.

165   Lucinda was a little female monkey with a prehensile tail. Her skin was
mauve and her fur miniver. She was of the species *Lagothryx,* commonly called
*barrigado,* because of its characteristic big belly. I got her when she was a few
weeks old, from a Nambikwara woman who had taken pity on her and carried
her, night and day, clamped to the head-dress which represented for the little
170   creature the furred backbone of her mother. (Mother monkeys carry their young

---

4.  *Tupi-Kawahibs:* Amazonian tribe studied by the author. (*ed.*)

on their backs.) I fed her on spoonfuls of condensed milk, and at night a drop or two of whisky would send her into the soundest of sleeps, leaving me free. But during the daytime I could get her to make, at most, a compromise: that she would leave go of my hair and settle for my left boot instead. And there she would cling, with all four paws, just above my toes, from morning till night. On horse-back this was all very well, and it was manageable when we were in our boats. But on foot it was quite a different matter, for at every bramble, every hollow in the ground, every low branch, she would give a loud cry. All my attempts to make her move to my arm, my shoulder, and even to my hair, were in vain. Only the left boot would do: it was her only protection, her sole point of security in the forest. She was a native of that forest, and yet a month or two in the company of human beings had made her as great a stranger to it as if she had grown up among the refinements of civilization. And so it was that, as I limped along with my left leg, doing my best not to lose sight of Abaitara's[5] back, my eardrums were pierced by Lucinda's cries of alarm. Abaitara forged ahead with a short and rapid step in the green half-light, working his way round trees so thick that I would think for a moment that he had disappeared, cutting a path through bushes and liana, and darting off to left or to right on an itinerary which, though unintelligible to the rest of us, took us ever deeper into the forest.

To forget my tiredness, I let my mind go free. Short poems formed in my head to the rhythm of our march and I would run over them, hour by hour, till they were like a mouthful of food so often chewed as to have no longer any flavour, and yet so acceptable, for its modest companionship, that one hesitates either to swallow it or to spit it out. The aquarium-like environment of the forest prompted this quatrain:[6]

> Dans la forêt céphalopode
> gros coquillage chevelu
> de vase, sur des rochers roses qu'érode
> le ventre des poissons-lune d'Honolulu

---

5. *Abaitara:* the author's native guide. (*ed.*)

6. The three quatrains are translated (by the editor) as follows:

In the mollusk forest
the big long-haired shellfish
of the ooze, on the red rocks that wear away
the belly of the Honolulu moon-fish.

One has cleaned the grass matting
the soaped pavements shine
on the avenue the trees are
great abandoned brooms.

Amazon, dear Amazon
you whose breast is dishonest
you tell us that all is well
but your paths are too narrow.

200    Or else, no doubt for the sake of contrast, I summoned up the dismal memory of a Parisian suburb:

> On a nettoyé l'herbe paillasson
> les pavés luisent savonnés
> sur l'avenue les arbres sont
205    de grands balais abandonnés

And then this last one, which never seemed to me quite finished, though it is
complete in form. Even today it torments me when I go for a long walk:

> Amazone, chère Amazone
> vous qui n'avez pas de sein droit
210    vous nous en racontez de bonnes
> mais vos chemins sont trop étroits

   Towards the end of the morning we were working our way round a big
bush when we suddenly found ourselves face to face with two natives who
were travelling in the opposite direction. The older of the two was about
215  forty. Dressed in a tattered pair of pyjamas, he wore his hair down to his
shoulders. The other had his hair cut short and was entirely naked, save for
the little cornet of straw which covered his penis. On his back, in a basket of
green palm-leaves tied tightly round the creature's body, was a large harpy-
eagle. Trussed like a chicken, it presented a lamentable appearance, despite
220  its grey-and-white-striped plumage and its head, with powerful yellow beak,
and crown of feathers standing on end. Each of the two natives carried a bow
and arrows.
   From the conversation which followed between them and Abaitara it
emerged that they were, respectively, the chief of the village we were hoping
225  to get to, and his right-hand man. They had gone on ahead of the other villagers, who were wandering somewhere in the forest. The whole party was
bound for the Machado with the object of paying their visit, promised a year
previously, to Pimenta Bueno. The eagle was intended as a present for their
hosts. All this did not really suit us, for we wanted not only to meet them, but
230  to meet them in their own village. It was only after they had been promised a
great many gifts when they got to the Porquinho camp that they agreed, with
the greatest reluctance, to turn in their tracks, march back with us, and make
us welcome in their village. This done, we would set off, all together, by
river. Once we had agreed on all this, the trussed eagle was jettisoned with-
235  out ceremony by the side of a stream, where it seemed inevitable that it
would very soon either die of hunger or be eaten alive by ants. Nothing more
was said about it during the next fifteen days, except that a summary "death
certificate" was pronounced: "He's dead, that eagle." The two Kawahib vanished into the forest to tell their families of our arrival, and we continued on
240  our way.

The incident of the eagle set me thinking. Several ancient authors relate that the Tupi breed eagles, feed them on monkeys' flesh, and periodically strip them of their feathers. Rondon had noted this among the Tupi-Kawahib, and other observers reported it among certain tribes of the Xingu and the Araguaya. It was not surprising, therefore, that a Tupi-Kawahib group should have pre-served the custom, nor that the eagle, which they considered as their most pre-cious property, should be taken with them as a gift, if these natives had really made up their minds (as I was beginning to suspect, and as I later verified) to leave their village for good and throw in their lot with civilization. But that only made more incomprehensible their decision to abandon the eagle to its pitiable fate. Yet the history of colonization, whether in South America or elsewhere, is marked by these radical renunciations of traditional values and repudiations of a style of life, in which the loss of certain elements at once causes all other ele-ments to be marked down: perhaps I had just witnessed a characteristic in-stance of this phenomenon.

We made a scratch meal of a few strips of grilled and still-salted *xarque*, en-livened with what we could get from the forest: some *tocari* nuts; the fruit—white-fleshed, acid in taste, foamy in texture—of the wild cocoa-plant; berries from the *pama* tree; fruit and seeds from the *caju* of the woods. It rained all night on the palm-leaf awnings that protected our hammocks. At dawn the for-est, silent during the day, was torn from end to end for several minutes by the cries of monkey and parrot. And on we went, trying never to lose sight of the back of the man immediately ahead of us, convinced that even a few yards "off course" would put us out of earshot, with no hope of retrieving the path. For one of the most striking characteristics of the forest is its way of seeming to merge into an element heavier than air: such light as gets through is greenish and enfeebled, and the human voice does not carry. The extraordinary silence which reigns—as a consequence, perhaps, of this condition—would communi-cate its example to the traveller if he were not already disinclined to speak, so intent is he upon not losing his way. His moral situation combines with his physical state to create an almost intolerable feeling of oppression.

From time to time our guide would lean over the edge of his invisible track, deftly lift the corner of a leaf, and show us the sharp point of a stick of bamboo that had been planted obliquely in the ground to pierce the foot of any enemy who happened to come by. These spikes are called *min* by the Tupi-Kawahib, who use them to protect the outskirts of their villages: the Tupi of former times used larger ones.

During the afternoon we reached a *castanhal*, or group of chestnut-trees around which the natives (who exploit the forest systematically) had opened up a little clearing, the better to collect such fruit as fell from the trees. The whole strength of the village had camped out there, the men naked save for the penis-cap which we had already encountered on the chief's lieutenant, and the women also naked, but for the slip of woven cotton round their loins: originally this was dyed red with urucu-dye, but with use it had faded to a russet colour.

285    There were in all six women and seven men, one of the men being an adolescent, and three little girls who seemed to be aged one, two, and three respectively. One could hardly conceive of a smaller group holding out for at least thirteen years (since the disappearance of Abaitara's village, that is to say), cut off
from any contact with the outer world. Among the company were two people
290    paralysed from the waist down: a young girl who supported herself on two sticks
and a man, also young, who dragged himself along the ground like a legless cripple. His knees stood out above his fleshless legs, which were swollen on their inner side and looked as if they were afflicted with serosity. The toes of the left foot
were paralyzed, but those of the right foot could still be moved. Yet these two
295    cripples managed to cover long distances in the forest with no apparent difficulty. Was it poliomyelitis, or some other virus, which had gone on ahead of any
real contact with civilization? When I was confronted with these unhappy people, who had been left to their own devices in the midst of a Nature as hostile as
any that men have to face, it was heart-rending to think back to the page on
300    which Thevet speaks with such admiration of the Tupi whom he visited in the
sixteenth century: "A people," he says, "made of the same stuff as ourselves, who
have never as yet been afflicted with leprosy, or paralysis, or lethargy, or chan-
cres, or other bodily ailments which are apparent to the eye." He had no idea that
he and his companions were the advance guard of these evils.

## AN AERIAL VIEW

### Looking Ahead

1. As you might remember from stories read to you in childhood, when animals speak,
   traditionally they tell secrets unknown to humans, speak unmentionable truths, or
   demonstrate qualities we flatter ourselves are confined to our own species.

2. A writing lesson: If the final item on a list or in a series differs radically from
   those preceding it, it can cast the whole list in an ironical light. See if that
   happens here.

3. Notice that *heck* is a euphemism for *hell*. **Euphemisms** are expressions that purposely soften the otherwise harsh or unpleasant impact of particular terms. We often criticize euphemisms as an evasion of reality, but test their criticism in the
   Audubon Society ad. How would it appear if a bird said "hell"?

## Looking Back

1. What characteristics of the heroic individual does Hesse ascribe to trees?

2. Can you say what Hesse means by his use of the terms *mother* and *home* in this context? How does he connect them to trees?

3. Which qualities of the sea and the mountains did Lévi-Strauss particularly appreciate at one time?

4. Why does he now regard the sea and the mountains less satisfying and the forest more so?

5. In what way might hearing and smell be senses "nearer to the spirit" than the other senses, as Lévi-Strauss claims in line 122?

6. How, in lines 140–158, do figures of speech and terms of comparison work to orient the reader to the "new planetary world" of the forest? Be specific.

7. Does the introduction of Lucinda the monkey seem digressive or integral in the narrative? Explain your answer.

8. What idea of Lévi-Strauss as a person do you get from his scattered comments on the impact of civilization on nature?

9. How would you compare Hesse and Lévi-Strauss in these readings? Whom do you prefer, and why?

10. The Audubon drawing bemoans with good reason the felling of the rain forests. Can you think of other examples of our squandering earth's natural resources?

## Writing Assignments (Linked Readings)

1. In a novel called *The Baron in the Trees,* by Italo Calvino (1923–1985), the eighteenth-century European continent is largely covered by forests. As a boy, the hero of the novel climbs a tree one day and perches on its top branches in rebellion against being forced to eat snails, which he hates. He swears never to come down, and he never does. The density and the proximity of the trees to each other allows him to move freely above ground. He leaves his father's estate and travels widely, living a full life out of reach of groundlings until the day of his death. If you wish, read the novel to follow his adventures, which are intellectual as well as physical. Here, dwelling solely on the topography basic to the plot, write an essay saying how you think the quality of life on ground level would be changed if your surroundings, and indeed the United States as a whole, were mostly tree-covered.

2. Lévi-Strauss several times criticizes the destruction of nature and the natural life by an encroaching civilization. His targets range from the tourist attractions that litter the shoreline to the intruders who introduced "European" diseases to the Amazonian natives. Resulting from these incursions are the loss of a true sense of liberty—the value that brings people to the sea in the first place—and the loss of stalwartness and health. To these ill effects, Lévi-Strauss adds the loss of "discovery—that greatest of joys" (line 104), meaning the ability to enter vast original states of existence, such as forests, there to experience a life that has not been merely invented, as machines and their products are. Focusing on the concepts of liberty, health, and discovery, write an essay that performs two major functions. First, further define these values and defend their human necessity. Second, explain how these values enable one to enter the kind of spiritual dimension of nature as home and holy place that Hesse describes. The first function should prepare the ground for the second.

3. Hermann Hesse and Claude Lévi-Strauss plunge into the woods in different ways and for different purposes. Hesse stays in Europe, singles out trees as individuals instead of the forest as a whole, and takes a basically religious approach to nature. Lévi-Strauss, on the other hand, travels to regions remote from Europe, views the forest as

a "collectivity," and is almost entirely secular, discovering in the forest satisfactions more of the self than of the soul. As if coming from the other side of the woods to meet these wanderers, the Audubon Society birds announce in sardonic tones the impending ruin of the groves the two writers think stretch endlessly before them. Clearly, however, the environmentalists who have sponsored these bitter birds do not consider it too late to save the forests. And doubtless they would argue that, in addition to practical measures restricting timber harvests, a general change of attitude toward nature is in order. We see before us two possibilities: the sacred view offered by Hesse, and the secular view described by Lévi-Strauss. Which do you prefer? Write an essay that, without ruling out either attitude completely, argues that one or the other would better preserve the forest, to quote the U.S. Forest Service, as "a refuge of biological diversity and an indicator of the health of the planet."

## Writing Assignments (Individual Readings)
### TREES

One of former president Ronald Reagan's most famous pronouncements was "If you've seen one redwood, you've seen them all." Reagan's view, like that of many other people, indicates a general willingness to exploit this natural resource to a virtually unlimited extent for economic purposes. The dismissive tone of Reagan's statement differs radically from the worshipful sense informing these lines from "Vacillation" by the Irish poet William Butler Yeats:

> A tree there is that from its topmost bough
> Is half all glittering flame and half all green
> Abounding foliage moistened with the dew.

In respect to redwood trees in particular, we read in the 1992 *World Almanac and Book of Facts* that some specimens date back 3,500 years. The tallest tree in the United States is a 362-foot redwood growing in Humboldt Redwoods State Park, California. Considering all these sources, we discover conflicting values. Jobs and industrial growth seem to demand clear-cutting. Beauty and dignity call for preservation. Which is the right path? Write an essay addressing this issue by analyzing Hesse's view of trees and evaluating it. If you favor it, you will tend in one direction; if you reject it, you will tend in the other.

### IN THE FOREST

Claude Lévi-Strauss explains the reasons for his initial attraction and long-lasting interest in the sea, the mountains, and the desert (represented by the arid landscape of Provence), and he goes on to describe his gradual loss of interest in them. No longer are they a refuge for him or an unqualified source of natural wonder. But as they retreat in significance, the forest advances, taking their place in his life to represent the "luxuriant Nature beloved of the ancients" (line 100). He is not alone in preferring one form of nature to another. Probably all of us do, and when we have a vacation or can get away, we tend to head in one direction. Write an essay saying which you prefer, and why: ocean, mountains, desert, forest, or some other natural environment.

## AN AERIAL VIEW

Animal fables are common in world literature. Those by Aesop and the Grimm brothers come to mind right away. Most often these stories point to a moral or illustrate a human situation with particular subtlety (see number 1 in Looking Ahead for this reading). As a literary form, these stories lie behind such uses as animals are put to in "An Aerial View." But these birds are very explicit. They are cute but scornful and, within limits, flay the conscience of us "higher animals." They have reason. We lay waste the planet, as is clear in these quotations from the 1992 *World Almanac and Book of Facts:*

> U.S. wildlife continued to suffer from the pressures of development and defor-estation in 1990. The northern spotted owl, considered to be a barometer of the irreplaceable old-growth woodlands of the Pacific Northwest, was officially listed as an endangered species.

> The chemical contamination of the Great Lakes, including PCBs, DDT, and dioxin, had been linked to reproductive problems in bald eagles and trout of the region, and had prompted concern for its possible effects on the develop-ment of children.

> Separate populations of a species, listed both as Endangered and Threat-ened, are . . . chimpanzee, grizzly bear . . . leopard, gray wolf, bald eagle, piping plover, roseate tern, Nile crocodile, green sea turtle, and olive ridley sea turtle.

Choose one of the situations described above and write your own animal fable to illustrate it. The general plot of your story should revolve around the discov-ery by the animal characters of a threat to their lives. Your animals, of course, should talk. You will have to stretch your imagination here, but if your animals criticize human practices in respect to nature—as they should—you will also be able to refer to the recognizable world you inhabit.

## Lauren Strutzel

# The Evolution of Allegiance to the Green Concern

Born in 1970 in Lincoln Park, New Jersey, Lauren Strutzel attended William Paterson State College before heading to Manhattan, where she is currently an English major at Hunter Col-lege. She plans to be a writer. Here, her praise of recycling as an ecological responsibility also defines the practice as a way to think critically about habits and, if appropriate, abandon them.

## Looking Ahead

1. You should notice here that, in recycling and writing both, concrete details make all the difference.

2. Although it is usually encountered in other contexts, the implicit claim here is that the personal is the political. Read critically to test this claim.

3. Note the way Strutzel discovers and acts on certain ecological principles that have to do with the individual's place in the world generally.

As far back as I can remember, when you were finished with something you threw it out in the big, yellow, plastic can in the kitchen; garbage was garbage. Then, one day my father announced that not all garbage was garbage: aluminum cans and glass bottles went in the brown bag next to the big, yellow plastic can.

I can mark the beginning of my "naturalist" thinking with that announcement; my father had introduced the "recycling idea" to his family but had never explained it to me. I knew where all the used bottles and cans went to; I had driven to the town dump with my Dad on Saturdays with our containers, the dump which had started out with only three bins: aluminum cans, glass bottles, and newspapers. But although I was sorting those particulars from our trash, I had no idea what happened to them after I dumped them. My father vaguely touched upon the concept that it all came back to us, but somehow cleaner than when we last left it.

Years passed. I got my driver's license and became the all too familiar "errand-girl" in my house. My father would often load my car full with paper bags and send me off to the dump to "recycle." By now, almost every family in town was at the dump "recycling," a Saturday morning ritual. Recycling had seemed to catch on in our town in some obedient, but rote fashion. It seemed we were setting out more than we could be throwing out, recycling plastic six pack rings, the plastic wrapper from the inside of the cookie boxes, tiny aspirin boxes, and used tin foil. The town dump grew from three dumpsters to nearly fifteen: one each for tin cans, plastic bottles, bags, aluminum, tires, batteries, magazines, books, cardboard, etc. Suddenly, I realized I hadn't been paying attention to this recycling scheme at all. I had been doing it for years as a family chore, and I still didn't know what happened to all these used products.

My seemingly trivial town, tucked away in the folds of New Jersey, began demonstrating its newfound green concern, making the connection between itself and this inaccessible earth. The local grocery store offered two cents for every paper bag its customers re-used. Pizza boxes were delivered to us coded for recycling. The stores carried recycled paper products, everything from notepads to toilet paper. This billow of recycled products carried me further into the idea of recycling. All of my cans and bottles were coming back to me brand new. I still had no idea about the process of recycling, but I found plenty

5

10

15

20

25

30

35   of information on gorged landfills, pollution from incinerators, and aimlessly wandering trash barges. Garbage became a political issue because it had been ignored for so long. I read that states were bargaining between themselves in order to find a closet to put it all in. To a young woman nearing high school graduation, all this news seemed absurd, not frightening. High school had tailored

40   my thinking to college and career options, and my family had groomed me for responsibility and security; there was little counseling on how to step into a world full of prizes and tragedies, and become an integral member. I had been educated to feel as if my own life were the whole world, and not a working part of the world. What was it about recycling that I needed to understand? Why

45   couldn't it just be a routine chore, something I could drop off on Saturdays and leave for someone else to take care of?

    My next endeavor helped to unfold some of the answers to my questions.

    I left my modest neighborhood to explore the bustling, adventuresome, urban life of Manhattan. I expected that New York City, a giant compared to my

50   minuscule community, would offer me ten times more experience regarding any issue. Concerning recycling, this theory proved true. Here we were, three young girls, sharing a one-bedroom apartment the size of my small town living room. Just the same, I set up my paper bag next to the blue plastic can in what we referred to as the kitchen. I continued reading information, asking ques-

55   tions, and listening to the responses of groups and individuals who were addressing environmental issues. I became involved in much more than recycling, and by being inquisitive, I found some answers.

    I learned how used paper is washed, turned into bits of wood pulp, and molded back into clean sheets of recycled paper. I learned that some paper is

60   too soiled to be recycled, and that the dyes in some colored paper render it unrecyclable. I learned that soy inks are preferred by earth-conscious consumers over toxic synthetic inks. My focus on recycling expanded to include the destruction of our forests and the production of toxic wastes due to dyes and inks. My concerns with the space we were overcrowding with trash were spilling into

65   what we were destroying and wasting to make new products that would eventually climb on top of the meandering trash wagon. I was busy consuming all of this information, but meanwhile back in the kitchen, my paper bag was spilling over.

    New York was less convenient than the suburbs, in that the town dump

70   was inaccessible to me. After several phone calls, I found the nearest recycling center was a twenty-five-minute walk from my apartment. I no longer had the convenience of a car to help me in transporting my collection. The suggestions from my peers were uninviting: to throw it out because it was inconvenient didn't solve my problem. I was confused now: Why was this so important to

75   me? If I was a blind and obedient citizen of my home town, persuaded by what I thought at the time to be my father's compliance to that town's decree, why did I need to bend over backwards to recycle, knowing I would not be fined according to my new community's legislation? I no longer recycled because it

was a family chore, I recycled out of fear! But if my father hadn't made it clear just what was at stake, then certainly this flood of information I had been un-  80 covering did. My shock was not that I had realized that I was frightened for my future, but that other people, citizens of my own generation, the very same young people who had just begun to open the doors to their lives and step out into the ungainly world, they were not yet frightened; and if they were scared, it wasn't enough to make them react, or maybe it was too much, and they be-  85 came paralyzed. One thing was clear, I had to decide what to do with what I had already used.

I spent a year of creative discarding; most of the time I bagged the recy- clables and brought them with me to New Jersey on the weekends, which be- came expensive and inconvenient. Several times I left bottles or cans on the  90 curb for the homeless to collect, and they did; it wasn't trash to them, it was in- come. I soon after moved, and found my new apartment was ten times more convenient. Recyclables were set out at the end of the hallway and taken care of by the building. One problem was that it was not clearly defined just what were the recyclables. Were the maintenance men just sorting out cardboard boxes,  95 plastic bottles, and aluminum cans, leaving the rest for the trash pile? I went around the apartment collecting anything resembling a recyclable. I picked plastic shampoo bottles out of the garbage can, and stole the tubes from inside the paper towel and toilet paper rolls. My fear was that all my picking and sav- ing was for naught; I had that old familiar feeling that I was dropping something  100 off at the dump and leaving it for someone else to take care of.

Even though I had been enlightened as to the details of the recycling process, and had come to think of recycling not as a chore, but as some insur- ance for my hazy future, something still gnawed at me. What about the citizens of my generation, and the citizens of all the other generations? What about their  105 fears, their ignorance, their paralyses? Will their choices challenge my efforts?

"Tell me, where to now, if your fight for a bearable life can be fought and lost in your backyard?"

Natalie Merchant's lyrics kept playing over and over in my head. I had been so anxious to know the specifics of recycling so that I could understand more,  110 but what good is one person's understanding? What about the individuals, out- side my intimate home, the ones with whom I have to share what space I am trying to save?

All that recycling at home had trained me so well that throwing away po- tential recycling material at work made me uneasy. We were wasting more at  115 my job than I could ever waste at home. But then, just by chance, I received a memo announcing the formation of a recycling committee at the office. Natu- rally, I joined, and soon found greater opportunity to understand the politics, the role of corporate practices, and the degree to which people want to be in- volved regarding recycling. I sent away for catalogs and brochures on how to  120 get started, and as a group, we learned how much paper was being wasted, the cost of purchasing recycled products, and the cost of storing and transporting collected recyclables.

125 Our first project, an easy victory in my mind, was to render our Styrofoam cup supply obsolete. Easy enough; Styrofoam has been taboo for quite a long time. It doesn't biodegrade and has harmful effects on the ozone layer. Since a great deal of media attention has recently been focused on the chemical assailants dismantling the ozone, it was fairly easy to wean our fellow workers away from Styrofoam cups.

130 It was another battle, however, trying to get the management committee to agree to subsidize one dollar per person for anyone without a coffee mug. Their final decision, which came after two months of debate, was no. Were they unwilling to commit a small donation, or more importantly, to demonstrate leadership and support for a committee they helped to conceive? Did they fail to see

135 the relationship between their weighted decision and the environment as a whole? Here was an example of the corporate boundaries, the hands-off policy. I say this, not with a cynic's tongue, but with a frightened voice, because I believe, despite the fact that as an individual I can make a difference, corporate and political barricades will be long and hard in falling.

140 So, the recycling committee marched on. We set up boxes by each photocopier to collect scrap paper, and asked everyone to use them when they could, so that we could reduce our paper supply. The boxes quickly became sloppy and overcrowded.

People were willing to dump their mistakes in, but were very reluctant to

145 take from it for their paper supply. A co-worker asked me, "How exactly does that box of paper get recycled?"

"That box of paper doesn't get recycled, it's for you to recopy on the clean side of the sheet."

"What would you recopy on it?"

150 "You can use it for anything that doesn't need to be circulated or mailed out; your files, notes, or private memos."

It made more sense to me as I said it aloud, and I was actually quite glad that someone was interested.

"To tell you the truth, no one wants to use dirty paper, they'd prefer a clean

155 sheet. Have a nice night."

So, the cardboard boxes are now bulging, but people are still very eager to toss their mistakes in. They probably feel good about being a part of the helping hand, but what good is being a part of a helping hand that does not alleviate, that simply rearranges? Do I explain my fears for the future to them? Do they

160 share my fears? Are environmental concerns as trivial as the decision to use a clean sheet of paper for your files, or are they a hassle?

I used to feel safe with my ingenuous understanding of the world; my provincial life in New Jersey was a safe haven from the ills of the wicked world. I could turn a blind eye to all of the insanity and convince myself that it would dissipate. Everything was under control because I *could* just drop the garbage off and wipe my hands clean of the problem. However, one day I was taken out of the safe haven on the curbside of the lunacy and made to dwell within it. It was at such a time that I began to muse on the idea that ignorance is bliss. Perhaps I'd be safer if I was clueless of my surroundings. Where I was once safe within my suburban confinements and had to interact with only a handful of people, I now had to invite the world in. I lost more control of the things that concern my daily actions once I had opened the doors to the community at my office and to society as a whole.

Recently our company received a letter written on the back of an envelope, from a doctor who very clearly stated that he would not do business with a company that did not use recycled paper. He went on to explain that the very business we were involved in, the medical community, depended on it. He gave the usual statistics on forest destruction, but then continued to point out the essential need for the marrow of this habitat: "The elements of the forest are used in developing new medicines." His focus turned from destroying the trees for paper to destroying the very building blocks of medical research. He ended the letter with plenty of addresses and phone numbers of companies that handled recycled products. My excitement swelled during the coming week before our next recycling meeting. It seemed only logical that we should be using recycled supplies, even if we started small.

Now that our Styrofoam conquest had been achieved, and our scrap paper bins were drooling out their contents, our agenda was empty and ready for a new endeavor. I read my news out loud and referred the members to my collection of recycled product catalogs. I waited for their responses, all the while thinking how much sense this made; that if we were going to be a recycling group we should explore the next logical step. I'd been reading a book by Debra Lynn Dadd about consumer products. Her new book, *Non-toxic, Natural and Earthwise,* like her previous book, *The Non-toxic Home,* reads somewhat like a catalog. She explained how she became interested in exploring product safety, but that her first book only focused on her private home, which she had been trying to keep in a protective bubble by using non-toxic products. However, her attempts to keep her home safe were in vain because the problems kept growing bigger. She then realized that she would have to head from the outside in. She had to help make her world safe, so that her home could be safe. If one wanted a cleaner water supply, then one has to start thinking in terms of what was polluting our soils and air, thus contaminating our wells, rather than attaching a filtering system to the faucets.

It occurred to me that as a recycling group we were suggesting that we were making a commitment to help the environment. It seemed hypocritical that we would clean up inside our office and pay no attention to the outside. If we couldn't help by reducing forest destruction through purchasing recycled products, then our bulging mistake box would have little effect at all. I was thinking

of all this when one member at the meeting finally spoke up. "If you want to please this doctor, you should show the letter to Ann and Eric. They handle the
210 mail lists." My colleagues, still locked within the corporate boundaries, missed the target. Surely my aim was not to please this doctor, nor was it to discontinue our mailing lists. Maybe they didn't see the next logical step, maybe they weren't afraid for their future. Maybe they were just crippled by their corporate mindset. No one even thumbed through my catalogs and the meeting was ad-
215 journed with a final statement, "I mention, now, that our company is on the cutting edge, and that we even have a recycling committee." I couldn't help but feel a bit apprehensive about this comment. It introduced a new barricade; different from the usual fear, frustration, ignorance, etc. Was it pride this member was expressing? Probably so; pride is nothing to be ashamed of, it is a reward
220 for our commitment and achievements. What else did I hear that kept that remark buzzing in my ears? Was I uneasy because my coworker coupled recycling with "cutting edge"? Perhaps so. What's so innovative about recycling?

Recycling is not a "trendy" thing to do. Environmentalism should not be considered fashionable. These two ideas suggest that something better may
225 come along. Something more efficient and polished that will help collect votes, or sell records, or instill a communal sense in the vagabonds of society. Recycling is a responsibility; environmentalism is a propensity. These two ideas suggest a little social reconditioning. So we stumble at first. Should we stop because of inconvenience, because paralysis, at the very least, allows us to remain un-
230 challenged and in "familiar" territory? A group of individuals embracing a concern may, someday, overcome the political and corporate walls that delay much needed progress. I am not suggesting a revolution of environmentalists; "cleaning up" is simple and though it may be, at times, inconvenient and fearful, it doesn't require that much muscle.

235 I'm also not suggesting that environmentalism is the only cause worth our concern. AIDS is another plague that is just as threatening as our environmental emergency, perhaps more so. No one should be expected to jump on either bandwagon, to save the world, or free it from disease; nor should they abandon their lives to fight for these causes. However, this trend of naivete, of con-
240 sciously turning our backs, for whatever reasons, can only be the path to catastrophe. People fail to see the connection between these global crises and their own lives. Committing myself to trying simply to understand these problems was a big first step, but taking the second step to do what ever I felt I could to help myself, and in turn, others, was an even bigger step. Maybe it's not enough
245 that we know how Styrofoam molecules can break apart ozone molecules and leave us unprotected from harmful sun rays. Maybe it means we should think twice before we order out for food, or think twice about how we package our products to be transported.

Essentially what I mean is, maybe it's necessary that we accompany our
250 thinking with action. It would be a shame to have to experience AIDS before we are able to massage our concern for the epidemic; and by the same token, it would be a crime to have to become infected with cancer or respiratory disease

in order to understand the very direct association between the environment and humans.

Recycling isn't the only issue in the realm of environmentalism that evokes responses. Several others come to mind—toxic waste dumping, vegetarianism, air pollution, natural preservation. I wanted to tell you about the time I mentioned to someone that I was going on a whale-watching trip in Massachusetts for the weekend and I was abruptly labeled as "one of those save-the-whales people." And about the time co-workers became hostile when I asked that we order a pizza only half covered in pepperoni. Two different stories, completely dissimilar from recycling, but the same responses: inconvenience, confusion, mistrust, misgivings.

I often think back to the beginning of my "green" thinking, and I wonder if I should consider my father a naturalist. I suppose it was he who introduced me to environmental concerns long before my naturalist thinking got a jump-start. My father was the one who taught me to recycle instead of waste. Though he did it as a reaction to town ordinances, as a chore, I'm certain he has a degree of understanding of the correlation between his life and the state of his environment. It was also my father who told me about the poisons in our water supply, triggered more by his keen interest in water filters, I think, than by his connection to toxic dumping. My father is a "gadgets man," and there was always a little boy's excitement when he examined the used filter for (harmful) particles. This said, why does my father still spray the trees, the lawn, and the garden with toxic pesticides? Is my father aware that the very chemicals he sprays on his half-acre of land will eventually become some residue he will inhale or consume? Is it not enough that he cleans his water supply if these chemicals will only leak into the soil to eventually pollute his rain and his river?

I suppose that all I, or anyone, can do is ask questions and pay attention to what's going on around us. You cannot convince people to change their habits if they do not feel they are directly involved with these global crises. I've come a long way from the paper bag in my kitchen, in that I have been happily awakened to the green concern. And, as I look around, I see that people are indeed paying attention. Colleges, restaurants, malls are all blooming with recycling bins. Environmental articles have been woven into the fabric of all kinds of journalism. The green concern has even shared stage time with other issues during presidential campaigns. These are achievements, rewards for the commitment, things to be proud of. I know that environmentalism has become an issue in my life because I realized I was a working piece of the world, that my life exists within the life of the environment. In the end, I know that I do not wonder if people know how or where to recycle; I do not wonder if people have thrown away their Styrofoam cup for a coffee mug; I do not wonder if they are sending letters on recycled paper; I do not wonder if they have installed a water filter in their kitchen faucet or chosen to buy bottled water. The details of their commitment do not concern me. My curiosity is awakened only when I think of the barricades, the trip-wires, and the plethora of hostile reactions to environmentalism. In fact, in the end, I only wonder if people have made the very definite connection between themselves and their waning world.

## Looking Back

1. What does Strutzel mean, in line 29, by "this inaccessible earth"?
2. According to the author, how was she raised to think of herself? When and how did she begin to change?
3. What quality as a writer does she exhibit in a phrase like "in what we referred to as the kitchen" (lines 53–54)? What other phrases stand out because of this quality?
4. What do you think she means by "I recycled out of fear!" (line 79)?
5. Do you think that a person can be *too* concerned for the future? Explain your answer.
6. Should the management committee have contributed money for coffee mugs, as Strutzel argues (lines 130–139)? Why or why not?
7. Assuming there are "corporate and political barricades" to ecology (lines 138–139), what form do they take?
8. Which ecological principle does the book Strutzel cites suggest to her?
9. Even though she is not insistent about it, do you think her view is correct that we should reform our daily routines to conform to environmentally sound habits? Explain your answer.
10. How, in the end, do her phrases "the green concern" (title and line 283) and "waning world" (line 298) work to make her essay a convincing personal testimony to social commitment?

## Writing Assignments

1. When it comes to recycling stationery, maybe Lauren Strutzel overlooks entirely the esthetic dimension of putting words on paper. After all, the idea of first and only use is an attractive one. No one before us has soiled the paper with meanings different from the ones we intend, meanings we might well find irrelevant, unrelated, even opposed to ours. And, if other people respect our view on using paper, no one coming after us will turn our page over and put a new face on things in their own scrawl. Is it silly to wish for these things? Or does the idea of exclusive use give us one of the few opportunities we have anymore to celebrate abundance? Is the aesthetic dimension mentioned above less important than the ecological urge to recycle? Write an essay on the issue of recycling stationery, taking up the above questions. Remember that this target of recycling efforts is a rather narrow focus for your writing. To expand on it, you should discuss the issues of esthetic quality, exclusivity, and abundance, in addition to environmental motives and concerns.

2. Strutzel thinks of herself as part of a world larger than herself. She opts for social conscientiousness, sharing, recycling, for a kind of collective responsibility in which she regards herself primarily as a member of a group—her fellow office workers, humanity at large—and not one person exercising the privileges of her education and

upbringing. Yet, the downside of all this (see lines 162–173) is that now her concern with other people forces her to give up some of her personal independence and control. She has to suffer the shortcomings of others. What course of action would you advise her to take? Is one course more in the nature of human beings than the other? Is one wise and the other foolish? Write an essay arguing for either individual achievement or collective responsibility, or some combination, as a general guideline to follow in life.

3. One strand of environmental thought is an altruistic concern for future generations. Yet, as number 5 in Looking Back suggests, the principle at the heart of this concern may contain the seed of self-neglect. We live here and now, not fifty or a hundred years off in the future, and if our actions deprive us of the enjoyment of an abundant life, may we be wasting our chance? This consideration is not confined to the environment but may carry over to other areas of life. One example is the decision to have children, which usually entails immense parental sacrifice. Other examples we might cite are working for political causes, saving money, and getting an education, all of which involve the subordination of the present to the future. Is such subordination worthwhile? Why or why not? In each, some, or none of the cases mentioned above? Write an essay answering these questions in order to discuss the link between the present and the future, and what the individual's position should be in respect to both.

# Beryl Markham

# Royal Exile

Beryl Markham (1902–1986) was four years old when her father took her to East Africa, where he farmed and raised horses. She became a horse breeder herself and also a pilot, both highly unusual occupations for women in those days. As a pilot, she flew mail planes and transported passengers in Kenya, Tanganyika, and other African countries. In 1936, she became the first pilot to cross the Atlantic solo east to west. Markham's books are *West with the Night,* from which "Royal Exile" is taken, and *The Splendid Outcast,* a collection of stories.

## Looking Ahead

1. How essential **point of view** (the position the writer takes when presenting the subject and the writer's attitude toward the subject) is to writing is made very clear here, as we encounter the "God's-eye" point of view. Note the great intimacy it gives us with the subject, greater than we might have thought possible: it sees all and knows all.

2. Notice that the charm of this memoir derives in part from the fact that the horse's consciousness exists somewhere between an animal's and a human's.

3. Read critically by defining for yourself the emotions referred to in the text and seeing if they are sufficient to produce the tension that both ties girl and horse together and keeps them apart.

To an eagle or to an owl or to a rabbit, man must seem a masterful and yet a forlorn animal; he has but two friends. In his almost universal unpopularity he
points out, with pride, that these two are the dog and the horse. He believes,
with an innocence peculiar to himself, that they are equally proud of this alleged confraternity. He says, "Look at my two noble friends—they are dumb,
but they are loyal." I have for years suspected that they are only tolerant.

Suspecting it, I have nevertheless depended on this tolerance all my life,
and if I were, even now, without either a dog or a horse in my keeping, I should
feel I had lost contact with the earth. I should be as concerned as a Buddhist
monk having lost contact with Nirvana.

Horses in particular have been as much a part of my life as past birthdays. I
remember them more clearly. There is no phase of my childhood I cannot recall
by remembering a horse I owned then, or one my father owned, or one I knew.
They were not all gentle and kind. They were not all alike. With some my father
won races and with some he lost. His black-and-yellow colours have swept past
the post from Nairobi to Peru, to Durban. Some horses he brought thousands of
miles from England just for breeding.

Camciscan was one of these.

When he came to Njoro, I was a straw-haired girl with lanky legs and he
was a stallion bred out of a stud book thick as a tome—and partly out of fire.
The impression of his coming and of the first weeks that followed are clear in
my mind.

But sometimes I wonder how it seemed to him.

He arrived in the early morning, descending the ramp from the noisy little train
with the slow step of a royal exile. He held his head above the heads of those
who led him, and smelled the alien earth and the thin air of the Highlands. It
was not a smell that he knew.

There was a star of white on his forehead; his nostrils were wide and
showed crimson like the lacquered nostrils of a Chinese dragon. He was tall,
deep in girth, slender-chested, on strong legs clean as marble.

He was not chestnut; he was neither brown nor sorrel. He stood uncertainly against the foreign background—a rangy bay stallion swathed in sunlight
and in a sheen of reddish gold.

He knew that this was freedom again. He knew that the darkness and the
terrifying movement of the ship that strained his legs and bruised his body
against walls too close together were gone now.

The net of leather rested on his head in those same places, and the long lines
that he had learned to follow hung from the thing in his mouth that could not be
bitten. But these he was used to. He could breathe, and he could feel the spring
of the earth under his hooves. He could shake his body, and he could see that
there was distance here, and a breadth of land into which he fitted. He opened
his nostrils and smelled the heat and the emptiness of Africa and filled his lungs
and let the rush of air go out of them again in a low, undulant murmur.

He knew men. In the three quick years of his life he had seen more of them than of his own kind. He understood that men were to serve him and that, in ex-   45
change, he was to concede them the indulgence of minor whims. They got upon his back and most often he let them stay. They rubbed his body and did things to his hooves, none of which was really unpleasant. He judged them by their smells and by the way they touched him. He did not like a hand with a tremor, or a hand that was hard, or one that moved too quickly. He did not trust the   50
smell of a man that had nothing of the earth in it nor any sweat in it. Men's voices were bad, but there were some not too loud that came to his ears slowly, without insistence, and these he could bear.

A white man came up to him now and walked around him. Other men, all of them very black—as black as his own mane—stood in a circle and watched   55
the first man. The stallion was used to this. It was always the same, and it made him impatient. It made him bend the sleek bow of his neck and jab at the earth with his hooves.

The white man put a hand on the stallion's shoulder and said a word that he knew because it was an old word and almost all men said it when they   60
touched him or when they saw him.

The white man said, "So you are Camciscan," and the black men repeated, more slowly, "Camciscan," one after another. And a girl, who was white too, with straw-coloured hair and legs like a colt's, said "Camciscan" several times.

The girl seemed foolishly happy saying it. She came close to him and said it   65
again and he thought her smell was good enough, but he saw that she was fa-miliar in her manner and he blew a little snort into her straw-coloured hair to warn her, but she only laughed. She was attended by a dog, ugly with scars, who never left her heels.

After a little while the girl tugged gently on the lines Camciscan had learned   70
to follow, and so he followed.

The black men, the white girl, the scarred dog, and the bay stallion walked along a dirt road while the white man rode far ahead in a buggy.

Camciscan looked neither to one side nor another. He saw nothing but the road before him. He walked as if he were completely alone, like an abdicated   75
king. He felt alone. The country smelled unused and clean, and the smells of the black men and the white girl were not outside of his understanding. But still he was alone and he felt some pride in that, as he always had.

He found the farm large and to his liking. It harboured many other horses in long rows of stables, but his box was separate from theirs.   80

He remembered the old routine of food and saddle and workout and rest, but he did not remember ever being attended before by a girl with straw-coloured hair and legs that were too long, like a colt's. He did not mind, but the girl was too familiar. She walked into his stall as if they had been old friends, and he had no need of friends.   85

He depended upon her for certain things, but, in turn, she got on his back in the morning and they went to a valley bigger than any he had ever seen, or sometimes up the side of a certain hill that was very high, and then they came back again.

90     In time he found himself getting used to the girl, but he would not let it be more than that. He could feel that she was trying to break through the loneliness that he lived by, and he remembered the reasons there were to mistrust men. He could not see that she was any different, but he felt that she was, and that disturbed him.

95     In the early morning she would come to his stable, slip his head-collar on and remove his heavy rug. She would smooth him down with a cloth and brush his black mane and his tail. She would clean the urine from his floor and separate the good bedding from that spoiled with manure. She did these things with care. She did them with a kind of intimate knowledge of his 100 needs and with a scarcely hidden sense of possession which he felt—and resented.

    He was by Spearmint out of Camlarge, and the blood flowed arrogantly in arrogant veins.

    Mornings came when Camciscan waited for the girl with his ears and with 105 his eyes, because he had learned the sound of her bare feet on the ground that was still unsoftened by any sun, and he could distinguish the tangle of straw-coloured hair among other things. But when she was in his stable, he retreated to a far corner and stood watching her work.

    He sometimes felt the urge to move closer to her, but the loneliness of 110 which he was so proud never permitted this. Instead, the urge turned often to anger which was, to himself, as unreasonable as the unprovoked anger of another might have been. He did not understand his anger; when it had passed, he would tremble as if he had caught the scent of something evil.

    The girl vaulted to his back one morning, as she always did when they went 115 to the hill or the valley, and the anger surged suddenly through his body like a quick pain. He threw her from him so that she fell against the root of a tree and lay there with blood running through the straw-coloured hair. Her legs that were too long, like a colt's, did not move even when the white man and the black men carried her away.

120     Afterward, Camciscan trembled and sweated in his box and let his mistrust of the men who tried to feed him boil into hate. For seven mornings the girl did not return.

    When she did return, he moved again to the farthest corner and watched her work, or stood still as death while she lifted his feet, one by one, and 125 cleaned them with a hard tool that never hurt. He was a Thoroughbred stallion and he knew nothing of remorse. He knew that there were things that made him tremble and things that filled him with anger. He did not know, always, what these things were.

    He did not know what the thing was that made him tremble on the morn-130 ing he saw the chestnut filly, or how it happened that there was suddenly a voice in his throat that came to his own ears unfamiliar and distant, startling him. He saw his dignity slip away like a blanket fallen from his back, and pride that had never before deserted him was in an instant shamefully vanished.

He saw the filly, smooth, young, and with a saunter in her pose, standing in an open field, under the care of four black men. Unaccountably, he had been led   135
to this field, and unaccountably he strained against restraint toward this filly.

Camciscan called to her in a tone as unfamiliar to him as it was to her, but there must have been danger in it. It was a new sound that he did not know himself. He went toward her, holding his head high, lifting his clean legs, and the filly broke from the kicking-straps that held her and fled, screaming, in a   140
voice as urgent as his own.

For the first time in his life he would have exchanged the loneliness he lived by for something else, but his willingness had gained him only the humility of rejection and disdain. He could understand this, but not more than this. He returned to his stable, not trembling. He returned walking with careful   145
steps, each as even as another.

When the girl came as she always did and kneaded the new dead hairs from his bright coat with supple fingers and ran the soft body-brush over him, he turned his head and watched her, accepting the soothing stroke of her hand, but he knew that the old anger was in him again. It had welled up in his heart   150
until now it burst and made him whirl round and catch her slender back with his teeth, biting until the brush dropped from her hand, flinging her bodily against the far wall of the box. She lay there huddled in the trampled bedding for a long time, and he stood over her, trembling, not touching her with any of his feet. He would not touch her. He would have killed any living creature that   155
touched her then, but he did not know why this was so.

After a while the girl moved and then crawled out of the box and he pawed through the bedding to the earthen floor, tossing his head up and down, letting the anger run out of him.

But the girl was there again, in the stable, the next day. She cleaned it as she   160
had cleaned it each other day and her touch on his body was the same, except there was a new firmness in it, and Camciscan knew, without knowing, that his strength, his anger, and his loneliness at last were challenged.

Nothing about the morning ride was different. The black men worked with the other horses and about the stables in their usual positions, with their usual   165
movements. The large tree against which he had thrown the girl was still there making the same little pond of shade, bees criss-crossed the unresisting air like golden bullets, birds sang or just dipped in and out of the sky. Camciscan knew that the morning was slow with peacefulness. But he also knew that this thing would happen; he knew that his anger would come and would be met by the   170
girl's anger.

By then he understood, in his own way, that the girl loved him. Also he understood now why it was that when she had lain hurt in his box, he could not

trample her with his hooves, nor allow any other living thing to touch her—and
175  the reason for this frightened him.

They came to a level spot on the green hill and he stopped suddenly with sweat stinging his blood-bay neck and his blood-bay flanks. He stopped because this was the place.

The girl on his back spoke to him, but he did not move. He felt the anger
180  again, and he did not move. For the first time her heels struck against his ribs, sharply, and he was motionless. He felt her hand relax the lines that held his head so that he was almost free. But she did not speak; she rapped him again with her heels, roughly, so that it hurt, and he whirled, baring his teeth, and tried to sink them into her leg.

185  The girl struck his muzzle with a whip, hard and without mercy, but he was startled by the act more than by the pain. The alchemy of his pride transformed the pain to anger that blinded him. He bit at her again and she struck again making the whip burn against his flesh. He whirled until their world was a cone of yellow dust, but she clung to his back, weightless, and lashed at him
190  in tireless rhythm.

He reared upward, cutting the dust cloud with his hooves. Plunging, he kicked at her legs and felt the thin whip bite at his quarters, time after time, until they glowed with pain.

He knew that his bulk could crush her. He knew that if he reared high
195  enough, he would fall backward, and this terrified him. But he was neither mastered by the girl nor by his terror. He reared until the ground fell away before him, and he saw only the sky, through bulging eyes, and inch by inch he went over, feeling the whip on his head, between his ears, against his neck. He began to fall, and the terror returned, and he fell.

200  When he knew that the girl was not caught under his weight, his anger left him as quickly as the wind had whisked the dust away. This was not reason, but it was so.

He got up, churning the air awkwardly, and the girl stood, watching him, still holding the lines and the whip, her straw-coloured hair matted with dust.

205  She came to him and touched the hurt places on his body and stroked his neck and his throat and the place between his eyes.

In a little time she vaulted again to his back and they went on along the familiar road, slowly, with no sound but the sound of his hooves.

Camciscan remained Camciscan. In relation to himself, nothing changed, noth-
210  ing was different. If there were horses on the farm that whinnied at the approach of certain men or forsook their peculiar nobility for the common gifts of common creatures, he was not one.

He held a heritage of arrogance, and he cherished it. If he had yielded once to a will as stubborn as his own, even this had left no bruise upon his spirit. The
215  girl had triumphed—but in so small a thing.

He still stood in the far corner of his stable each morning while she worked. Sometimes he still trembled, and once in the late evening when there was a storm outside and a nervous wind, she came and lay down in the clean bedding under his manger. He watched her while there was light, but when that failed, and she must surely have been asleep, he stepped closer, lowering his head a lit-    220
tle, breathing warmly through widened nostrils, and sniffed at her.

She did not move, and he did not. For a moment he ruffled her hair with his soft muzzle. And then he lifted his head as high as he had ever held it and stood, with the girl at his feet, all through the storm. It did not seem a strong storm.

When morning came, she got up and looked at him and spoke to him. But    225
he was in the farthest corner, where he always was, staring, not at her, but at the dawn, and at the warm clouds of his breath against the cold.

## Looking Back

1. What does Markham mean by saying that "without either a dog or a horse in my keeping, I should feel I had lost contact with the earth" (lines 8–9)?

2. Where does the introduction to this memoir end? How does it prepare us for what follows?

3. Since, to be consistent, Markham had to see herself as well as the horse from a God's-eye point of view, what is the effect of avoiding the first person singular?

4. How does the title, which is repeated in line 25, reveal the author's attitude toward Camciscan? How does the attitude emerge in lines 44–46 and 65–69?

5. Can pride in aloneness, which Camciscan feels (see lines 77–78), be a human quality as well? Why might some people value it in themselves?

6. Why does Camciscan feel so angry at the girl that he throws her?

7. What lesson about life does the stallion learn in his encounter with the filly (lines 129–146)?

8. Although Camciscan realizes the girl loves him, is it love or some other feeling for her that moves him?

9. What is the dramatic high point of this story? How does it work?

10. Can you sum up the overall relation between girl and horse?

## Writing Assignments

1. By establishing the God's-eye, or omniscient, point of view, Beryl Markham has hit upon a perfect strategy for revealing the beauty and nobility of a thoroughbred stallion. These qualities seem to be obvious properties of the horse instead of attributes resulting from a highly subjective appreciation. Further, this point of view enables us to become aware of Camciscan's consciousness of himself and the world, a knowledge we might otherwise be denied. Lastly, a difference occurs in the way Markham must view herself as a participant in the drama (see number 3 in Looking

Back). Write an essay in which you employ her writing strategy. Adopt the omniscient point of view to reveal as much as you can of the true nature of an animal. Attempt to express how the animal feels and thinks, and put yourself at the same distance from your subject as Markham puts herself from Camciscan.

2. Human beings are separated from nature, most especially from animals. Perhaps, during our eons-long struggle to achieve our present form, we developed faculties and capabilities that definitely set us off from the animal world. Not that some of us don't resemble animals, such as birds, giraffes, and cats; and not that we don't constantly find explanations of our behavior in similar animal patterns. Yet, these are weak ties. We *are* alone in the world, not only set off but cut off. It is this perception that leads Markham to point to our "universal unpopularity" and to value horses and dogs for the "contact" they provide. But now these questions arise: Exactly in what way are we separated from the world of creatures? What are we that they are not, and vice versa? Why do we seek to reestablish contact, through both household pets and other animals? How does this contact work? What does it give us? Does trying to make contact mean that human beings are not only alone but somehow incomplete, and that we need help from animals? Write an essay addressing these questions, imagining your audience as one not perfectly aware of the problem of human isolation.

3. Animals have always provided a rich source of comparisons with human beings. We know exactly what it means to be as dumb as an ox, brave as a lion, fat as a pig, and so on. Thus, when Markham refers to Camciscan's pride in aloneness, we know more than a fact about a horse. We recognize a significant human characteristic as well. Not everyone has this pride—many, going to the other extreme, have the herd instinct— but enough people demonstrate it to make it noteworthy. What do you think of it? What attitudes and forms of behavior does it imply? Can you put it in other words and thus amplify its meaning? What does it have to do with basic instincts, spontaneous behavior? With arrogance and loneliness? Is it valuable in human beings, or is it merely antisocial and snobbish? Does it repel or invite love? Starting with a definition of pride in aloneness, write an essay answering at least some of these questions. Refer to Camciscan throughout, and use examples from your own experience when you can.

# Annie Dillard

# Living Like Weasels

One of America's leading essayists, Annie Dillard (b. 1945) has branched out recently into fiction. In 1992, she published *The Living*, a novel that became an immediate best-seller. Her previous nonfiction books include *The Writing Life, Pilgrim at Tinker Creek, An American Childhood*, and *Teaching A Stone To Talk*, from which "Living Like Weasels" is taken. Currently, Dillard teaches writing at Wesleyan University. In this piece, Dillard's experience allows her to form a critical perspective on accustomed human attitudes and to imagine a different approach to living.

## Looking Ahead

1. Figures of speech are Dillard's stock in trade, so you should identify and carefully examine them. The way her figurative language works is a key to understanding her writing style in general.

2. Finding beauty even in horror, as Dillard does, may require paying special attention to the possibility that beauty has no moral content.

3. *Choice* and *necessity* are terms Dillard finds essential to discussing human reality. As you read, test her use of those terms as a source of her ideas; make sure you understand their meaning outside the text and their application within it.

A weasel is wild. Who knows what he thinks? He sleeps in his underground den, his tail draped over his nose. Sometimes he lives in his den for two days without leaving. Outside, he stalks rabbits, mice, muskrats, and birds, killing more bodies than he can eat warm, and often dragging the carcasses home. Obedient to instinct, he bites his prey at the neck, either splitting the jugular 5 vein at the throat or crunching the brain at the base of the skull, and he does not let go. One naturalist refused to kill a weasel who was socketed into his hand deeply as a rattlesnake. The man could in no way pry the tiny weasel off, and he had to walk half a mile to water, the weasel dangling from his palm, and soak him off like a stubborn label. 10

And once, says Ernest Thompson Seton—once, a man shot an eagle out of the sky. He examined the eagle and found the dry skull of a weasel fixed by the jaws to his throat. The supposition is that the eagle had pounced on the weasel and the weasel swiveled and bit as instinct taught him, tooth to neck, and nearly won. I would like to have seen that eagle from the air a few weeks or months be- 15 fore he was shot: was the whole weasel still attached to his feathered throat, a fur pendant? Or did the eagle eat what he could reach, gutting the living weasel with his talons before his breast, bending his beak, cleaning the beautiful airborne bones?

I have been reading about weasels because I saw one last week. I startled a 20 weasel who startled me, and we exchanged a long glance.

Twenty minutes from my house, through the woods by the quarry and across the highway, is Hollins Pond, a remarkable piece of shallowness, where I like to go at sunset and sit on a tree trunk. Hollins Pond is also called Murray's Pond; it covers two acres of bottomland near Tinker Creek with six inches of 25 water and six thousand lily pads. In winter, brown-and-white steers stand in the middle of it, merely dampening their hooves; from the distant shore they look like miracle itself, complete with miracle's nonchalance. Now, in summer, the steers are gone. The water lilies have blossomed and spread to a green horizontal plane that is terra firma to plodding blackbirds, and tremulous ceiling to 30 black leeches, crayfish, and carp.

This is, mind you, suburbia. It is a five-minute walk in three directions to rows of houses, though none is visible here. There's a 55 mph highway at one end of the pond, and a nesting pair of wood ducks at the other. Under every
35    bush is a muskrat hole or a beer can. The far end is an alternating series of fields and woods, fields and woods, threaded everywhere with motorcycle tracks—in whose bare clay wild turtles lay eggs.

So. I had crossed the highway, stepped over two low barbed-wire fences, and traced the motorcycle path in all gratitude through the wild rose and poi-
40    son ivy on the pond's shoreline up into high grassy fields. Then I cut down through the woods to the mossy fallen tree where I sit. This tree is excellent. It makes a dry, upholstered bench at the upper, marshy end of the pond, a plush jetty raised from the thorny shore between a shallow blue body of water and a deep blue body of sky.

45    The sun had just set. I was relaxed on the tree trunk, ensconced in the lap of lichen, watching the lily pads at my feet tremble and part dreamily over the thrusting path of a carp. A yellow bird appeared to my right and flew behind me. It caught my eye; I swiveled around—and the next instant, inexplicably, I was looking down at a weasel, who was looking up at me.

50    Weasel! I'd never seen one wild before. He was ten inches long, thin as a curve, a muscled ribbon, brown as fruitwood, soft-furred, alert. His face was fierce, small and pointed as a lizard's; he would have made a good arrowhead. There was just a dot of chin, maybe two brown hairs' worth, and then the pure white fur began that spread down his underside. He had two black eyes I didn't see,
55    any more than you see a window.

The weasel was stunned into stillness as he was emerging from beneath an enormous shaggy wild rose bush four feet away. I was stunned into stillness twisted backward on the tree trunk. Our eyes locked, and someone threw away the key.

60    Our look was as if two lovers, or deadly enemies, met unexpectedly on an overgrown path when each had been thinking of something else: a clearing blow to the gut. It was also a bright blow to the brain, or a sudden beating of brains, with all the charge and intimate grate of rubbed balloons. It emptied our lungs. It felled the forest, moved the fields, and drained the pond; the world
65    dismantled and tumbled into that black hole of eyes. If you and I looked at each other that way, our skulls would split and drop to our shoulders. But we don't. We keep our skulls. So.

He disappeared. This was only last week, and already I don't remember what shattered the enchantment. I think I blinked, I think I retrieved my brain
70    from the weasel's brain, and tried to memorize what I was seeing, and the weasel felt the yank of separation, the careening splash-down into real life and the urgent current of instinct. He vanished under the wild rose. I waited motionless, my mind suddenly full of data and my spirit with pleadings, but he didn't return.

Please do not tell me about "approach-avoidance conflicts." I tell you I've been in that weasel's brain for sixty seconds, and he was in mine. Brains are private places, muttering through unique and secret tapes—but the weasel and I both plugged into another tape simultaneously, for a sweet and shocking time. Can I help it if it was a blank?

What goes on in his brain the rest of the time? What does a weasel think about? He won't say. His journal is tracks in clay, a spray of feathers, mouse blood and bone: uncollected, unconnected, loose-leaf, and blown.

I would like to learn, or remember, how to live. I come to Hollins Pond not so much to learn how to live as, frankly, to forget about it. That is, I don't think I can learn from a wild animal how to live in particular—shall I suck warm blood, hold my tail high, walk with my footprints precisely over the prints of my hands?—but I might learn something of mindlessness, something of the purity of living in the physical senses and the dignity of living without bias or motive. The weasel lives in necessity and we live in choice, hating necessity and dying at the last ignobly in its talons. I would like to live as I should, as the weasel lives as he should. And I suspect that for me the way is like the weasel's: open to time and death painlessly, noticing everything, remembering nothing, choosing the given with a fierce and pointed will.

I missed my chance. I should have gone for the throat. I should have lunged for that streak of white under the weasel's chin and held on, held on through mud and into the wild rose, held on for a dearer life. We could live under the wild rose wild as weasels, mute and uncomprehending. I could very calmly go wild. I could live two days in the den, curled, leaning on mouse fur, sniffing bird bones, blinking, licking, breathing musk, my hair tangled in the roots of grasses. Down is a good place to go, where the mind is single. Down is out, out of your ever-loving mind and back to your careless senses. I remember muteness as a prolonged and giddy fast, where every moment is a feast of utterance received. Time and events are merely poured, unremarked, and ingested directly, like blood pulsed into my gut through a jugular vein. Could two live that way? Could two live under the wild rose, and explore by the pond, so that the smooth mind of each is as everywhere present to the other, and as received and as unchallenged, as falling snow?

We could, you know. We can live any way we want. People take vows of poverty, chastity, and obedience—even of silence—by choice. The thing is to stalk your calling in a certain skilled and supple way, to locate the most tender and live spot and plug into that pulse. This is yielding, not fighting. A weasel doesn't "attack" anything; a weasel lives as he's meant to, yielding at every moment to the perfect freedom of single necessity.

I think it would be well, and proper, and obedient, and pure, to grasp your one necessity and not let it go, to dangle from it limp wherever it takes you. Then even death, where you're going no matter how you live, cannot you part. Seize it and let it seize you up aloft even, till your eyes burn out and drop; let your musky flesh fall off in shreds, and let your very bones unhinge and scatter, loos-ened over fields, over fields and woods, lightly, thoughtless, from any height at

120    all, from as high as eagles.

## Looking Back

1. Why would the naturalist mentioned in line 7 rather endure pain than kill his assailant?
2. Does the image of the weasel's jawbone attached to the eagle's throat deserve the compliment Dillard gives it, "beautiful airborne bones" (lines 18–19)? Explain your answer.
3. Does "long glance" (line 21) instead of the expected *long look* seem right to you? Why or why not?
4. Which figure of speech describing the weasel in lines 50–55 do you like best? Why?
5. Is it probable that, as Dillard intimates in lines 60–67 and states outright later, that the weasel experienced what she did when they met? What reasoning supports your answer?
6. In what way does Dillard's confession, "I would like to learn, or remember, how to live" (line 83), seem shocking in the context? How does the word *remember* particu-larly contribute to this sensation?
7. What distinction does she draw between two ways of learning from animals (lines 83–93)?
8. Can you explain what she means by the weasel's living by necessity and the human being's living by choice?
9. Does the author contradict (in lines 94–101) her earlier assertion that she doesn't expect to "learn from a wild animal how to live in particular" (line 85)? Is the later passage **hyperbole**—intentional exaggeration? Explain your answer by referring to the text from line 94 to the end of the essay.
10. How does she manage to reconcile the two opposed concepts of choice and necessity?

## Writing Assignments

1. Most people would agree that fire is beautiful, yet once they imagine a house burn-ing, the idea of beauty dissipates. Imagine a person on fire and it becomes obscene to bring up beauty at all. Thus it seems to matter what is happening, what the con-text is, before we can say something is beautiful. Must something be good before it can be beautiful? If so, how can we judge a person's physical beauty unless we are in a position to know her or his moral character? Isn't this an unreal expectation? What about Benito Mussolini's aviator son's finding beautiful the fiery reds and oranges of his bombs exploding among Ethiopians armed with spears? What about Annie Dillard's finding the weasel's skull and clenched jawbone beautiful (see number 2 in both Looking Ahead and Looking Back)? These are questions to address as you write an essay exploring the relationship between morality and physical beauty.

2. Dillard has not so lost her head that she thinks she can model her life on the daily activities and routines of wild creatures. But she does think we all could learn some general lessons from them (see number 7 in Looking Back). These lessons, she says, have to do with "mindlessness . . . the purity of living in the physical senses and the dignity of living without bias or motive . . . open to time and death painlessly, noticing everything, remembering nothing . . ." (lines 87–93). This is an ambitious program for anyone who lives in society and who spends much time thinking—ambitious, but not necessarily impossible, and maybe highly desirable. To find out if it is desirable, these are some of the questions to ask: Are some of these aims more easily realizable than others? Should we pursue all or some of them? Is such a pursuit needed, not just to rev up the individual, but to revitalize the society as a whole? If so, that society must contain some serious inadequacies that require treatment. Which are they? If not, then how might such radical changes actually harm the possibility of living together in amity? Does it seem as if some people have already begun to move in this direction? If so, in what ways, and do their actions hold promise for the rest of us, or do they constitute a threat of some sort to society? Write an essay examining the merits of the Dillard program and addressing these questions and concerns.

3. Most of us dream of having freedom of choice, a freedom within which our life will flow on in interesting though not necessarily unchallenging courses of action. In this dream, as Dillard points out, necessity arrives when each of us faces the flat wall of death and cannot choose to go left or right. But Dillard recommends an earlier and happier meeting with necessity, one in which we fix on a particular way to live and do so wholeheartedly and without question. That is the weasel's way. Short of accepting her radical suggestion, people *do* adopt the idea of necessity when they make a career choice early in life. What happens when they do so? Is it worth it, or do we give up our dream of freedom? Is there an alternative? Perhaps the dream is false in the first place. Or perhaps not? Write an essay, extrapolating from Dillard's idea of necessity, that gives your view of making a permanent career choice while in college or just afterward. Discuss freedom and necessity as they pertain to such a decision. Be sure to specify your own plans (or those you refuse to make) and describe them in detail, especially since the shape of a particular career may modify the impact of choice and necessity on your life. Conceive of an audience consisting of people with a special interest in your future.

# Natalie Angier

# The Cockroach

Natalie Angier (b. 1958) won a Pulitzer Prize for science reporting in 1991. On March 12 of that year, "The Cockroach" appeared in *The New York Times,* where she has been a science reporter since 1990. Previously, she was on the staff of *Time* magazine. She has contributed articles to *The Atlantic, American Health, Mademoiselle,* and other magazines.

Angier is a specialist in biology and medicine. Her book *Natural Obsessions: The Search for the Oncogen* won the Lewis Thomas Award for excellence in 1988. Ed Koren, whose drawings illustrated this essay, appears chiefly in *The New Yorker*. Working in tandem, Angier and Koren demonstrate that, equally with scholarly articles and technical illustration, journalism and art may give an original conception of a subject and thus serve the interests of critical thinking to reevaluate traditional views and, perhaps, extend their limits.

## Looking Ahead

1. Although not usually considered the most delightful subject, the cockroach nonetheless has its own peculiar fascination, as you will see from this essay.
2. The history, variety, and biology of the cockroach all are topics here.
3. Since Angier also focuses on the complex relationship the insect has to human beings, test the authoritativeness of her ideas as a reliable source of any changing feelings you have about cockroaches.

If absence makes the heart grow fonder, then perhaps the moment has arrived to consider a modest celebration of the cockroach.

In recent times, many city dwellers have been able to stride into their kitchens at night with a newfound confidence that they can flick on the light,
5   take a glass from the cupboard, even grab a few cookies from a box on the counter—all without the odious sight of dozens of greasy brown cockroaches skittering for cover.

A new generation of insecticides, packed into discreet little disk-shaped bait traps called Combat or applied in more potent concentrations by profes-
10   sional exterminators, has helped bring the ubiquitous German cockroach to its six spindly knees.

The creature is far, far from nearing extinction, and indeed remains a serious pest in restaurants, hospitals and many inner-city housing projects. But entomologists and public health officials said that since the new insecticides, the
15   amidinohydrazones, were introduced in the mid-1980's, they have made a significant dent in the less extreme cases of infestations.

"Almost everyone I've talked to, both personally and on the job, has noticed a vast change in the roach population," said Roz Post, a spokeswoman for the Housing Preservation and Development Department in New York. "There
20   was a time when people were horrified at roaches running rampant, and now everybody keeps saying, Where did they go to?"

Entomologists report that the new chemicals will cut the German cockroach population by 50 percent to nearly 100 percent, depending on the severity of the infestation. More heartening still, the latest studies of cockroaches col-
25   lected from around the country indicate that the insect is showing no signs of developing resistance to the amidinohydrazones, as it has to nearly every other noxious compound leveled against it in the past.

"I've gathered up populations from a dozen or so geographical locations," said Dr. Donald G. Cochran, a cockroach and insecticide expert at Virginia Polytechnic Institute and State University in Blacksburg. "I haven't seen any indication of resistance, and I don't think you're going to find any."      30

And should the creature somehow manage to mutate beyond the might of the current pesticides, other new and highly effective compounds are being tested, many of them based on subtle understanding of the insect's biology and habits.      35

"We have some excellent materials coming up," said Dr. Austin Frishman, an entomologist and pest control consultant in Farmingdale, L.I., who travels around the world to help businesses suffering from cockroach infestations. "The chemistry is there to keep roaches under control for the next 10 years if we play our cards right."      40

So, now that humans no longer need share every meal and inch of shelf space with unwelcome squatters, entomologists hope they can instill, if not outright affection, at least a detached sense of admiration for cockroaches, which are among the oldest and most resourceful of all land animals.

In new studies of species found in the tropics—where the creatures know      45
their place and that place is not ours—researchers have discovered that the insects display a wide range of impressive behaviors. "Cockroaches do quite a few things that we normally associate more with mammals than with insects," said Dr. Colby Schal, an entomologist at the Cook College of Rutgers University in New Brunswick, N.J., who has studied cockroaches in Costa Rica and other      50
Central American countries.

Some female cockroaches are devoted mothers, carrying their offspring in little pouches, kangaroo-style, rather than simply dropping their eggs and leaving the nymphs to their own devices, as many insects do.

One scientist has recently discovered a type of cockroach that does the insect equivalent of breast-feeding.      55

In many animal species, the male's only contribution to the progeny's welfare is the donation of his genes. The male cockroach carries paternal care to a rather greater length. He will dine off bird droppings for the sole purpose of extracting precious nitrogen that he can bestow on his developing      60
offspring.

One kind of cockroach that lives in Central American tree bark turns out to be as social an insect as termites or bees. The males and females pair off to nurture their immature forms, known as nymphs, for the five or six years it takes the species to reach adulthood. All members of a nest maintain a sense of group      65
identity and cooperation through the use of mutual grooming, antennae stroking and placating pheromones, chemical signals that are secreted by glands on the thorax of one insect and detected by the antennae of another.

Cockroaches are exquisitely sensitive to the slightest breezes, a trait that accounts for their unusually long antennae. Such tactile sensitivity, combined      70

—Illustration by Ed Koren.

with a nervous system built of exceptionally large cells, makes the cockroach an ideal experimental organism for the study of how nerve cells work.

"Among neurobiologists, the cockroach has become the insect version of the white rat," said Dr. May R. Berenbaum, an entomologist at the  University of
75   Illinois at Urbana-Champaign.

Dr. Ivan Huber of Fairleigh Dickinson University in Madison, N.J., author of a book published last March by CRC Press called "Cockroaches as Models for Neurobiology," said that cockroaches are "beautifully easy" to study. Their receptors, which detect a single chemical molecule or a puff of air, are on the out-
80   side of the body, where they can be readily manipulated. And the cockroach's head will live and respond for at least 12 hours after the animal has been decapitated. Furthermore, few animal rights activists will disrupt a laboratory where the experimental organism is a cockroach.

"People get all worked up over using kittens and puppies for medical ex-
85   periments," said Dr. Berenbaum. "But nobody is going to shed any tears if you kill a few thousand cockroaches for the good of science."

—Illustration by Ed Koren.

Dr. Berenbaum has made it her particular mission to bolster the cockroach's reputation. Every year she holds an "insect fear film festival," using clips from movies to tweak the public's interest in insects and to dispel myths. The theme of the 1991 festival, presented last month, was the cockroach. 90

"There are a surprising number of cockroach-oriented films," she said, "probably because it's easy to breed them in large quantities."

In many of the shorter films, as well as in animated movies, she said, the cockroach is a sympathetic character. One offering, "All's Quiet in Sparkle City," an antiwar film from the early 1970's, equates efforts to eradicate cockroaches 95 with genocide. A 1989 comedy, "Dr. Ded Bug," is shot from the insect's perspective, as a frenzied chef attempts to hunt down and kill a cockroach. Cartoon cockroaches talk in high, chipper voices and rarely stop smiling. "They're modeled after Mickey Mouse," she said. "In animated films, vermin become your friends." 100

Whether or not cockroaches become one's bosom buddies, Dr. Berenbaum and other entomologists say the insects merit respect for their antiquity and their diversity. Fossils of cockroach-like species have been found dating to 280 million years ago, and some entomologists estimate that the creatures may be as old as 400 million years. By contrast, beetles are only about 150 million years 105 old, while butterflies are a youthful 60 million years.

Cockroaches are found in nearly every part of the world, but the great majority of the 4,000 known species live in the equatorial belt, and entomologists

believe another 6,000 tropical species remain to be discovered. Cockroaches
110   range in size from a quarter of an inch to the forbidding Megablatta of Central
America, which in length and girth approaches the dimensions of a small rat.
Universal to cockroaches are long, segmented antennae; a leathery pair of front
wings that allow many warm-weather species to fly but otherwise are vestigial,
and the famous cockroach head, which is tucked under and slightly pointed to-
115   ward the rear.
   Some smaller cockroaches are exquisitely colored, and may be deep crimson, spring green, a creamy white or a pale toffee. The most dazzling specimen
is a cobalt blue with bronze flecks and slim red stripes.
   "I thought it was a beetle when I first saw it," said Dr. William J. Bell of the
120 · University of Kansas in Lawrence, who has studied many tropical cockroach
species. "If it were any bigger, people might try to put it in a bird cage."

But only one type of cockroach is frequently kept as a pet: the three-inch Mada-
gascar hissing roach, which attempts to scare off predators by expelling a noisy
blast of air through holes in its upper thorax. The hissing roach is covered with
125   an armor-like cuticle that makes it far more appealing to hold and stroke than
many cockroach species. The German cockroach is coated with an oil that eases
its passage into cracks thinner than a paper match.
   The most advanced of all cockroaches, in terms of evolution's tree, is a
species known as Diploptera punctata, according to Dr. Barbara Stay, a biologist
130   at the University of Iowa in Iowa City. The female carries her embryos live,
rather than in an egg case, and she is the only insect known to nourish her
young in the uterus. The lining of the brood pouch, where about 12 baby cockroaches grow at a time, secretes a substance that Dr. Stay calls cockroach milk.
Like mammalian milk, it is rich in protein, carbohydrates and fat.
135   "The cockroach milk is not produced until the embryos have a fully developed digestive tract," said Dr. Stay. "Then they sit in the pouch drinking up the
milk right through their mouths."
   But while some cockroaches have evolved an elaborate system of maternal
care, others have opted for greater fecundity and the utmost behavioral flexibil-
140   ity, and these are the species that have become pests to humans. Only 20 types
of cockroaches are classified as pests, and only two of these, the German and
the American cockroaches, are broadly familiar, the three-inch American cockroach going by the name of palmetto bug in Florida and the water bug in New
York. And these two pest species have fared so successfully in their strategy of
145   taking up residence with humans that they no longer have an independent existence or any representatives of their kind in nature.
   "We've looked everywhere for their natural habitat," said Dr. Bell. "But
everytime we thought we had seen one in the wild, there's turned out to be
somebody's house nearby."

150   The smaller German cockroach is an especially prolific breeder, able to spawn
30 or 40 infant cockroaches every three weeks. If the population were left

unchecked, a single female German cockroach could theoretically give rise to about 40 million offspring in her two-year lifespan.

The insects grow to adulthood rapidly and molt frequently, which is why cockroaches can present a real health hazard for those with allergies. Dr. 155 Richard J. Brenner, a research entomologist with the Agricultural Research Service and Veterinary Entomology Research Laboratory in Gainesville, Fla., estimates that as many as 15 million Americans suffer from cockroach allergies, as their immune system mounts an overzealous defense against airborne particles of molted cockroach skin. 160

The allergies often worsen with time and continued exposure to cockroaches, and entomologists who work with the creatures said they, too, developed wheeziness, skin rashes and sinus troubles after years of pursuing their research.

"I love cockroaches, and I don't know where I'd be without them," said Dr. 165 Schal. "But unfortunately I'm starting to get slightly allergic to them."

For that reason, and because of the possibility that cockroaches may transmit the unsavory microbes piggybacked upon them, even entomologists who like the insects in the wild spend part of their time devising better ways to thwart cockroach pests. 170

To determine where cockroaches congregate and why, Dr. Brenner and his colleagues have designed an entire mock house. Its 200 sensors monitor the microclimate every 65 milliseconds and at every possible spot—behind walls, under the sink, up in the rafters. The researchers have learned that nothing will repel cockroaches as surely as ventilation. The animals use almost indetectable air 175 currents to sense the chemical signals of their mates, but any air movement approaching a draft will quickly and fatally dessicate the cockroach's coating. Dr. Brenner believes that by designing homes to have air circulating throughout, even in cupboards, the cockroach problem can be largely curtailed.

Others are encouraged by the new generation of pesticides, which differ 180 markedly from the older poisons, often used in the spray cans. Those pesticides, which include the organophosphates and carbamates, are potent nerve poisons that block the transmission of impulses from one nerve cell to the next. But because the older poisons work on only a single component of the nervous system, some cockroaches have turned out to have an inborn resistance to that one 185 means of attack. And those insects have been the ones that have survived to propagate entire legions of resistant nymphs.

By comparison, the newer pesticides seem to be more global in their activity, affecting so many parts of cockroach physiology that it is unlikely any one insect will have all the genetic traits necessary to withstand the assault. The ac- 190 tive ingredient found in Combat, for example, interferes with multiple steps in the biochemical pathway that allows a cell to use its stores of energy.

Of perhaps greater importance, the toxin works at extremely low concentrations. Dr. Cochran believes that one reason cockroaches may have trouble developing resistance to the chemical is that even those few insects able to 195 survive a nibble of poisoned bait become sterilized. Thus, they fail to pass along their detoxifying ability to offspring, as survivors of the older generation of pesticides were able to do.

But entomologists realize that, over the long term, the task of keeping cock-
200   roaches at bay is formidable.

"The insect has all the biological factors that help it survive," said Dr. Michael K. Rust, an entomologist at the University of California at Riverside. "It has a high reproductive rate and a fast life cycle. It has been living with man for thousands of years. So anytime I hear about a new chemical or bait I ask myself,
205   How long will this last?" Not long enough, surely, for people to start missing their nocturnal companions.

## Looking Back

1. How effective are the new methods of combating cockroaches in the home (see lines 8–31)? Why are these new methods so effective (see lines 188–198)?

2. Do you find it heartening or dispiriting that the cockroach seems to have met its match?

3. What features of mammals do some cockroaches have?

4. Do these similarities affect your understanding and sympathy for cockroaches in any way? Explain your answer.

5. What makes cockroaches such good candidates for laboratory study?

6. Do you share Dr. Berenbaum's sense, that "nobody is going to shed any tears if you kill a few thousand cockroaches for the good of science" (see lines 85–86)? Why or why not?

7. How do you view the cockroach in light of its antiquity and diversity (see lines 101–137)?

8. In what way might "greater fecundity and the utmost behavioral flexibility" result in cockroaches' being classified as pests (see lines 138–149)?

9. What cautionary note about the future of the cockroach do we hear at the end?

10. How do you interpret the view of cockroaches in Ed Koren's drawings?

## Writing Assignments

1. Angier, reporting how mammalian some cockroaches are, shows us how closely this insect approaches human beings. Ed Koren refers to this similarity, but he also shows—in the drawing of the cockroach prize-winner—how necessary it is to recognize the cockroach for what it is, a different species. The question that arises has to do with all animals: Do we understand them better when we discover how they are like us? Or do we understand them better by emphasizing how different they are from us, their *otherness*? Extrapolating from the cockroach facts Angier gives, but discussing other animals also, write an essay answering these questions.

2. Dr. May Berenbaum is quoted in this essay on clinical trials run on cockroaches. We may or may not agree with her that no animal rights activist cares about them (see number 6 in Looking Back). But her remarks do focus our attention on the issue of speciesism, which is the belief that the species you happen to belong to is superior to others. Such a belief—which only humans, it would seem, can hold—would justify humans' experimenting on animals to benefit themselves. Do you believe we are superior to other animals and thus have the right—or even the responsibility—to use them to further medical science? Do you believe that all creatures—human and nonhuman—are equal, and none should use the other? Write an essay defending a position on this issue.

3. The films featuring cockroaches to which Angier refers (see lines 91–100) are not the only examples of artistic sympathy and support for these insects. Don Marquis produced a regular newspaper column in verse about archy, a cockroach who tapped out messages by pressing his body against typewriter keys (though he was unable to make capital letters). And the Mexican song, "La Cucaracha" ("The Cockroach") advises the insect to "sing no matter where you are." Reading Angier, we can find reasons to admire the roach and never for a moment think it is beneath us. Write an essay collecting such reasons for this admiration from Angier's essay and expressing your own view on the matter.

✿

# (*The New York Times*, March 8, 1992)
# Animal Rights Raiders Destroy Years of Work

During the school year, *The New York Times* runs a regular Sunday feature reporting news from university campuses across the United States. The one reprinted here is about an occurrence at Michigan State University. Animal rights advocates have been quite active in this country for some years, opposing, in addition to animal research, the ill treatment of animals in factory farms, the trapping and killing of animals for their furs, and the practice of confining animals in zoos and aquariums. The methods of protest range from newspaper advertisements to marches to the kind of violent action described in this article.

## Looking Ahead

1. In newspaper articles, the headline and the subheads are editorial additions to the text that help shape reader response ("Animal Rights Raiders Destroy Years of Work" was the headline here). Examine these from that perspective.

2. Because space is limited in newspapers, articles are cut from the bottom up, meaning that the news is presented in order of importance. Recalling this fact can help you understand the reporter's evaluation of this news.

3. We expect of newspaper articles factual reportage in neutral language. Read critically to test whether that standard is met here.

East Lansing, Mich.—Animal rights advocates entered two research areas at Michigan State University on Feb. 28, set fire to one and destroyed 32 years' worth of animal science research, the university administration said. The vandals also inadvertently destroyed fertility research that could have helped both humans and endangered species.

5      The raid was directed against Richard J. Aulerich, an animal science professor, the university said. The raid destroyed equipment and property worth $75,000 to $125,000, said Maynard G. Hogberg, the chairman of the Animal Science Department at M.S.U.

Of the 32 years of data lost, two to three years' worth had not been pub-
10   lished, he said.

Karen Chou, an associate professor of animal science, said she lost 10 years' worth of data on the effects of chemicals in animal reproduction. Her research was aimed at testing the viability of sperm before fertilization and at studying the effects of chemicals on reproduction.

15     Professor Chou said her fertility research could have helped solve reproductive problems in endangered species. It could also have uncovered the effects chemicals have on human reproduction, she said.

## Raids at Other Campuses

The Animal Liberation Front, which conducted similar raids at Oregon State University one and one-half years ago and at Washington State University six
20   months ago, claimed responsibility for the acts in a press release. The group says it seeks to end all animal experimentation and in particular calls experimentation on minks, such as Professor Aulerich was doing, cruel and worthless.

Professor Aulerich had been conducting research on toxins and their effect on animals, Professor Hogberg said. The research involves feeding minks,
25   which are especially susceptible to toxics, food containing toxic chemicals or other contaminants. Professor Hogberg said the minks had recently been fed fish caught in Saginaw Bay in Michigan, which is contaminated by PCB's.

The research was intended to be used to benefit humans and other animals, he said.

30     Professor Hogberg said that he did not know how many of the 350 minks kept at the lab were euthanized each year, but said that the number was "very low." He said the animals were not maimed during the research.

Gregory Maas, the chairman of the Incurably Ill for Animal Research, based in Bridgeview, Ill., offered a $5,000 reward for information leading to the arrest
35   of the vandals. The group works for the continuation of animal research to aid human medical research, Mr. Maas said.

According to Bill Wardwell, a lieutenant with the Michigan State University Department of Public Safety, members of the Animal Liberation Front broke into Anthony Hall on campus about 5 A.M. and entered Professor Aulerich's of-

fice. Files and papers were strewn around the office and a fire was started, he      40
said.

The fire gutted Professor Aulerich's office and smoke extensively damaged
two other offices, a conference room and a reception area. Lieutenant Wardwell
said similar devices were used in the break-ins at both Washington State and
Oregon State. At the Poultry Research Facility, where Professor Aulerich con-      45
ducts his research, vandals destroyed research documents and poured sulfuric
acid into laboratory equipment, including devices used to feed the minks, Lieutenant Wardwell said. They also opened the minks' cages, but the animals remained inside, he said.

"Aulerich tortures minks" and "Fur is murder" were sprayed on the wall      50
with red paint. The slogans were signed "A.L.F.," for Animal Liberation Front.


## A Federal Case

Lieutenant Wardwell said a nationwide alert was sent to warn police depart-
ments of the possibility of similar actions. Increased security is planned for research laboratories on campus, he said, including more patrols.

The United States Bureau of Alcohol, Tobacco and Firearms and the Fed-      55
eral Bureau of Investigation have been brought in to investigate the case. Dennis
B. Anderson, the senior resident agent in Lansing, Mich., said the F.B.I. was involved because Professor Aulerich used Federal financing for his experiments
and because police suspect that the vandals crossed state lines to commit the
crime.
      60
The animal-rights group issues its press releases through People for the
Ethical Treatment of Animals, a national animal rights group in Washington,
D.C. Steven I. Simmons, a spokesman for People for Ethical Treatment of Animals, said his organization was not linked to the Animal Liberation Front. But
he said his group was usually alerted by the front before and after a raid.      65


## Looking Back

1. How does the headline reveal the editor's idea of what readers should focus on?
   How might you have worded it differently?

2. Is the subhead "A Federal Case" too sardonic, given that it's based on the old comedy line, "Don't make a federal case of it," or is it witty? Explain your answer.

3. Given the chance, what would the "raiders" probably rename the Animal Science
   Department?

4. What do you think of the term *vandals* applied to the raiders?

5. In what ways do the names of the two organizations—Animal Liberation Front
   (A.L.F.) and People for the Ethical Treatment of Animals—reflect differences in the
   groups' methods and ideology?

6. Do you think the A.L.F. is right to call for the end of *all* animal experimentation? Why or why not?

7. Does the spray-painted message "Aulerich tortures minks" accurately portray his research? Why or why not?

8. Is the slogan "Fur is murder" a fair or a biased statement? Explain your answer.

9. What conclusion about the use of violent means do you draw from the fact that the raiders destroyed research likely to benefit endangered species of animals?

10. Can violence ever lead to social reform, or does it result only in tougher security measures and bad publicity?

## Writing Assignments

1. The Animal Liberation Front, as we have seen, demands the end of all animal experimentation, no matter the type of animal, the method of research, the motives for it, or the possible benefits to be derived from it. Opposed to animal liberationists, however, the Americans for Medical Progress Educational Foundation points to advances in medicine made possible only by animal research. The organization cites, in particular, rabies, diphtheria, smallpox, tuberculosis, and polio, which have been virtually eliminated in the developed world (though TB is making a comeback), and diabetes, leukemia, and cystic fibrosis, which have been curtailed. Who is right? Should medical research using animals continue? Are there any kinds of research that should be abandoned? Which? Are animals equal to humans, or do humans rightly have dominion over them, including the right to use them for human purposes? Write an essay answering these questions in order to argue that animal research should or should not continue, in whole or in part. Think of addressing your remarks to an audience of future medical students.

2. The slogan that A.L.F. raiders spray-painted on the lab wall was "Fur is murder." This claim objects to killing animals to manufacture fur coats. The Humane Society of the United States, adding its voice to this complaint, criticizes the dual practices of trapping animals in the wild and raising them for the purpose of taking their pelts. The society's slogans are "Every Fur Coat Hurts" and "You Should Be Ashamed To Wear Fur." The two points with which the society supports its position invite these counterarguments:

| | |
|---|---|
| *Fur Advocates:* | Wearing fur is no different from eating meat and wearing leather. In both cases, animals are killed for what they can supply to humans. |
| *Humane Society:* | The meat industry is regulated, and therefore the way livestock is raised is monitored. Furthermore, fur coats are frivolous, not essential. |
| *Fur Advocates:* | Fur coats are warm and extremely attractive. Women wearing them become glamorous. They even seem more natural, as if they partook of the animal's wildness and original beauty. |

*Humane Society:*   Other materials can keep you warm. True beauty belongs to live animals in their original setting. It is uncivilized to take lives for the sake of fashion.

Adopting either the arguments or the counterarguments, and interpolating your own examples and explanations, write an essay that supports or opposes the use of animal fur in clothing.

3.  Here are reports of three protest actions:

One day, a man swaying from his strap in a crowded bus felt a sudden blow on his right shoulder. He looked up, startled, and received a muttered apology from a person moving to exit at the front door. When the man himself got off the bus later, he glanced at the shoulder that had been struck and saw there, in his nap-less, ancient, almost worn-out chamois jacket, the triangular slash a box-cutter makes. He had been targeted and hit by a righteous-minded animal liberationist.

Whispering conspiratorily and hilariously together, a group of animal libera-tionists descended late at night on a New Jersey chicken farm, a so-called fac-tory farm. They forced an entry into one of the large coops, roused the chick-ens from their slumbering perches, and hustled them out into the night. Then the gang broke up everything in sight within the building and disappeared into the countryside.

Members of the Animal Liberation Front torched offices at Michigan State Uni-versity's Animal Science Department and trashed research and lab equipment in the Poultry Research Facility.

In these three instances, the violence used to protect animals escalates and changes in both type and purpose. Within each passage, certain descriptive terms influence the reader's sympathies in definite ways. Do you approve of any of these actions? Write an essay explaining the reasons for your position. Be sure to make a critical distinction between the kinds of violence and to comment on the language used to describe them.

# Wallace Stegner

# Thoughts in a Dry Land[1]

Novelist, short story writer, and essayist, Wallace Stegner (1909–1993) wrote about the American West in books that ranged from *Remembering Laughter,* published in 1937, to his last, *Where the Bluebird Sings to the Lemonade Springs,* from which the essay here is taken.

---

1.  The title echoes the final line of T. S. Eliot's poem "Gerontion": "Thoughts of a dry brain in a dry season." To Eliot, aridity is a symbol of spiritual decline. Stegner is more literal, approaching aridity as a natural condition to cope with which requires human ingenuity. (*ed.*)

Stegner won the Pulitzer Prize for fiction in 1972, but perhaps his best-known novel is the earlier *The Big Rock Candy Mountain*. Stegner taught at the University of Utah, the University of Wisconsin, Harvard University, and Stanford University, where he led the creative writing program. As he points out here, settlers of previously unknown territory have a double task: to free themselves from ways of thinking unsuited to their new circumstances, and to discover totally fresh perspectives that will allow them to create the life they desire. Explorers, we see, are critical thinkers.

## Looking Ahead

1. The epigraph that introduces this essay, an excerpt from the essay itself, is a good piece of critical thinking advice for the reader as well as for the traveler.
2. To avoid getting lost, use a map to orient yourself to Stegner's numerous geographical references.
3. The author introduces historical and cultural concepts that you should note as keys to understanding the American West.

> *You have to get over the color green; you have to quit associating beauty*
> *with gardens and lawns; you have to get used to an inhuman scale.*

The western landscape is of the wildest variety and contains every sort of topography and landform, even most of those familiar from farther east. Bits of East and Middle West are buried here and there in the West, but no physical part of the true West is buried in the East. The West is short-grass plains, alpine moun-
5  tains, geyser basins, plateaus and mesas and canyons and cliffs, salinas and sinks, sagebrush and Joshua tree and saguaro deserts. If only by reason of their size, the forms of things are different, but there is more than mere size to differentiate them. There is nothing in the East like the granite horns of Grand Teton or Teewinot, nothing like the volcanic neck of Devil's Tower, nothing like the
10  travertine terraces of Mammoth Hot Springs, nothing like the flat crestline and repetitive profile of the Vermilion Cliffs. You know that these differences are themselves regional—that the West, which stretches from around the ninety-eighth meridian to the Pacific, and from the forty-ninth parallel to the Mexican border, is actually half a dozen subregions as different from one another as the
15  Olympic rain forest is from Utah's slickrock country, or Seattle from Santa Fe.
   You know also that the western landscape is more than topography and landforms, dirt and rock. It is, most fundamentally, climate—climate which expresses itself not only as landforms but as atmosphere, flora, fauna. And here, despite all the local variety, there is a large, abiding simplicity. Not all the West
20  is arid, yet except at its Pacific edge, aridity surrounds and encompasses it. Landscape includes such facts as this. It includes and is shaped by the way continental masses bend ocean currents, by the way the prevailing winds blow from the West, by the way mountains are pushed up across them to create well-watered coastal or alpine islands, by the way the mountains catch and store the

snowpack that makes settled life possible in the dry lowlands, by the way they literally create the dry lowlands by throwing a long rain shadow eastward. Much of the West except the narrow Pacific littoral lies in one or another of those rain shadows, such as the Great Basin and lower Colorado River country, or in the semi-arid steppes of the Montana, Dakota, Nebraska, Wyoming, Colorado, and New Mexico plains.

Aridity, more than anything else, gives the western landscape its character. It is aridity that gives the air its special dry clarity; aridity that puts brilliance in the light and polishes and enlarges the stars; aridity that leads the grasses to evolve as bunches rather than as turf; aridity that exposes the pigmentation of the raw earth and limits, almost eliminates, the color of chlorophyll; aridity that erodes the earth in cliffs and badlands rather than in softened and vegetated slopes, that has shaped the characteristically swift and mobile animals of the dry grasslands and the characteristically nocturnal life of the deserts. The West, Walter Webb said, is "a semi-desert with a desert heart." If I prefer to think of it as two long chains of mountain ranges with deserts or semi-deserts in their rain shadow, that is not to deny his assertion that the primary unity of the West is a shortage of water.

The consequences of aridity multiply by a kind of domino effect. In the attempt to compensate for nature's lacks we have remade whole sections of the western landscape. The modern West is as surely Lake Mead and Lake Powell and the Fort Peck reservoir, the irrigated greenery of the Salt River Valley and the smog blanket over Phoenix, as it is the high Wind River Range or the Wasatch or the Grand Canyon. We have acted upon the western landscape with the force of a geological agent. But aridity still calls the tune, directs our tinkering, prevents the healing of our mistakes; and vast unwatered reaches still emphasize the contrast between the desert and the sown.

Aridity has made a lot of difference in us, too, since Americans first ventured up the Missouri into the unknown in the spring of 1804. Our intentions varied all the way from romantic adventurousness to schemes of settlement and empire; all the way from delight in dehumanized nature to a fear of the land empty of human settlements, monuments, and even, seemingly, history. Let me call your attention to one book that contains most of the possible responses. It is called *The Great Lone Land,* and it is about the Canadian, not the American, West; it was written by an Irish officer in the British army, William F. Butler. But the report out of which the book grew was responsible for the creation of the Royal Northwest Mounted Police, and so had a big hand in the development of western Canada. Butler was also an intelligent observer, a romantic, and a man who loved both wild country and words. He is writing in 1872:

> The old, old maps which the navigators of the sixteenth century framed from the discoveries of Cabot and Cartier, of Verrazano and Hudson, played strange pranks with the geography of the New World. The coastline, with the estuaries of large rivers, was tolerably accurate; but the center of America was represented as a vast inland sea whose shores stretched far into the Polar

70 North; a sea through which lay the much-coveted passage to the long-sought treasures of the old realms of Cathay. Well, the geographers of that period erred only in the description of ocean which they placed in the central continent, for an ocean there is, and an ocean through which men seek the treasures of Cathay, even in our own times. But the ocean is one of grass, and the shores are the crests of the mountain ranges, and the dark pine forests of sub-Arctic

75 regions. The great ocean itself does not present more infinite variety than does this prairie-ocean of which we speak. In winter, a dazzling surface of purest snow; in early summer, a vast expanse of grass and pale pink roses; in autumn too often a wild sea of raging fire. No ocean or water in the world can vie with its gorgeous sunsets; no solitude can equal the loneliness of a night-shadowed

80 prairie; one feels the stillness, and hears the silence, the wail of the prowling wolf makes the voice of solitude audible, the stars look down through infinite silence upon a silence almost as intense. One saw here the world as it had taken shape and form from the hands of the Creator.

History builds slowly, starting from scratch, and understanding of a new coun-
85 try depends upon every sort of report, including some that are unreliable, biased, or motivated by personal interest—such a report, say, as Lansford Hastings's *The Emigrant's Guide to Oregon and California*. Across a century and three quarters since Lewis and Clark pushed off into the Missouri, we have had multitudinous reports on the West—Pike and Long; Catlin and Maximilian of Wied
90 Neuwied; Ashley and Jedediah Smith and Frémont; Bonneville and the Astorians and Nathaniel Wyeth; Spalding and Whitman; the random Oregon and California gold rush diarists; the historians of the compact Mormon migration; the Pacific Railroad Surveys of the 1850s, which for many areas were the basis of precise knowledge; the Powell, Hayden, King, and Wheeler surveys and the
95 U.S. Geological Survey that united and continued them. And the dime novels and the Currier and Ives prints; the reports of missionaries and soldiers; the reporters and illustrators for *Leslie's* and *Harper's Weekly*; the painters, from Catlin and Miller and Bodmer to Bierstadt and Moran; the photographers, from Jackson and Hillers and Haynes and Savage onward; the Fenimore Coopers, Mark
100 Twains, Bret Hartes, Dan de Quilles, Horace Greeleys; the Owen Wisters and Frederick Remingtons; the Andy Adamses and Zane Greys and Eugene Manlove Rhodeses.

True or false, observant or blind, impartial or interested, factual or fanciful, it has all gone into the hopper and influenced our understanding and response
105 at least as much as first-hand acquaintance has. But it took a long time. Even learning the basic facts—extents, boundaries, animals, ranges, tribes of men— took a long time. The physical exploration that began with Lewis and Clark was not completed until Almon Thompson led a Powell Survey party into Potato Valley in 1872, and discovered the Escalante River and verified the Henry
110 Mountains, which Powell had seen from a distance on his voyages down the Colorado. The surveying and mapping of great areas of the West was not completed for decades after real exploration had ended; and the trial and error (emphasis on the error) by which we began to be an oasis civilization was forced

upon us by country and climate, but against the most mule-headed resistance and unwillingness to understand, accept, and change.                                    115

In the actual desert, and especially among the Mormons, where intelligent leadership, community settlement, and the habit of cooperation and obedience were present, agricultural adaptation was swift. But in the marginal zone between humid Midwest and arid West it was easy to be deluded, for the difference of just one inch of rainfall or a slight variation in the seasonal distribution     120 would make the difference between success and failure. And delusion was promoted. The individualism of the frontier, the folklore and habit learned in other regions, the usual politics and boosterism, and land speculation encouraged settlement on terms sure sooner or later to defeat it. Cooperation was one lesson the West enforced, and it was learned hard. Bernard DeVoto once caustically re-    125 marked, in connection with the myth of western individualism, that the only real individualists in the West had wound up on one end of a rope whose other end was in the hands of a bunch of cooperators. But a lot of other individualists wound up in the hands of the bank, or trailed back eastward from the dry plains in wagons with signs reading, "In God we trusted, in Kansas we busted," leaving     130 a half-ruined land behind them.

John Wesley Powell submitted his *Report on the Lands of the Arid Region of the United States, with a More Detailed Account of the Lands of Utah,* on April 1, 1878. That early, partly from studying Mormon, Hispano, and Indian irrigation, he understood and accepted both the fact of aridity and the adaptations     135 that men, institutions, and laws would have to go through if we were ever to settle the West instead of simply raiding and ruining it. He comprehended the symbiotic relationship between highlands and lowlands; he understood rivers as common carriers, like railroads, which should not be encumbered by political boundaries. He knew that the Homestead Act and the rectilinear cadastral[2]     140 surveys that worked in well-watered country would not work in the West, and he advocated a change in the land laws that would limit irrigated farms to eighty acres—all a man needed and all he could work—and enlarge stock farms to four full sections, needed by a small farmer's herd in the way of range. He proposed surveys and political divisions not by arbitrary boundaries but by     145 drainage divides, and he and his pupils and associates virtually created the "Wyoming doctrine," which ties water rights to land.

A revolutionary. He might have spared the West the dust bowls of the 1890s, 1930s, and 1950s, as well as the worst consequences of river floods. He might have saved the lives and hopes of all the innocents who put their strad-    150 dlebugs on dryland homesteads in the Dakotas, Kansas, Nebraska, and Montana. But the boosters and the politicians always proclaimed that rain followed the plow; free land and movement westward were ingrained expectations. Habit, politics, and real estate boosterism won out over experience and good sense, and that is part of the history of the West, and of western landscape. Even     155

---

2. *cadastral:* refers to boundary lines. (*ed.*)

yet the battle, though to some extent won, is not universally understood. There are historians who grow so incensed over the "myth" of the Great American Desert, which began with Pike and Long, that they resent any admission of aridity, as well as all "deficiency terminology" in connection with the short-
160   grass plains.

Ultimately, the settlers of the shortgrass plains learned that water was more important to them than land. They became, by degrees, that oasis civilization and settled down to a relatively thin population because that was what the land would bear.

165   Karl Frederick Kranzel, in *The Great Plains in Transition,* even suggests that men in the Dakotas and elsewhere had to develop the same mobility that marked the buffalo, antelope, wolves, coyotes, and horse Indians in that country. They go as far for a swim or for shopping as an antelope will go for a drink, and for very similar reasons. They often go hundreds of miles to farm. There is a
170   kind of farmer called a suitcase farmer who spends the winter in some town or city, Grand Forks or Bismarck or Minneapolis, but who in early spring hitches his trailer-home to his pickup and takes off for the West—Dakota, Montana, or Saskatchewan. There he plants his wheat and works his summer fallow, living through the summer in his trailer and driving forty or fifty miles for his supplies
175   and entertainment. In the fall, he harvests and hauls his crop, does his fall plowing, hitches up his trailer again, and returns to the fleshpots of Bismarck. I know one who goes every winter to San Miguel d'Allende. His alternative would be what the early homesteaders attempted—to make a home out in the desolate plains and live there isolated through the worst winters on the continent. Hav-
180   ing lived that life as a boy, I can tell you his mobility, which is as natural as the mobility of the buffalo, is a sensible adaptation.

That is only one sample of how, as we have gone about modifying the western landscape, it has been at work and modifying us. And what applies to agricultural and social institutions applies just as surely to our pictorial and literary
185   representations. Perceptions trained in another climate and another landscape have had to be modified. That means we have had to learn to quit depending on perceptual habit. Our first and hardest adaptation was to learn all over again how to see. Our second was to learn to like the new forms and colors and light and scale when we had learned to see them. Our third was to develop new tech-
190   niques, a new palette, to communicate them. And our fourth, unfortunately out of our control, was to train an audience that would respond to what we wrote or painted.

Years ago I picked up an Iowa aunt of mine in Salt Lake City and drove her down to our cottage on Fish Lake. She was not looking as we drove—she was
195   talking—and she missed the Wasatch, and Mount Nebo, and the Sanpete Valley, and even Sigurd Mountain—the Pahvant—which some people down there call the Big Rock Candy Mountain and which is about as colorful as a peppermint stick. The first thing she really saw, as we turned east at Sigurd, was the towering, level front of the Sevier Plateau above Richfield—level as a rooftree,

steep as a cliff, and surging more than a mile straight up above that lush valley. 200
I saw it hit her, and I heard it too, for the talk stopped. I said, "How do you like
that, Aunt Min?" for like any Westerner I like to impress Iowans, and the easiest
way to do it is with size. She blinked and ruffled up her feathers and assembled
herself after the moment of confusion and said, "That's nice. It reminds me of
the river bluffs in the county park at Fort Dodge." 205

She couldn't even see it. She had no experience, no scale, by which to judge
an unbroken mountain wall more than a mile high, and her startled mental cir-
cuitry could respond with nothing better than the fifty-foot clay banks that her
mind had learned to call scenery. She was like the soldiers of Cárdenas, the first
white men who ever looked into the Grand Canyon. The river that the Indians 210
had said was half a league wide they judged was about six feet, until they
climbed a third of the way down and found that rocks the size of a man grew
into things taller than the great tower of Seville, and the six-foot creek, even
from four thousand feet above it, was clearly a mighty torrent.

Scale is the first and easiest of the West's lessons. Colors and forms are 215
harder. Easterners are constantly being surprised and somehow offended that
California's summer hills are gold, not green. We are creatures shaped by our
experiences; we like what we know, more often than we know what we like. To
eyes trained on universal chlorophyll, gold or brown hills may look repulsive.
Sagebrush is an acquired taste, as are raw earth and alkali flats. The erosional 220
forms of the dry country strike the attention without ringing the bells of appreciation. It is almost pathetic to read the journals of people who came west up
the Platte Valley in the 1840s and 1850s and tried to find words for Chimney
Rock and Scott's Bluff, and found and clung for dear life to the clichés of castles
and silent sentinels. 225

Listen to Clarence Dutton on the canyon country, whose forms and colors
are as far from Hudson River School standards as any in the West:

> The lover of nature, whose perceptions have been trained in the Alps, in
> Italy, Germany, or New England, in the Appalachians or Cordilleras, in Scot-
> land or Colorado, would enter this strange region with a shock, and dwell 230
> there for a time with a sense of oppression, and perhaps with horror. Whatso-
> ever things he had learned to regard as beautiful and noble he would seldom
> or never see, and whatsoever he might see would appear to him as anything
> but beautiful and noble. Whatsoever might be bold and striking would at first
> seem only grotesque. The colors would be the very ones he had learned to 235
> shun as tawdry and bizarre. The tones and shades, modest and tender, sub-
> dued yet rich, in which his fancy had always taken special delight, would be
> the ones which are conspicuously absent. But time would bring a gradual
> change. Some day he would suddenly become conscious that outlines which
> at first seemed harsh and trivial have grace and meaning; that forms which 240
> seemed grotesque are full of dignity; that magnitudes which had added enor-
> mity to coarseness have become replete with strength and even majesty; that
> colors which had been esteemed unrefined, immodest, and glaring, are as

245 expressive, tender, changeful, and capacious of effects as any others. Great in-
novations, whether in art or literature, in science or in nature, seldom take the
world by storm. They must be understood before they can be estimated, and
must be cultivated before they can be understood.

Amen. Dutton describes a process of westernization of the perceptions that
has to happen before the West is beautiful to us. You have to get over the color
250 green; you have to quit associating beauty with gardens and lawns; you have to
get used to an inhuman scale; you have to understand geological time.

Painters of the West have been hunting a new palette for the western landscape, from Miller and Bodmer to Georgia O'Keeffe, Maynard Dixon, and Mil-
lard Sheets. They have been trying to see western landforms with a clear eye
255 ever since the Baron von Egloffstein, illustrating the report of Lieutenant Ives,
showed the Grand Canyon with rims like puffs of cloud, exaggerated its narrowness and depth, and showed nothing of what the trained eye sees first—the
persistence of the level strata and the persistent profile of the cliffs. Writers have
been trying to learn how to see, and have been groping for a vocabulary better
260 than castles and silent sentinels, but often amateurs of a scientific bent, such as
Dutton, have had to show them how. And audiences, taught partly by direct
contact with the landscape and partly by studying its interpreters, have been
slowly acquiring a set of perceptual habits and responses appropriate to western
forms and colors. Perception, like art and literature, like history, is an artifact, a
265 human creation, and it is not created overnight.

The Westerner is less a person than a continuing adaptation. The West is
less a place than a process. And the western landscape that it has taken us a century and three quarters to learn about, and partially adapt our farming, our social institutions, our laws, and our aesthetic perceptions to, has now become
270 our most valuable natural resource, as subject to raid and ruin as the more concrete resources that have suffered from our rapacity. We are in danger of becoming scenery sellers—and scenery is subject to as much enthusiastic overuse
and overdevelopment as grass and water. It can lead us into an ill-considered
crowding on the heels of our resources. Landscape, with its basis of aridity, is
275 both our peculiar splendor and our peculiar limitation. Without careful controls and restrictions and planning, tourists can be as destructive as locusts—
can destroy everything we have learned to love about the West. I include you
and me among the tourists, and I include you and me in my warning to entrepreneurs. We should all be forced to file an environmental impact study before
280 we build so much as a privy or a summer cottage, much less a motel, a freeway,
or a resort.

Sometimes I wonder if Lewis and Clark shouldn't have been made to file
an environmental impact study before they started west, and Columbus before he ever sailed. They might never have got their permits. But then we
285 wouldn't have been here to learn from our mistakes, either. I really only want
to say that we may love a place and still be dangerous to it. We ought to file

that environmental impact study before we undertake anything that exploits or alters or endangers the splendid, spacious, varied, magnificent, and terribly fragile earth that supports us. If we can't find an appropriate government agency with which to file it, we can file it where an Indian would have filed it—with our environmental conscience, our slowly maturing sense that the earth is indeed our mother, worthy of our love and deserving of our care. That may be the last stage of our adaptation to the western landscape, and it may come too late.

290

## Looking Back

1. In general terms, how does the American West differ geographically from the East?
2. According to Stegner, what climatic condition did early settlers of the West discover to be so dominant that it determined all their efforts on the land?
3. Why do you think that what Stegner calls even "unreliable, biased" historical accounts of Western settlement have value (see lines 84–115)?
4. Which social practices and habits of mind does Stegner think were either valuable or useless in settling the West? What is the basis for his distinction between them?
5. Why was the willingness to adapt so essential to the success of nineteenth-century pioneers?
6. What does Stegner mean by an "oasis civilization" (lines 113 and 162)?
7. Can you put in your own words the lesson conveyed by the anecdote about Aunt Min (lines 193–205)?
8. What does the author mean when he says, "Perception . . . is an artifact, a human creation, and it is not created overnight" (lines 264–265)? How does he reach this conclusion?
9. Accepting Stegner's environmental warning as one with universal merit, how do you apply it to your own surroundings, rural or urban?
10. Do you agree that Americans have a "slowly maturing sense that the earth is our mother, worthy of our love and deserving of our care" (lines 291–292)? Explain your answer.

## Writing Assignments

1. "The Westerner," Stegner writes (line 266), "is less a person than a continuing adaptation." The adaptation to which he refers is to aridity, the overarching condition in the West that "calls the tune" (line 49). Generalizing from his insight, we can say that just about every environment has such a universal or dominant characteristic— social *or* physical, in urban centers *or* rural landscapes—that forces us to adapt in order to survive. Extrapolating from this cue, and referring to Stegner's West, write an essay on the dominant characteristic of the place you call home. Identify it, describe its influence, and explain how it necessitates adaptation.

2. Stegner contrasts individualism and cooperation as guiding principles of human action among the Western settlers in the nineteenth century (see number 4 in Looking Back). One of these principles, he argues, proved disastrous, while the other pointed to salvation. The same principles, with the same probable outcomes, apply today to the preservation of the environment. Write an essay that explains Stegner's distinction between individualism and cooperation in the lives of the settlers and demonstrates how these principles are relevant to the environmental problems the author discusses.

3. "We are creatures shaped by our experience; we like what we know . . ." (lines 217–218). With these words, Stegner alerts us to a common human tendency to resist what is new and unfamiliar because it is more comfortable to stick with what we have always thought. Write an essay that, first, refers to Stegner's treatment of this theme in his essay, then extrapolates from it to focus on an experience you have had that reflects the problem. What challenged your entrenched beliefs, how did it do so, and how did you resolve the conflict?

# Linked Readings

Leonardo da Vinci
## THE NATURE OF WATER

Fernand Braudel
## SOMETHING TO DRINK

Joan Didion
## HOLY WATER

Alain Robbe-Grillet
## REFLECTED VISION: THE WRONG DIRECTION

Painter, inventor, poet, and scientist, Leonardo da Vinci (1452–1519) is perhaps the epitome of the Renaissance Man, a term used to refer to persons who are multi-talented, human-centered, and infinitely curious about the world. He is best known for his paintings, *Mona Lisa* and *The Last Supper* chief among them. The selections printed here are from his notebooks and other manuscripts, one of which, the Codex Hammer, was sold at auction in 1994 for well over thirty million dollars. French historian Fernand Braudel (1902–1985) is perhaps best known for his massive three-volume work *Civilization and Capitalism: 15th–18th Century*. The excerpt printed here is from the first volume, *The Structure of Everyday Life: The Limits of the Possible,* a title that reveals much about the nature of water. Journalist and novelist Joan Didion (b. 1934) has, in recent years, moved to New York from California, an item of interest to readers of "Holy Water." Her books include *Slouching Toward Bethlehem, The White Album, Miami, Salvador, Play It As It Lays,* and, published in 1992, *After Henry.* Alain Robbe-Grillet (b. 1922) worked for six years in France and abroad as an agronomist. His fame rests, however, on his novels, which include *Erasers, The Voyeur,* and *In the Labyrinth.* He also wrote the film script of *Last Year at Marienbad* and is the author of *For A New Novel: Essays on Fiction.* These very different treatments of the same natural element combine to produce a novel contextual view of the subject. This is one of the prime functions of any critical thinking operation whose aim is to enable original and creative approaches to the matter at hand.

# THE NATURE OF WATER

## Looking Ahead

1. Leonardo's approach to water and its action is encyclopedic, but with a difference. His style is so open that it may seem almost childlike in the awe it demonstrates, which is not a bad quality in genius.

2. As you read, critically examine those places where the author brings to bear on description certain concepts that convey the meaning of nature as opposed to its mere existence.

3. At practically every turn here, it is possible to see in Leonardo the combined poet, natural scientist, engineer, and moralist.

This wears away the lofty summits of the mountains. It lays bare and carries away the great rocks. It drives away the sea from its ancient shores for it raises its base with the soil that it carries there. It shatters and devastates the high banks; nor can any stability ever be discerned in these which its nature does not suddenly bring to naught. It seeks out with its rivers every sloping valley    5
where it may carry off or deposit fresh soil. Wherefore many rivers may be said to be those through which all the element has passed, and the sea has gone back many times to the sea, and no part of the earth is so high but that the sea has been at its foundations, and no depth of the ocean is so low but that the loftiest mountains have their bases there. And so it is sometimes    10
sharp and sometimes strong, sometimes acid and sometimes bitter, sometimes sweet and sometimes thick or thin, sometimes it is seen bringing hurt or pestilence, sometimes health-giving, sometimes poisonous. So one would say that it suffers change into as many natures as are the different places through which it passes. And as the mirror changes with the colour of its object so it    15
changes with the nature of the place through which it passes:—health-giving, noisome, laxative, astringent, sulphurous, salt, incarnadined, mournful, raging, angry, red, yellow, green, black, blue, greasy, fat, thin. Sometimes it starts a conflagration, sometimes it extinguishes one; is warm and is cold; carries away or sets down, hollows out or raises up, tears down or establishes,    20
fills up or empties, raises itself up or burrows down, speeds or is still, is the cause at times of life or death, of increase or privation, nourishes at times and at times does the contrary, at times has a tang of salt, at times is without savour, at times submerges the wide valleys with great floods. With time everything changes.    25

At times it goes twisting to the northern parts, eating away the base of its bank; at times it overthrows the bank opposite on the south; at times it turns towards the centre of the earth consuming the base which supports it; at times leaps up seething and boiling towards the sky; at times revolving in a circle it confounds
30   its course; at times it extends on the western side robbing the husbandmen of their tilth; at times it deposits the soil it has carried away in the eastern parts. And thus at times it digs out, and at times fills in where it has taken away and where it has made a deposit. Thus without any rest it is ever removing and consuming whatever borders upon it. So at times it is turbulent and goes ravening
35   in fury, at times clear and tranquil it meanders playfully with gentle course among the fresh verdure. At times falls from the sky in rain or snow or hail; at times forms great clouds out of fine mist. At times moved of itself, at times by the force of others; at times gives increase to things that are born by its lifegiving moisture, at times shows itself either fetid or full of pleasant odours. Without it
40   nothing can exist among us. At times it is bathed in the hot element and dissolving into vapour becomes mingled with the atmosphere, and drawn upwards by the heat it rises until having found the cold region it is pressed closer together by its contrary nature, and the minute particles become attached together. And as when the hand under water squeezes a sponge which is well saturated so that
45   the water shut up in it as it escapes through the crevices is driven into the rest and drives this from its position by its wave, so it is with the cold which the warm moisture compresses, for when it has reduced it to a more solid form the air that is pent up within it breaks by force the weakest part, and hisses just as though it was coming out of bellows when they are pressed down by an insup-
50   portable weight. And thus in various positions it drives away the lighter clouds which form obstacles in its course.

Among straight rivers which occur in land of the same character, with the same abundance of water and with equal breadth, length, depth, and declivity of course, that will be the slower which is the more ancient.
55        This may be proved with straight rivers. That will be most winding which is the oldest, and that which winds will become slower as it acquires greater length.
        Of waters which descend from equal altitudes to equal depths that will be the slower which moves by the longer way.
        Of rivers which are at their commencement that will be the slower which is
60   the more ancient, and this arises from the fact that the course is continually acquiring length by reason of the additional meanderings of the river; and the reason of this is explained [later].

The cause which moves the humours in all kinds of living bodies contrary to the natural law of their gravity, is really that which moves the water pent up within
65   them through the veins of the earth and distributes it through narrow passages; and as the blood that is low rises up high and streams through the severed veins of the forehead, or as from the lower part of the vine the water rises up to where

its branch has been lopped, so out of the lowest depths of the sea the water rises
to the summits of the mountains, and finding there the veins burst open it falls
through them and returns to the sea below. Thus within and without it goes, 70
ever changing, now rising with fortuitous movement and now descending in
natural liberty.

So united together it goes ranging about in continual revolution.

Rushing now here now there, up and down, never resting at all in quiet either in its course or in its own nature, it has nothing of its own but seizes hold 75
on everything, assuming as many different natures as the places are different
through which it passes, acting just as the mirror does when it assumes within
itself as many images as are the objects which pass before it. So it is in a state of
continual change, sometimes of position and sometimes of colour, now enclosing in itself new scents and savours, now keeping new essences or qualities, 80
showing itself now deadly now lifegiving, at one time dispersing itself through
the air, at another suffering itself to be sucked up by the heat, and now arriving
at the region of cold where the heat that was its guide is restricted by it.

And as when the hand under water squeezes a sponge so that the water that
escapes from it creates a wave that passes through the other water, even so does 85
the air that was mingled with the water when the cold is squeezed out, flee away
in fury and drive out the other air; this then is the course of the wind.

And as the hand which squeezes the sponge under water when it is well
soaked, so that the water pent up within it is compelled to flee away and therefore is driven by force through the other water and penetrates it, and this sec- 90
ond mass perceiving itself to be struck departs in a wave from its position, even
so the new . . . makes . . .[1]

The sharp bends made in the embankments of rivers are destroyed in the great
floods of the rivers because the maximum current drives the water in a straight
course. But as this diminishes it resumes its winding course, during which it is 95
being continually diverted from one bank to another, and as it thus grows less
the embankment of the river becomes hollowed out.

But in this lesser depth the water does not move with uniform course, because the greater current leaps from one hollow to another of the opposite
banks, and the sides of the water which border upon the embankment have the 100
shortest course.

The rotundities in the islands of shingle formed by the angles of the embankment trace their origin to the chief eddies of the rivers, which extend with
their revolutions among the concavities and convexities which are found alternately in the embankments of the rivers; and from these spring the tiny brooks, 105
interposed between the sandbanks of the rivers and their embankments, and
placed opposite to the hollows of the embankments of these rivers.

---

1. Note the repeated mirror and sponge comparisons. Such repetitions are typical of an un-
completed and therefore unedited work. (*ed.*)

Among irremediable and destructive terrors the inundations caused by rivers in
flood should certainly be set before every other dreadful and terrifying move-
110    ment, nor is it, as some have thought, surpassed by destruction by fire. I find it
to be the contrary, for fire consumes that which feeds it and is itself consumed
with its food. The movement of water which is created by the slopes of the valleys does not end and die until it has reached the lowest level of the valley; but
fire is caused by what feeds it, and the movement of water by its wish to de-
115    scend. The food of the fire is disunited, and the mischief caused by it is disunited and separated, and the fire dies when it lacks food. The slope of the valley is continuous and the mischief done by the destructive course of the river
will be continuous until, attended by its valleys, it ends in the sea, the universal
base and only resting place of the wandering waters of the rivers.
120    But in what terms am I to describe the abominable and awful evils against
which no human resource avails? Which lay waste the high mountains with
their swelling and exulting waves, cast down the strongest banks, tear up the
deep-rooted trees, and with ravening waves laden with mud from crossing the
ploughed fields carry with them the unendurable labours of the wretched weary
125    tillers of the soil, leaving the valleys bare and mean by reason of the poverty
which is left there.
Among irremediable and destructive terrors the inundations caused by impetuous rivers ought to be set before every other awful and terrifying source of
injury. But in what tongue or with what words am I to express or describe the
130    awful ruin, the inconceivable and pitiless havoc, wrought by the deluges of
ravening rivers, against which no human resource can avail?

## SOMETHING TO DRINK

*Looking Ahead*

1. Compiling a history of drinking water may seem a bit strange; however, you will
   find here that water, as much a product of civilization as anything else, deserves its
   own chronicle.

2. Do you know where *your* water comes from? This is a question you might put to
   yourself as you read about the (often rudimentary) sources here.

3. Test the implicit reasoning here that differences in the historical development of
   potable water reveal differences between various cultures and civilizations.

Paradoxically we must begin with water. It was not always readily available and,
despite specific advice from doctors who claimed that one sort of water was
preferable to another for a particular disease, people had to be content with what
was on hand: rain, river, fountain, cistern, well, barrel or a copper receptacle in
5    which it was wise to keep some in reserve in every provident household. There
were some extreme cases. Sea water was distilled by alembic[1] in the Spanish *pre-*

_____
1. *alembic:* water purification apparatus. (*ed.*)

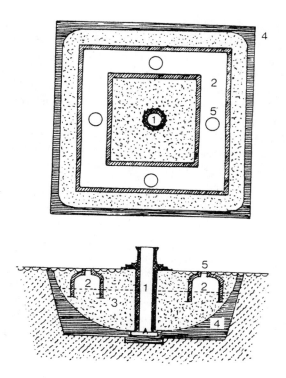

A Well-Cistern in Venice: Section and Elevation
1. Central well-shaft.   2. Rain-water tanks.   3. Sand for filtering.   4. Clay surround.
5. Mouths of rain-water tank, commonly known as *pilele* (literally fonts). The filtered water reappeared in the central well-shaft. Nowadays Venice has water mains, but the Venetian wells can still be seen in public squares or inside houses. (After E.R. Trincanato.)

*sidios* in North Africa in the sixteenth century; otherwise water would have been brought from Spain or Italy. And we hear of the desperate plight of some travellers across the Congo in 1648 who, starving, tired to death and sleeping on the bare ground, had to "drink water [which] resembled horse's urine." Another great problem was the lack of fresh water on board ship. There was no way of keeping it drinkable, despite so many recipes and jealously guarded secrets.    10

 Whole towns—and very wealthy ones at that—were poorly supplied with water. This applied to Venice where the wells in the public squares or the courtyards of palaces were not (as is often thought) dug right down to the underground fresh-water level, below the bed of the lagoon. They were cisterns half-filled with fine sand through which rain water was filtered and decanted and then oozed into the well running down through the centre. When no rain fell for weeks on end, the cisterns ran dry; this happened when Stendhal[2] was    15

<hr/>

 2. *Stendhal:* pen name of Marie-Henri Beyle (1783–1842), Swiss-born author of *The Red and the Black*, *The Charterhouse of Parma*, and *Lucien Leuwen.* (*ed.*)

20    staying in the city. If there was a storm they were tainted with salt water. Even
      in normal weather they were inadequate for the enormous population of the
      town. Fresh water had to be brought from outside, not by aqueduct but by
      boats filled in the Brenta and sent to Venice daily. These *acquaroli* of the river
      even formed an autonomous guild at Venice. The same unpleasant situation
25    prevailed in all the towns of Holland, reduced to using cisterns, shallow wells
      and dubious canal waters.
          There were few aqueducts in use: the deservedly famous ones at Istanbul,
      and the one at Segovia, the *puente* (repaired in 1481), which dated from Roman
      times and astounded visitors. Portugal had aqueducts at Coimbra, Tomar, Villa
30    do Conde and Elvas all functioning in the seventeenth century. The new Spring
      Water aqueduct built in Lisbon between 1729 and 1748, took water to the out-
      lying square of the Rato. The water of this fountain was much sought after, and
      it was here that the water carriers came to fill the red casks with iron handles
      which they carried on the backs of their necks. Sensibly, Martin V's first con-
35    cern when he reoccupied the Vatican after the Great Schism was to restore one
      of the demolished aqueducts of Rome. Two new aqueducts had to be built to
      supply the great city at the end of the sixteenth century: the *Aqua Felice* and the
      *Aqua Paola*. The fountains of Genoa were chiefly supplied by the aqueduct of La
      Scuffara, whose water also powered the mill-wheels inside the city walls and
40    was then distributed among the different quarters of the town. The western
      side, however, drew on water from springs and cisterns. In Paris the Belleville
      aqueduct was repaired in 1457; in conjunction with the one at Pré-Saint-
      Gervain it supplied the town until the seventeenth century. The Arcueil aque-
      duct, reconstructed by Maria de Medici, brought water from Rungis to the Lux-
45    embourg Palace. Large hydraulic wheels raised river water to supply towns in
      some places (Toledo 1526; Augsburg 1548) and drove powerful lift-and-force
      pumps for this purpose. The Samaritaine pump, built between 1603 and 1608,
      yielded 700 cubic metres of water every day, drawn from the Seine and redis-
      tributed to the Louvre and the Tuileries; in 1670 the pumps of the Notre Dame
50    bridge drew 2000 cubic metres from the same source. Water from aqueducts
      and pumps was distributed about the towns through terracotta pipes (as in Ro-
      man times) or wooden pipes (hollowed tree trunks fixed together, as in north-
      ern Italy from the fourteenth century and at Breslau from 1471). There was
      even some lead piping, but although the use of lead is recorded in England in
55    1236, it remained limited. In 1770, Thames water "which is not good" was car-
      ried to all the houses in London by underground wooden pipes, but this was
      not what we would usually think of as running water: it was "distributed regu-
      larly three times a week, according to the amount consumed per household . . .
      it was received and kept in great pipes bound with iron."
60        In Paris, the chief source of water remained the Seine. Its water, which was
      sold by carriers, was reputed to have all the virtues: it was supposed to bear
      boats well, being muddy and therefore heavy, as a Portuguese envoy reported in
      1641—not that this quality would recommend itself to drinkers; and it was

considered excellent for the health—which we may be allowed to doubt. "A number of dyers pour their dye three times a week into the branch of the river which washes the Pelletier quay and between the two bridges," said an eye witness (1771). "The arch which forms the Gêvres quai is a seat of pestilence. All that part of the town drinks infected water." It is true that this was soon remedied. And after all Seine water was better than water from the wells on the Left Bank, which were never protected from terrible infiltrations and with which the bakers made their bread. This river water was a natural purgative and of course "unpleasant for foreigners" but they could always add a few drops of vinegar or buy filtered and "improved" water—or better still, a product called the King's water, or the best and most expensive, the so-called Bristol water. These refinements were unknown before about 1760. "One drank water [from the Seine] without really bothering about it."

Twenty thousand carriers earned a living (though a poor one) supplying Paris with water, taking some thirty "loads" (two buckets at a time) even to the top floors at two sous a load. It was therefore the beginning of a revolution when the Périer brothers installed two steam pumps at Chaillot in 1782, "very curious machines," which raised water 110 feet from the low level of the Seine "by ordinary steam from boiling water." This was in imitation of London, which had had nine such pumps for several years. The Saint-Honoré district, the wealthiest and therefore the most able to pay for such progress, was the first to be served. But people were worried: what would happen to the twenty thousand water carriers if the number of machines increased? And furthermore, the venture shortly turned into a financial scandal (1788). But all the same, with the eighteenth century the problem of supplying drinkable water was clearly posed and the solutions seen and sometimes achieved. And as the proposed water supply for Ulm (1713) proves, this was not confined to capital cities.

Despite everything, progress was slow. In every town in the world the water carrier was indispensable. One Portuguese traveller in Valladolid in Philip III's time praised the excellent water sold in delightful demi-johns and ceramic jugs of all shapes and colours. In China the water carrier used two pails, as in Paris, balancing them at each end of his pole. But a drawing of Peking in 1800 also shows a large barrel on wheels, with a bung at the back. An engraving of about the same period explains "the way in which women carry water in Egypt" in two jars, reminiscent of ancient amphorae: a large one on the head supported by the left hand, a small one held flat on the right hand by a graceful movement of the bent arm. Many fountains were built in Istanbul as a result of the religious requirement to wash frequently every day under running water. The water drunk there was probably purer than anywhere else; which may be why Turks today still pride themselves on being able to recognize the taste of the water from the different springs—just as Frenchmen boast that they can tell the wine from different vineyards.

As for the Chinese, not only did they attribute different qualities to water according to its origin: ordinary rain water, storm water (dangerous), rainfall in

the early spring (beneficial), water from melted hailstones or frost in winter, water collected from stalactites in caves (a sovereign remedy), water from river,
110 well or spring—but they were also concerned about the dangers of pollution
and recommended boiling any suspect water. Hot drinks were in any case the
rule in China (vendors sold boiling water in the streets) and this habit no doubt
considerably contributed to the health of the Chinese population.

In Istanbul, by contrast, snow water was sold everywhere in the streets for a
115 small sum. It was also available in Valladolid where a Portuguese, Bartolomé
Pisheiro da Veiga, at the beginning of the seventeenth century was amazed that
it was possible to treat oneself to "cold water and iced fruit" during the hot
months. But snow water was mostly a great luxury, reserved for the wealthy.
This was the case in France, which only developed a taste for it at the time of
120 Henri III, and around the Mediterranean where boats loaded with snow sometimes made quite long voyages. The Knights of Malta were supplied by Naples;
one of their requests, in 1754, stated that they would die if they did not have
"this sovereign remedy" to break their fevers.

# HOLY WATER

## Looking Ahead

1. Didion's display of technical knowledge demonstrates not only the results of her
   own careful study but also the importance of factual information in the essay.
2. Weigh the effect of Didion's personal involvement in her subject and ask, if this had
   not been the case, would the essay—forgive the pun—have seemed dry.
3. By the end of this piece, you should understand that it is as much about California
   as it is about water.

Some of us who live in arid parts of the world think about water with a reverence others might find excessive. The water I will draw tomorrow from my tap
in Malibu is today crossing the Mojave Desert from the Colorado River, and I
like to think about exactly where that water is. The water I will drink tonight in
5 a restaurant in Hollywood is by now well down the Los Angeles Aqueduct from
the Owens River, and I also think about exactly where that water is: I particularly like to imagine it as it cascades down the 45-degree stone steps that aerate
Owens water after its airless passage through the mountain pipes and siphons.
As it happens my own reverence for water has always taken the form of this
10 constant meditation upon where the water is, of an obsessive interest not in the
politics of water but in the waterworks themselves, in the movement of water
through aqueducts and siphons and pumps and forebays and afterbays and
weirs and drains, in plumbing on the grand scale. I know the data on water projects I will never see. I know the difficulty Kaiser had closing the last two sluice-
15 way gates on the Guri Dam in Venezuela. I keep watch on evaporation behind

the Aswan in Egypt. I can put myself to sleep imagining the water dropping a thousand feet into the turbines at Churchill Falls in Labrador. If the Churchill Falls Project fails to materialize, I fall back on waterworks closer at hand—the tailrace at Hoover on the Colorado, the surge tank in the Tehachapi Mountains that receives California Aqueduct water pumped higher than water has ever been pumped before—and finally I replay a morning when I was seventeen years old and caught, in a military-surplus life raft, in the construction of the Nimbus Afterbay Dam on the American River near Sacramento. I remember that at the moment it happened I was trying to open a tin of anchovies with capers. I recall the raft spinning into the narrow chute through which the river had been temporarily diverted. I recall being deliriously happy.

I suppose it was partly the memory of that delirium that led me to visit, one summer morning in Sacramento, the Operations Control Center for the California State Water Project. Actually so much water is moved around California by so many different agencies that maybe only the movers themselves know on any given day whose water is where, but to get a general picture it is necessary only to remember that Los Angeles moves some of it, San Francisco moves some of it, the Bureau of Reclamation's Central Valley Project moves some of it and the California State Water Project moves most of the rest of it, moves a vast amount of it, moves more water farther than has ever been moved anywhere. They collect this water up in the granite keeps of the Sierra Nevada and they store roughly a trillion gallons of it behind the Oroville Dam and every morning, down at the Project's headquarters in Sacramento, they decide how much of their water they want to move the next day. They make this morning decision according to supply and demand, which is simple in theory but rather more complicated in practice. In theory each of the Project's five field divisions—the Oroville, the Delta, the San Luis, the San Joaquin and the Southern divisions—places a call to headquarters before nine A.M. and tells the dispatchers how much water is needed by its local water contractors, who have in turn based their morning estimates on orders from growers and other big users. A schedule is made. The gates open and close according to schedule. The water flows south and the deliveries are made.

In practice this requires prodigious coordination, precision, and the best efforts of several human minds and that of a Univac 418.[1] In practice it might be necessary to hold large flows of water for power production, or to flush out encroaching salinity in the Sacramento-San Joaquin Delta, the most ecologically sensitive point on the system. In practice a sudden rain might obviate the need for a delivery when that delivery is already on its way. In practice what is being delivered here is an enormous volume of water, not quarts of milk or spools of thread, and it takes two days to move such a delivery down through Oroville into the Delta, which is the great pooling place for California water and has

---

1. *Univac 418:* an early model of the supercomputer. (*ed.*)

been for some years alive with electronic sensors and telemetering equipment and men blocking channels and diverting flows and shoveling fish away from the pumps. It takes perhaps another six days to move this same water down the
60   California Aqueduct from the Delta to the Tehachapi and put it over the hill to Southern California. "Putting some over the hill" is what they say around the Project Operations Control Center when they want to indicate that they are pumping Aqueduct water from the floor of the San Joaquin Valley up and over the Tehachapi Mountains. "Pulling it down" is what they say when they want to
65   indicate that they are lowering a water level somewhere in the system. They can put some over the hill by remote control from this room in Sacramento with its Univac and its big board and its flashing lights. They can pull down a pool in the San Joaquin by remote control from this room in Sacramento with its locked doors and its ringing alarms and its constant print-outs of data from sensors out
70   there in the water itself. From this room in Sacramento the whole system takes on the aspect of a perfect three-billion-dollar hydraulic toy, and in certain ways it is: "LET'S START DRAINING QUAIL AT 12:00" was the 10:51 A.M. entry on the electronically recorded communications log the day I visited the Operations Control Center. "Quail" is a reservoir in Los Angeles County with a gross capac-
75   ity of 1,636,018,000 gallons. "OK" was the response recorded in the log. I knew at that moment that I had missed the only vocation for which I had any instinc-tive affinity: I wanted to drain Quail myself.

Not many people I know carry their end of the conversation when I want to talk about water deliveries, even when I stress that these deliveries affect their lives,
80   indirectly, every day. "Indirectly" is not quite enough for most people I know. This morning, however, several people I know were affected not "indirectly" but "directly" by the way the water moves. They had been in New Mexico shooting a picture, one sequence of which required a river deep enough to sink a truck, the kind with a cab and a trailer and fifty or sixty wheels. It so hap-
85   pened that no river near the New Mexico location was running that deep this year. The production was therefore moved today to Needles, California, where the Colorado River normally runs, depending upon releases from Davis Dam, eighteen to twenty-five feet deep. Now. Follow this closely: yesterday we had a freak tropical storm in Southern California, two inches of rain in a normally dry
90   month, and because this rain flooded the fields and provided more irrigation than any grower could possibly want for several days, no water was ordered from Davis Dam.
　　　No orders, no releases.
　　　Supply and demand.
95   　　　As a result the Colorado was running only seven feet deep past Needles to-day, Sam Peckinpah's desire for eighteen feet of water in which to sink a truck not being the kind of demand anyone at Davis Dam is geared to meet. The pro-duction closed down for the weekend. Shooting will resume Tuesday, provid-ing some grower orders water and the agencies controlling the Colorado release

it. Meanwhile many gaffers, best boys, cameramen, assistant directors, script su-    100
pervisors, stunt drivers and maybe even Sam Peckinpah are waiting out the
weekend in Needles, where it is often 110 degrees at five P.M. and hard to get
dinner after eight. This is a California parable, but a true one.

I have always wanted a swimming pool, and never had one. When it became
generally known a year or so ago that California was suffering severe drought,    105
many people in water-rich parts of the country seemed obscurely gratified, and
made frequent reference to Californians having to brick up their swimming
pools. In fact a swimming pool requires, once it has been filled and the filter has
begun its process of cleaning and recirculating the water, virtually no water, but
the symbolic content of swimming pools has always been interesting: a pool is    110
misapprehended as a trapping of affluence, real or pretended, and of a kind of
hedonistic attention to the body. Actually a pool is, for many of us in the West,
a symbol not of affluence but of order, of control over the uncontrollable. A
pool is water, made available and useful, and is, as such, infinitely soothing to
the western eye.
                                                                                 115
It is easy to forget that the only natural force over which we have any control out here is water, and that only recently. In my memory California sum-
mers were characterized by the coughing in the pipes that meant the well was
dry, and California winters by all-night watches on rivers about to crest, by
sandbagging, by dynamite on the levees and flooding on the first floor. Even    120
now the place is not all that hospitable to extensive settlement. As I write a
fire has been burning out of control for two weeks in the ranges behind the
Big Sur coast. Flash floods last night wiped out all major roads into Imperial
County. I noticed this morning a hairline crack in a living-room tile from last
week's earthquake, a 4.4 I never felt. In the part of California where I now live    125
aridity is the single most prominent feature of the climate, and I am not
pleased to see, this year, cactus spreading wild to the sea. There will be days
this winter when the humidity will drop to ten, seven, four. Tumbleweed will
blow against my house and the sound of the rattlesnake will be duplicated a
hundred times a day by dried bougainvillea drifting in my driveway. The ap-    130
parent ease of California life is an illusion, and those who believe the illusion
real live here in only the most temporary way. I know as well as the next person that there is considerable transcendent value in a river running wild and
undammed, a river running free over granite, but I have also lived beneath
such a river when it was running in flood, and gone without showers when it    135
was running dry.

"The West begins," Bernard DeVoto wrote, "where the average annual rainfall
drops below twenty inches." This is maybe the best definition of the West I have
ever read, and it goes a long way toward explaining my own passion for seeing
the water under control, but many people I know persist in looking for psycho-    140
analytical implications in this passion. As a matter of fact I have explored, in an

amateur way, the more obvious of these implications, and come up with nothing interesting. A certain external reality remains, and resists interpretation. The
West begins where the average annual rainfall drops below twenty inches. Wa-
145 ter is important to people who do not have it, and the same is true of control.
Some fifteen years ago I tore a poem by Karl Shapiro from a magazine and
pinned it on my kitchen wall. This fragment of paper is now on the wall of a
sixth kitchen, and crumbles a little whenever I touch it, but I keep it there for
the last stanza, which has for me the power of a prayer:

150         It is raining in California, a straight rain
        Cleaning the heavy oranges on the bough,
        Filling the gardens till the gardens flow,
        Shining the olives, tiling the gleaming tile,
        Waxing the dark camellia leaves more green,
155         Flooding the daylong valleys like the Nile.

    I thought of those lines almost constantly on the morning in Sacramento
when I went to visit the California State Water Project Operations Control Center. If I had wanted to drain Quail at 10:51 that morning, I wanted, by early afternoon, to do a great deal more. I wanted to open and close the Clifton Court Fore-
160 bay intake gate. I wanted to produce some power down at the San Luis Dam. I
wanted to pick a pool at random on the Aqueduct and pull it down and then re-
fill it, watching for the hydraulic jump. I wanted to put some water over the hill
and I wanted to shut down all flow from the Aqueduct into the Bureau of Reclamation's Cross Valley Canal, just to see how long it would take somebody over at
165 Reclamation to call up and complain. I stayed as long as I could and watched the
system work on the big board with the lighted checkpoints. The Delta salinity report was coming in on one of the teletypes behind me. The Delta tidal report was
coming in on another. The earthquake board, which has been desensitized to
sound its alarm (a beeping tone for Southern California, a high-pitched tone for
170 the north) only for those earthquakes which register at least 3.0 on the Richter
Scale, was silent. I had no further business in this room and yet I wanted to stay
the day. I wanted to be the one, that day, who was shining the olives, filling the
gardens, and flooding the daylong valleys like the Nile. I want it still.

## REFLECTED VISION: THE WRONG DIRECTION

### Looking Ahead

1. The abstractness of the description is as strong as or stronger than its concreteness, a
   novel characteristic.
2. Although this piece on the wrong direction may seem on the way to nowhere, it definitely arrives. Notice *where.*
3. Read critically to perceive the relation of persons to nature and the distinction between appearance and reality.

The rainwater has accumulated in the hollow of a shallow depression, forming among the trees a wide pond, roughly circular in shape, some ten yards in diameter. Round about, the earth is black, without the slightest trace of vegetation between the high, straight trunks. There is neither brush nor shrubs in this part of the woods. The ground is covered only with a uniform, feltlike layer made up of twigs and leaves reduced to their veins, from which a few patches of moss protrude slightly in spots, half decomposed. High above the tree trunks, the bare branches stand out sharply against the sky.

The water is transparent, though brownish in color. Bits of debris fallen from the trees—small branches, empty seed pods, pieces of bark—have lain at the bottom of the shallow pond, steeping there since the start of winter. But none of these fragments is light enough to float, to rise and break the surface, which is everywhere uniform and shiny. There is not the slightest breath of air to ruffle this immobility.

The sky has cleared. It is the end of the day. The sun is low, to the left, behind the tree trunks. Its shallowly slanting rays create, over the entire surface of the pond, narrow luminous bands alternating with wider dark bands.

Parallel to these strips, a row of thick trees runs along the water's edge, on the opposite bank; perfect cylinders, vertical, with no low branches, they run downward in a very brilliant reflection of much greater contrast than the real subject—which by comparison seems vague, even somewhat out of focus. In the black water, the symmetrical trunks shine as if varnished. A line of light emphasizes their outlines on the sides turned toward the setting sun.

Yet this admirable landscape is not only inverted, but also discontinuous. The hatching of the sun's rays over the surface of the mirror cuts through the picture with brighter lines, equally spaced and perpendicular to the reflected tree trunks; it is as if the view there was veiled by intense lighting, revealing innumerable particles suspended in the thin top layer of water. Only the shadowed zones, where these particles are invisible, are strikingly brilliant. Thus each tree trunk is cut off, at more or less equal intervals, by a series of uncertain rings (which nevertheless suggest their real models), giving this part of the "deep down" woods a checkered appearance.

Within a hand's grasp, close to the south edge of the pond, the reflected branches join with old, submerged leaves, reddish but still whole, whose intact lacework stands out against the muddy bottom—oak leaves.

Someone, walking noiselessly on the mulchy carpet of the woods, has appeared on the right, moving toward the water. He comes up to the edge and stops. Since the sun is shining directly into his eyes, he has to step to one side to shield his glance.

He then perceives the banded surface of the pond. But, for him, the reflections of the tree trunks merge with their shadows—at least partially, since the trees directly in front of him are not perfectly straight. Moreover, the sunlight prevents him from distinguishing anything clearly. And there are probably no oak leaves at his feet.

45    This was, then, the end of his walk. Or does he, only now, observe that he has gone in the wrong direction? After a few hesitant glances around, he turns back to the east through the woods, again walking silently, following the path that he had taken to reach this spot.

50    Once more the scene is empty. On the left, the sun is still at the same height; the light is unchanged. Opposite, the straight, smooth tree trunks are still reflected in the unwrinkled water, perpendicular to the rays of the sunset.

Deep in the shadowed zones shine the sectioned reflections of the columns, upside down and black, washed miraculously clean.

## Looking Back

1. How is one of Leonardo's themes echoed by the phrase *Of Time and the River,* title of a novel by Thomas Wolfe?

2. What would you say is the effect on Leonardo's prose of his sheer *looking* at things? What connection do the results of his gaze have with his thinking about these things?

3. What is the sense Braudel gives us of the historical importance of the water supply?

4. What picture does Braudel present of the connection between increase of populations and the availability of a natural resource, in this case water?

5. Is it surprising to learn about some refinements in the consumption of water, for example, the Chinese practice of drinking boiled water? Explain your answer with contemporary examples.

6. What do Didion in the first paragraph of her essay and Braudel in the first two paragraphs of his have in common?

7. In your opinion, why was Didion "deliriously happy" (line 26) when she was swept away by water?

8. Why does Didion want to be a hydraulic engineer?

9. What do you think Robbe-Grillet's view is of the link between appearance and reality?

10. By extracting key concepts from these readings, what synoptic view do you form of water? (A **synopsis** is a general sense of the subject matter; it often traces a common thread through different parts of a whole.)

## Writing Assignments (Linked Readings)

1. A research essay is a type of discourse that presents information gathered from a number of sources. Sometimes, the motive for writing it may be solely to put together what had been separated. Doing so produces a new set of meaningful relationships and a new way of knowing. At times, the researcher may also have in mind a particular idea or statement of fact whose reliability may be demonstrated only by joining bits of information from diverse sources. These related motives can be yours as you write an essay taking off from Leonardo's assertion about water that "Without it nothing can exist among us" (lines 39–40). Begin your essay by explaining what

he means. Go on in interpolative fashion to show how each of the readings on water demonstrates at least one of its essential qualities, values, or uses.

2. Three important themes or directions that the authors pursue with regard to water are liberty, utility, and beauty. However, in the United States, pollution or illegal dumping of waste may rule out bathing; chemical contaminants may harm the drinking supply; and human habitation and other marks of civilization may spoil the shoreline. Decide on one of the categories mentioned above—liberty, utility, or beauty—and make a relatively casual investigation of the state of water where you live. That is, go out and look, taste, smell, and so on. Write an essay that describes the problems relating to your topic and that points out what could and should be done to solve them.

3. Reflecting human cultures as they have developed over time, literary artists have portrayed nature in different guises. There is no necessary order to these portrayals within the history of a people, but the same notions and the same types of thinking recur. Several are relatively contemporary. One is of nature as a benign presence, the beneficence of God made manifest. Another, conversely, sees nature as hostile to human enterprise, a foe to be conquered and tamed, or else. And a third, retreating from these poles, returns nature's blank look of indifference: nature has nothing to do with us and spares or kills quite without knowing or caring. Which of these approaches to nature do you think rings most true? Which enables you to balance your need for security with your need to know the truth? Use the subject of water—ponds, streams, lakes, rivers, oceans—to focus your remarks on nature; think in terms of placid surfaces, raging floods, and forgetful deeps. Write an essay that generally opts for one of these ways of regarding nature and that explains the reasons for your choice. Extrapolate from the insights about water you have gained from the above readings and refer to your own experiences when pertinent.

## *Writing Assignments (Individual Readings)*
## THE NATURE OF WATER

In a poem entitled "Streams," poet W. H. Auden (1913–1973) begins,

> Dear water, clear water, playful in all your streams,
>   as you dash or loiter through life who does not love
>     to sit beside you, to hear you and see you,
>       pure being, perfect in music and movement?

A few stanzas later, he adds

> And not even man can spoil you: his company
>   coarsens roses and dogs but, should he herd you through a sluice
>     to toil at a turbine, or keep you
>       leaping in gardens for his amusement,
>
>   innocent still is your outcry, water . . .

Auden's vision of watercourses seems far from Leonardo's. Write an essay comparing their views of water. Follow your comparison by an overall evaluation, in which you state your own clear preference for one view or the other and your reasons for it.

## SOMETHING TO DRINK

It is certainly easy to take a glass of cold water for granted. You turn on the faucet and there it is: a finger-thick flow of transparent liquid laughing into your tumbler. Not a problem. It is beneath notice, uninteresting, reliably there. Or is it? Not if you live in the desert or if a long drought drops the water level in wells and reservoirs and brings the desert to you. Not if you have to go fetch it. Not if sewage and other contaminants sully the supply. And not if, thanks to normal local conditions, it just plain tastes bad. Then you probably begin to distinguish water here from water there, or to refine your usage by substituting a bottled type for tap water. But, as we see in Braudel, it has always been so, though past consumers seem to have had fewer alternatives to the raw real thing. Looking back to "Something to Drink," write an essay that interpolates your own examples to explain the distinctions and refinements in drinking water that we make in order to get something decent to wet our whistles.

## HOLY WATER

Two major principles guide Didion's thoughts about water: order and control. In discussing swimming pools, she seems to use one principle to explain the other ("order . . . control over the uncontrollable" in line 113), and the two certainly are related. But, taking it all in all, her essay goes into enough detail about waterworks and distribution systems to show how these principles can apply differently, and to account for different satisfactions she takes from the abundance of water. The principles are particularly comprehensible, in relation to each other and separately, when we examine what opposes each. Order is opposed by disarray, by chaos, by the lack of cultivation, by wilderness. Control is opposed by instinct and impulse, by vulnerability and by the freedom to have things happen to us without willing them to happen. Order and control are seen, for example, in a garden, in the orderly rows of plantings and in the gardener's control over blight, insects, and weeds. We are not gardens, however, and so we criticize over-orderly behavior as primness, and we coin such phrases as "control freaks." The questions for us are these: How much order should exist in our lives? What should be ordered? To what degree should we control the details of our lives, not to mention ourselves? Should our minds, like rooms, be tidy? From what should we hold ourselves back? Write an essay that tries to answer these questions.

## REFLECTED VISION: THE WRONG DIRECTION

Have you ever known anyone who, praising a particular book, admitted that he or she had "skipped the descriptions"? That would surely be a mistake reading this piece. Description is all there is. Furthermore, the meaning is in the description. We discover from it that the reflected scene is more vivid and more real than the original, and that the person who stumbles on the scene is incapable of perceiving this truth. Think of the pond as a mirror he looks into. Better yet, think of mirrors as water that our eyes sink into, finding there appearances we wish were reality but that may not be so. What is real? When we look in the mirror, how does the appearance we see there match the reality of ourselves? What happens between the lens of the eye and the surface of the mirror? What narcissism intervenes so that we flatter ourselves? Or what harsh self-judgment criticizes us (think, in extreme cases, of the anorexic individual)? Is looking in the mirror at all workable as a way to know ourselves? Write an essay about mirrors and the human image in them. You might experiment with different mirrors, in different rooms, at different times of day, in different lights, in different moods, and after different things happening.

# Loren Eiseley
# The Brown Wasps

Loren Eiseley (1907–1977) published a number of collections of essays in his lifetime, including *The Immense Journey* and *The Night Country*, in which "The Brown Wasps" appears. Eiseley headed the Sociology and Anthropology Department at Oberlin College. He also taught at the University of Kansas and the University of Pennsylvania, where he held several administrative posts. Elected to the National Institute of Arts and Letters, Eiseley was highly esteemed as both a naturalist and a humanist, a field and a persuasion that combine in his writing to link human beings to the environment in a manner demonstrating their mutual inextricability. Eiseley's critical thinking skills here form a new context for his subject from which emerges a creative understanding of it.

## Looking Ahead

1. Eiseley moves us swiftly back and forth between animal and human lives to reveal the same truth about each. Test the author's reasoning that notes their similarities, and try to discern Eiseley's point in showing them.

2. The author's sympathy for those he observes is perhaps the key to his ability to bring them so sharply into the reader's consciousness.

3. Eiseley is as much a participant as he is a witness, you may notice; as such, he never distances himself from the concerns he introduces.

There is a corner in the waiting room of one of the great Eastern stations where women never sit. It is always in the shadow and overhung by rows of lockers. It is, however, always frequented—not so much by genuine travelers as by the dying. It is here that a certain element of the abandoned poor seeks a refuge out of the weather, clinging for a few hours longer to the city that has fathered them. In a precisely similar manner I have seen, on a sunny day in midwinter, a few old brown wasps creep slowly over an abandoned wasp nest in a thicket. Numbed and forgetful and frost-blackened, the hum of the spring hive still resounded faintly in their sodden tissues. Then the temperature would fall and

5

10   they would drop away into the white oblivion of the snow. Here in the station it
is in no way different save that the city is busy in its snows. But the old ones
cling to their seats as though these were symbolic and could not be given up.
Now and then they sleep, their gray old heads resting with painful awkwardness on the backs of the benches.

15       Also they are not at rest. For an hour they may sleep in the gasping exhaustion of the ill-nourished and aged who have to walk in the night. Then a policeman comes by on his round and nudges them upright.

        "You can't sleep here," he growls.

        A strange ritual then begins. An old man is difficult to waken. After a mut-
20   tered conversation the policeman presses a coin into his hand and passes
fiercely along the benches prodding and gesturing toward the door. In his
wake, like birds rising and settling behind the passage of a farmer through a
cornfield, the men totter up, move a few paces, and subside once more upon
the benches.

25       One man, after a slight, apologetic lurch, does not move at all. Tubercularly
thin, he sleeps on steadily. The policeman does not look back. To him, too, this
has become a ritual. He will not have to notice it again officially for another
hour.

        Once in a while one of the sleepers will not awake. Like the brown wasps,
30   he will have had his wish to die in the great droning center of the hive rather
than in some lonely room. It is not so bad here with the shuffle of footsteps and
the knowledge that there are others who share the bad luck of the world. There
are also the whistles and the sounds of everyone, everyone in the world, starting
on journeys. Amidst so many journeys somebody is bound to come out all
35   right. Somebody.

        Maybe it was on a like thought that the brown wasps fell away from the old
paper nest in the thicket. You hold till the last, even if it is only to a public seat
in a railroad station. You want your place in the hive more than you want a
room or a place where the aged can be eased gently out of the way. It is the
40   place that matters, the place at the heart of things. It is life that you want, that
bruises your gray old head with the hard chairs; a man has a right to his place.

        But sometimes the place is lost in the years behind us. Or sometimes it is a
thing of air, a kind of vaporous distortion above a heap of rubble. We cling to a
time and a place because without them man is lost, not only man but life. This
45   is why the voices, real or unreal, which speak from the floating trumpets at spir-
itualist seances are so unnerving. They are voices out of nowhere whose only reality lies in their ability to stir the memory of a living person with some fragment of the past. Before the medium's cabinet both the dead and the living
revolve endlessly about an episode, a place, an event that has already been en-
50   gulfed by time.

        This feeling runs deep in life; it brings stray cats running over endless
miles, and birds homing from the ends of the earth. It is as though all living
creatures, and particularly the more intelligent, can survive only by fixing or

transforming a bit of time into space or by securing a bit of space with its objects immortalized and made permanent in time. For example, I once saw, on a flower pot in my own living room, the efforts of a field mouse to build a remembered field. I have lived to see this episode repeated in a thousand guises, and since I have spent a large portion of my life in the shade of a nonexistent tree I think I am entitled to speak for the field mouse.

One day as I cut across the field which at that time extended on one side of our suburban shopping center, I found a giant slug feeding from a runnel of pink ice cream in an abandoned Dixie cup. I could see his eyes telescope and protrude in a kind of dim uncertain ecstasy as his dark body bunched and elongated in the curve of the cup. Then, as I stood there at the edge of the concrete, contemplating the slug, I began to realize it was like standing on a shore where a different type of life creeps by and fumbles tentatively among the rocks and sea wrack. It knows its place and will only creep so far until something changes. Little by little as I stood there I began to see more of this shore that surrounds the place of man. I looked with sudden care and attention at things I had been running over thoughtlessly for years. I even waded out a short way into the grass and the wild-rose thickets to see more. A huge black-belted bee went droning by and there were some indistinct scurryings in the underbrush.

Then I came to a sign which informed me that this field was to be the site of a new Wanamaker suburban store. Thousands of obscure lives were about to perish, the spores of puffballs would go smoking off to new fields, and the bodies of little white-footed mice would be crunched under the inexorable wheels of the bulldozers. Life disappears or modifies its appearances so fast that everything takes on an aspect of illusion—a momentary fizzing and boiling with smoke rings, like pouring dissident chemicals into a retort. Here man was advancing, but in a few years his plaster and bricks would be disappearing once more into the insatiable maw of the clover. Being of an archaeological cast of mind, I thought of this fact with an obscure sense of satisfaction and waded back through the rose thickets to the concrete parking lot. As I did so, a mouse scurried ahead of me, frightened of my steps if not of that ominous Wanamaker sign. I saw him vanish in the general direction of my apartment house, his little body quivering with fear in the great open sun on the blazing concrete. Blinded and confused, he was running straight away from his field. In another week scores would follow him.

I forgot the episode then and went home to the quiet of my living room. It was not until a week later, letting myself into the apartment, that I realized I had a visitor. I am fond of plants and had several ferns standing on the floor in pots to avoid the noon glare by the south window.

As I snapped on the light and glanced carelessly around the room, I saw a little heap of earth on the carpet and a scrabble of pebbles that had been kicked merrily over the edge of one of the flower pots. To my astonishment I discovered a full-fledged burrow delving downward among the fern roots. I waited silently. The creature who had made the burrow did not appear. I remembered the wild field then, and the flight of the mice. No house mouse, no *Mus domesticus,* had kicked up this little heap of earth or sought refuge under a fern root in a flower pot. I thought of the desperate little creature I had seen fleeing from the wild-rose thicket. Through intricacies of pipes and attics, he, or one of his fellows, had climbed to this high green solitary room. I could visualize what had occurred. He had an image in his head, a world of seed pods and quiet, of green sheltering leaves in the dim light among the weed stems. It was the only world he knew and it was gone.

Somehow in his flight he had found his way to this room with drawn shades where no one would come till nightfall. And here he had smelled green leaves and run quickly up the flower pot to dabble his paws in common earth. He had even struggled half the afternoon to carry his burrow deeper and had failed. I examined the hole, but no whiskered twitching face appeared. He was gone. I gathered up the earth and refilled the burrow. I did not expect to find traces of him again.

Yet for three nights thereafter I came home to the darkened room and my ferns to find the dirt kicked gaily about the rug and the burrow reopened, though I was never able to catch the field mouse within it. I dropped a little food about the mouth of the burrow, but it was never touched. I looked under beds or sat reading with one ear cocked for rustlings in the ferns. It was all in vain; I never saw him. Probably he ended in a trap in some other tenant's room.

But before he disappeared I had come to look hopefully for his evening burrow. About my ferns there had begun to linger the insubstantial vapor of an autumn field, the distilled essence, as it were, of a mouse brain in exile from its home. It was a small dream, like our dreams, carried a long and weary journey along pipes and through spider webs, past holes over which loomed the shadows of waiting cats, and finally, desperately, into this room where he had played in the shuttered daylight for an hour among the green ferns on the floor. Every day these invisible dreams pass us on the street, or rise from beneath our feet, or look out upon us from beneath a bush.

Some years ago the old elevated railway in Philadelphia was torn down and replaced by a subway system. This ancient El with its barnlike stations containing nut-vending machines and scattered food scraps had, for generations, been the favorite feeding ground of flocks of pigeons, generally one flock to a station along the route of the El. Hundreds of pigeons were dependent upon the system. They flapped in and out of its stanchions and steel work or gathered in watchful little audiences about the feet of anyone who rattled the peanut-vending machines. They even watched people who jingled change in their hands, and prospected for food under the feet of the crowds who gathered between trains. Probably very few among the waiting people who tossed a crumb to an eager pigeon realized that this El was like a food-bearing river, and that the life which haunted its banks was dependent upon the running of the trains with their human freight.

I saw the river stop.

The time came when the underground tubes were ready; the traffic was transferred to a realm unreachable by pigeons. It was like a great river subsiding suddenly into desert sands. For a day, for two days, pigeons continued to circle over the El or stand close to the red vending machines. They were patient birds, and surely this great river which had flowed through the lives of unnumbered generations was merely suffering from some momentary drought.    145

They listened for the familiar vibrations that had always heralded an approaching train; they flapped hopefully about the head of an occasional workman walking along the steel runways. They passed from one empty station to another, all the while growing hungrier. Finally they flew away.    150

I thought I had seen the last of them about the El, but there was a revival and it provided a curious instance of the memory of living things for a way of life or a locality that has long been cherished. Some weeks after the El was abandoned workmen began to tear it down. I went to work every morning by one particular station, and the time came when the demolition crews reached this spot. Acetylene torches showered passers-by with sparks, pneumatic drills hammered at the base of the structure, and a blind man who, like the pigeons, had clung with his cup to a stairway leading to the change booth, was forced to give up his place.    155    160

It was then, strangely, momentarily, one morning that I witnessed the return of a little band of the familiar pigeons. I even recognized one or two members of the flock that had lived around this particular station before they were dispersed into the streets. They flew bravely in and out among the sparks and the hammers and the shouting workmen. They had returned—and they had returned because the hubbub of the wreckers had convinced them that the river was about to flow once more. For several hours they flapped in and out through the empty windows, nodding their heads and watching the fall of girders with attentive little eyes. By the following morning the station was reduced to some burned-off stanchions in the street. My bird friends had gone. It was plain, however, that they retained a memory for an insubstantial structure now compounded of air and time. Even the blind man clung to it. Someone had provided him with a chair, and he sat at the same corner staring sightlessly at an invisible stairway where, so far as he was concerned, the crowds were still ascending to the trains.    165    170    175

I have said my life has been passed in the shade of a nonexistent tree, so that such sights do not offend me. Prematurely I am one of the brown wasps and I often sit with them in the great droning hive of the station, dreaming sometimes of a certain tree. It was planted sixty years ago by a boy with a bucket and a toy spade in a little Nebraska town. That boy was myself. It was a cottonwood sapling and the boy remembered it because of some words spoken by his father and because everyone died or moved away who was supposed to wait and grow old under its shade. The boy was passed from hand to hand, but the tree for some intangible reason had taken root in his mind. It was under its branches that he sheltered; it was from this tree that his memories, which are my memories, led away into the world.    180    185

After sixty years the mood of the brown wasps grows heavier upon one. During a long inward struggle I thought it would do me good to go and look
190   upon that actual tree. I found a rational excuse in which to clothe this madness. I purchased a ticket and at the end of two thousand miles I walked another mile to an address that was still the same. The house had not been altered.

I came close to the white picket fence and reluctantly, with great effort, looked down the long vista of the yard. There was nothing there to see. For
195   sixty years that cottonwood had been growing in my mind. Season by season its seeds had been floating farther on the hot prairie winds. We had planted it lovingly there, my father and I, because he had a great hunger for soil and live things growing, and because none of these things had long been ours to protect. We had planted the little sapling and watered it faithfully, and I remembered
200   that I had run out with my small bucket to drench its roots the day we moved away. And all the years since it had been growing in my mind, a huge tree that somehow stood for my father and the love I bore him. I took a grasp on the picket fence and forced myself to look again.

A boy with the hard bird eye of youth pedaled a tricycle slowly up beside
205   me.

"What'cha lookin' at?" he asked curiously.

"A tree," I said.

"What for?" he said.

"It isn't there," I said, to myself mostly, and began to walk away at a pace
210   just slow enough not to seem to be running.

"What isn't there?" the boy asked. I didn't answer. It was obvious I was attached by a thread to a thing that had never been there, or certainly not for long. Something that had to be held in the air, or sustained in the mind, because it was part of my orientation in the universe and I could not survive without it.
215   There was more than an animal's attachment to a place. There was something else, the attachment of the spirit to a grouping of events in time; it was part of our mortality.

So I had come home at last, driven by a memory in the brain as surely as the field mouse who had delved long ago into my flower pot or the pigeons fly-
220   ing forever amidst the rattle of nut-vending machines. These, the burrow under the greenery in my living room and the red-bellied bowls of peanuts now hovering in midair in the minds of pigeons, were all part of an elusive world that existed nowhere and yet everywhere. I looked once at the real world about me while the persistent boy pedaled at my heels.
225   It was without meaning, though my feet took a remembered path. In sixty years the house and street had rotted out of my mind. But the tree, the tree that no longer was, that had perished in its first season, bloomed on in my individual mind, unblemished as my father's words. "We'll plant a tree here, son, and we're not going to move any more. And when you're an old, old man you can sit
230   under it and think how we planted it here, you and me, together."

I began to outpace the boy on the tricycle.

"Do you live here, Mister?" he shouted after me suspiciously. I took a firm grasp on airy nothing—to be precise, on the bole of a great tree. "I do," I said. I spoke for myself, one field mouse, and several pigeons. We were all out of touch but somehow permanent. It was the world that had changed.

235

## Looking Back

1. How are the old men in the railroad station like the brown wasps?

2. What does Eiseley mean by his remark, "We cling to a time and a place because without them man is lost, not only man but life" (lines 43–44)?

3. In what way do the disappearances and fast changes of certain forms of existence (see lines 73–81) emphasize the need of living things to have a definite place in the world?

4. What was the mouse in Eiseley's living room trying to accomplish?

5. How do you respond to the notion of the "invisible dreams" he refers to in line 127? Explain your answer.

6. Why is the one-sentence paragraph in line 142 so effective?

7. What do the pigeons and the blind man have in common?

8. At the beginning of the last section of "The Brown Wasps" (line 177), Eiseley looks backward and forward at the same time. How does this paragraph unify the essay?

9. What did the tree mean to Eiseley? How did discovering its nonexistence affect him?

10. Can we say that, after revisiting the tree that never grew, Eiseley is not lying to the little boy when he says he lives there? Explain your answer.

## Writing Assignments

1. Loren Eiseley builds his essay on thoughtful comparisons between animals and humans—wasps, a mouse, pigeons, a slug, and various people. Somehow, this seems more effective than finding similarities in behavior between different people. Why is it so effective? One way to find out is to extrapolate from Eiseley's method and make such a comparison yourself. Write an essay that does so. Bring to mind a specific or a general human characteristic, match it with a particular animal's behavior, and compare the two. Having done so, comment on the value of making such comparisons.

2. Throughout the essay, every example—animal or human—illustrates the need Eiseley says all creatures have to cling to a place in the world that they can recognize (and recognize themselves in), that they can call home (even if it's only a seat in a railroad station), that makes their life seem real (even if it's an illusory cottonwood tree). The author gives us bits and pieces of an explanation of why this "orientation to the universe" is so vital (line 192). But he doesn't produce a definitive statement that makes his point explicitly. Write an essay that interpolates your own explanations to illuminate his reasoning. Begin by referring to the efforts of the characters in the essay—animal and human—to keep the place their spirit recognizes.

3. Although "The Brown Wasps" was published over twenty years ago, long before the situation of the old men in the railroad station became all too familiar, in that part of the essay especially, Eiseley alerts the contemporary reader to the situation of the homeless in the United States. Because his sympathy (for humans and animals) is so pronounced, we who read his words today are moved to a greater understanding of the homeless population and a deeper feeling for them than we may previously have had. Write an essay that explains how Eiseley nurtures this growing sympathy, understanding, and pity for the homeless and go on to say what difference such strengthened feelings might make.

🌿

# D. H. Lawrence

# Reflections on the Death of a Porcupine

D(avid) H(erbert) Lawrence (1885–1930) was a coal miner's son and taught in a public school in England before his first novel, *Sons and Lovers,* made him famous. His other novels include *The Rainbow, Women in Love,* and *Lady Chatterley's Lover.* Also a poet, essayist, and short story writer, he traveled extensively, in part to discover a climate that might restore his frail health. He lived in the southwestern United States (the scene of this essay) as well as other places, and died at forty-five of tuberculosis in southern France. Among his travel books, which are as intensely personal as his fiction, are *Twilight in Italy* and *Etruscan Places.* "Reflections on the Death of a Porcupine," published posthumously, reveals his central concerns and passions as much as or more than anything else he wrote.

## Looking Ahead

1. Read critically to become aware of the logic in Lawrence's structural organization. It moves from narrative to meditation to analysis to dire prophecy, from the concrete to the abstract, sometimes looping back for a moment before going on again from the tangible to the conceptual.

2. Lawrence uses certain terms in special ways, and he defines them when he introduces them. Be alert to pick up his definitions of *vitality, fourth dimension, being,* and *the Holy Ghost.*

3. His passionate attachment to his subject matter may disguise the fact that he is conducting a rational argument, or a series of arguments that, like any such, you can read critically and test for logic and truth.

There are many bare places on the little pine trees, towards the top, where the porcupines have gnawed the bark away and left the white flesh showing. And some trees are dying from the top.

Everyone says porcupines should be killed; the Indians, Mexicans, Americans all say the same.

At full moon a month ago, when I went down the long clearing in the brilliant moonlight, through the poor dry herbage a big porcupine began to waddle away from me, towards the trees and the darkness. The animal had raised all its hairs and bristles, so that by the light of the moon it seemed to have a tall, swaying, moonlit aureole arching its back as it went. That seemed curiously fearsome, as if the animal were emitting itself demon-like on the air.

It waddled very slowly, with its white spiky spoon-tail steering flat, behind the round bear-like mound of its back. It had a lumbering, beetle's, squalid motion, unpleasant. I followed it into the darkness of the timber, and there, squat like a great tick, it began scrapily to creep up a pine-trunk. It was very like a great aureoled tick, a bug, struggling up.

I stood near and watched, disliking the presence of the creature. It is a duty to kill the things. But the dislike of killing him was greater than the dislike of him. So I watched him climb.

And he watched me. When he had got nearly the height of a man, all his long hairs swaying with a bristling gleam like an aureole, he hesitated, and slithered down. Evidently he had decided, either that I was harmless, or else that it was risky to go up any further, when I could knock him off so easily with a pole. So he slithered podgily down again, and waddled away with the same bestial, stupid motion of that white-spiky repulsive spoon-tail. He was as big as a middle-sized pig: or more like a bear.

I let him go. He was repugnant. He made a certain squalor in the moonlight of the Rocky Mountains. As all savagery has a touch of squalor, that makes one a little sick at the stomach. And anyhow, it seemed almost more squalid to pick up a pine-bough and push him over, hit him and kill him.

A few days later, on a hot, motionless morning when the pine-trees put out their bristles in stealthy, hard assertion; and I was not in a good temper, because Black-eyed Susan, the cow, had disappeared into the timber, and I had had to ride hunting her, so it was nearly nine o'clock before she was milked: Madame came in suddenly out of the sunlight, saying: "I got such a shock! There are two strange dogs, and one of them has got the most awful beard, all round his nose."

She was frightened, like a child, at something unnatural.

"Beard! Porcupine quills, probably! He's been after a porcupine."

"Ah!" she cried in relief. "Very likely! Very likely!"—then with a change of tone: "Poor thing, will they hurt him?"

"They will. I wonder when he came."

"I heard dogs bark in the night."

"Did you? Why didn't you say so? I should have known Susan was hiding—"

The ranch is lonely, there is no sound in the night, save the innumerable noises of the night, that you can't put your finger on; cosmic noises in the far deeps of the sky, and of the earth.

I went out. And in the full blaze of sunlight in the field, stood two dogs, a black-and-white, and a big, bushy, rather handsome sandy-red dog, of the

collie type. And sure enough, this latter did look queer and a bit horrifying,
50    his whole muzzle set round with white spines, like some ghastly growth; like
an unnatural beard.

The black-and-white dog made off as I went through the fence. But the red
dog whimpered and hesitated, and moved on hot bricks. He was fat and in good
condition. I thought he might belong to some shepherds herding sheep in the
55    forest ranges, among the mountains.

He waited while I went up to him, wagging his tail and whimpering, and
ducking his head, and dancing. He daren't rub his nose with his paws any more:
it hurt too much. I patted his head and looked at his nose, and he whimpered
loudly.

60    He must have had thirty quills, or more, sticking out of his nose, all the way
round: the white, ugly ends of the quills protruding an inch, sometimes more,
sometimes less, from his already swollen, blood-puffed muzzle.

The porcupines here have quills only two or three inches long. But they are
devilish; and a dog will die if he does not get them pulled out. Because they
65    work further and further in, and will sometimes emerge through the skin away
in some unexpected place.

Then the fun began. I got him in the yard: and he drank up the whole half-
gallon of the chickens' sour milk. Then I started pulling out the quills. He was a
big, bushy, handsome dog, but his nerve was gone, and every time I got a quill
70    out, he gave a yelp. Some long quills were fairly easy. But the shorter ones, near
his lips, were deep in, and hard to get hold of, and hard to pull out when you
did get hold of them. And with every one that came out, came a little spurt of
blood and another yelp and writhe.

The dog wanted the quills out: but his nerve was gone. Every time he saw
75    my hand coming to his nose, he jerked his head away. I quieted him, and
stealthily managed to jerk out another quill, with the blood all over my fingers.
But with every one that came out, he grew more tiresome. I tried and tried and
tried to get hold of another quill, and he jerked and jerked, and writhed and
whimpered, and ran under the porch floor.

80    It was a curiously unpleasant, nerve-trying job. The day was blazing hot.
The dog came out and I struggled with him again for an hour or more. Then we
blindfolded him. But either he smelled my hand approaching his nose, or some
weird instinct told him. He jerked his head, this way, that way, up, down, sideways, roundwise, as one's fingers came slowly, slowly, to seize a quill.

85    The quills on his lips and chin were deep in, only about a quarter of an inch
of white stub protruding from the swollen, blood-oozed, festering black skin. It
was very difficult to jerk them out.

We let him lie for an interval, hidden in the quiet cool place under the
porch floor. After half an hour, he crept out again. We got a rope round his
90    nose, behind the bristles, and one held while the other got the stubs with the
pliers. But it was too trying. If a quill came out, the dog's yelp startled every
nerve. And he was frightened of the pain, it was impossible to hold his head still
any longer.

After struggling for two hours, and extracting some twenty quills, I gave up. It was impossible to quiet the creature, and I had had enough. His nose on the top was clear: a punctured, puffy, blood-darkened mess; and his lips were clear. But just on his round little chin, where the few white hairs are, was still a bunch of white quills, eight or nine, deep in. [95]

We let him go, and he dived under the porch, and there he lay invisible: save for the end of his bushy, foxy tail, which moved when we came near. Towards noon he emerged, ate up the chicken-food, and stood with that doggish look of dejection, and fear, and friendliness, and greediness, wagging his tail. [100]

But I had had enough.

"Go home!" I said. "Go home! Go home to your master, and let him finish for you."

He would not go. So I led him across the blazing hot clearing, in the way I thought he should go. He followed a hundred yards, then stood motionless in the blazing sun. He was not going to leave the place. [105]

And I! I simply did not want him.

So I picked up a stone. He dropped his tail, and swerved towards the house. I knew what he was going to do. He was going to dive under the porch, and there stick, haunting the place. [110]

I dropped my stone, and found a good stick under the cedar tree. Already in the heat was that sting-like biting of electricity, the thunder gathering in the sheer sunshine, without a cloud, and making one's whole body feel dislocated. [115]

I could not bear to have that dog around any more. Going quietly to him, I suddenly gave him one hard hit with the stick, crying: "Go home!" He turned quickly, and the end of the stick caught him on his sore nose. With a fierce yelp, he went off like a wolf, downhill, like a flash, gone. And I stood in the field full of pangs of regret, at having hit him, unintentionally, on his sore nose. [120]

But he was gone.

And then the present moon came, and again the night was clear. But in the interval there had been heavy thunder-rains, the ditch was running with bright water across the field, and the night, so fair, had not the terrific, mirror-like brilliancy, touched with terror, so startling bright, of the moon in the last days [125] of June.

We were alone on the ranch. Madame went out into the clear night, just before retiring. The stream ran in a cord of silver across the field, in the straight line where I had taken the irrigation ditch. The pine tree in front of the house threw a black shadow. The mountain slope came down to the fence, wild and [130] alert.

"Come!" said she excitedly. "There is a big porcupine drinking at the ditch. I thought at first it was a bear."

When I got out he had gone. But among the grasses and the coming wild sunflowers, under the moon, I saw his greyish halo, like a pallid living bush, [135] moving over the field, in the distance, in the moonlit *clair-obscur*.[1]

---

1. *clair-obscur*: clear-obscure; a double phenomenon. (*ed.*)

We got through the fence, and following, soon caught him up. There he
lumbered, with his white spoon-tail spiked with bristles, steering behind almost
as if he were moving backwards, and this was his head. His long, long hairs
above the quills quivering with a dim grey gleam, like a bush.

140     And again I disliked him.
"Should one kill him?"
She hesitated. Then with a sort of disgust:
"Yes!"

145     I went back to the house, and got the little twenty-two rifle. Now never in
my life had I shot at any live thing: I never wanted to. I always felt guns very repugnant: sinister, mean. With difficulty I had fired once or twice at a target: but
resented doing even so much. Other people could shoot if they wanted to. Myself, individually, it was repugnant to me even to try.

150     But something slowly hardens in a man's soul. And I knew now it had
hardened in mine. I found the gun, and with rather trembling hands got it
loaded. Then I pulled back the trigger and followed the porcupine. It was still
lumbering through the grass. Coming near, I aimed.

155     The trigger stuck. I pressed the little catch with a safety-pin I found in my
pocket, and released the trigger. Then we followed the porcupine. He was still
lumbering towards the trees. I went sideways on, stood quite near to him, and
fired, in the clear-dark of the moonlight.

And as usual I aimed too high. He turned, went scuttling back whence he
had come.

160     I got another shell in place, and followed. This time I fired full into the
mound of his round back, below the glistening grey halo. He seemed to stumble
onto his hidden nose, and struggled a few strides, ducking his head under like a
hedgehog.

"He's not dead yet! Oh, fire again!" cried Madame.

165     I fired, but the gun was empty.

So I ran quickly, for a cedar pole. The porcupine was lying still, with subsiding halo. He stirred faintly. So I turned him and hit him hard over the nose;
or where, in the dark, his nose should have been. And it was done. He was
dead.

170     And in the moonlight, I looked down on the first creature I had ever shot.
"Does it seem mean?" I asked aloud, doubtful.

Again Madame hesitated. Then: "No!" she said resentfully.

And I felt she was right. Things like the porcupine, one must be able to
shoot them, if they get in one's way.

175     One must be able to shoot. I, myself, must be able to shoot, and to kill.

For me, this is a *volta face*.[2] I have always preferred to walk round my porcupine, rather than kill it.

Now, I know it's no good walking round. One must kill.

---

2. *volta face:* about face. (*ed.*)

I buried him in the adobe hole. But some animal dug down and ate him; for two days later there lay the spines and bones spread out, with the long skeletons of the porcupine-hands. 180

The only nice thing about him—or her, for I believe it was a female, by the dugs on her belly—were the feet. They were like longish, alert black hands, paw-hands. That is why a porcupine's tracks in the snow look almost as if a child had gone by, leaving naked little human footprints, like a little boy. 185

So, he is gone: or she is gone. But there is another one, bigger and blacker-looking, among the west timber. That too is to be shot. It is part of the business of ranching: even when it's only a little half-abandoned ranch like this one.

Wherever man establishes himself, upon the earth, he has to fight for his place against the lower orders of life. Food, the basis of existence, has to be 190 fought for even by the most idyllic of farmers. You plant, and you protect your growing crop with a gun. Food, food, how strangely it relates man with the animal and vegetable world! How important it is! And how fierce is the fight that goes on around it.

The same when one skins a rabbit, and takes out the inside, one realizes 195 what an enormous part of the animal, comparatively, is intestinal, what a big part of him is just for food-apparatus; for *living on* other organisms.

And when one watches the horses in the big field, their noses to the ground, bite-bite-biting at the grass, and stepping absorbedly on, and bite-bite-biting without ever lifting their noses, cropping off the grass, the young shoots 200 of alfalfa, the dandelions, with a blind, relentless, unwearied persistence, one's whose life pauses. One suddenly realizes again how all creatures devour, and *must* devour the lower forms of life.

So Susan, swinging across the field, snatches off the tops of the little wild sunflowers as if she were mowing. And down they go, down her black throat. 205 And when she stands in her cowy oblivion chewing her cud, with her lower jaw swinging peacefully, and I am milking her, suddenly the camomiley smell of her breath, as she glances round with glaring, smoke-blue eyes, makes me realize it is the sunflowers that are her ball of cud. Sunflowers! And they will go to making her glistening black hide, and the thick cream on her milk. 210

And the chickens, when they see a great black beetle, that the Mexicans call a *toro*, floating past, they are after it in a rush. And if it settles, instantly the brown hen stabs it with her beak. It is a great beetle two or three inches long: but in a second it is in the crop of the chicken. Gone!

And Timsy, the cat, as she spies on the chipmunks, crouches in another 215 sort of oblivion, soft, and still. The chipmunks come to drink the milk from the chickens' bowl. Two of them met at the bowl. They were little squirrely things with stripes down their backs. They sat up in front of one another, lifting their inquisitive little noses and humping their backs. Then each put its two little hands on the other's shoulders, they reared up, gazing into each 220 other's faces; and finally they put their two little noses together, in a sort of kiss.

But Miss Timsy can't stand this. In a soft, white-and-yellow leap she is after them. They skip, with the darting jerks of chipmunks, to the wood-heap, and
225   with one soft, high-leaping sideways bound Timsy goes through the air. Her snow-flake of a paw comes down on one of the chipmunks. She looks at it for a second. It squirms. Swiftly and triumphantly she puts her two flowery little white paws on it, legs straight out in front of her, back arched, gazing concentratedly yet whimsically. Chipmunk does not stir. She takes it softly in her
230   mouth, where it dangles softly, like a lady's tippet.[3] And with a proud, prancing motion the Timsy sets off towards the house, her white little feet hardly touching the ground.

But she gets shooed away. We refuse to loan her the sitting-room any more, for her gladiatorial displays. If the chippy must be "butchered to make a Timsy
235   holiday," it shall be outside. Disappointed, but still high-stepping, the Timsy sets off towards the clay oven by the shed.

There she lays the chippy gently down, and soft as a little white cloud lays one small paw on its striped back. Chippy does not move. Soft as thistle-down she raises her paw a tiny, tiny bit, to release him.
240   And all of a sudden, with an elastic jerk, he darts from under the white release of her paw. And instantly, she is up in the air and down she comes on him, with the forward thrusting bolts of her white paws. Both creatures are motionless.

Then she takes him softly in her mouth again, and looks round, to see if she
245   can slip into the house. She cannot. So she trots towards the wood-pile.

It is a game, and it is pretty. Chippy escapes into the wood-pile, and she softly, softly reconnoitres among the faggots.

Of all the animals, there is no denying it, the Timsy is the most pretty, the most fine. It is not her mere *corpus* that is beautiful; it is her bloom of aliveness.
250   Her "infinite variety"; the soft, snow-flakey lightness of her, and at the same time her lean, heavy ferocity. I had never realized the latter, till I was lying in bed one day moving my toe, unconsciously, under the bedclothes. Suddenly a terrific blow struck my foot. The Timsy had sprung out of nowhere, with a hurling, steely force, thud upon the bedclothes where the toe was moving. It was as
255   if someone had aimed a sudden blow, vindictive and unerring.

"Timsy!"

She looked at me with the vacant, feline glare of her hunting eyes. It is not even ferocity. It is the dilation of the strange, vacant arrogance of power. The power is in her.
260   And so it is. Life moves in circles of power and of vividness, and each circle of life only maintains its orbit upon the subjection of some lower circle. If the lower cycles of life are not *mastered,* there can be no higher cycle.

In nature, one creature devours another, and this is an essential part of all existence and of all being. It is not something to lament over, nor something to

---

3. *tippet:* fur stole. (*ed.*)

try to reform. The Buddhist who refuses to take life is really ridiculous, since if 265
he eats only two grains of rice per day, it is two grains of life. We did not make
creation, *we* are not the authors of the universe. And if we see that the whole of
creation is established upon the fact that one life devours another life, one cycle
of existence can only come into existence through the subjugating of another
cycle of existence, then what is the good of trying to pretend that it is not so? 270
The only thing to do is to realize what is higher, and what is lower, in the cycles
of existence.

It is nonsense to declare that there *is* no higher and lower. We know full
well that the dandelion belongs to a higher cycle of existence than the harts-
tongue fern, that the ant's is a higher form of existence than the dandelion's, 275
that the thrush is higher than the ant, that Timsy the cat is higher than the
thrush, and that I, a man, am higher than Timsy.

What do we mean by higher? Strictly, we mean more alive. More vividly
alive. The ant is more vividly alive than the pine-tree. We know it, there is no
trying to refute it. It is all very well saying that they are both alive in two differ- 280
ent ways, and therefore they are incomparable, incommensurable. This is also
true.

But one truth does not displace another. Even apparently contradictory
truths do not displace one another. Logic is far too coarse to make the subtle
distinctions life demands. 285

Truly, it is futile to compare an ant with a great pine-tree, in the absolute.
Yet as far as *existence* is concerned, they are not only placed in comparison to
one another, they are occasionally pitted against one another. And if it comes
to a contest, the little ant will devour the life of the huge tree. If it comes to a
contest. 290

And, in the cycles of *existence,* this is the test. From the lowest form of existence to the highest, the test question is: *Can thy neighbour finally overcome
thee?*

If he can, then he belongs to a higher cycle of existence.

This is the truth behind the survival of the fittest. Every cycle of existence is 295
established upon the overcoming of the lower cycles of existence. The real question is, wherein does *fitness* lie? Fitness for what? Fit merely to survive? That
which is only fit to survive will survive only to supply food or contribute in
some way to the existence of a higher form of life, which is able to do more than
survive, which can really *vive,* live. 300

Life is more vivid in the dandelion than in the green fern, or than in a palm
tree.

Life is more vivid in a snake than in a butterfly.

Life is more vivid in a wren than in an alligator.

Life is more vivid in a cat than in an ostrich. 305

Life is more vivid in the Mexican who drives the wagon than in the two
horses in the wagon.

Life is more vivid in me than in the Mexican who drives the wagon for me.

We are speaking in terms of *existence:* that is, in terms of species, race, or
310   type.

The dandelion can take hold of the land, the palm tree is driven into a corner, with the fern.

The snake can devour the fiercest insect.

The fierce bird can destroy the greatest reptile.

315   The great cat can destroy the greatest bird.

The man can destroy the horse, or any animal.

One race of man can subjugate and rule another race.

All this in terms of *existence.* As far as existence goes, that life-species is the
highest which can devour, or destroy, or subjugate every other life-species
320   against which it is pitted in contest.

This is a law. There is no escaping this law. Anyone, or any race, trying to
escape it will fall a victim: will fall into subjugation.

But let us insist and insist again, we are talking now of existence, of species,
of types, of races, of nations, not of single individuals, nor of *beings.* The dande-
325   lion in full flower, a little sun bristling with sun-rays on the green earth, is a
nonpareil, a nonsuch. Foolish, foolish, foolish to compare it to anything else on
earth. It is itself incomparable and unique.

But that is the fourth dimension, of *being.* It is in the fourth dimension,
nowhere else.

330   Because, in the time-space dimension, any man may tread on the yellow
sun-mirror, and it is gone. Any cow may swallow it. Any bunch of ants may an-
nihilate it.

This brings us to the inexorable law of life.

1. Any creature that attains to its own fullness of being, its own *living* self,
335   becomes unique, a nonpareil. It has its place in the fourth dimension, the
heaven of existence, and there it is perfect, it is beyond comparison.

2. At the same time, every creature exists in time and space. And in time
and space it exists relatively to all other existence, and can never be absolved.
Its existence impinges on other existences, and is itself impinged upon. And in
340   the struggle for existence, if an effort on the part of any one type or species or
order of life can finally destroy the other species, then the destroyer is of a more
vital cycle of existence than the one destroyed. (When speaking of existence we
always speak in types, species, not individuals. Species exist. But even an individual dandelion has *being.*)

345   3. The force which we call *vitality,* and which is the determining factor in
the struggle for existence, is, however, derived also from the fourth dimension.
That is to say, the ultimate source of all vitality is in that other dimension, or region, where the dandelion blooms, and which men have called heaven, and
which now they call the fourth dimension: which is only a way of saying that it
350   is not to be reckoned in terms of space and time.

4. The primary way, in our existence, to get vitality, is to absorb it from living creatures lower than ourselves. It is thus transformed into a new and higher

creation. (There are many ways of absorbing: devouring food is one way, love is often another. The best way is a pure relationship, which includes the *being* on each side, and which allows the transfer to take place in a living flow, enhancing the life in both beings.) 355

5. No creature is fully itself till it is, like the dandelion, opened in the bloom of pure relationship to the sun, the entire living cosmos.

So we still find ourselves in the tangle of existence and being, a tangle which man has never been able to get out of, except by sacrificing the one to the other. 360 Sacrifice is useless.

The clue to all existence is being. But you can't have being without existence, any more than you can have the dandelion flower without the leaves and the long tap root.

Being is *not* ideal, as Plato would have it: nor spiritual. It is a transcendent 365 form of existence, and as much material as existence is. Only the matter suddenly enters the fourth dimension.

All existence is dual, and surging towards a consummation into being. In the seed of the dandelion, as it floats with its little umbrella of hairs, sits the Holy Ghost in tiny compass. The Holy Ghost is that which holds the light and 370 the dark, the day and the night, the wet and the sunny, united in one little clue. There it sits, in the seed of the dandelion.

The seed falls to earth. The Holy Ghost rouses, saying: *"Come!"* And out of the sky come the rays of the sun, and out of earth come dampness and dark and the death-stuff. They are called in, like those bidden to a feast. The sun sits 375 down at the hearth, inside the seed; and the dark, damp death-returner sits on the opposite side, with the host between. And the host says to them: *"Come! Be merry together!"* So the sun looks with desirous curiosity on the dark face of the earth, and the dark damp one looks with wonder on the bright face of the other, who comes from the sun. And the host says: *"Here you are at home! Lift me up,* 380 *between you, that I may cease to be a Ghost. For it longs me to look out, it longs me to dance with the dancers."*

So the sun in the seed, and the earthy one in the seed take hands, and laugh, and begin to dance. And their dancing is like a fire kindled, a bonfire with leaping flame. And the treading of their feet is like the running of little 385 streams, down into the earth. So from the dance of the sun-in-the-seed with the earthy death-returner, green little flames of leaves shoot up, and hard little trickles of roots strike down. And the host laughs, and says: *"I am being lifted up! Dance harder! Oh wrestle, you two, like wonderful wrestlers, neither of which can win."* So sun-in-the-seed and the death-returner, who is earthy, dance faster and 390 faster and the leaves rising greener begin to dance in a ring above-ground, fiercely overwhelming any outsider, in a whirl of swords and lions' teeth. And the earthy one wrestles, wrestles with the sun-in-the-seed, so the long roots reach down like arms of a fighter gripping the power of earth, and strangles all intruders, strangling any intruder mercilessly. Till the two fall in one strange 395 embrace, and from the centre the long flower-stem lifts like a phallus, budded

with a bud. And out of the bud the voice of the Holy Ghost is heard crying: *"I am lifted up! Lo! I am lifted up! I am here!"* So the bud opens, and there is the flower poised in the very middle of the universe, with a ring of green swords be-
400    low, to guard it, and the octopus, arms deep in earth, drinking and threatening. So the Holy Ghost, being a dandelion flower, looks round, and says: *"Lo! I am yellow! I believe the sun has lent me his body! Lo! I am sappy with golden, bitter blood! I believe death out of the damp black earth has lent me his blood! I am incarnate! I like my incarnation! But this is not all. I will keep this incarnation. It is good! But oh! if I*
405    *can win to another incarnation, who knows how wonderful it will be! This one will have to give place. This one can help to create the next."*
        So the Holy Ghost leaves the clue of himself behind, in the seed, and wanders forth in the comparative chaos of our universe, seeking another incarnation.
410    And this will go on for ever. Man, as yet, is less than half grown. Even his flower-stem has not appeared yet. He is all leaves and roots, without any clue put forth. No sign of bud anywhere.
        Either he will have to start budding, or he will be forsaken of the Holy Ghost: abandoned as a failure in creation, as the ichthyosaurus was abandoned.
415    Being abandoned means losing his vitality. The sun and the earth-dark will cease rushing together in him. Already it is ceasing. To men, the sun is becoming stale, and the earth sterile. But the sun itself will never become stale, nor the earth barren. It is only that the *clue* is missing inside men. They are like flower-less, seedless fat cabbages, nothing inside.
420    Vitality depends upon the clue of the Holy Ghost inside a creature, a man, a nation, a race. When the clue goes, the vitality goes. And the Holy Ghost seeks for ever a new incarnation, and subordinates the old to the new. You will know that any creature or race is still alive with the Holy Ghost, when it can subordinate the lower creatures or races, and assimilate them into a new incarnation.
425    No man, or creature, or race can have vivid vitality unless it be moving towards a blossoming: and the most powerful is that which moves towards the as-yet-unknown blossom.
        Blossoming means the establishing of a pure, *new* relationship with all the cosmos. This is the state of heaven. And it is the state of a flower, a cobra, a
430    jenny-wren in spring, a man when he knows himself royal and crowned with the sun, with his feet gripping the core of the earth.
        This too is the fourth dimension: this state, this mysterious other reality of things in a perfected relationship. It is into this perfected relationship that every straight line curves, as if to some core, passing out of the time-space dimension.
435    But any man, creature, or race moving towards blossoming will have to draw immense supplies of vitality from men, or creatures below, passionate strength. And he will have to accomplish a perfected relation with all things.
        There will be conquest, always. But the aim of conquest is a perfect relation of conquerors with conquered, for a new blossoming. Freedom is illusory.
440    Sacrifice is illusory. Almightiness is illusory. Freedom, sacrifice, almightiness,

these are all human side-tracks, cul-de-sacs, bunk. All that is real is the over-whelmingness of a new inspirational command, a new relationship with all things.

Heaven is always there. No achieved consummation is lost. Procreation goes on for ever, to support the achieved revelation. But the torch of revelation itself is handed on. And this is all important.          445

Everything living wants to procreate more living things.

But more important than this is the fact that every revelation is a torch held out, to kindle new revelations. As the dandelion holds out the sun to me, say-ing: *"Can you take it!"*          450

Every gleam of heaven that is shown—like a dandelion flower, or a green beetle—quivers with strange passion to kindle a new gleam, never yet beheld. This is not self-sacrifice: it is self-contribution: in which the highest happiness lies.

The torch of existence is handed on, in the womb of procreation.          455

And the torch of revelation is handed on, by every living thing, from the protococcus to a brave man or a beautiful woman, handed to whomsoever can take it. He who can take it has power beyond all the rest.

The cycle of procreation exists purely for the keeping alight of the torch of perfection, in any species: the torch being the dandelion in blossom, the tree in          460
full leaf, the peacock in all his plumage, the cobra in all his colour, the frog at full leap, woman in all the mystery of her fathomless desirableness, man in the fulness of his power: every creature become its pure self.

One cycle of perfection urges to kindle another cycle, as yet unknown.

And with the kindling from the torch of revelation comes the inrush of vi-          465
tality, and the need to consume and *consummate* the lower cycles of existence, into a new thing. This consuming and this consummating means conquest, and fearless mastery. Freedom lies in the honourable yielding towards the new flame, and the honourable mastery of that which shall be new, over that which must yield. As I must master my horses, which are in a lower cycle of existence.          470
And they, they are relieved and *happy* to serve. If I turn them loose into the mountain ranges, to run wild till they die, the thrill of real happiness is gone out of their lives.

Every lower order seeks in some measure to serve a higher order: and rebels against being conquered.          475

It is always conquest, and it always will be conquest. If the conquered be an old, declining race, they will have handed on their torch to the conqueror: who will burn his fingers badly, if he is too flippant. And if the conquered be a bar-baric race, they will consume the fire of the conqueror, and leave him flameless, unless he watch it. But it is always conquest, conquered and conqueror, for          480
ever. The Kingdom of heaven is the Kingdom of conquerors, who can serve the conquest for ever, after their own conquest is made.

In heaven, in the perfected relation, is peace: in the fourth dimension. But there is getting there. And that, for ever, is the process of conquest.

485 　　When the rose blossomed, then the great Conquest was made by the Vegetable Kingdom. But even this conqueror of conquerors, the rose, had to lend
himself towards the caterpillar and the butterfly of a later conquest. A conqueror, but tributary to the later conquest.
　　There is no such thing as equality. In the kingdom of heaven, in the fourth
490 dimension, each soul that achieves a perfect relationship with the cosmos, from
its own centre, is perfect, and incomparable. It has no superior. It is a conqueror, and incomparable.
　　But every man, in the struggle of conquest towards his own consummation,
must master the inferior cycles of life, and never relinquish his mastery. Also, if
495 there be men beyond him, moving on to a newer consummation than his own,
he must yield to their greater demand, and serve their greater mystery, and so
be faithful to the kingdom of heaven which is within him, which is gained by
conquest and by loyal service.
　　Any man who achieves his own being will, like the dandelion or the butter-
500 fly, pass into that other dimension which we call the fourth, and the old people
called heaven. It is the state of perfected relationship. And here a man will have
his peace for ever: whether he serve or command, in the process of living.
　　But even this entails his faithful allegiance to the kingdom of heaven, which
must be for ever and for ever extended, as creation conquers chaos. So that my
505 perfection will but serve a perfection which still lies ahead, unrevealed and un-
conceived, and beyond my own.
　　We have tried to build walls round the kingdom of heaven: but it's no
good. It's only the cabbage rotting inside.
　　Our last wall is the golden wall of money. This is a fatal wall. It cuts us off
510 from life, from vitality, from the alive sun and the alive earth, as *nothing* can.
Nothing, not even the most fanatical dogmas of an iron-bound religion, can in-
sulate us from the inrush of life and inspiration, as money can.
　　We are losing vitality: losing it rapidly. Unless we seize the torch of inspiration, and drop our moneybags, the moneyless will be kindled by the flame of
515 flames, and they will consume us like old rags.
　　We are losing vitality, owing to money and money-standards. The torch in
the hands of the moneyless will set our house on fire, and burn us to death, like
sheep in a flaming corral.

## Looking Back

1. What prevents Lawrence from killing the porcupine straight off?
2. Can you discover any connection between his feelings toward the porcupine and the
   wounded dog?
3. Is he bloodthirsty when he says, "One must kill" (line 178), or is this statement
   purely symbolic? Explain your answer.
4. Do you find convincing Lawrence's comparison between human beings and animals
   in the struggle for existence (lines 189–203)? Why or why not?

5. Should we applaud or denounce Lawrence's question and answer in lines 292–294: "*Can thy neighbor finally overcome thee? If he can, then he belongs to a higher level of existence*"? Explain your answer.

6. How does his statement that life is more vivid in himself than in the Mexican wagoneer (lines 306–307) support his later statement that "There is no such thing as equality" (line 489)?

7. Is Lawrence a racist, as we use the term today, or is his meaning more subtle? Explain your answer.

8. How do fullness of being, vitality, and natural superiority produce the "inexorable law of life" mentioned in line 333? (To answer, construct a logical sequence from his numbered statements in lines 334–358.)

9. What political ideas might result from Lawrence's ideas about freedom, equality, sacrifice, "inspirational command" (line 442), mastery, and willingness to serve?

10. How do you interpret Lawrence's closing argument that money drains the vitality of human beings in their relationship to the cosmos?

## *Writing Assignments*

1. Robert Lowell, in a poem about being jailed as a conscientious objector during World War II, describes a fellow inmate who was "so vegetarian he wore rope shoes and preferred fallen fruit" ("Memories of West Street and Lepke"). Not all vegetarians carry matters this far, of course, but all by definition avoid eating meat, and many extend their dietary restrictions to eggs, poultry, and fish. Their motives range from nutrition to tender-heartedness to ideas of equality between "higher" and "lower" animals. Addressing the last-named motive, D. H. Lawrence mocks the vegetarian Buddhist in particular and states explicitly, "In nature, one creature devours another, and this is an essential part of all existence and all being" (lines 263–264). The word *all* includes human beings in this description, and the word *essential* implies that they should be included. Is Lawrence right? Write an essay taking the position either of Lawrence or of vegetarianism on the subject of eating other creatures. Imagine an audience composed of people whose persuasion is opposite from yours.

2. A formal belief in equality characterizes the political structure of the United States and of most other countries in the world. The modifier *formal* is important. It indicates that in some cases governments give only lip-service to equality, the practice being far different from the theory. And in some other cases, hierarchies are so entrenched that the people need to struggle constantly to achieve equality. However, for those who do believe in equality, its less-than-total presence is infinitely preferable to its complete absence—as in such states as Nazi Germany in contemporary times and many others that are ancient history. It is difficult to discuss equality without thinking in political and social terms, and these of course can extend to matters of religion, race, and ethnic origin, as well as to gender and sexual orientation. These concerns crop up when we encounter a remark like Lawrence's, "There is no such thing as equality" (line 489, and see number 6 in Looking Back). Are his ideas about equality destructive? Write an essay giving your view of Lawrence's po-

sition on equality. Begin by presenting the thinking that supports it, and end by saying what the likely consequences of agreeing or disagreeing with him would be.

3. Toward the end of his essay, Lawrence points out the need always to seek new fulfillments of "being," new and richer relationships with the created world that will ensure the growth of vitality. He complains, however, that we resist breaking out of our shell and expanding our horizons; we establish safe, narrow limits and stop at them; we build walls. One of these is "the golden wall of money" (line 509). Because Lawrence doesn't develop this topic very much, the commentary, including acceptance or rejection of his idea, is left to the reader. Write an essay interpolating your explanations of how money, as an individual's dominant aim in life, may prevent that person from going beyond himself or herself toward a greater, more fulfilling life. Or, in disagreement with Lawrence, give your explanation of how money can produce such fulfillment. Be as explicit as you can by defining what you take the fulfilled life to be and by describing how money can build either a barricade against it or a bridge to it.

# IV

## *Social Reality*

A n important theory of the self is that it is a social construction. That is, the individual's position in society is what ultimately shapes him or her. Obviously, the theory is broader than this brief definition, but our interest here is in its implication about society, namely that social reality is the most pressing and powerful reality.

Social structures have an undeniable impact on our lives. They have always had this, but now it seems overwhelming at times, as if the individual were no longer a deciding factor in social relations, but a product of them.

Nonetheless, however powerless he sometimes feels, the individual usually struggles out from under this unwelcome burden to persist as an agent of change in social structures. As such, he becomes an enduring theme of social analysis. You will meet that theme in this section of readings and thereby confront the individual in an expanding context. You will meet other themes and topics as well: institutions, groups, work, crime, politics, race, cities, and more. A list of social structures could include virtually every category in which ties exist between sizeable numbers of persons, joined together with or without their say-so. For instance, police and criminals are examples of separate yet linked interests out of which, as out of most social concerns, burning issues arise.

Think, for instance, of such issues as police brutality, welfare dependency, housing the homeless, or condom distribution in schools. As these examples make clear, it is difficult to mention "social reality" without adding "problems." Yet these are merely contemporary instances of what has always existed in different forms. Conflicting interests, the need for cooperative adjustments, the use of space and other scarce resources, and relationships between the dispensers and consumers of goods are types of problems that have always existed in proportion to the size and complexity of a given society.

Is the structure of society itself a problem? The question points to the dynamic interrelationships of people who live in an organized fashion in groups and who must deal with change. Societies are always shifting, though often in hidden ways, like tectonic plates under the surface of the earth. Even when

356 IV: Social Reality

everything seems settled, one group will change its political or cultural location, to see its interests differently, and by so doing will affect the interests and locations of contiguous groups.

The individual not only witnesses these movements but also participates in them by congregating with others in cities and towns, suburbs and villages, and seeking to be a part of a significant whole without losing sight of herself. She is a social being with a private life who sometimes goes public in order to ensure general recognition of the rights of the individual and a continued respect for autonomy. Perhaps in the "most real" social reality each of us stands alone and together at once.

As you read the selections that follow, keep these considerations in mind:

1. Although social forces seem to have a life unto themselves, and often are referred to as if they did, they originate partially as ideas that people put into practice, and as these readings make clear, people can have new ideas.

2. Social context is crucial to understanding. The particular environment, the history of a social group, the pressures for and against change, all contribute heavily to the meaning of events and either support or undermine the cogency of ideas.

3. Issues arise at every turn in every social setting. The need to decide issues points up the problematic relations of social groupings. To perceive the real issue, which is often disguised or not wholly apparent, is to grasp much of social reality.

# PRIMARY TEXTS

**Society** is now clear in two main senses: as our most general term for the body of institutions and relationships within which a relatively large group of people live; and as our most abstract term for the condition in which such institutions and relationships are formed. The interest of the word is partly in the often dif-
5 ficult relationship between the generalization and the abstraction. It is mainly in the historical development which allows us to say "institutions and relationships", and we can best realize this when we remember that the primary meaning of **society** was companionship or fellowship.

**Society** came into English in C14 from fw *société*, oF, *societas*, L, rw *socius*,
10 L—companion.[1] Its uses to mC16 ranged from active unity in fellowship, as in the Peasants' Revolt of 1381, through a sense of general relationship—"they have neede one of anothers helpe, and thereby love and soietie . . . growe

---

1. *C* means century; *fw* means French word; *oF* means Old French; *L* means Latin; *m* means mid; *l* means late. (*ed.*)

among all men the more" (1581) to a simpler sense of companionship or company—"your society" (1C16). An example from 1563, "society between Christ and us," shows how readily these distinguishable senses might in practice overlap. The tendency towards the general and abstract sense thus seems inherent, but until 1C18 the other more active and immediate senses were common. The same range can be seen in two examples from Shakespeare. In "my Riots past, my wilde Societies" (*Merry Wives of Windsor*, III, iv) **society** was virtually equivalent to relationship or to one of our senses of *associations*, whereas in "our Selfe will mingle with Society" (*Macbeth*, III, iv) the sense is simply that of an assembled company of guests. The sense of a deliberate association for some purpose (here of social distinction) can be illustrated by the "societe of saynct George" (the Order of the Garter, C15), and over a very wide range this particular use has persisted.

The general sense can be seen as strengthening from mC16. It was intermediate in "the yearth untilled, societie neglected" (1553) but clear though still not separate in "a common wealth is called a society or common doing of a multitude of free men" (1577). It was clear and separate in "societie is an assemblie and consent of many in one" (1599), and in C17 such uses began to multiply, and with a firmer reference: "a due reverence . . . towards Society wherein we live" (1650). Yet the early history was still evident in "the Laws of Society and Civil Conversation" (Charles I, 1642; *conversation*, here, had its earliest sense of mode of living, before additional (C16) familiar discourse; the same experience was working in this word, but with an eventually opposite specialization). The abstract sense also strengthened: "the good of Humane Society" (Cudworth, 1678) and "to the benefit of society" (1749). In one way the abstraction was made more complete by the development of the notion of "a society," in the broadest sense. This depended on a new sense of relativism but, in its transition from the notion of the general laws of fellowship or association to a notion of specific laws forming a specific society, it prepared the way for the modern notion, in which the laws of society are not so much laws for getting on with other people but more abstract and more impersonal laws which determine social institutions.

The transition was very complex, but can now be best seen by considering **society** with *state*. State had developed, from its most general and continuing sense of condition (*state of nature, state of siege*, from C13), a specialized sense which was virtually interchangeable with *estate* (both *state* and *estate* were from fw *estat*, oF, *status*, L—condition) and in effect with rank: "noble stat" (1290). The word was particularly associated with monarchy and nobility, that is to say with a hierarchical ordering of society: cf: "state of prestis, and state of knyghtis, and the thridd is staat of comunys" (1300). The *States* or *Estates* were an institutional definition of power from C14, while *state* as the dignity of the king was common in C16 and eC17: "state and honour" (1544); "goes with great state" (1616); "to the King . . . your Crowne and State" (Bacon, 1605). From these combined uses *state* developed a conscious political sense: "ruler of the state"

(1538); "the State of Venice" (1680). But *state* still often meant the association of a particular kind of sovereignty with a particular kind of rank. *Statist* was a common term for politician in C17, but through the political conflicts of that century a fundamental conflict came to be expressed in what was eventually a distinction between **society** and *state*: the former an association of free men, drawing on all the early active senses; the latter an organization of power, drawing on the senses of hierarchy and majesty. The crucial notion of **civil society** was an alternative definition of social order, and it was in thinking through the general questions of this new order that **society** was confirmed in its most general and eventually abstract senses. Through many subsequent political changes this kind of distinction has persisted: **society** is that to which we all belong, even if it is also very general and impersonal; the *state* is the apparatus of power.

The decisive transition of **society** towards its most general and abstract sense (still, by definition, a different thing from *state*) was an C18 development. I have been through Hume's *Enquiry Concerning the Principles of Morals* (1751) for uses of the word, and taking "company of his fellows" as sense (i) and "system of common life" as sense (ii) found: sense (i), 25; sense (ii), 110; but also, at some critical points in the argument, where the sense of **society** can be decisive, sixteen essentially intermediate uses. Hume also, as it happens, illustrates the necessary distinction as **society** was losing its most active and immediate sense; he used, as we still would, the alternative *company:*

> As the mutual shocks in *society,* and the oppositions of interest and self-love, have constrained mankind to establish the laws of justice . . . in like manner, the eternal contrarieties, in *company,* of men's pride and self-conceit, have introduced the rules of *Good Manners* or *Politeness* . . . (*Enquiry,* VIII, 211)

At the same time, in the same book, he used **society** for *company* in just this immediate sense, where we now, wishing for some purposes to revive the old sense, would speak of "face-to-face" relationships; usually, we would add, within a COMMUNITY.

By 1C18 **society** as a system of common life was predominant: "every society has more to apprehend from its needy members than from the rich" (1770); "two different schemes or systems of morality" are current at the same time in "every society where the distinction of rank has once been established" (Adam Smith, *Wealth of Nations,* **II**, 378–9; 1776). The subsequent development of both general and abstract senses was direct.

A related development can be seen in **social**, which in C17 could mean either associated or sociable, but by 1C18 was mainly general and abstract: "man is a Social creature; that is, a single man, or family, cannot subsist, or not well, alone out of all Society," . . . (though note that **Society** here, with the qualification *all,* is still active rather than abstract). By C19 **society** can be seen clearly enough as an object to allow such formations as **social reformer** (although **social** was also used, and is still used, to describe personal company; cf. **social life** and **social evening**). At the same time, in seeing **society** as an object (the objective sum of our relationships) it was possible, in new ways, to define the relationship of **man and society** or **the individual and society** as a problem. These formations measure the distance from the early sense of active fellowship. The problems they indicate, in the actual development of society, were signifi-cantly illustrated in the use of the word **social**, in eC19, to contrast an idea of   105 **society** as mutual co-operation with an experience of **society** (the **social system**) as individual competition. These alternative definitions of society could not have occurred if the most general and abstract sense had not, by this period, been firm. It was from this emphasis of **social**, in a positive rather than a neutral sense, and in distinction from INDIVIDUAL, that the political term SOCIALIST was to   110 develop.

One small specialized use of **society** requires notice if not comment. An early sense of **good society** in the sense of good company was specialized, by the norms of such people, to **Society** as the most distinguished and fashionable part of **society**: the *upper* CLASS. Byron (*Don Juan*, XIII, 95) provides a good ex-   115 ample of this mainly C19 (and residual) sense:

> Society is now one polish'd horde
> Formed of two mighty tribes, the *Bores* and *Bored.*

It is ironic that this special term is the last clear use of **society** as the active com-panionship of one's (class) fellows. Elsewhere such feelings were moving, for good   120 historical reasons, to COMMUNITY, and to the still active senses of **social.**

—Raymond Williams, from *Keywords*

Moreover, if I wanted to describe the differing ideas of justice, and the divergent institutions and customs and ways of life, that have prevailed, not only in vari-ous nations of the world, but even in this single city of our own, I could show you, also, that they have not remained the same, but have been changed in a thousand different ways. Take for example Manius Manilius here, our inter-   5 preter of the law. The advice that he generally gave you about women's legacies and inheritance when he was a young man, before the Voconian Law was passed, was not at all the same advice as he would give you now. (Yet that law, I might add, was passed for the benefit of males, and is very unfair to women. For why should a woman not have money of her own? And why should a Vestal   10 Virgin be permitted to have an heir, when her mother cannot? Nor can I see why, if a limit had to be set to the amount of property a woman could possess, the daughter of Publius Licinius Crassus Dives Mucianus, provided that she were her father's only child, should be authorized by law to own a hundred mil-lion *sesterces,* while three million is more than my own daughter is entitled to   15 own.) . . .

So laws, then, can vary considerably, and can be changed. If they had all come from God, that would not be so. For, in that case, the same laws would be

applicable to all, and, besides, a man would not be bound by one law at one
20 time of his life and by another later on. But what I ask, therefore, is this. Let us
accept that it is the duty of a just and good man to obey the laws. But *which* laws
is he to obey? All the different laws that exist?

There are difficulties here. Inconsistency, between laws, ought to be impermissible, since it is contrary to what nature demands. But the point is that laws
25 are *not* imposed on us by nature—or by our innate sense of justice. They are imposed by the fear of being penalized. In other words, human beings are not just,
by nature, at all.

Let us reject, moreover, the argument that, although laws vary, good men
naturally follow the true, authentic path of justice, and not merely what is
30 thought to be just. That argument maintains that what a good and just man
does is to give everyone his due. (One problem which arises in this connection
is what, if anything, we are to grant *dumb animals* as their due. Men of far from
mediocre calibre, indeed men of powerful learning such as Pythagoras and
Empedocles, insist that identical standards of justice apply to all living crea-
35 tures, and declare that inexorable penalties await those who ill-treat animals. To
do them harm, in other words, seems to them to be criminal.)

—Cicero, from *On Government*

In the dispute between realism and utopianism, the arguments against the latter
have been formulated so often and in such detail that I need not repeat them. I
shall, however, submit some "antirealist" propositions which for certain reasons
seem especially significant.
5 These premises are the following:

FIRST ASSUMPTION: *ethical individualism. Only human beings and their deeds
are subject to moral judgment.* There can be no moral evaluation without consideration of the intentions of the acting agent, and intentions can be ascribed only
to men. From this, in turn, one must infer that it is impossible to evaluate
10 morally the good or bad results of an anonymous historical process. It is equally
impossible to make a moral assessment, in the strict sense of the word, of a
group or social class, if by a social class we mean—and this definition seems to
us appropriate—not only a collection of individuals but a social "entity," a body
which behaves in such a way that the reactions of the human elements which
15 compose it are governed by the class as a whole and not vice versa.

It is important to stress that this does not imply that membership in a specific class or group—and, in general, this rather than any other kind of dependence in which every individual finds himself vis-à-vis the society in which he
lives—is not decisive in determining both his moral opinions and the part of his
20 behavior which is subject to moral judgment and which has been very differently circumscribed over the centuries. On the contrary, we assume hypotheti-
cally—although we lack sufficient proof—that this determination is absolute.

(I mean social determination and not determination resulting exclusively from membership in a class.) And we formulate this as our:

SECOND ASSUMPTION: *determinism.*   Opinions about good and evil and about the morality of people's behavior are determined by the way an individual participates in society. Under "participation" we include upbringing and the influence of tradition, as well as membership in all the social groups from whose confluence arises that unique thing called personality. (Of course tradition is also a social group, namely, a totality of people who remain within the sphere of influence of a given form of consciousness shaped before their time.)

We shall not dwell here on such questions as what share different forms of social life have in the molding of moral views; how many stem from universal aspects of social life and therefore assume an "elementary" nature of universal validity; how many derive from conditions particular to a class society and thus acquire, in any case, extreme longevity; and finally, which ones result from membership in a specific class, in a profession, and so on. (These questions summarize the main problems of the sociology of morality and, as such, lie outside the framework of this essay.)

Although many moralists hold these two assumptions to be contradictory, we maintain they are not. There is no logical contradiction between social determinism even more rigorously conceived than in our usage of the term, and the acceptance of moral responsibility. This results from the next premise:

THIRD ASSUMPTION: *the humanistic interpretation of values.*   Although a given person may accept the fact that his moral values and behavior are determined, nevertheless he cannot infer from his knowledge of the conditions that determine him any conclusions concerning the truth or falseness of values he has accepted. In other words, the fact that a person knows he judges something to be good or bad because specific circumstances inclined him to do so does not mean that this something is good or bad. Everyone has moral opinions, but he cannot justify them by claiming they result from certain ascertainable outside causes. Furthermore, to state that an individual can be judged morally means that *the right to judge him* has been given to others. This is a normative statement and consequently its negation is also normative. Thus when we affirm that the principle of determinism, which is a theoretical formula, proves that moral responsibility is impossible, we tacitly assume that moral values can be deduced from purely theoretical propositions. If we reject the possibility of this deduction, we are forced to admit that the question of determinism or nondeterminism of human activity has no logical connection with the confirmation or denial of man's moral responsibility, for neither the affirmation nor the denial is a theoretical proposition. In this manner our third assumption removes the supposed contradiction between our first two.

The third premise, therefore, would let us keep the concept of moral responsibility completely independent of our knowledge, or rather our postulates, about social or any other determination of human behavior, even if that knowledge were incomparably greater than it now is. Actually, it is rather meager in regard to individual cases, though it may be verifiable in general on a broad scale.

70    To say that an individual is morally responsible for his actions implies that his social environment has the right to make a moral evaluation of his acts and to approve or disapprove. It further implies that the environment is aware of this right. These reactions are determined as the very act to which they apply. To deny society this right is to judge its reactions morally and therefore to act in

75    a manner proscribed by the content of our action, in other words, to fall into a practical contradiction. We would then find ourselves in the situation of a Carthusian prior who loudly berates his brethren for breaking the vow of silence, or of someone who asks the death penalty for all who demand that the death penalty be retained.

—Leszek Kolakowski, from *Toward a Marxist Humanism*

# Laurie Anderson

## Politics & Music

Laurie Anderson (b. 1947) is a performance artist—a singer, poet, and musician—based in New York City. Her longer works include *U.S.A.* and *Empty Places;* this piece is an excerpt from the latter. Among her best-known albums are *Big Science, Mister Heartbreak,* and *Strange Angels.* Anderson's chief subject matter is American society, particularly its bizarre juxtapositions, its shams and illusions, but also its missing persons—individuals looking high and low for the place where they belong. Although social **satires** such as "Politics & Music" often employ direct language, their aims are indirect: to caricature reality in order to restore a lost but proper way of seeing it and to inspire people to act differently.

### Looking Ahead

1. Because this was originally a performance piece, read it aloud as speech (or even sing it!). Spoken language has different characteristics from written language, a distinction you should try to become aware of here.

2. Since even songs may employ reason, test this song as you read it for the ideas Anderson's logic produces.

3. This piece seems to end without truly concluding. The significance of the last words is their startling accuracy as comment on all the political leaders who figure here, not just on the last named. This type of sweeping commentary is a function of many hanging conclusions.

Good evening.
Tonight's topics are politics and music.
Now there are those who say that politics and art
just don't mix.
But before we begin, I just want to say a word about                    5
Sonny Bono. I mean the guy bothers me.
Ever since he was elected mayor
of Palm Springs,
it seems like singing politicians are everywhere.

I do have to say, however, I was happy to learn                         10
that the singer Alice Cooper is still running
for office and he's got a really great slogan.
His slogan is:

**"A troubled man
for troubled times."**                                                   15

Now he's got my vote on that slogan alone.

But of course now that so many singers
are doing politics,
a lot of politicians are starting to sing.
And lately it's been a really great time to study                       20
the political art song format.

I mean, just how do people convince each other of things
that are basically quite preposterous?
It's an art form. Listen carefully, and you discover these aren't speeches at all—
but quite sophisticated musical compositions.                           25

Now take a guy like Hitler. You listen to his speeches.
They're all rhythm—no pitch. I mean Hitler was a drummer.
A really good drummer.
And he'd always start with a really simple
kick/snare idea. You know:                                              30

**BOOM CHICK! BOOM CHICK!
BOOM CHICK! BOOM CHICK!!**

He'd lay down this really solid groove and people would start—
moving to it.
And then he'd add a few variations:                                     35

**BABABA BOOM CHICK
BABABA BOOM CHICK
BABACHICK BOOM CHICK!!**

And then he'd take a really wild solo and they'd all be yelling and dancing.
YEAH!                                                                   40
Now don't forget these were the people who invented the Christmas tree.

So in their minds, see, there's this fir tree out in the forest and they say:
YA! This tree must be inside the house!
We must go get it and bring it *inside* the house.

45    Inside! Inside!

They've got this thing about nature
and it's the same with music.
They've got to *do* something with it.
They've got to bring it on home.

50    So they're stomping and movin and groovin
and their feet are all synched up to those drums
and they're moving like one giant thing.
And pretty soon they've got to go somewhere
they've got to get out

55    they've got to go someplace
like Poland.

Or take Mussolini. You listen to his speeches.
And he's singing grand opera.
Doing all the parts. And he's hitting all those hard-to-reach

60    high notes.
**FRONTIERE! FRONTIERE!**
He was always singing about the frontier.
And all those fans with their ham sandwiches
up in the third mezzanine are going nuts

65    and it goes on for hours and hours.
Yeah, they go wild, those opera fans!

But of course the all-time American master of this art form was
Ron Reagan. And when Reagan wanted to make a point,
he would lean right into the mic

70    and get softer
and softer
until he was talking like
this.
And the more important it was,

75    the softer
and the more intimate
it would get.

With lots . . . .
and lots . . . . . . . . . of . . . . .

80    pauses.
Like he was trying to remember something that happened
a long time ago.
But he could never really *quite* put his
finger on it.

And when he talked
he was singing to you.
And what he was singing was

85

**"When You Wish
Upon a Star."**

## Looking Back

1. Why does announcing the topics seem odd in the context of this piece (see line 2)?
2. How does the sentence "I mean the guy bothers me" (line 6) demonstrate a characteristic that distinguishes speech from writing?
3. Would Alice Cooper's slogan (lines 14–15) get your vote too? Why or why not?
4. What verbal sleight of hand early in this piece allows Anderson to envision Hitler, Mussolini, and Reagan as singers?
5. Look up the word *drummer* (line 27) in a dictionary. What meaning other than "player of a musical instrument" do you find? How does this meaning tie in with Anderson's description of political speeches in lines 22–23?
6. How does Anderson's Christmas tree comment (line 41) strike you?
7. What specific criticism does Anderson aim at the Germans (see lines 39–56)?
8. What do you know about opera singing that sheds light on Anderson's description of Mussolini's speeches (line 57–66)?
9. How do the performance aspects of this piece become particularly evident in the remarks on former president Reagan?
10. What does the closing quotation imply about Reagan? About the author's attitude toward all politicians?

## Writing Assignments

1. Satirizing political speeches in order to criticize their use of emotional persuasion, Anderson particularly targets Ronald Reagan. In one campaign speech, Reagan declared "It's morning in America." A somewhat distant echo of this image appears in a speech by Ross Perot, as reported by *The New York Times* on July 9, 1992:

> Can we agree that we have work to do? Is there anybody here that's not willing to put his or her shoulder to the wheel and do it? Is there anybody here that can live with the fact that we are no longer the No. 1 economic superpower in the world? Is there any question in your minds that if we get off our seats and get in the ring, you and I can make the words "made in the U.S.A." once again the world standard for excellence?
>
> Is there any reason, as someone in the audience says, we don't need any morning glories that wilt by noon. I agree with that. Is there any reason we cannot outcrank, outcreate, and outwork anybody anywhere in the world, and beat them in economic competition?

Write an essay that analyzes Perot's language and its appeal to the emotions. What would be the probable response of his hearers? Do you see any intellectual content in the passage? What social value exists in political speeches built on emotional persuasion?

2. In the United States, an enormous proportion of registered voters stay home on election day. They cite different reasons for their refusal to vote—including despair over politicians—but one point of view holds that voting is the duty of *all* citizens who are of age, that it is irresponsible not to vote. What do you think? Write an essay arguing a position on voting as a civic duty. Consider the reasons that people do and do not vote. Should people be fined for not voting or, on the other hand, rewarded in some way for showing up at the polls? If you voted or decided not to in the last national election, refer in your essay to your own reasons. Conceive of your audience as people trying to decide whether to vote.

3. The fact that Anderson's culprits—Hitler, Mussolini, and Reagan—all are men brings up a question that increasingly Americans are asking: Would women be better office-holders than men? In the United States, women number over half of the population but make up only 5.8 percent of lawmakers in Congress; thus, the issue is equity. But we also wonder whether women would lie to us less and avoid war more, and whether in general they have qualities men lack that would be preferable in politics. Write an essay addressing the proposition that women would make better political leaders than men.

# Linked Readings

### Pauline Kael   Robert Gard   Chance Stoner
### CAMPUS LIFE (THE 1930s)

### Students for a Democratic Society
### THE PORT HURON STATEMENT (1962)

### Nicola Chiaromonte
### THE STUDENT REVOLT (1968)

As the above dates indicate, each linked piece has its origin in a specific historical period. Even the two 1960s dates point to dramatically different times in a decade that changed almost from one moment to the next. Documenting history is an important task, but here we benefit from another function of looking backward: the critical thinking function of discovering ideas and comprehending actions in their original context so we can apply them to our knowledge of present-day society. In these readings, the key topics are the social consciousness and political activism of college students.

Pauline Kael is a one-time movie critic for *The New Yorker* and the author of several books on film; Robert Gard is a professor of drama at the University of Wisconsin; Chance Stoner is a Wall Street financial consultant. Students for a Democratic Society (SDS), a political organization whose title reveals its aims, was founded in 1960 and was especially active during the Vietnam War. This piece was drawn up at its first convention, at Port Huron, Michigan, a town on Lake Huron. Nicola Chiaromonte (1901–1972) was an Italian literary and social critic. Having fled both Italian fascism and German Nazism, he fought in the Spanish Civil War, lived for a time in the United States, and eventually returned to Italy in the late 1940s.

# CAMPUS LIFE

## *Looking Ahead*

1. These recollections are part of an oral history of the Great Depression of the 1930s. See if you can detect how transcribed speech is frequently less perfected than writing, yet usually seems more natural.

2. Keep in mind the contrast between these authors' earlier political radicalism and their later conventional success in mainstream society. Ask yourself if the contrast affects your reading.

3. Try to perceive the relationship sketched here between poverty and deprivation on one hand and activism and revolt on the other.

When I attended Berkeley[1] in 1936, so many of the kids had actually lost their fathers. They had wandered off in disgrace because they couldn't support their families. Other fathers had killed themselves, so the family could have the insurance. Families had totally broken down. Each father took it as his personal failure. These middle-class men apparently had no social sense of what was going on, so they killed themselves.   5

It was still the Depression. There were kids who didn't have a place to sleep, huddling under bridges on the campus. I had a scholarship, but there were times when I didn't have food. The meals were often three candy bars. We lived communally and I remember feeding other kids by cooking up more   10 spaghetti than I can ever consider again.

There was an embarrassment at college where a lot of the kids were well-heeled. I still have a resentment against the fraternity boys and the sorority girls with their cashmere sweaters and the pearls. Even now, when I lecture at colleges, I have this feeling about those terribly overdressed kids. It wasn't a hatred   15 because I wanted these things, but because they didn't understand what was going on.

I was a reader for seven courses a semester, and I made $50 a month. I think I was the only girl on the labor board at Berkeley. We were trying to get the minimum wage on the campus raised to forty cents an hour. These   20 well-dressed kids couldn't understand our interest. There was a real division between the poor who were trying to improve things on the campus and the rich kids who didn't give a damn.

---

1. *Berkeley:* that is, the University of California at Berkeley. (*ed.*)

Berkeley was a cauldron in the late Thirties. You no sooner enrolled than
25   you got an invitation from the Trotskyites and the Stalinists.[2] Both were wooing
you. I enrolled at sixteen, so it was a little overpowering at the time. I remember
joining the Teachers Assistants Union. We had our own version of Mario Savio.[3]
He's now a lawyer specializing in bankruptcies. We did elect a liberal as president of the student body. It was a miracle in those days.

30       The fraternity boys often acted as strikebreakers in San Francisco—the athletes and the engineering students. And the poor boys were trying to get their
forty cents an hour. The college administration could always count on the frat
boys to put down any student movement.

It's different today, the fraternities and sororities having so much less
35   power. . . .

[Pauline Kael]


I set out for the University of Kansas on a September morning with $30 that I'd
borrowed from my local bank. I had one suit and one necktie and one pair of
shoes. My mother had spent several days putting together a couple of wooden
cases of canned fruits and vegetables. My father, a country lawyer, had taken as
5   a legal fee a 1915 Buick touring car. It was not in particularly good condition,
but it was good enough to get me there. It fell to pieces and it never got back
home anymore.

I had no idea how long the $30 would last, but it sure would have to go a
long way because I had nothing else. The semester fee was $22, so that left me
10   $8 to go. Fortunately, I got a job driving a car for the dean of the law school.
That's how I got through the first year.

What a pleasure it was to get a pound of hamburger, which you could buy
for about five cents, take it up to the Union Pacific Railroad tracks and have a
cookout. And some excellent conversation. And maybe swim in the Kaw River.

15       One friend of mine came to college equipped. He had an old Model T Ford
Sedan, about a 1919 model. He had this thing fitted up as a house. He lived in it
all year long. He cooked and slept and studied inside that Model T Ford Sedan.
How he managed I will never know. I once went there for dinner. He cooked a
pretty good one on a little stove he had in this thing. He was a brilliant student.
20   I don't know where he is now, but I shouldn't be surprised if he's the head of
some big corporation. (Laughs.) Survival. . . .

The weak ones, I don't suppose, really survived. There were many break-
downs. From malnutrition very likely. I know there were students actually
starving.

25       Some of them engaged in strange occupations. There was a biological company that would pay a penny apiece for cockroaches. They needed these in re-

---

2. *Trotskyites:* followers of Leon Trotsky (1879–1940), a leader of the 1917 Russian Revolution who was exiled and later assassinated; *Stalinists:* adherents to the ideology of Joseph Stalin
(1879–1953), Communist dictator of the Soviet Union from the 1920s until his death (*ed.*).
3. *Mario Savio:* student leader of the Free Speech Movement at Berkeley during the 1960s. (*ed.*)

search, I guess. Some students went cockroach hunting every night. They'd box 'em and sell them to this firm.

I remember the feverish intellectual discussion we had. There were many new movements. On the literary scene, there was something called the Proletarian Novel. There was the Federal Theater and the Living Newspaper.[4] For the first time, we began to get socially conscious. We began to wonder about ourselves and our society.

We were mostly farm boys and, to some extent, these ideas were alien to us. We had never really thought about them before. But it was a period of necessity. It brought us face to face with these economic problems and the rest. . . . All in all, a painful time, but a glorious time.

[Robert Gard]

*I actually in my own life did not see any difference between the Twenties and the Thirties. I was living in a small Virginia town, and it was poverty-stricken. You had five thousand rural bank failures in the Twenties. . . . My father was a typewriter salesman who did the best he could. . . .*

They gave me a $100 scholarship to the University of Virginia. That's in 1931, which was damn good. And my mother gave me $100. I had a pair of khaki pants, a pair of sneakers and a khaki shirt. That was it.

The first year on the campus, I organized a Marxist study class. The students fell into two groups. About nine hundred of them had automobiles. About nine hundred had jobs or scholarships. The other nine hundred fell in between. We had real class warfare. The automobile boys and the fraternities—we had thirty-three little Greek palaces on fraternity row—they had charge of the student government. So I organized the other nine hundred, and we took the student government away from them and rewrote the constitution.

I spent half my time on radical activities. I was trying to organize a union in Charlottesville—and bringing Negroes to speak on the campus. We had the first black man to speak there since Reconstruction.[5] He was an old Socialist.

This threw the dean into a fit. He still believed in slavery. He forbade the use of any university building. I was then writing a weekly column for the campus paper. So I attacked the dean: "What manner of small-minded men have inherited Mr. Jefferson's university?" (Laughs.) It was reprinted all over the Eastern seaboard. On the front pages of newspapers, including *The New York Times*. (Laughs.)

The president sent for me. He had a stack five inches high of clippings. He said, "Now look what you've done." (Laughs.) I said, "It's not my fault. The man's been properly invited, he's qualified and he's going to speak at the

30

35

5

10

15

20

---

4. *Proletarian . . . Newspaper:* Government-financed cultural activities for unemployed artists and other professionals. (*ed.*)

5. *Reconstruction:* the political and social rebuilding of the South after the Civil War. (*ed.*)

Episcopal Church chapel." The dean was one of the deacons of the church. So we had quite a time of it.

25 There were writings on the sidewalk of the university: "Down With Imperialistic War. Scholarships Not Battleships." Again I was invited to the president's office. He asked me if I couldn't stop people from writing all over the sidewalk. I said to him: We're perfectly willing to abide by a general rule. If the secret societies and fraternities aren't permitted to write on the steps or sidewalks, we

30 won't either. So he walked me to the window and outside in great purple letters was the slogan: "Down With Imperialist War." He said, "Couldn't you *please* at least get the spelling right?" (Laughs.)

In 1935, we had the first official shutdown of all university classes for a peace demonstration. Guess who the featured speaker was? J. B. Matthews. He

35 later ran the Un-American Activities Committee, as staff director for Martin Dies.[6] He was the man who invented the complete file and cross-reference system, and the theory of associations and fronts and all the rest of it. A very remarkable fella. He started out as a Protestant minister, came to socialism and wound up with Martin Dies. Joe McCarthy[7] was impossible without J. B.

40 Matthews. And we shut down the university for him. . . . Oh, well. . . .

I was a troublemaker then. (Laughs.) I wish I still were.

[Chance Stoner]

## THE PORT HURON STATEMENT

### Looking Ahead

1. It might be useful to list in one column SDS's particular criticisms of existing institutions and practices and, in a second column, its recommendations for change.

2. As you read, see if you can apply any of these political ideas to the current situation on your campus or in society at large.

3. The term *Negro,* the exclusive use of the masculine pronoun, and references to the Cold War as a current threat have all become outmoded since this document was drafted. See if the *reasons* they are now obsolete affect your reading.

## Introduction: Agenda for a Generation

We are people of this generation, bred in at least modest comfort, housed now in universities, looking uncomfortably to the world we inherit.

When we were kids the United States was the wealthiest and strongest country in the world; the only one with the atom bomb, the least scarred by

---

6. *Martin Dies:* chair of the U.S. House of Representatives committee that investigated so-called subversive political organizations in the 1950s. (*ed.*)

7. *Joseph McCarthy* (1908–1957): U.S. senator and communist hunter whose name is synonymous with political persecution. (*ed.*)

modern war, an initiator of the United Nations that we thought would distrib-  5
ute Western influence throughout the world. Freedom and equality for each
individual, government of, by, and for the people—these American values we
found good, principles by which we could live as men. Many of us began maturing in complacency.

As we grew, however, our comfort was penetrated by events too troubling  10
to dismiss. First, the permeating and victimizing fact of human degradation,
symbolized by the Southern struggle against racial bigotry, compelled most of
us from silence to activism. Second, the enclosing fact of the Cold War, symbolized by the presence of the Bomb, brought awareness that we ourselves, and our
friends, and millions of abstract "others" we knew more directly because of our  15
common peril, might die at any time. We might deliberately ignore, or avoid, or
fail to feel all other human problems, but not these two, for these were too immediate and crushing in their impact, too challenging in the demand that we as
individuals take the responsibility for encounter and resolution.

While these and other problems either directly oppressed us or rankled our  20
consciences and became our own subjective concerns, we began to see complicated and disturbing paradoxes in our surrounding America. The declaration
"all men are created equal . . ." rang hollow before the facts of Negro life in the
South and the big cities of the North. The proclaimed peaceful intentions of the
United States contradicted its economic and military investments in the Cold  25
War status quo.

We witnessed, and continue to witness, other paradoxes. With nuclear energy whole cities can easily be powered, yet the dominant nation-states seem
more likely to unleash destruction greater than that incurred in all wars of human
history. Although our own technology is destroying old and creating new forms  30
of social organization, men still tolerate meaningless work and idleness. While
two-thirds of mankind suffers undernourishment, our own upper classes revel
amidst superfluous abundance. Although world population is expected to double
in forty years, the nations still tolerate anarchy as a major principle of international conduct and uncontrolled exploitation governs the sapping of the earth's  35
physical resources. Although mankind desperately needs revolutionary leadership, America rests in national stalemate, its goals ambiguous and tradition-
bound instead of informed and clear, its democratic system apathetic and manipulated rather than "of, by, and for the people."

Not only did tarnish appear on our image of American virtue, not only did  40
disillusion occur when the hypocrisy of American ideals was discovered, but we
began to sense that what we had originally seen as the American Golden Age
was actually the decline of an era. The worldwide outbreak of revolution against
colonialism and imperialism, the entrenchment of totalitarian states, the menace of war, overpopulation, international disorder, supertechnology—these  45
trends were testing the tenacity of our own commitment to democracy and freedom and our abilities to visualize their application to a world in upheaval.

Our work is guided by the sense that we may be the last generation in
the experiment with living. But we are a minority—the vast majority of our

50   people regard the temporary equilibriums of our society and world as eternally-functional parts. In this is perhaps the outstanding paradox: we ourselves are imbued with urgency, yet the measure of our society is that there is no viable alternative to the present. Beneath the reassuring tones of the politicians, beneath the common opinion that America will "muddle through," beneath the stagna-
55   tion of those who have closed their minds to the future, is the pervading feeling that there simply are no alternatives, that our times have witnessed the exhaustion not only of Utopias, but of any new departures as well. Feeling the press of complexity upon the emptiness of life, people are fearful of the thought that at any moment things might be thrust out of control. They fear change itself, since
60   change might smash whatever invisible framework seems to hold back chaos for them now. For most Americans, all crusades are suspect, threatening. The fact that each individual sees apathy in his fellows perpetuates the common reluctance to organize for change. The dominant institutions are complex enough to blunt the minds of their potential critics, and entrenched enough to swiftly dis-
65   sipate or entirely repel the energies of protest and reform, thus limiting human expectancies. Then, too, we are a materially improved society, and by our own improvements we seem to have weakened the case for further change.
     Some would have us believe that Americans feel contentment amidst prosperity—but might it not be better be called a glaze above deeply-felt anxieties
70   about their role in the new world? And if these anxieties produce a developed indifference to human affairs, do they not as well produce a yearning to believe there *is* an alternative to the present, that something *can* be done to change circumstances in the school, the workplaces, the bureaucracies, the government? It is to this latter yearning, at once the spark and engine of change, that we di-
75   rect our present appeal. The search for truly democratic alternatives to the present, and a commitment to social experimentation with them, is a worthy and fulfilling human enterprise, one which moves us and, we hope, others today. On such a basis do we offer this document of our convictions and analysis: as an effort in understanding and changing the conditions of humanity in the late
80   twentieth century, an effort rooted in the ancient, still unfulfilled conception of man attaining determining influence over his circumstances of life. . . .

## The Students

In the last few years, thousands of American students demonstrated that they at least felt the urgency of the times. They moved actively and directly against racial injustices, the threat of war, violations of individual rights of conscience and,
85   less frequently, against economic manipulation. They succeeded in restoring a small measure of controversy to the campuses after the stillness of the McCarthy period. They succeeded, too, in gaining some concessions from the people and institutions they opposed, especially in the fight against racial bigotry.
     The significance of these scattered movements lies not in their success or
90   failure in gaining objectives—at least not yet. Nor does the significance lie in

the intellectual "competence" or "maturity" of the students involved—as some pedantic elders allege. The significance is in the fact that students are breaking the crust of apathy and overcoming the inner alienation that remain the defining characteristics of American college life.

If student movements for change are still rarities on the campus scene, what is commonplace there? The real campus, the familiar campus, is a place of private people, engaged in their notorious "inner emigration." It is a place of commitment to business-as-usual, getting ahead, playing it cool. It is a place of mass affirmation of the Twist, but mass reluctance toward the controversial public stance. Rules are accepted as "inevitable," bureaucracy as "just circumstances," irrelevance as "scholarship," selflessness as "martyrdom," politics as "just another way to make people, and an unprofitable one, too."

Almost no students value activity as citizens. Passive in public, they are hardly more idealistic in arranging their private lives: Gallup[1] concludes they will settle for "low success, and won't risk high failure." There is not much willingness to take risks (not even in business), no settling of dangerous goals, no real conception of personal identity except one manufactured in the image of others, no real urge for personal fulfillment except to be almost as successful as the very successful people. Attention is being paid to social status (the quality of shirt collars, meeting people, getting wives or husbands, making solid contacts for later on); much, too, is paid to academic status (grades, honors, the med school rat race). But neglected generally is real intellectual status, the personal cultivation of the mind.

"Students don't even give a damn about the apathy," one has said. Apathy toward apathy begets a privately-constructed universe, a place of systematic study schedules, two nights each week for beer, a girl or two, and early marriage; a framework infused with personality, warmth, and under control, no matter how unsatisfying otherwise.

Under these conditions university life loses all relevance to some. Four hundred thousand of our classmates leave college every year.

But apathy is not simply an attitude; it is a product of social institutions, and of the structure and organization of higher education itself. The extracurricular life is ordered according to *in loco parentis*[2] theory, which ratifies the Administration as the moral guardian of the young.

The accompanying "let's pretend" theory of student extracurricular affairs validates student government as a training center for those who want to spend their lives in political pretense, and discourages initiative from the more articulate, honest, and sensitive students. The bounds and style of controversy are delimited before controversy begins. The university "prepares" the student for "citizenship" through perpetual rehearsals and, usually, through emasculation of what creative spirit there is in the individual.

---

1. *George H. Gallup* (b. 1901): director of the Gallup poll. (*ed.*)

2. *in loco parentis:* in the place of a parent. (*ed.*)

135

140

145

150

155

160

165

170

The academic life contains reinforcing counterparts to the way in which extracurricular life is organized. The academic world is founded on a teacher-student relation analogous to the parent-child relation which characterizes *in loco parentis*. Further, academia includes a radical separation of the student from the material of study. That which is studied, the social reality, is "objectified" to sterility, dividing the student from life—just as he is restrained in active involvement by the deans controlling student government. The specialization of function and knowledge, admittedly necessary to our complex technological and social structure, has produced an exaggerated compartmentalization of study and understanding. This has contributed to an overly parochial view, by faculty, of the role of its research and scholarship, to a discontinuous and truncated understanding, by students, of the surrounding social order; and to a loss of personal attachment, by nearly all, to the worth of study as a humanistic enterprise.

There is, finally, the cumbersome academic bureaucracy extending throughout the academic as well as the extracurricular structures, contributing to the sense of outer complexity and inner powerlessness that transforms the honest searching of many students to a ratification of convention and, worse, to a numbness to present and future catastrophes. The size and financing systems of the university enhance the permanent trusteeship of the administrative bureaucracy, their power leading to a shift within the university toward the value standards of business and the administrative mentality. Huge foundations and other private financial interests shape the under-financed colleges and universities, not only making them more commercial, but less disposed to diagnose society critically, less open to dissent. Many social and physical scientists, neglecting the liberating heritage of higher learning, develop "human relations" or "morale-producing" techniques for the corporate economy, while others exercise their intellectual skills to accelerate the arms race.

Tragically, the university could serve as a significant source of social criticism and an initiator of new modes and molders of attitudes. But the actual intellectual effect of the college experience is hardly distinguishable from that of any other communications channel—say, a television set—passing on the stock truths of the day. Students leave college somewhat more "tolerant" than when they arrived, but basically unchallenged in their values and political orientations. With administrators ordering the institution, and faculty the curriculum, the student learns by his isolation to accept elite rule within the university, which prepares him to accept later forms of minority control. The real function of the educational system—as opposed to its more rhetorical function of "searching for truth"—is to impart the key information and styles that will help the student get by, modestly but comfortably, in the big society beyond.

## The Society Beyond

Look beyond the campus, to America itself. That student life is more intellectual, and perhaps more comfortable, does not obscure the fact that the fundamental qualities of life on the campus reflect the habits of society at large. The fraternity president is seen at the junior manager levels; the sorority queen has gone to Grosse Pointe;[3] the serious poet burns for a place, any place, to work; the once-serious and never-serious poets work at the advertising agencies. The desperation of people threatened by forces about which they know little and of which they can say less; the cheerful emptiness of people "giving up" all hope of changing things; the faceless ones polled by Gallup who listed "international affairs" fourteenth on their list of "problems" but who also expected thermonuclear war in the next few years; in these and other forms, Americans are in withdrawal from public life, from any collective effort at directing their own affairs.

Some regard these national doldrums as a sign of healthy approval of the established order—but is it approval by consent or manipulated acquiescence? Others declare that the people are withdrawn because compelling issues are fast disappearing—perhaps there are fewer bread-lines in America, but is Jim Crow[4] gone, is there enough work and work more fulfilling, is world war a diminishing threat, and what of the revolutionary new peoples? Still others think the national quietude is a necessary consequence of the need for elites to resolve complex and specialized problems of modern industrial society—but, then, why should *business* elites help decide foreign policy, and who controls the elites anyway, and are they solving mankind's problems? Others, finally, shrug knowingly and announce that full democracy never worked anywhere in the past—but why lump qualitatively different civilizations together, and how can a social order work well if its best thinkers are skeptics, and is man really doomed forever to the domination of today?

There are no convincing apologies for the contemporary malaise. While the world tumbles toward final war, while men in other nations are trying desperately to alter events, while the very future qua future is uncertain—America is without community, impulse, without the inner momentum necessary for an age when societies cannot successfully perpetuate themselves by their military weapons, when democracy must be viable because of the quality of life, not its quantity of rockets.

The apathy here is, first *subjective*—the felt powerlessness of ordinary people, the resignation before the enormity of events. But subjective apathy is encouraged by the *objective* American situation—the actual structural separation of people from power, from relevant knowledge, from pinnacles of decision-making. Just as the university influences the student way of life, so do major social institutions create the circumstances in which the isolated citizen will try hopelessly to understand his world and himself.

The very isolation of the individual—from power and community and ability to aspire—means the rise of a democracy without publics. With the great mass of people structurally remote and psychologically hesitant with respect to

---

3. *Grosse Pointe:* wealthy suburb of Detroit. (*ed.*)

4. *Jim Crow:* name given to laws and traditional practices that discriminate against African Americans. (*ed.*)

215  democratic institutions, those institutions themselves attenuate and become, in
the fashion of the vicious circle, progressively less accessible to those few who
aspire to serious participation in social affairs. The vital democratic connection
between community and leadership, between the mass and the several elites,
has been so wrenched and perverted that disastrous policies go unchallenged
220  time and again. . . .

## The Economy

American capitalism today advertises itself as the Welfare State. Many of us
comfortably expect pensions, medical care, unemployment compensation, and
other social services in our lifetimes. Even with one-fourth of our productive capacity unused, the majority of Americans are living in relative comfort—al-
225  though their nagging incentive to "keep up" makes them continually dissatisfied
with their possessions. In many places, unrestrained bosses, uncontrolled machines, and sweatshop conditions have been reformed or abolished and suffering tremendously relieved. But in spite of the benign yet obscuring effects of
the New Deal[5] reforms and the reassuring phrases of government economists
230  and politicians, the paradoxes and myths of the economy are sufficient to irritate our complacency and reveal to us some essential causes of the American
malaise.

We live amidst a national celebration of economic prosperity while poverty
and deprivation remain an unbreakable way of life for millions in the "affluent
235  society," including many of our own generation. We hear glib references to the
"welfare state," "free enterprise," and "share-holder's democracy" while military
defense is the main item of "public" spending and obvious oligopoly and other
forms of minority rule defy real individual initiative or popular control. Work,
too, is often unfulfilling and victimizing, accepted as a channel to status or
240  plenty, if not a way to pay the bills, rarely as a means of understanding and controlling self and events. In work and leisure the individual is regulated as part of
the system, a consuming unit, bombarded by hard-sell, soft-sell, lies and semi-
true appeals to his basest drives. He is always told that he is a "free" man because of "free enterprise." . . .

## Horizon

245  In summary: a more reformed, more human capitalism, functioning at three-
fourths capacity while one-third of America and two-thirds of the world goes
needy, domination of politics and the economy by fantastically rich elites, accommodation and limited effectiveness by the labor movement, hard-core

---

5. *New Deal:* the political and economic system installed by President Franklin Delano
Roosevelt to battle the Depression. (*ed.*)

poverty and unemployment, automation confirming the dark ascension of machine over man instead of shared abundance, technological change being intro-  250
duced into the economy by the criteria of profitability—this has been our inheritance. However, inadequate, it has instilled quiescence in liberal hearts—partly
reflecting the extent to which misery has been overcome, but also the eclipse of
social ideals. Though many of us are "affluent," poverty, waste, elitism, manipulation are too manifest to go unnoticed, too clearly unnecessary to go accepted.  255
To change the Cold War status quo and other social evils, concern with the
challenges to the American economic machine must expand. Now, as a truly
better social state become visible, a new poverty impends: a poverty of vision,
and a poverty of political action to make that vision reality. Without new vision,
the failure to achieve our potentialities will spell the inability of our society to  260
endure in a world of obvious, crying needs and rapid change. . . .

## Towards American Democracy

Every effort to end the Cold War and expand the process of world industrializa-
tion is an effort hostile to people and institutions whose interests lie in perpetuation of the East-West military threat and the postponement of change in the
"have not" nations of the world. Every such effort, too, is bound to establish  265
greater democracy in America. The major goals of a domestic effort would be:

1. *America must abolish its political party stalemate.*

Two genuine parties, centered around issues and essential values, demanding allegiance to party principles shall supplant the current system of organized
stalemate which is seriously inadequate to a world in flux. . . . What is desirable
is sufficient party disagreement to dramatize major issues, yet sufficient party  270
overlap to guarantee stable transitions from administration to administration.
Every time the President criticizes a recalcitrant Congress, we must ask that
he no longer tolerate the Southern conservatives in the Democratic Party. Every
time a liberal representative complains that "we can't expect everything at once"
we must ask if we received much of anything from Congress in the last gen-  275
eration. Every time he refers to "circumstances beyond control" we must ask
why he fraternizes with racist scoundrels. Every time he speaks of the "unpleas-
antness of personal and party fighting" we should insist that pleasantry with
Dixiecrats is inexcusable when the dark peoples of the world call for American
support.
280

2. *Mechanisms of voluntary association must be created through which political
information can be imparted and political participation encouraged.*

Political parties, even if realigned, would not provide adequate outlets for
popular involvement. Institutions should be created that engage people with

issues and express political preference, not as now with huge business lobbies which exercise undemocratic *power* but which carry political *influence* (appro-
285 priate to private, rather than public, groupings) in national decision-making enterprise. Private in nature, these should be organized around single issues (medical care, transportation systems reform, etc.), concrete interest (labor and minority group organizations); multiple issues or general issues. These do not exist in America in quantity today. If they did exist, they would be a signif-
290 icant politicizing and educative force bringing people into touch with public life and affording them means of expression and action. Today, giant lobby representatives of business interests are dominant, but not educative. The Federal government itself should counter the latter forces whose intent is often public deceit for private gain, by subsidizing the preparation and decentralized
295 distribution of objective materials on all public issues facing government.

   *3. Institutions and practices which stifle dissent should be abolished, and the promotion of peaceful dissent should be actively promoted.*

   The First Amendment freedoms of speech, assembly, thought, religion and press should be seen as guarantees, not threats, to national security. While society has the right to prevent active subversion of its laws and institutions, it has the duty as well to promote open discussion of all issues—otherwise it will be in
300 fact promoting real subversion as the only means of implementing ideas. To eliminate the fears and apathy from national life it is necessary that the institutions bred by fear and apathy be rooted out: the House Un-American Activities Committee, the Senate Internal Security Committee, the loyalty oaths on Federal loans, the Attorney General's list of subversive organizations, the Smith and
305 McCarran Acts.[6] The process of eliminating the blighting institutions is the process of restoring democratic participation. Their existence is a sign of the decomposition and atrophy of participation.

   *4. Corporations must be made publicly responsible.*

   It is not possible to believe that true democracy can exist where a minority utterly controls enormous wealth and power. The influence of corporate elites
310 on foreign policy is neither reliable nor democratic; a way must be found to subordinate private American foreign investment to a democratically-constructed foreign policy. . . .
   Labor and government as presently constituted are not sufficient to "regulate" corporations. A new re-ordering, a new calling of responsibility is neces-
315 sary: more than changing "work rules" we must consider changes in the rules of

---

   6. *Smith and McCarran Acts:* anti-immigration laws. (*ed.*)

society by challenging the unchallenged politics of American corporations. Before the government can really begin to control business in a "public interest," the public must gain more substantial control of government: this demands a movement for political as well as economic realignments. We are aware that simple government "regulation," if achieved, would be inadequate without increased worker participation in management decision-making, strengthened and independent regulatory power, balances of partial and/or complete public ownership, various means of humanizing the conditions and types of work itself, sweeping welfare programs and regional *public* development authorities. These are examples of measures to re-balance the economy toward public—and individual—control.

    5. *The allocation of resources must be based on social needs. A truly "public sector" must be established, and its nature debated and planned.*

    At present the majority of America's "public sector," the largest part of our public spending, is for the military. When great social needs are so pressing, our concept of "government spending" is wrapped up in the "permanent war economy." . . .

    The main *private* forces of economic expansion cannot guarantee a steady rate of growth, nor acceptable recovery from recession—especially in a demilitarizing world. Government participation will inevitably expand enormously, because the stable growth of the economy demands increasing "public" investments yearly. Our present outpour of more than $500 billion might double in a generation, irreversibly involving government solutions. And in future recessions, the compensatory fiscal action by the government will be the only means of avoiding the twin disasters of greater unemployment and a slackening rate of growth. Furthermore, a close relationship with the European Common Market will involve competition with numerous planned economies and may aggravate American unemployment unless the economy here is expanding swiftly enough to create new jobs.

    All these tendencies suggest that not only solutions to our present social needs but our future expansion rests upon our willingness to enlarge the "public sector" greatly. Unless we choose war as an economic solvent, future public spending will be of a non-military nature—a major intervention into civilian production by the government. . . .

    6. *America should concentrate on its genuine social priorities: abolish squalor, terminate neglect, and establish an environment for people to live in with dignity and creativeness.*

    A. A program against *poverty* must be just as sweeping as the nature of poverty itself. It must not be just palliative, but directed to the abolition of the

350  structural circumstances of poverty. At a bare minimum it should include a *housing* act far larger than the one supported by the Kennedy Administration, but one that is geared more to low- and middle-income needs than to the windfall aspirations of small and large private entrepreneurs, one that is more sympathetic to the quality of communal life than to the efficiency of city-split high-

355  ways. Second, *medical care* must become recognized as a lifetime human right just as vital as food, shelter and clothing—the Federal government should guarantee health insurance as a basic social service turning medical treatment into a social habit, not just an occasion of crisis, fighting sickness among the aged, not just by making medical care financially feasible but by reducing sickness among

360  children and younger people. Third, existing institutions should be expanded so the Welfare State cares for *everyone's* welfare according to need. *Social Security* payments should be extended to everyone and should be proportionately greater for the poorest. A *minimum wage* of at least $1.50 should be extended to all workers (including the 16 million currently not covered at all). Programs for

365  equal *educational opportunity* are as important a part of the battle against poverty.

B. A full-scale public initiative for civil rights should be undertaken despite the clamor among conservatives (and liberals) about gradualism, property rights, and law and order. The executive and legislative branches of the Federal

370  government should work by enforcement *and* enactment against any form of exploitation of minority groups. No Federal cooperation with racism is tolerable—from financing of schools, to the development of Federally-supported industry, to the social gatherings of the President. Laws hastening school desegregation, voting rights, and economic protection for Negroes are needed right

375  now. The moral force of the Executive Office should be exerted against the Dixiecrats specifically, and the national complacency about the race question generally. Especially in the North, where one-half of the country's Negro people now live, civil rights is not a problem to be solved in isolation from other problems. The fight against poverty, against slums, against the stalemated Congress,

380  against McCarthyism, are all fights against the discrimination that is nearly endemic to all areas of American life.

C. The promise and problems of long-range *Federal economic development* should be studied more constructively. It is an embarrassing paradox that the Tennessee Valley Authority is a wonder to most foreign visitors but a "radical"

385  and barely influential project to most Americans. The Kennedy decision to permit private facilities to transmit power from the $1 billion Colorado River Storage Project is a disastrous one, interposing privately-owned transmitters between publicly-owned generators and their publicly (and cooperatively) owned distributors. The contrary trend, to public ownership of power, should be gen-

390  erated in an experimental way.

The Area Redevelopment Act of 1961 is a first step in recognizing the underdeveloped areas of the United States. It is only a drop in the bucket financially and is not keyed to public planning and public works on a broad scale. It consists only of a few loan programs to lure industries and some grants to improve public facilities to lure these industries. The current public works bill in Congress is needed—and a more sweeping, higher-priced program of regional development with a proliferation of "TVAs" in such areas as the Appalachian region is needed desperately. However, it has been rejected already by Mississippi because of the improvement it bodes for the unskilled Negro worker. This program should be enlarged, given teeth, and pursued rigorously by Federal authorities. 395

400

D. We must meet the growing complex of "city" problems; over 90 percent of Americans will live in urban areas within two decades. Juvenile delinquency, untended mental illness, crime increase, slums, urban tenantry and non-rent controlled housing, the isolation of the individual in the city—all are problems of the city and are major symptoms of the present system of economic priorities and lack of public planning. Private property control (the real estate lobby and a few selfish landowners and businesses) is as devastating in the cities as corporations are on the national level. But there is no comprehensive way to deal with these problems now amidst competing units of government, dwindling tax resources, suburban escapism (saprophitic[7] to the sick central cities), high infrastructure costs and no one to pay them. 405

410

The only solutions are national and regional. "Federalism" has thus far failed here because states are rural-dominated; the Federal government has had to operate by bootlegging and trickle-down measures dominated by private interests, with their appendages through annexation or federation. A new external challenge is needed, not just a Department of Urban Affairs but a thorough national *program* to help the cities. The *model* city must be projected—more community decision-making and participation, true integration of classes, races, vocations—provision for beauty, access to nature and the benefits of the central city as well, privacy without privatism, decentralized "units" spread horizontally with central, regional democratic control—provision for the basic facility-needs, for everyone, with units of planned *regions* and thus public, democratic control over the growth of the civic community and the allocation of resources. 415

420

E. *Mental health institutions* are in dire need; there were fewer mental hospital beds in relation to the numbers of mentally-ill in 1959 than there were in 1948. Public hospitals, too, are seriously wanting; existing structures alone need an estimated $1 billion for rehabilitation. Tremendous staff and faculty needs exist as well, and there are not enough medical students enrolled today to meet the anticipated needs of the future. 425

430

F. Our *prisons* are too often the enforcers of misery. They must be either re-oriented to rehabilitative work through public supervision or be abolished

---

7. *saprophitic*: feeding on decay. (*ed.*)

for their dehumanizing social effects. Funds are needed, too, to make possible a decent prison environment.

435   G. *Education* is too vital a public problem to be completely entrusted to the province of the various states and local units. In fact, there is no good reason why America should not progress now toward internationalizing rather than localizing, its education system—children and young adults studying everywhere in the world, through a United Nations program, would go far to create mutual
440   understanding. In the meantime, the need for teachers and classrooms in America is fantastic. This is an area where "minimal" requirements should hardly be considered as a goal—there always are improvements to be made in the education system, e.g., smaller classes and many more teachers for them, programs to subsidize the education for the poor but bright, etc.

445   H. America should eliminate *agricultural policies* based on scarcity and pent-up surplus. In America and foreign countries there exist tremendous needs for more food and balanced diets. The Federal government should finance small farmers' cooperatives, strengthen programs of rural electrification, and expand policies for the distribution of agricultural surpluses throughout
450   the world (by Food-for-Peace and related UN programming). Marginal farmers must be helped to either become productive enough to survive "industrialized agriculture" or given help in making the transition out of agriculture—the current Rural Area Development program must be better coordinated with a massive national "area redevelopment" program.

455   I. *Science* should be employed to constructively transform the conditions of life throughout the United States and the world. Yet at the present time the Department of Health, Education, and Welfare and the National Science Foundation together spend only $300 million annually for scientific purposes in contrast to the $6 billion spent by the Defense Department and the Atomic En-
460   ergy Commission. One-half of all research and development in America is directly devoted to military purposes. Two imbalances must be corrected—that of military over non-military investigation, and that of biological-natural-physical science over the sciences of human behavior. Our political system must then include planning for the human use of science: by anticipating the political conse-
465   quences of scientific innovation, by directing the discovery and exploration of space, by adapting science to improved production of food, to international communications systems, to technical problems of disarmament, and so on. For the newly-developing nations, American science should focus on the study of cheap sources of power, housing and building materials, mass educational tech-
470   niques, etc. Further, science and scholarship should be seen less as an apparatus of conflicting power blocs, but as a bridge toward supra-national community: the International Geophysical Year is a model for continuous further cooperation between the science communities of all nations.

# THE STUDENT REVOLT

## Looking Ahead

1. Although Chiaromonte focuses on Italian society, his criticisms and proposals are international in scope.

2. Watch for the careful distinctions the author makes throughout; they are central to his purpose and misunderstanding them may distort the way you perceive his meaning.

3. Tracing the structure of this essay will help you see how Chiaromonte develops his thought and comes to his conclusions.

Some three years ago, in an article in *Tempo Presente* called "Rebellious Youth," I came to the conclusion that only one thing seems to have shaken the political inertia that characterizes our age and to have aroused political passions and a real sense of participation; and that is the idea of freedom. The Hungarian up- 5
rising, directed by intellectuals and fought by the young and the very young in the name of unadorned freedom, was the main and most memorable example of this. Before that there was Poznan and the "Polish October," where, in the main, intellectuals and young people were demanding their freedom. In Italy, there was July 1960; more significantly, there was the upsurge of action and opinion in France against the Algerian war. Then, in July 1963, there was the miners' 10
strike in Asturias,[1] in which the demand for freedom of association and of speech was raised before the question of wages, and was much the more important demand. And I also dealt at length in that article with the revolt of American students against racism and the war in Vietnam.

It was perfectly clear that freedom was again the leaven in the political 15
struggle, and that the young find themselves quite naturally in the vanguard of the movement, without waiting for the politicians to finish their calculations, organize their tactics, and put out their slogans.

But I felt that it was not enough to rejoice that a wave of rebellion (or rebelliousness), rather than some "realistic" conformity, seemed to have engulfed 20
young people immediately after the war: "We must also consider each manifestation of rebellion case by case. . . ."

All right, then, let us consider what is happening in this rebellion of the young—and not only of students. Since 1965 it has spread across Europe, indeed, across the world, from North and South America to China; in China, with 25
the approval of its intellectual hotheads and hangers-on, the remarkable event known as the "Cultural Revolution" has increasingly appeared to be an astute operation intended to unleash the rebelliousness of the young against the party machine, to the greater glory and support of Chairman Mao,[2] and with the army to prevent things getting too much out of hand. In Europe, the young are in re- 30

---

1. *Asturias:* a region in northwestern Spain. (*ed.*)

2. *Mao Zedong* (1893–1976): leader of the communist revolutionary movement in China and later head of state. (*ed.*)

volt in nearly all the countries of both East and West, including Scandinavia and Britain, on the one hand, and the Soviet Union and Poland, on the other.

But we must distinguish between these various forms of rebellion and consider their differences.

35   First, the Russian students' and intellectuals' protests against the regime's repressive refusal to listen and the open revolt of students, teachers, and intellectuals in Warsaw, to the cry of "freedom," are not at all the same as the uprisings of students in Turin, Milan, Florence, and Rome against their respective vice-chancellors, teachers, and ministers, even though the Italian students may
40   challenge the whole of society in their slogans and manifestoes, may talk about a "total rejection," refuse what they call "concessions," and declare their wish to change everything from top to bottom, independently, with their own methods and according to their own standards. The freedom the Polish students are demanding is a clear, specific challenge to a clearly and specifically oppressive
45   regime; whereas the "global confrontation" the Italian and German students are talking about is a formula as vague as it is violent. If we are speaking of the universities, then a challenge to their academic power means, at most, asking for the students' direct participation in discussions and decisions that affect their studies. Whereas if we are speaking of society as a whole—"the famous con-
50   sumer society"—then "total rejection" means rebellion against everything and against nothing.

In fact, apart from their extremely significant refusal to accept guidance from the political parties, what the rebellious Italian students seem to be protesting against is mainly the war in Vietnam, and what they approve of are
55   men and events wholly alien to the situation, both educational and political, in Italy—men like Guevara and Castro,[3] or exotic figures like Mao Tse-tung. Freedom, in fact, is the last thing they consider or even care about.

On the other hand, apart from violent clashes with the police (sometimes deliberately sought) and painfully confused stands taken by members of the
60   academic establishment—who are either warily submissive or toughly determined (and occasionally both, in quick succession)—the students have done as they pleased, and continue to do so. One is still waiting to see what direction their revolt is going to take and what objects it really aims at, and not merely who is going to lead it and in what direction. But it is obvious that there is no
65   question of seeking freedom—rather, its opposite: anger at the lack of authority and at the lack of any established order that commands respect.

We have yet to see what the Italian students are capable of doing, after this great wave of revolt in which indignation against the scandalous conditions of the universities and of schooling in general in Italy, and against the brutality and
70   madness of the American war in Vietnam, went with a cult (not unlike that of film-star fans) of Che Guevara and an enthusiasm for Mao Tse-tung, a dictator

---

3. *Ernesto "Che" Guevara* (1928–1967): guerrilla leader and later government minister in Cuba who was killed fighting in Bolivia; *Fidel Castro* (b. 1927): communist premier of Cuba. (*ed.*)

and thinker whose authority stems more from his power of command than from any qualities of his thought. It is impossible not to see in this revolt, however, an urge toward violence fatally combined with the idea of obtaining, at once and through direct action, what it is impossible to obtain at once and through direct action—namely, the reform of education and the reform of society. Impossible, that is, without total guidance by the hand of a dictator—and where that leads we know all too well.

The Italian students may have been doing as they pleased, but they have used this freedom of theirs for serious ends—or, at least, they are meant to be serious. Their revolt was a result of their anger toward and contempt for a so-called ruling class that primarily rules the affairs of the political parties into which it is divided and subdivided; and in this it was fully justified. But until now theirs have been mass riots, in which the voice of reason was drowned; and anyone who wanted to know what the whole thing was about had to go and listen to individuals, one by one.

But why was the students' revolt so confused, both in its ideas (or, rather, in its slogans) and in its behavior? It was justified by the facts, in particular by the Italian Parliament's shameful refusal to pass the reform that would have abolished the most scandalous privilege in present-day Italian universities—the right of deputies, senators, and ministers to hold academic chairs purely for prestige. Was it because of their youth? We are told to understand and not discourage the muddled enthusiasm of the young (because if we discourage it this means we want everything to continue as it is, corrupt, inert, torpid). And so we should, on condition that we reject absolutely the idea that the young must be right simply because they are young. It was on this principle that Fascism advanced, and something equally evil might grow out of it today, whether its label is socialist, anarchist, or simply humanitarian. We have already had the startling spectacle of teachers in their fifties rushing to join the rioting young, urging them on to "total rejection" and even to violence, in the certainty that they are marching with history.

But the young are in revolt not merely to reform the universities. As they themselves admit, their protest goes further than that. Indeed, it seems likely that the wretched conditions of education in Italy today, the teaching cliques, the academic charlatanism, the physical impossibility of following courses or even of seeing the professor's face except at exams, are all secondary reasons, excuses for rebellion, rather than its primary cause. That lies elsewhere, and it is, I think, very simple: it is the fact that the young—those born after 1940—find themselves living in a society that neither commands nor deserves respect, a society whose authority merely weighs on them and so seems to license every kind of lawlessness and rebellion, open or covert. This is so from the top of the social hierarchy (if there is still such a thing, apart from a hierarchy of power) down to the forms of political life and the circumstances of everyday Italian life. But the most irresponsible and corrupt group of all is, I would say unhesitatingly, today's intellectuals. They follow the crowd instead of setting an example, quibble instead of thinking, offer political factionalism instead of critical guidance, hold forth on undigested questions of ideology, and, in fact, instead of acting as the voice of a people of which they are part, themselves make up a special party, one that furthers their own particular aims and needs.

120 It is against this lack of moral guidance and of an authority worth respecting that young people are rebelling today, all over the world; and it is a serious matter, not to be answered by police attacks or tricky maneuvers. This explains why, in the absence of anyone or anything to respect—and of an authority that can be either respected or hated, but which at least exists—the Italian young,

125 like the young in France or Germany, create exotic myths out of Che and Ho[4] and Mao. These myths are by their very nature either empty or totalitarian; they lead either to nothing or to mass demagogy and, sooner or later, to a technocratic authoritarianism cloaked in ideology. This authoritarianism—which is today's, *not* yesterday's or the day before yesterday's, which is generally called

130 up as a bogey—does not even demand a charismatic leader; all it needs is the existing state of affairs, the endless complexity, the vast inertia, and the enormous, almost supernatural authority of industrial society, a society borne up not so much by the *capitalists,* as the current cliché maintains, as by the very ideas to which those in revolt have appealed. For has modern man, in his col-

135 lective existence, laid claim to any god or ideal but the god of possession and enjoyment and the limitless satisfaction of material needs? Has he put forward any reason for working but the reward of pleasure and prosperity? Has he, in fact, evolved anything but this "consumer society" that is so easily and so falsely repudiated?

140 In these conditions, it is suspiciously romantic to talk about "revolution." How will it be achieved except by a *coup d'état*[5] executed by a highly placed few, and in secret?

Are the young mistaken, then, in their revolt? No. But neither are they right. You can talk about right only when you talk reasonably, person to person.

145 A rioting crowd never reasons, nor can it ever be right; it is an explosion and nothing more, an event that may have its proper causes and reasons and so logically cannot be either approved or disapproved except in detail, case by case, individual by individual. You do not approve of an earthquake; you try to clear things up afterward. But as regards the earthquake of which the revolt of the

150 young is only *one* symptom, the present Italian ruling classes (indeed, the present rulers of the world in general, for the whole business is universal) show no sign of clearing anything up, only of aggravating the difficulties.[6]

If there is a remedy at all, it lies elsewhere and is a very long-term one. In my view, it consists of a determined secession from a society (or, rather, from

---

4. *Ho Chi Minh* (1890–1969): revolutionary leader and president of Vietnam. (*ed.*)

5. *coup d'état:* overthrow of the state, often by violent means. (*ed.*)

6. Chiaromonte is referring to the widespread, large-scale street demonstrations of college students at this time. (*ed.*)

a state of affairs, since "society" implies a community and a purpose, which is   155
exactly what collective life nowadays lacks) that is not actually evil by nature
(indeed, may well be improved), but which is neither good nor bad, only indifferent—and that is the worst thing of all, and the most deadening. From
this society—from this state of affairs—people must detach themselves, must
become resolute "heretics." They must detach themselves without shouting or   160
riots, indeed, in silence and secrecy; not alone but in groups, in real "societies" that will create, as far as is possible, a life that is independent and wise,
not utopian or phalansterian,[7] in which each man learns to govern himself
first of all and to behave rightly toward others, and works at his own job according to the standards of the craft itself, standards that in themselves are the   165
simplest and strictest of moral principles and, by their very nature, cut out deception and prevarication, charlatanism and the love of power and possession. This would not mean detaching oneself from either the life of like-
minded others or the life of politics in the real sense of the word. It would be,
all the same, a nonrhetorical form of "total rejection." The French student re-   170
volt, by sharply attacking the principle of centralized authority and demanding a reorganization of collective life from the ground up, has raised precisely
this question.

## Looking Back

1. How politically involved are the authors of these readings? How has the degree of involvement of each helped shape his or her ideas?

2. Which approach do you find most effective: the oral recollection of individuals, the joint statement of a committee, or the intellectual analysis of a single critic? Why?

3. What does the SDS manifesto mean by "the inner alienation that remains the defining characteristic of American college life" (lines 93–94)?

4. What criticisms of college education do these readings express?

5. Why are college students often expected—by themselves as much as by others—to bear special responsibility for understanding the causes of social ills and trying to remedy them?

6. On the basis of all three readings, do you agree with Chiaromonte's contention that student demonstrations are a mindless symptom of a diseased society rather than the result of the careful reasoning and decision-making power of individuals?

7. How do these authors view the excessive materialism that surrounds them? In what way is such criticism connected to the desire for social and political change?

8. Putting all three readings together, what picture do you draw of the alleged corruption, oppression, inefficiency, and injustice in the societies described here? Does the same picture hold true today? Explain.

---

7. *phalansterian:* characterized by small, cooperative communities. (*ed.*)

9. In what way do reform and revolution differ? How do these readings reflect this difference?

10. How does the revolutionary strategy of organizing groups to produce social change differ in the descriptions and proposals of these readings?

## Writing Assignments (Linked Readings)

1. On college campuses, the intensity of social awareness and political activism among students rises and falls from one historical era to the next. Very often, these shifts occur in response to pressing social and economic problems that at one point are burning issues and at the next seem to have disappeared. Examples of these problems as found in these readings are the 1930s Depression and the Vietnam War. But students may also concern themselves with ongoing social problems, like racial inequality, that may not be flaring in everybody's consciousness. Whether reacting to highly visible issues or acting on those that receive little attention, it is always possible, in the words of the Port Huron Statement, to "look beyond the campus, to America itself." Write an essay that does that. Define a current social or political problem and explain how students might organize to address it. Extrapolate from the readings by pointing out the similarities and differences between your insights and proposals and the ideas and actions of the students who are described.

2. Each of the readings criticizes some aspects of the way teachers and administrators educate college students. You should not be surprised to learn that students often are dissatisfied with their education. After all, the university is a social institution, and social institutions are conservative by nature: they are much slower to change in response to people's needs than people themselves are to feel these needs. So, for instance, the policy of *in loco parentis* referred to in the Port Huron Statement was the target of student criticism long before it finally dwindled to nothing. It is therefore quite likely that on your own campus all is not perfect, that students meet unnecessary obstacles that impede learning. Write an essay identifying and criticizing one or more such policies or practices, such as the unavailability of classes, or overcrowding, or impersonal lectures. Try to be fair in your criticism, since not everything we dislike is wholly avoidable. Say what you think ought to be done to minimize or eradicate the obstacle. If you are too new to your college to have seen and analyzed its educational problems, use your high school experience instead as a source for your essay.

3. Chiaromonte and the authors of the Port Huron Statement propose the formation of social and political groupings of students to effect specific political ends. Pauline Kael refers to living communally just to survive. In each case, by banding together, the members of a group are better equipped to reach their goals and to counter the isolation that is sometimes the fate of individuals. Note the leading characteristics and functions of each of these proposed or described groups (see your answer to question 10 in Looking Back, though you will have to imagine what must have been the case with Kael's group). Write an interpolative essay that evaluates the usefulness of such groups in solving a current social problem, like homelessness, or in reforming a negative political practice, like corruption in city government.

# Writing Assignments (Individual Readings)
## CAMPUS LIFE

Robert Gard explains that social consciousness was foreign to him and his fellow students when they entered college. At many points in our lives—not just on entering college and not just in hard times—we come face to face with new social reality. It may be a move to another locality; it may be sudden impoverishment resulting from a job loss; it may be taking on membership in a social group. At such times, we find ourselves having to form new ideas about ourselves and the world. Write an essay about one such transforming time in your life. Describe what you had to confront and say how your thinking about a new social reality changed and developed. Extrapolate from Gard's experience, and explain what lasting effects your own experience has had on you.

## THE PORT HURON STATEMENT

Writing more than thirty years ago, the authors envision a future "model city" (lines 418–424). In almost every respect, this projection has not become a reality in the United States. Could it ever be a reality? Focusing on your own locale and extrapolating from the authors' points, write an essay explaining what would have to be done to turn it into a model city. Be as concrete as possible in your description. For instance, precisely which "classes, races, vocations" (lines 419–420) would have to be integrated? What beauties could be provided? New plantings? If so, on what streets? As you move through the points of your essay, judge whether the Students for a Democratic Society utopia is really possible. Or would it be necessary to modify their vision? For example, can there be privacy without isolation ("privatism")? In the thesis of your essay, state whether such a model city—original or revised—seems likely in the future.

## THE STUDENT REVOLT

As the decade of the 1960s wore on and the war in Vietnam refused to go away, street demonstrations protesting U.S. policy galvanized the political energies of hundreds of thousands of people, especially young people, around the world. Political analysts like Nicola Chiaromonte had no choice, therefore, but to comment on these developments. On a number of grounds, Chiaromonte disapproves of demonstrations, particularly those that turn violent or have the potential to do so. At the time he was writing, however, other commentators insisted that taking to the streets effectively kept up the pressure on governmental policymakers. Certainly, street demonstrations have become commonplace practice since those days. But their proliferation does not necessarily prove Chiaromonte wrong. The legitimacy of street demonstrations remains an open question that you can address. Write an essay arguing for or against them. In your essay, introduce Chiaromonte's specific criticisms and comment on them.

❧

## Andrew L. Shapiro

## Reading, Writing, and Ignorance: Education and Achievement

A 1990 graduate of Brown University, Andrew L. Shapiro lives and works in New York City. He is a staff writer on *The Nation*, a weekly political magazine. This piece is a chapter from his book *We're Number One: Where America Stands—And Falls—in the New World Order*. In his introduction, Shapiro defines one function of critical thinking when he writes: "Some readers may find the book too critical of America. They may even call it unpatriotic. But I believe that it is only by facing our flaws and weaknesses that we can break out of our complacency, confront our massive problems, and surmount them."

### Looking Ahead

1. Echoing the book's title, Shapiro uses the formula "We're Number _____" throughout this piece, filling in the blank with the appropriate ranking. You should use these highlighted summaries to make a quick comparison between the United States and other industrialized nations.

2. Statistical charts, which Shapiro uses in abundance here to illustrate his points, show rather than tell the reality of a given situation. They do not, however, substitute for the text, which you should examine for the evidence supporting assertions and conclusions.

3. Bear in mind that, besides facts, Shapiro cites attitudes, beliefs, and practices that reflect to some degree American cultural values.

In 1983, the U.S. government released *A Nation At Risk*, a highly influential report whose most quoted line was: "If an unfriendly foreign power had attempted to impose on America the mediocre educational performance that exists today, we might well have viewed it as an act of war." The alarming rhetoric
5   of *A Nation At Risk* was answered with more alarm and then sputtering inaction: politicians huffed, the media gasped, task forces and blue ribbon panels were commissioned, and a new round of hollow manifestos was released to cure everything from early childhood education to teacher training. With a few exceptions, not much was done. As a result, America is now one stage past "at
10   risk": we are feeling the pain.
   Our high school dropout rate ranges from 10.5 percent for whites to 27.9 percent for Hispanics. By comparison, 94 percent of Japanese students and almost 100 percent of German students finish high school on time. For Americans who stay in school, things are not much better. High student-teacher ra-

tios, crumbling buildings, and insufficient materials make it nearly impossible   15
for many of our students to learn. Teachers in the United States spend more
time just trying to *control* their classes than do teachers in Japan, Germany, or
the United Kingdom.

The effects of a deteriorating educational system are already apparent.
Twenty-seven million American adults are functionally illiterate, according to   20
Laubach Literacy International. They cannot read to their children, or understand street signs or job applications. An additional forty million adults have
a difficult time reading newspapers, financial documents, and other complex
material.

Education has traditionally been the method by which a nation's future is   25
ensured. After the Soviet Union launched Sputnik in 1957, an increased emphasis on teaching math and science in the United States helped us stay competitive in the space race. In the 1960s and beyond, desegregation, busing, and
affirmative action helped alleviate racial discrimination—not only in schools,
but throughout society. Now, in its dilapidated state, American education ap-   30
pears to be more of an impediment than a safeguard of our collective fate.

## Spending

- **We're Number One in private spending on education.**
- **We're Number 17 in public spending on education.**

America's current education malaise has led many reformers to question
whether the United States is investing enough money to yield a strong return.
Are we slipping because we are not spending enough? If we spend more, will
education improve? These questions are well intentioned but wide of the mark.   35
America's primary concern should not be how *much* we spend on education,
but *how* we allocate the money we already spend. That's not because the former
issue isn't important, but because the latter is the cause of so many of the problems that beset American education.

Including public and private spending, the United States spends about   40
7 percent of its gross domestic product (GDP) on education annually, or
around $330 billion. By this measure, we do fairly well; only a few developed
nations spend more overall relative to the size of their economies. But as with
health care expenditures, the spending comparisons change dramatically
when we distinguish between public and private sources. The United States   45
is first in private spending on education among the nineteen major industrial
nations, but only seventeenth in public spending as a percentage of GDP.
The results also mirror those of health care spending: topflight resources are
generally available to those who can afford to pay for them, and the rest of
America scrapes by on a public contribution smaller than that of all but one   50
of the nineteen major industrial nations for which data is available.

Is our high private spending on education justified? It amounts to 1.7 percent of our GDP, almost a quarter of our total spending on education. Yet only 14 percent of students at all levels attend private schools. In addition,
55 many educators are challenging the conventional wisdom that private schools always provide a better education than public schools. Surely, there are some private schools that are leaps and bounds ahead of America's public schools. But "the fact is that both private and public education are doing a disastrously bad job," says Albert Shanker, president of the American Federation of Teach-
60 ers. "If we are serious about our students meeting world-class standards . . . private school choice is not the answer." Shanker's assessment, based on mathematics scores that show that private and public schools are not far apart in achievement, is particularly relevant given the Bush administration's emphasis on "school choice," which would most likely increase the privatization of Amer-
65 ican education.

Regarding America's low public spending relative to other nations, the United States is even worse off than the numbers show because of the arcane and grossly inequitable system by which public education is funded in the United States. In this respect as well, our public education system resembles
70 our public health system in that it leaves so many American's "uninsured" and exposed. Spending per student varies greatly from one school district to another because public contributions are linked to property taxes in these different areas. States are supposed to compensate for differences in property value by giving additional monies to the poorer districts according to a formula that is de-
75 signed to ensure that enough money is available to provide a minimal standard of education. But the numbers show that the equalization process is a sham. As Jonathan Kozol reports in his book *Savage Inequalities,* a wealthy suburb of New York City with high property values spends $15,000 per student annually, while the city itself spends $7,300 per student. Affluent Princeton, New Jersey,
80 spends $7,700 per pupil while poverty-stricken Camden, New Jersey, spends less than half that, $3,500 per pupil. In Texas, some districts spend as much as $19,000 per pupil annually, compared to just $2,100 in the poorest districts. Lawsuits have been initiated in many states to rectify these inequalities, and a few have been successful.

Spending on education from public and private sources
(and total), as a percentage of GDP, 1987

| Country | Public $ as a % of GDP | Private $ as a % of GDP | Total $ as a % of GDP |
|---|---|---|---|
| Denmark | 7.50 | 0.07 | 7.57 |
| Sweden | 7.19 | — | — |
| Netherlands | 6.99 | 0.34 | 7.33 |
| Norway | 6.82 | 0.17 | 6.99 |
| Canada | 6.53 | 0.59 | 7.12 |
| Austria | 5.91 | — | — |
| Ireland | 5.84 | 0.28 | 6.12 |
| France | 5.57 | 1.03 | 6.59 |
| New Zealand | 5.37 | — | — |
| Finland | 5.31 | 0.49 | 5.80 |
| Australia | 5.25 | 0.38 | 5.63 |
| Belgium | 5.12 | — | — |
| Switzerland | 5.01 | 0.10 | 5.11 |
| Japan | 4.98 | 1.41 | 6.38 |
| United Kingdom | 4.97 | — | — |
| Italy | 4.96 | — | — |
| **United States** | 4.77 | 1.68 | 6.44 |
| Germany | 4.24 | 0.17 | 4.41 |

Source: Organization for Economic Cooperation and Development, *Education in OECD Countries 1987–88* (Paris: OECD, 1990), p. 115. Note: Figures do not add up exactly due to rounding.

## Compulsory Education

- **We're Number One in providing compulsory education.**
- **We're Number 18 in providing compulsory education that meets the demands of a competitive economy.**

The United States provides as many years of free, full-time compulsory educa-    85
tion as any nation, and Americans attend school longer than do students in any
other nation for which data is available. American adults age 25 and over have
had 12.2 years of schooling on average, compared to 10.4 years in Japan and
8.8 years in Germany. Yet business leaders rate America behind all but one of
the nineteen major industrial nations in the ability of the compulsory education    90
system to effectively meet the needs of today's global economy. School systems
in Japan (75.5) and Germany (75.2) get the best ratings, far ahead of the United
States (47.6). The lesson to be learned is that quantity does not always guarantee quality.

Years of free, full-time compulsory education provided, 1989; and average rating (on an ascending scale of 1–100) of the effectiveness of the nation's compulsory education system in meeting the demands of a competitive economy, according to business executives in each country, 1991

| Country | Years Provided | Rating |
|---|---|---|
| Japan | 9 | 75.5 |
| Germany | 10 | 75.2 |
| Switzerland | 9 | 74.1 |
| Ireland | 9 | 72.2 |
| Austria | 9 | 71.2 |
| Finland | 10 | 65.6 |
| Denmark | 9 | 65.4 |
| Netherlands | 11 | 64.6 |
| Belgium | 10 | 64.4 |
| Australia | 9 | 60.2 |
| Canada | 9 | 58.2 |
| Sweden | 9 | 57.9 |
| Italy | 8 | 51.4 |
| France | 10 | 49.7 |
| Spain | 8 | 48.9 |
| New Zealand | 9 | 48.6 |
| Norway | 9 | 48.2 |
| **United States** | **11** | 47.6 |
| United Kingdom | 11 | 40.6 |

Sources: United Nations Development Programme, *Human Development Report 1991* (New York: Oxford University Press, 1991), p. 181; *World Competitiveness Report 1991,* published by IMD International, Lausanne, Switzerland, and World Economic Forum, Geneva, Switzerland, p. 338.

## Enrollment

- **We're Number 9 in early childhood education.**

Early childhood education is critically important to a child's development and
95   essential for society at large. Children gain important social and intellectual skills that ensure that they are ready to learn when they reach primary school. Each dollar spent on preschool education saves almost five dollars in later spending on special education, welfare, and crime control, according to the Children's Defense Fund. Despite the potential benefits, only 56 percent of
100   American four-year-olds are enrolled in school; eight of the nineteen major industrial nations do better. In France, Belgium, and the Netherlands, virtually all four-year-olds are enrolled in preschool.

In the mid 1960s, Congress implemented the Head Start program to pro- vide disadvantaged American preschoolers with an early boost. While Head Start's educational and social services have proven successful, only about one quarter of eligible children currently benefit from the program because it is se- verely underfunded. Congress has called for increased funding of Head Start so that all eligible three- and four-year-olds and some five-year-olds will be able to participate. Even if the monies are appropriated, many middle-class children will continue to be deprived of preschool education because they are ineligible for Head Start and their parents cannot afford private programs. 105 110

Percentage of four-year-olds enrolled in preprimary programs, 1987–90

| Country | Preprimary Enrollment | Country | Preprimary Enrollment |
|---|---|---|---|
| France | 100.0 | United States | 56.1 |
| Belgium | 98.1 | Japan | 54.6 |
| Netherlands | 97.9 | Ireland | 52.1 |
| Spain | 90.6 | Norway | 44.1 |
| Germany | 71.6 | Canada | 41.4 |
| New Zealand | 72.8 | Finland | 19.6 |
| United Kingdom | 69.2 | Switzerland | 18.7 |
| Austria | 63.4 | | |

Source: Organization for Economic Cooperation and Development, *Education in OECD Coun- tries 1987–88* (Paris: OECD, 1990), p. 107.

- **We're Number 15 in days spent in school each year.**

To kids in America, summer means lazy, playful days with no homework, no teachers . . . the stuff of Huck Finn and the juvenile American dream. Well, it may not last for long. Education policymakers increasingly believe that one reason why Johnny can't read (or multiply or spell) as well as some of his counterparts abroad is because he attends school for fewer days each year than students in many nations. The American school year is 180 days long on average, compared to 210 days in Germany, 211 days in the Soviet Union, and 243 days in Japan. 115

America's summer break from school dates "back to a time when family la- bor was vital to the late-summer harvest," says a recent *Time* magazine article. Now, as an ingrained part of American education, the summer break gives us the shortest school year of all countries (except Belgium) among nations for which data is available. Breaking with tradition, some American schools have experimented with school years as long as 220 days. The reasons have as much to do with inner-city survival as international competition. "This has nothing to do with competition with the Japanese and everything to do with urban reality," 120 125 says a school board member about one experiment. "This is eight hours when the drug addicts can't get at these kids."

Number of days in an average school year, 1991

| Country | Days in School | Country | Days in School |
|---|---|---|---|
| Japan | 243 | Canada | 191 |
| Israel | 216 | Finland | 190 |
| Soviet Union | 211 | New Zealand | 190 |
| Germany | 210 | Nigeria | 190 |
| Netherlands | 200 | France | 185 |
| Thailand | 200 | Ireland | 184 |
| Hungary | 192 | **United States** | **180** |
| United Kingdom | 192 | Belgium | 168 |

Source: Education Commission of the States' Information Clearinghouse, January 1991.

- **We're Number One in higher education enrollment.**

Many Americans believe that the United States has the best higher education system in the world. After all, more than 18 percent of Americans age 20 to 24 are enrolled full time in postsecondary education, the largest percentage of all nations for which data is available. We have the most universities of any nation, the most graduate programs, and the largest libraries. But these indicators measure the *quantity,* not *quality,* of American higher education.

In most industrialized nations, just attending college or university is considered a feat of educational achievement. Students are admitted only after taking grueling exams that test their knowledge in a variety of subjects; those who don't make the grade turn to vocational training or the job market. For example, about a third as many students per capita are enrolled in higher education in the United Kingdom as in the United States because in the U.K. most students do not pass the difficult exams required for entrance. While the United States has the infamous SAT and other standardized tests, there has essentially been a place for everyone who wanted to attend—between two-year colleges, community colleges, and larger universities—since the opening of American higher education during the postwar period. "About 95 percent of our high school graduates—private as well as public—would be unable to get into college in any other industrialized country," says Albert Shanker. "In the U.S., by contrast," says one recent study of American competitiveness, "even Bart Simpson would be able to find a college to admit him." In Japan or Germany, Bart the underachiever would be shut out.

Educational reformers have also argued recently that, because of a decline in standards in American secondary education, U.S. colleges and universities are now left to give students the skills and knowledge that high schools once provided. This argument makes sense, looking at the global picture. In Japan, half as many people go to college as in the United States, despite the fact that a *greater* percentage of Japanese students obtain the qualifications necessary to go on to postsecondary education. The logical conclusion, supported by comparisons of test scores (see test scores on the following pages), is that the Japanese students leave high school better educated than their American counterparts. Most, in fact, are ready to enter the job market without a college degree. As a result, Japanese students who do attend university are engaged in more advanced work, while many Americans are merely catching up. A good share of American college students, in fact, graduate with the same knowledge as a Japanese high school graduate—or less. "An average eighth grader in Japan knows more mathematics than a graduate of a master of business administration program in the United States," says Richard Lamm, former governor of Colorado, and an "average seventeen-year-old American knows half as much math as an average Swedish seventeen-year-old." 155

160

165

Percentage of population age 20 to 24 enrolled full time in institutions of higher education, 1986–90

| Country | Higher Ed. Enrollment | Country | Higher Ed. Enrollment |
|---|---|---|---|
| United States | 18.5 | Greece | 13.2 |
| Canada | 15.9 | Australia | 12.2 |
| France | 14.6 | Switzerland | 12.0 |
| Belgium | 14.1 | Sweden | 11.3 |
| Germany | 14.1 | Finland | 11.2 |
| Denmark | 13.9 | New Zealand | 6.9 |
| Netherlands | 13.8 | United Kingdom | 6.3 |
| Norway | 13.5 | Ireland | 4.6 |

Source: United Nations Development Programme, *Human Development Report 1991* (New York: Oxford University Press, 1991), p. 181.

## Teachers

- **We're Last in rewarding our teachers.**

Education policymakers have recognized the importance of rewarding committed educators. Yet veteran American teachers make less money than veteran teachers in seven other nations surveyed relative to per capita gross domestic product (GDP). At the starting level, American teachers make less than teachers in all seven nations except Japan. Switzerland leads in salaries for both starting 170

and veteran teachers; the maximum salary for a Swiss secondary teacher is
175  about three times the nation's per capita GDP.

Low wages discourage talented American college students from entering
teaching. Public school teachers in the United States start with a salary of
$20,529 on average, while their counterparts make $32,304 in entry-level positions in engineering, $27,408 in accounting, and $27,828 in sales. Recently, as
180  improving education has become a national priority and teachers' salaries have
increased, there has been renewed interest in teaching among young Americans. Still, we have a long way to go to catch up with teachers' salaries in other
countries.

Ratio of average teacher salary to per capita gross domestic product (GDP), 1988–90

| Country | Maximum Salary (Ratio to per Capita GDP) | Starting Salary (Ratio to per Capita GDP) |
|---|---|---|
| Switzerland | 2.97 | 1.69 |
| Austria | 2.60 | 0.98 |
| Canada | 2.22 | 1.10 |
| Japan | 2.21 | 0.75 |
| Germany | 2.19 | 1.37 |
| United Kingdom | 2.05 | 0.95 |
| Australia | 1.60 | 1.09 |
| United States | 1.58 | 0.94 |

Source: American Federation of Teachers.

## Math and Science

- **We're Number One in percentage of students who say they're good at math.**
- **We're Last in percentage of students who *are* good at math.**

Math is a priority for Americans—at least we say it is. Eighty-three percent of
185  Americans, more than any other nation surveyed, say it is absolutely necessary
to know something about mathematics in order to be a well-rounded person. In
fact, Americans are four times as likely to say this as the Japanese (21 percent)
and more than twice as likely as the Germans (36 percent).

In addition, more American students say that they are good at math than do
190  students from other nations surveyed. Sixty-eight percent of American thirteen-
year-olds agree with the statement "I am good at mathematics," three times as
many as in South Korea (23 percent), where the smallest percentage of students
say this. What's particularly alarming (or amusing) about our students' confidence is that they perform *worse* than any other nation included in this survey,

and the modest students, the Koreans, perform the best. Researchers in Korea    195
note that "it would be against their tradition of humility for many of their students to answer 'yes' to the question 'Are you good at math?'" But that humility
clearly doesn't exist among American students—and as the scores show, we
have reason to be humble.

The International Assessment of Educational Progress (the study men-    200
tioned above) finds the United States to be the only nation among six studied
where students perform *below* the mean average. According to the IAEP study,
97 percent of American thirteen-year-olds can add and subtract; 78 percent can
do simple math problems, like using a number line; 40 percent (about half as
many as in Korea) can do two-step problems; 9 percent (less than one quarter as    205
many as in Korea) understand measurement and geometry concepts; and only
1 percent can interpret data in more advanced math problems. A second international math study, conducted by the International Association for the Evaluation of Educational Achievement (IAE), also shows abysmal results for the
United States.    210

Percentage of thirteen-year-old students who agree with the
statement "I am good at mathematics," and math proficiency
on a scale ranging from 0 to 1,000, with 500 as the mean, 1988

| Country | Say They're Good at Math | Math Score |
|---|---|---|
| **United States** | 68 | 473.9 |
| Canada | 61 | 522.8 |
| Spain | 60 | 511.7 |
| Ireland | 49 | 504.3 |
| United Kingdom | 47 | 509.9 |
| South Korea | 23 | 567.8 |

Source: Educational Testing Service, *A World of Differences: An International Assessment of Mathematics and Science* (Princeton, N.J.: ETS, 1989), pp. 14, 24.

*And we'll balance the budget by then, too.*

"By the year 2000, U.S. students will be first in the world in science and mathematics achievement," says President Bush's National Goals for Education, developed with the fifty governors. But even Secretary of Education Lamar Alexander
is skeptical of the President's optimism. "If our aim is to be first in the world in
math and science by the year 2000," says Alexander, "there is an enormous    215
challenge ahead of us." Indeed, the challenge is so enormous as to make one
wonder whether the President and the nation's governors knew when they set
their goals just how badly America fares in international math and science comparisons. Maybe they should just shoot for a balanced budget.

- **We're Number One in percentage of young adolescents who DON'T think science is useful in everyday life.**
- **We're Last in science proficiency among young adolescents.**

220   Is what students learn in science relevant to everyday life? Only half of American thirteen-year-olds say it is, the smallest percentage of students in six nations surveyed. No wonder: American students also say they spend more time in science class *reading* their textbook and less time doing experiments than any other nation studied. Seventy percent say reading the text is a common activity, 225   while less than 20 percent say doing experiments is common.

Perhaps that explains why the United States performs so poorly in a study of science proficiency among fourteen-year-olds conducted by the International Association for the Evaluation of Educational Achievement. Out of seventeen nations tested, only the Philippines and Hong Kong perform more poorly than 230   the United States. America is outperformed by all of the nineteen major industrial nations tested, as well as Hungary and Poland, while Thailand and Singapore tie us.

Average science test scores among fourteen-year-olds in seventeen countries, 1983–86

| Country | Science Score | Country | Science Score |
|---------|---------------|---------|---------------|
| Hungary | 21.7 | Australia | 17.8 |
| Japan | 20.2 | Italy | 16.7 |
| Netherlands | 19.8 | United Kingdom | 16.7 |
| Canada | 18.6 | Singapore | 16.5 |
| Finland | 18.5 | Thailand | 16.5 |
| Sweden | 18.4 | **United States** | **16.5** |
| Poland | 18.1 | Hong Kong | 16.4 |
| South Korea | 18.1 | Philippines | 11.5 |
| Norway | 17.9 | | |

Source: International Association for the Evaluation of Educational Achievement, *Science Achievement in Seventeen Countries, A Preliminary Report* (New York: Pergamon Press, 1988).

- **We're Number 29 in scientists and technicians per capita.**

Egad! The United States has won the most Nobel prizes in science, but twenty-eight nations (including fourteen of the nineteen major industrial nations) have 235   more scientists and technicians per capita than we do. The United States has only 55 scientists and technicians per 1,000 persons, about six times fewer than Japan, which has 317 per 1,000 people. The average among industrial nations is 139 scientists and technicians per 1,000.

It's not surprising that we have so few scientists per capita, since only 30 240   percent of our college and university graduates major in science. Though the

United States graduates about three hundred thousand students annually with bachelor's degrees in natural and applied sciences, seventy-five countries (including Iran, Peru, Swaziland, Haiti, and Afghanistan) have a greater percentage of students graduating from postsecondary institutions with science degrees.

245

Scientists and technicians per 1,000 people, 1980–88

| Country | Scientists per 1,000 | Country | Scientists per 1,000 |
|---------|----------------------|---------|----------------------|
| Japan | 317 | Czechoslovakia | 130 |
| Austria | 268 | Spain | 130 |
| Sweden | 262 | Soviet Union | 128 |
| Canada | 257 | Bulgaria | 113 |
| Hungary | 251 | Norway | 103 |
| Ireland | 244 | Venezuela | 95 |
| Netherlands | 219 | France | 83 |
| Switzerland | 202 | Italy | 83 |
| Hong Kong | 200 | Israel | 82 |
| Yugoslavia | 192 | Peru | 76 |
| Poland | 168 | Argentina | 75 |
| Greece | 166 | Denmark | 63 |
| Cyprus | 158 | Kuwait | 63 |
| Australia | 157 | **United States** | 55 |
| Germany | 131 | New Zealand | 49 |

Source: United Nations Development Programme, *Human Development Report 1991* (New York: Oxford University Press, 1991), pp. 128, 174.

## Geography

- **We're Number One in percentage of people who say it is absolutely necessary to be able to read a map.**

- **We're Number One in ignorance of geography among young people.**

Where is the equator? The nearest mountain range? The next highway exit with a rest room? Americans place great value on the ability to read a map, according to a poll conducted by Gallup for the National Geographic Society. We lead nine countries surveyed in percentage of adults saying that being able to read a map is an "absolutely necessary" skill (69 percent). Map reading is more important to us than being able to write a business letter, or use a calculator or a personal computer. Ninety-five percent of Americans say that it is important for us to know at least as much geography as people in other countries.

250

Yet despite our cartographic compulsion, Americans age 18 to 24 rank dead last in geographic knowledge among the nine countries surveyed. On

255

average, young Americans are able to correctly identify about seven of the following sixteen places on a world map: Canada, Central America, Egypt, France, Italy, Japan, Mexico, the Pacific Ocean, the Persian Gulf, South Africa, Sweden, the United Kingdom, the United States, the Soviet Union, West Germany, and Vietnam. The most geographically knowledgeable young respondents, the Swedes, are able to locate about twelve of the sixteen places.

Results of the poll among other age groups show that our knowledge of geography is declining. Respondents age 55 and older scored the *best* comparatively of all U.S. age groups: they were fifth among nine countries in geographic prowess. Those age 35 to 44 and 45 to 54 were sixth; and Americans age 25 to 34 were seventh. In fact, the United States was the only country in which geographic knowledge among the oldest group of respondents was higher than that of the youngest. The face of the earth is becoming increasingly unrecognizable to Americans.

Mean number of correct answers (out of sixteen) in a geography test given in nine countries, 1988

| Country | Correct Answers, Age 18 to 24 | Correct Answers, Age 55 and over |
|---|---|---|
| Sweden | 11.9 | 10.3 |
| Germany | 11.2 | 10.9 |
| Japan | 9.5 | 7.9 |
| Canada | 9.3 | 8.7 |
| Italy | 9.3 | 5.5 |
| France | 9.2 | 8.8 |
| United Kingdom | 9.0 | 7.8 |
| Mexico | 8.2 | 5.7 |
| **United States** | 6.9 | 8.4 |

Source: The Gallup Organization, "Geography: An International Gallup Survey" (Princeton, N.J.: Gallup, 1988), p. 55.

### The United States . . . of Sweden?

Even if we don't know much about world geography, at least we know about our own country. Right? Wrong. Less than half of those Americans surveyed know that our population is between 150 million and 300 million people. In five other nations, more respondents know the population of the United States than we do. Only a third of young Americans know the approximate population of the United States, less than in all but one of the nations surveyed. At the top, young Swedes are 44 percent more likely to know the number of inhabitants in the United States than are the American inhabitants of the same age.

Percentage of population age 18 to 24 who know that the American population is between 150 million and 300 million people, 1988

| Country | Know U.S. Population | Country | Know U.S. Population |
|---------|---------------------|---------|---------------------|
| Sweden | 46 | France | 35 |
| Mexico | 46 | **United States** | 32 |
| Canada | 42 | United Kingdom | 32 |
| Germany | 42 | Italy | 25 |
| Japan | 41 | | |

Source: The Gallup Organization, "Geography: An International Gallup Survey" (Princeton, N.J.: Gallup, 1988), p. 59.

- **We're Number One in percentage of people who DON'T think it's important to be able to speak a foreign language.**

While it is true that Americans can usually make do with just English on tourist jaunts, the ability to speak foreign languages is essential as we move toward a global economy and as the United States itself becomes more diverse. The fact that fewer Americans than respondents in other nations surveyed think it is important to speak a foreign language does not augur well. *¿Comprendes?*

280

Percentage of population saying it is "absolutely necessary" or "not too important" to be able to speak a foreign language, 1988

| Country | Absolutely Necessary | Not Too Important |
|---------|---------------------|-------------------|
| Mexico | 59 | 8 |
| France | 51 | 9 |
| Italy | 45 | 7 |
| Germany | 35 | 14 |
| Sweden | 34 | 10 |
| Japan | 29 | 13 |
| Canada | 23 | 24 |
| United Kingdom | 16 | 34 |
| **United States** | 15 | 34 |

Source: The Gallup Organization, "Geography: An International Gallup Survey" (Princeton, N.J.: Gallup, 1988), p. 70.

## Work Habits

- **We're Number One in percentage of students who say they watch five or more hours of television a day.**

- **We're Number One in percentage of students who say they don't do their homework.**

American students are falling behind in math and science not only because of problems in school, but because few have home environments that are conducive to hard work and thinking. As with other age groups, young students in the United States watch more television than their foreign counterparts. They are also most likely to not do their homework.

285

Percentage of thirteen-year-old students who say they watch five or more hours of television a day, and percentage who say they don't do their homework, 1988

| Country | Watch 5+ Hours of TV Daily | Don't Do Homework |
|---|---|---|
| United States | 31 | 5 |
| United Kingdom | 27 | 2 |
| Canada | 19 | 3 |
| Ireland | 14 | 2 |
| Spain | 13 | 1 |
| Korea | 7 | 3 |

Source: Educational Testing Service, *A World of Differences: An International Assessment of Mathematics and Science* (Princeton, N.J.: ETS, 1989), pp. 55–57.

## Looking Back

1. What particular factors does Shapiro cite at the beginning (lines 11–18) to support his thesis that the American system is failing? How does each factor reveal failure?

2. How are property taxes and public spending related as a source of educational funding? Does the formal relation hold true in practice?

3. What do you infer from the table showing a low United States yield from compulsory education (p. 394)? Explain your answer.

4. In what way is the middle class at a disadvantage in the Head Start program?

5. Do you think keeping children off the streets is sufficient reason for increasing the length of the school year (see lines 123–128)? Why or why not?

6. Should colleges admit all high school graduates, even if the high schools could provide a better education than they presently do, or should admissions tests decide the issue (see lines 129–168)? Explain your answer.

7. What problem do students have who say they're good at math but in fact are not (see lines 184–219)?

8. Should students' lack of interest in science decide the place of science in the curriculum? Should the demands of international competition influence the science curriculum (see the table, p. 400)? Explain your answer.

9. What features do you think characterize "home environments that are conducive to hard work and thinking" (lines 285–286)?

10. In what areas does Shapiro distinguish between quantity and quality of education? Why does America tend to cultivate the first but not the second?

## Writing Assignments

1. "American education," comments Andrew L. Shapiro, "appears to be more of an impediment than a safeguard of our collective fate" (lines 30–31). This early statement acts as a thesis for the rest of his commentary. He intends the evidence he collects to bear him out and convince his readers that his thesis is true. This is exactly the need every thesis has. The question always is, Does it succeed? Write an essay interpolating your own critical commentary in order to say whether Shapiro succeeds in substantiating his thesis. Pay particular attention to the terms he uses in his thesis, try to evaluate his methods of argument, and weigh his evidence.

2. In the final table (p. 404) Shapiro demonstrates that among six nations for which figures have been compiled the United States is number one in thirteen-year-old students who watch television five or more hours a day *and* who don't do their homework. The connection seems obvious, but clearly a favorable home situation is essential for study and may well be more important than the distraction of television. Adopting this point of view, write an essay defining a good home environment for students. Be as specific as you can in pinpointing the necessary conditions and in describing their effects.

3. Since the late 1960s, many American colleges and universities have instituted a policy of admitting anyone holding a high school diploma. So many students have taken advantage of this policy—60 percent of the nation's high school graduates in 1990— that now the United States has the greatest proportion of college enrollment among people aged 20 to 24 of sixteen countries surveyed (see the table on p. 397). Number one again, but quantity not quality is the result, says Shapiro, who faults the open admissions policy for flooding colleges with "underachievers" (line 150). What do you think about his position? Write an essay stating your view on the matter. Discuss the points Shapiro makes, and include references to your own experience if relevant.

# Vera Brittain

# Women Workers, Today and Tomorrow

A pacifist and feminist throughout most of her life, Vera Brittain (1893–1970) was able, through force of character as much as through fortunate circumstances, to attend college at a time when few women did and thereafter to lead an independent economic existence. During World War I, she served as a Voluntary Aid Detachment nurse in London, Malta, and at the front in France. Her fiancé, her brother, and two close male friends died in the war, a traumatic experience described in her autobiographical volume *Testament of Youth*. Other writings include poems and novels, but she is best known for her autobiographical work and her journalism, such as the essay here, reprinted from *Testament of a Generation*. In it, she achieves a major aim of the critical thinker: to imagine a new and original way to regard her subject.

## Looking Ahead

1. Brittain's historical consciousness guides her thought in this piece. It is therefore important to keep pace with the references to particular events and different eras.

2. Test the effect on political advocacy of objective facts, including statistics, particularly as they influence the feminist case for equality.

3. More than fifty years have passed since Brittain penned this article, so you will do well to observe how the situation of women working has changed and how it has not.

For the second time within a generation, England's women workers are deeply involved in a world war.

There is one thing, and perhaps only one, to be said in favour of these gigantic conflicts, which have dictated the history of our time. They are convul-
5   sions which shake all life to its foundations; and though they destroy too much that is good, they bring down antiquated traditions and prejudices as well. Because war is a time of testing, it is also a period of opportunity. Of no section of our society is this truer than of its women.

The last war completed the struggle of women to escape from the tyranny
10  of Victorian homes. Before that war began, this country had witnessed such now historic conflicts as the fight for higher education, the struggle to enter hitherto masculine professions such as medicine and the law, and the campaign for the franchise. After so much preliminary spadework, the changes brought by the war came fast. Between 1914 and 1919, women had entered industry
15  and the professions in large numbers. They had shown ability in fields hitherto regarded as beyond their powers. Being required to move as well as to think quickly, they had discarded the voluminous garments and complicated coiffures of Edwardian fashion. They had already achieved emancipation in practice when the partial franchise was bestowed on them in 1918, and in 1919 the Sex
20  Disqualification (Removal) Act admitted them, at least theoretically, to the majority of professions.

So far as women exclusively are concerned, this war is unlikely to bring so many dynamic changes, but rather, by further establishing the right to equality and the capacity for full comradeship with men, to continue what the first cata-
25  clysm began. Women will find themselves part of a far greater revolution which will involve society as a whole in its results. As Ralph Ingersoll remarked of the dancers at the Dorchester in his wartime book, *Report on England*: "What is about to expire is not the breath in their bodies but their property rights in banks and mortgages. What is about to end is life as they knew it."

Students of history realize that we are now at the close of that epoch of modern European history which began with the Renaissance. We live in an era potentially as tremendous in its consequences as the fall of the Roman Empire. The first Great War started revolutionary changes in certain sections of society. The present war is likely to make them universal. A new page of history is about to be turned. How far are the women workers of today preparing for the chapters which they will share in writing?

Both industry and the professions clearly show the signs of the times. One of the most important developments has been the increasing use of compulsory powers by the Minister of Labour, culminating in the recent National Service Act which empowers him to direct women into the Auxiliary Services. The chief steps towards this compulsion have been the withdrawal of girls from 20 to 25 from the distributive trades (with the exception of the food trades), from the light clothing trade (women's underwear, children's clothes, millinery, etc.), and to some extent from the Civil Service. Since the Employment of Women (Control of Engagement) Order came into force on 16 February, women between 20 and 30 have only been able to obtain employment through the Labour Exchange.

In the great munition and engineering industries which now absorb so many women, there are three groups of female workers. These comprise the women doing work which was known as women's work before the war, the women who are doing men's work but are not recognized as thus engaged, and the women who are doing men's work, whether skilled, semi-skilled or unskilled. By no means all these women belong to what were commonly described as "the working classes" before the war. Quite a number of middle-class girls from secondary schools, called up under the National Service Act, are now going into factories. Some hope to use their experience after the war to obtain posts as factory inspectors and welfare officers. Although important supervisory positions are reserved for women with previous experience, many of these girls get promotion to the category of "charge hands" who supervise a number of workers.

There is now little segregation in industry between men and women workers as such. Any practical working division between the sexes is dictated by the nature of the work and not by prejudice. It is recognized that distinctions between "men's" work and "women's" work are largely arbitrary. Many women are naturally talented on the mechanical side of industry, and are often regarded as better at precision work through having more patience.

This does not mean that none of the old inequalities remain. The attitude of official England towards women was shown at a recent meeting of the International Labour Organization in New York, when the British delegation did not include one woman even in an advisory capacity. Discriminations against women exist throughout the field of compensation and insurance. Under the Personal Injuries (Civilian) Scheme a woman is paid 7s. [shillings] a week less than a man for civilian war injuries, and under the National Insurance system women's benefits and allowances are less than men's. For this reason a woman's

75   recovery from sickness is often retarded, since she cannot afford to buy nourishing food or to take sufficient rest.

But on the whole the main handicaps from which women suffer in industry, as in the professions, are the two from which, despite frequent promises of amendment, they have suffered since the last war—limited opportunity
80   and unequal pay. In wartime there is a tendency to exploit women and make patriotic appeals to them to sacrifice claims which have hitherto been regarded as excuses for denying them equal rights. Married women tend to be the chief sufferers from this policy. In many occupations, and notably in such professions as teaching and the Civil Service, women before the war were dis-
85   missed on marriage with the plausible excuses that the sacredness of family life would be impaired by a mother going out to work, and economic stability disturbed by two incomes coming into one home. But as soon as women's work is required on a large scale, both these excuses go by the board. The sacredness of family life has not prevented government pressure upon married
90   women to enter industry, leaving their children with neighbors or, if they are fortunate, in day nurseries. Nor does anybody—except perhaps magistrates concerned with cases of juvenile delinquency owing to excessive spending power—worry unduly about not only two, but five or six, incomes going into one home.

95   In munition factories the women doing men's work receive about four-fifths of a man's wages. "Munitions" now include every requirement of war in addition to the death-dealing and damage-inflicting weapons which are at present the main objects of production. Lorries, signalling sets, searchlights, the very tools themselves, all become munitions in wartime. Their makers are re-
100   cruited from such "non-essential" industries as dressmaking, cosmetics, jewellery, and the various branches of the tourist trade.

Under the Government Training Schemes, even more marked inequality of pay exists. Men of 21 and over receive a weekly wage of 65s. 6d. [pence], with a first and second increment of 5s., making a maximum "male" rate of 75s. 6d.
105   Women of 21 and over, though doing the same work, receive a weekly wage of 43s. with a first and second increment of 3s., making a maximum "female" rate of 49s.

At a Training Centre for three hundred women in London, I talked to a girl who had worked at Harrod's Stores, to the ex-proprietress of a dressmaking es-
110   tablishment in South Molton Street, and to an actress who had belonged to a repertory company. Later the woman superintendent sent me a list of occupations previously pursued by the trainees at the Institute. It read as follows: "Office workers, 58; housewife or no specified occupation, 138; dressmaker, milliner, tailor, 21; cutter or designer, 7; saleswoman, 23; teacher, 16; jour-
115   nalist, 13; beauty specialist, 11; supervisor, 14; artist, 10; actress, 8; catering or domestic, 17; ARP [Air Raid Precautions], 8; nurse, 5." There are now about forty Government Training Centres in different parts of the country, as well as a number of Emergency and Auxiliary Training Establishments.

Owing to the enormous development of mechanized warfare and to the existence of these training centres, engineering is the profession in which the position of women has most markedly changed. A woman with a gift for engineering has a much better chance of success than before the war, when women were not employed in engineering shops, and pioneers such as Amy Johnson and Caroline Haslett had considerable difficulty in acquiring the necessary training or finding it for others.

But engineering is not, of course, the only professional field for women affected by the war. In the Civil Service a large number of women of all ages are being taken on as temporary clerks, and many women graduates on coming down from the university become Temporary Assistant principals (Administrative Grade). In September last the Woman Power Committee of the House of Commons, led by Miss Thelma Cazalet, MP, took a deputation to Mr. Eden[1] on the subject of women's exclusion from the Diplomatic and Consular Services. In a letter to the committee some time afterwards, Mr. Eden explained that all regular entry into these services was suspended for the duration of the war, but agreed then to consider the appointment of a committee to examine the question again "in the light of existing conditions." Meanwhile, he said, as a wartime measure he was prepared to consider applications, "through normal channels," from women as well as men for temporary posts of the Administrative Grade in the Foreign Office whenever any vacancies arose.

Neither in the Foreign Office nor the Civil Service, judging from the wholesale demobilization of women holding clerical posts after the last war, does there seem to be much prospect for the future. The field of accountancy appears better; at present there is a great demand for accountants, and if a girl is articled to an accountant when she registers, she is allowed to remain and finish her articles.

All the professions which previously admitted women are still open, though the uncertainty of being allowed to continue their training is affecting the entry of women over 20. Owing to a change of outlook since the last war, women university graduates seldom go into the Services. One of the characteristics of the present younger generation, among men as well as women, is a desire to get out of uniform rather than into it. A specialist in the field of women's employment recently remarked that today the women anxious to wear uniform are mainly "the less educated rather than the college type."

We are still, perhaps, too far from the end of the war for any detailed prophecies about its effects upon the position of women as such. The chairwoman of a leading women's organization lately stated: "I do not think that the position of women will be as bad as it was after the last war, as I do not think that the government or employers will care to drop back to the old attitude to the same extent. We can make more fuss, or rather a more effective fuss, than

---

1. *Anthony Eden* (1897–1977): British statesman and prime minister of Great Britain from 1955–1957. (*ed.*)

160   we could then." The extension of the National Service Acts to women certainly includes all statutory safeguards, such as those of reinstatement or compensation on demobilization. If we lived in a wholly logical society it would seem obvious that one reply to Nazism, which regards women as auxiliaries, would be to treat them as equals.

165   After the last war, the often-repeated pious decision by public bodies—"We must have *a woman* on this committee"—gave expression to the public opinion which, still with some surprise, was praising women's achievements. When the present conflict ends, popular sentiment, having long taken for granted the presence of women in public life, is more likely to say: "We must have Mrs. X

170   on this committee because we need an expert accountant—or statistician—or legal adviser." If women, by training, fit themselves now to fill positions open to those with special qualifications, they will be ready to play their part in that unknown, difficult but adventurous future which lies beyond the end of this war.

## Looking Back

1. What saving grace does Brittain find in war?
2. Can you say, in reference to her remark about costume (lines 16–18), how women today free themselves from certain encumbering styles of dress and adopt others that suit their life-style or symbolize their independence?
3. What does Brittain mean by "full comradeship with men" (line 24)?
4. In lines 35–36, what structural function does the rhetorical question perform?
5. How, according to Brittain, have the minister of labor's directives helped women enter occupations previously reserved for men (see lines 37–47)?
6. Why might middle-class women want to continue factory work after the war, as Brittain claims they do (lines 56–57)?
7. As a principle of women's rights, can you reformulate the following declaration: "Any practical working division between the sexes is dictated by the nature of the work and not by prejudice. It is recognized that distinctions between 'men's' work and 'women's' are largely arbitrary" (lines 62–64)? Do you agree with this principle entirely, partly, or not at all?
8. What two "main handicaps" does industry impose on women? How do they injure women?
9. Which newly entered professions does the author think hold most promise for women in postwar Britain?
10. How would you define men's and women's equality, particularly as Brittain envisions it (see the last paragraph of the article)?

## Writing Assignments

1. Brittain tells us that during World War I, in order "to move as well as to think quickly," women "discarded the voluminous garments and complicated coiffures of

Edwardian fashion" (lines 16–18). The kind of freedom women gained then has continued to influence women's style of dress. These changes are applauded by many people yet have not met universal approval. Some criticize modern styles as making women into mere objects and puppets of fashion, enslaved to their appearance and losing in the bargain the freedom emancipated style was supposed to provide. What do you think? Write an essay addressing the issue of the general revolution in women's dress as one that has freed them, locked them up again, or done some of both. For essay material, look around you.

2. The headline tells the story in a *New York Times* op-ed column on June 25, 1992: "Let Women Fly in Combat." Arguing on behalf of women aviators, U.S. Army Captain Jamie Ann Conway compares Pentagon unwillingness to let women fight to the Army Air Corps' refusal to train African Americans as pilots for six crucial years prior to World War II. Is the comparison apt? What do you think Brittain's position would be? What is your considered opinion on the issue? Write an essay taking up the issue of whether women should be combat pilots. Particularly weigh Conway's final comment in her article, that the military's concern should "not be gender but the pilot's ability to put steel on target."

3. "If we lived in a wholly logical society," writes Vera Brittain, "it would seem obvious that one reply to Nazism, which regards women as auxiliaries, would be to treat them as equals" (lines 162–164). Women's equality is certainly more advanced than when Brittain wrote but equal status is by no means fully achieved. It continues to be necessary to imagine additional forms women's equality with men might take, and by so doing, help create personal and public goals for change. Write an essay in which you describe a new form of equality in a particular area of life. It can be the workplace, marriage, the family, the classroom, the political arena, or wherever women have a compelling interest. To help you do this, you may want to adopt the vision with which Brittain ends her article.

# Ronald Takaki

# Different Shores

Ronald Takaki (b. 1939), whose grandparents immigrated from Japan, is a professor of ethnic studies at the University of California, Berkeley. He has won Berkeley's Distinguished Teaching Award and was granted Cornell University's Goldwin Smith Union Lectureship. His concern with immigration patterns is personal as well as scholarly, as the tone of the following excerpt clearly demonstrates:

> Their dreams and hopes unfurled here before the wind, all of them—from the first Chinese miners sailing through the Golden Gate to the last Vietnamese people flying into Los Angeles International Airport—have been making history in America. And they have been telling us about it all along.

The following essay, whose critical purpose is to reevaluate the position of minority groups in the United States, is from the introduction to his edited volume, *From Different Shores: Perspectives on Race and Ethnicity in America.*

## Looking Ahead

1. Although this piece introduces a book on various aspects of race and ethnicity, Takaki pays most attention to the issue of affirmative action as a social response to historical developments. Read critically to test his reasoning on the subject.

2. Notice the author's structural decision—which may influence your own writing—to move from personal history to a general overview of origins, and from there to the particular issue of affirmative action.

3. As you read, keep in mind your own locale and its ethnic and racial make-up.

In the community where I lived as a child, my neighbors were Japanese, Chinese, Hawaiian, and Portuguese. Nearby there were Filipinos and Puerto Ricans. As I grew up, I did not ask why—why were we from so many "different shores," from Asia and Europe as well as Hawaii itself, living together in Palolo
5   Valley on the island of Oahu? My teachers and my textbooks did not explain the reasons why we were there.

After graduation from high school, I attended a college on the mainland where I found myself invited to dinners for "foreign students." I politely tried to explain to my kind hosts that I was not a foreign student; still they insisted that
10   I accept their invitations. My fellow students (and even my professors) would ask me where I had learned to speak English. "In this country," I would reply. And sometimes I would add, "I was born in America, and my family has been here for three generations." Like myself, they had been taught little or nothing about America's ethnic diversity, and they thought I looked like a foreigner.

15      The college curriculum itself contributed to their perception of me. Courses in American literature and history, by not including knowledge about racial minorities, had rendered them to be outsiders. "American," in effect, was "white." All of the readings assigned to my course on American literature, for example, were written by white authors. We did not read works by Richard Wright (*Native*
20   *Son*), Carlos Bulosan (*America Is in the Heart*), and Toshio Mori (*Yokohama, California*). Here was a course on the literature of America, but it did not teach the literature of all Americans.

For graduate study, I entered a Ph.D. program in American history. And there I studied the history of America as if there had been no racial minorities in
25   this country's past, certainly no Chicanos and no Asians. The war against Mexico was studied, and the Chinese were given a brief reference in discussions of the transcontinental railroad. Blacks were there, in the antebellum South, as slaves. And Indians were present, too, as obstacles to progress or as an ill-fated race. I was in an American history Ph.D. program, but I was not studying the
30   history of all the peoples of America.

But I felt the stirrings of protest and agitation happening outside the university as the civil rights movement of the sixties awakened America to the presence of blacks and the problem of racial inequality. I found myself deeply involved in the study of race relations in the Old South. After completing a dissertation on the Southern defense of slavery, I began teaching black history   35
but soon realized the need to study also the experiences of Native Americans, Chicanos, and Asian Americans. This awareness led me to broaden my focus and to write *Iron Cages: Race and Culture in 19th-Century America,* a comparative study of the experiences of the different racial groups (and also white workers and women) within the context of the culture and economy of the United   40
States.

While writing this book, I returned on a sabbatical to the place where I had grown up. There, on hot afternoons, I often visited an old retired uncle, and the two of us would sit in the backyard and "talk story." During one of these discussions, my uncle exclaimed, "Hey, why you no go write a book about us, huh?   45
After all, your grandfather came over here as a contract laborer. He worked on the plantation. And your mother was born on the plantation, and also all of your aunts and uncles." And I replied, "Why not?"

Some time after making this casual remark, I found myself examining old documents in archives and came across scores of business memoranda. One   50
of them, dated August 22, 1890, from Theo. H. Davies and Company to C. McClennan, manager of the Laupahoehoe plantation, acknowledged receipt of an order for:

    tobacco
    portuguese laborers. We have ordered 20 men for you.                55
    lumber
    7 ft. iron bar
    wool mattress
    olive oil

In another memorandum on July 2, 1890, the Davies Company wrote McClen-   60
nan regarding an order for bone meal, canvas, "Japanese laborers," macaroni, and a "Chinaman." A letter of May 5, 1908, from H. Hackfield and Company (now American Factors) to George Wilcox of the Grove Farm plantation listed alphabetically orders for "fertilizer" and "Filipinos." As I read these fading documents, I finally began to understand why peoples from all over the world lived   65
in my neighborhood.

Recently America's racial and ethnic diversity has been the focus of much attention by politicians and the press. In his acceptance speech before the 1984 Republican Convention, President Ronald Reagan referred to the Olympics to illustrate the multiple strands of America:
   70

We cheered in Los Angeles as the flame was carried in and the giant Olympic torch burst into a billowing fire in front of the teams. The youth of 140 nations assembled on the floor of the Coliseum. And in that moment, maybe you were

75 struck as I was with the uniqueness of what was taking place before 100,000 people in the stadium, most of the citizens in our country, and over a billion worldwide watching on television. There were athletes representing 140 countries here to compete in the one country in all the world whose people carry the bloodlines of all those 140 countries and more. Only in the United States is there such a mixture of races, creeds, and nationalities—only in our melting
80 pot . . . every promise, every opportunity is still golden in this land.


The next year, in July 1985, *Time* published a special issue on America's "Immigrants." Filled with photographs and statistical charts, *Time* noted the "changing face of America": "Twenty years ago, more than half of all immigrants came from Europe and Canada. Today, most are Mexicans, Filipinos, Viet-
85 namese, Koreans, Indians, Chinese, Dominicans, Jamaicans." The new face of America has a darker hue. And, according to *Time,* "Americans" are anxiously asking, "How long before the Third World overwhelms the First World?"

Of course, Americans have actually been both Third World (from Africa, Asia, and Latin America) and First World (from Europe) for a long time. The
90 first Africans arrived in the English colonies before the Pilgrims came on the *Mayflower*. The Chinese were already in America by the time Italian and Polish immigrants set foot on Ellis Island. And Mexicans in the Southwest found themselves incorporated into the United States after the war against Mexico in 1848.

But while America has been a cosmopolitan society for centuries, a sharp-
95 ened sense of its multiple racial and ethnic origins has emerged in the 1980s. Reagan's speech and *Time*'s special issue reflect this awareness, and their descriptions of our multiplicity are supported by census data and population projections. In 1980, American society was 76.7 percent white, 6.4 percent Hispanic, 11.7 percent black, 1.55 percent Asian and Pacific Islander, and other
100 races for the remainder. Of the white population, only 22 percent were of English ancestry, compared to 28.8 percent German and 24.4 percent Irish. Other whites included Italian (6.6 percent), Polish (4.7), Russian (1.9), Czechoslovakian (0.9), Hungarian (0.9), Greek (0.6), Swedish (2.7), and Norwegian (2.3). Concentrations of the Third World in the United States are especially evident in
105 urban areas. Blacks and Hispanics constitute close to or over 50 percent of the population of New York, Chicago, Atlanta, Detroit, Baltimore, Philadelphia, Cleveland, and Los Angeles. Hispanics alone represent sizable proportions of many metropolitan populations: 64 percent of Miami, 55 percent of San Antonio, 33 percent of Los Angeles, and 20 percent of Hartford. Three hundred
110 thousand Salvadorans reside in Los Angeles, nearly half the population of San Salvador. The City of Angels also has a population of 2 million Mexicans, more than any city except Mexico City. Twenty-two percent of the San Francisco population is Asian and Pacific Islander, and 200,000 Chinese live in New York, the largest Chinese community outside China itself. By the year 2000,
115 racial minorities will constitute over 30 percent of the U.S. population, with Hispanics and blacks each representing 13 percent. Reflecting this increase in

the minority population, 55 percent of the people of California will be white, 28 percent Hispanic, 7 percent black, and 10 percent Asian. Another projection, based on the racial composition of the school-aged population, predicts racial minorities will represent a majority of the people of California as early as the 1990s.

But what does it mean for America to have such a "rich mixture of races," and can racial inequality be overcome?

In *Ethnic America: A History* (1981), Thomas Sowell offers some answers. His scope is comprehensive. Though he overlooks Native Americans, he has chapters on the Irish, Germans, Jews, Italians, Chinese, Japanese, blacks, Puerto Ricans, and Mexicans. His report on ethnic America is cheerful and optimistic. "There are wide variations in the rates of progress among Americans," he states sanguinely, "but progress itself is pervasive." As Sowell notes, examples to support such a contention not only abound, they are also dramatic. Descendants of slaves today sit in Congress and on the Supreme Court, and O. J. Simpson is hailed as an American phenomenon.[1] Ethnic groups have made it or are making it into middle-class society. Many of them, especially Jews and Asian Americans, have family incomes above the national average. And even Puerto Ricans, Mexican Americans, and blacks are on the road to progress.

This new assessment has led Sowell to dismiss or deemphasize the importance of prejudice or group discrimination: "If bigotry alone was a sufficient causal explanation [for inequality], Jews and Japanese would not be among the most prosperous American ethnic groups." "Color," Sowell acknowledges, did play a "major role" in determining the fate of many Americans. But it was not an all-powerful determinant, he counters, and it has and can be overcome. How? Sowell examines different ethnic groups, one by one, in order to explain why ethnic Americans have been able to improve their lives.

Politics could not have been an important factor, Sowell contends, pointing out that "the Japanese, like the Chinese, studiously avoided political agitation for their rights." Neither was education the key to ethnic mobility and success: "The educational panacea is undermined by the history of groups like the Jews, the Chinese, and the Japanese, who first rose by their labor and their business sense and only later on could afford to send their children to college."

More important than their labor, Sowell argues, was their "middle class" orientation and values of discipline, obedience, politeness, hard work, thrift, industry, diligence, and self-reliance. Sowell sings high praises to the Chinese laundryman, the Japanese gardener, and the Jewish shopkeeper: "What made these humble occupations avenues to affluence was the effort, thrift, dependability, and foresight that built business out of 'menial' tasks and turned sweat into capital."

Sowell applauds the most successful ethnic groups—Jews and Japanese—as paragons of middle-class virtues. Jews, whose family incomes are the highest of any large ethnic group—72 percent above the national average—have a "very

---

1. Takaki wrote this about Simpson before the latter's murder trial in 1995. (*ed.*)

low rate of alcoholism" and a "traditional concern for cleanliness." The most important area of restraint, for Sowell, involves family size. Jewish families are
among the smallest, and the average Japanese American woman in the thirty-
five to forty-four age bracket has only 2.2 children compared to 3 children for
the average American woman in the same age category. On the other hand,
women of the less successful groups—blacks, Puerto Ricans, and Mexican
Americans—have the "highest fertility rates." Thus, they have less financial and
human resources to invest in individual children, enabling them to seize educational opportunities to advance themselves.

Sowell's historical study is mainly a prescription for the present. *Ethnic
America* seeks to describe the successful ethnic groups in order to offer instruction to groups still in poverty. Sowell advises discontented racial minorities to
avoid the "confrontationist" methods of "millitant" blacks. They should shun reliance on government intervention and welfare. They should instead follow the
example of the Japanese, whose "quiet persistence" and hard work have enabled
them to rise from the internment camps of World War II to a family-income status 32 percent above the national average. Sowell's "history" contains a conservative message: accommodation and self-help should be the strategy for racial
minorities.

But how seriously we consider Sowell's prescription should depend on our
assessment of his scholarship. Sowell reports ethnic "progress," but how
should progress be measured? In *Ethnic America,* we may have a case where the
means of measurement may be the message. *How* we calculate success may determine our conclusions. For example, in his discussion of Puerto Ricans, Sowell compares the incomes of Puerto Rican families headed by males in the
twenty-five to thirty-four age bracket with the incomes of "families of other
Americans of the same description," demonstrating that the income of such
Puerto Rican families is 96 percent of the other families and that Puerto Rican
"progress" has occurred. But we need to know what proportion of all Puerto
Rican families are headed by males: otherwise, we would be making conclusions based on families which do not represent the group itself. Furthermore,
two-thirds of the Puerto Rican population on the mainland lives in New York,
where both family incomes and the cost of living are higher than the national
average.

Similarly, Sowell calls the high family income of Japanese Americans remarkable. But he fails to underscore two crucial characteristics of this group.
First, more Japanese American families have two income earners than the average family. In 1970, both husbands and wives worked in over half of all Japanese American families, compared to 39 percent of all families in the country.
Hence the fact that Japanese American families have higher earnings than the
average family indicates that there are more members of each Japanese American family working. Second, Japanese Americans are concentrated in urban areas and also in Hawaii and California, states which have considerably higher average incomes and higher costs of living than the nation as a whole.

Even where Sowell's statistical analysis is accurate, his interpretation is sometimes open to question. According to Sowell, women of the less success- ful groups—blacks, Puerto Ricans, and Mexican Americans—have more chil- dren than women of the groups that have advanced themselves socially and economically. What does this finding mean? Here Sowell quips, "The rich get richer, and the poor have children." He views the high fertility rate of the women in these groups as a cause of their poverty: it "directly lowers the stan- dard of living of a group by spreading a given income more thinly among fam- ily members." But, we need to ask, is a high fertility rate an effect or a cause of poverty?

In *Ethnic America,* Sowell assumes that the experiences of white ethnic groups and racial minorities have been different in degree rather than in kind. They were all "ethnic." But only blacks were enslaved, only Native Americans were removed to reservations, only Chinese were singled out for exclusion, and only Japanese Americans (not Italian Americans or German Americans) were placed in concentration camps. This difference between "ethnic" and "racial" experiences can be seen in the Naturalization Law of 1790. Sowell does not even mention this law, which remained in effect until 1952 and which reserved naturalized citizenship for whites only.

Finally, what does Sowell's analysis of ethnic America mean in terms of public policy? Whereas Sowell does not explicitly relate his historical thesis to public policy, he questions the need for and the political wisdom of affirmative action. If Japanese Americans can succeed through their own efforts and with- out government intervention, then so can blacks and other racial minorities. "Controversial" affirmative action programs, Sowell contends, have had "little or no effect beyond what had already been achieved under 'equal opportunity' policies in the 1960s." Moreover, the "public perception" of affirmative action has engendered "strong resentment" among whites generally. Thus, what we have in Sowell's celebration of the "progress" of ethnic America is a criticism of affirmative action.

Curiously, Sowell seems to have found some support or tacit agreement in radical or left circles, recently from Christopher Jencks in the *New York Review of Books.* In the conclusion of his review of Sowell's *Ethnic America,* Jencks ob- serves: "In today's political environment the only argument that will persuade minorities not to seek protection from competition is prudential: certain short- term benefits, especially those that derive from reverse discrimination, may cost blacks more than the benefits are worth."

This statement is extraordinarily provocative, for Jencks considers himself a "radical" as opposed to a "conservative." Jencks identifies Sowell as the latter and explains what it means to be a conservative in terms of the affirmative ac- tion issue. Essentially, it involves an assessment of affirmative action as "reverse discrimination" and as "harmful" governmental efforts to eliminate discrimina- tion. But what does it mean to be a radical on this issue? Here, as it turns out, Jencks is not a radical.

In his evaluation of Sowell, Jencks assumes the validity of the theory of reverse discrimination. He states, for example, that it is a "fact" that affirmative action policies have sometimes led to discrimination against whites. But he fails to question whether this fact is really a fact—to substantiate the claim of reverse discrimination. More important, Jencks does not provide a definition of racial discrimination. The term, Jencks should have made clear, describes the historical and official, government-sanctioned categorization of a group based on race for the purpose of social subordination and economic exploitation. An attempt at a definition might have clarified the difference between the racial experience and the white "ethnic" experience, and offered a way to assess the prospects for racial minorities to overcome inequality without the government acting affirmatively to eliminate it.

To use the term *reverse discrimination* to describe affirmative action is both confusing and incorrect. Affirmative action, contrary to a popular notion, does not impose quotas. Rather, it requires employers to assess the racial composition of their workers and to develop timetables and goals for creating greater opportunities for the employment of racial minorities. Thus, affirmative action is actually designed to address the legacy of past racial discrimination and existing inequality by training and identifying qualified individuals of excluded racial minorities and allowing them greater access to equality of opportunity in education and employment.

What Jencks does instead is to give scholarly legitimacy to the theory and claim of reverse discrimination. He is a "radical," yet he turns out to agree with Sowell, a conservative." He presents his case in the progressive *New York Review of Books,* and does so as a "radical," advising racial minorities that affirmative action is not "prudential." However, his very analysis, by accepting Sowell's definition of racial discrimination and the validity of reverse discrimination, contributes in effect to the very "political environment" making affirmative action imprudent. Thus, in the end, Jencks, like Sowell, pushes upward the cost of benefits derived from affirmative action even as he asks racial minorities whether the price might not be too high.

"History," Sowell writes, "is what happened, not what we wish had happened. . . . History can sometimes help us to assess our beliefs about the past or about the present or future." All of this is true. But clearly, as this discussion of Sowell shows, there are different ways to study race and ethnicity in America's past and present. . . .

## Looking Back

1. How does your early education about the flow of immigrants to the United States compare to Takaki's (see lines 1–6)?

2. Lurking behind the assumption of Takaki's fellow students and professors that he was a foreign student are probably what attitudes?

3. Does Takaki's college education with respect to minorities resemble your own? Describe the similarities and differences.

4. What do the old documents Takaki finds reveal to him, and to us?

5. *Time* magazine reports Americans are concerned about changing immigration patterns. In your estimation, is the concern legitimate (see lines 86–87)?

6. Why does Sowell deemphasize political action as a path of escape from poverty?

7. Do you agree with Sowell that " 'middle class' orientation" (lines 150–151) and middle-class values are the key to immigrant success? Explain your answer.

8. What is Takaki's chief criticism of Sowell's method of argumentation (see especially lines 178–222)?

9. On the basis of Takaki's presentation, do you think that affirmative action is merely reverse discrimination or actually fair public policy? Explain your answer.

10. What is *your* answer to the questions Takaki poses echoing Reagan's allusion to the Olympics opening ceremony: "But what does it mean for America to have such a 'rich mixture of races,' and can racial inequality be overcome?" (lines 122–123)?

## Writing Assignments

1. In a major section of this essay, Ronald Takaki disputes Thomas Sowell on a number of points relating to the acceptability and prosperity of various ethnic and racial groups in the United States. Write an essay that summarizes the issues and the writers' respective positions in order to reach your own conclusions in support of one side or the other. Use any personal experience you think is relevant, but depend mostly on analysis and reasoned argument.

2. Here follow a publicly stated personal attitude and a political fact, both of which are related to race and ethnicity. The attitude was expressed in a statement made to the editor of this book by a guest at a dinner party he attended. The guest deplored the educational opportunities offered Asian immigrants by colleges and universities in the United States, since these people's admission to college is often at the expense of educating "real Americans." The political fact is that in Germany citizenship is almost always granted only to people whose racial stock is German; it is not automatically conferred by being born in Germany, nor can it be gained after immigration by nonracial Germans except by surmounting almost impossible obstacles. Write an essay saying what the personal attitude and the political practice have in common and what you think of them. Imagine an audience that will include members of the immigrant groups mentioned above.

3. Write an essay expanding on your answer to number 10 in Looking Back to Takaki's key questions, repeated here: "But what does it mean for America to have such a 'rich mixture of races,' and can racial inequality be overcome?" Note that the questions are related by more than a common topic. That is, the answer to the first question may well lead to the answer to the second question. Anticipating this connection will help you unify your essay.

✼

# Mary Man-Kong
# Memories of My Mother

Born in Trinidad, West Indies, in 1966, Mary Man-Kong lives in New York City where she attends Hunter College. She has worked in various publishing houses and after she graduates may either continue in publishing or pursue a teaching career. In this essay, Man-Kong's central purpose is to put her subject—her mother—in a new light in order to think freshly, and therefore creatively, about her.

## *Looking Ahead*

1. This essay acts as a reminder that, while eulogizing the dead, it is possible to show deep feelings without becoming sentimental and to make a realistic appraisal without being harsh.
2. Notice how subtly notions of the family and of male dominance mesh here with a sense of immigration patterns; Man-Kong gives us indirect evidence but no direct comment.
3. Integration as social policy is reflected in individual attitudes in this essay. Test the author's presentation of this idea to see if it helps you to understand in a better way social relations generally.

It happened so suddenly that sometimes I wonder if I dreamed it all. I still expect to hear my mother singing a Chinese song under her breath as she sews my father's shirt, to see her making a pan full of vegetables dance in hot oil with her chopsticks, to see her sitting in the living room watching TV and laughing with 5    us, or even hearing her complain about something I should have done. Nothing prepared me for her death last year from a massive stroke.

As I stood by my mother's bedside, I knew there would no longer be time to tell her how much she meant to me even though we had drifted apart these past few years. There would no longer be time to rectify our differences, or time 10    to tell my mother how much I owed her for giving up so much.

She was a mother and a wife, and we were her world. My mother never had an easy time raising five children. My father was a waiter in a Chinese restaurant, and since it was in New Jersey, he commuted home only once a week to Brooklyn. She had to take care of us on her own.

15    I remember, when I was ten, my mother telling us to be quiet because she had a headache, but being children, we decided to play a game of hide and seek instead. Just the other day she had let us jump rope and play ball in the apartment, so we thought she wouldn't mind.

The next thing we knew, however, there was the sound of glass popping 20    and cracking. My brother, William, screamed. We had trapped him behind the glass door in the living room, so he could be "It," but hadn't expected him to panic and push through the door. There was blood and glass everywhere.

Before any of us could react, we heard the pounding of my mother's footsteps on the linoleum floor as she raced from the kitchen where she was making dinner. Her plump frame was heaving and her salt and pepper hair was straggled around her perspiring face.

For a spilt-second I could tell she wanted to kill us for making her headache worse, but she controlled herself, and put down the meat cleaver she had been holding. She deftly stanched the flow of blood with a towel and bandaged William up.

We hurried to clean up the glass and blood, childishly thinking my mother would forget what happened if there wasn't any evidence. The wrinkles around her dark brown eyes tightened, and we knew better. Her words, when they came, tumbled over each other to get out. Her Chinese mixed with her English as she tried to express her anger.

My mother then hit us hard with the ruler she kept for such an occasion and sent us to our rooms. What was worse, however, was when she gave us the silent treatment for three whole days. That was a greater punishment to us because we had betrayed her trust. It took a while before she forgave us.

We must have been the constant source of her headaches. When we were children, I could not understand why we couldn't have those new jeans or clothes that everyone had on TV. Why did we have hand-me-downs? My mother's answer was, why waste when the clothes were still good to wear? She never told us we didn't have enough money. She didn't want us to feel as if we didn't have anything.

So we complained and begged, but my mother asked for nothing. I cannot recall my mother ever getting herself anything special to wear. The only dress that she bought, which stands out in my mind, was when she had to go to a banquet with my father. She bought a beautiful fuchsia dress with glass beads on it. When I asked her what the beads were made of, she playfully said they were diamonds. My mother never complained to my father, but appreciated whatever he brought home. I think as long as we were fed, clothed, and healthy, she was happy.

As we were growing up, we thought my mother was God. She was our savior from bullies and from each other. She was the disciplinarian when we misbehaved. She was the one we would turn to for guidance and approval.

My mother always encouraged us to do well in school. My older brother, Steven, was the "brainiac" of the family and we were all supposed to be like him. Poor Steven really had the worst luck being born the first male because my mother thought she knew what was best for him. To her, an engineer was better than an artist, which Steven wanted to be. It didn't matter that they were two different occupations with merits of their own.

An artist wasn't acceptable because artists didn't do any work. According to my mother, they just played with drawing. Since Steven refused to be an

65   engineer, my mother decided he should be an architect, so he could draw and make a lot of money working in an office. But my brother wanted none of that. He refused his scholarship to Columbia and dropped out of school until my mother stopped nagging him.

I was torn between doing well, and not doing well. If I didn't do well my
70   mother wouldn't take over my life. I wanted to do well, though, because when I got A's my mother would have the biggest smile on her face and give me a hug. When I got my first D in math, I couldn't stop crying, because I thought my mother was going to kill me. But she surprised me. Instead of yelling, she put her arms around me and squeezed me as if she were trying to take away all the
75   sadness and worry I had gone through.

My mother was also the source of information and communication with our father. My mother was like the United Nations between us; she held our entire family together.

Since my father was away most of the week at work, he was a stranger to his
80   children. We would all become quiet when he walked into a room, because he always wanted silence on his day off. When he tried to ask us a question it was mainly about our health and how we were doing in school. He didn't know what foods we liked, who our friends were, what grade we were in, not like our mother.

For many years I never knew where my father worked, until I asked my
85   mother. She would be the one to tell us my father had quit this job and moved to that restaurant. My mother also would be the one to tell my father if we were sick, behaving badly, or doing well in school.

My mother often sat between my father and myself when we would talk and act as a translator, because he spoke mostly Chinese and I spoke only Eng-
90   lish. He never learned English as well as my mother even though they both lived in America for over twenty years.

With my mother there, I always thought my father never really had to know us. He knew he could rely on my mother to find out what was going on. He didn't need to extend himself. Similarly, we never learned enough Chinese
95   to talk to him. My mother was less formidable and more familiar.

Somehow, as I got older my mother stopped being familiar and suddenly became the enemy. I don't know when I started disagreeing with my mother, but after a while my opinions clashed with hers. I stopped caring what she thought about me because I couldn't believe the things she did.
100   One of our most heated topics was race. When I was a teenager, we lived in a predominantly black neighborhood in Brooklyn and my best friend, Vanessa, was black. My mother would only have nice things to say about Vanessa while we were playing in my house, but once Vanessa left, my mother would tell me to not get close to black people. She said they were all muggers, burglars, and
105   criminals. She saw how they were portrayed on TV and believed all black people were like that.

When I tried to reason with her and tell her that not all black people were criminals, she wouldn't listen. I even brought up the fact that in Chinatown there were Chinese gangs and criminals, but she said they were different; they weren't black.

When my mother said that, I looked at her as if for the first time. Could this be my mother? All the things I had ever learned from her, like loving thy neighbor or giving people a chance, seemed to topple from where I held them.

In addition, all the things I had ever learned and believed from school differed from what she said and thought. It shocked me so that I felt winded. Didn't she know what black people had been through? I felt as if I were in the middle of the '60s and people were prejudiced against color. Didn't she hate being treated differently because we were Chinese? Could this be my mother? Could I sit there and try to be agreeable to keep the peace between us? I did not.

It was the beginning of many clashes that left us silently angry at each other. Our anger reached its height when my sister, Annie, starting dating Greg. A boyfriend, to my mother, should be healthy, rich, and preferably Chinese. Greg was black.

The first time my mother heard about Greg was when he called my sister on the telephone. Right away my mother's antennae went up and she wanted to know everything about him. My sister was no dummy, so she went out to meet Greg before my mother could ask her any questions. I was not so lucky.

"Who is this Greg?" my mother asked me. I couldn't believe the inquisition I was being given. Both my sister and I were in our twenties. I told her he was just a friend from work. "What kind of guy is he?" I knew my mother meant what race was he, but I just told her I didn't know much about him. She gave a huff and asked impatiently, "Is he white, is he black? You know what I mean." I told her Greg was black and a very nice person, but she stopped listening to me after I said black.

She started to voice her thoughts out loud and I wish she hadn't. My mother kept hoping Annie wouldn't go out with Greg anymore, because my mother would be so ashamed. She thought she wouldn't be able to walk down the street with her head held high because her daughter was dating a black person. Then she started mumbling something about the poor children that would come from such a mixture.

I'd known she wouldn't like the idea of my sister dating a black person, but I thought she was overly dramatic and her views were distorted. I tried to tell her what a friendly, hard-working, and nice person Greg was, but she wouldn't listen.

My mother even went so far as to ignore Greg's presence when Annie brought him up to meet her. When Annie introduced Greg, my mother left the room. Annie had to apologize for my mother's behavior, but Greg took it in stride and said good-humoredly, "Nice meeting you too." He and Annie quickly left after that.

I was so angry and embarrassed that I couldn't even speak when my mother returned. She kept muttering to herself, "Shame. Black. Shame." I kept trying to convince her, but nothing seemed to penetrate. I was so mad, I was tempted to go out with a black person just to spite her, for calling Annie and Greg shameful. I left her in the house alone and didn't speak to her for two days.

155    Even when I thought I was fighting for her sake, my mother would exasperate me by taking the other side. Like the time I tried to make her more independent of my father's control.

She became a different person when my father was around. The woman who shared in our jokes and spoke to us in English instead of Chinese disap-
160    peared when my father was home. She became a mouse and would always agree with him or change her mind if it was contrary to what he thought. She would agree to stay at home and take care of us all instead of doing what she wanted.

On her fifty-third birthday, however, my sisters and I decided to take her out to see the matinee performance of *A Chorus Line*. We knew my father
165    wouldn't like it because it meant she wasn't at home with the family, but we also knew my father would be away working so she would not object. In fact, when we told her, she couldn't wait to see her first Broadway show.

Unfortunately, my father surprised us all by coming home the day before our outing to the show. I told my mother he could take my ticket, so he
170    wouldn't object to her going.

It didn't work though. My mother was silent. When I asked her what was wrong, she got angry and said she didn't want to go and neither did my father. "Waste of time. Waste of money," she said. I could tell that was my father talking and not her, so I got really angry.

175    I thought if she wasn't going to stick up for herself, then I was. I went to my father and tried to be diplomatic. I started off by saying that I hoped he would celebrate my mother's birthday by going with her to a show. His response was, "No, no. Home is better. Wild and dangerous in New York City."

After trying to convince him for several minutes, I finally said, "Mommy's
180    been looking forward to this all week. Why don't you let her go?" He seemed to be waiting for this question, however, because he asked smugly, "Did you ask you Mommy? Did she say she wanted to go?" I looked at him and was ready to hit him because I was so exasperated. I stormed out of the room and slammed the door behind me.

185    I went back to the kitchen where my mother was cooking and told her she should go to the play because she wanted to. She just shook her head and continued to chop. "Too much work, too much work. I don't want to go. Not anything Daddy said."

I knew I wouldn't be able to change her mind. She was just as stubborn as I
190    was. My mother always used to think that the man was right, and the woman just agreed. She disapproved when my sisters and I argued volubly with our boyfriends and our brothers, but I also remember her laugh delightedly when we had the last word. She must have struggled between what she was taught in China and what she heard from her children, here in America.

195    Because I was brought up in America, I could not understand my mother. I would become angry and frustrated with the way my mother accepted the control my father had over her. I knew that I didn't want to be that way. I wanted to

be on equal terms. My mother's beliefs were too old-fashioned and they denied me my independence and self-worth.

We would fight and neither of us heard the words or listened for reason. 200
She had been brought up with different standards, and even though we lived in the same house, I had my own too. After a while the only way to relieve the tension was for one of us to leave the house. That one was normally me.

I spent most of my time at friends' houses or just going out to do other things. Every time I returned home, something would trigger an argument: a 205
program on television, a friend, the newspaper. Even my comings and goings got to be a subject of argument between us.

I never stopped to think about how she felt. She was raised to believe that a woman's place was, literally, behind her man. Also, being kept at home all day watching soap operas and news programs, she received unrealistic views of peo- 210
ple. I often wished she had taken a job or had more friends who could give her a different perspective.

As I write this essay, my thoughts of my mother move back and forth between good and bad just like our relationship was. I think each of us in our family has been deeply affected by her and through her death I have discov- 215
ered that we need to appreciate one another more and try to be tolerant of our differences.

My life without her makes me feel incomplete. Her ever-faithful presence does not hover over me, and that scares me. Even though we argued and fought, I always thought she would be there. A force to rely on or reckon with. 220

And yet her death, ironically enough, has brought our family closer together. We are more aware of the fragility of our own lives. We see the need to talk together. For the first time our father has really spoken to us, and we are finally getting to know one another because, in death, my mother is the bond.

## Looking Back

1. What picture of Man-Kong's mother do you form on the basis of details presented in lines 1–14.

2. What emotional ties must exist between people in order for the "silent treatment" (line 38) to hurt?

3. Are the roles of "savior," "disciplinarian," and counselor (lines 54–56) the ones you customarily expect in a mother? Explain you answer.

4. In the case of the author and her brother Steven, how do family standards and social possibilities conflict (see lines 57–75)?

5. What do you feel about Man-Kong's relationship to her father (see lines 79–83)? Is her description of their relationship effective?

6. How does her mother's unreasoning prejudice change Man-Kong's relation to her?

7. What can you generalize about racial attitudes based on the mother's response to Greg?

8. Why do you think Man-Kong's mother became "a different person when my father was around" (line 158)? What cultural attitude do you think this transformation reveals?

9. How does her mother's role as a wife affect the author?

10. Focusing on the last two paragraphs, state what solemn balance the author achieves in her thoughts about her mother.

## Writing Assignments

1. "She was a mother and a wife," Mary Man-Kong writes early in her essay. Although this seems a neutral description, it turns out to be such a limiting one that the author finds in it the source of considerable anguish. As the portrait of the mother becomes fuller, we discover three distinct themes in this anguish, each one relevant to the mother and wife's potential independence and freedom. These themes are (a) the behavior and attitudes of husbands, (b) the effects on daughters of relations between husbands and wives, and (c) the role of traditional culture in marriage. Extrapolating from Man-Kong's treatment of one of these themes, write an essay that examines it as fully as possible. Refer to "Memories of My Mother" and also to your own pertinent experience.

2. "Unreasoning prejudice" (see number 6 in Looking Back) is one of the most unattractive, even disfiguring, racial attitudes people may hold, but it is the source of all negative racial views, some of which may *seem* reasoned and logical. One of these views is that society does not approve of people from different races falling in love, marrying, and having children, and therefore people should avoid doing so. Taking into consideration Man-Kong's family situation and your own observations and ideas, write an essay explaining whether the logic opposing mixed marriages holds up.

3. Often, families seem to retreat into a defensive position in order to shield members, particularly children, from the attractions of outside life. In their view, society has become a threat because its values and behavior patterns so conflict with those of the family. We see this, for example, in the censorship of public library holdings on the grounds that parents ought to decide a child's reading matter. We also see this in several ways in Man-Kong's essay. Whatever the issue, the child is caught in the middle, and it is her position that may be most interesting. You may have been in such a position to some degree, but even if you haven't, it is possible to imagine it. Write an essay that both describes this position and prescribes the proper recognition that should be given a child who has reached the age of sixteen (the age after which education is no longer compulsory). Refer to Man-Kong and to issues such as the one cited above.

## Stanley Crouch

# Nationalism of Fools

A journalist and former jazz critic for the *Village Voice*, Stanley Crouch is the author of *Notes of a Hanging Judge: Essays and Reviews, 1979–1989*, from which this piece is taken. The title of the collection indicates the way the author regards himself: as a none-too-sympathetic critic whose keen eye and caustic tongue will allow few fools and scoundrels to go unscathed. As a sometimes dissident voice in the African-American community, however, he proves the value of critical thinking generally, which is not to be negative but rather to insist on truth and reason.

## Looking Ahead

1. Notice the essay structure Crouch employs. Making Louis Farrakhan's speech the central focus affords the opportunity to trace the history of his organization, the Nation of Islam, and to examine the themes Farrakhan introduces.

2. Crouch does not hide his opinions, but he does not believe they are worthwhile simply because they are his. As you read, test his reasoning and his presentation of evidence to see if they transform opinions into *considered* opinions and then into *balanced judgments* other people might also accept.

3. The author's criticism of Farrakhan's version of nationalism serves the purpose of proposing an alternative to it, an idea whose value you should in turn try to judge.

There again were the black suits and red ties, the bodyguards in blue uniforms, the women in white, the aloof cast of the eyes and the earthy manner: the Nation of Islam. Twenty-five years ago it was Malcolm X's show, though he could never have filled Madison Square Garden. On October 7, [1985] 25,000 people turned out to hear Louis Farrakhan.                                                                     5

They queued up outside—the poor and the young, the unemployed and the gang members, the middle-class Negroes. They were anxious to get in and hear someone attack the people they felt were responsible for their positions in the burgeoning illiterate mass; or they were there out of curiosity, intent on hearing for themselves what Farrakhan was about. Many came because they    10
were happy to support a black man the "white-controlled" media unanimously hated. Or because Mayor Koch had called Farrakhan "the devil," usurping the Muslims' term for the white enemy—if Koch hated him, he might be lovable, an understandable reaction given the long-standing antipathy between the mayor and New York's black community. I also think many    15
were there, especially the young, because they had never been to a mass black rally to hear a speaker who didn't appear to care what white people thought of him, a man who seemed to think their ears were more important than those of Caucasians.

The atmosphere at Madison Square Garden was unusual. Though the    20
speeches started two and half hours late, the audience was patient, partly out of respect and partly out of awareness that the Fruit of Islam doesn't play. A fool and his seat would soon have parted. I overheard one young black man saying that he could look at the Muslims with their neatness and their discipline, their sense of confidence and their disdain for white privilege,    25
and understand their appeal: "They look like the last thing they ever think about is kissing some white boody." After repeatedly telling a blond female

photographer that she couldn't sit in the aisle, one of the FOI said, to the joy
of the black people listening, "Miss, I asked you three times to *please* not sit
30   in the aisle. Now you will either get your behind over or you will get your behind *out*." And there was something else. As one woman put it, "Well, what
can you say? Nobody looks better than a black man in a uniform. Look at all
those handsome black men. I know I wouldn't want to be in the Nation, but
I wouldn't mind it if they lived on *my* block. I bet there wouldn't be any
35   mugging and dope dealing and all of *that*." From the outside, at least, Farrakhan's group projects a vision of restraint and morality. It's about smooth-
ing things out, upholding the family, respecting the woman, doing an honest
day's work, avoiding dissipation, and defining the difference between the
path of the righteous and the way of the wicked. At one point the comman-
40   der of the FOI came to the microphone and said that he could smell reefer
smoke. He asked that anyone who saw those guilty parties report them to
"the nearest brother." Wherever the puffing was going on, it stopped.

Beginning in 1959, when the press started bird-dogging Malcolm X, the Muslims' disdain for white people seared through the networks, eventually influ-
45   encing the tone, the philosophy, and the tactics of black politics. The Nation
of Islam offered a rageful revision that would soon have far more assenters
than converts. Though it seemed at first only a fanatical cult committed to a
bizarre version of Islam, Elijah Muhammad's homemade Nation was far from
an aberration. The Nation fit perfectly in a century we might appropriately
50   call "The Age of Redefinition." Its public emergence coincided with the assault on Western convention, middle-class values, and second-class citizenship that shaped the '60s in America. The whole question of what constituted
civilized behavior and civilized tradition was being answered in a variety of
wild ways. So Elijah Muhammad's sect was part of the motion that presaged
55   transcendental meditation, sexual revolution, LSD, cultural nationalism,
black power, the Black Panther Party, the anti-Vietnam War movement, feminism, and other trends that surely appalled the Muslims as thoroughly as the
Nation did its roughest critics. As much as anything else, those angry home-
grown Muslims foretold the spirit of what was later known as "the counter-
60   culture."
    But Elijah Muhammad's counterculture was black. Where others ex-
plained the world's problems with complex theories ranging from economic
exploitation to sexism, Muhammad simply pinned the tail on the white man.
In his view, black integrationists were only asking for membership in hell,
65   since the white man was a devil "grafted" from black people in an evil genetic
experiment by a mad, pumpkin-headed scientist named Yacub. That experiment took place 6,000 years ago. Now the white man was doomed, sentenced
to destruction by Allah. If "so-called American Negroes" separated themselves
from the imposed values of white culture, then moved into their own land,
70   black suffering would cease. In calling for five or six states as "back payment

for slavery," Muhammad reiterated a Negro Zionism rooted in the "back to Africa" schemes of the middle 19th century, which had last fizzled under the leadership of Marcus Garvey.[1]

In the context of prevailing media images and public racial struggle, this was all new. Here were Negroes who considered *themselves* the chosen people. They proclaimed that the black man was the original man, the angel, and that since the first devils to roll off Yacub's assembly line were the Jews, the idea of *their* being the chosen was a lot of baloney. By embracing Muhammad's version of Islam, his followers stepped outside of Judeo-Christian civilization, asserting their African roots at exactly the same time Africans were coming out from under colonialism and remarkable shifts in world power were in the offing. They declared the white man a thief and a murderer: he had ripped off the secrets of science from Africa. (Muhammad's ministers taught that Egypt was an acronym for "he gypped you.") Using the Africans' information, the blue-eyed devil went on to steal land all over the world, including America from the Indian. The Muslims "exposed" Christianity as no more than a tool to enslave black people, a way of getting them to deny their origins and worship a "white Jesus" (when the Savior was described in Revelations as having skin the color of burnished brass and hair akin to pure lamb's wool). They spoke of dark skin and thick lips as beautiful, charging that the mulatto look of light skin, thin lips, and "good" hair was the mark of shame, of rape on the plantation. In attacking the Caucasian standard of beauty, the Muslims foreshadowed the "black is beautiful" buttons and revisionist images of race and gender we would soon hear from all quarters.

Though most of what they said was no further out than the mythological tales of biblical heroes, their explanations lacked poetic grandeur. But their exotic integrity made that irrelevant. Just as there is a beauty in a well-made club or knife or rifle, there is a beauty in those who yield to nothing but their own ideals and the discipline necessary to achieve them. The Muslims had that kind of attraction, particularly for those who had known the chaos of drug addiction, prostitution, loneliness, abject poverty. Suddenly here were all these clean-cut, well-dressed young men and women—men, mostly. You recognized them from the neighborhood. They had been pests or vandals, thieves or gangsters. Now they were back from jail or prison and their hair was cut close, their skin was smooth, they no longer cursed blue streaks, and the intensity of their eyes remade their faces. They were "in the Nation" and that meant that new men were in front of you, men who greeted each other in Arabic, who were aloof, confident, and intent on living different than they had. Now the mention of a cool slice of ham on bread with mayonnaise and lettuce disgusted them. Consuming the pig was forbidden and food was eaten once a day because a single throe of digestion "preserved the intestines." Members didn't smoke, drink, use drugs, dance, go to movies or sports events.

---

1. *Marcus Garvey* (1887–1940): founder of the separatist Universal Negro Improvement Association in 1911. (*ed.*)

The Muslims' vision of black unity, economic independence, and "a true knowledge of self" influenced the spirit of black organization as the Civil Rights Movement waned. Few took notice that it was much easier to call white people names and sneer at voter registration drives from podiums in the North than to face the cattle prods, the bombings, and the murders in the South. Since the destruction of America was preordained, the Muslims scorned efforts to change the system. Theirs was the world of what the French call "the total no."

Though they were well mannered and reliable, the Muslims were too provincial and conservative to attract the kind of mass following that would pose a real political threat. Yet as chief black heckler of the Civil Rights Movement, Malcolm X began to penetrate the consciousness of young black people, mostly in the North. While his platform was impossible, a cockeyed racial vision of history that precluded any insights into human nature, young Negroes loved to watch him upset white people, shocking them no end with his attacks on their religion, their history, their morality, their political system, and their sense of superiority. He described nonviolence as nonsense. And he said it all with an aggressive, contemptuous tone that had never been heard from a black man on the air. What we witnessed was the birth of black saber rattling.

Malcolm quickly became what is now called a cult hero. But for all the heated, revisionist allusions to history and exploitation, Malcolm X's vision was far more conventional than King's. Where the Southern Christian Leadership Council and the Student Non-Violent Coordinating Committee [SNCC] were making use of the most modern forms of boycott, media pressure, and psychological combat, revealing the werewolf of segregation under a full moon, Malcolm X brought the philosophy of the cowboy movie into Negro politics: characters who turned the other cheek were either naive or cowardly. The Civil War had cost 622,500 lives; the Civil Rights Movement had brought about enormous change against violent opposition without losing 100 troops. But you could never have told that listening to Malcolm X, who made each casualty sound like 100,000. He talked like one of those gunfighters determined to organize the farmers against the violent, vicious cattlemen. One of his last speeches was even called "The Bullet or the Ballot." Hollywood had been there first.

In the wake of Malcolm X's assassination and canonization came the costume balls of cultural nationalism and the loudest saber rattlers of them all, the Black Panther Party. Both persuasions rose from the ashes of the urban riots, each dominated by egomaniacs who brooked no criticism, defining all skeptics as Uncle Toms. They gathered thunder as the Civil Rights Movement floundered. The remarkable Bob Moses of SNCC abdicated following the murders of Schwerner, Goodman, and Chaney.[2] The organization became a shambles as white support was driven out. Stokely Carmichael and Rap Brown devoted their efforts to inflammatory rabble rousing encouraging the anarchy of urban "revolts." King was felled in Memphis. America then endured the spectacles of Ron

---

2. *Schwerner, Goodman, and Chaney:* civil rights workers murdered in Mississippi during Freedom Summer, June 1964. (*ed.*)

Karenga and LeRoi Jones, Eldridge Cleaver and Huey Newton.[3] Hollywood
didn't miss the point: it turned pulp politics into pulp films. Black exploitation     155
movies saved a few studios as Negro heroes moved from scene to scene beating
up white villains, usually gangsters, in chocolate-coated James Bond thrillers. It
all wore thin as would-be radical black youth discovered that romanticizing
Africa and wearing robes or calling for the violent overthrow of the American
government led to little more than pretentious exotica and the discovery that     160
the police weren't paper tigers.

When Elijah Muhammad died in 1975, Louis Farrakhan was a member of
the Nation's upper echelon. He had seen the organization survive Malcolm X's
defection in 1964. So it must have been rough on him when Muhammad's son
Wallace repudiated his father's teachings, opting for regulation Islam. Suddenly,     165
Farrakhan was back in the world without a filter. Elijah Muhammad's vision had
created an extended family of believers destined to come out in front when Allah
gave the word and evil was struck down. Now Wallace was spurning seclusion
from society and the guarantees that come with apocalyptic prophecy. And there
was another problem. Elijah Muhammad had explicitly aimed his teachings at     170
the downtrodden black man in America, not Muslims in their own countries.
When charged with distorting Islam, he had explained that this was a special
medicine for a special case, a people who had "no knowledge of self." Submitting
to conventional Islam meant giving Middle Eastern Muslims the inside lane. But
Louis Farrakhan wasn't about to become just another one of millions of Muslims.     175
The Charmer, as he was known when he was a singer, wanted to lead. And he
did: he broke with Wallace to carry on Elijah Muhammad's teachings.

Now, after 30 years of watching others chased by reporters and interviewed
on national television, Farrakhan has his moment. Malcolm X is dead, King is
dead, the Panthers have been declawed, Eldridge Cleaver is born again, Ron     180
Karenga and LeRoi Jones are college professors, and the factions devoted to urban guerrilla warfare have been either snuffed out or chased into hiding. Now it
is all his, the mantle of extreme militance, and the media hang on his words, no
matter what they made of him. He is a national, if not an international, figure, a
man who can draw turn-away crowds, get $5 million from Qaddafi,[4] and sur-     185
round himself with a surprising array of supporters.

The appearance of Louis Farrakhan at this time seems to comment on the
failures of black, liberal, and conservative politics since the Nixon era, when
cultural nationalists started putting on suits and Marxist revolutionaries sought
the great leap forward of tenured professorships. Though black mayors were     190
elected in more and more cities, and many millions were spent to eradicate obstacles to Negro American success, the thrust of these attempts at social change
was no more accurate than Chester Himes's[5] blind man with the pistol. The

---

3. *Ron . . . Newton:* Ron Karenga and Leroi Jones (Amiri Baraka) are writers and poets.
Eldridge Cleaver and Huey Newton were leaders of the Black Panther party. (*ed.*)

4. *Col. Muammar al-Qaddafi* (b. 1942): Libya's head of state. (*ed.*)

5. *Chester Himes:* African American mystery writer and novelist. (*ed.*)

epidemic proportions of illiteracy, teenage pregnancy, and crime in Negro com-
195    munities across the nation tell us what went wrong. The schools became worse
and worse, the salaries for teachers less and less; there were no serious efforts
(including welfare cutbacks) to discourage teenage parenthood; and the courts
were absurdly lenient with criminals. The result is a black lower class perhaps
more despairing and cynical than we have ever seen.
200         But conservative programs have been equally deadly. While the administration chips away at the voting rights of black Southerners and panders to
religious fundamentalists, it ignores human nature by deregulating the business sphere with such vengeance that the profits of stockholders take precedence
over the environment. In this atmosphere, Farrakhan's broad attacks are political
205    rock and roll—loved more for the irritation they create than for their substance.

The guests who filled the podium gave the impression that Farrakhan had a
broader base than assumed. They included Christian ministers, American Indians, Palestinians, Stokely Carmichael, and Chaka Khan. Of Khan's presence,
one young man said, "She shouldn't have done that. Her record sales are going
210    to go down. Those Jews ain't going to like that. She might be through." I wasn't
so sure of that, but if black people were in equivalent positions in the record
business, I doubt they would think lightly of a white star sitting on a podium
with the Ku Klux Klan.
When things finally kicked off, a Christian choir opened with a song and
215    Stokely Carmichael spoke first. He bobbed and flailed, often pushing his head
past the microphone. The sound went up and down; some sentences came
through clearly, others were half-heard. He attacked Zionism, calling for war
against Israel and recognition of the "sacredness" of Africa, where Moses and Jesus were protected when in trouble. The intensity was so immediate and
220    Carmichael got carried away so quickly that the address seemed more a high-
powered act than anything else. In his white robe and white hair the lean and
tall West Indian looked much like the ghost of Pan-African nationalism past. As
Kwame Touré, he carried the names of fallen idols, African leaders who resorted
to dictatorial control when things didn't go the way they wanted, whether that
225    meant throttling the press or subjecting the opposition to the infamous "black
diet." But then much of what Carmichael has had to say since the black power
years has been itself a black diet, a form of intellectual starvation in which the
intricacies of international politics are reduced to inflammatory tribalism.
A Palestinian, Said Arafat, attacked Zionism as "a cancer" and called for "the
230    total liberation of Palestine." Russell Means, one of the founders of the American Indian Movement, gave a predictable address about an Indian taking his
tomahawk to an insulting white man. Then a golem popped out of his bandana:
"When we were in Los Angeles the Jews did a number on Mr. Farrakhan." He
concluded by saying, "I want you all to remember that Hollywood has deni-
235    grated and debased every race of people, but there are no plays or movies deni-
grating the Jewish people." (Half right, half wrong. As J. Hoberman points out,

many movies with Jewish stereotypes were made during the silent era, but the
moguls backed off when sound came in, yielding to community pressure. And
though Hollywood's contribution to "negative images" of ethnic groups is unar-
guable, it is also true that revisionist Westerns such as the classic *Fort Apache*     240
started appearing long before AIM [American Indian Movement] was founded.)
  All the speeches were short and made their points. Then the featured attraction was introduced. The audience rose to its feet and burst forth with a
heroic sound filling the Garden with a gigantic chord of collected voices. Very
soon, Farrakhan proved his shrewdness, highhandedly using the rhetoric of    245
social movements he would have opposed 25 years ago. When the applause
ended, Farrakhan called attention to the female bodyguards who surrounded
him and claimed that Elijah Muhammad was the first black leader to liberate the
woman. Point of fact, the Muslims used to say, "The black woman is the field in
which the black man sows his nation." But after all, the past is silly putty to men   250
like Farrakhan, who used the subject of women as the first of many themes he
would pass through or over. "The world is in the condition it is," he said, "because it doesn't respect women." Growing bolder, Farrakhan attacked the separation of the sexes in traditional Islam, saying women should be allowed into
the mosque. That will no doubt be quite a revelation in the Middle East, when   255
Farrakhan goes on his promised Third World tour.
  Farrakhan went on to be consistently incoherent for three hours, embodying
the phrase "Didn't he ramble?" He circled many topics, always ending on his favorite subject: Louis Farrakhan. He talked about how good he looked, how he
should be compared to Jesus, how the Jews were after him, how he was on a di-   260
vine mission, how he would go to the Southwest and die with the Indians if necessary, how "examples" should be made of black leaders who criticized men like
him, how black people needn't worry if they were called upon to go to war with
America, since Allah would do for them what he did for David when the boy
fought Goliath. He piled his points in Dagwood sandwiches of contradiction,   265
moving from the "fact" that whites were invented devils to the observation that if
America is hell, then those who run it must be devils; then obliquely referring to
the *Annacalyptus,* an occult history, with the remark that we have never seen
races evolve from light to dark, further proof that the "Asiatic black man" must
be the father of all races. To finish off that run, Farrakhan dug out the anthropo-   270
logical findings in East Africa, which suggest that man originated there. Rounding the bases of absurdity, metaphor, and the occult, he hook-slid into science.
  When Farrakhan wasn't talking about himself, he most frequently baited
Jews. When he does that, Farrakhan plumbs the battles that have gone on between black people and Jews for almost 20 years. He speaks to (though not for)   275
those who have fought with Jews over affirmative action, or have felt locked out
of discussions about Middle East policy by Jews as willing to bully and deflect
criticism with the term "anti-Semite" as black people were with "racist" 20 years
ago. I'm sure he scores points with those who argue that Jewish media executives are biased in favor of Israel; who say that films like *Exodus,* TV movies   280

about Entebbe, Golda Meir, Sadat,[6] the stream of documentaries, docudramas, and miniseries given over to "the final solution" are all part of a justification for Zionism; who were angry when Hollywood saluted Israel's 30th anniversary with a television special, and cynically wondered if "those Hollywood Jews" would salute any other country's birth.

I don't know of any other country Hollywood has saluted, but a propaganda ploy by a few executives does not a conspiracy of six million Jewish Americans make. (You can hear them whispering into the phone at your nearest deli. "Hey, Murray, I just got word we'll have another special coming up; spread the word in your block. But make sure no goyim are listening.") If such a conspiracy exists, how has it allowed South Africa, Israel's ally, to get such an overwhelming amount of bad press?

Of course, Israel's relationship to South Africa complicates the question. For all its moral proclamations, the Israelis supply arms to Botha's gang and refuse to cooperate with sanctions. This convinces certain quarters that Israel and its sympathizers support racial injustice and antidemocratic regimes, angering those who had a sense of international black struggle hammered into their minds by Malcolm X and his emulators. That sense of collective black effort was a sort of political evangelism, bent on saving the Third World from white savagery and exploitation, a racial variation on international revolutionary Marxism. (It was this sense of foreign destiny that inspired the back-to-Africa movements, which eventually led to the founding of Liberia, Israel's true forerunner—a country begun for free ex-slaves to the resentment of the 60 local tribes. One wonders how much Herzl[7] and associates knew about Liberia and whether or not they were inspired by its example.) At present, however, it seems to put more emphasis on the interests of a foreign country than on the conditions of black Americans, a tendency I doubt we would see in the Jewish community if it had the same degree of social, educational, and economic problems that burden millions of Negroes.

But screwed-up priorities are nothing new to black politics, nor, unfortunately, are anti-Semitic attacks loosely using that most dangerous article of speech: "the." Those three letters fan conspiracy theories and push us back to the 1960s, when LeRoi Jones brought a grotesque refinement to anti-white sentiment by reading poetry that baited Jews on college campus after college campus, to the cheers of black students. Such tours probably had had more than a little to do with intensifying the Zionist fervor of many Jews who had been told to get out of civil rights organizations.

---

6. *Entebbe:* refers to the Israeli commando raid at the Entebbe, Uganda, airport in 1973 to free Jewish hijack victims; *Golda Meir* (1898–1979): prime minister of Israel from 1969 to 1974; *Anwar al-Sadat* (1918–1981): president of Egypt from 1970 to his 1981 assassination, first Arab leader to make peace with Israel. (*ed.*).

7. *Theodor Herzl* (1860–1904): founder of Zionism, a movement to establish a Jewish homeland. (*ed.*)

The failure of Jones, Karenga, and other black nationalists to realize their separatist dreams made for a jealously that floats to the surface in the speeches of Louis Farrakhan, their heir. When Farrakhan makes references to Reagan "punking out" to the Jews or the Zionist lobby having "a stranglehold on the government of the United States," he is projecting the kind of power *he* wants onto the American-Israeli Public Affairs Committee [AIPAC], commonly called the Zionist lobby. In his version, however, Farrakhan feels free to make threats on the lives of black reporters, politicians, and anyone else who criticizes him.

The envy of AIPAC's influence reflects a nostalgia for the days when so much of the national dialogue was given over to the racial question and the quality of black life in the country was an issue at the front of the political bus. During those years, desegregation and racial double standards were the primary concerns. There was little room for anti-Jewish or anti-Zionist feeling, regardless of how deep they might have run in black nationalist circles. Now the judas goat of Jewish conspiracy is trotted out again as an explanation for the loss of concentrated attention on black problems.

Yet it would make more sense to emulate the efforts of activist Jews that have made AIPAC, as Paul Findley's *They Dare to Speak Out* documents, such a force on Capital Hill. Obviously, black leaders have failed to create a comparable force to lobby for interests of Negro Americans. The nationalist rhetoric backfired and made black problems seem more those of a group in a self-segregated world than central to the country at large. As one black woman, infuriated by Farrakhan, said, "We should be putting our feet in the pants of these politicians. Get this dope out of here. Get these schools working. Clean up these neighborhoods. Do what we need done." The Jews who work in Israel's interest know the secret: hard work, fund-raising, monitoring voting patterns, petitioning, telephoning, writing to elected officials. It's difficult and laborious work, but it can get results. As that angered black woman concluded, "We can get all this up off our backs if we want to do something besides listen to some fool who hates ham talk like he's bad enough to exterminate somebody."

But for all his muddled convolutions, Farrakhan's vision isn't small. He wants it all. The world. Who else would feel free to promise that he would tell the Muslims of the Middle East how they had distorted Islam? Who else would claim to be single-handedly raising a people from the death of ignorance and self-hatred?

Though Farrakhan's address was supposed to reveal his economic program, his ideas about black-produced mouthwash, toothpaste, and sanitary napkins took up only 10 or 15 of his 180-minute montage of misconceptions. They were cheered now and again, as was almost everything he said. I doubt, however, that the black people there rising to their feet, screaming themselves hoarse, roaring as though he was scoring baskets as he bounced his ideas off their heads, followed his content. What clarity there was had little connection to a black American point of view. Though his look and his podium style owe much to the black

church, his ideas were dominated by a bent Islamic fundamentalism that might get him more money from Arabs. But whatever the underlying goals, Farrakhan's cosmology has little chance of overthrowing the strong tradition of Negro culture, custom, and thought improvised in the "wilderness of North Amer-
365   ica," as Elijah Muhammad might say. Few black people will ever believe that Farrakhan is so divinely significant that if the Jews try to touch him Allah will bring down the blood of the righteous on America and they will all be killed outright. As a guy sitting near my row pointed out, "Anybody who uses the first person pronoun as much as he does can't be saying anything. If they were, they
370   would just say it, not keep telling you how great the one who is *about* to say it is."

But Farrakhan isn't just your garden-variety megalomaniac. "Louis Farrakhan," said one woman editor who lives in Harlem, "is a creep. He is a fascist and has nothing to say. Whenever people try to defend him by saying he's speaking out, I always wonder what the hell they mean. He has nothing to offer
375   but half-truths, he tries to intimidate the black press into a cheering squad or a bunch of silent lampposts. His exterior is clean and neat, but his insides are dirty and his talk is pure sloppiness. How can educated people like him? It's just laziness. All they want is to anger some white people, or pretend he's angering them in any way serious enough to warrant the attention he's getting.
380   Nowadays if you try to bring up a serious topic in a lot of middle-class black circles, people want to change the subject and treat you like you're causing trouble. This kind of thing is crazy."

The real deal is that few intellectually sophisticated black people are ever seen on television discussing issues. Reporters seem to prefer men like Louis
385   Farrakhan and Jesse Jackson over genuine thinkers and scholars. Farrakhan obviously reads little that gives him any substantive information, and Jackson admitted in his *Playboy* interview that he hates to read. As Playthell Benjamin, one of Harlem's finest minds, says, "There is a ban on black intellectuals in the media. As the '60s proved, if we were allowed back into the area of discussion, the
390   nature of the social vision would be radically changed, from politics to art. There are all kinds of men like Maynard Jackson, David Levering Lewis, Albert Murray, and others who could bring this sophistry and nonsense to a halt. They could make the dialogue more sophisticated." Benjamin is absolutely on the money. We rarely get to hear the ideas of black people who have spent many
395   years studying and thinking and assessing their American experience and the policies of this country around the world.

By and large, those were not the kinds of people who came to hear Louis Farrakhan, roaring and cheering until the evening was finished off by an overripe Chaka Khan singing, strangely, a song called "Freedom," a cappella and
400   quite beautifully. Beyond the podium and not far from Farrakhan's white limousine were the young women bodyguards, who had stood through the entire three-hour address, hardly moving and constantly scanning the crowd for assassins. They were hugging each other and crying, releasing the tension that had percolated through the long watch. Some were thanking Allah that their

leader hadn't been harmed. All of them were brown and their skin had a luxuri-    405
ant smoothness, their eyes the clarity of those who don't dissipate, and behind
what I'm sure was experience in martial arts, was the same tenderness a man always notices when women feel deep affection.

Yet one image remained in the front of my mind: this light-skinned young
man wearing a camouflage shirt and pants, brown fringe sewn across the shoul-    410
ders, studded black leather covering his forearms. Whenever Farrakhan said
something about "the Jews," that young man screamed or shouted, pushing
both fists into the air, frequently leaping to his feet. Near the end of the evening,
when I had moved down toward the stage and was preparing to leave, I looked
up and saw him once again. The front of his eight-inch-wide black belt bore a    415
large Star of David formed in studs.

## Looking Back

1. How does Crouch, up to line 42 (notice the line break signaling the end of a section), demonstrate the appeal of the Nation of Islam? Why, as a critic of Farrakhan,
   does he start on a positive note?

2. What were the principles and demands of the Black Muslims under Elijah Muhammad? How did his organization differ from the civil rights movement?

3. In comparing Malcolm X to Martin Luther King, Jr., whose ideas and methods does
   Crouch prefer? Why?

4. In what way do the italicized words in the following sentence beg the question (decide the issue by way of stating it): "In the wake of Malcolm X's assassination and
   *canonization* came the *costume balls* of cultural nationalism and the loudest *saber rattlers* of them all, the Black Panther Party" (lines 144–146; emphasis added)?

5. What empty place in American social reality does Crouch says Farrakhan is filling
   (see lines 187–205)?

6. How would you criticize the position Farrakhan is reported to have taken in
   speeches, as Crouch reports them in lines 257–272?

7. Can you say, on balance, how Crouch views Farrakhan's attack on Jews?

8. What does Crouch mean by "that most dangerous article of speech: 'the' " (lines
   311–312) and "the judas goat of Jewish conspiracy" (lines 331–332)?

9. In your estimation, are the criticisms voiced by the "woman editor" and Playthell
   Benjamin (lines 371–396) convincing or not? Explain your answer.

10. Crouch drives home his message at the end with a telling anecdote he has saved for
    last. What is that message? Why does he end the essay with the image of the zealous
    anti-Semite wearing a Star of David?

## Writing Assignments

1. As indicated by his outspoken title, "Nationalism of Fools," Stanley Crouch thinks
   little of Louis Farrakhan and his followers. However, nationalism may not always be

foolish; there may also be a wise nationalism. Or, for people seeking to improve their lot—African Americans, Native Americans, or any other beleaguered group— perhaps any kind of nationalism would be ineffective. What do you think? What basket should people put all their eggs in? Should it be nationalism with (as the essay brings out) its unswayable trust in the supreme value of its own cause, in the wrongdoing of a perceived oppressor, and in a definite set of fairly inflexible methods of achieving freedom? Or should it be the political arena, in which elected representatives propose legislation, lobby, engage in public debate in order to effect change? Write an essay arguing for one of these courses of action or, if you feel putting all your eggs in one basket is itself foolish, for some combination of courses.

2. Writing in *The New York Times* (July 20, 1992), Professor Henry Louis Gates, Jr., condemns black attempts to make Jews scapegoats. Quoting Professor Cornel West, he describes black anti-Semitism as "the bitter fruit of a profound self-destructive impulse, nurtured on the vine of hopelessness and concealed by empty gestures of black unity." No doubt, Crouch would agree. Extrapolating from his discussion of Louis Farrakhan's ideas, write an essay that defines and analyzes the particular function and appeal of demagogues and of scapegoating as a practice. Since virtually all minority groups have been made scapegoats at some time, you may want to use other examples as well to illustrate your discussion.

3. Whether the objective is separatist nationalism or racial integration, the means used to achieve either end and to defeat racism in the United States are always at issue. Martin Luther King, Jr., has been the figure chiefly associated with nonviolence as a philosophy and political method, and Malcolm X with using any means necessary. Crouch clearly prefers one leader and one approach to the other. Write an essay in which you summarize his opinions and declare your own general belief in one method or the other as the best means to ending what many people claim is the economic, social, and political oppression of African Americans. Give reasons for your conviction, and be as specific as possible in discussing the application of political methods. Conceive of your audience as one including people keenly interested in ending racism.

# Patricia Williams

# The Death of the Profane

Born in 1951, Patricia J. Williams is presently on the faculty of the Columbia University Law School. She has also taught at the University of Wisconsin. She is the great-great-granddaughter of a slave and a white southern lawyer. This essay comes from her collection *The Alchemy of Race and Right,* which the African American thinker Henry Louis Gates, Jr., calls "one of the most invitingly personal, even vulnerable books I've read.... Williams has a knack for keeping you just a bit off balance. ... Her readings invigorate familiar controversies." Williams, that is, is a model critical thinker.

## Looking Ahead

1. Let Williams's use of an incident from her life remind you that personal experience is a significant source of knowledge about social reality.

2. Affirmative action is a topic in this essay. You should look the term up in a current dictionary to understand its meaning. See also Takaki, p. 418, lines 260–267.

3. The structure of "The Death of the Profane" consists of three "tellings" of the same story. Read critically to become aware of how the sharp differences among them contribute to Williams's purpose in writing this essay.

Buzzers are big in New York City. Favored particularly by smaller stores and boutiques, merchants throughout the city have installed them as screening devices to reduce the incidence of robbery: if the face at the door looks desirable, the buzzer is pressed and the door is unlocked. If the face is that of an undesirable, the door stays locked. Predictably, the issue of undesirability has revealed itself to be a racial determination. While controversial enough at first, even civil-rights organizations backed down eventually in the face of arguments that the buzzer system is a "necessary evil," that it is a "mere inconvenience" in comparison to the risks of being murdered, that suffering discrimination is not as bad as being assaulted, and that in any event it is not all blacks who are barred, just "17-year-old black males wearing running shoes and hooded sweatshirts."[1]

The installation of these buzzers happened swiftly in New York; stores that had always had their doors wide open suddenly became exclusive or received people by appointment only. I discovered them and their meaning one Saturday in 1986. I was shopping in Soho and saw in a store window a sweater that I wanted to buy for my mother. I pressed my round brown face to the window and my finger to the buzzer, seeking admittance. A narrow-eyed, white teenager wearing running shoes and feasting on bubble-gum glared out, evaluating me for signs that would pit me against the limits of his social understanding. After about five second, he mouthed "We're closed," and blew pink rubber at me. It was two Saturdays before Christmas, at one o'clock in the afternoon; there were several white people in the store who appeared to be shopping for things for *their* mothers.

I was enraged. At that moment I literally wanted to break all the windows of the store and *take* lots of sweaters for my mother. In the flicker of his judgmental gray eyes, the saleschild had transformed my brightly sentimental, joy-to-the-world, pre-Christmas spree to a shambles. He snuffed my sense of humanitarian catholicity, and there was nothing I could do to snuff his, without making a spectacle of myself.

I am still struck by the structure of power that drove me into such a blizzard of rage. There was almost nothing I could do, short of physically intruding

5

10

15

20

25

30

---

1. "When 'By Appointment' Means Keep Out," *The New York Times*, December 17, 1986, p. B1. Letter to the Editor from Michael Levin and Marguerita Levin.

upon him, that would humiliate him the way he humiliated me. No words, no gestures, no prejudices of my own would make a bit of difference to him; his refusal to let me into the store—it was Benetton's, whose colorfully punnish ad
35   campaign is premised on wrapping every one of the world's peoples in its cottons and woolens—was an outward manifestation of his never having let someone like me into the realm of his reality. He had no compassion, no remorse, no reference to me; and no desire to acknowledge me even at the estranged level of arm's-length transactor. He saw me only as one who would take his money and
40   therefore could not conceive that I was there to give him money.

In this weird ontological imbalance, I realized that buying something in that store was like bestowing a gift, the gift of my commerce, the lucre of my patronage. In the wake of my outrage, I wanted to take back the gift of appreciation that my peering in the window must have appeared to be. I wanted to take
45   it back in the form of unappreciation, disrespect, defilement. I wanted to work so hard at wishing he could feel what I felt that he would never again mistake my hatred for some sort of plaintive wish to be included. I was quite willing to disenfranchise myself, in the heat of my need to revoke the flattery of my purchasing power. I was willing to boycott Benetton's, random white-owned busi-
50   nesses, and anyone who ever blew bubble gum in my face again.

My rage was admittedly diffuse, even self-destructive, but it was symmetrical. The perhaps loose-ended but utter propriety of that rage is no doubt lost not just to the young man who actually barred me, but to those who would appreciate my being barred only as an abstract precaution, who approve of those
55   who would bar even as they deny that they would bar *me*.

The violence of my desire to burst into Benetton's is probably quite apparent. I often wonder if the violence, the exclusionary hatred, is equally apparent in the repeated public urgings that blacks understand the buzzer system by putting themselves in the shoes of white storeowners—that, in effect, blacks
60   look into the mirror of frightened white faces for the reality of their undesirability; and that then blacks would "just as surely conclude that [they] would not let [themselves] in under similar circumstances."[2] (That some blacks might agree merely shows that some of us have learned too well the lessons of privatized intimacies of self-hatred and rationalized away the fullness of our public,
65   participatory selves.)

On the same day I was barred from Benetton's, I went home and wrote the above impassioned account in my journal. On the day after that, I found I was still brooding, so I turned to a form of catharsis I have always found healing. I typed up as much of the story as I have just told, made a big poster of it, put a
70   nice colorful border around it, and, after Benetton's was truly closed, stuck it to their big sweater-filled window. I exercised my first amendment right to place my business with them right out in the street.

---

2. *The New York Times*, January 11, 1987, p. E32.

So that was the first telling of this story. The second telling came a few months later, for a symposium on Excluded Voices sponsored by a law review. I wrote an essay summing up my feelings about being excluded from Benetton's and analyzing "how the rhetoric of increased privatization, in response to racial issues, functions as the rationalizing agent of public unaccountability and, ultimately, irresponsibility." Weeks later, I received the first edit. From the first page to the last, my fury had been carefully cut out. My rushing, run-on-rage had been reduced to simple declarative sentences. The active personal had been inverted in favor of the passive impersonal. My words were different; they spoke to me upsidedown. I was afraid to read too much of it at a time—meanings rose up at me oddly, stolen and strange.

A week and a half later, I received the second edit. All reference to Benetton's had been deleted because, according to the editors and the faculty adviser, it was defamatory; they feared harassment and liability; they said printing it would be irresponsible. I called them and offered to supply a footnote attesting to this as my personal experience at one particular location and of a buzzer system not limited to Benetton's; the editors told me that they were not in the habit of publishing things that were unverifiable. I could not but wonder, in this refusal even to let me file an affadavit, what it would take to make my experience verifiable. The testimony of an independent white bystander? (a requirement in fact imposed in U.S. Supreme Court holdings through the first part of the century).

Two days *after* the piece was sent to press, I received copies of the final page proofs. All reference to my race had been eliminated because it was against "editorial policy" to permit descriptions of physiognomy. "I realize," wrote one editor, "that this was a very personal experience, but any reader will know what you must have looked like when standing at that window." In a telephone conversation to them, I ranted wildly about the significance of such an omission. "It's irrelevant," another editor explained in a voice gummy with soothing and patience; "It's nice and poetic," but it doesn't "advance the discussion of any principle. . . . This is a law review, after all." Frustrated, I accused him of censorship; calmly he assured me it was not. "This is just a matter of style," he said with firmness and finality.

Ultimately I did convince the editors that mention of my race was central to the whole sense of the subsequent text; that my story became one of extreme paranoia without the information that I am black; or that it became one in which the reader had to fill in the gap by assumption, presumption, prejudgment, or prejudice. What was most interesting to me in this experience was how the blind application of principles of neutrality, through the device of omission, acted either to make me look crazy or to make the reader participate in old habits of cultural bias.

That was the second telling of my story. The third telling came last April, when I was invited to participate in a law-school conference on Equality and Difference. I retold my sad tale of exclusion from Soho's most glitzy boutique, focusing in this version on the law-review editing process as a consequence of an ideology of style rooted in a social text of neutrality. I opined:

120      Law and legal writing aspire to formalized, color-blind, liberal ideals. Neutrality is the standard for assuring these ideals; yet the adherence to it is often determined by reference to an aesthetic of uniformity, in which difference is simply omitted. For example, when segregation was eradicated from the American lexicon, its omission led many to actually believe that racism therefore no longer existed. Race-neutrality in law has become the presumed anti-
125 dote for race bias in real life. With the entrenchment of the notion of race-neutrality came attacks on the concept of affirmative action and the rise of reverse discrimination suits. Blacks, for so many generations deprived of jobs based on the color of our skin, are now told that we ought to find it demeaning to be hired, based on the color of our skin. Such is the silliness of simplistic
130 either-or inversions as remedies to complex problems.

     What is truly demeaning in this era of double-speak-no-evil is going on interviews and not getting hired because someone doesn't think we'll be comfortable. It is demeaning not to get promoted because we're judged "too weak," then putting in a lot of energy the next time and getting fired because we're
135 "too strong." It is demeaning to be told what we find demeaning. It is very demeaning to stand on street corners unemployed and begging. It is downright demeaning to have to explain why we haven't been employed for months and then watch the job go to someone who is "more experienced." It is outrageously demeaning that none of this can be called racism, even if it happens
140 only to, or to large numbers of, black people; as long as it's done with a smile, a handshake and a shrug; as long as the phantom-word "race" is never used.

     The image of race as a phantom-word came to me after I moved into my late godmother's home. In an attempt to make it my own, I cleared the bedroom for painting. The following morning the room asserted itself, came rush-
145 ing and raging at me through the emptiness, exactly as it had been for twenty-five years. One day filled with profuse and overwhelming complexity, the next day filled with persistently recurring memories. The shape of the past came to haunt me, the shape of the emptiness confronted me each time I was about to enter the room. The force of its spirit still drifts like an odor throughout the
150 house.

     The power of that room, I have thought since, is very like the power of racism as status quo: it is deep, angry, eradicated from view, but strong enough to make everyone who enters the room walk around the bed that isn't there, avoiding the phantom as they did the substance, for fear of bodily harm. They
155 do not even know they are avoiding; they defer to the unseen shapes of things with subtle responsiveness, guided by an impulsive awareness of nothingness, and the deep knowledge and denial of witchcraft at work.

     The phantom room is to me symbolic of the emptiness of formal equal opportunity, particularly as propounded by President Reagan, the Reagan Civil
160 Rights Commission and the Reagan Supreme Court. Blindly formalized constructions of equal opportunity are the creation of a space that is filled in by a meandering stream of unguided hopes, dreams, fantasies, fears, recollections.

They are the presence of the past in imaginary, imagistic form—the phantom-roomed exile of our longing.

It is thus that I strongly believe in the efficacy of programs and paradigms like affirmative action. Blacks are the objects of a constitutional omission which has been incorporated into a theory of neutrality. It is thus that omission is really a form of expression, as oxymoronic as that sounds: racial omission is a literal part of original intent; it is the fixed, reiterated prophecy of the Founding Fathers. It is thus that affirmative action is an affirmation; the affirmative act of hiring—or hearing—blacks is a recognition of individuality that re-places blacks as a social statistic, that is profoundly interconnective to the fate of blacks and whites either as sub-groups or as one group. In this sense, affirmative action is as mystical and beyond-the-self as an initiation ceremony. It is an act of verification and of vision. It is an act of social as well as professional responsibility.

The following morning I opened the local newspaper, to find that the event of my speech had commanded two columns on the front page of the Metro section. I quote only the opening lines: "Affirmative action promotes prejudice by denying the status of women and blacks, instead of affirming them as its name suggests. So said New York City attorney Patricia Williams to an audience Wednesday."[3]

I clipped out the article and put it in my journal. In the margin there is a note to myself: eventually, it says, I should try to pull all these threads together into yet another law-review article. The problem, of course, will be that in the hierarchy of law-review citation, the article in the newspaper will have more authoritative weight about me, as a so-called "primary resource," than I will have; it will take precedence over my own citation of the unverifiable testimony of my speech.

I have used the Benetton's story a lot, in speaking engagements at various schools. I tell it whenever I am too tired to whip up an original speech from scratch. Here are some of the questions I have been asked in the wake of its telling:

Am I not privileging[4] a racial perspective, by considering only the black point of view? Don't I have an obligation to include the "salesman's side" of the story?

Am I not putting the salesman on trial and finding him guilty of racism without giving him a chance to respond to or cross-examine me?

Am I not using the store window as a "metaphorical fence" against the potential of his explanation in order to represent my side as "authentic"?

How can I be sure I'm right?

What makes my experience the real black one anyway?

---

3. "Attorney Says Affirmative Action Denies Racism, Sexism," *Dominion Post* (Morgantown, W. V.), April 8, 1988, p. B1.

4. *privileging:* giving undue attention to. (*ed.*)

Isn't it possible that another black person would disagree with my experience? If so, doesn't that render my story too unempirical and subjective to pay
205   any attention to?

Always a major objection is to my having put the poster on Benetton's window. As one law professor put it: "It's one thing to publish this in a law review,
where no one can take it personally, but it's another thing altogether to put your
own interpretation right out there, just like that, uncontested, I mean, with
210   nothing to counter it."

## Looking Back

1. How does Williams's self-description of her "round brown face" (line 16), followed
   by her description of the store clerk, affect your reaction to the central incident?

2. Does Williams's instant rage at being excluded from the store seem justified to you?
   Might there be mitigating circumstances that explain the clerk's action? Explain.

3. What new perspective on the antisocial behavior called looting do we get from
   Williams (see lines 24–25)?

4. Can you describe in your own words the oppressive "structure of power" she discusses in lines 30–40?

5. What moral contradiction does she perceive in the thinking of people "who approve
   of those who would bar even as they deny that they would bar *me*" (lines 54–55)?

6. Was Williams's posting her story on Benetton's window a reasonable action? Why
   or why not?

7. How do you understand the topic of Williams's law review essay: " 'How the
   rhetoric of increased privatization, in response to racial issues, functions as the rationalizing agent of public unaccountability and, ultimately, irresponsibility' " (lines
   76–78)? (Use the dictionary if necessary.)

8. We normally regard "principles of neutrality" (line 111) as a sign of fairness. Why
   does Williams condemn them in the editorial treatment of her article?

9. Can you sum up the argument for affirmative action she conducts in her speech
   (lines 119–176)?

10. How would you answer the questions Williams tells us she often is asked (lines
    194–205)? How do you believe Williams would answer them?

## Writing Assignments

1. Williams's emotional pain and intellectual outrage at being excluded from the
   Benetton's store are clear and understandable. Yet she herself refers to the approval
   of such store policies by civil rights organizations (lines 6–11), and she reports that
   people ask about the salesman's side of the story (lines 197–198). What do you
   think of the policy excluding certain types of persons from stores according to a recognizable profile? Write an essay answering this question. Your essay can argue for
   or against the policy, or, interpolating your remarks into Williams's case, it can seek
   to explain the likely motive for such a policy and its probable consequences. Be sure
   to refer in your essay to the incident Williams discusses.

2. Forbidden to enter the store peaceably, "I was enraged," Williams writes. "At that moment I literally wanted to break all the windows of the store and *take* lots of sweaters for my mother" (lines 24–25). That is, the law professor suddenly feels the impulse to strike back at what she feels is discrimination on the basis of color by stealing what she had intended to buy. Her admission helps us to see in a new light the looting that accompanies so many urban riots (see number 3 in Looking Back). Not that we suddenly excuse what we previously condemned, but our understanding of looting may now be a fuller one. Write an essay that extrapolates from Williams's attitude in order to describe such a new way of understanding looting.

3. Now that you have defined affirmative action for yourself (see number 2 in Looking Ahead) and summed up Williams's argument for it (see number 9 in Looking Back), you are in a good position to address it as social policy. Write an essay doing so that particularly considers Williams's speech on the subject (lines 119–176) and the issues she brings up: neutrality, historical job discrimination against African Americans, reverse discrimination, and the possibility of being demeaned as the beneficiary of the policy.

# Follow-Up: An Essay for Analysis

## WEIGHT

When I first read Patricia Williams' "The Death of the Profane," the author's pain and outrage jumped off the pages and caught me off-guard. Her essay was not only angry but also hostile. I was immediately pulled into her story and forced to choose sides; I could not remain neutral. I reread Ms. Williams' story about not being buzzed into a Soho shop and thought about this ubiquitous, in Manhattan anyway, practice.     5

    I do not remember when this policy began, but it has been around for at least six years in the city. Because the owners of expensive boutiques had been complaining about robberies and assaults in their stores, they decided to install a buzzer system. The front doors remain locked so entry is restricted. One effect of this buzzer system has been the creation of an accepted form of discrimination based on the premise that people deemed suspicious-looking by shop owners and their clerks can be excluded. When a potential customer buzzes, the owner or clerk can look at who's seeking admission and either buzz the person in or not. Therein lies the author's anger and hostility.     10     15     20

Because some store owner or clerk has never not
25  buzzed me in, I have never experienced Ms. Williams'
pain and outrage. But, even though I get into the
store, I have felt the sting of discrimination in
certain exclusive shops because of my weight. The
clerks look down their noses at me while stating they
30  do not carry my size! I cannot browse or shop for
someone else; in the clerks' eyes, I am an undesirable. Just as Ms. Williams cannot leave her round,
brown face at home, I cannot leave my round, white
body at home either. I remember the first time a
35  store clerk handed me my purchase after stapling the
bag closed. The implication was clear. I had paid
for the item in the bag, but I wouldn't be able to
put anything else into it after I left the cash register. Based on instructions from the employer, the
40  clerk effectively stripped me of my integrity and
treated me a possible thief. I was incensed, ripped
open the bag and stormed out. My personal slights
aside, I cannot and do not support this arbitrary and
exclusionary buzzer practice.
45      How do the store owners determine who should be
admitted? In most cases I would say that exclusion
is based on race. Sex and age complete the formula.
The pronouncement is clear--if you fit this
race/sex/age profile, you are undesirable and, there-
50  fore, not admitted. You are no longer perceived as
an individual; you are judged based on a stereotype
established by a shop owner. And, what do shop owners tell their clerks about the policy? The owners
instruct their employees to follow certain guidelines
55  to keep their stores and customers out of harm's way.
So, the store owners and staff can don their imperial
togas and signal an effective "thumbs down." No
mercy shown here. One can see how this arbitrary
practice perpetuates racial fears and tensions and
60  causes more distrust.
    By telling and retelling her story and by writing
essays and articles about it, Ms. Williams has taken
positive steps to point out the obvious problems this
accepted form of discrimination has created. She is
65  forcing everybody to take another look at a practice
which is not only insensitive but also biased.

                    --Rosemary Waikuny, composition student

## Critical Inquiry

Rosemary Waikuny wrote the above essay in response to Patricia Williams's "The Death of the Profane," Writing Assignment 1 (p. 444). Waikuny's essay is an early draft. That is, it needs revision on several levels before it can be judged acceptable. To help you become more aware of your own writing needs as well as those of this student writer, use the following list of questions to analyze the essay. Before answering them, you should reread Williams's text and the writing assignment Waikuny responded to.

## Questions for Analysis

1. In your judgment, has Waikuny done what the writing assignment called for? If so, what supports your view? If not, what matters has she not addressed?

2. Has Waikuny referred to Williams's text sufficiently for someone who has *not* read it to understand Williams's intent and chief ideas? Why do you think this?

3. How would you evaluate the overall structure of this draft of Waikuny's essay? Is there a clear beginning, middle, and end? Do some materials need to be differently positioned in the essay?

4. Do the paragraphs connect with one another, or are more effective transitions needed?

5. Does Waikuny's logic hold up throughout, or are there places where it falls down? Be specific.

6. Would you suggest that, in later drafts, Waikuny develop some parts of the essay in greater detail? If so, which parts?

7. Is Waikuny's point of view generally convincing, or do you feel that she needs to make it more so? Be specific.

8. How would you evaluate Waikuny's word choice? Should she clarify or replace any language in the next draft? Are there any redundancies? Where, if at all, should she be more concise?

# Linked Readings

Aldous Huxley
## BRITISH HONDURAS

Katha Pollitt
## MEDIA GOES WILDING IN PALM BEACH

Anna Quindlen
## MAKING A CASE

The first of these three pieces—a travel report from what in 1934 was called British Honduras—may seem initially to have little to do with the other two, which have in common the subject of rape and the publicity given it. Actually, however, Huxley's disquisition on choice and its consequences is directly relevant to the issue and helps the critical thinking aim of creating a new context in which to view it. Aldous Huxley (1894–1963) was a British novelist, short story writer, and essayist. His most famous novels are *Brave New World, Point Counter Point, Eyeless in Gaza,* and *Time Must Have a Stop.* "British Honduras" is taken from his travel book, *Beyond the Mexique Bay.* Katha Pollitt is a poet and journalist whose books include *Antarctic Traveler* and *Reasonable Creatures: Essays on Women and Feminism.* She is a contributing editor of *The Nation* magazine, in which this article appeared (June 24, 1991). Along with another *Nation* piece, it won a National Magazine Award in 1992. The word *wilding* in the title refers to the practice of urban teenagers' roving in bands looking for and making trouble. Anna Quindlen is a novelist and former columnist for *The New York Times.* Her essay appeared in that journal on June 20, 1991. Among her books are *Living Out Loud, Thinking Out Loud, Object Lessons,* and *One True Thing.*

## BRITISH HONDURAS

### *Looking Ahead*

1. A writing lesson: As Huxley demonstrates, writers can move from personal observation and recorded fact to specific conclusions that themselves lead to more general insights.

2. Moral involvement in public life and human interdependence are key themes to keep in mind as you read.

3. It is useful to consider the extent, hinted at here, to which seemingly impersonal, abstract social and economic policies result from individual decisions. When they adversely affect millions of people, they likewise do so one person at a time.

When I was a boy there was hardly, in all my acquaintance, a single reputable family which did not eat off mahogany, sit on mahogany, sleep in mahogany. Mahogany was a symbol of economic solidity and moral worth. Just as in Barbados the hat proclaims the emancipated and no longer inferior negress, so, in
5   Victorian England, mahogany proclaimed the respectable man of substance. So loudly and unequivocally did it proclaim him, that those whose trade was in luxury could never be lavish enough with their mahogany. In Pullman cars, in liners—wherever, indeed, it was necessary to give clients the illusion that they were living like princes—mahogany fairly flowed like water.
10      Alas, how quickly such sacred symbols can lose their significance! For us, to-day, the highest luxury is a perfect asepsis.[1] The new casino at Monte Carlo Beach could be transformed at a moment's notice into a hospital. (Luxurious in the traditional manner, the old is almost infinitely unhygienic.) The Wagon Lit[2] Company's latest coaches are simply very expensive steel nursing-homes on
15   wheels. There is no place here for mahogany. There is hardly more place in the private house. I cannot think of a single modern high-bourgeois home, in which

---

1. *asepsis:* sterility. (*ed.*)

2. *Wagon Lit:* railroad sleeping car. (*ed.*)

mahogany plays more than a casual and inconspicuous part. My friends eat off glass and metal, sit on metal and leather, sleep on beds that are almost innocent of enclosing bedsteads. If they use wood at all for their furniture, they use one of the light-coloured varieties, or else a cheap soft-wood painted to harmonize with the general colour-scheme of the room. Never mahogany. The dark rich wood, so much beloved by our fathers and grandfathers, has not only lost its symbolic meaning; it is also (and the Marxians would say that this was directly due to the loss of prestige) regarded with aesthetic distaste. Mahogany, in a word, is now hopelessly out of fashion.

Here, so far as the historian of taste is concerned, the matter ends. For the social historian, however, it is only just beginning. British Honduras used to live on the export of mahogany. But we prefer the lighter woods, we prefer metal and glass and ripolin. Result: a falling off of Honduranean exports and a corresponding rise in the death-rate from tuberculosis. Increase of phthisis[3] in Belize has a contributory cause in the decline of gum-chewing in Chicago and New York. Chicle, like mahogany, but on a smaller scale, is a British Honduran staple. Financial stringency, and perhaps also a change of fashion, cause American typists to chew less than they did. Therefore the chicle-hunters and their dependents—like the mahogany-cutters and theirs—have less money to buy food and so less resistance to disease. Tubercle takes its opportunity.

The inadequacy of man's imagination and his immense capacity for ignorance are notorious. We act habitually without knowing what the more distant results of our actions are likely to be—without even caring to know. And our ability to imagine how other people think and feel, or how we ourselves should think and feel in some hypothetical situation, is strictly limited. These are defects in our make-up as mental beings. But they are defects which possess great biological advantages. Any considerable increase in our capacity for knowing and imagining would be likely to result in the paralysis of all our activities. Take, by way of example, this little matter of mahogany. If we knew precisely what were going to be the effects upon the British Honduraneans of our choice of metal instead of mahogany; if we could vividly imagine what it feels like to be chronically underfed, to die slowly of consumption; if our sympathy with them were what the word literally means, a genuine "withsuffering"—should we then ever have the courage to buy anything but mahogany? And if we bought nothing but mahogany, what about the people who live by the sale of soft-woods, glass and stainless steel? Knowing the effects on them, imaginatively realizing their sufferings, how could we resist *their* appeal? The final result would be a hopeless neurasthenia.

What is true of mahogany is true of everything else. Excess of knowledge and imagination leads to a kind of paralysis. (The tragedy of this excess has been written in *Hamlet*.) The confident capacity to choose depends on ignorance or, if knowledge is unescapable, on insentience and lack of imagination.

---

3. *phthisis:* a wasting, consumptive condition like tuberculosis. (*ed.*)

In practice we are able to do things with a light heart, because we never know
60   very clearly what we are doing, and are happily incapable of imagining how our
deeds will affect other people or our future selves. To rail against destiny because it has decreed that we shall live in darkness and insensibility is foolish.
We should rather be thankful that it has been made psychologically possible for
us to choose and to act. If we find that our acts and choices result in damage to
65   others, it is our duty, as human beings, to try to remedy the evil we have
caused. It is certainly not our duty to refrain from choice and action because all
choices and actions may—indeed must—result in some evil to somebody.

By remote delegation and proxy the English public is trying to make up for
the miseries it has unwittingly inflicted on the negroes of Belize. The British
70   Honduras government, for the existence of which we non-chewing despisers of
mahogany are at least theoretically responsible, is making great efforts to induce
the negro woodmen to go on the land. The task is not easy; for these woodmen
have been brought up in a traditional contempt for agriculture. The material
difficulties are also great. Still, there is plenty of fertile ground available, and the
75   country, which is about equal in area to Wales, has a population hardly if at all
larger than that of Nuneaton. The forests are filled with ruins, and in the palmy
days of the Maya Old Empire this territory which now supports, or rather does
not support, forty-five thousand people, may easily have had a million inhabitants. Intensely cultivated, it might again become populous and prosperous.
80   Our refusal to eat our dinners off mahogany is, for the moment, a disaster for
the Honduraneans. If it compels them to change their mode of life, it may perhaps some day turn out to have been the kindest thing that has ever been done
to them.

## MEDIA GOES WILDING IN PALM BEACH

*Looking Ahead*

1. A note on structure: After providing a background for the issue of publishing rape
victims' names without their consent, Pollitt announces her own view, her thesis,
reviews the arguments on either side, and comes to a general conclusion about rape
victims and the media.

2. In the act of citing an argument and answering it, Pollitt often introduces issues
broader than the one at the heart of her article. Try to detect these instances.

3. As you read, try to decide whether Pollitt's treatment of the issue is a fair or a biased
one. Then determine how that affects your response to her position.

I drink, I swear, I flirt, I tell dirty jokes. I have also, at various times, watched
pornographic videos, had premarital sex, hitchhiked, and sunbathed topless in
violation of local ordinances. True, I don't have any speeding tickets, but I
don't have a driver's license either. Perhaps I'm subconsciously afraid of my

"drives"? There are other things, too, and if I should ever bring rape charges 5
against a rich, famous, powerful politician's relative, *The New York Times* will
probably tell you all about them—along with, perhaps, my name. Suitably
adorned with anonymous quotes, these revelations will enable you, the public,
to form your own opinion: Was I asking for trouble, or did I just make the
whole thing up?

In April the media free-for-all surrounding the alleged rape of a Palm Beach 10
woman by William Smith, Senator Ted Kennedy's nephew, took a vicious turn
as the *Times*—following NBC, following the *Globe* (supermarket, not Boston,
edition), following a British scandal sheet, following *another* British scandal
sheet—went public with the woman's name, and a lot more: her traffic viola- 15
tions, her mediocre high school grades, her "little wild streak," her single motherhood, her mother's divorce and upwardly mobile remarriage. Pretty small
potatoes, really; she sounds like half my high school classmates. But it did make
a picture: bad girl, loose woman, floozy.

Or did it? In a meeting with more than 300 outraged staff members, na- 20
tional editor Soma Golden said that the *Times* could not be held responsible for
"every weird mind that reads [the paper]." NBC News chief Michael Gartner
was more direct: "Who she is is material in this. . . . You try to give viewers as
many facts as you can and let them make up their minds." Forget that almost
none of these "facts" will be admissible in court, where a jury will nonetheless 25
be expected to render a verdict.

In the ensuing furor, just about every advocate for rape victims has spoken
out in favor of preserving the longstanding media custom of anonymity, and in
large part the public seems to agree. But the media,[1] acting in its capacity as the
guardian of public interest, has decided that naming the victim is an issue up 30
for grabs. And so we are having one of those endless, muddled, two-sides-to-
every-question debates that, by ignoring as many facts as possible and by
weighing all arguments equally, gives us that warm American feeling that truth
must lie somewhere in the middle. Anna Quindlen, meet Alan Dershowitz.[2]
Thank you very much, but our time is just about up. 35

Sometimes, of course, the truth does lie somewhere in the middle. But not
this time. There is no good reason to publish the names of rape complainants
without their consent, and many compelling reasons not to. The arguments advanced in favor of publicity reveal fundamental misconceptions about both the
nature of the media and the nature of rape. 40

Let's take a look at what proponents of naming are saying.

---

1. I use "media" in the singular (rather than the strictly grammatical plural) because I am talking about the communications industry as a social institution that, while hardly monolithic (as the
debate over naming shows), transcends the different means—"media" plural—by which the news is
conveyed.

2. *Alan Dershowitz*: well-known lawyer and Harvard law professor; author of *Chutzpah*. (*ed.*)

*The media has a duty to report what it knows.*   Where have you been? The media keeps information secret all the time. Sometimes it does so on the ground of "taste," a waffle-word that means whatever an editorial board wants it to mean.
45  Thus, we hear about (some of) the sexual high jinks of heterosexual celebrities but not about those of socially equivalent closet-dwellers, whose opposite-sex escorts are portrayed, with knowing untruthfulness, as genuine romantic interests. We are spared—or deprived of, depending on your point of view—the gruesome and salacious details of many murders. (Of all the New York dailies,
50  only *Newsday* reported that notorious Wall Street wife-killer Joseph Pikul was wearing women's underwear when arrested. Not fit to print? I was *riveted.*) Sometimes it fudges the truth to protect third parties from embarrassment, which is why the obituaries would have us believe that eminent young bachelors are dying in large numbers only from pneumonia.
55      And of course sometimes it censors itself in "the national interest." The claim that the media constitutes a fourth estate, a permanent watchdog, if not outright adversary, of the government, has always been a self-serving myth. Watergate occurred almost twenty years ago and has functioned ever since as a kind of sentimental talisman, like Charles Foster Kane's Rosebud sled.[3] As we
60  saw during the gulf war, the media can live, when it chooses, quite comfortably with government-imposed restrictions. Neither NBC nor *The New York Times,* so quick to supply their audiences with the inside scoop on the Palm Beach woman, felt any such urgency about Operation Desert Storm.

*Anonymous charges are contrary to the American way.*   Anonymous charges are
65  contrary to American *jurisprudence.* The Palm Beach woman has not made an anonymous accusation. Her name is known to the accused and his attorney, and if the case comes to trial, she will have to appear publicly in court, confront the defendant, give testimony and be cross-examined. But the media is not a court, as the many lawyers who have made this argument—most prominently
70  Alan Dershowitz and Isabelle Pinzler of the American Civil Liberties Union's Women's Rights Project—ought to know.
    The media itself argues in favor of anonymity when that serves its own purposes. Reporters go to jail rather than reveal their sources, even when secrecy means protecting a dangerous criminal, impeding the process of justice or
75  denying a public figure the ability to confront his or her accusers. People wouldn't talk to reporters, the press claims, if their privacy couldn't be guaranteed—the same greater-social-good argument it finds unpersuasive when made about rape victims and their reluctance to talk, unprotected, to the police. The media's selective interest in concealment, moreover, undermines its vaunted
80  mission on behalf of the public's right to know. Might not the identity of an

---

3. *Charles Foster Kane:* newspaper tycoon of Orson Welles's classic film *Citizen Kane,* based on William Randolph Hearst; *Rosebud:* the mysterious last word of dying Kane, which turned out to be the name of the sled he had loved as a child. (*ed.*)

anonymous informant (one of those "sources close to the White House" or "highly placed observers," for instance) help the public "make up its mind" about the reliability of the statements? I don't want to digress here into the complex issue of protecting sources, but there can be little question that the practice allows powerful people, in and out of government, to manipulate information for their own ends. Interestingly, the *Times* story on the Palm Beach woman concealed (thirteen times!) the names of those spreading malicious gossip about her, despite the *Times*'s own custom of not using anonymous pejoratives. That custom was resuscitated in time for the paper's circumspect profile of William Smith, which did not detail the accusations against him of prior acquaintance rapes that have been published by *The National Enquirer* and the gossip columnist Taki, and which referred only vaguely to "rumors" of "a pattern of aggressiveness toward women in private." (These, the *Times* said, it could not confirm—unlike the accuser's "little wild streak.") 85

90

How *did* the *Times* manage to amass such a wealth of dirt about the Palm Beach woman so quickly? It's hard to picture the reporter, distinguished China hand Fox Butterfield, peeking into the window of her house to see what books were on her toddler's shelf. Could some of his information or some of his leads have come, directly or circuitously, from the detectives hired by the Kennedy family to investigate the woman and her friends—detectives who, let's not forget, have been the subject of complaints of witness intimidation? The *Times* denies it, but rumors persist. One could argue that, in this particular case, *how* the *Times* got the story was indeed part of the story—perhaps the most important part. 95

100

That anonymity is held to be essential to the public good in a wide variety of cases but is damned as a form of censorship in the Palm Beach case shows that what the media is concerned with is not the free flow of information *or* the public good. What is at stake is the media's status, power and ability to define and control information in accordance with the views of those who run the media. 105

110

Consider, for example, the case of men convicted of soliciting prostitutes. Except for the occasional athlete, such men receive virtual anonymity in the press. Remember the flap in 1979 when Manhattan D.A. Robert Morgenthau released a list of recently convicted johns and the *Daily News* and two local radio stations went public with it? Universal outrage! Never mind that solicitation is a crime, that convictions are a matter of public record, that the wives and girlfriends of these men might find knowledge of such arrests extremely useful or that society has a declared interest in deterring prostitution. Alan Dershowitz, who in his syndicated column has defended both the content of the *Times* profile and its use of the woman's name, vigorously supported privacy for johns, and in fact made some of the same arguments that he now dismisses. Reporting, he said, was vindictive, subjected ordinary people to the glaring light of publicity for a peccadillo, could destroy the johns' marriages and reputations, and stigmatized otherwise decent people. Dershowitz did not, however, think 115

120

125   privacy for johns meant privacy for prostitutes: They, he argued, have no reputation to lose. Although solicitation is a two-person crime, Dershowitz thinks
the participants have unequal rights to privacy. With rape, he treats the rapist
and his victim as *equally* placed with regard to privacy, even though rape is a
one-person crime.

130   *But here the woman's identity was already widely known.*   Well, I didn't know it. I
did, however, know the name of the Central Park jogger—like virtually every
other journalist in the country, the entire readership of *The Amsterdam News*
(50,000) and the listening audience of WLIB radio (45,000). Anna Quindlen, in
her courageous column dissenting from the *Times*'s profile naming the Palm
135   Beach woman, speculated that roughly equivalent large numbers of people
knew the identity of the jogger as knew that of William Smith's alleged victim
before NBC and the *Times* got into the act. Yet the media went to extraordinary
lengths to protect the remaining shreds of the jogger's privacy—film clips were
blipped, quotes censored.

140      What separates the jogger from the Palm Beach woman? You don't have to
be the Rev. Al Sharpton[4] to suspect that protecting the jogger's identity was
more than a chivalrous gesture. Remember that she too was originally blamed
for her assault: What was she doing in the park so late? Who did she think she
was? It's all feminism's fault for deluding women into thinking that their safety
145   could, or should, be everywhere guaranteed. But partly as a result of the severity
of her injuries, the jogger quickly became the epitome of the innocent victim,
the symbol, as Joan Didion[5] pointed out in *The New York Review of Books*, for
New York City itself (white, prosperous, plucky) endangered by the black un-
derclass. A white Wellesley graduate with a Wall Street job attacked out of
150   nowhere by a band of violent black strangers and, because of her comatose
state, unable even to bring a rape complaint—this, to the media, is "real rape."
The Palm Beach woman, on the other hand, is of working-class origins, a single
mother, a frequenter of bars, who went voluntarily to her alleged attacker's
house (as who, in our star-struck society, would not?). The jogger could have
155   been the daughter of the men who kept her name out of the news. But William
Smith could have been their son.

*Rape is like other crimes and should be treated like other crimes. Isn't that what you
feminists are always saying?*   As the coverage of the Palm Beach case proves,
rape isn't treated like other crimes. There is no other crime in which the charac-
160   ter, behavior and past of the complainant are seen as central elements in determining whether a crime has occurred. There are lots of crimes that could not
take place without carelessness, naiveté, ignorance or bad judgment on the part

---

4. *Al Sharpton:* African American community leader much criticized for his demagoguery. (*ed.*)

   5. *Joan Didion:* essayist and novelist; see her essays "Holy Water," p. 324, and "On Morality,"
p. 612. (*ed.*)

of the victims: mail fraud ("Make $100,000 at home in your spare time!"), con-
fidence games and many violent crimes as well. But when my father was bur-
glarized after forgetting to lock the cellar door, the police did not tell him he        165
had been asking for it. And when an elderly lady (to cite Amy Pagnozzi's example in the *New York Post*) is defrauded of her life savings by a con artist, the con
artist is just as much a thief as if he'd broken into his victim's safe-deposit box.
"The complainant showed incredibly bad judgment, Your Honor," is not a legal
defense.                                                                                   170

Why is rape different? Because lots of people, too often including the
ones in the jury box, think women really do want to be forced into sex, or by
acting or dressing or drinking in a certain way, give up the right to say no, or
are the sort of people (i.e., not nuns) who gave up the right to say no to one
man by saying yes to another, or are by nature scheming, irrational and            175
crazy. They also think men cannot be expected to control themselves, are entitled to take by force what they cannot get by persuasion and are led on by
women who, because they are scheming, irrational and crazy, change their
minds in mid-sex. My files bulge with stories that show how widespread
these beliefs are: the Wisconsin judge who put a child molester on probation       180
because he felt the 3-year-old female victim had acted provocatively; the
Florida jury that exonerated a rapist because his victim was wearing disco at-
tire; and so on.

In a bizarre column defending Ted Kennedy's role on the night in question,
William Safire took aim at the Palm Beach woman, who was "apparently" not         185
"taught that drinking all night and going to a man's house at 3:30 A.M. places
one in what used to be called an occasion of sin." (All her mother's fault, as
usual.) The other woman present in the Kennedy mansion that night, a waitress
named Michelle Cassone, has made herself a mini-celebrity by telling any reporter who will pay for her time that she too believes that women who drink      190
and date, including herself, are "fair game."

By shifting the debate to the question of merely naming victims, the media
pre-empts a discussion of the way it reports all crimes with a real or imaginary
sexual component. But as the *Times* profile shows, naming cannot be divorced
from blaming. When the victim is young and attractive (and in the tabloids *all*   195
female victims are attractive), the sexual element in the crime is always made its
central feature—even when, as in the case of Marla Hanson, the model who was
slashed by hired thugs and whose character was savaged in *New York*, there is
no sexual element. I mean no belittlement of rape to suggest it was one of the
lesser outrages visited on the Central Park jogger. She was also beaten so furi-   200
ously she lost 80 percent of her blood and suffered permanent physical, neuro-
logical and cognitive damage. Yet, paradoxically, it was the rape that seized the
imagination of the media, and that became the focus of the crime both for her
defenders and for those who defended her attackers.

*Naming rape victims will remove the stigma against rape.*   Of all the arguments in   205
favor of naming victims, this is the silliest, and the most insincere. Sure, NBC's

Michael Gartner told *Newsweek,* the consequences will be "extraordinarily difficult for this generation, but it may perhaps help their daughters and grand-
daughters." How selfish of women to balk at offering themselves on the altar of
210    little girls yet unborn! If Gartner wishes to make a better world for my descendants, he is amply well placed to get cracking. He could demand nonsensation-
alized reporting of sex crimes; he could hire more female reporters and producers; he could use NBC News to dispel false notions about rape—for example,
the idea that "who the woman is is material." Throughout the country there are
215    dozens of speakouts against rape at which victims publicly tell of their experiences. Every year there are Take Back the Night marches in Manhattan. Where
are the cameras and the reporters on these occasions? Adding misery to hundreds of thousands of women a year and—as just about every expert in the field
believes—dramatically lowering the already abysmal incidence of rape report-
220    ing (one in ten) will not help my granddaughter; it will only make it more likely
that her grandmother, her mother and she herself will be raped by men who
have not been brought to justice.

This argument is, furthermore, based on a questionable assumption. Why
would society blame rape victims less if it knew who they were? Perhaps its cen-
225    sure would simply be amplified. Instead of thinking, If ordinary, decent, conventional women get raped in large numbers it *can't* be their fault, people might
well think, Goodness, there are a lot more women asking for it than we thought.
After the invasion of Kuwait, in which scores of women were raped by Iraqi soldiers, there was no dispensation from the traditional harsh treatment of rape
230    victims, some of whom, pregnant and in disgrace, had attempted suicide, gone
into hiding or fled the country. One woman told *USA Today* that she wished she
were dead. America is not Kuwait, but here, too, many believe that a woman
can't be raped against her will and that damaged goods are damaged goods.
(Curious how publicity is supposed to lessen the stigma against rape victims but
235    only adds to the suffering of johns.)

One also has to wonder about the urgency with which Gartner and the
other male proponents of the anti-stigma theory, with no history of public concern for women, declare themselves the best judge of women's interests and advocate a policy that they themselves will never have to bear the consequences
240    of. Gartner cited, as did many others, the *Des Moines Register* profile of a named
rape victim but neglected to mention that the victim, Nancy Ziegenmeyer, vol-
unteered the use of her name, seven months after reporting the crime—in other
words, after she had had a chance to come to terms with her experience and to
inform her family and friends in a way she found suitable. (Ziegenmeyer, by the
245    way, opposes involuntary naming.) Why is it that, where women are concerned,
the difference between choice and coercion eludes so many? Rapists, too, persuade themselves that they know what women really want and need.

*William Smith's name has been dragged through the mud. Why should his accuser be
protected?*    Actually, William Smith has been portrayed rather favorably in the
250    media. No anonymous pejoratives for him: He is "one of the least spoiled and

least arrogant of the young Kennedys" (*Time*); an "unlikely villain" (*Newsweek*); "a man of gentleness and humor," "the un-Kennedy," "a good listener" (*The New York Times*); from a "wounded," "tragic" family (*passim*). Certainly he has been subjected to a great deal of unpleasant media attention, and even if he is eventually found innocent, some people will always suspect that he is guilty. But no one forced the media to sensationalize the story; that was a conscious editorial decision, not an act of God. Instead of heaping slurs on the Palm Beach woman in order to even things up, the media should be asking itself why it did not adopt a more circumspect attitude toward the case from the outset.   255

The tit-for-tat view of rape reporting appeals to many people because of its apparent impartiality. Feminists of the pure equal-treatment school like it because it looks gender neutral (as if rape were a gender-neutral crime). The non-feminist men like it because, while looking gender neutral, it would, in practice, advantage men. "Should the press be in the business of protecting certain groups but not others—," wrote *Washington Post* columnist Richard Cohen, "alleged victims (females), but not the accused (males)? My answer is no." Cohen, like Michael Gartner, presents himself as having women's best interests at heart: "If rape's indelible stigma is ever to fade, the press has to stop being complicitous in perpetuating the sexist aura that surrounds it." Thus, by some mysterious alchemy, the media, which is perhaps the single biggest promoter of the sexist aura surrounding crimes of violence against women, can redeem itself by jettisoning the only policy it has that eases, rather than augments, the victim's anguish.   260   265   270

Behind the tit-for-tat argument lies a particular vision of rape in which the odds are even that the alleged victim is really the victimizer—a seductress, blackmailer, hysteric, who is bringing a false charge. That was the early word on the Palm Beach woman, and it's hard not to conclude that publicizing her identity was punitive: She's caused all this trouble, is visiting yet more "tragedy" on America's royal family, and had better be telling the truth. In fact, the appeal of naming the victim seems to rest not in the hope that it "may perhaps" someday make rape reporting less painful but in the certainty that right now it makes such reporting *more* painful, thereby inhibiting false accusations. Although studies have repeatedly shown that fabricated rape charges are extremely rare, recent years have seen a number of cases: Tawana Brawley, for example, and Cathleen Crowell Webb, who recanted her testimony after finding Jesus and then hugged her newly freed, no-longer-alleged-assailant on the *Donahue* show. A year ago a Nebraska woman who admitted filing a false charge was ordered by a judge to purchase newspaper ads and radio spots apologizing to the man she had accused. (She was also sentenced to six months in jail.) It is not unknown for other criminal charges to be fabricated, but has anyone ever been forced into a public apology in those cases? The tenor of the equal-publicity argument is captured perfectly by the (female) letter writer to *Time* who suggested that newspapers publish both names and both photos too. Why not bring back trial by ordeal and make the two of them grasp bars of red-hot iron?   275   280   285   290   295

Fundamentally, the arguments about naming rape victims center around two contested areas: acquaintance rape and privacy. While the women's movement has had some success in expanding the definition of rape to include sexual violation by persons known to the victim—as I write, *The New York Times* is running an excellent series on such rape, containing interviews with women named or anonymous by their choice (atonement?)—there is also a lot of backlash.

The all-male editorial board of the *New York Post,* which rather ostentatiously refused to print the Palm Beach woman's name, has actually proposed a change in the law to distinguish between "real rape" (what the jogger suffered) and acquaintance rape, confusedly described as a "sexual encounter, forced or not," that "has been preceded by a series of consensual activities." *Forced or not?*

At the other end of the literary social scale, there's Camille (No Means Yes) Paglia, academia's answer to Phyllis Schlafly,[6] repackaging hoary myths about rape as a bold dissent from feminist orthodoxy and "political correctness." Indeed, an attack on the concept of acquaintance rape figures prominently in the many diatribes against current intellectual trends on campus. It's as though the notion of consensual sex were some incomprehensible French literary theory that threatened the very foundations of Western Civ. And, come to think of it, maybe it does.

Finally, there is the issue of privacy. Supporters of naming like to say that anonymity implies that rape is something to be ashamed of. But must this be its meaning? It says a great deal about the impoverishment of privacy as a value in our time that many intelligent people can find no justification for it but shame, guilt, cowardice and prudishness. As the tabloidization of the media proceeds apace, as the boundaries between the public and the personal waver and fade away, good citizenship has come to require of more and more people that they put themselves forward, regardless of the cost, as exhibit A in a national civics lesson. In this sense, rape victims are in the same position as homosexuals threatened with "outing" for the good of other gays, or witnesses forced to give painful and embarrassing testimony in televised courtrooms so that the couch potatoes at home can appreciate the beauty of the legal process.

But there are lots of reasons a rape victim might not want her name in the paper that have nothing to do with shame. She might not want her mother to know, or her children, or her children's evil little classmates, or obscene phone callers, or other rapists. Every person reading this article probably has his or her secrets, things that aren't necessarily shameful (or things that are) but are liable to misconstructions, false sympathy and stupid questions from the tactless and ignorant. Things that are just plain nobody's business unless you want them to be.

Instead of denying privacy to rape victims, we should take a good hard look at our national passion for thrusting unwanted publicity on people who are not

---

6. *Camille Paglia:* conservative literary critic, author of *Sexual Personae: Art and Decadence from Nefertiti to Emily Dickinson; Phyllis Schlafly:* antifeminist political lobbyist and organizer of the right-wing Eagle Forum. (*ed.*)

accused of wrongdoing but find themselves willy-nilly in the news. ("How did it *feel* to watch your child being torn to pieces by wild animals?" "It felt terrible, Maury, terrible.") I've argued here that society's attitudes toward rape justify privacy for rape complainants, and that indeed those attitudes lurk behind the arguments for publicity. But something else lurks there as well: a desensitization to the lurid and prurient way in which the media exploits the sufferings of any ordinary person touched by a noteworthy crime or tragedy. Most of the people who have spoken out against anonymity are journalists, celebrity lawyers, media executives and politicos—people who put themselves forward in the press and on television as a matter of course and who are used to taking their knocks as the price of national attention. It must be hard for such people to sympathize with someone who doesn't want to play the media game—especially if it's in a "good cause." 340 345

I'm not at all sure there is a good cause here. Titillation, not education, seems the likely reason for the glare on the Palm Beach case. But even if I'm unduly cynical and the media sincerely wishes to conduct a teach-in on rape, the interests of the public can be served without humiliating the complainant. Doctors educate one another with case histories in which patients are identified only by initials and in which other nonrelevant identifying details are changed. Lawyers file cases on behalf of Jane Doe and John Roe and expect the Supreme Court to "make up its mind" nonetheless. 350 355

If the media wants to educate the public about rape, it can do so without names. What the coverage of the Palm Beach case shows is that it needs to educate itself first. 360

## MAKING A CASE

### *Looking Ahead*

1. As is often the case with newspaper columns and "human interest" features alike, the focus here is personal but the import is public. The author attempts to give the personal its proper significance without robbing it of its unique character.
2. Although Quindlen usually states her own position in her columns, here she largely lets events and characters speak for themselves. Doing so increases the subtlety of a presentation, but you should recognize that what an author shows is also what she believes. Therefore test her belief according to the reasoning that lies behind it.
3. The chief topic is the rape victim's conscious decision to shed anonymity, but related topics emerge that you should note.

The moment of truth came for Carolyn Field when she was appearing on a television show. The producers had it all worked out; she would have her face shadowed and her voice distorted, as though she were a visitor from the witness protection program. Ms. Field refused the subterfuge. A man had raped her in

5    her Tulsa apartment while her daughter slept in the next room. She wanted the
lights and the cameras on her so she could make it personal.

"Those nameless women I'd read about, it never seemed real to me," she
says now. "I wanted people to know that I was a real person, that I had a face
and a name."

10    The crime of rape has moved into the light in this country, but anonymity
still shelters most of its victims, and when Ms. Field tried to step out of that
shelter in 1986, she found out how pervasive its assumption had become.
When she wanted a reporter to use her name, she had to fight with his editor
about her right to eschew anonymity. The story told of how the rapist nearly
15    severed her finger with his knife, how he took a gun she kept under her pillow
for protection and held it to her head while he raped her so violently that she
slid to the floor, how he said he knew her daughter was in the house.

"After he said that, I would have done anything he told me to," Ms. Field says.

We have made progress in the prosecution and perception of rape over the
20    last two decades. In 1969 there were 1,085 rape arrests in New York City—and
18 convictions. Today the number of convictions for the borough of Manhattan
alone is in the hundreds. Linda Fairstein, who runs the sex crimes unit in the
Manhattan D.A.'s office, says when she came on board 15 years ago, four
lawyers could comfortably handle the volume of cases. Today there are 16, with
25    an additional 8 handling only sex crimes against kids, and all are overworked.

One reason for the change was a change in state law, once the most strin-
gent in the country. It included a vestige of centuries-old common law, a corroboration requirement, which held rape prosecutions to a higher standard. A
woman could testify that she was robbed at knifepoint but could not prove that
30    the thief had raped her unless witnesses could testify to the attack.

It is a testimonial to progress that such a requirement seems not like a relic of
the 1970's, when it was overturned, but a reminder of the 1670's, as indeed it was.

Yet its underlying premise of some additional burden of proof still haunts
sexual assault prosecutions. The woman who took the stand this week in the St.
35    John's University case says her assailants talked of how no one would believe
her. Prosecutors sought corroboration through plea bargaining: two of those
implicated became prosecution witnesses, describing how the woman was
propped up half-conscious and half-naked while her fellow students pushed
their genitals into her face and mouth.

40    Carolyn Field's assailant was a neighbor she had never met; he was quickly
arrested and as quickly released on bail, in jail only slightly longer than his victim was in the emergency room. Ms. Field moved out of her own house, terrified to be on the same block as her rapist. But she began seeing his car following
her; by the time police arrived, the man would be gone. Everyone thought she
45    was imagining things until the day she frantically called the police to say that
the rapist was parked outside the phone company, where she was paying her
bill. When the police surrounded him he was carrying a gun, the same gun he
had taken the night of the rape, the gun she had to protect her family.

Her assailant, Reginald Phillips, was sentenced to 81 years in prison in 1986. His first parole hearing will be in 1994. Carolyn Field likes to use his name, too, "for the sake of other women out there." 50

With all the controversy about naming rape victims, Ms. Field is on a one-woman crusade to convince each of us that the way to shatter incredulity about rape is to voluntarily personify it. While the courtroom drawings in the St. John's case show the face of the alleged victim as a gray haze, Ms. Field says 55 anonymity makes us not just anonymous but nebulous. "The way to fight back is to show our faces," she says. "When they can see that we're people like their wives, their sisters, then they know we're telling the truth."

## Looking Back

1. What limits of knowledge and imagination does Huxley establish?

2. Why can't we be confident that our choices in life are the right ones? From reading Huxley, what do you think we should do about the problem?

3. Where does Pollitt state her thesis (identify by line number)?

4. How, according to Pollitt, do the first two arguments in favor of naming rape victims—the duty to report the news and the wrongness of anonymous charges—demonstrate the media's hypocrisy?

5. What is wrong with having "power and ability to define and control information in accordance with the views of those who run the media" (Pollitt, lines 108–110)?

6. Does Pollitt's distinction between the jogger case and the William Smith case ring true as an explanation of why the identity of the first was protected and the second disclosed? Explain your answer.

7. If rape is indeed different from other crimes (see Pollitt, lines 157–191), is its uniqueness sufficient cause to withhold even voluntary disclosure of the victim's name? Explain your answer.

8. Do you accept Pollitt's question—"Why would society blame victims less if they knew who they were?" (lines 223–224)—as a rhetorical question, one that implies society would not; or as a real question, one deserving an answer? If the first, why do you agree or disagree with her? If the second, what is your answer?

9. In your estimation, is the right to privacy compelling enough to override forced disclosure of rape victims' names (see lines 315–349)? Explain your answer.

10. Did Carolyn Field, the woman whose case history Anna Quindlen traces, make the right decision when she revealed her name? Why or why not?

## Writing Assignments (Linked Readings)

1. Katha Pollitt recalls that one rape victim, Nancy Ziegenmeyer, allowed newspaper publication of her name. Anna Quindlen describes Carolyn Field's television appearance. And the Smith trial plaintiff, Patricia Bowman, appeared on ABC after the trial ended in December 1991 with Smith's acquittal. Each woman went public for

virtually the same reason: publicity is a weapon to combat rape. Is it? It's a difficult choice, and as we learn from Huxley, choices are made uncertainly. Extrapolating from points made in the readings, write an essay arguing that names of rape victims should or should not be disclosed.

2. "Was I asking for trouble?" Pollitt says this question is one that the public would undoubtedly ask about her if she were raped. People do ask this question, but they more often phrase it as a statement. The assumption seems to be that, if men are brutes, women are fair game and better be careful. They must be realistic and not put themselves in danger, even if that means acting within certain permanent constraints on their freedom of movement, association, and choice of personal behavior. Is this reasoning correct? Write an essay that, referring to the readings, answers Pollitt's question as a way of saying how women should conduct themselves in public.

3. Many women these days are taking lessons in martial arts and/or arming themselves in order to be able to repel sexual and other assaults. Write an essay discussing this form of preparation. Is it wise, or do these women simply invite more violence from men? Is killing a rapist justifiable? What means of protection short of violence can women rely on? As you consider these questions, you may also want to keep in mind the following figures: from 1981 to 1990, rape has risen 24.3 percent nationwide; this increase is six times that of murders and negligent manslaughter cases in that period. And a recent survey shows that 21 percent of American women report that since they turned fourteen, they have been raped at least once.

## *Writing Assignments (Individual Readings)*
## BRITISH HONDURAS

Aldous Huxley consoles us that once we see the painful consequences of our actions, we can try to make up for any harm we may have caused. Thus we may redeem the fault that, to the extent we did not intend it, was not ours anyhow. Compensatory action of this sort is often a matter of social policy, in which the institutions of society act to remedy injustices. One such injustice is sexual harrassment, and one such institution is the university. Extrapolating from Huxley's logic, write an essay that defines the term *sexual harassment* by describing what constitutes the offense, what its consequences may be, and what the university can do to "remedy the evil."

## MEDIA GOES WILDING IN PALM BEACH

Acquaintance rape is a term Katha Pollitt defines as "sexual violation by persons known to the victim" (lines 298–299). Like all definitions, this one leaves some questions unanswered. For example: How well known to the victim must a person be to be an acquaintance? Does the degree of acquaintance make one rape different from another? Is partial consent an issue to consider? Does *no* mean "no"? Write an essay discussing acquaintance rape by responding to these questions and any others that occur to you. Pollitt reminds us that acquaintance rape is a "contested area" (line 297), meaning that some people do not consider it forcible rape, so be sure to express your own views on this issue.

## MAKING A CASE

The stalking of Carolyn Field by Reginald Phillips brings up the issue of penalties for sexual crimes in general and rape in particular. How should the courts deal with sexual violators? One answer is proposed by an attorney writing in *The New York Times* (January 5, 1993): "sexual predators" ought to be jailed for terms proportionate to the degree of violence they commit, with the toughest sentence being a life sentence with no chance of parole. Some people would go further and argue for the death penalty, while others would recommend standard terms aiming at rehabilitation. What is your view on the matter? Write an essay referring to the case Quindlen reports and giving your thoughts on the kinds of punishment deserved by rapists and other sexual violators.

# bell hooks

# Feminist Movement to End Violence

bell hooks (who never capitalizes her name) is the author of *Ain't I A Woman, And There We Wept, Yearning*, and *Feminist Theory*, from which this piece is taken. Hailing originally from Kentucky, hooks (born Gloria Watkins) formerly taught at Oberlin College and now is a member of the English department at City College in New York City. In this essay, the author approaches her subject by using the critical thinking technique of placing her immediate subject—violence against women—in the larger context of violence against any person, in order to establish a new perspective on her more limited subject and thus produce original thoughts on the matter.

## *Looking Ahead*

1. Sometimes it is useful to impose abstract concepts on totally concrete writing, and sometimes we have to imagine concrete instances in order fully to comprehend abstract writing. The latter procedure applies to hooks's essay.

2. hooks uses a number of key terms that you should look up in the dictionary if you cannot already define them or if you do not understand their meaning from context. Some of these are *hierarchy, patriarchy, sexism, imperialism,* and *dualism.*

3. Read critically to test the logical connections the author draws between hierarchy, social control, violence, and militarism.

Contemporary feminist movement successfully called attention to the need to end male violence against women. Shelters for abused and battered women were founded all around the United States by women activists dedicated to helping victimized women heal themselves and begin new lives. Despite years
5  of committed hard work, the problem of male violence against women steadily increases. It is often assumed by feminist activists that this violence is distinct from other forms of violence in this society because it is specifically linked to the politics of sexism and male supremacy: the right of men to dominate women. In Susan Schechter's thorough study of the battered women's move-
10  ment, *Women and Male Violence,* she continually emphasizes "that violence against women is rooted in male domination." Her chapter "Towards an Analysis of Violence Against Women in the Family" examines the extent to which the ideology of male supremacy both encourages and supports violence against women:

15      Theoretical explanations for battering are not mere exercises; by pinpointing
        the conditions that create violence against women, they suggest the directions
        in which a movement should proceed to stop it. Woman abuse is viewed here
        as an historical expression of male domination manifested within the family
        and currently reinforced by the institutions, economic arrangements, and sex-
20      ist division of labor within capitalist society. Only by analyzing this total con-
        text of battering will women and men be able to devise a long range plan to
        eliminate it.

While I agree with Schechter that male violence against women in the family is an expression of male domination, I believe that violence is inextricably
25  linked to all acts of violence in this society that occur between the powerful and the powerless, the dominant and the dominated. While male supremacy encourages the use of abusive force to maintain male domination of women, it is the Western philosophical notion of hierarchical rule and coercive authority that is the root cause of violence against women, of adult violence against chil-
30  dren, of all violence between those who dominate and those who are dominated. It is this belief system that is the foundation on which sexist ideology and other ideologies of group oppression are based; they can be eliminated only when this foundation is eliminated.
It is essential for continued feminist struggle to end violence against
35  women that this struggle be viewed as a component of an overall movement to end violence. So far feminist movement has primarily focused on male violence and as a consequence lends credibility to sexist stereotypes that suggest men are violent, women are not; men are abusers, women are victims. This type of thinking allows us to ignore the extent to which women (with men) in this soci-
40  ety accept and perpetuate the idea that it is acceptable for a dominant party or group to maintain power over the dominated by using coercive force. It allows us to overlook or ignore the extent to which women exert coercive authority over others or act violently. The fact that women may not commit violent acts as

often as men does not negate the reality of female violence. We must see both men and women in this society as groups who support the use of violence if we are to eliminate it.

The social hierarchy in white supremacist, capitalist patriarchy is one in which theoretically men are the powerful, women the powerless; adults the powerful, children the powerless; white people the powerful, black people and other nonwhite peoples the powerless. In a given situation, whichever party is in power is likely to use coercive authority to maintain that power if it is challenged or threatened. Although most women clearly do not use abuse and battery to control and dominate men (even though a small minority of women batter men) they may employ abusive measures to maintain authority in interactions with groups over whom they exercise power. Many of us who were raised in patriarchal homes where male parents maintained domination and control by abusing women and children know that the problem was often exacerbated by the fact that women also believed that a person in authority has the right to use force to maintain authority. Some of the women in these families exerted coercive authority over their children (as do women in families where men are not violent), sometimes with random acts of violent aggression for no clear reason or through systematic verbal abuse. This violence is not unlike male violence against children and women, even though it may not be as prevalent (which seems unlikely since 90% of all parents use some form of physical force against children). While it in no way diminishes the severity of the problem of male violence against women to emphasize that women are likely to use coercive authority when they are in power positions, recognizing this reminds us that women, like men, must work to unlearn socialization that teaches us it is acceptable to maintain power by coercion or force. By concentrating solely on ending male violence against women, feminist activists may overlook the severity of the problem. They may encourage women to resist male coercive domination without encouraging them to oppose all forms of coercive domination.

In a section of her theoretical chapter analyzing violence against women in the family, "Questions in Theory Building," Schechter acknowledges a need for further investigation of factors that cause battery. She points to the fact that women in lesbian relationships are sometimes battered to raise the question of how this information "fits" with a theory of battery that sees male domination as the cause. She answers, "One could theorize that models of intimate relationships based on power and domination are so pervasive in this society that they do, in fact, affect the nature of relationships between people of the same sex." Yet she is reluctant to accept this theory as it does not affirm male domination as the cause of battery. So she suggests that there must be greater research before the two forms of battery could be linked. However, if one assumes, as I do, that battery is caused by the belief permeating this culture that hierarchical rule and coercive authority are natural, then all our relationships tend to be based on power and domination, and thus all forms of battery are linked. In *The Cultural Basis of Racism and Group Oppression*, philosopher John Hodges suggests that it is in the context of the traditional Western family with its authoritarian male rule and its authoritarian adult rule that most of us are socialized to accept group oppression and the use of force to uphold authority. These patterns form the basis of all our relationships:

> Most personal relationships in Dualist culture take place within the established institutions. Consequently, most personal relationships contain a strong hierarchical element. Most personal interaction occurs within hierarchical structures and is shaped by these structures. We have just considered the relationship usually prevalent in the family where adult rule over non-adults and male rule over females is the accepted norm. In addition to these personal relationships, other personal interactions usually occur with the hierarchical framework of employer to employee, of boss or foreman to workers or crew, of producer or owner to user, of landlord to tenant, of lender to borrower, of teacher to student, of governor to governed—in short, of controller to controlled. . . .

In all these relationships, the power the dominant party exercises is maintained by the threat (acted upon or not) that abusive punishment, physical or psychological, could be used if the hierarchical structure is threatened.

Male violence against women in personal relationships is one of the most blatant expressions of the use of abusive force to maintain domination and control. It epitomizes the actualization of the concept of hierarchical rule and coercive authority. Unlike violence against children, or white racial violence against other ethnic groups, it is the violence that is most overtly condoned and accepted, even celebrated in this culture. Society's acceptance and perpetuation of that violence helps maintain it and makes it difficult to control or eliminate. That acceptance can be explained only in part by patriarchal rule supporting male domination of women through the use of force. Patriarchal male rule took on an entirely different character in the context of advanced capitalist society. In the precapitalist world, patriarchy allowed all men to completely rule women in their families, to decide their fate, to shape their destiny. Men could freely batter women with no fear of punishment. They could decide whom their daughters were to marry, whether they would read or write, etc. Many of these powers were lost to men with the development of the capitalist nation-state in the United States. This loss of power did not correspond with decreased emphasis on the ideology of male supremacy. However, the idea of the patriarch as worker, providing for and protecting his family, was transformed as his labor primarily benefited the capitalist state.

Men not only no longer had complete authority and control over women; they no longer had control over their own lives. They were controlled by the economic needs of capitalism. As workers, most men in our culture (like working women) are controlled, dominated. Unlike working women, working men are fed daily a fantasy diet of male supremacy and power. In actuality, they have very little power and they know it. Yet they do not rebel against the economic order nor make revolution. They are socialized by ruling powers to accept their dehumanization and exploitation in the public world of work and they are

taught to expect that the private world, the world of home and intimate relationships, will restore to them their sense of power which they equate with masculinity. They are taught that they will be able to rule in the home, to control
and dominate, that this is the big pay-off for their acceptance of an exploitative      135
economic social order. By condoning and perpetuating male domination of
women to prevent rebellion on the job, ruling male capitalists ensure that male
violence will be expressed in the home and not in the work force.

The entry of women into the work force, which also serves the interests of
capitalism, has taken even more control over women away from men. Therefore      140
men rely more on the use of violence to establish and maintain a sex role hierarchy in which they are in a dominant position. At one time, their dominance was
determined by the fact that they were the sole wage earners. Their need to dominate women (socially constructed by the ideology of male supremacy) coupled
with suppressed aggression towards employers who "rule" over them make the      145
domestic environment the center of explosive tensions that lead to violence.
Women are the targets because there is no fear that men will suffer or be severely punished if they hurt women, especially wives and lovers. They would be
punished if they violently attacked employers, police officers.

Black women and men have always called attention to a "cycle of violence"      150
that begins with psychological abuse in the public world wherein the male
worker may be subjected to control by a boss or authority figure that is humiliating and degrading. Since he depends on the work situation for material survival, he does not strike out or oppose the employer who would punish him by
taking his job or imprisoning him. He suppresses this violence and releases it in      155
what I call a "control" situation, a situation where he has no need to fear retalia-
tion, wherein he does not have to suffer as a consequence of acting violently.
The home is usually this control situation and the target for his abuse is usually
female. Though his own expression of violence against women stems in part
from the emotional pain he feels, the pain is released and projected onto the fe-      160
male. When the pain disappears he feels relief, even pleasure. His pain is gone
even though it was not confronted or resolved in a healthy way. As the psychology of masculinity in sexist societies teaches men that to acknowledge and express pain negates masculinity and is a symbolic castration, causing pain rather
than expressing it restores men's sense of completeness, of wholeness, or mas-      165
culinity. The fate of many young black men in this society, whose lives are characterized by cycles of violence that usually climax in the death of others or their
own deaths, epitomizes the peril of trying to actualize the fantasy of masculinity
that is socially constructed by ruling groups in capitalist patriarchy.

Unlike many feminist activists writing about male violence against women,      170
black women and men emphasize a "cycle of violence" that begins in the workplace because we are aware that systematic abuse is not confined to the domestic sphere, even though violent abuse is more commonly acted out in the home.
To break out of this cycle of violence, to liberate themselves, black men and
all men must begin to criticize the sexist notion of masculinity; to examine the      175

impact of capitalism on their lives; the extent to which they feel degraded, alienated, and exploited in the work force. Men must begin to challenge notions of masculinity that equate manhood with ability to exert power over others, especially through the use of coercive force. Much of this work has to be done by men who are not violent, who have rejected the values of capitalist patriarchy. Most men who are violent against women are not seeking help or change. They do not feel that their acceptance and perpetration of violence against women is wrong. How can it be wrong if society rewards them for it? Television screens are literally flooded daily with tales of male violence, especially male violence against women. It is glamorized, made entertaining and sexually titillating. The more violent a male character is, whether he be hero or villain, the more attention he receives. Often a male hero has to exert harsher violence to subdue a villain. This violence is affirmed and rewarded. The more violent the male hero is (usually in his quest to save or protect a woman/victim) the more he receives love and affirmation from women. His acts of violence in the interest of protection are seen as a gesture of care, of his "love" for women and his concern for humanity.

This equation of violence with love on the part of women and men is another reason it is difficult to motivate most people to work to end violence. In real life, the equation of love with violence is part of early childhood socialization. An article in the October 1982 issue of *Mademoiselle* magazine, "A Special Report on Love, Violence, and the Single Woman," by Jane Patrick calls attention to the fact that many women who are neither economically dependent on men nor bound to them through legal contracts do not reject males who are violent because they equate it with love. Patrick quotes Rodney Cate, professor of family studies, who links violence between parents and children to adult acceptance of violence in intimate relationships:

> When you examine the context in which parents suffer their children, it is easier to understand how the victim—and the abuser—equate the violence with love. It's not hard to see how over time we begin to pair some sort of physical punishment with love and to believe that someone is hurting us because they love us.

Many parents teach children that violence is the easiest way (if not the most acceptable way) to end a conflict and assert power. By saying things like "I'm only doing this because I love you" while they are using physical abuse to control children, parents are not only equating violence with love, they are also offering a notion of love synonymous with passive acceptance, the absence of explanation and discussions. In many homes small children and teenagers find their desire to discuss issues with parents sometimes viewed as a challenge to parental authority or power, as an act of "unlove." Force is used by the parent to meet this perceived challenge or threat. Again, it needs to be emphasized that the idea that it is correct to use abuse to maintain authority is taught to individuals by church, school, and other institutions.

Love and violence have become so intertwined in this society that many
people, especially women, fear that eliminating violence will lead to the loss of   220
love. Popular paperback romances, like the Harlequin series, that ten years ago
had no descriptions of male violence against women, now describe acts of hitting, rape, etc., all in the context of romantic love. It is interesting to note that
most women in these romances now have professional careers and are often
sexually experienced. Male violence, the romances suggest, has to be used to   225
subdue these "uppity" women who, though equal to men in the workplace,
must be forced to assume a subordinate position in the home. There is little
suggestion that women should stop working. Her work is depicted as a gesture
of defiance that adds passion to the sexual conflict at home, heightening sexual
pleasure when the male uses force to transform the "uppity" woman into a pas-   230
sive, submissive being. Of course, the man is always white, rich, and a member
of the ruling class.

These romances are read by millions of women who spend millions of
hard-earned dollars to read material that reinforces sexist role patterns and ro-
manticizes violence against women. It should be noted that they also uphold   235
white supremacy and Western imperialism. Women reading romances are being encouraged to accept the idea that violence heightens and intensifies sexual
pleasure. They are also encouraged to believe that violence is a sign of masculinity and a gesture of male care, that the degree to which a man becomes violently
angry corresponds to the intensity of his affection and care. Therefore, women   240
readers learn that passive acceptance of violence is essential if they are to receive
the rewards of love and care. This is often the case in women's lives. They may
accept violence in intimate relationships, whether heterosexual or lesbian, because they do not wish to give up that care. They see enduring abuse as the
price they pay. They know they can live without abuse; they do not think they   245
can live without care.

Speaking of why poor women may not leave violent relationships,
Schechter says "poor people experience so many different kinds of oppression,
violence may be responded to as one of many abuses." Certainly many black
women feel they must confront a degree of abuse wherever they turn in this so-   250
ciety. Black women as well as many other marginalized groups in graduate
schools are often psychologically abused by professors who systematically degrade and humiliate them for a period of years, as long as it takes for the woman
to finish her degree or to be so "messed up" that she drops out. Black women in
professional positions who appear to have "made it" are often the targets of   255
abuse by employers and co-workers who resent their presence. Black women
who work in service jobs are daily bombarded with belittling, degrading comments and gestures on the part of the people who have power over them. The
vast majority of poor black women in this society find they are continually subjected to abuse in public agencies, stores, etc. These women often feel that   260
abuse will be an element in most of their personal interactions. They are more
inclined to accept abuse in situations where there are some rewards or benefits,

where abuse is not the sole characteristic of the interaction. Since this is usually the case in situations where male violence occurs, they may be reluctant, even
265  unwilling to end these relationships. Like other groups of women, they fear the loss of care.

Until women and men cease equating violence with love, understand that disagreements and conflicts in the context of intimate relationships can be resolved without violence, and reject the idea that men should dominate
270  women, male violence against women will continue and so will other forms of violent aggression in intimate relationships. To help bring an end to violence against women, feminist activists have taken the lead in criticizing the ideology of male supremacy and showing the ways in which it supports and condones that violence. Yet efforts to end male violence against women will
275  succeed only if they are part of an overall struggle to end violence. Currently feminist activists supporting nuclear disarmament link militarism and patriarchy, showing connections between the two. Like analysis of violence against women, the tendency in these discussions is to focus on male support of violence—a focus which limits our understanding of the problem. Many
280  women who advocate feminism see militarism as exemplifying patriarchal concepts of masculinity and the right of males to dominate others. To these women, to struggle against militarism is to struggle against patriarchy and male violence against women. Introducing a recently published book of essays, *ain't no where we can run: a handbook for women on the nuclear mentality,*
285  Susan Koen writes:

It is our belief that the tyranny created by nuclear activities is merely the latest and most serious manifestation of a culture characterized in every sphere by domination and exploitation. For this reason, the presence of the nuclear mentality in the world can only be viewed as one part of the whole, not an iso-
290  lated issue. We urge the realization that separating the issue of nuclear power plants and weapons from the dominant cultural, social, and political perspectives of our society results in a limited understanding of the problem, and in turn limits the range of possible solutions. We offer then the argument that those male-defined constructs which control our social structures and rela-
295  tionships are directly responsible for the proliferation of nuclear plants and weapons. Patriarchy is the root of the problem, and the imminent dangers created by the nuclear mentality serve to call our attention to the basic problem of patriarchy.

By equating militarism and patriarchy, women who advocate feminism of-
300  ten structure their arguments in such a way as to suggest that to be male is synonymous with strength, aggression, and the will to dominate and do violence to others; to be female is synonymous with weakness, passivity, and the will to nourish and affirm the lives of others. Such dualistic thinking is basic to all forms of social domination in Western society. Even when inverted and em-
305  ployed for a meaningful purpose such as nuclear disarmament, it is nevertheless

dangerous because it reinforces the cultural basis of sexism and other forms of group oppression. It promotes a stereotypical notion of inherent differences between men and women, implying that women by virtue of their sex have played no crucial role in supporting and upholding imperialism (and the militarism that serves to maintain imperialist rule) or other systems of domination. Even if one argues that men have been taught to equate masculinity with the ability to do violence and women have been taught to equate femaleness with nurturance, the fact remains that many women and men do not conform to these stereotypes. Rather than clarifying for women the power we exert in the maintenance of systems of domination and setting forth strategies for resistance and change, most current discussion of feminism and militarism further mystifies women's role.

In keeping with the tenets of sexist ideology, women are talked about in these discussions as objects rather than subjects. We are depicted not as workers and activists, who, like men, make political choices, but as passive observers who have taken no responsibility for actively maintaining the value system of this society which proclaims violence and domination the most effective tools of communication in human interaction, a value system which advocates and makes war. Discussions of feminism and militarism that do not clarify for women the roles we have played and play in all their variety and complexity, make it appear that all women are against war, oppose the use of violence, that men are the problem, the enemy. This is a distortion of women's experience, not a clarification of it or a redefinition. Devaluing the roles women have played necessarily leads to a distorted perspective on women's reality. I use the word "devaluing" for it seems that the suggestion that men have made war and war policy while women passively watched represents a refusal to see women as active political beings even when we are subordinate to men. The assumption that to be deemed inferior or submissive necessarily defines what one actually is, or how one actually behaves, is a continuation of sexist patterns that deny the relative powers women have exercised. Even the woman who votes according to her husband's example is making a political choice. We need to see women as political beings.

An example of the distorted perception of women's reality that is being described by some activists who discuss women and militarism is the popular assumption that "women are natural enemies of war." Many female anti-war activists suggest that women as bearers of children, or the potential bearers of children, are necessarily more concerned about ending war than men—the implication being that women are more life-affirming. Leslie Cagan, in a recent interview in *South End Press News,* confirms that women participating in disarmament work often suggest that because they bear children, they have a "special relationship and responsibility to the survival of the planet." Cagan maintains that this is a "dangerous perspective" because it focuses on women's biology and "tends to reinforce the sexist notion that womanhood equals motherhood." She explains:

350 It may be that some, even many, women are motivated to activism through concern for their children. It may also be a factor for some fathers who don't want to see their kids blown up in a nuclear war either! But this simply doesn't justify a narrow and limiting perspective. It is limiting because it says that women's relationship to such an important issue as the future of our planet

355 rests on a single biological fact.

We who are concerned about feminism and militarism must insist that women (even those who are bearers of children) are not inherently non-violent or life-affirming. Many women who mother (either as single parents or in cama-raderie with husbands) have taught male children to see fighting and other

360 forms of violent aggression as acceptable modes of communication, modes that are valued more than loving or caring interaction. Even though women often as-sume nurturing, life-affirming roles in their relationship to others, they do not necessarily value or respect that role as much as they revere the suppression of emotion or the assertion of power through the use of force. We must insist that

365 women who do choose (even if they are inspired by motherhood) to denounce violence and domination and its ultimate expression, war, are political thinkers making political decisions and choices. If women who work against militarism continue to imply, however directly or indirectly, that there is an inherent pre-disposition in women to oppose war, they risk reinforcing the very biological

370 determinism that is the philosophical foundation of notions of male supremacy. They also run the risk of covering up the reality that masses of women in the United States are not anti-imperialist, are not against militarism, and do not op-pose the use of violence as a form of social control. Until these women change their values they must be seen as clinging, like their male counterparts, to a per-

375 spective on human relationships that embraces social domination in all its vari-ous forms and they must be held accountable for their actions.

Imperialism and not patriarchy is the core foundation of modern mili-tarism (even though it serves the interest of imperialism to link notions of mas-culinity with the struggle to conquer nations and peoples). Many societies in

380 the world that are ruled by males are not imperialistic; many women in the United States have made political decisions to support imperialism and mili-tarism. Historically, white women in the United States, working for women's rights, have felt no contradiction between this effort and their support of the Western imperialist attempt to conquer the planet. Often they argued that

385 equal rights would better enable white women to help in the building of this "great nation," i.e., in the cause of imperialism. Many white women in the early part of the twentieth century, who were strong advocates of women's libera-tion, were pro-imperialist.

Books like Helen Montgomery's *Western Women in Eastern Lands,* published

390 in 1910, outlining fifty years of white women's work in foreign missions, docu-ment the link between the struggle for the emancipation of white women in the United States and the imperialist, hegemonic spread of Western values and Western domination of the globe. As missionaries, white women traveled to

Eastern lands armed with psychological weapons that undermined the belief
systems of Eastern women and replaced them with Western values. In the clos-        395
ing statement of her work, Helen Montgomery writes:

> So many voices are calling us, so many goods demand our allegiance, that we
> are in danger of forgetting the best. To seek first to bring Christ's kingdom on
> the earth, to respond to the need that is sorest, to go out into the desert for that
> loved and bewildered sheep that the shepherd has missed from the fold, to         400
> share all of the privilege with the unprivileged and happiness with the un-
> happy, to see the possibility of one redeemed earth, undivided, unvexed, un-
> perplexed resting in the light of the glorious Gospel of the blessed God, this is
> the mission of the women's missionary movement.

Despite the fact that contemporary feminist movement against imperialism and        405
militarism is headed by white women, they are a small minority and do not represent the values of the majority of white women in this society or of women as
a whole. Many white women in the United States continue to wholeheartedly
support militarism. Feminist activists must hold these women accountable for
their political decisions and must also work to change their perspectives. We      410
avoid this challenge when we act as if men and patriarchy are the sole evils.

It is a quite blatant truth that men commit the majority of imperialist acts
globally, that men have committed the majority of violent acts in war. However,
we must remember that when called to do so in times of national crisis, women
fight in combat and are not necessarily opposed to war. We must also remem-        415
ber that war does not simply include fighting and that women's effort on the
home front and off the front lines has helped make war. At the end of her essay
discussing women's participation in war effort, "The Culture In Our Blood,"
Patty Walton writes:

> In conclusion, women have not fought in wars because of our material circum-     420
> stances and not because we are innately more moral than men or because of
> any biological limitation on our part. The work of women supports both a so-
> ciety's war and its peace activities. And our support has always derived from
> our particular socialization as women. In fact, the socialization of women and
> men complements the needs of the culture in which we live. It is necessary to    425
> recognize this because we need to change these material relationships and not
> just the sex of our work problem makers. Men are not more innately aggressive
> than women are passive. We have cultures of war, so we can have cultures of
> peace.

Sex role divisions of labor have meant that as parents women have sup-             430
ported war effort by instilling in their children an acceptance of domination and
a respect for violence as a means of social control. Implanting this ideology in
human consciousness is as central to the making of a militaristic state as the
overall control of males by ruling male groups who insist that men make war
and reward them for their efforts. Like men, women in the United States have a   435
high tolerance for witnessing violence, learned through excessive television

watching. To fight militarism, we must resist the socialization and brainwashing that teaches passive acceptance of violence in daily life, that tells us violence can be eliminated with violence. Women who are against militarism must withdraw
440 support for war by working to transform passive acceptance of violence as a means of social control in everyday life.

This means that we must no longer act as if men are the only people who act violently, who accept and condone violence, who create a culture of violence. As women we must assume responsibility for the role women play in
445 condoning violence. By only calling attention to male violence against women, or making militarism just another expression of male violence, we fail to adequately address the problem of violence and make it difficult to develop viable resistance strategies and solutions. While we need not diminish the severity of the problem of male violence against women or male violence against nations or
450 the planet, we must acknowledge that men and women have together made the United States a culture of violence and must work together to transform and recreate that culture. Women and men must oppose the use of violence as a means of social control in all its manifestations: war, male violence against women, adult violence against children, teen-age violence, racial violence, etc.
455 Feminist efforts to end male violence against women must be expanded into a movement to end all forms of violence. Broadly based, such a movement could potentially radicalize consciousness and intensify awareness of the need to end male domination of women in a context in which we are working to eradicate the idea that hierarchical structures should be the basis of human interaction.

## Looking Back

1. What does hooks mean by her claim that the "root cause of violence against women" is "hierarchial rule and coercive authority" (see lines 23–33)?

2. On what basis does hooks argue that women can be as violent as men (see lines 47–72)?

3. According to hooks, how did a developing capitalism promote male violence against women (see lines 105–138)?

4. Do you agree with hook's analysis of men's powerlessness in the workplace? Explain your answer.

5. In your view, has the rising tide of women working "taken even more control over women away from men" (line 140)?

6. Is it unmasculine for a man to admit emotional pain (see lines 160–169)? Explain your answer.

7. How does hooks trace the alleged connection between violence and love (see lines 188–266)?

8. Why do you think hooks goes to such lengths to criticize the "dualistic thinking" that says men are strong by nature and women weak (see lines 299–377)?

9. Why does the author maintain that "we need to see women as political beings" (lines 336–337)?

10. Do you accept hooks's thesis that the only way to stop men battering women is to work against *all* forms of violence? Explain your answer.

## Writing Assignments

1. A major component of hooks's argument is her assertion that "hierarchial rule and coercive authority" are at the heart of violence against women (see number 1 in Looking Back). Without necessarily accepting this connection, we can probably agree that the power some people have over others may not produce the most peaceful relationships. To do more than pay lip-service to this view, write an essay that refers to hooks and describes an alternative basis for relationship in *one* of the categories mentioned in the essay—women and men, "employer to employee, of boss or foreman to workers or crew, of producer or owner to user, of landlord to tenant, of lender to borrower, of teacher to student, of governor to governed" (lines 99–101).

2. Many men, hooks maintains, are threatened in their sense of masculinity and take out their humiliation and frustration on women, often by beating them. The problem may lie partially in the false notion men have of their masculinity. Thus, perhaps a new definition of masculinity is required. Write an essay that, extrapolating from hooks's reasoning on this issue, attempts to depict a "real man": what he would allow himself to feel, how he would regard violence, how he would define a woman's true status in the world, what he might think of tenderness, gentleness, and sympathy. You may want to conclude by stating how this new masculinity could change relations between women and men. Conceive of your audience as one consisting of men whose views on the issue you would like to influence.

3. "Feminist efforts to end male violence against women," hooks writes, "must be expanded into a movement to end all forms of violence" (lines 455–456, and see number 10 in Looking Back). Do you agree with the author that all forms of violence are connected and that the most effective way to end battery against women is to work against violence generally? Or should we regard acts of violence differently, according to the contexts in which they occur (war, sports, entertainment, whatever)? Perhaps some forms of violence (like football) may actually take the place of other forms (like wife-beating) and therefore be socially useful? Write an essay giving your view of hooks's point about violence.

# Randy Shilts

# Heterosexuals and AIDS

Randy Shilts was most recently the author of *Conduct Unbecoming*. Earlier, he wrote *And the Band Played On: Politics, People, and the AIDS Epidemic*, from which this chapter is reprinted. The book's subtitle is significant. Medical emergency, entrenched bureaucracy, and the varying status in society of different individuals frequently join to form a critical context that permits a new view of the matter. In the case of the AIDS epidemic, they do so tragically. Shilts, who covered the epidemic for the *San Francisco Chronicle*, interviewed over nine hundred people and traced the history of the disease from its onset in America to 1987, the book's publication date. Shilts died of AIDS in 1994.

## Looking Ahead

1. Notice how the chapter is structured as datelined reports from the front, greatly increasing the subject's dramatic urgency. This imperative nature is characteristic of the book as a whole.

2. As a reporter, Shilts observes people's activities and does research to gain factual knowledge. Test the way he combines and balances these two sources of information to form a critical view of his full presentation.

3. Catastrophes like AIDS always strain public and private resources, but handling such crises also often reveals institutional faults and personal defects that otherwise might not be exposed. As you read be on the lookout for these.

*January 1985*
*New York City*

At the emergency room of St. Vincent's Hospital in Greenwich Village, the patient lay on a gurney, wheezing from *Pneumocystis*. He had lain there for twenty-four hours, waiting for a room. Under normal circumstances, his doctor would have called the hospital and had the man admitted. But hospital administrators
5    preferred not to take any more AIDS patients; they already had so many. The man's doctor had told him to circumvent standard procedures and simply show up in the emergency room, where, under New York law, he could not be turned away.

    That's what doctors advised patients who needed hospitalization for AIDS
10   in New York City in early 1985. At Memorial Sloan-Kettering Cancer Center, Dr. Mathilde Krim fielded calls daily from doctors desperate to find hospital rooms for their ailing patients. Physicians were afraid to send their patients to a number of the city's hospitals, given the bad treatment AIDS patients had received in the past; institutions with good reputations for dealing with AIDS al-
15   ready were overwhelmed.

    Uptown at St. Luke's–Roosevelt Hospital, one of the largest medical centers in the world, half of the hospital's private rooms were filled with dying AIDS victims. In one well-known New York hospital, the vice-president of one of the largest corporations in New York City, who was suffering from Kaposi's sar-
20   coma, was denied a bed and had to check into the hospital through the emergency room. Even there, running a 104-degree fever, the executive had to wait seven hours for a room. There was talk among AIDS clinicians that one AIDS sufferer had already died while waiting for a room at one of Manhattan's most

prestigious university hospitals. Throughout the city, AIDS clinicians could not imagine what they would do in coming months when burgeoning numbers of patients overwhelmed the hospitals' finite resources. 25

"We're not talking about a nightmare that is going to happen," said St. Luke's–Roosevelt AIDS expert, Dr. Michael Lange. "It already is a nightmare."

At Jacobi Hospital in the Bronx, three-year-old Diana waved wanly at Dr. Arye Rubinstein, one of the only familiar faces she had known in her life. She 30 had lived in the hospital since 1983, not because she needed hospitalization but because New York City had no place else to put its AIDS patients. There were at least twenty-five children like her in the hospitals of New York and New Jersey, and every month, as the parents of such children died or abandoned them, there were more. Everybody had known this would happen, of course, but no- 35 body had really planned what to do when it did.

The crisis in New York AIDS treatment characterized the new phase the AIDS epidemic was entering. The unheeded warnings of 1983 and the lost opportunities of 1984 were materializing into the tragic stories of 1985. The future shock of the AIDS epidemic was arriving; the butcher's bill had come 40 due.

*January 3*
*The Tenderloin, San Francisco*

Street lights and blinking neon signs cast shadows across the young woman's face. She pouted histrionically when the undercover police asked for her identi- fication. The other women quickly hustled themselves off the dingy block of Ellis Street in the heart of San Francisco's sleazy hooker district. In this part of 45 town, of course, such arrests were not rare occasions.

Silvana Strangis ignored the stares of passing motorists while the arresting officer waited for the radio to tell him whether the thirty-four-year-old brunette had an arrest record. Her record, it turned out, was unusually impressive, even for this part of town. In the past five years, she had been busted thirty-two times 50 and charged with thirteen felonies and thirty-nine misdemeanors, from robbery and grand theft to tonight's offense, "obstructing a sidewalk."

When Silvana brushed her long straight hair out of her eyes, the arresting officer could see the dark brown puncture marks on her arm where she injected her heroin. He knew her story; it wasn't that different from the other prostitutes 55 who worked the Tenderloin.

Silvana was handcuffed and put in the back of the squad car. Right away, she noticed that the vice cops seemed inordinately chatty. Instead of reading her Miranda rights, they wanted to talk about Silvana's boyfriend and pimp, Tony Ford. They'd heard on the street that Tony had AIDS. Was it true? 60

Years of heroin addiction had undone whatever Silvana Strangis had learned of discretion, and she admitted that Tony had just been discharged from the AIDS Ward. She was worried that she had AIDS too, she added.

It was then that Silvana noticed that instead of turning toward the Hall of
Justice, the patrol car was heading through the Mission District. A little past
midnight, the police officers brought the handcuffed prisoner into the emergency room at San Francisco General Hospital.

"We want her to have the AIDS test," one of the officers said.

The hospital personnel were astonished at the request. They carefully explained that so far no AIDS test, per se, existed. The HTLV-III antibody test had
yet to be licensed, and that was not an AIDS test. Moreover, they could not force
a handcuffed prisoner to take any test so that the results could be turned over to
police officers. Maybe the woman should come back when the AIDS Clinic was
open and when she could decide for herself what she wanted to do.

The disappointed officers put Silvana back in the cruiser, wrote out a citation for obstructing a sidewalk, and drove back to the Tenderloin. Silvana
should go back to the AIDS Clinic, they instructed, and get whatever tests she
could. And she should get the results in writing. They'd be back to check up on
what the doctors had to say.

Silvana was shaken when she stepped out of the car. She searched out her
dealer, scored some heroin, and took it back to her seedy room, where Tony
Ford was waiting. They shot the heroin, sharing the needle, just as they always
had. Soon, the pair passed out.

The next morning, a *Chronicle* reporter, tipped off by an emergency room
attendant, knocked on Silvana's door.

"Tell him to get the hell out of here," Tony grumbled.

"I need a ride to the clinic," Silvana said, pulling a beat-up poncho over her
blue jeans.

At the AIDS Clinic, the head nurse, Gayling Gee, cleared her schedule to
talk to Silvana Strangis, although the hooker was too embarrassed about her
predicament to say much. Instead, she asked the reporter to tell Gee about her
profession and the vice cops and her urgent need for AIDS screening. Gee and
the other clinic staffers who heard the tale were dumbfounded. They wondered
about issues like confidentiality and civil rights.

Silvana didn't want to hear about this. All she wanted was a piece of paper
that said she didn't have AIDS. She could show it to the vice cops and get on
with the business of turning tricks and buying heroin. Gee gave her an appointment for the next week.

"How did you end up like this?" the reporter asked, as he drove Silvana
back to her Jones Street hotel room.

Silvana turned up the Moody Blues tape on the car stereo, sighed, and said
she had grown up in a nice Italian family in a San Francisco suburb. When she
had graduated from a Catholic high school in 1968, she was full of optimism
about a world that seemed on the brink of a New Age. The idealism faded in the
years that followed, and she started taking drugs, and then she met Tony and
bore his child. It was easy to make money by turning tricks, and life now went
from trick to trick, from fix to fix.

By the time the couple heard about AIDS and the threat posed by sharing needles and sexual relations, it was too late. Tony already had the first symptoms of immune disorder, and the threat of some distant health problem paled   110
in comparison to the urgency of getting that soothing rush of heroin. Nobody cared much about this disease in the Tenderloin, she added. When Tony lay in the AIDS Ward a few weeks ago, some of the other players from the neighborhood brought Tony's fixes to his bedside. They'd close the door, make jokes about the gay male nurses, and all shoot up together, sharing the same needle.   115

There was, of course, no question of what Silvana would do tonight. Tony couldn't work. He certainly didn't want her to stop working either; that would mean the end of his heroin.

"It's the drugs," she concluded. "It's like what they say on TV. You get in and you can't get out."   120

That was why Silvana was going back to the streets that night. Yes, she was worried about spreading AIDS. In fact, her lymph nodes were swollen, her sleep was disturbed by chronic nightsweats, and she felt dog-tired all the time. But she had to work. She didn't know any other way to make money.

The next morning's front-page story about a prostitute raised all the pro-   125
found public policy questions implicit in the case of a working hooker who almost certainly was an AIDS carrier. Dr. Paul Volberding talked about how the prostitute posed a "monster of a public health issue," with its classical conflict between public health and individual rights. Other news coverage of Silvana Strangis, however, was less delicate.   130

"A human time bomb is walking the streets of San Francisco," announced the grim anchor at the top of the local evening news that night. Another newscast likened her to "Typhoid Mary."

All weekend, television crews trolled the Tenderloin in their Instant Eye vans, trying to interview anxious streetwalkers. Frightened callers to talk shows   135
almost unanimously opined that the police should lock the woman up and quickly discard the key.

Silvana became such an instant persona non grata in her neighborhood that she was literally chased off the streets and into her residential hotel lobby by four angry prostitutes who threatened to have her stabbed to death if she left   140
her hotel again. The news stories, it turned out, hadn't done much for business. It seemed every john looking for action that weekend started negotiations by asking, "Are you the one with AIDS?"

The uproar illuminated the profound heterosexual male bias that dominates the news business. After all, thousands of gay men had been infecting   145
each other for years, but attempts to interest news organizations to pressure the city for an aggressive AIDS education campaign had yielded minimal interest. A single female heterosexual prostitute, however, was a different matter. She might infect a heterosexual man. That was someone who mattered; that was news.   150

Although evidence of heterosexual AIDS transmission could be dated back to the first epidemiological studies by the Centers for Disease Control in the summer of 1981, it was not until early 1985 that the straight links of the disease garnered much attention. The most disconcerting stories came from Central
155 Africa, where AIDS was simply called "the horror sex disease." Although image-conscious African governments swore to silence the researchers working within their borders, leaks confirmed that thousands of immune-suppressed people were dying in black Africa, usually from gastrointestinal parasites, the most common opportunistic infections of that region. Unaware of foreign acronyms,
160 Ugandans had dubbed AIDS "slim disease" because of the wasting away that marked the virulent parasitic diseases.

In the scientific forums, European researchers working closely with teams in Central Africa were the most outspoken about the heterosexual dimension of the epidemic. These doctors, largely in Belgium and France, had always consid-
165 ered the preoccupation with the gay angle of AIDS to be a strange American idiosyncrasy. Given the experiences of such nations as Zaire and Rwanda, these doctors warned that the Western world should not be complacent about the threat that this new sexually transmitted disease posed to all people.

In the United States, the most aggressive research on heterosexual AIDS
170 transmission came from a most unlikely source, the U.S. Army. From his work at the Walter Reed Army Institute in Washington, D.C., Dr. Robert Redfield had documented the ease of male-to-female sexual transmission of AIDS. Of seven married male sufferers of AIDS and ARC, for example, Redfield found that five had wives who were infected with HTLV-III. Of these five
175 wives, three were already showing clinical symptoms of ARC. The fact that one-third of military AIDS and ARC cases claimed that prostitute contact was their only risk behavior also made Redfield a passionate proponent of the threat posed by female-to-male AIDS transmission. His case, however, was problematical because the military was by now routinely dismissing gay ser-
180 vicemen suffering from the syndrome. That provided powerful motivation for military personnel to blame prostitutes rather than homosexual contacts for their infection.

The question of female-to-male AIDS transmission had exploded in San Francisco not long before, when Dr. Paul Volberding at the AIDS Clinic held a
185 press conference to announce the first two local AIDS cases among heterosexual men who claimed no other high-risk activity than sexual relations with intravenous drug-using prostitutes. In San Francisco, the new cases were something of a revelation because AIDS had remained an almost purely gay phenomenon in that city. More than 98 percent of the city's caseload were gay or bisexual
190 men; the transfusion AIDS cases and five drug addicts were the exception proving the rule that, in San Francisco, AIDS was a gay disease.

"We don't usually call a press conference to announce every new AIDS case," Volberding admitted when he announced that two straight men had contracted the disease from women. "But we shouldn't lose track that this might be
195 our last chance to halt an epidemic among heterosexuals."

Days later, Volberding's concern was underscored with the diagnosis of the first local woman to contract AIDS through a heterosexual liaison. Within days, she was in Ward 5B, the first woman on the AIDS Ward, staring at the stark landscape outside her window and wondering how a tryst with a bisexual man several years before had brought her here. 200

Dr. Mervyn Silverman, in his last weeks as health director, announced that the health department would start updating brochures to include risks to heterosexuals. A new task force was organized to start laying groundwork for more elaborate educational plans in the future. Volberding took things a step further when he suggested that city epidemiologists begin sexual contact tracing on 205 every heterosexual AIDS case. Dr. Dean Echenberg, who had replaced Selma Dritz in the Bureau of Communicable Disease Control, took what became the standard public health argument against such tracing, saying that even if the tracing turned up infected people, there was no medical treatment to offer them. "You might cause a tremendous amount of damage without doing any 210 good." Echenberg said. Volberding countered that the people who might later get infected from such contacts, however, would not see it that way.

This medical point of view did not prevail. AIDSpeak still dominated public health decision making, and those rules decreed that, even in a deadly epidemic, you weren't supposed to do anything that might hurt somebody's 215 feelings.

For all the concern about heterosexual transmission—and the role prostitutes might play in spreading the disease—there was probably no aspect of the epidemic in which the facts were more arguable. At this point, only 50 AIDS cases nationally were linked to heterosexual transmission. Of these, 45 were 220 women and only 5 were men who appeared to have no other risk except sexual contact with infected women. Five out of nearly 8,000 AIDS cases reported nationally did not constitute an epidemic. And there could be no certainty that those men, 2 of whom lived in San Francisco, were not gay men who were too ashamed to admit it. 225

The mechanics of female-to-male transmission also were problematical. Which female body fluids are as invasive to men as semen is during vaginal or anal intercourse? In Africa, transmission appeared possible when vaginal fluids connected with blood through open sores stemming from untreated venereal disease. In the United States, venereal disease was almost always treated, and 230 female-to-male transmission was rare. To be sure it did exist, and numbers would probably increase as more women became infected with the virus. However, heterosexuals had no amplification system comparable to the gay bathhouses to speed the virus throughout the country. In the future, heterosexual AIDS would remain a problem for the people it had already struck; sexual part- 235 ners of intravenous drug users, concentrated largely among poor and minorities in eastern urban cities. It seemed unlikely that the epidemic would suddenly become a heterosexual blight in the way it had swept the gay community.

Perhaps no single aspect of the epidemic was as instructive in this point than the AIDS-carrying prostitutes. Even while the Silvana Strangis story raged 240

on the front pages, UCSF researchers were completing their journal article on the first person in the United States known to have been infected with the AIDS virus. The first documented carrier was not a gay man, they said, but a San Francisco prostitute. This woman, like Strangis, had a long rap sheet of Tender-
245 loin arrests related to prostitution and intravenous drugs. In 1977, the woman, who was then twenty-five-years old, gave birth to a baby girl who began show-ing signs of immune deficiency eleven months later. While the infant's condi-tion deteriorated, the mother gave birth to a second girl in 1979. This child also showed signs of immune abnormalities, including chronic diarrhea and swollen
250 lymph glands. A third daughter was born in April 1982. Within two months, she had candidiasis in both her mouth and vagina. Three months later, doctors blamed her breathing problems on *Pneumocystis*. By 1984, two of the three chil-dren were dead. Any mystery about the source of their immune problems was resolved when UCSF researchers tested their stored blood samples for HTLV-III
255 antibodies. All three children were infected. The mother, who suffered from swollen lymph nodes in 1982, clearly was infected with the virus as early as 1977 and possibly 1976, shortly after the virus arrived in the United States.

During all these years of infection, the woman had been an active pros-titute in the Tenderloin, as she would continue to be until her death in May
260 1987. If she was easily spreading the virus to her clients, there had been plenty of time for the stricken men to surface. Yet, San Francisco counted only two male heterosexual cases. Similarly, New York City was not teeming with straight men blaming prostitutes, even though that city's legion of drug-shoot-ing hookers dwarfed the number of such women on the West Coast. Taken
265 together, it appeared there was more smoke than fire in the prostitution-AIDS debate.

Nevertheless, the outpouring of official attention to the handful of hetero-sexual AIDS cases in early 1985 proved a crucial event in determining the direc-tion of AIDS debate in the next two years. It instructed health officials and AIDS
270 researchers, who had had such a difficult time seizing government and media interest in the epidemic, that nothing captured the attention of editors and news directors like the talk of widespread heterosexual transmission of AIDS. Such talk could be guaranteed air time and news space, which, in the AIDS business, quickly translated into funds and resources. Thus, even though epidemiological
275 support for fears of a pandemic spread of AIDS among heterosexuals was scant, few researchers would say so aloud. There was no gain in taking such a posi-tion, even if it did ultimately prove to be honest and truthful. Five years of bitter experience had schooled just about everyone involved in this epidemic that truth did not count for much in AIDS policy.

*January 10*

280 Cathy Borchelt was at work in the San Francisco Police Department's record room when a co-worker handed her the morning *Chronicle* and asked about the

story on page eight. It was an announcement by the Irwin Memorial Blood Bank
that an ailing, unnamed woman at Seton Medical Center had contracted AIDS
through blood provided by Irwin in August 1983.

"Is that your mom?"

It was the first time anybody in the Borchelt family was informed that
Frances was indeed suffering from transfusion AIDS.

"I've been suspecting this because the doctors said she had *Pneumocystis*,"
Cathy said as she scanned the story.

"There's a lot of *Pneumocystis* going around," her colleague agreed.

Cathy knew her mother was an intensely private woman and would not
want to see anything about herself in the newspaper, even if it did not carry her
name. She called the hospital to make sure nobody put a copy of the *Chronicle*
in her room.

That evening at the hospital, Cathy was watching television with Frances
when the newscaster began talking about the new transfusion case in Seton
Medical Center. Frances Borchelt shook her head sadly at the news.

"That poor lady," she said. "If it were me, I'd sue."

Cathy was shocked. Obviously, nobody had told her mother yet that she
had AIDS. That night, Bob Borchelt insisted that the doctors tell Frances what
had happened.

The next day, Frances didn't say anything about the conversation she had
had with her doctor, although the family noted that she seemed depressed.

The woman in Seton Medical Center was the 100th American known to
have contracted AIDS through a blood transfusion, Irwin president Brian
McDonough said the next day. As part of a new policy of openness, Irwin was
now publicly announcing each new case of transfusion AIDS. The intent was to
allay any suspicion that the blood bank was whitewashing the transfusion-AIDS
problem. In revealing Frances's diagnosis, McDonough added that thirty-two
AIDS patients had donated blood to Irwin in recent years and that at least
seventy-two local people had received blood products from these donors. The
blood bank expected another two dozen AIDS cases from recipients of its products in the next year.

The Irwin policy of candor infuriated other blood bankers who were still
clinging to their one-in-a-million rhetoric, if not declining comment on the problem of transfusion AIDS altogether. Blood bankers were anxious to get the entire
AIDS problem behind them. That would happen with the release of the HTLV-III
antibody test, when at last they could pronounce the blood supply safe from AIDS.

The Food and Drug Administration had announced a February 15 release
date for the screening test. Local public health officials and gay organizations,
however, continued to be concerned about its vast policy implications. In few
issues had social, political, psychological, and medical variables converged to
create such a policy morass.

Surveys of gay men indicated that as many as 75 percent planned to take
the antibody test once it was available. Concern soared that, once blood banks
started screening, the men would go to a blood bank and donate blood in an effort to learn their antibody status.

Meanwhile, scientists were uncertain as to the accuracy of the test. Dr.
Robert Gallo said in early January that the test might not detect between 5 and
30 percent of AIDS virus carriers. The problem stemmed both from the test's accuracy and the fact that it did not appear that people developed detectable
HTLV-III antibodies until six weeks after infection. Thus, somebody recently
infected with the AIDS virus would not test positive on the antibody test. This
left health officials worried that if gay men donated blood to learn their antibody status, some infected blood might slip through the AIDS screening, further contaminating the blood supply.

Added to these fears was the growing anxiety about the civil liberties implications of blood testing among gay men. With as many as one-half of gay men
testing positive for HTLV-III in some studies, it appeared that the test could
well become a de facto test for sexual orientation. Access to test results could
possibly result in widespread discrimination against gays by employers, insur-
ers, or a government that might turn repressive toward gays in future years.

All this could happen even while the medical value of the test remained in
some doubt. Official estimates still put the number of antibody-positive people
who would develop AIDS at between 5 and 10 percent, although it was still not
possible to predict which group that might be. Because the test had little predic-
tive value, therefore, the newest axiom of AIDSpeak became "the test doesn't
mean anything."

Translating all these concerns to policy became the task of Dr. Mervyn
Silverman, who was president of the U.S. Conference of Local Health Officers.
Silverman put together a proposal that seemed to meet everyone's needs, seeking money for alternative test sites in which gay men and other concerned people could be tested outside the blood banks. Silverman also wanted the government to issue regulations assuring the confidentiality of blood bank test results,
so employers or government agencies could not subpoena them for purposes
unrelated to protecting the blood supply.

The proposals were greeted with enthusiasm at the Centers for Disease
Control, which had long grappled with the complexities of AIDS policy. In
meetings with federal officials, however, Silverman ran into a brick wall of resistance. The alternative test sites would cost money, he was told, and the federal
government had no plans to expend more money on AIDS. As it was, the Reagan administration still had not released the more than $8 million that Congress
had appropriated the October before to speed the antibody test to blood banks.
Moreover, the government would do nothing to assure confidentiality for blood
bank test results. That should be handled on the local level, officials said.

In a January 15 meeting with representatives from the Food and Drug Administration, Silverman got tough. If the government did not release funds for

the alternative test sites, he would publicly announce that federal officials were
fashioning a new threat to the blood supply. He gave the FDA a two-week deadline. Angry at being handed ultimatums, administration officials told Silverman    370
he was just looking for a way to line the pockets of his health department. The
charge amused Silverman, coming as it did on his last day as public health director of San Francisco.

The efficient social services department at the San Francisco AIDS Foundation
easily found Silvana Strangis a slot in a methadone program and quickly ob-    375
tained food stamps and general assistance funds, so she would not have to turn
tricks to pay rent. Silvana seemed repentant and ready for a new life. "Nobody
should have to see the kind of life I've lived in the Tenderloin," she said tear-
fully. "At least now I'm beginning to see an end to all this."

The end of Silvana's story, however, was no new life and was emblematic of    380
the complicated problems that intravenous drug users presented in the AIDS
epidemic. These people weren't optimistic gay men who would spend their last
days doing white-light meditations with their Shanti Project volunteer; they
were addicts.

With a terminal diagnosis, Tony Ford had little incentive to quit drugs, and    385
he provided little encouragement to Silvana. Within weeks, Silvana disappeared
from her drug rehabilitation program. Two months later, she was arrested for
petty theft, the first of five more arrests for prostitution and drug-related
charges in the next year.

Tony Ford survived four bouts with *Pneumocystis* before he died of kidney    390
failure on June 20, 1985.

Silvana Strangis died on January 24, 1986, during the eleventh day of her
first bout with cryptococcosis. Her remains were interred in the middle-class
San Francisco suburb where her story had started, back when she was the
beloved daughter of an Italian family and a New Age was dawning.    395

## Looking Back

1. What function does the short New York City segment of this chapter serve (lines
   1–41)?

2. Do you think that "confidentiality and civil rights" (line 94), the issues that worried
   the AIDS clinic head nurse, should apply to a person like Silvana Strangis? Explain
   your answer.

3. What insight into the mentality of addicts do we get from the needle sharing incident in the hospital room (lines 108–115)?

4. Can you summarize Shilts's criticisms of the media's coverage of AIDS (see lines
   125–150)?

5. Why does Shilts trace part of the history of the disease here?

6. Is the "AIDSpeak" Shilts refers to (line 213)—a variant of Newspeak, from George Orwell's novel *1984*, in which language is distorted for political ends—still common, or do bureaucrats now face facts more squarely and tell the truth about AIDS?

7. Do you think that being tested for the AIDS virus is a good idea? Why or why not?

8. In your view, is gays' suspicion of the test valid (see lines 337–340)?

9. Shilts reports the plain facts of Tony Ford's and Silvana Strangis's deaths (see lines 390–395). Do you think more comment is needed? Explain your answer.

10. Why does Shilts refer to "a New Age" at the end of the chapter (line 395)?

## Writing Assignments

1. Recently, a student said in a composition class, "I'm afraid of AIDS. I'm so afraid of it that I just don't do anything. I don't have anything to do with anything." Although no one would argue that AIDS is not to be feared, fear that races in the direction of terror ends in panic. It will hinder a person from taking rational measures. Further, self-willed isolation is counter to natural human tendencies. But if neither terror nor isolation seems a good choice, the need for self-protection is evident. How should a person conduct himself or herself to avoid contracting AIDS? Write an essay answering this question. Make your writing more than academic by putting yourself into it, just as the student quoted above does. Conceive of an audience that needs to know.

2. Under the title "A Casualty Report," an article appearing in *The New York Times* on June 28, 1992, reported that in the mid-1980s, the period Shilts writes about, the U.S. Centers for Disease Control issued AIDS bulletins fifty-two times a year. Now bulletins appear four times a year. AIDS has become, for all but those who suffer from it, routine. It is a routine, however, that in the United States results in fifty to sixty thousand new infections a year. By the year 2000, officials estimate that 40 million people will be infected worldwide. In such circumstances, with no vaccine or cure in sight, one approach is to try to prevent the spread of AIDS by controlling possible carriers, by placing certain restrictions on their activities. Write an essay that proposes what should be done, if anything, in this respect. In your essay, try to balance people's basic rights against the dangers of a raging epidemic.

3. A recent death notice contains this remark: The deceased "died of complications due to AIDS and the lack of care and funding for AIDS research by the Reagan/Bush Misadministrations" (*The New York Times,* July 13, 1992). An ad run by the Gay Men's Health Crisis (GMHC) and endorsed by local AIDS action committees nationwide reports government refusal to use the word "condoms" or even to mention sex in anti-AIDS campaigns. This refusal has been somewhat modified recently, however, and now warnings against unsafe sex do appear in public. But some people have argued that condoms are not foolproof, that abstinence is the safest policy, and that sex education merely encourages teenagers to have sex. What is your view on the matter of anti-AIDS public education? Write an essay discussing this issue and describing an appropriate and effective ad campaign.

# Linked Readings

George Orwell
## A HANGING

William Bradford
## ANNO DOM: *1638* [ENGLISHMEN EXECUTED FOR MURDERING AN INDIAN]

Most famous as the author of the novels *1984* and *Animal Farm*, George Orwell (1903–1950) was also an essayist and literary journalist, prolific letter writer, diarist, and radio commentator for the BBC during World War II. He was a socialist and fought for the Loyalist side against Franco in the Spanish Civil War (1936–1939), where he was gravely wounded in action. Years earlier, he was employed as a policeman in Burma while that country still lay under British imperial rule. "A Hanging" results from that experience. The account of an execution by William Bradford (1588–1657) is taken from his *Of Plymouth Plantation*, a history of the Massachusetts Bay Colony covering the years 1620–1647. Bradford, a historian by vocation, was born in Yorkshire, England, and with others fled religious persecution, arriving in Holland in 1608 and in Cape Cod aboard the *Mayflower* in 1620. A year later he was elected governor of Plymouth. Taken together, these readings provide a fuller context within which to think critically about capital punishment.

## A HANGING

## Looking Ahead

1. Read critically to detect how this intimate view of the accused and his execution contribute to an understanding of the event.

2. Keep in mind the position you hold on capital punishment, and note any changes in your opinion as you read.

3. Orwell does not reveal the hanged man's crime. Judge whether not knowing affects your sympathy or lack of it.

It was in Burma, a sodden morning of the rains. A sickly light, like yellow tinfoil, was slanting over the high walls into the jail yard. We were waiting outside the condemned cells, a row of sheds fronted with double bars, like small animal cages. Each cell measured about ten feet by ten and was quite bare within except for a plank bed and a pot of drinking water. In some of them brown silent     5
men were squatting at the inner bars, with their blankets draped round them. These were the condemned men, due to be hanged within the next week or two.

One prisoner had been brought out of his cell. He was a Hindu, a puny wisp of a man, with a shaven head and vague liquid eyes. He had a thick, sprouting moustache, absurdly too big for his body, rather like the moustache     10
of a comic man on the films. Six tall Indian warders were guarding him and

getting him ready for the gallows. Two of them stood by with rifles and fixed bayonets, while the others handcuffed him, passed a chain through his handcuffs and fixed it to their belts, and lashed his arms tight to his sides. They

15  crowded very close about him, with their hands always on him in a careful, caressing grip, as though all the while feeling him to make sure he was there. It was like men handling a fish which is still alive and may jump back into the water. But he stood quite unresisting, yielding his arms limply to the ropes, as though he hardly noticed what was happening.

20      Eight o'clock struck and a bugle call, desolately thin in the wet air, floated from the distant barracks. The superintendent of the jail, who was standing apart from the rest of us, moodily prodding the gravel with his stick, raised his head at the sound. He was an army doctor, with a grey toothbrush moustache and a gruff voice. "For God's sake hurry up, Francis," he said irritably. "The

25  man ought to have been dead by this time. Aren't you ready yet?"

Francis, the head jailer, a fat Dravidian[1] in a white drill suit and gold spectacles, waved his black hand. "Yes sir, yes sir," he bubbled. "All iss satisfactorily prepared. The hangman iss waiting. We shall proceed."

"Well, quick march, then. The prisoners can't get their breakfast till this

30  job's over."

We set out for the gallows. Two warders marched on either side of the prisoner, with their rifles at the slope; two others marched close against him, gripping him by arm and shoulder, as though at once pushing and supporting him. The rest of us, magistrates and the like, followed behind. Suddenly, when we

35  had gone ten yards, the procession stopped short without any order or warning. A dreadful thing had happened—a dog, come goodness knows whence, had appeared in the yard. It came bounding among us with a loud volley of barks, and leapt round us wagging its whole body, wild with glee at finding so many human beings together. It was a large woolly dog, half Airedale, half pariah. For a

40  moment it pranced round us, and then, before anyone could stop it, it had made a dash for the prisoner, and jumping up tried to lick his face. Everyone stood aghast, too taken aback even to grab at the dog.

"Who let that bloody brute in here?" said the superintendent angrily. "Catch it, someone!"

45      A warder, detached from the escort, charged clumsily after the dog, but it danced and gambolled just out of his reach, taking everything as part of the game. A young Eurasian jailer picked up a handful of gravel and tried to stone the dog away, but it dodged the stones and came after us again. Its yaps echoed from the jail walls. The prisoner, in the grasp of the two warders, looked on in-

50  curiously, as though this was another formality of the hanging. It was several minutes before someone managed to catch the dog. Then we put my handkerchief through its collar and moved off once more, with the dog still straining and whimpering.

---

1. *Dravidian:* member of an ancient race in southern India. (*ed.*)

It was about forty yards to the gallows. I watched the bare brown back of the prisoner marching in front of me. He walked clumsily with his bound arms, but quite steadily, with that bobbing gait of the Indian who never straightens his knees. At each step his muscles slid neatly into place, the lock of hair on his scalp danced up and down, his feet printed themselves on the wet gravel. And once, in spite of the men who gripped him by each shoulder, he stepped slightly aside to avoid a puddle on the path.

It is curious, but till that moment I had never realised what it means to destroy a healthy, conscious man. When I saw the prisoner step aside to avoid the puddle, I saw the mystery, the unspeakable wrongness, of cutting a life short when it is in full tide. This man was not dying, he was alive just as we were alive. All the organs of his body were working—bowels digesting food, skin renewing itself, nails growing, tissues forming—all toiling away in solemn foolery. His nails would still be growing when he stood on the drop, when he was falling through the air with a tenth of a second to live. His eyes saw the yellow gravel and the grey walls, and his brain still remembered, foresaw, reasoned—reasoned even about puddles. He and we were a party of men walking together, seeing, hearing, feeling, understanding the same world; and in two minutes, with a sudden snap, one of us would be gone—one mind less, one world less.

The gallows stood in a small yard, separate from the main grounds of the prison, and overgrown with tall prickly weeds. It was a brick erection like three sides of a shed, with planking on top, and above that two beams and a crossbar with the rope dangling. The hangman, a grey-haired convict in the white uniform of the prison, was waiting beside his machine. He greeted us with a servile crouch as we entered. At a word from Francis the two warders, gripping the prisoner more closely than ever, half led, half pushed him to the gallows and helped him clumsily up the ladder. Then the hangman climbed up and fixed the rope around the prisoner's neck.

We stood waiting, five yards away. The warders had formed in a rough circle round the gallows. And then, when the noose was fixed, the prisoner began crying out on his god. It was a high, reiterated cry of "Ram! Ram! Ram! Ram!"[2] not urgent and fearful like a prayer or a cry for help, but steady, rhythmical, almost like the tolling of a bell. The dog answered the sound with a whine. The hangman, still standing on the gallows, produced a small cotton bag like a flour bag and drew it down over the prisoner's face. But the sound, muffled by the cloth, still persisted, over and over again: "Ram! Ram! Ram! Ram! Ram!"

The hangman climbed down and stood ready, holding the lever. Minutes seemed to pass. The steady, muffled crying from the prisoner went on and on, "Ram! Ram! Ram!" never faltering for an instant. The superintendent, his head on his chest, was slowly poking the ground with his stick; perhaps he was counting the cries, allowing the prisoner a fixed number—fifty, perhaps, or a hundred. Everyone had changed colour. The Indians had gone grey like bad

---

2. *Ram:* name of a Hindu god. (*ed.*)

coffee, and one or two of the bayonets were wavering. We looked at the lashed, hooded man on the drop, and listened to his cries—each cry another second of life; the same thought was in all our minds: oh, kill him quickly, get it over, stop that abominable noise!

100 Suddenly the superintendent made up his mind. Throwing up his head he made a swift motion with his stick. "Chalo!" he shouted almost fiercely.

There was a clanking noise, and then dead silence. The prisoner had vanished, and the rope was twisting on itself. I let go of the dog, and it galloped immediately to the back of the gallows; but when it got there it stopped short,
105 barked, and then retreated into a corner of the yard, where it stood among the weeds, looking timorously out at us. We went round the gallows to inspect the prisoner's body. He was dangling with his toes pointed straight downwards, very slowly revolving, as dead as a stone.

The superintendent reached out with his stick and poked the bare body; it
110 oscillated, slightly. "*He's* all right," said the superintendent. He backed out from under the gallows, and blew out a deep breath. The moody look had gone out of his face quite suddenly. He glanced at his wrist-watch. "Eight minutes past eight. Well, that's all for this morning, thank God."

The warders unfixed bayonets and marched away. The dog, sobered and
115 conscious of having misbehaved itself, slipped after them. We walked out of the gallows yard, past the condemned cells with their waiting prisoners, into the big central yard of the prison. The convicts, under the command of warders armed with lathis, were already receiving their breakfast. They squatted in long rows, each man holding a tin pannikin, while two warders with buckets marched
120 round ladling out rice; it seemed quite a homely, jolly scene, after the hanging. An enormous relief had come upon us now that the job was done. One felt an impulse to sing, to break into a run, to snigger. All at once everyone began chattering gaily.

The Eurasian boy walking beside me nodded towards the way we had
125 come, with a knowing smile: "Do you know, sir, our friend (he meant the dead man), when he heard his appeal had been dismissed, he pissed on the floor of his cell. From fright.—Kindly take one of my cigarettes, sir. Do you not admire my new silver case, sir? From the boxwallah, two rupees eight annas. Classy European style."

130 Several people laughed—at what, nobody seemed certain.

Francis was walking by the superintendent, talking garrulously: "Well, sir, all hass passed off with the utmost satisfactoriness. It wass all finished—flick! like that. It iss not always so—oah, no! I have known cases where the doctor wass obliged to go beneath the gallows and pull the prisoner's legs to ensure de-
135 cease. Most disagreeable!"

"Wriggling about, eh? That's bad," said the superintendent.

"Ach, sir, it iss worse when they become refractory! One man, I recall, clung to the bars of hiss cage when we went to take him out. You will scarcely credit, sir, that it took six warders to dislodge him, three pulling at each leg.
140 We reasoned with him. 'My dear fellow,' we said, 'think of all the pain and

trouble you are causing to us!' But no, he would not listen! Ach, he wass very troublesome!"

I found that I was laughing quite loudly. Everyone was laughing. Even the superintendent grinned in a tolerant way. "You'd better all come out and have a drink," he said quite genially. "I've got a bottle of whisky in the car. We could   145
do with it."

We went through the big double gates of the prison, into the road. "Pulling at his legs!" exclaimed a Burmese magistrate suddenly, and burst into a loud chuckling. We all began laughing again. At that moment Francis's anecdote seemed extraordinarily funny. We all had a drink together, native and European   150
alike, quite amicably. The dead man was a hundred yards away.

Eric A. Blair[3]

## ANNO DOM: *1638* [ENGLISHMEN EXECUTED FOR MURDERING AN INDIAN]

### Looking Ahead

1. Read critically to note how Bradford's terseness affects the narrative.

2. Some seventeenth-century diction and syntax may pose slight problems here but should not block understanding. Among these, "falling to idle courses" (line 11) means doing things that have no value, and "murmured that any English should be put to death" (lines 50–51) means complained about its happening.

3. Notice how political considerations figure in the death sentence. Ask yourself whether these particular ones, or others like them, remain today as factors in calling for capital punishment.

This year Mr. Thomas Prence was chosen Governor.

Amongst other enormities that fell out amongst them; this year three men were after due trial executed for robbery and murder which they had committed. Their names were these: Arthur Peach, Thomas Jackson and Richard Stinnings. There was a fourth, Daniel Cross, who was also guilty, but he escaped   5
away and could not be found.

This Arthur Peach was the chief of them, and the ringleader of all the rest. He was a lusty and a desperate young man, and had been one of the soldiers in the Pequot War and had done as good service as the most there, and one of the forwardest in any attempt. And being now out of means and loath to work, and   10
falling to idle courses and company, he intended to go to the Dutch plantation; and had allured these three, being other men's servants and apprentices, to go with him. But another cause there was also of his secret going away in this manner. He was not only run into debt, but he had got a maid with child (which was not known till after his death), a man's servant in the town, and fear of punish-   15

---

3. *Eric A. Blair:* George Orwell's real name. (*ed.*)

ment made him get away. The other three complotting with him ran away from
their masters in the night, and could not be heard of; for they went not the ordinary way, but shaped such a course as they thought to avoid the pursuit of any.
But falling into the way that lieth between the Bay of Massachusetts and the
20   Narragansetts, and being disposed to rest themselves, struck fire and took tobacco, a little out of the way by the wayside.

At length there came a Narragansett Indian by, who had been in the Bay
atrading, and had both cloth and beads about him—they had met him the day
before, and he was now returning. Peach called him to drink tobacco with
25   them, and he came and sat down with them. Peach told the other he would kill
him and take what he had from him, but they were something afraid. But he
said, "Hang him, rogue, he had killed many of them." So they let him alone to
do as he would. And when he saw his time, he took a rapier and ran him
through the body once or twice and took from him five fathom of wampum and
30   three coats of cloth and went their way, leaving him for dead. But he scrambled
away when they were gone, and made shift to get home, but died within a few
days after. By which means they were discovered. And by subtlety the Indians
took them; for they, desiring a canoe to set them over a water, not thinking their
fact had been known, by the sachem's[1] command they were carried to Aquid-
35   neck Island and there accused of the murder, and were examined and committed upon it by the English there.

The Indians sent for Mr. Williams and made a grievous complaint; his
friends and kindred were ready to rise in arms and provoke the rest thereunto,
some conceiving they should now find the Pequots' words true, that the English
40   would fall upon them. But Mr. Williams pacified them and told them they
should see justice done upon the offenders, and went to the man and took Mr.
James, a physician, with him. The man told him who did it, and in what manner
it was done; but the physician found his wounds mortal and that he could not
live, as he after testified upon oath before the jury in open court. And so he died
45   shortly after, as both Mr. Williams, Mr. James and some Indians testified in
court.

The Government in the Bay were acquainted with it but referred it hither
because it was done in this jurisdiction; but pressed by all means that justice
might be done in it, or else the country must rise and see justice done; other-
50   wise it would raise a war. Yet some of the rude and ignorant sort murmured that
any English should be put to death for the Indians. So at last they of the Island[2]
brought them hither, and being often examined and the evidence produced,
they all in the end freely confessed in effect all that the Indian accused them of,

---

1. *Sachem:* North American Indian chief. (*ed.*)

2. *the Island:* Rhode Island. This is believed to have been the first case of Englishmen being
tried, found guilty and executed for the murder of an Indian. Crose or Cross, the murderer who escaped, was given sanctuary at the plantation he belonged to, Piscataqua, where (says Governor
Winthrop) "all such lewd persons as fled from us" were given "countenance."

and that they had done it in the manner aforesaid. And so, upon the forementioned evidence, were cast by the jury and condemned, and executed for the same, September 4. And some of the Narragansett Indians and of the party's friends were present when it was done, which gave them and all the country good satisfaction. But it was a matter of much sadness to them here, and was the second execution which they had since they came; being both for wilful murder, as hath been before related. Thus much of this matter. 55

60

## Looking Back

1. What sense of the condemned man do you get from the details Orwell provides in lines 8–19?

2. Why is the superintendent's exasperated statement, "For God's sake, hurry up, Francis. . . . The man ought to have been dead by this time" (Orwell, lines 24–25), so unintentionally horrifying?

3. How do you think the people accompanying the condemned man felt when the dog tried to lick his face? How is the dog's action possibly symbolic?

4. What connection exists between the prisoner's carefully stepping around a puddle on his way to the gallows and the sentiments that gesture aroused in Orwell (see lines 55–73)?

5. Can you explain Orwell's expressed belief in "the mystery, the unspeakable wrongness, of cutting a life short when it is in full tide" (lines 63–64)?

6. What does the superintendent mean by stressing the pronoun when he says, about the dangling corpse, "*He's* all right" (line 110)?

7. How do you account for everyone's laughter and friendly spirits after the hanging?

8. What picture of Arthur Peach's status in society do we get from Bradford's exposition of his crime (see lines 8–16)?

9. How do you balance factors like Peach's being a veteran of a war against the Indians and his betrayal of a particular Indian whom he had befriended?

10. Why do "some of the rude and ignorant sort" (line 50) complain about sentencing the men to death? Why does Mr. Williams go ahead with the execution?

## Writing Assignments (Linked Readings)

1. At one time, executions were public. Today, they are isolated within prisons and witnessed by a few, select individuals. They are reported in the newspapers and on television, but there are no pictures of the actual moment of death. Should there be? Should executions be open to the public, or even be broadcast live on TV? Write an essay addressing the issue of open executions. Refer to the death penalty carried out against the Hindu and the three Englishmen, and discuss reasons both for and against public executions. The weight of your arguments should lead you to one side or the other.

2. In 1990, over 2,000 inmates were living on death row in the United States. But this figure and others that might be cited cannot capture the actuality of executions or of

494    IV: Social Reality

the persons involved. Perhaps it is necessary to do so before we can understand the true nature of capital punishment. Comparing Orwell's and Bradford's accounts is one way to approach such an understanding. Write an essay that does this. Compare the two narratives on the basis of facts such as the author's intentions in writing, the psychological distance each maintains from the event, the social situation surrounding each hanging, the political factors involved, and the authors' descriptive styles. Try to delineate your own responses to the texts.

3. Orwell manages to enlist our sympathies for the condemned man, whereas Bradford does the same for the helpless murder victim. Orwell, however, never tells us what the crime the hanged man committed and so perhaps our sympathies are misplaced. Should sympathy for victim or criminal ever be a factor in capital punishment? How much weight should be put on the crime before it is reasonable to demand capital punishment? Write an essay addressing these questions by saying what particular kinds of crimes deserve the death penalty and what kind do not, and why. If you believe the state should never impose the death penalty, discuss your reasons for that belief.

## Writing Assignments (Individual Readings)
### A HANGING

Various states in the United States utilize different methods of execution. Often, but not always, the aim is to reduce suffering. The result of different views on this matter, as well as of the desire to retain traditional means of execution, is that at present the death penalty may be administered by hanging, firing squad, electrocution, gas chamber, or lethal injection. Write an essay that compares these different methods and evaluates them in terms of the pain and suffering caused. To some extent, you will have to imagine the procedures and their effects, but each is really so blunt that you should be able to produce a full enough picture to warrant a judgment.

## ANNO DOM: *1638* [ENGLISHMEN EXECUTED FOR MURDERING AN INDIAN]

In 1638, adherents of capital punishment no doubt approved in principle the death sentences handed the three men convicted for murder. But arguments could have arisen for commuting the death sentences to deportation back to England or banishment to the wilderness. One argument, which some colonists make, is that an Englishman should not be hanged for killing an Indian. The other argument is that the authorities ordered the sentences only to placate the Narragansett nation and avoid a bloody Indian uprising. Write an essay examining these grounds for commutation and, interpolating your own commentary on the case, decide whether or not they are convincing.

# Linked Readings

Vaclav Havel
THE END OF THE MODERN ERA

Herbert L. Meltzer    Stuart A. Newman
Felipe C. Cabello    Gregory Hedberg
WITH APOLOGIES TO HAVEL, LET REASON RULE

Vaclav Havel (b. 1936) was the first elected president of Czechoslovakia, now the Czech Republic, after the end of Communist rule. Primarily a playwright (*The Memorandum, Largo Desolato, Temptation*), his *Open Letters: Selected Writings* was published in 1991. He was jailed repeatedly as a political dissident by the Communist government. The piece below consists of remarks (excerpted) that Havel addressed to the World Economic Forum in Davos, Switzerland, in February 1992. They were published on the op-ed page of *The New York Times* on March 1 of that year. Responding to his speech in letters to the editor printed on March 17, Meltzer is a retired research scientist, Newman a professor of cell biology and Cabello of microbiology at New York Medical College, and Hedberg the Director of the New York Academy of Art. Perhaps no more interesting topic intrigues the critical thinker than the one discussed here: human reason and the uses to which it may be put. The interest lies in the fact that without reason there can of course be no critical thinking. Thus, these texts establish a forum for self-examination.

## THE END OF THE MODERN ERA

### Looking Ahead

1. Note the structure of this piece: the first half is devoted to stating the problem as Havel sees it, and the second half to suggesting a solution.
2. Havel's points are emphatically stated but largely unqualified, a factor to keep in mind when critically evaluating his argument.
3. Because Havel deals mainly in abstractions, try to think of concrete examples that might illustrate his ideas.

The end of Communism is, first and foremost, a message to the human race. It is a message we have not yet fully deciphered and comprehended. In its deepest sense, the end of Communism has brought a major era in human history to an end. It has brought an end not just to the 19th and 20th centuries, but to the modern age as a whole.

The modern era has been dominated by the culminating belief, expressed in different forms, that the world—and Being as such—is a wholly knowable system governed by a finite number of universal laws that man can grasp and rationally direct for his own benefit. This era, beginning in the Renaissance and

5

10 developing from the Enlightenment to socialism, from positivism to scientism, from the Industrial Revolution to the information revolution, was characterized by rapid advances in rational, cognitive thinking.

This, in turn, gave rise to the proud belief that man, as the pinnacle of everything that exists, was capable of objectively describing, explaining and

15 controlling everything that exists, and of possessing the one and only truth about the world. It was an era in which there was a cult of depersonalized objectivity, an era in which objective knowledge was amassed and technologically exploited, an era of belief in automatic progress brokered by the scientific method. It was an era of systems, institutions, mechanisms and statistical aver-

20 ages. It was an era of ideologies, doctrines, interpretations of reality, an era in which the goal was to find a universal theory of the world, and thus a universal key to unlock its prosperity.

Communism was the perverse extreme of this trend. It was an attempt, on the basis of a few propositions masquerading as the only scientific truth, to or-

25 ganize all of life according to a single model, and to subject it to central planning and control regardless of whether or not that was what life wanted.

The fall of Communism can be regarded as a sign that modern thought—based on the premise that the world is objectively knowable, and that the knowledge so obtained can be absolutely generalized—has come to a final cri-

30 sis. This era has created the first global, or planetary, technical civilization, but it has reached the limit of its potential, the point beyond which the abyss begins. The end of Communism is a serious warning to all mankind. It is a signal that the era of arrogant, absolutist reason is drawing to a close and that it is high time to draw conclusions from that fact.

35 Communism was not defeated by military force, but by life, by the human spirit, by conscience, by the resistance of Being and man to manipulation. It was defeated by a revolt of color, authenticity, history in all its variety and human individuality against imprisonment within a uniform ideology.

This powerful signal is coming at the 11th hour. We all know civilization is

40 in danger. The population explosion and the greenhouse effect, holes in the ozone and AIDS, the threat of nuclear terrorism and the dramatically widening gap between the rich north and the poor south, the danger of famine, the depletion of the biosphere and the mineral resources of the planet, the expansion of commercial television culture and the growing threat of regional wars—all

45 these, combined with thousands of other factors, represent a general threat to mankind.

The large paradox at the moment is that man—a great collector of information—is well aware of all this, yet is absolutely incapable of dealing with the danger. Traditional science, with its usual coolness, can describe the different

50 ways we might destroy ourselves, but it cannot offer us truly effective and practicable instructions on how to avert them. There is too much to know; the information is muddled or poorly organized; these processes can no longer be fully grasped and understood, let alone contained or halted.

We are looking for new scientific recipes, new ideologies, new control systems, new institutions, new instruments to eliminate the dreadful consequences   55
of our previous recipes, ideologies, control systems, institutions and instruments. We treat the fatal consequences of technology as though they were a technical defect that could be remedied by technology alone. We are looking for an objective way out of the crisis of objectivism.

Everything would seem to suggest that this is not the way to go. We cannot   60
devise, within the traditional modern attitude to reality, a system that will eliminate all the disastrous consequences of previous systems. We cannot discover a law or theory whose technical application will eliminate all the disastrous consequences of the technical application of earlier laws and technologies.

What is needed is something different, something larger. Man's attitude to   65
the world must be radically changed. We have to abandon the arrogant belief that the world is merely a puzzle to be solved, a machine with instructions for use waiting to be discovered, a body of information to be fed into a computer in the hope that, sooner or later, it will spit out a universal solution.

It is my profound conviction that we have to release from the sphere of pri-   70
vate whim such forces as a natural, unique and unrepeatable experience of the world, an elementary sense of justice, the ability to see things as others do, a sense of transcendental responsibility, archetypal wisdom, good taste, courage, compassion and faith in the importance of particular measures that do not aspire to be a universal key to salvation. Such forces must be rehabilitated.   75

Things must once more be given a chance to present themselves as they are, to be perceived in their individuality. We must see the pluralism of the world, and not bind it by seeking common denominators or reducing everything to a single common equation.

We must try harder to understand than to explain. The way forward is not   80
in the mere construction of universal systemic solutions, to be applied to reality from the outside; it is also in seeking to get to the heart of reality through personal experience. Such an approach promotes an atmosphere of tolerant solidarity and unity in diversity based on mutual respect, genuine pluralism and parallelism. In a word, human uniqueness, human action and the human spirit   85
must be rehabilitated.

The world today is a world in which generality, objectivity and universality are in crisis. This world presents a great challenge to the practice of politics, which, it seems to me, still has a technocratic, utilitarian approach to Being, and therefore to political power as well. Many of the traditional mechanisms of   90
democracy created and developed and conserved in the modern era are so linked to the cult of objectivity and statistical average that they can annul human individuality. We can see this in political language, where cliché often squeezes out a personal tone. And when a personal tone does crop up, it is usually calculated, not an outburst of personal authenticity.   95

Sooner or later politics will be faced with the task of finding a new, postmodern face. A politician must become a person again, someone who trusts not

only a scientific representation and analysis of the world, but also the world itself. He must believe not only in sociological statistics, but also in real people.
100 He must trust not only an objective interpretation of reality, but also his own
soul; not only an adopted ideology, but also his own thoughts; not only the
summary reports he receives each morning, but also his own feeling.

Soul, individual spirituality, first-hand personal insight into things: the courage
to be himself and go the way his conscience points, humility in the face of the
105 mysterious order of Being, confidence in its natural direction and, above all,
trust in his own subjectivity as his principal link with the subjectivity of the
world—these are the qualities that politicians of the future should cultivate.
      Looking at politics "from the inside," as it were, has if anything confirmed
my belief that the world of today—with the dramatic changes it is going
110 through and in its determination not to destroy itself—presents a great challenge to politicians.
      It is not that we should simply seek new and better ways of managing soci-
ety, the economy, and the world. The point is that we should fundamentally
change how we behave. And who but politicians should lead the way? Their
115 changed attitude toward the world, themselves and their responsibility can give
rise to truly effective systemic and institutional changes.

## WITH APOLOGIES TO HAVEL, LET REASON RULE

### Looking Ahead

1. You should be aware that because letters to the editor address a previously published text, they do not as a rule result in as worked-out a presentation as that they
   comment on.

2. Notice that the first two letters criticize Havel's main argument; the third, which applauds his essay, refers to only one aspect of his argument.

3. In response to controversial texts or events, the letters to the editor that are printed
   often represent the dominant public opinion. We may therefore assume that most
   reader reaction to Havel's proposition was negative.

To the Editor:
      "The End of the Modern Era,". . . is both eloquent and incomprehensible.
While the Czechoslovak playwright President points to major threats to our civilization, he misattributes some problems to science, which he believes "cannot
5 offer us truly effective and practicable instructions on how to avoid them." On
the contrary, science can provide the means to limit the population explosion
(one of the dangers he mentions), while all politicians find it more profitable to
pander to runaway emotions than advocate effective actions.
      The theme of distrust of scientific reasoning, which pervades Mr. Havel's
10 remarks, appears to me to represent misperceptions of science common to all

too many nonscientists. From the first day to the last day of my 45-year career as a research scientist, I never had either the reason or the inclination to believe that scientists were capable of "objectively describing, explaining and controlling everything that exists" or that "the world is a wholly knowable system."

Nor did most of my scientific colleagues, except, perhaps, for those who were the politicians of the scientific establishment. Science, for me, was always an adventure of human intellect, a search for partial understanding, which was occasionally rewarded by the emergence of theories that had the potential to improve the human condition.

The problem is not too much trust in objectivity, too much rationality, but rather that in more than 5,000 years of human civilization, not just the last 200, human irrationality has been the common denominator of human behavior. In this country, in our time, we are paralyzed by successful appeals to irrationality. Talk to someone about how an expanding population will someday outgrow the food supply, and the response is likely to be that such a problem will not occur for 500 years! Mention the need to make guns completely unavailable to unauthorized civilians, and you are told that we cannot infringe on the rights of hunters!

It is not some undefined journey to "the heart of reality through personal experience" or some even less definable, mystical trust in "the world itself" that will be our salvation, but rather a determined effort, guided by scientists in many disciplines and supported without reservation by politicians, to begin loosening the grip of human irrationality.

As the population expands and problems of survival increase, and people feel less and less important, less able to influence the events that impinge on their lives, they are more driven to respond irrationally to every perceived challenge. Human behavior has always been an unpredictable mix of thought and impulse, of hope and fear, tenderness and anger.

For the short term at least, we cannot eliminate the stresses that tip the equation toward destructive behavior. Perhaps, by recognizing that human behavior is not identical to immutable human nature, we can alter behavior so as to extend the residence time of human civilization on this earth.

[Herbert L. Meltzer]

To the Editor:

"The End of the Modern Era," Vaclav Havel's New Age maundering, would not be so ominous if he were not in charge of a newly democratized nation, and thus the focus of a certain hopeful expectancy. To Mr. Havel the end of Communism is a "message to the human race" that employing the scientific method and accumulated objective knowledge to help bring about commonly agreed-upon social goals is not the way to go.

Instead, he offers a wan spirituality in which we are led by a new breed of politicians, each with "trust in his own subjectivity as his principal link with the subjectivity of the world."

10 If this is how Mr. Havel views himself we are all in trouble. His call to irrationalism will be of little help against the population explosion, the greenhouse effect, holes in the ozone layer, the dramatically widening gap between the rich north and the poor south, the danger of famine, the depletion of the biosphere and the mineral resources of the planet, and the expansion of com-
15 mercial television culture, all of which he points to as signs that civilization is in danger.

Mr. Havel's embrace of the free market system, which many consider a major contributor to these disasters, can only be justified by a commitment to a scientific attitude in which policies are continually assessed in relation to
20 experience.

Few would begrudge the Czechoslovak people and other Eastern Europeans their newly won freedom to experiment with new social and economic directions. But in their attempts to avoid previous errors of both the communist and capitalist systems, they will not be helped, in our opinion, by the sort of
25 dangerous obscurantism represented by Mr. Havel's words.

[Stuart A. Newman]

[Felipe C. Cabello]

To the Editor:

Vaclav Havel's astute insights into how "the end of communism has brought a major era in human history to an end" also has important ramifications for art.
5 Not only 20th-century thought, but also modernism in art has "come to a final crisis." The first two decades of this century saw the rise of both communism and modernism from 19th-century positivism. Both systems held a deep faith in the future and called for a clean break with the past. Both proposed ideal structures—one for the economy and one for art—that could be applied
10 internationally with little need for local variations.

Both systems showed great early achievements. As lesser minds followed, both spawned true believers, who self-righteously condemned other systems and purged dissenters.

As our century draws to a close, communism has had the more dramat-
15 ic fall, while modernism in art is also crumbling, particularly in architecture, where the cold, inhuman international style is now passé. Nationalism is on the rise, and local and folk traditions are again being fostered, giving hope that in the 21st century modern art from Boise to Brazil will not all look alike.
20 As Mr. Havel points out, "communism was not defeated by military force, but by life, by the human spirit"; so too humanity calls out for a new humanism and less modernism in art.

[Gregory Hedberg]

## Looking Back

1. How would you paraphrase Havel's description of the spirit that has dominated the modern era (see especially lines 1–22)?

2. What distinction does Havel imply separates the communist system and "what life wanted" (line 26)?

3. Can you think of forces other than the ones Havel mentions that defeated communism (see lines 35–38)?

4. Do you agree with Havel that communism alone should be criticized, or with Newman and Cabello that capitalism also is at fault? Explain your answer.

5. In your estimation, is science as helpless to solve the world's problems as Havel indicates (see lines 47–53)? Explain your answer.

6. Can the human qualities Havel enumerates in lines 65–86 be trusted to substitute for a commitment to reason? Explain your answer.

7. Are politicians the wisest choice to lead and model new directions for humanity, as Havel thinks (lines 114–116)? Explain your answer.

8. The first two letters contend that mysticism, irrationality, and subjectivity are all unreliable guides to political action. Are they right or wrong? Explain your answer.

9. Do you agree with Hedberg's implication that the rise of nationalism is a positive outcome? Explain your answer.

10. On balance, who has the more accurate diagnosis and the most promising remedy for the ills of modern civilization, Havel or his critics? Explain your answer.

## Writing Assignments (Linked Readings)

1. Vaclav Havel condemns the human attempt at total control over the social and political environment through the use of "arrogant, absolutist reason" (line 33). Throughout his essay, he describes in abstract terms what he means by this, and what, in his view, have been the consequences. His critics take him to task on a number of grounds. For one, they say his ideas are "incomprehensible" (Meltzer, line 2) and result in "obscurantism" (Newman and Cabello, line 25). These scientists believe that a continued dependence on reason, not a retreat from it, is the answer. Extrapolating from these views in order to discuss the concrete uses of reason, write an essay that starts by saying which position you accept and why. Then apply that view to instances from social and political life.

2. Havel claims that "many of the traditional mechanisms of democracy created and developed and conserved in the modern era are so linked to the cult of objectivity and statistical average that they can annul human individuality" (lines 90–93). One kind of statistical analysis as a means of inquiry and an aid in setting public policy is the public opinion survey. For example, one poll shows a rising rate of discrimination on the job against women workers who become pregnant. Meltzer, Newman, and Cabello would no doubt support such surveys. Would they support a survey of voter opinion about a political candidate's love life? Write an essay

upholding or rejecting the value of surveys of public opinion, particularly addressing the idea of individuality that Havel introduces.

3. Havel and Meltzer agree that human behavior must be altered if we are to live decently and, in Meltzer's words, "extend the residence time of human civilization on this earth" (line 42). But these authors part company over *how* we should change and *what* we should become—a disagreement that is not surprising since they differ so radically about the uses of reason. Write an essay interpolating your own commentary on both authors' prescriptions. Present their views in your own language, but make sure your own ideas on the subject appear as well. You may agree with one side more than the other, or you may want to combine elements from both.

## Writing Assignments (Individual Readings)
### THE END OF THE MODERN ERA

Havel enumerates some of the afflictions of humankind (see lines 39–46) and prescribes the general attitude and behavior changes that he sees as the only antidote (see lines 65–110). He does not, however, draw a clear line between ills and remedies by showing in *concrete* terms how to resolve or diminish such problems. Write an essay that does this on a small scale. Take one of the cited dangers to civilization and attempt, in as much detail as possible, to say how his prescription might reverse it.

## WITH APOLOGIES TO HAVEL, LET REASON RULE

In a paragraph applauding the fall of communism and the decline of modernism in art, Gregory Hedberg mentions that "nationalism is on the rise" (lines 16–17). The context of this remark gives us reason to believe that he considers this a good thing. In fact, however, the current reassertion of nationalistic sentiment in various parts of the world remains extremely controversial as to its value. Write an essay on the subject, saying whether you believe nationalism is on the whole a positive or a negative force. Refer where you can to historical developments, but also try to see the phenomenon as a general political and human force.

# V

## *Moral Action and Spiritual Life*

*Fish live in streams,*
*Birds nest in trees;*
*Human beings dwell*
   *In Warm Hearts.*

Creatures have homes and so do human beings. But, according to this Japanese folk poem, our homes are not simply the physical places in which we dwell. Rather, our true homes, our essential homes, are in the sympathetic recognition we receive and give and the acts that confirm it. That is, either our spiritual life and our moral actions give meaning to the words we say to others, the objects we collect around us, and the things we do; or else our words, possessions, and actions are senseless, no more than what they are: they go nowhere and they have no future.

Spiritual life. Moral action. To define these is to know when we are at home. Unfortunately, although problems of definition are customary, here the best the dictionary can do with the term *spiritual* is to mention the soul and to oppose the spiritual to the physical or material. On the other hand, the term *moral* is apparently so hard and fast that it can be summed up in the dictionary as "right conduct." These definitions are not wrong but unsubtle; they leave too much unsaid. What, after all, is the soul? Where is the nonphysical? We catch sight of the tongue in a speaking mouth, but words go beyond sound to meaning. And meaning, though nonphysical, is not necessarily spiritual, as we realize when someone says, "I wouldn't vote for him in a million years," or "One lottery ticket, please," although the meaning may be spiritual when a person speaks of *mercy* or *remorse* or *forgiveness*.

And as for the definition of morality, surely this passage, from an interview with British philosopher Isaiah Berlin, leaves the dictionary in the dust:

The idea of human rights rests in the true belief that there are certain goods—freedom, justice, pursuit of happiness, honesty, love—that are in the interest of all human beings, as such, not as members of this or that nationality, religion, profession, character, and that it is right to meet these claims and to protect people against those who ignore or deny them. There are certain things which human beings require as such, not because they are Frenchmen, Germans, or medieval scholars, but because they lead human lives as men and women.

Rights, values, universal interest, protection, need—the concept of morality must include all these if we are to understand its true extension and importance.

Furthermore, as Berlin implies, a strong connection exists between the spiritual and the moral that, though not reducible to a formula, somehow ties in the perception of human meaning with the attempt to preserve it for everyone. Love, for example, is a spiritual value. It is not necessarily moral to love, but it is moral to recognize love and to respect its existence. Acting to do so, we refer ourselves both to an external ethics and to our internal conscience. We protect others' vulnerability and help meet their needs, thereby making love possible; that is, we go full circle and reproduce a spiritual value that itself puts the moral into play. When we live within this circle, we live well.

In the texts that follow, the moral and spiritual dimensions of human existence, whether woven into the texture of experience or stated outright, demand our undivided attention, not to mention our active participation. To help you understand these texts, here are some considerations to keep in mind:

1. Spiritual life and moral action are ordinary concerns. They are not reserved for special occasions, nor are they the exclusive domain of churches or other institutions. Therefore, it is necessary to scrutinize texts for definitions of the spiritual and moral that are unofficial, casual, mundane.

2. *Rights, values,* and *needs* figure more often in the vocabulary of certain writers than the words *moral* or *spiritual.* You will often have to make the translation yourself.

3. It is useful to look at our own thoughts and acts as well as those of these writers in order to find a common ground.

# PRIMARY TEXTS

Imagine a group of four people, each of whom is strenuously engaged in some charity work or some useful social or political activities, each from purely altruistic motives. Someone asks them: "Why do you work so hard helping your fellow man?" We get the following responses: The first says, "I regard it as my duty and moral obligation to help my fellow man." The second replies: "Moral obligations? To hell with moral obligations! It's just that I'll be God damned if I will stand around seeing my fellow man oppressed without *my* doing something about it!" The third replies: "I also have never been very much concerned with things like duties or moral obligations. It's just that I feel extremely sorry for these people and long to help them." The fourth says: "*Why* do I act as I do? To tell you the truth, I have absolutely no idea why. It is simply my nature to act as I act, and that's all I can say."

I should like to compare these four responses. The last one delights me utterly! He seems very Taoistic or Zen-like. He is the true Sage or saint who seems completely in harmony with the Tao. He is the one who is completely natural, spontaneous and unself-consciously helpful. If there is a God, I hope he lets him into heaven first! Close at his heels, I hope, would be the third man. He strikes me as sort of Buddhistic—not "moral" but compassionate, though perhaps a little too self-consciously so.

It is of interest to compare the first and second men. Both are being ego-assertive, but what a difference! The second, though somewhat gruff, is really kind of charming and humorous. He strikes me as the "tough man with a heart of gold" (like some of the roles played by Humphrey Bogart). He is really a very sympathetic person who is somehow ashamed to admit the fact and does not wish to appear sentimental. If I were God, I would, of course, let him into heaven too.

But the first man! Good heavens, what a monstrosity! I'm sorry to offend those readers brought up in a puritanical tradition, but I can no more help feeling as I feel than you can. People like the first man are so often pompous, vain, ego-assertive, puritanical, inhuman, self-centered, dominating and unsympathetic. They are the people who act out of "principles." In a way, they are even worse than people who don't help others at all! Now if I were God, I would, of course, let him into heaven too, but not for awhile! I would first send him back to earth for a few years for a little more "discipline."

Some pragmatic readers may well say: "Why this emphasis on how a person phrases it; does it not really all come to the same thing? Isn't the important thing how helpfully a person acts rather than his motives or reasons for doing so?" My answer is "No." I feel that if people's actions are helpful, but engaged in the wrong spirit, they can—in the long run—be as harmful as no helpful actions at all. I guess I have been very influenced by the Chinese proverb: "When the wrong man does the right thing, it usually turns out wrong."

—Raymond M. Smullyan, "Why Do You Help Your Fellow Man?"

The same applies to actions as well as to words: everyone should try to ensure that they contain more usefulness than showmanship, and are more concerned with truth than with display. If genuine love for a young man or for a woman does not seek witnesses, but reaps its harvest of pleasure even if it fulfils its

desire in secret, then it is even more likely that someone who loves goodness
and wisdom, who is intimate and involved with virtue because of his actions,
will be quietly self-assured within himself, and will have no need of an admiring
audience. There was a man who summoned his serving-woman at home and
shouted out, "Look at me, Dionysia: I have stopped being big-headed!" Analogous to this is the behavior of someone who politely does a favour and then
runs around telling everyone about it: it is obvious that he is still dependent on
external appreciation and drawn towards public recognition, that he does not
yet have virtue in his sights and that he is not awake, but is acting randomly
among the illusory shadows of a dream and then presents his action for viewing, as if it were a painting.

It follows that giving something to a friend and doing a favour for an acquaintance, but not telling others about it, is a sign of progress. And voting honestly when surrounded by corruption, rejecting a dishonourable petition from
an affluent or powerful person, spurning bribes and even not drinking when
thirsty at night or resisting a kiss from a good-looking woman or man, as Agesi-
laus did—quietly keeping any of these to oneself is also a sign of progress. A
man like this gains recognition from himself, and he feels not contempt, but
pleasure and contentment at being self-sufficient as a witness, and spectator
too, of his good deeds; this shows that reason is now being nourished within
and is taking root inside him, and that he "is getting used to being his own
source of pleasure," as Democritus puts it.

—Plutarch, from "On Being Aware of Moral Progress"


What *is* the gospel according to Jesus? Simply this: that the love we all long for
in our innermost heart is already present, beyond longing. Most of us can remember a time (it may have been just a moment) when we felt that everything
in the world was exactly as it should be. Or we can think of a joy (it happened
when we were children, perhaps, or the first time we fell in love) so vast that it
was no longer inside us, but we were inside it. What we intuited then, and what
we later thought was too good to be true, isn't an illusion. It is real. It is realer
than the real, more intimate than anything we can see or touch, "unreachable,"
as the Upanishads say, "yet nearer than breath, than heartbeat." The more
deeply we receive it, the more real it becomes.

Like all the great spiritual Masters, Jesus taught one thing only: presence.
Ultimate reality, the luminous, compassionate intelligence of the universe, is
not somewhere else, in some heaven light-years away. It didn't manifest itself
any more fully to Abraham or Moses than to us, nor will it be any more present
to some Messiah at the far end of time. It is always right here, right now. That is
what the Bible means when it says that God's true name is *I am.*

There is such a thing as nostalgia for the future. Both Judaism and Christianity ache with it. It is a vision of the Golden Age, the days of perpetual summer in a world of straw-eating lions and roses without thorns, when human life will be foolproof, and fulfilled in an endlessly prolonged finale of delight. I don't mean to make fun of the messianic vision. In many ways it is admirable, and it has inspired political and religious leaders from Isaiah to Martin Luther King, Jr. But it is a kind of benign insanity. And if we take it seriously enough, if we live it twenty-four hours a day, we will spend all our time working in anticipation, and will never enter the Sabbath of the heart. How moving and at the same time how ridiculous is the story of the Hasidic rabbi who, every morning, as soon as he woke up, would rush out his front door to see if the Messiah had arrived. (Another Hasidic story, about a more mature stage of this consciousness, takes place at the Passover seder. The rabbi tells his chief disciple to go outside and see if the Messiah has come. "But Rabbi, if the Messiah came, wouldn't you know it in here?" the disciple says, pointing to his heart. "Ah," says the rabbi, pointing to his own heart, "but in here, the Messiah has already come.") Who among the now-middle-aged doesn't remember the fervor of the Sixties, when young people believed that love could transform the world? "You may say I'm a dreamer," John Lennon sang, "but I'm not the only one." The messianic dream of the future may be humanity's sweetest dream. But it is a dream nevertheless, as long as there is a separation between inside and outside, as long as we don't transform ourselves. And Jesus, like the Buddha, was a man who had awakened from all dreams.

When Jesus talked about the kingdom of God, he was not prophesying about some easy, danger-free perfection that will someday appear. He was talking about a state of being, a way of living at ease among the joys and sorrows of *our* world. It is possible, he said, to be as simple and beautiful as the birds of the sky or the lilies of the field, who are always within the eternal Now. This state of being is not something alien or mystical. We don't need to earn it. It is already ours. Most of us lose it as we grow up and become self-conscious, but it doesn't disappear forever; it is always there to be reclaimed, though we have to search hard in order to find it. The rich especially have a hard time reentering this state of being; they are so possessed by their possessions, so entrenched in their social power, that it is almost impossible for them to let go. Not that it is easy for any of us. But if we need reminding, we can always sit at the feet of our young children. They, because they haven't yet developed a firm sense of past and future, accept the infinite abundance of the present with all their hearts, in complete trust. Entering the kingdom of God means feeling, as if we were floating in the womb of the universe, that we are being taken care of, always, at every moment.

—Stephen Mitchell, from *The Gospel According to Jesus*

# Linked Readings

Saint Matthew
## THE SERMON ON THE MOUNT

Martin Buber (ed.)
## WALKING THE TIGHT ROPE

Although the date of composition is uncertain, Saint Matthew's gospel was probably written about 70 C.E. Matthew was an apostle and a scholar of Jewish law, whose intention in writing a biography of Jesus was partially to persuade the Jewish community that Jesus was the Messiah. His work has long been considered the best written and most complete of the four gospels. The Sermon on the Mount is thought to be a compilation of Jesus' teachings, here given unity of time and place but probably delivered at different times and in different places. The sermon itself is a crystallization of Christian beliefs, and, like all succinct presentations of complex intellectual matters, is always in need of reinterpretation. The text produced here is Richmond Lattimore's translation. Lattimore, who translated Greek literature as well, was a professor emeritus at Bryn Mawr College at the time of his death in 1984. "Walking the Tight Rope" is from *Tales of the Hasidim,* a collection of stories and parables illustrating religious principles. The Hasidim, who still exist as a group today, are a mystical Jewish sect established in eighteenth-century Poland. They believe in a direct, joyful apprehension of spiritual truths. Martin Buber (1878–1965) fled the Nazis and emigrated to Israel, where he taught until his death. He studied philosophy at the University of Berlin and is best known for his work *I and Thou.* Making different approaches to living virtuously, those texts provide a new context in which to consider particular moral and spiritual problems, thereby setting the stage for original and creative thinking and writing about them.

## THE SERMON ON THE MOUNT

## Looking Ahead

1. The audience we write for or speak to is a crucial factor in our use of language. Our audience guides the tone we employ, the intellectual level of our discourse, our vocabulary, and more. Notice that Jesus addresses "the multitudes" as well as his disciples, and we speculate that each group might understand him differently.

2. Analogies, graphic images, and imaginative figures of speech abound, all requiring interpretation and application.

3. Pure motives, rigid morals, ethical paradox, social reform? Which concept you apply to these teachings will help decide the reception you give them, but best not to be too hasty in deciding.

And seeing the multitudes[1] he went up onto the mountain, and when he was seated, his disciples came to him, and he opened his mouth and taught them, saying:

Blessed are the poor in spirit, because theirs is the Kingdom of Heaven.

Blessed are they who sorrow, because they shall be comforted.

Blessed are the gentle, because they shall inherit the earth.

Blessed are they who are hungry and thirsty for righteousness, because they shall be fed.

Blessed are they who have pity, because they shall be pitied.

Blessed are the pure in heart, because they shall see God.

Blessed are the peacemakers, because they shall be called the sons of God.

Blessed are they who are persecuted for their righteousness, because theirs is the Kingdom of Heaven.

Blessed are you when they shall revile you and persecute you and speak every evil thing of you, lying, because of me. Rejoice and be glad, because your reward in heaven is great; for thus did they persecute the prophets before you.[2]

You are the salt of the earth; but if the salt loses its power, with what shall it be salted? It is good for nothing but to be thrown away and trampled by men. You are the light of the world. A city cannot be hidden when it is set on top of a hill. Nor do men light a lamp and set it under a basket, but they set it on a stand, and it gives its light to all in the house. So let your light shine before men, so that they may see your good works and glorify your father in heaven.

Do not think that I have come to destroy the law and the prophets. I have not come to destroy but to complete. Indeed, I say to you, until the sky and the earth are gone, not one iota or one end of a letter must go from the law, until all is done. He who breaks one of the least of these commandments and teaches men accordingly shall be called the least in the Kingdom of Heaven; he who performs and teaches these commandments shall be called great in the Kingdom of Heaven. For I tell you, if your righteousness is not more abundant than that of the scribes and the Pharisees, you may not enter the Kingdom of Heaven.

You have heard that it was said to the ancients: You shall not murder. He who murders shall be liable to judgment. I say to you that any man who is angry with his brother shall be liable to judgment; and he who says to his brother, fool, shall be liable before the council, and he who says to his brother, sinner, shall be liable to Gehenna.[3] If then you bring your gift to the altar, and there remember that your brother has some grievance against you, leave your gift before the altar, and go first and be reconciled with your brother, and then go and offer your gift. Be quick to be conciliatory with your adversary at law when you are in the street with him, for fear your adversary may turn you over to the

---

1. *the multitudes:* the crowds who, drawn by Jesus' fame and healing powers, gathered wherever he went in Palestine. (*ed.*)

2. This passage is referred to as the Beatitudes, or the blessings. (*ed.*)

3. *Gehenna:* Hebrew for "hell." (*ed.*)

40 judge, and the judge to the officer, and you be thrown into prison. Truly I tell
you, you cannot come out of there until you pay the last penny.

You have heard that it has been said: You shall not commit adultery. I tell
you that any man who looks at a woman so as to desire her has already committed adultery with her in his heart. If your right eye makes you go amiss, take it
45 out and cast it from you; it is better that one part of you should be lost instead of
your whole body being cast into Gehenna. And if your right hand makes you go
amiss, cut it off and cast it from you; it is better that one part of you should be
lost instead of your whole body going to Gehenna. It has been said: If a man
puts away his wife, let him give her a contract of divorce. I tell you that any man
50 who puts away his wife, except for the reason of harlotry, is making her the victim of adultery; and any man who marries a wife who has been divorced is committing adultery.[4] Again, you have heard that it has been said to the ancients:
You shall not swear falsely, but you shall make good your oaths to the Lord. I
tell you not to swear at all: not by heaven, because it is the throne of God; not
55 by the earth, because it is the footstool for his feet; not by Jerusalem, because it
is the city of the great king; not by your own head, because you cannot make
one hair of it white or black. Let your speech be yes yes, no no; more than that
comes from the evil one.

You have heard that it has been said: An eye for an eye and a tooth for a
60 tooth. I tell you not to resist the wicked man; but if one strikes you on the right
cheek, turn the other one to him also; and if a man wishes to go to law with you
and take your tunic, give him your cloak also, and if one makes you his porter
for a mile, go with him for two. Give to him who asks, and do not turn away one
who wishes to borrow from you. You have heard that it has been said: You shall
65 love your neighbor and hate your enemy. I tell you, love your enemies and pray
for those who persecute you, so that you may be sons of your father who is in
heaven, because he makes his sun rise on the evil and the good, and rains on the
just and the unjust. For if you love those who love you, what reward do you
have? Do not even the tax collectors do the same? And if you greet only your
70 brothers, what do you do that is more than others do? Do not even the pagans
do the same? Be perfect as your father in heaven is perfect.

Take care not to practice your righteousness publicly before men so as to be
seen by them; if you do, you shall have no recompense from your father in
heaven. Then when you do charity, do not have a trumpet blown before you, as
75 the hypocrites do in the synagogues and the streets, so that men may think well
of them. Truly I tell you, they have their due reward. But when you do charity,
let your left hand not know what your right hand is doing, so that your charity

---

4. About divorce, two religious scholars have this to say: "Mankind has found it necessary to
disagree with the rigidity of these bans, not only in practice but in principle, for even many religious
people regard divorce as on occasion a fundamental human and spiritual need" (Roy B. Chamberlin
and Herman Feldman, *The Dartmouth Bible*, p. 974). (*ed.*)

may be in secret, and your father, who sees what is secret, will reward you. And
when you pray, you must not be like the hypocrites, who love to stand up in the
synagogues and the corners of the squares to pray, so that they may be seen by      80
men. Truly I tell you, they have their due reward. But when you pray, go into
your inner room and close the door and pray to your father, who is in secret;
and your father, who sees what is secret, will reward you. When you pray, do
not babble as the pagans do; for they think that by saying much they will be
heard. Do not then be like them; for your father knows what you need before       85
you ask him. Pray thus, then: Our father in heaven, may your name be hal-
lowed, may your kingdom come, may your will be done, as in heaven, so upon
earth. Give us today our sufficient bread, and forgive us our debts, as we also
have forgiven our debtors. And do not bring us into temptation, but deliver us
from evil. For if you forgive men their offenses, your heavenly father will forgive   90
you; but if you do not forgive men, neither will your father forgive you your offenses. And when you fast, do not scowl like the hypocrites; for they make ugly
faces so that men can see that they are fasting. Truly I tell you, they have their
due reward. But when you fast, anoint your head and wash your face, so that
you may not show as fasting to men, but to your father, in secret; and your fa-     95
ther, who sees what is secret, will reward you.

Do not store up your treasures on earth, where the moth and rust destroy
them, and where burglars dig through and steal them; but store up your treasures in heaven, where neither moth nor rust destroys them, and where burglars
do not dig through or steal; for where your treasure is, there also will be your      100
heart. The lamp of the body is the eye. Thus if your eye is clear, your whole body
is full of light; but if your eye is soiled, your whole body is dark. If the light in
you is darkness, how dark it is. No man can serve two masters. For either he will
hate the one and love the other, or he will cling to one and despise the other;
you cannot serve God and mammon. Therefore I tell you, do not take thought      105
for your life, what you will eat, or for your body, what you will wear. Is not your
life more than its food and your body more than its clothing? Consider the birds
of the sky, that they do not sow or harvest or collect for their granaries, and your
heavenly father feeds them. Are you not preferred above them? Which of you by
taking thought can add one cubit to his growth? And why do you take thought      110
about clothing? Study the lilies in the field, how they grow. They do not toil or
spin; yet I tell you, not even Solomon in all his glory was clothed like one of
these. But if God so clothes the grass of the field, which grows today and tomorrow is thrown in the oven, will he not much more clothe you, you men of little
faith? Do not then worry and say: What shall we eat? Or: What shall we drink?     115
Or: What shall we wear? For all this the Gentiles study. Your father in heaven
knows that you need all these things. But seek out first his kingdom and his justice, and all these things shall be given to you. Do not then take thought of tomorrow; tomorrow will take care of itself, sufficient to the day is its own evil.

Do not judge, so you may not be judged. You shall be judged by that judgment      120
by which you judge, and your measure will be made by the measure by which

you measure. Why do you look at the straw which is in the eye of your brother, and not see the log which is in your eye? Or how will you say to your brother: Let me take the straw out of your eye, and behold, the log is in your eye. You

125 hypocrite, first take the log out of your eye, and then you will see to take the straw out of the eye of your brother. Do not give what is sacred to the dogs, and do not cast your pearls before swine, lest they trample them under their feet and turn and rend you. Ask, and it shall be given you; seek, and you shall find; knock, and the door will be opened for you. Everyone who asks receives, and

130 he who seeks finds, and for him who knocks the door will be opened. Or what man is there among you, whose son shall ask him for bread, that will give him a stone? Or ask him for fish, that will give him a snake? If then you, who are corrupt, know how to give good gifts to your children, by how much more your father who is in heaven will give good things to those who ask him. Whatever you

135 wish men to do to you, so do to them. For this is the law and the prophets.

Go in through the narrow gate, because wide and spacious is the road that leads to destruction, and there are many who go in through it; because narrow is the gate and cramped the road that leads to life, and few are they who find it. Beware of the false prophets, who come to you in sheep's clothing, but inside

140 they are ravening wolves. From their fruits you will know them. Do men gather grapes from thorns or figs from thistles? Thus every good tree produces good fruits, but the rotten tree produces bad fruits. A good tree cannot bear bad fruits, and a rotten tree cannot bear good fruits. Every tree that does not produce good fruit is cut out and thrown in the fire. So from their fruits you will

145 know them. Not everyone who says to me Lord Lord will come into the Kingdom of Heaven, but he who does the will of my father in heaven. Many will say to me on that day: Lord, Lord, did we not prophesy in your name, and in your name did we not cast out demons, and in your name did we not assume great powers? And then I shall admit to them: I never knew you. Go from me, for you

150 do what is against the law.

Every man who hears what I say and does what I say shall be like the prudent man who built his house upon the rock. And the rain fell and the rivers came and the winds blew and dashed against that house, and it did not fall, for it was founded upon the rock. And every man who hears what I say and does

155 not do what I say will be like the reckless man who built his house on the sand. And the rain fell and the rivers came and the winds blew and battered that house, and it fell, and that was a great fall.

And it happened that when Jesus had ended these words, the multitudes were astonished at his teaching, for he taught them as one who has authority,

160 and not like their own scribes.

# WALKING THE TIGHT ROPE

## Looking Ahead

1. Rabbi Israel's modesty and unassuming nature are keys to understanding the particular nature of some Jewish teaching.
2. Parables like this one produce equations between actual and constructed experience: you need to travel back and forth between the two.
3. Read critically to test the reliability of the uncertain, even experimental, sense of a spiritual life and morality given here as opposed to a definitive prescription.

Once the hasidim were seated together in all brotherliness, when Rabbi Israel joined them, his pipe in his hand. Because he was so friendly, they asked him: "Tell us, dear rabbi, how should we serve God?" He was surprised at the question and replied: "How should I know!" But then he went right on talking and told them this story:

There were two friends, and both were accused before the king of a crime. Since he loved them he wanted to show them mercy. He could not acquit them because even the king's word cannot prevail over a law. So he gave this verdict: A rope was to be stretched across a deep chasm and the two accused were to walk it, one after the other; whoever reached the other side was to be granted his life. It was done as the king ordered, and the first of the friends got safely across. The other, still standing in the same spot, cried to him: "Tell me, my friend, how did you manage to cross that terrible chasm?" The first called back: "I don't know anything but this: whenever I felt myself toppling over to one side, I leaned to the other."

5

10

15

## Looking Back

1. Judging from the Beatitudes (lines 1–16), what status in society did Jesus' hearers have?
2. What particular powers does Jesus refer to in his comparison of his followers to salt (lines 17–18)?
3. Remembering that Jesus was born a Jew, can you say what relation to Judaism he claims (lines 23–30)?
4. In the Hasidic tale, how does the friend's advice answer the question, "How should we serve God?"
5. Can you paraphrase Jesus' instruction, "Let your speech be yes yes, no no" (line 57)?
6. How does the admonition to "be perfect as your father in heaven is perfect" strike you (lines 70–71)? How does it compare with the advice the first friend gives about walking the tight rope (lines 14–15)?
7. In what way can seeking public acclaim for good deeds, acquiring possessions, and valuing creature comforts become spiritual problems (see lines 72–119)?

8. What lesson do you learn in lines 120–135 of the sermon? Explain your answer.

9. In terms of the spiritual life of human beings, how would you compare Buber's title and Lattimore's rendering: "Go in through the narrow gate" (line 136)?

10. What do you think of spiritual advice we receive from other people? Should we consider it seriously, or are we our own best teachers?

## Writing Assignments (Linked Readings)

1. "Tell us, dear rabbi, how should we serve God?" Rabbi Israel's disciples ask. This question, which he answers with a parable, also lies behind Jesus' longer sermon. The existence of God is taken for granted, a fact which holds particular interest in our later age, when belief in God is far from universal and individuals are more apt to decide the matter for themselves. Many people, in order to make such a decision, ask themselves why they should believe in a deity, what purpose doing so serves, and what evidence if any exists to support belief. Write an essay discussing these questions. Although you should not avoid personal opinion, your discussion will be fuller if you include the views of others to some extent.

2. Saint Matthew quotes Jesus directing his followers to "be perfect as your father in heaven is perfect" (line 71). Rabbi Israel, on the other hand, suggests meeting each new situation in life with the intent to keep or restore a moral and spiritual balance. Trying to think as critically as possible—that is, not simply urging on others, without analysis, what you may have been taught—write an essay that compares and evaluates these two prescriptions for action. To be as concrete as possible, consider using contemporary situations from your own experience or observations to which Israel's or Jesus' directives could be applied.

3. Both Jesus and Rabbi Israel teach that human character can be measured by its quotient of good and evil, and both Christianity and Judaism, as well as other religions, agree that the virtuous life is best. Assuming that this is so, select one of the virtues or sins discussed by Jesus and write an essay trying to define it, explaining how it affects people. You might attempt to discuss its implications for humanity at large. Be sure to report Jesus' view of the virtue or sin you choose, and consider whether his or the tight rope walker's approach is better and why.

## Writing Assignments (Individual Readings)

### THE SERMON ON THE MOUNT

As number 7 in Looking Back puts it, "seeking public acclaim for good deeds, acquiring possessions, and valuing creature comforts" are "spiritual problems," according to Jesus. Yet it seems we cannot help pursuing these aims to some degree, even though they may hurt the soul. Furthermore, in American society, these aims are regarded quite favorably. We may in fact ask if the value placed on them is really at the expense of spiritual life, or if we must update the sermon to accommodate worldly life. Can that be done, or is there an inevitable conflict of interest that we avoid addressing at our peril? Write an essay discussing the issue these questions raise, referring to the sermon and to relevant aspects of contemporary life.

## WALKING THE TIGHT ROPE

The spiritual leader or teacher is an ancient tradition in most religions. Priests, rabbis, immans—all are roles played by individuals who intervene between the people and God and interpret the Law in a satisfactory manner. Some, however, think that access to spiritual life and law requires no intercessor and that individuals themselves can go directly to the source. Which position do you think holds up better, particularly in light of this story and given the particular kind of teaching and the personal qualities of Rabbi Israel? Write an essay answering this question.

# Agnes Martin
# What We Do Not See If We Do Not See

Born in Saskatchewan, Canada, in 1912, painter Agnes Martin lived in New York City until 1967. After losing her subsidized apartment in Coenties Slip, an artistic community, she moved to New Mexico, where she now lives and paints in the town of Galisteo. Like her painting, which Martin describes as having "neither object nor space nor line," her writing is unencumbered by difficult concepts or complex reasoning. She addresses the reader directly and forthrightly, and readers meet her on her own ground, there to embrace or dissent from her views. This piece was originally given as a lecture in 1979 at Hunter College in New York City. It appears in *Writings/Schriften*, a bilingual book published to accompany a show of her work in Winterthur, Switzerland, in 1992. Partially disguised by the passion Martin displays in this text, her critical thinking nonetheless emerges when she exhorts readers to question received ideas. ("We feel that we should not live in the same way as our ancestors lived. We feel that we should take a step forward.")

## *Looking Ahead*

1. Martin uses the verb *see* in two ways in her title, which is a clue to understanding what follows.

2. You may balk at some of Martin's points—one, because she challenges "common sense," and two, because she is so assertive and convinced of being right. Be patient, let her language take over, and then judge.

3. The "conscious mind" is a constant theme in this piece. You should try to construct what she means by it and read critically to test the reliability of the conscious mind as a source of ideas.

> We all believe in life.
> We feel a certain devotion.
> We feel called upon to live as good a life as we can.
> We feel that we are in the dark and that even in darkness we must struggle to know what is best to do.
> Not altogether but each one every moment.
> We feel that we should not live in just the same way as our ancestors lived. We feel that we should take a step forward.

5

We know that this step will be in the dark and will require
courage.
Our tremendous urge forward has a grip of steel.
Because we are in the dark there is suffering and difficulty.

Life is an adventure and adventures are difficult.
They are hard work and one does not know how they will go on
or how they will end.
Nevertheless we have a tremendous appetite for the adventure
of life.
We are continually restless if we are not moving forward
according to our potential.
Although we are in the dark we are not without guidance.
Our guidance is called inspiration.
In crisis we say to ourselves: "What can I do", and miraculously
our mind answers and tells us what to do.
This miraculous answer is called an idea very often but it is not
an idea.

There are different parts of the mind.
When we are angry one part of the mind stands as though
outside and we see ourselves raving.
This part that stands as the outside of ourselves is *the conscious
mind.*
The conscious mind that is aware of perfection, happiness and
the sublime.
When we see ourselves with the conscious mind angry and
perhaps raving we feel guilty.
We recognize that we are off the path—We are off the path of
true life.
The conscious mind says *Yes* and *No.*
When it says: "Yes, go ahead, this is the way", we feel happy.
When it says: "You should not be here and you should not be
doing this". At those times we feel unhappy.
Our problem is not that we do not see or hear the conscious
mind but that we do not obey.
When we see ourselves angry and the conscious mind is saying
"No" we still go on.
And when it says: "You should not go" we rationalize and say:
"Everyone else is going".
We knowingly disobey the conscious mind.

In this life we are struggling from death into life.
This has been remarked by all sages of all times.
The adventure of life is the relinquishing of death and the
acceptance of life.
In the lives that we lead there is both life and death.
The conscious mind is life and happiness and all things sublime.

Death is all things anti-life and truth.
The most dangerous anti-life and destructive tendency is self
deception known as fantasy. Imagining that we are other than
we are.
The opposite of fantasy, *true knowledge of self,* is the greatest
wisdom.

55

The conscious mind is awareness of the sublime and it tells us
what to do by showing us when we are off the track.
Obedience to the conscious mind carries us forward to greater
awareness.
Disobedience of the conscious mind carries us backward to less
awareness.
With more accurate obedience we become rapidly more aware
of the sublime: of beauty and happiness in life.
We become more devoted to life.
With disobedience we become less and less aware with less
respect for life.

60

65

70

This is the side of death in the adventure of life versus death. We
will be disrespectful of life and everything in it, even of ourselves. We will be complaining and destructive and we will have
resistance to living our own life.
Other peoples lives will look better to us than our own life, more
interesting and more rewarding.
This is a very unnatural state of mind. If you have this state of
mind you must recognize at once that you are very far off the
track of life and happiness.
To correct this state of mind you must say to yourself: "*I want
to live a true life.*"
That is all you have to do to turn from death to life.
Asking for life and truth you will be on the side of life and
against death.
I will not speak any more of death because it does not count.
Reality is positive.
Art work is a celebration of reality of the positive.
A positive response to life (which we call happiness) is not a
single response. It is infinitely various and goes far beyond what
we are able to bear.
We cannot reproduce reality or represent it concretely. It is
ineffable.
In art work we represent our own happiness because of our
awareness of the infinite sublimity of reality.
Without awareness of beauty, innocence and happiness and
without happiness oneself one cannot make works of art.
Criticism and discontent expressed concretely are complaint and
destructiveness. All negative expression is anti-life and anti-art.

75

80

85

90

95

Besides recognition of the sublime there are two other elements
in life that must be recognized and lived.
They are *self knowledge* and *potential.*
If you have enough respect for yourself you will ask yourself:
"*What am I.*"
If the answer is "I am a man" then the question becomes: "*What
is a man.*"
When you come to the end of all ideas you will still have no
definitive knowledge on the subject. Then you will have to wait
for inspiration.
Until you can clear up your true identity you will be tied to a
repetition of this life.
I have come to tell you the easiest way to find an answer to this
question.
First you must say to yourself: "I want to live a true life." Then
you must watch your mind to see the response that it is making
to life.
You will discover the true response that you yourself make to
life undistorted by the ideas of others.
You will make discoveries every day and they will all be very
helpful.
Just as consciousness of the sublime is the path of life so is self
knowledge the path of life.
Neither consciousness nor self knowledge can be pursued
socially.
In groups we can compare our observations of life but life itself
is lived by individuals.
Changes in social living are the result of changes that take place
in individuals.
First some truth must be recognized by an individual (that is
what we call inspiration) and then it must be expressed concretely and responded to by others.
The cause of these changes is not with us but is a result of the
battle of life and death.
It is not just big inspirations that move life forward.
Every time an individual asks his mind what to do and receives
direction and acts upon it life moves forward.
Since we almost all live in this way life moves forward very
rapidly even though we have some tremendous setbacks.
It is up to us only in that our pursuit of awareness is on the side
of life.
As life is recognized death is overcome.
The only triumph in life is the triumph of life itself.
Our awareness of it we feel as happiness.
Art work represents this happiness.
It does not represent life because life is infinite, dimensionless. It
is consciousness of itself. And that cannot be represented.

But our positive response to life can be, has been, and is
represented in art work.

And now we come to the last element to be considered, our
individual potential.
We, each of us feels that our life is not like anyone else's life and          150
that is absolutely true, infinitely true.
To live an absolutely original life one has only to be oneself.
In nature there is no sameness anywhere. There are no two rocks
alike, no days alike, no moments alike even forever.
And no two people alike or any moment of their lives.          155
It follows from this that we cannot help one another since our
responses are not alike.
Since we are not alike the experience of others is of no use to us.
This is particularly obvious when we wish to know what to do.
We are all born with a certain potential. It is different from that          160
of anyone else and it is necessary to life.
We must unfold our potential as a contribution to life.
We are born to do certain things and we are born to fill a certain
need.
If there is a bare spot on the ground the best possible weed for          165
that environment will grow.
In the same way our lives are created out of necessity and we are
created with the potential to meet the necessity.
The resistance to function, that is our resistance to the unfolding
of our potential is due to the strength of the negative in life.          170
We are born as verbs rather than nouns.
We are born to function in life, to work and do all positive
actions that will carry out our potential.
When our potential is fully expended we will not be back. Our
concrete existence will come to an end.          175
Our ideas—deductions made from observed facts of life, are of
no use in the unfolding of potential.
Only obedience to the conscious mind counts. That is like saying
only inspiration counts.
Inspiration is a command. While you have a choice that is not          180
inspiration.
If a decision is required that is not inspiration and you should
not do anything by decision. It is simply a waste of time.
Things done by decision even if it is a summit decision are in-
effective and they will be undone.          185
Only actions carried out in obedience to inspiration are effective.

When we first begin art work we usually have a lot of ideas that
we have to try. But nothing that we do really satisfies us.
Finally we are absolutely defeated. We do not know what to do.

190     I want to try to explain to you that defeat is the beginning, not the end of all positive action.

A baby learning to walk knows that if he stands on his feet he will fall. He knows that he cannot walk. He is defeated and helpless.

195     This knowledge is an absolute prerequisite to inspiration. Defeated and helpless he receives the inspiration to get to his feet.

He is now defeated and helpless with regard to taking a step but again he is commanded forward.

200     At every moment we are helpless and defeated and at every moment we are commanded forward by inspiration.

There is no choice while we are on the true path.

Our inspirations come as a surprise to us.

Following them our lives are fresh and unpredictable.

205     But if in disobedience we imitate the lives of others or follow concepts or precepts our lives will be dull and unsatisfying and predictable.

The unfolding of potential in obedience to inspiration is happiness in this life. An arduous happiness in which we move

210     forward.

Disobedience is unhappiness and moving toward unconsciousness.

Happiness is self sought. It is life.

You can only bring happiness to others by being happy yourself.

215     You can only be happy by being on the path of your unfolding potential.

The path will be revealed to you by a request to your own mind.

If your mind is concerned with the political, with policies and

220     methods, with causes and reforms your work will not be in the art field.

The Greeks made a great discovery. They discovered that in Nature there are no perfect circles or straight lines or equal spaces.

225     Yet they discovered that their interest and inclination was in the perfection of circles and lines, and that in their minds they could see them and that they were then able to make them.

They realized that the mind knows what the eye has not seen but that what the mind knows is perfection.

230     They determined that with the help of the conscious mind to attain to perfection.

Because the Greeks sought the guidance of their conscious mind their work is very inspiring to us. Because they were inspired we are inspired by their work.

235     Work that is guided by the conscious mind is immediately responded to by others.

It is very easy to see how Greek art has been a very for-life-
against-death action.

Today we realize that perfection is out of reach for us because
we ourselves are a part of Nature but it is still our greatest
interest.                                                                240

What we see now is that the path pointed out to us by the
Greeks, the path guided by the conscious mind, is the path of life
and happiness and accomplishment in this world.

To discover the conscious mind in a world where intellect is held          245
to be valuable requires solitude—quite a lot of solitude.

We have been very strenuously conditioned against solitude. To
be alone is considered to be a grievous and dangerous condition.

So I beg you to recall in detail any times when you were alone
and discover your exact response at those times.                           250

I suggest to artists that you take every opportunity of being
alone, that you give up having pets and unnecessary
companions.

You will find the fear that we have been taught is not just one
fear but many different fears.                                             255

When you discover what they are they will be overcome.

Most people have never been alone enough to feel these fears.

But even without the experience of them they dread them.

I suggest that people who like to be alone, who walk alone will
perhaps be serious workers in the art field.                               260


All effective work in any field is dominated by the inspiration of
individuals. All other work is evanescent.

Inspiration is never destructive.

This has been pointed out most effectively by Gandhi and after
him by Martin Luther King.[1]                                              265

It never points to what someone else should do. It tells the
individual what he must do.

All of your inspirations will be related to your particular
potential.

Thus Martin Luther King suggested to the colored people that               270
they must not try to change the white people but must change
themselves. Not by policy or method but each one must change
himself.[2]

And I suggest to you that this way is not just for emergencies but
is the way of life.                                                        275

---

1. *Mohandas Gandhi* (1869–1948): Indian spiritual and political leader—assassinated; Martin
Luther King, Jr. (1929–1968): African American political leader—assassinated. (*ed.*)

2. The reference to "colored people" as late as 1979, when Martin delivered this lecture,
demonstrates the kind of political innocence that also accounts for the author's opinions about
King's aims. (*ed.*)

The individual by himself must move forward by inspiration in order to live. Not by help from others or with knowledge from the past. Real life is lived by Self Discovery.

In the night inspiration falls on the world like rain and pene-
280 trates our minds when we are asleep.

It is because of this that we are so eager, so desperate for sleep. It penetrates all clear minds.

People with such minds wake up eager to carry out the com-mands of inspiration.
285 They feel energetic, enthusiastic and are happy at the prospect of life.

They also feel contentment and spontaneous gratitude and are filled with the spirit of adventure.

If you think all night or if you are drugged inspiration cannot
290 penetrate. Then with reluctance you will be forced to live a life of habit.

If during the day you can keep from intellectualizing your life and keep from dreams you will double your possibility of being inspired. You will then move forward very quickly.
295 It is commonly believed that accomplishment follows dreams. Nothing could be further from the truth. Those who dream dream and those who can act are active.

The pretence of children is not a dream. They are playing and they know it.
300 Children make a perfect response to life. They see everything as beautiful and perfect, often telling their parents how beautiful and wonderful they are.

Children always love their parents with perfect love regardless of what the parents are like. They have to learn to bear
305 frustration which makes them seem unhappy at times.

Living without sufficient inspiration which is the incentive to life we tend to forget the perfect response we made as children and we become more and more blind.

It is necessary to make an absolute *about face* and search out
310 our true response.

You will be thinking: "It is easy enough for children because they have no responsibilities", but I assure you that you also can make a perfect response to life without worry or strain.

You have to see what you have to do in your mind's eye.
315 You have to give it time.

It is hard for your mind to get through to you because of the jumble it is in.

With seeing the direction the energy necessary to carry out the action is given. When it is carried out the energy is taken away
320 so that you can rest.

If you feel tired it is because you cannot see.

If you cannot see the next step you will take and the happiness you will know taking it. Then you cannot see.

If you cannot see you must withdraw yourself till you see what
your next action will be.
In confusion and blindness there is no help for you anywhere
except from your own mind.
From your own mind there is all the help you need.

325

## Looking Back

1. What can we surmise about Martin from her repeated use of *we* and *our* in her assertions?

2. How does she define "the conscious mind" and describe its functions?

3. Can you explain what Martin means by having a "true identity" (line 109)?

4. How do you interpret her statement, "Changes in social living are the result of changes that take place in individuals" (lines 126–127, and see also lines 266–273)? Do you agree?

5. How does Martin conceive of art work and the art worker (see lines 87–98, 143–147, 219–223, and 259–260)?

6. Is Martin convincing when she claims, "Since we are not alike the experience of others is of no use to us" (line 158)? Explain your answer.

7. According to Martin, what is the purpose of our lives (see lines 160–175)?

8. What distinguishes "a decision" from "inspiration" (see lines 180–185)?

9. What connection does Martin draw between perfection and solitude (see lines 221–260)?

10. How is your mind supposed to answer the needs of your self, according to Martin (see lines 314–328)?

## Writing Assignments

1. Agnes Martin describes the purpose of human life in no uncertain terms (see lines 160–175 and number 7 in Looking Back). Her view implies the high-order (very significant) concepts of uniqueness, destiny, necessity, and fate, all of which are summed up in her poetic claim, "We are born as verbs rather than nouns" (line 171). What does she mean by this grammatical simile? How does your own sense of human existence and purpose compare to hers? Write an essay that answers these questions by interpreting her points and expressing your own ideas on what it is to be human.

2. Martin is opposed to political activism. She believes that reforms in social relations, laws, and institutions result not from one group's trying to change another group, but from each person in every group changing himself or herself. She particularly applies this reasoning to race relations in the United States (see lines 126–127, 270–273, and number 4 in Looking Back). Write an essay examining her view when it comes to the situation of racism.

3. Connected to Martin's general ideas about purpose and change in life is her view on individualism. She contends, "Since we are not alike the experience of others is of no use to us" (line 158; and see number 6 in Looking Back). If she is right, it follows that we must carve out our own existence with little regard for what we might learn from others. If she is wrong, it means that we share a common condition with others and our lives can develop together. Write an essay weighing the reasonableness of her position and predicting the personal and social consequences of either or both situations.

# Helmuth James von Moltke
## Letters to Freya

Helmuth James von Moltke (1907–1945) was of German and English descent. On one side, his forebears were aristocrats and military officers; on the other, intellectuals and government officials. He himself was a lawyer, trained in both London and Berlin, and as the scion of a rich family, was the owner of a thousand-acre estate called Kreisau. This privileged background is important to keep in mind, for despite the protection it afforded him, he sacrificed his life in the anti-Nazi cause in Germany. Before World War II began, he actively helped Jews escape the Third Reich and later became a member of the Abwehr (German intelligence) to be in a position to continue such efforts. Arrested for suspected opposition to the government, he was imprisoned for a year and then executed. Throughout his military service and during his last year of life, he wrote to his wife Freya, who added the introductory remarks included here when his letters from prison were published.

## Looking Ahead

1. Note the poise and distinction of Moltke's prose. Read critically to see how these qualities contribute to the lucidity of his thinking in the face of death.

2. Freya von Moltke capitalizes the phrase "Year in Prison" (line 1) although it is not a title or proper name. Her doing so communicates the sense, which we may share, of the sacredness of her husband's mission.

3. Moltke's Christian faith reveals the depth of his convictions and his actions but is not, you should note, the sole motive for them, for his humanness seems to go beyond any specific set of beliefs.

*About the Year in Prison—January 19, 1944, to January 23, 1945—Freya von Moltke wrote the following account in August 1989:*
On 19 January 1944 Helmuth was arrested. He had warned a colleague, Otto Kiep, that he and a group of other persons would soon be imprisoned for having criticized the Nazi regime at a tea party in the presence of an agent provocateur. They were arrested soon afterwards. When the Gestapo learnt of the warning, they also arrested Helmuth, intent on finding out who had in turn warned

him. This was established without Helmuth, but they kept him in jail anyway. He was suspect as a person, and his base of work in the Oberkommando der Wehrmacht was also suspect. He was held in what was called "protective custody" in a prison which was part of the concentration camp Ravensbrück near Fürstenberg, about a hundred miles north of Berlin. The prison was built for the   10
inmates of the camp. Since it lay outside the radius of the Allies' bombing of Berlin, it served the SD[1] for political prisoners as well.

"Protective custody" allowed certain privileges. Helmuth wore his own clothes.—He continued to work for his office.—He could write to me twice a week, and he received letters from me. Those letters were censored, of course.—   15
I was allowed to visit him once a month. It took me about a day's travelling via Berlin from Kreisau.—I could bring additional food. Especially tea and coffee, great rarities in Germany at that time, were very helpful to him in many ways. We met about twenty miles away from Ravensbrück at a police training school, in a place called Drögen, where Helmuth was taken from Ravensbrück by car,   20
and where all interrogations of political prisoners also took place.

We met in the office room in a barrack. There was a bench and a table in one of the corners. The guard was sitting at his desk near the window, busy with his work. We could speak to each other quite freely. I brought a big ledger with me from the farm, pretending to talk business with Helmuth, and we did   25
to some extent. But we were also able to fit in unsupervised exchanges. The guards knew me after some time, also through my letters, which they obviously enjoyed reading. One of them once said how sorry he felt that I had had such bad luck with my geese. When I told Helmuth this, laughing and saying that they were really quite nice men, he said dryly, "Except that they pull out finger-   30
nails when they interrogate."

Then, on 20 July 1944, Claus von Stauffenberg attempted to kill Hitler. The attempt failed, along with the planned coup d'état. It had, however, exposed many conspirators, and hundreds of arrests followed. Through endless and cruel interrogations of the other prisoners, the SD had established by mid-   35
August that Helmuth had been closely associated with the conspirators for a long time. He lost his privileges and was interrogated as well, but not tortured.

I did not receive letters any more. I had visited Helmuth once more after the attempted coup; the situation was bad: we agreed on a code, and in one of his last letters Helmuth informed me that he was in grave danger. When, on 29   40
September 1944, I went from Kreisau to the police school, without a visiting permit, to try to obtain news and, maybe, get through to him, I was told that he had been transferred to Berlin the previous day to appear before the ominous judge Freisler and what was called the "People's Court." I found him at Tegel prison.
                                                                            45
This was the prison in Berlin where our friend Harald Poelchau happened to be prison chaplain. He belonged to our group, and had taken part in the

---

1. *SD:* the SS intelligence agency. (*ed.*)

group's first bigger meeting at Kreisau (Whitsun 1942). Throughout the Nazi
years he stood by countless political prisoners in his sober, unemotional, fear-
50 less way, yet feeling deeply. He accompanied Germans and prisoners from other
nations right to their execution. At that moment there was not even a glimmer
of hope. And there came this chance of close and immediate contact. What
luck! Of the many Berlin prisons, just that one! Poelchau had immediately
turned to assisting his own friends. Prison walls tend to be more transparent
55 than one would expect. They can be pierced at times; we found that out. For
just under four months Poelchau carried our letters in and out, almost daily,
and became very close to Helmuth. Because of the great number of cases before
the People's Court, it took this long before the case of Helmuth and those tried
with him came up. . . .

*[Helmuth von Moltke]*        *Tegel, 28 December 1944*

60     . . . A remarkable year is drawing to a close for me. I spent it predominantly
among people who were being prepared for a violent death and many of them
have suffered it meanwhile: Kiep, Frl. von Thadden,[2] Langbehn, Hassell, Peter,[3]
Schwerin, Schulenburg, Popitz, Maass, Leuschner, Wirmer, and certainly 10 or
11 concentration camp prisoners. With all these people I lived in the same
65 house, took part in their fate, listened when they were taken away for interrogations, or when they were removed altogether, talked with almost all of them
about their affairs, and saw how they coped with it all. And I think that here, at
Tegel, already about 10 of my group have been executed. Thus death has become a companion of the entire year. And if at first I got enormously excited
70 when "Emil" was asked to come for a "walk round the camp," these violent
killings simply became such an everyday matter that I accepted the disappearance of individual men sadly but as a natural event. And now, I tell myself, it is
my turn. Can I also accept it as a natural event in my own case? That's the frame
of mind in which I arrived here; in fact I thought the detour via the People's
75 Court just a nuisance, and if anyone had told me that death sentences could be
simply ordered after an application by the accused and carried out at once, I
would have applied for it at the end of September. That's how caught up I was
in the atmosphere that one must not make a *fuss*[4] about dying by execution.
And where am I now the landscape is unrecognisable. Now I definitely don't
80 want to die, there's no doubt about that. The constant work on arguments
aimed at avoiding it has been a mighty stimulus to my will to get round this
thing. When I think of the many steps, none of them earth-shaking, each one of

---

2. Elisabeth von Thadden (1890–1944), founder and head of a Protestant boarding school,
1929–41; after her dismissal on political grounds in 1941, active as a nurse, until her arrest as a result of a tea party she gave that was attended by a Gestapo spy.

3. Yorck.

4. English in the original.

which seen in retrospect only served the clarification of the arguments, I must say that after the event they prove to have a significant connection and have now produced a respectable defence. (I wonder what Hercher[5] will say about the new version.) All this is a miracle, but it doesn't mean that we can draw any conclusion about the future from it; I am far from doing that, apart from a few hours of weakness. But the accused who was psychologically prepared for non-defence and devoid of any exonerating arguments has turned into a man determined to do everything that can serve his defence and who has a defence worth discussing, which in any case has given him enough inner security that he does not hesitate to write quite impudent letters to H.H.[6]

So the year I spent in the immediate and quite familiar proximity of death ends in a will to resist which is much more determined than it was on 19 January or rather on the 24th of January.—And yet I must be gladly ready to die at any moment, I must maintain this feeling of readiness for it and accept it without any resistance against God, if he orders it. After this time of preparation I must not suddenly be surprised by it, even if it should come by a simple brazen bomb. That is why the admonition to "watch and pray" is so necessary, and yet I keep sinking into sleep when I see that there is still a week's or two week's time until the trial. It is really impossible, even for someone who spends as much time on it as I do, to feel the immediate presence of death every moment. Flesh and blood rebel against it wildly.

Now I sometimes think—a thing I haven't done for months—how everything would be if I stayed alive, and I wonder if I would forget it all again or if from this time one keeps a real relationship to death and thus to eternity. I come to the conclusion that in that case flesh and blood would stake all on repressing the insight again and that a constant battle would be needed to save the fruits of this time. We just are a miserable race, there's no doubt about it, only mostly we don't know how miserable we are. Now I know why Paul and Isaiah, Jeremiah and David and Solomon, Moses and the evangelists will never be obsolete: they were not so miserable; they had a stature unattainable by us, unattainable even by men like Goethe, even like Luther. What those men experienced and learnt we'll never understand entirely. One only asks oneself whether in those times such men existed in greater numbers. One has to assume that only a fraction of what existed has been handed down. But how was it possible for such men to exist then? They are like a different human species. And why among the Jews? And why today not among the Jews any more either? . . .

*Freya von Moltke:*

The letters from Tegel still exist, his and mine; and they belong together. At first Helmuth wrote them in handcuffs. They have as much to do with his death as

---

5. His defence lawyer.

6. Heinrich Himmler.

they have with my further life. They fitted me out for it, and our story still continues. The letters are personal, and I wish to keep them personal. At least as long as I live. When we wrote them, we found that we had almost four months in which to take leave of one another, two people, a man and a woman. The
125 summit of our lives—the hardest time of our lives.

After Helmuth's transfer to Berlin, we first expected that we had very few days left. We had no reason to doubt that he would be condemned to death, and at that time death sentences were mostly carried out on the day of the trial. Then we found we had more time. How much? We never knew for sure. Would
130 the case come up in November, before Christmas? Did we have time into the new year?

The days after the transfer from Ravensbrück, Helmuth was ready to die, ready to pay the price. We always knew this might be demanded. He was then completely free and at peace. As the days went by and more details of other
135 cases got known and the world outside changed, we began to hope again. Two of Helmuth's close friends were also in Tegel prison: Father Delp and Eugen Gerstenmaier. There was enough communication among them for Helmuth to know that they both believed they would survive. (Eugen Gerstenmaier did; Father Delp did not.) Was there a chance for a defence after all? How should it be
140 set up? New tensions arose. Hoping again, Helmuth lost that special peace and freedom; from prison he started to work on a possible defence. Countless steps had to be taken outside, which he suggested and which I carried out. Most of the time during those months, I was in Berlin always on the go or writing to Helmuth. I stayed with Helmuth's cousin Carl Dietrich von Trotha or with the
145 Poelchaus. Dorothee, Poelchau's wife, was just as brave as her husband—I was after all a person to be avoided. Other defendants still alive in other prisons, Helmuth's political friends, had to be informed of his line of defence, and theirs had to be integrated with his. None of those political prisoners were allowed lawyers except a very few days before the trial. And they were chosen and as-
150 signed from lawyers acceptable to the Nazi court.

Helmuth placed hope in an interview with Himmler's deputy, SS General Heinrich Müller. I went to the headquarters of the Gestapo in the Prinz-Albrecht-Strasse and arranged the interview with Müller. It felt like walking into the lion's mouth. He promised to see Helmuth, but left no doubt in my mind
155 that they were after his life. After the First World War, he said, "their" opponents survived and took over. They would see to it that this would not be possible this time. He was polite to me, even friendly, as if trying to separate me from Helmuth. No way!—I made that clear to him. Helmuth had his interview, but it was to no avail.

160 Freisler, the judge, also received me. He talked to me about the never-failing justice of the court. I saw members and employees of the court and the prosecution for different reasons, and asked for permission to visit Helmuth in prison. Four times I met him in prison. For some week-ends I went home to Kreisau to fetch food and get news of the children and the farm, where Hel-

muth's sister, Asta, was holding the fort. All this is discussed and reported in the      165
letters.

But there is more. There is also the struggle of Helmuth, ready to die and
yet hoping for life. There is my holding him yet having to let him go. The tension over so many months became at times unbearable, but we were grateful for
every day we had. For Helmuth there were days of deep depression, but he      170
overcame them every time. He became stronger, not weaker. We had always realized that it made sense to risk his life against the evil of the Nazis. We now became willing for him to die as well as to live. In all this we were supported by
our faith, faith that came and went like the ebb and flow of the tide. What lay
ahead of us was being decided neither by us nor by Freisler and his lot      175
alone. . . .

[*Helmuth von Moltke*]      *Tegel, 10 January 1945*

My dear heart, first I must say that quite obviously the last 24 hours of a life are
in no way different from any others. I always imagined that one would only feel
shock, that one would say to oneself: Now the sun sets for the last time for you,
now the clock only goes to 12 twice more, now you go to bed for the last time.      180
None of that is the case. I wonder if I am a bit high, for I can't deny that my
mood is positively elated. I only beg the Lord in Heaven that he will keep me in
it, for it is surely easier for the flesh to die like that. How merciful the Lord has
been to me! Even at the risk of sounding hysterical: I am so full of gratitude that
there is hardly room for anything else. He guided me so firmly and clearly these      185
2 days; the whole room could have roared like Herr Freisler and all the walls
could have shaken, it would have made no difference to me; it was truly as it
says in Isaiah 43,2: When thou passest through the waters, I will be with thee;
and through the rivers, they shall not overflow thee; when thou walkest
through the fire, thou shalt not be burned; neither shall the flame kindle upon      190
thee.—That is: your soul. When I was called upon for my final statement I almost felt like saying: There is only one thing I want to mention in my defence:
*nehmen sie den Leib, Gut, Ehr, Kind und Weib, lass fahren dahin, sie haben's kein
Gewinn, das Reich muss uns doch bleiben.*[7] But that would have harmed the others.
So I only said: I don't intend to say anything more, Herr Präsident.      195

Now there is still a hard bit of road ahead of me, and I can only pray that
the Lord will continue as gracious to me as he has been. For this evening Eugen
wrote down for us: Matthew 14, 22–33.[8] He meant it differently, but it remains
true that this was for me a day of a great draught of fishes and that tonight I am
justified in saying: "Lord, depart from me! I am a sinful man." And yesterday,      200

---

7. Last verse of Luther's hymn *"Ein' feste Burg"* ("A Mighty Fortress"): in the Carlyle translation: "And though they take our life, / Goods, honour, children, wife, / Yet is their power small. /
These things shall vanish all. / The city of God remaineth."

8. Marginal note: "I see that yesterday it was Luke 5,1–11."

my love, we read this beautiful passage: "But we have this treasure in earthen vessels, that the excellency of power may be of God, and not of us. We are troubled on every side, yet not distressed; we are perplexed, but not in despair; persecuted, but not forsaken; cast down, but not destroyed; always bearing about
205   in the body the dying of the Lord Jesus, that the life also of Jesus might be manifest in our body." Thanks be, my love, about all to the Lord. Thanks also to yourself, my love, for your intercessions, thanks to all the others who prayed for us and for me. Your husband, your weak, cowardly "complicated," very average husband, was allowed to experience all this. If I were to be reprieved now—
210   which under God is no more likely or unlikely than a week ago—I must say that I should have to find my way all over again, so tremendous was the demonstration of God's presence and omnipotence. He can demonstrate them to us, and quite unmistakably, when he does precisely what doesn't suit us. Anything else is rubbish.
215        Thus I can only say this, dear heart: may God be as gracious to you as to me, then even a dead husband doesn't matter at all. He can, after all, demonstrate his omnipotence even while you make pancakes for the boys or clean them up, though that is, I hope, a thing of the past. I should probably take leave of you—I cannot do it; I should probably deplore and lament your daily toil—
220   I cannot do it; I should probably think of burdens which now fall on you— I cannot do it. I can only tell you one thing: if you get the feeling of absolute protectedness, if the Lord gives it to you, which you would not have without this time and its conclusion, then I bequeath to you a treasure that cannot be confiscated, and compared with which even my life weighs nothing. These Ro-
225   mans, these miserable creatures of Schulze and Freisler and whatever the whole pack may be called: they couldn't even grasp how little they can take away!
        I shall write more tomorrow, but since one never knows what will happen, I wanted to touch on every subject in the letter. Of course I don't know if I'll be executed tomorrow. It may be that I'll be interrogated further, beaten up, or
230   stored away. Please scratch at the doors: perhaps it will keep them from beating me up too badly. Although after today's experience I know that God can also turn this beating to naught, even if there is no whole bone left in my body before I am hanged, although at the moment I have no fear of it, I'd rather avoid it.—So, good night, be of good cheer and undismayed. J.
235        [P.S.] Hercher, who really is a dear fellow, was a bit shocked at my good spirits; so you see that they were quite irrepressible.

*[continued]*     *11 January 1945*

My love, I just feel like chatting with you a little. I have really nothing to say. The material consequences we have discussed in detail. You will get through somehow, and if someone else settles in at Kreisau, you will master that too.
240   Just don't let anything trouble you. It really isn't worth it. I am definitely in favour of making sure that the Russians are informed of my death. That may

make it possible for you to stay in Kreisau. Wandering around what remains of Germany is ghastly in any case. Should the Third Reich last, contrary to all expectations, and I can't think so in my boldest imaginings, you must see how you keep the boys from the poison. I should naturally have no objections to your    245
leaving Germany in that case. Do what you think best, and don't consider yourself bound one way or the other by any wish of mine. I have told you again and again that the dead hand cannot govern.—You need to have no monetary worries either, as long as the Deichmann house pays and as long as you keep the Kreisau mortgage—but you must firmly insist that it was acquired with your    250
money, partly with the inheritance from Grandmother Schnitzler, partly with gifts from Aunt Emma[9] (Wodan); then you will always have enough to live on, and even if both should drop out, there will always be enough people to help you.

    I think with untroubled joy of you and the boys, of Kreisau and everybody there; the parting doesn't seem at all grievous at the moment. That may    255
still come. But it isn't a burden at the moment. I don't feel like parting at all. How this can be so, I don't know. But there isn't any trace of the feeling that overwhelmed me after your first visit in October, no, it must have been November. Now my inner voice says (a) God can lead me back there today just    260
as well as yesterday, and (b) if he calls me to himself, I'll take it with me. I haven't at all the feeling which sometimes came over me: Oh, I'd like to see it all again just once more. Yet I don't feel at all "other-worldly." You see that I am quite happy chatting with you instead of turning to the good God. There is a hymn—208,4—which says "for he to die is ready who living clings to Thee."    265
That is exactly how I feel. Today, because I live, I must cling to him while living; that is all he wants. Is that pharisaical? I don't know. But I think I know that I only live in his grace and forgiveness and have and can do nothing by myself.

    I am chatting, my love, just as things come into my head; therefore here is    270
something quite different. Ultimately what was dramatic about the trial was this: The trial proved all concrete accusations to be untenable, and they were dropped accordingly. Nothing remains of them. But what the Third Reich is so terrified of that it must kill 5, later it will be 7, people, is ultimately the following: a private individual, your husband, of whom it is established that he dis-    275
cussed with 2 clergymen of both denominations, with a Jesuit Provincial, and with a few bishops, *without the intention of doing anything concrete,* and this was established, things "which are the exclusive concern of the Führer." Discussed what: not by any means questions of organization, not the structure of the Reich—all this dropped away in the course of the trial, and Schulze said so ex-    280
plicitly in his speech for the prosecution ("differs completely from all other cases, because there was no mention of any violence or any organization"), but

---

9. Emma Schroeder, née Deichmann, wife of the London banker Bruno Schroeder.

discussions dealt with questions of the practical, ethical demands of Christianity. Nothing else; for that alone we are condemned. In one of his tirades,
285 Freisler said to me: "Only in one respect are we and Christianity alike: we demand the whole man!" I don't know if the others sitting there took it all in, for it
was a sort of dialogue—a spiritual one between F. and myself, for I could not
utter many words—in which we two got to know each other through and
through. Of the whole gang Freisler was the only one who recognized me, and
290 of the whole gang he is the only one who knows why he has to kill me. There
was nothing about a "complicated man" or "complicated thoughts" or "ideology," but "the fig leaf is off." But only for Herr Freisler. We talked, as it were, in
a vacuum. He made not a single joke at my expense, as he had done with Delp
and Eugen. No, this was grim earnest: "From whom do you take your orders?
295 From the Beyond or from Adolf Hitler?" "Who commands your loyalty and your
faith?" All rhetorical questions, of course.—Anyhow, Freisler is the first National Socialist who has grasped who I am, and the good Müller[10] is a simpleton
in comparison.

My love, your very dear letter has just arrived. The first letter, dear heart, in
300 which you did not grasp my mood and my situation. No, I don't occupy myself
with the good God at all or with my death. He has the inexpressible grace to
come to me and to occupy himself with me. Is that pride? Perhaps. But he will
forgive me so much tonight, that I may finally ask him for forgiveness for this
last piece of pride too. But I hope that it is not prideful, because I do not praise
305 the earthen vessel, no, I praise the precious treasure which has used this earthen
vessel, this altogether unworthy abode. No, dear heart, I am reading precisely
the passages of the Bible I would have read today if there had been no trial,
namely: Joshua 19–21, Job 10–12, Ezekiel 34–36, Mark 13–15, and our second
Epistle to the Corinthians to the end, also the short passages I wrote down on a
310 slip of paper for you. So far I have only read Joshua and our bit from Corinthians, which ends with the beautiful, familiar sentence, heard so often from childhood up: "The grace of Our Lord Jesus Christ and the love of God and the fellowship of the Holy Spirit be with you all. Amen." I feel, my love, as though I
had been authorized to say it to you and the little sons with absolute authority.
315 Am I then not fully entitled to read the 118th Psalm, which was appointed for
this morning? Eugen thought of it for a different situation, but it has become
much more true than we would ever have thought possible.

Therefore, dear heart, you'll get your letter back despite your request. I
carry you across with me and need no sign, no symbol, nothing. It isn't even
320 that I've been promised that I won't lose you; no, it is far more: I know it.

A long pause during which Buchholz[11] was here and I was shaved; also I
had some coffee and ate some cake & rolls. Now I am chatting on. The decisive

---

10. Obergruppenführer (General) Heinrich Müller, Gestapo chief.

11. Peter Buchholz, the Catholic prison chaplain. He was the last person to see M., who, as
Buchholz later reported to F.M., went to his execution "steadfast and calm—even with joy."

phrase of the trial was: "Herr Graf, one thing Christianity and we National Socialists have in common, and only one: we demand the whole man." I wonder if he realized what he was saying? Just think how wonderfully God prepared this, his unworthy vessel. At the very moment when there was danger that I might be drawn into active preparations of a putsch—it was in the evening of the 19th that Stauffenberg came to Peter—I was taken away, so that I should be and remain free from all connection with the use of violence.—Then he planted in me my socialist leanings, which freed me, as big landowner, from all suspicion of representing interests.—Then he humbled me as I have never been humbled before, so that I had to lose all pride, so that at last I understand my sinfulness after 38 years, so that I learn to beg for his forgiveness and to trust to his mercy.—Then he lets me come here, so that I can see you standing firm and I can be free of thoughts of you and the little sons, that is, of cares; he gives me time and opportunity to arrange everything that can be arranged, so that all earthly thoughts can fall away.—Then he lets me experience to their utmost depth the pain of parting and the terror of death and the fear of hell, so that all that should be over, too.—Then he endows me with faith, hope, and love, with a wealth of these that is truly overwhelming.—Then he lets me talk with Eugen & Delp and clarify things.—Then he lets Rösch[12] and König[13] escape, so that there aren't enough of them for a Jesuit trial and Delp is added to our case at the last moment.—Then he lets Haubach & Steltzer, whose cases would have introduced foreign matter, be dealt with separately, and finally puts together only Eugen, Delp, & me, for all practical purposes: and then he gives to Eugen and Delp, through the hope, the human hope they have, the weakness which makes their case secondary, and thereby removes the denominational factor; and then your husband is chosen, as a Protestant, to be above all attacked and condemned for his friendship with Catholics, and therefore he stands before Freisler not as a Protestant, not as a big landowner, not as a nobleman, not as a Prussian, not as a German—all that was explicitly excluded in the trial, thus for instance Sperr: "I thought what an astonishing Prussian"—, but as a Christian and nothing else. "The fig leaf is off," says Herr Freisler. Yes, every other category was removed—"a man whom others of his class are naturally bound to reject," says Schulze. For what a mighty task your husband was chosen; all the trouble the Lord took with him, the infinite detours, the intricate zigzag curves, all suddenly find their explanation in one hour on the 10th of January 1945. Everything acquires its meaning in retrospect, which was hidden. Mami and Papi, the brothers and sister, the little sons, Kreisau and its troubles, the work camps and the refusal to put out flags or to belong to the Party or its organizations, Curtis and the English trips, Adam and Peter and Carlo, it has all at last

---

12. Rösch was arrested on 23 January, but survived.

13. König went into hiding and was able to evade arrest, but he was very ill and died in 1948.

become comprehensible in a single hour. For this one hour the Lord took all that trouble.

And now, dear heart, I come to you. I have not mentioned you anywhere,
365 because you, my love, occupy a wholly different place from all the others. For you are not a means God employed to make me who I am, rather you are myself. You are my 13th chapter of the First Letter to the Corinthians. Without this chapter no human being is human. Without you I would have accepted love as a gift, as I accepted it from Mami, for instance, thankful, happy, grateful as one
370 is for the sun that warms one. But without you, my love, I would have "had not charity." I don't even say that I love you; that wouldn't be right. Rather, you are the part of me that, alone, I would lack. It is good that I lack it; for if I had it as you have it, this greatest of all gifts, my love, I could not have done a lot of things, I would have found it impossible to maintain consistency in some
375 things, I could not have watched the suffering I had to see, and much else. Only together do we constitute a human being. We are, as I wrote a few days ago, symbolically, created as one. That is true, literally true. Therefore, my love, I am certain that you will not lose me on this earth, not for a moment. And we were allowed finally to symbolize this fact by our shared Holy Communion, which
380 will have been my last.

I just wept a little, not because I was sad or melancholy, not because I want to return, but because I am thankful and moved by this proof of God's presence. It is not given to us to see him face to face, but we must needs be moved intensely when we suddenly see that all our life he has gone before us as a cloud
385 by day and a pillar of fire by night and that he permits us to see it suddenly in a flash. Now nothing more can happen.

Dear heart, this last week, above all yesterday, must have rendered some of my farewell letters out of date. They'll read like cold coffee in comparison. I leave it to you whether you want to send them off nevertheless, or whether you want
390 to add anything by word of mouth or in writing. Obviously I have the hope that the little sons will understand this letter some day, but I know that it is a question of grace, not of any influence from outside.—Obviously you are to give greetings to all, even such people as Oxé and Frl. Thiel and Frau Tharant. If it is an effort to call them up, don't do it: it makes no difference. I only mention them
395 because they are the extreme cases. Since God has the incredible mercy to be in me, I can take with me not only you and the boys, but all those whom I love, and a multitude of others who are much more distant. You can tell them that.

One more thing. This letter in many respects complements the report I wrote yesterday, which is much more sober. Both together must be made into a
400 legend, which, however, must be written as though Delp had told it about me. I must remain the chief character in it, not because I am or want to be, but because otherwise the story lacks its centre. For it is I who was the vessel for which the Lord has taken such infinite trouble.

Dear heart, my life is finished and I can say of myself: He died in the full-
405 ness of years and of life's experience. This doesn't alter the fact that I would

gladly go on living and that I would gladly accompany you a bit further on this earth. But then I would need a new task from God. The task for which God made me is done. If he has another task for me, we shall hear of it. Therefore by all means continue your efforts to save my life, if I survive this day. Perhaps there is another task.                                                          410

I'll stop, for there is nothing more to say. I mentioned nobody you should greet or embrace for me; you know yourself who is meant. All the texts we love are in my heart and in your heart. But I end by saying to you by virtue of the treasure that spoke from me and filled this humble earthen vessel:

> *The Grace of our Lord Jesus Christ*                                        415
> *and the love of God and the fellowship*
> *of the Holy Spirit be with you all.*

*Amen.*

J.

## Looking Back

1. What glimpses into Moltke's character do we get from the exchange between him and his wife that she reports in lines 29–31?

2. Can you identify the particular psychological obstacle to accepting the inevitability of death that Moltke describes (see especially lines 93–103)?

3. If he could claim for himself the "stature" of the biblical figures he names, what "real relationship to death and thus to eternity" would he keep (see lines 104–118)?

4. In his last days, for what does he eloquently express gratitude (lines 184–185)?

5. How do you interpret the biblical passage Moltke quotes in lines 201–206? What is its relation to his statements in lines 221–226?

6. Does his quite human aversion to pain surprise you in someone who believes in the supremacy of the soul (see lines 227–234)? Explain your answer.

7. What dimension is added to Moltke's martyrdom by the practical advice he gives his wife (lines 237–254) and by his affirmation of love for her (lines 364–380)?

8. How would you describe the moral significance of the issue raised by the trial judge: "From whom do you take your orders? From the Beyond or from Adolf Hitler?" (lines 294–295)?

9. What sense of Moltke's attitude toward dying do we get from his saying, "I feel, my love, as though I had been authorized to say [a blessing from Corinthians] to you and the little sons with absolute authority" (lines 313–314)?

10. Why does he want his letters to be "made into a legend" in which he "must remain the chief character" (lines 398–403)?

## Writing Assignments

1. Although he never employs the term *martyr,* Moltke clearly is one in the original Christian sense of the term: a person who dies for his or her faith. However, the term is not reducible to a cut-and-dried definition. In fact, we cannot truly understand what a martyr lives and dies for until we meet one face to face. Moltke recognizes at the end that he was "chosen . . . attacked and condemned . . . and stands before Freisler . . . as a Christian and nothing else" (lines 348–353). Taking this cue, write an essay defining *martyrdom* by referring to Moltke's life and death as described here.

2. "From whom do you take your orders? From the Beyond or from Adolf Hitler?" demands Judge Freisler of Moltke (see number 8 in Looking Back). The question is shocking; we expect that in a court of law the judge will not assume the role of prosecutor. Yet it is interesting that of all the Nazis bent on killing him, only Freisler understands the crucial issue: "Freisler is the first [Nazi] who has grasped who I am." It is an issue that although it refers to God or religion, most expressly concerns a certain view of humanity that Moltke thinks necessary to hold. Write an essay identifying this understanding of humanity and extrapolating from it to explain how it may be the key to avoiding evil and doing good in the world.

3. Write an essay attempting to judge the value to Moltke and, extrapolating from it, to all of us of a "real relationship to death and thus to eternity" (see number 3 in Looking Back). Questions you might take up are the following: What is a "real" relationship to eternity as opposed to an illusory one? What may it provide for the person whose situation is dire? How may that person begin to view not only death but also eternity—that is, the timeless span lying ahead? Does religious belief affect one's idea of eternity? How? Do you think it's worthwhile to ponder these issues long before facing death, or only then?

# Bertolt Brecht

# Two Sons

Poet, short story writer, and dramatist, Bertolt Brecht (1898–1956) fled Nazi Germany for the United States. He resettled in then East Germany after the war. His most famous works, perhaps, are operas and plays like *Galileo, The Three-Penny Opera, Mother Courage,* and *The Caucasian Chalk Circle,* and *Manual of Piety,* a book of poems. "Two Sons," which was made into a film in 1969, is taken from the only collection of his stories to appear in his lifetime.

## Looking Ahead

1. The sharp, quick, largely nondescriptive language of this brief story will tempt you to rush unobservantly. But take the time to pause and reflect, reading critically to see how the logic of events contributes to the overall meaning.

2. Although "Two Sons" is the title, the farmer's wife is the focus and the person who moves the action.

3. The Russian front, where the woman's son is stationed, was the scene of some of the fiercest fighting in the European theater of war. This fact, as much as anything, accounts for her anxious fears.

In January 1945, as Hitler's war was drawing to a close,[1] a farmer's wife in Thuringia[2] dreamt that her son at the front was calling her and, on going out into the yard dazed with sleep, she fancied she saw him at the pump, drinking. When she spoke to him she realized that it was one of the young Russian prisoners of war who were working as forced labour on the farm. A few days later    5
she had a strange experience. She was bringing the prisoners their food in a nearby copse, where they were uprooting tree-stumps. Looking back over her shoulder as she went away she saw the same young prisoner of war—a sickly creature—turning his face with a disappointed expression towards the mess-tin of soup someone was handing to him, and suddenly his face became that of her    10
son. During the next few days she repeatedly experienced the swift, and as swiftly vanishing, transformations of this particular young man's face into that of her son. Then the prisoner fell sick; he lay untended in the barn. The farmer's wife felt a rising impulse to take him something nourishing, but she was prevented by her brother who, disabled in the war, ran the farm and treated the    15
prisoners brutally, particularly now that everything was beginning to go to pieces and the village was beginning to feel afraid of the prisoners. The farmer's wife herself could not close her ears to his arguments; she did not think it at all right to help these sub-humans, of whom she had heard horrifying things. She lived in dread of what the enemy might do to her son, who was in the East. So    20
her half-formed resolve to help *this* prisoner in his forlorn condition had not yet been carried out when, one evening, she came unexpectedly upon a group of the prisoners in the little snow-covered orchard in eager conversation, held in the cold, no doubt, to keep it secret. The young man was there, too, shivering with fever and, probably because of his exceptionally weak condition, it was he    25
who was most startled by her. In his fright, his face now again underwent the curious transformation, so that she was looking into her son's face, and it was very frightened. She was greatly exercised by this and, although she dutifully reported the conversation in the orchard to her brother, she made up her mind that she would now slip the young man some ham-rind as she had planned.    30
This, like many a good deed under the Third Reich, proved to be exceedingly difficult and dangerous. It was a venture in which her own brother was her enemy, nor could she feel sure of the prisoners either. Nevertheless, she brought it off. True, it led her to the discovery that the prisoners really did intend to make

---

1. *a close:* Germany surrendered on May 7 of this year. (*ed.*)

2. *Thuringia:* a German province; the Red Army had crossed its eastern border and was now fighting in Germany. (*ed.*)

35   their escape, since each day, with the approaching Red Armies, there was greater danger that they would be moved westwards or simply massacred. The farmer's wife could not refuse certain requests, made clear to her in mime and a smattering of German by the young prisoner, to whom she was bound by her strange experience; and in this way she let herself be involved in the prisoners'
40   escape plans. She provided a jacket and a large pair of hand shears. Curiously enough, from that time on the change no longer occurred: she was now simply helping the young stranger. So it was a shock when, one morning in late February, there was a knock on her window and through the pane she saw in the half-light the face of her son. And this time it was her son. He wore the torn uniform
45   of the *Waffen S.S.*,[3] his unit had been cut to pieces and he said agitatedly that the Russians were now only a few kilometres from the village. His homecoming must be kept a dead secret. At a sort of war council held by the farmer's wife, her brother and her son in a corner of the loft, it was decided first and foremost that they must get rid of the prisoners, since they might have caught sight of the
50   S.S. man and in any case would presumably testify to their treatment. There was a quarry not far off. The S.S. man insisted that during that night he must lure them one by one out of the barn and kill them. The corpses could then be dumped in the quarry. Earlier they should be given some rations of alcohol; this would not strike them as too odd, the brother thought, since lately he, as well as
55   the farm-hands, had been downright friendly to the Russians, to put them in a favourable frame of mind at the eleventh hour. Whilst the young S.S. man expounded his plan, he suddenly saw his mother shudder. The menfolk decided not to let her go near the barn again in any circumstances. Thus, filled with horror, she awaited nightfall. The Russians accepted the brandy with apparent grat-
60   itude and the farmer's wife heard them drunkenly singing their melancholy songs. But when, towards eleven o'clock, her son went into the barn, the prisoners were gone. They had feigned drunkenness. It was precisely the new, unnatural friendliness of the farm people that had convinced them that the Red Army must be very close. The Russians arrived during the latter part of the
65   night. The son was lying drunk in the loft, while the farmer's wife, panic stricken, tried to burn his S.S. uniform. Her brother had also got drunk; it was she who had to receive the Russian soldiers and feed them. She did it with a stony face. The Russians left in the morning; the Red Army continued its advance. The son, haggard with sleeplessness, wanted more brandy and an-
70   nounced his firm intention of getting through to the German army units in retreat to go on fighting. The farmer's wife did not try to explain to him that to go on fighting now meant certain destruction. Desperate, she barred his way and tried to restrain him physically. He hurled her back on to the straw. As she got to her feet again she felt a wooden stake in her hand and, with a great heave, she
75   felled the frenzied man to the ground.

---

3. *Waffen S.S.*: an elite fighting unit in the German army, noted for their fanatical loyalty to Hitler and the Nazi state and for their murderous brutality in occupied lands. (*ed.*)

That same morning a farmer's wife drove a cart to Russian headquarters in the neighbouring hamlet and surrendered her son, bound with bullock-halters, as a prisoner of war, so that, as she tried to explain to an interpreter, he should stay alive.

## Looking Back

1. In respect to the woman's dream (lines 1–3), how far apart sometimes are night dreams and truth?
2. What do you know about the legality of using prisoners of war as forced labor?
3. How does the recurrence of the woman's hallucination several times affect its psychological significance?
4. What accounts for the brother's brutality toward the prisoners increasing as the war is being lost instead of decreasing?
5. Can you describe the mental processes that produce a term like *sub-humans* (line 19)?
6. Why does the woman accept that term? What does her acceptance demonstrate about its use and effectiveness?
7. How is it that the farmer's wife becomes a party to the prisoners' escape plans?
8. She now sees the "young stranger" (line 42) as just that, not as a soldier with the face of her son. How does this measure the extent of the change in her?
9. Do you think the son was worth saving? Explain your answer.
10. In the end, what idea have you formed of the woman?

## Writing Assignments

1. The farmer's wife thinks she sees her son when she looks at one of the Russian prisoners. However, once she begins to help him and his fellows, she no longer confuses him with her son but sees him for what he is. Her earlier hallucination or vision enables her to take action based on moral principle and itself has a kind of moral content. Her action is the result of conscious knowledge and choice. In more detailed terms, write an essay that interpolates a description of the moral progression she undergoes and the resultant transformation of her character. Although you will no doubt wish to recapitulate the plot, remember that your real subject is the meaning of the events as they propel, and are propelled by, the farmer's wife.

2. In "Two Sons," a clear division exists between the brother and son, on the one hand, and the woman, on the other. The men use their position to exploit, brutalize, and plot the murder of those who are weak; the woman counteracts their efforts. Thus, we discover two things: one, the exercise of power—by the woman as well as by the men—can be judged morally; and two, only the woman establishes moral limits on the use of power. The second point is the debatable one, for perhaps we have no right to extrapolate in this way from a single case. Write an essay that tries to establish the moral requirements in the use of power and that examines

the contention that women are more capable than men of acting morally in wielding power.

3. Theories of racial superiority and of subhumans are hardly confined to the Nazi era. Two current variants on such theories exist in respect to African Americans. One belief holds that, in light of standardized test results, African Americans are less intelligent on the average than Caucasians. Another theory says that the melanin in black skin pigment makes blacks better people and more intelligent than whites. The spiritual and moral damage such theories do both to those who hold them and to those condemned by them is considerable but not always clearly understood. Write an essay attempting to say what this damage is. Remember to discuss both those who promulgate these beliefs *and* those who are their targets.

# Julian Barnes
# The Visitors

Novelist Julian Barnes (b. 1946) was educated at Oxford University and lives in London. "The Visitors" is a chapter of his book *A History of the World in 10½ Chapters,* each part of which takes off from the story of Noah and the Ark. Barnes has written a number of other novels, the most famous of which is *Flaubert's Parrot.* In "The Visitors," by presenting a difficult and complicated moral situation, Barnes enables critical thinking on the part of the reader, who must judge actions and ideas in ways neither the characters nor the reader could have predicted.

## Looking Ahead

1. Since one character, Franklin Hughes, remains the focus throughout this narrative, we are meant to understand events through his presence on the scene. It is thus necessary to perceive his moral character and follow his reasoning as the story unfolds.

2. Although based on an actual incident (the 1985 hijacking by members of the Palestine Liberation Front of the cruise ship *Achille Lauro* and the murder of a passenger), "The Visitors" is fiction. As you read, try to detect what elements other than manipulation of facts distinguishes fiction from nonfiction.

3. Moral dilemmas point up the complexity of the human condition, which you should be able to observe in the choices afforded Franklin Hughes.

Franklin Hughes had come on board an hour earlier to extend some necessary bonhomie towards those who would make his job easier over the next twenty days. Now, he leaned on the rail and watched the passengers climb the gangway: middle-aged and elderly couples for the most part, some bearing an obvi-

ous stamp of nationality, others, more decorous, preserving for the moment a    5
sly anonymity of origin. Franklin, his arm lightly but unarguably around the
shoulder of his travelling companion, played his annual game of guessing where
his audience came from. Americans were the easiest, the men in New World
leisure-wear of pastel hues, the women unconcerned by throbbing paunches.
The British were the next easiest, the men in Old World tweed jackets hiding    10
short-sleeved shirts of ochre or beige, the women sturdy-kneed and keen to
tramp any mountain at the sniff of a Greek temple. There were two Canadian
couples whose towelling hats bore a prominent maple-leaf emblem; a rangy
Swedish family with four heads of blond hair; some confusable French and Italians whom Franklin identified with a simple mutter of *baguette* or *macaroni;* and    15
six Japanese who declined their stereotype by not displaying a single camera
among them. With the exception of a few family groups and the occasional lone
aesthetic-looking Englishman, they came up the gangway in obedient couples.

"The animals came in two by two," Franklin commented. He was a tall,
fleshy man somewhere in his forties, with pale gold hair and a reddish complex-    20
ion which the envious put down to drink and the charitable to an excess of sun;
his face seemed familiar in a way which made you forget to ask whether or not
you judged it good-looking. His companion, or assistant, but not, she would insist, secretary, was a slim, dark girl displaying clothes newly bought for the
cruise. Franklin, ostentatiously an old hand, wore a khaki bush-shirt and a pair    25
of rumpled jeans. While it was not quite the uniform some of the passengers
expected of a distinguished guest lecturer, it accurately suggested the origin of
such distinction as Franklin could command. If he'd been an American academic he might have dug out a seersucker suit; if a British academic, perhaps a
creased linen jacket the colour of ice-cream. But Franklin's fame (which was not    30
quite as extensive as he thought it) came from television. He had started as a
mouthpiece for other people's views, a young man in a corduroy suit with an af-
fable and unthreatening way of explaining culture. After a while he realized that
if he could speak this stuff there was no reason why he shouldn't write it as well.
At first it was no more than "additional material by Franklin Hughes," then a co-    35
script credit, and finally the achievement of a full "written and presented by
Franklin Hughes." What his special area of knowledge was nobody could quite
discern, but he roved freely in the worlds of archaeology, history and comparative culture. He specialized in the contemporary allusion which would rescue
and enliven for the average viewer such dead subjects as Hannibal's crossing of    40
the Alps, or Viking treasure hoards in East Anglia, or Herod's palaces. "Hannibal's elephants were the panzer divisions of their age," he would declare as he
passionately straddled a foreign landscape; or, "That's as many foot-soldiers as
could be fitted into Wembley Stadium on Cup Final Day"; or, "Herod wasn't
just a tyrant and a unifier of his country, he was also a patron of the arts—per-    45
haps we should think of him as a sort of Mussolini with good taste."

Franklin's television fame soon brought him a second wife, and a couple of
years later a second divorce. Nowadays, his contracts with Aphrodite Cultural

Tours always included the provision of a cabin for his assistant; the crew of the
Santa Euphemia noted with admiration that the assistants tended not to last from
one voyage to the next. Franklin was generous towards the stewards, and popular with those who had paid a couple of thousand pounds for their twenty days.
He had the engaging habit of sometimes pursuing a favourite digression so fer-
vently that he would have to stop and look around with a puzzled smile before
reminding himself where he was meant to be. Many of the passengers commented to one another on Franklin's obvious enthusiasm for his subject, how
refreshing it was in these cynical times, and how he really made history come
alive for them. If his bush-shirt was often carelessly buttoned and his denim
trousers occasionally stained with lobster, this was no more than corroboration
of his beguiling zeal for the job. His clothes hinted, too, at the admirable democracy of learning in the modern age: you evidently did not have to be a stuffy professor in a wing-collar to understand the principles of Greek architecture.

"The Welcome Buffet's at eight," said Franklin. "Think I'd better put in a
couple of hours on my spiel for tomorrow morning."

"Surely you've done that lots of times before?" Tricia was half-hoping he
would stay on deck with her as they sailed out into the Gulf of Venice.

"Got to make it different each year. Otherwise you go stale." He touched
her lightly on the forearm and went below. In fact, his opening address at ten
the next morning would be exactly the same as for the previous five years. The
only difference—the only thing designed to prevent Franklin from going
stale—was the presence of Tricia instead of . . . of, what was that last girl's
name? But he liked to maintain the fiction of working on his lectures beforehand, and he could easily pass up the chance of seeing Venice recede yet again.
It would still be there the following year, a centimetre or two nearer the water-
line, its pinky complexion, like his own, flaking a little more.

On deck, Tricia gazed at the city until the campanile of San Marco became a
pencil-stub. She had first met Franklin three months ago, when he'd appeared
on the chat-show for which she was a junior researcher. They'd been to bed a
few times, but not much so far. She had told the girls at the flat she was going
away with a schoolfriend; if things went well, she'd let on when she got back,
but for the moment she was a little superstitious. Franklin Hughes! And he'd
been really considerate so far, even allotting her some nominal duties so that
she wouldn't look too much like just a girlfriend. So many people in television
struck her as a bit fake—charming, yet not altogether honest. Franklin was just
the same offscreen as on: outgoing, jokey, eager to tell you things. You believed
what he said. Television critics made fun of his clothes and the tuft of chest-hair
where his shirt parted, and sometimes they sneered at what he said, but that
was just envy, and she'd like to see some of those critics get up and try to perform like Franklin. Making it look easy, he had explained to her at their first
lunch, was the hardest thing of all. The other secret about television, he said,
was how to know when to shut up and let the pictures do the work for you—
"You've got to get that fine balance between word and image." Privately,

Franklin was hoping for the ultimate credit: "Written, narrated and produced by Franklin Hughes." In his dreams he sometimes choreographed for himself a gigantic walking shot in the Forum which would take him from the Arch of    95
Septimius Severus to the Temple of Vesta. Where to put the camera was the only problem.

The first leg of the trip, as they steamed down the Adriatic, went much as usual. There was the Welcome Buffet, with the crew sizing up the passengers and the passengers warily circling one another; Franklin's opening lecture, in    100
which he flattered his audience, deprecated his television fame and announced that it was a refreshing change to be addressing real people instead of a glass eye and a cameraman shouting "Hair in the gate, can we do it again, love?" (the technical reference would be lost on most of his listeners, which was intended by Franklin: they were allowed to be snobbish about TV, but not to assume it    105
was idiots' business); and then there was Franklin's other opening lecture, one just as necessary to bring off, in which he explained to his assistant how the main thing they must remember was to have a good time. Sure he'd have to work—indeed, there'd be times when much as he didn't want to he'd be forced to shut himself away in his cabin with his notes—but mostly he felt they should    110
treat it as three weeks' holiday from the filthy English weather and all that back-stabbing at Television Centre. Tricia nodded agreement, though as a junior re-searcher she had not yet witnessed, let alone endured, any backstabbing. A more worldly-wise girl would have readily understood Franklin to mean "Don't expect anything more out of me than this." Tricia, being placid and optimistic,    115
glossed his little speech more mildly as "Let's be careful of building up false ex-pectations"—which to do him credit was roughly what Franklin Hughes in-tended. He fell lightly in love several times each year, a tendency in himself which he would occasionally deplore but regularly indulge. However, he was far from heartless, and the moment he felt a girl—especially a nice girl—need-    120
ing him more than he needed her a terrible flush of apprehension would break out in him. This rustling panic would usually make him suggest one of two things—either that the girl move into his flat, or that she move out of his life—neither of which he exactly wanted. So his address of welcome to Jenny or Cathy or in this case Tricia came more from prudence than cynicism, though    125
when things subsequently went awry it was unsurprising if Jenny or Cathy or in this case Tricia remembered him as more calculating than in fact he had been.

The same prudence, murmuring insistently at him across numerous gory news reports, had made Franklin Hughes acquire an Irish passport. The world was no longer a welcoming place where the old dark-blue British job, topped    130
up with the words "journalist" and "BBC," got you what you wanted. "Her Britannic Majesty's Secretary of State," Franklin could quote from memory, "Re-quests and requires in the Name of Her Majesty all those whom it may con-cern to allow the bearer such assistance and protection as may be necessary." Wishful thinking. Nowadays Franklin travelled on a green Irish passport with a    135
gold harp on the cover, which made him feel like a Guinness rep every time he

produced it. Inside, the word "journalist" was also missing from Hughes's largely honest self-description. There were countries in the world which didn't welcome journalists, and who thought that white-skinned ones pretending interest in archaeological sites were obviously British spies. The less compromising "Writer" was also intended as a piece of self-encouragement. If Franklin described himself as a writer, then this might nudge him into becoming one. Next time round, there was a definite chance for a book-of-the-series; and beyond that he was toying with something serious but sexy—like a personal history of the world—which might roost for months in the bestseller lists.

The *Santa Euphemia* was an elderly but comfortable ship with a courtly Italian captain and an efficient Greek crew. These Aphrodite Tours[1] brought a predictable clientèle, disparate in nationality but homogeneous in taste. The sort of people who preferred reading to deck quoits, and sun-bathing to the disco. They followed the guest lecturer everywhere, took most of the supplementary trips and disdained straw donkeys in the souvenir ships. They had not come for romance, though a string trio occasionally incited some old-fashioned dancing. They took their turn at the captain's table, were inventive when it came to fancy-dress night, and dutifully read the ship's newspaper, which printed their daily route alongside birthday messages and non-controversial events happening on the European continent.

The atmosphere seemed a little torpid to Tricia, but it was a well-organized torpor. As in the address to his assistant, Franklin had emphasized in his opening lecture that the purpose of the next three weeks was pleasure and relaxation. He hinted tactfully that people had different levels of interest in classical antiquity, and that he for one wouldn't be keeping an attendance book and marking down absentees with a black X. Franklin engagingly admitted that there were occasions when even he could tire of yet another row of Corinthian columns standing against a cloudless sky; though he did this in a way which allowed the passengers to disbelieve him.

The tail end of the Northern winter had been left behind; and at a stately pace the *Santa Euphemia* took its contented passengers into a calm Mediterranean spring. Tweed jackets gave way to linen ones, trouser-suits to slightly outdated sun-dresses. They passed through the Corinth Canal at night, with some of the passengers jammed against a porthole in their nightclothes, and the hardier ones on deck, occasionally letting off ineffectual bursts of flash from their cameras. From the Ionian to the Aegean: it was a little fresher and choppier in the Cyclades, but nobody minded. They went ashore at chichi Mykonos, where an elderly headmaster twisted his ankle while climbing among the ruins; at marbled Paros and volcanic Thira. The cruise was ten days old when they stopped at Rhodes. While the passengers were ashore the *Santa Euphemia* took

---

1. *Euphemia*: a name uncomfortably close to "euphemism"; the Italian captain and Greek crew may represent classical antiquity, as does the name of the tour company (*Aphrodite*, the goddess of love and beauty), but the essential character of that time is euphemized, laundered of its unpleasant features. (*ed.*)

on fuel, vegetables, meat and more wine. It also took on some visitors, although this did not become apparent until the following morning.

They were steaming towards Crete, and at eleven o'clock Franklin began his usual lecture on Knossos and Minoan Civilization. He had to be a little care- 180 ful, because his audience tended to know about Knossos, and some of them would have their personal theories. Franklin liked people asking questions; he didn't mind pieces of obscure and even correct information being added to what he had already imparted—he would offer thanks with a courtly bow and a murmur of "Herr Professor," implying that as long as some of us have an overall 185 grasp of things, it was fine for others to fill their heads with recondite detail; but what Franklin Hughes couldn't stand were bores with pet ideas they couldn't wait to try out on the guest lecturer. Excuse me, Mr. Hughes, it looks very Egyptian to me—how do we know the Egyptians didn't build it? Aren't you as- suming that Homer wrote when people think he (a little laugh)—or she—did? I 190 don't have any actual expert knowledge, yet surely it would make more sense if . . . There was always at least one of them, playing the puzzled yet reasonable amateur; unfooled by received opinion, he—or she—knew that historians were full of bluff, and that complicated matters were best understood using zestful intuition untainted by any actual knowledge or research. "I appreciate what 195 you're saying, Mr. Hughes, but surely it would be more logical . . ." What Franklin occasionally wanted to say, though never did, was that these brisk guesses about earlier civilizations seemed to him to have their foundation as of- ten as not in Hollywood epics starring Kirk Douglas or Burt Lancaster. He imag- ined himself hearing out one of these jokers and replying, with a skirl of irony 200 on the adverb, "Of course, you realize that the film of Ben Hur isn't *entirely* reli- able?" But not this trip. In fact, not until he knew it was going to be his last trip. Then he could let go a little. He could be franker with his audience, less careful with the booze, more receptive to the flirting glance.

The visitors were late for Franklin Hughes's lecture on Knossos, and he had 205 already done the bit in which he pretended to be Sir Arthur Evans when they opened the double doors and fired a single shot into the ceiling. Franklin, still headily involved in his own performance, murmured, "Can I have a translation of that?" but it was an old joke, and not enough to recapture the passengers' at- tention. They had already forgotten Knossos and were watching the tall man 210 with a moustache and glasses who was coming to take Franklin's place at the lectern. Under normal circumstances, Franklin might have yielded him the mi- crophone after a courteous inquiry about his credentials. But given that the man was carrying a large machine-gun and wore one of those red check head-dresses which used to be shorthand for lovable desert warriors loyal to Lawrence of 215 Arabia but in recent years had become shorthand for baying terrorists eager to massacre the innocent, Franklin simply made a vague "Over to you" gesture with his hands and sat down on his chair.

Franklin's audience—as he still thought of them in a brief proprietorial flurry—fell silent. Everyone was avoiding an incautious movement; each breath 220 was discreetly taken. There were three visitors, and the other two were guarding the double doors into the lecture room. The tall one with the glasses had an almost scholarly air as he tapped the microphone in the manner of lecturers everywhere: partly to see if it was working, partly to attract attention. The second half of this gesture was not strictly necessary.

"I apologize for the inconvenience," he began, setting off a nervous laugh or two. "But I am afraid it is necessary to interrupt your holiday for a while. I hope it will not be a long interruption. You will all stay here, sitting exactly where you are, until we tell you what to do."

A voice, male, angry and American, asked from the middle of the auditorium, "Who are you and what the hell do you want?" The Arab swayed back to the microphone he had just left, and with the contemptuous suavity of a diplomat, replied, "I am sorry, I am not taking questions at this juncture." Then, just to make sure he was not mistaken for a diplomat, he went on. "We are not people who believe in unnecessary violence. However, when I fired the shot into the ceiling to attract your attention, I had set this little catch here so that the gun only fires one shot at a time. If I change the catch"—he did so while holding the weapon half-aloft like an arms instructor with an exceptionally ignorant class—"the gun will continue to fire until the magazine is empty. I hope that is clear."

The Arab left the hall. People held hands; there were occasional sniffs and sobs, but mostly silence. Franklin glanced across to the far left of the auditorium at Tricia. His assistants were allowed to come to his lectures, though not to sit in direct line of sight—"Mustn't start me thinking about the wrong thing." She didn't appear frightened, more apprehensive about what the form was. Franklin wanted to say, "Look, this hasn't happened to me before, it isn't normal, I don't know what to do," but settled instead for an indeterminate nod. After ten minutes of stiff-necked silence, an American woman in her mid-fifties stood up. Immediately one of the two visitors guarding the door shouted at her. She took no notice, just as she ignored the whispers and grabbing hand of her husband. She walked down the central aisle to the gunmen, stopped a couple of yards short and said in a clear, slow voice suppurating with panic, "I have to go to the goddam bathroom."

The Arabs neither replied nor looked her in the eye. Instead, with a small gesture of their guns, they indicated as surely as such things can be that she was currently a large target and that any further advance would confirm the fact in an obvious and final way. She turned, walked back to her seat and began to cry. Another woman on the right of the hall immediately started sobbing. Franklin looked across at Tricia again, nodded, got to his feet, deliberately didn't look at the two guards, and went across to the lectern. "As I was saying . . ." He gave an authoritative cough and all eyes reverted to him. "I was saying that the Palace of Knossos was not by any means the first human settlement on the site. What we think of as the Minoan strata reach down to about seventeen feet, but below this there are signs of human habitation down to twenty-six feet or so. There was life where the palace was built for at least ten thousand years before the first stone was laid . . ."

It seemed normal to be lecturing again. It also felt as if some feathered cloak of leadership had been thrown over him. He decided to acknowledge this, glancingly at first. Did the guards understand English? Perhaps. Had they ever been to Knossos? Unlikely. So Franklin, while describing the council chamber at the palace, invented a large clay tablet which, he claimed, had probably hung    270
over the gypsum throne. It read—he looked towards the Arabs at this point— "We are living in difficult times." As he continued describing the site, he unearthed more tablets, many of which, as he now fearlessly began to point out, had a universal message. "We must above all not do anything rash," one said. Another: "Empty threats are as useless as empty scabbards." Another: "The tiger    275
always waits before it springs" (Hughes wondered briefly if Minoan Civilization knew about tigers). He was not sure how many of his audience had latched on to what he was doing, but there came an occasional assenting growl. In a curious way, he was also enjoying himself. He ended his tour of the palace with one of the least typically Minoan of his many inscriptions: "There is a great power    280
where the sun sets which will not permit certain things." Then he shuffled his notes together and sat down to warmer applause than usual. He looked across at Tricia and winked. She had tears in her eyes. He glanced towards the two Arabs and thought, that's shown you, now you can see what we're made of, there's some stiff upper lip for you. He rather wished he'd made up some Mi-    285
noan aphorism about people who wore red sea-towels on their heads, but recognized he wouldn't have had the nerve. He'd keep that one for later, after they were all safe.

They waited for half an hour in a silence that smelt of urine before the leader of the visitors returned. He had a brief word with the guards and walked    290
up the aisle to the lectern. "I understand that you have been lectured on the palace of Knossos," he began, and Franklin felt sweat burst into the palms of his hands. "That is good. It is important for you to understand other civilizations. How they are great, and how"—he paused meaningfully—"they fall. I hope very much that you will enjoy your trip to Knossos."    295

He was leaving the microphone when the same American voice, this time more conciliatory in tone, as if heedful of the Minoan tablets, said, "Excuse me, would you be able to tell us roughly who you are and roughly what you want?"

The Arab smiled. "I am not sure that would be a good idea at this stage." He gave a nod to indicate he had finished, then paused, as if a civil question at least    300
deserved a civil answer. "Let me put it this way. If things go according to plan, you will soon be able to continue your explorations of the Minoan Civilization. We shall disappear just as we came, and we shall seem to you simply to have been a dream. Then you can forget us. You will remember only that we were a small delay. So there is no need for you to know who we are or where we come    305
from or what we want."

He was about to leave the low podium when Franklin, rather to his own surprise, said, "Excuse me." The Arab turned. "No more questions." Hughes went on, "This is not a question. I just think . . . I'm sure you've got other things on your mind . . . if we're going to have to stay here you ought to let us go to the    310 lavatory." The leader of the visitors frowned. "The bathroom," Franklin explained; then again, "the toilet."

"Of course. You will be able to go to the toilet when we move you."

"When will that be?" Franklin felt himself a little carried away by his self-
315   appointed role. For his part the Arab noted some unacceptable lack of compliance. He replied brusquely, "When we decide."

He left. Ten minutes later an Arab they had not seen before came in and whispered to Hughes. He stood up. "They are going to move us from here to the dining-room. We are to be moved in twos. Occupants of the same cabin are to
320   identify themselves as such. We will be taken to our cabins, where we will be allowed to go to the lavatory. We are also to collect our passports, but nothing else." The Arab whispered again. "And we are not allowed to lock the lavatory door." Without being asked, Franklin went on, "I think these visitors to the ship are quite serious. I don't think we should do anything which might upset them."

325   Only one guard was available to move the passengers, and the process took several hours. As Franklin and Tricia were being taken to C deck, he remarked to her, in the casual tone of one commenting on the weather, "Take the ring off your right hand and put it on your wedding finger. Turn the stone round so that you can't see it. Don't do it now, do it when you're having a pee."

330   When they reached the dining-room their passports were examined by a fifth Arab. Tricia was sent to the far end, where the British had been put in one corner and the Americans in another. In the middle of the room were the French, the Italians, two Spaniards and the Canadians. Nearest the door were the Japanese, the Swedes and Franklin, the solitary Irishman. One of the last
335   couples to be brought in were the Zimmermanns, a pair of stout, well-dressed Americans. Hughes had at first placed the husband in the garment business, some master cutter who had set up on his own; but a conversation on Paros had revealed him to be a recently retired professor of philosophy from the Midwest. As the couple passed Franklin's table on their way to the American quarter,
340   Zimmermann muttered lightly, "Separating the clean from the unclean."

When they were all present, Franklin was taken off to the purser's office, where the leader was installed. He found himself wondering if the slightly bulbous nose and the moustache were by any chance attached to the glasses; perhaps they all came off together.

345   "Ah, Mr. Hughes. You seem to be their spokesman. At any event, now your position is official. You will explain to them the following. We are doing our best to make them comfortable, but they must realize that there are certain difficulties. They will be allowed to talk to one another for five minutes at each hour. At the same time those who wish to go to the toilet will be allowed to do
350   so. One person at a time. I can see that they are all sensible people and would not like them to decide not to be sensible. There is one man who says he cannot find his passport. He says he is called Talbot."

"Mr. Talbot, yes." A vague, elderly Englishman who tended to ask questions about religion in the Ancient World. A mild fellow with no theories of his
355   own, thank God.

"He is to sit with the Americans."

"But he's British. He comes from Kidderminster."

"If he remembers where his passport is and he is British he can sit with the British."

"You can tell he's British. I can vouch for him being British." The Aror looked unimpressed. "He doesn't talk like an American, does he?"     360

"I have not talked to him. Still, talking is not proof, is it? You, I think, talk like a British but your passport says you are not a British." Franklin nodded slowly. "So we will wait for the passport."

"Why are you separating us like this?"                                      365

"We think you will like to sit with one another." The Arab made a sign for him to go.

"There's one other thing. My wife. Can she sit with me?"

"Your wife?" The man looked at a list of passengers in front of him. "You have no wife."

"Yes I do. She's travelling as Tricia Maitland. It's her maiden name. We    370
were married three weeks ago." Franklin paused, then added in a confessional tone, "My third wife, actually."

But the Arab seemed unimpressed by Franklin's harem. "You were married three weeks ago? And yet it seems you do not share the same cabin. Are things   375
going so badly?"

"No, I have a separate cabin for my work, you see. The lecturing. It's a lux- ury, having another cabin, a privilege."

"She is your wife?" The tone gave nothing away.

"Yes she is," he replied, mildly indignant.                                 380

"But she has a British passport."

"She's Irish. You become Irish if you marry an Irishman. It's Irish law."

"Mr. Hughes, she has a British passport." He shrugged as if the dilemma were insoluble, then found a solution. "But if you wish to sit with your wife, then you may go and sit with her at the British table."                       385

Franklin smiled awkwardly. "If I'm the passengers' spokesman, how do I get to see you to pass on the passengers' demands?"

"The passengers' demands? No, you have not understood. The passengers do not have demands. You do not see me unless I want to see you."

After Franklin had relayed the new orders, he sat at his table by himself and   390
thought about the position. The good part was that so far they had been treated with reasonable civility; no-one had yet been beaten up or shot, and their cap- tors didn't seem to be the hysterical butchers they might have expected. On the other hand, the bad part lay quite close to the good part: being unhysterical, the visitors might also prove reliable, efficient, hard to divert from their purpose.   395
And what was their purpose? Why had they hijacked the *Santa Euphemia*? Who were they negotiating with? And who was steering the sodding ship, which as far as Franklin could tell was going round in large, slow circles?

From time to time, he would nod encouragingly to the Japanese at the next table. Passengers at the far end of the dining-room, he couldn't help noting,     400

would occasionally look up in his direction, as if checking that he was still there. He'd become the liaison man, perhaps even the leader. That Knossos lecture, in the circumstances, had been little short of brilliant; a lot more ballsy than he'd imagined possible. It was the sitting alone like this that got him down;
405 it made him brood. His initial burst of emotion—something close to exhilaration—was seeping away; in its place came lethargy and apprehension. Perhaps he should go and sit with Tricia and the Brits. But then they might take his citizenship away from him. This dividing-up of the passengers: did it mean what he feared it might mean?

410 Late that afternoon they heard a plane fly over, quite low. There was a muted cheer from the American section of the dining-room; then the plane went away. At six o'clock one of the Greek stewards appeared with a large tray of sandwiches; Franklin noted the effect of fear on hunger. At seven, as he went for a pee, an American voice whispered, "Keep up the good work." Back at his
415 table, he tried to look soberly confident. The trouble was, the more he reflected, the less cheerful he felt. In recent years Western governments had been noisy about terrorism, about standing tall and facing down the threat; but the threat never seemed to understand that it was being faced down, and continued much as before. Those in the middle got killed; governments and terrorists survived.

420 At nine Franklin was summoned again to the purser's office. The passengers were to be moved for the night: the Americans back to the lecture hall, the British to the disco, and so on. These separate encampments would then be locked. It was necessary: the visitors had to get their sleep as well. Passports were to be held ready for inspection at all times.

425 "What about Mr. Talbot?"
"He has become an honorary American. Until he finds his passport."
"What about my wife?"
"Miss Maitland. What about her?"
"Can she join me?"
430 "Ah. Your British wife."
"She's Irish. You marry an Irishman you become Irish. It's the law."
"The law, Mr. Hughes. People are always telling *us* what is the law. I am often puzzled by what they consider is lawful and what is unlawful." He looked away to a map of the Mediterranean on the wall behind Franklin. "Is it lawful to
435 drop bombs on refugee camps, for instance? I have often tried to discover the law which says this is permissible. But it is a long argument, and sometimes I think argument is pointless, just as the law is pointless." He gave a dismissive shrug. "As for the matter of Miss Maitland, let us hope that her nationality does not become, how shall I put it, relevant."
440 Franklin tried to damp down a shudder. There were times when euphemism could be much more frightening than direct threat. "Are you able to tell me when it might become . . . relevant?"
"They are stupid, you see. They are stupid because they think we are stupid. They lie in the most obvious way. They say they do not have the authority

to act. They say arrangements cannot be made quickly. Of course they can.   445
There is such a thing as the telephone. If they think they have learned something from previous incidents of this kind, they are stupid not to realize that we
have too. We know about their tactics, the lying and the delays, all this establishing of some kind of relationship with the freedom fighters. We know all
that. And we know about the limits of the body for taking action. So we are   450
obliged by your governments to do what we say we will do. If they started negotiating at once, there would be no problem. But they only start when it is too
late. It is on their heads."

"No," said Franklin. "It's on our heads."

"You, Mr. Hughes, I think, do not have to worry so soon."   455

"How soon is soon?"

"Indeed, I think you may not have to worry at all."

"How soon is soon?"

The leader paused, then made a regretful gesture. "Tomorrow some time.
The timetable, you see, is fixed. We have told them from the beginning."   460

Part of Franklin Hughes could not believe he was having this conversation.
Another part wanted to say he had always supported the cause of his captors—
whatever that cause might be—and incidentally the Gaelic on his passport
meant that he was a member of the IRA, and for Christ's sake could he please
go to his cabin and lie down and forget all about it. Instead, he repeated,   465
"Timetable?" The Arab nodded. Without thinking, Franklin said, "One an
hour?" Immediately, he wished he hadn't asked. For all he knew he was giving
the fellow ideas.

The Arab shook his head. "Two. A pair every hour. Unless you raise the
stakes they do not take you seriously."   470

"Christ. Just coming on board and killing people just like that. Just like that?"

"You think it would be better if we explained to them why we were killing
them?" The tone was sarcastic.

"Well, yes, actually."

"Do you think they would be sympathetic?" Now there was more mockery   475
than sarcasm. Franklin was silent. He wondered when the killing was due to
start. "Goodnight, Mr. Hughes," said the leader of the visitors.

Franklin was put for the night in a stateroom with the Swedish family and
the three Japanese couples. They were, he deduced, the safest group among the
passengers. The Swedes because their nation was famously neutral; Franklin   480
and the Japanese presumably because in recent times Ireland and Japan had
produced terrorists. How ludicrous. The six Japanese who had come on a cultural cruise in Europe hadn't been asked whether they supported the various
political killers in their own country; nor had Franklin been quizzed about the
IRA. A Guinness passport awarded through some genealogical fluke suggested   485
the possibility of sympathy with the visitors, and this was his protection. In fact,
Franklin hated the IRA, just as he hated any political group which interfered, or
might interfere, with the fulltime job of being Franklin Hughes. For all he

knew—and in accordance with his annual policy he had not asked—Tricia was
490   far more sympathetic to the various worldwide groups of homicidal maniacs indirectly committed to interrupting the career of Franklin Hughes. Yet she was
herded in with the diabolic British.

    There was little talk in the stateroom that night. The Japanese kept to them-
selves; the Swedish family spent the time trying to distract their children by
495   talking of home and Christmas and British football teams; while Franklin felt
burdened by what he knew. He was scared and sickened; but isolation seemed
to breed complicity with his captors. He tried thinking of his two wives and the
daughter who must be—what?—fifteen now: he always had to remember the
year of her birth and work it out from there. He should get down to see her
500   more often. Perhaps he could take her with him when they filmed the next series. She could watch his famous walking shot in the Forum; she'd like that.
Now where could he place the camera? Or perhaps a tracking shot. And some
extras in toga and sandals—yes, he liked it . . .

    Next morning Franklin was taken to the purser's office. The leader of the
505   visitors waved him to sit down. "I have decided to take your advice."

    "My advice?"

    "The negotiations, I fear, are going badly. That is to say, there are no nego-
tiations. We have explained our position but they are extremely unwilling to explain their position."

510      "They?"

    "They. So, unless things change very quickly, we shall be forced to put
some pressure on them."

    "Pressure?" Even Franklin, who could not have made a career in television
without skill in trading euphemisms, was enraged. "You mean killing people."

515      "That is the only pressure, sadly, which they understand."

    "What about trying other sorts?"

    "But we have. We have tried sitting on our hands and waiting for world
opinion to come to our help. We have tried being good and hoping that we
would be rewarded by getting our land back. I can assure you that these systems
520   do not work."

    "Why not try something in between?"

    "An embargo on American goods, Mr. Hughes? I do not think they would
take us seriously. A lack of Chevrolets being imported to Beirut? No, regrettably
there are people who only understand certain kinds of pressure. The world is
525   only advanced . . ."

    ". . . by killing people? A cheerful philosophy."

    "The world is not a cheerful place. I would have thought your investiga-
tions into the ancient civilizations would have taught you that. But anyway . . . I
have decided to take your advice. We shall explain to the passengers what is
530   happening. How they are mixed up in history. What that history is."

    "I'm sure they'll appreciate that." Franklin felt queasy. "Tell them what's
going on."

"Exactly. You see, at four o'clock it will become necessary to . . . to start killing them. Naturally we hope it will not be necessary. But if it is . . . You are right, things must be explained to them if it is possible. Even a soldier knows why he is fighting. It is fair that the passengers be told as well." 535

"But they're not fighting." The Arab's tone, as much as what he said, riled Franklin. "They're civilians. They're on holiday. They're not fighting."

"There are no civilians any more," replied the Arab. "Your governments pretend, but that is not the case. Those nuclear weapons of yours, they are only 540 to be let off against an army? The Zionists, at least, understand this. All their people are fighting. To kill a Zionist civilian is to kill a soldier."

"Look, there aren't any Zionist civilians on the ship, for Christ's sake. They're people like poor old Mr. Talbot who's lost his passport and has been turned into an American." 545

"All the more reason why things must be explained."

"I see," said Franklin, and he let the sneer come through. "So you're going to assemble the passengers and explain to them how they're all really Zionist soldiers and that's why you've got to kill them."

"No, Mr. Hughes, you misunderstand. I am not going to explain anything. 550 They would not listen. No, Mr. Hughes, *you* are going to explain things to them."

"Me?" Franklin didn't feel nervous. Indeed, he felt decisive. "Certainly not. You can do your own dirty work."

"But, Mr. Hughes, you are a public speaker. I have heard you, if only for a 555 short time. You do it so well. You could introduce a historical view of the matter. My second-in-command will give you all the information you require."

"I don't require any information. Do your own dirty work."

"Mr. Hughes, I really cannot negotiate in two directions at the same time. It is nine-thirty. You have half an hour to decide. At ten you will say that you do 560 the lecture. You will then have two hours, three hours if that is required, with my second-in-command for the briefing." Franklin was shaking his head, but the Arab continued regardless. "Then you have until three o'clock to prepare the lecture. I suggest that you make it last forty-five minutes. I shall listen to you, of course, with the greatest interest and attention. And at three-forty-five, 565 if I am satisfied with how you explain matters, we shall in return accept the Irish nationality of your recently married wife. That is all I have to say, you will send me your reply at ten o'clock."

Back in the stateroom with the Swedes and the Japanese, Franklin remembered a TV series about psychology he'd once been asked to present. It had 570 folded directly after the pilot, a loss nobody much regretted. One item in that show reported an experiment for measuring the point at which self-interest takes over from altruism. Put like this, it sounded almost respectable; but Franklin had been revolted by the actual test. The researchers had taken a female monkey who had recently given birth and put her in a special cage. The 575 mother was still feeding and grooming her infant in a way presumably not too

dissimilar from the maternal behaviour of the experimenters' wives. Then they turned a switch and began heating up the metal floor of the monkey's cage. At first she jumped around in discomfort, then squealed a lot, then took to stand-
580 ing on alternate legs, all the while holding her infant in her arms. The floor was made hotter, the monkey's pain more evident. At a certain point the heat from the floor became unbearable, and she was faced with a choice, as the experi- menters put it, between altruism and self-interest. She either had to suffer ex- treme pain and perhaps death in order to protect her offspring, or else place her
585 infant on the floor and stand on it to keep herself from harm. In every case, sooner or later self-interest had triumphed over altruism.

Franklin had been sickened by the experiment, and glad the TV series hadn't got beyond the pilot, if that was what he would have had to present. Now he felt a bit like that monkey. He was being asked to choose between two
590 equally repellent ideas: that of abandoning his girlfriend while retaining his in- tegrity, or rescuing his girlfriend by justifying to a group of innocent people why it was right that they should be killed. And would that rescue Trish? Franklin hadn't even been promised his own safety; perhaps the pair of them, reclassified as Irish, would merely be moved to the bottom of the killing list, but
595 still remain on it. Who would they start with? The Americans, the British? If they started with the Americans, how long would that delay the killing of the British? Fourteen, sixteen Americans—he translated that brutally into seven or eight hours. If they started at four, and the governments stood firm, by mid- night they would start killing the British. What order would they do it in? Men
600 first? Random? Alphabetical? Trish's surname was Maitland. Right in the middle of the alphabet. Would she see the dawn?

He imagined himself standing on Tricia's body to protect his own burning feet and shuddered. He would have to do the lecture. That was the difference between a monkey and a human being. In the last analysis, humans were capa-
605 ble of altruism. This was why he was not a monkey. Of course, it was more than probable that when he gave the lecture his audience would conclude the exact opposite—that Franklin was operating out of self-interest, saving his own skin by a foul piece of subservience. But this was the thing about altruism, it was al- ways liable to be misunderstood. And he could explain everything to them all
610 afterwards. If there was an afterwards. If there was a them all.

When the second-in-command arrived, Franklin asked to see the leader again. He intended demanding safe-conduct for Tricia and himself in exchange for the lecture. However, the second-in-command had only come for a reply, not for renewed conversation. Dully, Franklin nodded his head. He'd never
615 been much good at negotiating anyway.

At two-forty-five Franklin was taken to his cabin and allowed to wash. At three o'clock he entered the lecture hall to find the most attentive audience he had ever faced. He filled a glass from the carafe of stale water that nobody had bothered to change. He sensed below him the swell of exhaustion, a rip-tide of
620 panic. After only a day the men seemed almost bearded, the women crumpled.

They had already begun not to look like themselves, or the selves that Franklin had spent ten days with. Perhaps this made them easier to kill.

Before he got his own writing credit Franklin had become expert at presenting the ideas of others as plausibly as possible. But never had he felt such apprehension at a script; never had a director imposed such conditions; never had his fee been so bizarre. When first agreeing to the task he had persuaded himself that he could surely find a way of tipping off his audience that he was acting under duress. He would think up some ploy like that of the false Minoan inscriptions; or he would make his lecture so exaggerated, pretend such enthusiasm for the cause thrust upon him, that nobody could possible miss the irony. No, that wouldn't work. "Irony," an ancient TV producer had once confided to him, "may be defined as what people miss." And the passengers certainly wouldn't be on the lookout for it in their present circumstances. The briefing had made things yet harder: the second-in-command had given precise instructions, and added that any deviation from them would result not just in Miss Maitland remaining British, but in Franklin's Irish passport no longer being recognized. They certainly knew how to negotiate, these bastards.

"I had been hoping," he began, "that the next time I addressed you I would be taking up again the story of Knossos. Unfortunately, as you are aware, the circumstances have changed. We have visitors amongst us." He paused and looked down the aisle at the leader, who stood before the double doors with a guard on each side. "Things are different. We are in the hands of others. Our . . . destiny is no longer our own." Franklin coughed. This wasn't very good. Already he was straying into euphemism. The one duty, the one intellectual duty he had, was to speak as directly as he could. Franklin would freely admit he was a showman and would stand on his head in a bucket of herrings if that would raise viewing figures a few thousand; but there was a residual feeling in him—a mixture of admiration and shame—which made him hold in special regard those communicators who were deeply unlike him: the ones who spoke quietly, in their own simple words, and whose stillness gave them authority. Franklin, who knew he could never be like them, tried to acknowledge their example as he spoke.

"I have been asked to explain things to you. To explain how you—we— find ourselves in the position we are now in. I am not an expert on the politics of the Middle East, but I shall try to make things as clear as I can. We should perhaps begin by going back to the nineteenth century, long before the establishment of the state of Israel . . ." Franklin found himself back in an easy rhythm, a bowler pitching on a length. He felt his audience began to relax. The circumstances were unusual, but they were being told a story, and they were offering themselves to the story-teller in the manner of audiences down the ages, wanting to see how things turned out, wanting to have the world explained to them. Hughes sketched in an idyllic nineteenth century, all nomads and goat-farming and traditional hospitality which allowed you to stay in someone else's tent for three days before being asked what the purpose of your visit might be.

665 He talked of early Zionist settlers and Western concepts of land-ownership. The Balfour Declaration. Jewish immigration from Europe. The Second World War. European guilt over the Holocaust being paid for by the Arabs. The Jews having learned from their persecution by the Nazis that the only way to survive was to be like Nazis. Their militarism, expansionism, racism. Their pre-emptive attack
670 on the Egyptian air force at the start of the Six Day War being the exact moral equivalent of Pearl Harbor (Franklin deliberately did not look at the Japanese— or the Americans—at this moment, nor for some time thereafter). The refugee camps. The theft of land. The artificial support of the Israeli economy by the dollar. The atrocities committed against the dispossessed. The Jewish lobby in
675 America. The Arabs only asking from the Western powers for the same justice in the Middle East as had already been accorded to the Jews. The regrettable necessity of violence, a lesson taught the Arabs by the Jews, just as it had been taught the Jews by the Nazis.

Franklin had used up two thirds of his time. If he could feel a brooding
680 hostility in some parts of the audience, there was also, strangely, a wider drowsiness, as if they'd heard this story before and had not believed it then either. "And so we come to the here and now." That brought them back to full attention; despite the circumstances, Franklin felt a bubble of pleasure. He was the hypnotist who snaps his fingers. "In the Middle East, we must understand,
685 there are no civilians any more. The Zionists understand this, the Western governments do not. We, alas, are not civilians. The Zionists have made this happen. You—we—are being held hostage by the Black Thunder group to secure the release of three of their members. You may remember" (though Franklin doubted it, since incidents of this kind were frequent, almost interchangeable)
690 "that two years ago a civilian aircraft carrying three members of the Black Thunder group was forced down by the American air force in Sicily, that the Italian authorities in contravention of international law compounded this act of piracy by arresting the three freedom fighters, that Britain defended America's action at the United Nations, and that the three men are now in prison in France and
695 Germany. The Black Thunder group does not turn the other cheek, and this legitimate . . . hijack"—Franklin used the word carefully, with a glance at the leader as if to demonstrate how he disdained euphemism—"is in response to that act of piracy. Unfortunately the Western governments do not show the same concern for their citizens as the Black Thunder group shows for its free-
700 dom fighters. Unfortunately they are so far declining to release the prisoners. Regrettably the Black Thunder group has no alternative but to carry out its intended threat which was made very clear from the beginning to the Western governments . . . ."

At this moment a large, unathletic American in a blue shirt got to his feet
705 and started running down the aisle towards the Arabs. Their guns had not been set to fire only one shot at a time. The noise was very loud and immediately there was a lot of blood. An Italian sitting in the line of fire received a bullet in the head and fell across his wife's lap. A few people got up and quickly sat down again. The leader of the Black Thunder group looked at his watch and waved at

Hughes to continue. Franklin took a long swig of stale water. He wished it were 　710
something stronger. "Because of the stubbornness of the Western governments," he went on, trying to sound now more like an official spokesman than
Franklin Hughes, "and their reckless disregard for human life, it is necessary for
sacrifices to be made. You will have understood the historical inevitability of
this from what I have said before. The Black Thunder group has every con- 　715
fidence that the Western governments will swiftly come to the negotiating
table. In a final effort to make them do so it will be necessary to execute two of
you . . . of us . . . every hour until that point. The Black Thunder group finds
this course of action regrettable, but the Western governments leave them no alternative. The order of executions has been decided according to the guilt of the 　720
Western nations for the situation in the Middle East." Franklin could no longer
look at his audience. He dropped his voice, yet could not avoid being heard as
he went on. "Zionist Americans first. Then other Americans. Then British. Then
French, Italians and Canadians."

"What the fuck has Canada ever done in the Middle East? What the fuck?" 　725
shouted a man still wearing a towelling maple-leaf hat. He was restrained from
getting up by his wife. Franklin, who felt the heat from the metal floor of his
cage to be unendurable, shuffled his notes together automatically, stepped off
the podium without looking at anyone, walked up the aisle, getting blood on
his crêpe soles as he stepped past the dead American, ignored the three Arabs, 　730
who could shoot him if they wanted to, and went without escort or opposition
to his cabin. He locked the door and lay down on his bunk.

Ten minutes later there came the noise of shooting. From five o'clock to
eleven o'clock, punctually on the hour like some terrible parody of a municipal
clock, gunfire pealed. Splashes followed, as the bodies were flung over the rail 　735
in pairs. Shortly after eleven, twenty-two members of the American Special
Forces, who had been trailing the *Santa Euphemia* for fifteen hours, managed to
get on board. In the battle six more passengers, including Mr. Talbot, the honorary American citizen from Kidderminster, were shot dead. Out of the eight
visitors who had helped load supplies at Rhodes, five were killed, two after they 　740
had surrendered.

Neither the leader nor the second-in-command survived, so there remained
no witness to corroborate Franklin Hughes's story of the bargain he had struck
with the Arabs. Tricia Maitland, who had become Irish for a few hours without
realizing it, and who in the course of Franklin Hughes's lecture had returned 　745
her ring to the finger where it originally belonged, never spoke to him again.

## Looking Back

1. What sense of this voyage does Barnes establish with his references to "obedient
   couples" and "animals" in lines 18–19?

2. How does Barnes intend us to see Franklin Hughes in the early descriptive passages
   devoted to him (see lines 21–75)?

3. Prudence and self-restraint are regarded as positive qualities in most people. Are they positive when Hughes displays them (see lines 118–145 and 196–204)? Explain your answer.

4. Does the sudden takeover of the ship seem a sharp break with the cruise up to that point, or are there some links between what happens before and after that event? Explain your answer.

5. How do you interpret Zimmerman's remarks, "Separating the clean from the unclean" (line 340)?

6. Are the Arab leader's points about law and argument persuasively logical (see lines 432–437)? Why or why not?

7. What does he mean, "There are no civilians any more" (line 539)? Do you agree? Why or why not?

8. Do you believe Hughes makes the right decision in the face of his moral dilemma? How else might he have acted? Would the outcome have been any different?

9. What do you think of the history the Arabs put in Hughes's mouth?

10. Why does Tricia Maitland never speak to Franklin Hughes again?

## Writing Assignments

1. Freedom fighters or terrorists? The correct label depends on who makes the call. Partisan definitions aside, however, certain issues remain that the term we agree on cannot settle. One of these is the status of the innocent. The question that arises is whether any cause can ever justify the deliberate killing of innocent (that is, nonmilitary) persons on the other side. Write an essay that addresses this question by referring in detail to "The Visitors" and to any factual events you may be aware of. An important term to consider is *justify* since this is a moral question first and a political and military one second. Another term to consider at some length is *innocent*. In these respects, you might pay particular attention to Zimmerman's remark and to the Arab leader's comment about law and argument.

2. Franklin Hughes is a television personality, a phrase that once may have needed some explanation but that now brings immediately to mind the new breed of talk show hosts. The behavior of such people, for the most part, is calculated to captivate a large audience, almost all of which is unseen and unknown. As a result, we rarely get a look at who these people really are, which we might if we saw them respond to unrehearsed situations. As it is, we don't witness their moral character. Hughes, however, reveals himself to us through his decisions and actions as well as through his capsule biography; he is open to analysis. Write an essay that furthers our understanding of television personalities by interpolating an analysis of Hughes's moral character.

3. Moral dilemmas are crucial choices individuals are forced to make between unwelcome alternatives. Although neither alternative may be desirable, one may be worse than the other, or finally seem so. For instance, one may have dreadful immediate consequences, whereas the other has equally ruinous long-term effects. Both, however, have moral content, and hesitating between them, the individual is situated on the horns of a dilemma. This is where Franklin Hughes is in "The Visitors" before he

makes a choice. Write an essay in which you describe the terms of his dilemma and judge whether he makes the right choice. Be sure to weigh carefully the negative aspects of each alternative before reaching a judgment.

❦

# N. Scott Momaday
## The Priest of the Sun

N. Scott Momaday, a Kiowan Native American, is a poet and novelist. He is the author of *The Ancient Child, In the Presence of the Sun, The Names,* and *The Way to Rainy Mountain.* His novel *House Made of Dawn,* from which "The Priest of the Sun" is taken, won the Pulitzer Prize in 1968. Momaday is on the English Department faculty of the University of California at Santa Barbara.

## Looking Ahead

1. Tosamah, a character in *House Made of Dawn,* is described elsewhere in the novel as an orator—which we see here he is—and a physician; he presides over ceremonies in which the hallucinogen peyote is used. Peyote, he says, is "the vegetal representation of the sun." Hence his title, Priest of the Sun.

2. Biblical retellings, such as the one occurring here, shock some people because such retellings change enough of the original details to present a somewhat different story, but you should read critically to see to what degree this retelling puts the original story in a new context and so recharges it.

3. The **oral tradition**—the handing down of stories by word of mouth—is an important topic here.

The Priest of the Sun lived with his disciple Cruz on the first floor of a two-story red-brick building in Los Angeles. The upstairs was maintained as a storage facility by the A. A. Kaul Office Supply Company. The basement was a kind of church. There was a signboard on the wall above the basement steps, encased in glass. In neat, movable white block letters on a black field it read: 5

LOS ANGELES
HOLINESS PAN-INDIAN RESCUE MISSION
Rev. J. B. B. Tosamah, Pastor & Priest of the Sun
Saturday 8:30 P.M.
"The Gospel According to John" 10

Sunday 8:30 P.M.
"The Way to Rainy Mountain"
Be kind to a white man today

The basement was cold and dreary, dimly illuminated by two 40-watt bulbs
which were screwed into the side walls above the dais. This platform was made
out of rough planks of various woods and dimensions, thrown together without
so much as a hammer and nails; it stood seven or eight inches above the floor,
and it supported the tin firebox and the crescent altar. Off to one side was a
kind of lectern, decorated with red and yellow symbols of the sun and moon. In
back of the dais there was a screen of purple drapery, threadbare and badly
faded. On either side of the aisle which led to the altar there were chairs and
crates, fashioned into pews. The walls were bare and gray and streaked with water. The only windows were small, rectangular openings near the ceiling, at
ground level; the panes were covered over with a thick film of coal oil and dust,
and spider webs clung to the frames or floated out like smoke across the room.
The air was heavy and stale; odors of old smoke and incense lingered all
around. The people had filed into the pews and were waiting silently.

Cruz, a squat, oily man with blue-black hair that stood out like spines from
his head, stepped forward on the platform and raised his hands as if to ask for
the quiet that already was. Everyone watched him for a moment; in the dull
light his skin shone yellow with sweat. Turning slightly and extending his arm
behind him, he said, "The Right Reverend John Big Bluff Tosamah."

There was a ripple in the dark screen; the drapes parted and the Priest of
the Sun appeared, moving shadow-like to the lectern. He was shaggy and awful-
looking in the thin, naked light: big, lithe as a cat, narrow-eyed, suggesting in
the whole of his look and manner both arrogance and agony. He wore black like
a cleric; he had the voice of a great dog:

"'*In principio erat Verbum.*' Think of Genesis. Think of how it was before the
world was made. There was nothing, the Bible says. 'And the earth was without
form, and void; and darkness was upon the face of the deep.' It was dark, and
there was nothing. There were no mountains, no trees, no rocks, no rivers.
There was nothing. But there was darkness all around, and in the darkness
something happened. *Something happened!* There was a single sound. Far away
in the darkness there was a single sound. Nothing made it, but it was there; and
there was no one to hear it, but it was there. It was there, and there was nothing
else. It rose up in the darkness, little and still, almost nothing in itself—like a
single soft breath, like the wind arising; yes, like the whisper of the wind rising
slowly and going out into the early morning. But there was no wind. There was
only the sound, little and soft. It was almost nothing in itself, the smallest seed
of sound—but it took hold of the darkness and there was light; it took hold of
the stillness and there was motion forever; it took hold of the silence and there
was sound. It was almost nothing in itself, a single sound, a word—a word broken off at the darkest center of the night and let go in the awful void, forever
and forever. And it was almost nothing in itself. It scarcely was; but it *was*, and
everything began."

Just then a remarkable thing happened. The Priest of the Sun seemed
stricken; he let go of his audience and withdrew into himself, into some strange

potential of himself. His voice, which had been low and resonant, suddenly became harsh and flat; his shoulders sagged and his stomach protruded, as if he had held his breath to the limit of endurance; for a moment there was a look of amazement, then utter carelessness in his face. Conviction, caricature, callousness: the remainder of his sermon was a going back and forth among these. 60

"Thank you *so* much, Brother Cruz. Good evening, blood brothers and sisters, and welcome, welcome. Gracious me, I see lots of new faces out there tonight. *Gracious me!* May the Great Spirit—can we knock off that talking in the back there?—be with you always. 65

"'In the beginning was the Word.' I have taken as my text this evening the almighty Word itself. Now get this: 'There was a man sent from God, whose name was John. The same came for a witness, to bear witness of the Light, that all men through him might believe.' Amen, brothers and sisters, *Amen.* And the riddle of the Word, 'In the beginning was the Word. . . .' Now what do you suppose old John *meant* by that? That cat was a preacher, and, well, you know how it is with preachers; he had something big on his mind. On my, it was big; it was the *Truth,* and it was heavy, and old John hurried to set it down. And in his hurry he said too much. 'In the beginning was the Word, and the Word was with God, and the Word was God.' It was the Truth, all right, but it was more than the Truth. The Truth was overgrown with fat, and the fat was God. The fat was *John's* God, and God stood between John and the Truth. Old John, see, he got up one morning and caught sight of the Truth. It must have been like a bolt of lightning, and the sight of it made him blind. And for a moment the vision burned on in back of his eyes, and he *knew* what it was. In that instant he saw something he had never seen before and would never see again. That was the instant of revelation, inspiration, Truth. And old John, he must have fallen down on his knees. Man, he must have been shaking and laughing and crying and yelling and praying—all at the same time—and he must have been drunk and delirious with the Truth. You see, he had lived all his life waiting for that one moment, and it came, and it took him by surprise, and it was gone. And he said, 'In the beginning was the Word. . . .' And, man, right then and there he should have stopped. There was nothing more to say, but he went on. He had said all there was to say, everything, but he went on. 'In the beginning was the Word. . . .' Brothers and sisters, *that* was the Truth, the whole of it, the essential and eternal Truth, the bone and blood and muscle of the Truth. But he went on, old John, because he was a preacher. The perfect vision faded from his mind, and he went on. The instant passed, and then he had nothing but a memory. He was desperate and confused, and in his confusion he stumbled and went on. 'In the beginning was the Word, and the Word was with God, and the Word was God.' He went on to talk about Jews and Jerusalem, Levites and Pharisees, Moses and Phillip and Andrew and Peter. Don't you see? Old John *had* to go on. That cat had a whole lot at stake. He couldn't let the Truth alone. He couldn't see that he had come to the end of the Truth, and he went on. He tried to make it bigger and better than it was, but instead he only demeaned and encumbered 70 75 80 85 90 95 100

it. He made it soft and big with fat. He was a preacher, and he made a complex sentence of the Truth, two sentences, three, a paragraph. He made a sermon and theology of the Truth. He imposed his idea of God upon the everlasting
105   Truth. 'In the beginning was the Word. . . .' And that is all there was, and it was enough.

"Now, brothers and sisters, old John was a white man, and the white man has his ways. Oh gracious me, he has his ways. He talks about the Word. He talks through it and around it. He builds upon it with syllables, with prefixes
110   and suffixes and hyphens and accents. He adds and divides and multiplies the Word. And in all of this he subtracts the Truth. And, brothers and sisters, you have come here to live in the white man's world. Now the white man deals in words, and he deals easily, with grace and sleight of hand. And in his presence, here on his own ground, you are as children, mere babes in the woods. You
115   must not mind, for in this you have a certain advantage. A child can listen and learn. The Word is sacred to a child.

"My grandmother was a storyteller; she knew her way around words. She never learned to read and write, but somehow she knew the good of reading and writing; she had learned how to listen and delight. She had learned that in
120   words and in language, and there only, she could have whole and consummate being. She told me stories, and she taught me how to listen. I was a child and I listened. She could neither read nor write, you see, but she taught me how to live among her words, how to listen and delight. 'Storytelling; to utter and to hear. . . .' And the simple act of listening is crucial to the concept of language,
125   more crucial even than reading and writing, and language in turn is crucial to human society. There is proof of that, I think, in all the histories and prehistories of human experience. When that old Kiowa woman told me stories, I listened with only one ear. I was a child, and I took the words for granted. I did not know what all of them meant, but somehow I held on to them; I remem-
130   bered them, and I remember them now. The stories were old and dear; they meant a great deal to my grandmother. It was not until she died that I knew how *much* they meant to her. I began to think about it, and then I knew. When she told me those old stories, something strange and good and powerful was going on. I was a child, and that old woman was asking me to come directly into
135   the presence of her mind and spirit; she was taking hold of my imagination, giving me to share in the great fortune of her wonder and delight. She was asking me to go with her to the confrontation of something that was sacred and eternal. It was a timeless, *timeless* thing; nothing of her old age or of my childhood came between us.
140   "Children have a greater sense of the power and beauty of words than have the rest of us in general. And if that is so, it is because there occurs—or reoccurs—in the mind of every child something like a reflection of all human experience. I have heard that the human fetus corresponds in its development, stage by stage, to the scale of evolution. Surely it is no less reasonable to suppose that
145   the waking mind of a child corresponds in the same way to the whole evolution of human thought and perception.

"In the white man's world, language, too—and the way in which the white man thinks of it—has undergone a process of change. The white man takes such things as words and literatures for granted, as indeed he must, for nothing in his world is so commonplace. On every side of him there are words by the millions, an unending succession of pamphlets and papers, letters and books, bills and bulletins, commentaries and conversations. He has diluted and multiplied the Word, and words have begun to close in upon him. He is sated and insensitive; his regard for language—for the Word itself—as an instrument of creation has diminished nearly to the point of no return. It may be that he will perish by the Word.

"But it was not always so with him, and it is not so with you. Consider for a moment that old Kiowa woman, my grandmother, whose use of language was confined to speech. And be assured that her regard for words was always keen in proportion as she depended upon them. You see, for her words were medicine; they were magic and invisible. They came from nothing into sound and meaning. They were beyond price; they could neither be bought nor sold. And she never threw words away.

"My grandmother used to tell me the story of Tai-me, of how Tai-me came to the Kiowas. The Kiowas were a sun dance culture, and Tai-me was their sun dance doll, their most sacred fetish; no medicine was ever more powerful. There is a story about the coming of Tai-me. This is what my grandmother told me:

> Long ago there were bad times. The Kiowas were hungry and there was no food. There was a man who heard his children cry from hunger, and he began to search for food. He walked four days and became very weak. On the fourth day he came to a great canyon. Suddenly there was thunder and lightning. A Voice spoke to him and said, "Why are you following me? What do you want?" The man was afraid. The thing standing before him had the feet of a deer, and its body was covered with feathers. The man answered that the Kiowas were hungry. "Take me with you," the Voice said, "and I will give you whatever you want." From that day Tai-me has belonged to the Kiowas.

"Do you see? There, far off in the darkness, something happened. Do you see? Far, far away in the nothingness something happened. There was a voice, a sound, a word—and everything began. The story of the coming of the Tai-me has existed for hundreds of years by word of mouth. It represents the oldest and best idea that man has of himself. It represents a very rich literature, which, because it was never written down, was always but one generation from extinction. But for the same reason it was cherished and revered. I could see that reverence in my grandmother's eyes, and I could hear it in her voice. It was that, I think, that old Saint John had in mind when he said, 'In the beginning was the Word. . . .' But he went on. He went on to lay a scheme about the Word. He could find no satisfaction in the simple fact that the Word was; he had to account for it, not in terms of that sudden and profound insight, which must have devastated him at once, but in terms of the moment afterward, which was irrel-

190  evant and remote; not in terms of his imagination, but only in terms of his prejudice.

"Say this: 'In the beginning was the Word. . . .' There was nothing. There was *nothing!* Darkness. There was darkness, and there was no end to it. You look up sometimes in the night and there are stars; you can see all the way to the
195  stars. And you begin to know the universe, how awful and great it is. The stars lie out against the sky and do not fill it. A single star, flickering out in the universe, is enough to fill the mind, but it is nothing in the night sky. The darkness looms around it. The darkness flows among the stars, and beyond them forever. In the beginning that is how it was, but there were no stars. There was only the
200  dark infinity in which nothing was. And something happened. At the distance of a star something happened, and everything began. The Word did not come into being, but *it was.* It did not break upon the silence, but *it was older than the silence and the silence was made of it.*

"Old John caught sight of something terrible. The thing standing before
205  him said, 'Why are you following me? What do you want?' And from that day the Word has belonged to us, who have heard it for what it is, who have lived in fear and awe of it. In the Word was the beginning; *'In the beginning was the Word. . . .'*"

The Priest of the Sun appeared to have spent himself. He stepped back from
210  the lectern and hung his head, smiling. In his mind the earth was spinning and the stars rattled around in the heavens. The sun shone, and the moon. Smiling in a kind of transport, the Priest of the Sun stood silent for a time while the congregation waited to be dismissed.

"Good night," he said, at last, "and get yours."

## Looking Back

1. Why is the slogan on the signboard, "Be kind to a white man today" (line 13), ironic?

2. What does the description of Tosamah's basement church tell you about him and his congregation (see lines 14–27)?

3. Does Tosamah convince you in his first speech that a primal sound created light and motion (see lines 38–55)?

4. How do you think his tone, present in words like "can we knock off that talking in the back there?" (lines 65–66), affects his sermon and his listeners?

5. Can you say how, as with John, the idea of God can be an obstacle between a person and the Truth (see lines 75–106)?

6. In what way might the elaborations with which "the white man" surrounds the Word "subtract the Truth" from it (see lines 107–111 and lines 147–156)?

7. Why does Tosamah believe that storytelling is so significant? Can you add any details about telling stories and listening to them that would enhance Tosamah's valuation?

8. Do you think people could begin to revalue speech and language along the lines of the grandmother's practice (see lines 157–163)? What shape would this take?

9. How does Tosamah connect the oral art of storytelling and John's "In the beginning was the Word"?

10. By the end of the sermon, what is your overall view of the Priest of the Sun?

## Writing Assignments

1. In the age of the information superhighway, we may think the written word has largely superseded speech as a means of communication. Yet telephones, radio, and television all depend on talk. Oral histories, which are transcribed conversation, have become popular. Lectures and sermons have not ceased. And storytelling itself, at least as we can remember it from our childhood, remains a potent force. Why does human speech continue to hold such sway (see number 7 and 8 in Looking Back)? Picking up cues from Tosamah's discussion of the oral tradition, write an essay that attempts to answer this question.

2. Tosamah criticizes John for letting the idea of God block his view of the Truth (see number 5 in Looking Back). We can remove the capital letter from truth and omit mention of God, and yet agree with the Priest of the Sun that often enough the mental baggage people carry with them prevents them from experiencing the true nature of the world. In particular, this can happen when people hold various prejudices or when they cling too tightly to what is comfortable and familiar, to what is customary and acceptable. Write an essay extrapolating from Tosamah's criticism by citing concrete examples of how people can miss the truth in this way and commenting on the personal and social problems that can result.

3. Tosamah is the priest of a religion that uses the hallucinogenic drug peyote for ritual purposes. The Jamaican Rastifarians use marijuana for similar purposes. These, of course, are illegal drugs. Should their use for religious ceremonies be protected or forbidden by law? The question involves the separation of church and state, as well as the uses to which the drugs are put (here as part of the rituals in public religious ceremonies rather than for private recreation at parties or in the home). Write an essay arguing that the law should either protect or forbid such uses of drugs.

# Heinrich Böll

# Like a Bad Dream

A novelist and short story writer, Heinrich Böll (1917–1985) won the Nobel Prize for literature in 1972. Although a devout Catholic, his religious views enter only subtly into his writing; that is, he is concerned about moral and spiritual matters but is never heavy-handed. Among his most renowned works are *Billiards at Half-Past Nine*, *The Clown*, and *Group Portrait with Lady*. A collection of his short stories and novellas appeared shortly after his death. During World War II, Böll fought in the German army on both the Russian and

French fronts, was wounded four times, and was taken prisoner by the Americans. After the war, he devoted much of his energy to the cause of human rights and intellectual freedom.

## Looking Ahead

1. The title of this story is, in effect, the narrator's final comment on what happens in the plot, but it is up to you the reader to make the comparison stick.

2. Most of the time, moral issues arise in the way they do here, not sensationally, but as a result of ordinary events and speech. Read critically to discover the connection.

3. The distinction between morality and ethics, terms that are often confused, is one you should try to grasp as it emerges importantly in the story.

That evening we had invited the Zumpens over for dinner, nice people; it was through my father-in-law that we had got to know them: ever since we have been married he has helped me to meet people who can be useful to me in business, and Zumpen can be useful: he is chairman of a committee which places
5    contracts for large housing projects, and I have married into the excavating business.

I was tense that evening, but Bertha, my wife, reassured me. "The fact," she said, "that he's coming at all is promising. Just try and get the conversation round to the contract. You know it's tomorrow they're going to be
10   awarded."

I stood looking through the net curtains of the glass front door, waiting for Zumpen. I smoked, ground the cigarette butts under my foot, and shoved them under the mat. Next I took up a position at the bathroom window and stood there wondering why Zumpen had accepted the invitation; he couldn't be that
15   interested in having dinner with us, and the fact that the big contract I was involved in was going to be awarded tomorrow must have made the whole thing as embarrassing to him as it was to me.

I thought about the contract too: it was a big one, I would make 20,000 marks on the deal, and I wanted the money.
20       Bertha had decided what I was to wear: a dark jacket, trousers a shade lighter and a conservative tie. That's the kind of thing she learned at home, and at boarding school from the nuns. Also what to offer guests: when to pass the cognac, and when the vermouth, how to arrange dessert. It is comforting to have a wife who knows all about such things.
25       But Bertha was tense too: as she put her hands on my shoulders, they touched my neck, and I felt her thumbs damp and cold against it.

"It's going to be all right," she said. "You'll get the contract."

"Christ," I said, "it means 20,000 marks to me, and you know how we need the money."
30       "One should never," she said gently, "mention Christ's name in connection with money!"

A dark car drew up in front of our house, a make I didn't recognize, but it looked Italian. "Take it easy," Bertha whispered, "wait till they've rung, let them stand there for a couple of seconds, then walk slowly to the door and open it."

I watched Mr. and Mrs. Zumpen come up the steps: he is slender and tall,   35 with graying temples, the kind of man who fifty years ago would have been known as a "ladies' man"; Mrs. Zumpen is one of those thin dark women who always make me think of lemons. I could tell from Zumpen's face that it was a frightful bore for him to have dinner with us.

Then the doorbell rang, and I waited one second, two seconds, walked   40 slowly to the door and opened it.

"Well," I said, "how nice of you to come!"

Cognac glasses in hand, we went from room to room in our apartment, which the Zumpens wanted to see. Bertha stayed in the kitchen to squeeze some mayonnaise out of a tube onto the appetizers; she does this very nicely: hearts,   45 loops, little houses. The Zumpens complimented us on our apartment; they exchanged smiles when they saw the big desk in my study, at that moment it seemed a bit too big even to me.

Zumpen admired a small rococo cabinet, a wedding present from my grandmother, and a baroque Madonna in our bedroom.   50

By the time we got back to the dining room, Bertha had dinner on the table; she had done this very nicely too, it was all so attractive yet so natural, and dinner was pleasant and relaxed. We talked about movies and books, about recent elections, and Zumpen praised the assortment of cheeses, and Mrs. Zumpen praised the coffee and the pastries. Then we showed the Zumpens our honey-   55 moon pictures: photographs of the Breton coast, Spanish donkeys, and street scenes from Casablanca.

After that we had some more cognac, and when I stood up to get the box with the photos of the time when we were engaged, Bertha gave me a sign, and I didn't get the box. For two minutes there was absolute silence, because we had   60 nothing more to talk about, and we all thought about the contract; I thought of the 20,000 marks, and it struck me that I could deduct the bottle of cognac from my income tax. Zumpen looked at his watch and said: "Too bad, it's ten o'clock; we have to go. It's been such a pleasant evening!" And Mrs. Zumpen said: "It was really delightful, and I hope you'll come to us one evening."   65

"We would love to," Bertha said, and we stood around for another half-minute, all thinking again about the contract, and I felt Zumpen was waiting for me to take him aside and bring up the subject. But I didn't. Zumpen kissed Bertha's hand, and I went ahead, opened the doors, and held the car door open for Mrs. Zumpen down below.   70

"Why," said Bertha gently, "didn't you mention the contract to him? You know it's going to be awarded tomorrow."

"Well," I said, "I didn't know how to bring the conversation round to it."

"Now look," she said in a quiet voice, "you could have used any excuse to ask him into your study; that's where you should have talked to him. You   75 must have noticed how interested he is in art. You ought to have said: I have an eighteenth-century crucifix in there you might like to have a look at, and then . . ."

I said nothing, and she sighed and tied on her apron. I followed her into the
80  kitchen; we put the rest of the appetizers back in the refrigerator, and I crawled about on the floor looking for the top of the mayonnaise tube. I put away the remains of the cognac, counted the cigars: Zumpen had smoked only one. I emptied the ashtrays, ate another pastry, and looked to see if there was any coffee left in the pot. When I went back to the kitchen, Bertha was standing there with
85  the car key in her hand.

"What's up?" I asked.

"We have to go over there, of course," she said.

"Over where?"

"To the Zumpens," she said, "where do you think?"
90  "It's nearly half past ten."

"I don't care if it's midnight," Bertha said. "All I know is, there's 20,000 marks involved. Don't imagine they're squeamish."

She went into the bathroom to get ready, and I stood behind her watching her wipe her mouth and draw in new outlines, and for the first time I noticed how
95  wide and primitive that mouth is. When she tightened the knot of my tie I could have kissed her, the way I always used to when she fixed my tie, but I didn't.

Downtown the cafés and restaurants were brightly lit. People were sitting outside on the terraces, and the light from the street lamps was caught in the silver ice-cream dishes and ice buckets. Bertha gave me an encouraging look; but
100  she stayed in the car when we stopped in front of the Zumpens' house, and I pressed the bell at once and was surprised how quickly the door was opened. Mrs. Zumpen did not seem surprised to see me; she had on some black lounging pajamas with loose full trousers embroidered with yellow flowers, and this made me think more than ever of lemons.

105  "I beg your pardon," I said, "I would like to speak to your husband."

"He's gone out again," she said. "He'll be back in half an hour."

In the hall I saw a lot of Madonnas, gothic and baroque, even rococo Madonnas, if there is such a thing.

"I see," I said. "Well then, if you don't mind, I'll come back in half an hour."
110  Bertha had bought an evening paper; she was reading it and smoking, and when I sat down beside her she said: "I think you could have talked about it to her too."

"But how do you know he wasn't there?"

"Because I know he is at the Gaffel Club playing chess, as he does every
115  Wednesday evening at this time."

"You might have told me that earlier."

"Please try and understand," said Bertha, folding the newspaper. "I am trying to help you, I want you to find out for yourself how to deal with such things. All we had to do was call up Father and he would have settled the whole thing
120  for you with one phone call, but I want you to get the contract on your own."

"All right," I said, "then what'll we do: wait here half an hour, or go up right away and have a talk with her?"

"We'd better go up right away," said Bertha.

We got out of the car and went up in the elevator together. "Life," said Bertha, "consists of making compromises and concessions." 125

Mrs. Zumpen was no more surprised now than she had been earlier, when I had come alone. She greeted us, and we followed her into her husband's study. Mrs. Zumpen brought some cognac, poured it out, and before I could say anything about the contract she pushed a yellow folder toward me: "Housing Project Fir Tree Haven," I read, and looked up in alarm at Mrs. Zumpen, at Bertha, 130 but they both smiled, and Mrs. Zumpen said: "Open the folder," and I opened it; inside was another one, pink, and on this I read: "Housing Project Fir Tree Haven—Excavation Work." I opened this too, saw my estimate lying there on top of the pile; along the upper edge someone had written in red: "Lowest bid."

I could feel myself flushing with pleasure, my heart thumping, and I 135 thought of the 20,000 marks.

"Christ," I said softly, and closed the file, and this time Bertha forgot to rebuke me.

"*Prost,*" said Mrs. Zumpen with a smile, "let's drink to it then."

We drank, and I stood up and said: "It may seem rude of me, but perhaps 140 you'll understand that I would like to go home now."

"I understand perfectly," said Mrs. Zumpen. "There's just one small item to be taken care of." She took the file, leafed through it, and said: "Your price per square meter is thirty pfennigs below that of the next-lowest bidder. I suggest you raise your price by fifteen pfennigs: that way you'll still be the lowest and 145 you'll have made an extra four thousand five hundred marks. Come on, do it now!" Bertha took her pen out of her purse and offered it to me, but I was in too much of a turmoil to write; I gave the file to Bertha and watched her alter the price with a steady hand, re-write the total, and hand the file back to Mrs. Zumpen. 150

"And now," said Mrs. Zumpen, "just one more little thing. Get out your check book and write a check for three thousand marks; it must be a cash check and endorsed by you."

She had said this to me, but it was Bertha who pulled our check book out of her purse and made out the check. 155

"It won't be covered," I said in a low voice.

"When the contract is awarded, there will be an advance, and then it will be covered," said Mrs. Zumpen.

Perhaps I failed to grasp what was happening at the time. As we went down in the elevator, Bertha said she was happy, but I said nothing. 160

Bertha chose a different way home, we drove through quiet residential districts, I saw lights in open windows, people sitting on balconies drinking wine; it was a clear, warm night.

"I suppose the check was for Zumpen?" was all I said, softly, and Bertha replied, just as softly: "Of course." 165

I looked at Bertha's small, brown hands on the steering wheel, so confident and quiet. Hands, I thought, that sign checks and squeeze mayonnaise tubes, and I looked higher—at her mouth, and still felt no desire to kiss it.

That evening I did not help Bertha put the car away in the garage, nor did I
170  help her with the dishes. I poured myself a large cognac, went up to my study, and sat down at my desk, which was much too big for me. I was wondering about something. I got up, went into the bedroom and looked at the baroque Madonna, but even there I couldn't put my finger on the thing I was wondering about.

The ringing of the phone interrupted my thoughts; I lifted the receiver and
175  was not surprised to hear Zumpen's voice.

"Your wife," he said, "made a slight mistake. She raised the price by twenty-five pfennigs instead of fifteen."

I thought for a moment and then said: "That wasn't a mistake, she did it with my consent."

180  He was silent for a second or two, then said with a laugh: "So you had already discussed the various possibilities?"

"Yes," I said.

"All right, then make out another check for a thousand."

"Five hundred," I said, and I thought: It's like a bad dream—that's what
185  it's like.

"Eight hundred," he said, and I said with a laugh: "Six hundred," and I knew, although I had no experience to go on, that he would now say seven hundred and fifty, and when he did I said "Yes" and hung up.

It was not yet midnight when I went downstairs and over to the car to give
190  Zumpen the check; he was alone and laughed as I reached in to hand him the folded check. When I walked slowly back into the house, there was no sign of Bertha; she didn't appear when I went back into my study; she didn't appear when I went downstairs again for a glass of milk from the refrigerator, and I knew what she was thinking; she was thinking: he has to get over it, and I have
195  to leave him alone; this is something he has to understand.

But I never did understand. It is beyond understanding.

## Looking Back

1. Do you find Bertha's social know-how wholly admirable (see lines 20–24)? Why or why not?

2. Why doesn't the religious sentiment she expresses in lines 30–31 ring true?

3. What does the man's failure to bring up the contract at dinner reveal about him?

4. What does Bertha's communicating with her husband by a mere sign (lines 58–60) disclose about their relationship?

5. Why doesn't he kiss Bertha when she fixes his tie (see lines 93–96)?

6. In what way does the comparison to a lemon expose Mrs. Zumpen's character?

7. Is Bertha's urging her husband to be independent a good thing (see lines 117–120)? Why or why not?

8. Do you think she is right that life "consists of making compromises and concessions" (lines 124–125)? Explain your answer.

9. What deal does Mrs. Zumpen conclude with the narrator? What is the one he later negotiates with Mr. Zumpen?

10. What is it that the narrator finds "beyond understanding"?

## Writing Assignments

1. Both public ethics and private morality come into play in Bertha's comment that life "consists of making compromises and concessions" (lines 124–125). Is she right (see number 8 in Looking Back)? Write an essay answering this question by interpolating a discussion of the deals between the narrator and the Zumpens. Ask yourself whether anyone is cheated or hurt and why the narrator is so appalled by his own behavior. Try to discover whether there is a connection between morality and ethics that Bertha, despite her references to each, does not see.

2. It is difficult to criticize the desire to make money unless it outrageously supersedes other values, such as love, community, and faith in humanity. Böll seems to mount this particular criticism, but when we apply it to our own lives, it leaves us with certain questions about how much money we should have, how fiercely we should go after it, and what we ought to do with it. These questions are moral in character since answers to them shape the relationship between our resources and our values. Write an essay, referring to both "Like a Bad Dream" and relevant personal experience, that attempts to answer these questions and put values in their proper balance.

3. Bertha and her husband are a team. They help and support each other (even though Bertha is the more efficient of the two), as most of us believe married couples should. Yet their actions are immoral and probably illegal. So we get a double picture: couples stand together against the world in order to survive and prosper, and couples are part of a larger whole that has moral limits, which should be respected. Referring specifically to the fictional Bertha and her husband as well as to people you know, write an essay that attempts to make sense of the complicated situations couples often find themselves in. How should they see themselves, and how should such a view form the basis for their conduct? How much do they owe to themselves, and how much to the world? In such a situation, how would you balance moral and ethical considerations on the one hand, and personal needs and desires on the other?

# Eric Rohmer

# The Baker's Girl

Eric Rohmer is a French filmmaker whose work is regularly screened in American theaters. *My Night at Maud's* and *Claire's Knee* are perhaps his best-known movies. Like them, "The Baker's Girl" was first written as a short story and only later translated to cinema. Rohmer, while insisting for the record that he is not a moralist, nonetheless creates characters who, as we find in "The Baker's Girl," act on the basis of decisions that reflect moral principles and considerations. Always, however, Rohmer's subtle presentation of these choices reveals the way we confront them in even our smallest acts.

## Looking Ahead

1. Try to perceive the class relationships between the narrator and Sylvia on the one hand, and the narrator and the baker's assistant on the other. Consider how these relationships affect the action.
2. The narrator's character is revealed not only by his actions but also by his explanations of them. Read critically to see how, and if, action and explanation have a logical connection.
3. Egotism and betrayal are themes to become aware of as you read.

Paris, the Villiers intersection. To the east, the boulevard des Batignolles, with the outline of Sacré-Coeur[1] looming in the background. To the north, the rue de Lévis and its open market, the café du "Dôme" at the corner of the avenue de Villiers, then, on the sidewalk across the street, the Villiers subway stop, set
5 directly beneath a clock, among the trees of the center mall, which has been destroyed.
 To the west, the boulevard de Courcelles, which led to Monceau Park, on the fringe of which the former Cité-Club, a student center, used to occupy a building dating from Napoleon III, which was torn down in 1960. It was there I
10 ate dinner every night when I was in law school, for I lived nearby, on the rue de Rome. At the same time Sylvia, who worked in an art gallery on the rue de Monceau, used to walk through the park on her way home.
 At that point, I knew her only by sight. Once in a while our paths would cross somewhere along the three-hundred-yard length of the boulevard that
15 separated the intersection from the student center. We had exchanged a few furtive looks, but nothing more.
 My friend Schmidt was responsible for urging me to action.
 "Unfortunately, she's a little too tall for me. But why don't you see how you make out with her."
20 "What? Just go up and talk to her? Not me!"
 "Why not? You never know!"
 It was true: she wasn't a girl you could just go up and introduce yourself to on the street. And to confront her cold, just like that, was even less my style. Yet I assumed she would make an exception for me, as I would have made an ex-
25 ception for her. Despite these careful rationalizations I was afraid of making a

---

1. *Sacré-Coeur:* French for "sacred heart"; refers to a famous church in the Montmartre section of Paris. (*ed.*)

move too quickly. I opted for extreme caution, sometimes going so far as to avoid her gaze, leaving the task of sizing her up to Schmidt.

"Did she look over this way?"

"She did."

"For a long time?"

"Pretty long. Longer than usual; that I can safely say."

"Listen," I said, "I feel like following her. At least so I'll know where she lives."

"Go right up to her; don't follow her. If you do, you'll blow it."

"Go right up to her?"

I realized how strongly I felt about her. It was May, and the end of the school year was fast approaching. There was no question that she lived in the area. We had seen her once carrying a string basket, obviously doing her shopping. We had been sitting on the terrace of the Dôme, having an after-dinner coffee, when she walked by. It was only quarter to eight, and the stores were still open.

"Actually," I said after she had turned the corner, "she might live right around here somewhere."

"Don't go away," Schmidt said. "I'm going on a little reconnaissance mission."

A few moments later he was back.

"She went into one of the shops. I don't know which direction she'll take when she comes out. The risk is too great."

A short while later we saw her pass by again, "looking a little too straight in front her," as Schmidt was quick to note, "not to be aware of our presence."

"The hell with it!" I said, getting to my feet. "I'm going to follow her."

I abandoned all caution and followed hard on her heels up the rue de Lévis. But I had to beat a quick retreat, for she was zigzagging from one street stall to another in such a way that at any moment she might have caught sight of me. I came back to the Dôme, and for the rest of the evening didn't see her. But even if I had managed to follow her to her door, what good would that have done me? Schmidt was right: this skirmishing could not go on indefinitely. I was on the verge of taking the matter in hand—that is, of going straight up to her and saying hello—when, at long last, fortune smiled on me.

The corner clock said seven; we were on our way to dinner. I had stopped to buy the evening paper. Schmidt, instead of waiting for me, had gone ahead and crossed to the opposite sidewalk, from which he watched me as, head lowered, I ran to catch up with him. Just as I was about to start across the street I saw him signaling frantically to me, and at first I couldn't figure out what he wanted; I thought he was trying to warn me about some imminent danger in the street. Actually, it was toward the sidewalk behind me and to my right that he pointed. I turned my head, but the sun, which was low on the horizon, blinded me. I took a step or two back, the better to see, and when I did, I ran almost full tilt

into the object of Schmidt's gesticulations, which was none other than Sylvia
herself, striding up the boulevard. I began to apologize.

"Oh, I beg your pardon!"

"No problem. Don't give it another thought."

"You sure?"

"There's no marked damage, so far as I can tell."

"Luckily. . . . I don't know what's the matter with me today. Just a little
while ago I almost killed myself on those stupid things over there," I said, pointing toward a pile of rubbish stacked along the sidewalk.

She burst out laughing. "What I wouldn't have given to see that!"

"I said I *almost* killed myself."

"What?"

The traffic noises were so loud at that time of day we could barely make out
what we were saying. I raised my voice till I was almost shouting:

"I said I *almost*: I didn't really hurt myself. . . . Oh, these damn cars! You
can't hear yourself think!"

Any attempt at conversation was clearly futile. Sylvia began to leave, and
for the life of me I couldn't think of anything to say that might keep her.

"I'm going this way," she said.

"And I'm going that way," I said. Then I added, very quickly, "I owe you an
apology. What say we meet for coffee in an hour? You, my friend, and me."

I made it an hour from then because I was sure she wouldn't accept an invitation for here and now.

"I'm sorry, but I'm busy tonight. Maybe another time. We do seem to pass
each other in the street fairly often. 'Bye now."

"Good-bye!"

Without even watching her disappear into the distance, I ran to catch up
with Schmidt, smirking like a Cheshire cat.

During the brief minute our conversation had lasted I had kept but one
thought in mind: say something, anything, that would prevent her from leaving,
no matter what impression—and it could only be poor—I might make on her.
And yet there was no question that I had scored a victory. In all that rush-hour
hustle, something of myself had come through. She had not seemed put off by
it; on the contrary, she had seemed to relish it, to respond in kind to my remarks. That she had refused my invitation did not upset me in the least, since,
the way things were left, I felt free, when next we met, to take up our conversation where it had left off. And I had little doubt we would meet again soon.
What more could I ask?

Then something happened that I did not expect. The extraordinary stroke of
good luck that had thrown us together was followed by a stroke of bad luck.
Three days passed, a week, and not once did I so much as glimpse Sylvia in the
street. Schmidt, to concentrate on his upcoming written examination, had gone
home to his family to study. And no matter how madly in love I already was,
the idea of diverting some of my study time to go looking for Sylvia did not

even cross my mind. My only free moments were at mealtime. So I did without dinner.

I calculated that dinner took me thirty minutes. The trip to and from the student center took three. Thus, if I spent dinnertime looking for Sylvia, my chances of finding her would increase tenfold. But then arose the question of how best to use that time: stalking the boulevards had its virtues, but also its drawbacks, for since I did not know where she lived or from which direction she might come, she might well be taking other side streets, not to mention the Metro or the bus. One thing was certain: she still had to go shopping. And that was why I decided to broaden my investigations to include the rue de Lévis.

I have to confess that on these sultry late afternoons, patrolling the boulevard was dull and fatiguing. The market, on the contrary, offered variety, freshness, and the irresistible factor of food. My stomach, weary of student meals, was pestering me; in anticipation of the upcoming vacation it was clamoring for that gastronomical interlude that cherry time promised. The odors of the open market and the hurly-burly that went with it were more fun, and more relaxing for me, after so many hours of hitting the books and of memorizing the contents of the professors' lectures than were the noise of the student restaurant and the untantalizing whiffs of the student food.

And still my searches proved fruitless. Thousands of people lived in the area—probably one of the most densely populated sections of the city. Should I stay in one place? Or should I prowl? I was young, and doubtless thought, somewhat stupidly, that suddenly, in one of the windows that lined the streets, Sylvia would appear. Or perhaps she would emerge just as suddenly from one of the shops in the neighborhood and, as had happened the other day, literally run into me. So I opted to keep moving, to prowl.

It was in the course of my wanderings that I discovered, on the corner of the rue Lebouteux, a little bakery where I bought all kinds of cakes, which constituted the sum and substance of my daily fare. Two women ran the shop: the owner, or the wife of the owner, who at this time of day was almost always busy in the kitchen; and a rather pretty brunette, bright eyed and comely, with full, sensuous lips. The first days I visited the shop, if I remember correctly, I often found her coping with the young hoods of the area, who made a point of stopping in to horse around and show off in front of her. They hung around so long that she was never able to serve me promptly. Thus I had all the time in the world to decide what I wanted, though I almost never settled on anything but sugar cookies. The kind they made was neither better nor worse than one could find in any other bakery In fact, it was factory made, and distributed to all the stores and bakeries in Paris. On the one hand, the empty street down which I walked, the last lap in my peripatetic search, offered me the advantage of eating my purchase in peace, without Sylvia's seeing me, in case she might suddenly materialize out of the crowd without warning; on the other, the purchase of my sugar cookie had, after a certain time, turned into a kind of ceremony between the baker's assistant and me.

To tell the truth, it was she who started it. To irritate her young boy friend, she had at the height of one of their frequent arguments made a point of inti-
160    mating—by obvious winks and smiles, to which I responded with a face of marble—some tacit understanding between us.

I had bought only one cookie, and I began to eat it as I made my way from the bakery to the open market. When I got there, I wanted another one, and retraced my steps. The smile with which the baker's assistant greeted me, as
165    though she were welcoming a friend or acquaintance, only reinforced my coldness. At my age, if there is anything one hates to do it is run errands. I therefore made a point of avoiding the least semblance of familiarity with salespeople. I like to go into a shop as though I were there for the first time.

"I'd like a sugar cookie," I said, in my most neutral tone of voice.
170    Surprised, she did a kind of double-take, as though not quite sure she was seeing right, and her meaningful glance made me ashamed of myself. I found it impossible to play my little game any longer and, with the same ingenuous air, asked her how much I owed her. "Forty centimes?" I queried matter-of-factly.

"Forty even," she answered quickly, apparently having guessed the game I
175    was playing and having decided to play it, too.

And still no Sylvia anywhere on the horizon. Was she hiding from me? And, if so, why, in God's name? Could she have gone to the country? Was she sick? or dead? or married? I ran the full gamut of possibilities, all of which struck me as equally likely. By the end of the week my search had turned into a pure formal-
180    ity. I couldn't wait to return to my bakery, each day being more careful to prepare entrances and exits, my dilatory habits and bizarre conduct.

The mask of obsequiousness and commercial indifference that my baker's assistant sported only contributed, I could clearly see, to helping her play the game, and her distortions of the rule were not so many oversights, nor did they
185    stem from impatience, but were obviously meant to be provocative. If ever she happened to anticipate, by a movement of her hand or so much as a glance, the cake or cookie on which I had set my heart, I pretended to change my mind, even though I might eventually come back to my original choice.

"Two sugar cookies?"
190    "No . . . uh . . . Yes, one sugar cookie. . . . Uh . . . and, well, I think maybe I'll have . . . another. Yes, that's it: two."

She went about filling my order without the least trace of impatience, happy to find some excuse to keep me there in the shop with her, for at that late hour there were few customers. And the way she fluttered her eyelashes,
195    pressed her lips together—all sorts of little blunders she committed—betrayed feelings that were less and less unconscious. It hadn't taken me long to figure out that the pretty baker's assistant did not find me unattractive, but—call it vanity if you like—I somehow seemed to take it for granted that any girl would be attracted to me. Besides, not only was she not exactly what I would call my
200    type—which is the least you can say about her—but the fact is I was wholly preoccupied with Sylvia. . . .Yes, and it was precisely because I was thinking of

Sylvia that I did not disdain the advances of the baker's assistant—and there could be no question that they were advances. I in fact responded to them more warmly than I would have were I not in love with another girl.

And yet the comedy, impelled as it were by its own momentum, was emerging from the reserve in which it had been confined during the first few days, and threatened to turn into burlesque. Sure now of the girl's feelings about me, I took great delight in testing her malleability, making sure she yielded to my slightest whim. I watched her do a double-take when in contrast to my seemingly insatiable appetite of the previous day I would surprise her the following time by ordering in moderation. On my greedy visits I sometimes ordered as many as ten pastries at a time, far from sure I would be able to consume them. And yet somehow I did, although it might take me as long as fifteen minutes, standing there on the street corner munching away, only a stone's throw from the bakery, but now without the slightest fear of being seen.

So it was that each day I ventured a little farther, convinced it was but a game that could not go very far. Besides, I told myself, it was as good a way as any of whiling away the time, and also a method of getting even with Sylvia and being revenged for her absence. And yet I had the feeling that this vengeance was unworthy of me, and my way of reacting to it was to take out my irritation on the baker's girl. What upset me the most was not the notion that she might take a shine to me but, on the contrary, that it might enter her mind that I would end up liking her. And to justify myself in my own eyes I kept repeating, over and over again, that it was her fault and that I would have to punish her for daring to associate with her betters.

Matters had reached the point at which I decided to take the offensive. The bakery was empty. It was only a few minutes from closing time, and the baker herself was in the back checking the roast that she was preparing for supper. I remained in the shop while I munched on my pastries; I decided to offer one to the baker's assistant. She refused at first, but I knew she only wanted to be coaxed, and finally she chose a piece of pie that she swallowed as though she hadn't eaten in a week. I teased her.

"I always thought that anyone who worked in a bakery shop all day long would end up hating every kind of sweet or pastry there is."

"You know," she said, her mouth still full, "I've only been here a month, and I'm not staying on much longer. Come September I have a job in one of the big department stores."

"You work here all day long?"

"Yes."

"And what do you do with your evenings?"

She didn't reply. She was leaning back on the counter, her eyes lowered. I went on.

"How about going out with me one night?"

She took two steps forward, to the shop door, where she was framed in the waning light. Her square décolletage emphasized the line of her breast and shoulders. After a moment's silence she turned her head slightly.

"I'm only eighteen, you know."

I moved over to her and with one finger touched her bare back.

"So what? Don't your parents ever let you go out?"

250  The arrival of the baker enabled her to avoid a reply. Quickly she slipped back behind the counter.

My exams were almost over, and soon I would be going away on vacation. I assumed that Sylvia was lost forever. Force of habit alone made me continue my nocturnal rounds looking for her—plus, perhaps, the hope of extracting from

255  the baker's assistant the promise to go out with me, which I admit was meager consolation for my disappointment. Two days before my departure I ran into her in the street. She was carrying a basket of bread. I stopped her.

"Would you like me to help you?"

"Do I look as though I need help?"

260  "Am I bothering you? Are you afraid someone might see us?"

"Not at all. Anyway, I'm leaving in a month." She gave a slight smile, which she meant to be provocative. In order to dispel her embarrassment, I suggested we start walking.

"Would it bother you if I walked with you for a while?"

265  "Well, actually . . . "

Luckily I caught sight of a porte cochère.[2]

"Listen, let's step inside here, just for a second. I have something I want to tell you."

Like a little lamb, she followed me into an inside courtyard. She set down

270  her basket of bread and leaned up against the wall. Her solemn, questioning eyes looked up at me.

"Did I do something wrong? Something you took offense at?"

"No, I already told you, that's not the reason."

I looked her straight in the eye. I placed my hand on the wall just beside

275  her, at the height of her shoulders.

"What say we go out together some night? How about tomorrow?"

"Don't. . . . I should go now. I really should."

"Why?"

"I don't know. After all, I don't know you from Adam."

280  "That's precisely the point of going out; that way we can get to know each other. Do I look all that frightening?"

She smiled. "No, of course not."

I took her hand and began playing with her fingers.

"It's no big deal. We can go to a movie on the Champs-Elysées. Do you ever

285  go to the movies?"

"Sure. On Saturday."

"Then let's go on Saturday. . . ."

---

2. *porte cochère:* carriage entrance. (*ed.*)

"I usually go with some friends."

"Boy friends?"

"Boys and girls both. They're all so . . . stupid!"

"Another good reason to go with me. So are we all set for Saturday?" 290

"No, not Saturday."

"What about some other day? Do your parents keep you locked up?"

"Don't be silly. Of course they don't."

"All right, then, let's go out tomorrow. We'll have dinner in a good little 295
restaurant; then we'll go over to the Champs-Elysées. I'll wait for you at eight
o'clock at the café on the corner. The Dôme. You know the one, don't you?"

"Do I have to dress up?"

I slipped my hand beneath the strap of her dress and caressed her shoulder
with my fingertips. She didn't stop me, but I could feel her trembling. 300

"Of course you don't. You're fine just the way you are. Okay?"

"I don't know whether my mother will—"

"But you said that—"

"Yes, in principle. But—"

"Tell her you're going out with a girl friend."

"I suppose I could do that. I mean, maybe." 305

With a movement of her shoulder she forced me to withdraw my hand. Her
voice was thick. Mine, I have to confess, wasn't too self-assured either. I tried to
joke.

"Listen, are you romantic?"

"What?" 310

I enunciated each syllable carefully: "Ro-man-tic. I'll tell you what I'll do:
I'll come by the shop tomorrow night at seven-thirty. In case we can't talk
openly in the shop, here's what we'll do. I'll ask for a pastry. If you give me two,
it'll mean you're coming, in which case we'll meet as planned at the Dôme. 315
Okay?"

"Well . . . okay."

"Say it back to me, so we make sure you have it straight."

"If I give you two pastries, it means yes," she said with utter seriousness,
without the trace of a smile or that bit of ease that would have made me feel 320
more comfortable and eased my conscience to some degree.

What in the world had I got myself into?

The following day, a Friday, I took my oral examination and passed it. By now I
had lost all desire to keep my evening engagement, but the fellow students with
whom I might have celebrated my success were still bogged down in their ex- 325
ams, and the prospect of spending an evening alone was more than I could face.

When I got to the rue Lebouteux, it was already quarter to eight. As we had
agreed the day before, I asked for a pastry, and I watched as the baker's assistant
handed me one; then, after a second's hesitation, which I must admit upped her
in my esteem, a second. I exited and retraced my steps to the intersection, 330

munching on my pastries as I walked. But I had gone no more than a dozen yards when I gave a start. Yes, it was Sylvia walking toward me, clearly crossing the street to intercept me. Her ankle was bandaged, and she was walking with the help of a cane. I had just enough time to swallow what was in my mouth
335    and conceal the other pastry in the palm of my hand.

"Hi there!" she said, all smiles.

"Good evening! How are you? What happened? Did you have an accident?"

"Oh, nothing. I sprained my ankle. But it laid me up for three weeks."

"I was surprised not to have run into you again."

340    "I caught a glimpse of you yesterday, but you seemed lost in your thoughts."

"Oh, really?"

In a split second I had made my decision. Sylvia was there. Everything else vanished. All that mattered was getting away from this cursed place as soon as
345    possible.

"Have you had dinner yet?"

"No. In fact I didn't even have an afternoon snack today." And, so saying, she stared openly at the pastry in my hand.

"The heat makes me hungry," I said lamely, as though in answer to her
350    stare.

"You don't have to account for your eating habits," she said, laughing. But her sarcasm made no impression on me. My mind was filled with one idea and one idea only: to spirit her far away from where we were standing.

"What say we have dinner together?"

355    "Fine by me. But I must go back up to my place. Do you mind waiting. I only live on the second floor; I won't be a minute."

And I saw her disappear into the door of the building catercorner from where we had met, directly across from the bakery.

That minute she mentioned lasted fifteen, during which I had ample opportu-
360    nity to reflect on my imprudence. I doubtless ought to have invited Sylvia for another night, and kept to my plans with the baker's assistant for that evening. But my choice was, above all, *moral*. Having found Sylvia again, to have carried on with the baker's girl would have been worse than a vice: it would have been pure nonsense.

365    To make matters more complicated, it had begun to rain. And yet it was the rain that saved me. It was already past eight o'clock, but the baker's assistant was apparently waiting for the rain to let up before leaving the shop. The last drops were falling when Sylvia reappeared, a raincoat over her shoulders. I suggested I go look for a taxi.

370    "With the rain you'll never find one," she said. "I don't mind walking."

"Really?"

"Really."

I moved beside her and fell into step with her. The street was deserted, and if the baker's girl emerged from the shop, she might well see us. In any case, I thought to myself, realizing how cowardly the concern, she would be too far away to cause any trouble. I didn't dare turn to look, and the walk was interminable. Had she seen us, or was she pining away, waiting, in the café? I'll never know. 375

As for the conquest of Sylvia, it was a mere formality. The reason for it was revealed to me later that same night. 380

"During the time I was laid up I managed to find a few amusements," she said, looking at me with mocking air. "You probably don't know it, but my window looks out on the street. I saw everything." I felt myself trembling. She went on. "You're a terrible person! You came within a hairbreadth of making me jealous. Yet I obviously couldn't bring myself to let you know by some kind of signal. I loathe people who pace back and forth in front of my doorstep. Too bad for you if you want to ruin your stomach with all those silly little pastries." 385

"On the contrary, they're very good."

"I know. I tried them. Actually, I know all your vices!"

Six months later we were married, and for a while we lived on the rue Lebouteux. Sometimes we went to buy our bread together, but it was no longer the same baker's girl. 390

## Looking Back

1. Why does Rohmer have the narrator situate his café so precisely at the beginning of the story?

2. From what perspective must we view the story once the narrator has named Sylvia (line 11)?

3. What does his initial hesitation to "go right up to her" (line 35) reveal about him?

4. In your view, does Sylvia indeed "respond" to him when they first meet (lines 101–103)? Explain your answer.

5. How does he betray the baker's girl even at the outset?

6. Can you explain how, as he claims, his love for Sylvia makes him more rather than less responsive to the baker's girl's "advances" (see lines 201–204)?

7. What does his reference to the baker's girl's behaving "like a little lamb" (line 269) tell us about her?

8. Why does his conscience bother him when he makes a date with her (lines 319–322)?

9. How is he able to rationalize his decision to stand up to the baker's girl as "moral" (see lines 360–364)?

10. Is his last betrayal of her excusable? Explain your answer.

## Writing Assignments

1. Few of us, when we have done something bad, ever admit that it was bad. We deny it was our fault, or say that circumstances made it unavoidable, or justify it as necessary. But the people who suffer at our hands are unlikely to accept our defensive

reasoning—they feel the pain. And those who stand outside, as we do reading "The Baker's Girl," are also unlikely to excuse the perpetrator. We can see the bad conduct clearly, objectively, as well as the moral principle it violates and the negative effects it causes. To stand in moral judgment, therefore, is to objectify this kind of perception. Write an essay interpolating your judgment of the narrator's behavior toward the baker's assistant and extrapolating from this particular case to broader consideration of what is involved.

2. People respond to others for very different reasons. Some of these are natural and good, and others are downright harmful. Some motives for responding are suspect: one can begin to feel more like a bullseye than a human being. And some motives are so superficial that it becomes difficult to discover another's true character. Write an essay suggesting the best ways to respond to another person. Begin by examining the narrator's relations to the two women in his life and theirs to him; then expand on this to explain what ought to attract one person to another and the dangers of false responses. Use examples from your own and others' experience when it is useful to do so.

3. We suspect the narrator in "The Baker's Girl" of egotism. Although it may not be a sin, it is certainly a character fault of self-centeredness and conceit, and like all character faults, it is likely to hurt others as well as oneself. Faced with the egotist, we ask ourselves what causes such egotism, how it distorts personality and character, how it affects principles and perception of reality, what harm it may do, and so on. Referring to the story, write an essay that analyzes the phenomenon of egotism as exemplified by the narrator, and address these and any other related matters that occur to you. You may also want to use pertinent examples from your own observations.

---

# Albert Camus

# The Growing Stone

In his short lifetime, Albert Camus (1913–1960) produced outstanding works of fiction, drama, and philosophy. Most notable among his books are *The Stranger, The Plague, The Fall* (novels), *The Myth of Sisyphus, The Rebel* (philosophy), and *Caligula* (drama). Born in Algeria, he gained a degree in philosophy, became a journalist, and during World War II edited *Combat,* a resistance newspaper published in Paris during the Nazi occupation. He won the Nobel Prize for literature three years before his death in an automobile accident. This story is from *Exile and the Kingdom,* a collection of short fiction.

## Looking Ahead

1. Be alert to the cultural differences between the main character's European origins and his life in the Brazilian hinterlands.

2. Read critically to note the symbolic importance (and therefore the application to other situations in life) of actions to meaningful relationships, a moral concern of this story.

3. As you read, keep in mind the themes of penitence, sacrifice, fraternity, and rebirth.

The automobile swung clumsily around the curve in the red sandstone trail, now a mass of mud. The headlights suddenly picked out in the night—first on one side of the road, then on the other—two wooden huts with sheet-metal roofs. On the right near the second one, a tower of coarse beams could be made out in the light fog. From the top of the tower a metal cable, invisible at its      5
starting-point, shone as it sloped down into the light from the car before disappearing behind the embankment that blocked the road. The car slowed down and stopped a few yards from the huts.

The man who emerged from the seat to the right of the driver labored to extricate himself from the car. As he stood up, his huge, broad frame lurched a lit-      10
tle. In the shadow beside the car, solidly planted on the ground and weighed down by fatigue, he seemed to be listening to the idling motor. Then he walked in the direction of the embankment and entered the cone of light from the headlights. He stopped at the top of the slope, his broad back outlined against the darkness. After a moment he turned around. In the light from the dashboard he      15
could see the chauffeur's black face, smiling. The man signaled and the chauffeur turned off the motor. At once a vast cool silence fell over the trail and the forest. Then the sound of the water could be heard.

The man looked at the river below him, visible solely as a broad dark motion, flecked with occasional shimmers. A denser motionless darkness, far be-      20
yond, must be the other bank. By looking fixedly, however, one could see on that still bank a yellowish light like an oil lamp in the distance. The big man turned back toward the car and nodded. The chauffeur switched off the lights, turned them on again, then blinked them regularly. On the embankment the man appeared and disappeared, taller and more massive each time he came      25
back to life. Suddenly, on the other bank of the river, a lantern held up by an invisible arm swung back and forth several times. At a final signal from the lookout, the chauffeur turned off his lights once and for all. The car and the man disappeared into the night. With the lights out, the river was almost visible—or at least a few of its long liquid muscles shining intermittently. On each side of      30
the road, the dark masses of forest foliage stood out against the sky and seemed very near. The fine rain that had soaked the trail an hour earlier was still hovering in the warm air, intensifying the silence and immobility of this broad clearing in the virgin forest. In the black sky misty stars flickered.

But from the other bank rose sounds of chains and muffled plashings.      35
Above the hut on the right of the man still waiting there, the cable stretched taut. A dull creaking began to run along it, just as there rose from the river a faint yet quite audible sound of stirred-up water. The creaking became more regular, the sound of water spread farther and then became localized, as the lantern grew larger. Now its yellowish halo could be clearly seen. The halo      40

gradually expanded and again contracted while the lantern shone through the mist and began to light up from beneath a sort of square roof of dried palms supported by thick bamboos. This crude shelter, around which vague shadows were moving, was slowly approaching the bank. When it was about in the mid-
45 dle of the river, three little men, almost black, were distinctly outlined in the yellow light, naked from the waist up and wearing conical hats. They stood still with feet apart, leaning somewhat to offset the strong drift of the river pressing with all its invisible water against the side of a big crude raft that eventually emerged from the darkness. When the ferry came still closer, the man could see
50 behind the shelter on the downstream side two tall Negroes likewise wearing nothing but broad straw hats and cotton trousers. Side by side they weighed with all their might on long poles that sank slowly into the river toward the stern while the Negroes, with the same slow motion, bent over the water as far as their balance would allow. In the bow the three mulattoes, still and silent,
55 watched the bank approach without raising their eyes toward the man waiting for them.

The ferry suddenly bumped against something. And the lantern swaying from the shock lighted up a pier jutting into the water. The tall Negroes stood still with hands above their heads gripping the ends of the poles, which were
60 barely stuck in the bottom, but their taut muscles rippled constantly with a motion that seemed to come from the very thrust of the water. The other ferry-men looped chains over the posts on the dock, leaped onto the boards, and lowered a sort of gangplank that covered the bow of the raft with its inclined plane.

65 The man returned to the car and slid in while the chauffeur stepped on the starter. The car slowly climbed the embankment, pointed its hood toward the sky, and then lowered it toward the river as it tackled the downward slope. With brakes on, it rolled forward, slipped somewhat on the mud, stopped, started up again. It rolled onto the pier with a noise of bouncing planks,
70 reached the end, where the mulattoes, still silent, were standing on either side, and plunged slowly toward the raft. The raft ducked its nose in the water as soon as the front wheels struck it and almost immediately bobbed back to re-ceive the car's full weight. Then the chauffeur ran the vehicle to the stern, in front of the square roof where the lantern was hanging. At once the mulattoes
75 swung the inclined plane back onto the pier and jumped simultaneously onto the ferry, pushing it off from the muddy bank. The river strained under the raft and raised it on the surface of the water, where it drifted slowly at the end of the long drawbar running along the cable overhead. The tall Negroes relaxed their effort and drew in their poles. The man and the chauffeur got out of the car and
80 came over to stand on the edge of the raft facing upstream. No one had spoken during the maneuver, and even now each remained in his place, motionless and quiet except for one of the tall Negroes who was rolling a cigarette in coarse paper.

The man was looking at the gap through which the river sprang from the
85 vast Brazilian forest and swept down toward them. Several hundred yards wide

at that point, the muddy, silky waters of the river pressed against the side of the ferry and then, unimpeded at the two ends of the raft, sheered off and again spread out in a single powerful flood gently flowing through the dark forest toward the sea and the night. A stale smell, come from the water or the spongy sky, hung in the air. Now the slapping of the water under the ferry could be heard, and at intervals the calls of bullfrogs from the two banks or the strange cries of birds. The big man approached the small, thin chauffeur, who was leaning against one of the bamboos with his hands in the pockets of his dungarees, once blue but now covered with the same red dust that had been blowing in their faces all day long. A smile spread over his face, all wrinkled in spite of his youth. Without really seeing them, he was staring at the faint stars still swimming in the damp sky.

But the bird's cries became sharper, unfamiliar chatterings mingled with them, and almost at once the cable began to creak. The tall Negroes plunged their poles into the water and groped blindly for the bottom. The man turned around toward the shore they had just left. Now that shore was obscured by the darkness and the water, vast and savage like the continent of trees stretching beyond it for thousands of kilometers. Between the near-by ocean and this sea of vegetation, the handful of men drifting at that moment on a wild river seemed lost. When the raft bumped the new pier it was as if, having cast off all moorings, they were landing on an island in the darkness after days of frightened sailing.

Once on land, the men's voices were at last heard. The chauffeur had just paid them and, with voices that sounded strangely gay in the heavy night, they were saying farewell in Portuguese as the car started up again.

"They said sixty, the kilometers to Iguape. Three hours more and it'll be over. Socrates is happy," the chauffeur announced.

The man laughed with a warm, hearty laugh that resembled him.

"Me too, Socrates, I'm happy too. The trail is hard."

"Too heavy, Mr. D'Arrast, you too heavy," and the chauffeur laughed too as if he would never stop.

The car had taken on a little speed. It was advancing between high walls of trees and inextricable vegetation, amidst a soft, sweetish smell. Fireflies on the wing constantly crisscrossed in the darkness of the forest, and every once in a while red-eyed birds would bump against the windshield. At times a strange, savage sound would reach them from the depths of the night and the chauffeur would roll his eyes comically as he looked at his passenger.

The road kept turning and crossed little streams on bridges of wobbly boards. After an hour the fog began to thicken. A fine drizzle began to fall, dimming the car's lights. Despite the jolts, D'Arrast was half asleep. He was no longer riding in the damp forest but on the roads of the Serra that they had taken in the morning as they left São Paulo. From those dirt trails constantly rose the red dust which they could still taste, and on both sides, as far as the eye could see, it covered the sparse vegetation of the plains. The harsh sun, the pale mountains full of ravines, the starved zebus encountered along the roads, with a

tired flight of ragged urubus[1] as their only escort, the long, endless crossing of an endless desert . . . He gave a start. The car had stopped. Now they were in Japan: fragile houses on both sides of the road and, in the houses, furtive kimonos. The chauffeur was talking to a Japanese wearing soiled dungarees and a
135   Brazilian straw hat. Then the car started up again.

"He said only forty kilometers."

"Where were we? In Tokyo?"

"No. Registro. In Brazil all the Japanese come here."

"Why?"

140   "Don't know. They're yellow, you know, Mr. D'Arrast."

But the forest was gradually thinning out, and the road was becoming easier, though slippery. The car was skidding on sand. The window let in a warm, damp breeze that was rather sour.

"You smell it?" the chauffeur asked, smacking his lips. "That's the good old
145   sea. Soon, Iguape."

"If we have enough gas," D'Arrast said. And he went back to sleep peacefully.

Sitting up in bed early in the morning, D'Arrast looked in amazement at the huge room in which he had just awakened. The lower half of the big walls was newly painted brown. Higher up, they had once been painted white, and
150   patches of yellowish paint covered them up to the ceiling. Two rows of beds faced each other. D'Arrast saw only one bed unmade at the end of his row and that bed was empty. But he heard a noise on his left and turned toward the door, where Socrates, a bottle of mineral water in each hand, stood laughing. "Happy memory!" he said. D'Arrast shook himself. Yes, the hospital in which
155   the Mayor had lodged them the night before was named "Happy Memory." "Sure memory," Socrates continued. "They told me first build hospital, later build water. Meanwhile, happy memory, take fizz water to wash." He disappeared, laughing and singing, not at all exhausted apparently by the cataclysmic sneezes that had shaken him all night long and kept D'Arrast from closing an
160   eye.

Now D'Arrast was completely awake. Through the iron-latticed window he could see a little red-earth courtyard soaked by the rain that was noiselessly pouring down on a clump of tall aloes. A woman passed holding a yellow scarf over her head. D'Arrast lay back in bed, then sat up at once and got out of
165   the bed, which creaked under his weight. Socrates came in at that moment: "For you, Mr. D'Arrast. The Mayor is waiting outside." But, seeing the look on D'Arrast's face, he added: "Don't worry; he never in a hurry."

After shaving with the mineral water, D'Arrast went out under the portico of the building. The Mayor—who had the proportions and, under his gold-
170   rimmed glasses, the look of a nice little weasel—seemed lost in dull contemplation of the rain. But a charming smile transfigured him as soon as he saw

---

1. *zebus:* large, humped cattle; *urubus:* predatory birds. (*ed.*)

D'Arrast. Holding his little body erect, he rushed up and tried to stretch his arms around the engineer. At that moment an automobile drove up in front of them on the other side of the low wall, skidded in the wet clay, and came to a stop on an angle. "The Judge!" said the Mayor. Like the Mayor, the Judge was dressed in navy blue. But he was much younger, or at least seemed so because of his elegant figure and his look of a startled adolescent. Now he was crossing the courtyard in their direction, gracefully avoiding the puddles. A few steps from D'Arrast, he was already holding out his arms and welcoming him. He was proud to greet the noble engineer who was honoring their poor village; he was delighted by the priceless service the noble engineer was going to do Iguape by building that little jetty to prevent the periodic flooding of the lower quarters of town. What a noble profession, to command the waters and dominate rivers! Ah, surely the poor people of Iguape would long remember the noble engineer's name and many years from now would still mention it in their prayers. D'Arrast, captivated by such charm and eloquence, thanked him and didn't dare wonder what possible connection a judge could have with a jetty. Besides, according to the Mayor, it was time to go to the club, where the leading citizens wanted to receive the noble engineer appropriately before going to inspect the poorer quarters. Who were the leading citizens? 190

"Well," the Mayor said, "myself as Mayor, Mr. Carvalho here, the Harbor Captain, and a few others less important. Besides, you won't have to pay much attention to them, for they don't speak French."

D'Arrast called Socrates and told him he would meet him when the morning was over. 195

"All right," Socrates said, "I'll go to the Garden of the Fountain."

"The Garden?"

"Yes, everybody knows. Have no fear, Mr. D'Arrast."

The hospital, D'Arrast noticed as he left it, was built on the edge of the forest, and the heavy foliage almost hung over the roofs. Over the whole surface of 200 the trees was falling a sheet of fine rain which the dense forest was noiselessly absorbing like a huge sponge. The town, some hundred houses roofed with faded tiles, extended between the forest and the river, and the water's distant murmur reached the hospital. The car entered drenched streets and almost at once came out on a rather large rectangular square which showed, among numerous puddles in its red clay, the marks of tires, iron wheels, and horseshoes. 205 All around, brightly plastered low houses closed off the square, behind which could be seen the two round towers of a blue-and-white church of colonial style. A smell of salt water coming from the estuary dominated this bare setting. In the center of the square a few wet silhouettes were wandering. Along the 210 houses a motley crowd of gauchos, Japanese, half-breed Indians, and elegant leading citizens, whose dark suits looked exotic here, were sauntering with slow gestures. They stepped aside with dignity to make way for the car, then stopped and watched it. When the car stopped in front of one of the houses on the square, a circle of wet gauchos silently formed around it. 215

Line markers in right margin: 175, 180, 185, 190, 195, 200, 205, 210, 215

At the club—a sort of small bar on the second floor furnished with a bamboo counter and iron café tables—the leading citizens were numerous. Sugarcane alcohol was drunk in honor of D'Arrast after the Mayor, glass in hand, had wished him welcome and all the happiness in the world. But while D'Arrast was
220 drinking near the window, a huge lout of a fellow in riding-breeches and leggings came over and, staggering somewhat, delivered himself of a rapid and obscure speech in which the engineer recognized solely the word "passport." He hesitated and then took out the document, which the fellow seized greedily. After having thumbed through the passport, he manifested obvious displeasure.
225 He resumed his speech, shaking the document under the nose of the engineer, who, without getting excited, merely looked at the angry man. Whereupon the Judge, with a smile, came over and asked what was the matter. For a moment the drunk scrutinized the frail creature who dared to interrupt him and then, staggering even more dangerously, shook the passport in the face of his new in-
230 terlocutor. D'Arrast sat peacefully beside a café table and waited. The dialogue became very lively, and suddenly the Judge broke out in a deafening voice that one would never have suspected in him. Without any forewarning, the lout suddenly backed down like a child caught in the act. At a final order from the Judge, he sidled toward the door like a punished schoolboy and disappeared.
235 The Judge immediately came over to explain to D'Arrast, in a voice that had become harmonious again, that the uncouth individual who had just left was the Chief of Police, that he had dared to claim the passport was not in order, and that he would be punished for his outburst. Judge Carvalho then addressed himself to the leading citizens, who stood in a circle around him, and seemed to
240 be questioning them. After a brief discussion, the Judge expressed solemn excuses to D'Arrast, asked him to agree that nothing but drunkenness could explain such forgetfulness of the sentiments of respect and gratitude that the whole town of Iguape owed him, and, finally, asked him to decide himself on the punishment to be inflicted on the wretched individual. D'Arrast said that he
245 didn't want any punishment, that it was a trivial incident, and that he was particularly eager to go to the river. Then the Mayor spoke up to assert with much simple good-humor that a punishment was really mandatory, that the guilty man would remain incarcerated, and that they would all wait until their distinguished visitor decided on his fate. No protest could soften that smiling sever-
250 ity, and D'Arrast had to promise that he would think the matter over. Then they agreed to visit the poorer quarters of the town.
The river was already spreading its yellowish waters over the low, slippery banks. They had left behind them the last houses of Iguape and stood between the river and a high, steep embankment to which clung huts made of clay and
255 branches. In front of them, at the end of the embankment, the forest began again abruptly, as on the other bank. But the gap made by the water rapidly widened between the trees until reaching a vague grayish line that marked the beginning of the sea. Without saying a word, D'Arrast walked toward the slope, where the various flood levels had left marks that were still fresh. A muddy path
260 climbed toward the huts. In front of them, Negroes stood silently staring at the

newcomers. Several couples were holding hands, and on the edge of the mound, in front of the adults, a row of black children with bulging bellies and spindly legs were gaping with round eyes.

When he arrived in front of the huts, D'Arrast beckoned to the Harbor Captain. He was a fat, laughing Negro wearing a white uniform. D'Arrast asked him in Spanish if it were possible to visit a hut. The Captain was sure it was, he even thought it a good idea, and the noble engineer would see very interesting things. He harangued the Negroes at length, pointing to D'Arrast and to the river. They listened without saying a word. When the Captain had finished, no one stirred. He spoke again, in an impatient voice. Then he called upon one of the men, who shook his head. Whereupon the Captain said a few brief words in a tone of command. The man stepped forth from the group, faced D'Arrast, and with a gesture showed him the way. But his look was hostile. He was an elderly man with short, graying hair and a thin, wizened face; yet his body was still young, with hard wiry shoulders and muscles visible through his cotton pants and torn shirt. They went ahead, followed by the Captain and the crowd of Negroes, and climbed a new, steeper embankment where the huts made of clay, tin, and reeds clung to the ground with such difficulty that they had to be strengthened at the base and heavy stones. They met a woman going down the path, sometimes slipping in her bare feet, who was carrying on her head an iron drum full of water. Then they reached a small irregular square bordered by three huts. The man walked toward one of them and pushed open a bamboo door on hinges made of tropical liana. He stood aside without saying a word, staring at the engineer with the same impassive look. In the hut, D'Arrast saw nothing at first but a dying fire built right on the ground in the exact center of the room. Then in a back corner he made out a brass bed with a bare, broken mattress, a table in the other corner covered with earthenware dishes, and, between the two, a sort of stand supporting a color print representing Saint George. Nothing else but a pile of rags to the right of the entrance and, hanging from the ceiling, a few loincloths of various colors drying over the fire. Standing still, D'Arrast breathed in the smell of smoke and poverty that rose from the ground and choked him. Behind him, the Captain clapped his hands. The engineer turned around and, against the light, saw the graceful silhouette of a black girl approach and hold out something to him. He took a glass and drank the thick sugar-cane alcohol. The girl held out her tray to receive the empty glass and went out with such a supple motion that D'Arrast suddenly wanted to hold her back.

But on following her out he didn't recognize her in the crowd of Negroes and leading citizens gathered around the hut. He thanked the old man, who bowed without a word. Then he left. The Captain, behind him, resumed his explanations and asked when the French company from Rio could begin work and whether or not the jetty could be built before the rainy season. D'Arrast didn't know; to tell the truth, he wasn't thinking of that. He went down toward the cool river under the fine mist. He was still listening to that great pervasive sound he had been hearing continually since his arrival, which might have been made by the rustling of either the water or the trees, he could not tell. Having reached the bank, he looked out in the distance at the vague line of the sea, the thousands of kilometers of solitary waters leading to Africa and, beyond, his native Europe.

310     "Captain," he asked, "what do these people we have just seen live on?"

"They work when they're needed," the Captain said. "We are poor."

"Are they the poorest?"

"They are the poorest."

The Judge, who arrived at that moment, slipping somewhat in his best shoes,
315   said they already loved the noble engineer who was going to give them work.

"And, you know, they dance and sing every day."

Then, without transition, he asked D'Arrast if he had thought of the punishment.

"What punishment?"

320     "Why, our Chief of Police."

"Let him go." The Judge said that this was not possible; there had to be a punishment. D'Arrast was already walking toward Iguape.

In the little Garden of the Fountain, mysterious and pleasant under the fine rain, clusters of exotic flowers hung down along the lianas among the banana
325   trees and pandanus. Piles of wet stones marked the intersection of paths on which a motley crowd was strolling. Half-breeds, mulattoes, a few gauchos were chatting in low voices or sauntering along the bamboo paths to the point where groves and bush became thicker and more impenetrable. There, the forest began abruptly.

330     D'Arrast was looking for Socrates in the crowd when Socrates suddenly bumped him from behind.

"It's holiday," he said, laughing, and clung to D'Arrast's tall shoulders to jump up and down.

"What holiday?"

335     "Why, you not know?" Socrates said in surprise as he faced D'Arrast. "The feast of good Jesus. Each year they all come to the grotto with a hammer."

Socrates pointed out, not a grotto, but a group that seemed to be waiting in a corner of the garden.

"You see? One day the good statue of Jesus, it came upstream from the sea.
340   Some fishermen found it. How beautiful! How beautiful! Then they washed it here in the grotto. And now a stone grew up in the grotto. Every year it's the feast. With the hammer you break, you break off pieces for blessed happiness. And then it keeps growing and you keep breaking. It's the miracle!"

They had reached the grotto and could see its low entrance beyond the
345   waiting men. Inside, in the darkness studded with the flickering flames of candles, a squatting figure was pounding with a hammer. The man, a thin gaucho with a long mustache, got up and came out holding in his open palm, so that all might see, a small piece of moist schist, over which he soon closed his hand

carefully before going away. Another man then stooped down and entered the grotto.

D'Arrast turned around. On all sides pilgrims were waiting, without looking at him, impassive under the water dripping from the trees in thin sheets. He too was waiting in front of the grotto under the same film of water, and he didn't know for what. He had been waiting constantly, to tell the truth, for a month since he had arrived in this country. He had been waiting—in the red heat of humid days, under the little stars of night, despite the tasks to be accomplished, the jetties to be built, the roads to be cut through—as if the work he had come to do here were merely a pretext for a surprise or for an encounter he did not even imagine but which had been waiting patiently for him at the end of the world. He shook himself, walked away without anyone in the little group paying attention to him, and went toward the exit. He had to go back to the river and go to work.

But Socrates was waiting for him at the gate, lost in voluble conversation with a short, fat, strapping man whose skin was yellow rather than black. His head, completely shaved, gave even more sweep to a considerable forehead. On the other hand, his broad, smooth face was adorned with a very black beard, trimmed square.

"He's champion!" Socrates said by way of introduction. "Tomorrow he's in the procession."

The man, wearing a sailor's outfit of heavy serge, a blue-and-white jersey under the pea jacket, was examining D'Arrast attentively with his calm black eyes. At the same time he was smiling, showing all his very white teeth between his full, shiny lips.

"He speaks Spanish," Socrates said and, turning toward the stranger, added: "Tell Mr. D'Arrast." Then he danced off toward another group. The man ceased to smile and looked at D'Arrast with outright curiosity.

"You are interested, Captain?"

"I'm not a captain," D'Arrast said.

"That doesn't matter. But you're a noble. Socrates told me."

"Not I. But my grandfather was. His father too and all those before his father. Now there is no more nobility in our country."

"Ah!" the Negro said, laughing. "I understand; everybody is a noble."

"No, that's not it. There are neither noblemen nor common people."

The fellow reflected; then he made up his mind.

"No one works? No one suffers?"

"Yes, millions of men."

"Then that's the common people."

"In that way, yes, there is a common people. But the masters are policemen or merchants."

The mulatto's kindly face closed in a frown. Then he grumbled: "Humph! Buying and selling, eh! What filth! And with the police, dogs command."

Suddenly, he burst out laughing.

"You, you don't sell?"

"Hardly at all. I make bridges, roads."

"That's good. Me, I'm a ship's cook. If you wish, I'll make you our dish of
395    black beans."

"All right."

The cook came closer to D'Arrast and took his arm.

"Listen, I like what you tell. I'm going to tell you too. Maybe you will like."

He drew him over near the gate to a damp wooden bench beneath a clump
400    of bamboos.

"I was at sea, off Iguape, on a small coastwise tanker that supplies the harbors along here. It caught fire on board. Not by my fault! I know my job! No, just
bad luck. We were able to launch the lifeboats. During the night, the sea got
rough; it capsized the boat and I went down. When I came up, I hit the boat with
405    my head. I drifted. The night was dark, the waters are vast, and, besides, I don't
swim well; I was afraid. Just then I saw a light in the distance and recognized the
church of the good Jesus in Iguape. So I told the good Jesus that at his procession
I would carry a hundred-pound stone on my head if he saved me. You don't have
to believe me, but the waters became calm and my heart too. I swam slowly, I
410    was happy, and I reached the shore. Tomorrow I'll keep my promise."

He looked at D'Arrast in a suddenly suspicious manner.

"You're not laughing?"

"No, I'm not laughing. A man has to do what he has promised."

The fellow clapped him on the back.

415    "Now, come to my brother's, near the river. I'll cook you some beans."

"No," D'Arrast said, "I have things to do. This evening, if you wish."

"Good. But tonight there's dancing and praying in the big hut. It's the feast
for Saint George." D'Arrast asked him if he danced too. The cook's face hardened suddenly; for the first time his eyes became shifty.

420    "No, no, I won't dance. Tomorrow I must carry the stone. It is heavy. I'll go
this evening to celebrate the saint. And then I'll leave early."

"Does it last long?"

"All night and a little into the morning."

He looked at D'Arrast with a vaguely shameful look.

425    "Come to the dance. You can take me home afterward. Otherwise, I'll stay
and dance. I probably won't be able to keep from it."

"You like to dance?"

"Oh, yes! I like. Besides, there are cigars, saints, women. You forget everything and you don't obey any more."

430    "There are women too? All the women of the town?"

"Not of the town, but of the huts."

The ship's cook resumed his smile. "Come. The Captain I'll obey. And you
will help me keep my promise tomorrow."

D'Arrast felt slightly annoyed. What did that absurd promise mean to him?
435    But he looked at the handsome frank face smiling trustingly at him, its dark
skin gleaming with health and vitality.

"I'll come," he said. "Now I'll walk along with you a little."

Without knowing why, he had a vision at the same time of the black girl offering him the drink of welcome.

They went out of the garden, walked along several muddy streets, and reached the bumpy square, which looked even larger because of the low structures surrounding it. The humidity was now dripping down the plastered walls, although the rain had not increased. Through the spongy expanse of the sky, the sound of the river and of the trees reached them somewhat muted. They were walking in step, D'Arrast heavily and the cook with elastic tread. From time to time the latter would raise his head and smile at his companion. They went in the direction of the church, which could be seen above the houses, reached the end of the square, walked along other muddy streets now filled with aggressive smells of cooking. From time to time a woman, holding a plate or kitchen utensil, would peer out inquisitively from one of the doors and then disappear at once. They passed in front of the church, plunged into an old section of similar low houses, and suddenly came out on the sound of the invisible river behind the area of the huts that D'Arrast recognized.

"Good. I'll leave you. See you this evening," he said.

"Yes, in front of the church."

But the cook did not let go of D'Arrast's hand. He hesitated. Finally he made up his mind.

"And you, have you never called out, made a promise?"

"Yes, once, I believe."

"In a shipwreck?"

"If you wish." And D'Arrast pulled his hand away roughly. But as he was about to turn on his heels, he met the cook's eyes. He hesitated, and then smiled.

"I can tell you, although it was unimportant. Someone was about to die through my fault. It seems to me that I called out."

"Did you promise?"

"No. I should have liked to promise."

"Long ago?"

"Not long before coming here."

The cook seized his beard with both hands. His eyes were shining.

"You are a captain," he said. "My house is yours. Besides, you are going to help me keep my promise, and it's as if you had made it yourself. That will help you too."

D'Arrast smiled, saying: "I don't think so."

"You are proud, Captain."

"I used to be proud; now I'm alone. But just tell me: has your good Jesus always answered you?"

"Always . . . no, Captain!"

"Well, then?"

The cook burst out with a gay, childlike laugh.

"Well," he said, "he's free, isn't he?"

At the club, where D'Arrast lunched with the leading citizens, the Mayor told him he must sign the town's guest-book so that some trace would remain of the great event of his coming to Iguape. The Judge found two or three new expressions to praise, besides their guest's virtues and talents, the simplicity with
485   which he represented among them the great country to which he had the honor to belong. D'Arrast simply said that it was indeed an honor to him and an advantage to his firm to have been awarded the allocation of this long construction job. Whereupon the Judge expressed his admiration for such humility. "By the way," he asked, "have you thought of what should be done to the Chief of Po-
490   lice?" D'Arrast smiled at him and said: "Yes, I have a solution." He would consider it a personal favor and an exceptional grace if the foolish man could be forgiven in his name so that his stay here in Iguape, where he so much enjoyed knowing the beautiful town and generous inhabitants, could begin in a climate of peace and friendship. The Judge, attentive and smiling, nodded his head. For
495   a moment he meditated on the wording as an expert, then called on those present to applaud the magnanimous traditions of the great French nation and, turning again toward D'Arrast, declared himself satisfied. "Since that's the way it is," he concluded, "we shall dine this evening with the Chief." But D'Arrast said that he was invited by friends to the ceremony of the dances in the huts. "Ah
500   yes!" said the Judge. "I am glad you are going. You'll see, one can't resist loving our people."

That evening, D'Arrast, the ship's cook, and his brother were seated around the ashes of a fire in the center of the hut the engineer had already visited in the morning. The brother had not seemed surprised to see him return. He spoke
505   Spanish hardly at all and most of the time merely nodded his head. As for the cook, he had shown interest in cathedrals and then had expatiated at length on the black bean soup. Now night had almost fallen and, although D'Arrast could still see the cook and his brother, he could scarcely make out in the back of the hut the squatting figures of an old woman and of the same girl who had served
510   him. Down below, he could hear the monotonous river.
    The cook rose, saying: "It's time." They got up, but the women did not stir. The men went out alone. D'Arrast hesitated, then joined the others. Night had now fallen and the rain had stopped. The pale-black sky still seemed liquid. In its transparent dark water, stars began to light up, low on the horizon. Almost at
515   once they flickered out, falling one by one into the river as if the last lights were trickling from the sky. The heavy air smelled of water and smoke. Near by the sound of the huge forest could be heard too, though it was motionless. Suddenly drums and singing broke out in the distance, at first muffled and then distinct, approaching closer and closer and finally stopping. Soon after, one could
520   see a procession of black girls wearing low-waisted white dresses of coarse silk. In a tight-fitting red jacket adorned with a necklace of varicolored teeth, a tall Negro followed them and, behind him, a disorderly crowd of men in white pajamas and musicians carrying triangles and broad, short drums. The cook said they should follow the men.

The hut, which they reached by following the river a few hundred yards be-    525
yond the last huts, was large, empty, and relatively comfortable, with plastered
walls. It had a dirt floor, a roof of thatch and reeds supported by a central pole,
and bare walls. On a little palm-clad altar at the end, covered with candles that
scarcely lighted half the hall, there was a magnificent colored print in which
Saint George, with alluring grace, was getting the better of a bewhiskered    530
dragon. Under the altar a sort of niche decorated with rococo paper sheltered a
little statue of red-painted clay representing a horned god, standing between a
candle and a bowl of water. With a fierce look the god was brandishing an over-
sized knife made of silver paper.

The cook led D'Arrast to a corner, where they stood against the wall near    535
the door. "This way," he whispered, "we can leave without disturbing." Indeed,
the hut was packed tight with men and women. Already the heat was rising.
The musicians took their places on both sides of the little altar. The men and
women dancers separated into two concentric circles with the men inside. In
the very center the black leader in the red jacket took his stand. D'Arrast leaned    540
against the wall, folding his arms.

But the leader, elbowing his way through the circle of dancers, came toward them and, in a solemn way, said a few words to the cook. "Unfold your
arms, Captain," the cook said. "You are hugging yourself and keeping the saint's
spirit from descending." Obediently D'Arrast let his arms fall to his sides. Still    545
leaning against the wall, with his long, heavy limbs and his big face already
shiny with sweat, D'Arrast himself looked like some bestial and kindly god. The
tall Negro looked at them and, satisfied, went back to his place. At once, in a re-
sounding voice, he intoned the opening notes of a song that all picked up in
chorus, accompanied by the drums. Then the circles began to turn in opposite    550
directions in a sort of heavy, insistent dance rather like stamping, slightly emphasized by the double line of swaying hips.

The heat had increased. Yet the pauses gradually diminished, the stops became less frequent, and the dance speeded up. Without any slowing of the others' rhythm, without ceasing to dance himself, the tall Negro again elbowed his    555
way through the circles to go toward the altar. He came back with a glass of water and a lighted candle that he stuck in the ground in the center of the hut. He
poured the water around the candle in two concentric circles and, again erect,
turned maddened eyes toward the roof. His whole body taut and still, he was
waiting. "Saint George is coming. Look! Look!" whispered the cook, whose eyes    560
were popping.

Indeed, some dancers now showed signs of being in a trance, but a rigid
trance with hands on hips, step stiff, eyes staring and vacant. Others quickened
their rhythm, bent convulsively backward, and began to utter inarticulate cries.
The cries gradually rose higher, and when they fused in a collective shriek, the    565
leader, with eyes still raised, uttered a long, barely phrased outcry at the top of
his lungs. In it the same words kept recurring. "You see," said the cook, "he says
he is the god's field of battle." Struck by the change in his voice, D'Arrast looked
at the cook, who, leaning forward with fists clenched and eyes staring, was

570   mimicking the others' measured stamping without moving from his place. Then
he noticed that he himself, though without moving his feet, had for some little
time been dancing with his whole weight.

But all at once the drums began to beat violently and suddenly the big devil
in red broke loose. His eyes flashing, his four limbs whirling around him, he
575   hopped with bent knee on one leg after the other, speeding up his rhythm until
it seemed that he must eventually fly to pieces. But abruptly he stopped on the
verge of one leap to stare at those around him with a proud and terrible look
while the drums thundered on. Immediately a dancer sprang from a dark corner, knelt down, and held out a short saber to the man possessed of the spirit.
580   The tall Negro took the saber without ceasing to look around him and then
whirled it above his head. At that moment D'Arrast noticed the cook dancing
among the others. The engineer had not seen him leave his side.

In the reddish, uncertain light a stifling dust rose from the ground, making
the air even thicker and sticking to one's skin. D'Arrast felt gradually overcome
585   by fatigue and breathed with ever greater difficulty. He did not even see how the
dancers had got hold of the huge cigars they were now smoking while still
dancing; their strange smell filled the hut and rather made his head swim. He
merely saw the cook passing near him, still dancing and puffing on a cigar.
"Don't smoke," he said. The cook grunted without losing the beat, staring at the
590   central pole with the expression of a boxer about to collapse, his spine constantly twitching in a long shudder. Beside him a heavy Negress, rolling her animal face from side to side, kept barking. But the young Negresses especially
went into the most frightful trance, their feet glued to the floor and their bodies
shaken from feet to head by convulsive motions that became more violent upon
595   reaching the shoulders. Their heads would wag backward and forward, literally
separated from a decapitated body. At the same time all began to howl inces-
santly with a long collective and toneless howl, apparently not pausing to
breathe or to introduce modulations—as if the bodies were tightly knotted,
muscles and nerves, in a single exhausting outburst, at last giving voice in each
600   of them to a creature that had until then been absolutely silent. And, still howl-
ing, the women began to fall one by one. The black leader knelt by each one and
quickly and convulsively pressed her temples with his huge, black-muscled
hand. Then they would get up, staggering, return to the dance, and resume
their howls, at first feebly and then louder and faster, before falling again, and
605   getting up again, and beginning over again, and for a long time more, until the
general howl decreased, changed, and degenerated into a sort of coarse barking
which shook them with gasps. D'Arrast, exhausted, his muscles taut from his
long dance as he stood still, choked by his own silence, felt himself stagger. The
heat, the dust, the smoke of the cigars, the smell of bodies now made the air al-
610   most unbreathable. He looked for the cook, who had disappeared. D'Arrast let
himself slide down along the wall and squatted, holding back his nausea.

When he opened his eyes, the air was still as stifling but the noise had
stopped. The drums alone were beating out a figured bass, and groups in every

corner of the hut, covered with whitish cloths, were marking time by stamping. But in the center of the room, from which the glass and candle had now been 615 removed, a group of black girls in a semi-hypnotic state were dancing slowly, always on the point of letting the beat get ahead of them. Their eyes closed and yet standing erect, they were swaying lightly on their toes, almost in the same spot. Two of them, fat ones, had their faces covered with a curtain of raffia. They surrounded another girl, tall, thin, and wearing a fancy costume. D'Arrast 620 suddenly recognized her as the daughter of his host. In a green dress and a huntress's hat of blue gauze turned up in front and adorned with plumes, she held in her hand a green-and-yellow bow with an arrow on the tip of which was spitted a multicolored bird. On her slim body her pretty head swayed slowly, tipped backward a little, and her sleeping face reflected an innocent melan- 625 choly. At the pauses in the music she staggered as if only half awake. Yet the in- tensified beat of the drums provided her with a sort of invisible support around which to entwine her languid arabesques until, stopping again together with the music, tottering on the edge of equilibrium, she uttered a strange bird cry, shrill and yet melodious.

630

D'Arrast, bewitched by the slow dance, was watching the black Diana[2] when the cook suddenly loomed up before him, his smooth face now distorted. The kindness had disappeared from his eyes, revealing nothing but a sort of un- suspected avidity. Coldly, as if speaking to a stranger, he said: "It's late, Captain. They are going to dance all night long, but they don't want you to stay now." 635 With head heavy, D'Arrast got up and followed the cook, who went along the wall toward the door. On the threshold the cook stood aside, holding the bam- boo door, and D'Arrast went out. He turned back and looked at the cook, who had not moved. "Come. In a little while you'll have to carry the stone."

"I'm staying," the cook said with a set expression. 640

"And your promise?"

Without replying, the cook gradually pushed against the door that D'Arrast was holding open with one hand. They remained this way for a second until D'Arrast gave in, shrugging his shoulders. He went away.

The night was full of fresh aromatic scents. Above the forest the few stars in 645 the austral sky, blurred by an invisible haze, were shining dimly. The humid air was heavy. Yet it seemed delightfully cool on coming out of the hut. D'Arrast climbed the slippery slope, staggering like a drunken man in the potholes. The forest, near by, rumbled slightly. The sound of the river increased. The whole continent was emerging from the night, and loathing overcame D'Arrast. It 650 seemed to him that he would have liked to spew forth this whole country, the melancholy of its vast expanses, the glaucous light of its forests, and the noctur- nal lapping of its big deserted rivers. This land was too vast, blood and seasons mingled here, and time liquefied. Life here was flush with the soil, and, to iden- tify with it, one had to lie down and sleep for years on the muddy or dried-up 655

---

2. *Diana:* the Roman goddess associated with hunting and chastity. (*ed.*)

ground itself. Yonder, in Europe, there was shame and wrath. Here, exile or solitude, among these listless and convulsive madmen who danced to die. But through the humid night, heavy with vegetable scents, the wounded bird's outlandish cry, uttered by the beautiful sleeping girl, still reached his ears.

660     When D'Arrast, his head in the vise of a crushing migraine, had awakened after a bad sleep, a humid heat was weighing upon the town and the still forest. He was waiting now under the hospital portico, looking at his watch, which had stopped, uncertain of the time, surprised by the broad daylight and the silence of the town. The almost clear blue sky hung low over the first dull roofs. Yel-
665 lowish urubus, transfixed by the heat, were sleeping on the house across from the hospital. One of them suddenly fluttered, opened his beak, ostensibly got ready to fly away, flapped his dusty wings twice against his body, rose a few inches above the roof, fell back, and went to sleep almost at once.

    The engineer went down toward the town. The main square was empty,
670 like the streets through which he had just walked. In the distance, and on both sides of the river, a low mist hung over the forest. The heat fell vertically, and D'Arrast looked for a shady spot. At that moment, under the overhang on one of the houses, he saw a little man gesturing to him. As he came closer, he recognized Socrates.

675     "Well, Mr. D'Arrast, you like the ceremony?"

    D'Arrast said that it was too hot in the hut and that he preferred the sky and the night air.

    "Yes," Socrates said, "in your country there's only the Mass. No one dances." He rubbed his hands, jumped on one foot, whirled about, laughed up-
680 roariously. "Not possible, they're not possible." Then he looked at D'Arrast inquisitively. "And you, are you going to Mass?"

    "No."

    "Then, where are you going?"

    "Nowhere. I don't know."

685     Socrates laughed again. "Not possible! A noble without a church, without anything!"

    D'Arrast laughed likewise. "Yes, you see, I never found my place. So I left."

    "Stay with us, Mr. D'Arrast, I love you."

    "I'd like to, Socrates, but I don't know how to dance." Their laughter
690 echoed in the silence of the empty town.

    "Ah," Socrates said, "I forget. The Mayor wants to see you. He is lunching at the club." And without warning he started off in the direction of the hospital.

    "Where are you going?" D'Arrast shouted.

    Socrates imitated a snore. "Sleep. Soon the procession." And, half running,
695 he resumed his snores.

    The Mayor simply wanted to give D'Arrast a place of honor to see the procession. He explained it to the engineer while sharing with him a dish of meat and rice such as would miraculously cure a paralytic. First they would take their places on a balcony of the Judge's house, opposite the church, to see the procession come out. Then they would go to the town hall in the main street leading to the church, which the penitents would take on their way back. The Judge and the Chief of Police would accompany D'Arrast, the Mayor being obliged to take part in the ceremony. The Chief of Police was in fact in the clubroom and kept paying court to D'Arrast with an indefatigable smile, lavishing upon him incomprehensible but obviously well-meaning speeches. When D'Arrast left, the Chief of Police hastened to make a way for him, holding all the doors open before him. 700

Under the burning sun, in the still empty town, the two men walked toward the Judge's house. Their steps were the only sound heard in the silence. But all of a sudden a firecracker exploded in a neighboring street and flushed on every roof the heavy, awkward flocks of bald-necked urubus. Almost at once dozens of firecrackers went off in all directions, doors opened, and people began to emerge from the houses and fill the narrow streets. 710

The Judge told D'Arrast how proud he was to receive him in his unworthy house and led him up a handsome baroque staircase painted chalky blue. On the landing, as D'Arrast passed, doors opened and children's dark heads popped out and disappeared at once with smothered laughter. The main room, beautiful in architecture, contained nothing but rattan furniture and large cages filled with squawking birds. The balcony on which the Judge and D'Arrast settled overlooked the little square in front of the church. The crowd was now beginning to fill it, strangely silent, motionless under the heat that came down from the sky in almost visible waves. Only the children ran around the square, stopping abruptly to light firecrackers, and sharp reports followed one another in rapid succession. Seen from the balcony, the church with its plaster walls, its dozen blue steps, its blue-and-gold towers, looked smaller. 715 720 725

Suddenly the organ burst forth within the church. The crowd, turned toward the portico, drew over to the sides of the square. The men took off their hats and the women knelt down. The distant organ played at length something like marches. Then an odd sound of wings came from the forest. A tiny airplane with transparent wings and frail fuselage, out of place in this ageless world, came in sight over the trees, swooped a little above the square, and, with the clacking of a big rattle, passed over the heads raised toward it. Then the plane turned and disappeared in the direction of the estuary. 730

But in the shadow of the church a vague bustle again attracted attention. The organ had stopped, replaced now by brasses and drums, invisible under the portico. Black-surpliced penitents came out of the church one by one, formed groups outside the doors, and began to descend the steps. Behind them came white penitents bearing red-and-blue banners, then a little group of boys dressed up as angels, sodalities of Children of Mary with little black and serious faces. Finally, on a multicolored shrine borne by leading citizens sweating in their dark suits, came the effigy of the good Jesus himself, a reed in his hand and his head crowned with thorns, bleeding and tottering above the crowd that lined the steps. 735 740

745     When the shrine reached the bottom of the steps, there was a pause during which the penitents tried to line up in a semblance of order. Then it was that D'Arrast saw the ship's cook. Bare from the waist up, he had just come out under the portico carrying on his bearded head an enormous rectangular block set on a cork mat. With steady tread he came down the church steps, the stone

750 perfectly balanced in the arch formed by his short, muscular arms. As soon as he fell in behind the shrine, the procession moved. From the portico burst the musicians, wearing bright-colored coats and blowing into beribboned brasses. To the beat of a quick march, the penitents hastened their step and reached one of the streets opening off the square. When the shrine had disappeared be-

755 hind them, nothing could be seen but the cook and the last of the musicians. Behind them, the crowd got in motion amidst exploding firecrackers, while the plane, with a great rattle of its engine, flew back over the groups trailing behind. D'Arrast was looking exclusively at the cook, who was disappearing into the street now and whose shoulders he suddenly thought he saw sag. But at that

760 distance he couldn't see well.
    Through the empty streets, between closed shops and bolted doors, the Judge, the Chief of Police, and D'Arrast reached the town hall. As they got away from the band and the firecrackers, silence again enveloped the town and already a few urubus returned to the places on the roofs that they seemed to have

765 occupied for all time. The town hall stood in a long, narrow street leading from one of the outlying sections to the church square. For the moment, the street was empty. From the balcony could be seen, as far as the eye could reach, nothing but a pavement full of potholes, in which the recent rain had left puddles. The sun, now slightly lower, was still nibbling at the windowless façades of the

770 houses across the street.
    They waited a long time, so long that D'Arrast, from staring at the reverberation of the sun on the opposite wall, felt his fatigue and dizziness returning. The empty street with its deserted houses attracted and repelled him at one and the same time. Once again he wanted to get away from this country; at the same

775 time he thought of that huge stone; he would have liked that trial to be over. He was about to suggest going down to find out something when the church bells began to peal forth loudly. Simultaneously, from the other end of the street on their left, a clamor burst out and a seething crowd appeared. From a distance the people could be seen swarming around the shrine, pilgrims and penitents

780 mingled, and they were advancing, amidst firecrackers and shouts of joy, along the narrow street. In a few seconds they filled it to the edges, advancing toward the town hall in an indescribable disorder—ages, races, and costumes fused in a motley mass full of gaping eyes and yelling mouths. From the crowd emerged an army of tapers like lances with flames fading into the burning sunlight. But

785 when they were close and the crowd was so thick under the balcony that it seemed to rise up along the walls, D'Arrast saw that the ship's cook was not there.
    Quick as lightning, without excusing himself, he left the balcony and the room, dashed down the staircase, and stood in the street under the deafening

sound of the bells and firecrackers. There he had to struggle against the crowd   790
of merrymakers, the taper-bearers, the shocked penitents. But, bucking the human tide with all his weight, he cut a path in such an impetuous way that he
staggered and almost fell when he was eventually free, beyond the crowd, at the
end of the street. Leaning against the burning-hot wall, he waited until he had
caught his breath. Then he resumed his way. At that moment a group of men   795
emerged into the street. The ones in front were walking backward, and D'Arrast
saw that they surrounded the cook.

He was obviously dead tired. He would stop, then, bent under the huge
stone, run a little with the hasty step of stevedores and coolies—the rapid, flat-
footed trot of drudgery. Gathered about him, penitents in surplices soiled with   800
dust and candle-drippings encouraged him when he stopped. On his left his
brother was walking or running in silence. It seemed to D'Arrast that they took
an interminable time to cover the space separating them from him. Having almost reached him, the cook stopped again and glanced around with dull eyes.
When he saw D'Arrast—yet without appearing to recognize him—he stood still,   805
turned toward him. An oily, dirty sweat covered his face, which had gone gray;
his beard was full of threads of saliva; and a brown, dry froth glued his lips together. He tried to smile. But, motionless under his load, his whole body was
trembling except for the shoulders, where the muscles were obviously caught in
a sort of cramp. The brother, who had recognized D'Arrast, said to him simply:   810
"He already fell." And Socrates, popping up from nowhere, whispered in his
ear: "Dance too much, Mr. D'Arrast, all night long. He's tired."

The cook advanced again with his jerky trot, not like a man who wants to
progress but as if he were fleeing the crushing load, as if he hoped to lighten it
through motion. Without knowing how, D'Arrast found himself at his right. He   815
laid his hand lightly on the cook's back and walked beside him with hasty,
heavy steps. At the other end of the street the shrine had disappeared, and the
crowd, which probably now filled the square, did not seem to advance any
more. For several seconds, the cook, between his brother and D'Arrast, made
progress. Soon a mere space of some twenty yards separated him from the   820
group gathered in front of the town hall to see him pass. Again, however, he
stopped. D'Arrast's hand became heavier. "Come on, cook, just a little more," he
said. The man trembled; the saliva began to trickle from his mouth again, while
the sweat literally spurted from all over his body. He tried to breathe deeply and
stopped short. He started off again, took three steps, and tottered. And sud-   825
denly the stone slipped onto his shoulder, gashing it, and then forward onto the
ground, while the cook, losing his balance, toppled over on his side. Those who
were preceding him and urging him on jumped back with loud shouts. One of
them seized the cork mat while the others took hold of the stone to load it on
him again.   830

Leaning over him, D'Arrast with his bare hand wiped the blood and dust
from his shoulder, while the little man, his face against the ground, panted. He
heard nothing and did not stir. His mouth opened avidly as if each breath were
his last. D'Arrast grasped him around the waist and raised him up as easily as if

835 he had been a child. Holding him upright in a tight clasp with his full height leaning over him, D'Arrast spoke into his face as if to breathe his own strength into him. After a moment, the cook, bloody and caked with earth, detached himself with a haggard expression on his face. He staggered toward the stone, which the others were raising a little. But he stopped, looked at the stone with a

840 vacant stare, and shook his head. Then he let his arms fall at his sides and turned toward D'Arrast. Huge tears flowed silently down his ravaged face. He wanted to speak, he was speaking, but his mouth hardly formed the syllables. "I promised," he was saying. And then: "Oh, Captain! Oh, Captain!" and the tears drowned his voice. His brother suddenly appeared behind him, threw his arms

845 around him, and the cook, weeping, collapsed against him, defeated, with his head thrown back.

D'Arrast looked at him, not knowing what to say. He turned toward the crowd in the distance, now shouting again. Suddenly he tore the cork mat from the hands holding it and walked toward the stone. He gestured to the others to

850 hold it up and then he loaded it almost effortlessly. His head pressed down under the weight of the stone, his shoulders hunched, and breathing rather hard, he looked down at his feet as he listened to the cook's sobs. Then with vigorous tread he started off on his own, without flagging covered the space separating him from the crowd at the end of the street, and energetically forced his way

855 through the first rows, which stood aside as he approached. In the hubbub of bells and firecrackers he entered the square between two solid masses of onlookers, suddenly silent and gaping at him in amazement. He advanced with the same impetuous pace, and the crowd opened a path for him to the church. Despite the weight which was beginning to crush his head and neck, he saw the

860 church and the shrine, which seemed to be waiting for him at the door. He had already gone beyond the center of the square in that direction when brutally, without knowing why, he veered off to the left and turned away from the church, forcing the pilgrims to face him. Behind him, he heard someone running. In front of him mouths opened on all sides. He didn't understand what

865 they were shouting, although he seemed to recognize the one Portuguese word that was being constantly hurled at him. Suddenly Socrates appeared before him, rolling startled eyes, speaking incoherently and pointing out the way to the church behind him. "To the church! To the church!" was what Socrates and the crowd were shouting at him. Yet D'Arrast continued in the direction in

870 which he was launched. And Socrates stood aside, his arms raised in the air comically, while the crowd gradually fell silent. When D'Arrast entered the first street, which he had already taken with the cook and therefore knew it led to the river section, the square had become but a confused murmur behind him.

The stone weighed painfully on his head now and he needed all the

875 strength of his long arms to lighten it. His shoulders were already stiffening when he reached the first streets on the slippery slope. He stopped and listened. He was alone. He settled the stone firmly on its cork base and went down with a cautious but still steady tread toward the huts. When he reached them, his

breath was beginning to fail, his arms were trembling under the stone. He hastened his pace, finally reached the little square where the cook's hut stood, ran          880
to it, kicked the door open, and brusquely hurled the stone onto the still glowing fire in the center of the room. And there, straightening up until he was suddenly enormous, drinking in with desperate gulps the familiar smell of poverty
and ashes, he felt rising within him a surge of obscure and panting joy that he
was powerless to name.                                                                     885
    When the inhabitants of the hut arrived, they found D'Arrast standing with
his shoulders against the back wall and eyes closed. In the center of the room, in
the place of the hearth, the stone was half buried in ashes and earth. They stood .
in the doorway without advancing and looked at D'Arrast in silence as if questioning him. But he didn't speak. Whereupon the brother led the cook up to the          890
stone, where he dropped on the ground. The brother sat down too, beckoning
to the others. The old woman joined him, then the girl of the night before, but
no one looked at D'Arrast. They were squatting in a silent circle around the
stone. No sound but the murmur of the river reached them through the heavy
air. Standing in the darkness, D'Arrast listened without seeing anything, and the       895
sound of the waters filled him with a tumultuous happiness. With eyes closed,
he joyfully acclaimed his own strength; he acclaimed, once again, a fresh beginning in life. At that moment, a firecracker went off that seemed very close. The
brother moved a little away from the cook and, half turning toward D'Arrast but
without looking at him, pointed to the empty place and said: "Sit down with          900
us."

## Looking Back

1. What effect does the adjective *noble* have as it is used repeatedly to describe D'Arrast in lines 179–190?

2. By line 297, what socioeconomic picture of Iguape emerges?

3. How do we begin to think of D'Arrast differently once we learn that, like the pilgrims who arrived at Iguape, "He too was waiting" (lines 352–353)?

4. What, despite their class differences, do D'Arrast the engineer and the ship's cook have in common (see lines 378–396 and 458–469)?

5. Does the cook's vow (lines 407–408) make sense? Explain your answer.

6. In conversation with D'Arrast, what theological point does the cook make in line 480?

7. Can you explain the symbolic import of the conversation between D'Arrast and Socrates in lines 680–690?

8. What is the significance of D'Arrast's avoiding the church and instead carrying the stone to the huts?

9. Why is D'Arrast so joyful after he successfully delivers the stone?

10. Do the last spoken words in the story (lines 900–901) have a special significance? Explain your answer.

## Writing Assignments

1. Asked once by an interviewer what the artist can do to help relieve human suffering, Albert Camus's answer could apply to everyone, no matter his or her profession, job, or calling. He said: "Considered as artists, we perhaps have no need to interfere in the affairs of the world. But considered as men, yes." The assumption of human responsibility is a theme of "The Growing Stone." In his role not as an engineer but as a man does D'Arrast "interfere." It is easy to applaud such shouldering of others' burdens, but it is inordinately hard to do it. And before we can be expected to accept this task as a universal duty, it is necessary for us to imagine the results of *failing* to do so. Write an essay that does just that. Refer to D'Arrast and draw on your experience to illustrate your analysis.

2. "A man has to do what he has promised," says D'Arrast to the ship's cook, approving the latter's vow to Jesus (line 413). Is this true? Or can promises sometimes be excused? Are certain promises more binding than others? What makes them so? Do the motives for making promises figure in here? Are promises moral contracts? Do promises have a spiritual value that is destroyed if they are broken? What are the results of a broken promise? Write an essay taking up such questions as you analyze the phenomenon of making a promise. Consider the promise of the ship's cook's and others you know of that would shed light on this topic.

3. In effect, D'Arrast is no less a pilgrim than those who have made the trip to Iguape for more traditional reasons. His also is a spiritual journey, a quest to find himself again, and to make a fresh start, even though he is not fully aware of this motivation. Like him, all of us at some point feel the need to find for ourselves a new meaning in life. Write an essay that analyzes this quest. Here are some questions you might consider: Why is it often necessary to go far away to find oneself? Does one take the same self with one, or is it made different somehow by arriving elsewhere? Why is an ordeal of some sort often part of such a quest? What does it mean to make a fresh start? If you want to cite personal experiences, remember that such quests are not necessarily dramatic but can be part of ordinary life. You may have made one without knowing it at the time.

# Anonymous

# Is That So?

This is a Zen story. Zen is a branch of Buddhism that is particularly active in Japan. Paul Reps, the editor of *Zen Flesh Zen Bones*, the volume from which "Is That So?" is taken, describes Zen as follows: "A special teaching without scriptures, beyond words and letters, pointing to the mind essence of man, seeing directly into one's nature, attaining enlightenment." Zen's emphasis is on action rather than language; however, as Reps says further,

To study Zen, the flowering of one's nature, is no easy task in any age or civilization. Many teachers, true and false, have purposed to assist others in this accomplishment. It is from innumerable and actual adventures in Zen that these stories have evolved.

Paul Reps is a poet and painter as well as a Zen adept.

## Looking Ahead

1. Zen stories teach, but do so indirectly. You have to read critically to perceive their slow-working logic and thus learn the lesson.
2. Your understanding of this story will be enhanced if you note the contrast between the parents' behavior and Hakuin's, and how this difference characterizes each party.
3. Because the identical comment by Hakuin punctuates the key events in this story, you should look to this refrain for an idea of his character.

The Zen master Hakuin was praised by his neighbors as one living a pure life.

A beautiful Japanese girl whose parents owned a food store lived near him. Suddenly, without any warning, her parents discovered she was with child.

This made her parents angry. She would not confess who the man was, but after much harassment at last named Hakuin.

In great anger the parents went to the master. "Is that so?" was all he would say. 5

After the child was born it was brought to Hakuin. By this time he had lost his reputation, which did not trouble him, but he took very good care of the child. He obtained milk from his neighbors and everything else the little one needed. 10

A year later the girl-mother could stand it no longer. She told her parents the truth—that the real father of the child was a young man who worked in the fishmarket.

The mother and father of the girl at once went to Hakuin to ask his forgiveness, to apologize at length, and to get the child back again. 15

Hakuin was willing. In yielding the child, all he said was: "Is that so?"

## Looking Back

1. What do you think Hakuin's title of *master* means (line 1)?
2. How are we supposed to understand Hakuin's having lived "a pure life" (line 1)?
3. Why do you think the girl said Hakuin was the father?
4. Can you imagine why he doesn't defend himself against the charge?
5. What sense is conveyed by his answer, "Is that so?"
6. Hakuin's loss of reputation does not bother him. What are we to infer about the value of a reputation?

7. Can we value ourselves on any other basis than what people think about us?

8. What spiritual qualities does Hakuin demonstrate in caring for the child so responsibly?

9. How does the contrast between his behavior and the parents' behavior portray the difference between spiritual and material existence?

10. In what way are we enlightened by Hakuin's final speech, a repetition of his earlier one?

## Writing Assignments

1. Without a murmur, Hakuin assumes the burden of parenthood for a child not his own, yet we get the sense that it is not a burden at all. Why not? Something we cannot quite put our finger on motivates him to act, and he never sees fit to explain his action. What do you think is Hakuin's principle of action, his general approach to life? Write an essay interpolating your explanation of it as you understand it from his behavior. Try also to say how you might extrapolate from such a principle or approach and apply it to other situations; give examples of them from your own experience.

2. "But what will the neighbors think?" is a familiar question. People who ask it worry about the impression they make on others; they fear their reputation will suffer if some unflattering idea of them, true or false, gets around. Hakuin, however, does not harbor such fears, and his example may demonstrate to us that there is something more important than the way others see us. What is it? Write an essay developing a critique of the concern for personal reputation in order to identify what—in Hakuin's case and in life generally—might be more valuable. Be sure to explain in full how and why it is more valuable.

3. The pregnant girl in "Is That So?" suffers "much harrassment" (line 5) before she names the father of her child, and even then she tells a lie. Her lie protects the real father, but her reluctance to confess has also protected her sense of privacy, which has been described by writer Enid Starkie as a "spiritual quality." What makes privacy so precious? What does it preserve in our lives? What can happen to us if we lose it or if it is taken away from us? Are some parts of our lives more naturally private than others? Write an essay that, extrapolating from Starkie's view, answers the above questions to define privacy and describe its place in our lives. Be sure to refer to the unnamed girl's situation.

## Margot Olavarria

# Remembering John

Born in 1958 in Chile, Margot Olavarria grew up in Los Angeles. Between attending college there and in New York City, for ten years she toured with Brian Brain and other rock bands. That career behind her, she graduated from Hunter College in 1992 with a double major in writing and Latin American studies. She wrote "Remembering John" as a student.

In it, she demonstrates a determinedly solicitous yet clear-eyed and unsentimental attitude toward her friend that provides a new context in which to view him. The result is a critically acute idea of how the individual may become a member of the moral community.

## Looking Ahead

1. Notice how the original text Olavarria starts from helps structure her essay.
2. Read critically to see how the author's candid descriptions and forthright confession of her feelings contribute to the quality of this essay.
3. Given her subject matter, observe the particular value of Olavarria's tone of voice, and consider how a different tone might utterly distort the sense she wants to communicate.

### To the Memory of John Mangano

An old Chinese parable tells the story of a skillful harp player and a friend of his, who loved to listen to his music. When the musician played a song about the ocean, his friend would remark, "I hear the waves breaking!" When the harpist played a song about a mountain, his friend would exclaim, "I can see the mountain!" Then one day the listener became ill and died. In response, the musician cut his harp strings and never played again. In China, the cutting of harp strings has come to signify intimate friendship.  5

The special relationship illustrated by this parable is one in which both persons feel understood and appreciated. Both persons give and receive equally from the relationship. Thus the risk involved in reaching such intimacy, as there is inherent risk in baring one's soul, is ultimately worthwhile for both friends.  10

I was fortunate enough to have known such a friendship with my dying friend John Mangano in the last year of his life. We were both "musicians and listeners," as we were both writers who would read our work to each other.  15

John and I had been neighbors and friends, though not close friends, for about nine years before he learned he was HIV-positive. We had had a working relationship, as he was the president of our building's board of directors and I was vice-president. But our association didn't go beyond building business very often. We had separate social lives.  20

In the spring of 1989 John came over to talk to me about some building business. We chatted for a while and as he was leaving, John told me, in a matter of fact way, that he had tested positive. I was shocked and at a loss for words. The first thing that came to my mind was that John would die and I felt bad about jumping to that conclusion so quickly. I stood there feeling useless  25 and muttered, "I'm sorry."

A month or so later, John became intolerant of two of our neighbors regarding some contested building issues. He tried to smash down one of the apartment doors with a fire extinguisher. Other board members thought he should quit as president because his temper was out of control. My concern was  30 for his health and I urged him to quit, saying the stress involved in running the building was the last thing he needed. After much protest, he agreed.

    During that time, I and other neighbors sensed such anger from John that we interpreted it as personal hostility. What I didn't know was that John had al-
35 ready developed Kaposi's sarcoma, the skin cancer that can afflict persons with AIDS because of a faltering immune system. John's anger was not personal, but a reaction to the awareness that he was dying.

    When I would see John in the hallway, I would ask how he was doing and let him know that if there was anything I could do, all he had to do was ask. I
40 would usually get a cold response. I did not take offense; I knew he had to work things out and I also knew he had closer friends to rely on. He was still active and working at Theater for the New City as well as running the AIDS Theater Workshop, which he had helped start. I was comfortable with that distance since illness and hospitals, not to mention death, make me very nervous and
45 distressed. I had just lost another friend to AIDS that previous October and that experience was still painful for me.

    The next time I saw John, he had begun to show signs of KS—he had purple tumors over both of his eyes. This gave him the look of a panda bear and he was also puffy from the medication he was taking. I think he was scared of my
50 being scared by his looks. I tried to act normal, and sensing that John didn't want pity, I tried to suppress the pity I felt.

    A few weeks passed and I ran into one of John's friends who told me John had stopped working and was lonely. I planned to visit him, but John surprised me by ringing my buzzer the next Saturday afternoon. He invited me to go for a
55 walk. I was saddened to see that another purple mark had appeared on his balding head and that he needed a cane to walk with. We linked arms and walked around the corner to Tompkins Square Park. Now this is was when over 200 homeless were living in makeshift tents in the park and it was filthy. But John was utterly thrilled to see all that action taking place before his eyes. Guys were
60 cooking over garbage can fires. Groups were drinking and joking together. Others were fixing their blue tarp roofs. Taking in the scenery, John said, "Ah life! You don't know how lucky you are." I knew he not only meant me but all of us with a life ahead of us, even the hungry and homeless. I felt especially alive.

    That afternoon, John and I became very close very quickly. We had to,
65 there wasn't much time left. John laughed and told me how you know the end is near when everyone and their mother come to visit you. He hadn't lost his wry sense of humor. He confided that he missed sex, that he still got horny despite getting radiation on his penis. "Does it glow in the dark?" I asked and we both laughed. It seemed to me he needed a laugh.

70     John told me he was writing a play about AIDS called *AIDS Is Everybody.* I was taking writing at college and he said he would like me to read him my work. So I began to visit John in the evenings. I would help him clean up his apartment, which was cluttered and had gotten very messy and smelled of medicines. I would read him my essays and he always showed great interest and

would compliment and critique them afterwards. One essay was about my ex- 75
perience homesteading our building where I poked fun at some neighbors John
didn't like. He asked me for a copy and would read it to his visitors, laughing
and praising my astute characterization.

While I was reading him another essay, he stopped me and asked me to repeat a line describing the wind rustling through eucalyptus leaves. He said, 80
"Wow! You know not everyone can write like that; it takes a real gift." John gave
me encouraging praise about my writing. He had such an acute sense with
words; a comment like that really gave me confidence.

I learned a lot about John in those months. I learned that he grew up in
Long Island and had three sisters. His mother had died when he was in high 85
school, and his father still lived on the island. I once heard him on the phone
with him. John told his father he had bought a casket and I sensed that he had a
loving relationship with him. It was very touching. I also learned John had an
uncle who was a priest in Guatemala whom he was very fond of. I learned John
had gone to Carnegie Mellon University and won journalism and writing 90
awards. His love for the theater had inspired hopes for a career as a playwright.

John worked very hard to finish the play he was working on before his eyes
couldn't handle the word processor screen. When it was finished, some friends
arranged a reading at an off-Broadway theater. That night had all the excitement
of an opening night. There were roses and champagne and flashes of cameras. 95
The theater was full of John's friends and the actors did an excellent reading of
the play, which was extremely moving. After it was finished, everyone called,
"Author, author!" John went up to the stage to roaring applause and held up his
cane in triumph. It was a beautiful moment that filled me with pride and admiration for John. 100

John's health was deteriorating quickly but he didn't complain much and
never lost his sense of humor. Though nearly housebound, he kept himself
busy with little projects. He wrote funny film reviews for a bimonthly paper for
people with AIDS. He created a character, Sufferman, and had his picture taken
in a Superman suit (with cape) while standing on a table, holding up his cane. 105
We cut around his image and superimposed it on a Manhattan skyline photograph. The back cover of *PWA Newsline* that week was of John as Sufferman flying over Manhattan.

One of his favorite pastimes in those last months was taking pictures of all
his visitors as well as of his cats and himself. It was as if he was documenting his 110
last days. He took pictures of himself without a shirt on, graphically displaying
the worst tumors on his chest, which oozed liquid. His looks were shocking and
everytime I would get used to a certain stage, the following time I would see
him, he seemed more purple and more fragile. My old squeamishness would return and I would fight not to show it. 115

Everytime I would go upstairs to visit him, I would stand before his door
and feel extreme fear, near panic. I don't know if I was afraid that I would enter
and find John dead, or that he would die while I was there, or if John's physical

deterioration frightened me because it reminded me of my own mortality. I re-
120    member one evening being very frightened when John drifted off to sleep while
I was washing his dishes. At first he was moaning a lot, but then he was suddenly very quiet. I walked over to him, my heart racing, but was relieved to see
the slight movement of a Kleenex on his chest as he breathed.

Not long after that night, I called John and got a message on his machine
125    informing callers that he was in Beth Israel Hospital. I went to see him the
next day. As I walked down the hospital hallway, I noticed red stickers next
to most of the names by the doors. They bore the message "Think safe!" This
was the AIDS ward. I found John sitting up on his bed and looking yellow as
well as purple. His liver was malfunctioning and his belly was swollen. This
130    time I could tell he was in pain, yet he asked me if I had anything new to read
to him. I read him an essay about my days on the road with a band and he
laughed loudly. Afterwards he said he felt as though he'd been all over America in fifteen minutes and he was exhausted. The doctor had told him he now
had KS internally and that he would eventually fill up with liquid. There was
135    nothing they could do for him in the hospital and John wanted to come
home.

A few of us in the building rearranged John's apartment so he could have
maximum comfort during his last days. We boxed hundreds of books and
records and moved them to the basement. We set up his TV, video player,
140    stereo, and phone in the front room that had air conditioning. Then we moved
his recliner, which he preferred to his bed, into the center of the room. Thus,
John could hold court in this room, surrounded by all his comforts.

Our last visits took place in this room. By then John was pretty immobile
and on a catheter. Sunk into his big brown recliner, he looked like a newborn
145    bird, fragile and helpless. He was extremely thin, except for his belly and his
legs which had filled up with liquid. Nearly entirely purple from the knees
up, he looked very strange, like a starvation victim who had fallen into purple
paint. His feet felt rubbery, like an inflated toy, when I rubbed them. This
was needed to help his circulation since he couldn't move around much.
150    He was taking codeine tablets continuously, so he would drift in and out of
consciousness.

My last memory of John is saying goodbye to him in that room, in that
dreamy condition. I was about to leave on vacation to see my in-laws, a trip that
had been arranged a long time ago. Something told me John wouldn't be here
155    when I got back. I thanked him for his friendship and promised to dedicate
something to him should I ever be published. He died two days later, while I
was away.

That was just over a year ago, and I have not cut my harp strings in memory
of John. I don't see the sense in stopping the practice of the craft which the "lis-
160    tener" so appreciated. I feel that one should continue playing the harp in memory of the listener. I know that is what John would have wanted. I continue to
write and hopefully, one day I will be able to dedicate an essay or a story to the
memory of John Mangano, an intimate friend.

## Looking Back

1. How does Olavarria make the transition from an original text (the Chinese parable) to her chief topic (John Mangano)?

2. What do we learn about Olavarria's sensibility from her reaction to learning Mangano has the AIDS virus (see lines 23–26)?

3. Why does the anger Mangano feels (lines 27–37) seem universally to be a stage dying people go through?

4. Does Olavarria impress you as someone who seeks out the dying or who only reluctantly does so? What difference to your understanding of her experience does your answer make?

5. Is her comparing John to a panda bear (line 48) wise or unwise? effective or ineffective? Explain your answer.

6. How would you explain the connection between her remark, "I felt especially alive" (line 63), which might mean she felt distant from Mangano, and her very next comment, that there and then they became very close?

7. What does Mangano's reaction to Olavarria's writing and his own continued literary efforts tell us about him?

8. Do the services the author and other building residents perform for the dying man surprise you at all? Explain your answer.

9. What do you think the physical details of Mangano's deterioration, particularly those in lines 143–151, say about her as a writer?

10. How do you think Olavarria defines *friendship*? (Look especially at the final paragraph of her essay.)

## Writing Assignments

1. Proximity to death is a painful and highly unattractive experience for most people. Often, however, we feel morally obligated to attend closely to the dying. In Olavarria's case, the sense of duty grows into friendship. But for her, as for anyone, a problem still remains: how to act, as a healthy person whose life will go on, in the company of one whose life is about to end. Write an essay giving your sense of the attitudes and behavior appropriate in such a situation and assessing how Olavarria's conduct matches your ideas.

2. In this course, you probably are experiencing the ways writers can learn from and help each other. In "Remembering John," we observe that certain kinds of exchange and appreciation can take place even under the most dire circumstances, but at all times writers who are committed to their craft may join a community of like-minded people. They can do this simply by commenting on others' work and receiving comments on their own. Based on your own experience and extrapolating from Olavarria's, write an essay describing how such sharing best works and outlining its advantages. (If you believe there are also disadvantages to collaborative writing, include these as criticism.)

3. Olavarria begins her essay by citing a Chinese parable on the topic of true, or intimate, friendship. In her last paragraph, she takes issue with part of the parable.

Neither there nor at the beginning, however, does she interpret the parable itself by saying explicitly what its anonymous author considers a proof of true friendship. Write an essay defining true friendship. Interpret the parable, comment on Olavarria's objection to it, and expand by including your own ideas, based on personal experience, on the nature of true friendship.

⚜

# Joan Didion

# On Morality

Joan Didion is one of the finest practitioners of the personal essay in contemporary American literature. She treats important issues and leads readers to consider their general relevance and applicability. Yet her writing is full of concrete instances and physical detail. Furthermore, as in "On Morality," *she* is present in almost all of her nonfiction; that is, rarely are we separated from the voice of the author, a real person speaking to us, who is a witness and participant who takes personal responsibility for the views she professes. These views in "On Morality" are the result of Didion's effective critical thinking. She calls into question an idea most of us blindly accept—that our conscience is a guide that we can always count on. (See also her essay "Holy Water," p. 324, and the biographical and publication information given there.)

## Looking Ahead

1. The word *On* in the title means "about." It is a word traditionally used in the titles of essays to alert the reader to the subject.

2. Notice the relative informality of Didion's approach to her readers, and the effect it has on weakening any resistance we might have to such a ponderous subject as morality.

3. Read critically to test Didion's argument against one kind of moral thinking, one way of applying the term *morality,* and her defense of another kind.

As it happens I am in Death Valley,[1] in a room at the Enterprise Motel and Trailer Park, and it is July, and it is hot. In fact it is 119°. I cannot seem to make the air conditioner work, but there is a small refrigerator, and I can wrap ice cubes in a towel and hold them against the small of my back. With the help of the ice cubes I have been trying to think, because *The American Scholar* asked me to, in some abstract way about "morality," a word I distrust more every day, but my mind veers inflexibly toward the particular.

5

---

1. *Death Valley:* stretches between Nevada and California; it contains the lowest point below sea level in North America. (*ed.*)

Here are some particulars. At midnight last night, on the road in from Las
Vegas to Death Valley Junction, a car hit a shoulder and turned over. The driver,
very young and apparently drunk, was killed instantly. His girl was found alive      10
but bleeding internally, deep in shock. I talked this afternoon to the nurse who
had driven the girl to the nearest doctor, 185 miles across the floor of the Valley
and three ranges of lethal mountain road. The nurse explained that her husband, a talc miner, had stayed on the highway with the boy's body until the
coroner could get over the mountains from Bishop, at dawn today. "You can't       15
just leave a body on the highway," she said. "It's immoral."

It was one instance in which I did not distrust the word, because she meant
something quite specific. She meant that if a body is left alone for even a few
minutes on the desert, the coyotes close in and eat the flesh. Whether or not a
corpse is torn apart by coyotes may seem only a sentimental consideration, but       20
of course it is more: one of the promises we make to one another is that we will
try to retrieve our casualties, try not to abandon our dead to the coyotes. If we
have been taught to keep our promises—if, in the simplest terms, our upbringing is good enough—we stay with the body, or have bad dreams.

I am talking, of course, about the kind of social code that is sometimes       25
called, usually pejoratively, "wagon-train morality." In fact that is precisely
what it is. For better or worse, we are what we learned as children: my own
childhood was illuminated by graphic litanies of the grief awaiting those who
failed in their loyalties to each other. The Donner-Reed Party, starving in the
Sierra snows, all the ephemera of civilization gone save that one vestigial taboo,       30
the provision that no one should eat his own blood kin. The Jayhawkers, who
quarreled and separated not far from where I am tonight. Some of them died in
the Funerals and some of them died down near Badwater and most of the rest of
them died in the Panamints.[2] A woman who got through gave the Valley its
name. Some might say that the Jayhawkers were killed by the desert summer,       35
and the Donner Party by the mountain winter, by circumstances beyond control; we were taught instead that they had somewhere abdicated their responsibilities, somehow breached their primary loyalties, or they would not have
found themselves helpless in the mountain winter or the desert summer, would
not have given way to acrimony, would not have deserted one another, would       40
not have *failed*. In brief, we heard such stories as cautionary tales, and they still
suggest the only kind of "morality" that seems to me to have any but the most
potentially mendacious meaning.

You are quite possibly impatient with me by now; I am talking, you want to say,
about a "morality" so primitive that it scarcely deserves the name, a code that       45
has as its point only survival, not the attainment of the ideal good. Exactly. Particularly out here tonight, in this country so ominous and terrible that to live in

---

2. *Donner Party . . . Panamints:* reference is to western migrants whose wagon trains met disaster and to the places where they died. (*ed.*)

it is to live with antimatter, it is difficult to believe that "the good" is a knowable quantity. Let me tell you what it is like out here tonight. Stories travel at night
50 on the desert. Someone gets in his pickup and drives a couple of hundred miles for a beer, and he carries news of what is happening, back wherever he came from. Then he drives another hundred miles for another beer, and passes along stories from the last place as well as from the one before; it is a network kept alive by people whose instincts tell them that if they do not keep moving at
55 night on the desert they will lose all reason. Here is a story that is going around the desert tonight: over across the Nevada line, sheriff's deputies are diving in some underground pools, trying to retrieve a couple of bodies known to be in the hole. The widow of one of the drowned boys is over there; she is eighteen, and pregnant, and is said not to leave the hole. The divers go down and come
60 up, and she just stands there and stares into the water. They have been diving for ten days but have found no bottom to the caves, no bodies and no trace of them, only the black 90° water going down and down and down, and a single translucent fish, not classified. The story tonight is that one of the divers has been hauled up incoherent, out of his head, shouting—until they got him out of
65 there so that the widow could not hear—about water that got hotter instead of cooler as he went down, about light flickering through the water, about magma, about underground nuclear testing.

That is the tone stories take out here, and there are quite a few of them tonight. And it is more than the stories alone. Across the road at the Faith Com-
70 munity Church a couple of dozen old people, come here to live in trailers and die in the sun, are holding a prayer sing. I cannot hear them and do not want to. What I can hear are occasional coyotes and a constant chorus of "Baby the Rain Must Fall" from the jukebox in the Snake Room next door, and if I were also to hear those dying voices, those Midwestern voices drawn to this lunar country
75 for some unimaginable atavistic rites, *rock of ages cleft for me,* I think I would lose my own reason. Every now and then I imagine I hear a rattlesnake, but my husband says that it is a faucet, a paper rustling, the wind. Then he stands by a window, and plays a flashlight over the dry wash outside.

What does it mean? It means nothing manageable. There is some sinister
80 hysteria in the air out here tonight, some hint of the monstrous perversion to which any human idea can come. "I followed my own conscience." "I did what I thought was right." How many madmen have said it and meant it? How many murderers? Klaus Fuchs[3] said it, and the men who committed the Mountain Meadows[4] Massacre said it, and Alfred Rosenberg[4] said it. And, as we are rotely
85 and rather presumptuously reminded by those who would say it now, Jesus said it. Maybe we have all said it, and maybe we have been wrong. Except on the most primitive level—our loyalties to those we love—what could be more arro-

---

3. *Klaus Fuchs:* British atomic secrets spy. (*ed.*)

4. *Alfred Rosenberg:* Nazi Third Reich minister for the "occupied Eastern territory." (*ed.*)

gant than to claim the primacy of personal conscience? ("Tell me," a rabbi asked Daniel Bell[5] when he said, as a child, that he did not believe in God. "Do you think God cares?") At least some of the time, the world appears to me as a paint-  90 ing by Hieronymous Bosch,[6] were I to follow my conscience then, it would lead me out onto the desert with Marion Faye, out to where he stood in *The Deer Park* looking east to Los Alamos[7] and praying, as if for rain, that it would happen: " . . . *let it come and clear the rot and the stench and the stink, let it come for all of everywhere, just so it comes and the world stands clear in the white dead dawn.*"  95

Of course you will say that I do not have the right, even if I had the power, to inflict that unreasonable conscience upon you; nor do I want you to inflict your conscience, however reasonable, however enlightened, upon me. ("We must be aware of the dangers which lie in our most generous wishes," Lionel Trilling[8] once wrote. "Some paradox of our nature leads us, when once we have made  100 our fellow men the objects of our enlightened interest, to go on to make them the objects of our pity, then of our wisdom, ultimately of our coercion.") That the ethic of conscience is intrinsically insidious seems scarcely a revelatory point, but it is one raised with increasing infrequency; even those who do raise it tend to *segue* with troubling readiness into the quite contradictory position  105 that the ethic of conscience is dangerous when it is "wrong," and admirable when it is "right."

You see I want to be quite obstinate about insisting that we have no way of knowing—beyond that fundamental loyalty to the social code—what is "right" and what is "wrong," what is "good" and what "evil." I dwell so upon  110 this because the most disturbing aspect of "morality" seems to me to be the frequency with which the word now appears; in the press, on television, in the most perfunctory kinds of conversation. Questions of straightforward power (or survival) politics, questions of quite indifferent public policy, questions of almost anything: they are all assigned these factitious moral burdens.  115 There is something facile going on, some self-indulgence at work. Of course we would all like to "believe" in something, like to assuage our private guilts in public causes, like to lose our tiresome selves; like, perhaps, to transform the white flag of defeat at home into the brave white banner of battle away from home. And of course it is all right to do that; that is how, immemorially,  120 things have gotten done. But I think it is all right only so long as we do not delude ourselves about what we are doing, and why. It is all right only so long as we remember that all the *ad hoc* committees, all the picket lines, all the brave

---

5. *Daniel Bell:* American sociologist and author of *The End of Ideology.* (*ed.*)

6. *Hieronymous Bosch* (ca. 1450–1516): Dutch painter of grotesque human shapes and hideous scenes of hell. (*ed.*)

7. *Marion Faye:* a character in Norman Mailer's (b. 1923) novel *The Deer Park; Los Alamos:* atomic bomb testing site in New Mexico. (*ed.*)

8. *Lionel Trilling:* American literary critic and fiction writer. (*ed.*)

signatures in *The New York Times,* all the tools of agitprop[9] straight across the
125   spectrum, do not confer upon anyone any *ipso facto*[10] virtue. It is all right only
so long as we recognize that the end may or may not be expedient, may or
may not be a good idea, but in any case has nothing to do with "morality." Because when we start deceiving ourselves into thinking not that we want something or need something, not that it is a pragmatic necessity for us to have it,
130   but that it is a *moral imperative* that we have it, then is when we join the
fashionable madmen, and then is when the thin whine of hysteria is heard in
the land, and then is when we are in bad trouble. And I suspect we are already
there.

## Looking Back

1. What early sense do we get of Didion's approach to her assignment to write about "morality" (see lines 1–7)?
2. How are we intended to regard the behavior of the nurse and her husband (lines 11–16)?
3. Can you say, in a general way, what Didion means by "the promises we make to one another" (lines 20–21)?
4. What connection does the author make between the early life of children and their moral sense as adults?
5. Precisely how was Didion taught to interpret the fates of the Donner-Reed Party and the Jayhawkers? Whether you know the particulars of these disasters or not, does her interpretation seem likely? Explain your answer.
6. How would you define the terms *responsibility* and *loyalty,* which Didion contends are at the heart of moral action?
7. In what way does the carrying of stories through the desert seem to serve a moral purpose (see lines 46–67)?
8. Can you put in your own words Didion's critique of conscience as a guide to moral action (see lines 79–102)?
9. How do you account for the progression Lionel Trilling describes from interest to pity to wisdom to coercion (see lines 98–102)?
10. What final distinction does Didion make between true and false morality (see lines 108–133)?

## Writing Assignments

1. Joan Didion discovers the truest and most unfailing source of morality in what she calls the "social code," which has to do with loyalty and responsibility and "the

---

9. *agitprop:* propaganda activity usually associated with communist groups; often involves theatrical performance. (*ed.*)

10. *ipso facto:* Latin for "by its very nature." (*ed.*)

promises we make to one another" (lines 20–21, and see number 3 in Looking Back). These are all abstract concepts. Didion provides some positive and negative examples of them, but it remains for us to define the terms *social code, loyalty, responsibility,* and *promises;* and it remains for us to find in our own community the presence or absence of the moral relations they signify. Write an essay that defines the above terms and examines, to the extent that you are in a position to do so, the respect paid to the social code within your own community.

2. Personal conscience as a guide to moral action comes in for much criticism in "On Morality" (see lines 79–122, and number 8 in Looking Back). Write an essay that argues that the "ethic of conscience" Didion refers to is either unreliable or trustworthy. In your essay, report Didion's criticism of conscience, and say whether you think the social code surpasses it as a means of regulating behavior and teaching people how to act. Explain what you mean by *personal conscience* so that you and your readers get off on the same foot. Ask yourself, as well, if there is an alternative to either conscience or the social code that we may turn to for moral guidance.

3. Didion quotes Lionel Trilling as follows: "Some paradox of our nature leads us, when once we have made our fellow men the objects of our enlightened interest, to go on to make them the objects of our pity, then of our wisdom, ultimately of our coercion" (lines 100–102). Write an essay in which you do the following: (a) define Trilling's terms; (b) describe how this progression takes place; (c) explain what effect the move from interest to coercion might have on the general populace or on a particular group: and (d) extrapolate from his warning to apply it to some governmental social policies (see number 9 in Looking Back). Examples of social policies you might consider are welfare, shelter programs for the homeless, and Medicaid, but if you do not know enough about any of these, you can consider social policies from a more abstract perspective.

# *Follow-Up: An Essay for Analysis*

WORDS IN THE ENGLISH LANGUAGE

Social code, loyalty, responsibility, and promises. What do these words symbolize in a community? Are their meanings taken seriously or are they just terms that people use to be fashionable, to look good in the eyes of others? When you say I have re-         5
sponsibilities in life, I have made a promise to someone or he did a favor for me and helped me when I was in need therefore I must do the same for him, or she's my mother, I'm obligated to her, are there real intentions behind these statements? The sig-         10
nificance of it all depends upon the social code

that you have been raised by which grips these words
and places more than just a dictionary definition
behind them.

15    The social code is the code that one conducts his
life by, influenced less by what he believes in than
what society expects from him. You develop your own
identity and convictions as you grow older by what
experiences you go through in society but when
20    you're young, you follow the social code. You are
taught not to scratch in public, to speak English
correctly, to bathe and brush your teeth, to be kind
to others and do unto them as you would like them to
do unto you, no stealing or lying, and listening to
25    and respecting your elders (more within the community). These are just a few examples of things in
the social code which are impressed upon you as a
child but through the process of growing up, you
gradually acquire your own set of values which even-
30    tually makes this social code more complex than just
brushing your teeth.

One part of this complex social code is loyalty
which means faithful. Whether its family, friends,
country, or just other human beings it asks, "Do I
35    owe someone else something whether he's done anything
for me or not?" For instance in my own community we
can talk about being faithful to a husband or a wife.
If the wife disagrees with something one of her husbands relatives does regarding the treatment of the
40    wife's children, where does loyalty lie? Is the husband loyal to the family he has created or to the
family who has raised him?

Responsibility means to be morally, legally or
mentally responsible for your actions. As in Did-
45    ion's essay "On morality", we have a moral and mental
responsibility to take care of and help one another.
In my community if someone is a friend and needs borrow money or anything else tangible, you give it to
them as long as you know they are responsible people.
50    If they break or lose something of yours, they will
replace it or if they say they'll pay you back on
time, they'll do it.

Promise is a word that no one should utter because
it is the most difficult vow to keep due to the fact
55    that we are all human and make mistakes. But the

word has become so widely and generally used that it
has less and less meaning as time goes on. People
don't take it seriously because most that have been
around long enough know that promises are almost always broken and in my community promises tend to be       60
flung around.

Loyalty, responsibility and promises are words
that do have meaning in my community but it depends
on the individual and the social code he has decided
to live by. After all as Didion said, "We are what       65
we learned as children."

--Eileen Whitehead, composition student

## Critical Inquiry

Eileen Whitehead wrote the above essay in response to Joan Didion's "On Morality,"
Writing Assignment 1 (p. 616). Whitehead's essay is a preliminary draft. That is, it needs
revision on a number of levels before it can be judged acceptable. To help you become
more aware of your own writing needs as well as those of this student writer, use the following list of questions to analyze this essay. Before answering them you should reread
Didion's text and the writing assignment Whitehead responded to.

## Questions for Analysis

1. To what degree to you think Whitehead has absorbed and understood Didion's text?
   Why do you think so?

2. In your judgment, has Whitehead done what the writing assignment called for? If
   so, what supports your view? If not, what matters has she failed to address?

3. Has Whitehead referred to Didion's text sufficiently for someone who has *not* read it
   to understand Didion's intent and chief ideas? Why do you think this?

4. Does Whitehead's logic hold up throughout, or are there places where it falls down?
   Be specific.

5. Would you suggest that, in later drafts, Whitehead develop some parts of her essay
   in greater detail? If so, what parts?

6. How would you evaluate Whitehead's word choices? Does any language need elucidation or replacement in the next draft? Are there any redundancies? Where, if at
   all, should she be more concise?

7. Have you detected surface errors—grammar, sentence structure, punctuation,
   spelling, capitalization—that need editing? If so, correct them by marking up or
   rewriting the sentences.

8. Do you think Whitehead has come close, in this draft, to discussing the topic in a
   creative and original way? Would you have thought things out differently? Support
   your view.

❦

# Diana Tietjens Meyers

# Work and Self-Respect

Diana Tietjens Meyers (b. 1947) is a professor of philosophy at the University of Connecticut in Storrs. She is the author of *Inalienable Rights: A Defense* and *Self, Society, and Personal Choice* and is the co-editor of a number of collections of philosophical essays, among which is *Women and Moral Theory,* a volume widely used in college classrooms. Her most recent book, on psychoanalytic feminism and moral philosophy, is entitled *Subjection and Subjectivity.* The piece printed here is from a collection entitled *Moral Rights in the Workplace.* Here, Meyers's fresh approaches to personal integrity and human rights place self-respect in a new context and allow the author, through this critical thinking technique, to express original ideas about her subject.

## *Looking Ahead*

1. The author's thesis and purpose in writing this article are expressed early on. Read critically to test the logical flow of ideas from these statements.

2. As you read, be sure to keep track of key concepts, their definitions, and their relations to each other.

3. Note that the subheads designate both the topics of particular sections and the structural order of the whole piece.

## Meaningful Work and Self-Respect

To understand what makes work meaningful, it is necessary to ask what makes life worthwhile. But the latter question seems to have almost as many answers as there are people. For one person, it's becoming an astronaut; for another, it's caring for a child; for another, it's helping to alleviate world hunger; for still another, it's composing a popular song. Since this list could go on indefinitely, it
5   might seem futile to seek a single, comprehensive account of what makes life worthwhile. But the concept of self-respect provides a unifying theme.

Despite the remarkable diversity of their pursuits, people agree that self-respect helps to give life value. As John Rawls puts it, "Without it (self-respect), nothing may seem worth doing, or if some things have value for us, we lack the
10   will to strive for them." Self-respect protects people from despair while it enhances their resolve to carry out their plans and intensifies their satisfaction in fulfilling these plans. In view of this multiple function, the prevailing consensus that self-respect is desirable comes as no surprise. Still it is not at all obvious how self-respect is related to the myriad occupations that people engage in.
15   A person who has self-respect is able to lead a more rewarding life than a person who is burdened by self-contempt. But how do people gain self-respect?

Part of the explanation lies in our upbringing. Attentive, supportive parenting fosters self-respect. Yet since we have no control over this childhood experience, it is important to consider how as adults we can build upon this early care or, if necessary, overcome the lack of it. In this essay, I shall argue that personal integrity is necessary for self-respect and that rights can promote self-respect by allowing for personal integrity. Applying these results to the work world, I shall urge that employers ought to recognize certain work-related rights. For the right to employment, the right to equal opportunity, and the right to participate in job-related decisions encourage personal integrity. In so doing, these rights give persons the chance to make their work meaningful.

## Personal Integrity and Self-Respect

Self-respect appears to be a particularly elusive good. Like happiness, it is not the kind of thing that one can will into existence. Each person chooses to act in this way or that, to associate with this acquaintance or that, to strive for this virtue or that—in sum, to live a certain kind of life. Along the way, self-respect or self-contempt may accrue. There is no formula guaranteed to bring about one or the other. Still, since it is hardly accidental that some people have self-respect, we must consider how self-respect is gained.

To have personal integrity, a person must have stable beliefs and feelings that he or she expresses in practice. Personal integrity contrasts both with fickleness and with hypocrisy. Lacking firm convictions and abiding affections, the chameleonlike person tailors his or her views to fit changing circumstances. And though the hypocrite has lasting convictions and emotional bonds, this individual belies them in his or her conduct. Because of their respective failings, neither the chameleon nor the hypocrite can have self-respect.

A self-respecting person reflexively affirms the value of being a unique individual, that is, or having a distinctive mix of characteristics. Among them are the person's beliefs and feelings. Though Susan may share many convictions with others, she combines them in her own way. Like her friend James, Susan believes that more women should seek jobs in the construction industry; however, unlike James, Susan is fond of Linda. To respect herself, then, Susan must have beliefs and affections that taken together differentiate her from other individuals, and she must act in a manner that affirms the worth of this package.

Someone might object that because stable beliefs and feelings obstruct growth and improvement, they are inimical to self-respect. A self-respecting person must be free to develop his or her potential, and, to be free in the requisite way, a person must be open and flexible. Strong convictions and passions can freeze the self in foolish or outdated modes.

This objection confuses stability with rigidity and fanaticism. Saying that a self-respecting person's beliefs and feelings must be stable is not equivalent to saying that once formed they must never change. If Linda stops reciprocating Susan's friendship, Susan's warm feelings for Linda will gradually disappear,

60    and rightfully so. Stability is not immutability. But if Susan never felt any ongoing affection for Linda, her friendship was not genuine in the first place, and
stability could not be an issue.

If a person's beliefs and feelings shift constantly, the person can still approve or disapprove of these fleeting attitudes. However, momentary self-
65    satisfaction is not self-respect. Quite the contrary, self-respect is a steady self-
acceptance that endures through occasional self-blame, as well as occasional
self-congratulation. This foundational valuation would not be possible if personal characteristics all varied wildly. For only if the main lineaments of a person's character are stable can continuing acceptance (or continuing rejection) of
70    the self be warranted. While the scope of a self-respecting person's convictions
and affections could be extremely narrow—it could be limited to dedication to
a single cause or attachment to a single person—no one could have self-respect
without at least one enduring belief or feeling. After all, self-respect requires a
self to respect. An individual devoid of convictions and affections may be an ex-
75    periencer but is not a self.

It is important to recognize that a self-respecting person's conduct need not
be predetermined and routinized. A person might believe that in some areas it is
better not to form judgments, but, instead, to feel one's way and cope intu-
itively. However, this allowance for spontaneity does not license the hypocrite's
80    wiles. The hypocrite has lasting beliefs and feelings, but does not hew to them
in action. In order to curry favor with others, the hypocrite pretends to share
their views; thus betraying the ones he or she really holds. This self-suppression
prevents hypocrites from respecting themselves.

Frequently when a person silences beliefs or feelings, the reason is self-
85    doubt. But a person can suppress beliefs or feelings in order to shield them from
unsympathetic or even cruel audiences. John, who is gay, may deny these inclinations because he is ashamed of them and does not want to become the target
of what he regards as others' justified disdain. Or he may deny them because he
cherishes them and does not want them to be eroded by what he regards as oth-
90    ers' unjustified disdain. In the former case, it is clear that John suffers from self-
contempt. In the latter case, John's strategy may effectively preserve his integrity
despite widespread hostility to his predilections. Provided that John is part of a
supportive community in which he is free to discuss and act on his sexual pref-
erences, his selective self-censorship may well help him to retain his self-
95    respect. Unrelieved self-censorship, however, would be an entirely different
matter.

We have seen that a person who has no stable beliefs and feelings cannot
have self-respect because this individual lacks the kind of self that can be respected. The trouble with the person who has stable beliefs and feelings but re-
100  lentlessly suppresses them is that this individual cannot know himself or herself
well enough to have self-respect. Without self-knowledge, a person's respect
would be directed at an imagined self rather than at the real self. Consequently,
self-respect would be illusory. It would be like falling in love with a character in

a movie, but mistakenly believing it is the actor whom you love. Since self-knowledge is necessary for self-respect, the conditions under which self-knowledge is possible must be indicated.

Introspection alone is not sufficient for self-knowledge. Suppose Ann prides herself on being, at heart, an acute social critic and a steadfast supporter of oppressed minorities. Yet suppose also that Ann chooses never to reveal any of her insights to anyone else and deliberately hides her antagonism to racism. She has reason to doubt her self-concept. People discover who they are in part by observing themselves in action. To form a self-concept without the benefit of this testing ground is to run the risk of substituting a fictional self for the real one.

Both aspects of personal integrity—enduring convictions and affections and the expression of these beliefs and feelings in conduct—are inextricable from self-respect. Accordingly, self-respect is a highly individual good. Since no two persons have identical convictions and affections, no two persons can maintain their integrity and gain self-respect by following the same life plan. This explains why there can be no universal program for achieving self-respect and also why the private good of self-respect is often linked with the public good of liberty.

## Self-Respect and Rights

Human rights are commonly characterized as rights that all persons have simply in virtue of being human. The idea is that by itself humanity is a dignified station deserving of respect. Human rights articulate a set of moral requirements that specify the forms of respect humanity is owed. People have a right to life because of their capacities as human beings, not because of their personal talents or accomplishments. To respect a person's human rights, then, is to respect that person as a person.

Since compliance with a person's rights is obligatory regardless of special merits, rights may seem irrelevant to self-respect. As I have emphasized, self-respect presupposes intimate knowledge of the self and honors the unique self. We do not respect ourselves for being members of the human species, but rather for our distinctive qualities and achievements. Though it is difficult for a person to maintain self-respect if everyone else despises him or her, the fact that others accord a person his or her dignity as a human being cannot secure self-respect. What, then, is the contribution fundamental rights make to self-respect?

Rights give right-holders prerogatives in regard to specified benefits. A person who has a property right in a piece of land may use the land as he or she pleases, and a person who has a right to free speech may voice whatever ideas he or she chooses. Although right-holders are forbidden to violate others' rights while exercising their own, rights provide the persons who possess them with options. Even rights that do not explicitly confer liberties, such as

145    the right to medical care or to decent housing, nonetheless afford persons a
measure of discretion. Right-holders may avail themselves of existing rights-
implementing facilities. They may demand improved programs to deliver the
objects of their rights, or they may decide not to take advantage of their rights
at all.

150         The prerogatives rights afford are the key to the way rights support self-
respect. We have seen that personal integrity is necessary for self-respect and
that personal integrity requires that individuals form lasting convictions and
emotional ties that they act on. But without freedom, persons are likely to adopt
the views and attitudes the authorities prescribe. Moreover, if they have non-
155    conformist ideas, they will be forced to hide them or risk penalties. Only when
people are free to discover themselves and to express their distinctive personalities can personal integrity flourish. Because every right secures a measure of
such freedom, each right serves to foster self-respect.

         It might be objected that the superabundant freedom that rights grant is
160    detrimental to self-respect. When people are confronted by an unlimited array
of possibilities, they are apt to be uncertain and distraught about which direction to take. People need self-confidence before they can use their freedom to
secure personal integrity. For self-confidence gives people the courage to express themselves. But to have self-confidence, it could be urged, people need to
165    know their social role and what society expects of them. A person's secure
knowledge that he or she belongs in an assigned social role and shares socially
condoned values reinforces this person's self-confidence. Once this base of self-
assurance is established, a person can begin to form and carry out his or her
own ideas and feelings. Without this base, confusion and anxiety will preclude
170    personal integrity as well as self-respect.

         Undeniably, self-confidence is necessary for personal integrity. Neverthe-
less, funneling people into predetermined social roles and imposing values on
them is neither the only nor the best way to build self-confidence. Child-rearing
methods emphasizing delight in diversity, familiarity with a common heritage,
175    and emotional openness in a supportive atmosphere nurture self-confidence.
Also, associations of adults whose talents and interests overlap help to sustain
this sense of personal worth. In contrast, enforced social roles and values expand the self-confidence of some at the expense of the personal integrity of others. For example, Jane, who embraces the conventional feminine stereotype,
180    may find it gratifying to know that society applauds her activities as a housewife
and mother. But social ridicule may compel Brian, who would prefer a life as a
homemaker and father, to play the traditional masculine role of provider. Rigid
social attitudes rend Brian's personal integrity, and social tolerance would not
necessarily dissolve Jane's self-confidence.

185         The freedom human rights afford does not present people with so bewil-
dering a selection of options that self-confidence is inevitably destroyed. First,
each person's rights are limited by others' rights. Though some rights may be
exercised competitively, everyone has rights that prohibit, among other things,

assault, deception, and coercion. Since rights do not authorize persons to over-
turn these constraints, rights themselves set ground rules that narrow right-     190
holders' prerogatives. Furthermore, to the extent that parents and teachers give
children practice at imagining and evaluating options, adults become more
adept choosers. They become accustomed to deciding what to believe and
whom to associate with, and they automatically consult their own convictions
and feelings in deciding how to act. The worry and frustration many people suf-   195
fer when faced with free choice in strange situations can be alleviated through
education.

Widespread agreement about the importance of rights that allow for individuality goes hand in hand with respect for dissent and idiosyncrasy. Accordingly, conduct based on self-generated beliefs and feelings is not as likely to     200
meet with reflex condemnation in a society concerned with insuring human
rights. Insofar as self-confidence depends on popular acceptance, then a greater
variety of people will be able to enjoy this good if their rights are firmly established. Both by protecting self-confidence and by guaranteeing freedom, rights
promote personal integrity and, along with it, self-respect.                         205

## Rights and Meaningful Work

In authorizing persons to exercise a range of prerogatives, rights invite right-
holders to act in accordance with their settled beliefs and feelings. Unlike duties, which impose requirements, rights issue permissions. Each of these permissions defines an arena in which individuals may set personal objectives and
standards and seek to fulfill them. To the extent that right-holders grasp these    210
opportunities and succeed in projecting their values and inclinations, they gain
personal integrity and strengthen their self-respect. Though rights cannot endow persons with self-respect—no social mechanism can—denial of persons'
rights can crush self-respect. For this reason, it is important to consider how
rights support self-respect in major areas of life. Since work consumes a large    215
part of most people's lives, it is especially urgent to determine how rights figure
in work.

The concept of work is an evolving one. Work is traditionally associated
with onerous labor, and people work mainly in order to earn a living. Nevertheless, history reveals a broadening range of activities that count as work. During   220
the Middle Ages, workers were sharply differentiated from the nobility with
their stations in life as well as from the clergy with their callings to God's service. Workers performed physical, often dirty tasks, while the nobility wielded
political power and patronized the arts, and the clergy studied and prayed. Ves-
tiges of these divisions persist; however, with the democratization of political,   225
intellectual, and religious pursuits came an expanded concept of work. Today,
government officials, teachers, and spiritual leaders all work alongside servants,
factory workers, and farm hands. The category of work thus includes any socially useful occupation.

230      Accompanying this enlargement of the concept of work has been a humanization of the purposes work is thought to serve. As we have seen, a variety of personally rewarding occupations is now considered to be work. Also, unionization and labor law have provided greater job security and better salaries for many employees, while public education has afforded many people a more

235 egalitarian perspective on life. As a result, many people are not content to devote most of their time merely to earning a wage, and many workers have begun to demand more fulfilling work arrangements. Still, the problem of meaningful work has not been solved. Though meaningful work has become a widely discussed issue, many people remain unemployed or stuck in tedious jobs. I shall

240 argue, however, that full implementation of three rights would make the work world much more conducive to self-respect.

     The first difficulty a person encounters vis-a-vis work is finding employment. In our society, gainful employment is a badge of respectability; however, since World War II the official unemployment rate has never been lower than

245 2.8 percent and has ranged as high as 10.6 percent. Moreover, these government statistics do not count as "unemployed" those individuals who are unemployed because they have given up looking for jobs or have never wanted jobs. This distinction—the distinction between an unwilling, defeated dropout from the job market and a willing, happy dependent of another person or the state—

250 is crucial to the issue of self-respect. For a willing dependent does not need employment to respect himself or herself, but enforced unemployment is a direct threat to an unwilling dropout's personal integrity. The latter individual accepts conventional economic values, like effort and self-sufficiency. But a surplus of job candidates combines with rigidity in the economic sphere to prevent him or

255 her from acting on these beliefs. Structural unemployment compels its victims to jettison their values or sacrifice their self-respect.

     The right to employment is primarily a right to a fairly remunerated position. However, in a society where unemployment is chronic, it is important to see that this right implies a right to be recognized as a member of the work

260 force. As such, it provides right-holders with two kinds of leverage. First, this right entitles persons to the training they need in order to find a niche in the job market. Second, it justifies persons in demanding innovation in patterns of job and income distribution, such as part-time positions that pay decent wages and provide essential health and retirement benefits. Thus, the right to employment

265 denies that a class of permanently jobless, though able people is inevitable, and it authorizes right-holders who have been excluded from the job market to stand up for their values.

     The standard argument against the right to employment is that society cannot afford it: Training programs are costly; reliance on part-time labor is only

270 feasible when it can be bought cheap; the economy would falter because people would not strive to get ahead if jobs were guaranteed. The economic issues raised by this objection are too complex for adequate treatment here. Nevertheless, it should be said that it is an open question whether the proposed programs would be prohibitively expensive. In their support, it can be said that

savings on welfare and increased productivity would help to offset these costs.    275
Moreover, trimming the military budget could release funds to implement the
right to employment. Finally, it must be stressed that the right to employment
would not eliminate competition for jobs. Though everyone would be assured
of some job, candidates would compete for the more interesting and better paying positions. Accordingly, there is no reason to suppose that the right to em-    280
ployment would weaken the incentive to work.

At this point, the problem of how to distribute the more desirable positions
arises. The right to equal opportunity comes into play in education preparatory
to work, in the search for employment, and in consideration for promotion and
raises. At each of these stages, this right guarantees that no one's opportunities    285
will be limited by discrimination on grounds of race, creed, sex, or other irrelevant characteristics. In other words, this right requires that the best qualified
applicant be chosen for each available opening.

An obvious way in which the right to equal opportunity bears on self-
respect is that this right shields persons from arbitrary and humiliating rejec-    290
tions. Victims of discrimination may perceive that they are not being judged
fairly, yet it is difficult to avoid succumbing to self-doubt when one's endeavors
meet with repeated failure. The right to equal opportunity removes this source
of self-contempt. Moreover, in assuring all candidates that their credentials will
be reviewed impartially and taken seriously, this right implicitly affirms that    295
self-respect properly hinges on a person's effort and attainment, not on the accidents of one's birth. In effect, this right calls on individuals to assess their abilities, envisage a suitable career, and strive to bring it about. The right to equal
opportunity releases people from tradition-bound assumptions about the social
niches befitting them and offers them the chance to work at jobs of their own    300
choosing, if not their own design. Thus, a notable function of the right to equal
opportunity is to guarantee the possibility of self-expression in a person's initial
choice of an occupation.

Now it might be objected that self-respecting persons need not regard their
jobs as reflections of their selves. Persons can gain self-respect from performing    305
a socially designated task well. Perhaps, insisting that one's work match one's
personality is evidence of self-indulgence, not self-respect, for no viable economy can accommodate such adamant individualism. Whatever the merits of
equal opportunity, the objection concludes, workers must accede to the time-
honored compromises and strictures of the work world.    310

Of course, no right can promise that everyone's dreams will come true. Mature adults modulate their aspirations and expectations in light of a realistic
appraisal of what is possible. Graceless weaklings do not yearn to be ballerinas;
they turn to other enterprises. Nevertheless, if prejudice forces the members of
one social group to discard otherwise sensible career plans, while many indi-    315
viduals who do not belong to discriminated against groups can pursue the careers they prefer, personal integrity in employment goals becomes a privilege of
the advantaged class. Notoriously, there was never any good reason to bar the
great black pitcher Satchel Paige from major league baseball. The right to equal

320 opportunity prevents maldistribution of a central component of self-respect, namely, personal integrity in career direction.

Other rights protect personal integrity on the job. Prominent among them is the right to participate in job-related decisions. This is a right that is some-times dismissed out of hand because it seems to conflict with the rights of busi-

325 ness owners to delegate authority within their firms as they think best. How-ever, there are various ways to implement this right, and some of them do not usurp property owners' legitimate prerogatives. Moreover, all of these ways support personal integrity in the workplace.

First, it is important to recognize that business owners are not entitled to

330 wield absolute authority over workers during the workday. When laws or union contracts provide for such employee rights as the right to safe working condi-tions, rest periods, and job security, owners' rights are thereby eroded. Yet since the compelling needs of employees plainly justify many of these arrangements, property rights must yield to them. Likewise, the right to participate in job-

335 related decisions can be instituted in a manner that restricts but does not extin-guish owners' rights. For example, the right to participate in job-related deci-sions could be interpreted as requiring procedures for consulting with all concerned employees and a reorganization of work activities. Consultation in-volves soliciting and paying attention to employees' views before making deci-

340 sions. Reorganization may involve breaking up assembly lines, eliminating regi-mented, mass-production formats in offices, and replacing them with work groups that are responsible for handling particular projects. Experience has shown that such reforms can improve efficiency. Also, it is clear that these pro-grams do not preempt owners' rights.

345 Actually to democratize the workplace would be to grant employees the power to control, through their ballots, a firm's future course. Consultation procedures and reorganized work schedules do not redistribute economic power in so far-reaching a fashion and, therefore, are not tantamount to eco-nomic democracy. Nevertheless, a right exacting these reforms could have a

350 marked impact on employees' self-respect since both afford opportunities for constructive self-expression at the workplace. In discussions with supervisors and in cooperation with a self-contained work unit, individuals would be en-couraged to reflect on their occupations and to suggest changes. Workers' pro-posals must pass tests of practicality, but nothing would prevent workers from

355 putting forth sound suggestions based on their own values and feelings. Insofar as allowance for employees' personal integrity can be incorporated into the workplace, self-respect can be promoted in this context. Clearly the right to participate in job-related decisions serves this purpose.

Thinking about their lives, many people sharply divide work from leisure.

360 At work they maintain an appropriate facade, but at home they can be them-selves. Needless to say no one is equally at ease with loved ones and compara-tive strangers, and people will always have to adapt themselves to public situa-tions and be more guarded in this sphere. Still, none of this entails that the good of personal integrity must be confined to the private domain. The rights to

equal opportunity and to participate in job-related decisions provide employees     365
with the moral leverage they need to break down this compartmentalization of
life's reward. In authorizing employees to bring their convictions and feelings to
bear on their occupations, these rights respect the unity and independence of
persons. In recognizing the autonomy of employees, these rights make work a
source of self-respect and, as such, a site of personal meaning.     370

## Looking Back

1. Can you produce a graph or outline to demonstrate the author's thesis and purpose in writing, as those are noted in lines 21–27?

2. How, according to Meyers, is personal integrity essential to self-respect?

3. Applying her view to yourself, what "enduring belief or feeling" (line 73) do you hold?

4. How do hypocrisy and self-censorship hinder self-respect? How do self-knowledge and liberty encourage it?

5. How does Meyers define human rights?

6. What is the link she makes between freedom, rights, and self-respect (see lines 139–158)?

7. Does the right to employment have broader implications than merely having a job? What are they?

8. How does the right to equal opportunity promote self-respect?

9. What would it mean to "democratize the workplace" (line 345)?

10. In jobs you have held, have you experienced a clear connection between work and self-respect? Have you observed such a connection in the work of others? Explain your answer.

## Writing Assignments

1. Diana Tietjens Meyers makes the point that to acquire and maintain self-respect one must have meaningful work. For that to be the case, one must have certain rights. Among these are the right to employment itself, especially as it "justifies persons in demanding innovation in patterns of job and income distribution" (lines 262–263); the right to equal opportunity, here "consideration for promotion and raises" (lines 284–285), and the "right to participate in job-related decisions" (line 323). On the basis of your own work experience and your observation of your work conditions write an essay extrapolating from these rights, regarding them as principles that you may apply to a particular job to test its value (see number 10 in Looking Back).

2. "After all," writes Meyers, "self-respect requires a self to respect. An individual devoid of convictions and affections may be an experiencer but is not a self" (lines 73–75). It is hard to disagree with this view—that the self is no butterfly but a moral subject who acts on principle, makes decisions, and creates emotional bonds. Yet, our agreement may put us on the spot. That is, we may now need to identify our own "convictions and affections" and to describe the way they operate in our lives,

since, as we learn, self-knowledge has high value (see number 2 in Looking Back). Write an essay explaining this value in yourself by doing what is suggested above—identifying and describing your own convictions and affections.

3. Meyers tells us that liberty is essential to self-respect. "Since no two persons have identical convictions and affections," she writes, "no two persons can maintain their integrity and gain self-respect by following the same life plan" (lines 117–119). It follows, therefore, that we all must be free to develop along lines of our own choosing, and for this to take place we must be tolerant of one another's styles of life, associations, and activities. We grant people their liberty by not insisting that there is only one way to live. Write an essay that extrapolates from this line of reasoning by applying it to contemporary American society, discussing those people who deserve others' respect simply for being what they are, and who may earn their own respect by being able to choose and act without impediment.

## Gary Snyder

# Buddhism and the Coming Revolution

Gary Snyder (b. 1931) is a poet and essayist whose lifelong interest in Eastern religion, evident in this essay from his book *Earth House Hold*, has taken him to Japan to study Zen Buddhism. He won the Pulitzer Prize for poetry in 1975. Along with Allen Ginsberg, William Burroughs, and Jack Kerouac, Snyder was part of the beat generation, a group of artists who revolted against the tame literary standards of their day. He is the author of *No Nature: New and Selected Poems, Regarding Wave, Left Out in the Rain,* and *The Old Ways,* among other books. Snyder teaches at the University of California at Davis. In this essay, Snyder's critical thinking goal is a reevaluation of Western culture by submitting it to the test of Eastern ideals.

## Looking Ahead

1. As you will probably discover, Snyder's political references have as much relevance today as when he made them in 1969, before the Cold War ended and while the Vietnam War was raging.
2. Snyder proposes solutions to the problems he describes. It is necessary to consider his solutions seriously, if for no other reason than to understand fully the problems.
3. Read critically to decide whether Snyder is a utopian thinker—one who believes in the perfectibility of society—and whether his proposals seem capable of being realized.

Buddhism holds that the universe and all creatures in it are intrinsically in a state of complete wisdom, love and compassion; acting in natural response and mutual interdependence. The personal realization of this from-the-beginning state cannot be had for and by one-"self"—because it is not fully realized unless one has given the self up; and away.

In the Buddhist view, that which obstructs the effortless manifestation of this is Ignorance, which projects into fear and needless craving. Historically, Buddhist philosophers have failed to analyze out the degree to which ignorance and suffering are caused or encouraged by social factors, considering fear-and-desire to be given facts of the human condition. Consequently the major concern of Buddhist philosophy is epistemology[1] and "psychology" with no attention paid to historical or sociological problems. Although Mahayana Buddhism[2] has a grand vision of universal salvation, the *actual* achievement of Buddhism has been the development of practical systems of meditation toward the end of liberating a few dedicated individuals from psychological hangups and cultural conditionings. Institutional Buddhism has been conspicuously ready to accept or ignore the inequalities and tyrannies of whatever political system it found itself under. This can be death to Buddhism, because it is death to any meaningful function of compassion. Wisdom without compassion feels no pain.

No one today can afford to be innocent, or indulge himself in ignorance of the nature of contemporary governments, politics and social orders. The national polities of the modern world maintain their existence by deliberately fostered craving and fear: monstrous protection rackets. The "free world" has become economically dependent on a fantastic system of stimulation of greed which cannot be fulfilled, sexual desire which cannot be satiated and hatred which has no outlet except against oneself, the persons one is supposed to love, or the revolutionary aspirations of pitiful, poverty-stricken marginal societies like Cuba or Vietnam. The conditions of the Cold War have turned all modern societies—Communist included—into vicious distorters of man's true potential. They create populations of "preta"—hungry ghosts, with giant appetites and throats no bigger than needles. The soil, the forests and all animal life are being consumed by these cancerous collectivities; the air and water of the planet is being fouled by them.

There is nothing in human nature or the requirements of human social organization which intrinsically requires that a culture be contradictory, repressive and productive of violent and frustrated personalities. Recent findings in anthropology and psychology make this more and more evident. One can prove it for himself by taking a good look at his own nature through meditation. Once a person has this much faith and insight, he must be led to a deep concern with the need for radical social change through a variety of hopefully non-violent means.

---

1. *epistemology:* the study of the ways we know anything. (*ed.*)

2. *Mahayana Buddhism:* known not only for its religious teaching but also for its social concern. (*ed.*)

The joyous and voluntary poverty of Buddhism becomes a positive force. The traditional harmlessness and refusal to take life in any form has nation-shaking implications. The practice of meditation, for which one needs only "the
45   ground beneath one's feet" wipes out mountains of junk being pumped into the mind by the mass media and supermarket universities. The belief in a serene and generous fulfilment of natural loving desires destroys ideologies which blind, maim and repress—and points the way to a kind of community which would amaze "moralists" and transform armies of men who are fighters because
50   they cannot be lovers.

Avatamsaka (Kegon) Buddhist philosophy[3] sees the world as a vast interrelated network in which all objects and creatures are necessary and illuminated. From one standpoint, governments, wars, or all that we consider "evil" are uncompromisingly contained in this totalistic realm. The hawk, the swoop and the
55   hare are one. From the "human" standpoint we cannot live in those terms unless all beings see with the same enlightened eye. The Bodhisattva[4] lives by the sufferer's standard, and he must be effective in aiding those who suffer.

The mercy of the West has been social revolution; the mercy of the East has been individual insight into the basic self/void. We need both. They are both con-
60   tained in the traditional three aspects of the Dharma[5] path: wisdom (prajña), meditation (dhyāna), and morality (śīla). Wisdom is intuitive knowledge of the mind of love and clarity that lies beneath one's ego-driven anxieties and aggressions. Meditation is going into the mind to see this for yourself—over and over again, until it becomes the mind you live in. Morality is bringing it back out in
65   the way you live, through personal example and responsible action, ultimately toward the true community (sangha) of "all beings." This last aspect means, for me, supporting any cultural and economic revolution that moves clearly toward a free, international, classless world. It means using such means as civil disobedience, outspoken criticism, protest, pacifism, voluntary poverty and even gen-
70   tle violence if it comes to a matter of restraining some impetuous redneck. It means affirming the widest possible spectrum of non-harmful individual behavior—defending the right of individuals to smoke hemp, eat peyote, be polygynous, polyandrous[6] or homosexual. Worlds of behavior and custom long banned by the Judaeo-Capitalist-Christian-Marxist West. It means respecting
75   intelligence and learning, but not as greed or means to personal power. Working on one's own responsibility, but willing to work with a group. "Forming the new society within the shell of the old"—the I.W.W.[7] slogan of fifty years ago.

The traditional cultures are in any case doomed, and rather than cling to their good aspects hopelessly it should be remembered that whatever is or ever

---

3. *Avatamsaka . . . philosophy:* a set of doctrines studied by Buddhist adepts. (*ed.*)

4. *Bodhisattva:* an enlightened individual who lingers on earth to help others. (*ed.*)

5. *Dharma:* the key principles of our earthly existence. (*ed.*)

6. *polygynous, polyandrous:* having more than one female or male mate, respectively. (*ed.*)

7. *I.W.W.:* International Workers of the World, a political-labor organization which, in its heyday in the early 1900s, sought "one big union" as a way of radically altering American society. (*ed.*)

was in any other culture can be reconstructed from the unconscious, through    80
meditation. In fact, it is my own view that the coming revolution will close the
circle and link us in many ways with the most creative aspects of our archaic
past. If we are lucky we may eventually arrive at a totally integrated world culture with matrilineal descent, free-form marriage, natural-credit communist
economy, less industry, far less population and lots more national parks.    85

## Looking Back

1. Why might it be necessary to give the self up "and away" (line 5)? What would be the purpose?
2. What criticism does Snyder offer of traditional Buddhism (see lines 6–19)?
3. Can you find examples in American society supporting or refuting Snyder's complaints about the West (see lines 23–33 and 45–46)?
4. Given the author's social views, what do you think he means by "man's true potential" (lines 29–30)?
5. How do "faith and insight" (line 39) serve human ends?
6. Does Snyder's prescription of voluntary poverty, harmlessness, and pacifism seem feasible on a mass scale (see lines 42–44)?
7. What kind of community does Snyder envisage (see lines 46–50 and 64–69)?
8. Can you put in your own words his claim: "The Bodhisattva lives by the sufferer's standard, and he must be effective in aiding those who suffer" (lines 56–57)?
9. In what way does Snyder see the "mercy" of the East and West combining (see lines 58–77)?
10. Is Snyder's faith in the "coming revolution" of his title irrational? Why or why not?

## Writing Assignments

1. Gary Snyder's harsh criticisms of American society, particularly as found in lines 23–33, point to greed, exaggerated sexual desire, hatred, and ecocide. Later in the essay, he indicts "mountains of junk being pumped into the mind by the mass media and supermarket universities" (lines 45–46). Snyder does not give concrete examples of these spiritual and social failings, but you might (see number 3 in Looking Back). If you agree with his criticisms, choose *one* of the above problems, interpolate your own illustrations of it from American life, and point out its harmful consequences. If you disagree, do the same, only from a positive point of view.

2. The feeling for other human beings that motivates a Bodhisattva (see lines 56–57, and number 8 in Looking Back) is, according to Snyder, a potent force in the world. How is this so? What does it mean to "live by the sufferer's standard"? What kind of suffering is at issue here? Can the Bodhisattva actually relieve suffering or just make the sufferer better able to bear pain? Do you think suffering with others can become a widespread practice? What difference might it make in the world? Write an essay taking up these questions in order to find Snyder's faith in the Bodhisattva sensible or misplaced.

3. Snyder's possible utopianism (see number 3 in Looking Ahead and number 10 in Looking Back) is nowhere more evident than in the last paragraph of his essay. Here, he counts on a revolution to come—that is, a complete turnabout in social structures and relations—and lists a number of far-reaching changes he looks forward to. Granted, he says these will come "if we are lucky," but he nonetheless believes they can and should be achieved, for our good. Do you? Write an essay discussing all or some of his points, considering whether they make sense.

# Linked Readings

The Brothers Grimm
## THE WATER OF LIFE

Chuang Tzu
## SUPREME HAPPINESS

Jacob Grimm (1785–1863) and Wilhelm Grimm (1786–1859) were philologists and folklorists whose most famous publication was their collection of stories, *Folk Tales for Children and the Home.* Chuang Tzu, who lived in the fourth century B.C.E., was a philosopher whose personal name was Chou. The flavor of his writing is summed up by his translator, Burton Watson, this way: "The reader must learn to expect any opinion whatsoever from any source, to savor the outrageous incongruities, and to judge for himself which of the opinions offered represents the highest level of enlightenment." This textual need for interpretation is matched in the Grimms' folktales by a magic that is perhaps equally distant from us and that also taxes our sympathetic imagination. But from the authors on both sides we may gain a distinct sense of moral ideas and a recognizable picture of the human condition.

## THE WATER OF LIFE

*Looking Ahead*

1. Virtue is the subject matter here, but notice how it is associated with innocence.

2. The magical events in "The Water of Life" abbreviate more extended actions and also symbolize moral decisions and consequences. Try to formulate these for yourself as you read.

3. Consider how happy endings and moral rightness may be linked in some forms of literary imagination.

There was once a king who fell ill, and no one thought that he would survive. His three sons, however, were greatly distressed by this, went down into the palace garden, and wept. There they met an old man who asked what was troubling them. They told him that their father was so ill that he'd probably die, be-

cause nothing was doing him any good. "I know one remedy," said the old man,   5
"it's the Water of Life; if he drinks some of it, he'll get well again, but it's hard to
find." "I'll surely find it," said the eldest son. He went to the sick king and begged
him to let him set out in search of the Water of Life, for it alone could cure him.
"No," said the king, "it's too dangerous a task; I'd rather die." But the son begged
so long that the king finally assented. In his heart the prince thought, "If I bring   10
the Water, I'll be my father's favorite and inherit the kingdom."

So he set out, and when he'd been riding for a time, there was a dwarf
standing by the road who called out to him, saying, "Where are you going in
such a hurry?" "Stupid little shrimp," said the prince quite arrogantly, "that's
none of your business!" and rode on. The little dwarf had, however, got angry   15
and had made a bad wish. Soon after, the prince got into a mountain gorge and
the farther he rode, the more the mountains closed in, and finally the way got so
narrow that he couldn't go on another step. It was impossible to turn the horse
about or to get out of the saddle, and he sat there as if imprisoned. The sick king
waited a long time for him, but he didn't come. Then the second son said, "Fa-   20
ther, let me set out and search for the Water," thinking to himself, "If my
brother's dead, the kingdom will fall to me." At first the king was unwilling to
let him go either but finally gave in. Accordingly, the prince set out on the same
route his brother had taken and likewise met the dwarf, who stopped him and
asked where he was going in such a hurry. "Little shrimp," said the prince,   25
"that's none of your business!" and without further ado rode on. However, the
dwarf put a curse on him, and like his brother, he got into a mountain gorge
and could go neither forward nor back. But that's what happens to arrogant
people!

When the second son also failed to come back, the youngest offered to set   30
out and fetch the Water, and in the end the king had to let him go. When he
met the dwarf and the latter asked where he was going in such a hurry, he
stopped, talked to him, and answering his question, said, "I'm looking for the
Water of Life, for my father is mortally ill." "Do you happen to know where it's
to be found?" "No," said the prince. "Because you've behaved properly, not ar-   35
rogantly like your brothers, I'll give you the information and tell you how you
can get the Water of Life. It gushes from a spring in the courtyard of an enchanted castle, but you won't make your way inside unless I give you an iron
rod and two little loaves of bread. Strike three times with the rod on the iron
gate of the castle, then it will fly open; inside will be lying two lions with wide   40
open jaws. If, however, you toss a loaf to each, they'll quiet down. Then hurry
and fetch some of the Water of Life before it strikes twelve, otherwise the gate
will slam to again and you'll be shut in." The prince thanked him, took the rod
and the bread, and set out. When he got there, everything was as the dwarf had
said. The gate flew open at the third blow of the rod, and when he had pacified   45
the lions with the bread, he entered the castle and came into a large and handsome hall. In this hall were sitting enchanted princes, from whose fingers he
drew the rings. A sword and a loaf of bread were also lying there; these he took

with him. Then he got into a room where a beautiful maiden was standing. She
50  rejoiced when she saw him, kissed him, and said he'd disenchanted her and that
he should have her whole kingdom, and if he'd come back in a year, they would
celebrate their wedding. Then she further told him where the spring with the
Water of Life was, but he'd have to hurry and draw the Water before it struck
twelve. Then he went farther and at last came to a room where there was a beau-
55  tiful freshly made bed, and because he was tired, he thought he'd first take a little rest. So he lay down and fell asleep. When he awoke, it was striking quarter
to twelve. Then quite frightened he jumped up, ran to the spring, drew water
from it with a tumbler that was beside it, and hurried out. Just as he was going
out the iron gate, it struck twelve and the gate slammed so hard that it even
60  took off a bit of his heel.

He was happy, however, to have got the Water of Life, set out toward home
and again passed the dwarf. When the latter saw the sword and the bread, he
said, "With these objects you've acquired something very valuable: with the
sword you can slay whole armies, while the bread will never by used up." The
65  prince didn't want to go home to his father without his brothers and said, "Dear
dwarf, can't you tell me where my two brothers are? They set out for the Water
of Life ahead of me and haven't come back." "They're shut in between two
mountains," said the dwarf; "I cast a spell on them and set them there because
they were so arrogant." Then the prince entreated the dwarf until he released
70  them, but the latter warned him, saying, "Be on your guard against them,
they're evil-hearted."

When his brothers arrived, he was happy and told them how he had fared,
that he'd found the Water of Life and had brought along a tumbler full and he'd
disenchanted a beautiful princess; she was willing to wait a whole year for him,
75  and then their wedding would take place and he'd get the kingdom. After that
they rode on together and came to a country where there was famine and war,
and the king really believed he was doomed to die, so dire was the distress.
Then the prince went to him and gave him the bread with which he fed and satisfied his whole kingdom. Then the prince gave him the sword, too, and with
80  that he defeated the armies of his foes and was at last able to live in peace and
quiet. Then the prince took back his bread and sword, and the three brothers
rode on. They came to two more countries where famine and war prevailed, and
each time the prince gave the king his bread and sword, and by now had saved
three kingdoms. After that they boarded a ship and journeyed overseas. On the
85  voyage the two eldest said to one another, "It's the youngest who found the Water of Life, not we; in return for this our father will give him the kingdom that's
ours by right, and he'll deprive us of our good fortune." Then they plotted
vengeance and between them planned to ruin him. They waited till once when
he was fast asleep; then they poured the Water of Life out of the tumbler, took
90  that water for themselves, and poured bitter salt water into his tumbler.

When at last they reached home, the youngest brought the sick king his
tumbler so that he might drink and get well, but no sooner had he drunk a little
of the bitter salt water than he got sicker than ever. When he complained of

this, the two eldest sons came and accused the youngest of wanting to poison him, saying that they'd brought him the true Water of Life and handed it to him. No sooner had he drunk some of it than he felt his illness vanish and he became as strong and well as in the days of his youth. Then the two went to the youngest and mocked him, saying, "To be sure, you found the Water of Life, but you had the trouble and we the reward. You ought to have been smarter and kept your eyes open; we took it from you while you were asleep at sea, and when the year is up, one of us will fetch the beautiful king's daughter for himself. But watch out that you don't betray us. Father won't believe you anyway, and if you breathe a single word, you'll lose your life in the bargain. If, however, you keep quiet, we'll let you live." 95 100

The old king was angry at his youngest son and believed that he had designs on his life. Accordingly, he had the court assembled and passed a verdict against him that he should be secretly shot. Once when the prince was out hunting and suspected no harm; the king's huntsman had to accompany him. When they were all alone out there in the forest and the huntsman was looking very sad, the prince said to him, "Dear huntsman, what's the matter with you?" "I can't tell you," said the huntsman, "and yet I ought to." Then the prince said, "Speak up and say what it is; I'll pardon you for it." "Alas!" said the huntsman, "I'm to shoot you; the king ordered me to." Then the prince was frightened and said, "Dear huntsman, let me live. I'll give you my royal clothes, you give me your poor ones in exchange." "I'll do that gladly," said the huntsman, "I couldn't have shot at you anyway." Then they changed clothes, and the huntsman went home. The prince, however, went deeper into the forest. 105 110 115

After a time three carriages came to the old king, laden with gold and jewels for his youngest son. They'd been sent by the three kings who had defeated their foes with the prince's sword and had fed their countries with his bread and now wanted to show their gratitude. Then the old king thought, "Could my son have been innocent?" and said to his retainers, "If only he were still alive! It grieves me so that I had him killed." "He is still alive," said the huntsman, "I didn't have the heart to carry out your command," and told the king how it had gone. Then a great weight fell from the king's heart, and in every kingdom he had it proclaimed that his son might return and that he would be received into favor. 120 125

Before her palace the king's daughter had built a driveway that was all gold and glittering and told her people that whoever came riding to her straight up the road would be the right man and that they were to admit him. But whoever rode up off to the side of the road would not be the right man and that they were not to admit him. When the time was nearly up, the eldest son thought he'd hurry and go to the king's daughter and present himself as her redeemer; then he'd get her as his wife and the kingdom as well. Accordingly, he rode off, and when he got near the palace and saw the beautiful gold driveway, he thought, "It would be a crying shame to ride on it," turned off the road to the side on the right. But when he got outside the gate, the people told him he wasn't the right man and to go away again. 130 135

140  Shortly thereafter the second prince set out, and when he came to the gold driveway and the horse had set one foot down on it, he thought, "It would be a crying shame, it might wear some of it away," turned off it and rode to the side on the left. But when he got outside the gate, the people said he wasn't the right man and to go away again.

145  When the year was quite up, the third prince wanted to ride out of the forest and away to his beloved and forget his grief in her company. Accordingly, he set out and kept thinking of her and wishing he was already with her and didn't notice the gold driveway at all. Then his horse went right up the middle of it, and when he got outside the gate, it was opened, and the king's daughter received him joyfully and said he was her redeemer and lord of the kingdom. And

150  the wedding was celebrated with great happiness. When it was over, she told him that his father had summoned him to him and had pardoned him. Then he rode home and told the old king everything, how his brothers had deceived him and that he had nonetheless kept quiet about it. The old king was going to punish them, but they'd put to sea and sailed away and didn't come back as long as

155  they lived.

## SUPREME HAPPINESS

*Looking Ahead*

1. This piece consists of fragments, anecdotes, and miniature essays. Although the narrative link between them is weak at best, notice how they all reflect the same concern: how best to exist in the world.

2. From time to time, you may be puzzled over one sentence and then find the next one amazingly clear. Use the clear one as a key to the mysterious one.

3. Chuang Tzu is not only the author of this piece but a character in it, which demonstrates the author's freedom of invention, since this is not autobiography.

Is there such a thing as supreme happiness in the world or isn't there? Is there some way to keep yourself alive or isn't there? What to do, what to rely on, what to avoid, what to stick by, what to follow, what to leave alone, what to find happiness in, what to hate?

5  This is what the world honors: wealth, eminence, long life, a good name. This is what the world finds happiness in: a life of ease, rich food, fine clothes, beautiful sights, sweet sounds. This is what it looks down on: poverty, meanness, early death, a bad name. This is what it finds bitter: a life that knows no rest, a mouth that gets no rich food, no fine clothes for the body, no beautiful

10  sights for the eye, no sweet sounds for the ear.

People who can't get these things fret a great deal and are afraid—this is a stupid way to treat the body. People who are rich wear themselves out rushing around on business, piling up more wealth than they could ever use—this is a

superficial way to treat the body. People who are eminent spend night and day
scheming and wondering if they are doing right—this is a shoddy way to treat       15
the body. Man lives his life in company with worry, and if he lives a long while,
till he's dull and doddering, then he has spent that much time worrying instead
of dying, a bitter lot indeed! This is a callous way to treat the body.

Men of ardor[1] are regarded by the world as good, but their goodness
doesn't succeed in keeping them alive. So I don't know whether their good-          20
ness is really good or not. Perhaps I think it's good—but not good enough to
save their lives. Perhaps I think it's no good—but still good enough to save
the lives of others. So I say, if your loyal advice isn't heeded, give way and do
not wrangle. Tzu-hsü wrangled and lost his body.[2] But if he hadn't wrangled,
he wouldn't have made a name. Is there really such a thing as goodness or          25
isn't there?

What ordinary people do and what they find happiness in—I don't know
whether such happiness is in the end really happiness or not. I look at what ordinary people find happiness in, what they all make a mad dash for, racing
around as though they couldn't stop—they all say they're happy with it. I'm not   30
happy with it and I'm not unhappy with it. In the end is there really happiness
or isn't there?

I take inaction to be true happiness, but ordinary people think it is a bitter
thing. I say: the highest happiness has no happiness, the highest praise has no
praise. The world can't decide what is right and what is wrong. And yet inaction  35
can decide this. The highest happiness, keeping alive—only inaction gets you
close to this!

Let me try putting it this way. The inaction of Heaven is its purity, the inaction of earth is its peace. So the two inactions combine and all things are transformed and brought to birth. Wonderfully, mysteriously, there is no place they    40
come out of. Mysteriously, wonderfully, they have no sign. Each thing minds its
business and all grow up out of inaction. So I say, Heaven and earth do nothing
and there is nothing that is not done. Among men, who can get hold of this
inaction?

Chuang Tzu's wife died. When Hui Tzu went to convey his condolences, he           45
found Chuang Tzu sitting with his legs sprawled out, pounding on a tub and
singing. "You lived with her, she brought up your children and grew old," said
Hui Tzu. "It should be enough simply not to weep at her death. But pounding
on a tub and singing—this is going too far, isn't it?"

---

1. *men of ardor:* those who are willing to sacrifice their lives to save others or to preserve their
own honor. (*ed.*)

2. Wu Tzu-hsü, minister to the king of Wu, repeatedly warned the king of the danger of attack from the state of Yüeh. He finally aroused the king's ire and suspicion and was forced to commit suicide in 484 B.C.

50    Chuang Tzu said, "You're wrong. When she first died, do you think I didn't grieve like anyone else? But I looked back to her beginning and the time before she was born. Not only the time before she was born, but the time before she had a body. Not only the time before she had a body, but the time before she had a spirit. In the midst of the jumble of wonder and mystery a change took

55    place and she had a spirit. Another change and she had a body. Another change and she was born. Now there's been another change and she's dead. It's just like the progression of the four seasons, spring, summer, fall winter.

"Now she's going to lie down peacefully in a vast room. If I were to follow after her bawling and sobbing, it would show that I don't understand anything

60    about fate. So I stopped."

Uncle Lack-Limb and Uncle Lame-Gait were seeing the sights at Dark Lord Hill and the wastes of Kun-lun, the place where the Yellow Emperor rested.[3] Suddenly a willow sprouted out of Uncle Lame-Gait's left elbow.[4] He looked very startled and seemed to be annoyed.

65    "Do you resent it?" said Uncle Lack-Limb.

"No—what is there to resent?" said Uncle Lame-Gait. "To live is to borrow. And if we borrow to live, then the living must be a pile of trash. Life and death are day and night. You and I came to watch the process of change, and now change has caught up with me. Why would I have anything to resent?"

70    When Chuang Tzu went to Ch'u, he saw an old skull, all dry and parched. He poked it with his carriage whip and then asked, "Sir, were you greedy for life and forgetful of reason, and so came to this? Was your state overthrown and did you bow beneath the ax and so came to this? Did you do some evil deed and were you ashamed to bring disgrace upon your parents and family, and so came

75    to this? Was it through the pangs of cold and hunger that you came to this? Or did your springs and autumns pile up until they brought you to this?"

When he had finished speaking, he dragged the skull over and, using it for a pillow, lay down to sleep.

In the middle of the night, the skull came to him in a dream and said, "You

80    chatter like a rhetorician and all your words betray the entanglements of a living man. The dead know nothing of these! Would you like to hear a lecture on the dead?"

"Indeed," said Chuang Tzu.

The skull said, "Among the dead there are no rulers above, no subjects be-

85    low, and no chores of the four seasons. With nothing to do, our springs and au-

---

3. These are all places or persons associated in Chinese legend with immortality. The Yellow Emperor did not die but ascended to Heaven.

4. According to the more prosaic interpretation of Li Tz'u-ming, the character for "willow" is a loan for the word "tumor."

tumns are as endless as heaven and earth. A king facing south on his throne could have no more happiness than this!"

Chuang Tzu couldn't believe this and said, "If I got the Arbiter of Fate to give you a body again, make you some bones and flesh, return you to your parents and family and your old home and friends, you would want that, wouldn't you?" 90

The skull frowned severely, wrinkling up its brow. "Why would I throw away more happiness than that of a king on a throne and take on the troubles of a human being again?" it said.

When Yen Yüan went east to Ch'i, Confucius had a very worried look on his 95 face.[5] Tzu-kung got off his mat and asked "May I be so bold as to inquire why the Master has such a worried expression now that Hui has gone east to Ch'i?"

"Excellent—this question of yours," said Confucius, "Kuan Tzu[6] had a saying that I much approve of: 'Small bags won't hold big things; short well ropes won't dip up deep water.' In the same way I believe that fate has certain forms 100 and the body certain appropriate uses. You can't add to or take away from these. I'm afraid that when Hui gets to Ch'i he will start telling the marquis of Ch'i about the ways of Yao, Shun, and the Yellow Emperor, and then will go on to speak about Sui-jen and Shen-nung.[7] The marquis will then look for similar greatness within himself and fail to find it. Failing to find it, he will become dis- 105 traught, and when a man becomes distraught, he kills.

"Haven't you heard this story? Once a sea bird alighted in the suburbs of the Lu capital. The marquis of Lu escorted it to the ancestral temple, where he entertained it, performing the Nine Shao music for it to listen to and presenting it with the meat of the T'ai-lao sacrifice to feast on. But the bird only looked 110 dazed and forlorn, refusing to eat a single slice of meat or drink a cup of wine, and in three days it was dead. This is to try to nourish a bird with what would nourish you instead of what would nourish a bird. If you want to nourish a bird with what nourishes a bird, then you should let it roost in the deep forest, play among the banks and islands, float on the rivers and lakes, eat mudfish and 115 minnows, follow the rest of the flock in flight and rest, and live any way it chooses. A bird hates to hear even the sound of human voices, much less all that hubbub and to-do. Try performing the Hsien-ch'ih and Nine Shao music in the wilds around Lake Tung-t'ing—when the birds hear it they will fly off, when the animals hear it they will run away, when the fish hear it they will dive to the 120 bottom. Only the people who hear it will gather around to listen. Fish live in

---

5. Yen Yüan or Yen Hui, who has appeared earlier, was Confucius' favorite disciple.

6. Kuan Chung, a 7th-century statesman of Ch'i whom Confucius, judging from the *Analects*, admired.

7. Sui-jen and Shen-nung are mythical culture heroes, the discoverers of fire and agriculture respectively.

water and thrive, but if men tried to live in water they would die. Creatures differ because they have different likes and dislikes. Therefore the former sages never required the same ability from all creatures or made them all do the same

125 thing. Names should stop when they have expressed reality, concepts of right should be founded on what is suitable. This is what it means to have command of reason, and good fortune to support you."

Lieh Tzu was on a trip and was eating by the roadside when he saw a hundred-year-old skull. Pulling away the weeds and pointing his finger, he said, "Only

130 you and I know that you have never died and you have never lived. Are you really unhappy? Am I really enjoying myself?"

The seeds of things have mysterious workings. In the water they become Break Vine, on the edges of the water they become Frog's Robe. If they sprout on the slopes they become Hill Slippers. If Hill Slippers get rich soil, they turn into

135 Crow's Feet. The roots of Crow's Feet turn into maggots and their leaves turn into butterflies. Before long the butterflies are transformed and turn into insects that live under the stove; they look like snakes and their name is Ch'ü-t'o. After a thousand days, the Ch'ü-t'o insects become birds called Dried Leftover Bones. The saliva of the Dried Leftover Bones becomes Ssu-mi bugs and the Ssu-mi

140 bugs become Vinegar Eaters. Yi-lo bugs are born from the Vinegar Eaters, and Huang-shuang bugs from Chiu-yu bugs. Chiu-yu bugs are born from Mou-jui bugs and Mou-jui bugs are born from Rot Grubs and Rot Grubs are born from Sheep's Groom. Sheep's Groom couples with bamboo that has not sprouted for a long while and produces Green Peace plants. Green Peace plants produce

145 leopards and leopards produce horses and horses produce men. Men in time return again to the mysterious workings. So all creatures come out of the mysterious workings and go back into them again.

## Looking Back

1. Early in "The Water of Life," what character faults do we discover in the eldest and second sons?

2. In what way does the youngest son reveal his own good-heartedness?

3. From the king's behavior toward the slandered youngest son, what do we learn about judging another person's innocence or guilt?

4. What quality of mind allows the youngest son to reach the princess after the year is up, while his brothers are turned away?

5. What criticisms does Chuang Tzu make of people who derive their values from what "the world" says (see lines 1–26)? What is "the world"?

6. Why does Chuang Tzu decide to cease mourning his wife?

7. Who would you declare the winner in the debate between Chuang Tzu and the skull (lines 70–94)?

8. How would you describe the murderous impulse that Confucius—using the term *distraught*—ascribes to the marquis of Ch'i (lines 95–106)?

9. Can you express in a single sentence the moral of the story about the sea bird (lines 107–127)?

10. Using "The Water of Life" and "Supreme Happiness" as sources, list the virtues that the good (or happy) individual should have.

## Writing Assignments (Linked Readings)

1. How to be and how to act are questions that confront us throughout our lives. The considered, humane answers we give to these questions characterize our virtues. However, before we can answer, before we can be virtuous, we need to observe ways to be good (or supremely happy, to use Chuang Tzu's terms) and define them for ourselves. Sometimes we do this in our daily life and in our relationships; sometimes we do this by reading. Both "The Water of Life" and "Supreme Happiness" can afford the latter opportunity. Having read them, write an essay that names the virtues these texts elevate, defines them, and discusses at length their contributions to our humanity.

2. In "The Water of Life," the king accepts the majority opinion (that of two of his sons) that the youngest tried to poison him. In "Supreme Happiness," Chuang Tzu criticizes "what the world honors" (line 6), which is another way of referring to majority opinion. What is wrong with automatically accepting the opinion most others seem to hold about crucial issues? How can we resist the pressure to conform? What can we substitute for it? Write an essay attempting to answer these questions. Illustrate your points with references to your own and others' experience, as well as to the solutions offered in these readings.

3. The specific, personal reasons people perform actions and behave in ways that have importance in their lives vary tremendously, but general, overall motivation is more uniform. Self-interest, service, and absorption in the task might come to mind as chief motives. These may coexist, or one may give rise to another, but often one of them will predominate. In both "The Water of Life" and "Supreme Happiness," absorption in the task is seen as preferable to self-interest. Referring to these texts, and using your own experience where possible, write an essay describing what it means to be absorbed in a task that is important to you. Try to explain how such absorption may increase the spiritual happiness of a person and even be a force for good among others.

## Writing Assignments (Individual Readings)

### THE WATER OF LIFE

Arrogance is a vice that is offensive to others and harmful to the offender, as we see in the two elder sons' behavior toward the dwarf in this folk tale. The corresponding virtue is humility, as demonstrated by the youngest son. Write an essay that examines the traits of arrogance and humility. Define each, describe the attitudes and behaviors of arrogant versus humble people and speculate on the likelihood of lasting happiness for the person filled either with arrogance or with humility.

## SUPREME HAPPINESS

In his introduction to the *Basic Writings of Chuang Tzu,* Burton Watson declares that freedom is the central theme of the work. Most of us, when we think of freedom, imagine freedom from various forms of personal, social, or political oppression. Chuang Tzu, however, has in mind different obstacles to freedom. These are the names people impose on their world and the logic people use. These, he feels, prevent individuals from making carefully considered judgments. In virtually every section of "Supreme Happiness," Chuang Tzu discovers a particularly enslaving way of life and, happily, a way to be free. Write an essay that takes up two or three of these pairs that you consider most important, and describe both the problem Chuang Tzu poses and the solution he suggests. Follow each with your own commentary and evaluation of his point of view.

# VI

# *Further Writing Assignments*

*A*lthough it is convenient and frequently necessary to categorize kinds of knowledge and methods of inquiry, making such distinctions may disguise their real interconnections. If you look back over the contents of *Findings,* you will discover themes, ideas, events, and situations that cut across dividing lines and establish common bonds. Equally, original texts may spur your interest far beyond the borders of this book. Historical backgrounds, biographical data, and social application broaden the concerns these texts raise and increase their importance.

This final part of the book presents a series of paper assignments that will help you both to see such links and to make them explicit for other readers. For each part of the book, five writing projects are listed. Each of the first three assignments asks you to read (or reread with a new task in mind) two or more reading selections taken from different parts of the book. A brief discussion of a theme that connects these readings is followed by directions for writing. The last two assignments require outside research material that is related to a particular reading selection and sheds new light on it.

This light, which both types of research and writing generate, is global in character. The separate works enjoy an independent existence, a local fame, whose value is undeniable. That value can only grow, however, when you recognize the ties between them. Here you will see some of those ties. They may inspire you to see others, which is all to the good, since reading deeply and ranging widely—independently gaining intellectual power and creative freedom—are chief among the goals of learning.

## MYTHS OF EXISTENCE

1. It seems that human beings have always had a compelling need to tell the story of how their earth, and they themselves, came into existence. Most of

these stories are religious in nature. That is, they reflect beliefs in God and sacred matters that are dominant at the time of writing. These beliefs change over time and differ from culture to culture. Thus, though we find many points in common among the belief-based stories, we also find important and interesting cultural differences. A comparative study of creation myths can enlighten us about differing beliefs, cultures, and people's needs to understand the beginning. Write a paper making such a study by comparing the explanations of creation found in "The Creation" by Kevin Crossley-Holland (Myths of Existence, p. 47) and "The Priest of the Sun" by N. Scott Momaday (Moral Action and Spiritual Life, p. 559). Assume that you are writing to an audience unacquainted with these stories who would like to know what you think about the urge to explain creation.

2. The need to make money and the desire to do so are separate motivations, though so often combined that they may seem identical. It's hard to do something unless you want to, and you must have an income sufficient for the necessities of life. Still, there is a difference between earning money from your own labor and earning it from other people's, between living decently and getting rich, and—if you sell goods or services—between making a profit and making a killing. In these differences, desire enters as a consideration and with it the question of just how and how much the desire to make money ought to guide people's actions. Is there a limit? Where is the line? Who draws it? These questions arise in "The Bewitched Jacket" by Dino Buzzati (Myths of Existence, p. 85) and "Like a Bad Dream" by Heinrich Böll (Moral Action and Spiritual Life, p. 565). Write a paper explaining how each of these stories introduces and implicitly comments on the desire to make money. Do you agree with the authors' judgments? Compare them to your own.

3. C. J. Jung, in "On Life After Death" (Myths of Existence, p. 106), and Vaclav Havel, in "The End of the Modern Era" (Social Reality, p. 495), emerge as strong critics of human rationality. Although each is concerned with a different area of life, both denounce rationality as *the* guiding principle of belief and behavior. This attitude may surprise you. Rational action is generally thought to be wise, and irrationality at least self-defeating. However, pondering such challenges to widely held assumptions is useful; even if we don't change our minds as a result, our understanding of the idea is certainly more complete. Write a paper explaining your sense of human rationality and of just how necessary a function it is. Do so by referring explicitly to the views expressed by Jung and Havel and by delivering your own opinion on those views. As is the case with many abstract concepts, your readers might not share your idea of *rationality,* so be certain your discussion includes a thorough definition of the term.

4. *Did* a woman discover fire, as the woman in Al Ross's drawing claims (Myths of Existence, p. 77)? Lost in prehistory, that technological break-

through could owe to either gender, though it is instructive that Prometheus, a man, mythically gets the credit. This fact would not surprise many women who have gone without notice for their achievements or who have lost the status they gained once men began to desire it. A possible example of this latter situation occurred after World War II. With millions of male production workers drafted into the armed services, women moved into industry on a large scale. After the war, however, women lost many if not most of these jobs, to men, though not necessarily to the same workers who once had filled them. Further explore this situation by doing library research. Write a paper that describes this aspect of American social history for a hypothetical audience of readers entirely ignorant of it. In your paper, decide whether an injustice was done to women employees.

5. As you might gather from the readings in this book that deal with death, every culture makes its own approach to the subject (see "The Origin of Death: Krachi, Akamba, Hottentot," edited by Paul Radin; "The Origin of Death: Coeur D'Alêne," "Coyote and the Origin of Death: Caddo," and "A Speech to the Dead: Fox," edited by Margot Astrov; and "On Life After Death," by C. J. Jung, all in Myths of Existence, pp. 101–106). Cultures only *influence* belief, however; they don't *determine* it. Thus, we often find individuals with common cultural backgrounds entertaining quite different ideas about the same issue. One such issue is the possibility of an afterlife, and it is always interesting to see how people feel about this subject. Conduct a survey for this purpose by interviewing five to ten friends, acquaintances, or relatives. Ask them whether they believe in an afterlife, why they do or do not, and if they do, how they conceive of it. Write a paper that discloses your findings and that compares your (admittedly small) sample of opinion with the formal teaching of one major religion, which you should discover by library research.

# PERSONAL IDENTITY

1. The issue of free will versus determinism comes up in both "The Baby Boomer" (Personal Identity, p. 137) and Pär Lagerkvist's "Paradise" (Myths of Existence, p. 52). In the Lagerkvist tale, the issue has much greater repercussions than in the anonymous photograph and text. But in each the same problem is present: Can we do what we want in life, or are our actions determined by a force greater than us? This question is particularly relevant to our conception of God, our definition of evil, and our thinking about the possibility for moral decisions. After reading the above pieces, write a paper that first describes the ways that free will is an issue in each, and that then addresses these questions: If free will exists, then what does God seem to have in mind about the place of good and evil in the world? If we have no free will, then what? For

the purposes of this assignment, you are assuming the existence of God, but think of this writing as an exercise in critical thinking that does not automatically accept any particular religious belief associated with God.

2.  Everyone has a bad word to say about television programming and television viewing. Admittedly, much of this criticism is warranted, but a truly critical perspective—that is, one that examines the whole situation to discover the truth—would no doubt also cite positive factors. Taking as your starting point the negative commentary on television found in "Foul Shots" by Rogelio P. Gomez (Personal Identity, p. 163) and "Reading, Writing, and Ignorance" by Andrew L. Shapiro (Social Reality, p. 390), write a paper that provides a balanced view of the subject. Prepare for this task by watching one or more times a popular program that you like. Scrutinize it carefully in order to use it as the focus of your paper. Report the above authors' criticisms as they apply to your program, and describe those aspects of the show that both reflect and offset their criticisms. Evaluate the program in light of its positive and negative factors, and if you can, say what general conclusion you draw about television on the basis of your investigation.

3.  Both "The World According to Hsü" by Bharati Mukherjee (Personal Identity, p. 186) and "Different Shores" by Ronald Takaki (Social Reality, p. 411) reveal the personal and social problems associated with an ethnically mixed population. One of the chief problems is the isolation imposed on certain groups by others and, consequently, the obstacles to their fully entering society. These obstacles show some signs of disappearing when people are not ignorant of each other's ways, and so, to counter ignorance, many colleges and universities have instituted multicultural curricula, in which the intellectual products of various ethnic groups, not just one, are represented. These curricula have been both praised and condemned. One way of judging their worth is by imagining how people so educated might change their attitudes and behavior as a result of what they learn. Write a paper that makes such an approach by applying the idea of multiculturalism to the facts and events related in the Mukherjee and Takaki texts. How might multiculturalism make a difference? If such a curriculum exists at your school, you may want to refer to it specifically. If it does not, you can speculate about the effects such a curriculum might have on a course in, say, religion or literature.

4.  As the Vietnam War retreats into history and thus slips further from the consciousness of many Americans, it becomes more necessary than ever to recall the facts of our country's involvement in the war. This need is accentuated by the personal crises that every war produces for the young, crises that knowledge may help us prepare for but that may begin to seem unreal unless they are recollected. Tim O'Brien faces such a crisis in his story "On the Rainy River" (Personal Identity, p. 212). To better understand his and others' struggles at this time, write a paper that recounts the major events that occurred, both at home and abroad, in 1968, the year O'Brien was drafted and one of the most eventful years of the war and the decade. You will need to consult a selection of

the many books and articles that have been published about the war. Be sure to rely on more than one source so that you may acquaint yourself—and therefore your readers—with some of the divergent views on the same subject. Use your findings to provide an explanatory background to the O'Brien story, which you should refer to as extensively as you see fit.

5. At least since the 1960s, what was once the so-called youth culture, and what now probably doesn't need a name at all, has maintained its hold on the American imagination. Part of the reason is the commercial possibilities in youth as a market, but part is the widespread sense, which grew with the baby boom, that youth is a crucial time in everyone's life and should be represented within the culture as fully as possible. However, every age represents youth differently, and you can well imagine that, from the 1920s to the 1960s to the 1990s, great changes have occurred in the way young people view themselves. F. Scott Fitzgerald's "Early Success" (Personal Identity, p. 199), when we compare it with our own age, is a case in point. Beginning by describing his romantic sensibility, write a paper that attempts to show the differences and/or similarities between its picture of youth and the cultural attitudes about youth culture at later times. To research this information, you might focus on particular writers, musicians, or actors by finding books or articles about them in your college library.

# THE NATURAL WORLD

1. "Let your conscience be your guide" is a slogan few would disagree with. Yet even fewer, perhaps, have given thought to the definition of conscience; to the question of whether it must be personal or collective; and to the extent one may legitimately follow it in pursuit of rights and justice. These questions emerge as issues from a critical reading of the newspaper article "Animal Rights Raiders Destroy Years of Work" (The Natural World, p. 303), and the essay "The Death of the Profane" by Patricia Williams (Social Reality, p. 438). Read these texts, in which conscience functions—or fails to—in very different situations, though the word *conscience* is not even named. Write a paper that tries to establish general principles of conscience as a human faculty. Do this by using the texts to decide the issues raised above.

2. In "The Evolution of Allegiance to the Green Concern" by Lauren Strutzel (The Natural World, p. 274) and "On Morality" by Joan Didion (Moral Action and Spiritual Life, p. 612), the principle of social responsibility dominates. Write a paper that applies this principle to a specific problem you perceive in your community, town, school, club, or other locale or institution. Begin by forming a general idea of social responsibility as it is articulated in the two essays. How does it come up? Go on to describe the problem you have decided to focus on, and show how its solution requires peopl

assume responsibility in one way or another. To explain *why* the answer requires responsibility, you need to examine the extent to which people currently fail to pull together and the effects of that failure on the problematic situation.

3. Here are two excerpts from the readings:

> . . . the earth is our mother.

—Wallace Stegner, "Thoughts in a Dry Land" (The Natural World, p. 307)

> They've got this thing about nature
> and the same with music.
> They've got to do something with it.
> They've got to bring it on home.

—Laurie Anderson, "Politics & Music" (Social Reality, p. 362)

Each of these passages points to the same general attitude to the natural world, though Stegner affirms it and Anderson accuses people of not having it. Write a paper interpreting this attitude, explaining reasons for holding it, and applying it to a local situation you know about. How, in your situation (such as the building of a new highway through town or the restoration of a city park), is the sense the authors share violated or vindicated? What results can you see? Why is it important either to hold or to reject this attitude? In answering these questions, you should connect the quoted passages to others in which the authors reinforce them. Conceive of your essay as an attempt to sway your fellow citizens on the issue at hand.

4. In "Royal Exile" (The Natural World, p. 283), Beryl Markham introduces us to a particular horse of her acquaintance and, by means of lavish praise, to the virtues of horses generally. English satirist Jonathan Swift does the same thing, though at greater length and for different purposes, in *Gulliver's Travels,* when he compares horses (which he calls Houyhnhnms) to human beings (whom he calls Yahoos). Look up Swift's views on horses as he states them in the book and, adding Markham's to them, write a paper that discusses the horse from both authors' entirely positive viewpoints. You should include in this paper facts on the horse that you may research in an encyclopedia or other source book, and, of course, you may contribute any first-hand observations. Because the very familiarity of a subject like horses makes it difficult to know how much to say, write this paper to an audience that has never seen a horse (in the same way that some peoples living in the tropics have never seen snow).

5. The title of the newspaper article "Animal Rights Raiders Destroy Years of Work" (The Natural World, p. 303, and see assignment number 1, above) assumes a belief that not everyone adheres to: that animals have rights. Do they? Investigate this issue by looking up articles and books on the subject (most con-

tending views exist in the philosophical literature). Report the major points on each side of the issue and come to your own conclusions. Explain why you end up feeling the way you do, say whether your findings confirmed or contradicted your earlier views, and discuss the implications of the position you now hold. Try to address an audience that, at least partially, has a conviction different from your own. Doing so will require you to be not only clear but persuasive.

# SOCIAL REALITY

1. A persistent problem among the peoples of the world is the notion of racial superiority—the belief that the members of one group, who are identifiable according to a set of defined characteristics, are better endowed by nature than the members of another group. Although you are probably familiar with the phenomenon of racism, you may not have articulated for yourself the forms it may take, the power it may wield, and the consequences it may bring. These forms are various, the power subtle but mighty, the consequences wide-ranging, and you can see the phenomenon in action in different contexts if you read "Memories of My Mother" by Mary Man-Kong (Social Reality, p. 420), and "The Legendary Empire" by J. Alden Mason (The Myths of Existence, p. 58). Write a paper that identifies the symptoms of a belief in racial superiority as shown in each text. Compare the two readings on this basis, and discuss the effects of racism, both private and public, personal and historical.

2. Capital punishment has a long history, and so does the opposition to it. In the United States today, as in many countries over the years, a large number of people believe that the death penalty for convicted killers is necessary to prevent a repetition of their crimes. Other people hold that the death penalty is barbarous, that the state should not practice the very brutality of the people it seeks to punish, and that life sentences without parole should substitute for the death penalty. One question that comes up in this debate, however, is whether life behind bars actually is less cruel than death. Perhaps death would be preferable. Write a paper arguing that one form of punishment or the other is more cruel. For this purpose, read "A Hanging" by George Orwell (Social Reality, p. 487), and "Prometheus" by Franz Kafka (The Myths of Existence, p. 81). Analyze the probable torments of the condemned as they are illustrated by these texts, and extend your understanding of these to present-day penalties for capital crimes in order to take a position in your paper. To gather even more material on the issue, interview friends or classmates to get their opinions, which you may then also weigh in the balance.

3. Male dominance, resulting either in involuntary or habitual female subordination, is widely perceived today as a social evil. Women cannot achieve personal dignity or social worth if they are consistently viewed as lesser crea-

tures. Also, crimes and offenses against women—ranging from false promises to violent rape—will continue unabated as long as there is gender inequality. At least, many women believe this to be true. A majority of men might also subscribe to these views, but for men and women alike the problem is recognizing injurious male dominance when it occurs, a problem that arises sometimes because unequal relations between the sexes seem natural: people see nothing unusual and therefore see nothing wrong. To "denaturalize" male dominance and view the forms it may take, read "Media Goes Wilding in Palm Beach" by Katha Pollitt (Social Reality, p. 450), and "The Baker's Girl" by Eric Rohmer (Moral Action and Spiritual Life, p. 571). Write a paper that attempts to discover a connection between the incidence of male dominance described in each work. Then discuss the phenomenon as it is described in these texts and as it applies to the life of the society.

4. Often, our knowledge of social movements of great historical interest may be enhanced if we focus on the individuals who were the prime movers. Such a study is particularly useful in reference to "The Port Huron Statement" (Social Reality, p. 370), whose authorship is attributed to the Students for a Democratic Society, not an individual but a group that was politically active in the 1960s. Hidden in this anonymity is the figure of current California assemblyman Tom Hayden, a former SDS leader and primary crafter of the statement. Using your library, research Hayden and write a biographical study, the central purpose of which is to shed further light on the expressed principles and aims of "The Port Huron Statement," which you should read first.

5. In May 1993, the United States Air Force agreed to allow women to perform as combat pilots. Many people greeted this decision as serving the general interests of women. Others thought otherwise. Among them we can imagine would be bell hooks. Write a paper arguing that the opportunity for women to take on combat roles is or is not in their best interest. To prepare for this assignment, read hooks's "Feminist Movement to End Violence" (Social Reality, p. 463) and consult newspaper and magazine files, looking for articles, editorials, and letters to the editor on the subject.

# MORAL ACTION AND SPIRITUAL LIFE

1. Challenging unjust authority and, in order to do so, drawing a distinction between authority and authoritarianism, are important intellectual and political tasks. They involve careful observation, balanced judgment, subtle discernment, and moral courage. Among the questions we face are these: what is unjust as opposed to merely unwelcome about this or that authority, and when does authority go too far in exercising power and override the rights and prerogatives of citizens? Write a paper that seeks to define the proper limits of

authority. To help you do so, read "Letters to Freya" by Helmuth James von Moltke (Moral Action and Spiritual Life, p. 524) and "Prometheus and Pandora" by Thomas Bulfinch (The Myths of Existence, p. 67), and report the critique of authority you find in these works. Since both Prometheus and Moltke suffer in their persons as a result of their stand, include in your discussion the contrary views that rebellion against authority is either impractical or morally necessary.

2. Like all plagues throughout the history of civilizations, AIDS not only strikes the unfortunate but tests the capacity for human feeling of those whom it spares. Because the disease quickly draws the line between sufferers and nonsufferers, it may create a kind of them-and-us mentality wherein the "us" turn their backs on the "them." Is this an inevitable development? Is it justified in cases like AIDS? Or is it never right? What forms does such exclusion take? Are we mutually responsible for each other, or is that an unreal expectation? What effect on oneself might shunning another person have? Can you say what human virtues and what defects are involved in such a situation? How would you compare thinking of AIDS patients as alien beings to thinking likewise of an ethnic group, race, or religion different from your own? Write a paper addressing these questions, and any others that seem relevant, as a way of preparing a Manual of Behavior Toward AIDS Patients for the Well. In order that this manual be the product of reasoned analysis, and not just of raw opinion, base your thinking on the materials presented in "Remembering John" by Margot Olavarria (Moral Action and Spiritual Life, p. 606) and "Heterosexuals and AIDS" by Randy Shilts (Social Relations, p. 475).

3. Two schools of thought (at least) exist on the issue of the sources of principles of moral conduct. One school holds that these principles are stated or strongly implied in religious doctrine or traditional teachings, and that we should go to these sources to understand how to act. The other school holds that the situations we commonly find ourselves in present us with clear choices and that, on the basis of our past experience and our present perceptions—but without having to consult formal guides—we can discover what to do. Although we may never permanently decide between these two approaches, we usually tend in one direction or the other. Which is yours? Write a paper arguing that one of these schools represents generally the better method of making moral decisions and acting on them. The word *generally* here implies that neither position should be adopted absolutely, and so, as in all argumentation, you should grant to the other side what it deserves. Refer, if you wish, to your own experience, but use as objective material on which to base your thinking "The Sermon on the Mount" by Saint Matthew (Moral Action and Spiritual Life, p. 508), "Walking the Tight Rope" by Martin Buber (Moral Action and Spiritual Life, p. 512), and "Crystal" by Catherine S. Manegold (Personal Identity, p. 152).

4. In "What We Do Not See If We Do Not See" (Moral Action and Spiritual Life, p. 515), Agnes Martin makes these comments on Martin Luther King, Jr.:

> Inspiration is never destructive.
> This has been pointed out most effectively by Gandhi and Martin
> Luther King.

> Thus Martin Luther King suggested to the colored people that they
> must not try to change the white people but must change themselves.
> Not by policy or method but each one must change himself.

Agnes Martin's view of King enables her to use him as an example that serves the central argument of her piece. But because an argument is only as good as its reasoning and illustrations, and because every writer's duty is to be as historically accurate as possible, it is in the reader's interest to confirm or deny Martin's picture of King's political actions and principles. Write a paper limiting itself to just this function. Consult articles and/or books on King to find evidence for an argument—which you should make in your paper—that King either fits Martin's conception or does not.

5. Behind the events narrated in "The Visitors" by Julian Barnes (Moral Action and Spiritual Life, p. 540) lies a long history of hostility between Arabs and Jews in what was Palestine and is now Israel. Particularly relevant as a background to the story is the 1948 attack by every neighboring state on a newly independent Israel, the subsequent Arab defeat, and the flight of Palestinians from the land. With the help of appropriate historical sources in the library, write a paper that fills in the details of this sequence of events and, on the basis of your findings, examines the justice of the Palestinians' struggle to reclaim a homeland.

# ACKNOWLEDGMENTS

Roger D. Abrahams. "The Origin of Death" by Paul Radin, ed. from *African Folk Tales* by Roger D. Abrahams. Copyright © 1983 by Roger D. Abrahams. Reprinted by permission of Schocken Books, published by Pantheon Books, a division of Random House, Inc.

Laurie Anderson. "Politics and Music" pages 16–20 from *Empty Places* by Laurie Anderson. Copyright © 1991 by Laurie Anderson. Reprinted by permission of HarperCollins Publishers, Inc.

Natalie Angier. "Can You Like a Roach? You Might Be Surprised" by Natalie Angier from *The New York Times,* March 12, 1991. Copyright © 1991 by The New York Times Company. Reprinted by permission.

Diane Arbus. "My Favorite Thing is to Go Where I've Never Been" by Diane Arbus from *Diane Arbus,* Aperture Monograph, 1972, pp. 1–8. Copyright © Estate of Diane Arbus 1972. Image Copyright © Estate of Diane Arbus 1972.

Margot Astrov. Excerpts from *American Indian Prose and Poetry* by Margot Astrov. Copyright © 1946 by Margot Astrov. Copyright Renewed. Reprinted by permission of HarperCollins Publishers, Inc.

W. H. Auden. From "Streams" by W. H. Auden from *W. H. Auden: Collected Poems* by W. H. Auden, edited by Edward Mendelson. Copyright © 1955 by W. H. Auden. Reprinted by permission of Random House, Inc.

James Baldwin. "The Discovery of What It Is To Be An American" from *Nobody Knows My Name* by James Baldwin. Copyright © 1961; copyright renewed. Published by Vintage Books. Reprinted by permission of James Baldwin Estate.

Julian Barnes. "The Visitors" from *A History of the World in 10½ Chapters* by Julian Barnes. Copyright © 1989 by Julian Barnes. Reprinted by permission of Alfred A. Knopf, Inc.

Heinrich Böll. "Like a Bad Dream" by Heinrich Böll from *18 Stories*, McGraw-Hill, 1966. Reprinted by arrangement with Kiepenheurer & Witsch, c/o Joan Daves Agency as agent for the proprietor. Translated by Leila Vennewitz.

William Bradford. "Anno Dom 1688 [Englishman Executed for Murdering an Indian]" from *Of Plymouth Plantation* by William Bradford. Copyright © 1952 by Samuel Eliot Morison and renewed 1980 by Emily M. Bech. Reprinted by permission of Alfred A. Knopf, Inc.

Fernand Braudel. "Something to Drink" pages 227–231 and diagram "A Well Cistern in Venice" from *The Structures of Everyday Life* by Fernand Braudel. Copyright © 1979 by Librairie Armand Colin. English translation copyright © 1981 by William Collins Ltd. and Harper & Row Publishers, Inc. Reprinted by permission of HarperCollins Publishers, Inc.

Vera Brittain. "Women Workers, Today and Tomorrow" from *Testament of Generation: The Journalism of Vera Brittain and Winifred Holtby,* is included with the permission of Paul Berry, Literary executor and editor, Alan Bishop, editor, and Virago Press Ltd, publisher.

Martin Buber. "Walking the Tight Rope" from *Tales of the Hasidim* by Martin Buber, editor. Copyright © 1947, 1948 and renewed 1975 by Schocken Books, Inc. Reprinted by permission of Schocken Books, published by Pantheon Books, a division of Random House, Inc.

Thomas Bulfinch. "Prometheus and Pandora" by Thomas Bulfinch from *Bulfinch's Mythology: The Age of Fable,* Mentor, 1962, Penguin USA.

Albert Camus. "The Growing Stone" from *Exile of the Kingdom* by Albert Camus, translated by Justin O'Brien. Copyright © 1957, 1958 by Alfred A. Knopf, Inc. Reprinted by permission of Alfred A. Knopf, Inc.

Nicola Chiaromonte. "The Student Revolt" from *The Worm of Consciousness & Other Essays* by Nicola Chiaromonte, copyright 1976, by Miriam Chiaromonte, reprinted by permission of Harcourt Brace & Company.

Kevin Crossley-Holland. "The Creation" from *The Norse Myths* by Kevin Crossley-Holland. Copyright © 1980 by Kevin Crossley-Holland. Reprinted by permission of Pantheon Books, a division of Random House, Inc.

Stanley Crouch. "Nationalism of Fools" from *Notes of a Hanging Judge* by Stanley Crouch. Copyright © 1990 by Stanley Crouch. Reprinted by permission of Georges Borchardt, Inc. for the author.

Joan Didion. "Holy Water" from *The White Album* by Joan Didion. Copyright © 1979 by Joan Didion. "On Morality" from *Slouching Towards Bethlehem* by Joan Didion. Copyright © 1965, 1968 by Joan Didion. Reprinted by permission of Farrar, Straus & Giroux, Inc.

Annie Dillard. "Living Like Weasels" pages 11–17 from *Teaching a Stone to Talk* by Anne Dillard. Copyright © 1982 by Annie Dillard. Reprinted by permission of HarperCollins Publishers, Inc.

Loren Eiseley. "The Brown Wasps" reprinted with permission of Charles Scribner's Sons, an imprint of Macmillan Publishing Company from *The Night Country* by Loren Eiseley. Copyright © 1971 Loren Eisley.

Ida Fink. "Night of Surrender" by Ida Fink from *A Scrap of Time,* Schocken Books. Reprinted by arrangement with Ida Fink, c/o Liepman AG as agent for the proprietor.

F. Scott Fitzgerald. "Early Success" from *The Crack-Up* by F. Scott Fitzgerald. Copyright © 1945 by New Directions Publishing Corp. Reprinted by permission of New Directions Publishing Corp.

Rogelio P. Gomez. "Foul Shots" by Rogelio P. Gomez from *The New York Times Magazine,* October 13, 1991. Copyright © 1991 by The New York Times Company. Reprinted by permission.

The Brothers Grimm. "The Water of Life" by The Brothers Grimm from *German Folk Tales,* Francis P. Magoun, Jr. and Alexander H. Krappe, translators, Southern Illinois University Press, 1960. Reprinted by permission of Southern Illinois University Press.

Vaclav Havel. "The End of the Modern Era" by Vaclav Havel from *The New York Times,* March 1, 1992. Copyright © 1992 by The New York Times Company. Reprinted by permission.

Thomas Hayden. "The Port Huron Statement" by Students for a Democratic Society. Reprinted by permission of Senator Thomas Hayden.

bell hooks. "Feminist Movement to End Violence" from *Feminist Theory* by bell hooks, 1984. Reprinted by permission of South End Press.

Aldous Huxley. "British Honduras" from *Beyond the Mexique Bay* by Aldous Huxley, Harper & Bros., 1934. Reprinted by permission of The Aldous Huxley Literary Estate.

C. J. Jung. "On Life After Death" from *Memories, Dreams, Reflections* by C. J. Jung, edited by Anaila Jaffe. Translation copyright © 1961, 1962, 1963 by Random House, Inc. Copyright © renewed 1989, 1990, 1991 by Random House, Inc. Reprinted by permission of Pantheon Books, a division of Random House, Inc.

Franz Kafka. "Prometheus" from *The Great Wall of China* by Franz Kafka, translated by Willa and Edwin Muir. Copyright © 1936, 1937 by Heinr Mercy Sohn Prague. Copyright © 1946 and renewed 1974 by Schocken Books, Inc. Reprinted by permission of Schocken Books, published by Pantheon Books, a division of Random House, Inc.

Ed Koren. Two cartoons by Ed Koren which accompany the article "The Cockroach" by Natalie Angier from *The New York Times,* March 12, 1991. Copyright © 1991 by The New York Times Company. Reprinted by permission.

Pär Lagerkvist. "Paradise" from *The Marriage Feast* by Pär Lagerkvist. Published by agreement with Albert Bonniers Forlag, AB Stockholm.

Richmond Lattimore. "The Sermon on the Mount" excerpt from St. Matthew from *The Four Gospels and the Revelation,* translated by Richmond Lattimore. Copyright © 1962, 1979 by Richmond Lattimore. Reprinted by permission of Farrar, Straus & Giroux, Inc.

D. H. Lawrence. "Reflections on the Death of a Porcupine," copyright © 1925 by Centaur Press. Copyright © renewed 1953 by Frieda Lawrence from *Phoenix II: Uncollected Papers of D. H. Lawrence* by D. H. Lawrence, edited by Roberts and Moore. Used by permission of Viking Penguin, a division of Penguin Books USA, Inc.

Camara Laye. Chapter 6 from *The Dark Child* by Camara Laye, translated by James Kirkup and Ernest Jones. Copyright © 1954 and renewed © 1982 by Camara Laye. Reprinted by permission of Farrar, Straus & Giroux, Inc.

Claude Lévi-Strauss. "In the Forest" from *Tristes Tropiques* by Claude Lévi-Strauss. Copyright © 1955 by Librairie Plon. English translation copyright © 1973 by Jonathan Cape Limited. Reprinted by permission of Georges Borchardt, Inc.

Maynard Mack et al. "The Creation" from a blank verse translation of Ovid, *The Metamorphoses,* translated by Rolfe Humphries. Reprinted by permission of Indiana University Press.

Catherine S. Manegold. "To Crystal 12, School Serves No Purpose" by Catherine S. Manegold from *The New York Times,* April 8, 1993. Copyright © 1993 by The New York Times Company. Reprinted by permission.

Beryl Markham. "Royal Exile" from *West with the Night* by Beryl Markham. Copyright © 1942, 1983 by Beryl Markham. Reprinted by permission of North Point Press, a division of Farrar, Straus & Giroux, Inc.

J. Alden Mason. "The Legendary Empire" from *The Ancient Civilization of Peru* by J. Alden Mason (Penguin Books, 1957, Revised edition 1968). Copyright © J. Alden Mason, 1957, copyright © the Estate of J. Alden Mason, 1968.

Diana Tietjens Meyers. "Work and Self-Respect" by Diana Tietjens Meyers from *Moral Rights in the Workplace*, ed. Gertrude Ezorsky, State University of New York, 1987, pp. 18–27. Copyright © 1985 by Diana T. Meyers. Reprinted by permission of the author.

N. Scott Momaday. "The Priest of the Sun" pages 89–98 from *House Made of Dawn* by N. Scott Momaday. Copyright © 1966, 1967, 1968 by N. Scott Momaday. Reprinted by permission of HarperCollins Publishers, Inc.

Bharati Mukherjee. "The World According to Hsü" from *Darkness* by Bharati Mukherjee. Copyright © 1985 by Bharati Mukherjee. Reprinted by permission of the author.

New York Times. "Campus Life: Michigan State; Animal Rights Raiders Destroy Years of Work" from *The New York Times*, March 8, 1992. Copyright © 1992 by The New York Times Company. Reprinted by permission.

Stuart A. Newman, Felipe G. Cabello, Gregory Hedberg. Letter to the Editor: "With Apologies to Havel, Let Reason Rule" from *The New York Times*, March 17, 1992. Copyright © 1992. Reprinted by permission.

Tim O'Brien. "On the Rainy River" from *The Things They Carried* by Tim O'Brien. Copyright © 1990 by Tim O'Brien. Reprinted by permission of Houghton Mifflin Company/Seymour Lawrence. All rights reserved.

George Orwell. "A Hanging" from *Shooting an Elephant and Other Essays* by George Orwell, copyright © 1950 by Sonia Brownell Orwell and renewed 1978 by Sonia Pitt-Rivers, reprinted by permission of Harcourt Brace & Company.

Katha Pollitt. "Media Goes Wilding in Palm Beach" by Katha Pollitt from *The Nation,* January 24, 1991. Reprinted from *The Nation* magazine. © The Nation Company, Inc.

Anna Quindlen. "Public & Private; Making a Case" by Anna Quindlen from *The New York Times*, June 20, 1991. Copyright © 1991 by The New York Times Company. Reprinted by permission.

Alain Robbe-Grillet. "Reflected Vision: The Wrong Direction" by Alain Robbe-Grillet from *Snapshots,* Northwest University Press, 1986, pp. 13–15. Reprinted by permission of the publisher.

François duc de la Rochefoucauld. "Self-Portrait" from *Maxims* by François duc de la Rochefoucauld, translated by Leonard Tancock (Penguin Classics, 1959) copyright © Leonard Tancock, 1959.

Carl Sagan. From *Broca's Brain* by Carl Sagan. Copyright © 1974; 1975; 1976; 1977; 1978; 1979 by Carl Sagan. Reprinted by permission of the author.

Idries Shah. "The Fisherman and the Genie" from *Tales of the Dervishes* by Idries Shah. Copyright © 1967 by Idries Shah. Used by permission of Dutton Signet, a division of Penguin Books USA Inc.

Andrew Shapiro. "Reading, Writing, and Ignorance" from *We're Number One* by Andrew Shapiro. Copyright © 1991 by Andrew Shapiro. Reprinted by permission of Vintage Books, a Division of Random House, Inc.

Randy Shilts. "Heterosexuals and AIDS" from *And the Band Played On* by Randy Shilts, Penguin, 1988. Copyright © 1987 by Randy Shilts Agencies, Inc. Reprinted by permission of St. Martin's Press.

Gary Snyder.   "Buddhism and the Coming Revolution" from *Earth House Hold* by Gary Snyder. Copyright © 1969 by Gary Snyder. Reprinted by permission of New Directions Publishing Corp.

Wallace Stegner.   "Thoughts from a Dry Land" from *Where the Bluebird Sings to the Lemonade Springs* by Wallace Stegner. Copyright © 1992 by Wallace Stegner. Reprinted by permission of Random House Inc.

Ronald Takaki.   From *From Different Shores: Perspectives on Race and Ethnicity* by Ronald Takaki. Copyright © 1987 by Ronald Takaki. Reprinted by permission of Oxford University Press, Inc.

Studs Terkel.   "Campus Life" by Pauline Kael, Robert Gard, Chance Stoner from *Hard Times* by Studs Terkel. Copyright © 1970 by Studs Terkel. Reprinted by permission of Pantheon Books, a division of Random House, Inc.

Lewis Thomas.   "The Music of *This* Sphere," copyright © 1971 by The Massachusetts Medical Society, from *The Lives of a Cell* by Lewis Thomas. Used by permission of Viking Penguin, a division of Penguin Books USA, Inc.

Leo Tolstoy.   "Boyhood" from *Childhood, Boyhood & Youth* by Leo Tolstoy, McGraw-Hill, 1964, pp. 186–188. Copyright © by Michael Scammell, trans. Reproduced by permission of McGraw-Hill, Inc.

Chuang Tzu.   "Supreme Happiness" from *Chuang Tzu: Basic Writings* by Chuang Tzu, 1964. Copyright © Columbia University Press. Reprinted with permission of the publisher.

James Helmuth von Moltke.   "Letters to Freya" from *Letters to Freya 1939–1945* by James Helmuth von Moltke. Copyright © 1990 by Freya von Moltke. Reprinted by permission of Alfred A. Knopf, Inc.

Patricia Williams.   "The Death of the Profane" reprinted by permission of the publishers from *The Alchemy of Race and Rights* by Patricia Williams, Cambridge, Mass.: Harvard University Press, Copyright © 1991 by the President and Fellows of Harvard College.

William Butler Yeats.   Three lines from the poem "Vacillation" Part II from *The Poems of W. B. Yeats: A New Edition,* edited by Richard J. Finneran. Reprinted with permission of Simon & Schuster. Copyright © 1933 by Macmillan Publishing Company, renewed 1961 by Bertha Georgie Yeats.

# INDEX

*Abnormal Personality, The* (excerpt) (White), 134–135

adding (revision), 38

*Aerial View, An* (The Audubon Society), 270

*African Folktales* (excerpt) (Radin), 46–47

*Air Raid* (Galsworth), 167

Anderson, Laurie, 362

Angier, Natalie, 295–296

*Animal Rights Raiders Destroy Years of Work* (The New York Times), 303

*Anno Dom: 1638 [Englishmen Executed for Murdering an Indian]* (Bradford), 491

Anonymous, 137, 604

Anonymous Zen poet, 31, 32

aphorisms, 173

Arbus, Diane, 227

Aristotle, 244–245

*As a Baby* (Saint Augustine of Hippo), 139

Astrov, Margot, 100, 101

audience, 29–30

Audubon Society, The, 260

Augustine of Hippo, Saint, 137–138

Averill, Sarah, 32

*Baby Boomer, The* (Anonymous), 138

*Baker's Girl, The* (Rohmer), 571

Baldwin, James, 177

Barnes, Julian, 540

*Bewitched Jacket, The* (Buzzati), 85

Böll, Heinrich, 565–566

Booth, George, 31, 32

*Boyhood* (Tolstoy), 159

Bradford, William, 487

Braudel, Fernand, 316

Brecht, Bertolt, 536

*British Honduras* (Huxley), 448

Brittain, Vera, 405–406

*Brown Wasps, The* (Eiseley), 333

Buber, Martin, 508

*Buddhism and the Coming Revolution* (Snyder), 630

Bulfinch, Thomas, 66

Buzzati, Dino, 85

Cabello, Felipe C., 495

*Campus Life* (Kael, Gard, and Stoner), 367

Camus, Albert, 582

*Can We Know the Universe? Reflections on a Grain of Salt* (Sagan), 254

Capek, Karel, 66

Caras, Gwen, 183–185

Chiaromonte, Nicola, 366–367

Chuang Tzu, 634

Cicero, 359–360

*Cockroach, The* (Angier), 295

conferring with others, 28–29

Corey, Pamela, 252–253

*Coyote and the Origin of Death: Caddo* (Astrov), 104, 105

*Creation, The* (Crossley-Holland), 47

critical thinking, 22–25

Crossley-Holland, Kevin, 47

Crouch, Stanley, 426–427

*Crystal* (Manegold), 152

cutting (revision), 38

Czerwczak, Roman, 95

*Death of the Profane, The*
   (Williams), 438
*Debt to Animals, A* (Corey), 252
denouement, 78
*De Partibus Animalium* (excerpt)
   (Aristotle), 244–245
diction, 78
Didion, Joan, 316, 612
*Different Shores* (Takaki), 411
Dillard, Annie, 290
*Dirty Boulevard* (Caras), 183
*Discovery of What It Means to Be an
   American, The* (Baldwin), 177
drafting and revising, 30–32
   example of, 32–42
drafts, reading and discussing, 29

*Early Success* (Fitzgerald), 199
editing, 38
Eiseley, Loren, 333
Eliade, Mircea, 44–45
Emerson, Ralph Waldo, 245–246
*End of the Modern Era, The* (Havel),
   495
essay, 7–10
euphemisms, 270
*Evolution of Allegiance to the
   Green Concern, The* (Strutzel),
   274
extrapolating, 16

*Family One Evening in a Nudist
   Camp, A, Pa., 1965* (Arbus),
   227, 230
*Feminist Movement to End Violence*
   (hooks), 463
Fink, Ida, 205
*Fisherman and the Genie, The*
   (Shah), 91
Fitzgerald, F. Scott, 199
form, 8
*Foul Shots* (Gomez), 163

free writing, 27–28

Galsworth, Ondine, 167
Gard, Robert, 366
Gomez, Rogelio R., 163
*Gospel According to Jesus, The* (ex-
   cerpt) (Mitchell), 506–507
Grimm, The Brothers (Jacob and
   Wilhelm), 634
*Growing Stone, The* (Camus), 582
Guerber, H. A., 66

Hamilton, Edith, 45–46
*Hanging, A* (Orwell), 487
Havel, Vaclav, 495
Hedberg, Gregory, 495
Hesse, Hermann, 260
*Heterosexuals and AIDS* (Shilts),
   475
*Holy Water* (Didion), 324
hooks, bell, 463
Huxley, Aldous, 447–448

*Icon and Idea* (excerpt) (Read),
   136–137
ideas, generating, 28
inferences, 14
*Intelligence Does Not Equal Wisdom*
   (Muirhead), 56
interpolating, 17
*In the Forest* (Lévi-Strauss), 262
*Is That So?* (Anonymous), 604
"It seems useless, but" (Anony-
   mous Zen poet), 31
*I Was Very Young* (Laye), 142

Jung, C. G., 100, 101

Kael, Pauline, 366

Kafka, Franz, 66
*Keywords* (excerpt) (Williams),
356–359
Kolakowski, Leszek, 360–362
Koren, Ed, 298, 299
Kureishi, Harif, 31, 32

Lagerkvist, Pär, 52
language and meaning, changing,
38–39
La Rochefoucauld, François,
duc de, 173
Lawrence, D. H., 340
Laye, Camara, 142
*Legendary Empire, The* (Mason),
58
legend vs. myth, 81
*Letters to Freya* (von Moltke), 524
Lévi-Strauss, Claude, 260
*Like a Bad Dream* (Böll), 565
*Living Like Weasels* (Dillard), 290

*Making a Case* (Quindlen), 459
Manegold, Catherine S., 152
Man-Kong, Mary, 420
Markham, Beryl, 283
Martin, Agnes, 515
Mason, J. Alden, 58
Matthew, Saint, 508
*Media Goes Wilding in Palm Beach*
(Politt), 450
Meltzer, Herbert L., 495
*Memories of My Mother*
(Man-Kong), 420
*Metamorphoses* (excerpt) (Ovid),
243–244
Meyers, Diana Tietjens, 620
Mitchell, Stephen, 506–507
Moltke, Helmuth James von, 524
Momaday, N. Scott, 559
Muirhead, Sheryl, 56–57
Mukherjee, Bharati, 186

*Music of* This *Sphere, The*
(Thomas), 247
*My Favorite Thing Is to Go Where
I've Never Been* (Arbus), 227
*Myth and Reality* (excerpt)
(Eliade), 44–45
mythologizing, 44
*Mythology* (excerpt) (Hamilton),
45–46

narratives, 13
*Nationalism of Fools* (Crouch),
426
"Nature" (excerpt) (Emerson),
245–246
*Nature of Water, The* (Leonardo da
Vinci), 317
Neurohr, Fred, 11, 17
Newman, Stuart A., 495
*New York Times, The,* 152, 295,
303
*Night of Surrender* (Fink), 205
note taking, 26–27
*Now and Zen* (Neurohr), 17

O'Brien, Tim, 212–213
Olavarria, Margot, 606–607
"On Being Aware of Moral
Progress" (excerpt)
(Plutarch), 505–506
*On Government* (excerpt) (Cicero),
359–360
*On Life After Death* (Jung), 106
*On Morality* (Didion), 612
*On Moving On* (Averill), 32
*On the Rainy River* (O'Brien), 212
oral tradition, 559
*Origin of Death, The: Coeur d'Alêne*
(Astrov), 104
*Origin of Death, The: Krachi,
Akamba, Hottentot* (Radin),
101

Orwell, George, 487
Ovid, 243–244

*Parable, A* (Neurohr), 11
*Paradise* (Lagerkvist), 52
paraphrases, 15
personification, 101
Plutarch, 505–506
point of view, 85, 283
points, making connections between, 15–16
*Politics and Music* (Anderson), 362
Politt, Katha, 447, 448
*Port Huron Statement, The* (Students for a Democratic Society), 370
prewriting, 25–29
*Priest of the Sun, The* (Momaday), 559
*Prometheus* (Kafka), 81
*Prometheus and Pandora* (Bulfinch), 67
*Punishment of Prometheus, The* (Capek), 78

Quindlen, Anna, 447, 448

Radin, Paul, 46–47, 100, 101
Read, Herbert, 136–137
reading
    and discussing drafts, 29
    talking about, 28
*Reading, Writing, and Ignorance: Education and Achievement* (Shapiro), 390
redundancy, 38
*Reflected Vision: The Wrong Direction* (Robbe-Grillet), 328
*Reflections on the Death of a Porcupine* (Lawrence), 340
*Remembering John* (Olavarria), 606

revising, *see* drafting and revising
*Revolution from Within: A Book of Self-Esteem* (excerpt) (Steinem), 132–134
rhetorical questions, 139
Robbe-Grillet, Alain, 316–317
Rohmer, Eric, 571–572
Ross, Al, 66
*Royal Exile* (Markham), 283

Sagan, Carl, 254
satires, 362
selectivity, 15
*Self-Portrait* (La Rochefoucauld), 173
*Sermon on the Mount, The* (Saint Matthew), 508
Shah, J. Idries, 91
Shapiro, Andrew L., 390
Shilts, Randy, 475–476
Smullyan, Raymond M., 504–505
Snyder, Gary, 630
*Something to Drink* (Braudel), 320
"Some Time with Stephen" (Kureishi), 31
*Speech to the Dead, A: Fox* (Astrov), 125
Stegner, Wallace, 307–308
Steinem, Gloria, 132–134
Stoner, Chance, 366
*Story of Prometheus, The,* and *Deucalion and Pyrrha* (Guerber), 72
Strutzel, Lauren, 274
*Student Revolt, The* (Chiaromonte), 382
Students for a Democratic Society (SDS), 366–367
*Summer, A* (Czerwczak), 95
*Supreme Happiness* (Chuang Tzu), 634
syntax, 13, 67

Takaki, Ronald, 411–412
thematic unity, 9
"This is definitely the last time for Chapter Seventeen!" (drawing) (Booth), 31
Thomas, Lewis, 247
*Thoughts in a Dry Land* (Stegner), 307
Tolstoy, Leo, 159
"To the woman who discovered fire!" (drawing) (Ross), 77
*Toward a Marxist Humanism* (excerpt) (Kolakowski), 360–362
*Trees* (Hesse), 261
*Two Sons* (Brecht), 536

Vinci, Leonardo da, 316
*Visitors, The* (Barnes), 540
von Moltke, Helmuth James, *see* Moltke, Helmuth James von

Waikuny, Rosemary, 445–446
*Walking the Tight Rope* (Buber), 512

*Water of Life, The* (The Brothers Grimm), 634
*Weight* (Waikuny), 445
*What We Do Not See If We Do Not See* (Martin), 515
White, Robert W., 134–135
Whitehead, Eileen, 617–619
"Why Do You Help Your Fellow Man?" (excerpt) (Smullyan), 504–505
Williams, Patricia, 438
Williams, Raymond, 356–359
*With Apologies to Havel, Let Reason Rule* (Meltzer, Newman, Cabello, and Hedberg), 498
*Women Workers, Today and Tomorrow* (Brittain), 405
*Words in the English Language* (Whitehead), 617
*Work and Self-Respect* (Meyers), 620
*World According to Hsü, The* (Mukherjee), 186

Zen Buddhism, 604–605

# Instructor's Guide
# Findings
## *Readings for Critical Writing*

*Lewis Meyers*
Hunter College

D. C. Heath and Company
Lexington, Massachusetts    Toronto

Address editorial correspondence to:

D.C. Heath and Company
125 Spring Street
Lexington, MA 02173

Published simultaneously in Canada.

Printed in the United States of America.

International Standard Book Number: 0–669–33045–0

10   9   8   7   6   5   4   3   2   1

# CONTENTS

TO THE INSTRUCTOR    1
*Configuring Your Course*    *1*
    Teaching the Critical Faculty    1
    Teaching Argument    3
    Teaching Writing About Texts    4
    Teaching the Personal Essay    5
    Teaching the Rhetorical Mode Essay    6
    Teaching Writing as Process    7
*Practical Uses in the Classroom*    *8*
    Primary Texts    8
    Looking Ahead    8
    Looking Back    9
    Linked Readings    9
    Student Essay    10
    Part VI: Further Writing Assignments    11
*Writing Techniques in the Readings*    *11*
    Interpolation    12
    Extrapolation    12

THE CONTENTS OF *FINDINGS*    15
*Part I: Myths of Existence*    *15*
*Part II: Personal Identity*    *27*
*Part III: The Natural World*    *44*
*Part IV: Social Reality*    *60*
*Part V: Moral Action and Spiritual Life*    *81*

# To the Instructor

*F*indings: Readings for Critical Writing is, as the subtitle suggests, a collection of texts whose primary aim is to enable students' critical faculties in composition. However, critical thinking as it involves reading and writing can be viewed both as the specific intent of instruction and as a concert of abilities that underlie any mature intellectual enterprise. This book makes the former presentation explicitly and incorporates, through its apparatus, the latter one. The Introduction (pp. 7–42) uses a vocabulary whose key words later writing assignments echo as they point the way to critical writing. And, though students are asked to produce such diverse outcomes as narrative, argument, and comparison and contrast, the wording of introductions to specific texts, the pre-text suggestions for readings, and the posttext study questions most frequently enhance the possibility of critical thinking without sacrificing the pursuit of other purposes and modes.

Here, I would like first to describe—in a general way, and starting with the critical faculty—the varied instructional emphases *Findings* brings to bear, then turn to practical uses in the classroom, and finally discuss approaches to the readings themselves.

## CONFIGURING YOUR COURSE

You may wish to organize your composition course around a core of readings and writing assignments based on them that have a central purpose. Critical thinking is one such purpose, but writing as process, writing the personal essay, writing about texts, argumentation, and others are represented so strongly in *Findings* that they too may determine the direction of a course. I will take up some of these separately here. I do so, of course, knowing that you may want to make the equally valid approach of assigning readings that partake overall of a number of possibilities, especially since some of these overlap in one essay or story, or in one direction to write.

**Teaching the Critical Faculty.** As the Introduction makes clear, the basic aim of critical thinking is to assemble a sufficient quantity of charged facts, ideas, and perspectives to move an object of inquiry into a new context of understanding, one that is purportedly more availing than a previous one. In *Findings,* the formal preparation for such a move is reading, and the consolidation of the task is writing. In many instances, the headnotes to specific readings point up the particulars of an author's critical thinking in the piece at hand. Almost all of the Looking Ahead sections (see below, pp. 8–11, for a discussion of this and other parts of the instructional apparatus) include a suggestion to students that they test the reading for logic, basic assumptions, and reliability. The Looking Back, or study, questions include some that require the kind of interpretation that extends beyond basic comprehension to critical reading. The implication here is that students should not accept what they read at face value but should subject it, as the Introduction states, to the same scrutiny that they can expect their own writing to receive.

Added to the texts students read, whole-class discussion, small-group work, and your comments on their preliminary drafts will help produce a greater number of possible views to enable critical writing. That term we can apply to the handling of a theme or topic that produces ideas about it which you judge to be, within bounds, creative and original. Students' writing will meet these specifications when, as the Introduction also states, reevaluating ideas leads to fresh views, ones that are truly the students' own.

Most often, critical Writing Assignments (see, for instance, Writing Assignment 1 on p. 388) ask students to *extrapolate* from their reading. That is, students apply what they have read and given thought to, to an external but related topic. They do so to uncover the meaning and implications of such a topic by probing it with ideas that have become interpretative tools in their hands. Other assignments ask students to *interpolate* matter and by so doing help a given text to lift itself from the page, from what the author gives, to illuminate a new way of thinking about the subject matter. Another method of promoting critical thinking is the use of Linked Readings, a salient feature of *Findings* that is discussed in more detail on pp. 9–10.

From the start, a thematic reader such as this one presents a variety of universes, in each of which the readings are loosely affiliated by their mutual concern with the same general theme. It is pedagogically useful for these readings to retain their specificity, but also for some of them to reflect more closely on each other. In *Findings,* each thematic part of the book (Parts I through V) contains at least one set of such Linked Readings. These are directed toward the same subject, or they function in similar (but not identical) fashions. They tell the same story differently, join various aspects of the same reality, take up a given phenomenon from opposed or complementary viewpoints, discover the same teaching in diverse cultures.

This ordering of texts through Linked Readings will enable you to demonstrate, in a broadly humanistic way, both the disparate nature of human inquiry and the wisdom of an undogmatic search for truth. A critical interaction of ideas exists that will encourage students to form their own views, not simply choose between those presented to them. In addition to the normal tasks of making inferences and tracing logical paths, students must decide what individual texts say, what they have in common, how they differ in their approaches and conclusions, and what evaluative sense of the whole emerges from the comprehensive reading. Such a reading urges students to create their own patterns of ideas and to extrapolate from these (as well as from the ideas of others, as we have seen earlier) to address issues that Writing Assignments put to them on which they may now shed light.

**Teaching Argument.**    When, from time to time, instructors of other subjects have talked to me about the quality of student writing, it is not usually the grammar or vocabulary that they grieve over but, rather, students' inability to recognize and conduct an argument. This need of students is a compelling one, but it does not supersede the need for critical thinking, and exploring the connection between the two may be useful at this point.

It seems clear that the logical extension of critical thinking (from reading to writing) may readily take the form of argumentation. Once writers arrive at their own view of a particular matter, it becomes necessary to substantiate it by marshaling evidence for it and by employing the reasoned discourse that explains, qualifies, concedes, answers contending points, and makes the writer's own. Argumentation in this view therefore becomes synonymous with the *full* presentation of new ideas that, simply because they are new, because they are the writer's own (in the particular shape they have taken, if not absolutely), have a fragile existence that is in need of buttressing. Often, the students' hard evidence for a view will derive from the texts read and, particularly in Linked Readings, from a comparison of different or conflicting ideas found in them. At times, students' new evaluation will appear to be cogent only if it is seen as an actual position that must be supported by all or some of the methods of classical argumentation.

These points reveal the sense, I believe, that my colleagues have sought to convey to me. They certainly demonstrate the fact that instruction in discrete literate skills can always use a slight push toward synthesis to restore balance. But the direct, unconfined, indeed discrete approach to learning is also essential, and thus, in *Findings,* many Writing Assignments forthrightly ask students to adopt a definite standpoint on a controversial issue introduced in a particular reading.

Sometimes, the direction is a blunt one—yes or no, pro or con—but this becomes the case, I hope, only when to use less directive language would seem an evasion, when the issue at hand has already so divided opinion that expecting anyone not to take sides is unrealistic. But these assignments are relatively few in number, meaning that, especially to retrofit argumentation as a means of learning, it has seemed advisable to create more Writing Assignments that recognize that the truth of the matter is most often yet to be discovered. Further, truth should be discovered, as Montaigne said it should, by placing various views, including one's own, on trial. By no means, of course, do I wish students not to take a position finally, but "finally" is the key word here. And thus they do so more meditatively when the invitation extended to them employs phrases like "strike a balance" (between contending views that are extreme) or "answer the above questions" (which are pointed, to be sure, but whose collective answers cannot help but produce a more considered view).

As is the case with critical thinking, there is no part of the book in which Writing Assignments requiring argumentation are not present, and there is an abundance of readings in which the author conducts arguments that you may identify as such and ask students to examine.

***Teaching Writing About Texts.***   Writing critically *about* texts they have read instead of writing *from* them is an ability that any teacher who has read enough exams knows students need to develop. This book contains a sufficient number of Writing Assignments with this purpose in mind so that, if you wish, you may organize your course around it.

The Looking Back questions appended to every text test students' basic comprehension and interpretation ability, but naturally they do not require students to respond with a connected discourse. To do so, however, can be a means of commanding a text, or part of one (or two entire texts, as see the discussion of Part VI: Further Writing Assignments, below) in a much more complete manner. It is also a means of learning through practice the intellectual virtues of accuracy and precision (not to mention the skills of paraphrase, quotation, and summary) in reporting what a text actually states.

This purpose in writing takes students beyond response as reaction, however, and leads them to give evidence of their own thought about their reading. Doing so can take them even beyond interpretation—which still is centered on the text's contained meaning—to add to that meaning material that deepens or extends it, or calls it into question to diminish its importance. This process enriches the text (even if it challenges its validity) and therefore enhances the students' possession of it.

It is necessary to reiterate that, taking this direction, students at all times move *toward* the text at issue, and then *into* it. They are not using the text, as in critical thinking assignments, to drive understanding onto *other* intellectual terrain. It is sometimes a matter of emphasis, perhaps (who wants to be so Procrustean as to unnecessarily limit students' ambitions?), but the end result should not only largely match the original intent of the assignment, but it should give students a feeling of satisfaction that comes from learned response.

Taking up such assignments, which, again, are present in all parts of the book, students may use as particular resources their own experience and knowledge. These may not, at this stage of their lives, be as extensive as they later will be, but we disregard such knowledge and experience at our peril. Universally, and with good reason, people insist on mediating their understanding and their construals with the instruments, as it were, of their lives to date; that is, with their prior experience and accumulated knowledge. No less than anyone else, of course, students' ability to perform critical reading is limited by the finite nature of a single life, a fact teachers have no difficulty in recognizing, but one which, viewed as a problem, we can address.

The fact becomes a problem when students' responses are overdetermined, when language is unmodulated, and when viewpoints are too narrow to result in expanded meaning. These assignments, therefore, can afford you the opportunity to teach the arts of qualification and modification as a means of avoiding statements that are unrealistically absolute or that are not accompanied by the use of limiting characteristics or conditionals. And because the whole class responds to a common text, these assignments also are excellent candidates for small-group work to generate ideas, which will derive, it is to be hoped, from the experience and knowledge of more than the individual student.

Last, I should point up the fact that, since writing about texts is a largely interpolative function, the matter in the Introduction on this subject will be useful for students to review.

**Teaching the Personal Essay.**   At rather a remove from the aim of the critical essay, though equally stimulated by the reading selections in *Findings*, the personal essay is a type within the genre that students find quite engaging to write. The assignments to do so are less numerous than those cited above, but they are represented in all five thematic parts of the book. As well, there are thirteen essays that can be assigned as readings in the personal essay.

The personal essay is primarily one in which the author's presence is felt. This presence may be an autobiographical one, in the sense of a narrative that covers more than a single event in the life, or it may concentrate on an actual situation in the author's life, whether past or present. Or the personal essay may be so called because the author's voice—some unmistakably unique amalgam of syntax and verbalized attitudes—is dominant. Or the personal essay may be one in which the insistence on there being an actual person behind any commentary, no matter how abstruse or technical it may be, establishes the connected ideas of agency and responsibility. That is, we can trace logic, point of view, and critical insights to a particular writer—they are not lost in the ether of the impersonal third person pronoun—and therefore, recognizing the author, we can begin to solve the problem of deciding how much of the burden of meaning should rest on the approaches peculiar to the person writing and how much on the objective nature of the topic.

In *Findings*, the assignments to write personal essays follow the last of these descriptions more frequently than the earlier ones. For example, one assignment (in Moral Action and Spiritual Life, Writing Assignment 1, p. 666) asks students responding to an essay by Joan Didion first to define some of the crucial abstract terms she offers as a way of describing the moral community, and then to "examine, to the extent you are in a position to do so, the respect paid to the social code within your own community."

Such an assignment involves students in producing findings peculiar to their own experience and in making something of them (here, applying the terms Didion uses and students have defined) to gain knowledge. Viewed in this way, the personal essay is one that joins the thought to the object and the writer to the world. You should remember, however, that if the personal finds its converse in the social, the private is often betrayed by becoming public. It is useful, therefore, to caution students beforehand against choosing subject matter to write about that would embarrass them if it came to light and against treating it in such a way that would do likewise. Other students as well as their teacher might constitute an audience for a personal essay, since small-group discussion of preliminary drafts can help writers discover whether they have made accessible to others what is essential for communication and what they alone knew about.

***Teaching the Rhetorical Mode Essay.***   Narration, description, comparison and contrast, analysis, illustration by example, definition, and exposition (referring to making necessary explanations) are all modes that characterize an abundance of both readings and Writing Assignments in *Findings*. It is, of course, dubious that you would want to devote an entire composition course to any *one* of these modes, since in the essay—whose *raison d'être* is the production of ideas about a subject—each of these is a means toward that end, and several modes may be used in one written discourse. But you may draw up a syllabus that teaches these modes as separate units.

Emphasizing rhetorical modes is a traditional, even classical, approach to teaching a composition course. Although many teachers no longer configure courses in this way, there can be no doubt that such modes are the basic equipment of accomplished writers. It seems fitting, therefore, that this content occupy the attention to some degree—and conceivably, fully—of composition students. Having said that, I would suggest two further points for your consideration.

One is that the rhetorical modes often come naturally to writers, no matter their amount of experience. This seems clear when it comes to telling a story (though it can be done more or less effectively), but even the most abstract of these functions—definition—is largely reflexive. In speech as well as in writing, we commonly stake out our intended meaning, drawing verbal lines around it to prevent others' misconception. Intuiting the shape and uses of these means, your students probably are already halfway in command of them. But only halfway, perhaps. Instruction is still necessary to fix a given mode in its proper orbit (say, by showing how narrative may break to contemplate events), to distinguish functions (as, for example, comparison from analogy), and to give a new dimension to known quantities (such as by introducing the means of making an extended definition).

The other point is that, as you might guess, when the reading selections in *Findings* display the use of a rhetorical mode, they do not model it alone but others as well and, more, writing approaches that are broader in intent and effect than these modes. The Writing Assignments are similarly inclined. The result is that the rhetorical modes assume a clear but properly subordinate place in instruction: you may teach them without having to teach *only* them.

***Teaching Writing as Process.***   Just as the use of particular rhetorical modes is present in readings and Writing Assignments that are concerned with other composition approaches as well, so teaching writing as process is a potential for virtually every Writing Assignment, no matter its specific direction, and as a formal topic of study at a certain point in each part of the book.

It accords with the normal practice of experienced writers that their work moves toward completion through a series of stages. Writing teachers have long recognized that instruction itself should reflect this practice in order to be effective. As a consequence, most composition textbooks either include specific units teaching writing as process, or use it as a general organizing principle. Or they do both. Prewriting techniques, conferring with others (which recognizes the social dimension of writing), producing preliminary drafts, and the arts of revision, rewriting, and editing all are par for most courses.

The emphasis you place on these as you use *Findings,* like the choice to place any emphasis at all on them, is yours to decide, of course. The above approaches that singly engage students will, in any case, find their way into your course or not, without any direct urging on the part of this book. To give one example, no Writing Assignments actually mandate preliminary drafts because I believe to do so would force your hand as the instructor to an unacceptable degree. However, though again without enforcing the practice in instructions to write, the use of small groups in a workshop format to confer and generate ideas for writing becomes a definite possibility in *Findings.*

This happens particularly in the way many Writing Assignments pose a number of probing questions about the subject at hand for students to answer and, on the basis of their answers, to write knowledgeably about that subject. For example, part of Writing Assignment 2 following Beryl Markham's essay "Royal Exile," about a horse she owned as a child, reads as follows:

> But now these questions arise: Exactly in what way are we separated from the world of creatures? What are we that they are not, and vice versa? Why do we seek to reestablish contact, through both household pets and other animals? How does this contact work? What does it give us? Does trying to make contact mean that human beings are not only alone but somehow incomplete, and that we need help from animals? (p. 290)

Such queries can provide a definite structure for small groups, an element that is often required in workshops. As you might imagine, the answers to such questions will be various, reflecting individual experiences and thought processes, thus creating a wider view of the subject than one student alone could produce. The social context of intellect and craft, which exists outside the classroom, is in this way replicable within it as a natural approach to writing. The Looking Back questions can provide a similar occasion for conferring on reading and preparing for writing.

Recognizing the need for revision and thereby avoiding premature closure are essential to good writing practice. For this purpose, in each part of *Findings,* a preliminary draft of a student essay appears under the rubric Follow-Up: An Essay for Analysis. Each of these essays is a response to a text Writing Assignment, and each is itself followed by a list of questions about its clarity, coherence, need for development, and so on. By addressing these questions, students can not only practice the critical detachment necessary for the sake of revision, but also actually learn to recognize the specific editorial needs of a particular written discourse. The fact that the essay they analyze was written by a peer enhances this process.

## PRACTICAL USES IN THE CLASSROOM

Specific features of *Findings* deserve comment about their particular uses. These features, all of which are briefly discussed in the text preface to instructors, are the Primary Texts that begin each part of the book, the Looking Ahead and Looking Back sections, the Linked Readings, the student Follow-up Essays, and Part VI: Further Writing Assignments.

***Primary Texts.*** You will no doubt have students read the introduction to any part from which you are about to assign reading selections. At the same time, you can ask students to read these Primary Texts and discover in them themes from the introduction. The chief function of these texts is to precede a particular thematic focus with deeper, more philosophical, more abstract considerations and concerns that most often are also highly contrastive. These qualities should raise the general issue at hand to a higher level of abstraction, increasing its seriousness; they should give it more scope and thus should encourage students to have more latitude in viewing any particular topic; and they should provide a historical perspective, thus demonstrating the continuity of attention paid to it. If you wish, you can ask students to write a brief report on their reading of these texts, asking them to say how as a result they regard the subject and if their view now differs at all from what it had been.

***Looking Ahead.*** It is not merely convention that tables of contents are often used to synopsize chapters of a book. Readers want and often need some advance sense of what they are about to read. In lieu of such a notice, they sometimes review the pages they have already turned when they reach a point at which they require a general sense of direction. Without doing too much—as a synopsis might for those *studying* a text—or too little—as it might be to leave everything to the student—I have tried in the Looking Ahead sections to suggest concerns, problems, and particular points of significant interest that students will meet in the text.

When assigning a reading for the next class meeting (or before it comes up on your syllabus), you can take a few moments, if you wish, and point students to that place in the text to which one Looking Ahead item refers. Doing so will break open the crust of that reading, as it were, and alert students to the need to do a critical reading. You will note that usually one of the Looking Ahead suggestions explicitly points students in this direction by echoing language used in the pertinent section of the Introduction (see pp. 7–42). When you discuss a reading with your class, you may wish, before using the Looking Back questions, to make a more informal start by drawing attention to one of the Looking Ahead comments. At times, of course, students will turn a Looking Ahead item back on you, asking you to make plain what they were supposed to perceive. Although I have tried not to baffle students in their expectation, be prepared.

From time to time a Looking Back question or a writing assignment refers to a Looking Ahead item. It's wise to check for the possibility of such a cross-reference (it will come, if it does, *after* the reading) in case you want to emphasize in advance the importance of the original prereading suggestion.

**Looking Back.**   Most often, as the Preface to the student points out, these ten study questions that follow readings plot important concerns in the order of their appearance in the text. This method, though invariably it will abstract the text to some degree, does so much less than does the approach intended to wring from a text its thesis and one or two other ideas or authorial maneuvers alone. Certainly students are asked to pause at these, but in the context of their developing sense of the text, which I believe gives students a more organic sense of the whole. You should look to the Writing Assignments to see if, as sometimes is the case, they are based in part on the answer to a Looking Back question. In these instances, you may particularly want to emphasize that question in class discussion of the text.

Of course, you may not want to take up every question with your class. Depending on students' ability as you begin to experience and measure it, you may assume that your students can be depended on to have answered some questions by themselves. Other times, you may not make such an assumption. In either case, it is a good idea when assigning a reading to ask students to write out answers to one or two of the questions, selected for their important link to a critical reading or because the answer figures in a writing assignment. These written answers you can collect and grade or comment on, or they can serve students as a firmer basis than memory alone for small-group or whole-class discussion.

**Linked Readings.**   Above, I have described Linked Readings and explained their purpose to enable critical thinking. If you turn to any one set of linked readings in the book, you will notice that there is a single, inclusive biographical sketch and a single Looking Back section for all the readings. However, a different Looking Ahead section precedes each reading. Three Writing Assignments, the standard number for following a reading, call on students to answer—either directly or through accumulated knowledge more subtly informing their writing—for all texts that are linked. There is also, however, a separate Writing Assignment for each individual selection, in case you wish to disregard the linkage and assign a reading by itself.

Obviously, the Linked Readings assigned as a unit are a veritable project. They require students to balance an understanding of multiple texts and to write out of the new context that this understanding creates. The responsibility students thus take on is not only that of a larger assignment but also of a qualitatively more demanding one. You might therefore think of reserving the first of these projects to be assigned until that point in the semester when your class has gained experience in writing and, in particular, after they have acclimated themselves to the nature of the Writing Assignments in the book.

For discussion in class of Linked Readings, the Looking Back sections are key. They pose separate questions for each text and joint questions to tie readings together thematically. Depending on your perception of the difficulty of Linked Readings, you might want to devote an entire week to an assignment (or more, if you usually use a week for one reading) for discussion of the texts, freewriting, conferring to generate ideas and/or a preliminary draft. You might also have different groups of students in the class discuss different readings in small groups and present their answers to pertinent Looking Back questions to the whole class.

***Student Essay.***    Above, I refer to the existence of a student essay in each part that is a response to one of the Writing Assignments in an immediately prior reading. The analytic questions following the student essay will give your own students the opportunity to view and judge the kind of responses that are appropriate when evaluating a Writing Assignment. For this purpose, early in the semester or as you move from part to part of the book, you can have students read the particular text and Writing Assignment the student essay is based on as well as the student essay itself. After discussing the questions, you can then have your students move on to revise the student essay (or at least to make suggestions for doing so). You can ask your students to write their own response to the same assignment and then use the questions—privately on their own or in small-group discussion—to probe their own work critically in order to revise it. And they can certainly compare their product with the original student essay.

The purpose, then, is a triple one: first, to show students what a peer has done along the lines they are asked to work; second, to give them experience in revision; and third, to move students more capably into their own writing.

The first purpose is especially useful at the beginning of the semester, when a possibly inhibiting self-consciousness about writing is still pretty much intact. The student essay being judged was written by someone outside the class and thus "safe" to criticize. If students' judgments become overly harsh, they are nonetheless morally pressuring themselves to do better. If their judgments seem too lenient, you yourself can point out problems in the student essay and ask for solutions.

To have your students revise the student essay, it may be wise to isolate sentences or passages and work on them alone. Students can try to discover what is defective in some particular paragraph. In addition to general or small-group discussion, the class as a whole can be brought together on this task if you call on them to rewrite the weak passage. Working in that way can prime the class for a new approach to the writing assignment, and you may now want to have them reapproach it (and, moving through their own drafts, repeat the revision process, but on their own work).

***Part VI: Further Writing Assignments.***  Part VI offers twenty-five Writing Assignments, five for each thematic part of the book. Like the Writing Assignments following the Linked Readings, these too have sufficient scope and are sufficiently exacting to be called projects. Unlike the Linked Readings, however, the first three of each set of these projects ask students to read texts from *different* parts of the book and write on them. The texts are shown to be related, but the difference in original thematic intent demonstrates the universality of knowledge and the ultimate—if unavoidable—limitation of dividing knowledge into categories. The above description of approaches students can make to Linked Readings is equally relevant here.

The fourth and fifth assignments in each set also point students in two directions. Only one of these, however, is toward a reading in *Findings.* The other direction is toward the library, with instructions to do research that will add to the content of the previous reading. If the curriculum for your course includes a documented paper, these ten possibilities for writing give you choices that first-year students will find particularly useful. The research, because it supplements a regular reading selection and related study questions, has a base more solid than would exist if students received only a topic with which to work.

# WRITING TECHNIQUES
# IN THE READINGS

In the Introduction, I attempt generally to orient students to the arts of reading and writing. I do not, however, try to rival a rhetoric or steal the composition teacher's thunder by discussing writing techniques in detail. In the Introduction, only interpolation and extrapolation are treated at any length (see pp.

16–17). This is so because they are essential to critical thinking, a major instructional aim of the book. You might find useful a brief discussion of how texts in addition to those in the Introduction can be used to model interpolation and extrapolation.

**Interpolation.**   In his "Thoughts in a Dry Land" (The Natural World, p. 307), Wallace Stegner quotes a long passage that helps make his point and then comments on that passage so that the reader may form a fuller idea of its significance. On pp. 313–314 he quotes Clarence Dutton on the comparatively outrageous geography of the American West. In the paragraph following this passage, Stegner first interprets the text ("Amen. Dutton describes a process of westernization of the perceptions that has to happen before the West is beautiful to us"). Stegner then interpolates comments that go beyond interpretation to illuminate the text at the same time that they reveal its deepest implication:

> You have to get over the color green; you have to quit associating beauty with gardens and lawns; you have to get used to an inhuman scale; you have to understand geological time.

Whether you assign Stegner's essay or not, you can turn to this part of the text to show how interpolation works. This applies equally to extrapolation; both are displayed in the Introduction by Fred Neurohr's essay, p. 17. As is the case with all prose models, of course, it is advisable to move directly from them to the student's own application of the lesson, and for this purpose you might produce either your own sentences and propositions or some taken from *Findings.* Whatever your direction, you should make sure that, as in the Stegner example, students *add* to the original through their interpolation and do not simply put the same idea in other words.

**Extrapolation.**   James Baldwin jump-starts "The Discovery of What It Means to Be an American" (Personal Identity, p. 177) by quoting Henry James on the American character and then moving directly, by means of James's view ("'It is a complex fate to be an American'"), to the situation of the American writing in Europe. In his next sentence, Baldwin seems to shift to interpolative comments ("America's history, her aspirations, her peculiar triumphs, her even more peculiar defeats, and her position in the world . . ."), but we see in what follows that his real concern is to drive the James quotation harder. The third and final sentence in the paragraph refers again to the exportation of Americaness ("No one in the world seems to know exactly what it describes, not even we motley millions who call ourselves Americans"). Beginning with the next paragraph, the rest of the essay continues in this direction.

By helping students follow these movements, you can demonstrate the often necessary ties between interpolation and extrapolation as well as reveal the latter's possibilities alone. For these purposes, you can use merely this first paragraph. Teaching the full essay, of course, will make manifest the way the spirit of the James aphorism informs the discourse.

Another essay that models extrapolation is Margot Olavarria's "Remembering John" (Moral Action and Spiritual Life, p. 606). Like Baldwin, though here at more length, the author presents a text in the first paragraph that she will use as a springboard into her topic, a personal reminiscence of a deceased friend. Unlike Baldwin, Olavarria goes on not to interpolate but to interpret the Zen parable about friendship that she has cited. Here you can show the difference between interpreting and interpolating. Interpolation fills in a text with concrete details and/or implicit conceptual possibilities; interpretation points to a text and analyzes its meaning and the relations of its terms.

In the third paragraph, Olavarria extrapolates the type of relationship she has established to a particular friendship she had ("I was fortunate enough to have known such a friendship with my dying friend John Mangano in the last year of his life"). Describing this friendship continues in the essay. Through its depth of feeling (corresponding to the burden of meaning in the parable), we are impressed with the fact that one text has produced another. This extrapolative energy can inspire your students if you help them recognize it. Many students doubt their ability as writers to have anything to say, much less anything new. Extrapolating can give them a place to start. Obviously you should monitor the process to ensure that they are actually staking out new territory as they set off from given texts.

# The Contents of Findings

## PART I: MYTHS OF EXISTENCE

## Kevin Crossley-Holland

### The Creation

*Overview.*   Norse myths were current for at least one thousand years B.C.E. They provided the belief structure for the Vikings, or Northmen, or Rus, as they were variously called. This creation myth (every culture has its own) is elaborate and dramatic, but its seemingly bizarre events, such as a man and woman growing out of a sweaty armpit, are no more so than Eve's being lifted from Adam's side in Genesis. The strongest tie between this myth and others is perhaps the very human need it fulfills to account in narrative form for the Beginning, as if there were a story to tell that occurred within a limited space and time, a story populated by characters with names.

*In the Classroom.*   Cultural relativity is useful to cite (as above) if students familiar only with Genesis, and perhaps also regarding it as a sacred text, resist this myth on the grounds of credibility. Of course, various comic books feature Norse gods and heroes, so some students might be welcoming on that score, and in any event the direct language and the graphic images are appealing. It would be useful to have students read parts aloud since this text particularly lends itself to doing so, and early in the semester it is instructive to note reading ability in a class.

*Formal Considerations.*   The enlivening and enriching effect of concrete detail and the time signals and tense markers used in this narrative are particularly noticeable features. Pointing to them can serve a good purpose at the beginning of a writing course.

## Looking Back

1. Personification allows clearer recognition as well as identification.

2. The ice age thawing into a warm solution.

3. Accident in the sense of natural random events (melting and licking), but design in the sense of the subsequent creation of the world we know, as if that were ordained.

4. That this text was the result of a number of hands over time, beginning with oral rendering and going on to written transcription, but without emendation.

5. That it was harsh; that people had intimate ties to nature; that hierarchical relations were important in human society.

6. Out of the dead Ymir's body and blood.

7. Answers will vary, but one obvious difference is between monotheism and polytheism, and the social and cultural unity provided by the former.

8. Ymir is a hoodlum: he represents the forces of disorder and chaos, though paradoxically when dead he supplies material for the ordered world.

9. Immortality; a principle of vibrant life that flows through all forms and sustains them.

10. The answer obviously is yes. We hate mysteries; we desire order; we want an explanation that exalts our stature.

# Pär Lagerkvist

# Paradise

**Overview.**  With the influential tone of Norse sagas and myths, this story builds on the Old Testament tale of Adam and Eve and their expulsion from the Garden of Eden. The Lord is an artist-intellectual whose speech is commonplace. Like his original, he is susceptible to anger, not to mention *amour-propre*, though our ultimate impression is of his deep sorrow over human philistinism and vice. Human sinfulness is a theme, but so is the existence of free will, with a clear and significant relation between them. Notice key differences between this telling and its original: the Adam and Eve figures (unnamed here and not claimed as God's creation) are instructed to eat the fruit of the tree of knowledge, not eschew it; and a whole population grows up within Paradise, not just our first parents.

**In the Classroom.**  Students may be surprised at the Lord's natural speech patterns as well as by the departures from the original story. It will be helpful to refer to the universal practice of adapting myths to contemporary cultural requirements to give them new life. You can point to an example in the anachronistic reference to clocks (line 11) and in God's willingness not just to declare his will but to argue his intentions.

**Formal Considerations.**   This brief story depends for its meaning on various speeches. Selective use of speech can be effective in essays as well. Students can learn from the naturalness of speech in the story that overwriting and formality are not synonymous.

## Looking Back

1. These anachronisms telegraph the distance between present and biblical time.

2. Answers can vary, but rather like a gift giver.

3. The first terms suggest calm, poise, rationality, and compassion; the latter terms suggest egotism, manipulation, worldliness, and self-cultivation.

4. Although the humans follow God's directions, the fact that they turn out badly argues for some intrinsic defect in them.

5. Eating of its fruit conjoins free will and intelligence—that is, making wise choices, a hallmark of the mature human being.

6. You must have a mind of your own (which means, of course, not merely a reflection of God's).

7. That God is partially responsible for human failings and that there is therefore a closer familial bond between the deity and humans than the notion of the All Father or the Great Mother implies.

8. Humans have put their intelligence to destructive uses, have taken onto themselves godlike powers, and have made a hell on earth.

9. He has the artist's ego, his belief that his aesthetic decisions have independent value, his sense of personal and artistic irreplaceability, his resentment of those who don't appreciate or who misstate the significance of his works.

10. Answers will vary, but probably the tragic sorrowfulness of creativity and creating.

---

## J. Alden Mason

# The Legendary Empire

**Overview.**   As Mason writes elsewhere in his classic, "It is coming to be realized that, except for minor deviations, practically all of the great ancient civilizations of the world developed along more or less the same lines." This understanding is central to the themes that emerge from this chapter: the violent birth of empires (here, the Incas'), the place in this development of mythical figures as culture heroes, and the often blurred boundary line between mythical account and historical record. The respect owed to mythical tellings is never more evident than in Mason's straight narrative (lines 1–38). He doesn't show the slightest condescension to its (at least) semifictional character, despite his subsequent placement of the narrative in anthropological perspective.

***In the Classroom.*** From line 39 on, this is characteristically academic writing and thus is quite different from the first two selections in this book and most of those that follow in this part. You might point particularly to Mason's use of modifiers and qualifiers and his reliance on supportive evidence to substantiate his points. The move from fiction (or myth) to fact (or history) is also an object lesson in defining nonfiction.

***Formal Considerations.*** The objective tone of Mason's scholarship is exemplary (see lines 68–73, for instance). This tone accompanies the author's careful weighing of historical evidence and the ready concession he makes to logic and probability. These are all useful early lessons for composition students.

## Looking Back

1. The Incas' legitimacy is established by their deep roots if those who spring from the very earth share an identity with it.

2. Answers may vary, but a yes or no can still lead to the reasoning that a past culture defined its moral parameters differently.

3. A culture hero is positive, contributes to the arts of peace, promises an improved future; the conqueror imposes his will on reluctant, victimized inhabitants.

4. As in number 1, legitimacy; inevitable rightness; the merit of universal recognition.

5. Great nations start small, with a stature equal to others, and as combative as they; political unity from an early date (the possibility of hereditary rulers) favors the accession to power of one.

6. Inviting the cat in to squash a rival mouse is to let yourself be eaten also.

7. His son, though the father may never have existed.

8. Mythical stories are historically valuable for reflecting large events, like wars, that occurred before or during the lifetime of actual people and though not factually recorded, still influenced their activities.

9. Not people in succession, but stages; emergence from earth of first people; migration to Cuzco and conquest; expansion in immediate vicinity, though

timing is disputed; succession of emperors consolidating power; conquest of non-Inca peoples; final victory.

10. Answers may vary, but clearly the Incas are to be seen as warlike, ruthless, merciless, brave, inspired, clever, manipulative.

# Linked Readings

Thomas Bulfinch
PROMETHEUS AND PANDORA

H. A. Guerber
THE STORY OF PROMETHEUS

DEUCALION AND PYRRHA

Al Ross
TO THE WOMAN WHO DISCOVERED FIRE!

Karel Capek
THE PUNISHMENT OF PROMETHEUS

Franz Kafka
PROMETHEUS

*Overview.*   The concert of salient themes in these readings includes the nature of authority, forms of rebellion, the value of amelioration, cultural views of women, a creation myth, and the idea of global catastrophe. Bulfinch and Guerber tell the classic story. We encounter, besides the theft of fire to benefit the human race, Prometheus as creator, the origin of woman (Pandora) and her unfortunate curiosity about the jar full of plagues, the ages of human development, and after the deluge the survival of a just man and his pious wife. The chief differences between Bulfinch and Guerber have to do with implied cultural values, prose styles, and narrative techniques, which are commented on below. Having read these authors and then facing Ross's drawing, we are forced to see that a masculine bias has shaped the previous stories, not only of course in attributing to a man the discovery of fire, but also in depicting Pandora's weakness and even in relegating Pyrrha's virtue to faithfulness to the gods (Deucalion's sense of justice is one that, by contrast, is socially involved). Capek and Kafka continue the revisionist trend, Capek by dramatizing the authoritarian response to democratization, and Kafka by reviewing in an almost anthropologically neutral manner the mythic variants, though he ends with mystery and a confession of ignorance regarding it. Together, the standard and revised treatments of the Prometheus myth demonstrate the viability of myth generally, its continued power to shape our understanding and our responses to natural forces and human behavior.

***In the Classroom.*** For an early introduction to the difference in writing styles—a difference that is more clearly displayed when the similarities are greatest—contrast Bulfinch's syntactical elaboration and precise detail with Guerber's terser, more direct approach. You might want to select passages from each author about the same topic for students to examine. Another contrast lies between Bulfinch's obvious Christian bias (see his first paragraph) and its absence in Guerber. Narrative differences abound as well. Bulfinch reserves a description of Prometheus's punishment for scholarly comment out of chronological order, whereas Guerber follows the natural sequence. The authors reverse their descriptions of Pandora and of the ages of human civilization. Furthermore, Bulfinch rejects a version of the myth that Guerber embraces—that woman was made to punish man. The Ross drawing hits back here, and so the three takes can be a topic of discussion in preparation, if you wish, for the second writing assignment. The Kafka piece testifies not only to the cultural survival of myth but also to how variously it may approach one subject (also see Bulfinch and Guerber in this respect) and yet retain a bedrock truth.

***Formal Considerations.*** The Ross drawing, though obviously differing in form from the exclusive reliance on language of the other pieces, nonetheless requires a similar kind of interpretation. The second Looking Ahead item calls students' attention to such graphic particulars. Also interesting are the syntactical differences between Bulfinch and Guerber, the use in their texts of interpolated poems (and the consequent alteration of original material), the power of speech to convey meaning in Capek, and the dry, detached tone in Kafka.

## Looking Back

1. Answers clearly will vary, but students should cite textual passages.

2. Bulfinch: serious without being solemn; Guerber: not as formal or remote as Bulfinch, yet still serious; Ross: sardonic (text); whimsical (drawing); Capek: generally detached; Kafka: intense (particularly at the close).

3. Answers will vary, but mention that interpolated texts change the nature of the original and broaden scope.

4. Capek and Ross demonstrate that myths last because their original power to structure understanding is so great. Kafka tells us that myth is dissipated in interpretation but at the bottom contains a seed of truth that perhaps a new version of the myth can address.

5. Myth is fanciful; Scripture provides "information," that is, factual truth.

6. People cannot easily accept that the flawed human condition is all that is possible; they want to see our state as a falling off, implying a possible return to the original state.

7. Bulfinch: Pandora's perfect beauty is compromised by unhealthy curiosity, a weakness, with the obvious inference to be drawn about women generally; Guerber: women as punishment; misogyny; Ross: by implication, Ross would view Pandora as having gotten a bad press; women being oppressed by male domination; Capek and Kafka: no mention; their concern is with Prometheus alone; some might interpret this as exclusionary.

8. Future destruction is a fear we project backwards, thinking that what must happen must have happened before.

9. Answers will depend on views of modern technology and its uses; Capek is instructive here.

10. Answers will vary depending on views of authority, human solidarity and rights, and legality.

✦

# Dino Buzzati

# The Bewitched Jacket

*Overview.* Combining certain folktale elements (see number 3 in Looking Ahead), this story invests such contemporary topics as greed, the love of money, the profit motive, conspicuous consumption, and criminality with the universality that makes moral judgment convincing. At the same time, the contemporaneity of the dramatic situation produces a relevance that refuses to give moral judgment the vagueness and generality that often render it moot. The truly mythic figure is the devil. Folktale represents a communal reworking of original characters, events, and situations to make them responsive to what the teller and listener know and experience, thus producing the shock of recognition.

*In the Classroom.* As conservative logicians, your students may challenge the possible connection between the events the narrator becomes aware of and the money he gains. You can cite the terms suggested in number 2 in Looking Ahead, "suspending disbelief" and "fantasy," but you may also refer to the symbolic reality of these displacements in that, when one person gains, another loses (although the second in turn may profit at someone else's expense).

*Formal Considerations.* The style is minimalist, befitting a mythic telling but often leaving it to the reader to fulfill the author's description or narrative intent. Although students need instruction in development and amplification, the "less-is-more" lesson also is useful.

## Looking Back

1. Such "shining" is usually an attribution we make figuratively, never claiming it to be actual radiance.

2. Sadness at a dinner party seems incongruous; the oddness of his smile points to a mystery.

3. That he will have to pay in the end.

4. The casualness of such an action reinforces the sense we have that profiting is natural.

5. He feels guilt.

6. His conscience inhibits him less and less; he loses his moral sense.

7. Never satisfied, we have lost the sense of contentment with what is truly valuable.

8. He uses his wealth egotistically; he might have distributed it.

9. Answers will vary. He would still have gained his wealth at others' expense, but if he gave anonymously and kept nothing for himself, he might have expiated his sins.

10. You will lose your soul if you destroy others to enrich yourself.

# J. Idries Shah

# The Fisherman and the Genie

**Overview.**  Shah defines Sufism as mental activity leading to the "transcending of ordinary limitations," that is, a form of mysticism in which one tries to think beyond logical categories in order to reach wisdom. The author claims that ancient Sufi literature makes reference to such later theories as evolution and relativity. Like Aesop's tales, with which students may be more familiar, this story has a pedagogical intention and comments on the value of knowledge and wisdom and the decline of institutions as guarantors of those. As such, it is not only typical of Sufi tales but demonstrates the cultural subordination of entertainment to instruction, a moral aim that has infused some past literary efforts in their entirety and that is not completely absent today.

**In the Classroom.**  There are key passages that students should understand if they are to grasp the story's meaning. You might therefore emphasize the Looking Back questions that point to these passages (questions 1, 6, 7, and 10). Since, as is usual with moral tales, the ending is a fillip, you should make sure students understand how the conclusion reflects on the earlier, more conceptual points that are made.

**Formal Considerations.**    However minimal the telling here, its concrete language and precise diction contribute to the effectiveness of the story.

### Looking Back

1. Don't think you can profit from what you don't control.

2. Nature is temperament; capacity is ability.

3. That proverbial wisdom is considered a living source of advice on how to live.

4. They are "unacknowledged" in having taken themselves apart from mainstream culture, which is bound more to worldly success and therefore has no official place for them.

5. Lines 55–64 particularly display this quality. Notice how the wise man speculates on possible action.

6. Answers will differ, but at issue is the belief that ideas of true value and productive use are essential to a coherent life, a life that has a center.

7. Now we understand the decision to measure all things for their intrinsic value and distinguish what enriches us from that which thins us into meaninglessness (materialism).

8. He realizes the jinn will be of no further use to him.

9. He preaches a gospel based on the adage as it mediated his confrontation with the jinn.

10. The original message, as its source grows distant in time, becomes confused. Elaborate ceremonies are developed as substitutes for what now, because it is not fully understood, seems too bare and poor to convey the truth.

❀

# Roman Czerwczak

## A Summer

**Overview.**    Various topics emerge here: urban life, human isolation, death, the passing of time and the souvenirs it leaves behind. It is out of his experiences of all these that the author mythologizes his own life (described in the first writing assignment). Some of the impersonally orienting terms he uses early in the essay—*area, district,* and *zone*—transform the term *neighborhood*.

They both set the tone and establish the atmosphere for what follows by show-ing the inconsolability of certain forms of life. This is truly a gothic piece.

**In the Classroom.**   Because "A Summer" is such a dark work, it may not be to everyone's taste. You may want to prepare students by referring to the fact that life has a shadow side, whether we like it or not, and that personal testimony to its existence has been part of all great literature. This essay is the first in the book since the Introduction to extrapolate from another text (the Kafka parable), and so you may want to model this critical thinking technique here.

**Formal Considerations.**   The author's style is at one point philosophi-cally epigrammatic ("Nothing will alter the current of time which carries you to your end. And time is so precious that it might be better to focus on 'pure' exis-tence, unobstructed by any 'actions,' to 'reflect' rather than 'live.' "). The univer-sality so valuable to essay writing emerges here. Elsewhere, the author's con-creteness and figurative language produce the particularity of the situation. Essay writers strive for these qualities.

## Looking Back

1. The opening prefigures the desperate, impoverished, and somewhat sin-ister nature of his experience.

2. The sunny days find their obverse outrageous.

3. The family history in the photographs connects immediately with the grandfather Kafka mentions.

4. Yes. Both demonstrate the vanity of elaborating life in order to discover its center, its meaning.

5. Answers will vary, but the general idea is that life flourishes and then falls into decline, producing a general sense of the human condition as tragedy.

6. Answers will vary. No evidence for the view exists here, and so students will probably rely on speculation alone.

7. It becomes the symbol of his desperation and fear (lines 114–116).

8. Either answer is possible, depending on one's tolerance for self-produced fear as the occasion for metaphysical understanding.

9. People on the streets, ourselves included, whom we normally distin-guish sharply from the dead, but whom the author harbors doubts about.

10. Death, fear, and human tragedy crowded the author's life and his imagination that summer, and now that he's living in that notorious neighbor-hood, the Kafka parable renews the fear that, like the family photographs, a seemingly long, full life condenses to a bunch of faded images held by an indif-ferent hand.

# Linked Readings

Paul Radin (editor)
THE ORIGIN OF DEATH:
KRACHI, AKAMBA, HOTTENTOT

Margot Astrov (editor)
THE ORIGIN OF DEATH: COEUR D'ALÊNE

COYOTE AND THE ORIGIN OF DEATH: CADDO

C. G. Jung
ON LIFE AFTER DEATH

Margot Astrov (editor)
A SPEECH TO THE DEAD: FOX

*Overview.*   The major themes present in these readings are death and resurrection, the afterlife, the unconscious, the limits of human reason, and dreams and visions. Death, or more accurately, the end-state humans experience, is the central focus of these texts. The Native American and African texts are cultural products (their authors are unknown and they serve ritualistic purposes), but so, in a sense, is the prose by Jung. Not only does he subscribe explicitly to the necessity of myth (see particularly lines 142–156), but his ideas about archetypes and his belief in a collective unconscious point to the individual as the carrier of cultural reality. Thus, the seeming incongruity Jung represents in these linked readings is only superficial.

*In the Classroom.*   Some students might think the subject of death a harsh one, and it is true that generally it is. But we find in these texts not only that the forms death takes are never described but that the imagination is a consoling faculty. In regard to the African and Native American tales, you should try to elicit from students the realization that, however intricate the explanation, the inevitability and finality of death remain as facts, demonstrating the realism of the tellers. In Jung, students should grasp the view that dreams manifest the workings of the unconscious to raise the possibility of life after death. You might ask students to compare the Fox "Speech to the Dead" with graveside services they may be aware of.

*Formal Considerations.*   The African and Native American tales are simple narratives whose beauty lies in that simplicity. The last words of each, however, contain a twist of meaning that supplies the power and delivers the moral. Throughout, Jung is careful to modify his claims and qualify his statements in ways that put into practice his critique of rational narrowmindedness. The tone of the Fox speech is interesting for its wariness mixed with instruction and dismissal, perhaps demonstrating the psychological tension of the moment.

## Looking Back

1. The sense that death is intrusive, not simply the final state, and that therefore it is not an acceptable part of reality.

2. Krachi: magical, caused by death itself, though perhaps one time only; Akamba: no resurrection; Hottentot: no resurrection; Coeur D'Alène: after a seeming resurrection, no more, simply births and deaths; Caddo: no resurrection, though the dead go to another world.

3. According to Jung, myth allows people to entertain the idea of mystery. Pure rationality confines the imagination within narrow bounds, but the unconscious connects us with phenomena we otherwise would be oblivious of or reject. Thus he opens up for himself new ways of thinking about life and death as well as a method of thought not limited to fact or scientific proof.

4. Those who desire life after death find that belief makes their life on earth more pleasant, less foreboding; those who do not desire it do not want to stretch things out, sometimes because their present existence is painful.

5. Answers will vary. To the extent that New Age thinking has influenced students, they may be entirely sympathetic with Jung, and because Jung is skeptical of excessive rationality, you may find it necessary to elicit some argument heavily in favor of the use of reason.

6. Myth bridges conscious awareness and the unconscious. Myth allows humans to raise their consciousness in preparation for death.

7. He is warning against excess.

8. His version is a purely spiritual, or mental, one, not one in which the dead assume their earthly form.

9. We discard false selves and their ephemeral attachment (particularly to "false possessions"), and we regain our souls (the "essential"). We build up more consciousness, thereby becoming less prey to the irrelevant prejudices that tyrants and demagogues foster.

10. The attitude that the dead need to be guided carefully in their deportment.

# PART II: PERSONAL IDENTITY

## *Linked Readings*

Anonymous
THE BABY BOOMER

Saint Augustine of Hippo
AS A BABY

**Overview.** These two readings contrast with each other. The photograph and horoscope are obviously lighthearted; Saint Augustine's disquisition is, some might say, heavy-handed. But on grounds other than style and presentation, the authors have something in common. Both subscribe to ideas of predetermination, though to different degrees and with different "determinants." The photograph of the bouncing baby should actually complicate the conceptual picture offered by the author: she is so alert and cute that we resist ascribing to her—or to any infant—qualities that both texts suggest. Yet we all grow and develop from some predisposition, it seems.

**In the Classroom.** The connection described above between the photograph and the text is one that you might pursue; it certainly reflects on the issue of appearance versus reality, a favorite puzzler. It will be useful to focus on particular statements by both authors as tests of their general view. And see the issue of audience below.

**Formal Considerations.** Both texts address specific audiences: in "Baby Boomer," it's the newborn (probably her parents, in actuality); and "As A Baby," God. Because these are such different targets, the tone, attitude, vocabulary, and intent all differ, demonstrating the extent to which audience helps shape discourse.

## Looking Back

1. Answers will vary but innocence and openness might well be among them.

2. The way answers will vary is beyond conjecture.

3. Answers will vary, but because experience is sobering, students might think the advice would prevent later mistakes and pitfalls.

4. Unified: sane and sensible practices cohere with success.

5. An urgent, even desperate, need to do the impossible—recapture the moral character of his own infancy—convinces us of his sincerity.

6. Answers will vary depending on personal experience. If testimony supports both sides, we can say it depends on the individual or that the answer is a mixture.

7. Babies are not innocent.

8. Answers will vary.

9. If we owe all to God, we have a moral responsibility from the very beginning.

10. Answers will vary, but a Freudian would reject his view.

❀

# Camara Laye
# I Was Very Young

**Overview.**   College-age students are prone to harken back to their early school days, especially those students who are becoming increasingly self-conscious of their intellectual and emotional development. Generally, however, those days, with all their turmoil and only gradually—and painfully—understood meaning, haunt our memories, often convincing us that we were indelibly marked by our experiences then to become what we are now. Almost all autobiographies have something to say about these matters.

**In the Classroom.**   Obvious contrasts distinguish Laye's school in colonial Africa from our students' experience, either in the United States or in countries from which they may have recently emigrated. Still, similarities no doubt also are present, and it would be useful to ask students to identify these. Laye's use of initial topic sentences is a good model, by the way. Notice especially lines 45 and 57.

**Formal Considerations.**   Alert students to the interesting narrative pattern. Laye covers a lot of ground from the beginning until line 157; at that point, he begins to relate a particular series of connected events that extends to the end of the text and supplies the drama.

## Looking Back

1. It has slackened. Demands on students are fewer and softer. Corporal punishment has largely disappeared.

2. He moves without impediment; he has verve and energy.

3. Answers will vary. The director's authoritarianism might argue for exploitation, though sometimes valuable lessons can be taught by badly motivated people.

4. It can be argued that students' agricultural duties work against elitism and also that they represent the conservative burden of stifling tradition.

5. That history is social relations writ large, even those among schoolboys, and that perhaps, therefore, we never learn.

6. Laye ascribes to his people a growing desire for freedom that the bullying and subordination behind these beatings contravened.

7. She is emphatic and sensitive to his emotional fragility.

8. If yes, because the child is helpless and needs protection; if no, because the child needs to learn to stand up for himself or herself.

9. Answers will vary; this is a question designed to make students conscious of writing style.

10. Harsh, oppressive, demanding, cruel.

# Catherine S. Manegold

## Crystal

*Overview.* The "teen-age rage" Manegold refers to (line 5) appears more and more frequently as a description of the social malaise afflicting so many youths today. Yet we normally consider rage an emotional reaction to extreme, not mundane, events and circumstances. Crystal's situation does not seem to be extreme, so is the term *rage* mistaken? Or is it apt because the threshold for feeling it has been lowered? Is it that Crystal, like so many others, sees clearly into her own future, which is the present for teens somewhat older than she and is prefigured by a general societal indifference? Does she direct her rage legitimately against that scenario? Asking these questions, rather than making definitive statements here, is perhaps the best approach to Crystal's story.

*In the Classroom.* Students might recognize Crystal and even vicariously take her under their wing. Sympathy and compassion serve practical ends in reading and writing. You can ask students to decide what Crystal's problems are. How many problems are of her own making, and how many is she the helpless victim of?

*Formal Considerations.* The journalistic emphasis on facts here is worth students' attention (the places where facts emerge abound), since essayists of any stripe depend on such hard information to ground their ideas and insights. The brevity of the paragraphs is partly due to the typographical requirements of newspapers. The last paragraph is moving and shows careful structural decisions by the author.

## *Looking Back*

1. Her defensive hostility that yet craves the attention given those whom we cherish.

2. Answers will vary, but students can explain and justify.

3. There might be at least some inducement offered by role models.

4. Answers will vary, but her being tapped years earlier to enter a kindergarten for gifted students is an important datum.

5. That it presents a seemingly typical inner-city picture of students whose broken lives teach them that education is futile and that the socialization school imposes is counterproductive.

6. Because the chaos and danger of their lives psychologically overwhelmed them. Their life is obviously one of total insecurity.

7. A seeming contradiction, but perhaps it testifies to a surface order that, when no one is looking, yields to the violence lurking beneath it.

8. Answers will depend on students' own recent experience.

9. Answers will vary, but probably students will perceive the need for greater discipline and care.

10. The connections between community influences and school requirements should form this answer.

# Leo Tolstoy

# Boyhood

***Overview.*** First published in magazine form in the mid-1850s, *Childhood, Boyhood, and Youth* was originally meant to include a fourth volume, *Adolescence.* The book is an autobiographical novel, a fiction based on fact, and is composed of one hundred episodes bound thematically rather than through plot construction to detail the subject's intellectual and moral development. Despite its not being literal truth, the evident precosity of the narrator in the story is more than believable, though it points partially to a set of environmental conditions that surface parenthetically throughout and that students can become aware of.

***In the Classroom.*** If your students read "Crystal," the preceding selection, draw attention to the contrast between her and the present narrator to help isolate his particular situation and sensibility. Part of the latter is his obvious seriousness, his viewing himself less as a child than as a little man who must wrestle with adult problems. Students can comment on the wisdom of such a view.

**Formal Considerations.**    Familiarity with certain abstract concepts used by the narrator is crucial to understanding this piece. These are *symmetry, infinity, skepticism,* and *moral.* The narrative winds around them and shares their abstract character.

### Looking Back

1. "A man's situation," whatever it may be, makes behavior seem natural and inevitable, but "moral activity," despite such a situation, produces questioning and thus challenges an automatic acceptance of ourselves.

2. Answers will vary: a yes answer can point to the increase in human dignity and stature such questions make possible; a no answer may refer to unnecessary complication.

3. Answers will vary, depending on circumstances.

4. An awareness of limits.

5. An aesthetic attraction to symmetry, even assuming it to be inborn, does not logically imply its necessary contradiction of singleness, as in a single sun in the sky or a single life.

6. It makes him conscious of his own preciousness; the smile emanates from ordinary life, in which practical demands predominate.

7. Because his own mental activity seems so unreliable and wrong-headed.

8. It depleted his natural energies and clouded his vision.

9. He is embarrassed as if others know his self-exaltation and that it is at their expense.

10. Answers will vary.

# Rongelio R. Gomez

## Foul Shots

**Overview.**    The prevalent concern in this piece is the social, economic, and cultural dominance of the white population in the United States and the consequent ill effects on minorities. This issue never becomes abstract here, however, and the reasoning is never tendentious, as Gomez focuses almost entirely on a single concrete incident from his past life. The sharpness of his description argues implicitly that ordinary situations and events may contain wide-ranging significance that enables us to analyze general conditions at the same time we judge particular instances.

**In the Classroom.**   The fact, alluded to above, that Gomez's meaning arises largely from one event forces interpretation not only of that event but also of its incidentals—the actions, gestures, and speeches. Gomez does use conceptual language at times, such as the terms *racial, prejudice,* and *inferiority* (admittedly low-order concepts), and students should be clear on them.

**Formal Considerations.**   The structure of the essay is a useful model. Gomez begins by introducing the game, next furnishes background information that establishes the game's significance in his life, and then returns to the game to relate the central incident. The final paragraph is, like the first, retrospective but also completes its sense to give the essay symmetry.

## Looking Back

1. His present reconsiderations give the past event its significance.

2. Answers will vary, but perhaps if the boys had been separately and formally introduced to one another, if the coaches had stayed around, and so on, the strategy would have had some hope of working.

3. Answers will vary. The logic is elusive, but probably the rationale was to train them young; once in high school, they would be so much less malleable.

4. As a culturally imposed norm that individual selves must struggle against, a particular burden for children.

5. The origin of these feelings is an internalized sense that his language and culture are without value, but he is conscious of these feelings, which is a cause of further psychological pain and which increases his sense of valuelessness. If equal treatment were manifest in the schools, this sequence might never have begun.

6. The suffering one goes through by not living up to an impossible ideal.

7. He could not speak (or understand) English.

8. Their humiliation at the hands of the other team overwhelmed their victory on the scoreboard.

9. The bag of Fritos is the symbol of their humiliation. Concrete details such as this focus meaning and convince the reader that experience is authentic.

10. The past may infect the present with the memory of failure, pointing to its immense power to shape and influence us.

✤

# Ondine Galsworth

# Air Raid

*Overview.*   The mother-daughter relationship, in the past often considered less compelling than that between father and son, deserves the compensatory treatment it receives here. Although Galsworth's mother seems hardly "typical"—witness her mental illness, her great beauty, and her artistic bent—the mere existence of the typical when it comes to human beings, as well as its value, is dubious. We can learn without stint from this memoir, particularly as the focus is so much on the author herself and on her mother's early influences on her later life.

*In the Classroom.*   The double focus of this essay is important to establish. The mother dominates the first part and the child the second, but between those parts is a transition formed by Galsworth's recounting her mother's influence on her behavior. In today's conservative social climate, some students might think the author's upbringing was disastrous and insist she should have been separated from her mother. Others might notice there is no mention of a father. These are issues worthy of discussion.

*Formal Considerations.*   Numbers 2 and 3 in Looking Ahead point to two formal issues you can address explicitly in discussion.

## Looking Back

1. Like this one, titles may capture the most poignant sense of the essay and thus pinpoint its real subject.

2. Answers will vary, but this beginning is obviously engaging.

3. The staccato confessional quality of this repetition, insisting on the author's lack of innocence, creates in the reader a certain respect for her younger self and thus for the meaning of her experience.

4. She refers to her faculties of fantasy and imagination, which helped cushion the blows.

5. They show us it was close and warm, despite her mother's problems.

6. Answers will vary, but the American idiom is powerfully direct.

7. That her art and all else failed her.

8. Answers will vary.

9. Her attitude softens the sense that she has inherited some of her mother's peculiarities.

10. Answers will vary.

✸

# François, duc de La Rochefoucauld
## Self-Portrait

**Overview.**    As the biographical sketch notes, La Rochefoucauld is best known for his aphorisms. His *Maxims* were a formative influence on French culture, "giving it a feeling for aptness and precision," as Leonard Tancock says, and making wide use of the first-person plural pronoun for the purpose of universality. Examples to provide students with are "We are so used to disguising ourselves from others that we end by disguising ourselves from ourselves" and "Overeagerness to repay a debt is in itself a kind of ingratitude." As these examples show, La Rochefoucauld was, if not cynical, at least extraordinarily realistic and unsparingly candid, and always capable of deft insights and paradox. These qualities inform his "Self-Portrait."

**In the Classroom.**    Analysis yields to synthesis. In this piece, the first is the author's method; the second must be the students' task. Their problem will be to put together La Rochefoucauld's findings and revelations about himself and to form a general idea of the man's character and personality.

**Formal Considerations.**    La Rochefoucauld uses certain terms that are conceptually encompassing and yet, because they may be relatively foreign to students, should be isolated and examined. Some of these are "melancholic" (line 22), "a fluent tongue" (line 43), "frivolities" (line 49), "a noble soul" (line 83), and "austere virtue" (line 105).

## Looking Back

1. His report should seem doubly authentic.

2. That he is not addicted to self-regard, that he probably has little practice in looking in a mirror.

3. Answers will vary depending on experience, but the failure to examine oneself might lead to the inability to chart one's course through life successfully, since decisions might be based on self-deception.

4. Although used now almost exclusively to refer to comedy or preceded by the adjective *good, humor* is also a reference to a particular temperament (originally based on body fluid).

5. Some students might answer no, assuming an automatic identity between what we feel and how these feelings show on our faces; a more sophisticated approach would agree with La Rochefoucauld. But some stu-

dents might say he should consult others, not just himself, about these perceptions.

6. He knows he is intelligent and considers it a definite advantage over others, yet the expressions of his intelligence often are adversely affected by his depression.

7. To approach others' work critically alerts us to what our own work requires, and to learn to argue a case verbally is practice in defending a written position. Note that the author scorns his own tendency to go too far in criticism and argument.

8. Pity alleviates suffering and should be expressed, but emotion rather than reason produces it, so the intellectually superior person should not yield to its constraints.

9. His fear that the emotion of love will never dominate him testifies to his general sense of himself as primarily an intellectual who keeps the emotions in check.

10. Sincerity, honesty, integrity.

# James Baldwin

# The Discovery of What It Means to Be an American

***Overview.*** In recent years, separatist ideology and personal demagoguery have been the most visible forms the black struggle for rights and freedom has taken. Baldwin represents a different tendency: a militant belief that African Americans must claim a rightful place in American society. As he writes in an autobiographical note (in *Notes of a Native Son*): "I love America more than any other country in the world and, exactly for this reason, I insist on the right to criticize her perpetually." It is notable that, in the present essay, as in others, Baldwin integrates themes of personal identity, professional activity, and social life. His constant mediating principle is articulated in the note referred to above: "I want to be an honest man and a good writer."

***In the Classroom.*** Baldwin's reasoning tone, social and political insights, and statements of universal principles lift the essay above the purely confessional mode, even though autobiography forms the basis for his writing. Students need to be trained to find meaning in experience instead of remaining content with narrative, and so it will be entirely useful for them to identify and consider the above-named features.

**Formal Considerations.**   Baldwin's sentences are a thing of beauty, particularly in their varied syntax, frequent embedding, parallelism, and mounting intensities. The conclusion to this essay is quietly resonant, picking up preceding themes without merely drumming them back in.

## Looking Back

1. Fate is what dogs us; destiny, what beckons us. The complexity of an American's fate refers to the continuing need to discover personal identity; the destiny of the American, through such attempts at discovery, is to venture into new actual and mental places.

2. Although it is ideally imaginable that people be valued for their individuality, their special qualities, Baldwin's color—like that of African Americans generally—was a cause of his devaluation by whites. Further, he admits to internalizing white prejudices, which separated him from blacks as well. He belonged nowhere.

3. Despite his cultural influences, Baldwin still is African American, a fact his consciousness has suppressed but which remains nevertheless a fact, and one that can cause a personal crisis when for one reason or another it becomes important. The need then is to admit its existence and learn to live in its light.

4. In America, the intellect—and therefore the writer's profession—has a low standing (although this may be changing), but because Europeans believe that the writer can pose a challenge to the social order, writers enjoy an important place and status there.

5. They could experience a wide variety of common life-styles that would inform their writing.

6. People have self-respect, which translates into mutual respect without jealousy or resentment.

7. Answers will vary, but the freedom and new perspectives on self Baldwin says he gained seem valuable for anyone.

8. Freedom always brings one back to oneself since it entails self-responsibility, but also Baldwin the expatriate has discovered he is an American in Europe, not a European, and so must still contend with that personal identity.

9. Answers will vary, but Baldwin's terms—"rich confusion" and "unprecedented opportunities"—indicate his own positive reaction.

10. Paraphrases will vary, but at the heart of all should be the stated need to dispel myth in the interest of clearsightedness.

# Bharati Mukherjee
## The World According to Hsü

***Overview.***   Two traditions, one positive and one negative, stand in the background of Mukherjee's short story. One is the conscious position that numerous writers adopt in order to handle a situation they and millions of nonwriters experience: the position of critical sensitivity (and therefore armed vulnerability) to the reception (ranging from distaste to violent hostility) all too frequently given to immigrants and resident aliens. This xenophobia is the second, negative tradition. It exists on both national and community levels and constantly raises issues of "racial purity," ethnic isolation or diversity, assimilation, and others. The author demonstrates the international aspect of the problem, but we don't have to leave home to experience it.

***In the Classroom.***   To establish the immediate relevance of the story, you can ask students to cite any instances they know of or experiences they have had that reflect Ratna Clayton's problem. If this does not prove fruitful, you might ask students if America (or their more immediate locale) is indeed a "melting pot," or if that concept seems a myth.

***Formal Considerations.***   As in much fiction, the protagonist's past experience and present views come into focus slowly, over time. Readers feel and understand the full, combined impact of Hsü's geological description, Clayton Graeme's decision, and the words that end the story. The first is symbolic, the second a crucial plot element, and the third part of characterization.

### Looking Back

1. 1978.

2. They are a middle-class couple whose dominant member probably is the husband and who are seeking quite different results from their trip together— Ratna, a release from pressure, the husband, an experience he can shape into knowledge.

3. He seems callous and nationalistically egotistic in his disdain, and thus our sympathy for him lessens. Ratna's attitude is diametric.

4. Answers will vary, but a close parallel to Ratna's situation exists in the African American community in respect to lighter and darker complexions.

5. That the Indians are needed in the economy but despised, that the whites are the residue of former French colonialism (Vichy refers to the collaborationist

government during the Nazi occupation), and that blacks are the majority and—given their looting—the poorest population.

6. A truce suspends hostilities; peace makes a settlement. Ratna has not admitted that her fears of chauvinistic violence are groundless.

7. Because she is apprehensive and fearful, the most human and sympathic aspects of the others seem even more marked to her, as if the world were not dangerous for minorities after all.

8. She is asking why terrible things must occur and destroy unity.

9. Answers will vary but should chiefly be negative. Graeme cannot think beyond his own situation.

10. The ethnic integration on the island is one that will dissolve for Ratna in Toronto, where she will soon again be singled out as a despised foreigner.

# F. Scott Fitzgerald

# Early Success

***Overview.***    Fitzgerald's lifelong obsession with youth is reflected in the title of this piece. His nostalgia (sometimes for what hadn't even yet become the past) lasted to the moment of his death by heart failure while perusing an article about his alma mater Princeton University's football team. But as the headnote indicates, his was a critical nostalgia, and in his mature work Fitzgerald captured the pangs of loss, the irresistible need to redeem the time and its final impossibility, and the consequent suffering of a double loss. Anyone looking backward from the vantage point of this last stage is not simply prey to nostalgia and its obvious distortions but is measuring the tragic dimensions of a universally timebound existence. Whether in or out of fashion, Fitzgerald strikes some of the great themes in literature, and it is to be hoped that students will be drawn from this essay to his fiction.

***In the Classroom.***    The money Fitzgerald earned in 1920 may appear a quaint sum to your students, and they may be surprised that he saw it as sudden munificence; and added to that, other mentions may make this essay seem remote. But that is the fate of any writing—you might remind your students— whose author has the temerity to report social facts. Their historical importance remains, nonetheless, and it is clear that Fitzgerald's viewpoint about himself is partially ironic (that is, critically removed and not therefore merely reminiscent), viz. remarks such as "I retired, not on my profits, but on my liabilities" (line 3), "I was on the down-grade at twenty-two" (line 26), and his own sentence that he quotes, "'She was a faded but still lovely woman of twenty-seven'" (lines 99–100).

**Formal Considerations.**   "Early Success" teaches some lessons about the autobiographical personal essay. One is to be concrete, particular, and specific if readers are to believe it's your life. Another is to modulate your tone so that you don't seem to be so influenced by the fact it's your life that you overdramatize it. And a third is not merely to narrate events but to find meaning in them that you can express, at least in part, in universal terms.

## Looking Back

1. Should he quit work to write and thus lose his fiancee, or should he continue working and forgo the novel he counts on to make his name and fortune?

2. Answers will vary, but I have seen these words scrawled on walls by members of Generation X.

3. Like any mist, the mist of success casts a veil of illusion over matters, making them appear softened and friendly. When the mist disappears, the hard and hostile reality reemerges.

4. His advice is to think ahead so that your work rhythm will be uninterrupted; the writer is a worker, with routines and a production schedule, not merely an inspired artist.

5. These anecdotes support his claim of a new professionalism, in that now he is always on the lookout for material.

6. He determined to tell the story of this period according to his own analysis of its central truths, which derive from a wary, skeptical point of view.

7. Names, titles, and labels do not produce a new person but simply a new way for others to regard one.

8. Answers will vary, but clearly Fitzgerald identified closely with Princeton and felt betrayed.

9. At twenty, you delude yourself; at thirty, you know what different personal elements in yourself have contributed to the whole; at forty, you know that it has been a struggle (and thus a victory).

10. Then, the future was still ahead, not the present suffering, and he could still dream expectantly of it. Seeing himself again in that guise gives him a feeling of tenderness toward himself.

# Ida Fink

# Night of Surrender

**Overview.**   On the dust jacket of Fink's novel *The Journey,* the language of the Anne Frank Prize for Literature awarded her describes *A Scrap of Time* as a "powerful imaginative passage to an unimaginably infernal world." This description is a reminder of the position some hold that a fictional treatment of the Holocaust is a contradiction in terms. The implication is that artistic shaping, character invention, and invoked dramatic situations and dialogue distract from a terrible actuality comprehensible only as reported fact. Without joining this debate, we can nonetheless add to its terms that fiction by a survivor who limits her work to her own experience may escape such a limitation.

**In the Classroom.**    The reason for Ann/Klara's rejection of Mike—which is all but explicit—may not be immediately clear to your students. Mike is asking her to give up, on this "night of surrender," the identity that willy-nilly she has cherished by being persecuted for it and having to hide it from the Nazis; it has become identified with her own endangered life. After discussion, students should see that Mike is in effect asking her to give up herself, to be a different person.

**Formal Considerations.**    How can language that is simple and direct *hide* the human emotion it nonetheless expresses, and in doing so make its release even more powerful? Hemingway's less-is-more approach may be the answer, but it still needs explaining. Instead of conceptualizing dramatic conflict and emotion, Fink supplies their particulars and the reader experiences rather than knows them.

### Looking Back

1. She is understating the danger of having her real identity exposed.

2. As someone whose persecution has impoverished her of all but apprehension and survival skills.

3. They bare the soul.

4. He is educated, self-confident, powerful; she is afraid, cautious, weak.

5. Answers will depend on whether Mike or Ann/Klara is the focus; reasonable for him, but trust for her has been an impossibility, and she cannot be expected to yield to it as rapidly.

6. Ostensibly to spare her, but to her, it may seem that he wishes there were no Jews in the world to cause problems.

7. Answers will vary.

8. All her defenses go back up when she realizes he wants her to deny herself.

9. The river is the roaring flood of the old terror, the noise of murder that has threatened her, and now it is inside her.

10. Remember that she silently shakes her head (line 224). Answers will vary on whether her action was right.

舞

# Tim O'Brien

# On the Rainy River

*Overview.*    In his best work, O'Brien deals with the plight of the combat soldier in the Vietnam War, particularly the soldier's often reluctant status as a fighter and the moral ambiguity of his position at that time in that place. This story, which has its nonfictional counterpart in *If I Die in a Combat Zone,* concerns the kind of draftable youth who was not simply self-interested and certainly not bloodthirsty, but rather, sensitive, morally conflicted, pressured by circumstances. His decision to join the war would seem positive to officialdom but, to himself, would mark a failure of character. This paradox, the guts to go indicating moral cowardice, is at the heart of the story.

*In the Classroom.*    This story is easy to follow, but some students might take umbrage at O'Brien's final words: "I was a coward. I went to the war." Because as stated above, this admission captures the story's meaning, patriotism that blinds the reader to meaning should be disallowed. It is necessary, here as in any text, to understand character and event only within the given context.

*Formal Considerations.*    The author's plain language and confiding tone—"Now, perhaps, you can understand why I've never told this story before" (line 410)—are characteristic of his style. They demonstrate how unnecessary it is to strain for effects in order to communicate important meaning.

## *Looking Back*

1. We will have in store, unused but readily on hand, the necessary amount of courage called for.

2. That the leaders who had drawn us into war didn't know what they were doing.

3. Answers will vary, but they must be considered in the context of a nationwide draft.

4. He feels brutalized.

5. The war is wrong, he feels, but exile to avoid the war is disgrace.

6. He is, or has been, a person integrated into his community; to desert it would necessitate redefining himself.

7. Reflexive patriotism, which obviates knowledge and rejects argument.

8. Berdahl accepts him as he is, not as he should be according to others, and nurtures his moral crisis to the point where O'Brien attributes it to a base

motive, embarrassment, or what we might call shame before others that he anticipates (see lines 469–475).

9. He yielded to family and social pressure; he feared the disgrace exiling himself would bring.

10. Answers will vary.

🌿

## Diane Arbus

## My Favorite Thing Is to Go Where I've Never Been and A Family One Evening in a Nudist Camp, Pa., 1965

*Overview.* The *Aperture* monograph containing this piece and the photograph uses as an epigraph a statement by Arbus that, arguably, captures her entire project: "Nothing is ever the same as they said it was. It's what I've never seen before that I recognize." The "they" refers to the official version of everything, ranging from how things appear to how we should think. This normative view stifles individual perception and opposes art. In rejecting it, Arbus finds herself capable of looking for meaning in new places, not simply in those deemed acceptable. It is there that she discovers a correspondence between the world and her self. Hence the paradox of recognizing—that is, knowing again—what has never been seen—that is, never admitted as essentially known already, however strange in its particulars it still appears.

*In the Classroom.* So many of Arbus's statements are discretely resonant that it is useful to pause at particular ones and have students address their meaning. At the same time, you will no doubt want your students to become aware of her broader concerns with self, the other, and art itself.

*Formal Considerations.* The fragmentary nature of this transcript is obviously not a model for essay writing (not every text should be), but it *is* a model for journal keeping. You can alert students to the possibility of deriving from journal entries a continuous line of discourse reflecting a central concern or a constant sensibility. Arbus's language is often so colloquial that the reader seems to be thinking what she's saying. Speech has its place in writing.

### Looking Back

1. She's fascinated by their otherness, which alternately fades and reappears, and excited about the possibilities they offer.

2. People aim for a particular appearance but end up drawing attention to what it is about themselves that contradicts it.

3. Trying to be general, you lose the reality of a world of particulars as well as your own view. Being specific restores the particulars.

4. They have been ennobled by suffering, which refines the individual's sensibilities.

5. Photographs can be entirely artful yet miss an authentic sense of their subject, some inner meaning that reveals its essence, and thus not capture reality.

6. It is an understanding based on acceptance, which is a sine qua non.

7. The "everything else" is our external relations to the world; Arbus considers personal identity to be something existing prior to these, not a product of them.

8. These topics are covered in many places, but look particularly at lines 291–292: "I work from awkwardness. By that I mean I don't like to arrange things. If I stand in front of something, instead of arranging it, I arrange myself."

9. A prior mindset makes a person rigid and immune to new experience. In contrast, to feel your way into knowing is to be humble and open.

10. The nudists are physically unattractive; they seem isolated, as if thrown down onto the ground, not as if they had discovered a condition of paradise (see lines 112–117).

# PART III: THE NATURAL WORLD

✣

## Lewis Thomas

## The Music of *This* Sphere

*Overview.*   It would be to denigrate the virtues of clarity in writing and lucidity of vision to describe Thomas as a "popularizer" of science. Yet he easily penetrates what laypersons usually regard as the mysteries of science, and does so in a prose even cats and dogs can read. In line with these qualities, as Number 3 in Looking Ahead indicates, Thomas is an optimist about nature, which in other essays includes human beings. He is therefore positive about human potential, though he often speaks wryly about the actual character of human activities. We might call him a positive realist, certainly a humanist, and, we cannot help but suspect, a good man.

*In the Classroom.*   The first-person plural pronoun is a method Thomas uses—innocently enough—to tie audience and writer together and yet also to go beyond that exclusive use to include all humans. Both specific audience and universal appeal are lessons for students.

*Formal Considerations.*   The topic sentence and paragraph unity are much on display here for students. Note particularly paragraphs beginning on lines 43 and 61. Thomas uses many embedded sentences (those with inserted phrases and clauses), which are models for students whose sentences lack variety or complexity.

### Looking Back

1.  The music of the spheres usually is a celestial reference.

2.  We waste it.

3.  You have to be making the sound or know it from prior experience to assign meaning confidently and accurately.

4.  He admires the aesthetic quality, though he might have been deterred by the human bias against bats, thus showing his objective appreciation.

5.  He demonstrates the agency of animals in making sounds and thus producing meaning.

6.  Because earthworms are the most unlikely candidates for admiration, the audience is particularly impressed by his observations and claims.

7. This sound has no practical purpose but seems to exist solely for its own beauty. Thomas cites the examples of the thrush and the robin to further this sense of musical pleasure.

8. Otherwise, we could not discern the music in some creatures' sounds.

9. Fiction is one thing, but hypotheses such as Thomas engages in are legitimate in nonfiction (note his "might be" in line 118).

10. That the universal ordering of matter by a flow of solar energy has its counterpart in animal sounds, and that these sounds recall this order to us.

✿

# Carl Sagan

# Can We Know the Universe?
# Reflections on a Grain of Salt

**Overview.**    Science is a way of verifying knowledge about nature and codifying this knowledge, but this unexceptionable definition also carries a critical component. The general approach it implies not only to nature but also to such realms as social custom and political behavior challenges the automatic acceptance of received ideas and demonstrates the logical fallacy of relying blindly on authority. This essay, therefore, may make a particularly valuable contribution to our students' education: it may help erode their resistance to independent thinking, to new knowledge, and to unfamiliar experience. This resistance, which is part of the baggage many young people bring to college, needs to be dispelled so that students may make choices between alternative views and projects—that is, so they can be free. This is not to forget that Sagan also in this essay defines science and describes the scientific method.

**In the Classroom.**    Be sure students grasp the distinction Sagan draws between the scientific method of inquiry versus answers found through cultural inheritance or intuition.

**Formal Considerations.**    Notable features of Sagan's prose are the cohesiveness of his paragraphs, his use of series (see the second paragraph), and his interrogatory sentences (some but not all of which are rhetorical questions).

## Looking Back

1. Refer to lines 32–34, 37–40, and 99–103.

2. Answers will vary, but clearly they outfit the individual to meet, understand, and act positively with regard to new experiences.

3. Some believe that such customs are a cultural response to human nature, not a product of reason (with the latter's implied reversability).

4. Language style means choosing between alternatives to find the word that is appropriate and precise.

5. That it has been an introduction to science and the scientific method.

6. People fear such knowledge because it would dispel mystery and thus the possibility of attributing causes to other sources.

7. Regular formations can be known, explained, and confined to laws, but the universe as a whole is not knowable.

8. Answers will vary, depending on what is inferred from "belonging."

9. Common sense and intuition are based on experience and limited vision, not on experiment, and thus are misleading (think of the sun "rising" and "setting").

10. That we and the universe were made for each other.

# *Linked Readings*

### Hermann Hesse
### TREES

### Claude Lévi-Strauss
### IN THE FOREST

### The Audubon Society
### AN AERIAL VIEW

*Overview.* These readings combine three very different perspectives on the same subject—trees. Hesse is lyrical; Lévi-Strauss, though personal in his approach, writes as a social scientist; and the Audubon Society's cautionary note is delivered by ecological activists. Hesse's view of trees recalls the worship of nature and urge to wander (see line 37) that are often ascribed to romantic Germanic culture. For him, trees rise above both the actual and symbolic levels to exist almost as a variant species of humanity, which we might call the Comforters. Despite his different method of valuation, Lévi-Strauss is not unlike Hesse when he discovers in the forest (but not in the mountains or by the sea) "silence, coolness, peace" (line 124). The forest, he too feels, is restorative, yet the end of his essay strikes a note of warning that the white man's invasion spells the doom of nature. Lévi-Strauss, historical in a way that Hesse is not, also takes the reader into an actual landscape (the Amazonian forest) instead of contemplating an idealized one. The Audubon birds voice a concern for the Brazilian rain forest that Lévi-Strauss trekked and, in effect, complete the cycle of these pieces that ranges from piety to anxiety.

***In the Classroom.***    Defining and then explaining the merits of the tone of each of these pieces will not only point up their differences—and therefore the possibilities open to student writers—but will blunt any resistance to these texts based on a lack of understanding. Hesse is passionate and naive; Lévi-Strauss, dispassionate; the Audubon birds, querulous, wry, sarcastic. Hesse animates the tree, Lévi-Strauss explains the life of the forest, the birds plead. Which voice is most exigent?

***Formal Considerations.***    Given the above distinctions, it is useful to observe the different vocabularies at play here. Hesse's is simple, Lévi-Strauss's learned, the birds' deriving from the speech mode. Each is appropriate to authorial intent.

### Looking Back

1. Struggle, solitariness, self-fulfillment, endurance.

2. Mother nature, perhaps, but also the Great Mother, or Great Goddess, the matriarchal concept of the deity, who has designed the tree to "reveal the eternal" (line 25). But later (line 34) both *mother* and *home* are ordinary language, literal concepts. Trees comfort us when we think we have traveled far from home and mother.

3. The sea, its laying bare and casting up of detritus; the mountains, solitude.

4. The sea is invasive and monotonous, and the coastlines are spoiled; the mountains have lost their novelty and demand too much physical effort. The forest, however, is endlessly rich in rewards for the senses and the spirit.

5. Both are intimate senses, less detached and intellectual than sight and hence more capable of producing harmony.

6. These figures work to demonstrate the altitudes of layers of growth, starting from the height of humans and progressing to ships' masts and the tops of buildings, all of which are familiar and therefore help us measure and envision.

7. Lucinda's literal attachment to Lévi-Strauss helps him demonstrate the difficulty of walking through the forest.

8. He resents such inroads and values what is original; he also values the solitude and peace that nature can offer and that civilization sets no premium on.

9. See the Overview for this.

10. Answers will vary, but students may refer to stripmining, pollution of waterways and the sea, and destruction of the ozone layer.

※

## Lauren Strutzel

# The Evolution of Allegiance to the Green Concern

*Overview.*    Strutzel's specific concern is recycling to combat unnecessary waste. She patiently details her own development into an ecologically minded person, taking us into her home and acquainting us with the recycling habits of her family, and into the office where she has worked. By implication, however, she goes beyond her stated position on recycling to discover her place in a collectivity and accept social responsibilities that doubtless she did not originally imagine. For her, the personal is political in the sense that the connection between humans and nature argues for a social policy that registers and promotes the link.

*In the Classroom.*    Because the author's background seems to be a comfortable middle-class one, some students might regard her sense of interconnectedness, which she prefers to economic self-interest, as a luxury not possible for most. This is an issue worthy of discussion.

*Formal Considerations.*    The strength of Strutzel's writing is largely a result of her detailed explanation of various processes and her concreteness of language and example. These qualities give her larger statements their force and prevent them from being simply free-floating abstractions.

## *Looking Back*

1. Unknown, not previously investigated and therefore practically unreachable (*earth* referring to nature here).

2. She was raised to put herself and her own interests first; later she began to see herself as part of the whole.

3. Irony, wryness; see also "but meanwhile back in the kitchen, my paper bag was spilling over" (line 67), "the ungainly world" (line 84), and "creative discarding" (line 88), for instance.

4. Fear that she was helping to ruin the environment.

5. Answers will vary.

6. Answers will vary, depending on what one considers corporate responsibility (Strutzel is clear on this point).

7. Forms probably ranging from indifference to resistance to instituting costly measures.

8. The principle of "outside in" (line 198), taking social measures to effect personal change.

9. Answers will vary, though Strutzel's position is consistent with her prior reasoning.

10. These phrases are products of her own urgent speech, motivated by her perception that her fate is bound up with that of society, and vice-versa.

# Beryl Markham

# Royal Exile

***Overview.*** Revering an animal—not animals plural but one in particular—and paying homage to its qualities seem destined to produce sentimentality of the most appalling sort, and this story comes perilously close at the end to doing so. Yet Markham ultimately avoids that excess. Her proximity to it owes to the risk she takes in revealing the nature of the stallion Camciscan through his own perceptions. The gambit succeeds, though, and finally we feel that if it were our fate to be a horse, we would wish for the nobility and dignity of this one.

***In the Classroom.*** To focus the dominant point of view in the story (the omniscient one) and to reveal its effectiveness, you might ask students to contrast the first section (to line 30) with the rest.

***Formal Considerations.*** The narrative form and physical detail dominate, but conceptual language also surfaces: "the loneliness he lived by" (line 91), "the humility of rejection and disdain" (line 143), "a heritage of arrogance" (line 213). You can refer to the necessary and singular role of conceptualization in bearing the burden of meaning.

## *Looking Back*

1. That these animals, unlike humans, whose existences are so artificial, connect her to natural life.

2. Line 23 (see above); the introduction isolates horses, and Camciscan in particular, as being a vital part of Markham's life.

3. She is able to view herself more objectively and therefore more judiciously.

4. As a "royal exile," Camciscan is separated from his true noble domain to live among puny humans. His kingship comes out further as condescension (lines 45–46) and dignified reserve (lines 74–76).

5. Yes, pride is sometimes valued for its certification of originality and independence.

6. He resents her beginning to take possession of him.

7. He learns that he is subject to desire.

8. Maybe not love as we think of the word, but certainly the kind of protectiveness that responds to devotion.

9. When Camciscan rears up and falls with the girl (line 199); the rest is denouement.

10. Mutual respect—hers for his nobility, his for her fragile persistence.

# Annie Dillard

# Living Like Weasels

*Overview.*   Dillard introduces a number of important themes in this account of her accidental meeting with a weasel: wildness, the shock of recognition, human moderation, choice and necessity. At times here, her prose is calm, thoughtful, explanatory. But, characteristically, her chief intention is to dramatize what she considers virtually a mystical encounter (mystical meaning a lack of separateness between subject and object, herself and the weasel). At that point, her prose reaches a high pitch of violent figuration, as she skirts a passionate tendentiousness and goes further, perhaps, than we are willing to follow. That is, her emotion is beautiful but fanatical.

*In the Classroom.*   You may find your students taking either of two opposed positions on the essay. One supports the romanticism of Dillard's identification with the weasel; the other finds it unreal and wrong. You can steer a middle course by pointing out that her attitude permits us greater access to the secret life of wild creatures than we might otherwise have, and that—despite lines 94–107—her identification is largely metaphorical.

*Formal Considerations.*   Of structural interest are, first, Dillard's conclusion, which makes metaphorical use of the anecdote introduced in lines 5–19, and, second, the fact that the center of the essay is narrative (lines 20–82) but the center is not central; rather, her meditations on the experience are. You might point up Dillard's remarkable figures of speech, such as those in lines 9–10, 52, and 60.

## Looking Back

1. He valued the life of the innocent creature, whose assault was natural, not malign.

2. Answers will vary; students may see the image as strangely beautiful or grotesque.

3. The word *glance* connotes temporariness despite length.

4. Answers will vary.

5. Answers will vary, but the conflict between romanticism and realism may begin here.

6. It is shocking because it implies that the weasel, pursuing its secret subterranean life, has lessons to teach. *Remember* implies a primitive human state more valid and valuable than the present civilized one.

7. The distinction is between learning animality and learning to live in pure physicality.

8. The weasel's necessity is its basic instincts, appetites, needs; people elaborate on such things and choose among an array of possibilities they create, often leaving behind their original urgency.

9. Hyperbolic, but also symbolic of the spiritual state she desires. Note the more explicit statements in lines 108–109 and 114–115.

10. We can choose a course of action and follow it unswervingly as if it were a necessity, not a choice.

※

# Natalie Angier

# The Cockroach

**Overview.** Everything you never wanted to know about the cockroach is here. But to the disinterested eye, this seemingly unsavory subject (never so to the entomologist) is fascinating in its own right. After discussing potent methods of exterminating cockroaches as pests, which is probably of most interest to most readers (and which gives us a lesson in journalism), Angier moves into a detailed study of the cockroach as a species. The facts are interesting, often surprising. Ed Koren's accompanying drawings bring the insect closer to us, yet among the themes in the essay is the very "otherness" of the cockroach, as well as its likeness to our species. The writing assignments address this theme, along with specieism and the general sense emergent from the text that the cockroach is estimable.

**In the Classroom.** One approach to this article might be—no, not show and tell—to have students write down in advance of reading it their feelings about cockroaches. Then, after reading, have them explain how, if at all, their view of cockroaches has changed.

*Formal Considerations.* This article displays a number of journalistic features that capture and hold reader interest, including the prominent part played by facts, the results of interviews, careful explanation, and engaging prose (see especially the first two paragraphs and the final sentence).

## Looking Back

1. Devastatingly effective, because the new toxins attack the cockroach from many angles, work at low concentrations, and induce sterility.

2. Answers will surely vary.

3. Some nurture their offspring and "breastfeed."

4. Answers will vary, but a more positive leaning may result.

5. They have external receptors that can be manipulated, the head survives its separated torso for at least twelve hours, and animal activists don't disrupt cockroach studies.

6. Answers will vary. Most will probably agree with the statement, but an interesting view might be that, irrespective of specific qualities, every sentient being has inherent value.

7. Answers will vary, but again the intent of the question is to open new perspectives for students.

8. These factors have allowed cockroaches to flourish in human habitats more successfully than anywhere else, with the result that they no longer live in nature.

9. The cockroach has been around for so long that it well may outlast all attempts to exterminate it.

10. Answers will vary, but surely it's a cozy view.

---

## The New York Times

# Animal Rights Raiders Destroy Years of Work

*Overview.* This brief newspaper article reports a specific action by animal rights activists against a university science laboratory. Although the article seems to be straight journalism, some of its language and the fact that activists are represented mainly by the slogans they left behind raise questions of objectivity. Other questions, posed by the Writing Assignments, have to do with conflicts between medical research and animal use, the use of pelts, and degrees of violence used in protest actions (this last again bringing up the issue of charged language).

***In the Classroom.***   The chief aim of this reading is to open up the issue as widely as possible, not to close it down by means of possibly irreconcilable positions. One way to open the debate is to examine language use; another is to weigh the Animal Liberation Front's claims against Professor Aulerich's.

***Formal Considerations.***   The editorial decisions referred to in all three Looking Ahead items are translatable into student writing. The third, about language, is discussed above and as answers to Looking Back questions. The headline and subheads can be seen as essay titles, and the cutting of articles easily relates to the process of selecting important points for inclusion.

### Looking Back

1. The headline focuses on destructiveness. It could have read "Animal Rights Raiders Block Research."

2. Answers will vary.

3. Animal Extermination Department.

4. Answers will vary, but it does seem a biased term.

5. The first is militant, the second deliberative; the implication is that the first deals more in direct action, the second in persuasion.

6. Answers will vary.

7. Answers will vary, but the nature of his research should be taken under consideration.

8. Again, answers will vary, depending on one's basic position.

9. Perhaps that it's indiscriminate.

10. Answers will greatly vary.

# Wallace Stegner

# Thoughts in a Dry Land

***Overview.***   Stegner is never more a spokesperson for the American West than in this essay. He describes its geography and climate to demonstrate its strict difference from other regions and establishes the history of Americans' understanding of that difference. This understanding has come gradually, and achieved on an individual basis, it still takes time, as Stegner demonstrates, to produce this "process of westernization" (line 248). Two of the chief principles of this process are adaptation and cooperation. Adaptation is opposed to reverting to the familiar (as Stegner's visiting aunt did) simply because the known world is more comfortable. And cooperation replaces individuality as a guide to action. These themes inform the Writing Assignments for this reading.

**In the Classroom.**   Stegner is very history-minded and thus makes many references to people and places that might be obscure to your students. It is unnecessary to pause at these references and inadvisable to allow your students to worry over them (although Number 2 in Looking Ahead does recommend inspecting a map of the region). The main thing is to make sure students recognize the important themes (referred to above) that Stegner pursues.

**Formal Considerations.**   It is interesting to note in this piece the juncture of the critical and the personal essay. Stegner presents a scholarly study of western exploration and settlement, not to mention topography, but he also introduces his Aunt Min and, particularly in the last paragraph, talks directly to us in conversational tones. The mixture is salubrious.

## Looking Back

1. In its plains, deserts, mountains, and other land formations (see lines 4–11).

2. Aridity.

3. He doesn't say, so answers will vary, but he seems to assume there is always some connection between fact and fiction, myth, legend, and history that creates competing versions of a matter that eventually sort themselves out.

4. "[I]ntelligent leadership, community settlement . . . the habit of cooperation and obedience" were valuable (lines 116–117); individualism was not. The distinction between them is the social impulse implicit in the cooperation that was essential in the face of the West's harsh physical environment.

5. Without adaptation, newcomers would wrongly apply principles of settling and farming relevant to other conditions and thus would raid and ruin the West (see lines 132–147).

6. People could settle and build only near water; because water was scarce, they gathered together in so-called oases separated by waterless plains, mountains, and deserts.

7. She was too self-involved to see anything, and when she did look around, all she could do was to assimilate the new, strange sights to old, familiar ones, which is another way of not seeing.

8. The way we see truly matures through experience and effort, as he understands by reviewing particularly the early illustrations of Baron von Egloffstein, whose distortions owed to inexperience of the western terrain.

9. Answers will vary.

10. Answers will vary; there is evidence on both sides.

# Linked Readings

Leonardo da Vinci
THE NATURE OF WATER

Fernand Braudel
SOMETHING TO DRINK

Joan Didion
HOLY WATER

Alain Robbe-Grillet
REFLECTED VISION: THE WRONG DIRECTION

*Overview.*    As the titles indicate and the headnote confirms, water is the common topic about which different treatments create a new context in which to view it. Leonardo approaches water as if no one had thought about the subject before, or as if he were a visitor from another planet experiencing it for the first time. Such a view is exemplary in that it takes nothing for granted and risks being mocked for stating the obvious in order to be definitive. After we read this text, it is difficult for us not to look at bodies of water with different eyes. Complementing Leonardo's geological perspective is Braudel's historical treatment of water, drinking water in particular. He describes the great efforts necessary to ensure a supply of potable water on various continents, as well as the economic and city planning measures related to water. He also reviews different kinds of water and the value placed on them. Didion, like Wallace Stegner in the preceding reading, addresses aridity as the dominant climatic condition in the American West. She describes in precise detail, and with personal references, the operations of the California State Water Project. Robbe-Grillet invites us to look down into the water. Or does he? The individual who approaches the small pond he describes can't see straight and quickly turns away. At the end, if less grandiose, Leonardo's brutal, inhuman element remains.

**In the Classroom.**    Getting students to find a common denominator in these readings is important. The thread might be supplied by Didion's title, "Holy Water": a sacred monster (Leonardo), the faith we live by (Braudel), salvation (Didion) and eternal stillness (Robbe-Grillet). If students can say how each author evokes the sense he or she assigns to it, they will demonstrate both an understanding of each text and an appreciation of the total context.

*Formal Considerations.*    The nobility and power of Leonardo's prose owes to his syntax and his vocabulary. You can highlight the final paragraph for its near-biblical tone. The preceding paragraph is a model of unity. This is part of a chapter, not an essay, but it shares the characteristic tendency of essays to be nourished by facts. These facts may be the result of scholarship, as in

Braudel, but memory and investigation may also produce them, as we see in Leonardo and Didion. The second Looking Ahead item for Didion alerts students to her own involvement in her subject, an object lesson for writers of the personal essay. Robbe-Grillet's meticulous description tests students' reading ability. Particular words are crucial to the description, such as "feltlike" (line 5), "steeping" (line 11), "cylinders" (line 19), and "unwrinkled" (line 51).

## Looking Back

1. "With time everything changes," writes Leonardo (line 24), and we see that the preceding description, especially the initial sentence, finds its summation in that.

2. His observations form the basis for his insights and supply the details that authenticate them.

3. That population centers have always had to bend every effort to ensure a supply, sometimes taking desperate measures, and often not succeeding very notably.

4. As consumption inevitably grows with increased population density, availability of resources diminishes.

5. Yes or no, but contemporary examples are found on supermarket shelves holding the many varieties of bottled water.

6. Both show their deep concern with and remarkable knowledge of water delivery systems.

7. Answers will vary, but clearly any possible danger seemed less important than the thrilling sensation she experienced. Being moved involuntarily on the surface of a substance that parts to the touch is, perhaps, a form of spiritual transport.

8. She would like to exercise some control over a system that fascinates her, partially because it is at the heart of Californian reality.

9. Appearances, because they engage the viewer first, often stop that person from learning the reality behind them and thus become a substitute for reality.

10. That water is awe-inspiring and dangerous if uncontrolled but essential to human life and therefore necessary to control and refine.

# Loren Eiseley

# The Brown Wasps

**Overview.**   Eiseley, like the most appealing poets, finds not only correspondences between various forms of life but a unity among them that serves the overarching purpose of discovering and making known the *decent* permanencies of existence. As he says, "We cling to a time and a place because without them man is lost, not only man but life" (lines 43–44). Included in this statement are homeless old men, wasps (the title of the essay is symbolic of all), slugs, mice, pigeons, and the author himself. In a country whose inhabitants seem constantly on the move from one dwelling place to another, the concept of permanency—of home and, by implication, of values—seems more and more tenuous. For this reason, perhaps, its urgency is all the greater.

**In the Classroom.**  Eiseley moves his focus from one form of life to another, so it is important for students to grasp their binding element. For this purpose you can ask students to point out the places where the author looks back at what he has described and makes explicit points about his topic.

**Formal Considerations.**  Notable among Eiseley's subtle structural decisions is his initial mention of the "nonexistent tree" that has shaded him much of his life (line 58) and his return to that subject in the long conclusion (beginning on line 188); the tree framework puts his own existence squarely in the midst of those others he has described.

## Looking Back

1. They have come there to find not only warmth and shelter but, more important, a place to exist, however temporarily, among others of their kind.

2. We know ourselves in terms of where we have been most able to be ourselves.

3. The onslaught of such transfigurations of life half convinces us that any roots we put down are illusory. To counter such a situation, we need to consolidate our original position (spiritually as well as physically).

4. The field mouse was trying to reconstruct his original world.

5. Answers will vary depending on tenderness, which is Eiseley's most outstanding characteristic.

6. It is as terse as what it describes: form matches content.

7. The El was home to both, and both return to it.

8. See Formal Considerations above.

9. The tree was his one link to a safe world, a world in which love and care existed but which he lost early in life. Discovering that the tree no longer existed was a blow, but a sustainable one, since it was the idea of the tree more than its actual existence that mattered.

10. Eiseley is not lying; he lives there spiritually.

≈❧≈

# D. H. Lawrence

# Reflections on the Death of a Porcupine

*Overview.*    Perhaps no major British or American fiction writer in the twentieth century was more involved with nature—or less able to extricate himself from it, depending on your view—than D. H. Lawrence. Lawrence seems to write from *inside* natural phenomena and beings; he is never a mere observer or user (one remembers the shame he evinced at riding a horse, thinking maybe it should be the other way around). Yet it is what he surfaces with that gives his involvement meaning, a meaning that he wants the human species to have. Here, it is the need to face life directly, the necessity to struggle for existence against "the lower orders of life" (line 190), the importance "of power and of vividness" (line 260), and the unreality of equality.

*In the Classroom.*    Students should ultimately be able to discern Lawrence's principles of existence, first as they emerge from the experiences he describes in the first part of the essay, and second as they form a lengthy and independent philosophical statement (beginning with line 260). If students find Lawrence's reasoning offensive, you should remind them of his claim that he is discussing types of life, not individuals (see lines 323–327), although even this is not wholly convincing. Lawrence's is a voice not heard much anymore; listen to it for that reason alone.

*Formal Considerations.*    As noted above, the essay fairly breaks in two at line 260, the point at which the concrete segues into the abstract. The list of propositions he compiles (lines 301–317) is an interesting device, but students should notice that he supports these assertions; he does not simply make them. And notice his five-point "law of life," which has a similar function, though it is more fully elaborated.

## Looking Back

1. He found the porcupine repulsive and didn't want to get too near it.

2. The disgust he feels for the porcupine extends ultimately to the dog when the latter makes removing his quills so difficult.

3. Clearly symbolic; the statement means one must confront life, whatever its aspect, head on, not evade its reality.

4. Answers will vary, but students should at least hesitate to take this to the level of Social Darwinism.

5. Answers will vary, but one should delay in making these distinctions, especially when on the losing side, since their consequences seem all too permanent.

6. According to Lawrence, vividness is a quality that establishes superiority to the degree it characterizes a sentient being. By this logic, humans cannot be judged equal if they can be found to be more or less vivid (full of life).

7. Answers will vary, but surely he is not a racist as we commonly recognize this sociopathic type (that is, the Laurentian cast of mind is largely absent in American society). He does, however, seem to believe some races are superior to others, in the way some species of animals are thought to be superior (an extremely suspect belief), and this can argue for his racism.

8. Fullness of being creates uniqueness, yet the unique being relates to other beings against whom it must struggle for its very life. The winner is by definition the most vital, a quality that has its source both in the winner's species and in its own unique being. The vitality comes largely from the conquest of lower creatures and allows the fulfilled being, the winner, to enjoy a cosmic consciousness deserving of a unique being. The logic is circular.

9. Authoritarianism, dictatorship, superiority of a single caste, fascism.

10. Money-making as a life motive transforms the vital spirit into a material possession; it turns one's eyes to other human beings for the purpose of exploitation, instead of toward a world that cannot be bought or sold.

# PART IV: SOCIAL REALITY

❧

## Laurie Anderson
## Politics & Music

***Overview.***   One of the most versatile artists in America today, Laurie Anderson more frequently criticizes cultural and social forms than political behavior, but her sense of the absurd certainly has room for that target as well. This piece is satire of the lifted eyebrow sort; it is not savage, not partisan, simply a dismissal of self-interested and deceiving politicians generally, and of a few notorious figures in particular. Her position is pretty well summed up in her rhetorical question, "I mean, just how do people convince each other of things that are basically quite preposterous?" (lines 22–23).

***In the Classroom.***   As the headnote points out, satire typically aims at producing a new way of perceiving reality—a more accurate way, the satirist hopes— and at inspiring corrective action based on this new perception. You might ask your students if they think this satire succeeds in doing these things, and if so, what are their new perceptions and what actions do they think are called for.

***Formal Considerations.***   The first and third Looking Ahead items alert students to two important matters in prose writing. One is the distinction between writing and speech and the implied need to make this distinction in essays (see number 2 in Looking Back). The second is the type of conclusion practiced here. The excerpt from a popular song that ends this piece, though not exactly the way most students will conclude their work, crystallizes the author's criticism of politics to produce more a coda than a summary.

### Looking Back

1. It's a much more formal statement than a casual piece of this sort would usually include (this incongruity is typical of Anderson's style).

2. The "I mean" initial phrase is a common introductory maneuver in speech made by people who hesitate to discomfort their hearers by a bare statement. The word *guy* is characteristic of speech usage; the more formal *man* usually occurs in writing.

3. Answers will vary, but the evident humility is appealing.

4. If, like Sonny Bono and Alice Cooper, singers are becoming politicians, a simple reversal is all it takes to make politicians singers.

5. A traveling salesman. Hitler's speeches, described musically, were attempts to sell a bill of goods.

6. It should seem odd, though of course all customs are in some sense inventions.

7. She claims they loot nature (symbolized by the Christmas tree, once a simple fir) and that their tendency to mobilize music, as it were, instead of simply letting it be, excites their aggression.

8. Answers will vary, but opera singing usually is eloquent in its passion, not so coarse that it appeals to the hoi polloi.

9. Repetitions (in order better to play to the galleries), the use of *this* indicating speaker and listeners, literal pauses to refer to that behavior, final crescendo (indicated by boldface).

10. The closing quotation implies that Reagan and other politicians pander to people's unrealistic desires to have their fantasies come true instead of calculating plans on realistic bases.

## Linked Readings

### Pauline Kael  Robert Gard  Chance Stoner
### CAMPUS LIFE (THE 1930s)

### Students for a Democratic Society
### THE PORT HURON STATEMENT (1962)

### Nicola Chiaromonte
### THE STUDENT REVOLT (1968)

*Overview.*   Social malaise and how it is registered by college students are the elements that bind these readings, the first from the Depression era and the second two from the agitated and explosive 1960s. The 1930s students testifying in Studs Terkel's oral history of the Depression were poor; the SDS members and the students Chiaromonte criticizes were, according to the Port Huron Statement, "bred in at least modest comfort, housed now in universities, looking uncomfortably to the world we inherit." The language of this statement is telling. We may wish to conclude from it that mere discomfort—and nothing more—is the most likely outcome of this kind of upbringing. The thirties students, starting from a very different position, had a more radical analysis of class in America. Still, the SDS document eloquently states ideals of social justice, and it is necessary to remember that just a few years later these and other students were in the forefront of anti–Vietnam War activities that tested their resolve and often enough sent them down beneath police clubs. Were their activities, in this later incarnation, legitimate? Chiaromonte doesn't think so.

*In the Classroom.* Students may fail to recognize themselves in these readings; they may find the context remote. On the other hand, they may identify with the sixties students in a kind of false nostalgia for a time perhaps more vibrant than their own. Neither attitude is particularly useful as a way of absorbing and understanding these texts. Students should be able to recognize and deal with the intellectual energy apparent here and the social and political ideas that are enunciated. And they should be able to appreciate Chiaromonte's challenge to the actions fed by this energy and inspired by these ideas.

*Formal Considerations.* The contrast between speech and writing is clear in these texts; it is always useful to help students see what writers must do that speakers, in the presence of a listener, often feel no compulsion to. Notice the numbered program that comprises the last part of the Port Huron Statement. This is a useful structural variant, even in essay writing, wherein authors can conclude by itemizing what they have been driving at. Chiaromonte's piece demonstrates the compelling tie between analysis and argument: he minutely examines forms of student revolt and proposes a form different from those he sees.

## Looking Back

1. The authors in "Campus Life" testify to intense political involvement; the SDS authors' direct involvement is not made clear, but their intellectual attachment to political issues is quite apparent; Chiaromonte, in this piece, is a commentator; his ideas of "determined secession" (line 154) point to a certain detachment. How their degrees of involvement shape their politics is a matter of opinion; answers will vary.

2. Answers will vary, but students should be able to distinguish these different forms of response.

3. A self-willed separation from the greater life of the community.

4. Kael: political reaction on the part of the college administration; Stoner: likewise; SDS: student apathy is a result of "the structure and organization of higher education itself" (line 122); education falsely divides study and its application to the real world; academic bureaucracy defeats the possibilities of social criticism (see paragraph beginning with line 146); Chiaromonte: conditions in Italian universities are "scandalous" (line 90), though he doesn't explain further.

5. Answers will vary, but generally college students, in their studies and often as a function of their absence from the work force (a disappearing phenomenon), are in a position to produce critical analyses; that is, they can perform as intellectuals without undue hindrance.

6. Answers will vary, to say the least.

7. Kael: the rich clothing of some of the college students indicates their incomprehension of social and political realities; SDS: mere contentment with

prosperity is excessive, in that it is a self-deception; it hides actual anxieties about American society; Chiaromonte: "For has modern man, in his collective existence, laid claim to any god or ideal but the god of possession and enjoyment and the limitless satisfaction of material needs?" (lines 134–136); thus the author criticizes consumer society.

8. The "Campus Life" readings chiefly reveal academic authoritarianism; Chiaromonte reports a worldwide situation in the sixties in which the desire for freedom bespeaks not only a perception of its absence but the need for legitimate order. The SDS document conducts the most extensive analysis. "The Port Huron Statement" criticizes a society in which racism, poverty, unemployment, and waste of physical and human resources are common. Answers will vary as to whether this picture obtains today.

9. Reform normally works within the prevailing economic, social, and political systems; revolution seeks to change these systems radically on the grounds that they are dysfunctional and unjust. Kael seems to have lent her energies to political parties that profess revolution; Stoner, working to reform university policies, may have taken revolutionary measures to do so; so much depends on context. SDS actively sympathizes with revolution abroad (a sympathy Chiaromonte finds misdirected) and claims that "revolutionary leadership" is a worldwide need (line 36), but most of the SDS proposals seem reformist in nature.

10. The communal living and local unions glimpsed in "Campus Life" yield, in some respects, to SDS's national student movement with its numerous chapters. Chiaromonte refers to mass action only, but obviously mass action is organized by smaller political groups.

🌿

Andrew L. Shapiro

# Reading, Writing, and Ignorance: Education and Achievement

*Overview.* Shapiro's view of American education is a bleak one. He supports this view with statistical analyses that include comparisons of private and public spending for education within the United States and comparisons between America and other developed nations on the bases of spending, test scores, public policy, attitudes toward education and personal achievement, and more. Statistics, though they can be manipulated for devious ends (that does not seem to be the case here), are a particularly compelling kind of facts. Perhaps the most alarming use Shapiro puts them to here is to indicate certain disparities between belief and actuality.

**In the Classroom.**   The *number* of written and graphic findings in this study threatens to overwhelm the reader's grasp of the educational situation in the United States as a whole, so you should probably put some emphasis on students' producing a synthesis of Shapiro's discrete analyses. Do not assume in your students a perfect ability to read and understand charts; select at least one for your class to analyze together.

**Formal Considerations.**   Shapiro serves the purpose of clarity by using the "**We're Number** _____" formula, making abundant use of subheads, and employing boldface typography. These are of interest in themselves, but they also underscore the general aim of discourse: to make a lucid presentation. The charts are *inserts* in the normal text and as such model more than themselves (for instance, longer quotations and iconographic inserts that can enliven and change a text).

## Looking Back

1. High dropout rates, high student-teacher ratios, deteriorating physical plants, lack of educational materials, resulting in an uneducated populace on the one hand and a badly educated one on the other.

2. Public spending increases as property taxes go up; in districts with lower property taxes, states are expected to make up the difference. In practice, this seems not to be the case (see lines 66–85).

3. Answers may vary, but as Shapiro points out, "quantity does not always guarantee quality" (line 93).

4. Middle-class parents earn too much for their children to qualify for Head Start but not enough to afford private preschool education for them.

5. Answers will vary depending on personal experience, but, as shown in the relevant chart, the United States is near the bottom in number of days children attend school, below many countries whose children we probably think are safer on the streets than ours.

6. Answers will vary, but it should be noted that Shapiro speaks entirely to traditional measures of students' readiness for college, never to the democratization that open admissions policies attempt.

7. Self-deception, ostensibly based on believing that they can't be bad at what they're supposed to be good at.

8. Answers will vary, depending on how personal freedom competes in students' thinking with a possible obligation to serve national interests.

9. Answers will vary, but, given the chart demonstrating hours per day of television watching, this variable should be part of the discussion.

10. Compulsory school attendance and enrollment in colleges and universities. American culture values high production rates; overemphasis on quantity

often sacrifices the quality of what is produced. (In recent years, American-made automobiles were a case in point, though this situation seems to be changing.)

❋

# Vera Brittain

# Women Workers, Today and Tomorrow

**Overview.**   Writing during World War II, and looking back to the first world war, Brittain is especially conscious of how wars on this scale change social conventions and traditional assumptions, and how these changes give women new economic and social opportunities. She carefully details the transformation of women's working lives as well as the continued presence of wage and other inequalities. Although she denies the possibility of absolute prophecies about the development of women's position in the economy, she is generally optimistic. This particularly emerges in the closing distinction she draws between potential employers looking for *a* woman and employers looking for *the* woman.

**In the Classroom.**   It may be that much attention has been distracted in recent years from the basic feminist demand for equal work conditions and paid instead to women's cultural situation. This essay refocuses the original demand to good effect since the conditions producing it still exist. The purported unfairness of unequal wages for the same work is a topic most students can easily address.

**Formal Considerations.**   Brittain repeatedly uses subordinate clauses to open sentences throughout this essay. The results are left-branching sentences (a phrase or clause branching left from the main clause), with its particular capacity of setting conditions, establishing time, designating place, and so on. It is useful to make students consciously aware of this sentence form.

## Looking Back

1. War reveals the outmodedness of certain social and cultural traditions, whose foundations are now seen to have been baseless prejudices, and prepares the way for new possibilities.

2. Generally streamlined trends should inform these references, but answers will vary depending on observation and fashion.

3. Equal trust of the sort that eliminates discrimination bred by mistrust.

4. It opens the issue about to be discussed, which will now appear as an answer to the question, instead of as the fulfillment of a stated intention to proceed in this way.

5. His directives have used the force of law to remove women between certain ages from traditional employment and enlist them in occupations more necessary for the war effort.

6. Clearly, their wartime occupations offer them career opportunities unavailable in prewar days.

7. Sexual distinctions should not dictate the type of work people may do. Answers will vary on response to this principle.

8. "[L]imited opportunity and unequal pay" (lines 79–80), which result in the exploitation of women's labor and the denial of women's equal rights.

9. Engineering, Civil Service, Foreign Service.

10. See the last sentence of the Overview; students will also add their own definitions.

✼

# Ronald Takaki

## Different Shores

*Overview.*    Takaki's chief aim in this piece is to mount a defense of affirmative action, particularly as a rebuttal of the points Thomas Sowell makes against it. Takaki pursues this aim, however, only after having established the existence of a rich ethnic and racial diversity in the United States and the presence—seemingly correlated to this existence—of social and economic inequality. The fact that Takaki is thus politically engaged in what is, after all, the introduction to a collection of essays by other hands on race and ethnicity demonstrates the importance he believes affirmative action has for the future of equality in this country.

*In the Classroom.*    Since Takaki begins with personal and social history, both of which testify to the need for equality, students may accept his defense of affirmative action and his criticism of Sowell too easily; that is, their own critical discernment may have been softened by Takaki's appealing exordium. You may, therefore, want to urge them to examine affirmative action for merit dispassionately.

*Formal Considerations.*    As noted above and in the second Looking Ahead item, Takaki's structural decisions in this piece put him squarely in the situation he addresses. This refusal to separate self from objective conditions not only opposes psychological alienation but represents a formal nonfiction strategy to authenticate views and take personal responsibility for them.

## Looking Back

1. Answers will vary, but many students may confess total ignorance or a very truncated knowledge of this history.

2. That if you don't look like some fictional image of the American, you're a foreigner.

3. Answers will vary, but the spread of multiculturalism may affect responses.

4. Takaki merely comments on this evidence of the importation of laborers and America's resultant racial diversity. We might note the list's brutal lack of discrimination between things and human beings.

5. Answers will vary, but in recent years immigration has become a pressing concern for many Americans (remember Proposition 187 in California in 1994).

6. Sowell believes hard work and the Protestant ethic, not political action, enable success.

7. Answers will vary.

8. Takaki criticizes Sowell's use of unrepresentative samples, his neglect of crucial factors, and his faulty interpretation.

9. Answers will vary, but students should refer to the text to support their views.

10. Answers will surely vary.

⚜

# Mary Man-Kong

# Memories of My Mother

*Overview.* This essay is a measured yet heartfelt memorial tribute to the author's deceased mother. The style is plain, but the feeling is eloquent. The mother is at the center throughout, but the whole family is present as well. The existential anguish of a loss to death is the keynote, but the author uses it to bring in other themes that directly pertain to the greater community: the role of traditional culture in marriage, the effects of patriarchal attitudes in the family, the influence on daughters of their mothers' subordination, received values, and prejudice. As implied above, the virtue of this full bill is that Man-Kong does not introduce these themes in a heavy-handed or tendentious manner but, rather, as natural extensions of life in the family.

**In the Classroom.** The issues noted above, deriving ultimately as they always do from concrete situations in real life, require conceptualization if they are to apply to situations other than Man-Kong's. The wording of both the Looking Back questions and the Writing Assignments helps in this respect, but there is much for your students still to do. Because the danger of *over*conceptualization is to forget the particulars that gave rise to abstraction, you will probably want to maintain a strict tie between event and idea about it.

**Formal Considerations.** The introductory paragraph and the concluding three paragraphs are impressive models for essay writing. In the first paragraph, the lack of pronoun referent in the initial sentence, the concrete details, and the stark candor of the final sentence lock in the reader. The conclusion is contemplative. It draws attention to the writer's thinking, and yet it ends with a powerful attribution to the dead, who has been the central focus throughout.

## Looking Back

1. As a mother and wife, indeed; or nurturer and housewife.

2. We need that person's approval and warm presence.

3. The first two are perhaps normally ascribed to fathers, the third to mothers (at least in traditional families or in those in which a man is present).

4. The mother's ideas of what are legitimate occupations and reasonable achievements conflict with Steven's vocational plans and the author's aptitudes.

5. Answers will vary, but we're probably chilled by his distance from the children, and even more so because the author lets her description speak for itself.

6. She now doubts the sincerity of her mother's previous moral teaching; her mother seems a stranger.

7. Her mother stereotypes blacks; she thinks one's station in life is lowered by association with "inferiors."

8. Answers may vary, but clearly her traditional sense of deference to her husband is at work here; she recognizes the father as the head of the family.

9. She is alienated from her mother; she loses sympathy with her and thus cannot easily imagine her situation (though in retrospect she does).

10. Although her mother's spirit does not now console or help her (after all, her mother failed to do that sufficiently in life), the mother's loss has been so painful that her absence must be filled in by a renewal of family feeling.

# Stanley Crouch
# Nationalism of Fools

***Overview.***   As the headnote indicates and the title makes plain, Crouch does not suffer fools gladly. The question, of course, is whether the individuals he targets in his polemic truly are fools and whether the social tendencies he criticizes so acerbically go—as he seems to think—even beyond foolishness into confused irresponsibility. Louis Farrakhan and the Nation of Islam receive most of Crouch's ire, but his focus is not narrow; he mounts a critique of black nationalism generally. He takes up the theme of separatism versus integration, reviews the recent history of the civil rights movement in the United States, and examines black anti-Semitism. Ultimately, Crouch is more than a gadfly. He is pained by what he considers false rhetoric and misused intelligence and, in effect, the betrayal of the real needs of African Americans.

***In the Classroom.***   Although Crouch published this essay some ten years ago, its concerns are still pressing; in fact, they are perhaps even more so than they were then. Encourage students to respond to them not as part of the historic record but as present reality. It goes without saying that membership in one ethnic or racial group or another should not dictate the parameters of one's interest in social reality.

***Formal Considerations.***   The first Looking Ahead item draws students to one of Crouch's structural decisions. Note also that Crouch begins and ends with partial descriptions of the rally at Madison Square Garden, further unifying his essay.

## Looking Back

1. Crouch reports the enthusiastic response, in numbers and in both general and individual attitudes, to the rally. Individuals testify specifically to the Nation of Islam's appeal. Tactically it is wise to affirm the opposition (superficially) or to concede minor points to demonstrate your fairness before engaging critically. Also, the order of importance argues for your real intention to be presented last so as to avoid anticlimax or weaken the intensity of your argument.

2. The white man is the evil genius behind black suffering; blacks should separate themselves physically, culturally, and spiritually from whites; America should cede a number of states to African Americans for their exclusive settlement so that they can become economically as well as politically independent. This agenda differed radically from the integrationist policies of the civil rights movement.

3. Crouch prefers King to Malcolm X. In lines 130–143, he argues that King used modern methods of protest and successfully exposed the evils of segregation; Malcolm was melodramatic and "conventional."

4. *Canonization* declares Malcolm a (false) saint instead of arguing that is what his followers made him into; *costume balls* also assumes falsity instead of giving evidence for it; *saber rattlers* points to unprovoked warmongering instead of arguing the point.

5. He fills the place that the failure of liberal and conservative local and national social policies has left. Despite treasuries spent and black leaders elected, the plight of African Americans has worsened.

6. Answers will vary, but he seems egotistical, periphrastic, illogical, and obscurantist.

7. He views the attack as absurdly misplaced, though he notes the immoral aid Israel gives to South Africa (under its white apartheid government at the time).

8. *The* lumps everybody together; scapegoat.

9. Answers will vary, but one disagreement with these views might be that Farrakhan speaks to the "grass roots" in a way others cannot.

10. Answers will vary, but besides the structural felicity gained, Crouch picks an image that crystallizes the absurdity and self-contradiction he accuses Farrakhan and the Nation of Islam of.

# Patricia Williams

# The Death of the Profane

*Overview.* This essay on prejudice and discrimination stems from a particular incident in which the author was refused admission to a clothing store because she was black. Williams reports the aftermath of the incident as one devoted to attempts to tell the story, both to express her anger and to analyze the meaning of the event. The obstacles she met in these attempts are instructive: they seem to further the original injustice by holding her judgment up to unnecessarily rigid standards. Included in her account are remarks on the policy of affirmative action which, as number 2 in Looking Ahead points out, is also discussed by Ronald Takaki (see pp. 411–418).

*In the Classroom.* The outrage committed against Williams will perhaps be registered by most students. For a balanced presentation, therefore, you might particularly emphasize the final Looking Back question, which asks students to address the questions Williams says she most commonly receives after talking in public about the Benetton's incident. You might also point up the irony of this happening in connection with this chain, since Benetton's advertises their apparel as "united colors" worn by people of different races.

**Formal Considerations.**   Although Williams's anger supplies a topic rather than the tone of this essay, her language is biting at times and ought to be noted for that quality. See particularly lines 16–20 and (more abstractly) lines 56–65. Looking Ahead item number 3 alerts students to a matter of structural importance in the essay.

## Looking Back

1. Answers will vary, but a contrast exists between innocence and a kind of stupid meanness.

2. Answers will vary, though probably most students will agree with Williams's judgment.

3. Answers again will vary, but this question invites students to imagine the psychological motivation behind looting as opposed to the desire for material gain (notice that the second Writing Assignment takes up this question).

4. Paraphrases will differ, but the "structure of power" is a reference to the exclusionary attitudes and behavior of the store clerk whose power was exerted to put them into effect.

5. This refers to the common prejudicial attitude that excepts a present (known) person from a practice seen as justified in terms of the mass of persons she is part of (and who are unknown).

6. Answers will vary, though many students will admire such direct action.

7. The topic points out that social injustice is often avoided as a judgment, implying the need for changes in policy or law, since the offenses are viewed as personal decisions only.

8. In this context, adopting the neutrality principle distorts reality instead of restoring balanced judgment.

9. Racial difference exists and is a factor in employment and other decisions despite "race-neutrality in law." The denial of racial difference enshrines a racist status quo, which mere equal opportunity cannot successfully address. Affirmative action makes up for the historic "omission" of African Americans in varied employment and social life and recognizes individual worth.

10. Answers will vary.

# Linked Readings

· Aldous Huxley
BRITISH HONDURAS

Katha Politt
MEDIA GOES WILDING IN PALM BEACH

Anna Quindlen
MAKING A CASE

*Overview.*   Sexual violence against women and the measures they may take to combat it are the topics these readings address. As the headnote makes clear, Huxley's piece has no *direct* relation to the issue, but instead it bears on choices. The connection? Huxley increases the subtlety of decisions women might make in the context of violence against them by analyzing the complex tie between a choice of action and the consequences stemming from that choice. Katha Pollitt rebukes the press to take a definite stand against revealing the names of rape victims, which she considers a wrong decision in almost all circumstances. Carolyn Field, the rape victim Anna Quindlen writes about, did decide to publicize her case. Quindlen devotes her entire column to Field and her point of view because she obviously agrees with her position. Besides the main issue of publicity, these readings introduce other issues that the Writing Assignments take up. These are blaming the victim, women's forceful resistance to attempted rape, sexual harrassment, acquaintance rape, and penalties for rape. The number and variety of these topics should make it clear that sexual violation is a grave social concern; the statistics on rape in the United States demonstrate that its incidence has not abated and shows no sign of doing so. Thus discourse on the subject is ever more urgent.

*In the Classroom.*   The Huxley piece can act as a kind of fulcrum between Pollitt's and Quindlen's essays, not to neutralize their different arguments (Pollitt opposes *involuntary* disclosure) but to test their full implications by acting as a mediating principle. The principle is that choice is impossible to evade but that choices are often fateful, and thus we must be prepared to repair their worst results, which we often cannot foresee. Acting on this principle, you can avoid a pro-con approach to the central issue of publicity given rape victims and have your students discuss the worst possible consequences of either decision and how they could be handled. This does Huxley one better, of course, by indeed imagining these consequences.

*Formal Considerations.*   Huxley's essay is a model of extrapolation: he explores an economic situation and discovers in it a principle applicable to human action generally. The opening paragraph of Pollitt's essay is notable for its shock effects, translatable into the writing strategy of capturing the reader's attention immediately. Quindlen's journalistic use of cliché is a good negative lesson in language ("The moment of truth" [line 1]; "We have made progress" [line 19]; "a one-woman crusade" [line 52]).

## Looking Back

1. We can't know the ends of our actions, and our ability to imagine how other people will respond is strictly limited.

2. We can never be confident about choosing because we can't see ahead to the consequences of our choices. Huxley says we nonetheless must choose and act, and then, if we cause evil, we should do our best to compensate for it. Students will have different opinions about this solution to the problem, but remember Huxley is talking about significant choices and distant consequences.

3. Lines 37–38.

4. The media are selective in what they report, duty or no duty; and anonymous charges are impermissible only in courts of law, where names are known.

5. The implied point here is that the owners' and managers' views do not necessarily serve any interests except their own, yet the information they make available harms others.

6. Answers will vary, perhaps wildly (this question may motivate much discussion).

7. Answers will vary, though this fact should not necessarily damage Pollitt's argument.

8. Pollitt probably intends the question rhetorically, but for purposes of examination it can also be taken as a real question. However students take it, their explanations will vary.

9. Pollitt submits that privacy is a positive and affirmative value, not merely a negative and defensive one, though it is rightfully that as well. Further, unwanted publicity is exploitative and prurient. Students should consider these points in coming to a conclusion about the force of privacy versus involuntary disclosure.

10. Answers will vary, but here Huxley as well as Pollitt might be brought to bear on the answer.

☸

# bell hooks

# Feminist Movement to End Violence

***Overview.*** The subtitle of hooks's book is *From Margin to Center,* which is telling since hooks, an African American, maintains that the feminist movement has largely been the creation of privileged women, women already at the center, and that to be whole the movement must produce theory generated by previously marginalized women. They, hooks maintains, have been forced by necessity to learn the center as well as the margins of life. Incorporating their interests in those feminism addresses will, she believes, result in a more powerful and effective movement. As she says in the preface to her book, "Throughout the work my thoughts have been shaped by the conviction that feminism must become a mass based political movement if it is to have a revolutionary, transformative impact on society." The present essay is part of that project. hooks argues that the causes of violence against women are entrenched in American social relations and political behaviors. To end violence against women will require uprooting these causes of violence generally, violence that is not exclusively male but that stems chiefly from imperialism and militarism.

***In the Classroom.*** The best understanding of a text is not always evident in the ability to synopsize the author's main points; it is sometimes more effective to be able to move to real life from theories about it in order to grasp the theories themselves. The first Looking Ahead item encourages this procedure, which you might want to take selective advantage of. A case in point is this: "Male violence against women in personal relationships is one of the most blatant expressions of the use of abusive force to maintain domination and control. It epitomizes the actualization of the concept of hierarchial rule and coercive authority" (lines 105–108).

***Formal Considerations.*** Despite the point made above, this is academic writing and needs to be understood on its own abstract terms. hooks employs many high-order concepts, some of which students are directed to in Looking Ahead items 2 and 3; you will no doubt identify others as being in need of definition.

## *Looking Back*

1. Hierarchial rule is based on notions of domination and submission: rank, privilege, gender, and others may determine such an order. Coercive authority is the use of powerful position to make others bend to a particular will. Together, these two punish women, violently if women anger or compete with men whose sexist notions will not be challenged.

2. When women buy into the male idea that the powerful should dominate, they may act violently themselves toward those even less powerful, such as children.

3. Used badly and rendered powerless by capitalism in all places but the home, men are encouraged to exert control and maintain supremacy there to maintain the illusion of power.

4. Answers will vary. hooks's analysis seems too pat, certainly, but to deny its terms might be a natural defensive reaction. Personal experience will be useful here.

5. Answers will vary. Women in the class ought to have some sharp opinions about this.

6. Answers will vary, depending on cultural influence and degrees of enlightenment.

7. Early childhood socialization of boys encourages them to believe violence earns rewards (including the love of women) from a society grateful to its heroes, and that violence is the invariable path to power and control. Violence, hooks asserts, is also taught by societal institutions and is so much a part of popular culture (exemplified by romance fiction) that its victims accept it out of fear of losing the love it is equated with. Black women are particularly subjected to abuse in school and on the job; they are moved to accept it by their need for the positive benefits of the classroom or workplace.

8. Acceptance of such a dualism is fatal to women's ability to assert and free themselves from various forms of domination and stereotypical thinking; it deprives them of autonomy and political will by lending them qualities necessarily submissive to men; it falsely exempts women from the population that needs to be enlightened about forms of violence.

9. Politics, hooks implies, is the road to power; women can gain power if they make political choices, but to do that they need to be viewed—by themselves and others—as agents.

10. Answers will vary, but students should engage hooks's arguments throughout the essay.

## Randy Shilts

## Heterosexuals and AIDS

*Overview.*   This chapter from Shilts's book is devoted to the incidence of the disease among a population that drug use, bisexuality, or need for blood transfusions has made vulnerable. As an investigative reporter, Shilts goes directly into the homes and lives (and onto the streets they walk) of people afflicted with the disease. He gives us an unblushing picture of their actual condition, quoting their speech, describing their persons, and reporting their behavior. This is not a form of what often is called the *new journalism,* in which the reporter is an actor in the drama, yet Shilts's closeness to the scene and the people he writes about is unmistakable. His own ruefulness about the early indifference to the disease does enter in (see lines 144–150, for instance), and his commitment is evident. Notable also is the way he shifts from narrating the situations of individuals with AIDS to reporting relevant historical and social data and then back again.

**In the Classroom.**    The more sensational aspects of this text are so evident that, unless their attention is directed elsewhere at times, students might lose sight of the more abstract points Shilts makes. One, present in the paragraph referred to above, is that it took heterosexual affliction to alarm authorities. Another has to do with "unheeded warnings [about the disease] and the lost opportunities [to stop or hinder its spread]" (lines 38–39). A third is the growing routinization of the disease.

**Formal Considerations.**    The selective use Shilts makes of the present tense to increase dramatic urgency is instructive, as is Shilts's extreme flexibility in moving from the general to the particular and from the concrete to the abstract.

## Looking Back

1. It allows Shilts's reportage to span the country, but more important, he can quote a physician on the gravity of the plague and make his own point about lack of preparation.

2. Answers will vary, but this question opens the issue of health control versus rights, which AIDS has sometimes brought to the fore.

3. A certain fatalism, perhaps. Certainly they value drugs too much to be cautious, but caution is never a component of the addict's mentality.

4. That the media are sensational and exploitative (implied criticisms), that they have a "profound heterosexual male bias" (line 144) that traditionally had neglected homosexuals' health problems.

5. Partially to show that there was evidence in other countries that indicated the possibility of heterosexual infection; specifically to give background to infection through contact with prostitutes (remembering Silvana Stangis is one); also because Shilts's concern is with the disease itself, not just with individuals who have it.

6. Answers will vary depending on how informed students are, but most students should see some progress in this area.

7. Answers will vary, but students should take into consideration concerns referred to here: possibly inaccurate results, possible use of the test to certify sexual orientation, discrimination based on results.

8. Answers will vary, perhaps depending on the nature of the students' community.

9. Probably the bare mention of their deaths contains its own commentary. Particularly see Shilts's remark that Stangis's end was "emblematic" (line 380): the *emblematic* requires no editorial treatment.

10. This refers back to his first mention, in line 105, and is an ironic reminder that the idealistic hopes of the late sixties, including those for the sexual revolution, have been blasted.

# Linked Readings

### George Orwell
### A HANGING

### William Bradford
### ANNO DOM: *1638* [ENGLISHMEN EXECUTED FOR MURDERING AN INDIAN]

*Overview.*   At this writing, the American public seems largely to approve of the death penalty being meted out for murder. That fact alone might be reason to believe that capital punishment is not a controversial issue any longer (though I don't subscribe to this view), but perhaps there is a more compelling reason to address the issue differently. When pro and con arguments have neutralized each other, or when they are moot in the face of actual policy, or when all arguments are stale, it is still possible to analyze the practice and understand what we have consented to. That is the chief direction the Writing Assignments for these Linked Readings take. An interesting link between the readings is that, in each, a colonial power executes criminals. The political motivation in Plymouth is obvious; the political reality in Burma must be inferred. In both, politics dissolves the difference between the execution of a colonial and a native.

*In the Classroom.*   Each of these texts contains one place at which editorial comment breaks into the narrative. Refer students to these (see Looking Back number 5 for Orwell and number 10 for Bradford) in order to help them understand the meaning of the events related.

*Formal Considerations.*   There is no view of the man dying in "A Hanging," no physical details of his last agony. After all, he dies out of sight, beneath the platform. But we begin to think that such details would, in the end, be less effective than those that surround the execution. They evoke the reality of a day on which a man loses his life. You might particularly call students' attention to these details where they occur. In Bradford's bare-bones prose, two uses of language are vivid: "drink tobacco" (line 24) and "scrambled away" (line 30).

## Looking Back

1. That he is hardly threatening, but rather weak and innocuous.

2. The combination of deadlines (no pun intended) and death is grating; despite the real situation, one wants to think there is all the time in the world for death to occur.

3. They were probably appalled that innocent affection should be shown the condemned man, since such a demonstration calls one back to life. The symbolic nature of the event is that the merciful tongue of innocence finds out the person most in need of mercy.

4. Only those who still belong to life take such delicate measures as avoiding getting their feet wet.

5. Because there is no visible cause, such as disease, for the man's death, killing him seems entirely arbitrary; it is mysterious in the sense that the crime for which he will die seems so abstract and distant compared to his presence before death that it explains nothing.

6. Those who are dead have no more anxieties; those still alive, like the witnesses to the execution, must continue suffering the pains of life.

7. Hysterical relief as the execution retreats into even this small distance in time.

8. His status is low and he is disreputable.

9. Peach's quoted speech, "'Hang him, rogue, he had killed many of them'" (line 27, the *he* suspicious here) evokes the war veteran who continues his legalized practice of killing when it is no longer sanctioned; his befriending the Indian was insincere, and his betrayal is therefore of a piece with his practice in warfare.

10. They don't believe white men should be punished so severely for crimes against Indians. The execution proceeds to placate the Indians and ensure peace in the colony.

# Linked Readings

Vaclav Havel
THE END OF THE MODERN ERA

Herbert L. Meltzer    Stuart A. Newman
Felipe C. Cabello    Gregory Hedberg
WITH APOLOGIES TO HAVEL, LET REASON RULE

*Overview.*    Through their op-ed columns and answering letters to the editor, daily newspapers often perform a valuable service by producing a dialogue that all may share in. Although newspapers usually cut off such an exchange after the original statement and responses, readers may continue it, as here students can address themselves to the arguments introduced on one side and the counterarguments on the other. In his address, Havel criticizes the uses to which reason has been put as control mechanisms that rationalize human social existence and diminish the importance of the individual. The first two letters take Havel to task; the third applauds him.

***In the Classroom.***   As is befitting the last reading in this section of the book, Havel's essay is perhaps the most difficult (the twin assumptions here being that materials should be organized to move from the simple to the complex, and that complexity is naturally difficult). As Looking Ahead number 3 makes clear, Havel and his respondents mainly use abstract language. Therefore, you will probably want to single out particular statements and ask students to produce their concrete equivalents or applications. This does not mean, of course, that students do not need to grasp both the abstract concepts and the nature of the argument.

***Formal Considerations.***   Quite a number of terms used by these authors, like *technocratic* and *utilitarian* (Havel, line 89), need definition. As the first Looking Ahead item points out, Havel's piece is structurally divided between presentation of the problem and proposal of the solution.

### Looking Back

1. The spirit of intellectual and material domination.

2. Communism as Procrustean bed; life, with all its wildness and unpredictability, as that which goes beyond any systematic attempt to confine it within narrow bounds.

3. He might have mentioned the inefficiencies of a command economy and the ruinous expenses of a gigantic military machine.

4. Answers will vary, but students might easily find applications of Havel's criticism in capitalist societies.

5. Answers will vary, but it should be noted that the letter writers point up the use of scientific method as a means of understanding and the direct application of science to practical problems, matters Havel doesn't address here.

6. Answers will vary, but the point could be made that the human qualities Havel enumerates are not incompatible with reason (except perhaps in the way he defines its most dominant presence) but, on the contrary, depend on its full functioning.

7. Answers will vary, but note that Havel in lines 97–102 lists what politicians should "cultivate."

8. A loaded question. Students first have to accept that these terms accurately characterize Havel's approach. Then, they must understand what the terms mean and what a principled appeal to them might involve.

9. Because nationalism seems to have been a major factor in so many disasters in recent years (the war in the Balkans is a prime example), it might be difficult to argue on its behalf. But Hedberg seems to view it as a local antidote to the global poison of communism, and so we might also see it positively. And we must remember that nationalism is a traditional response to invasion or control by other countries of one's own land.

10. Answers will vary, but this is the occasion to explore the arguments on either side.

# PART V: MORAL ACTION AND SPIRITUAL LIFE

## *Linked Readings*

Saint Matthew
THE SERMON ON THE MOUNT

Martin Buber (ed.)
WALKING THE TIGHT ROPE

***Overview.*** There is an essential difference between the spiritual injunctions these texts contain. This difference lies in the extent to which, to live a virtuous life, the individual is instructed to live in the world. Indicting the wrongful *thought* behind the sinful deed, Jesus is instructing his followers to eschew the world's judgment, to avoid entanglement in the world's affairs whose circumstances will necessarily compromise the individual's moral decisions. It is in this way, perhaps, that Jesus' command, "Be perfect as your father in heaven is perfect" (line 71), should be understood. On the other hand, Rabbi Israel's message is to achieve balance as a way of continuing to exist. We can interpret the spiritual intent of his parable to mean that people should live in the world and lean *against* the pressure of society in order to make moral decisions, which only the individual can do, and only when free from constraint. The texts come together on the basis of this distinction between them.

***In the Classroom.*** When you are teaching texts held sacred by particular religions, it is necessary neither to subscribe to that valuation nor to deny it. Rather, you would do best to regard the text as such: a written discourse that exists in its own right and that is subject both to basic comprehension and to interpretation, without ideological manipulation to make the text accord with established institutions or received ideas. Jesus is a plain speaker, but he deals in paradox, and paradox is a difficult logical construction for students to grapple with. You should point out its existence and the problems it creates. Likewise, parables produce a certain amount of difficulty because they require interpretation and application. When these lead to extrapolation, readers are doing critical thinking.

***Formal Considerations.*** As Lattimore points out in his introductory remarks, this translation of the sermon does not attempt a contemporary idiom but, rather, tries to be more faithful than earlier attempts both to the sense and the style of the original Greek. You might sample the King James Version and have students compare it with the present translation. As the first Looking

Ahead item points out, audience is a crucial element in considering the sermon. You might ask students which parts you think are addressed exclusively to the disciples and which to the "multitudes." Because parables are allegorical in nature, they require some substitution of terms for interpretation, a point you might make to your students.

### Looking Back

1. We can conclude they were the common people, subservient to the ruling class.

2. Literally, its pungency as a condiment to produce its particular taste sensation; figuratively, the power to be worthy and thus live up to elemental capacity (Webster's Ninth International Dictionary defines the idiom "salt of the earth" as referring to "a scattered elite").

3. He upholds the law of Judaism but intends to refine its practice in order to preserve its true intent and value.

4. See the Overview.

5. Affirm or deny honestly; don't try to claim authority for your view by alluding to some greater power.

6. Answers will vary, but see the Overview.

7. Each of these is a way of entering the world and becoming beholden to it; doing so necessarily compromises one's ability to be free of material considerations when making spiritual decisions.

8. There are a number of "lessons" here, but the golden rule (lines 134–135) seems dominant.

9. Living virtuously seems a matter of fine adjustments and careful measurements in order to enter a life you have chosen bounded by certain moral standards; it is to be distinguished from the life lived without any moral considerations.

10. Answers will vary.

✳

## Agnes Martin

## What We Do Not See If We Do Not See

*Overview.* In his introduction to the collection of Martin's writings, Dieter Schwartz cites the "absoluteness and timelessness" of her work. He is referring primarily to her paintings, but we might adduce those terms to her prose and add others, like purity, lucidity, precision, bluntness, simplicity, naivete . . . The list could go on, but you may notice that not all its terms are equally praiseful. Like her paintings, which as Martin says, "have neither object nor space nor line nor anything—no forms," Martin's prose is a direct product of her solitudinous thinking and therefore exists in a world of its own. Not completely, of course—no human product can manage that—but sufficiently so that it is difficult not to weigh her unworldliness in a scale that faults as well as applauds it. This reading expresses her view that the purpose of life is to fulfill one's own (and therefore everyone's) potential for work and creativity. Individual conversion will improve the general quality of life.

**In the Classroom.**   Looking Ahead 2 calls students' attention to two difficulties they might have with this text: its possible lack of "common sense" (hers is uncommon, as in "In crisis we say to ourselves: 'What can I do', and miraculously our mind answers and tells us what to do"; lines 22–23); and its tone of infallibility. The advice to students is to read patiently and absorb her language. In this respect, you might point up that her language bears more than a passing resemblance to that of some Sunday preachers.

**Formal Considerations.**   The text appears to be more in stanzaic than paragraph form, more like lines of verse than connected discourse. Nevertheless, these *are* paragraphs and frequently manifest principles of good paragraph construction (see lines 48–59, for instance); you might want to emphasize this factor here in order to assimilate this text to "normal" discourse. Often her style is purely epigrammatical: maxims substitute for explanation. As with all maxims, aphorisms, and the like, the reader is called on for explication.

### Looking Back

1. That she believes she speaks for everybody.

2. The "conscious mind" seems to be that part of the total mind that is never involved with emotion; it is detached, intellectual, produces an awareness of spiritual states, seems to be the seat of conscience.

3. True identity is a product of self-knowledge and understanding one's capability; as such, it gives access to the human.

4. Answers will vary, but students should be aware of the total transfer of responsibility here from legislation to self-conversion (in the second line reference, this view has implications for civil rights).

5. Artists are positive by nature, reproducing in their work not "reality" but the spirit of their own happiness; they affirm life, do not criticize it, meaning they eschew political comment. Artists are solitary; they commune only with themselves.

6. Answers will vary, but this view seems to contradict her use of the first-person plural pronoun. Everything depends here on how we define *experience*. In its extreme, this principle could eliminate the possibility of social existence.

7. See the Overview.

8. Inspiration is a command of the conscious mind; decision seems the result of will, not of understanding.

9. The conscious mind is the source of perfection (which means to reproduce the inspired spirit) and can be discovered and cultivated only when the artist is free of the distractions of the intellect and extraneous activity, that is, in solitude.

10. The mind acts as a kind of television set for the person; on its screen one sees what is necessary to do next to help fulfill the self, returning us to the title idea of seeing.

# Helmuth James von Moltke
## Letters to Freya

***Overview.***   Except for the famous attempt to kill Hitler in July 1944, too little is known about the continuing anti-Nazi resistance within Germany before and during World War II. Moltke's name is closely associated with that resistance, and he is one of many oppositionists whom the Nazis executed. The former American diplomat George Kennan, who met with Moltke a number of times in 1940, had this to say of the man: "A tall, handsome, sophisticated aristocrat, in every sense a man of the world, Moltke was also, at the same time, everything that by logic of his official environment he might have been expected not to be: a man of profound religious faith and outstanding moral courage, an idealist and a firm believer in democratic ideals" (*Memoirs 1925–1950,* pages 120–121). The excerpts from this correspondence with his wife reveal these qualities, which stemmed from his belief that eternal (or spiritual) law supersedes human law when the latter covers for crimes against humanity. Moltke wrote these letters from prison during days of interrogation by the Gestapo and after he was sentenced to death.

***In the Classroom.***   To appreciate the significance of Moltke's religious beliefs and human sentiments, students should be reminded that he expressed them under the worst of conditions: in prison, first uncertain of his fate and then all too certain, when many individuals would be stunned into incoherence or speechless with misery. In such a situation, it is also noteworthy that he doesn't deny his own human fragility but, rather, allows for it and comes to terms with it.

***Formal Considerations.***   In line with the above, the poise, distinction, and lucidity of his prose are notable. Notable also is the way Moltke, without sacrificing these qualities, retains his passionate attachment to life and his contempt for the antihuman. As well as his principles, his style is an object lesson for writers of every stripe who feel the pressures of existence grinding down their language.

## Looking Back

1. He certainly is not easily taken in; he has a skeptical character; he can be sardonic.

2. When death is not imminent (and when the body is not suffering toward death, as see Orwell's "A Hanging," page 487), consciousness deserts the coming event and refuses to conduct the necessary preparation.

3. As he says, we can never fully understand the nature of these figures' relationship to death, but a partial sense must be that no essential difference existed between death and life, that the former was a continuation in another form of the latter, and that therefore they did not fear death but rather welcomed it.

4. He is grateful for having remained in the hands of God, of not having been forsaken by Him, and thus for having kept his soul intact.

5. To paraphrase, our bodies house souls that testify to the greatness of God, and our bodies themselves are sustained by faith in Christ. He bequeaths this "treasure" of truth to Freya.

6. Answers will vary, but if Moltke is a kind of saint, he is a humanly recognizable sort.

7. In the shadow of death, he belongs to life, for which, after all, he is being martyred.

8. The Nazi judge raises the issue of law that masks evil versus law—whether God's or other humans'—that preserves the human and the good. In literal terms, the state's or God's?

9. We get the sense that, dying for the cause of humanity, Moltke feels sanctified, convicted in the good.

10. He feels as if he is the Lord's instrument, and only if his story becomes known will God's work come to fruition.

*❀*

# Bertolt Brecht

# Two Sons

**Overview.**   Brecht himself described this story in his journal as about "a peasant woman who spends 2 days struggling with herself and her family (including a son who is on leave) to slip half a loaf of bread to a starving prisoner. She does so and brings her soldier son to the allies in a cart, bound with cattle-ropes—to make him safe." In the actual story, the bread is a ham-rind and the complexity of the woman's moral struggle is far greater than this bare outline indicates, which perhaps is a lesson about reducing narrative to plot. The woman's moral nature undergoes an interesting change here, pro-gressing from a helpless inability to see the Other as anyone but one's own (she sees her son's face in the Russian prisoner's) to taking action of the sort that recognizes the primacy of moral principles. Her tale is doubly impressive because often enough people who do enunciate such principles—which the woman, a peasant, does not and perhaps cannot do so—nevertheless fail to act on them.

**In the Classroom.**    The Writing Assignments for this reading selection di-rectly address the moral implications of the events in the story; therefore, you should emphasize interpretation of the woman's action in these terms. A lesser approach to her decisions and her actions might point to her being overcome by her vision and to her practicality, which her "frenzied" son lacks. Perceiving these is crucial, but students should move also on to the moral issue.

**Formal Considerations.**    Brecht's spare prose points up conciseness as a sterling language value: to be concise is to be economical and, more important, to take up the slack. A sentence like "She lived in dread of what the enemy might do to her son, who was in the East" (lines 19–20) could serve as an exam-ple of concise prose and a fine rendering of a hypothetical wordy sentence, such as "She was terribly afraid that her son, who was serving in the German infantry somewhere to the east, would be gravely wounded or even killed by the enemy soldiers."

## Looking Back

1. Answers will vary, but daytime anxiety registered in dreams often pro-vides the connection.

2. Students may know nothing about the Hague Convention of 1907, but the practice is clearly illegal; the postwar Nurenburg trials also declared it a crime.

3. Recurrence points to a deeper source within the psyche than a single event would and thus is a phenomenon with strong implications for the per-son's overall mental state.

4. He is afraid, and fear often lashes out. Behind his behavior is his cer-tainty that, once freed by the enemy, the prisoners will incriminate him.

5. Answers will vary, but the use of such a term stems from the kind of them-and-us thinking that relegates the former to an inferior status and elevates the latter to a privileged position.

6. She doesn't think for herself but is subject to social conventions, including those of language. The fact that she doesn't question the aptness of the term demonstrates its wide acceptance and thus its effectiveness in justifying certain mental attitudes and the individual actions and state policies they support.

7. She has moved from empathy and compassion to active succor in a manner that demonstrates the full moral involvement of an individual in a strong position with those whose weakness threatens their continued existence.

8. She now can recognize the difference and respect his humanity; she doesn't have to assimilate the stranger to what she already knows before she can express human feelings.

9. Answers will vary. Seen from some perspectives, he may not have been, but he was her son. In any event, she had to save him in order to complete her moral action, and so he is worth it for that reason.

10. Answers will vary, but obviously she has achieved full moral stature, including freedom from subordination to the brutal rule of the menfolk.

## Julian Barnes

## The Visitors

***Overview.***   The events of this story and the motives of the characters seem perennially relevant. Hardly a year passes without some similar situation: terrorists (a loaded word, we should realize) fulfilling an ideological mandate engage in killing and hostage-taking. This dramatic situation of the story supplies the topic for the initial Writing Assignment, which raises questions of innocence. The remaining Writing Assignments take up the issues of personal opportunism and fraudulence, and examine the nature of the protagonist's moral dilemma and his seeming betrayal of the other passengers. Of course, it is not at all clear that Franklin Hughes's decision to give a speech to the passengers professing the terrorists' position is immoral. But his own innocence seems compromised by the nature of his life to date with which this action seems consistent.

***In the Classroom.***   The protagonist's decision to represent the Arab terrorists' position is the climactic event of the story. It is also the culmination of Franklin Hughes's entire personality and its moral character. Students, therefore, need to see its relation to his past life in order to analyze his decision fully. The expertness with which he delivers his speech indicates he was made for the job and implies that his hypocrisy and falsity continue in this guise. The question arises whether one can escape one's past. The fact that no one survives who could attest to his bargain with the Arabs (and therefore present evidence for his innocence, although it would not be proof of innocence in itself) further complicates the moral situation. Are witnesses to goodness necessary if it is to be understood as that? Are personal motives, even when laudable, sufficient to justify action that has bad social consequences? Is it possible that in such a situation a heroic resolve to range oneself against evil, with no thought for one's own or a loved one's safety, is the only right conduct? These are questions to present to your students.

**Formal Considerations.**   The interpretative necessities of parables surface in the protagonist's recollection of a TV pilot; here the concepts of self-interest versus altruism are explicitly deduced instead of being left to the reader to puzzle out, but the possibility of such an interpretation is clearly modeled. Likewise, argumentation as a topic comes out of the Arab leader's examination of the case.

## Looking Back

1. It's Franklin Hughes's contemptuous sense of his clients; also, the reference is to Noah's Ark and that voyage. To Hughes, these passengers seem as mechanical and inevitable as those who had no leisure to reflect on the need to embark.

2. We are intended to see him as a fairly meretricious personality, someone who has found a niche in a not particularly meritorious occupation and who wins love through fame rather than through personal qualities.

3. These otherwise admirable qualities seem self-serving in Hughes, helping him to avoid responsibility and candor.

4. We've been prepared for the change partially by mention of Hughes's having taken out an Irish passport in case of such contingencies (see lines 127–145). There is a hint of trouble in lines 177–178. And when the "visitors" make their appearance (line 205), the reference to them is as if they had arrived to attend the lecture.

5. Corinthians 11.6:17. As also in the Dead Sea Scrolls, the prescribed separation of the holy community from those who are profane, or "unclean."

6. His logic seems to be that if the law is broken on one side, the other side has no obligation to respect it. If law is to operate universally, however, and function to condemn evildoers, there must be those who live by it no matter what others do. If you believe in law, he is illogical; but since he dismisses the very possibility of law, he is logical.

7. Everyone is at risk, everyone is endangered; therefore, everyone will take measures to protect themselves, and no one is an innocent bystander.

8. Answers will vary, but see In the Classroom.

9. Answers will vary, but there are compelling points.

10. Ignorant of his motive in making the bargain, she believes he has betrayed the passengers by speaking for the "visitors." Indeed he may have, but he did not betray her.

※

## Scott Momaday

# The Priest of the Sun

*Overview.*    Here is a demotic engagement with the Gospel, with special reference to John, who likewise cites the Word at the beginning. The contrast between the Priest of the Sun Tosamah's rough, colloquial manner and the abstract intellectuality of John's conception is telling. But Tosamah is an exponent of the spoken word as well as a living exemplar of it, and so his choice is appropriate. In fact, the oral tradition is a major topic in this chapter of *House Made of Dawn* (excerpted here because it can stand alone). Tosamah lauds John's enthusiasm, his "instant of revelation, inspiration, Truth" (line 83), yet criticizes his having yielded to a belief system and in doing so having lost his original insight into the heart of the matter. Tosamah's intent in his sermon is to restore that Truth. Along the way, he comments on the sacredness of his Kiowa ancestry (he stands between the old and the new religions, amalgamating both, in the way Jesus' disciples did), the white man's world, and the child's purported faculty to contain all human experience.

*In the Classroom.*    If students truly grasp Tosamah's point, they will see that he considers theology less important than the truth that comes before it is constructed, and not only less important but a positive hindrance to that truth (see lines 98–106). The Truth Tosamah preaches is a perception of the elemental universe. Students should understand this, and also Tosamah's indictment of John as a white man, a less palatable view that they can take issue with.

*Formal Considerations.*    The distinction is drawn here between the emotional directness of speech, particularly in its storytelling function, and the syntactical complexities—oversubtle and obscurantist ones, as Tosamah tells it—of writing. This is a topic of the chapter but also, in Tosamah's sermonizing (which seems transcribed rather than written), the reader's experience. The strongest critique of the written word—as its use has developed—occurs in lines 147–156.

## Looking Back

1. It reverses the majority-minority relation and relegates the white majority to the status of a pet or secretary or whomever a day or week is devoted to in patronizing respect.

2. Shared poverty, a primitive state one associates with the early church fathers, perhaps.

3. Answers will vary, but his description is powerful and eloquent. He does slip from sound to word without explanation of the customary distinction we draw between them.

4. Makes it human, convinces the congregation he's one of them.

5. Truth is revealed, not disclosed. The idea of God results from middlemen disclosing it to the congregation. The moment of revelation is lost in the resultant tangle of dogma and exegesis.

6. Too much language produces needless complexity and portentiousness, is finally decorative and smothers the purity and clarity of its object. In the white man's culture, words replace the Word and thus degrade the power of language to engage the truth.

7. Storytelling is a kind of spiritual communion between teller and listener (see lines 132–139). We can also imagine the magical evocation for children of a world beyond the four walls of their room, a beloved teller lending her presence to the narrative, her voice proof of tenderness, as well as the oral characteristics of tone, gesture, expression, and so on.

8. Obviously, we could hardly give up writing and depend on speech alone, but we could refine our use of words (advertisements and political speeches are the traditional examples of what to avoid). With help, we could throw a lot away without loss. Put students' imagination to work here with a few sentences which they could reduce to decency.

9. Reverence for language is the connecting element (see lines 204–208).

10. Answers will vary, but he's a gas.

# Heinrich Böll

# Like a Bad Dream

**Overview.**   Heinrich Böll is never more effective as a moralist than when he is portraying decent, well-bred, entirely pleasant people—as in this story—who bear none of the more sensational marks of evil and yet are thoroughly immoral. "Like a Bad Dream" is a story about corruption in business practices and the ensnaring by the profit motive of the previously innocent, uncomprehending, but available narrator. Berthe, the wife, is calculating and hypocritical, yet her hypocrisy, as hypocrisy always does, testifies to at least the residue of conscience (" 'One should never,' she said gently, 'mention Christ's name in connection with money!' "; lines 30–31). The Zumpens are aged in corruption, and the Madonna statues they own far outnumber the narrator's, as if their hypocrisy had to work especially hard to fill the vacuum conscience once inhabited. By the end of the story, not only is the unethical deal consummated to everyone's satisfaction, but the narrator has taken an active part in working it out to his advantage. Still, his final words, "It is beyond understanding," point to his continuing moral vulnerability.

**In the Classroom.**   The plot is simple and direct, but certain details are crucial to the psychology and moral stature of the characters, and students should be able to interpret their meaning. Particularly see the presence of the Madonnas in these Catholic households, the narrator's original failure to propose the deal to Mr. Zumpen (showing his relative innocence at this stage), the narrator's noticing the acquisitive contours of Berthe's "wide and primitive mouth" (see line 95), and Berthe's statement that life is a matter of "compromises and concessions" (line 125).

**Formal Considerations.**   Berthe and her husband and the Zumpens are alike in giving self-interest priority over ethics, but, as indicated above, they also are different. The Zumpens may represent a later development of the younger couple. That is, Böll shapes a comparison and contrast that is obviously less explicit than expository writing would produce but that can serve as a model and possible source of a student exercise.

## Looking Back

1. It seems entirely superficial, conventional, and unimaginative, as if she were dressing a display dummy.

2. See the Overview. Also, we normally distrust such convenient compartmentalization.

3. See In the Classroom: he is still somewhat innocent.

4. Among intimates who know each other inside out, words are a comparatively crude means of communication; a look or a gesture is often sufficient.

5. He can't show affection to one who has revealed a powerful urge to capitalize on human relations, whose fresh red lipstick, we can interpolate, looks to him like blood.

6. She has a certain tartness that constricts the mouth; that is, the antithesis of generosity and amplitude as perceived by the soul.

7. The economic independence she desires for him can only be gained by corrupt business practices; therefore, its value is disastrously compromised.

8. Answers will vary. The context of her remark is what destroys its validity; in other contexts, it might be reasonable.

9. Mrs. Zumpen allows the narrator to raise his bid by fifteen pfennigs per square meter and still be the lowest bid (though Berthe writes in twenty-five pfennigs); Mr. Zumpen has the narrator make up part of this difference by writing him a check for "seven hundred" (marks).

10. How all this has happened, what it means, how he finds himself radically changed, from a person who never dreamed that he was capable of corrupt practices.

---

# Eric Rohmer

# The Baker's Girl

**Overview.** The subtlest of moralists, Eric Rohmer here portrays, in a most commonplace situation, a betrayal of trust and incipient caring that, though we never see the effects on the person betrayed, we shudder to imagine. The nameless narrator has been smitten by a woman he sees who lives in his neighborhood but who, before he can get to know her, disappears from sight. He then dallies with a shopgirl whom he by no means considers the equal of the mysterious Sylvia. The baker's assistant is young and innocent, cautious yet grateful for his attentions, and obviously vulnerable. She agrees to a date, but before the agreed upon night arrives, the narrator meets Sylvia again, who returns his interest. He stands up the baker's girl and justifies his behavior in the following words: "But my choice was, above all, *moral*. Having found Sylvia again, to have carried on with the baker's girl would have been worse than a vice: it would have been pure nonsense" (lines 362–364). We can think of alternatives to not showing up for a date, but we must question his claim to be moral when he dissolves morality into a near-aesthetic view of logic. The self-justifying ego's sad triumph announces itself.

**In the Classroom.** The narrator's rationalization for his behavior is a key element for students to fix on. It explains the true moral dimensions of his behavior toward the baker's girl. Another important aspect of the dramatic situation, however, is never explicitly mentioned, and that too students should realize: it is the class differences between the shopgirl on the one hand and the narrator and Sylvia on the other. They live in the expensive neighborhood she merely works in. Further, Sylvia's employment in an art gallery is considered glamorous, and the narrator is a law student, whereas the baker's assistant has a dead-end job (one she is going to leave for another that seems only marginally better). Class difference affords the narrator the moral distance he uses so selfishly.

**Formal Considerations.**    The narrator's point of view is an important formal element that helps shape the story (point of view being, of course, key to all written discourse). We receive the sense through his various references that he is no longer a youth when he relates these events (see, for instance, line 135), though he is still probably relatively young. He is old enough by now for us to infer that, though time has not buried this story in oblivion for him—after all, he can still remember its smallest details—it has smoothed its rough edges and allows him to reflect on his behavior with equanimity. To suffer remorse of conscience, one may need to be nearer the events in question (although detailed memory and continued rationalization argue for his present uneasiness at least).

## *Looking Back*

1. Because it's on his way to this restaurant that he espies Sylvia and that he finally (literally) bumps into her.

2. From the perspective of a later relationship whose details we have not yet been treated to.

3. His feeling for her is too delicate, it seems, for a direct confrontation. Also, he doubts himself at this point, which is endearing in light of his later confidence.

4. Answers will vary. After all, she didn't turn him down flat, but she didn't seem too forthcoming, either. His sense of achievement seems mostly an inner conviction.

5. Despite earlier glances between them, he pretends that there has been no contact.

6. Because his real affection was toward Sylvia, it was safe for him to respond superficially to the baker's girl without committing himself emotionally; he could thus amuse himself with her.

7. That she was docile certainly, but also innocent like a lamb and, within bounds, trusting (see line 279 for one limit she draws).

8. He is not sincerely interested in her; his awareness of his own lack of sincerity is accentuated by the serious demeanor with which she accepts the appointment.

9. To act morally is to perform right conduct, but see above for his elaboration of this concept. He indicates that pretense is wrong but also that it would have been illogical in this case.

10. My view is that it is not, but students will argue both sides.

*❋*

# Albert Camus

# The Growing Stone

*Overview.*   Albert Camus has been both praised and criticized for being a moralist, and although we need not enter this debate over the artist's role (particularly when, as with Camus, others politicize it), we should recognize some of the great moral themes of philosophy and literature in this story. Briefly, these are penitence, sacrifice, fraternity, and rebirth (all cited in Looking Ahead 3). And we may mention as well shouldering others' burdens and keeping promises (see Writing Assignments 1 and 2, respectively) and the idea of spiritual pilgrimage (Writing Assignment 3). Despite the presence of these themes, "The Growing Stone" is hardly a tract. Doctrine has no place in Camus's art, nor does it appear to him a proper motivating power for human existence. Rather, as the story bears out, moral beliefs emerge from action, but not really *emerge* if we mean by that that they are abstracted from actual practice: they have their only life in it. The stone of penitence D'Arrast carries for the cook and his subsequent rejoining the human community are the whole story.

*In the Classroom.*   As indicated above, the moral principles present in this story are contained in the action, yet students should be able to move back and forth between references to belief and practice, not simply describe the action. Their ability to do this will depend largely on their understanding of the character of D'Arrast and the meaning to his character of the change his life has undergone by the end.

*Formal Considerations.*   Symbolic speech, which is crucial to fiction, can be discovered in the story, for instance, in the exchange between D'Arrast and Socrates in lines 680–690. Challenge students to discover the greater meaning of D'Arrast's confession that he doesn't know where he's going (not simply not to Mass) and that he doesn't know how to dance.

## Looking Back

1. It points up the awe in which the locals hold the foreign professional (ironically, it turns out D'Arrast *is* a former aristocrat).

2. Third world, impoverished, with a mixed race population.

3. This symbolically descriptive word tells us—despite its subsequent literal application—that his spiritual state is equally in question.

4. Neither profits from others nor seeks to control them; each is a productive worker; each has had a spiritual crisis.

5. Answers will vary. Besides the religious conviction, it is possible to say that psychologically his vow gave him a belief in himself that increased his physical endurance.

6. That Christ, not less than humans, has the free will to choose, that he is not bound by professions of faith on the part of human beings.

7. See In the Classroom.

8. The human solidarity that D'Arrast affirms through his act is not mediated through the church as an institution but is direct.

9. He not only has proved himself but also has been able to identify with the most common people ("he was suddenly enormous, drinking in with desperate gulps the familiar smell of poverty and ashes"; lines 882–884—the *drinking in* is key here).

10. They point to the people's acceptance of D'Arrast; he has succeeded in rejoining the human community.

⁂

# Anonymous

# Is That So?

*Overview.*    This is a story from the *Shaseki-shu* (*Collection of Stone and Sand*), a thirteenth-century compilation of anecdotes purportedly based on actual events in the lives of Chinese and Japanese Zen masters during the previous five centuries. The story demonstrates the virtuous equanimity of those, like the main character Hakuin, who trust the purity of their own actions and motives despite the opprobrium others may heap on their heads. Clearly, the story ties in with Western ideas of individualism, in which social pressures and collective demands do not eradicate the importance and validity of the person. But the story goes beyond such a sense to demonstrate the serenity of the achieved consciousness that takes neither offense in being falsely accused nor pleasure in being vindicated, but exists in lucid awareness in any situation.

*In the Classroom.*    The "achieved consciousness" referred to above is not a very well-understood concept in the West, and Hukuin's manifestation of it might particularly be obscure to students (although, depending on their idealism, it may not). It would be useful to ask students what they believe Hakuin is thinking when he is accused and when he is exonerated.

*Formal Considerations.*    Anecdotes like this one that act as parables are meant to yield to interpretation and application of their meaning. The events and situations, therefore, should be seen symbolically.

## Looking Back

1. That he is an accomplished practitioner of Zen and is recognized for his expertise and wisdom.

2. That he is chaste.

3. People are eager to believe the worst of those who appear to be the best; therefore, her accusation of Hakuin stood a greater chance of being believed.

4. His wisdom transcends such mechanisms as self-defense and professions of innocence: he knows he is innocent and doesn't need anyone else's witness to confirm it.

5. Bemusement.

6. That the kind of social acceptance it signifies has vastly less importance than the individual's own sense of his or her integrity.

7. Obviously. Formal principles enunciated in various places can legitimate our actions, as well as our own sense of their virtue.

9. He recognizes the baby's needs; he does not consider that the injustice done him exempts him from caring for others.

9. They believe justice demands punishment or assumption of responsibility, a material view; Hakuin believes that justice derives from right action under any circumstances, a spiritual view.

10. See the Overview.

# Margot Olavarria

# Remembering John

**Overview.**     This is an essay on friendship that uses as a springboard another Zen story, "True Friends," from the above collection. Olavarria writes about playwright John Mangano as he went through the last stages of AIDS. It is an essay in which, under the least propitious circumstances, friendship is discovered, tested, and certified. Although Olavarria never claims any special merit for herself, readers can observe her growth in moral stature through her faithfulness. Her description of her dying friend is unblinking (though when she made an oral presentation based on this essay in class, she wept). Because both she and Mangano are writers, it is not parenthetical, even if it seems so in context of his illness, that communication on the basis of craft is also a topic here; it leads, by the way, to Writing Assignment 2.

**In the Classroom.**     Students may feel squeamish reading Olavarria's description of Mangano's appearance (see lines 143–151), but the obvious point to make is that candor is a virtue and these details do justice to the subject (euphemistic treatment would, in effect, deny his present reality at that moment and thus humiliate his dying more than his symptoms did).

**Formal Considerations.**   The structural decisions Olavarria makes are instructive. She begins by paraphrasing the parable, goes on to interpret its meaning, and then extrapolates from that interpretation to launch an applicable narrative. At the end, she returns to the parable, not merely to repeat its sense, but originally, criticizing it and by so doing demonstrating the independence of her own writing. It is useful also to point to the simplicity and directness of Olavarria's prose.

## Looking Back

1. See Formal Considerations.

2. We see from her reaction that she is used to monitoring her own responses to other people to see if they are the right ones; she has a moral sensibility.

3. The dying feel their affliction is unjust.

4. Reluctantly, and therefore we credit her compassion more; if she were nurturing by nature, she would not seem to have made a *moral* decision.

5. The honesty of reporting the actual association—whether she made it at the time or only later—testifies to the general candor of her view and its influence on the quality of her prose. Nevertheless, answers will vary.

6. Her distance from him is only in terms of health. He has praised life, not her, and therefore her feeling especially alive is an acceptance of his valuation. Her closeness to him logically follows.

7. That he is a born—meaning lifelong—writer, so dedicated to the vocation that only death can interrupt.

8. Answers will vary, depending on students' view of mutual aid and any fear they have of coming in contact even with the personal effects of AIDS victims.

9. See In the Classroom. Olavarria is an honest reporter.

10. Friendship is faithfulness.

# Joan Didion

# On Morality

**Overview.**   Didion's essay goes beyond the classical formulation of her essay title, which promises mere exposition *about* the subject. She attempts a definition of *morality:* she says it is adherence to the social code. Along the way, she also defines what it is not and, in doing so, provides a critique of social and political action supposedly based on individual moral conscience. Conscience, according to Didion, is far too subjective a faculty to be a reliable moral instrument: anyone can justify any kind of action by appealing to conscience alone (these thoughts provide the basis for all three Writing Assignments). Written in 1965, this essay is politically conservative in tone (its context was the general upswell of student protest and the civil rights movement in the United States), but, as usual for Didion, it is not conservative in manner. Anecdotal, allusive, vividly detailed, it directly engages the reader with a ringing *you*.

***In the Classroom.*** This essay offers distinct challenges to two views that many first-year students bring to college: one is that religion is the exclusive source of moral principles, and the other is the one that Jiminy Cricket teaches Pinocchio: let your conscience be your guide. As we have seen, Didion directly criticizes the latter notion; she criticizes the first by omission and posits, instead, the social code as the key to right conduct. If your students find her views unsettling, you should nevertheless make sure—not that they agree with these views—but that they understand their exact sense and full import.

***Formal Considerations.*** "On Morality" is an excellent model of both the personal essay and the essay genre itself. On the first score, we feel the presence of the author throughout. Her voice is clear, the insights are her own, the ideas arise from situations she finds herself in and events she puts together. The genre is well represented by fulfilling the essential claim made for an essay—that it exists for the communication of ideas, that all else is finally subordinated to that end. (Notice in this regard how the essay grows increasingly abstract toward the conclusion.)

## Looking Back

1. That she is going to ground her ideas in concrete situations and not sacrifice her own presence to some high-minded goal of writing.

2. We're intended to admire these early instances of adherence to the social code: the nurse is faithful, the husband loyal.

3. In an unspoken way, the human community is based on the notion of preserving the dignity of all; it would be quite undignified to be eaten by coyotes.

4. She believes the lessons children are taught are what inform their adult moral sense.

5. She was taught to regard them as moral failures, people who abdicated their responsibility to each other and so brought on their collective doom. Answers will vary as to whether her interpretation is likely, but allowances might be made for the pioneers' extreme conditions.

6. Answers will vary, but *responsibility* seems to be our recognition of a moral duty toward someone or something else, a duty faithfully to care, uphold rights, and preserve humanness, perhaps. *Loyalty* is the bond of aid and support we form with others (or for a cause) that is based not necessarily on inherent objective value but on the perceived irreplaceability of the other.

7. The stories are the news; they tie the community together, no matter how scattered it is, and thus form something of a moral linkage.

8. Paraphrases will vary, but see the Overview.

9. The progression is a domineering and totalitarian one, in which early concern, intellectually and emotionally registered (as in analyzing the plight of the proletariat and sympathizing with them), leads to our philosophical certainty about what action will serve their interests best, and then to our making sure they do not resist our efforts.

10. She distinguishes between *interest* and *right conduct,* saying the former is often misinterpreted as the latter in order to justify our needs and desires.

※

# Diana Tietjens Meyers
# Work and Self-Respect

*Overview.*    This essay traces the serial, causal connections between basic human rights, personal integrity, meaningful work, and self-respect. It is self-respect that Meyers, agreeing with philosopher John Rawls, contends makes life worthwhile. But the question is how people gain self-respect. Particularly for the author, the question is how the prevalent condition of most adults—making a living—can sustain the human need for self-respect. Defining the various components of this good and showing their connections to each other, this essay is a model of good academic writing in that it is lucid, accessible, and—in its definitions, reasoning, and conclusions—highly applicable to the lives of real people in a real world. The Writing Assignments are based on this assumption, asking students to test their own work experience according to enumerated rights understood as principles; to identify their own personal convictions and affections that Meyers asserts help define the self; and to show how the right of liberty, essential to gaining self-respect, applies to people they choose to discuss.

*In the Classroom.*    The subheads used in this essay divide it into meaningful units that, though sequential within the general vector of the reasoning process, nonetheless can be conveniently taken up singly and understood as self-contained analyses. Doing so relieves the (light) burden on students of following the abstract reasoning of an entire discourse yet allows them to do just that in the end.

**Formal Considerations.**   Analysis, definition, and argument all are present in this essay and can be examined as such. As an example of argumentative procedures, note the author's taking account of an objection to her view and responding to it (lines 51–62); or her definition of the function of rights: "Rights give right-holders prerogatives in regard to specified benefits" (line 139). These are clear models of these rhetorical means.

## Looking Back

1. Rights (in the workplace, equal opportunity and participation in job-related decisions)  ⟶  personal integrity  ⟶  self-respect.

2. "Stable beliefs and feelings" (line 35)—the author's definition of personal integrity—consolidate the self, without which the personal acceptance necessary to self-respect is not possible.

3. Answers will vary, but everyone should come up (we hope) with something.

4. Hypocrites betray their own beliefs in order to profess those of others, producing a form of self-censorship that suppresses the very self that is to be respected. Self-knowledge divides fantasy from reality on the part of the self-perceiver so that self-respect can have a true foundation. Liberty is the condition of the true self, permitting a person individually to form the convictions and affections that selfhood requires.

5. "Human rights articulate a set of moral requirements that specify the forms of respect humanity is owed" (lines 125–126).

6. In different ways depending on the right in question, all rights create space around the person and a degree of freedom. The freedom to be and to act, "to discover themselves and to express their distinctive personalities" (lines 156–157), allows people personal integrity, which is essential to self-respect.

7. The right to decent pay; the "right to be recognized as a member of the work force" (lines 259–260); the subsidiary rights to proper training and improved conditions.

8. The right to equal opportunity combats discrimination and thus protects persons from the kind of humiliating treatment that leads to self-doubt and self-contempt, the opposite of self-respect. The fairness implicit in equal opportunity affirms the worth of the person's efforts and accomplishments against "the accidents of one's birth" (line 295).

9. To give employees a meaningful voice in directing the operations and setting the course of the firm they work for.

10. Answers will vary, but yes or no, students should trace the connections between work and self-respect Meyers makes in her discussion.

# Gary Snyder
# Buddhism and the Coming Revolution

***Overview.***   With almost synoptic brevity but with great effect, Gary Snyder in this essay levies a critical fine on Western civilization that, he intimates, it will pay in full in time and is perhaps unwittingly paying even now (see lines 20–33). This rejectionist posture is meant to serve his real discursive aim, which is to prescribe Buddhist practices and consciousness for all who wish to be truly human. Snyder believes we should give up the narrowness of our particular selves in order to realize the world's unity in love, naturalness, and wisdom. He himself is not narrowly focused on unworldliness and religious tradition, however, as we see in his approval of "any cultural and economic revolution that moves clearly toward a free, international, classless world" (lines 67–68). Utopianism may be said to characterize his conclusion, but, as he says, what he hopes for will only happen "[i]f we are lucky" (line 83).

***In the Classroom.***   Snyder's conciseness forces the reader to supply, in thought or in writing, the illustrations and definitions that he omits. I recommend working against a too hasty reading of this conceptually tight, short essay by pausing intermittently to have students define and give examples of the points Snyder makes.

***Formal Considerations.***   However much one sympathizes with Snyder's general views, and however animated his prose, his essay is a polemic more than it is a reasoned argument, meaning he does not take into consideration opposing positions, he doesn't concede points where it is appropriate to do so, and he doesn't support his views with evidence. Contrasting polemic with argument (say, with the previous essay by Diana Tietjens Meyers, which is equally humanistic) can be a useful exercise.

## Looking Back

1. The self limits vision by being defined, that is, separated from others by lines of demarcation; only by dissolving in the "All" can total states be perceived.

2. Traditional Buddhism has been elitist, unwilling to address itself to historical directions and social causes of the ignorance and suffering that its practice attempts to eliminate, and too ready to accept oppressive political regimes (probably in order to ensure its own survival).

3. Answers will vary.

4. The potential to live a harmonious life, free of avarice and unrealistic expectations and hatred, and to become whole by practicing compassion toward others.

5. *Faith* in the intrinsic beneficence of human nature and of the real needs of the human community, and *insight* into one's own innocent nature—these two lead one on the right path toward "harmlessness and the refusal to take life in any form" (line 43).

6. Answers will vary, depending on degrees of realism, cynicism, and idealism.

7. A loving community, in which people live in freedom, not divided from each other by the false barriers of ideological views, nationality, and class.

8. This is the ultimate of empathy, in which the enlightened person not only imagines the other's situation but subjects himself or herself to it in order not to be separated from any of humanity. By so doing, the Bodhisattva represents the sufferer and protects that person.

9. Personal change in consciousness (the East) leads one toward cooperating with others to produce social change (the West).

10. Answers will vary, but students should certainly address his concluding paragraph.

# Linked Readings

The Brothers Grimm
THE WATER OF LIFE

Chuang Tzu
SUPREME HAPPINESS

**Overview.** The themes that emerge from these combined readings are those of right conduct and goodness; humility and moral innocence; personal conviction based on moral feeling versus majority opinion as sole arbiter; and the freedom gained by seeing afresh, past the encrustations of mechanical routine. The link between these texts taken from entirely different times and cultures is perhaps best expressed by the first Looking Ahead item for the Chuang Tzu: they "reflect the same concern: how best to exist in the world." In "The Water of Life," the king is mortally ill. His three sons set out on a quest to find the only cure—the water of life. The two elder sons, however, fail in their mission because of their arrogance and malice. The youngest son succeeds, first in acquiring the elixir and later in winning love and respect, because he is innocently virtuous. "Supreme Happiness" mixes essayistic meditation and storytelling to comment memorably on wisdom, goodness, and true value.

**In the Classroom.**   The term *fairy tales* (the Grimm brothers collected *folk* tales, or *marchen*) can be used dismissively, so it is advisable to stress Looking Ahead 2 and ask students to interpret the symbolic action in "The Water of Life" (the rod, for instance, signifying power, and bread representing knowledge); the moral lesson is direct and simple to perceive. Although "Supreme Happiness" is unified in its pursuit of virtue, this discourse is broken into sections that can be taken up and understood discretely. The doctrinal point that might be most obscure to students is contained in lines 33–44. The key concept here is *inaction*. Another term for it might be *being*; it is opposed to mere doing, or action, and if we remember T. S. Eliot's animadversion that all actions lead to fatality (*Little Gidding*), we understand the desirable unchangeableness wrought by inaction. This is the "highest happiness" or good, and when Chuang Tzu says this happiness "has no happiness," he means that it is indivisible; it cannot be viewed apart from itself, no more than we could say life has or possesses life instead of saying it is itself.

**Formal Considerations.**   The formal symmetry of objects and events in "The Water of Life" is structurally interesting (see the departure of each son in turn, the sequential meetings with the dwarf, and the arrival of each son at the palace of the king's daughter). Balance of this sort helps produce unity and gives a text a sense of inevitability. The self-contained aspect of the sections in "Supreme Happiness" is commented on above; the idea of dividing an essay into sections by blank spaces is structurally useful, though in essays students obviously will want to provide tighter transitions between distinct sections.

## Looking Back

1. They're arrogant, contemptuous, self-serving.
2. He cares for his brothers even though he is told about their vices.
3. Hasty judgment brings regret.
4. Devotion to the truly valuable (the woman, not the gold).
5. Desiring to live, as opposed to truly living, is a waste; it is a product of wanting to live up to others' values instead of your own. Equally wasteful is spending energy in the attempt to become successful in the world's eyes.
6. Death, he avers, is one stage in a natural progression, and to mourn the dead overmuch is not to comprehend that progression.

7. Probably the skull: it rejects the ultimate temptation, to return to life, which Chuang Tzu has offered as his profession of what is good (the greatest happiness).

8. The marquis will become jealous of what he cannot have ("similar greatness") and turn from boiling resentment to murdering the one who caused this feeling in him.

9. We should measure differences and live in harmonious relations with others according to what is appropriate to each.

10. See the first sentence of the Overview.